The Awards of Science and Other Essays

Essays of an Information Scientist

This volume is one of a series published by ISI Press®. Each book in the series is a collection of Eugene Garfield's essays, which were orginally published in *Current Contents* under the title "Current Comments". The essays contain their author's personal observations about subjects which have caught his attention—from scientific research, librarianship, and information science to business, bureaucracy, journalism, and friendship. Volumes Six and Seven each contain an Appendix of papers, not previously published in *Current Contents,* but of interest to readers of the Series.

Beginning with Volume 7 in the *Essays of an Information Scientist* Series, each volume will have a unique title.

Books published in this series:

Essays of an Information Scientist, Volume 1: 1962 – 1973

Essays of an Information Scientist, Volume 2: 1974 – 1976

Essays of an Information Scientist, Volume 3: 1977 – 1978

Essays of an Information Scientist, Volume 4: 1979 – 1980

Essays of an Information Scientist, Volume 5: 1981 – 1982

Essays of an Information Scientist, Volume 6: 1983

Essays of an Information Scientist, Volume 7: 1984
   The Awards of Science and Other Essays

Essays of an Information Scientist: 1984

The Awards of Science and Other Essays

by
Eugene Garfield

with a foreword by
Gerald Holton

iSi PRESS

Published by

iSi PRESS ®A Subsidiary of the
Institute for Scientifc Information®
3501 Market Street, Philadelphia, PA 19104 U.S.A.

Library of Congress Cataloging in Publication Data
(Revised for v. 7)

Garfield, Eugene.
   Essays of an information scientist.

   Originally published in Current contents under the
title: Current comments.
   Includes bibliographical references and indexes.
   Contents: v. 1. 1962-1973—v. 2. 1974-1976—[etc.]
—v. 7. The awards of science and other essays.
      1. Communication in science—Collected works.
   2. Science—Abstracting and indexing—Collected works.
   3. Information science—Collected works.   I. Title.
   Z7405.C6G37Q223   507'.2   77-602

ISBN 0-89495-001-0 (Volume 1)
ISBN 0-89495-002-9 (Volume 2)
ISBN 0-89495-009-6 (Volume 3)
ISBN 0-89495-012-6 (Volume 4)
ISBN 0-89495-023-1 (Volume 5)
ISBN 0-89495-032-0 (Volume 6)
ISBN 0-89495-044-4 (Volume 7)

Printed in the United States of America

Dedicated to the Memory of
Anders Martinsson
Mort Mass
Knut R. Thalberg
Melvin Weinstock

TABLE OF CONTENTS

Volume 7

Contents

Contents

Appendix

Foreword

A tradition has emerged by which the writers of the Forewords of *Essays of an Information Scientist* must tell how they first met the author, Dr. Eugene Garfield. However perverse as it may seem, I would rather begin by referring to a moment during my most recent meeting with Garfield, just a few days ago.

I found he was passing through town, and he agreed to have lunch with me. I always look forward to such an occasion, which gives me at least a brief glimpse into the workshop of his mind. But this time there was a special celebratory air about him. He handed me a chocolate cigar to signal the birth of the latest addition to the Garfield family, Alexander Merton Garfield. He seemed the typical proud father; but it came to mind that his pleasure in a new son was also connected with his most abstract interest in children and childcare that I had noticed in many of his published essays, as well as in his dedication of Volume 5: "To all my children—past, present, and future."

In other regimes this successful joining of theory and praxis might give rise to ideological discussion; I prefer to put it forward as a metaphor—a metaphor for Garfield's part in the conception, nurturing, and efflorescence of Information Science since he started the Institute for Scientific Information, just 30 years ago.

With a little prodding from my side, he goes on to speak of the other "children" he expects to emerge soon: an index to 19th century science, including implicit citations (often included now in the Arts and Humanities *Citation Index*); an annual Atlas Encyclopedia of Science; a Newspaper of Science, first bi-weekly and then perhaps weekly; and other explorations, taking full advantage of the new technologies of computers and image-bearing disks.

I try to imagine how these new means will amplify the long list of research aids with which ISI has penetrated the working lives of the research community. Metaphors continue to present themselves. Who is this man with whom I am having a pleasant lunch? A Lazare Carnot, organizing the information revolution? A Diderot, encyclopedizing the findings of all the sciences, arts, and humanities?

There is much in both of these analogies, yet something essential is lacking. Garfield has not merely marshalled large pre-existing sets of forces, and has not only made a net with which to dredge the flood of information to find items which are wanted but disconnected from one another. He and his collaborators working with him in Philadelphia evidently have had to go much further, creating the ideas, methods, and actual material tools with which one can make meaningful connections between the atomized fragments of information that are washing over all of us, a torrent out of control.

The mere statistics of the flow of information through Garfield's hands—each a device for making the myriad of atoms individually accessible—are indeed awesome: Each month ANSA updates chemists on about 16,000 new compounds; the Arts and Humanities *Citation Index* annually covers literature in over 6,300 journals; every week the Automatic Subject Citation Alert sends out items culled from nearly 5,800 journals; the *Address Directory* formerly the *Current Bibliographic Directory of the Arts & Sciences* gives names, addresses, and descriptions of the output of nearly a million authors worldwide, every year; *Current Contents* is read by more than 350,000 persons weekly; the Index to Scientific & Technical Proceedings alerts the researcher to some 100,000 such conference papers published each year; the *Science Citation Index* keeps its eye on 3500 journals and indexes nearly nine million citations in 600,000 items yearly; and on and on. Or think of the extraordinary diversity of topics covered, week after week, in Garfield's lead essays in *Current Contents,* collected over the years in these volumes—essays on Nobel Prizes, agoraphobia, cystitis, entomology, gerontology, children's books, fine arts. . . .

In the history of science there have been persons who have loved an immense mass of detail for its own sake. Many of the 19th-century spectroscopists provide examples, such as Kaiser and his monumental volumes of data, wavelength by wavelength, obtained under every conceivable condition of pressure and potential difference. Garfield cannot be explained this way, of course. The fruitful analogy is not Kaiser, any more than it was Carnot or Diderot. Rather, the motivating force seems to me similar to that of an earlier figure, one who found himself at a similar point in the development of his field, when a few orderly and powerful regularities about the dynamics of the solar system were struggling to emerge out of the over-abundance of informational detail of the most diverse sort.

One need glance only at a few pages of Johannes Kepler's works to realize that the three laws that textbooks now selectively remember him for (and which he never so labelled) were quite hidden from the eye of the casual reader under all that diversity. They were obscure even to Galileo, who could not bear the seemingly scattered nature of Kepler's preoccupations. And to be sure, in terms of the range of what caught his attention, Kepler was generally thought to be too omniverous even in as mature a work as his *Epitome of Copernican Astronomy.* There he gives us, side by side with details of planetary positions and orderly motions, his disquisitions on Aristotle, on the Scriptures, on the geometry of the primary and secondary figures, on the hierarchy of densities and rarities, on the sounds the monochord plays in the minor and major modes, on soap bubbles, on magnets, on the question whether intelligences can act as motor forces, on light as *lux* and *lumen,* on pedagogy, and on the wars in Austria. It was all part of his "celestrial physics"—and the apparent chaos of minutiae is put to work in the service of a vision of simplicity and order that became evident to others only later.

Indeed, one of the characteristics marking the founders of any science is that their imagination should be able to embrace both the antitheticals, using the wealth of inchoate detail as raw material for the recognition of meaningful patterns. It must be so also among the founders of Information Science. Thus Garfield and his collaborators are showing us the patterns of evolution in the growth of sciences which are emerging from their layered "maps of science" and matrices of cluster co-citations.

As the field develops further, one can count on the continued prominence of Garfield's work in his pursuit of the Keplerian quest. There is also much benefit in the happy accident that in him are combined both productive scholar and industrial entrepreneur. It is a joining that can continue to bring into practice rather quickly ideas that otherwise might grow and become applicable much more slowly. In sum, all of us who are concerned with the social study of science will be keeping a keen eye on Philadelphia for many more stimulating volumes of the *Essays of an Information Scientist,* and on Garfield's many children, past, present, and future.

GERALD HOLTON

*Mallinckrodt Professor of Physics
  and Professor of History of Science
Harvard University
Cambridge, Massachusetts*

Preface

The sixth volume of *Essays of an Information Scientist* contained all of my essays published during the previous year in *Current Contents*. It also included an appendix containing many other papers never published in *Current Contents*, although they may have been discussed in one or more essays. Volume Seven continues this precedent. Indeed, by a perhaps not fortuitous yet unplanned occurrence, these eight publications cover most of the main projects that have been my preoccupation for over thirty years. My 1964 paper in *Science* was the culmination of a decade's work reported in that journal in 1955. The primordial paper was included in Volume Six of *Essays* along with a parallel paper on patent citation indexing, also matched in this volume. Very much related to these is the work on the *Genetics Citation Index*, which quite recently enabled me to do a revealing analysis of the work of Barbara McClintock in *Current Contents*. My only major published description of the *Permuterm Index* concept is included here. Finally, my algorithm for translation of chemical nomenclature is included. This was my doctoral dissertation at the University of Pennsylvania. By reprinting it here, I have resolved the chore of copying if for those occasional seekers after the original thesis. Chemists and historians are never really satisfied with surrogates.

Beginning this year, the titles of the books in the *Essays* series will change. The Series will retain the name *Essays of an Information Scientist* to preserve the Series identification. To emphasize the fact that each volume is unique in many ways, however, each book will now also have its own title. The title of the 1984 volume is *The Awards of Science and Other Essays*.

The essays for 1984 cover my "usual" assortment of citation studies, as well as topical articles on general science, health related concerns, and personality profiles. And of course, many describe ISI products and services such as *SciMate* microcomputer software. This personal database management system is now widely used by scientists.

The publication of the 1955-64 *Science Citation Index* cumulation in 1984 was a significant event. This permitted me to up-date several studies, including the list of all-time citation classics. The first five of a multi-part series discussing and listing the most-cited papers for 1961-1982 is included here. The first group of 100 is comparable to an earlier study in 1974, in which we identified the then most-cited papers. Citation aficionados should be interested in noting the changes in these lists.

In the same essays I described the process by which we select candidates for the autobiographical commentaries published in *Current Contents* under the rubric of *Citation Classics*. These commentaries are of significant interest not only to bench scientists and historians of science. They also serve as models of discovery for students and provide insights into the scientific process not discernible by simply reading the original papers. We plan to cumulate these commentaries in the future in separate volumes.

Our citation studies indicate that primordial articles in life sciences frequently appear in general medical journals. This volume includes essays in which we examine three groups of 100 classic articles published in the *New England Journal of Medicine,* the *Lancet,* and *Annals of Internal Medicine.* While these are among the highest impact journals, future essays will examine citation classics from other significant medical and scientific journals, especially multi-disciplinary publications like *Science* and *Nature.* Nevertheless, the latter journals are well represented by the studies already mentioned.

In addition to my essays on *Citation Classics,* this volume also contains a major two-part piece on Latin American Research. This study highlights the productivity and impact of Central and South American scientists. ISI's continuing interest in Third World research has helped draw further attention to this little-studied subject. Indeed, it will be the subject of discussion at a forthcoming NSF conference to be held in Philadelphia as well as a conference in Trieste sponsored by the Third World Academy.

The volume also contains several journal citation studies and numerous other lists of most-cited articles. My review of entomology journals also highlights the work of Dr. Miriam Rothschild, whose extraordinary life and research I describe in a subsequent personality profile. In addition to publishing more than 275 research works in fields ranging from marine biology to plant-insect interactions, she has written a biography of her uncle, Walter Rothschild, a noted naturalist. *Dear Lord Rothschild* depicts his colorful life against the backdrop of Victorian and Edwardian England.

As before, I have continued to analyze each year's crop of Nobel Prize winners, but not to the neglect of the numerous other prestigious awards—the non-Nobel prizes. The latter study, among others, represents a prodigious effort by my tireless assistants named in each essay. Given all the attention that is traditionally focused on the Nobel Prize and its recipients, other notable prizes of science are often overlooked. The essay identifies the many prestigious non-Nobel awards, names the recipients of these awards, identifies their most-cited and most-significant papers, and points out the multiplicity of awards given to the same person. It is noteworthy that Barbara McClintock, mentioned above, a 1983 Nobelist, also received three of the non-Nobel awards described in the article. However, a separate essay about her Nobel Prize appeared in *Current Contents* February 18, 1985. It shows in detail a different picture than was portrayed by the popular press. This essay will be included when the Eighth Volume of *Essays* appears.

My more controversial essays frequently prove to be almost too timely. At about the time that my comments on animal experimentation appeared, a vigilante group of animal rights advocates broke into a laboratory at the University of Pennsylvania School of Veterinary Medicine and attempted to destroy the laboratory's research records. Fortunately, the laboratory and all concerned survived this onslaught.

The essays about S. R. Ranganathan need no further elaboration except the expression of my gratitude to S. Arunachalam, editor of the *Indian Journal of Technology,* for his tireless efforts not only on my tour of India, but also in his quest to bring scientometrics and information technology of age in his country.

Volume Six was dedicated to the memory of my friend and colleague Derek J. deSolla Price. However, this volume contains my editorial tribute to him, which was extended in a festschrift volume of *Scien-*

tometrics, now in press. Recently, that journal honored me with the first Derek deSolla Price medal. More recently, Robert K. Merton and I have completed a Foreword to the forthcoming reprint of the classic *Little Science, Big Science,* to be published by Columbia University Press.

This volume is dedicated to the memory of four close friends. In 1984, my good friend and colleague Mort Mass died unexpectedly as did my good friend Anders Martinsson, the former editor of *Lethaia* and other journals and inventor of the *Biblid.* The loss of my friend and co-worker, Melvin Weinstock, added yet another sad note to an eventful year. And as I write this preface, I learned about the death of my classmate Knut Thalberg, the distinguished Director of the Libraries at the Norwegian Technical University in Trondheim.

It is tempting to recap the entire contents of this volume, but that is more simply done by reference to the Table of Contents. It is important to emphasize that I intentionally devote attention to several categories of topics each year, especially those that are of wide public interest but are treated less systematically by the popular press and more arcanely by the scientific journals. That I have achieved some success in this is reflected in the use of my essays by organizations that have a special interest in such topics as gerontology, twins, cystitis, anorexia, and agoraphobia. The typical media journalist cannot devote this kind of effort to each article, often published under pressure of a daily deadline. Short of an entire book on the research involved in each area, it is a special challenge to condense all this information in about eight to ten pages. This would not be possible without access to ISI's unique database, which I described in some detail when I introduced the *Atlas of Science.* My essays will increasingly reflect the use of historiographs and the research fronts they portray graphically as ISI moves towards its destiny of encyclopediaism in the electronic age.

On a recent trip to Boston, I made a pilgrimage to the subway to see the 100-foot-wide mural showing the origins of that institution created by Lilli Ann Killen Rosenberg. My essay on her work describes the marvelous mosaic-in-concrete mural she created for ISI's now famous Caring Center for Children and Parents. The insert that accompanied the essay is also included here. A limited number of reprints in color are still available.

The very last *Current Contents* essay for 1984 has already received attention in the press, indicating the wide public interest in the problem of selecting science books for children.

Finally, I would like to convey my appreciation to Gerald Holton, Professor of Physics and a Historian of Science at Harvard University, for contributing the Foreword to this volume. We share an interest in scholarship that explains how science and technology help shape industry and society. All scholars should be grateful to him not only for his contributions to the literature but also for his role in gaining for the History of Science Society a firm financial foundation for years to come. His wide intellectual and popular appeal is demonstrated by some of his more recent work in the *New York Review of Books* and the *Times Literary Supplement*.

Current Comments®

EUGENE GARFIELD
INSTITUTE FOR SCIENTIFIC INFORMATION®
3501 MARKET ST., PHILADELPHIA, PA 19104

Current Contents' New Clothes
for a New Year

Number 1   **January 2, 1984**

This issue of *Current Contents*® (*CC*®) includes a number of changes we think are important and beneficial. As you can see, the new *CC* cover is made of heavy, durable paper. For the past 26 years, *CC* used "self-covers," as they are known in the printing trade. A self-cover for a pamphlet or journal is made of the same paper used for the inside leaves or pages. We used such an integrated cover for many reasons, but especially for those of cost and time. The average issue of *CC* is used by many different readers. In some developing countries, a few hundred faculty and graduate students may scan a single copy. The new "separate cover" allows *CC* to circulate with a minimum of wear and tear. It will not only last for many years, but it also feels great.

All editions of *CC* will have essentially the same kind of cover, except for *CC/ Arts & Humanities* which will continue to have a self-cover. In addition, *CC/ Life Sciences* (*CC/LS*) will have a new type of binding. Called "perfect" binding, it gives us greater flexibility. We can now increase the number of pages in *CC*. When *CC/LS* was started,[1] it covered about 200 journals. Each issue contained about 30 pages. Today, *CC/LS* covers more than 1,100 journals containing more than 200,000 titles. The average issue contains about 320 pages, and often reaches 350. This is about the upper limit for using "saddle-stitch"

binding, that is, binding with staples. However, with perfect binding, we can stack as many signatures as required. The whole stack is then glued to the spine of the cover. All six other *CC* editions will continue to be bound with staples unless their size requires perfect binding. This is not unlikely, considering the continued growth of the literature.

In addition to being more durable, the new *CC* covers are, we hope, more informative. The titles of the *Citation Classics*™ and *Current Comments*® essays, which change from week to week, are highlighted on the covers. We believe it will be useful to many readers, including librarians and administrators, to have these features identified in this way. Placing the titles of essays and commentaries on the covers will be helpful when you're quickly trying to locate a specific work.

Based on many requests, the edition, date, volume, and number of each *CC* issue are printed along the back edge in large, easy-to-read type. This makes it easier to locate and file a particular issue, and to differentiate between the various *CC* editions. Also, since the binding for *CC/LS* is different, you should have no trouble telling it from the other editions you may receive.

We considered a complete change in the cover graphics, including the *CC* logo. We consulted with outside design experts, who prepared several prototype

Figure 1: Sample of alternative covers for *CC*®.

covers for *CC*. A sample of some alternative *CC* covers suggested by our own design staff is shown in Figure 1. Although some of the suggested layouts were visually attractive, we decided to compromise with a layout which retains the image familiar to most readers.

Our graphic design consultants, including our own Bob Ewing, manager, creative graphics, made several recommendations to improve the layout of *CC*'s text, and we've incorporated many of them. The inside front cover has been completely redesigned. Emphasis is placed on information directly needed by potential users. This includes information on how to obtain articles listed in *CC*, who to contact when you have questions, and how to order *CC* from anywhere in the world. The inside front cover also includes a succinct statement of *CC*'s purpose, and a description of the various weekly features, such as *Current*

Book Contents®, title word and author indexes, as well as author and publisher address directories.

The contents page section has a new look because we've added borderlines at the top and bottom of each page. The lines are intended to clearly define the margins. Lines are also drawn above and below each journal title in *CC/LS*. This makes it easier to identify where one journal ends and the next journal begins. Several contents pages of smaller journals often appear on a single *CC* page. Others carry over onto several pages. Similar lines will be introduced in the other *CC* editions in the near future. We think the borderlines will help you scan *CC* faster.

A standard bibliographic entry for the volume, issue, and year of each journal is set in new type. It is also offset by borderlines. It is essential to have this information delineated when requesting reprints or interlibrary loans, or writing to publishers. There has been no change made in the "oval" number used to identify each journal issue. Together with the article page number, this uniquely identifies the article for ordering through ISI®'s *Original Article Text Service (OATS®)*,[2] or for online access. All *CC* articles are available online through *Sci-Mate*™,[3] as well as other online systems. Any item can be downloaded into your personal files.

In the next few weeks, we will be adding a new feature. Special codes will follow the bibliographic information to indicate if a journal is covered in more than one *CC* edition. Individuals who subscribe to several *CC* editions with overlapping coverage sometimes find themselves scanning the same journal contents page twice. We hope to spare them that time by clearly indicating that a journal is covered in one or more *CC* editions.

The black vertical bars separating the various disciplines covered in *CC* have been eliminated. In the past, they appeared on the appropriate right-hand page along the outside vertical margin. During the final stages of binding, it was difficult to "trim" the margins in the exact spot. This also was a limitation of saddle-stitch binding. So a white margin sometimes showed through.

Furthermore, this method made it difficult to precisely delineate the disciplines. For example, the first journal in one category might share a page with the last journal in another category. This is solved by using horizontal bars. Nevertheless, we will never have a perfect system of categorizing journals that are inherently multidisciplinary. It is surprising how many readers write me about maintaining the subject integrity of their professional discipline.

One of the most important changes we have made is to increase the size of print in the author address directory for *CC/LS*. Figure 2 shows sample entries from the old and new directories. There is no greater bone of contention among *CC* readers. I regularly receive mail from lab assistants, secretaries, and others who type reprint request cards. To increase the type size by just one-half "point," we have had to increase the area used by more than 25 percent. So we've had to add many more pages to accommodate the larger type size. This could not be done before without modifying our binding procedure, as explained earlier. We are also planning to modify our procedures for listing addresses so that, in the future, we can include street addresses where necessary.

The new covers will also enable us to reduce the number of card inserts. The back cover of *CC* will be used for ads as well as subscription cards. The new cover also makes it possible to test the mailing of *CC* without envelopes. This would not only save the cost of envelopes, but also reduce the time and labor required

---

Figure 2: Sample entries from the old and new author address directory of *CC®/Life Sciences*. Entries on the left are printed in four point type. The new entries on the right have been enlarged to four and one-half point type.

DURANCEAU

DURANCEAU AC 56
HOTEL DIEU, DEPT
SURG, MONTREAL,
QUEBEC, CANADA H2W
1T8
DUROCHER LP 44
HOP MAISONNEUVE
ROSEMONT, DEPT SANTE
COMMUNAUTAIRE,
MONTREAL, QUEBEC,
CANADA H1T 2M4
DUTTON DA 115
VICTORIA INFIRM, DEPT
ANAESTHESIA, GLASGOW
G42 9TY, SCOTLAND
DVORAK AM 63
BETH ISRAEL HOSP,
DEPT PATHOL, BOSTON,
MA, 02215, USA
DWORKIN SF 39
UNIV WASHINGTON,
DEPT GEN MED,
SEATTLE, WA, 98195,
USA
EASON JR 25
WHIPPS CROSS HOSP,
LONDON E11 1NR,
ENGLAND
EDGREN RA 81
SYNTEX RES CORP, DIV
SCI AFFAIRS MED
AFFAIRS, 3401 MILLVIEW
AVE, PALO ALTO, CA,
94304, USA

DELATTRE M

DELATTRE M 193
SK&F INT CO,
PHILADELPHIA, PA,
19101, USA
DELENCASTRE H 89
REPRINT: PIGGOT PJ,
NATL INST MED RES,
DIV MICROBIOL, MILL
HILL, LONDON NW7
1AA, ENGLAND
DELGROSSO G 48
CITTA UNIV, IST
MATEMAT G
CASTELNUOVO, I-
00100 ROME, ITALY
DELIMA TCM 149
REPRINT:
PALERMONETO J,
UNIV SAO PAULO, FAC
MED VET & ZOOTECN,
FARMACOL APLICADA
& TOXICOL LAB, BR-
05340 SAO PAULO,
SP, BRAZIL
DELITALA G 174
UNIV SASSARI, IST
PATOL MED 1, CHAIR
ENDOCRINOL, I-
07100 SASSARI,
ITALY

for insertion. We know this is feasible in the US. But since *CC* is mailed to almost every country in the world, it isn't possible to assume that such methods will satisfy the postal regulations in other countries.

The goal of the changes I've described is to improve *CC* in a cost-effective manner. It is always easy to increase costs without regard to the benefits achieved.

We hope you'll be convinced that, unlike the fairy tale about the emperor's new clothes, the changes in *CC* are far from imaginary. If you don't agree, or if you have any other suggestions, please let us have your comments. We've always encouraged readers to comment on changes in our products and services.[4] That is one feature of ISI's service that will never change.

REFERENCES

1. **Garfield E.** On the 25th anniversary of *Current Contents/Life Sciences* we look forward to the electronic online microcomputing era. *Essays of an information scientist.* Philadelphia: ISI Press, 1983. Vol. 5. p. 380-6. (Reprinted from: *Current Contents* (4):5-11, 25 January 1982.)
2. --------------. While you're up, dial me an *OATS*—we're still waiting for the document delivery revolution. *Essays of an information scientist.* Philadelphia: ISI Press, 1983. Vol. 5. p. 779-84. (Reprinted from: *Current Contents* (50):5-10, 13 December 1982.)
3. --------------. Introducing *Sci-Mate*—a menu-driven microcomputer software package for online and offline information retrieval. Part 1. The *Sci-Mate Personal Data Manager*. Part 2. The *Sci-Mate Universal Online Searcher*. *Current Contents* (12):5-12, 21 March 1983 and (14):5-15, 4 April 1983.
4. --------------. Quality control at ISI: a piece of your mind can help us in our quest for error-free bibliographic information. *Current Contents* (19):5-12, 9 May 1983.

Current Comments®

Bringing the National Library of Medicine into the Computer Age: A Tribute to Frank Bradway Rogers

Number 2   January 9, 1984

In May 1983, the Medical Library Association (MLA) selected Frank Bradway Rogers to be the first recipient of the Information Advancement Award, which is sponsored by ISI®. The award recognizes the work of a "librarian who has made an outstanding contribution to the application of technology in delivering health sciences information."[1] Although many others have applied technology to advance medical librarianship, Rogers played a unique role in the application of mechanization and computers to medical information retrieval. In recognition of this, the MLA, with our blessing, decided that the award will henceforth be called the Frank Bradway Rogers Information Advancement Award.

Rogers was director of the National Library of Medicine (NLM) from 1949 to 1963, a crucial period in the life of that institution. The proliferation of medical literature in the postwar years posed a real challenge for the NLM. Rogers more than met that challenge, converting an old-fashioned institution into a modern organization, ready to enter the computer age.[2] During his splendid tenure, Rogers helped develop the Medical Literature Analysis and Retrieval System (MEDLARS), worked for passage of the National Library of Medicine Act, and spearheaded the successful drive to construct a new building for the NLM. Rogers was an energetic director, and personally tackled all the major problems that confronted the library.

Rogers was born in Norwood, Ohio, on December 31, 1914. After attending Walnut Hills High School, Cincinnati, he went on to Yale University, from which he received an AB degree in premedicine in 1936. During the next two years, Rogers worked at several different jobs,[3] first as a copyboy in New York for *Newsweek*, then as a bartender and bouncer back in Cincinnati. He later moved to Chicago, where he found employment as a claims adjuster for an insurance company. Finally, he was hired by Procter and Gamble, employed first to pass out coupons for products door-to-door, then as a field advertising crew manager. The fact that Rogers was able to obtain work time and again during the latter years of the Great Depression is evidence of one of his main virtues—perseverance.

In 1938, Rogers entered Ohio State University, where he received his MD in 1942. After working for a year as an intern at Letterman General Hospital, San Francisco, he took a commission in the US Army. Rogers served as a surgeon in the Philippines, for which he received the Bronze Star Medal. At the close of the war he spent two years in Japan as surgeon for the 25th Infantry Division. After returning to the US in 1947, he was assigned to Walter Reed Army Hospital, Washington, DC, as a resident in surgery. It was while he was at Walter Reed, in 1948, that Rogers noticed a job announcement that intrigued him. A new director was being sought for the Army Medical Library (AML), the predecessor of the NLM. Along with several other officers, he applied for the job. Rogers was subsequently interviewed by a commit-

Frank Bradway Rogers

tee consisting in part of Col. Joseph H. McNinch, the director of the library, Col. Harold Wellington Jones, director of the library from 1936 to 1945, and Luther Evans, the Librarian of Congress.[2,3] Although Rogers was concerned that he would be considered too young to assume such a responsible position, he was given the job. From then on, he could pursue the two things that he loved most: medicine and books.

The library at that time was changing rapidly. Accordingly, McNinch wanted Rogers to have an in-depth knowledge of librarianship, and to have the credentials needed to command respect among the medical library community.[2] McNinch subsequently sent Rogers to the Columbia University School of Library Service to pursue an MS in library service. Meanwhile, McNinch remained as director. In 1949, after receiving his degree, Rogers became the seventeenth director of the library.

Several problems required Rogers's immediate attention. A survey of the AML conducted for the American Library Association (ALA) between 1943 and 1944 had found almost every aspect of the century-old institution—from the services it provided to the building it was housed in—deficient.[4] Rogers's predecessors had begun to implement the recommended changes, but the modifications needed were far too radical and far-reaching to be accomplished quickly.

The library's funding was not always in line with its needs. The library was short on professional staff, and its post-1920 holdings were sparse.[5] Moreover, its card catalog was so deficient that the reference staff had to spend an inordinate amount of time just hunting for books.

By 1954, Rogers had successfully implemented many of the recommendations of the ALA committee. He hired additional staff, worked to have the library's budget increased, updated the reference services, and instituted in-service training.[4] Also, the AML was renamed the Armed Forces Medical Library.

However, the library's publication problems still remained unresolved. The staff compiled two of the three indexes to the medical literature then in use—the *Index Catalogue of the Library of the Surgeon General's Office* and the *Current List of Medical Literature*.[6] The coverage of these indexes overlapped with the American Medical Association's (AMA) *Quarterly Cumulative Index Medicus*. In addition, the *Index Catalogue* had been out of date for years. As far back as 1920 there was a backlog of one million references,[2] and by the early 1950s, the number was expected to reach two million. The indexing problems in particular had plagued all of the library's directors and eventually McNinch requested outside help.

This help came in the form of the Committee of Consultants for the Study of the Indexes to Medical Literature Published by the AML. Created in 1948, the committee was chaired by Lewis H. Weed, Johns Hopkins University and the National Research Council. Subsequently, the chairman was Chauncey D. Leake, then of the University of Texas.[7]

To undertake research for the committee, the so-called Welch Project was established at Johns Hopkins's Welch Medical Library, then directed by Sanford V. Larkey. The project, which I became a member of in 1951, concentrated on finding a solution to the AML's publication problems, and on evaluating machine methods for indexing.[8] It was during the course of my work on the Welch Project that I first met not only Rogers, but such dedicated people as Estelle Brodman, AML's head of reference; Seymour I. Taine, editor of the *Current List of Medical Literature*; and Samuel Lazerow, director of the library's acquisitions division.[9] The Lazerow Memorial Lectures, which are delivered annually at several universities, are named after Sam.[1]

The pattern in which the volumes were published was the primary reason that the *Index Catalogue* was so out of date. Following the format created in 1880 by John Shaw Billings, the library's first director, the citations were arranged in "dictionary" format, that is, in alphabetical order.[10] However, each volume of the *Index Catalogue* covered only a fraction of the alphabet. For example, the last volume, which was published in 1955, only included citations covering the letters Mh through Mn.[2] The volumes came out once a year at best and it usually took 20 years to cover the entire alphabet. Thus, at any one time, only five percent of the citations were current, while the rest were at least two to 20 years old.

The backlog of unindexed publications was increasing at a phenomenal rate. During the war years the library received few publications from war-torn nations.[10] But thanks to the acquisitions efforts of Rogers and the late Scott Adams,[11] publications from these countries began pouring in. Adding further to the library's backlog was the dramatic proliferation of scientific papers after the war. Given the hopelessness of the situation, it's no wonder that the Weed committee recommended that publication of the *Index Catalogue* stop.

With the *Index Catalogue* winding down, other publications such as the *Current List* and *Index Medicus* were receiving greater attention. The Welch Project had also devised a system for categorizing the subject headings used when indexing the medical literature.[8] By categorizing the subject headings and then sorting them by machine, we could more easily compare the AML's subject headings with those of other authorities, thus facilitating standardization. Larkey and I spent the days discussing these terms and sent recommendations to Taine. He and Rogers further refined the Subject Heading Authority List. In fact, the list was adopted by many other medical libraries and was the forerunner of the NLM's Medical Subject Headings (MeSH). Robert Hayne,[12] assistant editor of the *Current List*, was also heavily involved in this work as were Helen Field and Williamina Himwich, both members of the Welch Project.

Rogers has written that the study of subject headings and the elaboration of the concept of categorization was the Welch Project's "greatest achievement" and "their most important contribution to the development of medical bibliographic practice and the subsequent emergence of powerful new systems."[13]

If my days at the Welch Project were spent discussing medical history and subject headings, my nights were spent studying machine methods for indexing. To speed the compilation of the *Current List*, I developed a system employing IBM punched cards.[14] Later, this was modified and combined with the use of special Listomatic cameras. This system was formally implemented later when I acted as a consultant. The Index Mechanization Project, as it was called, is thoroughly described in a supplement to the *Bulletin of the Medical Library Association*,[15] prepared by Taine.

The punched-card system did not prove to be a practical method for retrieving bibliographic citations.[16] Nor were punched-card methods totally reliable for compiling the *Current List* or *Index Medicus*. There was always the chance that the huge stacks of sorted cards would be mixed-up.[17] Also, the machines did not sort as fast as desired to compile bibliographies regularly. This was a serious drawback, since selective bibliographies were becoming more and more important.

In an effort to solve these problems, Rogers learned as much as possible about computers. At that time, business and government agencies were just starting to use them. He took courses in computer operations and symbolic logic, and consulted with computer experts. In 1959, Rogers and Taine, then chief of the library's index division, drew up specifications for a system that would allow the library both to keep up with its indexing chores and quickly retrieve bibliographic information.[13] Thus, MEDLARS was born.

Taine and Rogers selected General Electric to design and implement MEDLARS. It required 30 man-years of programming effort to work out the best design for the system.[13] But the effort certainly paid off. MEDLARS, which began operation in January 1964, enabled users to search the library's vast data base much more quickly and comprehensively than before. The MEDLARS data base also provided the source data for more than two dozen publications such as *Index to Dental Literature* and *International Nursing*. In addition, it improved the currency of *Index Medicus*, which was being published again after a hiatus of several years. In 1960, *Current List of Medical Literature* was changed to *Index Medicus*. This title switch was accomplished when the AMA discontinued the *Quarterly Cumulative Index Medicus*. GRACE, for *GR*aphic *A*rts *C*omposing *E*quipment, was a high-speed printer specifically designed for the MEDLARS system by Photon Incorporated. In its day, GRACE was the world's fastest photocomposer—operating at a speed of 3,600 words per minute. As I mentioned in a previous essay,[6] GRACE laid the groundwork for much of the photocomposition in use today.

To permit greater access to its vast store of data, Adams recommended that MEDLARS be decentralized as soon as possible.[2] To accomplish this, the NLM created a network of MEDLARS centers throughout the US. Each center had its own copy of the MEDLARS tapes and could provide literature searches to local requesters. The NLM also helped establish MEDLARS centers in Canada, France, Federal Republic of Germany, Japan, Sweden, the UK, and at the World Health Organization in Geneva.[18]

By any reasonable measure, the MEDLARS project was successful. But in Rogers's view, MEDLARS was not his most significant accomplishment at the NLM.[3] Rogers feels that passage of the National Library of Medicine Act in 1956 was even more important. As a result of this bill, sponsored by then Senators Lister Hill and John F. Kennedy, the Armed Forces Medical Library became the NLM. According to Naomi C. Broering, Georgetown University Medical Center, the library was then authorized to function as the nation's primary collector and distributor of medical information.[19] The bill also bolstered the library's management by adding a knowledgeable and supportive board of regents.[5] And finally, the passage of the bill paved the way for the construction of the new NLM building in Bethesda, Maryland.

It's hard to exaggerate the importance of the new building. The previous building was obsolete and crowded within 30 years after its construction in 1887. During rainy weather it leaked, when temperatures dropped it became uncomfortably cold, and it was infested with birds and rodents.[5] Although as far back as 1920 the library had been promised a new building, construction was delayed time and again for lack of funds. But thanks to the National Library of Medicine Act, a new building was finally completed in 1962.

While at the NLM, Rogers also became an authority on Billings, who had been director of the AML's predecessor—the Library of the Surgeon General's Office—from 1865 to 1895. Rogers greatly admired Billings, who is widely credited for his efforts in organizing and developing the library that Rogers came to direct. In what he described as a "labor of love," Rogers compiled Billings's works in his 1965 book, *Selected Papers of John Shaw Billings*.[20] Heretofore, the papers had been widely scattered and nearly inaccessible to researchers.

Rogers also began a long professional relationship with Adams, whose career I discussed in a recent essay.[11] He first met Adams in 1948. At the time, Adams was filling in for the civilian head of the AML, which gave him the awkward title, Acting the Librarian. Although Adams left the AML in 1950 to become librarian of the National Institutes of Health, he returned in 1960 to work as deputy director under Rogers. Rogers and Adams collaborated on a number of projects. Perhaps the most significant was the *Guide to Russian Medical Literature*.[21] Rogers had great respect for Adams's talent as a librarian and writer. Recently, he wrote a moving obituary of Adams for the *Bulletin of the Medical Library Association*.[22]

Rogers's next career move came in 1963. In need of a change after 14 years at the helm,[23] he left the NLM to become librarian of the Denison Memorial Library, University of Colorado Medical Center. He continued in that position through 1974. When Rogers became librarian, there was little organizational structure to the institution. No one knew to whom they reported, there were no reference services of any kind, and the collection was small. At the end of his tenure there was a full-fledged reference section, a clear hierarchical staff order, and a respectable collection. Moreover, in 1965, the NLM awarded a contract to the University of Colorado to operate a MEDLARS search center.[24] This was the first operational peripheral MEDLARS center.

Never afraid to "get his hands dirty," Rogers was also heavily involved in the day-to-day operations of the library. For example, he revised the library's subject catalog to conform to the annual revisions in MeSH. In a 1968 paper, Rogers described the amount of work involved in making the changes. "[The project] required 240 man-hours, or six weeks," he wrote. "While I happen to find this kind of task congenial, I do begrudge the long hours involved."[25]

On occasion, Rogers also performed searches for MEDLARS users. In his 1974 paper, "Computerized bibliographic retrieval services,"[26] Rogers offers illuminating insights into "a day in the life of a search analyst." His clients that day included medical students, local physicians, and a graduate nursing student. While some of the search requests were specific, others were so broadly defined that much of his time had to be spent in question negotiation and in developing search strategies. During that typical day, he spent "only" 142 minutes actually at the terminal.

Throughout the years many organizations, apart from his employers, have tapped Rogers's expertise. From 1958 to 1961, he served as chairman of the Joint Committee on the Union List of Serials. In 1962, he was elected president of the MLA. Rogers has also served as chairman of the Library Technology Project Advisory Committee and as president of the American Association for the History of Medicine.

Rogers's many achievements have not gone unheralded. Besides the Information Advancement Award mentioned earlier, in 1961 he received the Marcia C. Noyes award from the MLA "for outstanding achievement in medical librarianship." In 1963, he received the Melvil Dewey Award of the ALA "for creative professional achievement." In 1964, he received the UK's Barnard Memorial Prize "for distinguished services to medical librarianship."

Although formally retired, Rogers is still an active contributor to his field. He is a member of the mid-continental chapter of the MLA and the Colorado Council of Medical Librarians. He has been working on some biographical sketches for the new edition of the *American Medical Biography*, and is preparing a short biography of Adams to be published in the *Encyclopedia of Library and Information Science*. But he spends most of his time these days repairing damaged medical books. This is a complex procedure that basically involves taking the book apart by separating it into its component sections, mending the torn pages, resewing, and then rebinding. Rogers has also attended many seminars on the craft of conservation bookbinding, and was taught by a professional bookbinder. He has repaired books for the Denver Botanical Garden, Denver Medical Society, Albany Medical College, and many other organizations. He has also restored at least one cookbook for his wife, Barbara.

It is characteristic of his unabated curiosity that Rogers has joined the personal computer generation and is now quite *au courant* with the abilities of the microcomputer. When I first demonstrated the *ISI/BIOMED®* system to him I felt as though we were transported back to those days 30 years ago in Baltimore when I first showed him what we had done with our primitive punched-card system. A lot has changed since those days but we still have a long way to go. As another one of my heroes, Vannevar Bush, once said, "Research is an endless frontier."

Recently, when discussing his admiration for Billings, Rogers noted that medical librarianship, like any field, needs heroes.[3] Unless one recounts the incredible accomplishments of a figure like Billings,[20] it is impossible to appreciate the implications of the assertion that Rogers more than amply lived up to the precedent established by Billings, a giant in the history of medicine and medical bibliography.[27] In addition to bringing the NLM into the computer age, Rogers authored numerous papers on various topics in medical librarianship, a selection of which appears in the references to this essay.[28-46]

Brad Rogers has remained one of my heroes. In spite of many differences of opinion, I was delighted that the MLA chose to honor him in a unique and permanent fashion.

* * * * *

My thanks to Brad Schepp and Amy Stone for their help in the preparation of this essay.

©1984 ISI

REFERENCES

1. **Garfield E.** The new ISI fellowships honor outstanding librarians and graduate students in the library and information sciences. *Current Contents* (11):5-10, 14 March 1983.
2. **Miles W D.** *A history of the National Library of Medicine: the nation's treasury of medical knowledge.* Bethesda, MD: National Library of Medicine, 1982. 531 p.
3. **Rogers F B.** Telephone communication. 14 October 1983.
4. **Brodman E, MacDonald M R & Rogers F B.** The National Medical Library: the survey and ten years' progress. *Bull. Med. Libr. Assn.* 42:439-46, 1954.
5. **Doe J.** The survey and after. *Bull. Med. Libr. Assn.* 49:361-8, 1961.
6. **Garfield E.** Some reflections on *Index Medicus. Essays of an information scientist.* Philadelphia: ISI Press, 1981. Vol. 4. p. 341-7. (Reprinted from: *Current Contents* (51):5-11, 17 December 1979.)
7. ⸺⸺⸺⸺⸺. To remember Chauncey D. Leake. *Essays of an information scientist.* Philadelphia: ISI Press, 1980. Vol. 3. p. 411-21. (Reprinted from: *Current Contents* (7):5-15, 13 February 1978.)
8. **Larkey S V.** The Welch Medical Library Indexing Project. *Bull. Med. Libr. Assn.* 41:32-40, 1953.
9. **Garfield E.** Introducing Samuel Lazerow, ISI's vice president for administration. *Essays of an information scientist.* Philadelphia: ISI Press, 1977. Vol. 1. p. 374-5. (Reprinted from: *Current Contents* (44):5-6, 1 November 1972.)
10. **Rogers F B & Adams S.** The Army Medical Library's publication program. *Tex. Rep. Biol. Med.* 8:271-300, 1950.

11. **Garfield E.** Scott Adams and *Medical bibliography in an age of discontinuity*—a tribute to a visionary leader in the field of medical information. *Current Contents* (26):5-11, 27 June 1983.
12. ---------------. To remember my brother, Robert L. Hayne. *Essays of an information scientist.* Philadelphia: ISI Press, 1980. Vol. 3. p. 213-4.
    (Reprinted from: *Current Contents* (34):5-6, 22 August 1977.)
13. **Rogers F B.** The origins of MEDLARS. (Stevenson L G, ed.) *A celebration of medical history.* Baltimore, MD: Johns Hopkins University Press, 1982. p. 77-84.
14. **Garfield E.** The preparation of printed indexes by automatic punched-card techniques. *Amer. Doc.* 6:68-76, 1955.
15. **Taine S I,** ed. The National Library of Medicine Index Mechanization Project. (Whole issue.) *Bull. Med. Libr. Assn.* 49(No. 1, Part 2), 1961. 96 p.
16. **Garfield E.** Preliminary report on the mechanical analysis of information by use of the 101 statistical punched-card machine. *Amer. Doc.* 5:7-12, 1954.
17. **Taine S I.** The Medical Literature Analysis and Retrieval System. *Bull. Med. Libr. Assn.* 51:157-67, 1963.
18. **McCarn D B & Leiter J.** On-line services in medicine and beyond. *Science* 181:318-24, 1973.
19. **Broering N C.** Medical libraries: laws and legislation. (Wedgeworth R, ed.) *ALA world encyclopedia of library and information services.* Chicago, IL: American Library Association, 1980. p. 352.
20. **Rogers F B,** ed. *Selected papers of John Shaw Billings.* Baltimore, MD: Medical Library Association, 1965. 300 p.
21. **Adams S & Rogers F B,** eds. *Guide to Russian medical literature.* Washington, DC: National Library of Medicine, 1958. 90 p.
22. **Rogers F B.** Obituaries: Scott Adams. *Bull. Med. Libr. Assn.* 71:245-8, 1983.
23. ---------------. Telephone communication. 2 December 1983.
24. ---------------. MEDLARS operating experience at the University of Colorado. *Bull. Med. Libr. Assn.* 54:1-10, 1966.
25. ---------------. Problems of medical subject cataloging. *Bull. Med. Libr. Assn.* 56:355-64, 1968.
26. ---------------. Computerized bibliographic retrieval services. *Libr. Trends* 23:73-88, 1974.
27. **Fulton J F.** *The great medical bibliographers.* Philadelphia: University of Pennsylvania Press, 1951. 107 p.
28. **Rogers F B.** A classification for the Army Medical Library. *Bull. Med. Libr. Assn.* 37:125-30, 1949.
29. ---------------. Cataloging and classification at the Army Medical Library. *Bull. Med. Libr. Assn.* 39:28-33, 1951.
30. ---------------. Report from the Army Medical Library. *Bull. Med. Libr. Assn.* 39:290-4, 1951.
31. ---------------. The National Medical Library. *Bull. Med. Libr. Assn.* 40:431-3, 1952.
32. ---------------. Application and limitations of subject headings: the pure and applied sciences. (Tauber M F, ed.) *The subject analysis of library materials.* New York: Columbia University School of Library Service, 1953. p. 73-82.
33. ---------------. Classification in the Armed Forces Medical Library. *Libri* 3:114-8, 1954.
34. ---------------. The Armed Forces Medical Library and medical education. *J. Med. Educ.* 30:529-32, 1955.
35. ---------------. Management improvement in the library. *Bull. Med. Libr. Assn.* 45:404-9, 1957.
36. **Schullian D M & Rogers F B.** The National Library of Medicine. I & II. *Libr. Quart.* 28:1-17; 95-121, 1958.
37. **Rogers F B & Charen T.** Abbreviations for medical journal titles. *Bull. Med. Libr. Assn.* 50:311-52, 1962.
38. **Rogers F B.** Stresses in current medical bibliography. *N. Engl. J. Med.* 267:704-8, 1962.
39. ---------------. John Shaw Billings: 1838-1913. *Libr. J.* 88:2622-4, 1963.
40. ---------------. The development of MEDLARS. *Bull. Med. Libr. Assn.* 52:150-1, 1964.
41. ---------------. The relation of library catalogs to abstracting and indexing services. *Libr. Quart.* 34:106-12, 1964.
42. ---------------. MEDLARS operating experience: addendum. *Bull. Med. Libr. Assn.* 54:316-20, 1966.
43. ---------------. Costs of operating an information retrieval service. *Drexel Libr. Quart.* 4:271-8, 1968.
44. ---------------. The rise and decline of the altitude therapy of tuberculosis. *Bull. Hist. Med.* 43:1-16, 1969.
45. ---------------. Billings, John Shaw. (Wedgeworth R, ed.) *ALA world encyclopedia of library and information services.* Chicago, IL: American Library Association, 1980. p. 87-9.
46. **Schullian D M & Rogers F B.** "Index Medicus" in the twentieth century. (Blake J B, ed.) *Centenary of Index Medicus.* Bethesda, MD: National Library of Medicine, 1980. p. 53-61.

Current Comments®

The 1982 Nobel Prize in Chemistry Goes to Structural Biologist Aaron Klug

Number 3   January 16, 1984

The 1982 Nobel prize in chemistry was awarded to Aaron Klug, Medical Research Council's (MRC) Laboratory of Molecular Biology, Cambridge, England. The purpose of this essay is to examine the impact of his research, with particular emphasis on citation analysis. We have examined each crop of annual Nobel prizes awarded since 1979.[1-3] Beginning with the 1982 awards, however, we have modified our discussion by including data based on the research fronts we identify each year for *Science Citation Index®* (*SCI®*). As will be seen here, this data bank is increasingly becoming a major tool for historical, retrospective, and prospective analyses of science and scholarship.

Briefly, a research front is a group of current papers that cite a cluster of older "core" papers in a specialty. Co-citation clustering procedures have been described in previous essays.[4] While the discussion that follows is not the typical *minireview* we produced for our prototype *Atlas of Science: Biochemistry & Molecular Biology, 1978/80*,[5] it does provide a more in-depth look at the core work involved than past Nobel essays. So we are covering the 1982 awards in four separate essays.

The first essay examined the 1982 Nobel prize in physics, awarded to Kenneth G. Wilson.[6] Future essays will cover the prizes in physiology or medicine, economics, and literature. Incidentally, the 1983 Nobel prize in chemistry was awarded to Henry Taube, Stanford University, California, for his work on electron transfer reactions in metal complexes.[7] This work now forms the basis of modern inorganic chemistry. Taube was among the 1,000 most-cited contemporary scientists we identified by examining *SCI* for the period 1965-1978.[8] His work will also be covered in a future essay.

A few cautionary notes concerning our Nobel studies are in order. These studies, as well as certain earlier papers,[9] have led some people to believe or assert that citation analysis can be used to *predict* Nobel prizewinners. This is, of course, an exaggeration. However, research front data are helpful in *forecasting* which *fields* may eventually be acknowledged with a Nobel prize. And citation analysis will certainly identify the individuals in those fields who are *of Nobel class*. It is characteristic of Nobel-quality work that it is generally highly cited over considerable periods of time. But to "predict" which individual will win a specific prize in a specific year is pure guesswork. One would have to be privy to confidential information concerning nominations, and the fields under consideration by the Nobel committees, to intelligently guess the outcome.

Klug received the 1982 chemistry prize "for his development of crystallographic electron microscopy, and his structural elucidation of biologically important nucleic acid-protein complexes."[10] The award citation thus takes note of the three major accomplishments of Klug's 25-year scientific career: his image reconstruction techniques for the electron microscope, his elucidation of the structure of numerous viruses, and his detailed analysis of the subunits of chromosomes.

Klug originally began his career in physics, which he still teaches at the undergraduate level at Peterhouse College, Cambridge.[11] In fact, his doctoral dissertation concerned phase transitions in solids—the same general field for which Wilson won his Nobel prize in 1982.[6] But Klug soon became interested in the structure of living matter—particularly in the study of macromolecular assemblies, which are the complex structures formed by interacting proteins and nucleic acids.[12] He became, in fact, a pioneer in structural molecular biology[13] by embarking on the X-ray diffraction analysis of complex viruses.[10] When the diffraction techniques of the day proved too indirect to produce a usable image, however, Klug turned to the electron microscope.

The conventional electron microscope is a direct analogue of an optical microscope, using a beam of electrons in place of light and an electric or magnetic field in place of lenses.[14] Since the wavelength of electrons is so much less than that of light, the resolving power of the electron microscope—that is, its ability to form images of very small objects—is hundreds of times that of an optical microscope.

Klug entered the field in its infancy, when electron micrographic images of organic molecules consisted merely of faint, coarse outlines,[10] due to the relatively large size of biological molecules and the low scattering power of organic nuclei.[15] Indeed, the relationship between the electron micrographic image and the reality of the target was not well understood. For one thing, the image was a two-dimensional projection of a three-dimensional object. The target's front and back sides were thus superimposed on one another, considerably confusing the interpretation of the image. So image interpretation was largely a subjective matter.

Klug overcame these inherent difficulties, however, by combining electron microscopy with some of the basic principles of X-ray diffraction. He also pioneered the use of densitometers and computers to manipulate electron micrographic images, making their interpretation quantitative and precise. Klug's combination of electron microscopy and X-ray diffraction, incidentally, established a new science, called Fourier microscopy—or crystallographic electron microscopy, as it is now more generally known.[10]

The extensive usefulness of Klug's optical and image processing techniques in numerous important applications cannot be overemphasized. An indication of the utility of Klug's work is provided by a 1971 paper he wrote with H.P. Erickson, MRC, entitled "Measurement and compensation of defocusing and aberrations by Fourier processing of electron micrographs."[16] The paper described a method of analyzing the structure of a target in an electron micrograph that has been enhanced in various ways. Klug regarded the paper as little more than an academic exercise.[17] Yet the method described in the paper formed the foundation of a 1975 paper by two other MRC workers, R. Henderson and P.N.T. Unwin.[18] Applying Klug's principles, Henderson and Unwin obtained a three-dimensional map of a specialized part of the cell membrane of *Halobacterium halobium* at a resolution of seven angstroms. As of 1983, this paper had been cited almost 600 times since its publication.

Klug developed his new image processing techniques over a period of ten years, during his early studies on the tobacco mosaic virus (TMV) and other biological assemblies. These approaches were accompanied by improved X-ray diffraction techniques, capable of tackling the very large biological molecules under study. One of the primary targets of Klug's new techniques was TMV, which attacks the leaves of tobacco and other plants and is the most widely studied of all known viruses. TMV consists of a spiral of RNA encased in a helical array of protein units—"arranged rather like corn-on-the-cob," according to Klug.[19] He discovered that the growth of the virus is initiated with the binding or attachment of a specific sequence of the viral RNA to a protein disk. And in perhaps one of his best-known accomplishments, Klug and colleagues determined the structure of those flat, doughnut-shaped protein disks to a resolution of better than three angstroms.[20] At the same time, they obtained a detailed atomic model.

Klug went on to analyze the general structures of a number of other viruses as well, including those that cause polio and warts in humans. Such viruses appear as fuzzy spheres in conventional electron micrographs. But using the techniques of image analysis, Klug was able to show that the protein shells encasing the nucleic acid component of all spherically shaped viruses were based on the symmetry of the icosahedron, a 20-sided regular polygon.[21] Viruses with such uniformly geometric protein shells are known as "regular" viruses.

Klug's intensive work with the structure and functional organization of the TMV RNA-protein complex led him to apply his image reconstruction techniques to a DNA-protein complex as well—specifically, to chromatin, chromosomal material after it has been extracted from a living cell.[12] Chromatin consists mainly of DNA and histones, as well as some RNA and other proteins. Histones are the proteins that make up nucleosomes, the chromosomal subunits that form the "scaffolding" about which the DNA double helix is wound into a further helix, called the superhelix. Indeed, these scaffolds are made up of precise aggregates of the histones, as dis-

covered by Klug's colleague Roger D. Kornberg, Stanford University.[22]

Nucleosomes are believed to be the smallest building blocks of chromosomes.[21] As such, Klug's elucidation of their structure and function has provided clues to the problem of gene expression, according to the Royal Swedish Academy.[23] The academy noted further that Klug's work will "undoubtedly be of crucial importance" for an understanding of how the genetic mechanisms of a cell malfunction and turn the cell cancerous. Changes in the structure of the chromatin may herald the metamorphosis of a normal cell into a cancerous cell.[24] Indeed, Klug's work has provided the basis for research into how DNA is incorporated into the chromosomes.

Klug's work, collectively, has been explicitly cited over 8,100 times since 1955. Not surprisingly, Klug is among the 1,000 most-cited authors.[8] His most-cited paper, "Physical principles in the construction of regular viruses"[25] (640 citations as of 1983), coauthored in 1962 with D.L.D. Caspar, Brandeis University, Waltham, Massachusetts, is a *Citation Classic* ™ by any reasonable standard. The paper reviews the structure and functional organization of regular viruses. It also discusses the use of X-ray diffraction and electron microscopy to elucidate how these viruses, including TMV, assemble themselves. The paper built on the results reported in an earlier review article they wrote entitled "The structure of small viruses"[26] (209 citations as of 1983).

As noted previously, Klug's early work on X-ray diffraction fueled his interest in optics, since both involved fundamental problems in image processing and interpretation. Indeed, these interests were mutually reinforcing, as evidenced by another early paper, coauthored by Klug, H.W. Wyckoff, Yale University, and Francis Crick, then at MRC and currently affiliated with the Salk Institute, La Jolla, California. (Crick shared the Nobel prize in physiology or medicine in 1962 with J.D. Watson and M.H.F. Wilkins.) "Diffraction by helical structures"[27] (202 citations as of 1983) reports a method for elucidating the structure of molecules such as RNA, and discusses how the method might be employed to solve the structure of the TMV helix.

A later paper, "An optical method for the analysis of periodicities in electron micrographs, and some observations on the mechanism of negative staining"[28] (215 citations as of 1983), by Klug and J.E. Berger, then at MRC and currently of the Roswell Park Memorial Hospital, Buffalo, New York, proposed a new method for analyzing image detail in electron micrographs of objects with regularly repeating features. It also included an interpretation of negative staining techniques in electron microscopy. These result in the formation of a light image against a dark background. Another paper, "Reconstruction of three-dimensional structures from electron micrographs"[29] (281 citations as of 1983), by Klug and D.J. DeRosier, Brandeis University, formulates general principles for the objective reconstruction of a three-dimensional object from a set of two-dimensional electron micrographic images. The paper applies the procedure to the calculation of a density map of the tail of bacteriophage $T4$, a type of virus which infects such bacteria as *Escherichia coli*. And in 1974, using classical imaging techniques, Klug and a number of MRC colleagues delineated the molecular "Structure of yeast phenylalanine tRNA at 3 Å resolution"[30] (294 citations as of 1983).

The explanation of the form and function of nucleosomes, now widely accepted, is reported in a series of highly cited articles published by Klug and a number of MRC colleagues between 1975 and 1979. The earliest of these was coauthored with Crick, and entitled "Kinky helix"[31] (198 citations as of 1983). It proposes that the superhelix of the DNA

formed by the chromatin might arise by regularly placed kinks in the chain of its cross-linked purine and pyrimidine base pairs—as opposed to the gradual, uniform bend which had previously been assumed to be the case.

In two early papers, Klug and several collaborators showed how nucleosomes are joined together to form higher-order structures of chromatin. The first, published in 1976 by Klug and J.T. Finch, an MRC colleague, described the nature of chromatin and was entitled "Solenoidal model for superstructure in chromatin"[32] (440 citations as of 1983). The second paper, "Structure of nucleosome core particles of chromatin"[33] (341 citations as of 1983), was published the following year and written by Klug in collaboration with numerous MRC colleagues, including Finch. It was among the most-cited 1977 life sciences papers we identified in a study covering from 1977 to 1979.[34] A later paper, "Involvement of histone H1 in the organization of the nucleosome and of the salt-dependent superstructures of chromatin"[35] (244 citations as of 1983), coauthored with F. Thoma and T. Koller, Institut für Zellbiologie, Eidgenössische Technische Höchschule, Zurich, Switzerland, greatly extended these results.

Figure 1 is a flowchart, or microhistory, of the field of nucleoproteins. It shows many research fronts we identified—a number of which included some of Klug's most influential papers on chromatin and nucleosomes. Each box represents a research front. Both the title of the front and the number of core articles on which each one is based is indicated, as well as the number of citing, current papers.

These research fronts are strung together by determining the "continuity" of the core literature from year to year.[36] For example, the paper on the kinky helix,[31] by Klug and Crick, is part of the core literature which helped identify the 1977 research front, "Chromatin struc-

Figure 1: Cluster string for the field of nucleoproteins. A cluster string enables us to track the evolution of a field backward or forward in time. A string is determined by the continuity a given research front's core literature exhibits from year to year. If any of the core documents of a given research front continue to achieve the required citation and co-citation thresholds for their field in an adjacent year, a cluster string is formed. Research fronts prior to 1977 have been included for historical background. Numbers at the bottom of each box refer to the number of cited/citing documents for each research front. Asterisks (*) indicate research fronts whose core literature includes some of the papers by Klug discussed in this essay. (Source of data: 1973-1978 *SCI®*; 1979-1982 *ISI/BIOMED®*.)

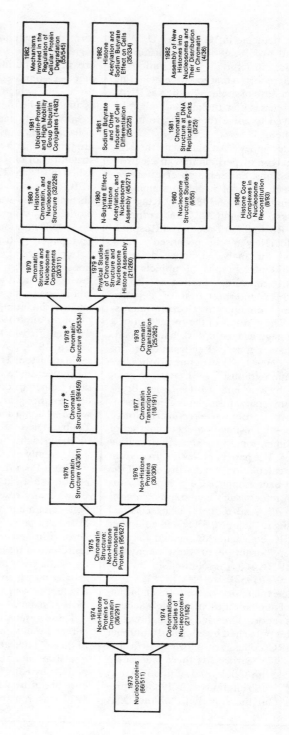

Figure 2: Multidimensional scaling map showing links between core papers of the 1980 *ISI/BIOMED®* research front #80-0096, "Histone, chromatin, and nucleosome structure." Authors with more than one paper have been marked by a letter. See accompanying key for bibliographic data. The box representing this research front in Figure 1 indicates that there were 32 core papers and 226 citing papers in 1980 alone. For clarity's sake, only 25 core papers were included in the map. The current literature for the research front can be identified on the ISI® *Search Network* by using the research front identification number.

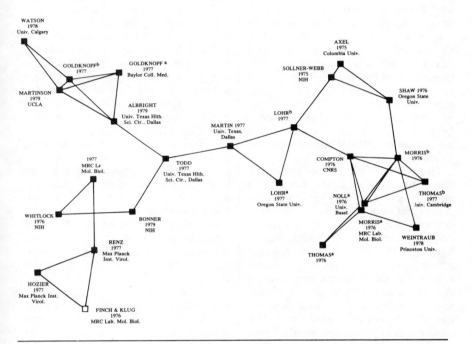

Key

Albright S C, Nelson P P & Garrard W T. *J. Biol. Chem.* 254:1065-73, 1979.
Axel R. *Biochemistry—USA* 14:2921-5, 1975.
Bonner W M & Stedman J D. *Proc. Nat. Acad. Sci. US* 76:2190-4, 1979.
Compton J L, Bellard M & Chambon P. *Proc. Nat. Acad. Sci. US* 73:4382-6, 1976.
Finch J T & Klug A. *Proc. Nat. Acad. Sci. US* 73:1897-901, 1976.
Goldknopf I L[a] & Busch H. *Proc. Nat. Acad. Sci. US* 74:864-8, 1977.
Goldknopf I L[b], French M F, Musso R & Busch H. *Proc. Nat. Acad. Sci. US* 74:5492-5, 1977.
Hozier J, Renz M & Nehls P. *Chromosoma* 62:301-17, 1977.
Lohr D[a], Kovacic R T & Van Holde K E. *Biochemistry—USA* 16:463-71, 1977.
Lohr D[b], Corden J, Tatchell K, Kovacic R T & Van Holde K E. *Proc. Nat. Acad. Sci. US* 74:79-83, 1977.
Martin D Z, Todd R D, Lang D, Pei P N & Garrard W T. *J. Biol. Chem.* 252:8269-77, 1977.
Martinson H G, True R, Burch J B E & Kunkel G. *Proc. Nat. Acad. Sci. US* 76:1030-4, 1979.
Morris N R[a]. *Cell* 8:357-63, 1976.
Morris N R[b]. *Cell* 9:627-32, 1976.
Noll M[a]. *Cell* 8:349-55, 1976. (See reference 46.)
Noll M[b] & Kornberg R D. *J. Mol. Biol.* 109:393-404, 1977. (See reference 48.)
Renz M, Nehls P & Hozier J. *Proc. Nat. Acad. Sci. US* 74:1879-83, 1977.
Shaw B R, Herman T M, Kovacic R T, Beaudreau G S & Van Holde K E. *Proc. Nat. Acad. Sci. US* 73:505-9, 1976.
Sollner-Webb B & Felsenfeld G. *Biochemistry—USA* 14:2915-20, 1975.
Thomas J O[a] & Furber V. *FEBS Lett.* 66:274-80, 1976. (See reference 49.)
Thomas J O[b] & Thompson R J. *Cell* 10:633-40, 1977. (See reference 50.)
Todd R D & Garrard W T. *J. Biol. Chem.* 252:4729-38, 1977.
Watson D C, Levy W B & Dixon G H. *Nature* 276:196-8, 1978.
Weintraub H. *Nucl. Acid. Res.* 5:1179-88, 1978.
Whitlock J P & Simpson R T. *Biochemistry—USA* 15:3307-14, 1976.

ture." Along with dozens of other papers, it continued as a core paper in 1978. In that year, two other Klug papers—"Solenoidal model for superstructure in chromatin,"[32] coauthored with Finch, and "Structure of nucleosome core particles of chromatin,"[33] written with Finch and others—were also core papers. In turn, the solenoidal model paper[32] was "core" to the 1979 research front entitled "Physical studies of chromatin structure and nucleosome histone assembly." It then turns up in the 1980 *ISI/BIOMED®* research front, "Histone, chromatin, and nucleosome structure." This illustrates the continuity phenomenon.

Twenty-five of the 32 core papers for the 1980 research front have been mapped in Figure 2. The seven core papers that were linked by co-citation to only one other core paper each were excluded from the map.[37-43] Incidentally, Klug and Caspar's paper on physical principles in the construction of regular viruses[25] is one of three core papers in the 1982 research front entitled "Structure of virus capsid; coat-protein structure of southern bean mosaic virus." The other two core papers concern the structure of southern bean mosaic virus,[44] by C. Abadzapatero and colleagues, Purdue University, and tomato bushy stunt virus,[45] by S.C. Harrison and colleagues, then of Harvard University, Cambridge, Massachusetts, and MRC.

In his Nobel lecture, given on December 8, 1982, in Stockholm, Klug acknowledged his intellectual indebtedness to numerous other scientists, including coauthors Caspar, DeRosier, Kornberg, and Finch.[12] Three of the coworkers he mentioned are identified in Figure 2: Markus Noll, MRC, Kornberg, and Jean O. Thomas, University of Cambridge, England. A 1976 *Cell* paper by Noll[46] concerned the differences and similarities in the structure of various types of chromatin, and built on the work he presented in an earlier paper in *Nature*.[47] The other core paper in Figure 2 by Noll is a 1977 article coauthored with Kornberg. It concerned the regularity of the structure of chromatin and the location of a particular histone protein.[48] A 1976 paper in *FEBS Letters* by Thomas and Valerie Furber, University of Cambridge, compared the structure of chromatin found in yeast cells with that found in higher organisms.[49] A 1977 paper coauthored by Thomas and R.J. Thompson, Welsh National School of Medicine, Cardiff, Wales, found variation in the structure of the chromatin in two cell types from the same tissue.[50] The cluster map in Figure 2 illustrates the pervasive influence of the Klug group at Cambridge. Space does not permit similar expansions of the core literature for the dozens of other research fronts in which Klug and his colleagues have made lasting impact.

Caspar and DeRosier note that part of Klug's genius lies in his ability to surmount the conceptual barriers that often separate various scientific specialties and disciplines.[10] They also believe that the success of Klug's work may lie to a great extent in his talent for productive collaborations with people who possess abilities complementary to his own. The list of his associates is indeed long and distinguished. But the breadth and depth of Klug's multidisciplinary investigations involving mathematics, physics, chemistry, and biology all bear the unmistakable imprint of his insight and thoroughness. In view of the transcendent importance of the structures of proteins and nucleic acids in so many branches of modern science, and considering the strength of the foundation Klug's work has provided, it seems safe to expect that the field of structural biology has not seen its last Nobel prizewinner in Aaron Klug.

* * * * *

My thanks to Stephen A. Bonaduce and Terri Freedman for their help in the preparation of this essay.   ©1984 ISI

REFERENCES

1. **Garfield E.** Are the 1979 prizewinners *of Nobel class? Essays of an information scientist.*
   Philadelphia: ISI Press, 1981. Vol. 4. p. 609-17.
   (Reprinted from: *Current Contents* (38):5-13, 22 September 1980.)
2. --------------. The 1980 Nobel prizewinners. *Essays of an information scientist.*
   Philadelphia: ISI Press, 1983. Vol. 5. p. 189-201.
   (Reprinted from: *Current Contents* (31):5-17, 3 August 1981.)
3. --------------. Were the 1981 Nobel prizewinners in science, economics, and literature anticipated by
   citation analysis? *Essays of an information scientist.* Philadelphia: ISI Press, 1983.
   Vol. 5. p. 551-61. (Reprinted from: *Current Contents* (23):5-15, 7 June 1982.)
4. --------------. ABCs of cluster mapping. Parts 1 & 2. Most active fields in the life and physical
   sciences in 1978. *Essays of an information scientist.*
   Philadelphia: ISI Press, 1981. Vol. 4. p. 634-49.
   (Reprinted from: *Current Contents* (40):5-12, 6 October 1980 and (41):5-12, 13 October 1980.)
5. --------------. Introducing the *ISI Atlas of Science: Biochemistry and Molecular Biology,*
   1978/80. Essays of an information scientist. Philadelphia: ISI Press, 1983. Vol. 5. p. 279-87.
   (Reprinted from: *Current Contents* (42):5-13, 19 October 1981.)
6. --------------. The 1982 Nobel prize in physics. *Current Contents* (50):5-14, 12 December 1983.
7. **Milgrom L & Anderson I.** Understanding the electron. *New Sci.* 100:253-5, 1983.
8. **Garfield E.** The 1,000 contemporary scientists most-cited 1965-1978. Part I. The basic list and
   introduction. *Essays of an information scientist.* Philadelphia: ISI Press, 1983. Vol. 5. p. 269-78.
   (Reprinted from: *Current Contents* (41):5-14, 12 October 1981.)
9. **Sher I H & Garfield E.** New tools for improving and evaluating the effectiveness of research.
   (Yovits M C, Gilford D M, Wilcox R H, Stavely E & Lerner H D, eds.) *Research program*
   effectiveness. New York: Gordon & Breach, 1966. p. 135-46.
10. **Caspar D L D & DeRosier D J.** The 1982 Nobel prize in chemistry. *Science* 218:653-5, 1982.
11. Magic, matter and money. *Time* 120(18):88-9, 1982.
12. **Klug A.** From macromolecules to biological assemblies. (Nobel lecture.)
    Angew. Chem. Int. Ed. 22:565-636, 1983.
13. ---------. The assembly of tobacco mosaic virus: structure and specificity.
    Harvey Lect. 74:141-72, 1980.
14. **Crewe A V.** Electron microscopy. (Lerner R G & Trigg G L, eds.) *Encyclopedia of physics.*
    Reading, MA: Addison-Wesley, 1981. p. 256-7.
15. **Schwarzschild B M.** Aaron Klug wins Nobel prize in chemistry. *Phys. Today* 36(1):17-9, 1983.
16. **Erickson H P & Klug A.** Measurement and compensation of defocusing and aberrations by Fourier
    processing of electron micrographs. *Phil. Trans. Roy. Soc. London B* 261:105-18, 1971.
17. **Caspar D L D.** Telephone communication. 19 December 1983.
18. **Henderson R & Unwin P N T.** Three-dimensional model of purple membrane obtained by electron
    microscopy. *Nature* 257:28-32, 1975.
19. **Klug A.** Telephone communication. 14 December 1983.
20. **Miller J A & Thomsen D E.** Biological structure, nature of matter are topics of Nobel prizes.
    Sci. News 122:261, 1982.
21. **Schmeck H M.** Chemistry prize goes for research into intimate details of virus structure.
    NY Times 19 October 1982, p. C6.
22. **Kornberg R D.** Chromatin structure: a repeating unit of histones and DNA.
    Science 184:868-71, 1974.
23. A Nobel for developing electron microscopy. *Chem. Week* 131(17):16-7, 1982.
24. U.S., British scientists win Nobels. *Phila. Inquirer* 19 October 1982, p. 4-B.
25. **Caspar D L D & Klug A.** Physical principles in the construction of regular viruses.
    Cold Spring Harbor Symp. 27:1-24, 1962.
26. **Klug A & Caspar D L D.** The structure of small viruses. *Advan. Virus Res.* 7:225-325, 1960.
27. **Klug A, Crick F H C & Wyckoff H W.** Diffraction by helical structures.
    Acta Crystallogr. 11:199-213, 1958.
28. **Klug A & Berger J E.** An optical method for the analysis of periodicities in electron micrographs,
    and some observations on the mechanism of negative staining. *J. Mol. Biol.* 10:565-9, 1964.
29. **DeRosier D J & Klug A.** Reconstruction of three dimensional structures from electron micrographs.
    Nature 217:130-4, 1968.
30. **Robertus J D, Ladner J E, Finch J T, Rhodes D, Brown R S, Clark B F C & Klug A.** Structure of
    yeast phenylalanine tRNA at 3 Å resolution. *Nature* 250:546-51, 1974.
31. **Crick F H C & Klug A.** Kinky helix. *Nature* 255:530-3, 1975.
32. **Finch J T & Klug A.** Solenoidal model for superstructure in chromatin.
    Proc. Nat. Acad. Sci. US 73:1897-901, 1976.

33. **Finch J T, Lutter L C, Rhodes D, Brown R S, Rushton B, Levitt M & Klug A.** Structure of nucleosome core particles of chromatin. *Nature* 269:29-36, 1977.
34. **Garfield E.** The 1977 articles most cited from 1977 to 1979. Part 1. Life sciences. *Essays of an information scientist.* Philadelphia: ISI Press, 1981. Vol. 4. p. 528-41. (Reprinted from: *Current Contents* (29):5-18, 21 July 1980.)
35. **Thoma F, Koller T & Klug A.** Involvement of histone H1 in the organization of the nucleosome and of the salt-dependent superstructures of chromatin. *J. Cell Biol.* 83:403-27, 1979.
36. **Garfield E.** Computer-aided historiography—how ISI uses cluster tracking to monitor the "vital signs" of science. *Essays of an information scientist.* Philadelphia: ISI Press, 1983. Vol. 5. p. 473-83. (Reprinted from: *Current Contents* (14):5-15, 5 April 1982.)
37. **Carpenter B G, Baldwin J P, Bradbury E M & Ibel K.** Organization of subunits in chromatin. *Nucl. Acid. Res.* 3:1739-46, 1976.
38. **Goldstein G, Scheid M, Hammerling U, Schlesinger D H, Niall H D & Boyse E A.** Isolation of a polypeptide that has lymphocyte-differentiating properties and is probably represented universally in living cells. *Proc. Nat. Acad. Sci. US* 72:11-5, 1975.
39. **Kiryanov G I, Manamshjan T A, Polyakov V Y, Fais D & Chentsov J S.** Levels of granular organization of chromatin fibers. *FEBS Lett.* 67:323-7, 1976.
40. **Spadafora C, Bellard M, Compton J L & Chambon P.** DNA repeat lengths in chromatins from sea-urchin sperm and gastrula cells are markedly different. *FEBS Lett.* 69:281-5, 1976.
41. **Stratling W H, Muller U & Zentgraf H.** Higher-order repeat structure of chromatin is built up of globular particles containing 8 nucleosomes. *Exp. Cell Res.* 117:301-11, 1978.
42. **Thoma F & Koller T.** Influence of histone H1 on chromatin structure. *Cell* 12:101-7, 1977.
43. **Varshavsky A J, Bakayev V V & Georgiev G P.** Heterogeneity of chromatin subunits in vitro and location of histone H1. *Nucl. Acid. Res.* 3:477-92, 1976.
44. **Abadzapatero C, Abelmeguid S S, Johnson J E, Leslie A G W, Rayment I J, Rossman M G, Suck D & Tsukihara T.** Structure of southern bean mosaic virus at 2.8 Å resolution. *Nature* 286:33-9, 1980.
45. **Harrison S C, Olson A J, Schutt C E, Winkler F K & Bricogne G.** Tomato bushy stunt virus at 2.9 Å resolution. *Nature* 276:368-73, 1978.
46. **Noll M.** Differences and similarities in chromatin structure of Neurospora crassa and higher eucaryotes. *Cell* 8:349-55, 1976.
47. ---------. Subunit structure of chromatin. *Nature* 251:249-51, 1974.
48. **Noll M & Kornberg R D.** Action of micrococcal nuclease on chromatin and the location of histone H1. *J. Mol. Biol.* 109:393-404, 1977.
49. **Thomas J O & Furber V.** Yeast chromatin structure. *FEBS Lett.* 66:274-80, 1976.
50. **Thomas J O & Thompson R J.** Variation in chromatin structure in two cell types from the same tissue: a short DNA repeat length in cerebral cortex neurons. *Cell* 10:633-40, 1977.

Current Comments®

The ASIS Outstanding Information Science Teacher Award for 1983: Ching-chih Chen Wins the Fourth Award

Number 4   January 23, 1984

Last October, at its forty-sixth annual meeting, the American Society for Information Science (ASIS) presented the 1983 Outstanding Information Science Teacher Award to Ching-chih Chen. She is professor and associate dean of the Graduate School of Library and Information Science at Simmons College, Boston, Massachusetts. ISI® sponsors the award, donates the $500 honorarium, and also covers the administrative costs. However, neither I nor anyone else at ISI was consulted on Chen's selection.

Information science is still a young field, and its intellectual boundaries are not sharply defined.[1] The next generation of information professionals will play a crucial role in shaping the field. Thus, today's teachers will have great influence in developing future information scientists and technologists.

In 1979, ISI proposed to ASIS the establishment of an award which would honor excellence in teaching rather than research. The following year, F. Wilfrid Lancaster, University of Illinois, was named the first winner of the new award.[2] Pauline Atherton Cochrane, Syracuse University, New York, received the award in 1981.[3] The 1982 winner was Belver C. Griffith, Drexel University, Philadelphia.[4] This past year, the ASIS Education Committee named Chen.

The award certificate presented to Chen honors her "for her dedication and deep commitment to education and training in library and information science through her teaching, publications, research and professional involvement, for her enthusiastic ability to inspire, challenge and generate excitement among her students, and for her leadership in the international information arena."

A native of China, Chen received a bachelor's degree from the National Taiwan University, which presented her with the Distinguished Alumnus Award in June 1983. In 1961, she obtained an MA in library science from the University of Michigan. She received a Distinguished Alumnus Award from that institution in March 1981. After earning her MA, Chen held positions in the University of Michigan library. She also worked at the public library in Windsor, the McMaster University library in Hamilton, and the University of Waterloo library—all three in Ontario, Canada. This was followed by a position at the Massachusetts Institute of Technology (MIT) Science Library, Cambridge, Massachusetts. In 1971, Chen joined the Simmons faculty as an assistant professor. While at Simmons, she continued work on a PhD in library and information science. In 1974, she received her PhD from Case Western Reserve University. In 1979, she was named professor and associate dean at Simmons.

In teaching her courses, Chen uses a balance of theory and practice. However, whenever appropriate, she stresses theory over practice. She believes that this produces more versatile information professionals, who are able to adapt

Ching-chih Chen

their knowledge to different circumstances.[5] Among those who nominated Chen for the ASIS award were a number of her former students, who testified to her energetic, enthusiastic, and knowledgeable delivery of lessons and her deep devotion to her students.

Frances Berger, assistant to the dean at Simmons's Graduate School of Library and Information Science, told the ASIS Education Committee, at registration time, "[Chen's] courses are filled within a few days...with long waiting lists for each course."[6] Willie Hardin, Chen's former doctoral student and now associate librarian at the University of Central Arkansas, Conway, asserts: "No matter how busy Chen was doing research or writing, she was always able to apply her extraordinary talent and time with her doctoral students."[7]

Chen's teaching experience has not been limited to the US. She has conducted seminars and special training courses in information management and technology in various parts of the world such as China, India, Israel, Mexico, and Taiwan. In 1979, Chen was invited to deliver a series of lectures in the People's Republic of China. Her experience prompted her to write on the state of information science there.[8,9] Since then, she has traveled frequently to China in different capacities. These included trips as a consultant to the World Health Organization (WHO).

Chen's dedication to teaching has not prevented her from doing active research. She is also a prolific author. In a recent study by Robert M. Hayes, Graduate School of Library and Information Science, University of California, Los Angeles, of the most-cited ten percent of 411 tenured library and information science faculty, Chen ranked fourth. Using *Social Sciences Citation Index®* (*SSCI®*), Hayes derived the ranking from a "normalized" frequency of citations to substantive articles.[10] This study is an important addition to the literature on faculty evaluation, recently reviewed in *Current Contents®* (*CC®*).[11,12]

Among Chen's earliest papers is a 1972 study of the use patterns of physics journals at the MIT Science Library.[13] In this study, Chen observed which physics journals were left lying on study tables and trucks in the library over a period of time. From her observations, she concluded that a core of 49 journals supplied 90 percent of the user needs. With 47 citations in *SSCI* and *Science Citation Index®* (*SCI®*), this paper ranks among the three or four most-cited articles published in the *Journal of the American Society for Information Science*. Chen's results, by the way, demonstrate once again the pervasiveness of the Bradford distribution.[14]

Another early Chen project focused on book reviews published in scientific journals. Librarians depend on these book reviews to help them make acquisitions decisions. Chen evaluated the quality and timeliness of book reviews published in issues of biomedical, scientific, and technical journals in the early 1970s. Results of this study formed the basis of her book *Biomedical, Scientific & Technical Book Reviewing*.[15] In fact, this work was well known to us when we started the *Index to Book Reviews in the Sciences* .[16] However, there is a great gap in the perceived needs of librarians and the ability of existing book review mechanisms to satisfy these needs. We subsequently had to abandon this service.[17]

The time lag between publication of a book and appearance of a review was the biggest problem Chen found. She noted that the value of a book review is inversely proportional to the length of that time lag. According to Chen, chemistry periodicals appeared to be the most prompt, with nearly 75 percent of the reviews appearing within a year.[15] (p. 76) But Chen asserts that for book reviews to be truly useful to librarians, the time lag should be just three or four months. Although Chen has not updated her findings, she recently stated that the situation in scientific book reviewing is probably no better today.[5]

Chen also performed two major, multiyear research projects with sourcebooks on subject literature that led to the publication of reference books by MIT Press—*Scientific and Technical Information Sources*[18] and *Health Sciences Information Sources*.[19] Listings in both volumes, which consist of annotated bibliographic information and sources for reviews of the books, are grouped by type of sourcebook—abstract, dictionary, encyclopedia, etc.—and then by subject.

A more recent investigation by Chen was designed to help determine what role libraries should play in today's changing information environment. Together with Peter Hernon, a former faculty member at Simmons, Chen surveyed the information needs of the general public in the Boston area. The results of this study, which was funded by the US Department of Education, were published in the book *Information Seeking*.[20] Commenting on this work, Chen noted that libraries are just one part of a society's total information system. In a pluralistic society, private as well as governmental agencies are providers of information. According to Chen, in truly effective information systems, all relevant information providers work in concert to satisfy the needs of consumers. We can expect that, one day, combinations of these providers will be integrated into formal networks.[5]

Currently, Chen is researching the use of video disks for information storage and processing. The National Endowment for the Humanities has awarded Chen a planning grant for Project Emperor I. The project will use video disk technology to present and interpret information about the archaeological dig at the tomb of Ching Shih Huang Ti—the first emperor of a united China.[5]

In addition to teaching and research, Chen has authored or edited a dozen books, several of which have been mentioned here. Her first book, *Applications of Operations Research Models to Libraries*,[21] shows librarians how to apply analytical methods to assist them in effective management. This book was first runner-up for the ASIS Best Information Science Book in 1977. She edited *Quantitative Measurement and Dynamic Library Service*,[22] in which 18 papers by 23 authors explain the application of statistical techniques to library management. In 1980, she authored *Zero-Base Budgeting in Library Management*.[23] This method of budgeting requires that a detailed justification for every item be provided for each new year. Zero-base budgeting is widely used in business, especially in lean years, because it forces managers to reevaluate their objectives and costs for each operation.

More recently, Chen and Susanna Schweizer, Simmons College, wrote a do-it-yourself manual for noninformation professionals who want to perform online searches.[24] She coedited with Stacey E. Bressler, currently with Apple Computers, Inc., *Microcomputers in Libraries*.[25] The book describes the fundamentals of microcomputers and the hardware and software available for library use. She also coedited with Hernon *Numeric Databases*,[26] which explains how data bases featuring statistics, tables, and other data can be useful to librarians. Chen is the editor of a monographic series, *Applications in Information Management and Technology in Libraries* published by Neal-Schuman Publishers. She serves as editor in chief of a new quarterly international journal, *Microcomputers for Information Management*, to be published by Ablex Publishing Corp. beginning in March 1984.

Chen is active in numerous professional organizations. Currently she is the director of the board of ASIS, councillor-at-large of the American Library Association, and chairs the Program Planning Committee of the American Association for Library and Information Science Education (ALISE). She is the past president of the New England chapter of ASIS, and chaired the Statistics and Survey Committee of the Medical Library Association. Chen is an active consultant in the US and abroad. She has worked with the Southeast Asia and Western Pacific regions of WHO, Engineering Information, Inc., Abt Associates, the National Library of Medicine, and Berkshire Community College.

The ASIS Outstanding Information Science Teacher Award is but one of several awards that ISI sponsors. With Annual Reviews, Inc., we cosponsor the National Academy of Sciences (NAS) Award for Excellence in Scientific Reviewing.[27] The Society for Social Studies of Science presents the ISI-sponsored John Desmond Bernal Prize for an outstanding scholarly achievement in the social studies of science.[28] And the Medical Library Association presents the ISI-sponsored Frank Bradway Rogers Information Advancement Award.[29]

In memory of Sam Lazerow, ISI's late senior vice president of administration, we initiated a fellowship and a series of lectureships.[30] The Samuel Lazerow Fellowship for Outstanding Contributions to Acquisitions or Technical Services in an Academic or Research Library is given annually. Four Lazerow lectures are presented each year at Drexel, Columbia, and Indiana Universities and the University of Pittsburgh. These universities invite outstanding practitioners to speak to information science students and faculty. Beginning this year, ISI will provide a £600 prize for the Aslib/ISI Award for Innovation in Information Management. ISI has established several fellowships for doctoral students of information science.[30] At the October ASIS meeting, Barbara Rapp, Drexel University, and Carol Tenopir, University of Illinois, Urbana, received such fellowships.

In order to publicize these awards and the importance of the role of librarians and information scientists, we have arranged to run an ad about the awards we sponsor in this issue of *CC*. A similar ad has been published in numerous journals including the *Bulletin of the Medical Library Association, Choice, Chronicle of Higher Education, College and Research Libraries, College and Research Libraries News, Journal of Information Science, Library Journal, Online, RQ, Special Libraries, Who's Who in Special Libraries*, and *Wilson Library Bulletin*.

I urge anyone who wishes to nominate a candidate for the next ASIS Outstanding Information Science Teacher Award to write to: Outstanding Information Science Teacher Award, ASIS, 1010 16th Street, NW, Washington, DC, 20036. We at ISI are gratified by the results of the ASIS Outstanding Information Science Teacher Award. I would like to take this opportunity to personally congratulate Ching-chih Chen. For the benefit of her Chinese colleagues, the following expresses my heartiest congratulations:

给 Ching-chih Chen 道 喜

* * * * *

My thanks to Lillian Spangler and Amy Stone for their help in the preparation of this essay.

REFERENCES

1. **Garfield E.** Information science education—an ivory Tower of Babel?
   Essays of an information scientist. Philadelphia: ISI Press, 1981. Vol. 4. p. 494-502.

2. ------------. The ASIS Outstanding Information Science Teacher Award: F. Wilfrid Lancaster is the first winner. *Essays of an information scientist*. Philadelphia: ISI Press, 1983. Vol. 5. p. 1-3.
3. ------------. The ASIS Outstanding Information Science Teacher Award: Pauline Atherton Cochrane wins the second award. *Essays of an information scientist*. Philadelphia: ISI Press, 1983. Vol. 5. p. 331-4.
4. ------------. The ASIS Outstanding Information Science Teacher Award: Belver C. Griffith wins the third award. *Essays of an information scientist*. Philadelphia: ISI Press, 1983. Vol. 5. p. 774-8.
5. **Chen C.** Telephone communication. 6 December 1983.
6. **Berger F.** Personal communication. 17 November 1983.
7. **Hardin W.** Personal communication. 17 November 1983.
8. **Chen C.** Education and training in information science in the People's Republic of China. *Bull. Amer. Soc. Inform. Sci.* 6(4):16-8, 1980.
9. ----------. Recent developments in library and information science in China. *Bull. Amer. Soc. Inform. Sci.* 6(4):10-1, 1980.
10. **Hayes R M.** Citation statistics as a measure of faculty research productivity. *J. Educ. Libr.* 23:151-72, 1983.
11. **Garfield E.** How to use citation analysis for faculty evaluations, and when is it relevant? Part 1. *Current Contents* (44):5-13, 31 October 1983.
12. ------------. How to use citation analysis for faculty evaluations, and when is it relevant? Part 2. *Current Contents* (45):5-14, 7 November 1983.
13. **Chen C.** The use patterns of physics journals in a large academic research library. *J. Amer. Soc. Inform. Sci.* 23:254-70, 1972.
14. **Garfield E.** Bradford's law and related statistical patterns. *Essays of an information scientist*. Philadelphia: ISI Press, 1981. Vol. 4. p. 476-87.
15. **Chen C.** *Biomedical, scientific & technical book reviewing*. Metuchen, NJ: Scarecrow Press, 1976. 186 p.
16. **Garfield E.** Introducing *Index to Book Reviews in the Sciences*. *Essays of an information scientist*. Philadelphia: ISI Press, 1981. Vol. 4. p. 280-4.
17. ------------. A swan song for *IBRS*. *Essays of an information scientist*. Philadelphia: ISI Press, 1983. Vol. 5. p. 327-30.
18. **Chen C.** *Scientific and technical information sources*. Cambridge, MA: MIT Press, 1977. 519 p.
19. ----------. *Health sciences information sources*. Cambridge, MA: MIT Press, 1981. 767 p.
20. **Chen C & Hernon P.** *Information seeking: assessing and anticipating user needs*. New York: Neal-Schuman, 1982. 205 p.
21. **Chen C.** *Applications of operations research models to libraries*. Cambridge, MA: MIT Press, 1976. 212 p.
22. ----------, ed. *Quantitative measurement and dynamic library service*. Phoenix, AZ: Oryx Press, 1979. 290 p.
23. ----------. *Zero-base budgeting in library management: a manual for librarians*. Phoenix, AZ: Oryx Press, 1980. 293 p.
24. **Chen C & Schweizer S.** *Online bibliographic searching: a learning manual*. New York: Neal-Schuman, 1981. 227 p.
25. **Chen C & Bressler S E,** eds. *Microcomputers in libraries*. New York: Neal-Schuman, 1982. 259 p.
26. **Chen C & Hernon P,** eds. *Numeric databases*. Norwood, NJ: Ablex, 1984. (In press.)
27. **Garfield E.** The NAS James Murray Luck Award for Excellence in Scientific Reviewing: G. Alan Robison receives the first award for his work on cyclic AMP. *Essays of an information scientist*. Philadelphia: ISI Press, 1981. Vol. 4. p. 127-31.
28. ------------. J.D. Bernal—the sage of Cambridge. 4S award memorializes his contributions to the social studies of science. *Essays of an information scientist*. Philadelphia: ISI Press, 1983. Vol. 5. p. 511-23.
29. ------------. Bringing the National Library of Medicine into the computer age: a tribute to Frank Bradway Rogers. *Current Contents* (2):3-9, 9 January 1984.
30. ------------. The new ISI fellowships honor outstanding librarians and graduate students in the library and information sciences. *Current Contents* (11):5-10, 14 March 1983.

Current Comments®

Animal Experimentation—When Do the Ends Justify the Means?

Number 5   January 30, 1984

In 1977, I became involved in the animal experimentation controversy[1] when Nicholas Wade, then a reporter for *Science*, used *Science Citation Index*® data to assess the impact of some research that had been questioned in the press.[2] Antivivisectionists accused a scientist at the American Museum of Natural History of mutilating cats for trivial scientific gain. His experiments involved removing endocrine glands, sectioning nerves, and ablating brain tissues of domestic cats and observing their subsequent sexual behavior. Our own citation analysis showed that the literature reporting that work was reasonably well cited, and therefore had some impact upon the research community.[1] But although citation analysis can help us to evaluate the impact of basic research, it cannot, alas, answer moral or ethical questions, whether on animal experimentation or other issues.

There's no question that experiments with animals have greatly advanced the frontiers of medicine over the years. For example, the discovery of insulin, which has proved so beneficial to diabetics, was accomplished in part through experiments on dogs.[3] Advances in the treatment of pediatric vision disorders resulted from Hubel and Wiesel's experiments with monkeys and cats.[4] A recent paper by Neal E. Miller, Rockefeller University, New York, describes how experiments with animals led to the development of new drugs for the treatment of mental illness.[5] And this listing is by no means exhaustive.

Nevertheless, medical researchers today find their work threatened by an "animal rights" movement, which seeks to curtail the use of animals in research. Some of the observations by animal rightists are outlined by prominent activist Peter Singer in his book, *Animal Liberation*. Singer suggests that most animal experiments are unnecessary.[6] He and other activists assert that animal lab work often replicates already documented experiments, is not innovative enough to merit publication, could be replaced by alternative methods, is performed for trivial purposes, or is inappropriate because the results cannot be translated to humans. Moreover, these activists claim that some experiments and tests are unnecessarily cruel, causing animals great pain and suffering for little scientific gain. They add that facilities used may not be adequate for the proper care of the animals, and that scientists have little regard for the animals they use.[7]

To refute such charges and promote the scientific community's point of view, the National Society for Medical Research (NSMR, 1029 Vermont Avenue, NW, Suite 700, Washington, DC 20005) was founded in 1946.[8] More recently, scientists established the Association for Biomedical Research (ABR, 400-2 Totten Pond Road, Suite 200, Waltham, Massachusetts 02154) in 1979. Both groups promote freedom for researchers to use laboratory animals without excessively restrictive regulations. To this end, they monitor pending legislation concerning laboratory animals in the US, and lobby on behalf of the scientific community's viewpoint. Membership in NSMR consists of research institutions and concerned individuals, while membership in ABR is limited to institutions. More will be said about these organizations later in this essay.

The problem addressed by both sides in the controversy is not trivial. It is difficult to accurately determine how many animals are used in scientific research around the world, but one estimate puts the figure at about 250 million each year.[9] In the US alone, according to the National Institutes of Health (NIH), about 20 million animals per year are acquired by various research institutions for scientific studies. This includes about 18,500,000 rodents, 400,000 rabbits, 240,000 cats and dogs, 450,000 birds, and 30,000 primates.[10] These animals are used in basic research; applied biomedical research; the development of drugs; and the testing of consumer goods for toxicity, safety, irritation, mutations, cancer, or birth defects. In addition, animals are the subjects of psychological experiments and are also used in medical and veterinary schools to demonstrate diseases or for surgery practice.

The ethics of humankind's treatment of animals has been the subject of discussion throughout the ages. Philosophers, scholars, and scientists—among them Aristotle, René Descartes, Voltaire, Immanuel Kant, Thomas Aquinas, and Charles Darwin—grappled with such moral and ethical questions as: Do animals have rights? How do humans differ from other animals? Do animals possess language, rational thinking, or self-consciousness? Do animals feel pain or suffer? Essays by these venerable scholars have been compiled into a book edited by Tom Regan, North Carolina State University, Raleigh, and Singer.[11] More will be said about these questions later in this essay.

Real public debate over animal experiments did not surface until the seventeenth and eighteenth centuries, when European scientists began performing surgery to advance their knowledge of physiology.[12,13] Samuel Johnson summed up the public outcry when he wrote:

> I know not that by living dissections any discovery has been made by which a single malady is more easily cured. And if knowledge of physiology has been somewhat increased, he surely buys knowledge dear...at the expense of his humanity.[11]

In 1871, the British Association for the Advancement of Science issued guidelines stating, among other things, that anesthesia would be used wherever possible during animal experiments. This self-regulation mollified the critics until 1873, when a manual was published describing experiments for the laboratory. The manual neglected to mention that anesthesia should be used, and public furor ignited once again.[12,13] By 1876, animal welfare groups had pressured the British Parliament into passing the Cruelty to Animals Act. The law required experimenters to be licensed by the Home Secretary. Many kinds of animal experiments required special certification. However, by 1884 responsibility for licensing recommendations was placed in the hands of a scientific body, the Association for the Advancement of Medicine by Research, and licenses were subsequently issued in large numbers.[12,13]

In the US, Henry Bergh founded the American Association for the Prevention of Cruelty to Animals in 1866.[13] In 1883, the first antivivisectionist society was established in Philadelphia. Animal welfare proponents concentrated their efforts on state legislatures where, thanks to scientific lobbying, restrictive bills consistently failed to pass. In the first decade of this century, the American Medical Association developed a voluntary code regulating laboratory experimentation.[13] In 1966, the US Congress passed the Animal Welfare Act. Amended in 1970, the act regulates laboratory animal use by licensing research facilities and establishing minimum standards for the care of experimental animals.

Today, animal rights organizations continue to lobby for stronger measures. At least 400 different animal rights organizations now exist in the US, each with different concerns. Some oppose all animal experimentation, while others are interested solely in the protection of household pets. Still others target specific procedures as objectionable and attempt to change them.

Recently, debate has focused sharply on two standard tests used extensively by industry—the Draize test for eye irritation and the lethal dose 50 percent (LD_{50}) test for toxicity. Both of these procedures use large numbers of laboratory animals.

The Draize test measures the extent of injury a substance may cause to the eyes. It was developed in 1944 in response to the Federal Drug and Cosmetic Act of 1938.[14] This act requires that cosmetics be free of substances which might injure the user. Rabbits are the subjects of the Draize test. One-tenth of a milliliter of a substance is instilled in the conjunctival sac of the rabbit's eye. The eyelids are held together for one second. The rabbit is then released and examined periodically thereafter.[15] Although the law does not specifically require the Draize test for new cosmetics, the test is nevertheless routinely performed. This is because the law *does* require cosmetic manufacturers to label their products as "untested" if the Draize test, or some other approved assay, is not performed.

Animal welfare groups object to the Draize test on a number of grounds. Andrew N. Rowan, Tufts School of Veterinary Medicine, Boston, Massachusetts, asserts that the differences in physiology between the rabbit eye and the human eye render test results invalid. Other critics of the test charge that the scale used to judge irritation is subjective and the results are open to interpretation.[16,17] Still others make the arguable point that cosmetics are too frivolous to justify subjecting animals to pain.

Another testing procedure found objectionable by critics is the LD_{50} test, which measures toxicity—the degree to which substances are poisonous. LD_{50} is the amount of a substance required to kill half the test animals within 14 days. The American biometrician Chester I. Bliss is sometimes credited with standardizing the test in its present form while a student at University College London in 1935.[18]

Critics of the LD_{50} note that a hundred animals may be used each time a substance is tested, of which half will die. Since the test measures acute toxicity only, and cannot predict the long-term effects of small doses, it may not apply to drugs taken over a long period of time. Further, hundreds of variables affect the outcome of the test, including the sex, age, and health of the animals—and even the lab's caging practices. Finally, according to Rowan, the test does not indicate the cause of death, "which sometimes, in the case of a relatively benign substance like distilled water, results merely from the sheer bulk of the dose."[19]

In the US, LD_{50} has been used extensively in the pharmaceutical industry where it is generally believed that the test is mandated by federal law. However, at a recent Food and Drug Administration (FDA) meeting there was considerable confusion on the matter.[20] Industry and animal rights groups were both represented. Both were under the impression that the LD_{50} test is required by the FDA. FDA officials denied this, however, and asserted that other tests may comply with regulations.[20] In this connection, the scientific community's efforts to reduce the number of animals used in the Draize and LD_{50} tests are relevant.

A major criticism of animal experiments is that they don't always apply to humans. One relevant controversy concerns Depo-Provera, an injected contraceptive. Depo-Provera is used in 82 countries to control population growth and is approved by the World Health Organization. In the US, however, it may be prescribed only as a treatment for inoperable endometrial cancer. Proponents of the drug say that it is safe, and they point to the experience of thousands of women who have already taken it.[21] Opponents point to animal studies, which show the development of tumors and other abnormalities.

Beagles were used to test the drug as a contraceptive. Many of them developed breast tumors. But researchers now believe that the healthy beagle's breast may contain a reservoir of microscopic tumors. Over a long period of time, these tumors can grow and become malignant if stimulated by progesterone, an ingredient of Depo-Provera.[21] Humans do not exhibit this trait, and in fact dogs are no longer used to test contraceptive hormone preparations in the US.

When results from a ten-year study of rhesus monkeys were released, two out of 52 animals had developed endometrial cancer after receiving Depo-Provera.[22] This was surprising, since the drug is used to treat this disease. Nevertheless, the drug's proponents assert that the onset of endometrial cancer in monkeys differs from that in humans, and that the drug is safe and effective.[23]

Animal rightists sometimes cite the thalidomide case as one in which the results of animal studies did not apply to humans. Thalidomide, of course, is the tranquilizer which resulted in thousands of birth deformities before its removal from the market. There's a popular misconception that thalidomide had been extensively tested, and its teratogenic ef-

fects went undetected.[9] (p. 103) The sad truth is that the manufacturer of the drug performed no tests at all on pregnant animals.[24] Numerous tests of the drug on animals, after it had already been taken by thousands of pregnant women, clearly demonstrated the drug's teratogenicity. Some animal rightists would have us eliminate such testing.

Another focus of debate over the validity of animal studies is the recent saccharin controversy.[25] Studies on rats sufficed to convince the FDA that saccharin may cause cancer in humans. But critics charged that a person would have to drink about 800 12-oz. bottles of diet soda daily to consume the equivalent amount administered to the test rats. Toxicological testing routinely relies on giving large doses to small groups of animals. Scientists reason that if large doses cause tumors in a significant number of animals during their short lifetimes, a small dose administered over a longer period can cause tumors in some people.[25]

Some of the more emotional rhetoric from animal rights activists concerns the treatment of laboratory animals. In 1981, Edward Taub, Institute for Behavioral Research, Silver Spring, Maryland, was prosecuted for the alleged mistreatment of the primates in his laboratory.[26] Photographs offered at his trial showed animals with mutilated limbs and open wounds.

Taub was investigating how monkeys cope with the loss of sensation when their forelimb sensory nerves are severed. His work would presumably be used to develop better rehabilitation techniques for human stroke victims. One consequence of Taub's research was that the monkeys inflicted wounds on themselves. Although Taub was recently exonerated of all charges,[27] his case served to focus public attention on laboratory conditions.

Scientists are often criticized for not trying alternatives to animal research. One reason they don't may be inadequate training in the alternative design of experiments. Biologists, for example, may not know which problems are good candidates for nonanimal experiments.[28] Bernard Dixon notes that researchers stick with established techniques. Doctoral students must be sure that the methods they use are sanctioned by advisers. Thus, an adviser must be familiar with the approach being tried. This works against using novel experimental methods.[29]

In response to pressures exerted by animal rights activists, the scientific community is looking for ways to alleviate animal suffering. Many universities, including Tufts, Medical College of Pennsylvania, Johns Hopkins, and Rockefeller, have established research programs to study alternatives to animal testing.[30] The Johns Hopkins Center for Alternatives to Animal Testing was established with a $1 million grant from the Cosmetics, Toiletry and Fragrances Association and $300,000 from Bristol-Myers. A $750,000 grant from Revlon, Inc., the cosmetics firm, supports the quest for alternatives to animal research at Rockefeller University's Laboratory Animal Research Center.

The Rockefeller scientists are working toward creating a replacement for the Draize test. Their efforts involve the development of cell culture assays that mimic the complexities of the living animal. According to Ellen Borenfreund, Rockefeller University, the assays have several requirements: they must be easy to standardize so that reproducibility among laboratories is assured, and "they must be capable of detecting toxicity over a large spectrum of chemically differing toxicants and target tissues."[31] The reproducibility of assays is a difficult problem. Two different types of cell cultures are used in this kind of research—cell lines and primary cultures.[31] Cell lines isolated from tumors can be maintained over generations and exchanged between laboratories. However, they may not have the specific metabolic systems needed to develop accurate assays. Primary cell cultures are isolated directly from living animals. They can be maintained for only a few days, but do retain most complex metabolic activity. Rockefeller scientists are working on both types of cultures in their search for alternatives.[32]

One approach under study is based on a characteristic of inflammatory response—macrophages, cells that engulf and consume foreign material, migrate to areas of injury. This migration can be measured *in vitro* in a specially designed chamber. D.M. Stark, Laboratory Animal Research Center, Rockefeller University, is studying how cultured macrophages react to fluids from cell cultures which have been exposed to various irritants. Ideally, the migratory response toward these culture fluids can be correlated with the already established *in vivo* response.[32]

Another approach involves the development of a preliminary screening test for irritants. Borenfreund exposed five different cell lines to a group of about 40 potentially toxic agents. Her results correlated well with already published Draize data, but the test might be difficult to standardize. Her colleague, J. Walberg, uses another approach.[33] He collects cells shed in the washing of eyes from rabbits exposed to various alcohols of known irritancy. The cells are recovered by centrifugation, counted, fixed, stained, and examined by microscope. Again, results were found to parallel the Draize test. In this case, although animals were still used, a standard could be developed eliminating the need for repeated testing, thus reducing the number of rabbits exposed.[33]

Several researchers have recently published methods for reducing the number of animals used in the LD_{50} test. E. Schütz and H. Fuchs, Hoerst Company, Frankfurt, Federal Republic of Germany, found that three male animals per dose were all that are needed to determine toxicity rather than the five animals of each sex now used.[34] H. Müller and H.-P. Kley, Byk Gulden Lomberg Co., Konstanz, Federal Republic of Germany, assert, "A 50-75 percent reduction of expenditure in animal material is possible in most LD_{50} determinations."[35] Other researchers are pursuing cell culture alternatives to the LD_{50}.

Culture assays have already proved a successful alternative to some types of animal testing. The Ames test is one well-known example.[36] This test is an unobtrusive alternative to direct exposure. Bacteria in an extract of rat liver are exposed to potential carcinogens. These bacteria cannot make a certain amino acid, histidine. If, after exposure, histidine is detected, it is assumed that the chemical under study affected the DNA and caused the change. It therefore could cause changes in living things. The Ames test has been discussed in a previous essay.[37]

In addition to cell culture alternatives, scientists are working on replacement techniques that rely on computer modeling. Corwin Hansch, Pomona College, California, uses "quantitative structure activity relation analysis," a method that makes preliminary estimations of the toxicity or efficacy of compounds. Hansch converts structural characteristics into numbers allowing for more precision than do pictures of molecules. Comparison of the numbers can tell researchers which differences between two compounds are significant.[28]

To efficiently use this technique, a large data base containing the chemical structures of known molecules is required. For example, the National Cancer Institute uses structure activity analysis to find new antitumor drugs. All new reported compounds are compared with the structures of 55,000 known compounds. Any compound with an unusual structure is analyzed chemically. If accepted as a potential new drug, it is tested on cancerous mice. This eliminates about half of the new compounds before they have to be tested on mice.[30] In a recent article, Nancy L. Geller, Memorial Sloan-Kettering Cancer Center, New York, notes that statistical methods can minimize the number of animals needed by contributing to the adequate design of experiments.[38]

A recent article in *Chemical & Engineering News*[39] reviewed many alternatives to animal research. Many of the scientists quoted in this article express optimism that the number of animals used in research can be significantly reduced. They are not, however, sanguine about the chances of replacing animal experiments entirely. Their sentiments are echoed by NSMR. Testifying on behalf of the society before a committee of the US House of Representatives, S.M. Wolff, Tufts University School of Medicine, pointed out that the word "alternative" is really a misnomer describing adjunct methodologies to be used side by side with traditional animal testing, not replacing it entirely.[40]

Thus, the new techniques will still leave us with the ethical question of whether we have the right to use animals for experiments at all. A related and more profound question is whether or not animals possess "consciousness" in the sense that humans do. Does human consciousness differ from that of animals in kind, or only in degree? Donald R. Griffin, Rockefeller University, an ethologist, examines these questions in his 1981 book, *The Question of Animal Awareness*.[41]

Griffin begins by summing up the prevailing scientific orthodoxy regarding animal consciousness: "The current scientific *Zeitgeist* almost totally avoids consideration of mental experience in other species, while restricting attention to overt and observable behavior and physiological mechanisms."[41] (p. 1) Throughout the book, Griffin cites a huge body of literature which reflects the assumption that nonhuman animals, with the possible exception of the great apes, are incapable of any thought or behavior which has not been genetically programmed.

Griffin does not share this assumption, although he does not argue the opposite view. He merely demonstrates that experimental evidence gives us no reason to assume that evolutionary development is anything but a continuum. According to Griffin, a view of the animal kingdom which has humankind somehow qualitatively detached from other species is not necessarily supported by the evidence.[41]

Griffin examines those human attributes alleged by philosophers and scientists to set the human species apart from all others. These include symbolic communication, self-awareness, anticipation of future events, and so on. Griffin shows that experimental evidence either suggests that even such "lower" species as honeybees possess some or many of these attributes or that no conclusions about the presence or absence of these attributes can be drawn.[41]

Nowhere in his book does Griffin address the implications of his work on the ethics of using animals in scientific research. Still, one wonders if an animal's possession of awareness would endow it with "rights" which exempt it from being the subject of scientific experiments.

A recent unsigned editorial in *Nature* presents a defense of the use of laboratory animals that does not depend on the question of consciousness. The anonymous author writes: "We should resist the temptation of viewing the natural world as a blissful, magical kingdom, save only for man, a clod with heavy boots trampling the flowers. The 'sentient, purposeful' creatures of the wild lead difficult, violent, parasitized and short lives. Man's exploitation of animals for his own survival is hardly a perverse departure from the natural order."[42]

The anonymous author (the Washington office of *Nature* says that editor John Maddox did not write the essay) concludes with a statement most scientists would find reasonable: "None of this implies that human beings can treat animals as they choose. Perversion—and corruption of human values—undeniably comes from pointless cruelty to animals.... But there are simply no consistent or universal principles that imbue animals with 'rights' as exercised by humans."[42]

The scientific community recognizes that it must be conscientious in providing humane care for experimental animals, or else lose public credibility. Most scientists make every reasonable effort to keep their laboratory animals comfortable and disease free. However, other motivations exist. As C.R. Coid, Clinical Research Center, Harrow, Middlesex, England, points out, "Scientists can do without the frustrations and additional costs arising from the use of animals infected with pathogens or harboring microorganisms which may interfere with experiments."[43]

Under the Animal Welfare Act, the US Department of Agriculture's Animal and Plant Health Inspection Service (APHIS) insures that laboratories follow humane standards. This service, consisting of diligent, well-trained inspectors, has been threatened with budget cutbacks. NSMR in concert with four other scientific organizations fought to maintain APHIS intact.[44]

Responsible laboratories follow guidelines outlined in *Guide for the Care and Use of Laboratory Animals* prepared for NIH by the Institute of Laboratory Animal Resources, National Research Council.[45] The purpose of the guide is "to assist scientific institutions in using and caring for laboratory animals in ways that are judged to be professionally appropriate."[45] Topics covered are quite diverse. The guide is very specific. For example, it recommends the amount of caging space required for different animal species, exercise, etc.

By adhering to the guide's criteria, animal research facilities can be accredited by the American Association for Accreditation of Laboratory Animal Care (AAALAC), 2317 Jefferson Street, Suite 135, Joliet, Illinois 60434.[46] A nonprofit corporation, the Council on Accreditation reviews applications for accreditation and conducts on-site visitor's inspections. Criteria are so stringent that relatively few—only 422—laboratories have achieved it. However, full accreditation by AAALAC is accepted by NIH as assurance that animal facilities follow Department of Health and Human Services policy on laboratory animals when evaluating research grants. The National Science Foundation, the Department of Defense, and other federal funding agencies require that grantees performing research on warm-blooded animals comply with the standards established by the Animal Welfare Act of 1966 and the NIH guide.[47]

While the scientific community accepts voluntary controls, most scientists adamantly oppose any further legislation that interferes with the design or progress of experimentation. Walter C. Randall, president, American Physiological Society, called "unfortunate" the notion that restrictive federal legislation was needed despite easily verifiable trends that marked reductions have taken place in the use of animals in research and testing.[48] In recent years, several versions of a bill designed to put more teeth into laboratory regulation have been introduced in the US Congress.[49,50] Rats and mice, exempt from regulation under the present Animal Welfare Act, would be included under most new versions. One provision directed government agencies to look for and use methods of research and testing that reduce the use of warm-blooded animals—a design scientists regard as "clumsy interference with the conduct of research."[49] In addition, animal care requirements would be made stricter.

The establishment of an "animal experiment review board" at each institution, staffed by scientists and at least one nonscientist not connected with the institution, was also proposed. Several versions called for all federally supported research facilities to be accredited by the AAALAC.[49] Universities fear that it would cost $500 million to bring all NIH supported laboratories up to AAALAC standards. An additional provision states that a 50 percent share of NIH funds now going to work involving animals be diverted to fund nonanimal substitutes, a move that could severely restrict research.[51]

As we noted earlier, scientists have also responded by establishing NSMR and ABR. In its early days, NSMR defended scientists against antivivisectionist publicity by the Hearst newspaper chain. Subsequently, through its assistance in the founding of the AAALAC, and its watch over legislation affecting scientific freedom, NSMR has effectively combated the emotional rhetoric characterizing this controversy. NSMR takes a reasoned approach. It stands for the use of nonanimal methods when these have been proved effective. But it believes that these techniques will nearly always be used as *adjuncts* to animal testing. It is against restrictive legislation but for responsible laboratory animal care. In addition, NSMR documents the benefits to humankind of laboratory animal experimentation.[8]

To keep its members abreast of its activities, NSMR publishes a newsletter, the *NSMR Bulletin*, ten times a year. Recent issues analyzed the proposed legislation affecting lab animal management, announced upcoming conferences of interest, reported on the outcome of the Taub case, and followed antivivisectionist activities.[52,53]

The ABR keeps its member organizations abreast of legislative developments through two newsletters. One, *Regulatory Alert*, is published at irregular intervals, whenever new legislation is proposed in Congress. Recent issues have discussed the so-called Walgren Amendment which, if it becomes law, would give the recommendations in the NIH guide the force of law;[54] and the recent efforts of animal rights groups to push legislation which would divert huge sums of federal research money from experiments on animals to investigations into whether those experiments actually duplicate previous work.[55]

The other ABR newsletter, *Update*, is published about twice a month. It provides follow-up information on the progress of legislation previously reported in *Regulatory Alert*. Recent *Updates* have reported on a request from several US senators to the General Accounting Office to study the enforcement of the Animal Welfare Act,[56] and the progress of a bill which would forbid the Department of Defense from using dogs and cats to train combat surgeons.[57]

Another organization, the Scientists' Center for Animal Welfare (SCAW, P.O. Box 3755, Washington, DC 20007), was established by scientists and social scientists to "provide scholarly input, collect scientific facts and make objective analysis of animal welfare issues." SCAW has sponsored its own conference on review procedures for animal experimentation.[58] One speaker at the conference, Michael W. Fox, Institute for the Study of Animal Problems, Washington, DC, has suggested that journal editors should reject papers reporting research which used inhumane methodology.[58] He suggests that journals publish guidelines for the proper use of laboratory animals. At least one journal, the *American Journal of Physiology*, does publish such guidelines.

Several journals deal with laboratory animal issues. The *Journal of Animal Science* covers animal welfare topics on occasion, as does the *Journal of the American Veterinary Medical Association*. The *Annals of the New York Academy of Sciences* recently devoted an entire issue to the role of animals in biomedical research,[59] while as far back as 1967 the *American Journal of Public Health* devoted part of an issue to the benefits of using animals in research.[60] Information on cell culture alternatives can be found throughout the biological and biomedical journal literature.

It may seem obvious to many *Current Contents*® readers that research on laboratory animals has contributed greatly to the advance of medical science and the well-being of humankind. Unfortunately, these contributions may be too obvious for our own good. Randall correctly identifies the activities of the animal rights activists as posing a major threat to the future of medical research.[61] Yet in reviewing the literature for this essay, I was surprised at how the critics of animal research dominate the popular literature on this subject. While one can find cogent defenses of animal research in the scholarly literature, it is in the political arena where the battle is being fought.

While the existence of NSMR and ABR is encouraging, what is needed is for more individual scientists to become involved in public education, lest regulations interfering with experimental design are imposed on us. It is clear that scientists can never be complacent on the issue of laboratory animals.

* * * * *

My thanks to Terri Freedman and Esther Surden for their help in the preparation of this essay.

©1984 ISI

REFERENCES

1. **Garfield E.** Citation analysis and the anti-vivisection controversy, part I. An assessment of Lester R. Aronson's citation record, part II. *Essays of an information scientist.* Philadelphia: ISI Press, 1980. Vol. 3. p. 103-8; 316-25.
2. **Wade N.** Animal rights: NIH cat sex study brings grief to New York museum. *Science* 194:162-7, 1976.

3. **Banting F G & Best C H.** The internal secretion of the pancreas.
   J. Lab. Clin. Med. 7:251-66, 1922.
4. **Lettvin J Y.** "Filling out the forms": an appreciation of Hubel and Wiesel.
   Science 214:518-20, 1981.
5. **Miller N E.** Understanding the use of animals in behavioral research: some critical issues.
   Ann. NY Acad. Sci. 406:113-8, 1983.
6. **Singer P.** *Animal liberation.* New York: New York Review, 1975. 301 p.
7. **Fox M W.** *Returning to Eden: animal rights and human responsibility.*
   New York: Viking Press, 1980. 281 p.
8. **Grafton T S.** The founding and early history of the National Society for Medical Research.
   Lab. Anim. Sci. 30:759-64, 1980.
9. **Rollin B E.** *Animal rights and human morality.* Buffalo, NY: Prometheus, 1981. 182 p.
10. **National Academy of Sciences.** *National survey of laboratory animal facilities and resources.*
    Bethesda, MD: National Institutes of Health, March 1980. NIH Publ. No. 80/2091.
11. **Regan T & Singer P,** eds. *Animal rights and human obligations.*
    Englewood Cliffs, NJ: Prentice-Hall, 1976. 250 p.
12. **French R D.** *Antivivisection and medical science in Victorian society.*
    Princeton, NJ: Princeton University Press, 1975. 425 p.
13. **Sechzer J A.** Historical issues concerning animal experimentation in the United States.
    Soc. Sci. Med. 15F:13-8, 1981.
14. **Draize J H, Woodard G & Calvery H O.** Methods for the study of irritation and toxicity of
    substances applied topically to the skin and mucous membranes.
    J. Pharmacol. Exp. Ther. 82:377-90, 1944.
15. **Rowan A.** The Draize test: political and scientific issues. *Cosmet. Technol.* 3(7):32-7, 1981.
16. ------------. *The Draize test: a critique and proposals for alternatives.*
    Washington, DC: Humane Society of the United States. (Brochure.) March 1980. 16 p.
17. ------------. *The Draize test: the search for alternatives. Cosmet. Technol.* 4(6):30-3, 1983.
18. **Bliss C I.** The calculation of the dosage-mortality curve. *Ann. Appl. Biol.* 22:134-67, 1935.
19. **Rowan A N.** The LD_{50} test: a critique and suggestions for alternatives.
    Pharmaceut. Technol. 5(4):65-6; 80-6; 89-94, 1981.
20. **Sun M.** Lots of talk about LD_{50}. *Science* 222:1106, 1983.
21. **Benagiano G & Fraser I.** The Depo-Provera debate. Commentary on the article "Depo-Provera,
    a critical analysis." *Contraception* 24:493-528, 1981.
22. **International Research and Development Corporation.** *Long-term intramuscular study in monkeys.*
    Unpublished report, 17 September 1979.
23. **Sun M.** Depo-Provera debate revs up at FDA. *Science* 217:424-8, 1982.
24. **The Sunday Times, London.** *Suffer the children: the story of thalidomide.*
    New York: Viking Press, 1979. 309 p.
25. **Culliton B J.** Fight over proposed saccharin ban will not be settled for months.
    Science 196:276-8, 1977.
26. NIH suspends funding of researcher charged with animal cruelty.
    Bioscience 31:714-5, 1981.
27. Maryland Appeals Court clears Dr. Taub of animal cruelty charge.
    Nat. Soc. Med. Res. Bull. 34(7):1; 3, 1983.
28. **Hansch C.** A quantitative approach to biochemical structure-activity relationships.
    Account. Chem. Res. 2:232-9, 1969.
29. **Dixon B.** Animal experiments: time for a new approach. (Paterson D & Ryder R D, eds.)
    Animals' rights—a symposium. Arundel, UK: Centaur Press, 1979. p. 178-86.
30. **Holden C.** New focus on replacing animals in the lab. *Science* 215:35-8, 1982.
31. **Borenfreund E.** Progress in alternatives to Draize testing. Lecture at the seminar for science
    writers on *Progress in alternatives to animal testing.* 2 June 1983. New York. 4 p.
32. **Stark D M.** Introduction. Lecture at the seminar for science writers on *Progress in alternatives to
    animal testing.* 2 June 1983. New York. 6 p.
33. **Walberg J.** Exfoliative cytology as a refinement of the Draize eye irritancy test.
    Toxicol. Lett. 18:49-55, 1983.
34. **Schütz E & Fuchs H.** A new approach to minimizing the number of animals used in acute toxicity
    testing and optimizing the information of test results. *Arch. Toxicol.* 51:197-220, 1982.
35. **Müller H & Kley H-P.** Retrospective study on the reliability of an "approximate LD_{50}" determined
    with a small number of animals. *Arch. Toxicol.* 51:189-96, 1982.
36. **Ames B N, McCann J & Yamasaki E.** Methods for detecting carcinogens and mutagens with the
    salmonella/mammalian microsome mutagenicity test. *Mutat. Res.* 31:347-64, 1975.
37. **Garfield E.** Risk analysis, part 2. How we evaluate the health risks of toxic substances in the
    environment. *Essays of an information scientist.* Philadelphia: ISI Press, 1983. Vol. 5. p. 659-65.
38. **Geller N L.** Statistical strategies for animal conservation. *Ann. NY Acad. Sci.* 406:20-31, 1983.
39. **Dagani R.** Alternative methods could cut animal use in toxicity tests.
    Chem. Eng. News 61(44):7-13, 1983.

40. US House of Representatives, Committee on Science and Technology. *Use of animals in medical research and testing*, 97th Cong., 1st. Sess. (October 13-14, 1981.) (Testimony of Wolff S M.) Y4. Sci. 2:97/68.
41. Griffin D R. *The question of animal awareness.* New York: Rockefeller University Press, 1981. 209 p.
42. What rights for animals? *Nature* 306:522, 1983.
43. Coid C R. Selection of animals suitable for biomedical investigations. *J. Roy. Soc. Med.* 71:675-7, 1978.
44. Reynolds O E. Statement for American Institute of Biological Sciences et al. to the Committee on Appropriations, Subcommittee on Agriculture, Rural Development & Related Agencies, US House of Representatives. 30 March 1982. Washington, DC. 7 p.
45. Committee on Care and Use of Laboratory Animals, Institute of Laboratory Animal Resources, National Research Council. *Guide for the care and use of laboratory animals.* (Brochure.) NIH Publ. No. 80-23, April 1980.
46. American Association for Accreditation of Laboratory Animal Care. (Information pamphlet.) Joliet, IL: AAALAC. 11 p.
47. Use of animals in research: a reminder. *Nat. Sci. Foundation Bull.* 10(1):2, 1982.
48. Randall W C. Testimony for American Physiological Society on S.657. "Improved Standards for Laboratory Animals Act" presented to the US Senate Committee on Agriculture, Nutrition, and Forestry. 20 July 1983. Washington, DC. 5 p.
49. Animal-welfare legislation stirring in Congress. *Sci. Govt. Rep.* 13(2):5, 1983.
50. Fields C M. House panel approves new limits on use of animals in research. *Chron. High. Educ.* 26(5):15-6, 1983.
51. Budiansky S. Congress in sight of compromise. *Nature* 298:6-7, 1982.
52. National Society for Medical Research. *Nat. Soc. Med. Res. Bull.* 34(7), 1983. (Newsletter.)
53. --. *Nat. Soc. Med. Res. Bull.* 34(8), 1983. (Newsletter.)
54. Association for Biomedical Research. *Regulatory Alert* 5(2), 1983. (Newsletter.)
55. --. *Regulatory Alert* 5(4), 1983. (Newsletter.)
56. --. *Update* 4(17), 1983. (Newsletter.)
57. --. *Update* 4(18), 1983. (Newsletter.)
58. Fox M W. Summary of workshop on editorial responsibilities. (Dodds W J & Orlans F B, eds.) *Scientific perspectives on animal welfare.* New York: Academic Press, 1982. p. 107-8.
59. Sechzer J A, ed. The role of animals in biomedical research. (Whole issue.) *Ann. NY Acad. Sci.* 406, 1983. 227 p.
60. Vivisection-vivistudy: the facts and the benefits to animal and human health. *Amer. J. Public Health* 51:1597-626, 1967.
61. Randall W C. Is medical research in jeopardy? *Hosp. Pract.* 18:144A-144N, 1983.

Current Comments®

Number 6   February 6, 1984

Not long ago, I was invited to deliver the sixth series of Ranganathan Memorial Lectures at the Documentation Research and Training Centre, Bangalore, India. These lectures are sponsored by the Sarada Ranganathan Endowment for Library Science, a trust founded by the late Shiyali Ramamrita Ranganathan in honor of his wife. The purpose of the endowment is to promote and publish research in library science.

My lectures covered three basic topics—the use of citation indexes, co-citation analysis and clustering, and Third World research. I covered the same subjects again at Madras University. However, there I presented a fourth talk that related my work to Ranganathan's. The occasion of the Madras talks was the unveiling of a new portrait of Ranganathan, who was the librarian at Madras University for more than 20 years.

These original invitations quickly evolved into a full-scale lecture tour of academic and governmental institutions in several major cities of India. Many invitations to speak were generated by my recent article on Third World research, published in *Science & Public Policy* and reprinted in *Current Contents®*.[1,2] Ultimately, my itinerary included New Delhi, Hyderabad, and Bombay. I'm deeply indebted to Subbiyah Arunachalam, editor of the *Indian Journal of Technology*, for his prodigious efforts in arranging this itinerary. He made it possible for me to meet personally with many leading Indian scientists and media representatives.

The entire tour proved very rewarding. But it was particularly gratifying to help honor Ranganathan, who is, without question, one of the luminaries of library science and library classification. Not only did he do more than any other single individual to modernize and professionalize library science in India, he also had a revolutionary impact on international classification theory.

I had the pleasure of meeting Ranganathan only once, in Dorking, England, at the International Study Conference on Classification for Information Retrieval in 1957.[3] Ranganathan gave the opening address, and I contributed my views on citation indexing. We shared many conversations during the conference. At the time, Ranganathan was riding the crest of a career that spanned almost 50 years (from 1924 to 1972), and from which he never really retired.

Ranganathan was born in 1892 in Shiyali in the Tanjur district of Madras state. His family belonged to the Brahman community. Ranganathan's father died when the boy was only six. He was brought up under the influence of his grandfather, who was a schoolteacher, and two of his elementary schoolteachers. These men, who were steeped in Hindu religious lore, invested Ranganathan with a lifelong love of Hindu sacred literature that is plainly evident in his writings.[4] Most of his library science

Shiyali Ramamrita Ranganathan

works are liberally sprinkled with allusions to the Hindu scriptures.

In 1909, Ranganathan managed to secure one of the few seats available at Madras Christian College. He received his BA in 1913, and an MA in mathematics in 1916. In 1917, he received a professional teaching certificate from Teacher's College, Saidapet, Madras. He then taught physics and mathematics at Government College, Mangalore; Government College, Coimbatore; and Presidency College, Madras. But his teaching positions paid poorly. When his attempts to get higher pay for teachers failed, Ranganathan was reluctantly persuaded by a friend to apply for the well-paid post of Madras University librarian.[5] To his surprise, he won the appointment, although he lacked any library training. Ranganathan, however, found the library's quiet atmosphere stultifying after the liveliness of the classroom. Within a week he was back at Presidency College, begging to be reinstated. The college principal urged Ranganathan to return to the library, but agreed to hold his teaching position open until his library training in London

was completed. It's ironic that this man, who later became so single-mindedly devoted to library science, was practically forced into the field against his will.

His reluctance to embrace librarianship was understandable considering the ill-organized, poorly attended, and understaffed institution he inherited. In fact, his first days at the library were passed in tedious inactivity. Yet he slowly began to perceive that his library's backwardness constituted a monumental challenge. Indeed, upon his return from London in 1925, he launched a full-scale reform program to implement his ideas for staffing and furnishing the library as well as classifying and cataloging its contents.

He gleaned many of these ideas from his nine-month stay in London. There he studied at the School of Librarianship, University College, London, under W.C. Berwick Sayers, the chief librarian of the Croydon Public Library. Ranganathan received an honors certificate from the school at the end of his stay. In addition, he visited over a hundred libraries to observe their operation. He was profoundly impressed by the community orientation of these libraries. Unlike those in India, British libraries made every effort to serve all strata of society equally. But positively impressed as he was in many ways, he was dismayed by the welter of different services, techniques, buildings, and equipment that he observed in the libraries he visited. He felt that each library was developing in its own independent direction, rather than all developing according to common principles. So Ranganathan set himself the task of defining some unifying principles.

These were published in 1931 in a seminal work, *The Five Laws of Library Science*.[6] Ranganathan himself considered this to be the wellspring of the 50 books he produced over his long career.[6] (p. 382) The five laws are the following deceptively simple statements: 1) books are for use, 2) every reader his book, 3) every book its reader, 4) save the time of the reader, and 5) a library is a growing organism.

Although these statements might seem self-evident today, they certainly were not to librarians in the early part of this century. After all, the democratic library tradition we currently enjoy had arisen in America and England only in the latter part of the nineteenth century.[7] Previously, many libraries restricted their services to paying subscribers from the moneyed classes. Often libraries served primarily a custodial function. The libraries of India, as a colony and a developing country, were hardly among the most progressive. In Ranganathan's day, they were usually associated only with universities and other academic institutions.[8] There was no public library system as such. But even given a well-established public library system, the tendency toward bureaucratic entrenchment must always be guarded against. The five laws help ensure that libraries are service-oriented.

For Ranganathan and his followers, the five laws were a first step toward putting library work on a scientific basis. These laws provided general principles from which all library practices could be deduced. Thus, the first law—books are for use—leads naturally to a library system in which libraries are centrally located, open long hours, hospitably furnished, and staffed by trained, service-oriented, and adequately compensated workers. (Of course, the term "books" here stands for all information items.) The second law—every reader his book—dictates that libraries serve all readers, regardless of social class, sex, age, or any other factor. The third law—every book its reader—stipulates that a book exists for every reader, and that books should be well described in the catalog, displayed in an attractive manner, and made readily available to readers. This law leads naturally to such

practices as open access rather than closed stacks, a coherent shelf arrangement, an adequate catalog, and a reference service. The fourth law—save the time of the reader—emphasizes efficient service, which implies an expeditious book-charging system and easy-to-understand guides to the stacks. This law has a corollary—save the time of the staff—which requires the use of those techniques and technology that enable the staff to perform most efficiently. The fifth law—a library is a growing organism—recognizes that growth will undoubtedly occur and must be planned for systematically. From the physical facilities to administrative practices, the library must be open-ended, always ready to expand.

Besides encouraging formulation of the five laws, Ranganathan's visit to England stimulated another important line of thought. The more he learned about the orthodox Anglo-American library classification systems, the more convinced he became that they were seriously flawed. Library classification is the systematic arrangement of documents by subject.[9] As such, it may determine the arrangement of books on library shelves or of documents in an information retrieval system. However, in many libraries, particularly in Europe, classification determines only the order of the catalog cards describing information items, rather than the physical arrangement of the items themselves.

Ranganathan's objection to the prevailing classification systems, such as Dewey Decimal Classification and Library of Congress Classification, was that they tried to enumerate all possible subjects and provide preconceived pigeonholes to accommodate all documents.[10] But this enumerative approach made little allowance for the addition of new topics. Thus, these systems couldn't easily accommodate the explosion of knowledge occurring in the twentieth century. Of course, any new enumerative scheme that simply incorporated contemporary topics would itself be quickly outmoded. Rather, what Ranganathan sought was an entirely novel, more flexible, approach.

As so often happens in scientific discovery, this vague notion was fully conceptualized only with the help of an unlikely catalyst. For Isaac Newton, according to legend, the catalyst was a falling apple. For Friedrich Kekulé, discoverer of the benzene ring, it was a snake with its tail in its mouth that appeared to him in a dream. For Ranganathan, it was a toy erector set at Selfridge's, the London department store.[11] There he saw a salesperson create an entirely new toy with each new combination of metal strips, nuts, and bolts. This experience made Ranganathan realize that his classification scheme should likewise consist of elements that could be freely combined to meet the needs of each specific subject.

But this eureka experience in 1924 would require many years' gestation before it came to fruition. Not until 1933 did Ranganathan publish his first major work on his new classification system, *The Colon Classification*.[12] Since then, Colon Classification has undergone several revisions. Its basic principles, however, require the *analysis* of a subject to determine its various aspects, called *facets*, and the *synthesis* of a class number (call number) from the numbers assigned in published schedules to different facets. Thus, Colon Classification is known as an *analytico-synthetic* classification system. Part 2 of this essay will include an appendix with a detailed discussion of Colon Classification.

According to Bernard I. Palmer, formerly of the Library Association, London, England, the major distinction between enumerative and analytico-synthetic classification is that "enumerative classification lists composite subjects, built up from a number of basic ideas. Facet classification lists the basic terms and leaves the building of derived composite terms to the classifier."[13] (p. 37) This frees the deviser of the classification scheme from the burden of specifying all conceivable subjects. By stringing together the appropriate facets, the classifier using Colon Classification can precisely specify new subjects as they arise. Therefore, in Colon Classification, a subject category with a ready-made class number never preexists without a document to occupy it.[14]

Actually, this feature, known as "literary warrant," is not unique to Colon Classification. Colon Classification shares this characteristic with the Library of Congress Classification system. Also, certain aspects of facet analysis and synthesis had been anticipated to some degree in Dewey Decimal Classification[15] and even more so in other classification systems, such as Universal Decimal Classification.[9] Furthermore, as Phyllis Richmond, Baxter School of Information and Library Science, Case Western Reserve University, Cleveland, Ohio, pointed out in reviewing this essay, the ideas of W.C. Berwick Sayers, Henry Evelyn Bliss, and Ernest Richardson further strengthened the foundation for facet theory.[16] But Ranganathan was the first to fully explicate facet theory, and his work has had a major impact on modern classification schemes.[9]

In 1934, just a year after *The Colon Classification* came out, Ranganathan published another important work, the *Classified Catalogue Code*.[17] This book grew out of Ranganathan's strong objection to the commonly used dictionary-type catalog. In the dictionary catalog, subjects, authors, and titles are merely listed in alphabetic order. Ranganathan maintained, however, that a catalog should consist of two components. One part should be classified by subject, reflecting the library's classification system, with class number entries. The other should be a dictionary catalog, including author, title, series, and similar identifiers, as well as alphabetized subject entries.

The function of a catalog is to itemize works so they can be found by author, title, series, and so forth. It must also allow readers to review the selection of works on a given subject. Traditionally, as a practical matter, the alphabetical catalog was considered easiest for the ordinary reader to use. But Ranganathan thought that, although most readers are unfamiliar with classified systems, the alphabetized dictionary catalog could be used to guide readers to the correct location in the classified catalog. Once in the classified system, the reader would be exposed to the depth and breadth of material on the subject of interest. This would help pinpoint the most relevant material.

To determine subject entries for the dictionary catalog, Ranganathan devised an ingeniously simple method called *chain indexing*.[18] This method simply uses each facet of a subject, together with its immediately preceding facets, as an index entry. Thus, all important aspects of the subject, from the most general to the most specific, are automatically covered. Chain indexing can be adapted to other classification systems as well. The British National Bibliography used it in conjunction with its version of the Dewey Decimal Classification, from 1950 until 1971, when the preserved context index system (PRECIS) was substituted.[19,20]

Although Ranganathan's works on classification and cataloging are his best-recognized contributions, he published over 50 books and 1,000 papers on all aspects of library science.[21] In addition, he founded and edited three periodicals: *Abgila*, the Indian Library Association *Annals*, *Bulletin*, and *Granthalaya* (the Hindi component of the journal); the *Annals of Library Science*; and *Library Science with a Slant to Documentation*. He also involved himself in every aspect of library work in India. In the course of

his career, he was a member or chairman of more than 25 committees which addressed such issues as library administration, education of librarians, and library legislation.

In 1935, he published the first edition of his influential book, *Library Administration*,[22] in which he broke down library work into approximately 1,000 component jobs. By precisely identifying many different library functions, he was able to simplify and streamline library routine. He also wrote extensively on the physical layout and furnishings of libraries.[23,24]

Ranganathan worked tirelessly to professionalize library education in India. One of his first achievements, in 1929, was to found a library school that was later incorporated into the University of Madras. He also instituted a master of library science degree in 1948 and a doctoral program in 1950, both at the University of Delhi. These were the first higher degree programs in library science offered in India, and probably in any of the Commonwealth countries.[25] Ranganathan greatly influenced the curricula and textbooks for such courses. In fact, a student of Ranganathan's, Asha Kaula, has stated, "In India, the advanced professional education is nothing but an interpretation of Dr. Ranganathan's ideas."[26] (p. 556) Ranganathan's crowning accomplishment in library education was to found the Documentation Research and Training Centre at Bangalore, under the auspices of the Indian Statistical Institute. The center, where I presented the Ranganathan lectures, is devoted solely to research and advanced training in documentation and information science.

Ever since his return from England, Ranganathan had hoped to establish a Western-style network of public libraries throughout India. His first step toward achieving this end was to form the Madras Library Association in 1928, to promote development of public libraries in the state of Madras. He also drafted specific legislation to extend the public library system beyond the state of Madras into other areas of India. In 1950, he published an influential work detailing plans for a system of national, state, university, public, and school libraries for the entire country.[27] As he told Pauline Atherton Cochrane, School of Information Studies, Syracuse University, New York, this plan was brought forward at the request of Indian government leaders whom Ranganathan helped during the struggle for independence from the UK. He brought these men books while they were in prison. Later, when they assumed responsible positions in the new Indian government, they came to him for advice on developing the nation's library system.[28]

Ranganathan held several important offices in India during his long career. He served as president of the Indian Library Association from 1944 to 1953 and as president of the Madras Library Association from 1958 to 1967. He also served as vice president of the Governing Council of the Indian Standards Institute from 1965 to 1972.

Although Ranganathan is widely acknowledged as the father of library science in India, his activities extended well beyond his country's borders. In addition to attending many international library and information science conferences, he traveled extensively on lecture tours to library science schools throughout the US and Europe. He also participated in the activities of such international organizations as UNESCO, the International Federation of Library Associations, and the International Standards Organization. He played a key role in setting policy for the United Nations Library and he devoted much effort to international standardization of documentation. He was particularly active in the International Federation for Documentation (FID).[29] He founded the FID committee on classification theory,

served as vice president of the FID council, and was elected an honorary member of FID. He also became honorary chairman of the FID committee on classification research.

Ranganathan's contributions were acknowledged many times over, both in India and abroad, by similar honorary offices and fellowships. For example, in 1964, he was named honorary president of the Second International Conference on Classification Research, held in Elsinore, Denmark. He also received a number of other high honors. In 1935 and 1957, respectively, the Indian government bestowed on him the honorific title Rao Sahib and the public service award Padmashri. In 1948, he received an honorary doctorate of literature from the University of Delhi. In 1964, he received the same degree from the University of Pittsburgh. In 1965, he was made a national research professor by the Indian government, and in 1970, he received the Margaret Mann Citation in Cataloging and Classification of the American Library Association (ALA). In 1965, and in 1967, in honor of his seventy-first birthday, his colleagues published two volumes of a *festschrift* dedicated to him.[30,31] After his death, the FID, in 1976, established the Ranganathan award in his memory. This certificate of merit is awarded biennially for a recent outstanding contribution in the field of classification.

Ranganathan's activity level throughout his lifetime reflects a total, selfless commitment to library science. P.N. Kaula, Banaras Hindu University, Varanasi, India, a fellow library scientist and a close associate of Ranganathan, observed that Ranganathan lived and breathed library science, talking of nothing else from when he arose until late at night.[32] Co-workers testify to Ranganathan's long working hours, which averaged 16 hours a day, seven days a week.[33] During his 20 years of service as librarian of the University of

Madras, he took no leave. He worked even on his wedding day, returning to the library shortly after the ceremony.[34] When he retired from the Madras University library, it was only to accept a series of appointments at other Indian universities and to step up his involvement in international activities. He remained actively engaged in research until his death in 1972 at the age of 80.

Again, Cochrane provides a salient anecdote.[28] When she visited him at his bedside one Sunday in 1970, there were ten or more Indian librarians present who had traveled more than 250 miles to spend the afternoon discussing library developments with him. This was a weekly occurrence until his death.

Besides his great capacity for work, Ranganathan was renowned for his abstemious life-style. In spite of the good salary he earned, he adopted a Ghandilike simplicity in diet and dress. He ate only lightly, shunned coffee and tea, and wore plain homespun garments. He usually walked barefoot to the library and worked there barefoot, saying that the library was his home, and no one wears shoes in his own home.[33] As for his real home, it was sparsely furnished and lacked electricity, although he could have easily afforded these amenities. The money he saved through years of frugal living, he gave away twice: once in 1925 to endow a mathematics fellowship at Madras Christian College in honor of his mathematics professor, Edward B. Ross, and again in 1956 to endow the Sarada Ranganathan chair of library science at the University of Madras in honor of his wife.

This self-abnegation and devotion to work were grounded in a deep spirituality. As T.R. Seshadri, an associate of Ranganathan, writes, "Ranganathan was born and brought up at a time when spirituality and religion still continued to be the mainsprings of life."[35] Some of his followers viewed him as a yogi.[35,36] He concentrated his whole body, mind, and soul on the discipline of library science, so they felt he had embraced it as a path to spiritual perfection.

Part 2 of this essay will examine Ranganathan's impact both on Indian and international library science, draw some parallels between Ranganathan's work and co-citation clustering, and discuss colon classification.

* * * * *

My thanks to Terri Freedman and Patricia Lawson for their help in the preparation of this essay.

©1984 ISI

REFERENCES

1. **Garfield E.** Third World research. Part 1. Where it is published and how often it is cited. *Current Contents* (33):5-15, 15 August 1983.
2. ---------------. Third World research. Part 2. High impact journals, most-cited articles, and most active areas of research. *Current Contents* (34):5-16, 22 August 1983.
   (Reprints of **Garfield E.** Mapping science in the Third World.
   Sci. Public Policy 10(3):112-27, 1983, are included in Parts 1 & 2.)
3. **Aslib.** *Proceedings of the International Study Conference on Classification for Information Retrieval,* 13-17 May 1957, Dorking, UK. New York: Pergamon Press, 1957. 151 p.
4. **Gopinath M A.** Ranganathan, Shiyali Ramamrita. (Kent A, Lancour H & Daily J E, eds.) *Encyclopedia of library and information science.* New York: Dekker, 1978. Vol. 25. p. 58-86.
5. **Ranganathan S R.** A librarian looks back. *Herald Libr. Sci.* 2:1-7; 127-30, 1963.
6. ----------------------. *The five laws of library science.* London: Blunt, 1957. 456 p.
7. **Sayers W C B.** Introduction to the first edition. (Ranganathan S R.) *The five laws of library science.* London: Blunt, 1957. p. 13-7.
8. **Saksena R S.** India's contribution to library science. (Kaula P N, ed.) *Library science today: Ranganathan festschrift.* New York: Asia Publishing House, 1965. Vol. 1. p. 625-31.
9. **Wellisch H H.** Classification. (Wedgeworth R, ed.) *ALA world encyclopedia of library and information services.* Chicago: American Library Association, 1980. p. 146-50.

10. **Ranganathan S R.** Impact of growth in the universe of subjects on classification. (International Federation for Documentation, Committee on Classification Research.) *Ranganathan memorial issue.* Copenhagen: Danish Centre for Documentation, 1972. FID/CR Report No. 12. p. 1-20.

11. ----------------------. Introduction to the Colon Classification. *The Colon Classification.* New Brunswick, NJ: Rutgers Graduate School of Library Service, 1965. Vol. 4. p. 9-23.

12. ----------------------. *The Colon Classification.* New Brunswick, NJ: Rutgers Graduate School of Library Service, 1965. Vol. 4.

13. **Palmer B I & Wells A J.** The process of division. *The fundamentals of library classification.* London: George Allen & Unwin, 1961. p. 35-41.

14. **Palmer B I.** A short introduction to Colon. *Libr. World* 51:123-5, 1949.

15. **Chan L M.** Colon Classification by Shiyali Ramamrita Ranganathan. *Cataloging and classification: an introduction.* New York: McGraw-Hill, 1981. p. 312-5.

16. **Matthews G O.** *The influence of Ranganathan on faceted classification.* PhD dissertation. Cleveland: Case Western Reserve University, 1980. p. 100-2.

17. **Ranganathan S R.** *Classified catalogue code.* New York: Asia Publishing House, 1964. 644 p.

18. **Palmer B & Wells A J.** The chain procedure for subject indexing and featuring. *The fundamentals of library classification.* London: George Allen & Unwin, 1961. p. 101-7.

19. **Wells A J.** Ranganathan's influence on bibliographical services. (Dudley E, ed.) *S.R. Ranganathan, 1892-1972.* London: Library Association, 1974. p. 13-5.

20. **Sørensen J.** Austin, Derek William. (Wedgeworth R, ed.) *ALA world encyclopedia of library and information services.* Chicago: American Library Association, 1980. p. 64.

21. **Kaula P N.** A new era of library science. *Herald Libr. Sci.* 1:160-6, 1962.

22. **Ranganathan S R.** *Library administration.* Bombay: Asia Publishing House, 1959. 678 p.

23. ----------------------. Library buildings and furniture. *Mod. Libr.* 14:121-4, 1944.

24. ----------------------. Style and character in library buildings. *Mod. Libr.* 15:87-9, 1945.

25. **Singh M.** Progress in librarianship in India, 1911-1978. *Libri* 29:158-68, 1969.

26. **Kaula A.** Dr. Ranganathan and library education. (Kaula P N, ed.) *Library science today: Ranganathan festschrift.* New York: Asia Publishing House, 1965. Vol. 1. p. 553-7.

27. **Ranganathan S R.** *Library development plan: thirty-year programme for India.* Delhi: University of Delhi, 1950. 464 p.

28. **Cochrane P A.** Personal communication. 3 January 1984.

29. **Mölgaard'H R.** Editorial. (International Federation for Documentation, Committee on Classification Research.) *Ranganathan memorial issue.* Copenhagen: Danish Centre for Documentation, 1972. FID/CR Report No. 12.

30. **Kaula P N,** ed. *Library science today: Ranganathan festschrift.* New York: Asia Publishing House, 1965. Vol. 1.

31. **Das Gupta A K.** *An essay in personal bibliography: Ranganathan festschrift.* London: Asia Publishing House, 1967. Vol. 2.

32. **Kaula P N.** Ranganathan: a study. (Kaula P N, ed.) *Library science today: Ranganathan festschrift.* New York: Asia Publishing House, 1965. Vol. 1. p. 649-76.

33. **Ghatak B N.** Dr. Ranganathan in Banaras. (Kaula P N, ed.) *Library science today: Ranganathan festschrift.* New York: Asia Publishing House, 1965. Vol. 1. p. 725-8.

34. **Kaula P N.** Back from my mind: anecdotes from Dr. Ranganathan's life. *Herald Libr. Sci.* 1:179-90, 1962.

35. **Seshadri T R.** Dr. Ranganathan: a karmayogin. (Kaula P N, ed.) *Library science today: Ranganathan festschrift.* New York: Asia Publishing House, 1965. Vol. 1. p. 737-8.

36. **Thakore A V.** Ranganathan: the magic man. (Kaula P N, ed.) *Library science today: Ranganathan festschrift.* New York: Asia Publishing House, 1965. Vol. 1. p. 764-5.

Current Comments®

A Tribute to S. R. Ranganathan, the Father of Indian Library Science. Part 2. Contribution to Indian and International Library Science

Number 7   February 13, 1984

Last week's essay presented a biographical account of Shiyali Ramamrita Ranganathan, the father of Indian library science.[1] This week's essay will attempt to evaluate his contribution to library science, and discuss some parallels between his work and co-citation clustering. At the end of the essay, you'll find an appendix that describes his classification system, Colon Classification.

Any evaluation of Ranganathan's work must consider both his impact on Indian *and* on international library science. That Ranganathan made an enormous contribution to Indian library science is indisputable. An article by Mohinder Singh, Regional Research Laboratory, Bhuboneswar, Orissa, India, singles out the year 1925, when Ranganathan joined the library profession, as the advent of an important new era in Indian library science.[2] Before Ranganathan's time, he notes, libraries were simple book repositories, open access was unheard of, and the average librarian worked for little pay under poor conditions. No Indian university offered any library science certificate, diploma, or degree. It was Ranganathan who spearheaded the movement to professionalize librarianship and to expand the Indian library system. It was he who propelled Indian librarianship into the twentieth century.

Ranganathan's contribution to international library science, although significant, is more difficult to determine. Colon Classification, for example, is rarely used in libraries in the Western world.[3,4] Even in India, where Ranganathan's ideas have had tremendous impact, use of Colon Classification is not as widespread as might be expected.[3,5] In American library science schools, Colon Classification is usually covered only briefly. One study[6] found that of 48 schools accredited by the American Library Association (ALA), 73 percent (35 schools) include facet theory in their curricula (see appendix for an explanation of facet classification). But of these, only 20 percent (seven schools) cover it in any depth. And although 50 percent of the schools include Colon Classification in their curricula, only about eight percent (two schools) conduct any practice exercises in it. A related study[7] indicates that Dewey Decimal Classification is the dominant system in the US, being taught in all ALA-accredited schools. The Library of Congress system is a close second. Next comes the Universal Decimal Classification system, taught in just over half the schools. Colon Classification, in fourth place, is also taught in just over half the schools. Although, according to this study, the number of schools in which Colon Classification is covered seems to be increasing, coverage is cursory.

Ranganathan's international contribution is measured, however, not in the actual application of Colon Classification, but in its influence on classification and indexing theory. According to the *ALA World Encyclopedia of Library and Information Services*, Colon Classifica-

Figure 1: Portrait of S.R. Ranganathan included in the ISI® mural "Cathedral of Man."

System of Ordering commissioned by UNESCO and promoted by the International Federation for Documentation (FID) allows the combination of subject subdivisions according to faceted classification principles.[5]

A partial indicator of Ranganathan's international impact is the number of citations to his work in *Science Citation Index*® (*SCI*®) and *Social Sciences Citation Index*® (*SSCI*®). Over 400 publications cited his work over a 20-year period. *Prolegomena to Library Classification*,[12] his comprehensive work on classification theory, is his most-cited publication. But, for a number of reasons, these citations are only a fraction of what a thorough search would establish. Not·the least of these reasons is that our coverage of the field in the early days of *SCI* and *SSCI* was rather selective and limited. Still, when compared to other library notables, it is remarkable how often Ranganathan's work is cited. Indeed, when I began my recent talk at the Madras University library, I was moved to tell the audience that Ranganathan is to library science what Einstein is to physics. Considering the many honors Ranganathan received, examination of his citation record only confirms the widespread subjective impression of his impact. We acknowledged Ranganathan's contributions several years ago when we included his portrait in the mural at ISI® entitled "Cathedral of Man."[13] (See Figure 1.)

I was particularly pleased to honor Ranganathan's memory by giving the Ranganathan lectures. I've felt a special kinship with the man ever since I heard a fellow student lecture on Colon Classification at Columbia University, New York, in 1953. At a time when documentation was a dirty word, I had joined forces with several other radicals at Columbia to form the Documentation Club. Although none of the faculty attended, at one of our meetings a member of the club named Gupta gave a

tion, in spite of its infrequent use, has had a major impact on library classification, affecting all existing or newly revised schemes except the Library of Congress system.[5] One author even suggests that the Library of Congress system is showing an increasing use of synthesis, which is the combining of notation symbols to create a class number, as in faceted classification.[4] Also, over the past few decades, many specialized faceted classification schemes have been developed by the members of the Classification Research Group, London, England.[8,9] Similar developments based on faceted classification principles include the natural language subject heading system of the British Technology Index and Thesaurofacet. Preserved Context Index System (PRECIS), the indexing system devised by Derek W. Austin for use with the British National Bibliography, also owes much to Ranganathan's influence.[10,11] Of the few generalized classification schemes developed in recent years, the USSR's Bibliothecal-Bibliographic Classification scheme has a faceted component, while the Broad beautiful description of Ranganathan's system.

Unfortunately, for very practical reasons, Ranganathan had to compromise in constructing his system. The limited topics he chose for his system's classification schedules were not enduring ones. For example, there was no way Ranganathan could anticipate that such broad subjects as biochemistry would not be adequate to cover the growth of molecular biology information.

Regardless of the shortcomings of his system, it must be emphasized that Ranganathan's work anticipated the need for an automatic self-generating system of classification, of which co-citation clustering based on citation indexing is one important example. Indeed, one might consider each citation as a "facet" of the document citing it, because each citation represents a subject addressed in the document. These facets may be considered linked by implicit colons. For example, a document could be described as: 78JBC456:77PNAS1234:51JBC234:12JICS456:49SCI567. At the next hierarchical level of description, one could substitute for each of these citation facets the research front number we assign to documents through co-citation clustering. Each of these numbers represents a class of core papers identified by co-citation clustering. No doubt one could even determine Ranganathan's fundamental categories of personality, matter, energy, space, or time for each cited document, and organize the research front numbers by his facet formula.

As an automatic classification system, co-citation clustering answers Ranganathan's objections to the inflexible enumerative systems by allowing prompt identification of new research topics. Being completely algorithmic, co-citation clustering automatically reflects new directions in research, without depending on the "eventual" recognition of change in scientific terminology.

I must admit, I'd always thought of Ranganathan in terms of book classification and not in terms of indexing journal literature. But the arbitrary distinction between indexing and classification is based only on the tradition that articles are indexed, but books are classified or cataloged. This separation by form is, however, alien to scientists. At ISI, we index both journals and articles as well as multiauthor books. We also index cited articles, books, patents, or whatever may be cited. Furthermore, Ranganathan's formulation of the term *depth classification* (the symbolic representation of minute units of information), his involvement in the FID, and his founding of the Documentation Research and Training Centre all reflect his active interest in the documentation of journal articles.

In addition to co-citation clustering, more automatic classification systems will undoubtedly follow as computers make it possible to immediately expand and modify a classification schedule to accommodate new books and papers added to a collection. That will be one of the prime advantages of the electronically stored library. It is this responsiveness of computerized systems that's made it possible for us to produce a new *Index to Research Fronts* for our *Index to Scientific Reviews™* and other data bases each year.[14] In the future, we expect to make such an index available for any time period desired. In this way, I like to think that we at ISI have fulfilled some ideas that are implicit, if not articulated, in Ranganathan's work. And I'm happy to acknowledge the debt that all workers in classification and indexing owe this revolutionary thinker.

* * * * *

My thanks to Terri Freedman and Patricia Lawson for their help in the preparation of this essay.

REFERENCES

1. **Garfield E.** A tribute to S.R. Ranganathan, the father of Indian library science. Part 1. Life and works. *Current Contents* (6):3-10, 6 February 1984.
2. **Singh M.** Progress in librarianship in India, 1911-1978. *Libri* 29:158-68, 1969.
3. **Bakewell K G B.** Ranganathan, Shiyali Ramamrita. (Wedgeworth R, ed.) *ALA world encyclopedia of library and information services.* Chicago: American Library Association, 1980. p. 467-8.
4. **Chan L M.** Colon Classification by Shiyali Ramamrita Ranganathan. *Cataloging and classification: an introduction.* New York: McGraw-Hill, 1981. p. 312-5.
5. **Wellisch H H.** Classification. (Wedgeworth R, ed.) *ALA world encyclopedia of library and information services.* Chicago: American Library Association, 1980. p. 146-50.
6. **Thomas A R.** The influence of S.R. Ranganathan on basic instruction in subject analysis of ALA-accredited library schools. *Indian Librarian* 32:51-3, 1977.
7. ---------------. Colon Classification in North American library education. *Indian Librarian* 31:153-6, 1977.
8. **Crossley C A.** New schemes of classification: principles and practice. (Kaula P N, ed.) *Library science today: Ranganathan festschrift.* New York: Asia Publishing House, 1965. Vol. 1. p. 113-29.
9. **Foskett D J.** The Classification Research Group, 1952-1962. *Libri* 12:127-38, 1962.
10. **Vickery B C.** Ranganathan's contribution to indexing. (Dudley E, ed.) *S.R. Ranganathan, 1892-1972.* London: Library Association, 1974. p. 9-11.
11. **Sorensen J.** Austin, Derek William. (Wedgeworth R, ed.) *ALA world encyclopedia of library and information services.* Chicago: American Library Association, 1980. p. 64.
12. **Ranganathan S R.** *Prolegomena to library classification.* New York: Asia Publishing House, 1967. 640 p.
13. **Garfield E.** Fine art enhances ISI's new building: a ceramic mural by Guillermo Wagner Granizo and a sgraffito mural by Joseph Slawinski. *Essays of an information scientist.* Philadelphia: ISI Press, 1983. Vol. 5. p. 15-9.
14. -------------. ISI's "new" *Index to Scientific Reviews* (*ISR*): applying research front specialty searching to the retrieval of the review literature. *Essays of an information scientist.* Philadelphia: ISI Press, 1983. Vol. 5. p. 695-702.

Colon Classification

The Colon Classification system, like enumerative classification systems, divides the universe of knowledge into a number of main classes, such as agriculture, philosophy, and literature. Dewey Decimal Classification, for example, has ten main classes, labeled zero through nine. The Colon Classification system has 42 main classes, most labeled with one or two letters of the alphabet. A few are labeled with numbers or Greek letters. (See Table 1.) But Colon Classification, rather than simply dividing the main classes into a series of subordinate classes, as most systems do, subdivides each main class by particular characteristics into facets. The facets, which are labeled in the Colon Classification system by Arabic numbers, are then combined to make subordinate classes as needed. For example, literature may be divided by the characteristic "language" into the facet of language, including English, German, and French. It may also be divided by "form" which yields the facet of form, including poetry, drama, and fiction.

Colon Classification contains both *basic subjects* and their facets, which contain *isolates*. A basic subject can stand alone, for example, "literature" in the subject "English literature." An isolate, in contrast, is a term that modifies a basic subject, such as the term "English." To create a class number, the basic subject is named first. The isolates follow ordered according to a *facet formula.* This formula states that every isolate in every facet is a manifestation of one of five fundamental categories: personality, matter, energy, space, and time. Personality is the distinguishing characteristic of a subject. Matter is the physical material of which a subject may be composed. Energy is any action that occurs with respect to the subject. Space is the geographic component or the location of a subject. And time is the period associated with a subject.

Thus, the basic subject "handicrafts" of the topic "19th-century woven wool Peruvian clothing handicrafts" would have the isolate from the personality facet, "clothing";

Table 1: The main classes of S.R. Ranganathan's Colon Classification system.

z	Generalia	HZ	Mining	O	Literature
1	Universe of Knowledge	I	Botany	P	Linguistics
2	Library Science	J	Agriculture	Q	Religion
3	Book Science	K	Zoology	R	Philosophy
4	Journalism	KZ	Animal Husbandry	S	Psychology
A	Natural Sciences	L	Medicine	Σ	Social Sciences
β	Mathematical Sciences	LZ	Pharmocognosy	T	Education
B	Mathematics	M	Useful Arts	U	Geography
Γ	Physical Sciences	Δ	Spiritual Experience and	V	History
C	Physics		Mysticism	W	Political Science
D	Engineering	μ	Humanities and Social	X	Economics
E	Chemistry		Sciences	Y	Sociology
F	Technology	ν	Humanities	YZ	Social Work
G	Biology	N	Fine Arts	Z	Law
H	Geology	NZ	Literature and Language		

From: **Ranganathan S R.** *Colon Classification. Part 2. Schedules of Classification.*
New York: Asia Publishing House, 1960. p. 2.4.

from the matter facet, "wool"; from the energy facet, "woven"; from the space facet, "Peru"; and from the time facet, "19th century." Some topics have fewer than five fundamental categories. And some have more than one facet in a given fundamental category. Isolates are always arranged in order of decreasing concreteness, based on the fundamental categories. Personality is considered the most concrete and time the least concrete. The acronym PMEST helps the classifier remember the formula and its order.

To avoid confusion when combining several facet numbers, the classifier needs a device for stringing facets together. The *colon*, from which Colon Classification takes its name, was the first such device in the system. Later, Ranganathan introduced the comma, semicolon, period, inverted comma, and other punctuation marks. Each of these introduces a new fundamental category of facet, such as space or time.

How does a classifier go about synthesizing a class number? Suppose the book to be classified is entitled *The Management of Elementary Education in the United Kingdom in the 1950s*. For this topic, "education" is the basic subject facet. It is also one of the main classes and is indicated by a capital T. "Elementary" is the personality facet. It is indicated by the number 15. There is no matter facet for this topic. Therefore, a colon follows to introduce the energy facet "management," indicated by an eight. A period introduces the space facet, "United Kingdom," indicated by 56. The space facet is followed by an inverted comma, which always introduces time. In this case, the time facet is the 1950s, or N5. When we string together the letters, numbers, and punctuation marks, we obtain the class number T15:8.56'N5. This number will appear on the spine of the book.

Besides its greater flexibility in determining new subjects and subject numbers, Colon Classification improves on the enumerative systems in several other ways. One such improvement is the concept of *phases*. This allows the classifier to readily combine both main classes in a subject such as "mathematics for the biologist." Such a subject is considered "bi-phased" and Colon Classification supplies a specific notation to indicate this condition. However, single-class-number enumerative systems, which predominate in US libraries, tend to force the classifier to choose either "mathematics" or "biology" as the main subject.

Current Comments®

Sci-Mate 1.1: Improved Customer Services and a New Version of the Software for Personal Text Retrieval and Online Searching

Almost a year has passed since we announced ISI®'s new microcomputer software package, *Sci-Mate*™.[1] Briefly, *Sci-Mate* consists of two components: the *Personal Text Manager* (formerly the *Personal Data Manager*) and the *Universal Online Searcher*. The *Personal Text Manager* is a data base management system designed specifically to accommodate textual material—especially bibliographic material. It allows scientists to keep tabs on reprints, correspondence, lab notes, and even patient records. The *Universal Online Searcher* allows users to search any of the hundreds of data bases mounted on several large commercial vendors, without learning any special command languages. Using both *Sci-Mate* components, one can "offload" items retrieved through the *Universal Online Searcher* (from data bases which permit downloading) for permanent storage in the *Personal Text Manager*. See the appendix following this essay for a summary of this software system's principal features. (A revised version of the original *Sci-Mate* description[1] is in preparation. This will take into account changes in the system.)

Enough time has now elapsed for us to evaluate our first venture into microcomputer software. *Sci-Mate* has been well received by users. But even though we anticipated that providing support to customers would be an important factor in its success, we underestimated just how important it would be.

If you're one of those who has used a personal computer, surely you remember your first encounter with it. Who could forget the instruction manual's "technogibberish" and the repeated error messages caused by seemingly minor mistakes? For the moment, "booting-up" a microcomputer is not as simple as plugging the electric cord into an outlet. Clearly, most people can quickly learn what is involved, but no thanks to the manuals generally provided.

The fact is, like many hardware and software manufacturers, we at ISI overestimated scientists' sophistication in the use of microcomputers. Although we expected to have some novice users, we underestimated the number of individuals who would buy their microcomputers just to use *Sci-Mate*. Therefore, many scholars were sitting down to their microcomputers for the first time when they received their *Sci-Mate* diskettes and manuals.

In spite of the complexity of hardware and software systems, manufacturers continue to advertise their use as virtual child's play. Certainly that's the message conveyed by ads showing cute six-year-olds playing the latest video games with computer keyboards. With products as potentially intimidating as digital computers, this desire to exaggerate the ease and downplay the difficulties is understandable. But the result is a legion of frustrated users. They've been primed to expect immediate gratification. In reality, beginning to use these systems demands some hours of contemplation. Alphonse Chapanis, Communications Research Laboratory, Johns Hopkins University, Baltimore, Maryland, recently commented to the effect that "computers are not quite as easy to work as the glossy brochures suggest. Most systems have languages that are too cryptic, too difficult to remember and too large."[2] He went on to note that users can't communicate their difficulties to designers and that systems don't warn the inexperienced of potentially serious mistakes. Similarly, an editorial in *Info World* notes, "There is a communication barrier between manufacturers and consumers.... The people who buy the machines, in general, do *not* know what they are buying and, in general, the people who make computers can *not* explain to the consumers what it is that they are buying."[3]

User difficulties are compounded by the current shakeout in the microcomputer market. With apparently well-established companies such as Osborne folding, support services cannot always be relied upon. As a well-written article in *Monitor* aptly puts it, "The only thing that is safe to predict in this emerging industry is that, in two years' time, it will all be different."[4] That article emphasizes the dizzying choices available to the consumer and attempts to provide some rough guidelines for buyers. These boil down to: (1) go ahead and buy something now—who knows when the market will finish shaking out? and (2) talk to other users rather than relying on manufacturers' literature, which will only dazzle and confuse you. Again, the information gap between user and manufacturer is emphasized. And this prob-

lem can certainly be generalized to the software market.

It is this information gap that ISI has made every effort to close. If we've learned nothing else in the past year, we've learned that the quality of customer support is just as important as the quality of the actual software. Selling software is simply not enough. Often we must first virtually teach people how to operate their microcomputers, as well as such basics as Boolean logic, field definition, etc. Then we can help them install and use *Sci-Mate*.

In addition, as with *Current Contents®* (*CC®*) or any other ISI service, we must carefully evaluate the feedback we receive from *Sci-Mate* users to continually improve our product. The commitment to customer service at ISI begins with yours truly. ISI takes pride in the quality of its products, as I have repeatedly explained.[5] Customer support for *Sci-Mate* is an extension of this philosophy. It begins with the relevant ISI director, Catheryne Stout, and continues with the manager, Cynthia Lopata. Among other departments at ISI, there is also the Customer Service Department's *Sci-Mate* Hotline. This service is staffed from 8 a.m. to 6 p.m., Monday through Friday. The senior customer service representative is Robert Rodgers. He has worked for several years in quality control of ISI's online systems. He's supported by several experienced assistants.

The hotline deals with dozens of calls every day. Questions range from the most elementary to the extremely technical. As indicated earlier, problems encountered by novice users in installing and using *Sci-Mate* are quite common. Some questions may require referral to one of our specialists in research and development. Scientists have a propensity for demanding profound explanations. Many questions have no direct bearing on *Sci-Mate* software, yet we endeavor to answer them all. Customer service representatives are often asked how to formulate search strategy, or how to design records. Since we have handled thousands of calls by now, we have accumulated a bank of valuable information on particular applications of *Sci-Mate* and its installation on various hardware systems. We have even served as a go-between with users and their hardware manufacturers.

When we first launched *Sci-Mate*, our user's manual assumed that users knew how to operate their own computers well enough to install any new software package. Since this was a mistaken assumption, many hotline calls concern *Sci-Mate* installation in the different hardware systems our customers own. (See the appendix for a list of hardware systems with which *Sci-Mate* is compatible.)

We have completely revised the installation section of the manual. It is written in simple language, in a step-by-step format that makes no confusing conceptual leaps. Our manual no longer refers users to their microcomputer manuals. For example, to copy the *Sci-Mate* diskettes, we guide you through every step involved. There is a separate section specifically geared to each of the hardware systems. Incidentally, the manual is sold separately, and many *Sci-Mate* users acquired it first before ordering the software.

One of the most significant sociological aspects of the microcomputer revolution is the growth of users' groups or clubs. Emulating software organizations such as SHARE, these consumer groups have become an important source of market feedback. We will be encouraging the formation of local *Sci-Mate* clubs. In the meantime, we have launched *Sci-Mate Matters*, a free, bi-monthly publication available to all customers. It is designed to help scholars, physicians, and others use *Sci-Mate* to best advantage.

In *Sci-Mate Matters* we discuss specific applications, such as using *Sci-Mate* as a reprint file, or to keep track of lab notes. *Sci-Mate Matters* also covers data base development and maintenance. For example, in the first issue we thoroughly review "templating." This is the procedure used to customize your record formats in *Sci-Mate*. Also covered are the fine points of Boolean searching. *Sci-Mate Matters* will also keep you informed about new and proposed improvements. Finally, we intend to make *Sci-Mate Matters* a user's forum, through which you can share experiences. Most scientists I've encountered are eager to tell colleagues and fellow *Sci-Mate* users about their own information retrieval systems.

In my previous essay,[1] I cautioned you not to expect *Sci-Mate* to be the ultimate intelligent software. Every important program must be continually improved. *Sci-Mate 1.1*, the first revised version of *Sci-Mate*, has now become available. Among other features, *Sci-Mate 1.1* includes a multiple-line report generator. Columnar formats, as shown in Figure 1, can be extremely useful. Many report generators are limited to printing one format. *Sci-Mate*'s multiple-line report generator allows you to vary your report formats so that fields are listed in any order you choose. In addition, it allows you to print the entire entry in each field. *Sci-Mate 1.1* also includes a number of programming changes that further simplify the system.

We are working on a variety of other improvements. Among them is an optional bibliographic formatter. This package will not only allow you to print out the references you cite in a manuscript, it will also tailor the format to a

Figure 1: Sample multiple-line report showing full entries under fields for author, title, citation, and Original Article Text Service (*OATS®*) number.

AUTHOR	TITLE	CITATION	OATS #
ABER M; SALLE G	HISTO-CYTOLOGICAL STUDY OF THE PRINCIPAL PHENOCY TOLOGICAL STAGES OF ORBA NCHE-CRENATA FORSK	BIOLOGY OF THE CELL 44(1):A021 —A021, 1982	NX753
HAMZA R; TOUIBI S; ZAOUCHE A; KAMMOUN M; ELLOUZE R; BARDI I	CANCER OF THE CAVUM IN TUNISIAN CHILDREN — A HI STO-RADIOTOMODENSITOMETR IC CORRELATION REVIEW OF 47 CASES	PEDIATRIC RADIO LOGY 12(6):311- 312, 1982	PW387
JOLY R; CHAPUY MC; ALEXANDRE C; MEUNIER PJ	OSTEOPOROSIS AT HIGH REM ODELING AND PARATHYROID FUNCTION — HISTO-BIOLOGI CAL CONFRONTATIONS	PATHOLOGIE BIOL OGIE 28(7):417- 424, 1980	KJ588
LAGERON A	LIVER STORAGES INDUCED BY PERHEXILINE-MALEATE — HISTOLOGICAL, HISTO-EN ZYMOLOGICAL, BIOCHEMICAL DATA	THERAPIE 36(3): 289-291, 1981	LZ046
MEYER WW; KAUFFMAN SL; HARDYSTASHIN J	STUDIES ON HUMAN AORTIC BIFURCATION .1. HISTO-AR CHITECTURE OF THE BIFURC ATION	ATHEROSCLEROSIS 37(3):377-388, 1980	KR778
MIYAYAMA Y; FUJIMOTO T	FINE-STRUCTURE AND HISTO -CYTOCHEMICAL STUDY OF NEURAL CREST CELLS IN CH ICK-EMBRYO	JOURNAL OF ELEC TRON MICROSCOPY 31(1):113-113, 1982	NR451

given journal's style. You could prepare your first draft for submission to the *Journal of Biological Chemistry*, and then, if necessary, revise it for resubmission to the *Journal of the American Chemical Society*, *Nature*, or *Science*.

Obviously, it is not my intent to discourage anyone from purchasing a microcomputer for *Sci-Mate* or any other purpose. In the long run, our sensitivity to problems encountered by users should help them to overcome unnecessary apprehensions about computers. It is not necessary to soft-pedal the commitment required to use a new software system. On the contrary, a realistic attitude about the long-term benefits versus the short-term problems of developing a computerized information system will overcome these fears.

An automobile dealer can't assume that you're a mechanic. We can't assume that you're either a computer programmer or an information specialist. But we carry our understanding a step further than a used car salesman. He can assume you know how to drive. But he may not know the traffic laws where you will drive, or the terrain. We don't assume you're thoroughly familiar with your hardware system. Not only will we help you make the most of *Sci-Mate*'s sophisticated search, storage, and retrieval functions, we'll also do our best to help you avoid simple mishaps.

In the *InfoWorld* editorial I referred to earlier,[3] there is an anecdote about someone who obtained excellent advice from computer experts. He bought a computer, set it up as instructed, and turned it on. His next step was, with the best of intentions, to peel off the protective paper cover of the floppy disk, inadvertently destroying it. The whole field

Figure 2: Sample format for record in the *Personal Text Manager*.

```
USER File Accession Number 3

Data Base    SOCIAL SCISEARCH 197
Acc. No.     1630144
Title        THEY STAND ON THE SHOULDERS OF GIANTS—SOL SPIEGELMAN, A PIONEER
             IN MOLECULAR BIOLOGY
Language     EN
Doctype      ARTICLE
Author       GARFIELD E
Address      INST SCI INFORMAT/PHILADELPHIA//PA/19104
Citation     CURRENT CONTENTS, MAY 23, #21, P5-12
Year         83
No. Refs     11 REFS
OATS No.     QP 603
Refs.        SHAPIRO A (J GENET, V34, P237, 193.,
             SPIEGELMAN S (SCIENCE, V104, P581, 1946)
             SPIEGELMAN S (CANCER RES, V7, P42, 1947)
             HALL BD (P NAT ACAD SCI US, V47, P137, 1961)
             HAYASHI M (P NAT ACAD SCI US, V50, P664, 1963)
             DOI RH (SCIENCE, V138, P1270, 1962)
             TEMIN HM (NATURE, V226, P1211, 1970)
             HARUNA I (P NAT ACAD SCI US, V50, P905, 1963)
             MILLS DR (P NAT ACAD SCI US, V60, P713, 1968)
             LEVISOHN R (P NAT ACAD SCI US, V60, P866, 1968)
             BISHOP DHL (BIOCHEMISTRY US, V7, P3744, 1968)
Res Spec
Notes
```

of microcomputer use is mined with such potential errors. That's why diligent customer support is essential to user success.

Perhaps the best thing I can do is share with you my own experience with *Sci-Mate*. As you know, I've been writing essays for some time. I decided to experiment with my file of essays. I wanted even better access than using the indexes to the five volumes published until now. I could have asked my secretary to keyboard all the bibliographic data for my essays. Instead, I decided to use *Social SCISEARCH®*. To do this, I used *Sci-Mate's Universal Online Searcher* to automatically dial up the *Social Sciences Citation Index®* files on DIALOG. By going through a quick succession of multiple-choice screens, I did an author search on my own name. At 1,200 baud, or 120 characters per second, I downloaded or offloaded over 650 records. Each record included not only the title, journal, pagination, etc., for each

paper, but also a condensed list of every reference I had cited. Once the downloading onto the temporary file was completed, I transferred the records into my permanent file. Figure 2 shows an example of a record templated in the permanent file.

Since that time, I have used my *Sci-Mate* file almost daily. I don't often have the time or the inclination to browse through the filing cabinet outside my office. Whether at my desk at home or in the office, I can now quickly answer questions like, "In what paper did I cite an editorial in *Lancet* or *Journal of the American Medical Association?*" or "When did I evaluate Italian research?" or "Where did I discuss scientific dictionaries?"

As has often been documented by researchers and clinicians with access to mainframes or minicomputers, the flexibility of a *Sci-Mate* microcomputer system can change the way you function. You may have to change your habits somewhat but the greater flexibility in using your own information system will be worth the initial effort. Those of you who, like me, can easily afford a *Sci-Mate* system may not have the time to get started. You can turn the start-up task over to an assistant. With the help of the *Sci-Mate* manual you can be operational overnight.

But don't take my word for it. If you are planning to attend the annual meeting of the American Society for Microbiology, March 4-9, in St. Louis, or of the Federation of American Societies for Experimental Biology, April 1-6, also in St. Louis, drop by our *Sci-Mate* exhibit and we'll give you a demonstration of the software, and show you how you can begin *SCISEARCH*ing with a minimum of effort.

For more information about *Sci-Mate*, call the hotline at 800-523-4092. Back-up numbers include 800-523-1850, 800-523-1851, or 215-386-0100. When using these last three numbers, ask for extension 1418. After hours or on weekends, you may leave a recorded message at 800-523-4092. A customer service representative will call back as soon as possible. *CC* readers in all European countries except Scandinavia can contact our UK office at 132 High Street, Uxbridge, Middlesex UB8 1DP, UK; telephone: 44-895-30085; or telex: 933693 UKISI. In Scandinavia, contact Lab Comp—Laboratory Computing AB, Gelbgjutarevägen 4, 17148 Solna, Sweden; telephone 46-8-7303598.

©1984 ISI

REFERENCES

1. **Garfield E.** Introducing *Sci-Mate*—a menu-driven microcomputer software package for online and offline information retrieval. Part 1. The *Sci-Mate Personal Data Manager*. Part 2. The *Sci-Mate Universal Online Searcher*. *Current Contents* (12):5-12, 21 March 1983 and (14):5-15, 4 April 1983.
2. **Joyce C & Wingerson L.** Can we adjust to computer culture? *New Sci.* 98(1353):72-3, 1983.
3. **Swaine M.** Go ahead and gripe. *InfoWorld* 5(32):30, 1983.
4. Micros: envy, or pity, the buyer? *Monitor* (33):8-10, 1983.
5. **Garfield E.** Quality control at ISI: a piece of your mind can help us in our quest for error-free bibliographic information. *Current Contents* (19):5-12, 9 May 1983.

The *Sci-Mate* Software System

Sci-Mate™ is a menu-driven microcomputer software package for offline and online information retrieval. *Sci-Mate* consists of two components, the *Personal Text Manager* and the *Universal Online Searcher*. The offline component, the *Personal Text Manager*, is intended to accommodate bibliographic references, lab notes, correspondence, abstracts, and other forms of textual material. The online component, the *Universal Online Searcher*, allows searching of data bases mounted on several large commercial vendors using a universal command language.

Although both the *Personal Text Manager* and the *Universal Online Searcher* are available as separate packages, they are also in-tended for use as an integrated system. Using both components, items can be retrieved through the *Universal Online Searcher* from data bases that permit downloading, for permanent storage in the *Personal Text Manager*.

Sci-Mate is designed to be "user-friendly." It has a menu-driven (or multiple-choice) command system with a tutorial subsystem. At each step, the computer asks you a question and presents a short list of options. If any choice needs clarification, you can ask *Sci-Mate* for help by entering a question mark.

The *Personal Text Manager* has a variety of text-handling functions. One of its major uses is as a reprint filing system. Of course, the bibliographic records kept are representations of the original reprints. The actual reprints are filed separately. The same holds true for storage of lab notes or correspondence, unless the full text is so small that it constitutes the entire document.

The *Personal Text Manager* actually consists of two interrelated files. Users can temporarily store and manipulate records retrieved online or read from a word processor or any other text file in the *temporary work file*. The *permanent user file* is a free-text searchable system where information is permanently stored. Information in the user file can be stored as free text, or by using one of 20 customized, self-generated formats, or templates. Variable-length records of up to 1,900 characters can be used. Records can be linked to extend record capacity. Any record is searchable as soon as it is entered.

Menu-driven searches of stored records can be refined through Boolean logic. This means that "and" and "or" can be used to combine search terms. For example, two title words could be combined, or an author's name could be combined with a journal title and year of publication. Truncation can also be used to allow stem searching, e.g., bronch# for bronchitis, bronchial, etc. A search string can consist of 255 consecutive characters. Ironically, the longer the string, the faster the search.

The *Personal Text Manager* has several special features for manipulating textual material. Bibliographic or other material can be flagged to indicate action taken, such as a reprint ordered or a letter answered. You can review these records periodically to determine their status. Also, the multiple-line report generator feature allows you to print lists of authors, titles, and other elements of records in a columnar format.

Sci-Mate's Universal Online Searcher allows you to search data base hosts such as DIALOG, BRS, MEDLINE, ISI, or SDC. *Sci-Mate's* menu-driven language frees you from the need to know numerous command languages, but the "host" language can be used, if desired. For all host systems, the *Universal Online Searcher* will "logon" automatically. It will also automatically dial up the system if an automatic modem is used. In addition to *Sci-Mate's* search functions, such as Boolean logic and truncation, you retain all of the important search functions offered by the host system. Transferring information into the *Personal Text Manager*, from data bases that permit downloading, allows you to create data bases that are free-text searchable.

Sci-Mate is available for the Apple II (IIe and II+), Vector 3 and 4, TRS-80 Models II and 12, Kaypro 4 and 10, IBM PC and XT (using the PCDOS operating systems), and CP/M-80 systems with Z-80 microprocessors and eight-inch disk drives. A modem is necessary to use the *Universal Online Searcher*. The *Sci-Mate Personal Text Manager* costs $540. The *Universal Online Searcher* costs $440. If purchased together, they cost $880.

Current Comments®

Introducing *Science Citation Index, Abridged Edition*: A Professional Quality Search Tool for Science Students

Number 9   February 27, 1984

More than 20 years ago, ISI® introduced *Science Citation Index®* (*SCI®*). Then, as now, *SCI* employed citation indexing[1] to help searchers retrieve information. When the concept of citation indexing was first proposed,[2] many people were skeptical of its usefulness. But *SCI* has gradually achieved worldwide acceptance during the past two decades. This acceptance grew as we applied citation indexing to virtually every field of scholarship. In 1973, we introduced *Social Sciences Citation Index®* (*SSCI®*). In 1978, *Arts & Humanities Citation Index™* (*A&HCI™*) appeared.

ISI's citation indexes use the cited references in published articles as "subject" indexing terms. Current papers are uniquely linked to their predecessors. By avoiding reliance on arbitrary subject headings, citation indexing simplifies multidisciplinary searching. *SCI* now covers more than 3,000 source journals and over 200 monographic serials annually. Since I recently reviewed the how and why of using *SCI*,[3] it is not necessary to repeat all that here.

Although *SCI* is designed for the working scientist, students who major in science can certainly make good use of it as well. However, *SCI*'s journal coverage is far more exhaustive than most undergraduate students require. Thus, libraries at junior and four-year undergraduate colleges, as well as two-year technical schools and most public libraries, often cannot justify purchasing *SCI*. Thus, students and patrons at these institutions have been deprived of the searching power citation indexes offer.

To date, undergraduate students of science have had little in the way of information retrieval tools to help guide and focus their research. They are often forced to rely on a very limited range of readily available popular sources, such as encyclopedias, magazines, and newspapers. So we developed a retrieval tool especially suited to the needs of the undergraduate student. *Science Citation Index, Abridged Edition* is that tool. It provides students, faculty, and librarians with the search capabilities enjoyed by working scientists.

Like *SCI*, the *Abridged Edition* has a *Citation Index* and an *Author Index*. It also has a specially prepared *Subject Index*. It offers precise access to a multidisciplinary selection of popular periodicals, trade journals, and key journals from the primary literature of science. *SCI, Abridged Edition* employs the same indexing methods used in *SCI*. But the *Abridged Edition*'s coverage has been carefully tailored to fill the needs of students and the faculty that serves them. It comprehensively indexes more than 500 general and popular science periodicals. These cover such fields as engineering, life sciences, technology and applied sciences, earth sciences, physics, mathematics and computer sciences, clinical medicine, chemistry, agriculture, environmental sciences, and social and behavioral sciences, including psychology. Numerous trade and vocational journals are also covered. A categorized list is presented in Table 1. Table 2 shows some high-impact journals indexed by *SCI, Abridged Edition*, arranged by subject.

Rock Products
Welding Design & Fabrication
Wire Journal International

Table 2: Some high-impact journals covered by *SCI®, Abridged Edition*, arranged according to subject.

Table 1: List of trade and vocational journals covered by *SCI®, Abridged Edition*, categorized by subject.

AERONAUTICS & ASTRONAUTICS
  Aviation Week & Space Technology
  Business & Commercial Aviation
CHEMISTRY
  Cosmetics & Toiletries
CIVIL & ENVIRONMENTAL ENGINEERING
  Design News
  Public Roads
  Public Works
  Specifying Engineer
COMPUTER SCIENCES
  Computers in Industry
  EDP Analyzer
CONSTRUCTION & BUILDING TECHNOLOGY
  Concrete Construction
  Construction Contracting
  EC&M—Electrical Construction & Maintenance
  Heating—Piping—Air Conditioning
  Highway & Heavy Construction
ELECTRICAL & ELECTRONIC ENGINEERING
  EDN Magazine—Electrical Design News
  Electrical World
  EPRI Journal
ENERGY & FUELS
  Offshore
  Pipeline & Gas Journal
  Pipe Line Industry
  Power
  Solar Age
INDUSTRIAL ENGINEERING & MANUFACTURING
  Industrial Design Magazine
  Industrial Finishing
  Industrial Wastes
  Material Handling Engineering
  Modern Machine Shop
  Modern Materials Handling
  Package Engineering
  Plant Engineering
  Process Engineering
  Robotics Age
  Tooling & Production
  Turbomachinery International
MATERIALS SCIENCE
  Ceramic Industry
  Modern Paint & Coatings
  PIMA Magazine—Paper Industry Management
    Association
  Plastics Design & Engineering
  Plastics World
  Textile World
  Wood & Wood Products
MECHANICAL ENGINEERING
  Hydraulics & Pneumatics
  Machine Design
METALLURGY & MINING
  American Machinist
  Iron Age
  Light Metal Age
  Metal Finishing
  Modern Casting

AERONAUTICS & ASTRONAUTICS
  AIAA Journal
  Astronautics & Aeronautics
AGRICULTURE/HORTICULTURE/FORESTRY
  Crop Research
  Journal of Forestry
  Journal of Soil Science
ASTRONOMY & ASTROPHYSICS
  Astronomy
  Astrophysical Journal
BIOCHEMISTRY & BIOPHYSICS
  Biochemistry
  Biophysical Journal
  Journal of Biological Chemistry
BIOLOGICAL SCIENCES
  Anatomical Record
  Cell
  Evolution
  Genetics
  Physiological Reviews
BOTANY
  Phytopathology
  Plant Physiology
CHEMICAL ENGINEERING
  AIChE Journal—American Institute of Chemical
    Engineers
  Chemical & Engineering News
CHEMISTRY
  Angewandte Chemie—International Edition in English
  Journal of the American Chemical Society
CIVIL & ENVIRONMENTAL ENGINEERING
  Civil Engineering
  IEEE Journal of Oceanic Engineering
  Journal of Water Resources Planning and Management
  Transportation
COMPUTER SCIENCES
  ACM Transactions on Database Systems
  IEEE Transactions on Computers
CONSTRUCTION & BUILDING TECHNOLOGY
  ASHRAE Journal—American Society of
    Heating, Refrigerating and Air-Conditioning
    Engineers
  Journal of Construction Engineering and
    Management—ASCE
ELECTRICAL & ELECTRONIC ENGINEERING
  Bell Laboratories Record
  IBM Journal of Research and Development
  IEEE Journal of Solid-State Circuits
ENERGY & FUELS
  Journal of Petroleum Technology
  Journal of Solar Energy Engineering—Transactions of
    the ASME
ENVIRONMENTAL SCIENCES
  Environmental Research
  Journal of Ecology
FIRE SCIENCE
  Combustion Science and Technology
  Fire Engineering
FOOD SCIENCE & TECHNOLOGY
  CRC Critical Reviews in Food Science and Nutrition
  Journal of Food Science

GEOGRAPHY
  Geographical Review
  Journal of Geography
GEOSCIENCES
  AAPG Bulletin—American Association of Petroleum
    Geologists
  Journal of Geophysical Research
INDUSTRIAL ENGINEERING & MANUFACTURING
  IEEE Transactions on Industry Applications
  Industrial Engineering
INSTRUMENTS & INSTRUMENTATION
  Instrumentation Technology
  Review of Scientific Instruments
MATERIALS SCIENCE
  Journal of the American Ceramic Society
  TAPPI Journal
MATHEMATICS & STATISTICS
  American Journal of Mathematics
  Journal of the American Statistical Association
  SIAM Review
MECHANICAL ENGINEERING
  Journal of Applied Mechanics—Transactions of the
    ASME
  Proceedings of the Institution of Mechanical Engineers
    Part A—Power and Process Engineering
MEDICAL & HEALTH SCIENCES
  JAMA—Journal of the American Medical Association
  Lancet
  New England Journal of Medicine
  Nursing Research
METALLURGY & MINING
  CIM Bulletin
  International Journal of Powder Metallurgy & Powder
    Technology
METEOROLOGY & ATMOSPHERIC SCIENCES
  Bulletin of the American Meteorological Society
  Journal of the Atmospheric Sciences
MICROBIOLOGY
  Microbiological Reviews
  Virology
MULTIDISCIPLINARY SCIENCES
  Nature
  Proceedings of the National Academy of Sciences of
    the United States of America—Biological Sciences
  Proceedings of the National Academy of Sciences of
    the United States of America—Physical Sciences
  Science
NUCLEAR SCIENCE & TECHNOLOGY
  Nuclear Engineering International
  Nuclear Technology
OCEANOGRAPHY & MARINE BIOLOGY
  Journal of Experimental Marine Biology and Ecology
  Journal of Marine Research
PHYSICS
  Journal of Applied Physics
  Physical Review A—General Physics
PSYCHOLOGY
  American Psychologist
  Journal of General Psychology
TELECOMMUNICATIONS
  Bell System Technical Journal
  IEEE Transactions on Communications
TESTING & QUALITY CONTROL
  Journal of Research of the National Bureau of
    Standards
  Journal of Testing and Evaluation
VETERINARY SCIENCES
  Animal Production
  Journal of the American Veterinary Medical
    Association

ZOOLOGY
  Animal Behaviour
  Annals of the Entomological Society of America

SCI, Abridged Edition's initial coverage was based primarily on the needs of American institutions. Our experience with it will determine whether we can consider supplements or other editions for other countries. Coverage of medicine, for example, is highly selective and includes such journals as the *New England Journal of Medicine* and *Lancet*. These journals are often featured prominently in the worldwide media. It is therefore not uncommon for public libraries to need access to medical articles quoted in the press. The same is true of *Science* and *Nature*, as well as *Scientific American*, *Science News*, *Discover*, and many other popular journals I have discussed in *Current Contents*® (*CC*®) on numerous occasions.

Most of these journals are covered in *SCI, SSCI*, or *A&HCI*. Although a main university library can make good use of *SCI, Abridged Edition*, it may prefer to consider its use at satellite or department libraries, where an additional subscription to *SCI* cannot presently be justified. As a matter of fact, in the near future, we are considering the inclusion of cross-reference information that will tell the user that additional references may be found by searching *SCI* in print, or *SCISEARCH*® online. This feature is already provided in *SSCI* and *SCI*.

SCI, Abridged Edition indexes all the material contained in every periodical issue covered, from general articles, book reviews, editorials, letters, meetings, notes, and reviews to chronologies, corrections, discussions, and biographical items. Each monthly issue will cover more than 8,000 articles. Each semiannual cumulation will index more than 50,000 items. Annual coverage therefore exceeds 100,000—less than 20 percent of *SCI* itself.

Like *SCI*, the *Abridged Edition* is easy to use. The *Citation Index* of *SCI, Abridged Edition* is arranged alphabetically, by the first author of the *cited* paper or book. Below the abbreviated bibliographic description of each work is a list of the current articles that cite it. These are also arranged alphabetically, by first author. Once you have identified the *citing* authors, you can locate the full bibliographic description of their work by looking them up in the *Author Index*. In the discussion which follows, all examples are taken from the 1983 annual *SCI, Abridged Edition*.

Suppose a biology major at a four-year undergraduate school was taking an introductory biology course. It is not unlikely that such a student would hear about Gregor Mendel, discoverer of the basic principles of heredity. Indeed, it is quite possible that such a student or his or her teacher would know of Mendel's landmark 1866 article, "Experiments with plant hybrids."[4] So they might be

Figure 1: Sample *Citation Index* entry from 1983 annual *SCI®, Abridged Edition*. The first *cited* author is S.B. Mende. Listed beneath this author's name is the paper that was cited in a 1983 journal. Beneath the paper appears the condensed citation for the *citing* paper. Then under "MENDEL G," we find his 1866 paper in *Verhandlungen des Naturforschenden*. This was cited in 1983 by J.B. Reid and I. Kohane. Indicated to the right of each citing author's name is the journal title, volume, first page, and the year in which the citing article was published.

		VOL	PG	YR
MENDE SB				
83 GEOPHYS RES LETT	**10**	**122**		
RYCROFT MJ	NATURE	E	303	282 83
MENDEL CW				
** COMMUNICATION				
JOHNSON DJ	J APPL PHYS		54	2230 83
75 REV SCI INSTRUM	**46**	**847**		
SHILOH J	REV SCI INS		54	46 83
77 J APPL PHYS	**48**	**1004**		
ADLER RJ	REV SCI INS		54	940 83
HUMPHRIE.S	J APPL PHYS		54	4629 83
79 2ND P IEEE INT PULS				
81 JUL P INT C HIGH POW				
JOHNSON DJ	J APPL PHYS		54	2230 83
81 JUL P INT C HIGH POW		**45**		
MENDEL CW	PHYS REV A		27	3258 83
81 4TH P INT C HIGH POW				
PRESTWIC.KR	NUCL TECH-F		4	945 83
82 J APPL PHYS	**53**	**7265**		
MENDEL CW	PHYS REV A		27	3258 83
MENDEL G				
1866 VERHANDLUNGEN NATURF	**4**	**3**		
KOHANE I	J HEREDITY		74	175 83
REID JB	PLANT PHYSL		72	759 83
MENDEL JE				
73 BNWL1761 PAC NW LAB		**16**		
WEBER WJ	NUCL TECH	R	60	178 83
73 USAEC BNWL1765 NTIS				
NEILSON RM	NUCL SAFETY		24	213 83
76 1976 P S MAN RAD WAS	**2**	**49**		
WEBER WJ	NUCL TECH	R	60	178 83
77 BNWL2252 PAC NW LAB				
STRACHAN DM	NUCL CH WAS		4	177 83
WEBER WJ	NUCL TECH	R	60	178 83
78 PNLSA2764 PAC NW LAB				
MCVAY GL	J AM CERA			170 83

Figure 2: Sample *Author Index* entries from *SCI®, Abridged Edition*. In addition to full bibliographic information, the *Author Index* indicates the number of references each article contains. The sample shows that I. Kohane published an article during the 1983 indexing period, coauthored with J.F. Kidwell. Their affiliation, Brown University, follows the journal citation. The entry for J.B. Reid is also shown. The language of the original work, if other than English, is indicated by a two-letter abbreviation in parentheses immediately preceding the title. The code following the number of references refers to the ISI® journal accession number, for ordering reprints from *OATS®* (*Original Article Text Service*).

```
KOH W
 ● SILVERMA.H  KEM K—STRUCTURE CHARACTERIZATION OF
   SULFONATED POLYSULFONE MEMBRANES ● MEETING
   J ELCHEM SO  130(3):C112          83  NO R    QF826
     DURACELL INC, BURLINGTON, MA  01803, USA

KOHANE I
 ● KIDWELL JF—EFFECT OF SELECTION, MUTATION, AND
   LINKAGE ON THE EQUILIBRIUM STRUCTURE OF SELFING
   SYSTEMS
   J HEREDITY   74(3):175-180        83    9R   QR882
     BROWN UNIV,DIV BIOL & MED, PROVIDENCE, RI  02912, USA

KOHANSKI RA
 ● LANE MD—BINDING OF INSULIN TO SOLUBILIZED INSULIN-
   RECEPTOR FROM HUMAN-PLACENTA - EVIDENCE FOR A
   SINGLE CLASS OF NONINTERACTING BINDING-SITES
   J BIOL CHEM  258(12):7460-7468    83   64R   QV928
     JOHNS HOPKINS UNIV,SCH MED,DEPT PHYSIOL CHEM, BALTIMORE,
     MD  21205, USA

REID IR
 ● BLUETONGUE ● LETTER
   J AM VET ME  182(2):100           83    3R   PY410
     AGR CANADA,DIV ANIM HLTH, OTTAWA K1A 0Y9, ONTARIO, CANADA

REID JB
 ● INTERNODE LENGTH IN PISUM - DO THE INTERNODE LENGTH
   GENES EFFECT GROWTH IN DARK-GROWN PLANTS
   PLANT PHYSL  72(3):759-763        83   29R   RA527
     UNIV TASMANIA,DEPT BOT, HOBART, TAS 7001, AUSTRALIA

REID L
 ● MCKINLAY AP—WHITESMITH C-COMPILER ● REVIEW
   BYTE         8(1):330             83    5R   PW617
     DATATEC COMP SYST LTD,344 2ND AVE S, SASKATOON S7K 1L1,
     SASKATCHEWAN, CANADA
```

interested in finding out what the recent literature has to say about it.

To determine whether or not Mendel's paper had been cited recently, you simply look under "MENDEL G" in the *Citation Index*, as illustrated in Figure 1. As it turns out, the paper was cited twice in 1983: by J.B. Reid, University of Tasmania, Hobart, Australia, in *Plant Physiology*, and by I. Kohane, Brown University, Providence, Rhode Island, in a recent issue of the *Journal of Heredity*. The full bibliographic descriptions of these papers are found under their respective authors' names in the *Author Index*, as shown in Figure 2.

The *Author Index* includes all the articles indexed during the period covered. It is arranged alphabetically, and has an entry for every author. Each first-author entry contains the complete bibliographic information needed to locate the article. Entries for coauthors refer you back to the main entry under the first author's name. Each first-author entry also lists the ISI journal accession

60

number, so users can order tear sheets or high quality photocopies from *OATS®* (*Original Article Text Service*),[5] ISI's document delivery service. Furthermore, the author's address is provided, so that reprints can be requested. This can be especially important to small libraries in the US, as well as in the Third World.

It is possible, however, that a college student just beginning a science education will be unaware of even the best-known authors in a field. That was our original rationale for designing the *SCI's Permuterm® Subject Index* (*PSI*). In the *PSI*, every significant title word is paired with every other significant word in the same title to produce a list of all possible pairs of terms. However, to address the specific needs of undergraduate science students and faculty, the *Subject Index* of *SCI, Abridged Edition* has been modified. Every significant title word from each indexed article still becomes a primary entry. However, under each primary entry, only one or two of the other significant title words are listed. The co-terms have been selected by computer on the basis of their proximity to the primary entry word. The names of the authors using these terms appear beside each co-term. So if you know a few words that are relevant, you can quickly locate current papers. As with the *Citation Index*, the full bibliographic description of the articles whose title words appear in the *Subject Index* can be found in the *Author Index*.

Continuing with our previous example, the student could have begun a search by selecting a few keywords. Turning to the *Subject Index*, he or she looks up the word "MUTATION." The student would note that it has been used together with 70 other terms (see Figure 3). Each term has been used in the title of an article, together with the main entry word, by the authors listed down the right-hand side of the column. Kohane's paper, "Effect of selection, mutation, and linkage on the equilibrium structure of selfing systems," can be found next to the term "SELECTION."

Figure 3: Sample *Subject Index* entry from *SCI®*, *Abridged Edition*. The main entry, "MUTATION," has been paired with numerous other terms. Alongside each co-term is found the name of an author who used both words in the title of an article.

MUTATION

POLALX1	- - - WAHL AF
REGULATORY	- SPARROW CP
RESISTANCE	- MARK LG
RNA	- - - - - - WEISSBRU.B
RNA2	- - - - - TEEM JL
RPOB	- - - - - LITTLE R
SELECTION	- - KOHANE I
SITE	- - - - - - DOBKIN C
SPONTANEOUS	DASSARMA S
STANLEYVIL.	- RHODA MD
STRAINS	- - - CHANG YY
STREPTOCOC.	- GRIST RW
SUPPRESS	- - GROSSMAN AD
TARGETED	- - FIX D
TS15	- - - - - GULLETTA E
TYPE	- - - - UHM JY

Those interested in technical or math-related topics, rather than in the life sciences, will also find *SCI, Abridged Edition* useful, since it is a multidisciplinary tool. One topic of great current interest in the computer sciences community is "artificial intelligence."[6] A key concept in this field is "fuzzy sets," introduced by Lofti A. Zadeh, University of California, Berkeley, in 1965.[7] Fuzzy sets are a mathematical method of dividing complex, real-world problems into sequences of simpler questions.

A student majoring in computer science might well be acquainted with Zadeh's primordial paper on fuzzy sets. In the *Citation Index*, the student learns that Zadeh's paper was cited in 1983 by Colin B. Brown, University of Washington, Seattle (see Figure 4). To find the full bibliographic description of the paper by Brown, he or she checks the *Author Index* under Brown's name (see Figure 5). For students not familiar with Brown or Zadeh, the Brown article can also be found under "FUZZY SETS" in the *Subject Index* (see Figure 6). A current article by Zadeh himself is listed under the entry, "FUZZY LOGIC." Figure 7 shows the *Author Index* entry which could also have been the starting point of a search.

Figure 4: Sample entry from *SCI®*, *Abridged Edition*'s *Citation Index*, showing the names of the cited author, L.A. Zadeh, and the citing authors, including C.B. Brown.

ZADEH LA		VOL	PG	YP
50 P IRE 38				
TSAO YH	J ACOUST SO		74	827 83
63 LINEAR SYSTEM THEORY				
FISH AJ	J DYN SYST		105	83 83
KUH ES	CC/ENG TECH		1983	20 83
MIYAZAWA Y	AIAA J		21	163 83
63 LINEAR SYSTEMS THEOR				
KABAL P	IEEE COMMUN	N	31	430 83
65 INFORMATION CONTROL 8 338				
BROWN CB	J STRUC ENG		109	1211 83
69 SYSTEM THEORY				
BILARDI G	IEEE COMMUN		31	853 83
69 SYSTEMS THEORY				
FISH AJ	J DYN SYST		105	83 83
72 ERLM325 U CAL MEM				
73 I ELECTRICAL ELECTRO 3 28				
DAS TK	AIAA J	N	21	786 83
75 SYNTHESE 30 407				
ZADEH LA	COMPUTER		16	61 83
78 FUZZY SETS SYSTEMS 1 3				
DUDA RO	SCIENCE		220	261 83
79 MACHINE INTELLIGENCE 9				
QUINLAN JR	COMPUTER J		26	255 83
79 MACHINE INTELLIGENCE 9 149				
81 247 SRI INT AI CTR T				
83 COMPUTERS MATH 9 149				
83 ERL M8326 U CAL MEM				
ZADEH LA	COMPUTER		16	61 83

Figure 5: Sample *Author Index* entry from *SCI®*, *Abridged Edition*, showing the full bibliographic description of the paper by C.B. Brown and J.T.P. Yao.

BROWN CA
● BURNS FC KNOLL W SWALEN JD FISCHER A—UNUSUAL MONOLAYER BEHAVIOR OF A GEMINALLY DISUBSTITUTED FATTY-ACID - CHARACTERIZATION VIA SURFACE-PLASMONS AND X-RAY PHOTOELECTRON-SPECTROSCOPY STUDY
J PHYS CHEM 87(19):3616-3619   83   21R   RG485
IBM CORP,RES LAB, SAN JOSE, CA 95193, USA

BROWN CB
● YAO JTP—FUZZY-SETS AND STRUCTURAL-ENGINEERING
J STRUC ENG 109(5):1211-1225   83   15R   QN167
UNIV WASHINGTON, SEATTLE, WA 98195, USA

BROWN CC
● LEARNING ABOUT TOXICITY IN HUMANS FROM STUDIES ON ANIMALS
CHEMTECH US 13(6):350-358   83   49R   QT367
NCI,BIOMETRY BRANCH,LANDOW BLDG,RM 5C03, BETHESDA, MD 20205, USA
● KOZIOL JA—STATISTICAL ASPECTS OF THE ESTIMATION OF HUMAN RISK FROM SUSPECTED ENVIRONMENTAL CARCINOGENS ● REVIEW
SIAM REV 25(2):151-181   83   148R   QK788
NCI,BIOMETRY BRANCH, BETHESDA, MD 20205, USA

SCI, Abridged Edition began regular publication in January 1984. It will appear in softcover volumes each month, except for June and December. These months will be included, respectively, in two-volume, semiannual cumulations published each July and January. Thus, students, faculty, librarians, and others will be able to identify and retrieve the most current articles on topics in science and technology each month, while the information is new, and reprints still readily available from authors.

I have stressed the usefulness of *SCI, Abridged Edition* to undergraduate students. It may one day fill a special niche in college and university libraries

Figure 6: Sample *Subject Index* entry from *SCI®*, *Abridged Edition*, showing various entries, including, "FUZZY SETS," used in an article by C.B. Brown, and "FUZZY LOGIC," used by L.A. Zadeh.

FUZZY
| ALGORITHM - - DAS TK
| CONTEXT - - - SMITH TA
| OBJECTIVE - - WANG PH
| TECHNIQUES - CAULFIEL.HJ

FUZZY-LOGIC
| BASED - - - - ZADEH LA

FUZZY-SETS
| STRUCTURAL. - BROWN CB

FV
| REGION - - - - GONI F

throughout the world. There is additional emphasis on applied science and technology in the *Abridged Edition*. Those institutions that are not yet ready to acquire the full *SCI* can use the *Abridged Edition* as an entry point to the key literature. Third World nations certainly have a need for "appropriate technology," but may not be able to afford the journal coverage available to the larger institutions.

The price of *SCI, Abridged Edition* is comparable to the cost of a dozen or so average journals in its coverage. This means that the *Abridged Edition* may even be within the budget of a department library. Since the *Abridged Edition* has been geared toward student needs, a user in a research setting would obtain only a sampling of key articles, compared to the exhaustive list of references a comprehensive search of

Figure 7: *SCI®*, *Abridged Edition*'s *Author Index* entry showing the bibliographic description of the 1983 article in *Computer* by L.A. Zadeh.

ZACZEK R
● KOLLER K. COTTER R HELLER D COYLE JT—N-ACETYLASPARTYLGLUTAMATE - AN ENDOGENOUS PEPTIDE WITH HIGH-AFFINITY FOR A BRAIN GLUTAMATE RECEPTOR
P NAS BIOL 80(4):1116-1119   83   25R   QD167
JOHNS HOPKINS UNIV,SCH MED,DEPT PSYCHIAT & BEHAV SCI,DIV CHILD PSYCHIAT, BALTIMORE, MD 21205, USA

ZADEH LA
● COMMONSENSE KNOWLEDGE REPRESENTATION BASED ON FUZZY-LOGIC
COMPUTER 16(10):61-65   83   12R   RK103
UNIV CALIF BERKELEY,DEPT EECS & ERL, BERKELEY, CA 94720

ZADIK FR
● LATE DETECTION OF HIP DISLOCATION ● LETTER
LANCET 2(8345):340   83   1R   RB259

SCI would yield. But *SCI, Abridged Edition* can provide an excellent start to a search before going to the main library. An examination of the topics covered in the *Abridged Edition* will demonstrate that the most influential journals in most fields have been included. (See Table 2.) It will also remind you that the borderline between science and technology is indeed narrow. *SCI* itself has always covered the major journals in engineering, science, and technology. By including many of these journals in *SCI, Abridged Edition* and adding some "trade" journals to this coverage, we enhance its usefulness in an age of rapid technological advances.

It should be apparent that were it not for the existence of the larger and comprehensive *SCI*, the *Abridged Edition* would not have been possible at these prices. The 1983 annual is clearly a bargain. We want to encourage the use of the *Abridged Edition* in undergraduate institutions—even in high schools. All such places of learning have their share of future Nobel prizewinners as well as future science teachers. They should all learn how to use libraries and *SCI* at the earliest possible stage of their careers.

The 1983 annual *SCI, Abridged Edition* is available at the introductory price of $380. An annual subscription for 1984 is $780. For more information about the *Abridged Edition*, or for a free sample issue, call ISI Customer Services at (215) 386-0100, extension 1359, telex: 84-5305, or write us at 3501 Market Street, Philadelphia, Pennsylvania 19104. Subscribers in Europe and elsewhere can contact ISI at 132 High Street, Uxbridge, Middlesex UB8 1DP, UK. The Uxbridge office's phone number is 44-895-30085 (telex: 933693 UKISI).

* * * * *

My thanks to Stephen A. Bonaduce for his help in the preparation of this essay. ©1984 ISI

REFERENCES

1. **Garfield E.** *Citation indexing—its theory and application in science, technology, and humanities.* Philadelphia: ISI Press, 1983. 274 p.
2. --------------. Citation indexes for science. *Science* 122:108-11, 1955.
3. --------------. How to use the *Science Citation Index (SCI).* *Current Contents* (9):5-14, 28 February 1983.
4. **Mendel G.** Versuche über Pflanzen-Hybriden (Experiments with plant hybrids). *Verhand. Naturforsch. Ver. Brünn* 4:3-47, 1866.
5. **Garfield E.** While you're up, dial me an *OATS*—we're still waiting for the document delivery revolution. *Essays of an information scientist.* Philadelphia: ISI Press, 1983. Vol. 5. p. 779-84.
6. --------------. Artificial intelligence: using computers to think about thinking. Part 1. Representing knowledge. Part 2. Some practical applications of AI. *Current Contents* (49):5-13, 5 December 1983 and (52):5-17, 26 December 1983.
7. **Zadeh L A.** Fuzzy sets. *Inform. Contr.* 8:338-53, 1965.

Current Comments®

What Does *Current Contents Online* Mean to You?

Number 10

March 5, 1984

In 1981, we announced the first of several new online data bases including *ISI/BIOMED®*.[1] Since then, we have added several other data bases to the ISI® Search Network: *ISI/CompuMath®*, *ISI/GeoSciTech™*, and *Index to Scientific & Technical Proceedings & Books (ISI/ISTP&B®)*. The data bases were stored on a host computer in Washington, DC. By the time you read this essay, those files will be closed. We are now continuing with a long-range development effort to "renovate" and reopen our files, perhaps on our own computer in Philadelphia.

Over the years, ISI files have been available via several "third party vendors," such as DIALOG and DIMDI. However, the development of software directly relevant to our needs is crucial. This is especially true for readers of *Current Contents®* (*CC®*). The new *ISI/NET* system will, in fact, provide simultaneous access to all editions of *CC*, including *CC/Arts & Humanities*.

During the transition from the ISI Search Network to *ISI/NET*, we intend to test our system extensively. In another essay, I will provide a detailed analysis of this three-year experiment. ISI Search Network passholders have received a letter describing in more detail the new changes. If you use any of the data bases mentioned here, and did not receive this letter, you should direct questions to Barbara Schreiber-Coia, ISI's online commitments administrator, at 800-523-1850, ext. 1288. Overseas clients should contact the nearest ISI office.

The decision to make *CC* available online, or in some electronic form, was always a long-term goal. Even with considerable experience with online searching, we do not want to mount any new files until we have fully tested our premises and our software. In planning for *CC Online*, we know that only a fraction of our readers have their own microcomputers. But that number is increasing rapidly. A significant number of *CC* readers have acquired *Sci-Mate™*,[2-4] and many of them have asked, "Why don't you put *CC* online?" This was confirmed in a recent telephone poll. This study confirms a high degree of interest and also a wide diversity in perceptions of costs and features.

This brings me to the main point of this essay. In designing this new service, we wish to be guided by comments from as many readers as possible. As a *CC* reader, you are invited to participate in our planning. We'd like you to tell us your vision or version of *CC Online*. Tell us the features you'd expect the service to include.

Our reliance on user feedback in designing ISI services is not new. By now, many of you are familiar with our "Piece of Your Mind" (POYM) questionnaires.[5] Through these periodic surveys, we keep our finger on the pulse of user needs. Over the years, most POYM responses expressed satisfaction with *CC* as it is. There are always those, however, who suggest ways *CC* could be made "better." Most of their suggestions involve journal coverage, and reflect the eternal dilemma in information systems: should it be all-inclusive, or highly selective? Should it be a mass product or personalized?

There are always readers who want *more* journals and features added to *CC*. Many of them have forgotten the time when *CC* contained nothing but contents pages. There was no subject index or author address directory. The journals we covered then numbered but a few hundred. Today, a typical *CC* edition covers about 800 to 1,200 journals, and lists from 100,000 to 200,000 articles per year.

On the other hand, there are those who want *fewer* journals. They would reduce the number of journals covered in *CC*, but not their favorite journals. These "economizers" are rarely in agreement about which journals should go. Acceding to their wishes would offend others. To paraphrase Abraham Lincoln: You can't please all of the people all of the time. However, in designing *CC Online*, we are going to try.

Of course, there's been a "customized *CC*" of sorts available for the past 20 years. Our weekly *Automatic Subject Citation Alert* (*ASCA*®)[6] can tell you about a select group of articles or journals. *ASCA* users themselves provide us with highly individualized interest profiles. These profiles can consist of keywords, author names, cited references, institutions, journals, countries of origin, or any combination of these. Each week, you receive a printout of all the latest articles which match your profile. As effective as *ASCA* is, many feel that it cannot replace the aesthetic *satisfaction* of browsing contents pages. So a large percentage of *ASCA* users also scan *CC*. When *CC* goes online, many readers will want to combine the best features of both systems.

CC Online can have many different meanings. For some readers, this is interpreted literally to mean exactly what it implies. Such readers visualize using their personal microcomputer or other intelligent terminals for direct access to the ISI central computer. They want to browse or search intermittently. They would turn from page to page, checking carefully their favorite journals. They would scan the contents pages and check off interesting article titles. Then they would execute a command to generate a reprint request, interlibrary loan, or a purchase order.

Those of you who have already adopted the *Sci-Mate*[2-4] software system, or its equivalent on minicomputers and mainframes, could take the literal interpretation of the *CC Online* idea a step further. You would download or offload the bibliographic information retrieved *online* into your personal microcomputer files. This would not only make it easier to retrieve the references in the future, it would also permit you to do all the housekeeping (file management, annotations, etc.) *offline*.

The literal *CC Online* idea is possible, but not necessarily inexpensive. The fact is that any national online system involves a "connect charge" of 50 cents to a dollar per minute. Even if you can browse a contents page in 60 seconds, you can run up quite a bill going through dozens of contents pages each week. The fact that *CC Online* is not necessarily cheaper than the printed version will surprise many readers. Many of you believe that electronic journals will somehow be cheaper than their printed counterparts.

Electronic versions of journals or *CC* may be cheaper in the long run, especially if you take into account all costs. It depends upon your particular situation. The initial cost of selecting and obtaining an individual electronic record may seem high. But the long-term benefits may be higher. Once your personal file is stored electronically, you can access it free of charge. On the other hand, if you never download records, you must pay connect time whenever you access a document.

There are other electronic alternatives. Instead of accessing *CC Online* over networks such as Tymnet, Telenet, or Euronet one could obtain *CC* each week on floppy disks. Each floppy disk could contain a category of *CC* journals (biochemistry, mathematics, neuroscience, etc.). This is a variation on the theme of *CC* magnetic tapes, which have been available for 20 years.[7] Some of the world's leading information centers use them to provide selective dissemination of information services to their clients. These include centers in such countries as Canada, Hungary, Israel, and Sweden.[8]

The advent of minicomputers added a new dimension to the use of ISI tapes. Several pharmaceutical and chemical firms use them, as do such institutions as the Imperial Cancer Research Fund in London. There, the contents of the tapes are stored online for a short period. Readers can access them on the basis of predetermined profiles. This eliminates the cost of long-distance telephone networks. Access is provided free to anyone on the local area network. Browsing online becomes cost effective. It is not the aesthetic equivalent, however, of browsing the printed version of *CC*. So it is not unusual to use this system selectively. This is combined with browsing the printed version of *CC*.

Indeed, preliminary market research confirms that most readers intend to continue reading and browsing the printed *CC*. For such readers, *CC Online* means the ability to search retrospectively. Sometimes, you may want to retrieve a paper noted earlier in *CC*. You recall the particular journal in which it appeared, as well as a keyword, but you may not remember the exact title or author. It was in such situations that readers often used the *Quarterly Index to Current Contents®/Life Sciences* (*QUICC™/LS*).[9] However, this print service has been discontinued. *CC Online* could provide all the access points we provided in *QUICC/LS*, and a lot more.

Some readers might want to use *CC Online* in another way. They would continue to scan *CC* each week, marking off particular items of interest. They would then want to go online to ISI to record the author's address and/or the entire bibliographic record. This could be done by simply using the *Original Article Text Service* (*OATS®*) number which appears in the oval in the left-hand corner of each *CC* page. This number uniquely identifies each issue of each journal covered in *CC*.

In combination with the journal page and, for error-checking redundancy, the first author's initials, a unique code is created. This code is sufficient to capture complete bibliographic information including, if desired, the list of references cited in that article. Preparing the list of article codes *offline* on your *Sci-Mate* controlled microcomputer can minimize the time spent *online*. Using 1,200 baud lines, it will take about one minute to download from ten to 20 records. The telecommunications cost would be small compared to the nominal "hit" charge for downloading a record.

How would one pay for such a service? The online industry has dozens of charging systems, most of them complex. We hope to provide *CC Online* for use by the individual scientist subscriber or small lab. For larger groups or institutions, group rates will be worked out. Clearly, we want to provide you with bibliographic records that are timely and accurate. If we tried to charge you more than what it would cost you to do it yourself, you would create your own bibliographic records. Depending upon your own local circumstances, this may be the best solution. However, using ISI's verified records should be more convenient and economical in the long run. ISI has no particular commitment to a particular technology. Printed journals have a long-term future. So do their electronic counterparts. Scientists and librarians have an insatiable appetite for information. Each new medium offers new opportunities. According to the circumstances, titles, citations, abstracts, and even full texts are useful and necessary. Selective critical reviews and/or mini-reviews will also be necessary and increasingly useful as the volume of literature continues to grow. But each has a price.

As long as the worldwide population of research scientists and scholars continues to grow, the volume of useful information in electronic and print media will increase. Aesthetic and intellectual, as well as economic, factors will determine how rapidly *CC* or other journals or indexes will make the transition to electronic form. As we develop *CC Online*, we also see videodiscs on the horizon. The popularity of these new technologies will be conditioned by the quality and resolution of television screens.

Adaptations to these new media will not take place overnight. It required a generation for *CC* to reach the stage where it is now taken for granted. Certainly it will take at least half that time for the scientific community worldwide to adapt to the new computer and information age. Those of us who are enamored of each new information technology "breakthrough" want things to happen overnight. A few do seem to happen that quickly. But most require endurance, patience, and persistence.

CC could never please all of the people all of the time. Perhaps neither will *CC Online*. But if you will continue to give us a piece of your mind, we will continue to listen. And we will continue to satisfy most of you most of the time. In a world where specialization is the hallmark of scholarly endeavor, this may be overly optimistic. But we must try.

Please let us know how you envision *CC Online*. You can be sure that I'll be reporting the results of these developmental efforts as soon as we have something really new to report.

REFERENCES

1. **Garfield E.** ISI's on-line system makes searching so easy even a scientist can do it: introducing METADEX automatic indexing & ISI/BIOMED SEARCH. *Essays of an information scientist.* Philadelphia: ISI Press, 1983. Vol. 5. p. 11-4.
2. --------------. Introducing *Sci-Mate*—a menu-driven microcomputer software package for online and offline information retrieval. Part 1. The *Sci-Mate Personal Data Manager. Current Contents* (12):5-12, 21 March 1983.
3. --------------. Introducing *Sci-Mate*—a menu-driven microcomputer software package for online and offline information retrieval. Part 2. The *Sci-Mate Universal Online Searcher. Current Contents* (14):5-15, 4 April 1983.
4. --------------. *Sci-Mate 1.1*: improved customer services and a new version of the software for personal text retrieval and online searching. *Current Contents* (8):3-9, 20 February 1984.
5. --------------. Quality control at ISI: a piece of your mind can help us in our quest for error-free bibliographic information. *Current Contents* (19):5-12, 9 May 1983.
6. --------------. You don't need an online computer to run SDI profiles offline! So why haven't you asked for *ASCA*—the ISI selective citation alert. *Current Contents* (13):5-12, 28 March 1983.
7. --------------. *Current Contents* is available on tape. *Essays of an information scientist.* Philadelphia: ISI Press, 1977. Vol. 1. p. 47.
8. --------------. Library of the Hungarian Academy of Sciences builds computerized information services on ISI's data base. *Essays of an information scientist.* Philadelphia: ISI Press, 1983. Vol. 5. p. 4-6.
9. --------------. Introducing ISI's *Quarterly Index to Current Contents/Life Sciences (QUICC/LS). Essays of an information scientist.* Philadelphia: ISI Press, 1981. Vol. 4. p. 338-40.

Current Comments®

Journal Citation Studies. 41.
Entomology Journals—What They Cite
and What Cites Them

Number 11
March 12, 1984

In a recent essay on ISI Press®,[1] I gave a brief description of *Dear Lord Rothschild*,[2] a biographical memoir on Walter Rothschild by his niece, Miriam Rothschild. It is gratifying to report that the scientific and popular press agree that this is an exceptional book that bridges many cultures.[3-5]

In my review, I promised to tell you more about the extraordinary Miriam Rothschild. The book that tells the story of her scientist-conservationist uncle is just the tip of the iceberg. At age 74, Miriam Rothschild has demonstrated just one more facet of her polymathic talents.

We often speak about the two cultures of art and science. But within science there are many separate cultural groups. One group of biologists, for example, is represented by the Federation of American Societies for Experimental Biology (FASEB). Another kind of biology is that taught in high schools and colleges. This "traditional" biology is better exemplified by the American Institute of Biological Sciences (AIBS). FASEB and AIBS represent two cultures of biology. The full spectrum of biology, or life science as we call it in *Current Contents*® (*CC*®), runs the gamut from preclinical medicine to agriculture.

While the readership of *CC* includes many botanists, zoologists, and even an occasional paleontologist, fields such as entomology have only occasionally received attention here. We did touch on the firefly,[6] spiders,[7] and a few other diversions of biological interest, but the most definitive study involved a citation analysis of botany journals.[8]

When I met Miriam Rothschild, I became conscious of the fact that we had never specifically discussed the field of entomology. We have published several *Citation Classics*™ by entomologists,[9,10] including one in the current issue of *CC/Life Sciences*.[11] I decided to analyze the entomology journals indexed in *Science Citation Index*® (*SCI*®). The analysis follows the pattern in our studies of other fields, such as earth science[12] and biochemistry.[13] I believe the study will enable us to better appreciate the contributions of such entomologists as Miriam Rothschild. In the near future, we intend to discuss the research of this entomologist *extraordinaire* in an essay.

Entomology is the study of insects, the largest class of living things on Earth. In the fourth century BC, Aristotle used the word "entoma," or insect, to describe the animals he observed to have three basic body sections. Today, there are about 850,000 known species of insects, and entomologists continue to discover new species. In fact, it has been estimated that another 850,000 species of insects are still unknown to scientists.[14]

Table 1 lists 36 entomology journals indexed in *SCI* that are included in this study. The year each of these "core" journals began publication is also shown. Fifteen of the journals in Table 1 are published in the US. The UK accounts for six core entomology journals. Canada, France, and Japan each publish two core journals. Australia, Czechoslovakia, the Federal Republic of Germany, India, the Netherlands, New Zealand, People's Republic of China, South Africa, and Switzerland each publish one of the journals listed in Table 1.

As in our previous journal citation studies, we will treat the 36 core journals as if they were a single "Macro Journal of Entomology." That is, we'll pool their references to see what journals they collectively cite. Conversely, we are interested in identifying what journals cite this macro journal. Data reported here are taken from the 1982 *Journal Citation Reports®* (*JCR™*), which is volume 14 of *SCI*.

The 36 core journals published 2,600 articles in 1982. This represents less than one percent of the 378,000 articles included in the 1982 *JCR*. Keep in mind that *JCR* excludes items such as editorials, news reports, and obituaries. The core journals cited 42,000 references in 1982, or about half of one percent of the eight million references processed in *JCR* that year. Thus, the average 1982 entomology article cited 16 references, lower than the 21 cited in the average *SCI* article.

The core entomology journals *received* 23,500 citations in 1982, less than half of one percent of all *JCR* citations that year. Just four journals account for 50 percent of these citations: *Annals of the Entomological Society of America* (2,150 citations), *Canadian Entomologist* (1,950), *Journal of Economic Entomology* (4,000), and *Journal of Insect Physiology* (3,700). Thus, citations to the entomology journals follow the "law of concentration," discussed previously.[15]

Table 2 lists the 50 journals that were most frequently cited *by* the core group in 1982. They are listed in descending order of number of citations from the core entomology journals (column A). Also shown are citations received from all *JCR*-covered journals (column B), self-citations (column C), impact factors (column G), immediacy indexes (column H), and the number of articles each journal published in 1982 (column I). Impact factors indicate how often a journal's articles were cited in the past few years. Immediacy indicates how frequently a journal's articles were cited in the same year that they were published. We'll say more about impact in this essay.

The 50 journals in Table 2 received 17,000 citations from the core group, or 41 percent of all references cited by the

Table 1: Core entomology journals indexed by *SCI®* and the year each began publication.

Acta Entomologica Bohemoslovaca—1965
Acta Entomologica Sinica—1950
Annales de la Societe Entomologique de France—1832
Annals of the Entomological Society of America—1908
Annual Review of Entomology—1956
Applied Entomology and Zoology—1966
Bulletin of Entomological Research—1910
Canadian Entomologist—1868
Ecological Entomology—1976
Entomologia Experimentales et Applicata—1958
Entomon—1976
Entomophaga—1956
Environmental Entomology—1972
Florida Entomologist—1917
Great Lakes Entomologist—1966
Insect Biochemistry—1971
Insectes Sociaux—1954
International Journal of Insect Morphology and Embryology—1971
Japanese Journal of Applied Entomology and Zoology—1957
Journal of Arachnology—1972
Journal of Economic Entomology—1908
Journal of Insect Physiology—1957
Journal of Medical Entomology—1964
Journal of the Australian Entomological Society—1967
Journal of the Entomological Society of Southern Africa—1939
Journal of the Georgia Entomological Society—1966
Journal of the New York Entomological Society—1893
Mosquito News—1941
New Zealand Entomologist—1951
Pacific Insects—1959
Physiological Entomology—1976
Proceedings of the Entomological Society of Ontario—1959
Proceedings of the Entomological Society of Washington—1884
Proceedings of the Hawaiian Entomological Society—1905
Systematic Entomology—1976
Zeitschrift fur Angewandte Entomologie—Journal of Applied Entomology—1914

core in 1982. Twenty are themselves members of the core. They are indicated by asterisks. These 20 journals received 22,000 citations in 1982, of which 51 percent were from core citing journals. The 30 *non*-core journals on the list received 617,000 citations, of which just one percent were from the core group.

Several entomologists who reviewed this study suggested that a journal's age affects the number of citations it re-ceives. That is, the longer a journal has been in publication, the greater the number of its citable articles and, thus, the more citations it receives. Presumably, the same "advantage" is enjoyed by journals that publish a large number of articles each year. However, the advantage of a journal's age or size varies from field to field.

For example, consider the top two journals in Table 2. The *Journal of Eco-*

nomic Entomology received about 4,000 citations from all *JCR*-covered journals in 1982. The *Journal of Insect Physiology* received 3,700 citations. The first journal has been in publication since 1908 while the second started in 1957, a difference of 50 years. Also, in 1982 the first journal published twice as many articles as the second journal (column I). Despite the great differences in age *and* size, both journals received about the same number of citations.

But in general, any journal with a long history will accumulate a larger number of citations regardless of the average quality of its articles, now or in the past. However, impact is how we differentiate journals that are highly cited for *historical* reasons from those producing articles of great *current* relevance and quality. Historical or "cumulative" impact is yet another measure we can study by showing what particular years of a journal's publications are cited. *JCR* reports such data over a ten-year period for each journal it indexes. For example, the *Annual Review of Entomology* received 1,255 citations in 1982, of which 16 were to articles it published that year; 63 to its 1981 articles; 108 to 1980; 132 to 1979; 68 to 1978; 75 to 1977; 76 to 1976; 84 to 1975; 56 to 1974; 64 to 1973; and 513 to 1972 and earlier years.

The five core journals that ranked highest in impact appear in Table 2. *Annual Review of Entomology* had an impact of 4.75. Review journals generally have the highest impact. *Journal of Insect Physiology* follows with an impact of 1.58. *Insect Biochemistry* had an impact of 1.48; *Physiological Entomology*, 1.35; and *Ecological Entomology*, 1.25. When we consider all 36 core journals as a group, the Macro Journal of Entomology has an impact of .61. This compares to 1.06 in our study of botany journals[8] and 3.36 for biochemistry.[13]

In the 1982 *JCR*, impact is calculated by adding the number of articles a journal published in 1980 and 1981. The number of citations these articles received in 1982 is also tabulated. Divid-

ing the latter by the former, we find how often the average article from the *previous two years* is cited in the current year.

Of course, the relevance of this two-year base depends on the lag time for each field's literature. That is, the core journals might have higher impacts if a two-year base *earlier* than 1980-1981 is used. Table 3 lists the top ten high-impact entomology journals, showing how their impacts vary when different two-year bases are used. For example, *Annual Review of Entomology* has an impact of 4.75 when 1982 citations to its 1980-1981 articles are considered. But its impact rises to 6.49 when we consider 1982 citations to its 1979-1980 articles. This pattern is generally followed by the other entomology journals. So this two-year base would perhaps be more relevant if we were comparing the impact of entomology journals to those in other fields. But the relative rankings of the journals in Table 3 does not change significantly, whichever two-year period is used.

The peak years for the entomology journals can be determined by examining their "half-lives," also shown in Table 3. Cit*ed* half-life indicates the median age of articles from each journal that were cited in 1982. For example, the core journal with the shortest half-life is *Ecological Entomology*. It has a cited half-life of 3.1 years. That is, half of the citations this journal *received* in 1982 were to articles it published from 1980 through 1982.

Cit*ing* half-life indicates the median age of the literature cited *by* each journal. *Mosquito News* has the shortest citing half-life of the core journals in this study at 6.6 years. Half of its 1982 references cited articles published from 1976 through 1982.

As you can see, a few of the core journals in Table 3 have citing and cited half-lives greater than ten years. The data indicate that the entomology literature remains useful and significant for a fairly long period of time. In the future, *JCR* will provide complete data on any half-

Table 3: 1982 impact factors of selected entomology journals across various two-year bases. Cited and citing half-lives for each journal appear at the far right.

Journal	1980-81	1979-80	1978-79	1977-78	1976-77	Cited Half-Life	Citing Half-Life
Annu. Rev. Entomol.	4.75	6.49	5.00	3.11	3.68	8.1	8.7
Ecol. Entomol.	1.25	1.30	1.30	1.15	.99	3.1	8.8
Entomol. Exp. Appl.	.67	.88	1.19	1.08	.58	7.4	7.6
Environ. Entomol.	.72	.95	.91	.86	.82	5.5	8.3
Insect Biochem.	1.48	1.68	1.35	1.18	.97	3.9	7.4
Int. J. Insect Morph.	.71	1.02	.87	.65	.79	5.2	>10.0
J. Econ. Entomol.	.72	.89	.90	.80	.75	>10.0	7.6
J. Insect Physiol.	1.58	2.19	2.12	1.47	1.25	8.5	8.0
J. Med. Entomol.	.61	.66	.50	.51	.63	6.6	>10.0
Physiol. Entomol.	1.35	1.46	1.54	1.26	.73	3.4	8.3

lives greater than ten years. However, we have determined that the average half-life for the core journals in this study, taken as a group, is between 11 and 12 years, whether cit*ing* or cit*ed*.

The *Annual Review of Entomology* ranks first in immediacy as well as impact—.89 (Table 2, column H). Immediacy is calculated by dividing the number of citations to a journal's 1982 articles by the total number of articles it published that year. *Ecological Entomology* has the second highest immediacy at .65. *Journal of Insect Physiology* is next at .41, followed by *Entomologia Experimentales et Applicata* at .37. *Insect Biochemistry* and *Journal of Medical Entomology* are virtually tied for fifth place with an immediacy of .32 and .31, respectively. The Macro Journal of Entomology has an immediacy of .18.

Table 4 lists 50 journals that most frequently cit*ed* the core entomology journals in 1982. Although these 50 journals represent seven percent of the 711 journals that cited the core group that year, they account for 68 percent of all citations received by the core in 1982.

Twenty-five journals in Table 4 are members of the core group. Again, they are indicated by asterisks. These 25 journals cited 39,000 references in 1982, of which 29 percent were to the core journals in this study. In contrast, the noncore journals in Table 4 cited 140,000 references, only three percent of which were to the core.

As is our custom, we also have looked at the specific content of these journals. Table 5 lists the 44 most-cited articles from the core entomology journals. They are arranged alphabetically by first author. The number of citations each article received from 1961 through 1982 in *SCI* is also shown. Only those papers which were cited more than 100 times are listed. When this study was begun, citation data from the 1955-1964 *SCI* cumulation were not available. However, we were later able to add citations, in parentheses, to those papers on the list published in 1960 and earlier.

Seven of the 36 core journals are represented in the table. *Annual Review of Entomology* accounts for 16 of the 44 papers listed. *Journal of Economic Entomology* and *Journal of Insect Physiology* each published ten of the most-cited entomology articles. *Annals of the Entomological Society of America* and *Canadian Entomologist* each account for three articles. *Bulletin of Entomological Research* and *Mosquito News* each account for one paper. Our search service can provide editors with complete lists of the most-cited articles published in any journals they desire.

The most-cited paper, by W.S. Abbott, US Department of Agriculture, Washington, DC, is also the oldest paper on the list. Published in 1925 in *Journal of Economic Entomology*, Abbott's paper discusses a method for calculating the effectiveness of insecticides. In par-

Table 4: The 50 journals which most frequently cited core entomology journals in 1982. An asterisk indicates a core journal. A = citations to core journals. B = citations to all journals. C = self-citations. D = percent of total citations that are core journal citations (A/B). E = percent of total citations that are self-citations (self-citing rate C/B). F = percent of citations to core journals that are self-citations (C/A). G = impact factor. H = immediacy index. I = 1982 source items.

	A	B	C	D	E	F	G	H	I
*Environ. Entomol.	1461	3559	398	41.1	11.2	27.2	.72	.17	270
*J. Econ. Entomol.	1233	2973	764	41.5	25.7	62.0	.73	.18	283
*J. Insect Physiol.	888	3393	488	26.2	14.4	55.0	1.58	.41	143
*Ann. Entomol. Soc. Amer.	770	2197	232	35.1	10.6	30.1	.53	.18	128
*Z. Angew. Entomol.—J. Appl. Entom.	678	2459	180	27.6	7.3	26.6	.45	.08	125
*Can. Entomol.	657	2003	276	32.8	13.8	42.0	.54	.16	140
*J. Med. Entomol.	653	2262	191	28.9	8.4	29.3	.61	.31	109
J. Chem. Ecol.	610	2727	—	22.4	—	—	1.86	.54	129
*Entomol. Exp. Appl.	601	1790	116	33.6	6.5	19.3	.67	.37	75
*Annu. Rev. Entomol.	565	3010	48	18.8	1.6	8.5	4.75	.89	18
*Insect Biochem.	466	2510	168	18.6	6.7	36.1	1.48	.32	88
*Mosq. News	445	985	234	45.2	23.8	52.6	.60	.07	94
*J. Ga. Entomol. Soc.	393	989	54	39.7	5.5	13.7	.24	.17	98
*Appl. Entomol. Zool.	359	1112	86	32.3	7.7	24.0	.37	.15	85
*Bull. Entomol. Res.	345	1105	177	31.2	16.0	51.3	.54	.28	69
*Fla. Entomol.	337	1133	57	29.7	5.0	16.9	.45	.17	81
*Physiol. Entomol.	336	1115	55	30.1	4.9	16.4	1.35	.11	53
Can. J. Zool.	325	9544	—	3.4	—	—	.88	.30	373
Comp. Biochem. Physiol. Pt. A	261	8742	—	3.0	—	—	.82	.17	334
Parasitology	247	3789	—	6.5	—	—	1.99	.54	113
Oecologia	236	7603	—	3.1	—	—	1.38	.27	259
Cryo-Lett.	197	1135	—	17.4	—	—	.95	.23	30
Comp. Biochem. Physiol. Pt. B	186	10,556	—	1.8	—	—	.90	.17	387
*Ecol. Entomol.	180	1070	35	16.8	3.3	19.4	1.25	.65	52
*Entomon	177	902	20	19.6	2.2	11.3	.11	.03	104
J. Comp. Physiol.	175	6831	—	2.6	—	—	1.81	.51	245
Experientia	174	10,697	—	1.6	—	—	.79	.15	679
*Insectes Soc.	165	828	84	19.9	10.1	50.9	.60	.14	42
Residue Reviews	163	1302	—	12.5	—	—	.83	.10	10
J. Invertebr. Pathol.	160	1765	—	9.1	—	—	.89	.31	123
*Acta Entomol. Bohemoslov.	159	743	45	21.4	6.1	28.3	.26	.10	58
Science	159	27,145	—	.6	—	—	6.81	1.73	988
*J. Aust. Entomol. Soc.	155	599	29	25.9	4.8	18.7	.21	.10	59
Res. Pop. Ecol.	155	667	—	23.2	—	—	.59	.29	28
Ecology	141	7552	—	1.9	—	—	2.45	.62	205
*J. N.Y. Entomol. Soc.	132	521	13	25.3	2.5	9.9	.25	.06	36
*Int. J. Insect Morphol. Embryol.	129	832	27	15.5	3.3	20.9	.71	.10	30
*Pac. Insects	125	544	53	23.0	9.7	42.4	.18	.15	41
J. Morphol.	123	3507	—	3.5	—	—	.91	.33	98
Gen. Comp. Endocrinol.	122	5582	—	2.2	—	—	1.80	.48	193
J. Exp. Zool.	121	6628	—	1.8	—	—	1.34	.31	275
Pestic. Biochem. Physiol.	113	1806	—	6.3	—	—	1.45	.32	79
Z. Pflanzenkr. Pflanzensch.	111	1511	—	7.4	—	—	.39	.11	82
Aust. J. Zool.	109	2069	—	5.3	—	—	.74	.32	71
Amer. J. Trop. Med. Hyg.	108	3652	—	3.0	—	—	1.55	.46	185
Advan. Nutr. Res.	104	1649	—	6.3	—	—	2.80	.50	10
Ann. Appl. Biol.	99	2334	—	4.2	—	—	.63	.29	138
Comp. Biochem. Physiol. Pt. C	99	4781	—	2.1	—	—	1.18	.30	182
*Great Lakes Entomol.	98	431	19	22.7	4.4	19.4	.13	.06	35
Amer. Naturalist	96	5248	—	1.8	—	—	2.00	.58	137

ticular, it describes how researchers can account for insects that died of "natural causes" when samples of insects treated and untreated with insecticides are compared. This paper was cited at least 650 times between 1955 and 1982. Despite its age, it continues to be highly cited. In 1982, it received 32 citations; in 1981, 38 citations; in 1980, 42; in 1979, 33; etc.

The second most-cited paper is by W.H. Telfer, University of Pennsylva-nia, Philadelphia, and was published in *Annual Review of Entomology* in 1965. This review describes the mechanism and control of yolk formation in insects. It was cited 262 times from 1965 to 1982. The author commented on this *Citation Classic* in 1979.[16] Eight other papers in Table 6 were designated *Citation Classics*.[9,10,17-22]

The third most-cited paper is by C.S. Holling, Forest Insect Laboratory, Sault

Table 5: The 44 most-cited articles from the core entomology journals cited 100 or more times, 1961-1982 *SCI*®, in alphabetical order by first author. At the time these data were collected, the 1955-1964 *SCI* was not yet available. We have added (in parentheses) the additional cites for the papers published in 1960 or earlier.

Citations 1961-1982		Bibliographic Data
604	(55)	**Abbott W S.** A method of computing the effectiveness of an insecticide. *J. Econ. Entomol.* 18:265-7, 1925.
119	(0)	**Adkisson P L, Vanderzant E S, Bull D L & Allison W E.** A wheat germ medium for rearing the pink bollworm. *J. Econ. Entomol.* 53:759-62, 1960.
120		**Auclair J L.** Aphid feeding and nutrition. *Annu. Rev. Entomol.* 8:439-90, 1963.
115	(20)	**Baumhover A H, Graham A J, Bitter B A, Hopkins D E, New W D, Dudley F H & Bushland R C.** Screw-worm control through release of sterilized flies. *J. Econ. Entomol.* 48:462-6, 1955.
162		**Beck S D.** Resistance of plants to insects. *Annu. Rev. Entomol.* 10:207-32, 1965.
129		**Berger R S.** Isolation, identification, and synthesis of the sex attractant of the cabbage looper, *Trichoplusia ni*. *Ann. Entomol. Soc. Amer.* 59:767-71, 1966.
111	(5)	**Bonhag P F.** Ovarian structure and vitellogenesis in insects. *Annu. Rev. Entomol.* 3:137-60, 1958.
126		**Bursell E.** Aspects of the metabolism of amino acids in the tsetse fly, *Glossina* (Diptera). *J. Insect Physiol.* 9:439-52, 1963.
104		**Craig G B & Vandehey R C.** Genetic variability in *Aedes aegypti* (Diptera: culicidae). I. Mutations affecting color pattern. *Ann. Entomol. Soc. Amer.* 55:47-58, 1962.
128		**Cummins K W.** Trophic relations of aquatic insects. *Annu. Rev. Entomol.* 18:183-206, 1973.
123	(0)	**Dethier V G, Browne L B & Smith C N.** The designation of chemicals in terms of the responses they elicit from insects. *J. Econ. Entomol.* 53:134-6, 1960.
112		**Fraenkel G & Hsiao C.** Bursicon, a hormone which mediates tanning of the cuticle in the adult fly and other insects. *J. Insect Physiol.* 11:513-56, 1965.
112		**Highnam K C, Lusis O & Hill L.** The role of the corpora allata during oocyte growth in the desert locust, *Schistocerca gregaria* Forsk. *J. Insect Physiol.* 9:587-96, 1963.
135		**Hill L.** Neurosecretory control of haemolymph protein concentration during ovarian development in the desert locust. *J. Insect Physiol.* 8:609-19, 1962.
245	(1)	**Holling C S.** The components of predation as revealed by a study of small-mammal predation of the European pine sawfly. *Can. Entomol.* 91:293-320, 1959.
213	(1)	**Holling C S.** Some characteristics of simple types of predation and parasitism. *Can. Entomol.* 91:385-8, 1959.
103	(20)	**Hoskins W M & Gordon H T.** Arthropod resistance to chemicals. *Annu. Rev. Entomol.* 1:89-122, 1956.
104		**Ignoffo C M.** A successful technique for mass-rearing cabbage loopers on a semisynthetic diet. *Ann. Entomol. Soc. Amer.* 56:178-82, 1963.
110		**Karlson P & Bode C.** Die Inaktivierung des Ecdysons bei der Schmeissfliege *Calliphora erythrocephala* Meigen. (Ecdysone inactivation in the blow-fly *Calliphora erythrocephala* Meigen.) *J. Insect Physiol.* 15:111-8, 1969.
154	(4)	**Karlson P & Butenandt A.** Pheromones (ectohormones) in insects. *Annu. Rev. Entomol.* 4:39-58, 1959.
148	(14)	**Knipling E F.** Possibilities of insect control or eradication through the use of sexually sterile males. *J. Econ. Entomol.* 48:459-62, 1955.
139		**Krishnakumaran A, Berry S J, Oberlander H & Schneiderman H A.** Nucleic acid synthesis during insect development—II. Control of DNA synthesis in the cecropia silkworm and other saturniid moths. *J. Insect Physiol.* 13:1-57, 1967.
106		**Kroeger H & Lezzi M.** Regulation of gene action in insect development. *Annu. Rev. Entomol.* 11:1-22, 1966.
103		**LaBrecque G C.** Studies with three alkylating agents as house fly sterilants. *J. Econ. Entomol.* 54:684-9, 1961.
112		**Lichtenstein E P & Schulz K R.** The effects of moisture and microorganisms on the persistence and metabolism of some organophosphorous insecticides in soils, with special emphasis on parathion. *J. Econ. Entomol.* 57:618-27, 1964.
103		**Mayer R J & Candy D J.** Control of haemolymph lipid concentration during locust flight: an adipokinetic hormone from the corpora cardiaca. *J. Insect Physiol.* 15:611-20, 1969.
109		**McMorran A.** A synthetic diet for the spruce budworm, *Choristoneura fumiferana* (Clem.) (Lepidoptera: tortricidae). *Can. Entomol.* 97:58-62, 1965.
101		**Noirot C & Quennedey A.** Fine structure of insect epidermal glands. *Annu. Rev. Entomol.* 19:61-80, 1974.
156		**Salt R W.** Principles of insect cold-hardiness. *Annu. Rev. Entomol.* 6:55-74, 1961.
147		**Satir P & Gilula N B.** The fine structure of membranes and intercellular communication in insects. *Annu. Rev. Entomol.* 18:143-66, 1973.
140		**Shaaya E & Karlson P.** Der Ecdysontiter wahrend der Insektenentwicklung—II. Die postembryonale Entwicklung der Schmeissfliege *Calliphora erythrocephala* Meig. (The ecdysone titer during insect development—II. The post-embryo development of the blow-fly *Calliphora erythrocephala* Meig.) *J. Insect Physiol.* 11:65-9, 1965.
243		**Shorey H H & Hale R L.** Mass-rearing of the larvae of nine noctuid species on a simple artificial medium. *J. Econ. Entomol.* 58:522-4, 1965.
162		**Slifer E H.** The structure of arthropod chemoreceptors. *Annu. Rev. Entomol.* 15:121-42, 1970.
178	(9)	**Solomon M E.** Control of humidity with potassium hydroxide, sulphuric acid, or other solutions. *Bull. Entomol. Res.* 42:543-54, 1951.
101		**Staal G B.** Insect growth regulators with juvenile hormone activity. *Annu. Rev. Entomol.* 20:417-60, 1975.
141		**Sudia W D & Chamberlain R W.** Battery-operated light trap, an improved model. *Mosq. News* 22:126-9, 1962.
262		**Telfer W H.** The mechanism and control of yolk formation. *Annu. Rev. Entomol.* 10:161-84, 1965.
203	(0)	**Thorsteinson A J.** Host selection in phytophagous insects. *Annu. Rev. Entomol.* 5:193-218, 1960.
149		**Vanderzant E S, Richardson C D & Fort S W.** Rearing of the bollworm on artificial diet. *J. Econ. Entomol.* 55:140, 1962.

Citations 1961-1982	Bibliographic Data

111   **Waters T F.** The drift of stream insects. *Annu. Rev. Entomol.* 17:253-72, 1972.
105   **Wigglesworth V B.** Chemical structure and juvenile hormone activity: comparative tests on *Rhodnius prolixus. J. Insect Physiol.* 15:73-94, 1969.
194   **Wyatt G R.** The biochemistry of insect hemolymph. *Annu. Rev. Entomol.* 6:75-102, 1961.
118   **Yamamoto R T.** Mass rearing of the tobacco hornworm. II. Larval rearing and pupation. *J. Econ. Entomol.* 62:1427-31, 1969.
129   (4)   **Yamasaki T & Narahashi T.** The effects of potassium and sodium ions on the resting and action potentials of the cockroach giant axon. *J. Insect Physiol.* 3:146-58, 1959.

Table 6: Sample of highly cited entomology articles published in non-core journals, in alphabetical order by first author.

Total SCI® Citations 1955-1982	Bibliographic Data

136   **Bollenbacher W E, Vedeckis W V, Gilbert L I & O'Connor J D.** Ecdysone titers and prothoracic gland activity during the larval-pupal development of *Manduca sexta. Develop. Biol.* 44:46-53, 1975.
58   **Bowers W S & Martinez-Pardo R.** Antiallatotropins: inhibition of corpus allatum development. *Science* 197:1369-71, 1977.
168   **Bowers W S, Ohta T, Cleere J S & Marsella P A.** Discovery of insect antijuvenile hormones in plants. *Science* 193:542-7, 1976.
61   **de Barjac H.** Une nouvelle variete de Bacillus thuringiensis tres toxique pour les moustiques: B. thuringiensis var. israelensis serotype 14. (A new subspecies of Bacillus thuringiensis very toxic for mosquitoes: Bacillus thuringiensis var israelensis new variety serotype 14.) *C.R. Acad. Sci. Ser. D* 286:797-800, 1978.
251   **Feeny P.** Seasonal changes in oak leaf tannins and nutrients as a cause of spring feeding by winter moth caterpillars. *Ecology* 51:565-81, 1970.
174   **Hagedorn H H, O'Connor J D, Fuchs M S, Sage B, Schlaeger D A & Bohm M K.** The ovary as a source of γ-ecdysone in an adult mosquito. *Proc. Nat. Acad. Sci. US* 72:3255-9, 1975.
79   **Kennedy J S & Marsh D.** Pheromone-regulated anemotaxis in flying moths. *Science* 184:999-1001, 1974.
87   **Nijhout H F & Williams C M.** Control of moulting and metamorphosis in the tobacco hornworm, *Manduca sexta* (L.): growth of the last-instar larva and the decision to pupate. *J. Exp. Biol.* 61:481-91, 1974.
64   **Nijhout H F & Williams C M.** Control of moulting and metamorphosis in the tobacco hornworm, *Manduca sexta* (L.): cessation of juvenile hormone secretion as a trigger for pupation. *J. Exp. Biol.* 61:493-501, 1974.
74   **Reichstein T, von Euw J, Parsons J A & Rothschild M.** Heart poisons in the monarch butterfly. *Science* 161:861-6, 1968.
71   **Scriber J M.** Limiting effects of low leaf-water content on the nitrogen utilization, energy budget, and larval growth of *Hyalophora cecropia* (Lepidoptera: Saturniidae). *Oecologia* 28:269-87, 1977.
84   **Slansky F & Feeny P.** Stabilization of the rate of nitrogen accumulation by larvae of the cabbage butterfly on wild and cultivated food plants. *Ecol. Monogr.* 47:209-28, 1977.
116   **Truman J W.** Physiology of insect rhythms. I. Circadian organization of the endocrine events underlying the moulting cycle of larval tobacco hornworms. *J. Exp. Biol.* 57:805-20, 1972.
87   **Wyatt G R & Pan M L.** Insect plasma proteins. *Annu. Rev. Biochem.* 47:779-817, 1978.

Ste. Marie, Ontario. It discusses factors involved in the predation of sawfly cocoons by small mammals, such as the population density of the prey. Published in *Canadian Entomologist* in 1959, this paper received 246 citations from 1959 to 1982. Holling currently is the director of the Institute of Resource Ecology, Vancouver, British Columbia.

It is important to remember that Table 5 does *not* include entomology articles published in *non*-core journals, such as *Nature, Science, Journal of Experimental Biology, Ecology,* etc. We identified a sample of entomology articles published in these journals that were cited at least six times by the core group in 1982. We then tabulated their citations from 1955 through 1982 in *SCI.* Table 6 lists the 14 most-cited entomology articles from this sample. Incidentally, Miriam Rothschild is coauthor with T. Reichstein and colleagues on the paper published in *Science* in 1968. This fascinating paper discussed heart poisons in the monarch butterfly. It is important to stress that we attribute no specific *qualitative* differences between these papers—that's why they are arranged alphabetically rather than in order of citations. We would have liked to create a map of entomology showing how these papers interact, but we are constrained by time.

Comparing Tables 2 and 4, we see that ten journals appear among the top 20 on both lists. They are: *Annals of the Entomological Society of America, Annual Review of Entomology, Bulletin of Entomological Research, Canadian Entomologist, Entomologia Experimentales et Applicata, Environmental Entomology, Insect Biochemistry, Journal of Economic Entomology, Journal of Insect Physiology,* and *Journal of Medical Entomology.* These journals rank highest in terms of their references *to* the core

literature, and the number of citations received *from* the core. The same ten journals also ranked among the top 20 in terms of impact and immediacy.

This concludes our look at the core journals of entomology. In the weeks to come, the journal citation studies series will continue with an examination of the core journals of analytical chemistry.

* * * * *

My thanks to John Dale and Alfred Welljams-Dorof for their help in the preparation of this essay. ©1984 ISI

REFERENCES

1. **Garfield E.** Science communication and the continuing mission of ISI Press. *Current Contents* (51):5-11, 19 December 1983.
2. **Rothschild M.** *Dear Lord Rothschild: birds, butterflies and history.* Philadelphia/London: ISI Press/Hutchinson, 1983. 398 p.
3. **Ryan A.** Zoological fairyland in Tring. Review of "Dear Lord Rothschild: birds, butterflies and history" by M. Rothschild. *New Sci.* 100:937, 1983.
4. **Cain A J.** Natural history and the rogue elephant. Review of "Dear Lord Rothschild: birds, butterflies and history" by M. Rothschild. *Nature* 306:506-7, 1983.
5. **Schudel M.** Review of "Dear Lord Rothschild: birds, butterflies and history" by M. Rothschild. *Wash. Post Book World* 8 January 1984, p. 6; 10.
6. **Garfield E.** William D. McElroy and the illuminating story of bioluminescence. *Essays of an information scientist.* Philadelphia: ISI Press, 1983. Vol. 5. p. 731-41.
7. ——————. Spiders and the cobwebs of myth about them. *Current Contents* (31):5-14, 1 August 1983.
8. ——————. Journal citation studies. 33. Botany journals, part 1: what they cite and what cites them. Part 2: growth of botanical literature and highly-cited items. *Essays of an information scientist.* Philadelphia: ISI Press, 1981. Vol. 4. p. 555-73.
9. **Knipling E F.** Citation Classic. Commentary on *J. Econ. Entomol.* 48:459-62, 1955. *Current Contents/Agriculture, Biology & Environmental Sciences* 14(50):22, 12 December 1983.
10. **Lichtenstein E P.** Citation Classic. Commentary on *J. Econ. Entomol.* 57:618-27, 1964. *Current Contents/Agriculture, Biology & Environmental Sciences* 14(28):18, 11 July 1983.
11. **Fraenkel G S.** Citation Classic. Commentary on *Science* 129:1466-70, 1959. *Current Contents/Life Sciences* 27(11):00, 12 March 1984.
12. **Garfield E.** Journal citation studies. 38. Earth sciences journals: what they cite and what cites them. *Essays of an information scientist.* Philadelphia: ISI Press, 1983. Vol. 5. p. 791-800.
13. ——————. The number of biochemical articles is growing, but why also the number of references per article? *Essays of an information scientist.* Philadelphia: ISI Press, 1981. Vol. 4. p. 414-25.
14. Entomology. *Encyclopaedia Britannica. Micropaedia.* Chicago: H.H. Benton, 1974. Vol. III. p. 909-10.
15. **Garfield E.** Citation analysis as a tool in journal evaluation. *Science* 178:471-9, 1972.
16. **Telfer W H.** Citation Classic. Commentary on *Annu. Rev. Entomol.* 10:161-84, 1965. *Current Contents/Agriculture, Biology & Environmental Sciences* 10(45):10, 5 November 1979.
17. **Berger R S.** Citation Classic. Commentary on *Ann. Entomol. Soc. Amer.* 59:767-71, 1966. *Current Contents/Agriculture, Biology & Environmental Sciences* 13(39):20, 27 September 1982.
18. **Shaaya E.** Citation Classic. Commentary on *J. Insect Physiol.* 11:65-9, 1965. *Current Contents/Agriculture, Biology & Environmental Sciences* 13(6):22, 8 February 1982.
19. **Slifer E H.** Citation Classic. Commentary on *Annu. Rev. Entomol.* 15:121-42, 1970. *Current Contents/Agriculture, Biology & Environmental Sciences* 13(28):12, 14 July 1980.
20. **Solomon M E.** Citation Classic. Commentary on *Bull. Entomol. Res.* 42:543-54, 1951. *Current Contents/Agriculture, Biology & Environmental Sciences* 13(29):18, 19 July 1982.
21. **Sudia W D.** Citation Classic. Commentary on *Mosq. News* 22:126-9, 1962. *Current Contents/Agriculture, Biology & Environmental Sciences* 12(37):20, 14 September 1981.
22. **Thorsteinson A J.** Citation Classic. Commentary on *Annu. Rev. Entomol.* 5:193-218, 1960. *Current Contents/Agriculture, Biology & Environmental Sciences* 11(45):14, 10 November 1980.

Current Comments®

The 1982 Nobel Prize in Medicine Recognizes the Impact of Prostaglandin Research by S. K. Bergström, B. I. Samuelsson, and J. R. Vane

Number 12   March 19, 1984

The 1982 Nobel prize in physiology or medicine was shared by Sune K. Bergström, age 66, and Bengt I. Samuelsson, age 48, both of the Karolinska Institutet, Stockholm, Sweden, and by John R. Vane, age 55, Wellcome Research Foundation, Beckenham, England.

Previous reports on Nobel prizes[1-3] used citation analysis to provide a documentary account of the field represented. Recently, we amplified these discussions by using research front data to determine the place the award-winning work occupies on the worldwide map of science. Briefly, research fronts are identified by groups of current papers that cite clusters of earlier, "core" papers.[4]

We are covering the 1982 awards in five separate essays. The first dealt with the work of physics laureate Kenneth G. Wilson.[5] The second focused on the work of chemistry prizewinner Aaron Klug.[6] Future essays will cover the prizes in economics and in literature.

Before discussing the 1982 prize in medicine, let me reiterate that citation analysis cannot *predict* Nobel laureates. It is true that citation analysis can help identify those individuals *of Nobel class*. And co-citation analysis does provide a modeling technique for forecasting the growth and development of specialties or disciplines. Indeed, we have seen that research front analysis helps identify the fields that are *eventually* acknowledged with a Nobel prize. But without confidential information it would be difficult to predict which field or individual will be recognized in a particular year.

Bergström, Samuelsson, and Vane were awarded the 1982 prize for their discoveries involving prostaglandins (PGs) and related substances.[7] As is often the case, they previously shared (in 1977) the Albert Lasker Basic Medical Research Award.[8]

PGs, of which there are many types, are hormone-like fatty acids. They are formed in the membranes of cells throughout the body—especially during times of illness, stress, or injury.[9] PGs affect the nervous, reproductive, gastrointestinal, and renal systems, as well as the regulation of body fluids and temperature and the body's defense mechanisms, such as inflammation.

PGs were first discovered in 1930 by two gynecologists, Raphael Kurzrok and Charles C. Lieb, both of Columbia University.[10] They observed a marked responsiveness of uterine smooth muscle to an as yet unidentified substance in semen.[11] However, they believed that the activity they were measuring was due to acetylcholine. It was Ulf S. von Euler, Karolinska Institutet, who first realized that this bioactivity was not due to any known mediator or catalyst.[12] By 1935, von Euler showed that the mysterious substance in semen affected numerous types of smooth muscles, and could lower the blood pressure of laboratory animals.[13,14] At that time, von Euler thought its presence in semen resulted from its production in the prostate. Thus, he named the compound "prostaglandin."[15] It was von Euler who, in 1947, urged Bergström to take up the formidable task of characterizing prostaglandin's chemical structure.[16] Significantly, von Euler shared a 1970 Nobel prize with Julius Axelrod, National Institutes of Health, Bethesda, Maryland, and Bernard Katz, University College, London, for work on neurotransmitters.

Bergström quickly demonstrated that the active principle in PGs was a new type of highly active, lipid-soluble, unsaturated fatty acid.[17] Later known as arachidonic acid, this chain of hydrocarbon molecules forms part of the structure of cellular membranes. It took Bergström and his colleagues about ten years to isolate pure crystals of two types of PG.[18-21] In 1962, he and his colleagues at Karolinska reported the chemical structure of three PGs.[22] It was this crucial breakthrough for which Bergström was recognized by the Nobel committee.[7]

One of the coauthors of the landmark 1962 paper was Bergström's student, Bengt Samuelsson, who subsequently participated in the structural elucidation of other types of PGs. In 1962, Samuelsson, Bergström, and others also collaborated on procedures by which all known prostaglandins can be isolated and identified.[23] A year later, Samuelsson reported improvements in these procedures,[24] and in 1964 he and Krister Gréen, Karolinska, succeeded in developing a method of quantifying the production of PGs in the body by measuring their metabolites—the products of their breakdown—in blood or urine.[25] That same year, Samuelsson again collaborated with Bergström, as well as with Henry Danielsson, Karolinska, on a detailed elucidation of the oxygenation of arachidonic acid.[26]

After setting up his own laboratory, Samuelsson began a series of investigations into the formation of PGs, and their consumption by enzymes after only a few minutes of existence.[27] This direction was suggested in part by a 1967 paper[28] coauthored by John R. Vane and Sergio H. Ferreira, University of São Paulo, Brazil, and a 1969 paper[29] by Vane and Priscilla J. Piper, then of Royal College of Surgeons, London. The former paper showed that PGs were inactivated in a few seconds upon passage through the pulmonary circulation. The latter paper reported the discovery of an unidentified substance that caused contractions in strips of aorta material from laboratory rabbits. Vane and Piper also found that anti-inflammatory agents, such as aspirin, inhibited the release of PGs.[29]

Acting on these and other results, in 1973 Samuelsson coauthored a paper with Mats Hamberg, Karolinska, showing that an endoperoxide compound is formed as an intermediate step in the process of prostaglandin synthesis.[30] Another paper by Samuelsson and several Karolinska colleagues, published in 1974, reported the isolation of two endoperoxides, and elucidated their structure.[31] These endoperoxides caused blood platelets to clump together, or aggregate. They also caused a strip of rabbit aorta to contract—although hundreds of times less strongly than the "rabbit-aorta contracting substance" found by Vane and Piper.[29,31] Later that same year, the results of an investigation by Samuelsson and Hamberg on the oxygenation of arachidonic acid in human platelets provided evidence that endoperoxides play a direct role in the regulation of cellular functions.[32] We reported this paper as one of the 1974 articles most cited during 1974.[33] This type of study, incidentally, has proved to be one of the strongest predictive indicators derived from chronological citation studies.

Hamberg, Samuelsson, and Jan Svensson, also of Karolinska, next went on to show that PG synthesis stops almost completely at the endoperoxide stage when aspirin or indomethacin, an aspirin-like drug, is taken.[34] In early 1975, Samuelsson and colleagues reported the results of a further study into the mechanism of action of endoperoxides in platelet aggregation.[35] By mid-1975, Samuelsson's years of research on PG intermediates bore fruit in a breakthrough paper entitled "Thromboxanes: a new group of biologically active compounds derived from prostaglandin endoperoxides."[36] Coauthored with Hamberg and Svensson, the paper reported the discovery of thromboxane A_2, the unstable intermediate formed during the conversion of prostaglandin G_2 into thromboxane B_2. From the time of its publication through 1983, it has received 1,330 citations, according to *Science Citation Index*® (*SCI*®). This paper was featured as a *Citation Classic*™ last year in *Current Contents*® /*Life Sciences*.[37] Thromboxane A_2 proved to be the mysterious substance that so powerfully contracted rabbit aorta tissue and caused blood platelets to clump together, as reported in the 1974 paper on the isolation and structure of two new endoperoxides.[31]

While Samuelsson studied and clarified the biological processes of PG formation, Vane was investigating the role PGs play in the body. The 1967 paper on the disappearance of PGs in the pulmonary circulation,[28] a *Citation Classic*,[38] also confirmed that PGs are released into the venous bloodstream when the spleen contracts. As a direct result of his interest in the release and fate of PGs in the body, and of his discovery of the rabbit-aorta contracting substance in 1969,[29] Vane was led to the idea that aspirin might interfere with the biosynthesis of PGs.[39] In a 1971 article in *Nature New Biology*, he clearly demonstrated this inhibition in cell-free preparations, and proposed that the therapeutic effects of aspirin and aspirin-like drugs are due to their ability to inhibit the enzymes that generate PGs.[40] This *Citation Classic*[41] was cited over 2,570 times by the end of 1983. It was also among the 25 1971 articles most cited in 1971 and 1972.[42]

Another article published in the same issue of *Nature New Biology*, coauthored by Vane, Ferreira, and Salvadore Moncada while they were at the Royal College of Surgeons, London, showed that aspirin and indomethacin prevent the release of PGs from the spleen, providing further support, *in vivo*, for the finding in isolated enzyme preparations.[43] This paper was also among the 25 most-cited papers of 1971.[42] The discovery of the basis of aspirin's therapeutic activity is one of the major accomplishments for which Vane was cited by the Nobel committee, which credited him with providing a powerful approach to understanding the possible role PGs play in a variety of biological events, including, for example, rheumatoid arthritis.[44]

Vane's other major accomplishment cited by the Nobel committee was his discovery of prostacyclin and its properties. Prostacyclin is also a PG derived from arachidonic acid, but has the opposite effect of thromboxane—rather than promoting the aggregation of platelets, it inhibits their clumping together.[44] Thromboxane and prostacyclin carry on a delicate balancing act to regulate clot formation. They are under study for possible use in the prevention of heart disease and stroke.

As already indicated by data for specific papers, it is somewhat redundant to say that these scientists are highly cited. Bergström's work, collectively, has been cited at least 3,600 times since 1955. He was among the 250 most-cited primary authors for the period from 1961 through 1975.[45] Among his most-cited works, Bergström's earliest papers deal with rat liver bile acids[46] and steroids.[47] By 1959, however, he had published a paper on the effects of an infusion of prostaglandin E in volunteer subjects,[48] coauthored with von Euler and several other Karolinska colleagues. In 1963, Bergström collaborated with Samuelsson, J. Sjövall, and R. Ryhage on a paper elucidating the structures of three types of prostaglandin.[49] Bergström's most-cited paper is a major review of the PG literature[50] that has received 660 citations since its publication in 1968. The paper was also among the most-cited articles of the 1960s.[51] A year earlier, Bergström wrote a comprehensive review for *Science*.[52]

Samuelsson's work has been cited explicitly over 17,000 times since 1955, the earliest year for which *SCI* data is available at present. He was identified as one of the 300 most-cited authors for the period 1961 to 1976,[53] and also one of the 1,000 authors most-cited from 1965 through 1978.[54] Together with several Karolinska colleagues, he, too, has written a major review of PGs, covering their biosynthesis, how they are metabolized, general considerations concerning their quantitative analysis, and other characteristics.[55] He is also responsible for describing the most recently discovered members of the arachidonic acid family: leukotrienes, which contribute to inflammation, antibody production, and immune response. A paper he coauthored in 1979 with Robert C. Murphy, University of Colorado Medical School, Denver, and Sven Hammarström, Karolinska, identifies a chemical found in tumor cells as a leukotriene.[56] The paper is one of the most-cited 1979 life sciences articles.[57]

Vane's work has received over 15,400 citations from 1955 through 1983. Like Samuelsson, Vane was also identified in two of our earlier studies of most-cited authors.[53,54] Among the earliest of Vane's highly cited papers is a 1957 article reporting an improved method of detecting the presence of an amine compound (5-hydroxytryptamine) in solution.[58] He continued in this line of research, and in 1960 published an article on tryptamine receptors.[59] In 1969, Vane reviewed the development of his biological assay method known as the "blood-bathed organ technique."[60] In this technique, preparations of isolated organs are continuously bathed in a stream of blood from an anesthetized animal. The article discusses the application of the technique in the determination of the distribution and eventual fate of various hormones released into the bloodstream.

The paper reporting the discovery of prostacyclin, published in *Nature* in 1976, was coauthored by Vane and Wellcome Research Laboratory colleagues Moncada, R. Gryglewski, and S. Bunting.[61] It has been cited over 1,325 times. It is one of the most-cited papers published in 1976.[62] Indeed, it is already

among the 20 most-cited articles *Nature* has ever published.[63] In fact, three more articles by Vane and colleagues,[64,65] including one reporting that prostacyclin protects arterial walls from the deposition of platelet thrombi,[66] were also identified in our study of the 1976 literature.[62] Another *Citation Classic*[67] is on a 1977 paper by Vane and colleagues that discussed the function of prostacyclin in the body.[68] Along with three others by his group,[69-71] it was among the most-cited 1977 articles.[72] Other papers by Vane's group[73,74] were included in our list of 1978 papers,[75] while still another paper[76] appears in the list for 1979.[57]

Figure 1 presents a flowchart, or microhistory, of the field of prostaglandins. Each box in the figure represents a research front. Both the title of the front and the number of core articles on which each front is based are indicated. The number of citing documents is also shown. Briefly, the configuration of the string is determined by the continuity of the core literature from year to year.[77] If any core document in a research front continues to achieve the required thresholds in an adjacent year, a cluster string is formed.

The paper on the enzymatic formation of prostaglandin E_2 by Bergström, Samuelsson, and Danielsson[26] is part of the core literature in the following research fronts: "Prostaglandin synthesis" (1977), "Synthesis and biological properties of prostaglandins and thromboxanes" (1978), "Pharmacology of prostaglandins" (1979), "Prostaglandin effect on inflammation" (1980), and "Factors affecting prostaglandin synthesis" (1981).

A 1965 article by Samuelsson on prostaglandin E_1[78] appears in the 1978 research front mentioned above. An article coauthored by Samuelsson[79] is part of the core literature for the research front "Prostaglandin biosynthesis" (1976). Another paper coauthored by Samuelsson[80] appears in the following research fronts: "Prostaglandin hydroperoxidase and prostaglandin endoperoxide synthetase" (1979), "Free radical

Figure 1: A microhistory of the field of prostaglandins. Numbers at the bottom of each box refer to the number of cited/citing documents for each research front. a=research fronts whose core literature includes papers by Bergström; b=those fronts whose core literature includes papers by Samuelsson; c=those fronts whose core literature includes papers by Vane.

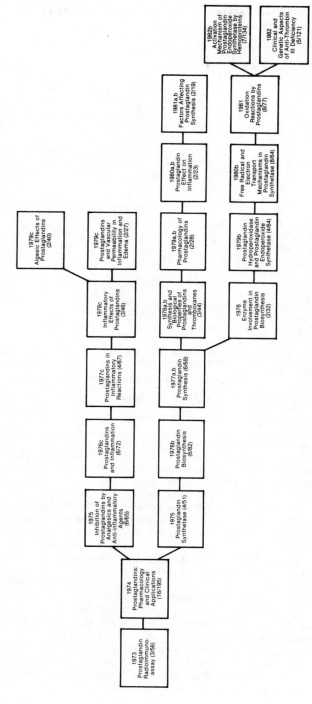

Figure 2: Multidimensional scaling map showing co-citation links between core papers of the 1976 *SCI®* research front #76-0869, "Prostaglandins and inflammation." See key for bibliographic data.

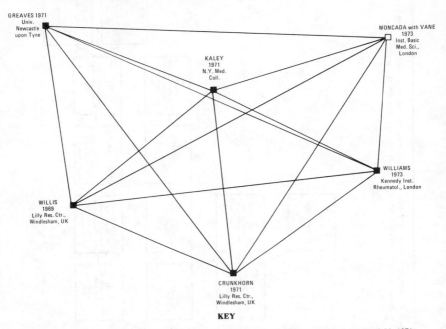

KEY

Crunkhorn P & Willis A L. Cutaneous reactions to intradermal prostaglandins. *Brit. J. Pharmacol.* 41:49-56, 1971.
Greaves M W, Sondergaard J & McDonald-Gibson W. Recovery of prostaglandins in human cutaneous inflammation. *Brit. Med. J.* 2:258-60, 1971.
Kaley G & Weiner R. Prostaglandin E_1: a potential mediator of the inflammatory response. *Ann. NY Acad. Sci.* 180:338-50, 1971.
Moncada S, Ferreira S H & Vane J R. Prostaglandins, aspirin-like drugs and the oedema of inflammation. *Nature* 246:217-9, 1973.
Williams T J & Morley J. Prostaglandins as potentiators of increased vascular permeability in inflammation. *Nature* 246:215-7, 1973.
Willis A L. Letter to editor. (Parallel assay of prostaglandin-like activity in rat inflammatory exudate by means of cascade superfusion.) *J. Pharm. Pharmacol.* 21:126-8, 1969.

and electron transport mechanisms in prostaglandin synthetase" (1980), and "Activation mechanism of prostaglandin endoperoxide synthetase by hemoproteins" (1982). Data for 1983 research fronts were not available at the time this essay was written.

Two papers by the Vane group also occur in the core literature of research fronts in Figure 1, from 1976 through 1979. One[81] is included in the core literature of the following fronts: "Prostaglandins and inflammation" (1976), "Prostaglandins in inflammatory reactions" (1977), "Inflammatory effects of prostaglandins" (1978), and "Prostaglandins and vascular permeability in inflam-

mation and edema" (1979). The other paper by the Vane group[82] occurs in the core literature of the 1979 front, "Algesic effects of prostaglandins."

A multidimensional scaling map of the core literature of the 1976 *SCI* front, "Prostaglandins and inflammation," is presented in Figure 2. The map includes a paper by Vane and colleagues.[81] Figure 3 presents a similar map for the 1977 *SCI* front named "Prostaglandin synthesis," which includes the enzymatic formation paper by Bergström, Samuelsson, and Danielsson.[26]

In their Nobel lectures, the 1982 laureates mention several of the workers whose papers appear in Figures 2 and 3:

Figure 3: Multidimensional scaling map of the 1977 *SCI*® research front #77-0535, "Prostaglandin synthesis," showing links between core papers. Consult key for bibliographic information.

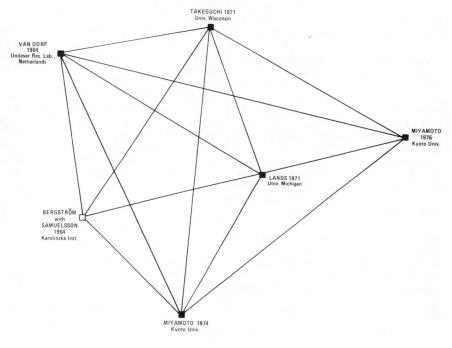

KEY

Bergström S, Danielsson H & Samuelsson B. The enzymatic formation of prostaglandin E$_2$ from arachidonic acid. Prostaglandins and related factors. 32. *Biochim. Biophys. Acta* 90:207-10, 1964.
Lands W, Lee R & Smith W. Factors regulating the biosynthesis of various prostaglandins. *Ann. NY Acad. Sci.* 180:107-22, 1971.
Miyamoto T, Ogino N, Yamamoto S & Hayaishi O. Purification of prostaglandin endoperoxide synthetase from bovine vesicular gland microsomes. *J. Biol. Chem.* 251:2629-36, 1976.
Miyamoto T, Yamamoto S & Hayaishi O. Prostaglandin synthetase system—resolution into oxygenase and isomerase components. *Proc. Nat. Acad. Sci. US* 71:3645-8, 1974.
Takeguchi C, Kohno E & Sih C J. Mechanism of prostaglandin biosynthesis. I. Characterization and assay of bovine prostaglandin synthetase. *Biochemistry* 10:2372-6, 1971.
Van Dorp D A, Beerthuis R K, Nugteren D H & Vonkeman H. The biosynthesis of prostaglandins. *Biochim. Biophys. Acta* 90:204-7, 1964.

D.A. Van Dorp, R.K. Beerthuis, D.H. Nugteren, and H. Vonkeman, Unilever Research Laboratory, the Netherlands, and A.L. Willis, Syntex Research, Palo Alto, California. The core paper by the Van Dorp group,[83] listed in Figure 3, puts forward essentially the same hypothesis concerning the synthesis of prostaglandins as did Bergström, Samuelsson, and Danielsson in the enzymatic formation paper.[26] Willis has two core papers in Figure 2. One, coau-

thored with P. Crunkhorn when they were together at the Lilly Research Centre, Windlesham, England, concerned the effects of PGs on the blood vessels in the skin.[84] The other, authored by Willis alone, describes modifications of Vane's cascade bioassay procedure, used to detect the presence of PGs.[85]

Almost 40 years have elapsed since von Euler convinced Bergström to keep prostaglandin research alive, despite the inherent difficulties of working with such a transient substance—and in spite of such distractions as antibiotics, steroid hormones, and World War II.[10] The perseverance of basic research pioneers such as Bergström, Samuelsson, and Vane has paid off. This is reflected in the explosive growth of the field of prostaglandins. And it is remarkable that, as more research is done, the more diverse and crucial the function of PGs seems to be. Indeed, the study of PGs has provided a basis for the development of new knowledge and therapy in many fields of medicine.

Those who select the Lasker and other awards take special pride in anticipating the Nobel prize selections. It is with some understandable pride, then, that we recall that the many citational indicators in which the work of this new crop of winners appeared long preceded their selection by the Nobel committee. Undoubtedly, there is always an element of self-consciousness in choosing candidates from one's own country or institution. But unless the number of Nobel prizes is significantly expanded, there will frequently be a considerable time gap between the award and the earliest indications that the candidates are *of Nobel class*.

This may not always be the case. Considering the widespread notion that the discoveries of the 1983 Nobel prizewinner Barbara McClintock were "premature,"[86] our analysis of her work should prove interesting. Incidentally, like Bergström, Samuelsson, and Vane, McClintock also was awarded the Albert Lasker Basic Medical Research Award (in 1981)[87] prior to receiving the Nobel prize.

* * * * *

My thanks to Stephen A. Bonaduce and Terri Freedman for their help in the preparation of this essay. ©1984 ISI

REFERENCES

1. **Garfield E.** Are the 1979 prizewinners *of Nobel class*? *Essays of an information scientist.*
   Philadelphia: ISI Press, 1981. Vol. 4. p. 609-17.
2. --------------. The 1980 Nobel prizewinners. *Essays of an information scientist.*
   Philadelphia: ISI Press, 1983. Vol. 5. p. 189-201.
3. --------------. Were the 1981 prizewinners in science, economics, and literature anticipated by citation analysis?
   Essays of an information scientist. Philadelphia: ISI Press, 1983. Vol. 5. p. 551-61.
4. --------------. ABCs of cluster mapping. Parts 1 & 2. Most active fields in the life and physical sciences in 1978.
   Essays of an information scientist. Philadelphia: ISI Press, 1981. Vol. 4. p. 634-49.
5. --------------. The 1982 Nobel prize in physics. *Current Contents* (50):5-14, 12 December 1983.
6. --------------. The 1982 Nobel prize in chemistry goes to structural biologist Aaron Klug.
   Current Contents (3):3-11, 16 January 1984.
7. **Oates J A.** The 1982 Nobel Prize in Physiology or Medicine. *Science* 218:765-8, 1982.
8. **Schmeck H M.** Five pioneers in medicine get Lasker awards. *NY Times* 17 November 1977, p. 23.
9. **Altman L K.** 2 Swedes and Briton win Nobel for clues to body's chemistry. *NY Times* 12 October 1982, p. A1; C3.
10. **Shodell M.** The prostaglandin connection. *Science 83* 4(2):78-82, 1983.
11. **Kurzrok R & Lieb C C.** Biochemical studies of human semen. II. The action of semen on the human uterus.
    Proc. Soc. Exp. Biol. Med. 28:268-72, 1930.
12. **Vane J R.** Personal communication. 10 February 1984.
13. **von Euler U S.** Zur Kenntnis der pharmakologischen Wirkungen von Nativsekreten und extrakten mannlicher
    accessorischer Geschlechtsdrusen. (Toward an understanding of the pharmacological effects of the natural
    secretions and extracts of the male accessory sex glands.) *Arch. Exp. Pathol. Pharmakol.* 175:78-84, 1934.
14. --------------. A depressor substance in the vesicular gland. *J. Physiol.—London* 84:21P-2P, 1935.
15. --------------. Kurze wissenschaftliche Mitteilungen. Uber die spezifische blutdrucksenkende Substanz des
    menschlichen Prostata- und Samenblasensekretes. (Short scientific notes. On the specific blood pressure
    lowering substance in human prostate and semen vesicle secretions.) *Klin. Wochenschr.* 14:1182-3, 1935.
16. **Sattaur O.** On the trail of prostaglandins. *New Sci.* 96:82-3, 1982.
17. **Bergström S.** Prostaglandinets kemi. (Chemistry of prostaglandin.) *Nord. Med.* 42:1465-6, 1949.
18. **Bergström S & Sjövall J.** The isolation of prostaglandin. *Acta Chem. Scand.* 11:1086, 1957.
19. --------------. The isolation of prostaglandin F from sheep prostate glands.
    Acta Chem. Scand. 14:1693-700, 1960.
20. --------------. The isolation of prostaglandin E from sheep prostate glands.
    Acta Chem. Scand. 14:1701-5, 1960.

21. **Bergström S, Krabisch L & Sjövall J.** Smooth muscle stimulating factors in ram semen.
    Acta Chem. Scand. 14:1706-10, 1960.
22. **Bergström S, Ryhage R, Samuelsson B & Sjövall J.** Short communications. (The structure of prostaglandin E, F_1 and F_2.) *Acta Chem. Scand.* 16:501-2, 1962.
23. **Bergström S, Dressler F, Ryhage R, Samuelsson B & Sjövall J.** The isolation of two further prostaglandins from sheep prostate glands. Prostaglandin and related factors. 8. *Ark. Kem.* 19:563-7, 1962.
24. **Samuelsson B.** Letter to editor. (Prostaglandins and related factors. 17. The structure of prostaglandin E_3.) *J. Amer. Chem. Soc.* 85:1878-9, 1963.
25. **Gréen K & Samuelsson B.** Prostaglandins and related factors: XIX. Thin-layer chromatography of prostaglandins. *J. Lipid Res.* 5:117-20, 1964.
26. **Bergström S, Danielsson H & Samuelsson B.** The enzymatic formation of prostaglandin E_2 from arachidonic acid. Prostaglandins and related factors. 32. *Biochim. Biophys. Acta* 90:207-10, 1964.
27. **Miller J A.** Nobel prize in medicine for prostaglandin discoveries. *Sci. News* 122:245, 1982.
28. **Ferreira S H & Vane J R.** Prostaglandins: their disappearance from and release into the circulation. *Nature* 216:868-73, 1967.
29. **Piper P J & Vane J R.** Release of additional factors in anaphylaxis and its antagonism by anti-inflammatory drugs. *Nature* 223:29-35, 1969.
30. **Hamberg M & Samuelsson B.** Detection and isolation of an endoperoxide intermediate in prostaglandin biosynthesis. *Proc. Nat. Acad. Sci. US* 70:899-903, 1973.
31. **Hamberg M, Svensson J, Wakabayashi T & Samuelsson B.** Isolation and structure of two prostaglandin endoperoxides that cause platelet aggregation. *Proc. Nat. Acad. Sci. US* 71:345-9, 1974.
32. **Hamberg M & Samuelsson B.** Prostaglandin endoperoxides. Novel transformations of arachidonic acid in human platelets. *Proc. Nat. Acad. Sci. US* 71:3400-4, 1974.
33. **Garfield E.** The 1974 articles most cited in 1974. *Essays of an information scientist.* Philadelphia: ISI Press, 1977. Vol. 2. p. 426-9.
34. **Hamberg M, Svensson J & Samuelsson B.** Prostaglandin endoperoxides. A new concept concerning the mode of action and release of prostaglandins. *Proc. Nat. Acad. Sci. US* 71:3824-8, 1974.
35. **Malmsten C, Hamberg M, Svensson J & Samuelsson B.** Physiological role of an endoperoxide in human platelets: hemostatic defect due to platelet cyclo-oxygenase deficiency. *Proc. Nat. Acad. Sci. US* 72:1446-50, 1975.
36. **Hamberg M, Svensson J & Samuelsson B.** Thromboxanes: a new group of biologically active compounds derived from prostaglandin endoperoxides. *Proc. Nat. Acad. Sci. US* 72:2994-8, 1975.
37. **Hamberg M.** Citation Classic. Commentary on *Proc. Nat. Acad. Sci. US* 72:2294-8, 1975. *Current Contents/Life Sciences* 26(2):19, 10 January 1983.
38. **Ferreira S H.** Citation Classic. Commentary on *Nature* 216:868-73, 1967. *Current Contents/Life Sciences* 26(51):18, 19 December 1983.
39. **Vane J R.** Adventures and excursions in bioassay: the stepping stones to prostacyclin. (Nobel lecture.) *Brit. J. Pharmacol.* 79:821-38, 1983.
40. ------------. Inhibition of prostaglandin synthesis as a mechanism of action for aspirin-like drugs. *Nature New Biol.* 231:232-5, 1971.
41. ------------. Citation Classic. Commentary on *Nature New Biol.* 231:232-5, 1971. *Current Contents/Life Sciences* 23(42):12, 20 October 1980.
42. **Garfield E.** The 25 most cited 1971 papers reveal a great deal about research in 1971. *Essays of an information scientist.* Philadelphia: ISI Press, 1977. Vol. 1. p. 496-9.
43. **Ferreira S H, Moncada S & Vane J R.** Indomethacin and aspirin abolish prostaglandin release from the spleen. *Nature New Biol.* 231:237-9, 1971.
44. **Check W A.** Prostaglandin research captures Nobel prize. *J. Amer. Med. Assn.* 248:2212-3, 1982.
45. **Garfield E.** The 250 most-cited primary authors, 1961-1975. Part I. How the names were selected. *Essays of an information scientist.* Philadelphia: ISI Press, 1980. Vol. 3. p. 326-36.
46. **Bergström S & Danielsson H.** On the regulation of bile acid formation in the rat liver. *Acta Physiol. Scand.* 43:1-7, 1958.
47. **Bergström S & Gloor U.** Studies on the 7α-hydroxylation of taurodesoxycholic acid in rat liver homogenates. Bile acids and steroids. 18. *Acta Chem. Scand.* 9:34-8, 1955.
48. **Bergström S, Duner H, von Euler U S, Pernow B & Sjövall J.** Observations on the effects of infusion of prostaglandin E in man. *Acta Physiol. Scand.* 45:145-51, 1959.
49. **Bergström S, Ryhage R, Samuelsson B & Sjövall J.** Prostaglandins and related factors. 15. The structures of prostaglandin E_1, $F_{1\alpha}$, and $F_{1\beta}$. *J. Biol. Chem.* 238:3555-64, 1963.
50. **Bergström S, Carlson L A & Weeks J R.** The prostaglandins: a family of biologically active lipids. *Pharmacol. Rev.* 20:1-48, 1968.
51. **Garfield E.** Most-cited articles of the 1960s. 3. Preclinical basic research. *Essays of an information scientist.* Philadelphia: ISI Press, 1981. Vol. 4. p. 370-8.
52. **Bergström S.** Prostaglandins: members of a new hormonal system. *Science* 157:382-91, 1967.
53. **Garfield E.** The 300 most-cited authors, 1961-1976, including co-authors at last. 1. How the names were selected. *Essays of an information scientist.* Philadelphia: ISI Press, 1980. Vol. 3. p. 538-50.
54. ------------. The 1,000 contemporary scientists most-cited 1965-1978. Part I. The basic list and introduction. *Essays of an information scientist.* Philadelphia: ISI Press, 1983. Vol. 5. p. 269-78.
55. **Samuelsson B, Granström E, Gréen K, Hamberg M & Hammarström S.** Prostaglandins. *Annu. Rev. Biochem.* 44:669-95, 1975.
56. **Murphy R C, Hammarström S & Samuelsson B.** Leukotriene C: a slow-reacting substance from murine mastocytoma cells. *Proc. Nat. Acad. Sci. US* 76:4275-9, 1979.
57. **Garfield E.** The 1979 articles most cited from 1979 to 1981. 1. Life sciences. *Essays of an information scientist.* Philadelphia: ISI Press, 1983. Vol. 5. p. 575-90.
58. **Vane J R.** A sensitive method for the assay of 5-hydroxytryptamine. *Brit. J. Pharm. Chem.* 12:344-9, 1957.
59. ------------. The actions of sympathomimetic amines on tryptamine receptors. (Vane J R, Wolstenholme G E W & O'Connor M, eds.) *Ciba Foundation Symposium on Adrenergic Mechanisms.* Boston: Little, Brown, 1960. p. 356-72.

60. -----------. The release and fate of vaso-active hormones in the circulation. *Brit. J. Pharmacol.* 35:209-42, 1969.

61. **Moncada S, Gryglewski R, Bunting S & Vane J R.** An enzyme isolated from arteries transforms prostaglandin endoperoxides to an unstable substance that inhibits platelet aggregation. *Nature* 263:663-5, 1976.

62. **Garfield E.** The 1976 articles most cited in 1976 and 1977. Part I. Life sciences. *Essays of an information scientist.* Philadelphia: ISI Press, 1981. Vol. 4. p. 81-99.

63. -----------. *Nature:* 112 years of continuous publication of high impact research and science journalism. *Essays of an information scientist.* Philadelphia: ISI Press. 1983. Vol. 5. p. 261-8.

64. **Johnson R A, Morton D R, Kinner J H, Gorman R R, McGuire J C, Sun F F, Whittaker N, Bunting S, Salmon J, Moncada S & Vane J R.** The chemical structure of prostaglandin X (prostacyclin). *Prostaglandins* 12:915-28, 1976.

65. **Needleman P, Moncada S, Bunting S, Vane J R, Hamberg M & Samuelsson B.** Identification of an enzyme in platelet microsomes which generates thromboxane A_2 from prostaglandin endoperoxides. *Nature* 261:558-60, 1976.

66. **Gryglewski R J, Bunting S, Moncada S, Flower R J & Vane J R.** Arterial walls are protected against deposition of platelet thrombi by a substance (prostaglandin X) which they make from prostaglandin endoperoxides. *Prostaglandins* 12:685-713, 1976.

67. **Moncada S.** Citation Classic. Commentary on *Lancet* 1:18-21, 1977. *Current Contents/Life Sciences* 25(41):22, 11 October 1982.

68. **Moncada S, Higgs E A & Vane J R.** Human arterial and venous tissues generate prostacyclin (prostaglandin X), a potent inhibitor of platelet aggregation. *Lancet* 1:18-21, 1977.

69. **Dusting G J, Moncada S & Vane J R.** Prostacyclin (PGX) is the endogenous metabolite responsible for relaxation of coronary arteries induced by arachidonic acid. *Prostaglandins* 13:3-15, 1977.

70. **Moncada S, Bunting S, Mullane K, Thorogood P, Vane J R, Raz A & Needleman P.** Imidazole: a selective inhibitor of thromboxane synthetase. *Prostaglandins* 13:611-8, 1977.

71. **Tateson J E, Moncada S & Vane J R.** Effects of prostacyclin (PGX) on cyclic AMP concentrations in human platelets. *Prostaglandins* 13:389-97, 1977.

72. **Garfield E.** The 1977 articles most cited from 1977 to 1979. Part 1. Life sciences. *Essays of an information scientist.* Philadelphia: ISI Press, 1981. Vol. 4. p. 528-41.

73. **Armstrong J M, Lattimer N, Moncada S & Vane J R.** Comparison of the vasodepressor effects of prostacyclin and 6-oxo-prostaglandin $F_{1\alpha}$ with those of prostaglandin E_2 in rats and rabbits. *Brit. J. Pharmacol.* 62:125-30, 1978.

74. **Moncada S, Korbut R, Bunting S & Vane J R.** Prostacyclin is a circulating hormone. *Nature* 273:767-8, 1978.

75. **Garfield E.** The 1978 articles most cited in 1978 and 1979. 2. Life sciences. *Essays of an information scientist.* Philadelphia: ISI Press, 1981. Vol. 4. p. 686-95.

76. **Moncada S & Vane J R.** Arachidonic acid metabolites and the interactions between platelets and blood-vessel walls. *N. Engl. J. Med.* 300:1142-7, 1979.

77. **Garfield E.** Computer-aided historiography—how ISI uses cluster-tracking to monitor the "vital signs" of science. *Essays of an information scientist.* Philadelphia: ISI Press, 1983. Vol. 5. p. 473-83.

78. **Samuelsson B.** Letter to editor. (On the incorporation of oxygen in the conversion of 8,11,14-eicosatrienoic acid to prostaglandin E_1.) *J. Amer. Chem. Soc.* 87:3011-3, 1965.

79. **Hamberg M & Samuelsson B.** On the mechanism of the biosynthesis of prostaglandins E_1 and $F_{1\alpha}$. *J. Biol. Chem.* 242:5336-43, 1967.

80. **Marnett L J, Wlodawer P & Samuelsson B.** Co-oxygenation of organic substrates by the prostaglandin synthetase of sheep vesicular gland. *J. Biol. Chem.* 250:8510-7, 1975.

81. **Moncada S, Ferreira S H & Vane J R.** Prostaglandins, aspirin-like drugs and the oedema of inflammation. *Nature* 246:217-9, 1973.

82. **Ferreira S H, Moncada S & Vane J R.** Prostaglandins and the mechanism of analgesia produced by aspirin-like drugs. *Brit. J. Pharmacol.* 49:86-97, 1973.

83. **Van Dorp D A, Beerthuis R K, Nugteren D H & Vonkeman H.** The biosynthesis of prostaglandins. *Biochim. Biophys. Acta* 90:204-7, 1964.

84. **Crunkhorn P & Willis A L.** Cutaneous reactions to intradermal prostaglandins. *Brit. J. Pharmacol.* 41:49-56, 1971.

85. **Willis A L.** Letter to editor. (Parallel assay of prostaglandin-like activity in rat inflammatory exudate by means of cascade superfusion.) *J. Pharm. Pharmacol.* 21:126-8, 1969.

86. **Cherfas J & Connor S.** How restless DNA was tamed. *New Sci.* 100:78-9, 1983.

87. **Altman L K.** Lasker awards go to geneticist and a lab head. *NY Times* 19 November 1981, p. B2.

Current Comments®

Journal Citation Studies. 42.
Analytical Chemistry Journals—
What They Cite and What Cites Them

Number 13   March 26, 1984

We've published many studies of journal citation patterns covering various fields of science, social sciences, and arts and humanities. Recently, we presented data on journals in entomology,[1] anthropology,[2] and earth sciences.[3] I've often commented on different aspects of the chemical literature, since ISI® publishes *Current Abstracts of Chemistry and Index Chemicus®* (*CAC&IC®*).[4] In earlier studies, we looked at citation patterns in individual journals, such as *Journal of the American Chemical Society, Biochemistry,* and *Journal of Chemical Physics,* for example,[5,6] rather than groups of journals. This study of analytical chemistry journals is the first time we've done the type of in-depth analysis where we treat the "core" journals in a unified manner. In the near future, we'll do the same type of analysis for physical chemistry as well as astrosciences.

This study coincides with the centennial of the Association of Official Analytical Chemists (AOAC). The AOAC has scheduled a spring workshop to be held in Philadelphia from April 30 to May 2. Among the topics to be discussed at this meeting are: immunoligand, chromatographic, and instrumental techniques; drug delivery systems; drug metabolism; genetic toxicology; environmental contamination; robotics in laboratory automation; forensic science; and adulteration and food analysis. The last topic is especially relevant in light of the current controversy surrounding grains treated with ethylene di-

bromide (EDB), a cancer-causing agent. For more information on the AOAC spring workshop, contact the program chairman, Walter Fiddler, US Department of Agriculture, 600 East Mermaid Lane, Philadelphia, Pennsylvania 19118; telephone: (215) 233-6502.

Analytical chemistry deals with the characterization and measurement of the composition of matter in solid, liquid, or gaseous form. One of the earliest applications of analytical chemistry was to determine the purity of gold and silver samples. Crude analytical methods have been traced back to ancient Babylonian times—as early as 2600 BC. More sophisticated methods, including titration, flame tests, bead tests, etc., were developed in Britain, France, and Germany in the seventeenth through nineteenth centuries. The methods were used to analyze a wide variety of elements, metals, alloys, and compounds.[7]

In the US, analytical chemistry developed in the late nineteenth century, when chemical fertilizers were first introduced. Certain states passed laws requiring manufacturers to provide labels showing the amounts of nitrogen, potash, and phosphorus in their fertilizers. The AOAC, then known as the Association of Official *Agricultural* Chemists, was established in 1884 to standardize the methods of chemical fertilizer analyses. Harvey Wiley, one of the founders of AOAC, was also a central figure in the passage of the Pure Food and Drug Act of 1906. One of its main objectives was to combat the adulteration or contamination of food and drugs.[8]

So analytical chemistry has a long and international history. This is reflected in the list of 28 analytical chemistry journals indexed in *Science Citation Index®* (*SCI®*) that are included in this study (see Table 1). Nine of these "core" journals are published in the US. The Federal Republic of Germany, the Netherlands, Switzerland, and the UK each publish three of the journals listed. Spain accounts for two journals, while Austria, France, Japan, Poland, and the USSR each publish one of the core journals. *Journal of Analytical Chemistry of the USSR* is a cover-to-cover translation of *Zhurnal Analiticheskoi Khimii*.

Table 1 also shows the year each journal began publication. Several existed before the dates shown but under different titles, or as parts of a larger journal that subsequently split into separate sections. For example, the *Journal of the Association of Official Agricultural Chemists* began publication in 1915 but changed its name to *Journal of the Association of Official Analytical Chemists* in 1966. In this study, journals that changed names or split are combined under the current title.

As in previous studies, we'll consider the core journals analyzed here as if they were a single "Macro Journal of Analytical Chemistry." We'll examine what this macro journal cites and, in turn, what cites it. Data are taken from the 1982 *Journal Citation Reports®* (*JCR™*), which is volume 14 of *SCI*. Incidentally, this volume can be purchased separately.

The 28 core analytical chemistry journals published 6,000 articles in 1982. This represents 1.6 percent of the 380,000 research articles included in the 1982 *JCR*. The core journals cited about 115,600 references that year, or 1.5 percent of the eight million references processed in *JCR*. Thus, the average analytical chemistry article cited about 19

Table 1: Core analytical chemistry journals indexed by *SCI®* and the year each began publication.

Afinidad—1924
Anales de Quimica Serie B—Quimica Inorganica y Quimica Analytica—1980
Analusis—1972
Analyst—1877
Analytica Chimica Acta—1947
Analytical Chemistry—1947
Analytical Letters Parts A & B—1967
Bunseki Kagaku—1952
Chemia Analityczna—1956
Chromatographia—1968
CRC Critical Reviews in Analytical Chemistry—1970
Fresenius Zeitschrift für Analytische Chemie—1947
International Journal of Environmental Analytical Chemistry—1971
Journal of Analytical Chemistry of the USSR—1952
Journal of Chromatographic Science—1969
Journal of Chromatography—1958
Journal of Electroanalytical Chemistry and Interfacial Electrochemistry—1967
Journal of High Resolution Chromatography & Chromatography Communications—1978
Journal of Liquid Chromatography—1978
Journal of Radioanalytical Chemistry—1968
Journal of the Association of Official Analytical Chemists—1966
Microchemical Journal—1957
Mikrochimica Acta—1966
Radiochemical and Radioanalytical Letters—1969
Separation and Purification Methods—1972
Separation Science and Technology—1978
Talanta—1958
TRAC—Trends in Analytical Chemistry—1981

references, as compared to 21 for the average *JCR* article.

Articles in the core *received* nearly 82,000 citations in 1982—about one percent of the total processed in *JCR*. Just two core journals account for 52 percent of these citations—*Analytical Chemistry* (23,500) and *Journal of Chromatography* (18,300). The same two journals also account for 36 percent of all papers published by the core group in 1982. The analytical chemistry journals dramatically demonstrate the "concentration effect" that applies to the scientific literature in general—a small number of journals accounts for the majority of citations and published articles.[9]

Table 2 shows the 50 journals most frequently cited *by* the core analytical chemistry journals in 1982. They are ranked by the number of core citations they received (column A). Also shown are the number of citations from *all* journals (column B), each journal's self-citations (column C), impact factor (column G), immediacy index (column H), and the number of source items each journal

published in 1982 (column I). Impact indicates how often articles published in the previous two years were cited in the year studied. Immediacy measures the impact of a journal's articles in the same year they were published.

The 50 journals in Table 2 *received* about 57,200 citations from the core analytical chemistry journals. This represents 50 percent of all references cited

Table 2: The 50 journals most cited by core analytical chemistry journals in 1982. An asterisk indicates a core journal. A=citations received from core journals. B=citations received from all journals. C=self-citations. D=percent of citations from all journals that are core journal citations (A/B). E=percent of citations from all journals that are self-citations (self-cited rate, C/B). F=percent of core citations that are self-citations (C/A). G=impact factor. H=immediacy index. I=1982 source items.

	A	B	C	D	E	F	G	H	I
*Anal. Chem.	10,243	23,406	3910	43.8	16.7	38.2	3.71	.59	691
*J. Chromatogr.	9833	18,259	5064	53.9	27.7	51.5	2.00	.45	1454
*Anal. Chim. Acta	3874	6667	953	58.1	14.3	24.6	2.45	.25	430
*J. Electroanal. Chem. Interfac.	2612	6557	1859	39.8	28.4	71.2	2.15	.45	371
J. Amer. Chem. Soc.	2296	111,901	—	2.1	—	—	4.72	.90	1835
*Fresenius Z. Anal. Chem.	1641	3048	499	53.8	16.4	30.4	1.23	.32	267
*Talanta	1625	2784	349	58.4	12.5	21.5	1.40	.18	218
*J. Chromatogr. Sci.	1588	2469	156	64.3	6.3	9.8	3.43	.25	99
*Analyst	1468	2970	301	49.4	10.1	20.5	1.40	.19	229
*J. Anal. Chem.—USSR	1216	1995	410	61.0	20.6	33.7	.54	.04	222
Anal. Biochem.	1157	22,737	—	5.1	—	—	2.88	.36	572
*J. Assn. Offic. Anal. Chem.	1081	2665	543	40.6	20.4	50.2	.84	.18	240
*Chromatographia	1008	1410	192	71.5	13.6	19.1	1.69	.18	206
Clin. Chem.	956	10,120	—	9.5	—	—	3.16	.69	408
*J. High Res. Chromatogr.	824	995	273	82.8	27.4	33.1	—	—	—
*J. Radioanal. Chem.	821	1412	419	58.1	29.7	51.0	.69	.15	232
J. Phys. Chem.	813	22,314	—	3.6	—	—	2.44	.57	898
J. Pharm. Sci.	719	7201	—	10.0	—	—	1.16	.25	349
*Bunseki Kagaku	670	985	119	68.0	12.1	17.8	.54	.10	265
*Anal. Lett. Pts. A & B	612	1248	39	49.0	3.1	6.4	1.18	.15	134
*J. Liq. Chromatogr.	607	1026	134	59.2	13.1	22.1	1.90	.15	188
J. Biol. Chem.	573	131,922	—	.4	—	—	5.87	1.18	2380
Nature	533	110,923	—	.5	—	—	8.75	2.10	1362
*Mikrochim. Acta	526	872	86	60.3	9.9	16.4	.94	.11	100
J. Electrochem. Soc.	521	10,401	—	5.0	—	—	1.95	.33	602
Clin. Chim. Acta	504	8973	—	5.6	—	—	1.78	.27	379
J. Chem. Phys.	502	71,173	—	.7	—	—	2.95	.63	1714
Spectrochim. Acta Pt. B—At. Spec.	496	1166	—	42.5	—	—	2.47	.22	96
Science	495	70,867	—	.7	—	—	6.81	1.73	988
Appl. Spectrosc.	491	1693	—	29.0	—	—	2.42	.24	140
Biochim. Biophys. Acta	467	71,656	—	.7	—	—	2.65	.48	2213
J. Inorg. Nucl. Chem.	427	6102	—	7.0	—	—	.68	—	—
Electrochim. Acta	423	2969	—	14.3	—	—	1.14	.20	256
Amer. Lab.	403	630	—	64.0	—	—	1.05	.09	143
J. Agr. Food Chem.	403	5385	—	7.5	—	—	1.20	.34	320
Bull. Chem. Soc. Jpn.	387	10,452	—	3.7	—	—	.99	.27	912
Biochem. J.	365	38,440	—	1.0	—	—	3.38	.69	791
Nucl. Instrum. Method. Phys. Res.	365	8035	—	4.5	—	—	1.17	.35	1058
Environ. Sci. Technol.	353	3345	—	10.6	—	—	1.81	.32	213
*Radiochem. Radioanal. Lett.	348	749	168	46.5	22.4	48.3	.48	.13	207
Biomed. Mass. Spectrom.	344	1250	—	27.5	—	—	2.32	.36	92
Zavod. Lab.	332	970	—	34.2	—	—	.18	.02	163
*Separ. Sci. Technol.	310	563	146	55.1	25.9	47.1	.76	.36	88
Elektrokhimiya	308	1784	—	17.3	—	—	.34	.18	208
Inorg. Chem.	302	22,487	—	1.3	—	—	2.90	.56	888
J. Chem. Soc.	283	13,236	—	2.1	—	—	—	—	—
Biochemistry—USA	268	46,682	—	.6	—	—	4.50	.86	1045
Collect. Czech. Chem. Commun.	268	3936	—	6.8	—	—	.59	.32	366
*Chem. Anal.	255	449	—	56.8	—	—	.32	—	—
Surface Sci.	254	13,318	—	1.9	—	—	3.59	.65	538

by the core in 1982. Twenty of these journals are themselves members of the core group. They are indicated by asterisks. Fifty-one percent of the citations these 20 journals received in 1982 came from the core journals. *Journal of High Resolution Chromatography & Chromatography Communications* is the core journal with the highest percentage of its overall citations from core journals—83 percent of the 995 citations it received in 1982.

Analytical Chemistry has the highest impact of the 28 core journals—3.7. *Journal of Chromatographic Science* follows at 3.4, followed by *Analytica Chimica Acta* (2.5), and *Journal of Electroanalytical Chemistry and Interfacial Electrochemistry* (2.2). *CRC Critical Reviews in Analytical Chemistry* (2.0) does not appear in Table 2. It was cited only 91 times by the core group in 1982. This is 163 short of the 254 cutoff.

Impact is determined by dividing the number of 1982 citations to a journal's 1980 and 1981 articles by the combined number of articles it published in those two years. We are aware that the way impact is calculated may be biased in favor of "fast moving" fields, such as biochemistry or molecular biology. Papers in some fields are cited very soon after publication, but the same may not be true of other fields, such as mathematics or geosciences. That is, the "peak" citation year may be later than the two-year base used in this study.

The *JCR* reports data on a journal's "half-life," which indicates the median age for a given field's cited and citing literature. Table 3 shows half-lives for the core analytical chemistry journals. Column A gives each journal's *cited* half-life—that is, the median age of articles from each journal which were cited in 1982. For example, *Afinidad*'s cited half-life is 3.1 years. Thus, half of the citations this journal *received* in 1982 were to articles it published over the past three years, from 1980 to 1982. One has

Table 3: 1982 *SCI*® cit*ed* and cit*ing* half-lives of core analytical chemistry journals. Journals with no listing either received less than 100 citations in 1982, or gave out less than 100 citations in 1982. A = cit*ed* half-life. B = cit*ing* half-life. C = core analytical chemistry journal.

A	B	C
3.1	>10.0	Afinidad
—	>10.0	An. Quim. B—Inorg. Anal.
3.8	6.7	Analusis
8.2	8.2	Analyst
5.0	5.6	Anal. Chim. Acta
7.6	2.8	Anal. Chem.
5.1	6.4	Anal. Lett. Pts. A & B
5.4	7.3	Bunseki Kagaku
6.9	—	Chem. Anal.
5.0	5.2	Chromatographia
4.3	6.0	CRC Crit. Rev. Anal. Chem.
5.3	5.7	Fresenius Z. Anal. Chem.
3.1	5.4	Int. J. Environ. Anal. Chem.
7.0	7.5	J. Anal. Chem.—USSR
4.3	5.0	J. Chromatogr.
5.2	5.8	J. Chromatogr. Sci.
5.3	7.3	J. Electroanal. Chem. Interfac.
—	—	J. High Res. Chromatogr.
2.6	4.5	J. Liq. Chromatogr.
5.0	8.3	J. Radioanal. Chem.
7.1	5.8	J. Assn. Offic. Anal. Chem.
4.5	9.6	Microchem. J.
6.6	>10.0	Mikrochim. Acta
4.5	8.6	Radiochem. Radioanal. Lett.
—	5.6	Separ. Purif. Method.
4.9	8.2	Separ. Sci. Technol.
7.3	8.1	Talanta
—	—	TRAC—Trend. Anal. Chem.

to be careful in interpreting half-life. Many journals are now much larger than they were even a decade ago.

Cit*ing* half-life, shown in column B in Table 3, indicates the age of the literature that each journal cites. Again, cit*ing* half-life is the median age of the literature cited *by* a journal. A figure greater than ten means that more than 50 percent of a journal's 1982 references cited articles published before 1973, as is the case with *Afinidad*. *Analytical Chemistry* has the shortest citing half-life of all the core journals. Half of its 1982 references were to articles published between 1980 and 1982.

Analytical Chemistry ranks first in immediacy, at .59, as well as in impact. Immediacy is calculated by dividing the number of citations a journal's 1982 articles received by the number of articles published in 1982. The *Journal of Chromatography* (.45) and *Journal of Electroanalytical Chemistry and Interfacial Electrochemistry* (.45) are followed by

90

Table 4: The 50 journals which most frequently cited core analytical chemistry journals in 1982. An asterisk indicates a core journal. A=citations to core journals. B=citations to all journals. C=self-citations. D=percent of total citations that are core journal citations (A/B). E=percent of total citations that are self-citations (self-citing rate, C/B). F=percent of citations to core journals that are self-citations (C/A). G=impact factor. H=immediacy index. I=1982 source items.

	A	B	C	D	E	F	G	H	I
*Anal. Chem.	9113	27,006	3910	33.7	14.5	42.9	3.71	.59	691
*J. Chromatogr.	8381	24,013	5064	34.9	21.1	60.4	2.00	.45	1454
*Anal. Chim. Acta	3387	8082	953	41.9	11.8	28.1	2.45	.25	430
*J. Electroanal. Chem. Interfac.	2278	7968	1859	28.6	23.3	81.6	2.15	.45	371
*Talanta	1923	4589	349	41.9	7.6	18.2	1.40	.18	218
*Chromatographia	1656	3123	192	53.0	6.2	11.6	1.69	.18	206
*Fresenius Z. Anal. Chem.	1537	4254	499	36.1	11.7	32.5	1.23	.32	267
*Analyst	1395	3289	301	42.4	9.2	21.6	1.40	.19	229
*J. Liq. Chromatogr.	1393	3466	134	40.2	3.9	9.6	1.90	.15	188
*Bunseki Kagaku	1062	2127	119	49.9	5.6	11.2	.54	.10	265
*J. High Res. Chromatogr.	948	1987	273	47.7	13.7	28.8	—	—	—
*J. Assn. Offic. Anal. Chem.	936	2697	543	34.7	20.1	58.0	.84	.18	240
*J. Radioanal. Chem.	899	4020	419	22.4	10.4	46.6	.69	.15	232
*J. Chromatogr. Sci.	757	1621	156	46.7	9.6	20.6	3.43	.25	99
Chem. Listy	724	4122	—	17.6	—	—	.41	.10	80
*CRC Crit. Rev. Anal. Chem.	697	2012	3	34.6	.2	.4	2.03	.25	8
Anal. Biochem.	672	10,987	—	6.1	—	—	2.88	.36	572
Electrochim. Acta	641	5102	—	12.6	—	—	1.14	.20	256
Prog. Anal. Atom. Spectrosc.	585	1653	—	35.4	—	—	—	—	—
*J. Anal. Chem.—USSR	579	2976	410	19.5	13.8	70.8	.54	.04	222
J. Amer. Chem. Soc.	568	56,674	—	1.0	—	—	4.72	.90	1835
Pure Appl. Chem.	563	7906	—	7.1	—	—	2.03	.45	188
*Anal. Lett. Pt. A & Pt. B	544	1814	39	30.0	2.1	7.2	1.18	.15	134
*Analusis	530	1374	47	38.6	3.4	8.9	.54	.18	73
Clin. Chem.	478	9400	—	5.1	—	—	3.16	.69	408
J. Electrochem. Soc.	436	11,564	—	3.8	—	—	1.95	.33	602
*Mikrochim. Acta	422	1117	86	37.8	7.7	20.4	.94	.11	100
Appl. Spectrosc.	419	2182	—	19.2	—	—	2.42	.24	140
Spectrochim. Acta Pt. B—At. Spec.	401	1815	—	22.1	—	—	2.47	.22	96
Bull. Chem. Soc. Jpn.	395	15,759	—	2.5	—	—	.99	.27	912
J. Pharm. Sci.	374	6691	—	5.6	—	—	1.16	.25	349
Biochim. Biophys. Acta	368	68,118	—	.5	—	—	2.65	.48	2213
*Radiochem. Radioanal. Lett.	356	2120	168	16.8	7.9	47.2	.48	.13	207
*Separ. Sci. Technol.	355	1659	146	21.4	8.8	41.1	.76	.36	88
J. Water Pollut. Contr. Fed.	348	8448	—	4.1	—	—	.89	.16	178
J. Biol. Chem.	347	79,759	—	.4	—	—	5.87	1.18	2380
*Microchem. J.	337	918	84	36.7	9.2	24.9	.83	.11	79
Int. J. Mass Spectrom. Ion Phys.	329	3076	—	10.7	—	—	1.81	.39	111
J. Agr. Food Chem.	325	5410	—	6.0	—	—	1.20	.34	320
Environ. Sci. Technol.	324	5089	—	6.4	—	—	1.81	.32	213
Collect. Czech. Chem. Commun.	299	6372	—	4.7	—	—	.59	.32	366
Inorg. Chem.	287	25,350	—	1.1	—	—	2.90	.56	888
J. Phys. Chem.	284	28,408	—	1.0	—	—	2.44	.57	898
ACS Symp. Ser.	279	16,457	—	1.7	—	—	.56	.14	616
J. Indian Chem. Soc.	273	5716	—	4.8	—	—	.27	.03	384
Biomed. Mass Spectrom.	272	1904	—	14.3	—	—	2.32	.36	92
*Int. J. Environ. Anal. Chem.	267	989	19	27.0	1.9	7.1	1.27	.12	57
Bull. Soc. Chim. Fr.	262	3895	—	6.7	—	—	.54	.13	132
Indian J. Chem. Sect. A	261	4917	—	5.3	—	—	.38	.06	354
Ind. Lab.—Engl. Tr.	232	1945	—	11.9	—	—	.01	.00	163

Separation Science and Technology (.36), *Fresenius Zeitschrift für Analytische Chemie* (.32), and *Analytica Chimica Acta*, *CRC Critical Reviews in Analytical Chemistry*, and *Journal of Chromatographic Science*, each with an immediacy of .25.

Table 4 lists the 50 journals that most frequently cited the core analytical chemistry journals in 1982. These 50 represent just two percent of the 2,200 journals that cited the core that year. Yet they account for 62 percent of the 82,000 citations received by the core in 1982.

Twenty-three of the journals in Table 4 are core journals. Again, they are indicated by asterisks. Of the 113,000 references these 23 journals cited in 1982, 35 percent were to the core group. *Chro-*

matographia has the highest percentage of its references to the core group. Of the 3,100 references cited in its 1982 articles, 53 percent were to the core journals. The 27 *non*-core journals in Table 4 cited 400,000 references in 1982, and only three percent of these were to the core journals.

Another important factor in journal analyses is the number of "superstar" articles they publish. The 62 most-cited articles from the core analytical chemistry journals are listed in Table 5 in alphabetical order by first author. Also shown are the number of citations each received from 1961 through 1982 in *SCI*. We were also able to add citations from 1955

through 1960 to papers published in 1960 and earlier, shown in parentheses.

Table 5 includes only those 62 articles cited 300 times or more. Six of the 28 core journals met or exceeded this threshold. *Analytical Chemistry* dominates the list, accounting for 48 papers. *Analyst* and *Journal of Chromatography* each published five of the most-cited papers, the *Journal of the Association of Official Analytical Chemists* published two, and *Analytica Chimica Acta* and *Fresenius Zeitschrift für Analytische Chemie* each account for one paper.

The most-cited paper, by D.H. Spackman, W.H. Stein, and S. Moore, Rockefeller Institute for Medical Research,

Table 5: The 62 most-cited articles from the core analytical chemistry journals cited 300 or more times, 1961-1982 *SCI*®, in alphabetical order by first author. We have added (in parentheses) the additional citations to the papers published in 1960 and earlier.

Citations 1961-1982		Bibliographic Data
301		**Albee A L & Ray L.** Correction factors for electron probe microanalysis of silicates, oxides, carbonates, phosphates, and sulfates. *Anal. Chem.* 42:1408-14, 1970.
678	(16)	**Bencze W L & Schmid K.** Determination of tyrosine and tryptophan in proteins. *Anal. Chem.* 29:1193-6, 1957.
395		**Bergman I & Loxley R.** Two improved and simplified methods for the spectrophotometric determination of hydroxyproline. *Anal. Chem.* 35:1961-5, 1963.
581		**Bruno G A & Christian J E.** Determination of carbon-14 in aqueous bicarbonate solutions by liquid scintillation counting techniques. *Anal. Chem.* 33:1216-8, 1961.
3809	(48)	**Chen P S, Toribara T Y & Warner H.** Microdetermination of phosphorus. *Anal. Chem.* 28:1756-8, 1956.
353	(60)	**Cifonelli J A & Smith F.** Detection of glycosides and other carbohydrate compounds on paper chromatograms. *Anal. Chem.* 26:1132-4, 1954.
371		**Currie L A.** Limits for qualitative detection and quantitative determination. *Anal. Chem.* 40:586-93, 1968.
351	(60)	**Dixon J S & Lipkin D.** Spectrophotometric determination of vicinal glycols. *Anal. Chem.* 26:1092-3, 1954.
6052	(63)	**Dubois M, Gilles K A, Hamilton J K, Rebers P A & Smith F.** Colorimetric method for determination of sugars and related substances. *Anal. Chem.* 28:350-6, 1956.
600	(1)	**Gelotte B.** Studies on gel filtration: sorption properties of the bed material Sephadex. *J. Chromatogr.* 3:330-42, 1960.
359	(31)	**Gordon H T, Thornburg W & Werum L N.** Rapid paper chromatography of carbohydrates and related compounds. *Anal. Chem.* 28:849-55, 1956.
564	(17)	**Gran G.** Determination of the equivalence point in potentiometric titrations. Part II. *Analyst* 77:661-71, 1952.
521		**Hamilton P B.** Ion exchange chromatography of amino acids. *Anal. Chem.* 35:2055-64, 1963.
556		**Hatch W R & Ott W L.** Determination of sub-microgram quantities of mercury by atomic absorption spectrophotometry. *Anal. Chem.* 40:2085-7, 1968.
478	(2)	**Herberg R J.** Determination of carbon-14 and tritium in blood and other whole tissues. *Anal. Chem.* 32:42-6, 1960.
335		**Huang T C, Chen C P, Wefler V & Raftery A.** A stable reagent for the Liebermann-Burchard reaction. *Anal. Chem.* 33:1405-7, 1961.
529		**Huisman T H J & Dozy A M.** Studies on the heterogeneity of hemoglobin. IX. The use of tris-(hydroxymethyl)aminomethane-HCl buffers in the anion-exchange chromatography of hemoglobins. *J. Chromatogr.* 19:160-9, 1965.
334		**Hutchison W C & Munro H N.** The determination of nucleic acids in biological materials—a review. *Analyst* 86:768-813, 1961.
447		**Jeffay H & Alvarez J.** Liquid scintillation counting of carbon-14. *Anal. Chem.* 33:612-5, 1961.
316	(11)	**Johnson C M & Nishita H.** Microestimation of sulfur in plant materials, soils, and irrigation waters. *Anal. Chem.* 24:736-42, 1952.
348	(3)	**Kissinger H E.** Reaction kinetics in differential thermal analysis. *Anal. Chem.* 29:1702-6, 1957.
397	(17)	**Lang C A.** Simple microdetermination of Kjeldahl nitrogen in biological materials. *Anal. Chem.* 30:1692-4, 1958.
1041		**Laurent T C & Killander J.** A theory of gel filtration and its experimental verification. *J. Chromatogr.* 14:317-30, 1964.

341   **Lindeman L P & Adams J Q.** Carbon-13 nuclear magnetic resonance spectrometry. *Anal. Chem.* 43:1245-52, 1971.

1394 (115) **Martin J B & Doty D M.** Determination of inorganic phosphate. *Anal. Chem.* 21:965-7, 1949.

313   (22)   **McCready R M, Guggolz J, Silviera V & Owens H S.** Determination of starch and amylose in vegetables. *Anal. Chem.* 22:1156-8, 1950.

956   **Metcalfe L D & Schmitz A A.** The rapid preparation of fatty acid esters for gas chromatographic analysis. *Anal. Chem.* 33:363-4, 1961.

625   **Metcalfe L D, Schmitz A A & Pelka J R.** Letter to editor. (Rapid preparation of fatty acid esters from lipids for gas chromatographic analysis.) *Anal. Chem.* 25:514-5, 1966.

495   (130) **Miller F A & Wilkins C H.** Infrared spectra and characteristic frequencies of inorganic ions. *Anal. Chem.* 24:1253-94, 1952.

1149   (2)   **Miller G L.** Protein determination for large numbers of samples. *Anal. Chem.* 31:964, 1959.

327   (1)   **Miller G L.** Use of dinitrosalicylic acid reagent for determination of reducing sugar. *Anal. Chem.* 31:426-8, 1959.

319   (0)   **Miwa T K, Mikolajczak K L, Earle F R & Wolff I A.** Gas chromatographic characterization of fatty acids. *Anal. Chem.* 32:1739-42, 1960.

1896 (125) **Moore S, Spackman D H & Stein W H.** Chromatography of amino acids on sulfonated polystyrene resins. *Anal. Chem.* 30:1185-90, 1958.

572   **Munro H N & Fleck A.** Recent developments in the measurement of nucleic acids in biological materials. *Analyst* 91:78-88, 1966.

1085   **Murphy J & Riley J P.** A modified single solution method for the determination of phosphate in natural waters. *Anal. Chim. Acta* 27:31-6, 1962.

327   (7)   **Nelsen F M & Eggertsen F T.** Determination of surface area. *Anal. Chem.* 30:1387-90, 1958.

316   **Nicholson R S.** Theory and application of cyclic voltammetry for measurement of electrode reaction kinetics. *Anal. Chem.* 37:1351-5, 1965.

1210   **Nicholson R S & Shain I.** Theory of stationary electrode polarography. *Anal. Chem.* 36:706-23, 1964.

540   (1)   **Parker C A & Rees W T.** Correction of fluorescence spectra and measurement of fluorescence quantum efficiency. *Analyst* 85:587-600, 1960.

1360   **Patterson M S & Greene R C.** Measurement of low energy beta-emitters in aqueous solution by liquid scintillation counting of emulsions. *Anal. Chem.* 37:854-7, 1965.

478   (86)   **Pearson S, Stern S & McGavack T H.** A rapid, accurate method for the determination of total cholesterol in serum. *Anal. Chem.* 25:813-4, 1953.

305   (15)   **Peterson E A & Sober H A.** Variable gradient device for chromatography. *Anal. Chem.* 31:857-62, 1959.

599   (87)   **Peterson R E, Karrer A & Guerra S L.** Evaluation of Silber-Porter procedure for determination of plasma hydrocortisone. *Anal. Chem.* 29:144-9, 1957.

338   **Randerath K & Randerath E.** Ion-exchange chromatography of nucleotides on poly-(ethyleneimine)-cellulose thin layers. *J. Chromatogr.* 16:111-25, 1964.

303   (36)   **Saltzman B E.** Colorimetric microdetermination of nitrogen dioxide in the atmosphere. *Anal. Chem.* 26:1949-55, 1954.

888   **Savitzky A & Golay M J E.** Smoothing and differentiation of data by simplified least squares procedures. *Anal. Chem.* 36:1627-39, 1964.

696   **Sawardeker J S, Sloneker J H & Jeanes A.** Letter to editor. (Quantitative determination of monosaccharides as their alditol acetates by gas liquid chromatography.) *Anal. Chem.* 37:1602-4, 1965.

812   (1)   **Schlenk H & Gellerman J L.** Esterification of fatty acids with diazomethane on a small scale. *Anal. Chem.* 32:1412-4, 1960.

674   (50)   **Scott T A & Melvin E H.** Determination of dextran with anthrone. *Anal. Chem.* 25:1656-61, 1953.

8813 (100) **Spackman D H, Stein W H & Moore S.** Automatic recording apparatus for use in the chromatography of amino acids. *Anal. Chem.* 30:1190-206, 1958.

408   (39)   **Spies J R & Chambers D C.** Chemical determination of tryptophan. *Anal. Chem.* 20:30-9, 1948.

994   (61)   **Spies J R & Chambers D C.** Chemical determination of tryptophan in proteins. *Anal. Chem.* 21:1249-66, 1949.

359   **Stahl E & Kaltenbach U.** Dunnschicht-Chromatographie. VI. Mitteilung. Spurenanalyse von Zuckergemischen auf Kieselgur G-Schichten. (Thin-layer chromatography. VI. Trace analysis of sugar mixtures on Kieselgur G layers.) *J. Chromatogr.* 5:351-5, 1961.

678   (24)   **Stoffel W, Chu F & Ahrens E H.** Analysis of long-chain fatty acids by gas-liquid chromatography. *Anal. Chem.* 31:307-8, 1959.

601 (136) **Toennies G & Kolb J J.** Techniques and reagents for paper chromatography. *Anal. Chem.* 23:823-6, 1951.

650   **Van Soest P J.** Use of detergents in the analysis of fibrous feeds. II. A rapid method for the determination of fiber and lignin. *J. Assn. Offic. Agr. Chem.* 46:829-35, 1963.

476   **Van Soest P J & Wine R H.** Use of detergents in the analysis of fibrous feeds. IV. Determination of plant cell-wall constituents. *J. Assn. Offic. Anal. Chem.* 50:50-5, 1967.

303   **Walker J L.** Ion specific liquid ion exchanger microelectrodes. *Anal. Chem.* 43:89A-91A, 1971.

349   **Werner W, Rey H G & Wielinger H.** Properties of a new chromogen for the determination of glucose in blood according to the GOD/POD (glucose oxidase-peroxidase) method. *Fresenius Z. Anal. Chem.* 252:224-8, 1970.

1193   **Whitaker J R.** Determination of molecular weights of proteins by gel filtration on Sephadex. *Anal. Chem.* 35:1950-3, 1963.

302   **Willis J B.** Determination of calcium and magnesium in urine by atomic absorption spectroscopy. *Anal. Chem.* 33:556-9, 1961.

1044 (100) **Yemm E W & Cocking E C.** The determination of amino-acids with ninhydrin. *Analyst* 80:209-13, 1955.

New York, was published in *Analytical Chemistry* in 1958. It describes an instrument used to automatically record results from chromatographic analyses of amino acids. This paper has been explicitly cited about 9,000 times. The second and third most-cited papers were also published in *Analytical Chemistry*, both in 1956. The paper by

M. Dubois and colleagues, University of Minnesota, St. Paul, "Colorimetric method for determination of sugars and related substances," was cited in over 6,100 publications from 1956 through 1982.

The paper by P.S. Chen, T.Y. Toribara, and H. Warner, University of Rochester School of Medicine and Den-

Table 6: The 26 most-cited articles from *Journal of the Association of Official Analytical Chemists* cited 80 or more times, 1961-1982 *SCI®*, in alphabetical order by first author. We have added (in parentheses) the additional citations to the papers published in 1960 and earlier.

Citations 1961-1982		Bibliographic Data
183		**Armour J A & Burke J A.** Method for separating polychlorinated biphenyls from DDT and its analogs. *J. Assn. Offic. Anal. Chem.* 53:761-8, 1970.
93		**Bowman M C & Beroza M.** Extraction *p*-values of pesticides and related compounds in six binary solvent systems. *J. Assn. Offic. Agr. Chem.* 48:943-52, 1965.
81		**Burke J A & Holswade W.** A gas chromatographic column for pesticide residue analysis: retention times and response data. *J. Assn. Offic. Anal. Chem.* 49:374-85, 1966.
153		**Eppley R M.** Screening method for zearalenone, aflatoxin, and ochratoxin. *J. Assn. Offic. Anal. Chem.* 51:74-8, 1968.
93		**Fazio T, White R H, Dusold L R & Howard J W.** Food additives. Nitrosopyrrolidine in cooked bacon. *J. Assn. Offic. Anal. Chem.* 56:919-21, 1973.
97		**Firestone D, Ress J, Brown N L, Barron R P & Damico J N.** Determination of polychlorodibenzo-*p*-dioxins and related compounds in commercial chlorophenols. *J. Assn. Offic. Anal. Chem.* 55:85-92, 1972.
99		**Giuffrida L.** A flame ionization detector highly selective and sensitive to phosphorus—a sodium thermionic detector. *J. Assn. Offic. Agr. Chem.* 47:293-300, 1964.
131		**Hoffman I, Westerby R J & Hidiroglou M.** Metals and other elements. Precise fluorometric microdetermination of selenium in agricultural materials. *J. Assn. Offic. Anal. Chem.* 51:1039-42, 1968.
87		**Howard J W, Fazio T & Watts J O.** Food additives. Extraction and gas chromatographic determination of N-nitrosodimethylamine in smoked fish: application to smoked nitrite-treated chub. *J. Assn. Offic. Anal. Chem.* 53:269-74, 1970.
89		**Kamm L, McKeown G G & Smith D M.** Food additives. New colorimetric method for the determination of the nitrate and nitrite content of baby foods. *J. Assn. Offic. Agr. Chem.* 48:892-7, 1965.
136		**Kovacs M F.** Thin-layer chromatography for chlorinated pesticide residue analysis. *J. Assn. Offic. Agr. Chem.* 46:884-93, 1963.
88		**Magos L & Clarkson T W.** Atomic absorption determination of total, inorganic, and organic mercury in blood. *J. Assn. Offic. Anal. Chem.* 55:966-71, 1972.
85		**Mills P A.** Collaborative study of certain chlorinated organic pesticides in dairy products. *J. Assn. Offic. Agr. Chem.* 44:171-7, 1961.
167	(7)	**Mills P A.** Detection and semiquantitative estimation of chlorinated organic pesticide residues in foods by paper chromatography. *J. Assn. Offic. Agr. Chem.* 42:734-40, 1959.
231		**Mills P A, Onley J H & Gaither R A.** Rapid method for chlorinated pesticide residues in nonfatty foods. *J. Assn. Offic. Agr. Chem.* 46:186-91, 1963.
81	(7)	**Mitchell L C.** Separation and identification of chlorinated organic pesticides by paper chromatography. XI. A study of 114 pesticide chemicals: technical grades produced in 1957 and reference standards. *J. Assn. Offic. Agr. Chem.* 41:781-816, 1958.
159		**Olson O E.** Plants. Fluorometric analysis of selenium in plants. *J. Assn. Offic. Anal. Chem.* 52:627-34, 1969.
160		**Pons W A, Cucullu A F, Lee L S, Robertson J A, Franz A O & Goldblatt L A.** Aflatoxins. Determination of aflatoxins in agricultural products: use of aqueous acetone for extraction. *J. Assn. Offic. Anal. Chem.* 49:554-62, 1966.
118		**Stoloff L, Nesheim S, Yin L, Rodricks J V, Stack M & Campbell A D.** A multimycotoxin detection method for aflatoxins, ochratoxins, zearalenone, sterigmatocystin, and patulin. *J. Assn. Offic. Anal. Chem.* 54:91-7, 1971.
116		**Van Soest P J.** Feeds. Use of detergents in the analysis of fibrous feeds. I. Preparation of fiber residues of low nitrogen content. *J. Assn. Offic. Agr. Chem.* 46:825-9, 1963.
650		**Van Soest P J.** Use of detergents in the analysis of fibrous feeds. II. A rapid method for the determination of fiber and lignin. *J. Assn. Offic. Agr. Chem.* 46:829-35, 1963.
83		**Van Soest P J.** Use of detergents in the analysis of fibrous feeds. III. Study of effects of heating and drying on yield of fiber and lignin in forages. *J. Assn. Offic. Agr. Chem.* 48:785-90, 1965.
476		**Van Soest P J & Wine R H.** Use of detergents in the analysis of fibrous feeds. IV. Determination of plant cell-wall constituents. *J. Assn. Offic. Anal. Chem.* 50:50-5, 1967.
127		**Van Soest P J & Wine R H.** Determination of lignin and cellulose in acid-detergent fiber with permanganate. *J. Assn. Offic. Anal. Chem.* 51:780-5, 1968.
133		**Verrett M J, Marliac J-P & McLaughlin J.** Use of the chicken embryo in the assay of aflatoxin toxicity. *J. Assn. Offic. Agr. Chem.* 47:1003-6, 1964.
113		**Walker K C & Beroza M.** Thin-layer chromatography for insecticide analysis. *J. Assn. Offic. Agr. Chem.* 46:250-61, 1963.

tistry, New York, entitled "Microdetermination of phosphorus," was cited 3,850 times from 1956 through 1982. Chen gave his personal views on the development of this paper, and suggested why it is highly cited, in a *Citation Classic*™ commentary published in *Current Contents*® (*CC*®).[10] Authors of twelve other papers in Table 5 also contributed *Citation Classic* commentaries.[11-22]

Editors should keep in mind that complete lists of the most-cited articles from any journal can be obtained through the ISI Search Service. In honor of AOAC's centennial celebration, we've prepared a list of highly cited articles originally published in the *Journal of the Association of Official Analytical Chemists*. Table 6 lists 26 articles cited 80 or more times. This journal also published 14 articles cited between 70 and 79 times, eight cited from 60 to 69 times, and 14 cited 50 to 59 times.

The most-cited article in Table 6 is by P.J. Van Soest, US Department of Agriculture, Beltsville, Maryland. It is the second part of a four-part paper entitled "Use of detergents in the analysis of fibrous feeds." Parts one and two were published in 1963, part three in 1965, and part four in 1967. Taken together, this four-part article was cited more than 1,300 times. Van Soest commented on this article in a *Citation Classic* in 1979.[20]

Comparing Tables 2 and 4, we see that 19 core analytical chemistry journals appear in both tables. Seven journals are among the top ten on both lists. They are: *Analyst, Analytica Chimica Acta, Analytical Chemistry, Fresenius Zeitschrift für Analytische Chemie, Journal of Chromatography, Journal of Electroanalytical Chemistry and Interfacial Electrochemistry*, and *Talanta*. These seven journals rank highest in terms of their references *to* the core group, and the number of citations received *from* the core. With one exception, these same journals ranked among the top ten core journals in impact *and* immediacy.

Fresenius Zeitschrift für Analytische Chemie ranked twelfth on impact at 1.2.

Interested readers should refer to the excellent studies of the analytical chemistry literature by Tibor Braun and Erno Bujdosö, Hungarian Academy of Sciences.[23-25] Braun is also managing editor of *Scientometrics* as well as editor of *Journal of Radioanalytical Chemistry*. One study occupied an entire issue of *CRC Critical Reviews in Analytical Chemistry*.[23] It is a comprehensive report on the volume and growth of the literature, its distribution with respect to countries and languages of publication, the exchange of information between analytical chemistry and other fields of science, etc. The authors also analyzed the 100 articles most cited from 1961 through 1972 that ISI identified in 1974.[26,27] Although that list was independent of discipline, they found that 47 percent of the papers were on the subject of analytical chemistry. They concluded that there was no "better proof for the...viability and importance of this subject field."[23] However, it is important to note that, while this may be true for a tiny percentage of the *super*-cited papers, the percentage of such "method" papers would be much smaller in a longer list of highly cited articles.

In conclusion, we extend congratulations to the AOAC on its 100th anniversary. Its 700 volunteer members around the world do much to verify industrial compliance with international regulations and standards. They also help ensure the reliability of analytical data reported in the research literature. We would also like to thank the many journal editors who refereed this study of analytical chemistry. In the near future, we'll report on journals in physical chemistry.

*   *   *   *   *

My thanks to Abigail W. Grissom and Alfred Welljams-Dorof for their help in the preparation of this essay.

REFERENCES

1. **Garfield E.** Journal citation studies. 41. Entomology journals—what they cite and what cites them. *Current Contents* (11):3-11, 12 March 1984.
2. --------------. Journal citation studies. 40. Anthropology journals—what they cite and what cites them. *Current Contents* (37):5-12, 12 September 1983.
3. --------------. Journal citation studies. 39. Earth sciences journals: what they cite and what cites them. *Essays of an information scientist*. Philadelphia: ISI Press, 1983. Vol. 5. p. 791-800.
4. --------------. Chemical information for the man who has everything. *Essays of an information scientist*. Philadelphia: ISI Press, 1980. Vol. 3. p. 465-73.
5. --------------. What is the "core" literature of biochemistry as compared to the "core" of chemistry? *Essays of an information scientist*. Philadelphia: ISI Press, 1977. Vol. 1. p. 262-5.
6. --------------. What is the "core" literature of chemical physics? *Essays of an information scientist*. Philadelphia: ISI Press, 1977. Vol. 1. p. 274-7.
7. **Anderson D M W.** Chemical analysis. *Encyclopaedia Britannica. Macropaedia.* Chicago: H.H. Benton, 1974. Vol. 4. p. 76-84.
8. **Helrich K.** *The great collaboration: the first 100 years of the Association of Official Analytical Chemists.* Arlington, VA: AOAC. (In press.)
9. **Garfield E.** Citation analysis as a tool in journal evaluation. *Science* 178:471-9, 1972.
10. **Chen P S.** Citation Classic. Commentary on *Anal. Chem.* 28:1756-8, 1956. *Current Contents* (9):7, 28 February 1977.
11. **Bencze W L.** Citation Classic. Commentary on *Anal. Chem.* 29:1193-6, 1957. *Current Contents/Life Sciences* 24(8):20, 23 February 1981.
12. **Hatch W R.** Citation Classic. Commentary on *Anal. Chem.* 40:2085-7, 1968. *Current Contents/Physical, Chemical & Earth Sciences* 22(48):18, 29 November 1982.
13. **Huisman T H J.** Citation Classic. Commentary on *J. Chromatogr.* 19:160-9, 1965. *Current Contents/Life Sciences* 23(39):22, 29 September 1980.
14. **Metcalfe L D.** Citation Classic. Commentary on *Anal. Chem.* 33:363-4, 1961. *Current Contents/Life Sciences* 24(2):16, 12 January 1981.
15. **Miller G L.** Citation Classic. Commentary on *Anal. Chem.* 31:964, 1959. *Current Contents/Life Sciences* 23(9):14, 3 March 1980.
16. **Parker C A.** Citation Classic. Commentary on *Analyst* 85:587-600, 1960. *Current Contents/Engineering, Technology & Applied Sciences* 12(12):20, 23 March 1981.
17. **Randerath K.** Citation Classic. Commentary on *J. Chromatogr.* 16:111-25, 1964. *Current Contents/Life Sciences* 24(5):16, 2 February 1981.
18. **Shain I & Nicholson R S.** Citation Classic. Commentary on *Anal. Chem.* 36:706-23, 1964. *Current Contents/Physical, Chemical & Earth Sciences* 21(6):18, 9 February 1981.
19. **Spies J R.** Citation Classic. Commentary on *Anal. Chem.* 21:1249-66, 1949. *Current Contents* (25):13, 20 June 1977.
20. **Van Soest P J.** Citation Classic. Commentary on *J. Assn. Offic. Agr. Chem.* 46:829-35, 1963. *Current Contents/Agriculture, Biology & Environmental Sciences* 10(16):12, 16 April 1979.
21. **Whitaker J R.** Citation Classic. Commentary on *Anal. Chem.* 35:1950-3, 1963. *Current Contents/Life Sciences* 24(12):21, 23 March 1981.
22. **Gordon H T.** Citation Classic. Commentary on *Anal. Chem.* 28:849-55, 1956. *Current Contents/Life Sciences* 27(13):18, 26 March 1984.
23. **Braun T & Bujdosó E.** The growth of modern analytical chemistry as reflected in the statistical evaluation of its subject literature. (Whole issue) *CRC Crit. Rev. Anal. Chem.* 13(3), 1982. 89 p.
24. --------------------------. Some tendencies of the radioanalytical literature. Statistical games for trend evaluation. Part I. Distribution of the information sources. *Radiochem. Radioanal. Lett.* 23:195-203, 1975.
25. --------------------------. Gatekeeping patterns in the publication of analytical chemistry research. *Talanta* 30:161-7, 1983.
26. **Garfield E.** Selecting the all-time Citation Classics. Here are the fifty most-cited papers for 1961-1972. *Essays of an information scientist*. Philadelphia: ISI Press, 1977. Vol. 2. p. 6-9.
27. --------------. The second fifty papers most cited from 1961-1972. *Essays of an information scientist*. Philadelphia: ISI Press, 1977. Vol. 2. p. 21-5.

Current Comments®

Social Gerontology. Part 1.
Aging and Intelligence

Number 14   April 2, 1984

A previous essay discussed the biology of prolongevity, including genetic, cellular, immunological, neuroendocrine, and free radical theories on aging.[1] That essay also addressed the question of why aging evolved and what purpose it serves. At that time, I noted that the social and economic consequences of a major breakthrough in aging research would be tremendous.

Many of the theories discussed in the prolongevity essay are fairly speculative. Also speculative are estimates of the effects a much longer life span—say, 110 years—might have on society. What is known, however, is that the number of US citizens over 65 grew fourfold during the first half of this century.[2] And this growth is already placing considerable demands on our social and political institutions.

This two-part essay on social gerontology examines the sociological and psychological aspects of aging. There is a considerable literature on this topic, so we can only highlight two aspects of this field in these essays. Perhaps we will be able to extend our coverage of social gerontology in the future. This week the effects of aging on intelligence, memory, and learning will be reviewed. In a future essay, some of the effects of having a larger proportion of aged people in the population will be discussed. At that time, we will also discuss some of the steps individual nations are taking to cope with growing elderly populations.

During various periods in history, and among different societies, attitudes toward the elderly and the process of aging have differed considerably. The fifth-century BC Greek historian Herodotus reported that the Issedonians gilded the heads of their elderly and offered sacrifices to them.[3] The people of Bactria, in contrast, fed their elderly to flesh-eating dogs.[4] And the ancient Sardinians hurled their elders from a high cliff and shouted with laughter as they fell on the rocks.[5]

Today, we outwardly treat our elderly with more respect than did the Bactrians or Sardinians. But we've also moved precariously far from the reverence of the Issedonians. This is confirmed by attitude studies carried out in the US in the past three decades.[6-9] These studies reveal that many people view the elderly as predominantly sick, tired individuals who are often grouchy, withdrawn, and self-pitying. According to this stereotype, older people are mentally slow, have trouble learning and remembering, and have little or no interest in sex.[6] Robert N. Butler, the founding director of the National Institute on Aging (NIA) who is now at Mount Sinai Hospital, New York, refers to this stereotyping, and the discrimination that accompanies it, as "ageism." He likens ageism to racism and sexism, noting that it allows young people to "cease to identify with their elders as human beings."[10] (p. ix)

Why has ageism come about? There are a number of reasons, not the least of them being our own fears about growing old. This fear, no doubt, has prompted much of the prolongevity research mentioned earlier.[1] But social gerontologists—sociologists, psychologists, economists, and others who study aging—offer a number of other explanations as well. Robert F. Almeder, Georgia State University, Atlanta, attributes ageism to materialism. Almeder notes that in a materialistic society, where people are judged according to their productivity and wealth, it is not surprising to find that "the elderly lose their right to respect" as they abandon their economically productive role.[11]

Donald O. Cowgill, University of Missouri, Columbia, claims that "modernization" has lowered the status of aged individuals. Cowgill reports that the elderly tend to be revered in the more primitive societies where they're relatively rare, and where their experience can benefit younger people. As a society modernizes, technological advances increase the proportion of aged individuals while making their talents obsolete.[12]

One of the most harmful outcomes of this obsolescence may be that it reinforces the stereotype that the elderly are less intelligent than the young. Such stereotypes, particularly regarding elderly people's supposed inflexibility and inability to learn new things, can cause job-related discrimination.[13,14]

Until recently, many researchers agreed that certain intellectual skills decline with age. Now, according to Matilda White Riley, NIA, they are finding that intellectual decline is not inevitable. Riley notes that much of the age-related decline observed in earlier studies may have actually been the result of poor health or the use of medications that impair intellectual functioning. A lack of intellectual and social stimulation, and an absence of opportunities and incentives for cognitive functioning, are also coming to be recognized as causes for the decline observed among some elderly people.[15] Granted, declines may be found in some individuals, but these declines appear to be so minor that they have almost no effect on the daily lives of physically and mentally healthy older adults. Moreover, those declines that do occur are not irreversible.[16]

Since intelligence involves such diverse skills as problem-solving, reasoning, and numerical facility, researchers have developed classification systems to describe various types of intelligence.[17] John L. Horn, University of Denver, Colorado, and Raymond B. Cattell, working at University of Hawaii, Honolulu, and University of Illinois, Urbana, described two general forms of intelligence that are now widely used in the gerontological literature.[18-20] *Crystallized* intelligence is somewhat like knowledge. It results from education, experience, and acculturation and is measured with tests of verbal comprehension, vocabulary, and numerical skill. *Fluid* intelligence represents the ability to solve new problems, reason abstractly, and adjust one's thinking to unfamiliar situations. Fluid intelligence appears to be influenced by one's physiological and neurological health. It is measured through performance tests that involve solving new types of problems and using perceptual motor skills.

In numerous studies done in the past three decades, fluid intelligence was found to peak and decline earlier than crystallized intelligence. Consequently, elderly individuals tended to score higher on tests of crystallized intelligence. However, for healthy people the decline in fluid intelligence does not have any practical effect until their mid-70s or early 80s. At this point, gains in crystallized intelligence also become smaller.[21]

Despite the large amount of research that has been done on aging and intelligence, researchers continue to debate whether an age-related decline occurs in healthy individuals, as well as the extent of this decline. During the mid-1970s, in fact, a well-known debate over age and intelligence took place, most notably in the pages of *American Psychologist.* Briefly, K. Warner Schaie, working at the University of Southern California, Los Angeles, and Paul B. Baltes, working at Pennsylvania State University, University Park, took the position that a decline in intelligence was not inevitable with age.[22,23] In contrast, Horn and Gary Donaldson, University of Denver, argued that a substantial decline in fluid intelligence does occur.[24,25] Much of this controversy has, in the past, centered on the different results reported with different study designs.

The earliest studies of aging were cross-sectional—different age groups were compared at a single point in time. In these studies, researchers found small but significant differences with age, particularly in fluid intelligence, beginning in late adolescence. Horn reports that these range from three to seven intelligence quotient (IQ) points per decade from ages 30 to 70.[26] But later longitudinal studies, which measured changes among the same group of people over time, suggested that these changes began later in life.[27] They indicated that at least some of the decrement noted in cross-sectional studies was caused by the lower educational levels of the older groups, or cohorts, in these studies. Furthermore, the tests used in these studies were designed for college students and others seeking entry-level jobs.[16] So they may not have measured cognitive processes that are more critical later in life, such as decision-making and other tasks that make use of accumulated experience.[16]

While cross-sectional studies seemed to magnify age changes, longitudinal studies tended to minimize them. Jack Botwinick, Washington University, St. Louis, maintains that people who perform poorly on standardized tests tend to be less available for repeat testing than people who perform well.[28] Consequently, median scores in longitudinal studies are often spuriously high because they reflect the scores of the more able older people who agree to be retested. In reanalyzing data from one of the most comprehensive longitudinal studies of aging and intelligence,[29] Botwinick found median test scores actually increased with age due to selective dropout.[28] As less intelligent members of the group dropped out of the test sample, the brighter members brought the average score up.

In the 1950s, Schaie, Baltes, and colleagues began using a methodology that attempted to resolve the discrepancies between cross-sectional and longitudinal studies.[30-33] They used a "sequential analysis" design that incorporated both types of studies. The group initially tested in 1956 included individuals aged 22 to 67. The same group was retested every seven years until 1977. The cross-sectional analysis of test data showed a downward trend in test scores. But the longitudinal analysis showed a decrease on only one of the five dimensions of intelligence measured—the ability to shift from familiar to unfamiliar patterns in visual-motor tasks. Schaie and Christopher Hertzog, Pennsylvania State University, concluded that generational differences in intellectual performance resulted in "an overestimation of the magnitude and age of onset of intellectual decline."[32]

Schaie also found that scores on tests of crystallized intelligence improved for each successive generation. He suggested that each group performed better because its members were better educated. In an earlier study of the relationship between education and intelligence, James E. Birren, now at the University of Southern California, and D.F. Morrison, working at the National Institute of Mental Health, Bethesda, Maryland, found that education had an even greater effect on test scores than did occupation, which would seem more relevant to the maintenance of intellectual function among older people.[34]

Finally, Schaie also found wide variability in the performance of individuals 80 and older. He traced this variability to such factors as the different economic status, intellectual stimulation, and health of test subjects.[16]

While most researchers acknowledge at least some decline in fluid intelligence, the gerontological community has been split on the significance of this decline. On one side of the argument are investigators who believe that factors unrelated to intelligence cause older people to perform poorly on tests of fluid intelligence. Chief among these factors is the slower response of older people. This may cause them to take longer to evaluate and respond to test questions. This slowdown may make it more difficult for elderly persons to do well on fluid intelligence tests because these tests often require rapid responses. Two other important factors affect performance on these tests. The elderly are reluctant to take risks—they tend to sacrifice speed for accuracy. And the older person experiences high anxiety in unfamiliar testing situations.[35]

On the other side of this debate are researchers who argue that response speed is an integral component of intelligence. They maintain that the slower response is a normal part of aging. Therefore, declining scores on fluid intelligence tests reflect real intellectual decline.[28] Studies attempting to isolate response speed from intellectual competence have provided mixed results.[36-38]

Gerontologists have investigated the reasons for the slowdown in response. Although the precise physical causes still remain a mystery, by the mid-1960s, researchers such as Alfred D. Weiss,[39] Harvard Medical School, Cambridge, Massachusetts, and Botwinick and Larry W. Thompson,[40] working at Duke University Medical Center, Durham, North Carolina, had found that the slowdown affects the transmission and integration of information in the central nervous system (CNS). Robert C. Atchley, Miami University, Oxford, Ohio, explains that older people tend to make more errors on speed-based tests because "too little information can be processed between the time the sensory input is received and the time action must be taken."[41] (p. 48)

Also contributing to delayed response, but to a lesser extent than the slowdown in the CNS, is the fact that older people generally require more sensory stimulation before they are aroused. For example, a noise must be louder or last longer before an elderly person perceives it. A.T. Welford, University of Hawaii, Honolulu, attributes the higher sensory threshold to "anatomical deterioration of the sense organs" and, more importantly, to increased random activity in the CNS, also called "neural noise."[42] Sensory information must compete with this background neural noise to gain an individual's attention.

Some investigators believe that a "terminal drop," a decline in intelligence a few months or years before death, may explain lower test scores among the elderly. In a 1972 study examining the relationship between test performance and survival, Klaus F. and Ruth M. Riegel, working at the University of Michigan, Ann Arbor, found an individual's test score tended to drop markedly within five years before death.[43] Similarly, in an earlier study on this theme, R.W. Kleemeier, working at Moosehaven Research Laboratory, Orange Park, Florida, found that elderly subjects who died soonest after a test also tended to be those with the lowest scores.[44] A number of investigators suspect that some neurophysiological processes, probably related to dying, may cause a drop in intelligence. In the 1960s and 1970s, researchers suggested that this terminal drop, rather than aging *per se*, might be responsible for lower intelligence test scores among the people who are oldest, and therefore closest to death.[28] Atchley notes that more recent research on this topic, while not entirely discrediting the terminal drop theory, has indicated that the drop may occur primarily in people with multiple chronic conditions, such as atherosclerosis and diabetes.[45]

Much of the most current research on aging and intelligence focuses on the effects of educational intervention. Studies by Baltes,[46] now at the Max Planck Institute for Human Development and Education, Berlin, by Schaie,[33] and by Sherry L. Willis,[47] Pennsylvania State University, indicate that training elderly people, or giving them an opportunity to use their minds, can improve their performance on intelligence tests appreciably. In a study in which elderly people received training in spatial orientation and inductive reasoning—skills in which most elderly people are likely to show declines—more than three-fourths of the subjects showed improvement which lasted at least six months.[46] Riley notes that many subjects raised their performance to the level they performed at some 20 years earlier.[16] Schaie was asked to comment on this intervention research. He observed, "The use-it-or-lose-it principle applies not only to the maintenance of muscular flexibility, but to the maintenance of a high level of intellectual performance as well."[21]

Riley[15] asserts that these educational intervention studies[33,46,47] are having an enormous impact on the gerontology community. So are other recent studies in which elderly people are provided with incentives to perform well on tests.[48] These studies are calling into question assumptions about intellectual decline by suggesting that environmental factors may far outweigh any age-related effects on intelligence. Also being reexamined in recent years is the validity of the tests administered to elderly people. As mentioned earlier, many of these tests are inappropriate for the elderly,

because they may not be measuring the skills that become better developed and more useful with advanced age. Riley says that the NIA is beginning to examine more relevant components of intelligence "such as experience-based decision-making, interpersonal competence, or 'wisdom.' "[16] If methods for measuring these components can be found, they may be used in designing intelligence tests that will be "valid across the entire life course."[16] According to Riley, this recent work on motivation, test validity, and educational intervention is also calling into question earlier findings on the effects of reaction time on cognitive performance. She has found, "Even reaction time can be improved by giving people hints and cues on speeding up their performance."[15]

Closely related to the intellectual performance of elderly people—and to a large extent, underlying it—are age-related changes in learning and memory. For example, poor test performance could result from failure to learn the material adequately in the first place, to retain it in memory, or to retrieve it from memory within the time limit provided.[17] It is difficult to isolate memory loss from learning decrements, since you must learn material before you can remember it, and remember it to show you've learned it. But gerontologists generally agree that learning ability does decline with age, though not noticeably until past middle age. As with other intellectual skills, learning seems to be affected by a general slowdown in response. When given enough time to memorize or learn material, learning in the elderly improves considerably. Recent work by Michael Perone, University of North Carolina, Wilmington, and Alan Baron, University of Wisconsin, Milwaukee, has shown that training and practice can also improve learning ability, even under time constraints.[48]

Researchers have attributed age-related declines in learning to a number of factors. These range from a lack of recent experience in learning situations to a lack of motivation to learn.[17] William J. Hoyer and Dana J. Plude, Syracuse University, New York, found that learning ability in the aged may be restricted by a decreased ability to distinguish relevant material from irrelevant material.[49] Carl Eisdorfer, Montefiore Hospital, Bronx, New York, found learning was also restricted by elderly people's anxiety in learning situations.[50,51] In a study in which he monitored the fatty acid levels of younger and older subjects to determine autonomic (involuntary) nervous system arousal during tests, Eisdorfer found that the nervous system in older persons became aroused as the test progressed.[50] This arousal—perhaps resulting from frustration with their performance—may have interfered with their performance. In another study in which he administered propranolol, a drug which blocks autonomic nervous system activity, Eisdorfer found that elderly subjects had much higher test scores than a control group not given the drug.[51]

A.E. David Schonfield, University of Calgary, Alberta, Canada, mentions several other factors that affect ability to learn in the elderly. One is the difficulty they experience switching their concentration from one aspect of a situation to another. Another is the ease with which they are distracted by irrelevant details. He also notes that the elderly tend to have a harder time translating thoughts or words into action. For example, it might take an older person longer to convert the mental note "an octagonal sign means stop" into the automatic act of stopping at an octagonal sign.[52]

Since learning is the first or "acquisitional" step, many of the factors that impair learning in the aged also impede their ability to memorize new material. The effect of aging on memory is one of the most controversial areas of aging research, and is confounded by the different categories of memory described by individual investigators. In a 1977 review of aging and memory, Fergus I.M. Craik, University of Toronto, Canada, says that "primary" memory, or memory for material still at the focus of attention, declines negligibly with age unless the material memorized has to be reorganized, or attention has to be divided between several mental operations at one time.[53]

More substantial age differences occur with "secondary" memory—material already learned, but in the not too distant past. Craik maintains that the decrease in secondary memory stems from older people's failure to effectively and permanently transfer information from short- to long-term memory. He also reports that age differences in recall—retrieving material from memory—are greater than those for recognition.[53] According to Craik, researchers disagree over whether memory for events from the distant past declines with age.

Atchley reports that a greater age-related loss occurs with short-term or recent memory than with remote or old memory. He adds that older people are better at remembering things heard than seen, and are best at remembering things both heard and seen.[41]

Finally, John C. Cavanaugh, Bowling Green State University, Ohio, and Jayne G. Grady and Miriam Perlmutter, University of Minnesota, Minneapolis, concede that older people experience more memory failures in their daily lives. However, they note that older people may also report proportionately more memory loss because they are more sensitive to memory problems.[54]

Some researchers attribute age-related memory loss to poor initial learning. Others point to the failure to use information stored in memory. Another theory proposes that newly learned material interferes with the recall of old information. And material already stored interferes with memorizing new information.[17] Barry D. McPherson, University of Waterloo, Canada, suggests that the stereotype of memory loss with old age may contribute to this loss by becoming a self-fulfilling prophecy.[17]

Since relatively little is known about the neurophysiological effects of aging on learning, memory, and intellectual competence, biological theories to explain declines in these areas are somewhat tentative. Until recently, the loss of brain tissue, particularly nerve cells, was widely assumed to be a partial explanation for age-related declines in healthy people.[21] Gerontologists attributed this tissue loss to poorer cardiovascular circulation in the elderly, which might starve the brain of oxygen.

The question of aging and intelligence has in recent years received considerable attention from sociologists and historians of science. This is because economic retrenchment at universities has resulted in fewer opportunities for young scientists. It is commonly assumed that scientists are most productive and creative when young. According to Mark Oromaner, Hudson County Community College, North Bergen, New Jersey, if true, a reduced percentage of young scholars in academia would affect the quality of work produced in universities.[55]

One of the earliest and most-quoted works on this subject is a 1953 study in which H.C. Lehman, Ohio University, Athens, examined histories of science to determine the age of various scientists when their most outstanding discoveries were made. He concluded that, although productivity persists into old age, scientists do their highest quality work before the age of 40.[56]

Lehman's study has been challenged by a number of researchers. Harriet Zuckerman and Robert K. Merton, Columbia University, New York, suggest that scientists make their most important contributions at a young age in fields that are highly codified.[57] In such fields, it takes less time for students to master the discipline's theoretical framework, since this framework takes the form of fairly condensed, interrelated laws, rather than voluminous factual material. And Stephen Cole, State University of New York, Stony Brook, notes that Lehman failed to consider that science has been growing exponentially for the past few centuries. The reason for the disproportionate number of contributions from young people is that this growth has meant science has been disproportionately populated by young scientists.[58] Another variation on this theme is Derek J. de Solla Price's oft quoted statement, "80 to 90 percent of all the scientists that have ever lived are alive now."[59] (p. 1)

In his own study of the effects of aging on scientific creativity and productivity, Cole examined the citations and publications of chemists, geologists, mathematicians, physicists, psychologists, and sociologists. He found that productivity peaked in all fields except mathematics—which showed no age effect—from ages 40 to 45, and then declined gradually. Scholars over age 50 were only slightly less productive than those under age 35. Scientists did their highest quality, or most-cited, work from ages 35 to 44, with scholars over 45 slightly less likely to publish highly cited work than those under 35. Cole also did a longitudinal study of mathematicians in which he found that their productivity and creativity remained fairly stable throughout their careers.[58]

Cole believes the reward system of science is partially responsible for scientists' increased productivity with age. He explains, "Since the members of an age cohort who continue to be prolific publishers after the age of 50 are the scientists who have in the past produced significant work and been rewarded, their current research will be of relatively high quality."[58] Of course, as mentioned in an

Table 1: 1978-1980 *SSCI®* derived research fronts on social gerontology. A=research front name. B=number of core papers in the research front. C=number of citing papers in the research front.

A	B	C
Research in developmental psychology and the aged	3	42
Issues in life-span developmental psychology	3	33
Educational gerontology and cognitive performance	5	67
Effect of age on reaction time	2	24
Age differences in fluid and crystallized intelligence	5	102
Study of attitudes toward the aged	8	65
Methodologies in life-span developmental research	2	72

earlier essay on using citation analysis to evaluate faculty,[60] the positive relationship Cole found between age and publication output may not hold if a scholar is diverted to administration.

The effects of aging on cognition represent just a fraction of the social gerontology research now under way. Even so, numerous research fronts on this topic were identified in the *Social Sciences Citation Index®* (*SSCI®*) data base between 1978 and 1980. Table 1 provides a list of these research fronts, which are specialty areas identified when a group of current papers cites one or more core papers for that topic. Each of the core papers was cited at least 11 times between 1978 and 1980, and at least 35 percent of its citations were co-citations with other papers in the cluster. Although the papers in these fronts represent only a few of the hundreds of key documents on aging and intelligence, many proved invaluable when writing this essay. The research front entitled "Effect of age on reaction time," for example, provided two core papers on age-related changes in the nervous system that affect response speed.[39,40] Core publications[19,20,61-63] in the research front, "Age differences in fluid and crystallized intelligence," report studies in which the theory of fluid and crystallized intelligence, mentioned earlier in this essay, is tested and refined.

The role practice and training play in improving cognitive performance in the elderly is discussed in the papers in the research front entitled "Educational gerontology and cognitive performance."[28,64-67] The question of whether declines in intelligence test scores are the result of aging itself, or differences between generations, is discussed in the core papers in the research front, "Research in developmental psychology and the aged."[23-25] The two core documents in the research front, "Methodologies in life-span developmental research," are the seminal studies[30,31] in which sequential analysis, the technique combining cross-sectional and longitudinal study designs, was used. Baltes commented on his paper[31] in a *Citation Classic ™* in *Current Contents®*.[68]

The research front, "Issues in lifespan developmental psychology," focuses on a relatively new research perspective in which aging is viewed as another step in development, and the events of childhood and adulthood are considered part of the aging process.[69-71] The research front entitled "Study of attitudes toward the aged"[6-9] focuses on the way different age, race, professional, and ethnic groups view the elderly.

The fact that certain aspects of cognition decline with age should not be taken to mean that intellectual decline is inevitable for all people. The many who do not suffer from senile dementia[72] and other age-related diseases maintain their intellectual functions well into old age. Many of the declines reported here can be avoided or minimized by maintaining good health, by exercising intellectual faculties, by staying socially active, and by allowing the aged more time to learn.[21] Even those changes that do occur with age don't seem to interfere with meeting the personal and professional demands of life. Rather, the elderly develop strategies for adapting to slower response speeds and other age-related declines. In a 1969 survey of successful professional people, Birren found that these older people coped by becoming more flexible in their goals, recognizing when advice should be taken, conserving their time and resources, and making an effort to "distinguish between critical and extraneous tasks and demands."[73] Patrick Rabbitt, University of Oxford, England, concludes from Birren's study, "In considering the real-life performance of older people, it is naive to regard them as passive victims of a cognitive degeneration of which they are helplessly aware."[74] (p. 623)

For more information on social sciences research fronts, contact Yvonne McGee at the ISI® Search Service; telephone: (800) 523-1850, extension 1274. In clustering for 1983, we are identifying research fronts in social sciences by clustering a combined file for *SSCI* and *Science Citation Index*®. This combined approach is needed in fields such as social gerontology where the artificial and arbitrary separation of the social sciences from the life sciences is unwarranted.

In part two, the economic, social, and political effects of population, or demographic, aging will be reviewed. At that time, social gerontology journals and organizations will be discussed.

* * * *

My thanks to Joan Lipinsky Cochran and Terri Freedman for their help in the preparation of this essay.
©1984 ISI

REFERENCES

1. **Garfield E.** The dilemma of prolongevity research—must we age before we die, or if we don't, will we? *Current Contents* (15):5-18, 11 April 1983.
2. **Tibbitts C,** ed. *Handbook of social gerontology.* Chicago: University of Chicago Press, 1960. 770 p.
3. **Herodotus.** (Rawlinson G, transl.) *The history of Herodotus.* New York: Tudor Publishing, 1936. p. 212.
4. **Strabo.** (Hamilton H C & Falconer W, transls.) *The geography of Strabo.* London: Henry G. Bohn, 1856. Vol. II. p. 253.
5. **Fischer D H.** *Growing old in America.* New York: Oxford University Press, 1977. 242 p.
6. **McTavish D G.** Perceptions of old people: a review of research methodologies and findings. *Gerontologist* 11:90-101, 1971.
7. **Tuckman J & Lorge I.** Attitudes toward old people. *J. Soc. Psychol.* 37:249-60, 1953.
8. **Hickey T & Kalish R A.** Young people's perceptions of adults. *J. Gerontol.* 23:215-9, 1968.
9. **Kogan N.** Attitudes toward old people: the development of a scale and an examination of correlates. *J. Abnormal Soc. Psychol.* 62:44-54, 1961.
10. **Butler R N & Lewis M I.** *Aging & mental health.* St. Louis: Mosby, 1973. 306 p.
11. **Almeder R F.** Materialism and the future of aging in America. *Int. J. Aging Human Develop.* 16:161-5, 1983.
12. **Cowgill D O.** A theory of aging in cross-cultural perspective. (Cowgill D O & Holmes L D, eds.) *Aging and modernization.* New York: Appleton-Century-Crofts, 1972. p. 1-13.
13. **Rosen B & Jerdee T H.** The nature of job-related age stereotypes. *J. Appl. Psychol.* 61:180-3, 1976.
14. --------------------------. The influence of age stereotypes on managerial decisions. *J. Appl. Psychol.* 61:428-32, 1976.
15. **Riley M W.** Telephone communication. 1 March 1984.
16. ---------------. *Aging and society: notes on the development of new understandings.* Unpublished lecture delivered at the University of Michigan School of Social Work. 12 December 1983. Ann Arbor, MI. 18 p.
17. **McPherson B D.** The aging process: adaptation to psychological changes. *Aging as a social process.* Boston: Butterworth, 1983. p. 197-221.
18. **Horn J L & Cattell R B.** Age differences in fluid and crystallized intelligence. *Acta Psychol.* 26:107-29, 1967.
19. **Cattell R B.** Theory of fluid and crystallized intelligence: a critical experiment. *J. Educ. Psychol.* 54:1-22, 1963.
20. **Horn J L & Cattell R B.** Refinement and test of the theory of fluid and crystallized general intelligences. *J. Educ. Psychol.* 57:253-70, 1966.
21. **Goleman D.** The aging mind proves capable of lifelong growth. *NY Times* 21 February 1984. p. C1; C5.

22. **Baltes P B & Schaie K W.** The myth of the twilight years. *Psychol. Today* 7(10):35-40, 1974.
23. ----------------------------------. On the plasticity of intelligence in adulthood and old age. *Amer. Psychol.* 31:720-5, 1976.
24. **Horn J L & Donaldson G.** On the myth of intellectual decline in adulthood. *Amer. Psychol.* 31:701-19, 1976.
25. **Horn J L.** Faith is not enough. *Amer. Psychol.* 32:369-73, 1977.
26. **Horn J L, Donaldson G & Engstrom R.** Apprehension, memory and fluid intelligence decline in adulthood. *Res. Aging* 3:33-84, 1981.
27. **Schaie K W.** Translations in gerontology—from lab to life. *Amer. Psychol.* 29:802-7, 1974.
28. **Botwinick J.** Intellectual abilities. (Birren J E & Schaie K W, eds.) *Handbook of the psychology of aging.* New York: Van Nostrand Reinhold, 1977. p. 580-605.
29. **Schaie K W, Labouvie G V & Barrett T J.** Selective attrition effects in a fourteen-year study of adult intelligence. *J. Gerontol.* 28:328-34, 1973.
30. **Schaie K W.** A general model for the study of developmental problems. *Psychol. Bull.* 64:92-107, 1965.
31. **Baltes P B.** Longitudinal and cross-sectional sequences in the study of age and generation effects. *Hum. Develop.* 11:145-71, 1968.
32. **Schaie K W & Hertzog C.** Fourteen-year cohort-sequential analyses of adult intellectual development. *Develop. Psychol.* 19:531-43, 1983.
33. **Schaie K W, ed.** *Longitudinal studies of adult psychological development.* New York:Guilford Press, 1983. 332 p.
34. **Birren J E & Morrison D F.** Analysis of the WAIS subtests in relation to age and education. *Gerontology* 16:363-9, 1961.
35. **Botwinick J.** Disinclination to venture response *versus* cautiousness in responding: age differences. *J. Genet. Psychol.* 115:55-62, 1969.
36. **Klodin V M.** *Verbal facilitation of perceptual-integrative performance in relation to age.* PhD dissertation, Washington University, 1975.
37. **Doppelt J E & Wallace W L.** Standardization of the Wechsler Adult Intelligence Scale for older persons. *J. Abnormal Soc. Psychol.* 51:312-30, 1955.
38. **Schaie K W, Rosenthal F & Perlman R M.** Differential mental deterioration of factorially "pure" functions in later maturity. *J. Gerontol.* 8:191-6, 1953.
39. **Weiss A D.** The locus of reaction time change with set, motivation, and age. *J. Gerontol.* 20:60-4, 1965.
40. **Botwinick J & Thompson L W.** Components of reaction time in relation to age and sex. *J. Genet. Psychol.* 108:175-83, 1966.
41. **Atchley R C.** *The social forces in later life.* Belmont, CA: Wadsworth, 1980. 468 p.
42. **Welford A T.** Sensory, perceptual, and motor processes in older adults. (Birren J E & Sloane R B, eds.) *Handbook of mental health and aging.* Englewood Cliffs, NJ: Prentice-Hall, 1980. p. 192-213.
43. **Riegel K F & Riegel R M.** Development, drop, and death. *Develop. Psychol.* 6:306-19, 1972.
44. **Kleemeier R W.** Intellectual change in the senium. *Proceedings of the Social Statistics Section of the American Statistical Association,* 7-10 September 1962, Minneapolis, MN. Washington, DC: ASA, 1962. p. 290-5.
45. **Atchley R C.** Telephone communication. 18 January 1984.
46. **Baltes P B & Willis S L.** Plasticity and enhancement of intellectual functioning in old age: Penn State's Adult Development and Enrichment Project (ADEPT). (Craik F I M & Trehub S E, eds.) *Aging and cognitive processes.* New York: Plenum Press, 1982. p. 353-89.
47. **Willis S L, Blieszner R & Baltes P B.** Intellectual training research in aging: modification of performance on the fluid ability of figural relations. *J. Educ. Psychol.* 73:41-50, 1981.
48. **Perone M & Baron A.** Age-related effects of pacing on acquisition and performance of response sequences: an operant analysis. *J. Gerontol.* 37:443-9, 1982.
49. **Hoyer W J & Plude D J.** Attentional and perceptual processes in the study of cognitive aging. (Poon L W, ed.) *Aging in the 1980s.* Washington, DC: American Psychological Association, 1980. p. 227-38.
50. **Eisdorfer C.** Arousal and performance: experiments in verbal learning and a tentative theory. (Talland G A, ed.) *Human aging and behavior.* New York: Academic Press, 1968. p. 189-216.
51. **Eisdorfer C, Nowlin J & Wilkie F.** Improvement of learning in the aged by modification of autonomic nervous system activity. *Science* 170:1327-9, 1970.
52. **Schonfield A E D.** Learning, memory, and aging. (Birren J E & Sloane R B, eds.) *Handbook of mental health and aging.* Englewood Cliffs, NJ: Prentice-Hall, 1980. p. 214-44.
53. **Craik F I M.** Age differences in human memory. (Birren J E & Schaie K W, eds.) *Handbook of the psychology of aging.* New York: Van Nostrand Reinhold, 1977. p. 384-420.
54. **Cavanaugh J C, Grady J G & Perlmutter M.** Forgetting and use of memory aids in 20 to 70 year olds everyday life. *Int. J. Aging Human Develop.* 17:113-22, 1983.

55. **Oromaner M.** The quality of scientific scholarship and the "graying" of the academic profession: a skeptical view. *Res. High. Educ.* 15:231-9, 1981.
56. **Lehman H C.** *Age and achievement.* Princeton, NJ: Princeton University Press, 1953. 359 p.
57. **Zuckerman H & Merton R K.** Age, aging, and age structure in science. (Merton R K.) *The sociology of science.* Chicago: University of Chicago Press, 1973. p. 497-559.
58. **Cole S.** Age and scientific performance. *Amer. J. Sociol.* 84:958-77, 1979.
59. **Price D J D.** *Little science, big science.* New York: Columbia University Press, 1963. 118 p.
60. **Garfield E.** How to use citation analysis for faculty evaluations, and when is it relevant? Part 2. *Current Contents* (45):5-14, 7 November 1983.
61. **Cattell R B.** *Abilities: their structure, growth, and action.* Boston: Houghton Mifflin, 1971. 583 p.
62. **Horn J L.** Organization of abilities and the development of intelligence. *Psychol. Rev.* 75:242-59, 1968.
63. ------------. Organization of data on life-span development of human abilities. (Goulet L R & Baltes P B, eds.) *Life-span developmental psychology.* New York: Academic Press, 1970. p. 423-66.
64. **Hoyer W J, Labouvie G V & Baltes P B.** Modification of response speed deficits and intellectual performance in the elderly. *Hum. Develop.* 16:233-42, 1973.
65. **Furry C A & Baltes P B.** The effect of age differences in ability-extraneous performance variables on the assessment of intelligence in children, adults, and the elderly. *J. Gerontol.* 28:73-80, 1973.
66. **Baltes P B & Labouvie G V.** Adult development of intellectual performance: description, explanation, and modification. (Eisdorfer C & Lawton M P, eds.) *The psychology of adult development and aging.* Washington, DC: American Psychological Association, 1973. p. 157-219.
67. **Labouvie-Vief G & Gonda J N.** Cognitive strategy training and intellectual performance in the elderly. *J. Gerontol.* 31:327-32, 1976.
68. **Baltes P B.** Citation Classic. Commentary on *Hum. Develop.* 11:145-71, 1968. *Current Contents/Social & Behavioral Sciences* 13(18):16, 4 May 1981.
69. **Baltes P B & Willis S L.** Toward psychological theories of aging and development. (Birren J E & Schaie K W, eds.) *Handbook of the psychology of aging.* New York: Van Nostrand Reinhold, 1977. p. 128-54.
70. **Overton W F & Reese H W.** Models of development: methodological implications. (Nesselroade J R & Reese H W, eds.) *Life-span developmental psychology.* New York: Academic Press, 1973. p. 65-86.
71. **Reese H W & Overton W F.** Models of development and theories of development. (Goulet L R & Baltes P B, eds.) *Life-span developmental psychology.* New York: Academic Press, 1970. p. 115-45.
72. **Garfield E.** Senility: a major health problem in need of a solution. *Essays of an information scientist.* Philadelphia: ISI Press, 1983. Vol. 5. p. 138-42.
73. **Birren J E.** Age and decision strategies. *Interdisciplin. Top. Gerontol.* 4:23-36, 1969.
74. **Rabbitt P.** Changes in problem solving ability in old age. (Birren J E & Schaie K W, eds.) *Handbook of the psychology of aging.* New York: Van Nostrand Reinhold, 1977. p. 606-25.

Current Comments®

The 1982 Nobel Prize for Economic Science Goes to George J. Stigler for His Work on Industrial Structure, Markets, the Effects of Regulation, and the Economics of Information

Number 15   April 9, 1984

Since 1979, we have discussed the significant work of each of the Nobel prizewinners in science, economics, and literature.[1-3] While these essays will never qualify as up-to-the-minute science journalism, we believe that *Current Contents®* (*CC®*) readers appreciate the in-depth approach we have adopted. Through citation analysis, our main purpose is to evaluate the impact of an author's most significant publications. As pointed out recently in discussing faculty evaluation,[4] this type of analysis is not performed overnight, nor is it merely a matter of consulting a computer printout. We are also interested in learning, in each case, whether the data anticipate or confirm the decisions of the Nobel committee.

We are covering the 1982 awards in five separate essays. The first dealt with the work of physics laureate Kenneth G. Wilson.[5] The second focused on the work of chemistry prizewinner Aaron Klug.[6] The third covered the work of the 1982 laureates in medicine: Sune K. Bergström, Bengt I. Samuelsson, and John R. Vane.[7] A discussion of the economics award follows here. An essay on the 1982 prize in literature will appear shortly. A future essay will discuss the work of the 1983 Nobel prizewinner in economics, Gerard Debreu, University of California, Berkeley.

The 1982 Nobel prize for economic science was awarded to George J. Stig-ler, age 71, University of Chicago, Illinois, for his studies of industrial structures, the functioning of markets, and the causes and effects of public regulation.[8] Instrumental in all these contributions was his pioneering work in the "economics of information," which concerns the effects on the marketplace of consumers' knowledge of what they're buying, producers' knowledge of what their competitors are selling, and the cost of acquiring such knowledge. Stigler's work, collectively, has been cited over 4,800 times from 1955 through 1983, according to *Science Citation Index®* (*SCI®*) and *Social Sciences Citation Index®* (*SSCI®*).

In the discussion that follows, we have indicated the number of citations received by each of Stigler's ten most-cited publications. All citation data were obtained from the *SSCI* and *SCI* data bases.

Incidentally, Stigler is not the inventor of Stigler's Law of Eponymy,[9] which states that an eponym is *never* named after its originator or discoverer.[10] The law was impishly formulated by his son, statistician Stephen M. Stigler.

Stigler's early work reflected his interest in numerous areas of economic science. For instance, while at the University of Minnesota, Minneapolis, his work included a paper on production and distribution,[11] a critical review of a statistical method,[12] and a theoretical paper on duopoly[13]—a situation in which two sellers dominate but cannot gain control of a given market. Also among his earliest publications was an article[14] on a subject which would interest Stigler throughout his career: price theory, the study of the factors affecting the value set by sellers on their goods.

Stigler began empirical work in price theory in the mid-1940s, soon after moving to Columbia University, New York. Indeed, he published what was perhaps the first example of linear programming in a paper entitled "The cost of subsistence."[15] His work also included the statistical investigation of a specialized theory of rigid price structures,[16] and a paper on the factors governing the delivered prices of commodities.[17] In 1946, he published a landmark book, *The Theory of Price*.[18] After two revisions, in 1952 and again in 1966, it is still used in graduate schools throughout the US. It has been cited over 260 times through 1983.

Stigler also coauthored another important empirical study of prices in 1970, *The Behavior of Industrial Prices*[19] (75 citations through 1983). This book examines the question of price stability and presents meticulous data collected by Stigler and his colleague James K. Kindahl, University of Massachusetts, Amherst. The book's statistical evidence helped undermine the long-standing economic maxim that a major segment of the economy sets prices by management decision rather than in reaction to market factors.

While pursuing his interest in price theory, Stigler continued to be active in other areas of economics as well. During the post-World War II housing shortage, for example, he wrote a controversial pamphlet entitled *Roofs or ceilings?*[20] with Milton Friedman, University of Chicago. The pamphlet used an avalanche of statistics to argue that rent controls had the inevitable effect of distorting the rental market, bringing about severe shortages of apartments. Friedman won the 1976 Nobel prize for his work concerning monetary economics and statistics.

Stigler matured as a scholar during his years at Columbia, and his reputation as a clear-sighted, empirically oriented scientist grew. He wrote several books, including one on the expansion of employment opportunities in the service sector of the economy[21] and one on job prospects in science.[22] He also published numerous papers on a variety of subjects, including: monopolies;[23,24] utility theory, the study of how the consumer's use of a product affects the way in which that product is marketed;[25] the limits on the division of labor in a given market;[26] and historical accounts of the lives and works of early economists.[27,28] But much of Stigler's most important work lay ahead of him, upon his move to the University of Chicago in 1958.

The theoretical foundation for this work was laid in Stigler's most-cited paper, "The economics of information,"[29] published in 1961 and cited over 370 times through 1983. This *Citation Classic* ™ discusses the costs and the benefits to both producers and consumers of supplying and obtaining information about commodities. Stigler's commentary on this article appears in this week's issue of *CC/Social & Behavioral Sciences*.[30] A later paper applies this theoretical framework to the description of the ways in which members of an oligopoly—a situation similar to a duopoly, but with more participants—interact and monitor one another[31] (120 citations). Another paper extends the economics of information to the job market, discussing the cost-efficiency of various methods of locating prospective employers for workers entering a labor pool[32] (135 citations).

It should be mentioned here that Stigler's good friend, Fritz Machlup, Princeton and New York Universities, was instrumental in bridging the "gap" between information science and economics. Although Machlup was an expert on international currency problems, he published a monumental work on knowledge production[33] in 1962. It has been cited in over 230 publications through 1983. Moreover, three volumes of a multivolume work on the economics of knowledge and information[34] were completed before Machlup died last year, shortly after his eightieth birthday.

Stigler's work in the economics of information and his interest in the public regulation of industry spurred his study of economic and political institutions and industrial organization. Among his first efforts in this area, he confirmed a correlation between a given industry's profit margin and the degree to which that industry is concentrated in a few large firms[35] (155 citations). In addition, he coauthored a paper with Claire Friedland, University of Chicago, on the effects of regulation on rates and profits in electric utilities[36] (85 citations). The paper showed that nonregulated electric utilities of the 1930s tended to behave in similar fashion to their regulated counterparts. Later, his numerous articles on industrial organization were reprinted in *The Organization of Industry*[37] (220 citations).

Stigler's skepticism of the notion that government regulation makes a positive difference in the behavior of regulated industries is reflected in subsequent work. For example, he showed that even when regulation did affect industrial behavior, it usually produced more costs than benefits.[38,39] Indeed, according to Stigler, it is not necessarily true that regulatory agencies pursue the broad, common interest. In a paper entitled "The theory of economic regulation"[40] (315 citations), in which he argued that standard economic theory can be applied to determine when and how regulation will take place, he also found regulatory agencies were liable to be "captured" by the very industries they were supposed to regulate. They tended to protect the interests of the regulated industry to the disadvantage of the consumer.

According to 1970 Nobel prizewinning economist Paul Samuelson, Massachusetts Institute of Technology, Cambridge, not all of Stigler's conclusions are universally accepted.[8] In the utility rate study, for example, the evidence could also be interpreted to support the view that the unregulated industries kept their rates competitive out of fear of regulation. But it is important to note that Stigler's emphasis on statistical documentation has been no less than revolutionary. Previously, regulatory agencies were frequently judged by their original intentions or their self-proclaimed successes—indeed, by almost any standard but the verifiable results of their actions. Much of the credit for the growing interest in the empirical verification of economic theory must be given to Stigler.

Perhaps the best example of Stigler's combination of theory and hard data is provided by a paper entitled "De gustibus non est disputandum"[41] (85 citations), coauthored in 1977 with Gary S. Becker, University of Chicago. The title is roughly translated as, "There's no accounting for taste." It refers to the belief among traditional economists that certain economic phenomena are due solely to the vagaries of personal taste and are therefore unsuitable for scientific scrutiny. In this paper, however, Stigler rejects the traditional view and proposes that standard economic logic and analysis be applied as extensively as possible. He asserts that it is not tastes that change, but levels of economic information.

Stigler's conclusions yield useful predictions about behavior, even in such seemingly unpredictable industries as fashion and advertising. But perhaps even more significant than the paper's results is its combination of theory and confirmation by observational data.

Stigler's work establishes the paradigms for four different *SSCI* research fronts. Briefly, a research front consists of a group of current papers that cite a cluster of earlier, "core" papers.[42] Three of these research fronts were identified through our *SSCI* cluster analyses for 1978 through 1980. The first, entitled "Electoral conditions and economic outcomes," is based in part on a paper in which Stigler questions the traditional assumptions about the ways economic conditions influence voters.[43] The core of the second *SSCI* research front, entitled "Economics of crime," contains a paper in which Stigler discusses a theory of the constraints on the rational enforcement of the laws in society, given the inherent shortcomings of law enforcement agencies and the limitations imposed on them from without.[44] Stig-

ler's highly cited paper on the theory of economic regulation[40] forms part of the core literature of the third *SSCI* front, "Economic theory of regulation." The fourth research front is derived from the *ISI/CompuMath®* data base, and is entitled "Consumer search, industrial search, market information, and adaptive expectations." Its core literature includes Stigler's most-cited paper, "The economics of information."[29]

Although it was Stigler's tangible work on the causes and consequences of economics and political institutions that was recognized by the Nobel committee, his intangible contributions to economics may be just as important. He has raised the standards of industrial economics far beyond those found in the work of earlier scholars. Moreover, Stigler has made sterling contributions to the history and sociology of economic thought. His recognition by the Nobel committee is a testament to his rigorous, clear-thinking style.

* * * * *

My thanks to Stephen A. Bonaduce and Terri Freedman for their help in the preparation of this essay.

©1984 ISI

REFERENCES

1. **Garfield E.** Are the 1979 prizewinners *of Nobel class? Essays of an information scientist.* Philadelphia: ISI Press, 1981. Vol. 4. p. 609-17.
2. --------------. The 1980 Nobel prizewinners. *Essays of an information scientist.* Philadelphia: ISI Press, 1983. Vol. 5. p. 189-201.
3. --------------. Were the 1981 Nobel prizewinners in science, economics, and literature anticipated by citation analysis? *Essays of an information scientist.* Philadelphia: ISI Press, 1983. Vol. 5. p. 551-61.
4. --------------. How to use citation analysis for faculty evaluations, and when is it relevant? Parts 1 & 2. *Current Contents* (44):5-13, 31 October 1983 and (45):5-14, 7 November 1983.
5. --------------. The 1982 Nobel prize in physics. *Current Contents* (50):5-14, 12 December 1983.
6. --------------. The 1982 Nobel prize in chemistry goes to structural biologist Aaron Klug. *Current Contents* (3):3-11, 16 January 1984.
7. --------------. The 1982 Nobel prize in medicine recognizes the impact of prostaglandin research by S.K. Bergström, B.I. Samuelsson, and J.R. Vane. *Current Contents* (12):3-12, 19 March 1984.
8. **Williams W.** Nobel won by Chicago economist. *NY Times* 21 October 1982, p. D1; D7.
9. **Stigler S M.** Stigler's law of eponymy. (Gieryn T F, ed.) *Science and social structure: a festschrift for Robert K. Merton.* New York: NY Academy of Sciences, 1980. p. 147-57.

---

10. **Garfield E.** What's in a name? The eponymic route to immortality.
    Current Contents (47):5-16, 21 November 1983.
11. **Stigler G J.** Production and distribution in the short run. *J. Polit. Econ.* 47:305-27, 1939.
12. --------------. The limitations of statistical demand curves. *J. Amer. Statist. Assn.* 34:469-81, 1939.
13. --------------. Notes on the theory of duopoly. *J. Polit. Econ.* 48:521-41, 1940.
14. --------------. Social welfare and differential prices. *J. Farm Econ.* 20:573-86, 1938.
15. --------------. The cost of subsistence. *J. Farm Econ.* 27:303-14, 1945.
16. --------------. The kinky oligopoly demand curve and rigid prices. *J. Polit. Econ.* 55:432-49, 1947.
17. --------------. A theory of delivered price systems. *Amer. Econ. Rev.* 39:1143-59, 1949.
18. --------------. *The theory of price.* New York: Macmillan, 1966. 355 p.
19. **Stigler G J & Kindahl J K.** *The behavior of industrial prices.*
    New York: National Bureau of Economic Research, 1970. 202 p.
20. **Friedman M & Stigler G J.** *Roofs or ceilings? The current housing problem.*
    Irvington-on-Hudson, NY: Foundation for Economic Education, 1946. (Pamphlet.) 22 p.
21. **Stigler G J.** *Trends in employment in the service industries.*
    Princeton, NJ: Princeton University Press, 1956. 167 p.
22. **Blank D M & Stigler G J.** *The demand and supply of scientific personnel.*
    New York: National Bureau of Economic Research, 1957. 200 p.
23. **Stigler G J.** Monopoly and oligopoly by merger. *Amer. Econ. Rev.* 40(Suppl.):23-34, 1950.
24. --------------. The statistics of monopoly and merger. *J. Polit. Econ.* 64:33-40, 1956.
25. --------------. The development of utility theory. Part I. *J. Polit. Econ.* 58:307-27, 1950.
26. --------------. The division of labor is limited by the extent of the market.
    J. Polit. Econ. 59:185-93, 1951.
27. --------------. Sraffa's *Ricardo*. *Amer. Econ. Rev.* 43:586-99, 1953.
28. --------------. Schumpeter's *History of economic analysis*. *J. Polit. Econ.* 62:344-5, 1954.
29. --------------. The economics of information. *J. Polit. Econ.* 69:213-25, 1961.
30. --------------. Citation Classic. Commentary on *J. Polit. Econ.* 69:213-25, 1961.
    Current Contents/Social & Behavioral Sciences 16(15):14, 9 April 1984.
31. --------------. A theory of oligopoly. *J. Polit. Econ.* 72:44-61, 1964.
32. --------------. Information in the labor market. *J. Polit. Econ.* 70(Suppl. No. 5 Pt. 2):94-105, 1962.
33. **Machlup F.** *The production and distribution of knowledge in the United States.*
    Princeton, NJ: Princeton University Press, 1962. 416 p.
34. --------------. *Knowledge: its creation, distribution, and economic significance.*
    Princeton, NJ: Princeton University Press, 1980-1984. Vols. 1-3.
35. **Stigler G J.** *Capital and rates of return in manufacturing industries.*
    Princeton, NJ: Princeton University Press, 1963. 229 p.
36. **Stigler G J & Friedland C.** What can regulators regulate? The case of electricity.
    J. Law Econ. 5:1-16, 1962.
37. **Stigler G J.** *The organization of industry.* Homewood, IL: Richard D. Irwin, 1968. 328 p.
38. --------------. Public regulation of the securities markets. *J. Bus.* 37:117-42, 1964.
39. --------------. The economic effects of the antitrust laws. *J. Law Econ.* 9:225-58, 1966.
40. --------------. The theory of economic regulation. *Bell J. Econ. Manage. Sci.* 2:3-21, 1971.
41. **Stigler G J & Becker G S.** De gustibus non est disputandum. *Amer. Econ. Rev.* 67:76-90, 1977.
42. **Garfield E.** ABCs of cluster mapping. Parts 1 & 2. Most active fields in the life and physical
    sciences in 1978. *Essays of an information scientist.* Philadelphia: ISI Press, 1981.
    Vol. 4. p. 634-49.
43. **Stigler G J.** General economic conditions and national elections.
    Amer. Econ. Rev. (Papers Proc.) 63:160-7, 1973.
44. --------------. The optimum enforcement of laws. *J. Polit. Econ.* 78:526-36, 1970.

Current Comments®

Gabriel García Márquez Receives the 1982 Nobel Prize in Literature

Number 16

April 16, 1984

It surprises most readers of *Current Contents®* (*CC®*) to learn that ISI® covers the arts and humanities literature. Obviously, readers of *CC/Arts & Humanities* (*CC/A&H*) know that we do. Nevertheless, as far as these essays are concerned, *CC/A&H* readers must often feel that we neglect their interests. The fact is, however, that our readers in the sciences outnumber those in the humanities by at least 100 to one. This ratio may not be characteristic of the typical academic institution, but it is a fact of life we cannot ignore.

I say this by way of introducing this atypical essay about an important literary figure. From long experience, I have learned that even the most single-minded organic chemist or engineer may appreciate an occasional reminder that there is something in the world besides science or technology. Furthermore, I like to remind them that there are important connections between the two cultures. And besides, ISI is also the purveyor of *Arts & Humanities Citation Index™* (*A&HCI™*) and *Social Sciences Citation Index®* (*SSCI®*). These tools permit us to study scholars in a unique way. They also provide me with the hubris to comment upon a figure such as Gabriel José García Márquez. Of course, there will be some readers who will feel that this essay is no more daring than my forays into other fields in which I am not an expert.

But in these exercises, we perceive our role as that of an investigative journalist. With considerable help from many ISI colleagues, we have discussed the significant work of each of the Nobel prizewinners in science, economics, and literature since 1979.[1-3] We are covering the 1982 awards in five separate essays.[4-6] Recently, we discussed the work of economist George J. Stigler.[7] This concluding essay for the 1982 awards discusses the prize in literature. García Márquez was honored for his stories about the imaginary village of Macondo. These stories reflect, with bewildering, surrealistic, yet convincing authenticity, the human riches and poverty of Latin America.[8]

The Nobel prize in literature is awarded annually by the Swedish Academy in Stockholm. The academy is the literary counterpart of the Royal Swedish Academy of Sciences, which presents the awards in chemistry and physics. The Swedish Academy's literature selections have sometimes been the subject of criticism and debate in the past. Certainly, not all of the literature prizewinners are among those writers most often cited in the scholarly literature. But it should be pointed out that the output of even great artists and writers may be more erratic than that of Nobel laureates in the sciences, who are generally known for the steady production of important articles throughout their careers. For example,

Elias Canetti, the 1981 literature prize-winner, published his first novel, *Die Blendung* (*Auto-da-Fé*),[9] in 1935. But between 1938 and 1960, he published almost nothing at all.[10] It is unsurprising, therefore, that he did not appear in our study of the 100 most-cited literary figures of the twentieth century.[11]

But the Nobel prize itself often serves as a spur to scholarship concerning the winner. Indeed, it is common for literary authors to become increasingly cited as their work is studied and appreciated by scholars. Thus, literature laureates may *eventually* become highly cited. In Canetti's case, most of the 100 citations to his work came in the period just prior to and immediately after his selection for the literature prize. This is not to imply that citation data do not have validity in the humanities. Among the 100 most-cited literary authors in our last study,[11] 24 have already been awarded the Nobel prize. Many more are still eligible.

No elaborate explanations, however, are required to justify the selection of García Márquez as the 1982 literature prizewinner. You might even say that we told you so much in previous essays. The world's best-selling author in the Spanish language, García Márquez was identified as eligible for the Nobel prize in our study of the twentieth century's most-cited literary figures.[11]

Much of García Márquez's writing is political satire, and has aroused interest in scholars throughout the world. Not surprisingly then, citations to his work are not restricted to scholars in the humanities. Social scientists often refer to his stories as well. Thus, according to *A&HCI* and *SSCI*, García Márquez has been explicitly cited over 300 times since 1966, the earliest year for which such data are available. Almost 20 percent of these citations were found in social sciences journals. Over 175 were to the original Spanish-language editions. Almost 120 cited the English translations, while the rest were divided among French, Italian, Russian, German, and Portuguese versions. Over 80 citations came from journals published in Spanish.

The number of citations to García Márquez's work is unusually high for a literary author. But it is especially so for one publishing primarily in Spanish, since neither the *A&HCI* nor the *SSCI* claims to be comprehensive for Spanish-language journals. Even so, his best-known work, *Cien Años de Soledad* (*One Hundred Years of Solitude*), 1967,[12] which has sold ten million copies in 32 languages, has been cited over 175 times since 1967 in various editorials, interviews, critiques, book reviews, notes, and biographical items. One hundred of these citations were to the Spanish-language edition, 65 to the English, and the rest divided among the French, German, Italian, and Russian versions. Over 50 came from Spanish-language journals. In the discussion that follows, we have indicated the number of citations received by each of García Márquez's novels and certain of his other works. All data were obtained from the *A&HCI* and *SSCI* data bases.

García Márquez was born on March 6, 1928, in the village of Aracataca, near the northern Caribbean coast of Colombia. The eldest of 16 children, he was raised until age eight by his maternal grandparents. His grandmother's stories of ghosts, spirits, and ancestors, combined with the military tales of his grandfather, a retired army colonel, greatly influenced García Márquez's development as a writer.

His first efforts at writing came at the age of five, when he was given a toy printing press. Little hindered by his inability to spell, García Márquez turned out a page of gibberish daily, which he sold to his indulgent grandfather for one centavo. Later, he began to write down his grandparents' stories in comic strip form. In high school, García Márquez acquired a reputation as a writer, although he "never in fact wrote anything" of consequence, as he put it in a 1981 interview for the literary journal *Paris Review*.[13] Still, he continued, "If there was a pamphlet to be written or a letter of petition, I was the one to do it because I was supposedly the writer." It wasn't until García Márquez read Franz Kafka's *The Metamorphosis*[14] in 1946, while attending the University of Bogotá, that he began writing seriously. His first short story was published a year later in the literature supplement of the Bogotá newspaper *El Espectador*.

On April 9, 1948, the assassination in Bogotá of a national political leader touched off a civil war that sputtered for a decade. Referred to as *la violencia*, the war bled the country and took the lives of perhaps 300,000 people. The war affected García Márquez deeply, politicizing his writing and serving as source material for three books, including *One Hundred Years of Solitude*.

The war forced García Márquez to leave Bogotá for Cartagena, where he resumed his studies and took up journalism. In 1950, he moved to Barranquilla, where he wrote a column for the daily *El Heraldo*. The experience of rubbing elbows with other journalists and writers in local cafés and bookstores continued his literary development. It was during this period that he first read the authors who were to influence his later writing: William Faulkner, Ernest Hemingway, Virginia Woolf, and James Joyce.

The influence of Faulkner is evident in the first of García Márquez's major works, a novella entitled *La Hojarasca* (*Leaf Storm*, first published in 1955; translated into English and published in the collection *Leaf Storm and Other Stories*[15] in 1979). The story centers on the funeral of a reclusive village physician and the desire of the town's citizens to avenge themselves on his corpse for a wrong they believe he committed. According to many literary critics, the complexity of *Leaf Storm*'s narrative and its gothic phrasing and atmosphere are clearly Faulknerian.[16-18] So too is the imaginary village of Macondo, introduced in this story, which is often compared to Faulkner's "Yoknapatawpha County." However, according to Peruvian writer Mario Vargas Llosa, author of perhaps the most searching and authoritative critical study of García Márquez's work to date,[19] García Márquez's stories are far more accessible to the average reader than many of Faulkner's works. They benefit from an exuberant sense of humor wholly absent from Faulkner's stories.[19] Vargas Llosa, a great novelist in his own right, is best known for his novels, *The Green House*[20] and *Conversation in the Cathedral*.[21]

While writing *Leaf Storm* in 1955, García Márquez moved back to Bogotá and took a job as a film critic and reporter for *El Espectador*, which continued to publish his short stories over the years. During the year of *Leaf Storm*'s publication, he was assigned to a beat in Europe that eventually took him to Paris. There he wrote *La Mala Hora* (*In Evil Hour*),[22] which he made little effort to have published. (An edited version appeared in 1962; an authorized edition did not appear until 1966.) *In Evil Hour* is a story of political oppression in a small town during the days of *la violencia*. (We could find only a few dozen citations to this work, possibly because our data is limited to the post-1966 period.) One of the characters in the book is a retired army colonel who spends his days awaiting the arrival of his pension in the mail. The character so intrigued García Márquez that he put *In Evil Hour* aside to write a novella devoted to the colonel. The resulting work, *El Coronel No Tiene Quien Le Escriba* (*No One Writes to the Colonel*),[23] was first published in a Colombian magazine, *Mito*, in 1958, and as a book in 1961. After finishing it in 1957, he went to Caracas, Venezuela, where he worked for various periodicals and continued to write short stories.

Although *Leaf Storm* and García Márquez's other early work had brought him recognition among critics as a writer of extraordinary talent, he had not yet attracted much attention outside literary circles. That changed, however, with the publication of *One Hundred Years of Solitude* in 1967. In a 1973 interview with William Kennedy for the *Atlantic*,[24] he said that the complete first chapter of the book suddenly came to him while driving his car between Acapulco and Mexico City, where he had moved in 1961 and where he still makes his home. Upon his return home, he instructed his wife not to distract him with any problems—especially concerning the state of their finances—and shut himself away eight to ten hours a day for the next 18 months. "I didn't know what my wife was doing," he said, "and I didn't ask any questions.... We...lived as if we had money. But when I was finished writing, my wife said, 'Did you really finish it? We owe $12,000.' "[24]

One Hundred Years of Solitude spans six generations of the Buendía family, founders of the mythical town of Macondo. In this spectral village, flower petals fall like raindrops from the sky, children are born with little pigs' tails, dictators seem immortal, and memory vanishes from one day to the next. In one of the more memorable scenes in the book, Rebeca Buendía is levitated heavenward while folding bedsheets outdoors near her washline. Her sister-in-law can only grumble that the sheets, which rose with Rebeca, are now lost forever.

More recent works by García Márquez include: a novella entitled *La Increíble y Triste Historia de la Cándida Eréndira y de Su Abuela Desalmada*[25] (*The Incredible and Sad Tale of Innocent Eréndira and Her Heartless Grandmother*, 1972, republished in 1978 in the collection, *Innocent Eréndira, and Other Stories*);[26] *El Otoño del Patriarca* (*The Autumn of the Patriarch*, 1975);[27] and *Cronica de una Muerte Anunciada* (*Chronicle of a Death Foretold*),[28] published in its entirety in the March 1983 issue of *Vanity Fair*,[29] and more recently in book form as well. *Autumn of the Patriarch* has been cited in at least 75 editorials, interviews, book reviews, critiques, and notes since its publication. Over 35 quoted the Spanish edition, and 25 quoted the English translation. The rest are divided among the French, Italian, and Russian editions. Almost 20 of these came from journals published in Spanish—undoubtedly only a fraction of the possible sources. *Chronicle of a Death Foretold*, in spite of the recent date of its publication, has already received more than 20 citations, of which almost half were to the Spanish edition.

In the humanities literature, the majority of the articles citing García Márquez's work consists of book reviews, editorials, and interviews. A significant number also came from in-depth analyses, commentaries, and essays concerning various facets of García Márquez's work. For example, an article by García Márquez's English translator, Gregory Rabassa, Queens College, New York, discusses the blending of the literary and journalistic traditions in much of García Márquez's writings, and in *Chronicle of a Death Foretold* in particular.[30] "What unites so much of García Márquez's writing," according to Rabassa, "is the sense of inexorability, of fatefulness. Things often come to an end that has been there all the while—in spite of what might have been done to avoid it—and often [do so] mysteriously and inexplicably.... [*Chronicle*] shows many aspects of life and literature and how one is essentially the same as the other: life imitates art."[30]

A 1981 article in *Latin American Literary Review* by Gene H. Bell-Villada, Williams College, Williamstown, Massachusetts, discusses the significance of the names of García Márquez's characters and his narrative patterns.[31] Bell-Villada notes that the repetition of names in *One Hundred Years of Solitude* helps illustrate the personality traits linking the book's characters. Michael Sexson, Montana State University, Bozeman, argues that García Márquez's juxtaposition of realism and fantasy denotes an attempt to write in the style of various former periods without adopting the cultural assumptions of those periods.[32] A 1982 article by Eduardo González, Johns Hopkins University, Baltimore, Maryland, in *Modern Language Notes*, published by Johns Hopkins, analyzes the structure of García Márquez's prose.[33]

Many literary articles which cite García Márquez do not deal with strictly literary concerns. Such articles include, for instance, a comparison of García Márquez's treatment of death and mourning in *One Hundred Years of Solitude* with the way death is experienced in the real world.[34] It was written by Laurence M. and Laura Porter, both of Michigan State University, East Lansing, for a special issue of *Mosaic*, a literary journal published by the University of Manitoba, Canada. The issue was devoted to topics concerning death and dying. An article by Howard M. Fraser, College of William and Mary, Williams-burg, Virginia, discusses ritualistic violence in society, and examines the motif of cockfighting in Latin American literature[35]—including García Márquez's *No One Writes to the Colonel*. An essay[36] by S. Meckled, University of Essex, Colchester, England, in *Crane Bag*, a literary review journal, examines the psychological elements in *One Hundred Years of Solitude*, *Leaf Storm*, *Autumn of the Patriarch*, and García Márquez's earliest short stories. One of these is the psychic split of the self by the ego as a defense mechanism against the fear of death.

A number of authors in the social sciences also refer to the works of García Márquez. These include articles on the role of literature in Latin American and Third World politics.[37-39] One article in *Social Praxis* by E. San Juan, Brooklyn College, New York, notes that literature reflects the dynamic political processes in the developing countries.[37] The relationship between Latin America and the developed world is explored in two other articles,[40,41] including another by Bell-Villada. His paper discusses the communication gap between the intellectuals of North and Latin America.[40] The use of literary works in teaching Latin American geography[42] is discussed by Don R. Hoy, University of Georgia, Athens, and Gary S. Elbow, Texas Tech University, Lubbock. The authors argue that properly selected literary works can spark student interest in regional geography.

Fundamentally a storyteller in the tradition of his grandparents, García Márquez stresses that he is not interested in conveying deep, hidden messages or in handing down moral judgments, but simply in reporting the behavior of his characters.[13] Thus, his early stories were written for his friends. "In general," he told *Paris Review*, "I think you usually do write for someone. When I'm writing,

I'm always aware that this friend is going to like this, or that another friend is going to like that paragraph or chapter—always thinking of specific people."[13] But *One Hundred Years of Solitude* has made writing "terribly hard work, more so all the time," as he told journalist Rita Guibert in an interview for her book on major Latin American literary figures, entitled *Seven Voices*.[43] Much of his difficulty stemmed from an acute awareness that, after the astonishing success of *One Hundred Years of Solitude*, he was no longer writing only for friends, but for millions of strangers. This upsets and inhibits him so much that "every letter I write weighs me down, you can't imagine how much."[43] Indeed, in his interview with *Paris Review*, García Márquez confessed, "On a good working day, working from nine o'clock in the morning until two or three in the afternoon, the most I can write is a short paragraph of four or five lines—which I usually tear up the next day."[13]

One hopes that in spite of these difficulties, García Márquez can continue to write of the magical Latin America he created almost 30 years ago. As Rabassa

notes, "Of contemporary Latin American writers, García Márquez is probably the most accomplished. Certainly, he is at the forefront of the new, original novelists coming out of Latin America today."[44] Rabassa believes that the literature prize recognizes not only García Márquez but also the entire group of contemporary Latin American writers represented by García Márquez and others, such as Carlos Fuentes and the late Julio Cortázar. "García Márquez and the others have taken the novel to places it had never gone before," says Rabassa. "The Latin American novel had not really come into its own until this group—and García Márquez in particular—revolutionized it."[44]

This completes our look at the 1982 Nobel prizewinners in science and literature. In the near future we will begin our series on the 1983 Nobel prizes, including the literature award to William K. Golding.

* * * * *

My thanks to Stephen A. Bonaduce and Terri Freedman for their help in the preparation of this essay. ©1984 ISI

REFERENCES

1. **Garfield E.** Are the 1979 prizewinners *of Nobel class? Essays of an information scientist.* Philadelphia: ISI Press, 1981. Vol. 4. p. 609-17.
2. -------------. The 1980 Nobel prizewinners. *Essays of an information scientist.* Philadelphia: ISI Press, 1983. Vol. 5. p. 189-201.
3. -------------. Were the 1981 Nobel prizewinners in science, economics, and literature anticipated by citation analysis? *Essays of an information scientist.* Philadelphia: ISI Press, 1983. Vol. 5. p. 551-61.
4. -------------. The 1982 Nobel prize in physics. *Current Contents* (50):5-14, 12 December 1983.
5. -------------. The 1982 Nobel prize in chemistry goes to structural biologist Aaron Klug. *Current Contents* (3):3-11, 16 January 1984.
6. -------------. The 1982 Nobel prize in medicine recognizes the impact of prostaglandin research by S.K. Bergström, B.I. Samuelsson, and J.R. Vane. *Current Contents* (12):3-12, 19 March 1984.
7. -------------. The 1982 Nobel prize for economic science goes to George J. Stigler for his work on industrial structure, markets, the effects of regulation, and the economics of information. *Current Contents* (15):3-7, 9 April 1984.
8. **Salisbury S.** García Márquez of Colombia wins Nobel prize for literature. *Phila. Inquirer* 22 October 1982, p. 1C; 4C.
9. **Canetti E.** *Die Blendung.* (*Auto-da-Fé.*) Munich: Willi Weismann Verlag, 1935. 504 p.
10. **Sontag S.** Mind as passion. *NY Rev. Books* 25 September 1980, p. 47-52.
11. **Garfield E.** The 100 most-cited authors of 20th century literature. Can citation data forecast the Nobel prize in literature? *Essays of an information scientist.* Philadelphia: ISI Press, 1981. Vol. 4. p. 363-9.

12. **García Márquez G.** *Cien años de soledad.* (*One hundred years of solitude.*) Buenos Aires: Editorial Sudamericana, 1967. 351 p.
13. **Stone P H.** The art of fiction LXIX: Gabriel García Márquez. *Paris Rev.* (82):44-73, 1981.
14. **Kafka F.** *The metamorphosis.* New York: Vanguard Press, 1946. 98 p.
15. **García Márquez G.** *Leaf storm and other stories.* New York: Harper & Row, 1979. 146 p.
16. **Kiely R.** Memory and prophecy, illusion and reality are mixed and made to look the same. Review of "One hundred years of solitude" by G. García Márquez. *NY Times Book Rev.* 8 March 1970, p. 5; 24.
17. **Christ R.** A novel mythologizes a whole continent. Review of "One hundred years of solitude" by G. García Márquez. *Commonweal* 91:622-3, 1970.
18. **Vargas Llosa M.** A morbid prehistory (the early stories). *Books Abroad* 47:451-60, 1973.
19. --------------------. *García Márquez: historia de un deicidio.* (Story of a deicide.) Barcelona: Barral, 1971. 667 p.
20. --------------------. *The green house.* New York: Harper & Row, 1968. 405 p.
21. --------------------. *Conversation in the cathedral.* New York: Harper & Row, 1975. 601 p.
22. **García Márquez G.** *La mala hora.* (*In evil hour.*) Mexico City: Ediciones Era, 1966. 198 p.
23. ----------------------. *El coronel no tiene quien le escriba.* (*No one writes to the colonel.*) Medellín: Aguirre, 1961. 90 p.
24. **Kennedy W.** The yellow trolley car in Barcelona, and other visions. *Atlantic* 231:50-9, 1973.
25. **García Márquez G.** *La increíble y triste historia de la cándida Eréndira y de su abuela desalmada.* (*The incredible and sad tale of innocent Eréndira and her heartless grandmother.*) Barcelona: Barral, 1972. 163 p.
26. ----------------------. *Innocent Eréndira, and other stories.* New York: Harper & Row, 1978. 183 p.
27. ----------------------. *El otoño del patriarca.* (*The autumn of the patriarch.*) Barcelona: Plaza & Janes, S.A., 1975. 271 p.
28. ----------------------. *Chronicle of a death foretold.* New York: Ballantine, 1984. 143 p.
29. ----------------------. Chronicle of a death foretold. *Vanity Fair* 46(1):122-224, 1983.
30. **Rabassa G.** García Márquez's new book: literature or journalism? *World Lit. Today* 56:48-51, 1982.
31. **Bell-Villada G H.** Names and narrative pattern in *One hundred years of solitude.* *Lat. Amer. Lit. Rev.* 9(18):37-46, 1981.
32. **Sexson M.** Postmodern paradigms: the enchantment of realism in the fiction of Italo Calvino and Gabriel García Márquez. *J. Soc. Biol. Struct.* 6:115-21, 1983.
33. **González E.** Beware of gift-bearing tales: reading García Márquez according to Mauss. *MLN—Modern Lang. Notes* 97:347-64, 1982.
34. **Porter L M & Porter L.** Relations with the dead in *Cien años de soledad.* *Mosaic—J. Interdiscipl. Study Lit.* 15:119-27, 1982.
35. **Fraser H M.** The cockfight motif in Spanish-American literature. *Revista Interamericana Bibliogr.—Inter-American Review Bibliogr.* 31:514-23, 1981.
36. **Meckled S.** The theme of the double: an essential element throughout García Márquez works. *Crane Bag* 6(2):108-17, 1982.
37. **San Juan E.** Literature and revolution in the Third World. *Social Praxis* 6(1/2):19-34, 1979.
38. **Mena L I.** Bibliografía anotada sobre el ciclo de la violencia en la literatura Colombiana. (Annotated bibliography on the cycle of violence in Colombian literature.) *Lat. Amer. Res. Rev.* 13(3):95-107, 1978.
39. **Milenky E S.** Lateinamerika und die Dritte Welt. (Latin America and the Third World.) *Europa-Archiv* 32:441-52, 1977.
40. **Bell-Villada G H.** Two Americas, two worldviews, and a widening gap. *Monthly Rev.* 34(5):37-43, 1982.
41. **Vargashidalgo R.** United States and Latin America under President Carter. *Revista Política Internacional* (155):7-43, 1978.
42. **Hoy D R & Elbow G S.** The use of literary works in teaching Latin American geography. *J. Geogr.* 75:556-69, 1976.
43. **Guibert R.** *Seven voices.* New York: Knopf, 1973. 436 p.
44. **Rabassa G.** Telephone communication. 20 March 1984.

Current Comments®

A Tribute to Miriam Rothschild: Entomologist *Extraordinaire*

Number 17   April 23, 1984

In a recent essay, I reviewed the latest publications of ISI Press®.[1] Among these is a biography of the turn-of-the-century British zoologist, Walter Rothschild, entitled *Dear Lord Rothschild: Birds, Butterflies and History*.[2] The book was written by Miriam Rothschild, a distinguished entomologist who is also Walter's niece. She has produced a most entertaining and informative account of his life and scientific achievements.

Dear Lord Rothschild has been well received by the scientific and lay press.[3-6] The book establishes beyond a doubt that significant contributions to zoological systematics, nomenclature, and microevolution were made at Tring Museum, which Walter Rothschild founded and administered for 50 years. Yet for all its value as science history, the book is leavened with entertaining insider's anecdotes about some of the most powerful people in Victorian and Edwardian England. And as the only book about a Rothschild written by a Rothschild, the work has special authority.

Meeting Miriam Rothschild prompted me to analyze, for the first time, the entomology journals indexed in *Science Citation Index®* (*SCI®*).[7] It also confirmed my feeling that the work of this remarkable scientist merited a thorough review. In this essay, I will discuss her most important research in several areas of entomology. I will also try to convey

some sense of Rothschild the individual, for she is a dynamic and unconventional personality with a boundless range of interests.

Rothschild was born into the eminent Rothschild family on August 5, 1908. Her father, Charles Rothschild (Walter's brother), was an enthusiastic amateur zoologist. In free time snatched from the demands of the family business, he managed to publish over 150 scientific papers on fleas. He was also one of Tring Museum's major collectors.

For 27 years, Rothschild lived at Tring Park, Hertfordshire, northwest of London. Tring Park was the site of her uncle's natural history museum. This museum housed the largest collection of animal specimens assembled by one person. It contained more than two million butterflies and moths, 300,000 bird skins, 144 giant tortoises, and 200,000 birds' eggs. Given this environment and her father's influence, it's not surprising that the young Rothschild evinced a passionate attachment to insects, birds, and all other animals. She began breeding ladybirds when she was only four years old.

Like most women of her day, Rothschild was educated at home. In fact, the Rothschild family did not favor formal education for either sex. Her uncle endured only the minimum of university rote learning before breaking away to conduct independent zoological re-

Miriam Rothschild

searches. Similarly, her father had maintained that formal education stifled intellectual creativity.

Rothschild gleaned her education from her parents, her uncle's museum, and her own wide reading. Her own attitude toward formal education might be summed up by her statement, "The types of tests devised by the appropriate authorities in Britain today assess the size of the child's bottom rather than that of its head."[8] Although she did take courses at the University of London, she has never received a formal degree. Instead, she chose to work outside the educational system. The academic credentials Rothschild has acquired, such as the honorary doctor of science degree she received from the University of Oxford in 1968, she wrested from the educational establishment by the sheer compelling merit of her research. Her work also earned her the status of honorary fellow, St. Hugh's College, Oxford. Despite her lack of formal credentials, she served as visiting professor of biology at the Royal Free Hospital School of Medicine, London, from 1968 to 1973.

Lack of conventional education has in no way curbed Rothschild's research output. She has published over 275 works in fields ranging from marine biology to plant/insect interactions. As a child, Rothschild studied butterflies and ladybirds, but her zoological interests later crystallized around marine biology. Indeed, her earliest publications include a series of papers on the effects of flatworm parasites (trematodes) on a species of marine snail.[9-11] These papers showed that parasitism by larval trematodes causes abnormal growth in the marine snail. Trematode infestation also causes variations in shell development. These findings had important implications for snail taxonomy.

Rothschild inherited from her father an interest in fleas. Charles Rothschild had amassed at Tring Museum the largest collection of fleas in existence. He coauthored many papers with Karl Jordan, a curator of Tring Museum and a respected entomologist. Among these was a paper identifying the plague-carrying rat flea *Xenopsylla cheopis*.[12]

Initially, however, fleas were a sideline for Rothschild. Although she occasionally published descriptions of new species, she did not study fleas in depth until the 1950s. Then she began cataloging her father's flea collection. The first of the six-volume series covering the taxonomy and morphology of the collection was published in 1953. Rothschild coauthored five of these volumes with G. Harry Hopkins.[13] She has recently coauthored another work based on her father's collection.[14]

Around this time Rothschild also published jointly with Theresa Clay, formerly of the British Museum of Natural History, a popular work entitled *Fleas, Flukes & Cuckoos*.[15] This was part of a series intended to promote neglected facets of British natural history such as parasitology. In it Rothschild explained for the lay reader parasitism, symbiosis, and other species interrelationships. The book incorporated many of her interests, as it discussed fleas, protozoa, flatworms, flies, mites, microparasites, the fauna of birds' nests, skuas (gull-like seabirds), and European cuckoos. Clay contributed a chapter on feather lice. *Fleas, Flukes & Cuckoos* proved that Rothschild could communicate science in a very palatable fashion. Characteristically, she served up the facts with a generous measure of levity. For example, she introduced her discussion of avian fleas by saying: "Birds' fleas and feather lice do not sing. Nor do they fly about flashing brilliantly coloured wings in the sunshine. It is scarcely surprising that in Britain bird and butterfly enthusiasts number thousands, but the collectors of fleas and lice can be counted on the fingers of one hand."[15] (p. 56)

But Rothschild's most important work on fleas was yet to come. In the early 1950s, the British Ministry of Agriculture formed a committee (which Rothschild was invited to join) to study the flea's role in transmitting myxomatosis, a viral disease of South American rabbits. The disease had reached England and was devastating the British rabbit population. To conduct the study, it was necessary to breed the rabbit flea in captivity. Other flea species bred readily in the laboratory, but the rabbit flea would not cooperate. Rothschild suggested that the host's hormone cycle might influence the flea's sexual maturation. This hunch was borne out when an associate demonstrated that the ovaries of the female rabbit flea matured only on pregnant rabbits.[16]

Rothschild then conducted a series of experiments to determine which hormones were at work. She and an associate, Bob Ford, showed that corticosteroids produced by the adrenal glands during late pregnancy, as well as estrogens, are the most influential hormones controlling ovarian maturation.[17,18] It was also found that in nature rabbit fleas copulate only on newborn rabbits, although they mature sexually on the pregnant doe. The fleas transfer from the mother to the newborns at parturition of the host. This ensures a food supply for the flea larvae, which feed on debris in the rabbit nest. Rothschild, Ford, and M. Hughes identified a pheromone, an airborne chemical stimulus produced by the newborn rabbits, that aids sexual maturation.[19] But they concluded that a simple change of host actually induces copulation of the sexually mature, egg-bearing fleas. The rabbit flea was the first known case of an insect parasite whose reproductive cycle is dependent on that of its host.[20]

Rothschild's flea studies included an elucidation of their jumping mechanism. In a series of articles published in the early 1970s, Rothschild and associates used high-speed photography combined with precise morphological studies to determine the exact jumping mechanism of *Xenopsylla cheopis*, the vector of plague.[21-23] Their findings suggest that fleas are descended from winged ancestors, since the jumping mechanism employs modified flight structures. These include the presence of resilin, a rubber-like protein, in the pleural arch of the flea's thorax.

Rothschild's flea research features prominently in the citation accompanying her honorary degree from Oxford.[24] The citation refers to her coming "to this our Capitol, not by degrees, but by one leap as of her fleas, in a triumphal chariot, so to speak, drawn not by Venus' doves, Juno's peacocks, Alexander's gryphons, Pompey's elephants, but by her sixty-odd species of avian parasites." The citation goes on to itemize her work on fleas, saying, "One flea (of the genus [sic *irritans*) is enough for most of us, but she has faced some twenty-two thousand and despatched them."

Although Rothschild's work in ornithology is not as extensive as her work in fleas, to some extent these studies overlap. A number of her papers discuss bird fleas specifically.[25,26] In addition, she has studied the wood pigeon,[27] the black-headed gull,[28] and the mountain chough (a relative of the crow).[29] Perhaps her most arresting discovery was that wood pigeons with darkened plumage, which appeared in England in the winter months, were suffering from tuberculosis of the adrenal glands. Previously, they were thought seasonal migrants from another country. This discovery was economically important, because wood pigeons were a major source of avian tuberculosis among cattle. Unfortunately, Rothschild's discovery was made during World War II and wartime censorship prohibited publication of these findings.[30,31]

Rothschild never completely abandoned her childhood interest in butterflies. When she married in 1942 and began having children of her own, this interest was resurrected. After all, children are most easily introduced to natural history through these colorful creatures. Rothschild had four children and adopted two more. Her oldest son, Charles Lane, is now a biochemist. She credits him with inspiring, at the age of ten, many ideas for the new field of plant/insect interactions she pioneered through butterfly studies.[30]

One of Rothschild's major contributions to this field was her research on the defensive use by insects of toxic plant secondary substances. Secondary substances are plant products other than those necessary to sustain growth. Some of these substances are used in plant defense, but the function of many is unknown. Caffeine and digitalis are examples of plant secondary substances useful to humans.

According to *SCI* for the period 1955-1983, Rothschild's most-cited experimental paper in this field, cited 75 times, concerns heart poisons in the monarch butterfly.[32] This was published jointly with Tadeus Reichstein and Josef von Euw, both of the University of Basel, Switzerland, and J.A. Parsons, National Institute for Medical Research, London. Reichstein received the Nobel prize in physiology or medicine in 1950 for his work on the hormones of the adrenal cortex, including the isolation of cortisone.

This highly cited paper shows that heart poisons, which are present in some species of the milkweed plant family, are ingested and stored by the monarch butterfly species that feeds on milkweeds. These butterflies, having developed an immunity to the heart poisons, use them for defense. The poisons make the insect indigestible (or at least distasteful) to many predators such as birds and spiders. The presence of these poisons in milkweeds also reduces competition for this food plant from species without immunity.

Rothschild and associates have discovered toxic or distasteful secondary substances in many insects. For example, they have found cardiac glycosides in aphids,[33] aristolochic acids in swallowtail butterflies,[34] and pyrrolizidine alkaloids in tiger moths.[35] In addition, Rothschild has shown that many butterflies secrete toxic substances themselves. One example is the burnet moth, which secretes the potent toxin hydrocyanic acid in all stages of its life cycle.[36]

Rothschild's most-cited paper is a review of secondary plant substances and warning coloration in insects.[37] This *Citation Classic™*[38] has been cited by at least 80 researchers in the past decade. Insects with warning coloration are known as *aposematic* insects. Their bright colors alert predators to their toxicity, so predators will avoid ingesting them. Rothschild discusses the information available on those aposematic insects that take up and store toxins from food plants.

A related area of research is mimicry among insects.[39] Certain species evolve the same warning coloration, and even store the same toxins, as a successful insect "model" species. Warning coloration is directed against birds and other predators that hunt by sight. Rothschild observed that insects also produce defensive *odors* directed against predators that hunt by smell.[40] Since a number of these odors resemble each other, she concluded that mimicry of scent can occur as well as mimicry of warning coloration.

Rothschild's work in warning coloration and mimicry has vindicated the evolutionary insights of such nineteenth-century naturalists as Alfred Wallace, Henry Bates, and Fritz Müller, whose work had been wrongly discredited.[37] These scientists had intuited the presence of toxic substances in insects, but the methods of chemical analysis available at the time were too primitive to provide proof.

Through her research on butterflies, Rothschild has investigated the role of carotenoid pigments in warning or attracting other species or for camouflage. She showed that the pupae of the large white butterfly failed to match their background when their diet lacked carotenoids.[41] Normally this species is highly responsive to the color of background foliage. Also, when monarch pupae were deprived of carotenoids, they developed silver- rather than gold-flecked pupal cases.[42] In her review of carotenoids in the evolution of signaling,[43] Rothschild points out that since carotenoids are involved in both photoreception and vision throughout the animal kingdom, they must be an important factor in signal reception. She also reviews cases of both plants and animals using carotenoids in body parts displayed to warn or attract other species.

Behavior is another aspect of Rothschild's butterfly studies. She has demonstrated the large white butterfly's ability to assess the egg load on a plant or leaf.[44] The butterfly responds to visual cues, such as damaged foliage or the presence of feeding larvae. It also responds to such olfactory cues as an airborne emanation from eggs already laid on a leaf. When the butterfly detects these cues, it switches to another leaf, plant, or species. In this way, it avoids overloading the host plant and ensures an adequate food supply for the new generation.

Rothschild's fresh and startling observations put her at the forefront of a new wave of ecological research in the 1970s. Jeffrey Harborne, University of Reading, England, identified ecological biochemistry as a new interdisciplinary field that has grown up since the late 1960s. He credits Rothschild with playing a seminal role in developing this field: "By her own pioneering experiments with aposematic insects and equally her encouragement of other scientists, Dr. Rothschild has contributed more than anyone else to this new subject...."[45] (p. vi) Similarly, E.B. Ford, University of Oxford, in describing another relatively new field, ecological genetics, also cites Rothschild's contributions.[46] Ecological genetics is the experimental study of evolution and adaptation conducted in both the field and the laboratory. Ford notes, "It is to Rothschild and Clay (1952) that we owe the general analysis of brood parasitism in birds; one which has demonstrated the principles of its evolution."[46] (p. 259) He also cites her work in mimicry, plant toxins, maturation of fleas on hosts, poisons in aposematic insects, and toxic butterflies.

Rothschild has received many honors for her scientific contributions. These include the H.H. Bloomer Medal from the Linnean Society of London, which she received in 1968. She has also been made an honorary fellow of the Royal Entomological Society of London and an honorary fellow of the American Society of Parasitology. In recognition of her scientific merit, she was made a Commander of the British Empire in 1983.

Rothschild has recently been invited to deliver the Romanes Lecture for 1984-1985 at the University of Oxford. This lecture was first given in 1892 by William Gladstone. Since then, the long list of illustrious Romanes lecturers has included John Masefield, Winston Churchill, and Peter Medawar, among others.

Rothschild's memberships in professional associations include the American Academy of Arts and Sciences, the Royal Entomological Society of London, the Zoological Society of London, the Marine Biological Association of the United Kingdom, and the Linnean Society of London. She has also been a trustee of the British Museum of Natural History.

Rothschild edited *Novitates Zoologicae*, the official publication of Tring Museum, from 1938 to 1941. She has also been a member of the publications committees of the Zoological Society of London and the Marine Biological Association of the United Kingdom. She has generously edited the work of many individual scientists as well.

Rothschild's diverse scientific interests would be enough to occupy several lifetimes. But, in addition, she has supported herself, her family, and her scientific researches through farming. She considers herself a farmer as well as an experimental biologist. Her farm is situated at Ashton Wold, Peterborough, Northamptonshire, England, on an estate established by her father. Over the years, she has received a number of gold medals from the Royal Horticultural Society for fruit and vegetable cultivation. Also, the walls of one of her rooms at Ashton Wold are papered with ribbons and awards for raising prizewinning domestic animals. Her farming success has enabled her to finance all her scientific activities. In the past 60 years, she has accepted only one grant of any kind, a travel grant to a conference.

Rothschild has also been active in a broad range of civic and social causes. During World War II she joined with a group of distinguished scientists working in cryptography to crack the German secret code. She received a Defence Medal from the British Government for her work. She also aided refugee Jewish scientists during and after the war, often housing them in her own home.

Her humanitarian activities include founding the Schizophrenia Research Fund, based in London. This fund is dedicated to promoting the understanding, treatment, and cure of schizophrenia and other mental illnesses. She also helped marshal scientific evidence on homosexuality for the Wolfenden committee. This government committee produced a report[47] in 1957 that helped decriminalize homosexuality in England.

Rothschild is a strong proponent of natural resource conservation. Her latest conservation effort is to cultivate the native flora of the British Isles. To counteract the increasing encroachment of monoculture grain crops on native meadowland, she has been experimenting with growing wildflowers from seed.

Wildflowers are difficult to cultivate on a large scale, but Rothschild has developed special techniques that permit seeds to be harvested and sown elsewhere. She has recreated a Northamptonshire primitive flowering meadow containing 100 species. The Royal Horticultural Society has awarded her a gold medal for wildflower cultivation. Her efforts have generated tremendous public interest, and she is supplying seeds to other farmers and gardeners. She hopes that public bodies will adopt the practice of sowing wildflower seeds in parks and along roadsides. She recently published a book on growing wildflowers in small gardens.[48]

For some time now, it's been fashionable to deplore the specialization of scientists and other professionals in narrow subfields. Yet, as with the weather, everybody talks about overspecialization, but nobody does anything about it. Most people simply conform. Rothschild, in contrast, has dedicated her life to the untrammeled pursuit of a wide front of intellectual interests. By following her own path, she found herself at the forefront of some of the most interesting ecological researches of the 1970s. Her entire career is testimony to that most essential ingredient of original scientific research—imagination. It is a great pleasure for me to pay her a small measure of the tribute that is her due.

* * * * *

My thanks to Patricia Lawson and Amy Stone for their help in the preparation of this essay.   ©1984 ISI

REFERENCES

1. **Garfield E.** Science communication and the continuing mission of ISI Press. *Current Contents* (51):5-11, 19 December 1983.
2. **Rothschild M.** *Dear Lord Rothschild: birds, butterflies and history.* Philadelphia/London: ISI Press/Hutchinson, 1983. 398 p.
3. **Ryan A.** Zoological fairyland in Tring. Review of "Dear Lord Rothschild: birds, butterflies and history" by M. Rothschild. *New Scientist* 100:937, 1983.
4. **Cain A J.** Natural history and the rogue elephant. Review of "Dear Lord Rothschild: birds, butterflies and history" by M. Rothschild. *Nature* 306:506-7, 1983.
5. **Cannadine D.** Family fortunes. Review of "The English Rothschilds" by R. Davis and "Dear Lord Rothschild: birds, butterflies and history" by M. Rothschild. *Sunday Times* (London) 12 February 1984, p. 43.
6. **FitzGibbon F.** Dear Lord Rothschild. Review of "Dear Lord Rothschild: birds, butterflies and history" by M. Rothschild. *Evening Telegraph* 3 December 1983, p. 9.
7. **Garfield E.** Journal citation studies. 41. Entomology journals—what they cite and what cites them. *Current Contents* (11):3-11, 12 March 1984.
8. **Rothschild M.** Hooked on histology. *Natur. Hist.* 77(6):44-5, 1968.
9. ------------------. Gigantism and variation in *Peringia ulvae* Pennant 1777, caused by infection with larval trematodes. *J. Mar. Biol. Assn. UK* 20:537-46, 1936.
10. ------------------. Further observations on the effect of trematode parasites on *Peringia ulvae* (Pennant) 1777. *Novitat. Zool.* 41:84-102, 1938.
11. ------------------. Observations on the growth and trematode infections of *Peringia ulvae* (Pennant) 1777 in a pool in the Tamar saltings, Plymouth. *Parasitology* 33:406-15, 1941.
12. **Rothschild N C.** New species of *Siphonaptera* from Egypt and the Soudan. *Entomol. Mon. Mag.* 39:83-7, 1903.
13. **Hopkins G H E & Rothschild M.** *An illustrated catalogue of the Rothschild collection of fleas (Siphonaptera) in the British Museum.* London: Trustees of the British Museum (Natural History), 1953-1971. 5 vols.
14. **Traub R, Rothschild M & Haddow J F.** *The Rothschild collection of fleas. The Ceratophyllidae: key to the genera and host relationships.* London: Academic Press, 1983. 288 p.
15. **Rothschild M & Clay T.** *Fleas, flukes & cuckoos.* London: Collins, 1952. 304 p.
16. **Mead-Briggs A R & Rudge A J B.** Breeding of the rabbit flea, *Spilopsyllus cuniculi* (Dale): requirement of a factor from a pregnant rabbit for ovarian maturation. *Nature* 187:1136-7, 1960.

17. **Rothschild M & Ford B.** Maturation and egg-laying of the rabbit flea (*Spilopsyllus cuniculi* Dale) induced by the external application of hydrocortisone. *Nature* 203:210-1, 1964.
18. ------------------------------. Factors influencing the breeding of the rabbit flea (*Spilopsyllus cuniculi*): a spring-time accelerator and a kairomone in nestling rabbit urine with notes on *Cediopsylla simplex*, another "hormone bound" species. *J. Zool.* 170:87-137, 1973.
19. **Rothschild M, Ford B & Hughes M.** Maturation of the male rabbit flea (*Spilopsyllus cuniculi*) and the oriental rat flea (*Xenopsylla cheopis*): some effects of mammalian hormones on development and impregnation. *Trans. Zool. Soc. London* 32:105-88, 1970.
20. **Rothschild M & Ford B.** Breeding of the rabbit flea (*Spilopsyllus cuniculi* (Dale)) controlled by the reproductive hormones of the host. *Natur* 201:103-4, 1964.
21. **Rothschild M, Schlein Y, Parker K & Stern J** . Jump of the oriental rat flea *Xenopsylla cheopis* (Roths.). *Nature* 239:45-8, 1972.
22. **Rothschild M & Schlein J.** The jumping mechanism of *Xenopsylla cheopis*. I. Exoskeletal structures and musculature. *Phil. Trans. Roy. Soc. London B* 271:457-90, 1975.
23. **Rothschild M, Schlein J, Parker K, Neville C & Sternberg S.** The jumping mechanism of *Xenopsylla cheopis*. III. Execution of the jump and activity. *Phil. Trans. Roy. Soc. London B* 271:499-515, 1975.
24. *Honorary Degree of Doctor of Science for the Honorable Mrs. Miriam Lane.* Unpublished speech delivered at the University of Oxford, UK. 24 February 1968. 1 p.
25. **Rothschild M.** A collection of fleas from the bodies of British birds, with notes on their distribution and host preferences. *Bull. Brit. Museum (Natur. Hist.) Ser. Entomol.* 2:185-232, 1952.
26. ------------------. The bird fleas of Fair Isle. *Parasitology* 48:382-412, 1958.
27. ------------------. Some problems connected with the wood-pigeon (*Columba palumbus* L.) and its control in Britain. *XIIIe Congrès International de Zoologie. Comptes rendus*, 21-27 July 1948, Paris. Paris, 1949. p. 480-1.
28. ------------------. Development of paddling and other movements in young black-headed gulls. *Brit. Birds* 55:114-7, 1962.
29. ------------------. Diurnal movements of the mountain chough (*Pyrrhocorax graculus*) in the Wengen and Kleine Scheidegg (Bernese Oberland) areas during the months of January, February and March. *Acta XI Congressus Internationalis Ornithologici*, 29 May-5 June 1954, Basel. Basel: Berhäuser Verlag, 1955. p. 611-7.
30. ------------------. Telephone communication. 5 March 1984.
31. **McDiarmid A.** The occurrence of tuberculosis in the wild wood-pigeon. *J. Comp. Pathol. Ther.* 58:130-3, 1948.
32. **Reichstein T, von Euw J, Parsons J A & Rothschild M.** Heart poisons in the monarch butterfly. *Science* 161:861-6, 1968.
33. **Rothschild M, von Euw J & Reichstein T.** Cardiac glycosides in the oleander aphid, *Aphis nerii*. *J. Insect Physiol.* 16:1141-5, 1970.
34. --. Aristolochic acids stored by *Zerynthia polyxena* (Lepidoptera). *Insect Biochem.* 2:334-43, 1972.
35. **Rothschild M, Aplin R T, Cockrum P A, Edgar J A, Fairweather P & Lees R.** Pyrrolizidine alkaloids in arctiid moths (Lep.) with a discussion on host plant relationships and the role of these secondary plant substances in the Arctiidae. *Biol. J. Linn. Soc.* 12:305-26, 1979.
36. **Jones D A, Parsons J & Rothschild M.** Release of hydrocyanic acid from crushed tissues of all stages in the life-cycle of species of the Zygaeninae (Lepidoptera). *Nature* 193:52-3, 1962.
37. **Rothschild M.** Secondary plant substances and warning colouration in insects. (van Emden H F, ed.) *Insect/plant relationships.* Oxford: Blackwell Scientific Publishers, 1972. p. 59-83.
38. ------------------. Citation Classic. Commentary on *Insect/plant relationships*. Oxford: Blackwell Scientific Publishers, 1972. p. 59-83. *Current Contents/Life Sciences* 27(17):17, 23 April 1984.
39. ------------------. Mimicry, butterflies and plants. *Symbol. Botan. Upsal.* 22(4):82-99, 1979.
40. ------------------. Defensive odours and Müllerian mimicry among insects. *Trans. Roy. Entomol. Soc. London* 113:101-21, 1961.
41. **Rothschild M, Gardiner B, Valadon G & Mummery R.** Lack of response to background colour in *Pieris brassicae* pupae reared on carotenoid-free diet. *Nature* 254:592-4, 1975.
42. **Rothschild M, Gardiner B & Mummery R.** The role of carotenoids in the "golden glance" of danaid pupae (Insecta: Lepidoptera). *J. Zool.* 186:351-8, 1978.
43. **Rothschild M.** Remarks on carotenoids in the evolution of signals. (Gilbert L E & Raven P H, eds.) *Coevolution of animals and plants.* Austin: University of Texas Press, 1975. p. 20-50.
44. **Rothschild M & Schoonhoven L M.** Assessment of egg load by *Pieris brassicae* (Lepidoptera: Pieridae). *Nature* 266:352-5, 1977.
45. **Harborne J B.** *Introduction to ecological biochemistry.* New York: Academic Press, 1977. 243 p.
46. **Ford E B.** *Ecological genetics.* London: Chapman and Hall, 1971. 410 p.
47. **Great Britain. Committee on Homosexual Offenses and Prostitution.** *The Wolfenden report.* New York: Stein and Day, 1963. 243 p.
48. **Rothschild M & Farrell C.** *The butterfly gardener.* London: Michael Joseph/Rainbird, 1983. 128 p.

Current Comments®

Why Is the Ancient and Prevalent Disorder Called Agoraphobia a Neglected Research Topic?

Number 18   April 30, 1984

In previous essays, we've covered a number of psychiatric illnesses including autism,[1] schizophrenia,[2] and depression.[3] Depression, we noted, is a particularly disturbing problem because it is so widespread, and so debilitating. Like depression, agoraphobia is an incapacitating illness. Agoraphobia, however, is less known to the general public.

The third edition of the American Psychiatric Association's *Diagnostic and Statistical Manual of Mental Disorders* (*DSM III*)[4] defines phobias as "persistent and irrational fears of an object or situation." To date, scientists have identified phobias ranging from acrophobia, fear of high places, to zoophobia, fear of animals. There is even a phobiaphobia, or fear of fear. But according to the *DSM III*, no phobia is as "severe or pervasive" as agoraphobia.[4] (p. 225)

The term agoraphobia is derived from two Greek words: *agora*, meaning marketplace or place of assembly, and *phobos*, meaning terror or flight.[5] Robert Burton, the British scholar and writer, first described agoraphobia's symptoms in his 1621 work, *The Anatomy of Melancholy*.[6] It wasn't until 1871, however, that C. Westphal coined the term to describe several of his patients who experienced severe anxiety when walking through streets or squares.[5] According to historical accounts, recounted by Isaac M. Marks, Maudsley Hospital, London, in his book *Fears and Phobias*,[7] the French mathematician Blaise Pascal suffered from agoraphobia, as did the Italian writer Alessandro Manzoni. Manzoni, in fact, carried a bottle of concentrated vinegar with him whenever he left home so that he could revive himself if he felt faint.

In her review of the symptomatology of agoraphobia, Diane L. Chambless, Department of Psychiatry, American University, Washington, DC, writes that the primary symptom of agoraphobia is a fear of being away from home, or in any public place from which escape is viewed as difficult.[8] To an agoraphobic, escape can be "blocked" by physical constraints such as those imposed by crowds, or by social constraints that call for highly ritualized, regimented behavior. For instance, acting as a bridesmaid or being the "mother of the bride" would make many agoraphobics very anxious.

Agoraphobics need to feel that they can escape from any situation readily, because for many, panic attacks can strike anytime. During a panic attack, agoraphobics feel dizzy, nauseous, weak in the limbs, and short of breath.[8] Throughout these attacks, agoraphobics may worry that their pounding heart or dizziness will cause them irreparable harm. Typical thoughts include, "I am going crazy," or "I am having a heart attack (or stroke)."[9]

Agoraphobics, therefore, often find that home is the only place where they feel safe, since even if an attack strikes there it will go unobserved, sparing them public embarrassment. Consequently, although their symptoms may wax and wane, some agoraphobics are housebound for years, sometimes for their entire lives. Obviously, this prevents them from working or maintaining a normal social life. Other agoraphobics can leave home, but only if their spouses or other trusted companions accompany them. J.A. Mullaney and C.J. Trippett, St. Patrick's Hospital, Gosforth, Newcastle upon Tyne, England, now suspect that some alcoholics actually suffer from agoraphobia.[10] In such cases, agoraphobics first turn to alcohol because it relieves the anxiety they feel when venturing outside,[11] according to physician Arthur B. Hardy, a former agoraphobic, who is now director of TERRAP (for *TERR*itorial *AP*prehensiveness), a nonprofit organization which assists agoraphobics. Although they may eventually seek treatment for their alcoholism, their real problem—agoraphobia—will likely remain untreated.

For most agoraphobics, the onset of the illness is sudden. If panic attacks are part of the disorder, the first one usually occurs between ages 18 and 35. Common sites for attacks include supermarkets, elevators, escalators, parties, crowds, tunnels, bridges, airplanes, and theaters.[12] After the attack, the agoraphobic avoids returning to the place where it occurred for fear of triggering another episode. This phobic avoidance then increases to include other places.

In the last few years, a large volume of literature on agoraphobia has appeared in the scientific as well as the popular press. Marks traces the emergence of this interest to a 1965 BBC radio broadcast about agoraphobia.[7] After the broadcast, 300 listeners wrote to the station for further information. The program generated such interest that eventually an organization to help agoraphobics was established—the Open Door Organization. Within a few months, 1,600 people had joined the group.[7] Incidentally, we did a search of *Science Citation Index*® (*SCI*®) and *Social Sciences Citation Index*® (*SSCI*®): Marks's book, *Fears and Phobias*,[7] which reviews the phenomenology and treatment of phobias, including agoraphobia, has been cited over 325 times since its publication in 1969, qualifying it as a *Citation Classic*™.[13]

According to a study by Stewart Agras, Department of Psychiatry, University of Vermont, Burlington, and colleagues, from one to two million people in the US alone suffer from agoraphobia,[14] although the actual number of victims may be much higher. Since agoraphobics are reluctant to leave home, many are never identified. Often ashamed or embarrassed by their symptoms, they may become so adept at avoiding fear-inducing situations that even their spouses may not realize they have the disorder,[15] according to Claire Weekes, Rachel Forster Hospital, Cremorne Point, Australia.

There are several theories regarding the etiology of agoraphobia. One prominent view is supported by Weekes, Chambless, and Alan J. Goldstein, Department of Psychiatry, Temple University Medical School, Philadelphia. They believe that stress precipitates the first panic attack.[16,17] Events which can trigger an attack include the death of a loved one, a miscarriage, or a divorce. Even happy events such as childbirth or marriage can elicit an attack, since they can also promote stress.[9]

For years, the etiology of agoraphobia was described in terms of psychoanalytic theory, as Wallace H. Vale and Sylvester R. Mlott, Department of Psychiatry, Medical University of South Carolina, Charleston, note in their review of agoraphobia.[18] This rests upon the premise that earlier, usually infantile, traumas account for adult neuroses. In his review of psychoanalytic theories, John Bowlby, Tavistock Clinic, London, noted that some adherents of a psychoanalytic viewpoint believed that an agoraphobic's fear of leaving home indicated a need to return to the security provided by one's parents.[19] Freud, on the other hand, believed that agoraphobia, like all phobias, was part of an "anxiety neurosis" and had a sexual origin.[20] However, such psychoanalytic theories lack empirical support.[21]

Many behavioral scientists now use one of several etiological models to explain the onset of the disease. Some view the onset of the disorder in terms of operant conditioning, whereby behaviors are acquired or eliminated depending on their consequences.[17] Accordingly, behavior that is rewarded or *positively reinforced* will be acquired, whereas behavior that is punished will be eliminated.

In the view of Kathleen A. Brehony, Department of Psychology, Virginia Polytechnic Institute and State University, Blacksburg, behavior theory may help explain why approximately 85 percent of all known agoraphobics are women. She believes that societal conditioning of women serves as a powerful backdrop for the development of agoraphobic behavior.[22] In her classic paper,[23,24] Sandra L. Bem, Department of Psychology, Stanford University, California, asserts that males are reinforced for behavior that is aggressive, independent, and competent. Females, however, are reinforced for submissive, passive, fearful, and nonassertive behavior[23]—behavior that is characteristic of agoraphobics. After reviewing the literature linking agoraphobia with women, Brehony was prompted to ask, " 'Why are not all women agoraphobic?' rather than, 'Why are some women agoraphobic?' "[22]

Male agoraphobics are less likely to be as severely homebound as their female counterparts. This may also be due to societal stereotyping. Traditionally, men are expected to be the breadwinners, which usually requires them to work outside the home. Most male agoraphobics learn to tolerate the trip to and from work, but venturing elsewhere makes them anxious. Weekes calls this the "city-bound executive syndrome."[16]

Other researchers are investigating a possible biochemical basis for agoraphobia. In the mid-1970s, D. Eugene Redmond, Department of Psychiatry, Yale University, New Haven, Connecticut, and colleagues discovered that victims of panic attacks produced an excess of brain norepinephrine and other neurotransmitters.[25] Neurotransmitters are chemical carriers that transport message impulses across nerve synapses. Indeed, certain drugs such as imipramine and phenelzine, which decrease norepinephrine production, also block panic attacks. Although these drugs have complex effects, in their review of the literature, Dennis S. Charney, Yale University School of Medicine, and colleagues report some scientists believe that their antipanic effects may be due to their effect on norepinephrine.[26]

As with other psychiatric illnesses, there may be a genetic basis for agoraphobia. Several studies found a higher incidence of phobias among family members than among the general public. In a study by R.C. Bowen and J. Kohout, Department of Psychiatry, University of Saskatchewan, Saskatoon, Canada, 84 percent of the agoraphobics questioned could identify a close relative who suffered from an emotional disorder.[27] Moreover, a study by Gregory Carey, University of Minnesota, Minneapolis, found that agoraphobia was more prevalent among identical twins than among fraternal twins.[28]

For agoraphobia to be effectively treated it must, of course, be accurately diagnosed. But this can take years. Seventy percent of the agoraphobics participating in a study by David V. Sheehan, Department of Psychiatry, Massachusetts General Hospital, Boston, and colleagues reported seeing ten or more physicians before a correct diagnosis was made.[29]

Typically, agoraphobics first approach their family physician after experiencing one or more panic attacks. Often, physicians focus on the physiological components such as the patient's pounding heart or dizziness.[21] They may then prescribe diazepam (Valium) or another antianxiety agent. In fact, a nationwide survey of agoraphobics by E.H. Uhlenhuth, Department of Psychiatry, University of Chicago, Illinois, and colleagues found that a full 55 percent had used an antianxiety agent.[30] Ninety-eight percent of the patients participating in the Sheehan study said that they had been treated with what were often very high doses of tranquilizers for up to 15 years.[29] Whether these agents actually reduce panic attacks is still under debate. While the prevailing opinion has been that these agents are ineffective against panic attacks,[31] a recent paper by Russell Noyes and colleagues, Department of Psychiatry, University of Iowa, College of Medicine, Iowa City, reports the results of a study which found that "diazepam reduced the number and severity of panic attacks."[31]

Diagnosed agoraphobics rarely recover from the disorder without professional assistance. And since misdiagnosis is prevalent, the outlook for most patients has been bleak,[32] according to Lars Jansson and Lars-Göran Öst, Psychiatric Research Center, Ulleråker Hospital, Uppsala, Sweden. However, for those who do receive competent professional help, at least partial recovery is likely.

Up until the early 1960s, psychiatrists usually treated agoraphobics with psychotherapy. This is not surprising considering psychotherapy's popularity at the time, and the paucity of other available treatments. Chambless and Goldstein, however, believe that psychotherapy by itself is impotent against agoraphobia.[9] By the way, they are the editors of *Agoraphobia: Multiple Perspectives on Theory and Treatment*,[33] a comprehensive overview of agoraphobia which was used heavily in preparing this essay.

In the mid-1960s, some therapists began treating agoraphobia with systematic desensitization which, as Matig Mavissakalian, Western Psychiatric Institute and Clinic, and University of Pittsburgh School of Medicine, Pennsylvania, and David H. Barlow, Department of Psychology, State University of New York, Albany, note in their review of phobias, was then being used to successfully treat many other phobias.[34] Systematic desensitization involves exposing the phobic to the objects or places feared after relaxation exercises are mastered. The exposure is graduated. In several steps, a snake phobic, for example, would progress from just viewing a picture of a snake, to actually handling one. In their review of agoraphobia, however, Jansson and Öst cite studies indicating that systematic desensitization is not effective in treating agoraphobia,[32] probably because it does not allow the patient to experience anxiety in the phobic situation.[17] Although following systematic desensitization agoraphobics may think they are cured, panic attacks usually recur.

The primary behavioral treatment now used is exposure therapy, of which there are two types: imaginal exposure and exposure *in vivo*. During imaginal exposure, the therapist describes in detail situations that the patient previously stated were fearful. When this is done gradually, following relaxation exercises, the therapy closely approximates systematic densensitization. Imaginal exposure, however, can also be conducted rapidly, in which case the therapist forces the patient to visualize the fearful situation until reported anxiety decreases.[32] Rapid exposure is sometimes called "flooding."

In vivo exposure, on the other hand, involves real-life practice. The agoraphobic actually enters the dreaded situations. As with imaginal exposure, *in vivo* exposure can be conducted either gradually or rapidly.[32]

Exposure methods are not only effective, they work quickly and patients can learn them easily. A homebound person treated by exposure may be able to enter a local shop on the first session, a suburban shopping center during the second, and center city on the third.[35] And, in a study of agoraphobics treated by exposure, Paul M.G. Emmelkamp, Academic Hospital, Department of Clinical Psychology, Groningen, the Netherlands, found that once improvements are made, they last. Relapses are rare. Emmelkamp also found that four years after *in vivo* exposure, patients remained improved.[36]

For financial reasons, therapists often administer exposure therapy to a group of patients rather than to individuals.[9] Group therapy also gives agoraphobics the chance to meet each other, and thus learn that their affliction is not unique. As with Alcoholics Anonymous, they can share coping methods, and form close friendships which they so desperately need.

Not all agoraphobics can be treated with exposure therapy. *In vivo* therapy, in particular, can be very hard on some patients, especially men. A study by R. Julian Hafner, Flinders Medical Centre, Australia, found that of 18 male patients offered graded exposure *in vivo*, 44 percent refused or dropped out prematurely.[37] Only 12 percent of the women subjects refused or terminated treatment prematurely. The study also found, however, that those men who did follow through with the treatment benefited from it as much as the women.

Overall, 60 to 70 percent of patients who undergo exposure therapy improve.[32,38] It is likely that as a result of a therapeutic regimen based on exposure therapy, a patient will be able to lead a life relatively free of panic attacks. Occasionally, however, he or she will probably still be troubled by some of agoraphobia's symptoms. In fact, residual disability is the norm.[38]

Drug therapy is the other major treatment that clinicians use. The successful use of drugs to treat agoraphobia was first reported in a 1962 paper by Donald F. Klein, US Public Health Service, and Max Fink, Hillside Hospital, Glen Oaks, New York.[39] Between October 1958 and July 1961, Klein and Fink treated 125 agoraphobics with imipramine, a tricyclic antidepressant. They found that the drug effectively eliminated the panic attacks associated with the disorder.[39]

Since that time, Klein, Sheehan, and others have found that two classes of antidepressants are effective against the panic attacks associated with agoraphobia: the tricyclic antidepressants and the monoamine-oxidase (MAO) inhibitors.[40] Imipramine remains the most commonly used tricyclic, and is usually prescribed first. If imipramine should fail, psychiatrists may prescribe phenelzine, the most commonly used MAO inhibitor. According to Robert Pohl, Department of Psychiatry, Wayne State University, Detroit, Michigan, and colleagues, imipramine is usually tried first because it does not place the harsh restrictions on one's diet that phenelzine does.[41] Patients taking MAO inhibitors can experience severe and even lethal high blood pressure if they eat foods containing the amino acid tyramine. Examples of such foods are pickled herring, aged cheese, chicken liver, and certain wines.[42]

Antidepressants do not work immediately. It may take up to six weeks of treatment before their effectiveness is apparent.[41] After attacks are relieved, therapists usually continue treatment for six months. Although at that point the patient may be free of panic attacks, it's likely that eventually they will recur. Renewed treatment, however, will once again halt the attacks.

The existence of *ISI/BIOMED®* research front #82-3495, "Clonidine and imipramine and tricyclic antidepressant clinical psychotherapeutic drugs for treating depression, agoraphobia, and panic attacks," is evidence of the current interest in using drug therapy to treat agoraphobia and other affective disorders. Two core papers are associated with this front: "Treatment of agoraphobia with group exposure in vivo and imipramine,"[43] by Klein, Charlotte M. Zitrin, and Margaret G. Woerner, Long Island Jewish-Hillside Medical Center, Glen Oaks, New York, and "Treatment of endogenous anxiety with phobic, hysterical, and hypochondriacal symptoms,"[29] by Sheehan, James Ballenger, University of Virginia School of Medicine, Charlottesville, and Gary Jacobsen, Westwood Lodge Hospital, Westwood, Massachusetts. To date, over 50 publications have cited one or both of these papers, which were published in 1980 in the same issue of *Archives of General Psychiatry*. The first paper gives the results of a double-blind study that compared the effectiveness of group exposure *in vivo*, combined with the use of either imipramine or a placebo. The study found that while a majority of patients in both groups showed at least moderate improvement, imipramine-treated patients fared better than placebo-treated patients. In the study reported in the second paper, in addition to a placebo and imipramine group, a third group received the MAO inhibitor phenelzine sulfate. Patients assigned to the imipramine and phenelzine groups improved much more than the patients in the placebo group. In addition, phenelzine-treated patients showed more improvement than the imipramine-treated patients.

Given these results, it's not surprising that Klein and several other researchers enthusiastically recommend the use of antidepressants for agoraphobia. In addition to the studies described here, they cite others that show these drugs often block panic attacks, and that 70 percent of the patients treated improve to some extent.[44]

Although these results are encouraging, there are many critics of drug therapy. Imipramine, for example, can have side effects. Even small doses of the drug can produce insomnia, jitteriness, irritability, and palpitations, and will exacerbate panic attacks in one in five agoraphobics.[45] Although in such cases other drugs can be used,[45] many agoraphobics refuse to use these drugs at all.

Chambless and Goldstein have reported that over 25 percent of their agoraphobic patients refuse to take imipramine "because of hypochondriacal concerns, fears of drug-induced discontrol, or adverse reactions to previous drugs."[9] Moreover, they report that most of the remaining 75 percent of their patients are afraid or otherwise hesitant to use the medication. One patient had a full-blown panic attack on the first two nights when it was time for her to take the medication.

In their review of the literature, Michael J. Telch, Blake H. Tearnan, and C. Barr Taylor, Stanford University School of Medicine, California, found that of those who do go through with drug therapy, 35 to 40 percent drop out.[46] This compares to a drop out rate of about ten percent for drug-free behavioral treatments. Also, the relapse rate following discontinuation of drugs is much higher than for exposure therapy. They found that between 27 and 50 percent of patients who improve after drug therapy relapse after withdrawal.[46]

Current therapeutic regimens often comprise elements of both drug and behavior therapy, which seems to reflect a coming together of the two camps. In fact, S. Rovner for the *Washington Post* described a May 1983 meeting on phobia treatments held in White Plains, New York, as "a veritable love feast between the behaviorists and medical model proponents."[47] Many behaviorists, however, still use drugs only for particularly stubborn cases, or for patients who don't wish to take part in behavior therapy. Goldstein has written that the great majority of his patients "cease having panic attacks without the use of medication."[48] On the other hand, some drug proponents such as Klein and Michael R. Liebowitz, Department of Psychiatry, Columbia University, New York, will only use behavior therapy by itself when patients are no longer experiencing spontaneous panic attacks.[49]

While most psychiatrists treat agoraphobics with either drug or behavioral therapy or a combination of both, some recommend a self-help program of treatment. Such programs have appeal because they greatly reduce the need for a therapist's costly time. One of the best-known proponents of self-help therapy for agoraphobics is Weekes. Between 1966 and 1974, Weekes treated 2,000 agoraphobics through "remote direction."[16] This is basically exposure therapy. But instead of personally accompanying patients when they leave home, Weekes encourages them by telephone to conduct the exposure sessions on their own. Then, throughout the therapy program, patients periodically call in to report on their progress. Weekes's patients can also receive instruction through her three books,[15,50,51] a record album, cassettes, and a quarterly magazine.[16]

Recently, Arthur E. Holden, Center for Stress and Anxiety Disorders, State University of New York, Albany, and colleagues have criticized self-help strategies for agoraphobia. They found that subjects in a self-help program consisting of *in vivo* therapy did not perform the practice required by the manual given them.[52] They also criticized Weekes's claims that her strategies were effective since she used questionnaires to assess effectiveness and her improvement criteria were not made clear.[52]

Through drug and behavior therapy, therapists can now control the most severe symptoms of the disease. But few scientists currently feel the disorder can be cured. Agoraphobics can be brought to the point where they are "in control," but remnants of the disorder commonly persist.[53]

If scientists are to improve on this success rate, they must find new drugs that do not present imipramine's side effects. One promising drug which is receiving increasing attention in the literature is alprazolam (marketed by Upjohn Company under the trade name Xanax). According to Guy Chouinard, Department of Psychiatry, McGill University, Montreal, Canada, and colleagues, alprazolam seems to be effective against panic attacks.[54] Moreover, alprazolam does not seem to cause the side effects associated with antidepressants although, like other benzodiazepines, it may induce drowsiness.[54]

But therapists may also have to view agoraphobia in a larger context. Previously, most therapists did not consider the effect family members might have. A number of researchers have found that family members can help agoraphobics. But in other cases, the spouse can severely impede progress.

Frank Milton, Kenley Ward Kingston Hospital, Kingston-on-Thames, Surrey, England, and Hafner, then at St. George's Hospital Medical School, London, studied 15 agoraphobics. They found that in nine cases, when symptoms improved, marriages deteriorated.[55] In a study of 25 patients, Chambless and Goldstein found that only those that divorced their spouses remained improved.[9] However, a former agoraphobic, Ruth Mass, Miami, Florida, has formed several self-help groups for agoraphobics. Out of 50 members, only one out of six married patients divorced after treatment.[56]

Table 1: A selected list of organizations that counsel agoraphobics.

Agoraphobia and Anxiety Center
Temple University
3975 Conshohocken Avenue
Philadelphia, PA 19131

Freedom from Fear Foundation
Box 261
Etobicoke, Ontario M9C 4V3
Canada

Jovicin Foundation for Agoraphobic Recovery
6569 Cleomoore Avenue
Canoga Park, CA 91307

P.A.S.S. Group Inc.
1042 East 105th Street
Brooklyn, NY 11236

Phobia Clinic
Long Island Jewish-Hillside Medical Center
76th Avenue and 266 Street
Glen Oaks, NY 11004

Phobia Clinic
White Plains Hospital Medical Center
Davis Avenue at East Post Road
White Plains, NY 10601

Phobia Society of America
6191 Executive Boulevard
Rockville, MD 20852

Phobics Society
4 Cheltenham Road
Chorlton-cum-Hardy
Manchester M21 1QN
UK

TERRAP
T.S.C. Corporation
1010 Doyle Street
Menlo Park, CA 94025

Part of the problem may be that agoraphobics often choose mates that they know will care for them as a parent would.[57] Subsequently, a symbiotic relationship can form where the spouse needs the agoraphobic as much as the agoraphobic needs the spouse. In one case, the husband of an agoraphobic developed a paranoid psychosis one month after the successful treatment of his wife. He recovered shortly after his wife resumed her agoraphobic ways.[55]

Other family members can also hamper the agoraphobic's progress by overprotection. They may insist on accompanying the agoraphobic on forays outside the "circle of safety,"[32] thus keeping the patient from coming to terms with the disorder. To prevent such problems, Hafner recommends that members of an agoraphobic's immediate family also undergo treatment. This therapy should include education as to the nature of agoraphobia, advice on dealing with the effect the disorder has on family life, and help in coping with the changes that will occur after the agoraphobic's symptoms improve.[57]

Agoraphobics can now turn to a number of organizations for help. The most prominent of these is TERRAP, mentioned earlier. TERRAP was organized in 1964 by Hardy and several other former agoraphobics. Since that time, Hardy and other TERRAP therapists have treated 5,000-6,000 agoraphobics through their 43 treatment centers located in 26 states. The treatment usually consists of exposure *in vivo*, conducted in groups. Another well-known organization that specializes in treating agoraphobics is the Phobia Clinic, White Plains Hospital Medical Center, New York. The treatment at White Plains is termed "contextual therapy," and was developed by clinic director Manuel D. Zane.[58] Contextual therapy is very similar to exposure therapy. The therapist travels with the agoraphobic to a setting where the phobic reaction occurs. At the setting, the therapist works with the patient to help replace anxious feelings with more constructive ones. They then make as many trips as are needed for the phobic reaction to be extinguished.

Despite the efforts of the organizations cited here, and other groups listed in Table 1, most agoraphobics remain untreated. They find that they cannot drive to the treatment center, or that treatment is too expensive, or unavailable locally. Some 60 to 70 percent of the agoraphobics that contact TERRAP remain afflicted for these reasons.[59] TERRAP director Hardy is now forming a corps of improved agoraphobics who can provide inexpensive help to those unable to visit a TERRAP center.[59] But it will take further bold and creative steps on the part of those in a position to help before the many victims of this disorder can lead normal lives.

* * * * *

My thanks to Brad Schepp and Amy Stone for their help in the preparation of this essay.

REFERENCES

1. **Garfield E.** Autism: few answers for a baffling disease. *Essays of an information scientist.* Philadelphia: ISI Press, 1983. Vol. 5. p. 406-16.
2. --------------. What do we know about the group of mental disorders called schizophrenia? Part 1: etiology. Part 2: diagnosis and treatment. *Current Contents* (25):5-13, 20 June 1983 and (27):5-16, 4 July 1983.
3. --------------. What do we know about depression? Part 1: etiology. Part 2: diagnosis and treatment. Part 3: children and adolescents. *Essays of an information scientist.* Philadelphia: ISI Press, 1983. Vol. 5. p. 100-15; 157-63.
4. **American Psychiatric Association.** *Diagnostic and statistical manual of mental disorders.* Washington, DC: APA, 1980. 494 p.

5. **Westphal C.** Die Agoraphobia, Eine neuropathische Erscheinung. (Agoraphobia, a neuropathological symptom.) *Arch. Psychiat. Nervenkr.* 3:138-61, 1871.
6. **Burton R.** *The anatomy of melancholy.* New York: Tudor, 1927. 1036 p.
7. **Marks I M.** *Fears and phobias.* New York: Academic Press, 1969. 302 p.
8. **Chambless D L.** Characteristics of agoraphobics. (Chambless D L & Goldstein A J, eds.) *Agoraphobia: multiple perspectives on theory and treatment.* New York: Wiley, 1982. p. 1-18.
9. **Chambless D L & Goldstein A J.** Clinical treatment of agoraphobia. (Mavissakalian M & Barlow D H, eds.). *Phobia: psychological and pharmacological treatment.* New York: Guilford Press, 1981. p. 103-44.
10. **Mullaney J A & Trippett C J.** Alcohol dependence and phobias: clinical description and relevance. *Brit. J. Psychiat.* 135:565-73, 1979.
11. **Hardy A B.** *Agoraphobia: symptoms, causes, treatment.* (Brochure.) Menlo Park, CA: TERRAP, 1976. 42 p.
12. **Vose R H.** *Agoraphobia.* London: Faber and Faber, 1981. 204 p.
13. **Marks I M.** Citation Classic. Commentary on *Fears and phobias.* New York: Academic Press, 1969. 302 p. *Current Contents/Social & Behavioral Sciences* 12(48):10, 1 December 1980.
14. **Agras S, Sylvester D & Oliveau D.** The epidemiology of common fears and phobia. *Compr. Psychiat.* 10:151-6, 1969.
15. **Weekes C.** *Hope and help for your nerves.* New York: Bantam, 1981. 212 p.
16. ----------. Simple, effective treatment of agoraphobia. *Amer. J. Psychother.* 32:357-69, 1978.
17. **Goldstein A J & Chambless D L.** A reanalysis of agoraphobia. *Behav. Ther.* 9:47-59, 1978.
18. **Vale W H & Mlott S R.** Agoraphobia: a review for the physician. *Southern Med. J.* 73:1607-10, 1980.
19. **Bowlby J.** Anxious attachment and "agoraphobia." *Attachment and loss. Volume II. Separation: anxiety and anger.* New York: Basic, 1973. p. 292-312.
20. **Freud S.** Obsessions and phobias. (Strachey J, ed.) *The standard edition of the complete psychological works of Sigmund Freud.* London: Hogarth Press, 1962. Vol. III. p. 74-84.
21. **Brehony K A & Geller E S.** Agoraphobia: appraisal of research and a proposal for an integrative model. *Progr. Behav. Modif.* 12:1-66, 1981.
22. **Brehony K A.** Women and agoraphobia: a case for the etiological significance of the feminine sex-role stereotype. (Franks V & Rothblum E D, eds.) *The stereotyping of women.* New York: Springer, 1983. p. 112-28.
23. **Bem S L.** The measurement of psychological androgyny. *J. Consult. Clin. Psychol.* 42:155-62, 1974.
24. ----------. Citation Classic. Commentary on *J. Consult. Clin. Psychol.* 42:155-62, 1974. *Current Contents/Social & Behavioral Sciences* 13(41):22, 12 October 1981.
25. **Redmond D E.** New and old evidence for the involvement of a brain norepinephrine system in anxiety. (Fann W E, Karacan I, Pokorny A D & Williams R, eds.) *Phenomenology and treatment of anxiety.* New York: Spectrum, 1979. p. 153-203.
26. **Charney D S, Heninger G R, Hafstad K M, Capelli S & Redmond D E.** Neurobiological mechanisms in human anxiety: recent clinical studies. *Psychopharmacol. Bull.* 19:470-5, 1983.
27. **Bowen R C & Kohout J.** The relationship between agoraphobia and primary affective disorders. *Can. J. Psychiat.* 24:317-22, 1979.
28. **Carey G.** *A clinical-genetic twin study of obsessional and phobic states.* PhD dissertation, University of Minnesota, 1978.
29. **Sheehan D V, Ballenger J & Jacobsen G.** Treatment of endogenous anxiety with phobic, hysterical, and hypochondriacal symptoms. *Arch. Gen. Psychiat.* 37:51-9, 1980.
30. **Uhlenhuth E H, Balter M B, Mellinger G D, Cisin I H & Clinthorne J.** Symptom checklist syndromes in the general population. *Arch. Gen. Psychiat.* 40:1167-73, 1983.
31. **Noyes R, Anderson D J, Clancy J, Crowe R R, Slymen D J, Ghoneim M M & Hinrichs J V.** Diazepam and propranolol in panic disorder and agoraphobia. *Arch. Gen. Psychiat.* 41:287-92, 1984.
32. **Jansson L & Öst L-G.** Behavioral treatments for agoraphobia: an evaluative review. *Clin. Psychol. Rev.* 2:311-36, 1982.
33. **Chambless D L & Goldstein A J,** eds. *Agoraphobia: multiple perspectives on theory and treatment.* New York: Wiley, 1982. 227 p.
34. **Mavissakalian M & Barlow D H.** Phobia: an overview. (Mavissakalian M & Barlow D H, eds.) *Phobia: psychological and pharmacological treatment.* New York: Guilford Press, 1981. p. 1-33.
35. A treatment outline for agoraphobia: the quality assurance project. *Aust. N. Z. J. Psychiat.* 16:25-33, 1982.
36. **Emmelkamp P M G.** *In vivo* treatment of agoraphobia. (Chambless D L & Goldstein A J, eds.) *Agoraphobia: multiple perspectives on theory and treatment.* New York: Wiley, 1982. p. 43-76.
37. **Hafner R J.** Behaviour therapy for agoraphobic men. *Behav. Res. Ther.* 21:51-6, 1983.
38. **Chambless D L.** Telephone communication. 30 December 1983.

39. **Klein D F & Fink M.** Psychiatric reaction patterns to imipramine. *Amer. J. Psychiat.* 119:432-8, 1962.
40. **Sheehan D V.** Current concepts in psychiatry: panic attacks and phobias. *N. Engl. J. Med.* 30:156-8, 1982.
41. **Pohl R, Berchou R & Rainey J M.** Tricyclic antidepressants and monoamine oxidase inhibitors in the treatment of agoraphobia. *J. Clin. Psychopharmacol.* 2:399-407, 1982.
42. **Blackwell B.** Hypertensive crisis due to monoamine-oxidase inhibitors. *Lancet* 2:849-51, 1963.
43. **Zitrin C M, Klein D F & Woerner M G.** Treatment of agoraphobia with group exposure in vivo and imipramine. *Arch. Gen. Psychiat.* 37:63-72, 1980.
44. **Mavissakalian M.** Antidepressants in the treatment of agoraphobia and obsessive-compulsive disorder. *Compr. Psychiat.* 24:278-84, 1983.
45. ----------------------. Pharmacologic treatment of anxiety disorders. *J. Clin. Psychiat.* 43:487-91, 1982.
46. **Telch M J, Tearnan B H & Taylor C B.** Antidepressant medication in the treatment of agoraphobia: a critical review. *Behav. Res. Ther.* 21:505-17, 1983.
47. **Rovner S.** When panic pervades. *Wash. Post* 27 May 1983, p. E5.
48. **Goldstein A J.** Agoraphobia: treatment successes, treatment failures, and theoretical implications. (Chambless D L & Goldstein A J, eds.) *Agoraphobia: multiple perspectives on theory and treatment.* New York: Wiley, 1982. p. 183-213.
49. **Liebowitz M R & Klein D F.** Agoraphobia: clinical features, pathophysiology, and treatment. (Chambless D L & Goldstein A J, eds.) *Agoraphobia: multiple perspectives on theory and treatment.* New York: Wiley, 1982. p. 153-81.
50. **Weekes C.** *Peace from nervous suffering.* New York: Hawthorn, 1972. 206 p.
51. --------------. *Simple, effective treatment of agoraphobia.* New York: Hawthorn, 1976. 168 p.
52. **Holden A E, O'Brien G T, Barlow D H, Stetson D & Infantino A.** Self-help manual for agoraphobia: a preliminary report of effectiveness. *Behav. Ther.* 14:545-56, 1983.
53. **Chambless D L, Foa E B, Groves G A & Goldstein A J.** Exposure and communications training in the treatment of agoraphobia. *Behav. Res. Ther.* 20:219-31, 1982.
54. **Chouinard G, Annable L, Fontaine R & Solyom L.** Alprazolam in the treatment of generalized anxiety of panic disorders: a double-blind, placebo-controlled study. *Psychopharmacol. Bull.* 1:115-6, 1983.
55. **Milton F & Hafner R J.** The outcome of behavior therapy for agoraphobia in relation to marital adjustment. *Arch. Gen. Psychiat.* 36:807-11, 1979.
56. **Mass R.** Telephone communication. 1 April 1984.
57. **Hafner R J.** The marital context of the agoraphobic syndrome. (Chambless D L & Goldstein A J, eds.) *Agoraphobia: multiple perspectives on theory and treatment.* New York: Wiley, 1982. p. 77-117.
58. **Zane M D & Seif M N.** Agoraphobia: contextual analysis and treatment. (Chambless D L & Goldstein A J, eds.) *Agoraphobia: multiple perspectives on theory and treatment.* New York: Wiley, 1982. p. 119-52.
59. **Hardy A B.** Telephone communication. 3 January 1984.

Current Comments®

Latin American Research. Part 1.
Where It Is Published and
How Often It Is Cited

Number 19   May 7, 1984

Last January, I addressed the fifth congress of the National Academy of Medicine of Mexico on the productivity and impact of Latin American research. Naturally, new data were generated for this occasion, but this was not the first citation analysis of Latin American science. A number of excellent studies based on ISI® data have been conducted by Latin American researchers.[1-5] However, these studies concentrated on one field, one scientist, or one nation. The present talk provided data across all fields of science in Central and South America. The main purpose was to review Latin American research in an international context, much as we had done in our earlier report on Third World science.[6]

The data on Latin American science were based on a special file we created from the 1978 *Science Citation Index®* (*SCI®*). This file contains about 3,100 articles whose first authors are affiliated with institutions located in Central and South America. We also determined in what journals and languages these articles were published. Then we used the cumulated *SCI* files for 1978-1982 to find how often each article was cited.

We also kept track of the nationality and language of the *citing* articles. This gives us a unique perspective on international and interlingual citation patterns in the world scientific press. In addition, we identified those specialties in which Latin American researchers had published in 1981. These research front analyses provide insights into *current* areas of research activity in Latin America. They are one example of several modeling techniques one can use to "map" Latin American science.

In Part 1 of this essay, we'll discuss productivity and impact—the number of 1978 *SCI* articles authored in Central and South America, and the number of citations they received from 1978 to 1982. We'll compare these results to similar data for the totality of countries represented in *SCI*. We'll also indicate the journals that published Latin American papers and in what languages. In Part 2, we'll list and discuss the most-cited articles as well as fields of science in which the Latin American contribution is concentrated. That discussion will include maps of the fields in which Latin American scientists were most active.

In 1978, *SCI* indexed more than 500,000 articles published in 2,600 journals. While most of these articles listed an author's address, many were anonymous editorials, obituaries, correction notes, etc. The latter were omitted, as were some substantive articles published in journals that do not provide author affiliations, or give only incomplete addresses. I've discussed the problem of missing or incomplete addresses previously.[7] However, even after all of the above items were removed from the study, more than 388,000 articles remained.

In this study, an article's "nationality" is defined by the country given for the *first* author's address. For example, if an article lists a first author based in Brazil, it is considered a Brazilian paper even though it was coauthored with researchers from other countries. Although this method is not perfect, the "bias" it introduces is minimal. Only four percent of 1979 and 1980 *SCI* articles were internationally coauthored.[8] (p. 229)

Of course, a higher percentage of Latin American papers may be multinationally coauthored. In recent years, the US and Europe have established cooperative scientific agreements with many developing nations, including those in Latin America—joint research projects, exchange of scientists, funding of regional laboratories, etc.[8] (p. 27) The number of collaborative articles produced as a result of such programs is a small proportion of the very large number of articles from the US and Europe. But these articles may represent a significant percentage of Latin American publications because the total output of Latin American science is much smaller compared to that of the US and Europe.

About 3,100, or one percent, of 1978 *SCI* articles listed first authors from Central and South America. Table 1 shows the geographic distribution and impact of all *SCI* articles. The Latin American proportion has remained constant at one percent from 1973 to 1982.

Other indexing services report similar proportions. According to Richard Sharpe, *Chemical Abstracts*, one percent of their 1982 file was from Latin America.[9] And Cathy Ferrere, *Physics Abstracts*, says that Latin American articles account for less than one percent of their current file.[10] As early as 1972, *SCI*'s coverage of the world's literature was shown to be in close agreement, in terms of national distribution, with that of other abstracting services including *Biological Abstracts*, *Psychological Abstracts*, and *Engineering Abstracts*.[11]

Table 1: Percentage and impact of 1978 *SCI®* articles by country. A = geographical region. B = percent of 1978 *SCI* articles. C = 1978-1982 impact.

	A	B	C
US	44	5.7
Western Europe	17	4.5
UK	9	5.2
USSR	6	1.5
Japan	5	4.0
Canada	4	4.9
Third World Nations	4	1.7
Eastern Europe	3	2.3
Scandinavia	3	6.4
Australia	2	4.4
Latin America	1	2.9
All Others	2	4.0

Table 2: Productivity and impact of Latin American countries. A = country. B = 1978 articles. C = 1978-1982 impact.

A	B	C
Brazil	1060	2.6
Argentina	643	3.1
Mexico	611	3.1
Chile	312	3.3
Venezuela	261	3.0
Colombia	64	2.5
Peru	35	1.5
Costa Rica	35	2.8
Uruguay	25	2.4
Guatemala	23	3.3
Cuba	22	2.4
Ecuador	13	.8
Panama	7	4.0
Honduras	5	.8
Bolivia	4	1.0
El Salvador	4	1.3
Haiti	1	0
Dominican Republic	1	7.0
Total	3126	2.9

The 388,000 articles in the 1978 *SCI* received about two million citations between 1978 and 1982. Thus, the average *SCI* article had a five-year impact of 4.8. Impact was calculated by dividing the number of 1978-1982 citations to 1978 articles by the number of articles published in 1978. The 3,100 Latin American articles received 9,000 citations, giving an impact of 2.9.

Table 2 provides details on the 18 Latin American countries represented in this study. Data on the number of articles and their impacts are given for each nation. The top five countries—Brazil, Argentina, Mexico, Chile, and Venezuela—account for 92 percent of the Latin American articles indexed in the 1978 *SCI*.

The same five countries are the leaders in Latin America in terms of the number of their articles in the 1973, 1978, and 1982 *SCI*. However, their *relative* rankings have changed over the years, as shown in Table 3. Argentina slipped from first place in 1973 to second in 1978 and 1982, trading places with Brazil. Mexico advanced from fifth place in 1973 to third in 1978, but slipped to fourth in 1982. These changes may be a reflection of economic or political events. Increases in foreign debts, for example, might result in austerity measures that reduce science budgets. Thus, fewer funds are available to support basic research, and the number of published articles declines.[12]

M.J. Moravcsik and J. Blickenstaff, Institute of Theoretical Science, University of Oregon, Eugene, used ISI data to study the number of publishing scientists in the Third World from 1971 to 1976.[13] They found that countries with stable political systems have a steady and fast "growth rate" of science. Moravcsik explained that many people, including scientists, emigrate abroad during domestic political upheavals. Venezuela often is the *recipient* of refugee scientists from Central and South America because of its relative stability. Thus, both the number of scientists and articles fluctuate sharply over time for Venezuela. Moravcsik notes that this "inter-regional mi-

Table 4: Impact of articles for Latin American countries that produced at least 35 articles in 1978. A=country. B=impact. C=1978 articles. D=1978-1982 citations.

A	B	C	D
Chile	3.3	312	1017
Argentina	3.1	643	1987
Mexico	3.1	611	1871
Venezuela	3.0	261	789
Costa Rica	2.8	35	97
Brazil	2.6	1060	2720
Colombia	2.5	64	157
Peru	1.5	35	51

gration" is characteristic of Latin America, and is less frequently observed in Africa and Asia.[14]

Table 4 gives the impacts for eight Latin American nations that produced at least 35 articles, or one percent of all Latin American publications in the 1978 *SCI*. Although Brazil ranked first on the number of articles it produced, it ranks sixth in impact. Articles from Chile had the greatest impact at 3.3, followed closely by Argentina and Mexico.

Latin American articles in our 1978 "sample" were published in seven languages. They are shown in Table 5. More than 80 percent were in English, and they had the greatest impact. Although Spanish and Portuguese are the major domestic languages in Latin America, only 17 percent of Latin American research articles were published in these languages. In the 1982 *SCI*, about 80 percent of Latin American articles were in English.

Clearly, English is the dominant language of Latin American research reported in the international scientific journals. This statement shouldn't be surprising. English is the dominant language of *all* *SCI* articles, and its use has increased. Table 6 shows the major languages of publication for *SCI* articles in 1973, 1978, and 1982. The number of articles indexed in *SCI* grew by 26 percent from 1973 to 1982. English-language articles accounted for 83 percent of the 1973 *SCI* file, and 89 percent in 1982. Span-

Table 3: Most productive Latin American nations in 1973, 1978, and 1982 *SCI*®. A=country. B=1973 articles. C=1978 articles. D=1982 articles.

A	B	C	D
Argentina	1526	643	1217
Brazil	812	1060	1531
Venezuela	589	261	318
Chile	565	312	822
Mexico	535	611	735

Table 5: Languages of publication and impact for 1978 Latin American articles. A=language. B=1978 articles. C=percent of total. D=impact.

A	B	C	D
English	2520	81	3.4
Spanish	450	14	.6
Portuguese	91	3	.2
German	30	1	2.5
French	30	1	.7
Russian	4	—	.3
Italian	1	—	1.0
Total	3126	100	2.9

Table 6: Languages of publication for all *SCI*® articles in 1973, 1978, and 1982. A=language. B=1973 articles. C=1978 articles. D=1982 articles.

A	B	C	D
English	292,261	343,640	394,281
Russian	19,477	15,011	17,360
German	18,140	14,651	15,702
French	16,020	10,168	10,219
All Others	7350	4806	6193
Total	353,248	388,276	443,755

Table 7: Countries that published at least 12 Latin American articles in 1978. A=publishing country. B=1978 articles. C=1978-1982 citations. D=impact. E=number of Latin American countries.

A	B	C	D	E
US	1317	4884	3.7	17
UK	369	1233	3.3	14
Netherlands	231	1128	4.9	12
Mexico	217	87	.4	3
Brazil	144	46	.3	2
Switzerland	140	408	2.9	8
FRG	138	428	3.1	9
Chile	122	79	.7	1
Argentina	78	79	1.0	2
France	73	91	1.3	10
Denmark	36	74	2.1	8
Italy	31	44	1.4	6
Venezuela	31	18	.6	3
GDR	29	65	2.2	6
Japan	28	49	1.8	5
Costa Rica	23	13	.6	7
Spain	23	16	.7	7
Canada	19	43	2.3	6
Austria	15	42	2.8	3
USSR	12	2	.2	5
All Others	50	106	2.1	
Total	3126	8935	2.9	

ish- and Portuguese-language articles accounted for less than one percent of *SCI* articles in 1973, 1978, and 1982. *Chemical Abstracts* reported the same percentage for Spanish and Portuguese articles in its 1982 file.[9]

English dominates Latin American science publication because the majority of Latin American articles in the 1978 *SCI* were published in English-language journals. Table 7 lists 20 nations that published at least 12 Latin American articles. Fifty-five percent of the 3,100 Latin American articles were published in the US, UK, and Canada, where English is the most common language of publication. In fact, English accounts for the majority of articles published in Switzerland, the Federal Republic of Germany (FRG), Denmark, Italy, the Netherlands, and other countries whose native language is *not* English.

The US published more Latin American articles than any other nation—1,300. This amounts to only one percent of all articles published in the US. But it represents 42 percent of the 1978 *SCI* articles from Latin America. The US also published articles from 17 Latin American nations. Thus, more Latin American authors found a publishing opportunity in the US than in any other country.

Table 7 shows that Latin American articles published in the Netherlands had the greatest impact—4.9. The average Latin American article published in the US received 3.7 citations from 1978 to 1982. For the UK, this figure is 3.3 and for the FRG 3.1. Latin American articles published in Argentina had an impact of 1.0, the highest of all six Latin American publishers in Table 7.

However, only 700 articles published in Latin American journals were indexed in the 1978 *SCI*. Conclusions on the relative impact of Latin America as a scientific publisher drawn from such a small sample must be tentative. Clearly, the processing of more Latin American publications *might* increase the impact

Table 8: Journals that published at least ten 1978 Latin American articles.* A=journal. B=Latin American articles. C=Latin American impact. D=total articles. E=total impact.

A	B	C	D	E
Rev. Invest. Clin.	157	.1	161	.1
Rev. Med. Chile	122	.7	128	.6
An. Acad. Brasil Cienc.	106	.3	112	.3
Medicina—Buenos Aires	78	1.0	79	1.0
Arch. Invest. Med.	48	1.4	67	1.9
Rev. Brasil Pesquisas Med. Biol.	38	.4	40	.4
Acta Cient. Venez.	31	.6	32	.6
Bull. Amer. Phys. Soc.	27	.1	5765	.3
Solid State Commun.	26	2.4	991	6.5
J. Chem. Phys.	25	7.8	1668	11.5
Biochim. Biophys. Acta	23	8.0	2079	13.7
Phytochemistry	22	4.6	584	6.2
Turrialba	21	.6	28	.5
Biochem. Biophys. Res. Commun.	20	9.9	1095	13.2
Experientia	20	2.8	1364	2.6
Phys. Rev. B—Condensed Matter	20	3.8	947	11.6
Sangre	20	.7	382	.1
Trans. Roy. Soc. Trop. Med. Hyg.	20	1.6	194	3.4
Amer. J. Trop. Med. Hyg.	18	3.8	178	6.5
Pediat. Res.	18	1.4	1511	1.3
C.R. Acad. Sci. Ser. II—Mec. Phys.	17	.3	478	.5
Fed. Proc.	17	.5	7144	1.2
Phys. Rev. D—Part. Fields	17	4.1	784	10.2
Abstr. Pap. Amer. Chem. Soc.	16	0	4290	0
Astrophys. J.	16	12.1	1191	12.6
Agent. Action.	15	1.1	148	4.6
IEEE Trans. Power App. Syst.	15	.3	501	.7
Fert. Steril.	14	5.7	294	6.4
Lett. Nuovo Cim.	14	1.9	417	2.5
FEBS Lett.	13	7.5	1210	11.2
J. Phys.—C—Solid State Phys.	13	2.1	562	5.9
Nature	13	17.4	2252	20.1
Phys. Rev. A—Gen. Phys.	13	8.3	883	6.6
Publ. Astron. Soc. Pac.	13	1.8	167	3.0
Brain Res.	12	9.8	983	16.4
Chem. Phys. Lett.	12	3.9	988	8.4
Int. J. Androl.	12	0	216	1.4
J. Food Sci.	12	2.4	516	3.9
J. Opt. Soc. Amer.	12	.7	1116	1.2
J. Org. Chem.	12	6.3	1360	8.8
Patol.—Mex.	12	.3	12	.3
Phys. Status Solidi B—Basic Re.	12	2.0	713	3.4
Plant Dis. Report.	12	2.0	336	1.5
Amer. J. Phys.	11	.7	304	1.1
Arch. Biochem. Biophys.	11	9.3	441	12.0
J. Math. Phys.—NY	11	2.6	409	3.9
J. Membrane Biol.	11	7.0	131	15.4
Phys. Lett. A	11	3.1	782	4.4
Plant Physiol.	11	1.1	1074	5.1
Trans. Amer. Geophys. Soc.	11	.1	2724	.1
Exp. Parasitol.	10	5.7	77	6.2
J. Appl. Phys.	10	2.6	1149	6.5
J. Electrochem. Soc.	10	2.7	1417	2.3
J. Sound Vib.	10	1.9	601	1.9
J. Steroid Biochem.	10	1.8	556	2.7
Life Sci.	10	3.7	533	13.9
Plast. Reconstr. Surg.	10	1.9	255	4.5
Trans. Amer. Nucl. Soc.	10	.6	1384	.6

*Data for *Acta Physiologica Latino-Americana* are not available because its 1978 issues were processed in 1979.

Table 9: Journals that published high-impact Latin American articles in 1978. A=journal. B=Latin American impact. C=Latin American articles. D=total impact. E=total articles.

A	B	C	D	E
Gene	162.0	1	20.7	40
J. Immunol.	40.3	3	21.1	867
J. Clin. Invest.	35.0	2	34.1	353
Biochimie	31.0	1	6.1	142
J. Physiol.—London	30.3	3	7.8	1028
Proc. Roy. Soc. London Ser. B	29.0	1	13.8	102
Proc. Soc. Exp. Biol. Med.	25.0	3	6.3	353
Proc. Nat. Acad. Sci. US	24.0	4	40.6	1208
J. Volcanol. Geotherm. Res.	23.0	1	7.0	26
Amer. Heart J.	21.5	2	6.1	315
Parasitology	19.7	3	1.7	346
Eur. J. Biochem.	19.3	4	17.2	740
J. Cell Sci.	19.0	1	13.4	148
Nature	17.4	13	20.1	2252
Phys. Rev. Lett.	17.3	4	19.7	1099
Naturwissenschaften	17.0	1	5.0	171
Artery	17.0	1	4.4	43
Annu. Rev. Biophys. Bioeng.	16.0	1	48.8	18
J. Exp. Med.	15.0	1	50.5	300
Photochem. Photobiol.	15.0	2	11.5	254

of particular journals or articles, but their overall impact could *de*crease. Assuming that the journals we do not cover are of lower impact than those we already index, adding more of them to our data base can only lower even further the average impact of any group of low impact journals.

The 3,100 Latin American articles in the 1978 *SCI* were published in about 850 journals. Table 8 lists 58 journals that published at least ten Latin American articles. Eight of them are Latin American journals. Mexico and Brazil account for two journals each. Argentina, Chile, Costa Rica, and Venezuela have one journal each. Thirty of the journals were published in the US, seven in the UK, five in the Netherlands, and two in Switzerland. Denmark, France, the FRG, German Democratic Republic, Italy, and Spain account for one journal each.

Table 9 lists 20 journals with the greatest impact for the Latin American articles they published. No Latin American journal is listed. The US accounts for ten journals. Six were published in the UK, two in the Netherlands, and one each in

France and the FRG. Although only 52 Latin American articles were published in these 20 journals, they received almost 1,300 citations. That is, these 52 articles account for 15 percent of all 1978-1982 citations to Latin American articles in the 1978 *SCI*. Most of these journals are in biomedicine or clinical medicine. These fields tend to produce more "superstar" papers than earth sciences, botany, or mathematics. This is primarily due to the great number of papers published in biomedicine. Also, in biochemistry, the average number of references cited per paper is very high and increasing.[15]

In Part 2, we'll identify the 1978 Latin American articles that were most cited from 1978 to 1982. We'll continue our journal analysis and describe the fields of science that Latin American literature is concentrated in. An analysis of research fronts that include Latin American papers published in 1981 provides an interesting insight into their research emphases.

* * * * *

My thanks to Abigail W. Grissom and Alfred Welljams-Dorof for their help in the preparation of this essay.

©1984 ISI

REFERENCES

1. **Sandoval A M & Núñez A.** The biomedical manuscripts drain from Latin America. *UNESCO Bull. Libr.* 28:10-6, 1974.
2. **Büttenklepper A, Maffey L & Delgado H.** International impact of research in Mexico. Bibliometric study on the works of Jesus Romo Armeria. *Rev. Latinoamer. Quim.* 9:11-6, 1978.
3. **Morel R L D M & Morel C M.** Um estudo sobre a produção científica Brasileira, segundo os dados do Institute for Scientific Information, ISI. (A study on Brazilian scientific production, based on information provided by the Institute for Scientific Information, ISI.) *Cienc. Inform.* 6(2):99-109, 1977.
4. **Morel C M & Morel R L D M.** Estudo sobre a produção científica Brasileira, segundo os dados do ISI. (Study on Brazilian scientific production, based on information provided by ISI.) *Cienc. Inform.* 7(2):79-83, 1978.
5. **Martínez-Palomo A & Aréchiga H.** Biomedical research in Mexico. 1. Basic research. *Gaceta Med. Mex.* 115:65-70, 1979.
6. **Garfield E.** Third World research. Part 1. Where it is published, and how often it is cited. Part 2. High impact journals, most-cited articles, and most active areas of research. *Current Contents* (33):5-15, 15 August 1983 and (34):5-16, 22 August 1983. (A reprint of **Garfield E.** "Mapping science in the Third World. Parts 1 & 2." *Sci. Public Policy* 10(3):112-27, 1983, is included.)
7. --------------. Is your journal "up front" with your address? Or, the saga of the incomplete address. Parts 1 & 2. *Current Contents* (42):5-13, 17 October 1983 and (43):5-11, 24 October 1983.
8. **National Science Board.** *Science indicators, 1982. Report of the National Science Board, 1983.* Washington, DC: National Science Foundation, 1983. 344 p.
9. **Sharpe R.** Telephone communication. 11 October 1983.
10. **Ferrere C.** Telephone communication. 11 October 1983.
11. **Narin F & Carpenter M P.** National publication and citation comparisons. *J. Amer. Soc. Inform. Sci.* 26:80-93, 1975.
12. **Powledge T.** Mexican science in money trouble. *Nature* 299:99-100, 1982.
13. **Blickenstaff J & Moravcsik M J.** Scientific output in the Third World. *Scientometrics* 4:135-69, 1982.
14. **Moravcsik M J.** Telephone communication. 11 April 1984.
15. **Garfield E.** The number of biochemical articles is growing, but why also the number of references per article? *Essays of an information scientist.* Philadelphia: ISI Press, 1981. Vol. 4. p. 414-25.

Current Comments®

Latin American Research. Part 2.
Most-Cited Articles, Discipline Orientation,
and Research Front Concentration

Number 20   May 14, 1984

In Part 1 data were provided on 3,100 Latin American articles found in the 1978 *Science Citation Index®* (*SCI®*). The average Latin American article received about three citations from 1978 through 1982. In comparison, the five-year impact of the average *SCI* article was five. Brazil, Argentina, Mexico, Chile, and Venezuela accounted for 92 percent of the Latin American articles indexed in the 1978 *SCI*. The same five countries dominated Latin American scientific output in the 1973 and 1982 *SCI*.

Our discussion of Latin American science continues with a list of most-cited articles and a discipline analysis—life sciences, physics, chemistry, etc. An analysis of the specific clusters of research cited by Latin American scientists in 1981 helps us identify the particular research fronts in which they are active.

Table 1 lists 24 1978 articles that received at least 30 citations from 1978 through 1982. Ten papers list first authors based in Mexico, five in Brazil, four in Chile, three in Argentina, and two in Venezuela. Of course, it's possible that some of the first authors on these high-impact papers listed different institutional affiliations outside of Latin America on other articles. That is, some may have been visiting researchers at institutions in Europe or North America. Or they may have been researchers from Europe or North America who worked at Latin American laboratories for a while. We checked ISI®'s *Current Bibliographic Directory of the Arts & Sciences®* (*CBD®*) to determine what addresses were listed for the first authors of the high-impact 1978 Latin American papers in later years. Six authors were found to have listed addresses at other institutions outside of Latin America—E.R. Abney, F. Bolivar, R. Bravo, D.E. Richards, J.L. Ochoa, and L.C. Vaz. In addition, five of the 24 highly cited articles were *co*authored with researchers from the US and UK.

We've also provided details on the "nationality" of the citations to these high-impact Latin American articles in Table 1. That is, we show the number of citations given by authors based in the same Latin American nation as the cited first author, those based in other Latin American nations, and those from non-Latin American countries. These 24 articles received about 1,200 citations from 1978 through 1982. Eighty-nine percent were from *non*-Latin American papers. Ten percent were "self-citations" from the cited author's own country. Only one percent were from other Latin American countries. Apparently, there is little inter-citation *between* Latin American scientists, at least as it is reflected in the international journals indexed in *SCI*. Thus, whether or not a Latin American article is highly cited depends on the recognition it gets from scientists *outside of* Central and South America.

This point is better illustrated when we identify the countries that most frequently cited the 1978 *SCI* Latin American articles. These articles received about 9,000 citations from 1978 to 1982.

Table 1: 1978 Latin American articles cited at least 30 times from 1978 to 1982. A=bibliographic data. B=total citations. C=citations from first author's own country. D=citations from other countries in Latin America. E=citations from all other countries.

A	B	C	D	E
Bolivar F. Construction and characterization of new cloning vehicles. III. Derivatives of plasmid pBR322 carrying unique *Eco* RI sites for selection of *Eco* RI generated recombinant DNA molecules. *Gene* 4:121-36, 1978. Natl. Autonomous Univ. Mexico (UNAM), Inst. Biomed. Res., Mexico City, Mexico.	162	5	2	155
Abney E R, Cooper M D, Kearney J F, Lawton A R & Parkhouse R M E. Sequential expression of immunoglobulin on developing mouse B lymphocytes: a systematic survey that suggests a model for the generation of immunoglobulin isotype diversity. *J. Immunol.* 120:2041-9, 1978. Natl. Autonomous Univ. Mexico (UNAM), Facult. Med.: Natl. Polytech. Inst. (IPN) Res. Ctr., Mexico City, Mexico; Univ. Alabama, Dept. Pediat., Microbiol. & Compr. Cancer Ctr., Birmingham, AL.	120	0	0	120
Borgono J M, McLean A A, Vella P P, Woodhour A F, Canepa I, Davidson W L & Hilleman M R. Vaccination and revaccination with polyvalent pneumococcal polysaccharide vaccines in adults and infants (40010). *Proc. Soc. Exp. Biol. Med.* 157:148-54, 1978. Natl. Hlth. Serv., Sect. Epidemiol., Santiago, Chile; Merck Inst. Ther. Res., Div. Virus Cell Biol. Res. & Corp. Med. Dept.-Occup. Hlth., West Point, PA.	67	0	0	67
Peimbert M, Torres-Peimbert S & Rayo J F. Abundance gradients in the galaxy derived from H_{11} regions. *Astrophys. J.* 220:516-24, 1978. Natl. Autonomous Univ. Mexico (UNAM), Inst. Astron., Mexico City, Mexico.	62	3	1	58
DiPolo R. Ca pump driven by ATP in squid axons. *Nature* 274:390-2, 1978. Sci. Res. Inst. (IVIC), Ctr. Biophys. Biochem., Caracas, Venezuela.	52	5	1	46
Alarcon-Segovia D & Ruiz-Arguelles A. Decreased circulating thymus-derived cells with receptors for the Fc portion of immunoglobulin G in systemic lupus erythematosus. *J. Clin. Invest.* 62:1390-4, 1978. Natl. Inst. Nutr., Dept. Immunol. Rheumatol., Mexico City, Mexico.	50	13	0	37
Alarcon-Segovia D, Ruiz-Arguelles A & Fishbein E. Antibody to nuclear ribonucleoprotein penetrates live human mononuclear cells through Fc receptors. *Nature* 271:67-9, 1978. Natl. Inst. Nutr., Dept. Immunol. Rheumatol., Mexico City, Mexico.	50	18	0	32
Didyk B M, Simoneit B R T, Brassell S C & Eglinton G. Organic geochemical indicators of palaeoenvironmental conditions of sedimentation. *Nature* 272:216-22, 1978. Natl. Petroleum Enterprise, Concon, Chile; Univ. California, Inst. Geophys. Planet. Phys., Los Angeles, CA; Univ. Bristol, Sch. Chem., Bristol, UK.	45	0	0	45
Hopp H E, Romero P A, Daleo G R & Pont Lezica R. Synthesis of cellulose precursors. *Eur. J. Biochem.* 84:561-71, 1978. Bariloche Fdn., Dept. Biol., San Carlos de Bariloche, Argentina.	43	3	0	40
Padial N, Csanak G, McKoy B V & Langhoff P W. Photoabsorption in carbon monoxide: Stieltjes-Tchebycheff calculations in the separated-channel static-exchange approximation. *J. Chem. Phys.* 69:2992-3004, 1978. State Univ. Campinas, Inst. Phys., Campinas, Brazil; Calif. Inst. Technol., Arthur Amos Noyes Lab. Chem. Phys., Pasadena, CA; Indiana Univ., Dept. Chem., Bloomington, IN.	43	3	0	40
Bravo R, Otero C, Allende C C & Allende J E. Amphibian oocyte maturation and protein synthesis: related inhibition by cyclic AMP, theophylline, and papaverine. *Proc. Nat. Acad. Sci. US* 75:1242-6, 1978. Univ. Chile, Facult. Med., Santiago, Chile.	40	8	0	32
Cuccovia I M, Schroter E H, Monteiro P M & Chaimovich H. Effect of hexadecyltrimethylammonium bromide on the thiolysis of *p*-nitrophenyl acetate. *J. Org. Chem.* 43:2248-52, 1978. Univ. Sao Paulo, Inst. Chem., Sao Paulo, Brazil.	38	4	0	34
Llados F & Zapata P. Effects of dopamine analogues and antagonists on carotid body chemosensors *in situ*. *J. Physiol.* 274:487-99, 1978. Catholic Univ. Chile, Dept. Neurobiol., Santiago, Chile.	38	6	0	32
Sanchez J A & Stefani E. Inward calcium current in twitch muscle fibres of the frog. *J. Physiol.* 283:197-209, 1978. Natl. Polytech. Inst. (IPN) Res. Ctr., Mexico City, Mexico.	38	6	1	31
Staneloni R J & Leloir L F. Oligosaccharides containing glucose and mannose in glycoproteins of the thyroid gland. *Proc. Nat. Acad. Sci. US* 75:1162-6, 1978. Inst. Biochem. Res. "Fundacion Campomar"; Coll. Exact Natur. Sci., Buenos Aires, Argentina.	38	11	0	27
Mortara R A, Quina F H & Chaimovich H. Formation of closed vesicles from a simple phosphate diester. Preparation and some properties of vesicles of dihexadecyl phosphate. *Biochem. Biophys. Res. Commun.* 81:1080-6, 1978. Univ. Sao Paulo, Inst. Chem., Sao Paulo, Brazil.	36	3	0	33
Ferreira S H, Nakamura M & Castro M S A. The hyperalgesic effects of prostacyclin and prostaglandin E_2. *Prostaglandins* 16:31-7, 1978. Ribeirao Preto Facult. Med., Dept. Pharmacol., Sao Paulo, Brazil.	35	10	0	25
Zepeda A. Mass of the up quark. *Phys. Rev. Lett.* 41:139-41, 1978. Natl. Polytech. Inst. (IPN) Res. Ctr., Mexico City, Mexico.	35	1	0	34
Carrasco H A, Fuenmayor A, Barboza J S & Gonzalez G. Effect of verapamil on normal sinoatrial node function and on sick sinus syndrome. *Amer. Heart J.* 96:760-71, 1978. Los Andes Univ. Hosp., Cardiovasc. Ctr., Merida, Venezuela.	34	0	0	34

Vaz L C & Alexander J M. Systematics of fusion barriers obtained with a modified proximity potential. *Phys. Rev. C—Nucl. Phys.* 18:2152-61, 1978. IFUFRJ Cidade Univ., Dept. Nucl. Phys., Rio de Janeiro, Brazil; SUNY, Dept. Chem., Stony Brook, NY.   34   0   0   34

Perez-Tamayo R. Pathology of collagen degradation. *Amer. J. Pathol.* 92:509-66, 1978. Natl. Inst. Nutr., Dept. Pathol., Mexico City, Mexico.   32   6   1   25

Ochoa J-L. Hydrophobic (interaction) chromatography. *Biochimie* 60:1-15, 1978. Natl. Autonomous Univ. Mexico (UNAM), Inst. Chem., Mexico City, Mexico.   31   2   0   29

Ramos C, Lamoyi E, Feoli M, Rodriguez M, Perez M & Ortiz-Ortiz L. *Trypanosoma cruzi:* immunosuppressed response to different antigens in the infected mouse. *Exp. Parasitol.* 45:190-9, 1978. Natl. Autonomous Univ. Mexico (UNAM), Inst. Biomed. Res., Mexico City, Mexico.   31   2   9   20

Richards D E, Rega A F & Garrahan P J. Two classes of site for ATP in the Ca^{2+}-ATPase from human red cell membranes. *Biochim. Biophys. Acta* 511:194-201, 1978. Univ. Buenos Aires, Facult. Pharmacol. Biochem., Buenos Aires, Argentina.   30   7   0   23

Totals 1184   116   15   1053

Source of data on articles: 1978 *SCI®*.
Source of data on citations: 1978-1982 *SCI*.

Table 2 shows 21 countries that account for at least one percent of citations to Latin American research. Twenty-nine percent were from US citing papers. West European articles account for 14 percent. The UK accounts for eight percent. All Latin American countries combined account for 32 percent.

Table 3 provides details on these Latin American citations to Latin American research. A pattern of high national "self-citation" is obvious. For example, 971 of the citations to Latin American research came from Brazilian papers. Yet 917 of these were "self-citations" to Brazilian research. In this study, "self-citation" refers to citations by any author from one country to the work of any authors in that same *nation*. It should not be confused with the usual meaning of self-citation as an *author* citing his or her own work. Thus, national self-citations indicate a form of "provinciality" or "insularity," even though the authors in question may not be known to each other.

This high level of "insularity" is observed in other Latin American nations. Ninety-one percent of Argentina's citations to Latin American research cited Argentinean papers; Mexico, 98 percent; Chile, 93 percent; Venezuela, 91 percent, and so on. These data indicate that Latin American researchers are not aware of, or choose not to cite, papers from neighboring countries in Central and South America. Keep in mind that this statement is based on the inter-

Table 2: Countries that most frequently cited 1978 *SCI®* Latin American articles. Asterisks (*) indicate Latin American countries. A=citing country. B=citations to Latin American articles. C=percent of all citations to Latin American articles. D=citations to all articles.

A	B	C	D
US	2605	29	833,933
*Brazil	971	11	3960
*Argentina	787	9	3302
UK	700	8	188,323
*Mexico	436	5	2289
FRG	374	4	117,817
France	334	4	94,919
*Chile	290	3	1696
*Venezuela	259	3	1120
Canada	243	3	80,894
Japan	219	3	94,149
Australia	177	2	38,099
Italy	153	2	36,509
USSR	145	2	48,459
Switzerland	111	1	30,873
Netherlands	100	1	35,180
Sweden	85	1	34,336
India	80	1	20,312
Belgium	78	1	18,102
Israel	69	1	18,040
Denmark	66	1	17,139
All Others	653	7	137,385
Total	**8935**		

national journals covered in *SCI*. A citation analysis of regional journals might reveal a different pattern.

The finding that there is little inter-citation between Latin American scientists raises important science policy questions. Much has been done to increase contacts between Latin American scientists and those in the US and Europe. As a result, scientific information from the US and Europe is more accessible to Latin American scientists, and vice versa. Similar programs should be

Table 3: Inter-Latin American self-citations. Self-citation is defined as the number of references in a nation's literature that cited that same nation's papers divided by the number of references to all Latin American papers. A=citing country. B=Latin American citations. C=self-citations. D=percent of self-citations.

A	B	C	D
Brazil	971	917	94
Argentina	787	716	91
Mexico	436	425	98
Chile	290	269	93
Venezuela	259	235	91
Colombia	46	40	87
Costa Rica	22	15	68
Guatemala	13	7	54
Cuba	11	11	100
Uruguay	9	9	100
Peru	8	6	75
Ecuador	3	3	100
Bolivia	1	0	0
El Salvador	1	1	100
Honduras	1	1	100
Panama	1	0	0
Total	2859	2655	93

Table 4: Distribution of 1973 *SCI®* articles from Brazil and Mexico by field. A=Brazilian articles. B=percent of all Brazilian articles. C=impact of Brazilian articles. D=Mexican articles. E=percent of all Mexican articles. F=impact of Mexican articles.

Field	A	B	C	D	E	F
Life Sciences	449	55	2.5	390	73	2.6
Physics*	137	17	3.2	58	11	2.1
Chemistry	58	7	4.4	41	8	2.1
Engineering/Technology	55	7	.9	12	2	1.5
Mathematics	31	4	.9	8	1	4.1
All Others**	82	10	.8	26	5	4.2

* Includes Geophysics and Astrophysics.
** Includes articles from multidisciplinary journals.

designed to intensify contacts between scientists in Central and South America—travel grants, exchange programs, cooperative research projects, regional laboratories and journals, etc. This could lead to a greater awareness among Latin American nations of each other's useful scientific contributions.

By examining the journals that published Latin American research, we can get a rough idea of the fields of science they concentrate in. Several studies have indicated that Latin American science in general is concentrated in the life sciences.[16] In comparison to the distribution of the world's literature, Latin American science is underrepresented in physics and chemistry.

J. Davidson Frame, Department of Management Science, George Washington University, Washington, DC, combined 1973-1975 *SCI* data for a study of Latin American and world science.[16] He found that 60 percent of the world literature was in the life sciences, compared to 73 percent for Latin American publications. Nineteen percent was in chemistry—for Latin America, this figure was 11 percent. Physics, including geophysics and astrophysics, accounted for 21 percent of the world literature but only 16 percent of Latin American articles. Frame concluded that Latin American research is "peripheral" to world or "mainstream" scientific output.

But when we examine individual Latin American nations, we see that some are more "mainstream" than others. Table 4 shows the distribution of 1973 *SCI* articles from Brazil and Mexico by broad discipline, and their five-year impacts. About 52 percent of the world literature covered in *SCI* that year was in the life sciences. For Brazil, this figure is 55 percent, very close to the world average. A much larger proportion of Mexican publications—73 percent—is in the life sciences.

Brazilian publications in physics are also roughly proportional to the world output—18 percent in 1973. Four percent of Brazil's articles were in mathematics, compared to three percent for the world literature. Mexico is underrepresented in both physics and mathematics—11 and one percent, respectively. (Both Brazil and Mexico published much smaller proportions of articles in chemistry and engineering than the world as a whole. In 1973, 17 percent of the world's literature was in chemistry, and 11 percent in engineering.)

Table 5 shows how Brazilian and Mexican articles in the 1978 *SCI* are distributed by discipline. The Brazilian proportion of articles in the life sciences declined to 46 percent in 1978, *lower* than the world average of 55 percent that year. But the impact of Brazilian life sciences articles increased from 2.5 in

147

Table 5: Distribution of 1978 *SCI®* articles from Brazil and Mexico by field. A=Brazilian articles. B=percent of all Brazilian articles. C=impact of Brazilian articles. D=Mexican articles. E=percent of all Mexican articles. F=impact of Mexican articles.

Field	A	B	C	D	E	F
Life Sciences	483	46	2.9	410	67	3.1
Physics*	229	22	3.0	87	14	4.8
Chemistry	96	9	3.6	30	5	1.3
Engineering/Technology	76	7	1.3	51	8	.7
Mathematics	38	4	1.4	9	1	2.9
All Others**	138	13	.9	24	4	3.6

* Includes Geophysics and Astrophysics.
** Includes articles from multidisciplinary journals.

1973 to 2.9 in 1978. The percentage of Brazil's output in physics increased from 17 percent in 1973 to 22 percent in 1978, which is *higher* than the world average of 17 percent. The impact of Brazilian physics articles was stable at about three in 1973 and 1978. The proportion of Brazilian articles in chemistry also grew, from seven percent in 1973 to nine percent in 1978. This is still lower than the world average—16 percent of the world's literature was in chemistry in 1978. Brazil's proportionate productivity in chemistry increased, but its average impact declined from 4.4 in 1973 to 3.6 in 1978.

Mexico's emphasis on the life sciences in 1978 is still strong, accounting for 67 percent of Mexico's publications—down from 73 percent in 1973. The impact of Mexico's life sciences publications increased from 2.6 in 1973 to 3.1 in 1978. The percentage of Mexico's output in physics grew from 11 percent in 1973 to 14 percent in 1978, closer to the world average of 17 percent. Significantly, the impact of Mexican physics articles more than doubled, from 2.1 in 1973 to 4.8 in 1978. Only five percent of 1978 Mexican articles were in chemistry, lower than its 1973 proportion of eight percent and far lower than the 1978 world average of 16 percent. The impact of Mexico's chemistry articles also declined, from 2.1 in 1973 to 1.3 in 1978.

Of course, analyses of field distributions are too broad to give us an idea of the *specific* subjects of research a nation's scientists specialize in. It is useful to know how much of a nation's literature is devoted to life sciences, but it is more relevant to know what disciplines within this field are stressed—biomedicine, biochemistry, clinical medicine, botany, etc. It is even more interesting to know what specific research problems are addressed within these disciplines—erythrocyte membrane proteins, cell-mediated cytotoxicity, T-cell responses to tuberculosis, etc.

ISI has developed a method to automatically classify the scientific literature into thousands of discrete, highly specific "clusters" of research. The method relies on co-citation analysis to identify "core" documents in these clusters, and the current "research front" papers that cite them. This method has been described previously.[17]

For this study, we used the 1981 *SCI* file to see what clusters of research were cited by Latin American articles. This helps us identify the *current* areas of Latin American research. In brief, we examined more than 2,300 research fronts that included at least one Latin American paper. Obviously, we can't discuss all of them here. So we set a threshold to obtain a manageable number for analysis.

Figure 1 shows a map of 37 clusters of research cited by at least eight Latin American articles in the 1981 *SCI*. Each circle represents a single cluster of research. The connecting lines indicate co-citation links between research specialties. Each cluster is identified by a number. The full name for each research front is provided in the table and corresponds to the number on the map. We have explained previously how the research fronts are named.[17] After each research front name, the number of 1981 citing papers is shown, as well as the percentage from Latin America.

Before we discuss Latin American research specialization, a few comments about the map itself are needed. The map does not show the relative "sizes" of the specialty areas it depicts. The number of citing articles in these research

Figure 1: Multidimensionally scaled map of reseach clusters cited by at least eight 1981 *SCI®* Latin American articles. Numbers correspond to accompanying index of research front names.

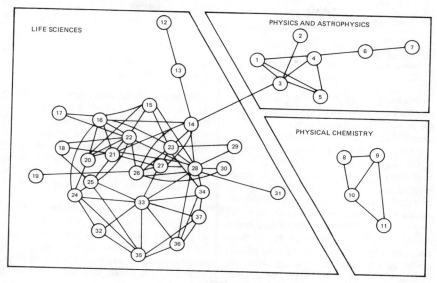

Physics & Astrophysics

A	B	C	D
1	Spectroscopic studies of Wolf-Rayet stars		
2	Interacting boson model	75	17
3	Neutrino masses, neutral currents, and other factors involved in unified field theories	133	7
4	Chemical composition and structure of globular clusters	288	15
5	Mass, photometric abundances, and colors of cepheids, carbon stars, and super giants; stellar evolution	205	5
6	Monte Carlo and other studies of renormalization, roughening transitions, and expansions in lattice-gauge theories	108	8
		225	4
7	Renormalization group studies of percolation behavior in lattice models		
		77	16

Physical Chemistry

A	B	C	D
8	Intermediate valence states		
9	Auger spectron and self-consistent band structure theory of metals	118	9
10	Electronic structure, magnetism, conductivity, and related properties of solid surfaces described by the Hubbard, Anderson, and other models	276	3
		105	8
11	Self-consistent field X-alpha-scattered wave calculations of electronic structure and magnetic properties of molecules		
		134	7

Life Sciences

A	B	C	D
12	Macrophage activation and intercellular infection		
13	Development and structure of trypanosoma	63	19
14	Enzymes which control DNA conformation and the effect of interactions with intercalating drugs	38	24
15	Analysis of tight junctions in various tissue	988	1
16	Transmembrane electrical potentials and membrane permeability	244	3
17	Ecological and adaptation strategies in community stability	383	3
18	Kallikrein and hypertension	315	3
19	Serodiagnosis and subtyping of arbovirus diseases	126	9
20	Mechanisms of ion exchange and transport ATP	88	10
21	Sarcoplasmic reticulum ATPase	337	3
22	Renal physiology and ion transport	263	4
23	Methods for the analysis and characterization of proteins	419	2
24	Effects of anti-arrythmic drugs on cardiovascular disease	1034	3
25	Adrenoreceptors and physiology of neurotransmission	314	3
26	Etiology and pathology of viral gastroenteritis	567	3
27	Glycoprotein biosynthesis	495	4
		180	6

fronts range from 20 to more than 1,000 but they are all shown on the map as single points. However, the map *is* multidimensionally scaled[18]—the distances *between* clusters reflect how close or far apart they are in subject matter. In effect, the map depicts the *cognitive* structure of the research areas shown. Keep in mind that the scaling is multidimensional—when it is reproduced on a flat page, the distances between some clusters are altered to prevent overlapping. Ideally, a three-dimensional model could be built for these maps, like the ball and stick models used by chemists.

The research fronts numbered one through seven on the map in Figure 1 deal with physics and astrophysics. They discuss the interacting boson model, lattice-gauge theories, unified field theories, stellar evolution, and studies of various types of stars. More than 1,100 1981 citing papers are included in these seven research fronts, and 104, or nine percent, are from Latin America.

The concentration of Latin American citing papers was particularly high in three of these research fronts in physics and astrophysics. Of the 75 papers published in 1981 that cited research front number one, "Spectroscopic studies of Wolf-Rayet stars," 17 percent were from Central or South America. Sixteen percent of the 77 papers in research front number seven, "Renormalization group studies of percolation behavior in lattice models," were from Latin America. In research front number three, "Neutrino masses, neutral currents, and other factors involved in unified field theories," Latin America accounts for 15 percent of the 288 papers published.

Latin American scientists were also active in four research fronts in physical

chemistry. They are numbered eight to 11 on the map. These research fronts concentrate on valence states, band structure theory of metals, properties of solid surfaces, and properties of molecules. However, of the 633 1981 citing papers in these research fronts, only 36, or six percent, were from Central or South America.

The research fronts numbered 12-37 are in the life sciences. About 8,100 citing papers published in 1981 are included in these 26 research fronts. Only 315, or four percent, are from Latin America. However, several individual research fronts show a high concentration of papers from Latin America. For example, research front number 29, "Effects of dietary cholesterol on the plasma and arterial wall of undernourished rats," includes 21 papers—38 percent of these were from Central or South America. Latin America accounts for 24 percent of the 38 published papers in research front number 13, "Development and structure of trypanosoma." Of the 63 papers in research front number 12, "Macrophage activation and intercellular infection," 19 percent were from Latin America.

This map shows, at a glance, that Latin American science in 1981 continued to place a heavy emphasis on the life sciences. Physics, astrophysics, and physical chemistry are other areas of specialization. Of course, Latin American scientists do work in areas that do not appear on the map—mathematics and engineering, for example. But they are *most* active in the research areas shown here. Also, the research fronts we've discussed were identified *quantitatively* by determining the number of 1981 papers and the percentage from

Latin America. The map shows those research areas in which Latin American scientists published most frequently. They are not necessarily the "best" or highest-impact areas of Latin American science.

This concludes our analysis of Latin American science. As you can see, ISI's data bases can provide unique insights into the scientific output of any nation or group of nations—its productivity, impact, internationality, interlinguality, and areas of specialization. The data we've presented are relevant and important measures of a nation's scientific "economy." In fact, the US National Science Board has used ISI's data in its *Science Indicators* reports since the early 1970s. While these reports provide several international comparisons, they primarily focus on the US. This study demonstrates that ISI's data can be used to compile science indicators reports for any country or region desired. Indeed, a proposal to compile such data may be discussed at a conference sponsored by the United Nations, to be held this May in Graz, Austria. For more information, contact M. Anandakrishnan, Room 1040, 1 United Nations Plaza, New York, New York, 10017.

In the coming weeks, we plan to publish more studies of the scientific literature from various other geographic regions. Interested readers should also refer to earlier studies of highly cited articles and journals from France,[19] Scandinavia,[20] and Italy.[21]

* * * * *

My thanks to Abigail W. Grissom and Alfred Welljams-Dorof for their help in the preparation of this essay.

©1984 ISI

REFERENCES

16. **Frame J D.** Mainstream research in Latin America and the Caribbean. *Interciencia* 2:143-8, 1977.
17. **Garfield E.** ABCs of cluster mapping. Parts 1 & 2. Most active fields in the life and physical sciences in 1978. *Essays of an information scientist.* Philadelphia: ISI Press, 1981. Vol. 4. p. 634-49.
18. **Kruskal J B.** Multidimensional scaling by optimizing goodness of fit to a nonmetric hypothesis. *Psychometrika* 29:1-27, 1964.
19. **Garfield E.** Le nouveau défi Américain. I & II. *Essays of an information scientist.* Philadelphia: ISI Press, 1980. Vol. 3. p. 88-102.
20. --------------. Journal citation studies. 28. Scandinavian journals. *Essays of an information scientist.* Philadelphia: ISI Press, 1977. Vol. 2. p. 599-605.
21. --------------. Highly cited articles. 34. Articles from Italian journals and from Italian laboratories. *Essays of an information scientist.* Philadelphia: ISI Press, 1980. Vol. 3. p. 34-41.

ERRATUM

In the *Current Comments®* essay, "Is your journal 'up front' with your address? Or, the saga of the incomplete address. Part 1," *Current Contents®* (42):5-13, 17 October 1983, I stated, "The signers of the now famous Vancouver Declaration did not consider the issue of author addresses." This statement is indeed true of the original declaration.

However, Edward Huth, North American correspondent, International Committee of Medical Journal Editors, points out that the declaration was intended to define manuscript requirements, not to specify publication format. The latest version of the declaration[1] does specify that the manuscript carry the address of the author responsible for correspondence about the manuscript and the address of the author to whom reprint requests should be addressed.

My thanks to Dr. Huth, who is also editor of *Annals of Internal Medicine*, for his correction.

1. **International Committee of Medical Journal Editors.** Uniform requirements for manuscripts submitted to biomedical journals. *Ann. Intern. Med.* 96:766-71, 1982.

Current Comments®

Journal Citation Studies. 43.
Astrosciences Journals—
What They Cite and What Cites Them

Number 21   May 21, 1984

Over the years, we've published numerous studies identifying the significant journals from various fields in the sciences, social sciences, and arts and humanities. Most recently, we investigated the journals of anthropology,[1] entomology,[2] and analytical chemistry.[3] This essay examines the literature of the astronomical sciences, or "astrosciences," which are comprised of the disciplines of astronomy and astrophysics. It expands on a study we did ten years ago on the *Astrophysical Journal*.[4]

A persistent theme links each of these journal studies: the distinction between the literature *of* a field and the literature *of interest* to the scientists in that field. The literature of a field consists of the articles reporting results pertinent to that specialty. The literature of interest to researchers in a field may be another matter, however. In addition to their own specialty journals, researchers will also cite a common set of basic research journals cited by scientists in other specialties. This is what links the work of agricultural scientists, for instance, to that of other life scientists or biotechnologists.

The degree to which this is true varies from field to field. The literature of some fields is relatively narrow—that is, its authors cite papers mainly from the field's own specialized journals. An example is the dentistry literature, which we found to be relatively self-con-

tained.[5] The literature of other fields, such as anthropology,[1] cite many diverse sources. As is shown in this essay, astronomers generally cite the same group of journals in which they publish.

The literature of the astrosciences includes not only astronomy and astrophysics, but non-optical astronomy, solar physics, and planetary science as well. Astronomy, by far the oldest science in the group, is the study of the motions, positions, and physical properties of celestial bodies. The term "astrophysics" refers to the study of the physical and chemical properties of celestial objects, including their origins and evolution. It is a relatively recent development of nineteenth- and twentieth-century astronomy. In fact, "astronomy" and "astrophysics" are often used interchangeably. Non-optical astronomy encompasses the collection and interpretation of radio frequency, gamma ray, X-ray, and infrared data, rather than the traditional type of information gathered by means of visible light. Solar physics concerns itself with the study of our sun. And with the advent of space exploration, astronomy has also grown to include planetary science, the study of the components of our solar system other than the sun, including the solid, liquid, and gaseous parts of other planets.

Table 1 lists the 25 "core" astrosciences journals used to initiate this study. Eight of the journals are published by

US organizations. Five each are published in the UK and the Netherlands. Canada, Czechoslovakia, the Federal Republic of Germany, India, Japan, and the USSR published one each. One journal, *Astronomy and Astrophysics*, may be considered a European, multinational publication.

Fourteen of these journals publish exclusively in English. The other 11 are multilingual, but English is the predominant language of four of these—*Icarus*, *Moon and the Planets*, *Solar Physics*, and *Space Science Reviews*. Incidental-

ly, as of the first 1984 issue, *Moon and the Planets* changed its name to *Earth, Moon, and Planets*.

This basic or starting list of 25 journals does not include every astronomy journal published today. Nor does it include journals from other disciplines that publish research in the astrosciences. The *Journal of Geophysical Research— Space Physics* should be regarded as a core journal. Unfortunately, many scientists simply cite "*J. Geophys. Res.*," no matter which edition they are referring to. Thus, we are unable to include citation data on the *Space Physics* section of this journal, and did not treat it as a core journal. We face precisely the same problem with journals that split into several separate editions. Such journals provide nothing more than subtitles or letters to distinguish the new parts.[6] Citations to all three editions of the *Journal of Geophysical Research* have been combined for the purposes of this essay. We did the same thing in our study of the earth sciences.[7] Had we included *Journal of Geophysical Research—Space Physics* as a core journal we could at least have reported that it published over 370 items in 1982, as compared to 1,310 for *Astrophysical Journal*.

The oldest astrosciences journals covered in *Science Citation Index®* (*SCI®*) were established in the nineteenth century. They include: *Monthly Notices of the Royal Astronomical Society*, founded in England in 1827; *Astronomical Journal*, founded in 1849 by Benjamin A. Gould, and *Astrophysical Journal*, founded in 1895 by George E. Hale and James E. Keeler, which are both publications of the American Astronomical Society; *Observatory*, established by the Royal Greenwich Observatory in England in 1877; and *Publications of the Astronomical Society of the Pacific*, established in 1889 by the Astro-

Table 1: Core astrosciences journals indexed by *SCI®* and the year each began publication.

Annual Review of Astronomy and Astrophysics—1963
Annual Review of Earth and Planetary Sciences—1973
Astronomical Journal—1849
*Astronomicheskii Zhurnal—1924
Astronomy and Astrophysics—1969
**Astrophysical Journal—1895
Astrophysical Letters—1967
Astrophysics and Space Science—1968
Bulletin of the Astronomical Institutes of Czechoslovakia—1947
Celestial Mechanics—1969
Geophysical and Astrophysical Fluid Dynamics—1970
Icarus—1962
Indian Journal of Radio & Space Physics—1972
Journal of the Royal Astronomical Society of Canada—1907
Monthly Notices of the Royal Astronomical Society—1827
Moon and the Planets—1969
Observatory—1877
Publications of the Astronomical Society of Japan—1949
Publications of the Astronomical Society of the Pacific—1889
Quarterly Journal of the Royal Astronomical Society—1960
Sky and Telescope—1941
Solar Physics—1967
Space Science Reviews—1962
Vistas in Astronomy—1955
Zeitschrift fur Naturforschung Teil A—Physik, Physikalische Chemie, Kosmophysik—1946

*Includes Soviet Astronomy—1957
**Includes Astrophysical Journal Supplement Series—1954

nomical Society of the Pacific, headquartered in San Francisco.

As in all our previous journal citation studies, we will consider the core journals of this field as if they comprised a single "Macro Journal of the Astrosciences." In other words, we'll pool their references to see which journals they collectively cite, and which journals cite them. Data were taken from the 1982 *Journal Citation Reports*® (*JCR*™), which is volume 14 of the 1982 *SCI*.

The 25 core journals in the astrosciences published about 4,500 articles in 1982, or about one percent of the 378,000 articles indexed in the 1982 *JCR*. Keep in mind that *JCR* does not include such items as editorials, news reports, obituaries, etc. By comparison, *Astronomy and Astrophysics Abstracts* indexed over 17,250 papers in 1982. The core journals cited 116,000 references in 1982, or about 1.5 percent of the eight million references processed by *JCR* during that year. The average 1982 astrosciences article cited 26 references, whereas the average *SCI* article cited 21.

The core astrosciences journals received 85,000 citations in 1982, or about one percent of all *JCR* citations that year. Just two journals account for over 60 percent of these citations: *Astrophysical Journal*, which received 41,500 citations, or almost half of all core citations, and *Astronomy and Astrophysics*, which received 11,200.

Table 2 lists the 50 journals that were most frequently cited by the core astrosciences journals in 1982. They are ranked in descending order by the number of citations received from the core group (column A). The table also shows the number of citations each journal received from all journals (column B), each journal's self-citations (column C), journal impacts (column G), immediacy indexes (column H), and the number of source items each journal published in 1982 (column I). Impact indicates how often, on average, an article published by a certain journal in a given two-year period was cited during a particular year. The 1982 impact in column G was arrived at by dividing the number of a journal's 1982 citations to articles published in 1980-1981 by the total number of 1980-1981 articles published by that journal. Immediacy is a measure of how often a journal's articles were cited in the same year in which they were published.

The 1982 source item counts, as well as impact and immediacy data, are unavailable for several journals in Table 2, for many reasons. Three are not yet included in *SCI*'s coverage: *Acta Astronomica*, *Bulletin of the American Astronomical Society*, and *Information Bulletin on Variable Stars*. The first two are being evaluated for future coverage. *Astronomische Nachrichten* was recently added to *SCI*'s coverage.

Memoirs of the Royal Astronomical Society ceased publication in 1978. However, articles published in it are still cited. *Zeitschrift für Astrophysik*, the *Bulletin of the Astronomical Institutes of the Netherlands*, and *Annales d'Astrophysique* merged to form *Astronomy and Astrophysics* in 1969. *Physical Review*, as it appears in Table 2, is the pre-1975 version. In that year it split into several editions, each of which now has its own separate source and citation information. In fact, *Physical Review A—General Physics* and *Physical Review D—Particles and Fields* also appear in Table 2.

The 50 journals in Table 2 received 80,000 citations from the core astrosciences journals, or almost 69 percent of all the references cited by the core group in 1982. Eighteen of the journals in Table 2 are themselves members of the core, and are indicated by asterisks. Altogether, these 18 journals received

Table 2: The 50 journals most cited by core astrosciences journals in 1982. An asterisk indicates a core journal. A=citations received from core journals. B=citations received from all journals. C=self-citations. D=percent of citations from all journals that are core journal citations (A/B). E=percent of citations from all journals that are self-citations (self-cited rate, C/B). F=percent of core citations that are self-citations (C/A). G=impact factor. H=immediacy index. I=1982 source items.

	A	B	C	D	E	F	G	H	I
*Astrophys. J.[1]	34,526	41,464	17,544	83.3	42.3	50.8	4.07	1.20	1310
*Astron. Astrophys.	10,061	11,206	3390	89.8	30.3	33.7	2.28	.54	683
*Mon. Notic. Roy. Astron. Soc.	6965	8144	1754	85.5	21.5	25.2	2.39	.76	401
*Astron. J.	3228	3558	690	90.7	19.4	21.4	1.81	.34	199
*Sol. Phys.	2693	3341	1155	80.6	34.6	42.9	1.75	.67	212
J. Geophys. Res.	2409	25,430	—	9.5	—	—	2.84	1.02	1045
Nature	2348	110,293	—	2.1	—	—	8.75	2.10	1362
*Publ. Astron. Soc. Pac.	1713	1857	256	92.2	13.8	14.9	1.16	.27	188
*Annu. Rev. Astron. Astrophys.	1354	1711	61	79.1	3.6	4.5	11.96	1.45	20
*Astrophys. Space Sci.	1326	1814	458	73.1	25.3	34.5	.80	.34	287
*Icarus	1279	2386	672	53.6	28.2	52.5	1.92	.86	125
Science	769	70,867	—	1.1	—	—	6.81	1.73	988
*Astron. Zh. SSSR	755	1039	258	72.7	24.8	34.2	.48	.30	153
J. Chem. Phys.	569	71,173	—	.80	—	—	2.95	.63	1714
Bull. Amer. Astron. Soc.	523	647	—	80.8	—	—	—	—	—
*Publ. Astron. Soc. Jpn.	483	578	81	83.6	14.0	16.8	1.14	.44	41
*Space Sci. Rev.	456	1167	97	39.1	8.3	21.3	1.35	.78	41
Phys. Rev. Lett.	425	44,487	—	1.0	—	—	6.20	1.34	1036
*Z. Naturforsch. Teil A	411	3740	370	11.0	9.9	90.0	.88	.32	223
*Astrophys. Lett.	395	472	4	83.7	.9	1.0	1.36	.12	26
Phys. Fluids	365	5731	—	6.4	—	—	1.32	.26	339
Planet. Space Sci.	330	2303	—	14.3	—	—	1.63	.56	129
Geophys. Res. Lett.	325	3491	—	9.3	—	—	2.01	.53	341
Phys. Rev.	315	31,568	—	1.0	—	—	—	—	—
Austral. J. Phys.	313	886	—	35.3	—	—	.64	.24	63
Acta Astron.	312	357	—	87.4	—	—	—	—	—
*Celest. Mech.	304	386	211	78.8	54.7	69.4	.44	.30	104
J. Atmos. Sci.	280	6272	—	4.5	—	—	2.69	.70	234
*Bull. Astron. Inst. Czech.	278	297	140	93.6	47.1	50.4	.52	.30	53
J. Fluid Mech.	262	7094	—	3.7	—	—	1.47	.42	311
Sov. Astron. Lett.—Engl. Tr.	253	410	—	61.7	—	—	—	—	76
Z. Astrophys.	249	330	—	74.5	—	—	—	—	—
Rev. Geophys. Space Phys.	238	2028	—	11.7	—	—	4.46	.89	47
Bull. Astron. Inst. Neth.	233	254	—	91.7	—	—	—	—	—
Proc. Roy. Soc. London Ser. A	233	11,155	—	2.1	—	—	1.60	.20	164
Mem. Roy. Astron. Soc.	227	244	—	93.0	—	—	—	—	—
J. Phys.—B—At. Mol. Phys.	222	8749	—	2.5	—	—	2.89	.90	401
J. Quant. Spectrosc. Radiat.	218	1662	—	13.1	—	—	1.03	.31	121
*Observatory	213	237	16	89.9	6.8	7.5	.66	.17	29
Phys. Rev. D—Part. Fields	205	16,752	—	1.2	—	—	2.87	.65	837
Astron. Nachr.	203	232	—	87.5	—	—	—	—	—
*Moon Planets	202	394	87	51.3	22.1	43.1	1.14	.41	42
Rev. Mod. Phys.	200	6074	—	3.3	—	—	20.71	2.41	22
Phys. Scr.	194	2303	—	8.4	—	—	1.62	.30	280
Appl. Opt.	192	8262	—	2.3	—	—	1.74	.36	716
Ann. Astrophys.	184	224	—	82.1	—	—	—	—	—
J. Atmos. Terr. Phys.	184	1753	—	10.5	—	—	.98	.24	111
Phys. Rev. A—Gen. Phys.	182	16,706	—	1.1	—	—	2.58	.67	849
J. Amer. Chem. Soc.	179	111,901	—	.2	—	—	4.72	.90	1835
Inf. Bull. Variable Stars	177	177	—	100.0	—	—	—	—	—

[1]Includes Astrophys. J. Suppl. Series

about 84,000 citations in 1982, of which about 80 percent were from core citing journals. By comparison, the 32 *non-core* journals in the table received a total of about 570,000 citations, of which just two percent came from the astrosciences core group.

In general, a journal with a long history will accumulate a larger number of citations than a more recently established one, regardless of the current quality of the older journal's articles. The longer a journal has been in print, the greater the number of citable articles it has published, and, thus, the more citations it receives. Much the same type of cumulative advantage is enjoyed by newer journals that publish a large number of articles each year. The top two journals in Table 2 perhaps illustrate these points. *Astrophysical Journal* has been in print since 1895. Even though it "only" published 1,300 items in 1982, it received 41,500 citations. *Astronomy and Astrophysics* received about 11,200 citations. It was started in 1969—a difference of almost 75 years. However, it published "only" 680 items in 1982.

Table 3 lists the 50 journals that most frequently *cited* the core astrosciences

Table 3: The 50 journals which most frequently cited core astrosciences journals in 1982. An asterisk indicates a core journal. A=citations to core journals. B=citations to all journals. C=self-citations. D=percent of total citations that are core journal citations (A/B). E=percent of total citations that are self-citations (self-citing rate C/B). F=percent of citations to core journals that are self-citations (C/A). G=impact factor. H=immediacy index. I=1982 source items.

	A	B	C	D	E	F	G	H	I
*Astrophys. J.[1]	27,144	40,382	17,544	67.2	43.5	64.6	4.07	1.20	1310
*Astron. Astrophys.	11,633	17,634	3390	66.0	19.2	29.1	2.28	.54	683
*Mon. Notic. Roy. Astron. Soc.	7350	10,551	1754	69.7	16.6	23.9	2.39	.76	401
*Astron. J.	3537	5168	690	68.4	13.4	19.5	1.81	.34	199
*Astrophys. Space Sci.	3279	6348	458	51.7	7.2	14.0	.80	.34	287
*Sol. Phys.	2333	4006	1155	58.2	28.8	49.5	1.75	.67	212
*Annu. Rev. Astron. Astrophys.	2227	3225	61	69.1	1.9	2.7	11.96	1.45	20
*Publ. Astron. Soc. Pac.	2145	3329	256	64.4	7.7	11.9	1.16	.27	188
Nature	1426	36,347	—	3.9	—	—	8.75	2.10	1362
*Astron. Zh. SSSR	1366	2749	258	49.7	9.4	18.9	.48	.30	153
J. Geophys. Res.	1246	30,880	—	4.0	—	—	2.84	1.02	1045
*Icarus	1184	4236	672	28.0	15.9	56.8	1.92	.86	125
*Space Sci. Rev.	819	3262	97	25.1	3.0	11.8	1.35	.78	41
Rev. Mod. Phys.	810	7313	—	11.1	—	—	20.71	2.41	22
Ann. N.Y. Acad. Sci.	587	19,644	—	3.0	—	—	1.65	.43	798
*Publ. Astron. Soc. Jpn.	528	782	81	67.5	10.4	15.3	1.14	.44	41
*Celest. Mech.	470	1228	211	38.3	17.2	44.9	.44	.30	104
*Moon Planets	416	1328	87	31.3	6.6	20.9	1.14	.41	42
*Z. Naturforsch. Teil A	408	4337	370	9.4	8.5	90.7	.88	.32	223
Sov. Astron. Lett.—Engl. Tr.	406	907	—	44.8	—	—	—	—	76
Science	398	27,145	—	1.5	—	—	6.81	1.73	988
Rev. Geophys. Space Phys.	375	5006	—	7.5	—	—	4.46	.89	47
*Vistas Astronomy	374	866	8	43.2	.9	2.1	—	—	19
J. Chem. Phys.	363	48,059	—	.8	—	—	2.95	.63	1714
*Bull. Astron. Inst. Czech.	351	906	140	38.7	15.5	39.9	.52	.30	53
*Astrophys. Lett.	296	415	4	71.3	1.0	1.4	1.36	.12	26
Phys. Rev. D—Part. Fields	291	19,806	—	1.5	—	—	2.87	.65	837
Phil. Trans. Roy. Soc. London A	287	5234	—	5.5	—	—	1.43	.17	149
Planet. Space Sci.	279	3155	—	8.8	—	—	1.63	.56	129
Phys. Rev. A—Gen. Phys.	273	19,758	—	1.4	—	—	2.58	.67	849
Geochim. Cosmochim. Acta	262	9756	—	2.7	—	—	3.06	.72	224
Rep. Progr. Phys.	261	4399	—	5.9	—	—	7.08	.48	27
Prog. Theor. Phys. Kyoto	255	7491	—	3.4	—	—	1.44	.54	294
*Quart. J. Roy. Astron. Soc.	249	909	9	27.4	1.0	3.6	1.12	.20	20
*Observatory	231	414	16	55.8	3.9	6.9	.66	.17	29
*Geophys. Astrophys. Fluid Dynam.	209	1032	34	20.3	3.3	16.3	.99	.46	57
J. Phys.—B—At. Mol. Phys.	199	10,527	—	1.9	—	—	2.89	.90	401
J. Quant. Spectrosc. Radiat.	196	2291	—	8.6	—	—	1.03	.31	121
Phys. Rep.—Rev. Sect. Phys. Lett.	188	11,682	—	1.6	—	—	6.39	.57	62
*J. Roy. Astron. Soc. Can.	186	454	40	41.0	8.8	21.5	.19	.18	28
Phys. Rev. Lett.	186	17,005	—	1.1	—	—	6.20	1.34	1036
Geophys. Res. Lett.	184	5037	—	3.7	—	—	2.01	.53	341
Nucl. Instrum. Method. Phys. Res.	181	15,520	—	1.2	—	—	1.17	.35	1058
*Annu. Rev. Earth Planet. Sci.	180	1834	8	9.8	.4	4.4	3.39	.16	19
J. Phys.—Paris	174	6332	—	2.8	—	—	1.13	.40	276
Nucl. Phys. A	147	20,385	—	.7	—	—	2.43	.89	572
Chem. Phys. Lett.	140	20,180	—	.7	—	—	2.19	.44	1110
Origins Life	139	1438	—	9.7	—	—	1.50	.35	26
Phys. Lett. A	134	9740	—	1.4	—	—	1.26	.34	837
J. Phys. Chem.	128	28,408	—	.5	—	—	2.44	.57	898

[1]Includes Astrophys. J. Suppl. Series

journals in 1982. Although these journals represent only a little over six percent of the 800 journals which cited the "Macro Journal of the Astrosciences" in 1982, they account for 90 percent of all the citations received by the core group that year. Almost half of the 50 journals in Table 3 are members of the core literature themselves, and, as in Table 2, these are indicated by asterisks. These 23 journals cited over 115,000 references in 1982, of which 58 percent were to the core literature in this study. In contrast, the non-core journals in Table 3 cited about 400,000 references, only two percent of which were to the core group.

Of the five core journals that rank highest in impact, four appear in both Tables 2 and 3. The other appears in Table 3 only. Since review journals in general have high impact, it is unsurprising to find that a review journal, the *Annual Review of Astronomy and Astrophysics*, is highest with an impact of about 12. In fact, its impact ranks fifteenth out of the 4,173 journals studied in the 1982 *JCR*. The second-ranked journal included in the core literature was *Astrophysical Journal*, with an impact of 4.1. The *Annual Review of Earth and Planetary Sciences*, which was the only one of the top five journals to appear only in Table 3, had an impact of 3.4. *Monthly Notices of the Royal Astronomical Society* was fourth among all core journals, with an impact of 2.4. Finally, *Astronomy and Astrophysics* had an impact of 2.3. By comparison, the average article in the "Macro Journal of the Astrosciences" had a 1982 impact of 1.1. The median impact of all the *SCI* journals in that year's *JCR* was .6.

Incidentally, an article in *Le Journal des Astronomes Français* reports that the journals which merged to form *Astronomy and Astrophysics* had a collective 1969 impact of only .8.[8] Apparently, in the case of *Astronomy and Astrophys-*

ics at least, the whole is greater than the sum of its parts. The increase in the impact of *Astronomy and Astrophysics* may be due at least in part to the growth of the astrosciences and space-related fields in continental Europe. However, greater visibility and circulation seem to be correlated with better quality papers.

The relevance of using 1980 and 1981 as the base years for obtaining a 1982 impact factor depends on what the "peak" citation period may be for astrosciences journals. In other words, the core journals might have higher impact factors if we use a two-year base *earlier* than 1980-1981. Table 4 lists ten high-impact astrosciences journals, showing how their impacts vary when different two-year bases are used. The *Annual Review of Astronomy and Astrophysics'* impact of 12 rises to 16 when we consider 1982 citations to its articles published in 1979-1980. A majority of the other core journals in the table also increase in impact when the 1979-1980 baseline is used. So that baseline might be more relevant if we were comparing the impact of astrosciences journals to those in other fields. Whichever two-year base period is chosen, however, the *relative* rankings of the journals in Table 4 would not change significantly.

Table 4: 1982 impacts of selected astrosciences journals using various two-year bases. A=journal title. B=1980-1981. C=1979-1980. D=1978-1979. E=1977-1978. F=1976-1977.

A	B	C	D	E	F
Annu. Rev. Astron. Astrophys.	11.96	16.4	11.75	8.13	8.46
Astron. Zh. SSSR	0.33	0.29	0.27	0.21	0.14
Astron. J.	1.81	1.88	1.92	1.68	1.41
Astron. Astrophys.	2.28	2.35	2.23	2.03	1.66
Astrophys. J.	4.07	4.14	3.68	3.07	2.68
Astrophys. Space Sci.	0.80	0.67	0.77	0.68	0.57
Icarus	1.92	1.75	1.66	1.45	1.02
Mon. Notic. Roy. Astron. Soc.	2.39	2.28	2.29	2.04	1.79
Publ. Astron. Soc. Pac.	1.16	1.19	0.93	0.80	1.04
Sol. Phys.	1.75	1.87	1.61	1.37	1.40

The peak citation period for the core astrosciences journals can be determined by examining their cit*ed* and cit*ing* "half-lives." These half-lives are shown in Table 5. The cit*ed* half-life of a journal refers to the median age of its articles that were cited in a given year. For example, the core journal with the shortest cit*ed* half-life for 1982 is *Geophysical and Astrophysical Fluid Dynamics*, at 3.1 years. This means that half of the citations this journal received in 1982 were to articles published from 1980 through 1982.

The cit*ing* half-life of a journal indicates the age of the material it cites. It is calculated by determining the median year of publication for the items cited by a given journal in the current year. Going back from the current year, then, a journal's cit*ing* half-life is defined as the period to which half of its citations were given. A figure greater than ten indicates that more than 50 percent of the cita-

tions given by a journal in 1982 were to articles published before 1973. In the future, *JCR* will provide more precise data on half-lives for such journals. A few of the core astrosciences journals have cit*ed* and cit*ing* half-lives greater than ten years. This indicates that the astrosciences literature, in general, remains useful and significant over a long period of time. However, the journal with the shortest cit*ing* half-life is *Moon and the Planets*, at 3.2 years. This means that in half of its 1982 references, the articles cited were published from 1980 through 1982.

A glance at Table 5 tells you that both the cit*ed* and cit*ing* half-lives of the astrosciences core journals cluster around four to seven years. In fact, a 1981 paper in the *Publications of the Astronomical Society of the Pacific* on the long-term citation rates of 326 astrosciences articles published in 1961 concluded that, on the average, citations reached a maximum rate five years after publication.[9] The study, by Helmut A. Abt, Kitt Peak National Observatory, Tucson, Arizona, showed that theoretical and observational papers were cited with equal frequency, and exhibited the same rate of decline. Abt also showed that the most frequently cited papers are almost invariably long ones, although only half of the long papers are cited frequently. According to Abt, it takes about 27 years for the citation frequency of highly cited astrosciences articles to decline to half the maximum rate.

Among the core journals, the *Annual Review of Astronomy and Astrophysics* ranks first in immediacy as well as in impact—1.45. *Astrophysical Journal* follows with 1.20; *Icarus*, .86; *Space Science Reviews*, .78; and *Monthly Notices of the Royal Astronomical Society*, .76. The "Macro Journal of the Astrosciences" has a 1982 immediacy of .32, which compared with a median of .17 for

Table 5: 1982 *SCI*® cit*ed* and cit*ing* half-lives of core astrosciences journals. Journals with no listing either received less than 100 citations in 1982, or gave out less than 100 citations in 1982. A = cit*ed* half-life. B = cit*ing* half-life. C = core astrosciences journal.

A	B	C
5.4	3.9	Annu. Rev. Astron. Astrophys.
4.6	6.0	Annu. Rev. Earth Planet. Sci.
5.3	5.7	Astron. J.
6.5	7.1	Astron. Zh. SSSR
4.4	5.0	Astron. Astrophys.
4.9	4.6	*Astrophys. J.
9.9	5.2	Astrophys. Lett.
5.1	6.3	Astrophys. Space Sci.
7.2	7.8	Bull. Astron. Inst. Czech.
6.0	9.2	Celest. Mech.
3.1	7.5	Geophys. Astrophys. Fluid Dynam.
4.4	4.8	Icarus
—	>10.0	Indian J. Rad. Sp. Phys.
>10.0	>10.0	J. Roy. Astron. Soc. Can.
5.3	5.4	Mon. Notic. Roy. Astron. Soc.
4.2	3.2	Moon Planets
8.9	6.2	Observatory
5.4	5.9	Publ. Astron. Soc. Jpn.
6.5	6.2	Publ. Astron. Soc. Pac.
6.7	5.3	Quart. J. Roy. Astron. Soc.
—	—	Sky Telesc.
6.8	6.3	Sol. Phys.
4.6	6.5	Space Sci. Rev.
—	—	Vistas Astronomy
>10.0	8.4	Z. Naturforsch. Teil A

*Includes Astrophys. J. Suppl. Ser.

Table 6: Articles from the core astrosciences journals cited 300 or more times, according to 1961-1983 *SCI®*, in alphabetical order by first author. A=total *SCI* citations, 1961-1983. Additional citations to papers published in 1960 and earlier, based on data from the 1955-1964 *SCI* cumulation, appear in parentheses. B=bibliographic data.

A		B
421	(3)	**Abell G O.** The distribution of rich clusters of galaxies. *Astrophys. J. Suppl. Ser.* 3(31):211-88, 1958.
394		**Anders E.** Origin, age, and composition of meteorites. *Space Sci. Rev.* 3:583-714, 1964.
328		**Bless R C & Savage B D.** Ultraviolet photometry from the orbiting astronomical observatory. II. Interstellar extinction. *Astrophys. J.* 171:293-308, 1972.
378		**Brocklehurst M.** Calculations of the level populations for the low levels of hydrogenic ions in gaseous nebulae. *Mon. Notic. Roy. Astron. Soc.* 153:471-90, 1971.
340	(2)	**Burgess A & Seaton M J.** A general formula for the calculation of atomic photo-ionization cross sections. *Mon. Notic. Roy. Astron. Soc.* 120:121-51, 1960.
477		**Cameron A G W.** Abundances of the elements in the solar system. *Space Sci. Rev.* 15:121-46, 1970.
338		**Colgate S A & White R H.** The hydrodynamic behavior of supernovae explosions. *Astrophys. J.* 143:626-81, 1966.
367		**Cox D P & Tucker W H.** Ionization equilibrium and radiative cooling of a low-density plasma. *Astrophys. J.* 157:1157-67, 1969.
327		**Eggen O J, Lynden-Bell D & Sandage A R.** Evidence from the motions of old stars that the galaxy collapsed. *Astrophys. J.* 136:748-66, 1962.
338	(29)	**Forster T.** Experimentelle und theoretische Untersuchung des zwischenmolekularen Ubergangs von Elektronenanregungsenergie. (Experimental and theoretical study of the intramolecular surface of electron-stimulated energy.) *Z. Naturforsch. Teil A* 4:321-7, 1949.
350		**Giacconi R, Murray S, Gursky H, Kellogg E, Schreier E, Matilsky T, Koch D & Tananbaum H.** The third *Uhuru* catalog of X-ray sources. *Astrophys. J. Suppl. Ser.* 27(237):37-64, 1974.
522		**Gingerich O, Noyes R W, Kalkofen W & Cuny Y.** The Harvard-Smithsonian reference atmosphere. *Sol. Phys.* 18:347-65, 1971.
324		**Goldberg L, Muller E A & Aller L H.** The abundances of the elements in the solar atmosphere. *Astrophys. J. Suppl. Ser.* 5(45):1-138, 1960.
366		**Goldreich P & Julian W H.** Pulsar electrodynamics. *Astrophys. J.* 157:869-80, 1969.
321		**Hayes D S.** An absolute spectrophotometric calibration of the energy distribution of twelve standard stars. *Astrophys. J.* 159:165-76, 1970.
343		**Herbst E & Klemperer W.** The formation and depletion of molecules in dense interstellar clouds. *Astrophys. J.* 185:505-33, 1973.
333	(37)	**Hiltner W A.** Photometric, polarization, and spectrographic observations of O and B stars. *Astrophys. J. Suppl. Ser.* 2(24):389-462, 1956.
681	(68)	**Humason M L, Mayall N U & Sandage A R.** Redshifts and magnitudes of extragalactic nebulae. *Astron. J.* 61:97-162, 1956.
389		**Iben I.** Stellar evolution within and off the main sequence. *Annu. Rev. Astron. Astrophys.* 5:571-626, 1967.
1090		**Johnson H L.** Astronomical measurements in the infrared. *Annu. Rev. Astron. Astrophys.* 4:193-206, 1966.
596	(245)	**Johnson H L & Morgan W W.** Fundamental stellar photometry for standards of spectral type on the revised system of the Yerkes spectral *Atlas*. *Astrophys. J.* 117:313-52, 1953.
493		**Jordan C.** The ionization equilibrium of elements between carbon and nickel. *Mon. Notic. Roy. Astron. Soc.* 142:501-21, 1969.
500		**Kellermann K I, Pauliny-Toth I I K & Williams P J S.** The spectra of radio sources in the revised 3C catalogue. *Astrophys. J.* 157:1-34, 1969.
542	(3)	**Maier W & Saupe A.** Eine einfache molekular-statistische Theorie der nematischen kristallinflussigen Phase. Teil I. (A simple molecular-statistical theory of the nematic crystalline-liquid phase. Part I.) *Z. Naturforsch. Teil A* 14:882-9, 1959.
540	(2)	**Maier W & Saupe A.** Eine einfache molekular-statistische Theorie der nematischen kristallinflussigen Phase. Teil II. (A simple molecular-statistical theory of the nematic crystalline-liquid phase. Part II.) *Z. Naturforsch. Teil A* 15:287-92, 1960.
420	(62)	**Moliere G.** Theorie der Streuung schneller geladener. Teilchen I. Einzelstreuung am abgeschirmten Coulomb-Feld. (Theory of the scattering of rapid charged particles. I. Single scattering in the shielded Coulomb-field.) *Z. Naturforsch. Teil A* 2:133-45, 1947.
308		**Morton D C & Adams T F.** Effective temperatures and bolometric corrections of early-type stars. *Astrophys. J.* 151:611-21, 1968.
458		**Oke J B & Schild R E.** The absolute spectral energy distribution of Alpha Lyrae. *Astrophys. J.* 161:1015-23, 1970.
384		**Panagia N.** Some physical parameters of early-type stars. *Astron. J.* 78:929-34, 1973.
402	(22)	**Parker E N.** Dynamics of the interplanetary gas and magnetic fields. *Astrophys. J.* 128:664-76, 1958.
389		**Penzias A A & Wilson R W.** Letter to editor. (A measurement of excess antenna temperature at 4080 Mc/s.) *Astrophys. J.* 142:419-21, 1965.
349		**Pringle J E & Rees M J.** Accretion disc models for compact X-ray sources. *Astron. Astrophys.* 21:1-9, 1972.
336		**Reifenstein E C, Wilson T L, Burke B F, Mezger P G & Altenhoff W J.** A survey of H 109 recombination line emission in galactic H II regions of the northern sky. *Astron. Astrophys.* 4:357-77, 1970.
323		**Schraml J & Mezger P G.** Galactic H II regions. IV. 1.95-cm observations with high angular resolution and high positional accuracy. *Astrophys. J.* 156:269-301, 1969.

417   **Shakura N I & Sunyaev R A.** Black holes in binary systems. Observational appearance. *Astron. Astrophys.* 24:337-55, 1973.

345   **Van Regemorter H.** Rate of collisional excitation in stellar atmospheres. *Astrophys. J.* 136:906-15, 1962.

321   **Wagoner R V, Fowler W A & Hoyle F.** On the synthesis of elements at very high temperatures. *Astrophys. J.* 148:3-49, 1967.

344   (6)   **Whitford A E.** The law of interstellar reddening. *Astron. J.* 63:201-7, 1958.

all *SCI* journals included in the 1982 *JCR*.

While statistical analyses of journals are revealing, it is always fascinating to look at the individual articles that have contributed to their high impact and long-term cumulative counts. Table 6 lists articles from the core astrosciences journals that have been cited 300 or more times. They are arranged alphabetically by first author. The number of citations each article received from 1961 through 1983 is shown. At the time we began this study, data from the 1955-1964 *SCI* cumulation were not available. Since it is now published, we have added, in parentheses, the counts for 1955-1960 when relevant.

Eight of the 25 core journals are represented in Table 6. *Astrophysical Journal* accounts for 20 of the 38 papers listed. *Zeitschrift für Naturforschung Teil A—Physik, Physikalische Chemie, Kosmophysik* published four of the most-cited astrosciences articles. The *Astronomical Journal, Astronomy and Astrophysics*, and the *Monthly Notices of the Royal Astronomical Society* each account for three articles. The *Annual Review of Astronomy and Astrophysics* and *Space Science Reviews* each published two of the most-cited papers, while *Solar Physics* published one.

The most-cited paper is by H.L. Johnson, then of the Lunar and Planetary Laboratory, University of Arizona, Tucson. Published in 1966 in the *Annual Review of Astronomy and Astrophysics*, it discusses the development of the field of infrared astronomy, and the various methods used to make observations us-

ing the long-wavelength radiation in the infrared part of the electromagnetic spectrum. The paper has been cited almost 1,100 times since its publication. Johnson also has the second most-cited paper on the list. It was coauthored with W.W. Morgan when they were both affiliated with Yerkes and McDonald Observatories. Yerkes is in Williams Bay, Wisconsin, and is administered by the University of Chicago, Illinois. The McDonald Observatory is located in Fort Davis, Texas, and is operated by the University of Texas, Austin. The paper describes a method of classifying stars by their spectral type, or the way in which the components of the light given off by an object relate to that object's physical and chemical composition. It has been cited over 840 times from 1953 to 1983.

The third most-cited paper was coauthored in 1956 by M.L. Humason, N.U. Mayall, and A.R. Sandage. Humason and Sandage were affiliated, at the time, with Mount Wilson and Palomar Observatories, operated jointly by the Carnegie Institution of Washington, Washington, DC, and the California Institute of Technology, Pasadena. Mayall was at the Lick Observatory, Mount Hamilton, California. Incidentally, Mount Wilson and Palomar Observatories were renamed the Hale Observatories in 1969. The paper, published in the *Astronomical Journal*, contains observational data on the redshifts of numerous galaxies. Redshift refers to the relationship between an object's distance from the Earth, the speed and direction of its travel, and how these factors affect the spectral pattern of the light emitted by that object. The paper has been cited over 750 times.

The 1971 paper in *Solar Physics* was coauthored by O. Gingerich, R.W. Noyes, and W. Kalkofen, all of the Smithsonian Astrophysical Observatory and Harvard College Observatory, Cambridge, Massachusetts; and Y. Cuny, Observatoire de Paris, Section d'Astrophysique, Meudon, France. It was discussed by Gingerich in 1981 in *Current Contents*®.[10] Four other papers in Table 6 have also been reviewed in *Citation Classics* ™ commentaries.[11-14]

Table 7 lists the most-cited article from each core journal in this study that does not already appear in Table 6. Only those journals that published at least one paper cited 50 or more times from 1961 through 1983 are listed. Twenty-three of the 25 core journals in this study met or exceeded this threshold. Table 7 also includes the number of papers published by each journal cited 50 or more times.

Data for *Astronomicheskii Zhurnal* and its translation, *Soviet Astronomy*, have been combined. Incidentally, *Moon and the Planets* was called simply *Moon* in 1971, when it published the article included in this table.

It is important to remember that Tables 6 and 7 do not include highly cited astrosciences articles published in non-core journals, such as *Science, Nature, Reviews of Modern Physics, Philosophical Transactions of the Royal Society of London Series A—Mathematical and Physical Sciences*, etc. We have identified a sample of astrosciences articles published in these non-core journals which have been cited at least 15 times by the core group in 1982. We then counted their citations from 1955 through 1983 in *SCI*. Table 8 lists the 18 most-cited astrosciences articles from this sample. It is also important to stress that we attribute no qualitative significance to the differences in citation frequency of the high-impact papers in this

Table 7: Most-cited articles from core astrosciences journals cited 50 or more times, 1961-1983 *SCI*®, in alphabetical order by journal title. Articles already listed in Table 6 are not repeated in this table. A = total *SCI* citations, 1961-1983. Additional citations to papers published in 1960 and earlier, based on data from the 1955-1964 *SCI* cumulation, appear in parentheses. B = bibliographic data. C = total number of papers from that journal cited 50 or more times.

A		B	C
95		Karig D E. Evolution of arc systems in the western Pacific. *Annu. Rev. Earth Planet. Sci.* 2:51-75, 1974.	7
134		Syrovat-skii S I. Dynamic dissipation of a magnetic field and particle acceleration. *Astron. Zh.* 43:340-55, 1966. (*Sov. Astron.* 10:270-80, 1966.)	9
110		Radhakrishnan V & Cooke D J. Magnetic poles and the polarization structure of pulsar radiation. *Astrophys. Lett.* 3:225-9, 1969.	16
168		Arnett W D. A possible model of supernovae: detonation of 12C. *Astrophys. Space Sci.* 5:180-212, 1969.	17
123		Plavec M & Kratochvil P. Tables for the Roche Model of close binaries. *Bull. Astron. Inst. Czech.* 15:165-70, 1964.	2
90		Deprit A. Canonical transformations depending on a small parameter. *Celest. Mech.* 1:12-30, 1969.	1
114		Garrett C & Munk W. Space-time scales of internal waves. *Geophys. Astrophys. Fluid Dynam.* 3:225-64, 1972.	12
231		Irvine W M & Pollack J B. Infrared optical properties of water and ice spheres. *Icarus* 8:324-60, 1968.	52
64		van den Bergh S. The galaxies of the local group. *J. Roy. Astron. Soc. Can.* 62:145-80, 1968.	1
72		Hartmann W K & Wood C A. Moon: origin and evolution of multi-ring basins. *Moon* 3:3-78, 1971.	2
130	(1)	Unno W. Line formation of a normal Zeeman triplet. *Publ. Astron. Soc. Jpn.* 8:108-25, 1956.	8
270		Robinson L B & Wampler E J. The Lick Observatory image-dissector scanner. *Publ. Astron. Soc. Pac.* 84:161-6, 1972.	27
127		Stromgren B. Problems of internal constitution and kinematics of main sequence stars. *Quart. J. Roy. Astron. Soc.* 4:8-36, 1963.	5
162		Iriarte B, Johnson H L, Mitchell R I & Wisniewski W K. Five-color photometry of bright stars. *Sky Telesc.* 30:21-4, 1965.	1
65		Pottasch S R. The diffuse emission nebulae. *Vistas Astronomy* 6:149-204, 1965.	6

A	B
80	Batten A H, Fletcher J M & Mann P J. Seventh catalogue of the orbital elements of spectroscopic binary systems. *Publ. Dominian Astrophys. Observ.* 15:121-295, 1978.
222	Boggess A, Carr F A, Evans D C, Fischel D, Freeman H R, Fuechsel C F, Klinglesmith D A, Krueger V L, Longanecker G W, Moore J V, Pyle E J, Rebar F, Sizemore K O, Sparks W, Underhill A B, Vitagliano H D, West D K, Macchetto F, Fitton B, Barker P J, Dunford E, Gondhalekar P M, Hall J E, Harrison V A W, Oliver M B, Sandford M C W, Vaughan P A, Ward A K, Anderson B E, Boksenberg A, Coleman C I, Snijders M A J & Wilson R. The IUE spacecraft and instrumentation. *Nature* 275:372-7, 1978.
167	Boggess A, Bohlin R C, Evans D C, Freeman H R, Gull T R, Heap S R, Klinglesmith D A, Longanecker G R, Sparks W, West D K, Holm A V, Perry P M, Schiffer F H, Turnrose B E, Wu C C, Lane A L, Linsky J L, Savage B D, Benvenuti P, Cassatella A, Clavel J, Heck A, Macchetto F, Penston M V, Selvelli P L, Dunford E, Gondhalekar P, Oliver M B, Sandford M C W, Stickland D, Boksenberg A, Coleman C I, Snijders M A J & Wilson R. In-flight performance of the IUE. *Nature* 275:377-85, 1978.
379	Brown R L & Gould R J. Interstellar absorption of cosmic X-rays. *Phys. Rev. D—Part. Fields* 1:2252-6, 1970.
91	Davidson K & Netzer H. The emission lines of quasars and similar objects. *Rev. Mod. Phys.* 51:715-66, 1979.
84	Gabriel A H. A magnetic model of the solar transition region. *Phil. Trans. Roy. Soc. London A* 281:339-52, 1976.
91	Hanel R, Conrath B, Flasar F M, Kunde V, Maguire W, Pearl J, Pirraglia J, Samuelson R, Herath L, Allison M, Cruikshank D, Gautier D, Gierasch P, Horn L, Koppany R & Ponnamperuma C. Infrared observations of the Saturnian system from Voyager 1. *Science* 212:192-200, 1981.
46	Ku W H-M, Helfand D J & Lucy L B. X-ray properties of quasars. *Nature* 288:323-8, 1980.
226	Lynden-Bell D. Galactic nuclei as collapsed old quasars. *Nature* 223:690-4, 1969.
70	Milne D K. A new catalogue of galactic SNRs corrected for distance from the galactic plane. *Aust. J. Phys.* 32:83-92, 1979.
41	Nandy K, Morgan D H, Willis A J, Wilson R, Gondhalekar P M & Houziaux L. Interstellar extinction in the Large Magellanic Cloud. *Nature* 283:725-9, 1980.
300	Paczynski B. Evolution of single stars. I. Stellar evolution from main sequence to white dwarf or carbon ignition. *Acta Astron.* 20:47-58, 1970.
64	Rees M J. Accretion and the quasar phenomenon. *Phys. Scr.* 17:193-200, 1978.
267	Ross J E & Aller L H. The chemical composition of the sun. *Science* 191:1223-9, 1976.
110	Scheuer P A G & Readhead A C S. Superluminally expanding radio sources and the radio-quiet QSOs. *Nature* 277:182-5, 1979.
138	Smith B A, Soderblom L A, Beebe R, Boyce J, Briggs G, Bunker A, Collins S A, Hansen C J, Johnson T V, Mitchell J L, Terrile R J, Carr M, Cook A F, Cuzzi J, Pollack J B, Danielson G E, Ingersoll A, Davies M E, Hunt G E, Masursky H, Shoemaker E, Morrison D, Owen T, Sagan C, Veverka J, Strom R & Suomi V E. Encounter with Saturn: Voyager 1 imaging science results. *Science* 212:163-91, 1981.
177	Smith B A, Soderblom L A, Johnson T V, Ingersoll A P, Collins S A, Shoemaker E M, Hunt G E, Masursky H, Carr M H, Davies M E, Cook A F, Boyce J, Danielson G E, Owen T, Sagan C, Beebe R F, Veverka J, Strom R G, McCauley J F, Morrison D, Briggs G A & Suomi V E. The Jupiter system through the eyes of Voyager 1. *Science* 204:951-72, 1979.
122	Vogt S S, Tull R G & Kelton P. Self-scanned photodiode array: high performance operation in high dispersion astronomical spectrophotometry. *Appl. Opt.* 17:574-92, 1978.

study. That's why they've been arranged alphabetically by first author—or, as in the case of Table 7, by journal title—rather than by number of citations.

Comparing Tables 2 and 3, we see that 13 core journals appear among the top 20 in both. They are: *Annual Review of Astronomy and Astrophysics*; *Astronomical Journal*; *Astronomicheskii Zhurnal*; *Astronomy and Astrophysics*; *Astrophysical Journal*; *Astrophysics and Space Science*; *Icarus*; *Monthly Notices of the Royal Astronomical Society*; *Publications of the Astronomical Society of Japan*; *Publications of the Astronomical Society of the Pacific*; *Solar Physics*;

Space Science Reviews; and *Zeitschrift für Naturforschung Teil A—Physik, Physikalische Chemie, Kosmophysik*. These journals ranked highest in terms of their references to the core and in the number of citations they received from the core. They also ranked among the top 20 journals in this study in terms of their impact and immediacy. However, there is considerable variation in their production of superstar papers, or should I say superastronomical!

In a look backward at our original small-scale study of astrophysics in 1974,[4] it is interesting to observe that a citation analysis of the obvious and central journal in the field can often provide a remarkably accurate picture of that field. Examination of the 1982 citing journal *JCR* entry for the *Astrophysical Journal* provides a remarkable confirmation of the complete census for the field. This concludes our look at the core literature of the astrosciences. In the weeks to come, our journal citation series will continue with an examination of the core journals in physical chemistry.

* * * * *

My thanks to Stephen A. Bonaduce and Abigail W. Grissom for their help in the preparation of this essay.

©1984 ISI

REFERENCES

1. **Garfield E.** Journal citation studies. 40. Anthropology journals—what they cite and what cites them. *Current Contents* (37):5-12, 12 September 1983.
2. --------------. Journal citation studies. 41. Entomology journals—what they cite and what cites them. *Current Contents* (11):3-11, 12 March 1984.
3. --------------. Journal citation studies. 42. Analytical chemistry journals—what they cite and what cites them. *Current Contents* (13):3-12, 26 March 1984.
4. --------------. Journal citation studies. XII. *Astrophysical Journal* and its *Supplements*. *Essays of an information scientist*. Philadelphia: ISI Press, 1977. Vol. 2. p. 120-4.
5. --------------. Journal citation studies. 34. The literature of dental science *vs.* the literature used by dental researchers. *Essays of an information scientist*. Philadelphia: ISI Press, 1983. Vol. 5. p. 373-9.
6. --------------. What a difference an "A" makes. *Essays of an information scientist*. Philadelphia: ISI Press, 1981. Vol. 4. p. 208-15.
7. --------------. Journal citation studies. 38. Earth sciences journals: what they cite and what cites them. *Essays of an information scientist*. Philadelphia: ISI Press, 1983. Vol. 5. p. 791-800.
8. **Steinberg J L.** *Astronomy and Astrophysics*, ou comment publier? (*Astronomy and Astrophysics*, or how to publish it?) *J. Astron. Franc.* (3):5-7, 1978.
9. **Abt H A.** Long-term citation histories of astronomical papers. *Publ. Astron. Soc. Pac.* 93:207-10, 1981.
10. **Gingerich O.** Citation Classic. Commentary on *Sol. Phys.* 18:347-65, 1971. *Current Contents/Physical, Chemical & Earth Sciences* 21(26):18, 29 June 1981.
11. **Anders E.** Citation Classic. Commentary on *Space Sci. Rev.* 3:583-714, 1964. *Current Contents/Physical, Chemical & Earth Sciences* 19(11):14, 12 March 1979.
12. **Colgate S A.** Citation Classic. Commentary on *Astrophys. J.* 143:626-81, 1966. *Current Contents/Physical, Chemical & Earth Sciences* 21(4):16, 26 January 1981.
13. **Iben I.** Citation Classic. Commentary of *Annu. Rev. Astron. Astrophys.* 5:571-626, 1967. *Current Contents/Physical, Chemical & Earth Sciences* 22(13):20, 29 March 1982.
14. **Penzias A A.** Citation Classic. Commentary on *Astrophys. J.* 142:419-21, 1965. *Current Contents/Physical, Chemical & Earth Sciences* 21(18):16, 4 May 1981.

Current Comments®

Social Gerontology. Part 2. Demography. The Effects of an Aging Population on Society

Number 22　　　　　　　　　　　　　　　　　　May 28, 1984

Part 1 of this essay discussed the effects of aging on intelligence.[1] The most recent research indicates that aging has a minimal effect on the mental functioning of healthy adults. These findings are significant because they contradict the stereotype of the aged person as a mentally impaired and dependent individual. The findings also add important information on the question of the compulsory retirement age. This is but one aspect of the many ways in which an aging population affects society.

So, in this second part of the essay we will discuss the factors that have caused tremendous growth in the world's elderly population. Also discussed are the steps individual nations are taking to cope with the social and economic burdens of this major demographic shift.

Emily Grundy, Department of Health Care of the Elderly, University of Nottingham, England, defines demography as the "numerical portrayal of human populations." This field is concerned with the "mechanisms of population change and with the structure and composition of populations. Demographers," she continues, "also study the causes of population trends, their consequences, and techniques for measuring them."[2]

One of the most important worldwide population trends of this century is increasing numbers and proportions of aged citizens. In the US alone, the number of persons aged 80 and older is expected to grow from the extant 5.6 million to more than ten million by the year 2000.[3] Demographers determine the reasons for this growth and project how many people will be in the elderly population in the future. Economists, politicians, and gerontologists use demographic data to plan social services and facilities for the elderly and determine if present services meet current needs.

Demographers generally agree that three basic processes affect population structure—fertility, mortality, and immigration. Jacob S. Siegel, Center for Population Research, Georgetown University, Washington, DC, notes that a common misperception among laypersons and social scientists is that increased longevity, resulting from lower mortality rates among the elderly, largely accounts for the growing elderly population.[4] In fact, fertility is the most important factor. It determines the number of people born within a given time period. Each group born within a specific interval, usually five to ten years, is referred to by demographers as a "birth cohort." This concept was incorporated into sociology at least partially as a result of research by Norman B. Ryder, Office of Population Research, Princeton University, New Jersey.[5] In his commentary on that *Citation Classic*™, Ryder suggests that his paper may have become well-cited because the cohort approach "may have provided some insight into how to think demographically about non-demographic subjects."[6]

Shirley H. Rhine, an economist with the Conference Board, New York, notes that the US now has a large number of people aged 65 and older because of high fertility rates during the late 1800s and early 1900s.[7] This group's relative *share* of the population—about 11.6 percent in 1980—was determined by the fertility rates of the cohorts that preceded and followed it.

In many developed countries, especially the US, one of the most noteworthy demographic trends of this century was the high birth rate from about 1945 to the mid-1960s. This period is frequently referred to as the baby boom. Due to the "baby bust" or drop in fertility that followed,[8] baby boomers will continue to represent a disproportionately large percentage of the population. The size of this group, which is now aged from about 25 to 40, has caused major social changes in the US. When this group reached school age, thousands of new facilities had to be built for them. In the early 1970s, when they entered the labor force, they faced stiff competition and limited opportunities for advancement. Mary Beard Deming and Neal E. Cutler, Ethel Percy Andrus Gerontology Center, University of Southern California, Los Angeles, report that by the 2010-2020 decade, the baby boom cohort will become the "gerontic boom."[9] Politicians, economists, and gerontologists are already investigating the effects this growth of the elderly population will have on social security, private pensions, long-term care, education, and other social institutions.

Another process that influences population aging is the mortality, or death, rate. Infant mortality rates affect the size of a cohort by setting a limit on the number of members who survive. The im-

provement in infant mortality rates during the first half of this century played an important role in the rising number of elderly people. According to Grundy, "Elderly people in the West today represent the very first generations in which there was a reasonable chance of surviving infancy and living on to reach old age."[2]

Until the 1950s, mortality rates for individuals 65 and older dropped only slightly. Between 1900 and 1949 average life expectancy at age 65 rose from 11.9 to 12.8 years in the US.[9] Eli Ginzberg, Conservation of Human Resources Project, Columbia University, New York, reports that in 1980, however, life expectancy for a 65-year-old reached about 15 years for men and 20 for women.[10] As medical science gains better control over the primary killers of elderly people—heart disease, cancer, and stroke—mortality rates among older persons will continue to decline.

Immigration is the third process influencing population age. Historically, immigrants have largely been young males. Immigration tends to bring the average age of a population down while increasing the proportion of men. The wave of some 27.6 million immigrants to the US between 1881 and 1930 brought about changes in the male-female ratio and age of the population.[9] However, at present levels, legal immigration is unlikely to have any widespread demographic effect on the US as a whole. Richard Suzman, Behavioral Sciences Research Branch, National Institute on Aging, Bethesda, Maryland, suggests immigration may, in the long-term, affect the population structure of states experiencing heavy illegal immigration, such as Texas, California, and Florida.[11]

On a more local level, though, the migration of young people from the cities to the suburbs and rural areas has left increasingly older inner-city populations in the US and UK. Charles F. Longino,

Center for Social Research on Aging, University of Miami, Florida, and Jeanne C. Biggar, Department of Sociology, University of Virginia, Charlottesville, note that elderly people who had migrated to the southern US after retirement are returning to their home states. This generally occurs after they become widowed, ill, and in need of financial and other assistance.[12] Longino reports that this "return migration" often benefits Sunbelt states, since people moving to such states as Florida are usually younger, healthier, and more affluent than those returning home.[13] In many developing countries, immigration of the young to urban areas has produced older populations in rural districts.[2]

Although the worldwide population is aging, Western nations presently tend to have the oldest populations. This can be explained, at least partially, by changes associated with the demographic transition. Developed by F.W. Notestein, then of the Office of Population Research, Princeton University,[14] and colleagues and W.S. Thompson, then of the Department of Gerontology, Miami University, Oxford, Ohio,[15] the demographic transition theory holds that, with modernization, nations shift from high to low birth and death rates. In the preindustrial stage, high birthrates are accompanied by high death rates from famine, epidemics, and wars. During the transition, or second stage, high birthrates continue, but the mortality rate, especially for infants and children, declines significantly. This decline results from economic and technology-related improvements such as better nutrition, sanitary water, and better and more accessible health care. A country enters the third stage when it becomes industrialized. Since infants have a greater chance of survival, parents have fewer children. Death rates also drop because of medical and other technological improvements. Countries in this stage of the aging cycle may reach zero population growth, or even population decline.

Suzman says that a fourth stage in the demographic transition—the postindustrial stage—occurs when a country has gained control over infectious diseases and can turn its attention to the chronic diseases that typically afflict the elderly.[11] At this stage, the population includes many elderly people with heart disease, cancer, and stroke—diseases that earlier would have killed them. Suzman notes that a major question facing nations in this stage is whether chronic diseases will be curable or whether society will be faced with increasing proportions of disabled, dependent elderly.[11] This question is the subject of an interesting debate between James F. Fries, Department of Medicine, Stanford University Medical Center,[16] and Edward L. Schneider, Biomedical Research and Clinical Medicine, and Jacob A. Brody, Epidemiology, Demography, and Biometry Program, National Institute on Aging,[17] on the "compression of morbidity" into very old age. Kenneth G. Manton, Center for Demographic Studies, Duke University, Durham, discusses the implications of a decline or delay in chronic disease among the elderly for predicting mortality trends in the US.[18]

Barry D. McPherson, Department of Kinesiology, University of Waterloo, Ontario, Canada, says that many developing countries started to enter the transition stage after World War II.[19] In these countries, high birth and death rates and short life expectancies had produced fairly young populations. According to Philip M. Hauser, Population Research Center, University of Chicago, in 1976 the median age in less developed countries was 23, compared to 33 in the developed countries.[20] The governments of many of these countries are supporting programs to lower fertility rates. If these birth control efforts are successful, the less developed countries will witness an increase in the proportion of elderly people. In fact, the aged population of developing countries worldwide is projected to grow 77 percent by the year 2000. Developed nations, in contrast, are expected to experience only a 30 percent increase.[21]

The situation of the elderly in these developing countries can be much more difficult than that of the aged in industrialized nations. According to Burkhard Schade, Department of Psychology, University of Dortmund, Federal Republic of Germany, Third World elderly generally are not supported by public institutions, as are their Western counterparts. Instead, most depend on their families, or their own ability to live self-sufficiently. If their families do not support them, they must rely on charity.[22] Their situation is exacerbated by the fact that they have to compete with other needy groups for limited funds.[23]

Further along in the population aging cycle are the US, USSR, Canada, Japan, Australia, and most of Southern and Eastern Europe. These countries are in the process of "aging." In contrast, the countries of northwestern Europe have already seen great increases in the proportion of elderly people and can be described as "aged."[2] Aged countries include the UK, Sweden, Austria, and the Federal Republic of Germany, where the elderly comprise at least 15 percent of the population.[24]

One of the most noteworthy characteristics of the present world, but especially elderly, population is a higher ratio of women to men. William Reichel, Department of Family Practice, Franklin Square Hospital, Baltimore, Maryland, notes that for persons aged 85 or older in the US, this ratio exceeds two to one.[25] This has been attributed to men's greater susceptibility to heart disease, cancer, and stroke, as well as their higher death rates from wars and accidents. In Europe, emigration of young men to the US in the 1920s and 1930s also contributed to uneven male-female ratios.[2] Since women in most developed nations tend to retire with lower pensions and social security benefits than men, large numbers of elderly women in the population will place increasing pressure on the social institutions that support them.

Another characteristic of the worldwide elderly population is the rapid growth in the number of people, particularly women, aged 80 and older. In the next 20 years, the world population will include 24 million additional people who are 80 and over.[21] Suzman says that individuals aged 85 and older comprise America's fastest growing population.[11] George L. Maddox, director, Center for the Study of Aging and Human Development, Duke University, notes that these very old people are at the greatest risk of long-term chronic illness and disability. Nearly half of them also need assistance in carrying out the activities of daily life.[21] And, according to the American Association of Retired Persons, more than 20 percent of those over age 85 in the US live in institutions.[26] Moreover, Social Security and most pension benefits in the US are based to a certain extent on preretirement income. According to Ann Foner, Department of Sociology, Rutgers University, New Brunswick, New Jersey, and Karen Schwab, US Social Security Administration, Washington, DC, the benefits of people who retired many years ago when salaries were much smaller are generally lower than those of more recent retirees.[27] As a result, these very old persons draw on a disproportionately large share of public services, particularly health services. Gerontologists are currently looking for ways to increase independence among these very old, and often disabled, people by offering home-based, rather than institutional, care. They are also investigating the future costs of income support and long-term, or nursing home, care for this larger population of very old people, and estimating the need for specialized housing and transportation.

Demographic change is prompting government officials to reexamine their retirement policies and the types of income and social support provided senior citizens. The old-age dependency ratio—the ratio of retired to working persons—is climbing worldwide, forcing governments to question the ability of future workers to finance income and social support for the elderly. According to the US Census Bureau's projections for moderate population growth, the aged dependency ratio (number of persons 65 and older per 100 persons 15 to 64) in the USSR and Eastern Europe is expected to increase from 14.6 in 1975 to 18.6 by the year 2000. In Latin America, this ratio is expected to increase from 7.1 to 7.5 during the same period.[28] In 1945, shortly after the US government began paying out Social Security benefits, each beneficiary was supported by the relatively smaller taxes of about 50 workers. Now each beneficiary is supported by higher taxes from about three workers. The situation looks even bleaker for the year 2035, when many members of the baby boom cohort will have retired.[10] Ginzberg reports that at that point, the ratio could be less than two taxpayers per beneficiary.[10]

The fact that people are living longer *after* retirement has also been a major factor in the precarious position of national pension systems. Partially as a result of this longer benefit payout period, nearly 28 percent of the US government's 1981 budget went to income support and social services for the elderly. Walter M. Beattie, School of Social

Work, Syracuse University, New York, notes that even at this rate nearly 15 percent of the US elderly, mostly women and minorities, remained below the poverty line.[29] The situation in the US parallels that of many European nations. In the Federal Republic of Germany, the cost of social security has multiplied sevenfold in the past 20 years. Italy expects its pension costs to double by 1989.[30]

Many social scientists believe that we will have to work to an older age in the future if benefits are to remain at present levels. In an effort that many hoped would reduce the benefit payout period and increase the amount of money collected for the Social Security fund, the US government in 1979 raised the mandatory retirement age from 65 to 70.[31] Most reports indicate, however, that this has not had the desired effects.[7] Rather, the trend toward earlier retirement that began after World War II and accelerated in the 1960s continues. Only 19 percent of men 65 and older are in the US labor force now, compared to 48 percent in 1947.[7] The number of men aged 65 and up in the work forces of many other Western nations has also dropped dramatically—from 50 percent in 1931 to about 11 percent in 1981 in the UK, and from 30 percent in 1968 to 16 percent in 1978 in France.[7]

A variety of factors account for the trend toward early retirement in Western nations. These include a diminution of the stigma associated with abandoning an economically productive role. The growing availability of private pensions—at least partly attributable to the desire of management and labor to bring in "new blood"—has also made retirement more attractive. Robert L. Clark, Department of Economics, North Carolina State University, Raleigh, believes governmental retirement policies are also responsible.[32] In the US, one such policy was the expansion and earlier availability of Social Security benefits. Since its passage in 1935, hospital and medical benefits (Medicare) and disability insurance have been added to Social Security. Benefit levels have risen several times and, in 1972, the government added automatic cost-of-living adjustments. The availability of early retirement at age 62 with reduced benefits has prompted people to leave the work force before age 65. And the Social Security "earnings test"—in which $1 of Social Security is forfeited for every $2 earned above an exempt amount—has discouraged people eligible for Social Security from continuing to work.

In several European countries, early retirement is encouraged as a deliberate government policy. Mary J. Gibson, associate editor, *Ageing International*, reports that many European governments, faced with high unemployment rates among youth, are offering attractive early retirement benefits in order to open more jobs for young people. In the Netherlands, individuals who have worked for the same firm for the preceding ten years may retire at age 62 at about 85 percent of their full-time wage. In France, workers who are laid off at age 60 or later, or who resign and agree not to take another job, can collect about 70 percent of their last salary. Although the goal of these programs is to reduce unemployment, Gibson says that such schemes generally have not opened up many jobs for young unemployed people.[33]

Although most governments of industrialized nations are faced with serious challenges to their social security systems, private pensions are mitigating the problem in a few countries. In Finland and Switzerland, private firms are legally required to provide retirement pensions. And some 80 to 90 percent of wage and salary workers are covered by pensions under industry-wide collective bargaining agreements in France and Sweden.[29] Legislation has been passed in the US to encourage companies to offer pensions.[34] But, in 1980, only about 21 percent of the retired population received private pension income.[29] The situation is appreciably better for US government workers, 90 percent of whom are covered by private pensions.

But, given present laws, pensions are unlikely to fill the growing needs of America's burgeoning and increasingly long-lived nonworking population. What seems to be needed, particularly in preparation for the gerontic boom predicted for the years 2010-2020, are major structural changes in the Social Security and pension system, and in work and retirement patterns.

Many changes in this direction were recently enacted through the Social Security Amendments of 1983.[35] These include a gradual rise in the retirement age to 67 by the year 2027, coverage of newly hired federal employees who had earlier been exempt from the system, and the taxation of Social Security benefits for retirees with higher incomes. The amendments also delayed the annual cost-of-living adjustment for 1983 benefits and increased the 1984 Social Security payroll tax.

McPherson says that other options discussed include paying a portion of Social Security benefits out of general tax revenues, rather than just out of the Social Security tax levied on employees and employers.[36] Some commentators have suggested that workers pay taxes to be applied to their future Social Security benefits. Social Security benefits are now paid out of taxes from current workers.

Whichever approaches are taken, it is evident that the early retirement trend is becoming too expensive and will have to be changed. On a more optimistic note, though, the majority of respondents in a 1979 Harris poll of US citizens indicated they would be more willing to work beyond retirement age if flexible work options were available.[37] However, most would not work if it meant forfeiting benefits. Older persons said they would be most interested in part-time work, usually the same as or similar to their full-time jobs. M.H. Morrison, Department of Public Policy and Management, Wharton School, University of Pennsylvania, Philadelphia, notes a considerable response in firms that have offered part-time work to older workers. Unfortunately, few firms offer this opportunity.[38]

More flexible work options are available in Europe. The governments of France, Sweden, and Norway have enacted legislation to help older workers ease into retirement by working fewer hours and days over a period of weeks, months, or even years.[33,39] Some of these programs provide for partial pension benefits to offset earnings lost by reducing work schedules. In her survey of phased retirement in the UK, France, Belgium, and the Federal Republic of Germany, Constance Swank, National Council for Alternative Work Patterns, a Washington, DC-based organization that concerns itself with work scheduling, discusses several companies that have established programs to reduce the working time of older workers before full retirement.[39] In general, one can participate in these programs with little or no reduction in benefits or compensation.

Linda G. Martin, Department of Economics, University of Hawaii, Honolulu, says many Japanese companies allow post-retirement age workers to stay on at lower salaries, often in less responsible positions.[40] Although a few US companies, most notably Polaroid, John Deere, and Grumman, offer phased re-

tirement or part-time work for older employees, such programs are very much the exception.[41] However, some economists are predicting that the number of new entrants into the labor force will decline in the next few decades, due to the declining fertility rate that followed the baby boom.[7] This may provide more and better opportunities for older workers, particularly those willing to take entry-level jobs.[8]

Demographic research has had an important influence on the many disciplines contributing to social gerontological research. Consequently, papers on the effects of population aging appear in a wide variety of journals, particularly, of course, those devoted to aging and to demography. John Balkema, librarian, National Council on the Aging, notes that major social gerontology libraries find it necessary to subscribe to over 400 journals in order to cover the field.[42] It is not possible to name all the journals covering gerontological research here. However, the journals covered in *Social Sciences Citation Index®* (*SSCI®*) that are devoted exclusively to aging and demography are listed in Tables 1 and 2, respectively.

A few of the journals not devoted exclusively to aging which carry many articles on the effects of age on intelligence, discussed in the first part of this essay, are *Journal of Educational Psychology*, *Journal of Abnormal Psychology, Amer-*

Table 1: Journals covered in the 1983 *SSCI®* devoted to aging research.

Aging and Work
Educational Gerontology
Gerontologist
International Journal of Aging & Human Development
Journal of Geriatric Psychiatry
Journal of Gerontology
Journal of the American Geriatrics Society
Research on Aging
Zeitschrift für Gerontologie

ican Psychology, Human Development, Developmental Psychology, and *Journal of Social Psychology.* Papers on the effects of population aging on the labor force are carried in such journals as *Monthly Labor Review, International Labor Review,* and *Population Research and Policy Review.* However, the only journal devoted solely to age and work is *Aging and Work,* formerly published as *Industrial Gerontology.* All these journals are covered in *SSCI* and *Current Contents®/Social & Behavioral Sciences.*

Much of the important literature on social gerontology has appeared in books. Some of the most prominent of these are *Why Survive? Being Old in America*,[43] by Robert N. Butler, Department of Geriatrics and Adult Development, Mt. Sinai Hospital, New York; *Handbook of Aging and the Social Sciences*,[44] edited by Robert H. Binstock, Program in the Economics and Politics of Aging, Brandeis University, Waltham, Massachusets, and Ethel Shanas, Department of Sociology, University of Illinois, Chicago; and *The Economics of Individual and Population Aging*,[45] by R.L. Clark and Joseph J. Spengler, Department of Economics, Duke University. Three important sociological vol-

umes, edited by Matilda White Riley, National Institute on Aging, and colleagues, were published under the overall title, *Aging and Society*.[46-48] Historical accounts of old age in the US are available in *Growing Old in America*,[49] by David H. Fischer, Department of History, Brandeis University, and *Old Age in the New Land*,[50] by W.A. Achenbaum, Department of History, Carnegie Mellon University, Pittsburgh.

Some of the demographic research now under way deals with predicting population growth and aging trends. Many of the predictive models appear in the mathematical literature and are discussed in papers identified through our analysis of research fronts in the *Compu-Math Citation Index®*. Research fronts are specialty areas identified by clustering current papers that cite one or more core papers for that topic. The 15 core papers[51-65] in the front entitled "Nonnegative matrices and ergodicity of age structure in populations with Markov vital rates" discuss models for predicting the age structure of a population based on the recent history of birth and death rates. The four core papers[66-69] in the front "Nonlinear age dependent population growth" discuss models for predicting population growth when fertility and mortality rates respond to environmental factors. These models attempt to deal with situations in which, for example, the death rate rises as the population grows. Linear models, in contrast, would hold the death rate constant regardless of population density. Since it is not our main purpose to identify this area of research in detail, we have not identified the many institutions where this research is done.

Since population aging has already had a major effect on society, it is not surprising that organizations concerned with the rights and welfare of senior citi-

Table 3: A selected list of organizations devoted to promoting the interests of elderly people.

American Association of Retired Persons
1909 K St., NW
Washington, DC 20049
202-872-4700

Asociación Nacional Pro Personas Mayores
1730 West Olympic Blvd., Suite 401
Los Angeles, CA 90015
213-487-1922

Gray Panthers
3635 Chestnut St.
Philadelphia, PA 19104
215-382-3300

International Federation on Aging
1909 K St., NW
Washington, DC 20049
202-872-4700

National Caucus and Center on Black Aged, Inc.
1424 K St., NW, Suite 500
Washington, DC 20005
202-637-8400

National Council of Senior Citizens
925 15th St., NW
Washington, DC 20005
202-347-8800

National Council on the Aging, Inc.
600 Maryland Ave., SW
West Wing 100
Washington, DC 20024
202-479-1200

National Indian Council on Aging, Inc.
P.O. Box 2088
Albuquerque, NM 87103
505-766-2276

---

zens abound. According to Henry J. Pratt, Department of Political Science, Wayne State University, Detroit, Michigan, excluding local chapters of national organizations, some 1,000 individual groups promote the interests of the elderly.[70] The most visible and active among these are the Gray Panthers, the American Association of Retired Persons, the National Council of Senior Citizens, the National Council on Aging, and the National Association of Retired Federal Employees. Other smaller caucus-like bodies serve subgroups of the old. These include the National Council on Black Aged and Asociación Nacional Pro Personas Mayores (National Association of Hispanic Elderly). Several of these organizations are listed in Table 3.

The changing age structure of the worldwide population will obviously have a tremendous impact in the future, as it already has. By the year 2020, when elderly US citizens outnumber teenagers by two to one, we will probably see a shift away from the present emphasis on youth. Instead of watching commercials for hamburgers, sneakers, and tight jeans, we may see a marketplace oriented more toward retirement communities, continuing education, and other interests of what is predicted to be a more educated, affluent, and healthier elderly population.

Other societal changes may not be benign. In the US, as in most developed nations, people may have to work to an older age before retirement. Depending on your work, this may or may not be good news. An earlier essay on prolongevity research[71] noted that very few people are working on increasing the human life span. Leonard Hayflick, Center for Gerontological Studies, University of Florida, one of our primary information sources on that topic, notes in a *New York Times* interview that such research may not even be desirable. Unless plans are made soon to cope with it, a ten- or 20-year increase in longevity could have "absolutely catastrophic" social effects.[72]

* * * * *

My thanks to Joan Lipinsky Cochran and Terri Freedman for their help in the preparation of this essay. ©1984 ISI

REFERENCES

1. **Garfield E.** Social gerontology. Part 1. Aging and intelligence. *Current Contents* (14):3-13, 2 April 1984.
2. **Grundy E.** Demography and old age. *J. Amer. Geriat. Soc.* 31:325-32, 1983.

3. **Harris D.** USA tomorrow: the demographic factor. *Finan. World* 152:16-20, 1983.
4. **Siegel J S.** On the demography of aging. *Demography* 17:345-64, 1980.
5. **Ryder N B.** The cohort as a concept in the study of social change. *Amer. Sociol. Rev.* 30:843-61, 1965.
6. --------------. Citation Classic. Commentary on *Amer. Sociol. Rev.* 30:843-61, 1965. *Current Contents/Social and Behavioral Sciences* 13(51):22, 21 December 1981.
7. **Rhine S H.** *America's aging population: issues facing business and society.* New York: Conference Board, 1980. Report No. 785. 60 p.
8. Drastic demographic shifts seen. *NY Times* 23 January 1979, p. B12.
9. **Deming M B & Cutler N E.** Demography of the aged. (Woodruff D S & Birren J E, eds.) *Aging.* Monterey, CA: Brooks/Cole, 1983. p. 18-51.
10. **Ginzberg E.** The Social Security system. *Sci. Amer.* 246(1):51-7, 1982.
11. **Suzman R.** Telephone communication. 1 May 1984.
12. **Longino C F & Biggar J C.** The impact of population redistribution on service delivery. *Gerontologist* 22:153-9, 1982.
13. **Fine M J.** After years of sunny retirement, a one-way ticket here. *Phila. Inquirer* 15 April 1984, p. 1-A; 12-A.
14. **Notestein F W, Taeuber I B, Kirk D, Coale A J & Kiser L K.** *The future population of Europe and the Soviet Union.* Geneva: League of Nations, 1944. 316 p.
15. **Thompson W S.** Population. *Amer. J. Sociol.* 34:959-75, 1929.
16. **Fries J F.** Aging, natural death, and the compression of morbidity. *N. Engl. J. Med.* 303:130-5, 1980.
17. **Schneider E L & Brody J A.** Aging, natural death, and the compression of morbidity: another view. *N. Engl. J. Med.* 309:854-6, 1983.
18. **Manton K G.** Changing concepts of morbidity and mortality in the elderly population. *Milbank Mem. Fund Quart.—Heal. S.* 60:183-244, 1982.
19. **McPherson B D.** Demographic, social and environmental aspects of aging. *Aging as a social process.* Toronto: Butterworths, 1983. p. 75-103.
20. **Hauser P M.** Aging and world-wide population change. (Binstock R H & Shanas E, eds.) *Handbook of aging and the social sciences.* New York: Van Nostrand Reinhold, 1976. p. 59-86.
21. **Maddox G L.** Aging people and aging populations: a framework for decision making. (Thomae H & Maddox G L, eds.) *New perspectives on old age.* New York: Springer, 1982. p. 19-30.
22. **Schade B.** Aging and old age in developing countries. (Thomae H & Maddox G L, eds.) *New perspectives on old age.* New York: Springer, 1982. p. 98-112.
23. **Ginzberg E.** The elderly: an international policy perspective. *Milbank Mem. Fund Quart.—Heal. S.* 61:473-88, 1983.
24. **Ross V.** The graying of the north. *World Press Rev.* 30(3):59, 1983.
25. **Reichel W.** Demographic aspects of aging. (Reichel W, ed.) *Clinical aspects of aging.* Baltimore, MD: Williams & Wilkins, 1983. p. 518-21.
26. **American Association of Retired Persons.** *A profile of older Americans.* (Pamphlet—PF3049/383.)
27. **Foner A & Schwab K.** *Aging and retirement.* Monterey, CA: Brooks/Cole, 1981. 132 p.
28. **US Bureau of the Census.** *Illustrative projections of world populations to the 21st century.* Washington, DC: US Department of Commerce, 1979. Series P-23, No. 79.
29. **Beattie W M.** Economic security for the elderly: national and international perspectives. *Gerontologist* 23:406-10, 1983.
30. How Europe will cope with lag in population. *US News World Rep.* 89(11):82-3, 1980.
31. **US Congress.** *The Age Discrimination Act of 1975.* 29 USC § 631(a) (Suppl. II 1978).
32. **Clark R L.** Aging, retirement, and the economic security of the elderly: an economic review. *Annu. Rev. Gerontol. Geriat.* 2:299-319, 1981.
33. **Gibson M J.** Early retirement a widespread phenomenon in western countries. *Ageing Int.* 9(2):15-7, 1982.
34. **US Congress.** *Employee Retirement Income Security Act of 1974.* 29 USC § 1001-1381 (1976).
35. --------------. *Social Security Amendments of 1983.* 42 USCA § 1305. (1983).
36. **McPherson B D.** Work, retirement, economic status and aging. *Aging as a social process.* Toronto: Butterworths, 1983. p. 367-406.
37. **Louis Harris and Associates, Inc.** *Aging in the eighties: America in transition.* Washington, DC: National Council on the Aging, 1981. 169 p.
38. **Morrison M H.** The aging of the U.S. population: human resource implications. *Mon. Lab. Rev.* 106(5):13-9, 1983.
39. **Swank C.** *Phased retirement: the European experience.* Washington, DC: National Council for Alternative Work Patterns, 1982. 228 p.
40. **Martin L G.** Japanese response to an aging labor force. *Pop. Res. Policy Rev.* 1:19-41, 1982.
41. **Cowan W M.** The aging work force: implications for tomorrow's office. *Admin. Manage.* 43:22-3; 76; 78, 1982.

42. **Balkema J.** Social gerontology periodicals. *Behav. Soc. Sci. Libr.* 2:63-79, 1981.
43. **Butler R N.** *Why survive? Being old in America.* New York: Harper & Row, 1975. 496 p.
44. **Binstock R H & Shanas E,** eds. *Handbook of aging and the social sciences.*
    New York: Van Nostrand Reinhold, 1976. 684 p.
45. **Clark R L & Spengler J J.** *The economics of individual and population aging.*
    New York: Cambridge University Press, 1980. 211 p.
46. **Riley M W & Foner A.** *Aging and society. Vol. 1. An inventory of research findings.*
    New York: Russell Sage, 1968. 636 p.
47. **Riley M W, Riley J W & Johnson M E,** eds. *Aging and society, Vol. 2. Aging and the professions.*
    New York: Russell Sage, 1969. 410 p.
48. **Riley M W, Johnson M & Foner A.** *Aging and society. Vol. 3. A sociology of age stratification.*
    New York: Russell Sage, 1972. 652 p.
49. **Fischer D H.** *Growing old in America.* New York: Oxford University Press, 1977. 242 p.
50. **Achenbaum W A.** *Old age in the new land: the American experience since 1790.*
    Baltimore. MD: Johns Hopkins University Press, 1978. 237 p.
51. **Golubitsky M, Keeler E B & Rothschild M.** Convergence of the age structure: applications of the
    projective metric. *Theor. Pop. Biol.* 7:84-93, 1975.
52. **Cohen J E.** Ergodicity of age structure in populations with Markovian vital rates. I. Countable
    states. *J. Amer. Statist. Assn.* 71:335-9, 1976.
53. ------------. Ergodicity of age structure in populations with Markovian vital rates. II. General
    states. *Advan. Appl. Probab.* 9:18-37, 1977.
54. ------------. Ergodicity of age structure in populations with Markovian vital rates. III. Finite-state
    moments and growth rate; an illustration. *Advan. Appl. Probab.* 9:462-75, 1977.
55. **Demetrius L.** Primitivity conditions for growth matrices. *Math. Biosci.* 12:53-8, 1971.
56. **Hajnal J.** On products of non-negative matrices. *Math. Proc. Cambridge Phil. Soc.* 79:521-30, 1976.
57. **Furstenberg H & Resten H.** Products of random matrices. *Ann. Math. Statist.* 31:457-69, 1960.
58. **Hajnal J.** The ergodic properties of non-homogeneous finite Markov chains.
    Proc. Cambridge Phil. Soc. 52:67-77, 1956.
59. ----------. Weak ergodicity in non-homogeneous Markov chains.
    Proc. Cambridge Phil. Soc. 54:233-46, 1958.
60. **Lopez A.** *Problems in stable population theory.*
    Princeton, NJ: Princeton University Press, 1961. 107 p.
61. **Parlett B.** Ergodic properties of populations I: the one sex model.
    Theor. Pop. Biol. 1:191-207, 1970.
62. **Pollard J H.** *Mathematical models for the growth of human populations.*
    Cambridge, England: Cambridge University Press, 1973. 186 p.
63. **Seneta E.** *Non-negative matrices; an introduction to theory and applications.*
    London: Allen & Unwin, 1973. 214 p.
64. -----------. On the historical development of the theory of finite inhomogeneous Markov chains.
    Proc. Cambridge Phil. Soc. 74:507-13, 1973.
65. **Sykes Z M.** On discrete stable population theory. *Biometrics* 25:285-93, 1969.
66. **Langhaar H L.** General population theory in the age-time continuum.
    J. Franklin Inst. 293:199-214, 1972.
67. **Gurtin M E & MacCamy R C.** Non-linear age-dependent population dynamics.
    Arch. Ration. Mech. Anal. 54:281-300, 1974.
68. **Griffel D H.** Age-dependent population growth. *J. Inst. Math. Appl.* 17:141-52, 1976.
69. **Von Foerster H.** Some remarks on changing populations. (Stohlman F, ed.) *The kinetics of cellular
    proliferation.* New York: Grune and Stratton, 1959. p. 382-407.
70. **Pratt H J.** National interest groups among the elderly: consolidation and constraint. (Browne W P
    & Olson L K, eds.) *Aging and public policy.* Westport, CT: Greenwood Press, 1983. p. 145-79.
71. **Garfield E.** The dilemma of prolongevity research—must we age before we die, or if we don't,
    will we? *Current Contents* (15):5-18, 11 April 1983.
72. **Boffey P M.** Longer lives seen as threat to nation's budget. *NY Times* 31 May 1983, p. 17.

Current Comments®

The 100 Most-Cited Papers Ever and How We Select *Citation Classics*

Number 23

June 4, 1984

Each week for the past seven and a half years, we have published in *Current Contents®* (*CC®*) personal commentaries by authors of *Citation Classics™*.[1,2] In these commentaries, authors of high-impact work discuss the roles they and their coworkers played in the evolution of their milestone papers and books. They also offer opinions on why their work proved important. We have now published more than 1,800 of these commentaries.

We are often asked how these commentaries are selected. Ideally, we would like to have published a commentary for every highly cited classic—certainly those among the top thousand. We would also want a fairly even representation of the classics from each major discipline or research specialty. In reality, however, a number of pragmatic considerations prevent us from achieving the ideal. This is an important point to keep in mind.

Citation Classics have been the basis for at least one study of scientific productivity. For example, E.O. Schulz-DuBois recently published an interesting analysis of the *Citation Classics* published by German scientists.[3] While his conclusions about the quality of research in postwar Germany may be valid, we cannot be sure that our "sampling" is random. It is quite possible that we might have selected more foreign scientists had we emphasized selection by journal on a country-by-country basis. I hope we have been unbiased, but in reviewing our selections to date we certainly could not claim that each country is adequately represented.

The fact is that we use citation frequency as the first criterion in selecting *Citation Classics* candidates. This almost invariably leads to articles published in the well-known international journals. As reported earlier, we have identified about 2,000 papers cited over 500 times in *Science Citation Index®* (*SCI®*). Table 1 provides a frequency distribution for articles cited between 1961 and 1980.

We have invited most of the first authors of the 1,000 most-cited papers to write commentaries. About 40 percent of them have done so. A small percentage have explicitly refused our invitations. However, we don't know how many simply failed to receive our invitations. Many authors moved long before our invitations were mailed. Occasionally, we used the address provided on the original paper. Many authors have died or are in retirement. One of my own professors, now 90, wrote that he no longer writes papers. We are systematically attempting to send invitations to coauthors, or other colleagues who might be in a position to comment on the highly cited work. This essay, and new letters we are sending out, are intended to facilitate location of at least one qualified commentator.

The 100 most-cited papers for the period 1961-1982 are provided in Table 2. The asterisks indicate those papers that have been featured as *Citation Classics*. If you are an author of one of the "missing" papers, please consider this an open invitation to write a commentary. If you were a colleague of any of the deceased authors, and if you are willing and able to write 500 words about the topic, please contact me. The benefits to students, historians, and others would be significant. These commentaries provide insights into the process of discovery that cannot be obtained by simply reading the original papers.

In future essays, we will catalog the additional candidates for *Citation*

175

Table 1: Citation frequency distribution for papers in *SCI*®, 1961-1980. A=number of citations. B=approximate number of items receiving that number of citations. C=approximate percent of the entire *SCI* file.

A	B	C
>5000	20	*
4000-4999	11	*
3000-3999	25	*
2000-2999	44	*
1000-1999	334	*
500-999	1500	*
100-499	54,000	.3
50-99	145,000	.7
25-49	393,000	2.0
15-24	558,000	2.9
10-14	656,000	3.4
5-9	1,690,000	8.8
2-4	4,562,000	23.7
1	11,228,000	58.2
	19,287,934	

*equals <.01 percent of total *SCI* file, 1961-1980.

Classics. While any paper cited over 400 times will probably qualify, citation frequencies will vary from field to field. A paper from the *Journal of Symbolic Logic* that has been cited over 50 times is a classic for that small field. This does not prevent superstar papers in small fields that have wide multidisciplinary impact. Commentaries on a well-cited review paper in even a relatively small discipline may tell the rest of us much about the early development of that field.

To facilitate selection of candidates, we have created many files at ISI®. One file provides a list of about 200,000 papers that have been cited over 50 times. For many high-impact journals, that threshold is quite low. Since these are frequency-ranked lists, the number of papers in each rank for a particular journal can tell us something about its size and just how unusual the citation frequency is.

In recent times, we have accumulated multi-year impact data on most journals. These data confirm that the lifetime citation expectancy of articles in certain journals will exceed 100 citations.[4] Articles published in the *Proceedings of the National Academy of Sciences* (*PNAS*), will reach that figure after 20 years. In fact 2,400 papers from *PNAS* have already been cited more than 100 times.

In order to obtain as wide a representation of journals as possible, we made a concerted effort to obtain commentaries for the most-cited paper in each specialty journal. As a result of this policy, we have identified hundreds of "small field" papers and journals. Unless we did this, papers from the superstar journals would predominate. While we could easily have justified selecting many more, we have so far published only 30-35 classics from journals like *PNAS*, *Science*, *Journal of the American Chemical Society*, *Lancet*, *Psychological Reviews*, etc.

Table 3 provides a partial list of the more than 500 journals that have been represented in *Citation Classics* to date. Space considerations forced us to limit this list to those represented by three or more commentaries. Thus, it includes many well-known, superstar journals. However, this almost defeats the point of the listing, which is intended to show that small fields are represented by journals such as *Nursing Research*, *Economic Geology*, and *Public Administration Review*.

A key factor which has tended to distort journal and field representation is the arbitrary decision to treat the articles published in journals covered in each *CC* edition as a "separate" population of papers. By publishing one classic each week in *CC/Agriculture, Biology & Environmental Sciences*, we in fact have an overrepresentation from plant science. Considering the number of papers published in biochemistry and other life sciences, we could easily justify four or more *Citation Classics* in *CC/Life Sciences* (*CC/LS*) each week. Similarly, the distribution for *CC/Engineering, Technology & Applied Sciences* and *CC/Physical, Chemical & Earth Sciences* (*CC/PC&ES*) is distorted. In order to reduce this bias, we recently reduced the number of engineering papers. This has irritated some readers. In addition, we found that it was difficult to convince engineering scientists to write about their classic papers. Furthermore, in engineering, as in the social sciences, books rather than journal articles are often the classic or primordial publications. Even a few technical reports surfaced, as would patents if we searched for them.

When I first read the Schulz-DuBois paper,[3] I found it hard to believe that more papers from *Chemische Berichte*

176

Table 2: The 100 most-cited *SCI*® articles listed in alphabetical order by first author. An asterisk (*) indicates that the paper was featured as a *Citation Classic*™ in *Current Contents*® (*CC*®). The issue number, year, and edition of *CC* in which the classic appeared are indicated in parentheses. (In 1977 and 1978, the same *Citation Classic* was featured in each edition of *CC*.) Two asterisks (**) indicate that the paper did not appear on the 1974 list of most-cited articles.

Citations	Bibliographic Data

2286 ** *Ames B N, McCann J & Yamasaki E. Methods for detecting carcinogens and mutagens with the salmonella/mammalian-microsome mutagenicity test. *Mutat. Res.* 31:347-64, 1975. (12/84/LS)

3533 Andrews P. Estimation of the molecular weights of proteins by sephadex gel-filtration. *Biochem. J.* 91:222-33, 1964.

2535 ** Andrews P. The gel-filtration behaviour of proteins related to their molecular weights over a wide range. *Biochem. J.* 96:595-606, 1965.

3921 Arnon D I. Copper enzymes in isolated chloroplasts. Polyphenoloxidase in *Beta vulgaris*. *Plant Physiol.* 24:1-15, 1949.

2161 Bardeen J, Cooper L N & Schrieffer J R. Theory of superconductivity. *Phys. Rev.* 108:1175-204, 1957.

2489 *Barker S B & Summerson W H. The colorimetric determination of lactic acid in biological material. *J. Biol. Chem.* 138:535-54, 1941. (46/83/LS)

5772 Bartlett G R. Phosphorus assay in column chromatography. *J. Biol. Chem.* 234:466-8, 1959.

2342 ** Bitter T & Muir H M. A modified uronic acid carbazole reaction. *Anal. Biochem.* 4:330-4, 1962.

5117 *Bligh E G & Dyer W J. A rapid method of total lipid extraction and purification. *Can. J. Biochem. Physiol.* 37:911-7, 1959. (52/78)

3911 ** *Bonner W M & Laskey R A. A film detection method for tritium-labelled proteins and nucleic acids in polyacrylamide gels. *Eur. J. Biochem.* 46:83-8, 1974. (1/83/LS)

8654 ** *Boyum A. Isolation of mononuclear cells and granulocytes from human blood. *Scand. J. Clin. Lab. Inv.* 21(Suppl.):77-89, 1968. (45/82/LS)

4550 ** Bradford M M. A rapid and sensitive method for the quantitation of microgram quantities of protein utilizing the principle of protein-dye binding. *Anal. Biochem.* 72:248-54, 1976.

2114 Bratton A C & Marshall E K. A new coupling component for sulfanilamide determination. *J. Biol. Chem.* 128:537-50, 1939.

9305 *Bray G A. A simple efficient liquid scintillator for counting aqueous solutions in a liquid scintillation counter. *Anal. Biochem.* 1:279-85, 1960. (2/77)

9803 *Burton K. A study of the conditions and mechanism of the diphenylamine reaction for the colorimetric estimation of deoxyribonucleic acid. *Biochem. J.* 62:315-22, 1956. (26/77)

3809 *Chen P S, Toribara T Y & Warner H. Microdetermination of phosphorus. *Anal. Chem.* 28:1756-8, 1956. (9/77)

3090 *Conney A H. Pharmacological implications of microsomal enzyme induction. *Pharmacol. Rev.* 19:317-66, 1967. (3/79/LS)

2419 ** Cromer D T. Anomalous dispersion corrections computed from self-consistent field relativistic Dirac-Slater wave functions. *Acta Crystallogr.* 18:17-23, 1965.

2325 ** Cromer D T & Liberman D. Relativistic calculation of anomalous scattering factors for X-rays. *J. Chem. Phys.* 53:1891-8, 1970.

3464 ** Cromer D T & Mann J B. X-ray scattering factors computed from numerical Hartree-Fock wave functions. *Acta Crystallogr. A* 24:321-5, 1968.

3464 Cromer D T & Waber J T. Scattering factors computed from relativistic Dirac-Slater wave functions. *Acta Crystallogr.* 18:104-9, 1965.

2043 ** *Cuatrecasas P. Protein purification by affinity chromatography. *J. Biol. Chem.* 245:3059-65, 1970. (22/80/LS)

13,222 Davis B J. Disc electrophoresis—II. Method and application to human serum proteins. *Ann. NY Acad. Sci.* 121:404-27, 1964.

2255 *de Duve C, Pressman B C, Gianetto R, Wattiaux R & Appelmans F. Tissue fractionation studies. 6. Intracellular distribution patterns of enzymes in rat-liver tissue. *Biochem. J.* 60:604-17, 1955. (12/77)

3379 Dole V P. A relation between non-esterified fatty acids in plasma and the metabolism of glucose. *J. Clin. Invest.* 35:150-4, 1956.

6052 Dubois M, Gilles K A, Hamilton J K, Rebers P A & Smith F. Colorimetric method for determination of sugars and related substances. *Anal. Chem.* 28:350-6, 1956.

2580 Dulbecco R & Vogt M. Plaque formation and isolation of pure lines with poliomyelitis viruses. *J. Exp. Med.* 99:167-82, 1954.

6013 *Duncan D B. Multiple range and multiple *F* tests. *Biometrics* 11:1-42, 1955. (4/77)

3448 *Eagle H. Amino acid metabolism in mammalian cell cultures. *Science* 130:432-7, 1959. (5/77)

4287 Ellman G L. Tissue sulfhydryl groups. *Arch. Biochem. Biophys.* 82:70-7, 1959.

2591 ** *Ellman G L, Courtney K D, Andres V & Featherstone R M. A new and rapid colorimetric determination of acetylcholinesterase activity. *Biochem. Pharmacol.* 7:88-95, 1961. (22/77)

4737 ** Fairbanks G, Steck T L & Wallach D F H. Electrophoretic analysis of the major polypeptides of the human erythrocyte membrane. *Biochemistry—USA* 10:2606-17, 1971.

11,162 Fiske C H & Subbarow Y. The colorimetric determination of phosphorus. *J. Biol. Chem.* 66:375-400, 1925.

13,974 Folch J, Lees M & Sloane Stanley G H. A simple method for the isolation and purification of total lipides from animal tissues. *J. Biol. Chem.* 226:497-509, 1957.

3019 Germain G, Main P & Woolfson M M. The application of phase relationships to complex structures. III. The optimum use of phase relationships. *Acta Crystallogr. A* 27:368-76, 1971.

3669 ** Gilman A G. A protein binding assay for adenosine 3':5'-cyclic monophosphate. *Proc. Nat. Acad. Sci. US* 67:305-12, 1970.

8777 *Gornall A G, Bardawill C J & David M M. Determination of serum proteins by means of the biuret reaction. *J. Biol. Chem.* 177:751-66, 1949. (13/79/LS)

Citations   Bibliographic Data

3927 **Graham R C & Karnovsky M J.** The early stages of absorption of injected horseradish peroxidase in the
** proximal tubules of mouse kidney: ultrastructural cytochemistry by a new technique. *J. Histochem.
Cytochem.* 14:291-302, 1966.

4875 ***Greenwood F C, Hunter W M & Glover J S.** The preparation of ^{131}I-labelled human growth hormone of high
** specific radioactivity. *Biochem. J.* 89:114-23, 1963. (15/77)

2590 ***Hales C N & Randle P J.** Immunoassay of insulin with insulin-antibody precipitate. *Biochem. J.*
88:137-46, 1963. (49/80/LS)

2225 **Hamburger V & Hamilton H L.** A series of normal stages in the development of the chick embryo.
** *J. Morphol.* 88:49-92, 1951.

2074 **Higgins G M & Anderson R M.** Experimental pathology of the liver. I. Restoration of the liver of the white
rat following partial surgical removal. *Arch. Pathol.* 12:186-202, 1931.

2264 ***Hodgkin A L & Huxley A F.** A quantitative description of membrane current and its application to
** conduction and excitation in nerve. *J. Physiol.—London* 117:500-44, 1952. (28/81/LS)

2203 **Hoffmann R.** An extended Huckel theory. 1. Hydrocarbons. *J. Chem. Phys.* 39:1397-412, 1963.

3838 **Hunter W M & Greenwood F C.** Preparation of iodine-131 labelled human growth hormone of high specific
** activity. *Nature* 194:495-6, 1962.

2690 **Jacob F & Monod J.** Genetic regulatory mechanisms in the synthesis of proteins. *J. Mol. Biol.* 3:318-56, 1961.

2239 ***Jaffe H H.** A reexamination of the Hammet equation. *Chem. Rev.* 53:191-261, 1953. (33/77)

2507 **Jondal M, Holm G & Wigzell H.** Surface markers on human T and B lymphocytes. 1. A large population of
** lymphocytes forming nonimmune rosettes with sheep red blood cells. *J. Exp. Med.* 136:207-15, 1972.

2208 **Julius M H, Simpson E & Herzenberg L A.** A rapid method for the isolation of functional thymus-derived
** murine lymphocytes. *Eur. J. Immunol.* 3:645-9, 1973.

4101 **Karnovsky M J.** A formaldehyde-glutaraldehyde fixative of high osmolality for use in electron microscopy.
J. Cell Biol. 27:137A-8A, 1965.

2075 **Karplus M.** Contact electron-spin coupling of nuclear magnetic moments. *J. Chem. Phys.* 30:11-5, 1959.

2572 ***Krebs H A & Henseleit K.** Untersuchungen uber die Harnstoffbildung im Tierkorper. (Studies on urea
** formation in the animal organism.) *Hoppe-Seylers Z. Physiol. Chem.* 210:33-66, 1932. (52/80/LS)

16,872 **Laemmli U K.** Cleavage of structural proteins during the assembly of the head of bacteriophage T4. *Nature*
** 227:680-5, 1970.

2164 ***Laskey R A & Mills A D.** Quantitative film detection of ^{3}H and ^{14}C in polyacrylamide gels by fluorography.
** *Eur. J. Biochem.* 56:335-41, 1975. (13/83/LS)

2391 ***Laurell C-B.** Quantitative estimation of proteins by electrophoresis in agarose gel containing antibodies.
** *Anal. Biochem.* 15:45-52, 1966. (51/80/LS)

2268 **Layne E.** Spectrophotometric and turbidimetric methods for measuring proteins. *Meth. Enzymology*
3:447-9, 1957.

6772 **Lineweaver H & Burk D.** The determination of enzyme dissociation constants. *J. Amer. Chem. Soc.*
56:658-66, 1934.

4143 ***Litchfield J T & Wilcoxon F A.** A simple method of evaluating dose-effect experiments. *J. Pharmacol.
Exp. Ther.* 96:99-113, 1949. (7/77)

100,639 ***Lowry O H, Rosebrough N J, Farr A L & Randall R J.** Protein measurement with the Folin phenol reagent.
J. Biol. Chem. 193:265-75, 1951. (1/77)

9480 ***Luft J H.** Improvements in epoxy resin embedding methods. *J. Biophys. Biochem. Cytol.* 9:409-14, 1961.
(20/77)

6793 **Mancini G, Carbonara A O & Heremans J F.** Immunochemical quantitation of antigens by single radial
immunodiffusion. *Immunochemistry* 2:235-54, 1965.

4862 **Marmur J.** A procedure for the isolation of deoxyribonucleic acid from micro-organisms. *J. Mol. Biol.*
3:208-18, 1961.

4469 **Martin R G & Ames B N.** A method for determining the sedimentation behaviour of enzymes: application to
protein mixtures. *J. Biol. Chem.* 236:1372-9, 1961.

2522 **Maxam A M & Gilbert W.** A new method for sequencing DNA. *Proc. Nat. Acad. Sci. US* 74:560-4, 1977.
**

2850 **Monod J, Wyman J & Changeux J P.** On the nature of allosteric transitions: a plausible model. *J. Mol. Biol.*
12:88-118, 1965.

2139 **Moore S.** On the determination of cystine as cysteic acid. *J. Biol. Chem.* 238:235-7, 1963.
**

3456 ***Moorhead P S, Nowell P C, Mellman W J, Battips D M & Hungerford D A.** Chromosome preparations of
leukocytes cultured from human peripheral blood. *Exp. Cell Res.* 20:613-6, 1960. (7/83/LS)

2610 ***Murashige T & Skoog F.** A revised medium for rapid growth and bioassays with tobacco tissue cultures.
** *Physiol. Plant.* 15:473-97, 1962. (43/78)

2083 ***Murphy B E P.** Some studies of the protein-binding of steroids and their application to the routine micro and
** ultramicro measurement of various steroids in body fluids by competitive protein-binding radioassay.
J. Clin. Endocrinol. Metab. 27:973-90, 1967. (3/81/LS)

4485 ***Nelson N.** A photometric adaptation of the Somogyi method for the determination of glucose. *J. Biol. Chem.*
** 153:375-80, 1944. (3/77)

3178 ***O'Farrell P H.** High resolution two-dimensional electrophoresis of proteins. *J. Biol. Chem.* 250:4007-21, 1975.
** (51/82/LS)

3236 **Omura T & Sato R.** The carbon monoxide-binding pigment of liver microsomes. 1. Evidence for its
** hemoprotein nature. *J. Biol. Chem.* 239:2370-8, 1964.

3414 **Ornstein L.** Disc electrophoresis—I. Background and theory. *Ann. NY Acad. Sci.* 121:321-49, 1964.

2333 **Ouchterlony O.** Diffusion-in-gel methods for immunological analysis. *Progr. Allergy* 5:1-78, 1958.
**

2369 **Palade G E.** A study of fixation for electron microscopy. *J. Exp. Med.* 95:285-97, 1952.

4706 **Reed L J & Muench H.** A simple method of estimating 50 percent endpoints. *Amer. J. Hyg.* 27:493-7, 1938.

Citations	Bibliographic Data
2058 **	*Reisfeld R A, Lewis U J & Williams D E. Disk electrophoresis of basic proteins and peptides on polyacrylamide gels. *Nature* 195:281-3, 1962. (6/81/LS)
13,907	*Reynolds E S. The use of lead citrate at high pH as an electron-opaque stain in electron microscopy. *J. Cell Biol.* 17:208-12, 1963. (32/81/LS)
3941	Sabatini D D, Bensch K, Barrnett R J. Cytochemistry and electron microscopy. *J. Cell Biol.* 17:19-58, 1963.
6985 **	Scatchard G. The attractions of proteins for small molecules and ions. *Ann. NY Acad. Sci.* 51:660-72, 1949.
4755	Scheidegger J J. Une micro-methode de l'immuno-electrophorese. (A micro-method for immunoelectrophoresis.) *Int. Arch. Allergy* 7:103-10, 1955.
2416	Schmidt G & Thannhauser S J. A method for the determination of deoxyribonucleic acid, ribonucleic acid, and phosphoproteins in animal tissues. *J. Biol. Chem.* 161:83-9, 1945.
3046	Shapiro A L, Vinuela E & Maizel J V. Molecular weight estimation of polypeptide chains by electrophoresis in SDS-polyacrylamide gels. *Biochem. Biophys. Res. Commun.* 28:815-26, 1967.
2966 **	*Singer S J & Nicolson G L. The fluid mosaic model of the structure of cell membranes. *Science* 175:720-31, 1972. (46/77)
2513	Smithies O. Zone electrophoresis in starch gels: group variations in the serum proteins of normal human adults. *Biochem. J.* 61:629-41, 1955.
2295	Somogyi M. Notes on sugar determination. *J. Biol. Chem.* 195:19-23, 1952.
3941 **	Southern E M. Detection of specific sequences among DNA fragments separated by gel-electrophoresis. *J. Mol. Biol.* 98:503, 1975.
8813	Spackman D H, Stein W H & Moore S. Automatic recording apparatus for use in the chromatography of amino acids. *Anal. Chem.* 30:1190-206, 1958.
4526 **	*Spurr A R. A low-viscosity epoxy resin embedding medium for electron microscopy. *J. Ultrastruct. Res.* 26:31-43, 1969. (50/79/LS)
5657 **	*Stewart R F, Davidson E R & Simpson W T. Coherent x-ray scattering for the hydrogen atom in the hydrogen molecule. *J. Chem. Phys.* 42:3175-87, 1965. (48/77)
2155 **	Studier F W. Sedimentation studies of the size and shape of DNA. *J. Mol. Biol.* 11:373-90, 1965.
3276	*Trevelyan W E, Procter D P & Harrison J S. Detection of sugars on paper chromatograms. *Nature* 166:444-5, 1950. (6/77)
2556 **	*Vane J R. Inhibition of prostaglandin synthesis as a mechanism of action for aspirin-like drugs. *Nature New Biol.* 231:232-5, 1971. (42/80/LS)
3487	*Venable J H & Coggeshall R. A simplified lead citrate stain for use in electron microscopy. *J. Cell Biol.* 25:407-8, 1965. (10/77)
2302	Warburg O & Christian W. Isolierung und Kristallisation des Garungsferments Enolase. (Isolation and crystallization of the enzyme enolase.) *Biochem. Z.* 310:384-421, 1941.
4742	*Warren L. The thiobarbituric acid assay of sialic acids. *J. Biol. Chem.* 234:1971-5, 1959. (36/77)
3308	Watson M L. Staining of tissue sections for electron microscopy with heavy metals. *J. Biophys. Biochem. Cytol.* 4:475-8, 1958.
15,189	Weber K & Osborn M. The reliability of molecular weight determinations by dodecyl sulfate-polyacrylamide gel electrophoresis. *J. Biol. Chem.* 244:4406-12, 1969.
2428 **	Weinberg S. A model of leptons. *Phys. Rev. Lett.* 19:1264-6, 1967.
2772	Yphantis D A. Equilibrium ultracentrifugation of dilute solutions. *Biochemistry—USA* 3:297-317, 1964.

and other German journals did not qualify. But clearly, the heyday of the *Berichte* was in the years before World War II. Undoubtedly, had we been able to gain access to our 1955-1964 data much sooner, we would have identified many more German papers of earlier vintage.

Table 4 lists the publication dates by decade of the 100 most-cited papers. Now that the 1955-1964 *SCI* has been published, we can identify many of the earlier classics. Although, in some cases, 40 years have passed since original publication, we hope many of the authors will still be available for comment. If not, we may solicit a commentary from a colleague as we did in the case of Karl G. Jansky's paper in *Proceedings of the IRE*.[5,6]

Contrary to widespread belief, the most-cited paper in a particular specialty does not always turn up in a specialist journal. The primordial articles in many specialties will turn up in a multidisciplinary journal like *Nature* or *Science*, or in some general medical journal such as *New England Journal of Medicine* or *Lancet*. Having selected a highly cited paper in a specialist journal, we often find that the author mentions another paper that is clearly the primordial one for that topic. While the commentary submitted concerns the most-cited paper in the leading journal of its field, it would not be fair to ignore other important papers, often cited more frequently, which appeared in another journal. In such cases, we invite the author of the other important paper to write a commentary. We have found that the authors themselves often prevent unfair selection because we encourage them to mention those papers that had an impor-

Table 3: Journals represented by three or more *Citation Classics*™, in alphabetical order by journal. A = journal title. B = total number of *Citation Classics*.

A	B	A	B	A	B
Acta Chem. Scand.	3	Cancer Res.	12	J. Histochem. Cytochem.	5
Acta Crystallogr.	8	Carbohyd. Res.	4	J. Lab. Clin. Med.	8
Acta Metall.	12	Chem. Eng. Sci.	10	J. Mater. Sci.	4
Acta Physiol. Scand.	4	Chem. Ind. London	4	J. Mol. Biol.	7
Advan. Agron.	3	Chem. Rev.	6	J. Nat. Cancer Inst.	6
Advan. Ecol. Res.	3	Child Develop.	3	J. Nutr.	3
Advan. Insect Physiol.	3	Circulation	8	J. Opt. Soc. Amer.	11
Advan. Phys.	6	Comput. J.	4	J. Pediat.	4
Advan. Prot. Chem.	8	Crop Sci.	4	J. Personal. Soc. Psychol.	13
AIChE J.	5	Diabetes	4	J. Petrol.	4
Amer. Econ. Rev.	3	Ecology	5	J. Pharmacol. Exp. Ther.	3
Amer. J. Bot.	8	Electroencephalogr. Clin. Neuro.	9	J. Sci. Food Agr.	5
Amer. J. Cardiol.	6			J. Sci. Instrum.	3
Amer. J. Clin. Nutr.	4	Eur. J. Biochem.	5	J. Vac. Sci. Technol.	5
Amer. J. Clin. Pathol.	7	Evolution	3	J. Verb. Learn. Verb. Behav.	4
Amer. J. Hyg.	3	Exp. Cell Res.	3		
Amer. J. Med.	17	Gastroenterology	6	Lancet	35
Amer. J. Obstet. Gynecol.	7	Genetics	7	Limnol. Oceanogr.	8
Amer. J. Pathol.	4	Gut	4	Medicine	5
Amer. J. Psychiat.	4	Ibis	3	Nature	14
Amer. Naturalist	10	IBM J. Res. Develop.	4	N. Engl. J. Med.	28
Amer. Psychol.	7	IEEE Trans. Automat. Contr.	4	New Phytol.	3
Amer. Sociol. Rev.	14	IEEE Trans. Inform. Theory	3	Nucl. Instrum. Method.	5
Anal. Biochem.	7	Ind. Eng. Chem.	8	Nucl. Phys.	8
Anal. Chem.	9	Ind. Eng. Chem. Anal. Ed.	3	Pediatrics	10
Anesthesiology	3	Int. J. Appl. Radiat. Isotop.	3	Percept. Psychophys.	3
Anim. Behav.	3	J. Abnormal Psychol.	6	Pharmacol. Rev.	4
Ann. Intern. Med.	7	J. Abnormal Soc. Psychol.	6	Phys. Rev.	23
Ann. Math.	4	J. Acoust. Soc. Amer.	4	Phys. Rev. A—Gen. Phys.	3
Ann. Surg.	4	J. Amer. Chem. Soc.	31	Phys. Rev. Lett.	4
Annu. Rev. Biochem.	3	JAMA—J. Am. Med. Assn.	7	Physiol. Plant.	5
Annu. Rev. Entomol.	5	J. Amer. Oil Chem. Soc.	7	Phytochemistry	4
Annu. Rev. Plant Physiol.	20	J. Amer. Statist. Assn.	3	Phytopathology	4
Appl. Opt.	3	J. Anim. Ecol.	3	Planet. Space Sci.	3
Arch. Biochem. Biophys.	7	J. Appl. Behav. Anal.	7	Plant Physiol.	29
Arch. Dis. Child.	4	J. Appl. Phys.	9	Planta	11
Arch. Gen. Psychiat.	8	J. Biol. Chem.	28	Proc. IEEE	21
Arch. Hydrobiol.	3	J. Biophys. Biochem. Cytol.	4	Proc. IRE	8
Aust. J. Exp. Biol. Med. Sci.	4	J. Cell Biol.	10	Proc. Nat. Acad. Sci. US	31
Behav. Res. Ther.	17	J. Cell. Physiol.	3	Proc. Soc. Exp. Biol. Med.	6
Bell Syst. Tech. J.	17	J. Chem. Phys.	35	Psychol. Bull.	23
Biochem. Biophys. Res. Commun.	4	J. Chem. Soc.	10	Psychol. Monogr.	3
Biochem. J.	21	J. Clin. Endocrinol. Metab.	14	Psychol. Rep.	5
Biochem. Pharmacol.	3	J. Clin. Invest.	12	Psychol. Rev.	31
Biochemistry—USA	7	J. Clin. Pathol.	5	Psychometrika	6
Biochim. Biophys. Acta	8	J. Consult. Clin. Psychol.	6	Quart. Rev. Biol.	3
Biometrics	6	J. Dairy Sci.	3	Quart. Rev. Chem. Soc.	3
Biometrika	6	J. Electrochem. Soc.	9	Radiat. Res.	6
Blood	7	J. Exp. Anal. Behav.	5	RCA Rev.	6
Bot. Rev.	5	J. Exp. Bot.	5	Rev. Mod. Phys.	12
Brit. J. Exp. Pathol.	4	J. Exp. Med.	10	Rev. Sci. Instr.	9
Brit. J. Haematol.	3	J. Exp. Zool.	5	Science	30
Brit. J. Psychiat.	8	J. Fish. Res. Board Can.	6	Soil Sci.	3
Brit. Med. J.	6	J. Fluid Mech.	7	Solid State Electron.	5
Can. J. Chem.	3	J. Food Sci.	3	Trans. ASME	5
Cancer	4	J. Geophys. Res.	13	Trans. Metall. Soc. AIME	12
				Transplant. Rev.	3

tant influence on their work. This fact is often revealed in editing when we add the citation frequencies to many of the author's own references. Quite often, we do this mischievously since we can often demonstrate when an author was wrong in thinking that a certain paper was ignored or little known. On the other hand, citation data may prove dramatically that he or she is right.

In addition to the systematic review of frequency-ranked author and journal lists, there are also other subjective inputs. Any reader is free to suggest that a paper is a classic in its field. I am not loathe to question such an assertion but am more than happy to confirm it. And there are many random inputs that remind us that a particular paper is a classic.

Table 4: Chronological distribution of publication dates of the 100 most-cited articles. A=publication date. B=number of papers.

A	B
1920s	1
1930s	5
1940s	8
1950s	28
1960s	41
1970s	17
	100

As of 1984, more than 500 different journals and 129 books have been represented in *Citation Classics*. Consider that there have been at least 20,000,000 papers published, and at least 10,000,000 of them since 1950. Therefore, there are at least 10,000 candidate publications if we limit our selections to one for each 1,000 published. If we continue to publish about 300 per year, it will take 30 years to cover another 10,000.

Since I would like to benefit from reading at least another 5,000 over the next decade, we will have to do something to accelerate the process. An expansion of the *Citation Classics* feature in *CC/LS* and *CC/PC&ES* is one obvious solution. Another is to create a new supplementary publication called the "Journal of *Citation Classics*." Yet another is to publish commentaries in other journals. There is always the danger of too much of a good thing, but considering the size of the scientific enterprise, we have only scratched the surface. Derek J. de Solla Price used to talk about the "Journal of Really Important Papers." I

think he might have accepted the "Journal of *Citation Classics*" as a compromise for the science historian, if not the working scientist.

We are also planning to publish collections of *Citation Classics* in separate volumes as interesting models of discovery. While collections of highly cited papers may not provide a uniform selection of the "best" in any field you care to mention, they do provide an amazing sample of high-impact research. Although certain journals have their usual expected list of methods classics, most do not, as can be demonstrated by an article-by-article examination of the classics for many leading journals.

It has been some time since we have published a list of the all-time *Citation Classics*.[7,8] Most of the papers in Table 1 have been mentioned before, in one essay or another. No need to comment further on the ubiquitous anomaly of the Lowry method.[9] However, since we last looked at the top 100 back in 1974, a number of newcomers have turned up. Of the original 100 list, only 44 of the same papers appear in Table 1. Two asterisks (**) indicate that the paper did not appear in the earlier list. This is a rather large shift. It remains to be seen whether the remaining group of 56 classics turn up in our future lists. Old classics rarely die. They don't even fade away. What makes them so different from papers that are "obliterated" is part of the exciting dynamics of the human process we call research.

©1984 ISI

REFERENCES

1. **Garfield E.** Introducing *Citation Classics*: the human side of scientific reports. *Essays of an information scientist*. Philadelphia: ISI Press, 1980. Vol. 3. p. 1-2.
2. --------------. *Citation Classics*—four years of the human side of science. *Essays of an information scientist*. Philadelphia: ISI Press, 1983. Vol. 5. p. 123-34.
3. **Schulz-DuBois E O.** Arbeiten deutscher Wissenschaftler, die weltweit am häufigsten zitiert wurden. (The most frequently quoted publications by German scientists.) *Umschau* 84(1):21-5, 1984.
4. **Geller N L, de Cani J S & Davies R E.** Lifetime-citation rates to compare scientists' work. *Soc. Sci. Res.* 7:345-65, 1978.
5. **Jansky K G.** Electrical disturbances apparently of extraterrestrial origin. *Proc. IRE* 21:1387-98, 1933.
6. **Hey J S.** Citation Classic. Commentary on *Proc. IRE* 21:1387-98, 1933. *Current Contents/Engineering, Technology & Applied Sciences* 15(23):16, 4 June 1984 and *CC/Physical, Chemical & Earth Sciences* 24(23):16, 4 June 1984.
7. **Garfield E.** Selecting the all-time Citation Classics. Here are the fifty most cited papers for 1961-1972. *Essays of an information scientist*. Philadelphia: ISI Press, 1977. Vol. 2. p. 6-9.
8. --------------. The second fifty papers most cited from 1961-1972. *Essays of an information scientist*. Philadelphia: ISI Press, 1977. Vol. 2. p. 21-5.
9. --------------. Citation frequency as a measure of research activity and performance. *Essays of an information scientist*. Philadelphia: ISI Press, 1977. Vol. 1. p. 406-8.

Current Comments®

The 1984 NAS Award for Excellence in Scientific Reviewing: E. R. Hilgard Receives Sixth Award for His Work in Psychology

Number 24

June 11, 1984

On April 30, 1984, the National Academy of Sciences (NAS) presented the 1984 NAS Award for Excellence in Scientific Reviewing to Ernest R. Hilgard, Department of Psychology, Stanford University. Hilgard was honored at an awards ceremony during the academy's 121st annual meeting in Washington, DC. This is the sixth year the award has been presented to an outstanding author of scientific reviews.

ISI® and Annual Reviews, Inc. have sponsored this award and co-donated its $5,000 honorarium since its establishment in 1979.[1] The award was originally named in honor of the founder of Annual Reviews, James Murray Luck, who served as that organization's editor-in-chief until his retirement in 1969. Luck continues to serve on the editorial committee of the *Annual Review of Biochemistry*, which he started in 1932. I should mention that neither ISI nor Annual Reviews was consulted on Hilgard's selection by a committee of the academy.

The disciplines from which outstanding reviewers are chosen for the NAS award rotate annually among the life sciences, the physical sciences, and the social and behavioral sciences. This year, Hilgard was selected from among a number of outstanding candidates in the social and behavioral sciences. The previous winner from this area of scholarship was economist John S. Chipman, University of Minnesota, for his reviews of international trade theories.[2]

In honoring Hilgard, the NAS cited his "creative synthesis of the literature on conditioning and learning theory, which shaped the field for decades, and his reviews in the difficult areas of hypnosis, suggestibility, and consciousness." His interpretation of the literature of *two* major fields of psychology is a remarkable contribution. Just as remarkable is that he continues his work today in this, his eightieth year.

The son of a horse-and-buggy doctor, Hilgard earned a degree in chemical engineering from the University of Illinois. Upon graduation, he served as an officer in the YMCA and studied at Yale Divinity School. Eventually, he decided that psychology might best address his interest in religion and science.

After receiving his PhD in experimental psychology from Yale University in 1930, Hilgard remained at the university as an instructor in psychology until 1933. In that year, he accepted a position at Stanford, where he has remained ever since. From 1942 to 1951, he served as chairman of Stanford's Department of Psychology. Since 1969, he has been emeritus professor of psychology, and director of Stanford's Laboratory of Hypnosis Research.

His numerous memberships and offices held in professional and honorary societies include the American Psychological Association (APA), the International Society of Hypnosis, and the Society for the Psychological Study of Social Issues, all of which he has served as president. His previous awards include the Warren Medal in Experimental Psychology and the Distinguished Scientific Contribution Award, presented to him by the APA.

Ernest R. Hilgard

Hilgard has authored more than 200 original research papers and reviews, plus numerous book reviews, biographies, etc. According to *Science Citation Index®* (*SCI®*) and *Social Sciences Citation Index®* (*SSCI®*) his work has amassed over 4,000 citations from 1955 to the present. Someday we will fill in the missing citation data for the pre-1955 years. His publications reveal a broad background in the laboratory and a lively concern for linking experimental results with theory. This breadth of interest has undoubtedly helped to make him a preeminent synthesizer and scientific reviewer. A selected bibliography of Hilgard's reviews appears in Table 1.

Most of Hilgard's work from the 1930s through the 1950s concerned one important area of psychology—conditioning and learning theory. Conditioning, the process by which a response becomes automatic as a result of reinforcement, was the subject of his early papers. A form of learning, conditioning opened the door for Hilgard to explore learning theories. His investigations led to his first series of major reviews.[3-7] One of these[4] appeared in the first volume of the *Annual Review of Physiology* in 1939.

One of the most influential of his reviews (with 334 citations) is *Conditioning and Learning*, published in 1940. The book had its inception in the fact that "theories of learning which make use of conditioning principles are not related in a simple manner to the facts from conditioning experiments."[5] Hilgard and his coauthor Donald G. Marquis, Yale, thus attempted to synthesize facts and theories. Their critical review pointed up inconsistencies and gaps in knowledge and thus helped to stimulate further research.

In another influential review,[6] Hilgard outlined the rigorous experimental designs needed to bring the study of learning into the laboratory. In keeping with his concern for theory, he addressed much more than laboratory techniques. Hilgard also discussed the importance of the "context" of any experiment—the conceptual framework that gives rise to useful laboratory work. This review, published in *Handbook of Experimental Psychology*, in 1951, has been cited in at least 250 publications over the past three decades.

Hilgard's reviews on learning were capped in 1948 by *Theories of Learning*.[7] Covering all the major theories in the first half of the century, the book explained each one, and also revealed gaps and suggested areas for further investigation. Hilgard's review had a momentous impact on this area of psychology. The NAS award committee stated that the book "almost instantaneously cast learning theory into the form that was taught and investigated for the next twenty years." *Theories of Learning* has been revised four times since its publication, the latest appearing in 1981.[8] As might be expected, the five editions of this book comprise Hilgard's most-cited work—over 650 citations.

In the late 1950s, Hilgard's research interests seemed to veer away from his previous work into the realms of suggestibility, hypnosis, and consciousness. Hilgard himself sees no great division between his earlier work and his later research on hypnosis. He feels that his in-

Table 1: A selected list of Ernest R. Hilgard's review publications.

Hilgard E R. The relationship between the conditioned response and conventional learning experiments. *Psychol. Bull.* 34:61-102, 1937.
Hilgard E R. Physiological psychology. Part I. The conditioned reflex. *Annu. Rev. Physiol.* 1:471-86, 1939.
Hilgard E R & Marquis D G. *Conditioning and learning.* New York: Appleton-Century-Crofts, 1940. 429 p.
Hilgard E R. *Theories of learning.* New York: Appleton-Century-Crofts, 1948. 409 p.
Hilgard E R. Methods and procedures in the study of learning. (Stevens S S, ed.) *Handbook of experimental psychology.* New York: Wiley, 1951. p. 517-67.
Hilgard E R. Impulsive versus realistic thinking: an examination of the distinction between primary and secondary processes in thought. *Psychol. Bull.* 59:477-88, 1962.
Hilgard E R. Hypnosis. *Annu. Rev. Psychol.* 16:157-80, 1965.
Hilgard E R. Hypnosis. *Annu. Rev. Psychol.* 26:19-44, 1975.
Hilgard E R & Hilgard J R. *Hypnosis in the relief of pain.* Los Altos, CA: William Kaufmann, 1975. 262 p.
Hilgard E R. *Divided consciousness: multiple controls in human thought and action.* New York: Wiley, 1977. 300 p.
Hilgard E R. Consciousness in contemporary psychology. *Annu. Rev. Psychol.* 31:1-26, 1980.

terest in the subject can be traced to some of his earliest publications.[9] Hypnosis, or autosuggestion, bears certain similarities to the conditioned response.

Others, however, perceive his venture into hypnosis as a courageous act. In the late 1950s, Hilgard, his reputation assured by *Theories of Learning*, could easily have waited for an honored retirement. Instead, he chose to investigate an area that was sometimes viewed as the purlieu of amateurs at best, charlatans at worst. According to colleague Lynn S. Johnson, Mental Health Center, Great Falls, Montana, "He was one of the first to really risk his reputation" on hypnosis. That reputation is not only intact today but has additional luster because Hilgard is "really an uncompromising scientist" who has studied hypnosis "as a scientist and not as a hypnotist."[10]

Hilgard has been responsible for numerous experimental reports on hypnosis and has also investigated theoretical explanations for the phenomenon. This work spawned his second series of major reviews.[9,11-15] The importance of these reviews to the field is acknowledged by the NAS award committee in their summary statement on Hilgard: "His critical, judicious, and painstaking reviews and analysis of the literature have done much to put a scientific stamp on the field that has often, with reason, been considered on the fringe of science."

This statement is backed up by the objective evidence from citation analysis, which shows that hypnosis is hardly "on the fringe of science" these days. "Clinical study of the significance and use of hypnosis" was one of the active research fronts of science in 1982 according to *ISI/BIOMED®* data. Four of the five core publications for the research front were written by Hilgard.[15-18] They include Hilgard's 1975 "review," *Hypnosis in the Relief of Pain*,[15] published in collaboration with his wife, Josephine R. Hilgard, a practicing psychiatrist and clinical investigator. The book was updated in 1984.[19]

It's hard to overstate the importance of review articles or books to the advancement of science. Hilgard himself suggested that "without scientific literature, we couldn't have science. And to make that literature accessible is an obligation on the part of scientists to one another."[20] I have advocated that review writing be considered a profession in its own right.[21] *SCI*'s *Journal Citation Reports®* repeatedly reveal that review journals achieve high impact.

Although it is agreed that good reviews are an essential aid to research, getting people to write them has always been difficult. To write reviews, they must put aside their own immediate research efforts and expend a great amount of time and effort in analyzing, synthesizing, and evaluating information in a limited subject area. In return, they have received very small financial reward. Research funding agencies should find a way to sponsor these efforts on a regular basis. While citation analysis and other methods can help identify important areas for reviewing, the role of the critical interpretive review will never be supplanted.

Until recently, there existed no formal award to recognize the contributions made by the most capable scientific reviewers. The cosponsorship of the NAS award by ISI and Annual Reviews is intended to encourage more scientists to try their hand at reviewing. The large number of *Citation Classics*™ which turn out to include reviews of the literature demonstrates all too well how useful reviews are to science in the continuing process of condensation.

I was delighted to be present, along with Bill Kaufmann, editor-in-chief of Annual Reviews, and Luck, on the occasion of this award. Not only has Hilgard made outstanding contributions to the field of psychology, he gave many long years of service as a member of the board of Annual Reviews.

Since the field of the award rotates annually, next year's presentation will be made to a reviewer from the life sciences. Nominations should be submitted before September 15, 1984 to the Office of the Home Secretary, National Academy of Sciences, 2101 Constitution Avenue, Washington, DC 20418.

* * * * *

My thanks to Tom Isenberg and Amy Stone for their help in the preparation of this essay. ©1984 ISI

REFERENCES

1. **Garfield E.** The NAS James Murray Luck Award for Excellence in Scientific Reviewing: G. Alan Robison receives the first award for his work on cyclic AMP. *Essays of an information scientist.* Philadelphia: ISI Press, 1981. Vol. 4. p. 127-31.
2. --------------. The 1981 NAS James Murray Luck Award for Excellence in Scientific Reviewing: John S. Chipman receives third award for his reviews in economics. *Essays of an information scientist.* Philadelphia: ISI Press, 1983. Vol. 5. p. 96-9.
3. **Hilgard E R.** The relationship between the conditioned response and conventional learning experiments. *Psychol. Bull.* 34:61-102, 1937.
4. --------------. Physiological psychology. Part I. The conditioned reflex. *Annu. Rev. Physiol.* 1:471-86, 1939.
5. **Hilgard E R & Marquis D G.** Conditioning and learning. New York: Appleton-Century-Crofts, 1940. 429 p.
6. **Hilgard E R.** Methods and procedures in the study of learning. (Stevens S S, ed.) *Handbook of experimental psychology.* New York: Wiley, 1951. p. 517-67.
7. --------------. Theories of learning. New York: Appleton-Century-Crofts, 1948. 409 p.
8. **Bower G H & Hilgard E R.** *Theories of learning.* Englewood Cliffs, NJ: Prentice-Hall, 1981. 647 p.
9. **Hilgard E R.** *Divided consciousness: multiple controls in human thought and action.* New York: Wiley, 1977. 300 p.
10. **Johnson L S.** Telephone communication. 3 May 1984.
11. **Hilgard E R.** Impulsive versus realistic thinking: an examination of the distinction between primary and secondary processes in thought. *Psychol. Bull.* 59:477-88, 1962.
12. --------------. Hypnosis. *Annu. Rev. Psychol.* 16:157-80, 1965.
13. --------------. Hypnosis. *Annu. Rev. Psychol.* 26:19-44, 1975.
14. --------------. Consciousness in contemporary psychology. *Annu. Rev. Psychol.* 31:1-26, 1980.
15. **Hilgard E R & Hilgard J R.** *Hypnosis in the relief of pain.* Los Altos, CA: William Kaufmann, 1975. 262 p.
16. **Hilgard E R.** *Hypnotic susceptibility.* New York: Harcourt, Brace & World, 1965. 434 p.
17. **Weitzenhoffer A M & Hilgard E R.** *Stanford hypnotic susceptibility scale. Forms A and B.* Palo Alto, CA: Consulting Psychologists Press, 1959. 56 p.
18. --. *Stanford hypnotic susceptibility scale. Form C.* Palo Alto, CA: Consulting Psychologists Press, 1962. 48 p.
19. **Hilgard E R & Hilgard J R.** *Hypnosis in the relief of pain.* Los Altos, CA: William Kaufmann, 1984. 302 p.
20. **Hilgard E R.** Telephone communication. 26 April 1984.
21. **Garfield E.** Proposal for a new profession: scientific reviewer. *Essays of an information scientist.* Philadelphia: ISI Press, 1980. Vol. 3. p. 84-7.

Current Comments®

100 Classics from
the *New England Journal of Medicine*

Number 25   June 18, 1984

Recently, we identified the 100 most-cited papers of all time,[1] and indicated which of them were the subjects of *Citation Classics*™ [2] commentaries. We now plan to publish a series of essays listing the most-cited articles from several leading multidisciplinary or multispecialty journals. Publication of these lists constitutes an open invitation to the authors of these *Citation Classics* to submit commentaries if they have not done so already. Simultaneously, we are sending letters of invitation to the authors involved.

This essay examines the classic articles published by the *New England Journal of Medicine* (*NEJM*). Numerous studies have shown this journal to be one of the most influential medical journals in the world. Indeed, it ranks among the highest impact journals regardless of discipline.

Of the thousands of articles published in *NEJM* since its inception in 1812, many hundreds would qualify as *Citation Classics*. Table 1 shows the frequency distribution for the 3,100 papers from *NEJM* cited 50 or more times between 1961 and 1982. Over 250 papers have been cited at least 200 times.

NEJM is famous for the "Ingelfinger rule." The present editor, Arnold Relman, believes that *NEJM* is so well-respected because of his strict enforcement of the rule, among other reasons. Formulated by his predecessor, Franz Ingelfinger,[3] the rule prohibits prior disclosure to the media of papers submitted to *NEJM*. When an author submits a paper, he or she may *not* disclose its substance prior to publication in *NEJM*. The rule undoubtedly protects the "newsworthiness" of *NEJM*. Presumably, it also protects the public. Otherwise, we might be misled by reports that had not been rigorously refereed by medical experts.[4] The Ingelfinger rule has been the subject of considerable debate,[5-10] too extensive to be reviewed here. The public visibility of *NEJM* was recently reinforced when "Bud" Relman was interviewed by Hugh Downs on *20/20*, an American television "magazine."

The 100 most-cited articles from *NEJM* are listed alphabetically by first author in Table 2. Column A shows the number of citations we found for each paper in *Science Citation Index®* (*SCI®*) from 1961 to 1983. These papers were cited at least 270 times during this period. For the papers published before 1961, we added data from the recently published 1955-1964 *SCI* cumulation. Additional *Citation Classics* published in the first half of the twentieth century will be identified when our source data base is extended even further to include pre-1955 material. Many of these could also be identified by limiting the analysis to citation data in the 1955-1964 *SCI* cumulation. In fact, a list of the 250 most-cited publications for that period is included in the introductory *Guide and Lists of Source Publications*[11] to the cumulation. We'll discuss these classics in the near future.

An asterisk in column B of Table 2 indicates that the paper has already been featured as a *Citation Classic* in *Current*

Table 1: Citation frequency distribution, 1961-1982 *SCI®*, for *NEJM* articles with 50 or more citations. A=number of citations. B=number of items receiving that number of citations. C=percent of group.

A	B	C
≥ 500	17	.6
400-499	13	.4
350-399	23	.8
300-349	29	.9
250-299	48	1.6
200-249	130	4.2
150-199	242	7.8
100-149	627	20.3
75-99	734	23.8
50-74	1222	39.6
	3085	100.0

Contents® (*CC®*). The issue number, year, and edition of *CC* in which the commentary appeared are shown in parentheses. Of the 23 *Citation Classics* included, all but one appeared in *CC/Clinical Practice*. In addition, they were mentioned in the list of *Citation Classics* published each week in six *CC* editions.

ISI® 's many detailed studies of *NEJM* confirm in many ways its importance to clinical practice and research. In unpublished article-by-article analyses, we have examined the many components of the impact of such journals as *NEJM*, *Lancet*, *British Medical Journal*, *Journal of the American Medical Association*, *Annals of Internal Medicine*, etc. These analyses confirm that letters to the editors of medical journals play an important role in the progress of medicine. David Spodick, St. Vincent Hospital, Worcester, Massachusetts, and Robert Goldberg, University of Massachusetts Medical School, have recently done an interesting analysis of the four basic types of such correspondence—letters concerning articles, those concerning editorials or essays, letters about letters, and letters presenting cases or original investigations.[12]

In the future, we intend to publish a separate analysis of most-cited "letters." The difficulty of doing so is complicated by the ambiguity of the term "letters." For example, "letters to the editor" of *Nature* report original research. There are also "letters" journals in physics, chemistry, etc. Then there are the corre-

spondence sections of many weekly journals such as *Science*, *NEJM*, *Lancet*, etc. We believe that *SCI* is the only indexing or abstracting service that indexes all of these items comprehensively. And the large number of citations to these letters can affect the impacts we calculate for journals, especially those with large correspondence sections, such as *NEJM* and *Lancet*.

In Table 3 we have provided the chronological distribution of the papers in this study. It is surprising how many of them were published in the 1970s. However, the dynamics of the literature explosion are such that the old is rapidly displaced by the new literature. A different method of analysis is needed to properly identify the *Citation Classics* for each year of the older literature. Most of the classics in Table 2 are core papers in ISI research fronts. For example, the most-cited paper, by D.S. Fredrickson and colleagues, was part of the core literature of a research front entitled "Metabolic derangements and clinical aspects of apolipoprotein disorders" included in our 1983 *Index to Research Fronts in ISI/BIOMED®*.[13] A more detailed discussion of Fredrickson's paper follows here.

Table 4 lists the countries where the authors of the most-cited papers in this study are based. For US papers, we also show the number of authors from individual states. As the official publication of the Massachusetts Medical Society, it is not altogether surprising that so many *NEJM* papers are by authors from that state. In fact, all are from the city of Boston. With the exception of one author from Connecticut, however, no other New England state is represented. A much more detailed study would be needed to determine if there is a "bias" in publications selected by this journal of international impact.

The oldest article in Table 2 was published in 1948 by a team of researchers from the Children's Medical Center, Boston: S. Farber, L.K. Diamond, R.D. Mercer, R.F. Sylvester, and J.A. Wolff. The article describes the effects of

Table 2: Most-cited articles from *NEJM*, 1961-1982 *SCI*®, in alphabetic order by first author. Asterisks indicate articles with *Citation Classics*™ commentaries. The issue number, year, and edition of *Current Contents*® in which these commentaries appeared are in parentheses. A=total citations, 1961-1983 *SCI*. B=bibliographic data.

A | | B

358 **Adams R D, Fisher C M, Hakim S, Ojemann R G & Sweet W H.** Symptomatic occult hydrocephalus with "normal" cerebrospinal-fluid pressure. *NEJM* 273:117-26, 1965. Mass. Gen. Hosp.; Harvard Med. Sch., Boston, MA; Military Hosp.; Nat. Univ., Bogota, Colombia.

380 *__Aisenberg A C & Bloch K J.__ Immunoglobulins on the surface of neoplastic lymphocytes. *NEJM* 287:272-6, 1972. Harvard Univ.; Mass. Gen. Hosp., Boston, MA. (24/82/CP)

380 *__Alfrey A C, LeGendre G R & Kaehny W D.__ The dialysis encephalopathy syndrome. *NEJM* 294:184-8, 1976. Univ. Colorado Med. Ctr., Denver, CO. (7/83/CP)

584 **Babior B M.** Oxygen-dependent microbial killing by phagocytes. *NEJM* 298:659-68, 1978. New Engl. Med. Ctr. Hosp. and Tufts Univ. Sch. Med., Boston, MA.

628 *__Baehner R L & Nathan D G.__ Quantitative nitroblue tetrazolium test in chronic granulomatous disease. *NEJM* 278:974-6, 1968. Children's Hosp. Med. Ctr.; Harvard Med. Sch., Boston, MA. (44/82/CP)

663 **Bast R C, Zbar B, Borsos T & Rapp H J.** BCG and cancer. *NEJM* 290:1413-20; 1458-69, 1974. NIH, NCI, Bethesda, MD.

399 **Beller G A, Smith T W, Abelmann W H, Haber E & Hood W B.** Digitalis intoxication. *NEJM* 284:989-97, 1971. Boston City Hosp; Mass. Gen. Hosp.; Harvard Med. Sch., Boston, MA.

330 **Bendixen H H, Hedley-Whyte J, Chir B & Laver M B.** Impaired oxygenation in surgical patients during general anesthesia with controlled ventilation. *NEJM* 269:991-6, 1963. Harvard Med. Sch., Boston, MA.

432 **Bonadonna G, Brusamolino E, Valagussa P, Rossi A, Brugnatelli L, Brambilla C, De Lena M, Tancini G, Bajetta E, Musumeci R & Veronesi U.** Combination chemotherapy as an adjuvant treatment in operable breast cancer. *NEJM* 294:405-10, 1976. Ist. Naz. Tumori, Milan, Italy.

430 **Borer J S, Bacharach S L, Green M V, Kent K M, Epstein S E & Johnston G S.** Real-time radionuclide cineangiography in the noninvasive evaluation of global and regional left ventricular function at rest and during exercise in patients with coronary-artery disease. *NEJM* 296:839-44, 1977. NIH, NHLBI, Bethesda, MD.

376 *__Boyd A E, Lebovitz H E & Pfeiffer J B.__ Stimulation of human-growth-hormone secretion by L-dopa. *NEJM* 283:1425-9, 1970. Duke Univ. Med. Ctr., Durham, NC. (33/82/CP)

287 **Brady R O, Gal A E, Bradley R M, Martensson E, Warshaw A L & Laster L.** Enzymatic defect in Fabry's disease. *NEJM* 276:1163-7, 1967. NIH, NINDB, NIAMD, Bethesda, MD.

497 **Brescia M J, Cimino J E, Appel K & Hurwich B J.** Chronic hemodialysis using venipuncture and a surgically created arteriovenous fistula. *NEJM* 275:1089-92, 1966. Vet. Admin. Hosp., Bronx, NY.

325 **Broder S, Humphrey R, Durm M, Blackman M, Meade B, Goldman C, Strober W & Waldmann T.** Impaired synthesis of polyclonal (non-paraprotein) immunoglobulins by circulating lymphocytes from patients with multiple myeloma. *NEJM* 293:887-92, 1975. NIH, NCI, Bethesda; Johns Hopkins Univ., Baltimore, MD.

288 **Brouet J-C, Flandrin G & Seligmann M.** Indications of the thymus-derived nature of the proliferating cells in six patients with Sezary's syndrome. *NEJM* 289:341-4, 1973. Hop. St.-Louis, Paris, France.

504 *__Brunner H R, Laragh J H, Baer L, Newton M A, Goodwin F T, Krakoff L R, Bard R H & Buhler F R.__ Essential hypertension: renin and aldosterone, heart attack and stroke. *NEJM* 286:441-9, 1972. Columbia Univ., Coll. Physic. Surg.; Presbyterian Hosp., New York, NY. (40/82/CP)

685 **Buhler F R, Laragh J H, Baer L, Vaughan E D & Brunner H R.** Propranolol inhibition of renin secretion. *NEJM* 287:1209-14, 1972. Columbia Univ., Coll. Physic. Surg.; Presbyterian Hosp., New York, NY.

352 **Cahill G F.** Starvation in man. *NEJM* 282:668-75, 1970. Harvard Med. Sch.; Diabetes Fdn., Inc.; Peter Bent Brigham Hosp., Boston, MA.

598 **Claman H N.** Corticosteroids and lymphoid cells. *NEJM* 287:388-97, 1972. Univ. Colorado Sch. Med., Denver, CO.

329 **Clements J A, Platzker A C G, Tierney D F, Hobel C J, Creasy R K, Margolis A J, Thibeault D W, Tooley W H & Oh W.** Assessment of the risk of the respiratory-distress syndrome by a rapid test for surfactant in amniotic fluid. *NEJM* 286:1077-81, 1972. Univ. California, San Francisco & Los Angeles, CA.

339 *__Cohen A S.__ Amyloidosis. *NEJM* 277:522-30, 1967. Boston Univ. Sch. Med., Boston, MA. (21/83/CP)

286 **Cohen S & Harris L D.** Does hiatus hernia affect competence of the gastroesophageal sphincter? *NEJM* 284:1053-6, 1971. Univ. Hosp.; Boston Univ. Sch. Med., Boston, MA.

587 **Cotzias G C, Papavasiliou P S & Gellene R.** Modification of Parkinsonism—chronic treatment with L-dopa. *NEJM* 280:337-45, 1969. Brookhaven Nat. Lab., Upton, NY.

524 **Cotzias G C, Van Woert M H & Schiffer L M.** Aromatic amino acids and modification of Parkinsonism. *NEJM* 276:374-9, 1967. Brookhaven Nat. Lab., Upton, NY.

402 *__Danzinger R G, Hofmann A F, Schoenfield L J & Thistle J L.__ Dissolution of cholesterol gallstones by chenodeoxycholic acid. *NEJM* 286:1-8, 1972. Mayo Clin.; Mayo Fdn., Rochester, MN. (29/82/CP)

296 **Dietschy J M & Wilson J D.** Regulation of cholesterol metabolism. *NEJM* 282:1128-38, 1970. Univ. Texas Southwestern Med. Sch., Dallas, TX.

336 **DuPont H L, Formal S B, Hornick R B, Snyder M J, Libonati J P, Sheahan D G, LaBrec E H & Kalas J P.** Pathogenesis of *Escherichia coli* diarrhea. *NEJM* 285:1-9, 1971. Univ. Maryland Sch. Med.; Walter Reed Army Inst. Res., Baltimore, MD.

389 **Farber S, Diamond L K, Mercer R D, Sylvester R F & Wolff J A.** Temporary remissions in acute leukemia in children produced by folic acid antagonist, 4-aminopteroyl-glutamic acid (aminopterin). *NEJM* 238:787-93, 1948. Children's Med. Ctr., Boston, MA.

500 **Fisher B, Carbone P, Economou S G, Frelick R, Glass A, Lerner H, Redmond C, Zelen M, Band P, Katrych D L, Wolmark N & Fisher E R.** I-phenylalanine mustard (L-PAM) in the management of primary breast cancer. *NEJM* 292:117-22, 1975. Univ. Pittsburgh Sch. Med., Pittsburgh, PA.

333 **Frantz A G & Rabkin M T.** Human growth hormone. *NEJM* 271:1375-81, 1964. Mass. Gen. Hosp.; Harvard Med. Sch., Boston, MA.

A   B

330   Fraser D W, Tsai T R, Orenstein W, Parkin W E, Beecham H J, Sharrar R G, Harris J, Mallison G F, Martin S M, McDade J E, Shepard C C, Brachman P S & Field Invest. Team. Legionnaires' disease. *NEJM* 297:1189-97, 1977. Ctr. Dis. Control, Atlanta, GA.

6399 *Fredrickson D S, Levy R I & Lees R S. Fat transport in lipoproteins—an integrated approach to mechanisms and disorders. *NEJM* 276:34-44, 94-103; 148-56; 215-25; 273-81, 1967. NIH, NHI, Bethesda, MD. (3/78)

290   Gallus A S, Hirsh J, Tuttle R J, Trebilcock R, O'Brien S E, Carroll J J, Minden J H & Hudecki S M. Small subcutaneous doses of heparin in prevention of venous thrombosis. *NEJM* 288: 545-51, 1973. St. Joseph's Hosp.; McMaster Univ., Hamilton, Canada.

428   Gavras H, Brunner H R, Turini G A, Kershaw G R, Tifft C P, Cuttelod S, Cavras I, Vukovich R A & McKinstry D N. Antihypertensive effect of the oral angiotensin converting-enzyme inhibitor SQ 14225 in man. *NEJM* 298:991-5, 1978. Boston Univ. Med. Ctr., Boston, MA; Hop. Cantonal Univ., Lausanne, Switzerland; Squibb Res. Inst., Princeton, NJ.

292   Gianelly R, von der Groeben J O, Spivack A P & Harrison D C. Effect of lidocaine on ventricular arrhythmias in patients with coronary heart disease. *NEJM* 277:1215-9, 1967. Stanford Univ. Sch. Med.; Palo Alto-Stanford Hosp., Palo Alto, CA.

352   Giles J P, McCollum R W, Berndtson L W & Krugman S. Viral hepatitis. *NEJM* 281:119-22, 1969. New York Univ. Sch. Med., New York, NY; Yale Univ. Sch. Med., New Haven, CT.

391   Goodwin J S, Messner R P, Bankhurst A D, Peake G T, Saiki J H & Williams R C. Prostaglandin-producing suppressor cells in Hodgkin's disease. *NEJM* 297:963-8, 1977. Univ. New Mexico Sch. Med.; Bernalillo County Med. Ctr., Albuquerque, NM.

353   Gorbach S L & Bartlett J G. Anaerobic infections. *NEJM* 290:1177-84, 1974. Vet. Admin. Hosp., Sepulveda; Univ. California Sch. Med., Los Angeles, CA.

308   Graw R G, Herzig G, Perry S & Henderson E S. Normal granulocyte transfusion therapy. *NEJM* 287:367-71, 1972. NIH, NCI, Bethesda, MD.

339   Greenblatt D J & Koch-Weser J. Drug therapy. *NEJM* 293:702-5, 1975. Mass. Gen. Hosp., Boston, MA; Ctr. Rech. Merrell Intl., Strasbourg, France.

502   Gregory G A, Kitterman J A, Phibbs R H, Tooley W H & Hamilton W K. Treatment of the idiopathic respiratory-distress syndrome with continuous positive airway pressure. *NEJM* 284:1333-40, 1971. Univ. California, San Francisco, CA.

296   Harker L A & Slichter S J. Studies of platelet and fibrinogen kinetics in patients with prosthetic heart valves. *NEJM* 283:1302-5, 1970. Univ. Washington Sch. Med., Seattle, WA.

456   Harker L A & Slichter S J. Platelet and fibrinogen consumption in man. *NEJM* 287:999-1005, 1972. Univ. Washington Sch. Med; King County Central Blood Bank, Seattle, WA.

346   Haussler M R & McCain T A. Basic and clinical concepts related to vitamin D metabolism and action. *NEJM* 297:974-83, 1977. Univ. Arizona, Tucson, AZ.

721   Herbst A L, Ulfelder H & Poskanzer D C. Adenocarcinoma of the vagina. *NEJM* 284:878-81, 1971. Vincent Mem. Hosp., Boston, MA.

525   Herman M V, Heinle R A, Klein M D & Gorlin R. Localized disorders in myocardial contraction. *NEJM* 277:222-32, 1967. Peter Bent Brigham Hosp.; Harvard Med. Sch., Boston, MA.

404   *Hersh E M & Oppenheim J J. Impaired in vitro lymphocyte transformation in Hodgkin's disease. *NEJM* 273:1006-12, 1965. NIH, NCI, Bethesda, MD. (13/83/CP)

370   *Hogg J C, Macklem P T, Thurlbeck W M & Path M C. Site and nature of airway obstruction in chronic obstructive lung disease. *NEJM* 278:1355-60, 1968. McGill Univ.; Royal Victoria Hosp., Montreal, Canada. (52/82/CP)

310   Jaffe E S, Shevach E M, Frank M M, Berard C W & Green I. Nodular lymphoma—evidence for origin from follicular B lymphocytes. *NEJM* 290:813-9, 1974. NIH, NCI, NIAID, Bethesda, MD.

380   Jaffe N, Frei E, Traggis D & Bishop Y. Adjuvant methotrexate and citrovorum-factor treatment of osteogenic sarcoma. *NEJM* 291:994-7, 1974. Sidney Farber Cancer Ctr.; Children's Hosp. Med. Ctr.; Harvard Med. Sch.; Harvard Sch. Publ. Hlth., Boston, MA.

317   Kahn C R, Flier J S, Bar R S, Archer J A, Gorden P, Martin M M & Roth J. The syndromes of insulin resistance and acanthosis nigricans. *NEJM* 294:739-45, 1976. NIH, NIAMDD, Bethesda, MD; Georgetown Univ. Sch. Med., Washington, DC.

365   *Kellermann G, Shaw C R & Luyten-Kellerman M. Aryl hydrocarbon hydroxylase inducibility and bronchogenic carcinoma. *NEJM* 289:934-7, 1973. Univ. Texas; M.D. Anderson Hosp.; Tumor Inst., Houston, TX. (42/82/CP)

349   Kleinberg D L, Noel G L & Frantz A G. Galactorrhea: a study of 235 cases, including 48 with pituitary tumors. *NEJM* 296:589-600, 1977. Columbia Univ. Coll. Physic. Surg.; Presbyterian Hosp.; Vet. Admin. Hosp.; New York Univ. Sch. Med., New York, NY.

339   Koenig R J, Peterson C M, Jones R L, Saudek C, Lehrman M & Cerami A. Correlation of glucose regulation and hemoglobin A_{Ic} in diabetes mellitus. *NEJM* 295:417-20, 1976. Rockefeller Univ.; Cornell Univ. Med. Coll., Ithaca; Beth Israel Med. Ctr., New York, NY.

304   Kumar A, Falke K J, Geffin B, Aldredge C F, Laver M B, Lowenstein E & Pontoppidan H. Continuous positive-pressure ventilation in acute respiratory failure. *NEJM* 283:1430-6, 1970. Harvard Med. Sch., Mass. Gen. Hosp., Boston, MA.

381   *Lerner P I & Weinstein L. Infective endocarditis in the antibiotic era. *NEJM* 274:199-206, 1966. New Engl. Med. Ctr. Hosp.; Tufts Univ. Sch. Med., Boston, MA. (19/82/CP)

377   Lindner A, Charra B, Sherrard D J & Scribner B H. Accelerated atherosclerosis in prolonged maintenance hemodialysis. *NEJM* 290:697-701, 1974. Univ. Washington Sch. Med.; Vet. Admin. Hosp., Seattle, WA.

312   Lipschitz D A, Cook J D & Finch C A. A clinical evaluation of serum ferritin as an index of iron stores. *NEJM* 290:1213-6, 1974. Univ. Washington Sch. Med., Seattle, WA.

477   Lo Gerfo P, Krupey J & Hansen H J. Demonstration of an antigen common to several varieties of neoplasia. *NEJM* 285:138-41, 1971. Columbia Univ. Coll. Physic. Surg.; Inst. Cancer Res., New York, NY; McGill Univ. Med. Clin.; Montreal Gen. Hosp., Montreal, Canada; Hoffmann-La Roche, Inc., Nutley, NJ.

291 **Lotz M, Zisman E & Bartter F C.** Evidence for a phosphorus-depeletion syndrome in man. *NEJM* 278:409-15, 1968. Georgetown Univ. Sch. Med. and Distr. Columbia Gen. Hosp., Washington, DC.; NIH, NHI, Bethesda, MD.

425 **Lukes R J & Tindle B H.** Immunoblastic lymphadenopathy. *NEJM* 292:1-8, 1975. Univ. Southern California Sch. Med. & Los Angeles County Med. Ctr., Los Angeles, CA.

378 **McCaffrey R, Harrison T A, Parkman R & Baltimore D.** Terminal deoxynucleotidyl transferase activity in human leukemic cells and in normal human thymocytes. *NEJM* 292:775-80, 1975. Mass. Inst. Technol.; Children's Hosp. Med. Ctr.; Sidney Farber Cancer Ctr.; Harvard Med. Sch., Boston, MA.

369 **McDade J E, Shepard C C, Fraser D W, Tsai T R, Redus M A, Dowdle W R & Lab. Invest. Team.** Legionnaires' disease. *NEJM* 297:1197-203, 1977. Ctr. Dis. Control, Atlanta, GA.

383 **Mitenko P A & Ogilvie R I.** Rational intravenous doses of theophylline. *NEJM* 289:600-3, 1973. Montreal Gen. Hosp.; McGill Univ., Montreal, Canada.

300 **Nahmias A J & Roizman B.** Infection with herpes-simplex viruses 1 and 2. *NEJM* 289:667-74, 1973. Emory Univ. Sch. Med., Atlanta, GA.

380 **Nash G, Blennerhassett J B & Pontoppidan H.** Pulmonary lesions associated with oxygen therapy and artificial ventilation. *NEJM* 276:368-74, 1967. Harvard Med. Sch.; Mass. Gen. Hosp., Boston, MA.

430 *****Northway W H, Rosan R C & Porter D Y.** Pulmonary disease following respirator therapy of hyaline-membrane disease. *NEJM* 276:357-68, 1967. Stanford Univ. Sch. Med., Stanford, CA. (25/82/CP)

300 **O'Brien J S, Okada S, Chen A & Fillerup D L.** Tay-Sachs disease. *NEJM* 283:15-20, 1970. Univ. California San Diego, Sch. Med., La Jolla, CA.

319 **Okada K, Kamiyama I, Inomata M, Imai M, Miyakawa Y & Mayumi M.** e-Antigen and anti-e in the serum of asymptomatic carrier mothers as indicators of positive and negative transmission of hepatitis B virus to their infants. *NEJM* 294:746-9, 1976. Okubo Municip. Hosp.; Jichi Med. Sch.; Univ. Tokyo, Japan.

469 **Oliva P B, Potts D E & Pluss R G.** Coronary arterial spasm in Prinzmetal angina. *NEJM* 288:745-51, 1973. Denver Gen. Hosp.; Univ. Colorado Med. Ctr., Denver, CO.

421 *****Page D L, Caulfield J B, Kastor J A, DeSanctis R W & Sanders C A.** Myocardial changes associated with cardiogenic shock. *NEJM* 285:133-7, 1971. Mass. Gen. Hosp.; Harvard Med. Sch., Boston, MA. (3/84/CP)

483 **Parrish J A, Fitzpatrick T B, Tanenbaum L & Pathak M A.** Photochemotherapy of psoriasis with oral methoxsalen and longwave ultraviolet light. *NEJM* 291:1207-11, 1974. Harvard Med. Sch.; Mass. Gen. Hosp., Boston, MA.

323 **Payne F E, Baublis J V & Itabashi H H.** Isolation of measles virus from cell cultures of brain from a patient with subacute sclerosing panencephalitis. *NEJM* 281:585-9, 1969. Univ. Michigan, Sch. Publ. Hlth. & Sch. Med., Ann Arbor, MI.

417 **Perry T L, Hansen S & Kloster M.** Huntington's chorea. *NEJM* 288:337-42, 1973. Univ. British Columbia, Vancouver, Canada.

378 *****Pincus T, Schur P H, Rose J A, Decker J L & Talal N.** Measurement of serum DNA-binding activity in systemic lupus erythematosus. *NEJM* 281:701-5, 1969. NIH, NIAID, NIAMDD, Bethesda, MD; Robert Breck Brigham Hosp., Boston, MA. (2/83/CP)

551 *****Rhoads G G, Gulbrandsen C L & Kagan A.** Serum lipoproteins and coronary heart disease in a population study of Hawaii Japanese men. *NEJM* 294:293-8, 1976. NHLI, Honolulu, HI. (43/82/CP)

1172 *****Ross R & Glomset J A.** The pathogenesis of atherosclerosis. *NEJM* 295:369-77, 420-5, 1976. Univ. Washington Sch. Med. & Region. Primate Res. Ctr., Seattle, WA. (1/83/LS; 34/82/CP)

306 **Ruddy S, Gigli I & Austen K F.** The complement system of man. *NEJM* 287:489-95, 1972. Harvard Med. Sch.; Robert Breck Brigham Hosp., Boston, MA.

420 **Salmon S E, Hamburger A W, Soehnlen B, Durie B G M, Alberts D S & Moon T E.** Quantitation of differential sensitivity of human-tumor stem cells to anticancer drugs. *NEJM* 298:1321-7, 1978. Univ. Arizona Coll. Med., Tucson, AZ.

510 **Schlosstein L, Terasaki P I, Bluestone R & Pearson C M.** High association of an HL-A antigen, W27, with ankylosing spondylitis. *NEJM* 288:704-6, 1973. Wadsworth Vet. Admin. Hosp.; Univ. California Sch. Med., Los Angeles, CA.

380 **Schur P H & Sandson J.** Immunologic factors and clinical activity in systemic lupus erythematosus. *NEJM* 278:533-8, 1968. Rockefeller Univ.; Bronx Municip. Hosp. Ctr.; Albert Einstein Coll. Med., New York, NY.

352 **Sen L & Borella L.** Clinical importance of lymphoblasts with T markers in childhood acute leukemia. *NEJM* 292:828-32, 1975. St. Jude Children's Res. Hosp., Memphis, TN.

395 **Smith D C, Prentice R, Thompson D J & Herrmann W L.** Association of exogenous estrogen and endometrial carcinoma. *NEJM* 293:1164-7, 1975. Univ. Washington, Seattle, WA.

610 *****Smith T W, Butler V P & Haber E.** Determination of therapeutic and toxic serum digoxin concentrations by radioimmunoassay. *NEJM* 281:1212-6, 1969. Harvard Med. Sch.; Mass. Gen. Hosp., Boston, MA; Columbia Univ. Coll. Physic. Surg., New York, NY. (47/79/CP)

483 **Stewart G L, Parkman P D, Hopps H E, Douglas R D, Hamilton J P & Meyer H M.** Rubella-virus hemagglutination-inhibition test. *NEJM* 276:554-7, 1967. US Publ. Hlth. Serv., NIH, Bethesda, MD.

295 **Stossel T P.** Phagocytosis. *NEJM* 290:717-23, 1974. Children's Hosp. Med. Ctr.; Harvard Med. Sch., Boston, MA.

727 *****Swan H J C, Ganz W, Forrester J, Marcus H, Diamond G & Chonette D.** Catheterization of the heart in man with use of a flow-directed balloon-tipped catheter. *NEJM* 283:447-51, 1970. Cedars-Sinai Med. Ctr.; Univ. California, Los Angeles, CA. (1/82/CP)

309 **Terasaki P I, Mottironi V D & Barnett E V.** Cytotoxins in disease. *NEJM* 283:724-8, 1970. Univ. California Sch. Med., Los Angeles, CA.

1076 *****Thomas E D, Storb R, Clift R A, Fefer A, Johnson F L, Neiman P E, Lerner K G, Glucksberg H & Buckner C D.** Bone-marrow transplantation. *NEJM* 292:832-43; 895-902, 1975. Univ. Washington Sch. Med.; Providence Med. Ctr.; Fred Hutchinson Cancer Res. Ctr., Seattle, WA. (21/82/CP)

282 **Tripodi D, Parks L C & Brugmans J.** Drug-induced restoration of cutaneous delayed hypersensitivity in anergic patients with cancer. *NEJM* 289:354-7, 1973. Johns Hopkins Hosp., Baltimore, MD.

A

421   **Trivelli L A, Ranney H M & Lai H-T.** Hemoglobin components in patients with diabetes mellitus. *NEJM* 284:353-7, 1971. Albert Einstein Coll. Med.; Bronx Municip. Hosp. Ctr., New York, NY.

361   **Vecchio T J.** Predictive value of a single diagnostic test in unselected populations. *NEJM* 274:1171-3, 1966. Upjohn Co., Kalamazoo, MI.

385   **Wacker W E C, Ulmer D D & Vallee B L.** Metalloenzymes and myocardial infarction. *NEJM* 255:449-56, 1956. Harvard Med. Sch.; Peter Bent Brigham Hosp., Boston, MA.

358   **Weiss H J.** Platelet physiology and abnormalities of platelet function. *NEJM* 293:531-41, 1975. Roosevelt Hosp.; Columbia Univ. Coll. Physic. Surg., New York, NY.

271   **Weissmann G.** Lysosomes. *NEJM* 273:1084-90, 1965. New York Univ. Sch. Med., New York, NY.

353   *Weller T H.** The cytomegaloviruses: ubiquitous agents with protean clinical manifestations. *NEJM* 285:203-14, 1971. Harvard Sch. Publ. Hlth, Boston, MA. (17/83/CP)

325   *Weller T H & Hanshaw J B.** Virologic and clinical observations on cytomegalic inclusion disease. *NEJM* 266:1233-44, 1962. Harvard Sch. Publ. Hlth.; Children's Hosp. Med. Ctr., Boston, MA. (39/79/CP)

335   **Whitley R J, Soong S, Dolin R, Galasso G J, Ch'ien L T & Alford C A.** Adenine arabinoside therapy of biopsy-proved herpes simplex encephalitis. *NEJM* 297:289-94, 1977. Univ. Alabama, Birmingham, AL; NIH, NIAID, Bethesda, MD.

296   **Zacest R, Gilmore E & Koch-Weser J.** Treatment of essential hypertension with combined vasodilation and beta-adrenergic blockade. *NEJM* 286:617-22, 1972. Mass. Gen. Hosp.; Harvard Med. Sch., Boston, MA.

369   *Ziel H K & Finkle W D.** Increased risk of endometrial carcinoma among users of conjugated estrogens. *NEJM* 293:1167-70, 1975. Kaiser Permanente Med. Ctr.; Kaiser Fdn. Hlth. Plan, Los Angeles, CA. (26/82/CP)

aminopterin on children with acute leukemia. It was cited more than 300 times from 1955 to 1983. For 30 consecutive years, this article was cited between four and 27 times. We hope one of the authors can approximate how often it was cited in the pre-1955 period. By the way, the first author of this paper, who died in 1973, is the same Sidney Farber for whom the famous cancer center in Boston is named. Two papers from this institution are included on the list (see N. Jaffe and R. McCaffrey).

W.E.C. Wacker, D.D. Ulmer, and B.L. Vallee, Peter Bent Brigham Hospital, Boston, collaborated on the next oldest paper. Published in 1956, the article demonstrates how blood levels of metalloenzymes can be used to diagnose myocardial infarction. It was cited between five and 26 times for 28 consecutive years.

The most-cited article was published in five parts in four 1967 issues of *NEJM*. Fredrickson, R.I. Levy, and R.S. Lees were then affiliated with the National Heart Institute, Bethesda, Maryland. Fredrickson is now at the National Academy of Sciences, Washington, DC, and Lees is affiliated with the Massachusetts Institute of Technology, Cambridge. Levy, still with the National Institutes of Health, explained in his commentary[14] that "up to the time the articles were published, specialists in the field who attempted to treat patients

Table 3: Frequency distribution of publication dates for the 100 most-cited articles from *NEJM, SCI®* 1961-1982. A=publication date. B=number of articles.

A	B
1940-1949	1
1950-1959	1
1960-1964	3
1965-1969	24
1970-1974	44
1975-1979	27
	100

Table 4: Geographic areas represented by the 100 most-cited papers published in *NEJM*, listed in descending order of the number of papers produced.

United States	
Massachusetts	30
Maryland	16
New York	14
California	13
Washington	7
Colorado	3
Georgia	3
Arizona	2
Michigan	2
New Jersey	2
Texas	2
Washington, DC	2
Alabama	1
Connecticut	1
Hawaii	1
Minnesota	1
New Mexico	1
North Carolina	1
Pennsylvania	1
Tennessee	1
Canada	5
France	2
Colombia	1
Italy	1
Japan	1
Switzerland	1

with hyperlipidemia had to grapple with complicated classifications that often proved contradictory and misleading in clinical practice. The system of classifying blood lipid disorders that we introduced was...a simpler, more convenient code than the existing classifications."

As to why the article was cited so often, Levy suggests, "Perhaps one of the intrinsic reasons for the volume of citation received by our articles is that they drew attention to an important group of diseases that are common and often potentially fatal.... Our objective was to break down some of the conventional clichés and approaches to the management of these patients by providing a more rational and workable alternative. Perhaps the frequency with which our work is cited is proof that in some measure we succeeded."[14] It should be noted that, while this five-part paper received 6,400 citations, the number of unique citing publications involved is "only" about 1,900 since most authors cited several or all parts of the study.

The second most-cited paper, by R. Ross and J.A. Glomset, University of Washington School of Medicine, Seattle, is also a multipart review paper. It was cited about 1,200 times in 800 papers from 1976 to 1983. The authors reviewed three major hypotheses on the fatty degeneration of the inner lining of arteries, or "atherogenesis." In a recent commentary,[15] Ross observed, "One unique feature of the school of medicine at the University of Washington was the fact that at particular points in time at least three hypotheses of atherogenesis had been developed, surprisingly, all emanating from the same department! Since all three...had generated a fair amount of interest, we decided that... those notions should be related...."

The third most-cited article is another multipart review paper. Published in 1975, the article reviews the literature on bone marrow transplantation. About 740 papers cited it more than 1,000 times. The paper was coauthored by nine researchers based at the University of Washington School of Medicine. E.D. Thomas describes the article as a "potpourri of topics including a brief history of the field, a review of the more significant advances based on work in animals...and a review of the developments that set the stage for marrow transplantation in man."[16] In his commentary, Thomas offers a partial explanation for the frequent citation of this paper. "Unlike most reviews, the article contained a great deal of clinical data and interpretation that had not been published previously.... Of even greater importance, perhaps, is the fact that [it] appeared at that junction in time marking the emergence of marrow transplantation from an experimental laboratory procedure and/or a desperate clinical undertaking to an accepted form of therapy for selected patients...."[16] I can't agree completely with his assumption that most reviews do not contain clinical data and interpretation. It is quite possible that this may in fact be characteristic of highly cited reviews. But data compilations do tend to be highly cited.

Citation Classics commentaries provide interesting background information on how significant scientific advances were developed and carried out. More than 1,800 scientists have already accepted our invitation to write a personalized account of their papers. We believe this collection constitutes an important sociological statement about scientific activity. We are most grateful to those authors who have already responded. So that papers from *NEJM* may be appropriately represented in this collection, we now extend our invitation to the new group of authors identified here. And we will follow up this study with lists of most-cited articles from other superstar journals in medicine as well as the life, physical, and social sciences.

As I have explained on numerous occasions, many of these papers are not considered to be the most important or significant work produced by the individuals involved. The impact or utility to science of a particular well-cited paper may have little to do with the level of creativity required. We often publish more than one commentary by a prolific author. Any author is free to point out the utilitarian nature of a particular work. But throughout science there is often an inseparable bond between theory and practice. Behind some of the most important "simple" discoveries may lie years of significant theoretical or experimental research or contemplation. On the other hand, clinical problems or technological breakthroughs often open the way to basic discoveries.

But scientific journals are not designed to communicate either history, sociology, or biography. For the objective purposes they serve, especially with the need for precision and condensation, journals cannot allow adequate space for personal history or interpretation. Even if they did, they could not provide the hindsights of these *Citation Classics*. These commentaries are written long after the original work is published. It is difficult to imagine that this kind of hindsight would be possible even if journals were willing to include accounts of the author's prepublication trials and tribulations.

Authors of the articles in Table 2 who have not yet received letters of invitation, and anyone who wants more information on *Citation Classics*, should call (215) 386-0100, extension 1381. ©1984 ISI

REFERENCES

1. **Garfield E.** The 100 most-cited papers ever and how we select *Citation Classics*. *Current Contents* (23):3-10, 4 June 1984.
2. --------------. *Citation Classics*—four years of the human side of science. *Essays of an information scientist*. Philadelphia: ISI Press, 1983. Vol. 5. p. 123-34.
3. **Ingelfinger F.** Definition of "sole contribution." *N. Engl. J. Med.* 281:676-7, 1969.
4. **Relman A S.** The Ingelfinger rule. *N. Engl. J. Med.* 305:824-6, 1981.
5. **Huth E J.** Medical journals and urgent medical news. *Ann. Intern. Med.* 99:559-61, 1983.
6. **Sackler A M.** On the freedom of scientific communication. *Med. Tribune* 22(16):15, 1981.
7. The Ingelfinger rule. *Time* 115(9):74, 1980.
8. Publish and be silenced. *New Sci.* 88:75, 1980.
9. **Grouse L D.** The Ingelfinger rule. *JAMA—J. Am. Med. Assn.* 245:375-6, 1981.
10. **Morgan P P.** Scientific journals and the news media: partners or competitors? *Can. Med. Assn. J.* 130:252, 1982.
11. **Institute for Scientific Information.** 250 most-highly cited items. *SCI Science Citation Index 1955-1964, ten year cumulation. Guide and lists of source publications.* Philadelphia: ISI, 1984. Vol. 1. p. 22-31.
12. **Spodick D H & Goldberg R J.** The editor's correspondence: analysis of patterns appearing in selected specialty and general journals. *Amer. J. Cardiol.* 52:1290-2, 1983.
13. **Institute for Scientific Information.** *Index to research fronts in ISI/BIOMED 1983.* Philadelphia: ISI, 1983. 544 p.
14. **Levy R I.** Citation Classic. Commentary on *N. Engl. J. Med.* 276:34-44; 94-103; 148-56; 215-25; 273-81, 1967. *Current Contents* (3):11, 16 January 1978.
15. **Ross R.** Citation Classic. Commentary on *N. Engl. J. Med.* 295:369-77; 420-5, 1976. *Current Contents/Clinical Practice* 10(34):18, 23 August 1982.
16. **Thomas E D.** Citation Classic. Commentary on *N. Engl. J. Med.* 292:832-43; 895-902, 1975. *Current Contents/Clinical Practice* 10(21):20, 24 May 1982.

Current Comments®

Index Chemicus Goes Online with Graphic Access to Three Million New Organic Compounds

Number 26   June 25, 1984

Those *Current Contents*® (*CC*®) readers who are chemists know that we cover all the significant journals of chemistry in either of our two most widely used editions—*CC/Life Sciences* or *CC/Physical, Chemical & Earth Sciences*. For most readers of *CC*, scanning article titles is adequate for their current awareness needs. But for many scientists in organic chemistry, pharmacology, and other disciplines, there is a crucial need for browsing and searching at another level—the chemical compound. Since 1960, therefore, we have produced *Index Chemicus*® (*IC*®). At first, *IC* was a monthly, and then a biweekly, publication. But in 1970, it became a weekly listing of and index to newly reported compounds. Since each *IC* graphic record also includes the author's abstract when available, we changed its name to *Current Abstracts of Chemistry and Index Chemicus*® (*CAC&IC*®). In the past 24 years, *IC* has covered over 350,000 articles and listed over 3,000,000 new organic compounds.

It was inevitable that this data base would be accessible electronically. It has been available on magnetic tapes for many years, but with little fanfare we mounted *Index Chemicus Online*™ earlier this year and it became available this month. The file is stored on the host computer of the Paris-based online vendor Telesystemes. This organization has pioneered the development of the *Questel* and *DARC* software systems, which

handle bibliographic and structural data, respectively.

Index Chemicus Online covers the same information reported in *CAC&IC* each week. Its main virtues are both bibliographic and structural. Two additional ISI® services, the *CAC&IC* 22-year Microform Cumulation, available since December 1983, and the *Chemistry Citation Index*™ (*CCI*™), which we'll introduce later this year, are designed to complement *Index Chemicus Online*.

By the end of 1984, *Index Chemicus Online* will include information on over 350,000 articles published 1962 to date. These papers first reported more than 3,000,000 new organic compounds. The inclusion of compounds reported between 1962 and 1964 is noteworthy since structural information for that period is not readily available online from any other source.

Index Chemicus Online covers over 90 percent of the new organic compounds reported worldwide in chemistry journals. The thoroughness of this service is due, in part, to ISI's staff of 23 professional chemists. During the course of a year, they carefully read every item, including footnotes and references, in more than 100 key journals. From a total of at least 35,000 articles, they prepare entries for the approximately 15,000 articles which report new compounds and synthetic methods. When preparing these entries, our chemists often contact authors to clarify ambiguities or correct errors reported in the journals. This information then becomes part of the "record."

One of the features which *CAC&IC* readers find most valuable is the structural diagram included for each compound reported. Chemists find them to be a real time saver, since they are readily familiar with such diagrams. Users of *Index Chemicus Online* can also view these diagrams, *while online*, if they have a graphics terminal. These graphic displays overcome the ambiguity and complexity of chemical nomenclature. This was the original inspiration for *IC*.

Each *Index Chemicus Online* record contains the standard bibliographic data, including authors and their addresses, journal name, and article title. In addition, "flags" or "alerts" to scientific data reported in the original article appear in relevant records from 1968 to date. Of special interest is the flag for the analytical instrumentation used to isolate and identify the new compounds. These include infrared spectroscopy, nuclear magnetic resonance, and gas chromatography. Other alerts flag data on biological activities, explosive reactions, isotopically labeled compounds, and new synthetic methods. Experimental details regarding these synthetic methods are available in our printed publication *Current Chemical Reactions*®.[1] Table 1 lists the displayable fields in *Index Chemicus Online*.

Just as the *New York Times* does not report "all the news that's fit to print," neither does any single service catch everything. At the urging of our readers, we have gone to great lengths to identify many "intermediates" in organic synthesis that are not indexed elsewhere. Consequently, many intermediates (i.e., unisolated reaction intermediates) indexed for *Index Chemicus Online* cannot be retrieved through any other chemical information service.

As with our other services, we expect that the heaviest users of *Index Chemi-*

Table 1: Displayable fields in *Index Chemicus Online* ™

AF—AUTHOR AFFILIATION
AU—AUTHOR
*BA—BIOLOGICAL ACTIVITY
CP—COMPOUND-RELATED DATA (SEQUENCE NUMBER AND COMPOUND NUMBER)
DT—DOCUMENT TYPE
*ED—LEVEL OF EXPERIMENTAL DETAIL
*EX—EXPLOSIVE REACTION ALERT
FC—MICROFICHE COORDINATES TO THE *CURRENT ABSTRACTS OF CHEMISTRY AND INDEX CHEMICUS*® (*CAC&IC*®) MICROFORM CUMULATION
FL—MICROFILM COORDINATES TO THE *CAC&IC* MICROFORM CUMULATION
*IM—INSTRUMENTAL METHOD
*ISO—ISOTOPE
*IT—INDEX TERM
*LA—LANGUAGE OF DOCUMENT
*MA—MAILING ADDRESS
MF—MOLECULAR FORMULA
NO—*CAC&IC* ABSTRACT NUMBER AND *THE GENUINE ARTICLE* ™ (FORMERLY *OATS*®) ORDER NUMBER
*NSM—NEW SYNTHETIC METHOD ALERT
SO—SOURCE
TI—TITLE
WLN—WISWESSER LINE NOTATION

*These fields do not appear in every record.

cus Online initially will be those who already subscribe to *CAC&IC*. While it will be possible to browse online, we expect that its main use will be for retrieval. For current awareness, *CAC&IC* along with *CC* would still be used weekly. This is not to say that *Index Chemicus Online* would never be used for browsing. The chemist does browse retrospectively. For example, if you want to explore the data base for classes of compounds that exhibit a particular biological activity, a search could be performed in the bibliographic file and compounds viewed on the structure file. In this way, the graphics capabilities of *Index Chemicus Online* are vital. You can explore the literature in creative ways not previously practical.

Although *Index Chemicus Online* is an interesting file that is fun to use, it was designed as a sophisticated search and display tool for chemists and information specialists, typically employed in pharmaceutical or chemical research. This applies in academia as well as in industry. We fully expect that educators will use *Index Chemicus Online* to demonstrate state-of-the-art methods of chemical information retrieval to students. Indeed, those students who are not at least familiar with such methods may find themselves at a disadvantage once they become working scientists.

As mentioned here earlier, Telesystemes is the vendor for *Index Chemicus Online*. Telesystemes is a private company which receives considerable support from the French government.[2] It is a major vendor and has mounted many other data bases. In fact, Telesystemes was the first vendor to provide graphic substructure access to the original *Chemical Abstracts* file. In short, they are experienced in operating an online system. Although Telesystemes's main computer is based in Valbonne, on the French Riviera, all US and European customers can reach it via a telephone call to their local Telenet, Tymnet, or other telecommunications hosts.

There are key software packages and command languages involved in using Telesystemes's files. The *Questel* software deals with bibliographic data. The *DARC* system, pioneered originally by Jacques Dubois, at the University of Paris,[3] deals with chemical structure data. We chose Telesystemes as a vendor because it included *DARC*'s superior graphics capabilities. Through *DARC*, you can view full-screen diagrams of the compounds you retrieve from a search.

You can also use diagrams of compounds to *search* with *DARC*. This can be done by using any of several graphic input techniques or by text input. Figure 1 shows a sample search query, while Figure 2 provides an example of a structure "hit" that was subsequently retrieved in response to the query.

You can search the bibliographic, or *Questel*, portion of the file by the traditional access modes including author, journal source, and keyword. Figure 3 shows a sample bibliographic hit for the query given in Figure 1. Additionally, the alerts to biological activities or new synthetic methods can be used as access modes. For example, a search for new methods for synthesizing dihydrobenzofuran retrieved the bibliographic record shown in Figure 4. A corresponding structure record from the *DARC* file is shown in Figure 5.

If you do not have a graphics terminal, you can still search for chemical information using text input, molecular formulae, or Wiswesser Line Notation

Figure 1: Sample structural search query. The search query is: Have any derivatives of 11H-dibenz(b,f)-1,4-oxathiepin been made?

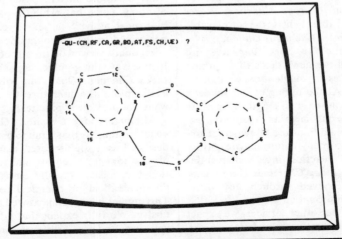

Figure 2: Display of first answer from substructure search on 11H-dibenz(b,f)-1,4-oxathiepin.

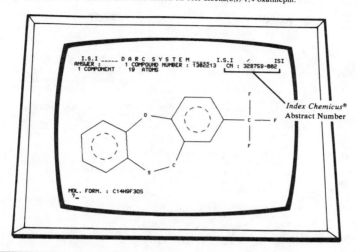

```
      I.S.I ___ D A R C  S Y S T E M ___ I.S.I  /        ISI
      ANSWER :        1 COMPOUND NUMBER : 1302213  CN : 328759-002
        1 COMPONENT     19 ATOMS
```

Index Chemicus®
Abstract Number

MOL. FORM. : C14H9F3OS
?_

Figure 3: Bibliographic record corresponding to structural record shown in Figure 2.

Index Chemicus® Abstract Number

-1- 122861 C.ISI IC ONLINE
NO   : 328759   OATS ORDER: NN659
TI   : NEUROTROPIC AND PSYCHOTROPIC AGENTS. 164. TRICYCLIC PSYCHOTROPIC
       AGENTS CONTAINING TWO CHALCOGEN ATOMS IN THE CENTRAL RING:
       DERIVATIVES OF 11H-DIBENZ(B,F)-1,4-OXATHIEPIN.
AU   : SINDELAR K.; HOLUBEK J.; RYSKA M.; DLABAC A.; METYSOVA J.; SCATEK E.;
       HRUBANTOVA M.; PROTIVA J.; PROTIVA M.
AF   : RES INST PHARM & BIOCHEM, 130 60 PRAGUE 3, CZECHOSLOVAKIA.
SO   : COLLECT CZECH CHEM COMMUN; V47(3); P.967-83; 1982
LA   : ENG (ENGLISH)
DT   : J (ARTICLE)
IT   : — DIBENZOXATHIEPIN(B.F)(1.4): 11H, DERIVS, PSYCHOTROPIC AGENTS, SYN
BA   : ANTIRESERPINE ACTIVITY; ANTIAPOMORPHINE ACTIVITY; ANTIDEPRESSANT
       ACTIVITY; ANTIBACTERIAL ACTIVITY; ANTIFUNGAL ACTIVITY
IM   : THIN LAYER CHROMATOGRAPHY; INFRARED SPECTRA; NUCLEAR MAGNETIC
       RESONANCE; MASS SPECTRA; ULTRAVIOLET SPECTRA; COLUMN
       CHROMATOGRAPHY
CP   : — 001(1B)
       — MF : C13H9ClOS
       — WLN: T_C676_BO_IS_JHJ_MG
       — 002(IC)
       — MF : C14H9F3OS
       — WLN: T_C676_BO_IS_JHJ_MXFFF
       — 003(2A)
       — MF : C14H10O3S
       — WLN: T_C676_BO_IS_JHJ_JVQ
       — 004(3A)
       — MF : C16H15NO2S
       — WLN: T_C676_BO_IS_JHJ_JVN1&1
       — 005(4A)
       — MF : C16H17NOS
       — WLN: T_C676_BO_IS_JHJ_J1N1&1
       — 006(5A)
       — MF : C17H19NOS
       — WLN: T_C676_BO_IS_JHJ_J2N1&1
       — 007(6A)
       — MF : C18N21NOS
       — WLN: T_C676_BO_IS_JHJ_J3N1&1
       — 008(6B)
       — MF : C18H20C1NOS
       — WLN: T_C676_80_IS_JHJ_J3N1&1_MG
FC   : 00793-B13
FL   : 2047M817G
```
```

Figure 4: Bibliographic record from a search for a new synthetic method and dihydrobenzofuran.

Accession
Number

```
  ?. . SH MAX
  -1- 106213 C.ISI IC ONLINE
 NO   :    312111      OATS ORDER: . . . . .
  TI   :    THE SYNTHESES AND ABSOLUTE CONFIGURATIONS OF FOMANNOXIN,
            (—)-5-ACETYL-2-(1-HYDROXYMETHYLVINYL)-2,3-DIHYDROBENZOFURAN, AND
            ANODENDROIC ACID.
  AU   :    KAWASE Y.; YAMAGUCHI S.; INOUE O.; SANNOMIY M.; KAWABE K.
  AF   :    TOYAMA UNIV, FAC SCI, DEPT CHEM, TOYAMA 930, JAPAN.
  SO   :    CHEM LETT; (12); P.1581-4; 1980
  LA   :    ENG (ENGLISH)
  DT   :    J (ARTICLE)
  IT   :    — FOMANNOXIN: SYN & ABS CONFIG DETERMINATN
            — BENZOFURAN: 5-AC-2-(1-OH-ME-VINYL)-2,3-DI-H, SYN & ABS CONFIG DETERMINATN
            — ANODENDROIC ACID: SYN & ABS CONFIG DETERMINATN
  IM   :    INFRARED SPECTRA
  NSM  :    NEW SYNTHETIC METHOD
  CP   :    — 001(7)
            — MF  : C13H1403
            — WLN: T56__BOT&J__CYU1&1OV1
            — 002(8)
            — MF  : C15H1604
            — WLN: T56__BOT&J__CYU1&1OV1__GV1
            — 003(9)
            — MF  : C13H1603
            — WLN: T56__BOT&J__CX1&1&OV1
            — 004(10)
            — MF  : C14H1604
            — WLN: T56__BOT&J__CX1&1&OV1__GVH
  FL   :    2461M016G
  FC   :    00749-D11
```

Figure 5: Structural record corresponding to bibliographic record shown in Figure 4.

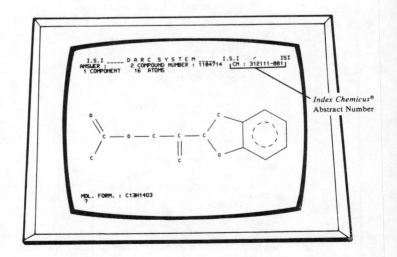

Index Chemicus®
Abstract Number

Figure 6: *CAC&IC®* record corresponding to sample *Index Chemicus Online™* hits shown in Figures 2 and 3.

328759

NEUROTROPIC AND PSYCHOTROPIC AGENTS. 164. TRICYCLIC PSYCHOTROPIC AGENTS CONTAINING TWO CHALCOGEN ATOMS IN THE CENTRAL RING: DERIVATIVES OF 11H-DIBENZ(B,F)—1,4-OXATHIEPIN.

SINDELAR K, HOLUBEK J, RYSKA M, DLABAC A, METYSOVA J, SVATEK E, HRUBANTOVA M, PROTIVA J, PROTIVA M.
RES INST PHARM & BIOCHEM, 130 60 PRAGUE 3, CZECHOSLOVAKIA.

COLLECT CZECH CHEM COMMUN 47(3), 967-83(1982).

CC IR MS NMR TLC UV

Reactions of 2-bromobenzyl bromide and its analogues *XVII* and *XXV* with 2-hydroxythiophenol resulted in 11*H*-dibenz[*b,f*]-1.4-oxathiepin (*Ia*) and its 2-chloro (*Ib*) and 2-trifluoromethyl derivative (*Ic*). Treatment of the lithium compounds derived from *Ia* and *Ib* with carbon dioxide and dimethylaminoalkyl chlorides gave compounds *IIa*, *Va* and *VIab*; modification of the side chains led to amines *IVa*, *VIIa* and *VIIIa*. 11-(1-Methyl-4-piperidyl) derivatives *Xbc* were obtained by chlorination of compounds *Ibc* with sulfuryl chloride or N-chlorosuccinimide and the following treatment with 1-methyl-4-piperidylmagnesium chloride. Compound *Ib* was transformed by oxidation to the sulfone *XX* affording by treatment with sodium hydride and tert-aminoalkyl chlorides the basic sulfones *XXI* and *XXII*. While the nuclearly unsubstituted amines with the aliphatic side chains (*IVa* and *VIIa*) have intensive antireserpine activity and are potential antidepressants, the 11-(1-methyl-4-piperidyl) derivatives with a substituent in position 2 of the skeleton (*Xbc*) are potential neuroleptics; the trifluoromethyl derivative *Xc* especially has outstanding cataleptic and antiapomorphine efficacy.

ANTIRESERPINE ACTIVITY
ANTIAPOMORPHINE ACTIVITY
ANTIDEPRESSANT ACTIVITY
ANTIFUNGAL ACTIVITY
ANTIBACTERIAL ACTIVITY

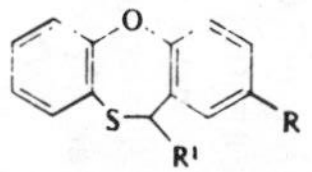

I(a,b,c),IIa-Va,VI(a,b),
VIIa,VIIIa,IX(b,c),
X(b,c),XIb,XXVIa

	R	R^1
Ia:	H	H
b:	Cl	H
c:	CF_3	H
IIa:	H	COOH
IIIa:	H	$CONMe_2$
IVa:	H	CH_2NMe_2
Va:	H	$(CH_2)_2NMe_2$
VIa:	H	$(CH_2)_3NMe_2$
b:	Cl	$(CH_2)_3NMe_2$
VIIa:	H	$(CH_2)_2NHMe$
VIIIa:	H	$(CH_2)_3NHMe$
IXb:	Cl	Cl
c:	CF_3	Cl
Xb:	Cl	1-Me-4-piperidyl
c:	CF_3	1-Me-4-piperidyl
XIb:	Cl	1-Me-4-HO-4-piperidyl
XXVIa:	H	COCl

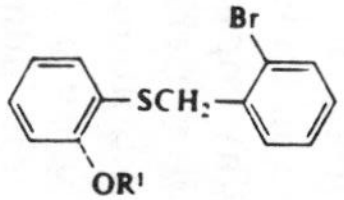

XII,XIII

	R^1
XII:	Me
XIII:	H

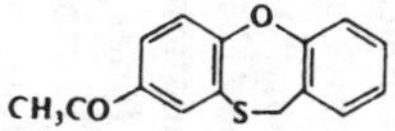

XV

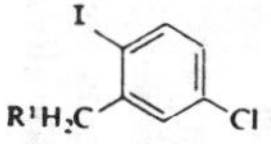

XVI-XVIII

	R^1
XVI:	OH
XVII:	Br
XVIII:	$2\text{-}HOC_6H_4S$

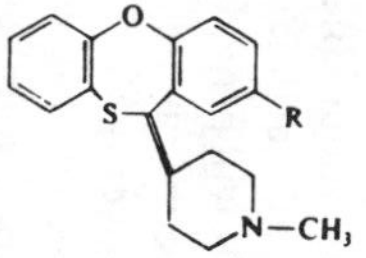

XIX(a,b,c)

	R
XIXa:	H
b:	Cl
c:	CF_3

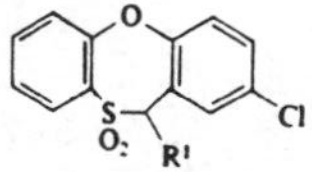

XX-XXII

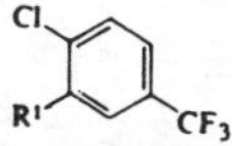

XXIII-XXV,XXVII

	R^1
XX:	H
XXI:	$(CH_2)_2NMe_2$
XXII:	$(CH_2)_3$piperidino
XXIII:	CHO
XXIV:	CH_2OH
XXV:	CH_2Cl
XXVII:	$NN^+ Cl^-$

(WLN) in the bibliographic file. As described on many earlier occasions, ISI has pioneered the use of this notation. WLN permits you to do many types of substructure or parent compound searches. We have encoded over 3,000,000 compounds to date and continue to input structural information to the data base in this manner. In order to provide graphic display of these compounds through the *DARC* system, we have developed programs to convert these WLNs to a format compatible with the *DARC* software. Therefore, we can encode private files as well, and convert them to formats compatible with *DARC* and other in-house graphics software packages.

The *Index Chemicus Online* data base was designed to be used in concert with other ISI services. For example, our new *CCI* will be cross-referenced with *Index Chemicus Online*. The *CCI*, which will be a separate online file, will include entries for all articles abstracted in *CAC&IC*. It will provide full coverage of about 300 core chemistry journals, and selective coverage from the rest of the *SCI* file. Each article will be tagged with its *IC* abstract number when appropriate. For example, if you have done a search in *CCI* and found a key relevant article, you can use the *IC* abstract number to retrieve and examine the structural diagrams for the compounds reported. Additionally, you can perform a cited reference search of articles retrieved in *Index Chemicus Online*. The *CCI* file will also have the research front capability that will add an interesting new dimension to the retrieval of chemical compounds. It will be a modern complement to *Beilstein*.

The *CAC&IC* 22-year Microform Cumulation will also be cross-referenced with *Index Chemicus Online*. By using the microform coordinate numbers which are included in each *Index Chemicus Online* record (see Table 1), you can go to the cumulation to retrieve the author's abstract and a hard copy of the structures shown. This feature would be particularly useful if your initial system does not have graphic capabilities. The cumulation, incidentally, covers the entire *CAC&IC* printed file from 1960 to 1981. (Annual cumulations are available for 1982 on.) Available in both microfiche and microfilm, it provides archival quality copy. Its price is $10,000 for industrial users, and $5,000 for educational institutions.

Figure 6 shows the *CAC&IC* record corresponding to the query given in Figure 1. For the time being, there is only one major difference between the coverage of *CAC&IC* and *Index Chemicus Online*. *CAC&IC* includes the author's abstract when available, while *Index Chemicus Online* does not.

To use an online system, you ordinarily need to learn a new command language. We have designed the *Sci-Mate*™ software package to overcome this requirement.[4] *Sci-Mate* is a microcomputer-based software system for maintaining private files and interacting directly with large online data bases. By the end of this year, we expect to introduce a new version of *Sci-Mate* that will include *Questel* as one of the many "host" options to search bibliographically.

We believe that the cost of *Index Chemicus Online* is quite reasonable. Bibliographic searching costs $70 per hour. Structure searching costs $160 per hour. The average search is approximately six to ten minutes and costs about $20. In addition, there is a charge of $.16 per record display.

There is no subscription fee, monthly minimum, or initiation charge. All you need to get started is a Telesystemes password. In the US, phone 800-424-9600, or write Questel Inc., 1625 I Street, Washington, DC 20006. In Europe, phone 33-1-544 38 13, or write Telesystemes, 40 Rue du Cherche Midi, 75006 Paris, France. Specify that you want access to *Index Chemicus Online.* After you complete and return the user agreement you will receive your account number, password(s), and a complete set of *DARC/Questel* manuals, usually within one week.

A do-it-yourself kit for *Index Chemicus Online* will soon be available. It will include a primer which introduces the data base and a step-by-step tutorial manual for programmed instruction. The manual is designed to be used while you are sitting at the terminal. Half of each page shows what is on the screen, while the other half provides notes and instructions.

ISI will offer training sessions in major cities in the US and Europe. Whenever possible, these sessions will run concurrently with Telesystemes's training workshops.

So far, we have demonstrated *Index Chemicus Online* at several major conventions. It was first introduced at the International Online meeting held in London in December 1983. It was then demonstrated at the April National Online Meeting, in New York City, and the spring meeting of the American Chemical Society (ACS), in St. Louis, Missouri. In each case, *Index Chemicus Online* was very well received. Many chemists learned of ISI's long-term involvement in chemical information for the first time. The next meeting of the ACS will be held from August 26 to 31 in Philadelphia, Pennsylvania. You can be sure ISI and *Index Chemicus Online* will be there.

We have established a special hotline strictly for *Index Chemicus Online*-related inquiries. In the US, the number is 800-523-1857. Readers outside of the US should call 215-386-0100, ext. 1291. *Index Chemicus Online* subscribers will also receive Telesystemes's *DARC* and *Questel* newsletters, *Tel-a-Chem* and *Questel-a-Gram*. These newsletters will provide a user's forum, and feature sample searches, announcements, pricing information, and the like.

We have designed *Index Chemicus Online* to make it possible to use organic chemical information as part of the dynamic process of designing new molecular entities in medical, agricultural, and other applications. Whether you are a pharmaceutical chemist, microbiologist, or organic chemist you will want to test out this new methodology. Simply call our hotline, or write to Keri Luiso, Chemical Information Division Marketing, ISI, 3501 Market Street, Philadelphia, PA 19104.

* * * * *

My thanks to Brad Schepp for his help in the preparation of this essay. ©1984 ISI

REFERENCES

1. **Garfield E.** Introducing *Current Chemical Reactions. Essays of an information scientist.* Philadelphia: ISI Press, 1981. Vol. 4. p. 12-5.
2. **Bonnet J C.** *Questel/DARC* as an important service to the chemical industry. *Inform. Chim.* 231:243-5, 1982.
3. **Dubois J E.** French national policy for chemical information and the DARC system as a potential tool of this policy. *J. Chem. Doc.* 13:8-13, 1973.
4. **Garfield E.** Introducing *Sci-Mate*—a menu-driven microcomputer software package for online and offline information retrieval. Part 1. The *Sci-Mate Personal Data Manager.* Part 2. The *Sci-Mate Universal Online Searcher. Current Contents* (12):5-12, 21 March 1983 and (14):5-15, 4 April 1983.

Current Comments®

How to Use the *Social Sciences Citation Index (SSCI)*

Number 27   July 2, 1984

Most readers of *Current Contents®* are research scientists in the life and physical sciences. A significant number are interested in the social or behavioral sciences. In addition, there is an important group of readers who work directly in the social sciences. Some day we hope to demonstrate by detailed "connectivity" studies how important the social sciences are in the conduct not only of research in biomedicine, but also in providing answers to important policy issues in the physical sciences.

Several of our journal citation studies have uncovered links between the social and natural sciences. For example, an analysis of citation patterns in anthropology journals revealed a close relationship between anthropology and human anatomy, biology, genetics, and dentistry.[1] In the early days, *Science Citation Index®* (*SCI®*) covered fields—like psychology—at the border between the social and natural sciences. However, when we created a separate file called *Social Sciences Citation Index®* (*SSCI®*),[2] the majority of journals in these borderline fields were assigned to either *SCI* or *SSCI*. Although psychology journals were assigned to *SSCI*, *SCI* still covers those major journals in this and other borderline fields.

My first paper on the need for a citation index in the social and behavioral sciences was published in 1964.[3] It wasn't until 1973 that ISI® launched *SSCI* to meet that need.[2] However, we eventually extended *SSCI* coverage back to 1966. These and subsequent annual volumes now provide coverage of two million journal articles, books, and book chapters from 1966 to 1983 and the 20 million references they cited. We also plan to publish an 11-year cumulation for *SSCI* covering 1955-1965 to match its chronological coverage with the 1955-1964 *SCI* cumulation we recently published.[4]

Since their inception, both *SCI* and *SSCI* were recognized by information scientists and sociologists as important tools to help study the history, evolution, and sociology of science. Some of these potential uses were forecast as early as 1955.[5] Although the sociometric and other nonbibliographic uses of citation indexes may one day exceed their use for information retrieval, the primary purpose of *SCI*, *SSCI*, and *Arts & Humanities Citation Index™* (*A&HCI™*) is to help you search the literature. As I stressed recently, there is a continuing need to educate scholars in these uses.

The basic function of any well-designed index ought to be readily self-evident. But there are numerous strategies for searching which can turn the index into an active and dynamic research tool. While I have recently reviewed these strategies for *SCI*,[6] it is equally important to review these methods as they apply to the social sciences.

For those of you who prefer a briefer review, turn to the summary table entitled "How to use the *Social Sciences Citation Index (SSCI)*" at the end of this essay.

Before discussing details, let me point out some of the differences between *SSCI* and conventional subject indexes. In the traditional indexing or cataloging process, indexers or bibliographers assign subject headings or terms to articles to facilitate their retrieval. These indexes depend upon the expertise and consistency of the indexers involved. Editors also attempt to control the vocabulary used for indexing, and terms tend to be general rather than specific. In general, economic as well as intellectual considerations limit the number of terms that can be used to index individual papers.

In *SSCI* there are several approaches to subject analysis. In the *Permuterm®️ Subject Index (PSI)*, every significant title word or phrase is indexed. And in the *Citation Index* section, each cited reference becomes a symbolic representation for the "subject" of the item cited. Thus, you can retrieve citing articles independent of their titles by using any one of the references they cited instead.

Conventional scholarly indexes also focus on the literature of one field or discipline—history, psychology, sociology, etc. But *SSCI* is *multi*disciplinary, covering about 1,400 journals in more than 25 major fields of the social and behavioral sciences (see Table 1). In addition, *SSCI* selectively covers articles relevant to the social sciences from about 3,100 journals in the natural and physical sciences which are fully covered in *SCI*. This selection procedure is done automatically by computer, and is based on citation patterns of the articles in these selectively covered journals. Most scholars would agree that the divisions between the social science disciplines are arbitrary. Yet *SSCI* is one of the few information retrieval tools that is truly multidisciplinary.

Conventional discipline-oriented indexes are also quite selective in what they choose to index even for the most important journals. If you can't find an article on a given topic, you can't be sure whether it doesn't exist or simply wasn't selected. *SSCI* indexes every significant

Table 1: Disciplines in the social and behavioral sciences covered by *SSCI®️*.

Anthropology
Archaeology
Area Studies
Business & Finance
Communication
Community Health
Criminology & Penology
Demography
Economics
Educational Research
Ethnic Group Studies
Geography
History
Information & Library Science
International Relations
Law
Linguistics
Management
Marketing
Philosophy
Political Science
Psychiatry
Psychology
Sociology
Statistics
Urban Planning & Development

item a journal publishes—articles, literature reviews, book reviews, editorials, letters, meeting reports, correction notes, discussions, etc. If you are trying to verify a reference and can't find it in *SSCI*, you can be sure that it has not been published in one of the journals *SSCI* indexes.

Also, conventional indexes give access to only one year of published literature. That is, they do not provide cross-references to relevant publications that appeared before or after the particular annual index you are searching. By indexing reference citations, *SSCI* breaks the "time barrier." Whatever particular volume you use, *SSCI* enables you to move forward or backward in time to identify literature relevant to your topic.

For example, let's assume you are interested in one or more authors who have published articles of interest to you. They can be located in either the *Source Index* or *Citation Index* sections of *SSCI*. The *Source Index* corresponds to the traditional author index. *All* authors who published articles during the indexing period are arranged alphabetically in the *Source Index. Full* bibliographic descriptions of their articles are given. In addition, all references cited in the article are listed with the source article. This allows you to identify *previously* published sources that the author found useful to the research he or she addressed. Many of these cited publications should also be relevant to you. I should point out that *A&HCI* also lists cited references with each indexed source item. This unique feature of *SSCI* and *A&HCI* is not provided in *SCI* strictly because of space considerations. In the online version of *SSCI*, this feature is retained and is sometimes called the "citation abstract." You can learn a great deal about an article by examining the list of papers and books it cited.

You can also locate the authors you are looking for in the *Citation Index* section of *SSCI*. The first author of each cited item is listed alphabetically here. Under that author's name is a separate line for every paper or book that was cited. This is arranged in chronological order, as in *SCI*. However, in *A&HCI*, cited works are listed alphabetically. Full bibliographic information on these current sources is obtained by referring to the *Source Index*.

Of course, you may not be familiar with specific authors who are working on a particular subject. In that case, you can identify them through *PSI*. In this keyword index, every significant word or phrase in each article title is paired with all others in the same title. The first term of each main entry is printed in boldface in *PSI*. Directly under that word is listed every other word that was paired with it, in alphabetic order. The first authors of papers that used these words in their titles follow.

This general introduction summarizes the three basic uses of *SSCI* in retrieving information. We'll now illustrate each of these with several searches to demonstrate the simplicity of the system.

Suppose you are interested in self-efficacy theories. This subject is a part of psychology that deals with people's perceptions of their own capabilities and

how these perceptions affect their behaviors and emotions when confronted with a task. For example, if you aren't confident about your driving ability you may feel overly anxious about hazardous road conditions such as rain or snow. Or, you may avoid demanding traffic situations or winding mountain roads. On the other hand, overconfident drivers take unnecessary risks they can't handle, such as passing cars on blind curves.

It is possible that you know that a prominent researcher in this field is Albert Bandura. You might even recall or have a reprint of his paper, "Gauging the relationship between self-efficacy judgement and action," published in 1980 in *Cognitive Therapy and Research*. You ask yourself, "What has happened since that paper was published? Has he or anyone else done any further work?"

To quickly answer these questions, you simply turn to the *Citation Index* section of *SSCI* and look under "Bandura A." Using the latest index available, it is easy to determine that this paper was cited in five articles in 1983, shown in Figure 1. These five current citing papers, involving over a half dozen authors, have commented on Bandura's 1980 article and they will probably add to your knowledge of self-efficacy theories. Of course, you could do the same search for the many other articles Bandura has published on this and other subjects. For example, Bandura's 1981 paper in *Journal of Personality and Social Psychology* has been cited by him and others in papers they published in 1983. The illustration in Figure 1 is an *abridged* sample of Bandura's cited works. In fact, the 1983 *SSCI Citation Index* includes six columns on his cited publications.

Figure 2 gives complete bibliographic data for each of the five papers that cited Bandura's 1980 article in *Cognitive Therapy and Research*, including the title, author, journal, etc. They were obtained from the *Source Index* of the 1983 *SSCI* annual. As you can see, the *Source Index* lists all the references each of these papers cited. Many of these citing publications deal directly with various aspects of the theory of self-efficacy, while others support points made in Bandura's article. Thus, in a simple two-step procedure involving the *Citation Index* and *Source Index* you now have a current bibliography of five relevant publications related to self-efficacy theory. Through the references these authors have cited, you could identify several dozen earlier papers.

If you are not familiar with this literature or the subject, you will not be aware of Bandura or any other author in the field. In that case, you would choose the appropriate keyword or phrase to start your search with *PSI*. In Figure 3, the entries for the term "self-efficacy" in the 1983 *PSI* are shown. This term has been used in combination with many other keywords. In fact you can see an entry for Bandura under each of the terms "determinants," "fears," "calamities," etc. When you turn to the *Source Index*, you find his 1983 papers that used these words in their titles.

The arrowheads in the column preceding the author entry in Figure 3 are used to limit your scanning if you want to identify all the articles that use self-efficacy in their titles. By checking only those authors with this symbol you can avoid repetitive look-ups of the same article or author. The arrowhead quickly tells you the number of unique first authors who have published articles on self-efficacy. Twenty-three first authors discussed various aspects of self-efficacy theory in the 1983 *SSCI*. Two of them— D.H. Schunk and J. Barling—wrote more than one article using the same primary and co-terms listed in *PSI*. They are indicated by an "@" sign.

Incidentally, had you looked up these 23 authors, you would have also found an additional group of 26 coauthors in the *Source Index*, all of whom are cross-referenced to the first authors. While the *Source Index* supports the other sections of *SSCI*, its main purpose is to help you determine what an author has published. This allows you to track the work of a specific author over time. By using the *Source Indexes* for the last 20 years, you can follow the publication history of that individual. While Bandura has published many earlier papers, which can best be

Figure 2: 1983 *SSCI® Source Index* entries for authors citing Bandura's 1980 paper, "Gauging the relationship between self-efficacy judgement and action," *Cognitive Therapy and Research.* The cited paper is indicated by boxes.

BARLING J
ABEL M—SELF-EFFICACY BELIEFS AND TENNIS PERFORMANCE
COGN THER R 7(3):265-272   83   21R
UNIV WITWATERSRAND,SCH PSYCHOL, JOHANNESBURG 2001, SOUTH AFRICA

(ANON)	78 ADV BEHAVIOUR RES TH	1	137
"	79 MAGAZINE RACQUE 0501		
BANDURA A	77 COGNITIVE THERAPY RE	1	287
"	77 J PERS SOC PSYCHOL	35	125
"	77 PSYCHOL REV	84	191
"	80 COGNITIVE THERAPY RE	4	39
"	80	4	263
BARLING J	80 UNPUB SELF EFFICACY		
"	83 J ORG BEHAVIOR MANAG		
GRAVEL R	80 COGNITIVE THERAPY RE	4	83
HOROWITZ LM	79 J CONSULT CLIN PSYCH	47	453
KAZDIN AE	78 ADV BEHAVIOUR RES TH	1	177
"	78 COGNITIVE THERAPY RE	2	105
"	79 J CONSULT CLIN PSYCH	47	725
"	80 BEHAV RES THER	18	191
KENDALL PC	80 COGNITIVE THERAPY RE	3	1
KEYSER V	81	5	29
KIRSCH I	80		
MAHONEY MJ	79 UNPUB BEHAVIORAL		
PATZ M	81 UNPUB SELF EFFICACY		
WOOLFOLK RL	79 COGNITIVE THERAPY RE	3	239

KIRSCH I
WICKLESS CV—CONCORDANCE RATES BETWEEN SELF-EFFICACY AND APPROACH BEHAVIOR ARE REDUNDANT
COGN THER R 7(2):179-188   83   7R
UNIV CONNECTICUT,DEPT PSYCHOL, STORRS, CT 06268, USA

BANDURA A	77 COGNITIVE THERAPY RE	1	287
"	77 PSYCHOL REV	84	191
"	79 COMMUNICATION		
"	80 COGNITIVE THERAPY RE	4	263
KIRSCH I	80	4	259
"	82 UNPUB ROLE EXPECTANC		
NIE NH	70 STATISTICAL PACKAGE		

see COUNCIL JR   J CONS CLIN   51   432 83

MANNING MM
WRIGHT TL—SELF-EFFICACY EXPECTANCIES, OUTCOME EXPECTANCIES, AND THE PERSISTENCE OF PAIN CONTROL IN CHILDBIRTH
J PERS SOC 45(2):421-431   83   36R
CATHOLIC UNIV AMER,DEPT PSYCHOL, WASHINGTON, DC 20064

BANDURA A	77 COGNITIVE THERAPY RE	1	287
"	77 J PERS SOC PSYCHOL	35	125
"	77 PSYCHOL REV	84	191
"	78 ADV BEHAVIOUR RES TH	1	237
"	80 COGNITIVE THERAPY RE	4	39
"	80	4	263
BORKOVEC TD	78 ADV BEHAVIOUR RES TH	1	163
BRACKBILL Y	74 AM J OBSTET GYNECOL	118	377
BRADLEY R	65 HUSBAND COACHED CHIL		
BROWN I	78 J PERS SOC PSYCHOL	36	900
CHAMBLISS CA	79 COGNITIVE THERAPY RE	3	91
"	79	3	349
COGAN R	76 J PSYCHOSOM RES	20	523
COHEN J	75 APPLIED MULTIPLE REG		
CROWNE DP	60 J CONSULTING PSYCHOL		
DAVENPORTSLACK B	74 PSYCHOSOM MED	36	215
ENKIN M	72 PSYCHOSOMATIC MED OB		
FELTON GS	78 BIRTH FAMILY J	5	141
HUGHEY MJ	78 OBSTET GYNECOL	51	643
HUTTEL FA	72 J PSYCHOSOM RES	16	81
JACOBSON E	59 RELAX HAVE YOUR BABY		
KARMEL M	65 THANK YOU LAMAZE		
KAZDIN AE	78 ADV BEHAVIOUR RES TH	1	177
"	79 J CONSULT CLIN PSYCH	47	725
KEYSER V	81 COGNITIVE THERAPY RE	5	29
KLAUS MH	76 MATERNAL INFANT BOND		
KLUSMAN LE	75 J CONSULT CLIN PSYCH	43	162
MANNING MM	80 UNPUB SELF EFFICACY		
READ GD	59 CHILDBIRTH FEAR PRIN		
ROTTER JB	66 PSYCHOL MONOGRAPHS	80	
SCOTT JR	76 NEW ENGL J MED	294	1205
TEASDALE JD	78 ADV BEHAVIOUR RES TH	1	211
VELVOUSKI I	72 MODERN PERSPECTIVES		
WHITELY N	72 B AM COLLEGE NURSE M		
WILLMUTH L	78 J OBSTETRICAL GYNECO	7	33
ZAX M	75 AM J OBSTET GYNECOL	123	185

LEFEBVREPINARD M
QUESTIONS ABOUT THE RELATIONSHIP BETWEEN SOCIAL COGNITION AND SOCIAL-BEHAVIOR - THE SEARCH FOR THE MISSING LINK
CAN J BEH S 14(4):323-337   82   49R
UNIV QUEBEC,DEPT PSYCHOL, MONTREAL H3C 3P8, QUEBEC, CANADA

ASHER SR	76 DEV PSYCHOL	12	132
"	81 CHILDRENS ORAL COMMU		
BANDURA A	80 COGNITIVE THERAPY RE	4	263
EISENBERGBERG N	80 CHILD DEV	51	552
ENRIGHT RD	80	51	156
FLAVELL JH	68 DEV ROLE TAKING COMM		
"	81 CHILDRENS ORAL COMMU		
"	81 SOCIAL COGNITIVE DEV		
FOOT HC	77 J PERS SOC PSYCHOL	35	401

GARVEY C	73 CHILD DEV	44	562
"	75 J CHILD LANGUAGE	2	41
GLUCKSBERG S	67 MERRILL PALMER QUART	13	309
HIGGINS ET	81 DEV ROLE TAKING COMM		
KRASNOR LR	81 COGNITIVE ASSESSMENT		
KURDEK LA	75 DEV PSYCHOL	11	643
LANGER EJ	78 NEW DIRECTIONS ATTRI	2	
LEFEBVREPINARD M	INT J BEHAVIORAL DEV		
"	79 B PSYCHOL	33	593
"	79 CANADIAN J BEHAVIOUR	11	305
"	80 CHILD DEV	51	179
"	80 INT J PSYCHOLINGUIST	7	59
"	80 SOCIAL COGNITION COM		
"	82 J EXPT CHILD PSYCHOL	34	174
"	82 J PSYCHOL	110	133
LEVIN EA	CHILDRENS LANGUAGE	4	
MARATSOS MP	73 CHILD DEV	44	697
MARVIN RS	76	47	511
MEISSNER JA	76 DEV PSYCHOL	12	245
MENIGPETERSON CL	75 CHILD DEV	46	1015
MUELLER E	72	43	930
"	75 FRIENDSHIP PEER RELA		
NEWCOMB AF	79 CHILD DEV	50	878
NUCCI LP	78	49	400
PATTERSON CJ	81 DEV PSYCHOL	17	379
REVELLE GL	81 APR BIENN M SOC RES		
RUBIN KH	73 CHILD DEV	44	661
SELMAN RL	80 GROWTH INTERPERSONAL		
SHANTZ CU	72 CHILD DEV	43	643
"	75 REV CHILD DEV RES	5	
"	81 CHILDRENS ORAL COMMU		
SHATZ M	73 MONOGRAPHS SOC RES C	38	
"	78 NEBRASKA S MOTIVATIO		
STRAYER FF	80 SOCIAL COGNITION COM		
STRAYER J	80 CHILD DEV	51	815
URBERG KA	76 DEV PSYCHOL	12	198
WELLMAN HM	77 CHILD DEV	48	1052
WHITEHURST GJ	76	47	473
WICKLUND RA	80 SELF SOCIAL PSYCHOL		
ZAHNWAXLER C	77 DEV PSYCHOL	13	87

UNDERSTANDING AND AUTO-CONTROL OF COGNITIVE FUNCTIONS - IMPLICATIONS FOR THE RELATIONSHIP BETWEEN COGNITION AND BEHAVIOR
INT J BEHAV 6(1):15-35   83   69R
UNIV QUEBEC,DEPT PSYCHOL, MONTREAL H3C 3P8, QUEBEC, CANADA

ABELSON RP	76 COGNITION SOCIAL BEH		
ASHER SR	DEV CHILDRENS FRIEND		
BAKER L	HOB READING RES		
BANDURA A	80 COGNITIVE THERAPY RE	4	263
"	81 COGNITIVE SOCIAL DEV		
BELMONT JM	77 PERSPECTIVES DEV MEM		
BRANSFORD JD	77 SCH ACQUISITION KNOW		
BROWN AL	78 ADV INSTRUCTIONAL PS		
"	78 APPLICATION BASIC RE		
"	78 CHILDRENS THINKING W		
"	79 CHILD DEV	50	501
"	79 SRCD MONOGRAPHS	44	
CARR TH	79 ASPECTS CONSCIOUSNES		
CASE R	78 ADV INSTRUCTIONAL PS	1	
CAVANAUGH JC	79 J GENERAL PSYCHOL	101	161
"	80 DEV PSYCHOL	16	441
CHANOWITZ B	80 HUMAN HELPLESSNESS		
"	81 J PERS SOC PSYCHOL	41	1051
CHARLESWORTH WR	78 OBSERVING BEHAVIOR	1	
DUCKWORTH E	79 HARVARD EDUC REV	49	297
DUVAL S	72 THEORY OBJECTIVE SEL		
EISENBERGBERG N	79 DEV PSYCHOL	15	228
"	80 CHILD DEV	51	552
ERICSSON KA	80 PSYCHOL REV	87	215
FENIGSTEIN A	75 J CONSULT CLIN PSYCH	43	522
FLAVELL HJ	81 CHILDRENS ORAL COMMU		
FLAVELL JH	77 PERSPECTIVES DEV MEM		
"	79 AM PSYCHOL	34	906
KENDALL CR	80 INTELLIGENCE	4	255
KIMBLE GA	70 PSYCHOL REV	77	361
KOBASIGAWA A	80 ALBERTA J ED RES	26	169
KREUTZER MA	75 MONOGRAPHS SOC RES C	40	
KUHN D	79 GENETIC EPISTEMOLOGI	8	1
"	79 HARVARD EDUC REV	49	340
"	79 INTELLECTUAL DEV CHI		
"	80 UNPUB DEV DEV PSYCHO		
LACHMANN JL	79 DEV PSYCHOL		543
LAGRECA AM	80 CHILD DEV	51	572
LANGER EJ	PERSONALITY SOCIAL P	2	
"	76 J PERS SOC PSYCHOL	34	191
"	78 NEW DIRECTIONS ATTRI		
"	80 J PERS SOC PSYCHOL	37	2014
"	80 OLD AGE ARTIFACT BIO		
LEFEBVREPINARD M	80 INT J PSYCHOLINGUIST	7	59
"	80 MAY U WAT C CHILD DE		
"	80 REV QUEBECOISE PSYCH	1	53
"	82 CANADIAN J BEHAVIORA	14	323
"	82 J PSYCHOL	110	133
LUNZER EA	79 ASPECTS CONSCIOUSNES		
LURIA AR	61 ROLE SPEECH REGULATI		
MEICHENBAUM D	GROWTH INSIGHT		
"	77 COGNITIVE BEHAVIOR M		
"	77 COGNITIVE BEHAVIORAL		
"	80 OCT NIE LRDC C THINK		
MEICHENBAUM DH	71 J ABNORMAL PSYCHOLOG	77	115
MILLER PH	79 MERRILL PALMER Q	25	235
MISCHEL W	79 AM PSYCHOL	34	740
MYERS M	78 J EDUC PSYCHOL	70	680
NISBETT R	80 HUMAN INFERENCE STRA		
NISBETT RE	77 PSYCHOL REV	84	231
PASCUALLEONE J	80 DEV MODELS THINKING		
PATTERSON CJ	78 UNPUB DEV LISTENER C		
PIAGET J	74 PRISE CONSCIENCE		
"	74 REUSSIR COMPRENDRE		
SMITH ER	78 PSYCHOL REV	85	355
SNYDER M	SOCIAL PSYCHOL BEH		
VYGOTSKY LS	62 THOUGHT LANGUAGE		
WICKLUND RA	80 SELF SOCIAL PSYCHOL		
ZIVIN G	79 DEV SELF REGULATION		

206

Figure 3: 1983 *SSCI®* *PSI*. The main entry, "self-efficacy," has been paired with all other significant terms. The co-terms Bandura used with "self-efficacy" in his 1983 papers are indicated by boxes.

SELF-DISSOLVING
INJUNCTION -◆BLOCK DJ
TIME - - - - - "

SELF-DOUBT
ATTENTION - -◆TESSER A
CONFORMITY - "
PRESSURE - - "
ROLE - - - - "
SOCIAL - - - "
STIMULUS - - "

SELF-EFFICACY
◆STOLTE JF
ACADEMIC - -◆BARLING J
ACHIEVEMENT ◆SCHUNK DH@
ADJUSTMENT -◆HOLAHAN CK
AGING - - - - "
ANTICIPATED -◆BANDURA A
APPLICATIO. -◆TAYLOR KM
APPROACH - -◆KIRSCH I
-◆REBOK GW
ASSERTIVEN. -◆LEE C
ASSESSING - - BARLING J
ASSESSMENT -◆POSER EG
ASSISTANCE - "
ATTITUDES - -◆CROWDER RL
ATTRIBUTIO. "
AUTONOMIC - -◆FELTZ DL
BANDURA - - "
BEHAVIOR - - - KIRSCH I
- - LEE C
BELIEFS - -◆BARLING J@
CALAMITIES - BANDURA A
CAREER - - -◆TAYLOR KM
CAUSAL - - - CROWDER RL
- - FELTZ DL
CESSATION - -◆MCINTYRE KO
-◆PROCHASK.JO
CHILDBIRTH -◆MANNING MM
CHILDRENS - -◆FELTZ DL
-◆SCHUNK DH@
CLINICIANS -◆RUDOLF SR
COGNITIVE -◆DITTMANN.F
COMPETITIVE -◆MCAULEY E
CONCORDANCE KIRSCH I
CONSTRUCT-. -◆SHERER M
CONTINGENC. SCHUNK DH
CONTROL - - MANNING MM
COUNSELING -◆CLIFFORD JS
DEPRESSION -◆KANFER R
DETERMINAN. BANDURA A
BARLING J
DEVELOPING - SCHUNK DH
DEVELOPMENT "
DIFFERENTI. "
EFFECTS - -◆BANDURA A
-◆SCHUNK DH
ELDERLY - - - DITTMANN.F
ELEMENTS - FELTZ DL
EXPECTANCI. - MANNING MM
FACILITATI. -◆GOLDFRIE.MR
FACILITATOR -◆SCHUNK DH
FEARS - - - - BANDURA A
GOAL - - - - "
GOVERNING - - "
GROUP - - - POSER EG
HEROIN - - - - CROWDER RL
INDECISION - - TAYLOR KM
INFLUENCE - - FELTZ DL
INTERPERSO. - KANFER R
INTERVENTI. - POSER EG
JUDGMENTS - KANFER R

SELF-EFFICACY (CONT)
LIFE - - - - - HOLAHAN CK
MAINTENANCE CLIFFORD JS
PROCHASK.JO
MECHANISMS - BANDURA A
MOTIVATION -◆MADDUX JE
MOTIVATION. - BANDURA A
OUTCOME - - MANNING MM
PAIN - - - - "
PATH-ANALY. - FELTZ DL
PEER - - - - POSER EG
PERCEPTION - FELTZ DL
PERFORMANCE BARLING J
PERSISTENCE - MANNING MM
PHYSICAL - - - MCAULEY E
PRE-RETIRE. - POSER EG
PREDICTORS - LEE C
PROCESSES - PROCHASK.JO
PROTECTION - MADDUX JE
PSYCHOLOGI. - HOLAHAN CK
RATES - - - - KIRSCH I
REDUNDANT - "
RELAPSE - - - MCINTYRE KO
- - PROCHASK.JO
RELATIONSH. - HOLAHAN CK
RELIABILITY - MCAULEY E
REPLICATION - FELTZ DL
REWARD - - - SCHUNK DH
SCALE - - - - MCAULEY E
- - SHERER M
SCALING - - - RUDOLF SR
SELF-CHANGE PROCHASK.JO
SELF-CONCE. - "
SELF-EVALU. - BANDURA A
SELF-REGUL. - SCHUNK DH
SETTING - - - KANFER R
- - MCAULEY E
SKILLS - - - - SCHUNK DH@
SMOKING - - - MCINTYRE KO
- - PROCHASK.JO
SOBRIETY - - - CLIFFORD JS
SPORT - - - - MCAULEY E
STANDARD - - KANFER R
STRESS - - - HOLAHAN CK
STUDENT - - RUDOLF SR
SUBSEQUENT - LEE C
SYSTEMS - - - BANDURA A
TENNIS - - - - BARLING J
THEORY - - - FELTZ DL
- - - TAYLOR KM
TRAINING - - DITTMANN.F
- - RUDOLF SR
TRAINING-P. - TAYLOR KM
TREATMENT - TAYLOR KM
UNDERSTAND. "
USE - - - - - RUDOLF SR
VALIDITY - - - MCAULEY E
VERBAL - - - SCHUNK DH

SELF-EMPLOYED
AGE - - - - -◆DORNBUSC.HL
EARNINGS - -◆HENDERSO.JW
-◆TEILHETW.S
EVIDENCE - -◆MOORE RL
FUNCTIONS - HENDERSO.JW
INCOME-TAX - DORNBUSC.HL
INFORMAL - - TEILHETW.S
RELATIOUSH. - DORNBUSC.HL
SECTOR - - - TEILHETW.S
TREATMENT - DORNBUSC.HL
WORKERS - - - MOORE RL

thor. Thus, if you remember having seen an article on self-efficacy by Cervone, the *Source Index* would direct you to look under "Bandura A" for complete information. This is illustrated in Figure 5.

These cross-references serve a useful purpose in helping you to verify partially remembered citations. This function is crucial because it is extremely important to supply an accurate and complete set of references when you submit a manuscript for publication. Even if you don't remember in what year a particular paper was published, you can use the five-year cumulations of *SSCI* to scan the complete lists of papers for an author. If it was published from 1966 onward, you can find it in *SSCI*.

If you are so inclined, you can also use the *Citation Index* to identify papers published even more than 20 years ago. As long as the paper or book in question has been cited even once from 1966 to 1983, a condensed citation for it will appear in the *Citation Index* of *SSCI*. To obtain full bibliographic data you can go to the library and retrieve any of the current publications that have cited it and look in their reference lists.

You can also use the *Citation Index* of any annual or cumulated *SSCI* edition to compile a partial bibliography of an author's works. This list will usually include the author's most influential papers or books, as shown in Figure 1.

Indexes are not always used to do comprehensive searches. Very often we simply want to retrieve a partially remembered citation. As long as you can recall part of the title, you can use *PSI* for those keywords. Once you recognize the author's name, you can confirm you have the right paper by examining its title in the *Source Index*. You can then either check your reprint collection or the journal itself in your library if you are still unsure that this is indeed the right paper.

The *Corporate Index* section of *SSCI* is still another option for identifying authors and their publications. It is arranged by country and city, and subdi-

identified using the five-year cumulations, Figure 4 shows that in 1983 he published two articles on self-efficacy, one of which he coauthored with D. Cervone. Bandura also wrote two shorter pieces, an editorial in the *Journal of Japanese Psychological Research* and a "short" note in *Psychological Review*.

I should point out that full bibliographic data for an article in the *Source Index* are listed only under the entry for the *first* author. However, a cross-reference is provided for *every* coau-

Figure 4: 1983 *SSCI®* *Source Index* entries for Bandura's 1983 papers. In addition to full bibliographic information, the *Source Index* indicates the number of references each article contained and provides condensed citations for each. The sample shows that Bandura published two articles, an editorial, and a note in 1983. "Self-efficacy determinants of anticipated fears and calamities" was published in *Journal of Personality and Social Psychology*, volume 45, issue 2, pages 464 through 469, 1983, and contained 34 references. The second article, coauthored with D. Cervone, "Self-evaluative and self-efficacy mechanisms governing the motivational effects of goal systems," was published in *Journal of Personality and Social Psychology*, volume 45, issue 5, pages 1017 through 1028, 1983, and contained 26 references. Bandura's affiliation and address are repeated beneath each of the entries.

Figure 5: 1983 *SSCI®* *Source Index*, showing an example of a cross-reference for D. Cervone (in box), a coauthor of Bandura's 1983 article published in *Journal of Personality and Social Psychology*. The entry directs you to look under the primary author, "BANDURA A," for complete bibliographic information on this article, which is included in Figure 4.

```
CERULLO FM
   see GOTTESMA.RL       ELEM SCH J          83    239 83
CERUTTI F
   (GE) THE LIVING AND THE DEAD IN THE THEORY OF MARX,
   KARL
      ARGUMENT    25(MAR):231-238            83     NO R
CERVELLATI R
   see BENEDETT.L        EUR J SCI E          5    439 83
┌─────────────────────────────────────────────────────────┐
│ CERVONE D                                                 │
│   see BANDURA A        J PERS SOC          45   1017 83   │
└─────────────────────────────────────────────────────────┘
CESA I
   see MACKINNO.A        B PSYCHON S         21    362 83
```

vided by organization and department. Under the department heading are listed all papers published by members of that department. A condensed citation for each article is provided. Figure 6 shows that Bandura is listed under the Department of Psychology, Stanford University, Stanford, California. The *Source Index* will give you full bibliographic information for each of his papers, as shown in Figure 4.

You'll also notice in Figure 6 that each publication is coded by type—note, meeting, editorial, letter, etc. Original, substantive research articles are not coded simply because they are the most common type of publication indexed.

However, in the social sciences and humanities, book reviews are quite common. Indeed, *SSCI* is the *only* information retrieval service for the social sciences that indexes book reviews comprehensively. The reviewer is treated as an author in the *Source Index*. For example, Figure 6 indicates that C.N. Jacklin wrote a review in *Contemporary Psychology* of a book by J. Sayers. Figure 7a shows the *Source Index* entry for this review from the 1983 *SSCI*. In addition, the author of the *book* is listed in the *Citation Index*, as shown in Figure 7b.

Book reviews and the monographs and books they discuss are crucial forms of communication in the social and behavioral sciences. Critical reviews of these books and monographs are useful and important information sources for social scientists. From 1966 to date,

```
BANDRAGE A
  CORRECTION ◊ CORRECTION
     B CON AS SC      15(1):71                    83        1R
  BANDRAGE A          82 B CON AS SC       14   17
BANDU I
  see VASAVADA BC      CLIN RES           31  A674 83
BANDURA A
  SELF-EFFICACY DETERMINANTS OF ANTICIPATED FEARS AND
  CALAMITIES
     J PERS SOC       45(2):464-469                83       34R
     STANFORD UNIV,DEPT PSYCHOL, STANFORD, CA 94305, USA
  AVERILL JR          73 PSYCHOL BULL          80   286
  BANDURA A           77 COGNITIVE THERAPY RE    1   287
                      77 J PERS SOC PSYCHOL     35   125
                      77 PSYCHOL REV            84   191
                      80 COGNITIVE THERAPY RE    4    39
                      82 AM PSYCHOL             37   122
                      82 J PERS SOC PSYCHOL     43     5
  BARLOW DH           69 BEHAV RES THER          7   191
  BECK KH             81 J APPLIED SOCIAL PSY   11   401
  BIRAN M             81 J CONSULT CLIN PSYCH   49   886
  BLACK AH            65 CLASSICAL CONDITIONI
  BOLLES RC           75 LEARNING THEORY
  COLLINS J           82 MAN M AM ED RES ASS
  HERRNSTEIN RJ       69 PSYCHOL REV            76    49
  KIRSCH I            82 J PERS SOC PSYCHOL     42   132
  LANGER EJ           79 CHOICE PERCEIVED CON
  LAZARUS RS          80 THEORETICAL BASES PS
  LEE C               83 UNPUB EFFICACY EXPEC
                      83 COGNITIVE THERAPY RE
  LEITENBERG H        71 J ABNORM PSYCHOL       78    59
  LELAND EI           83 THESIS STANFORD U
  MILLER SM           79 BEHAV RES THER         17   287
                      81 ADV EXPT SOCIAL PSYC   14
  NOTTERMAN JM        52 J ABNORMAL SOCIAL PS   47   674
  OBRIEN GT           77 J BEHAVIOR THERAPY E    8   359
  ORENSTEIN H         75 BEHAV RES THER         13   177
  RAPPOPORT A         81 OCT M PHOB SOC AM SA
  RESCORLA RA         67 PSYCHOL REV            74   151
  RINM DC             69 BEHAVIOUR RESEARCH      7   349
  SCHROEDER HE        76 J CONSULT CLIN PSYCH   44   191
  SCHWARTZ B          78 PSYCHOL LEARNING BEH
  TELCH MJ            82 THESIS STANFORD U
  WEINBERG RS         79 J SPORT PSYCHOL         1   320
  WORTMAN CB          76 J EXP SOC PSYCHOL      12   301
  CERVONE D—SELF-EVALUATIVE AND SELF-EFFICACY
  MECHANISMS GOVERNING THE MOTIVATIONAL EFFECTS OF
  GOAL SYSTEMS
     J PERS SOC       45(5):1017-1028             83       26R
     STANFORD UNIV,DEPT PSYCHOL, STANFORD, CA 94305, USA
  ATKINSON JW         64 INTRO MOTIVATION
                      74 MOTIVATION ACHIEVEME
  BANDURA A           77 COGNITIVE THERAPY RE    1   177
                      77 PSYCHOL REV            84   191
                      77 SOCIAL LEARNING THEO
                      78 AM PSYCHOL             33   344
                      81 J PERS SOC PSYCHOL     41   586
                      81 PSYCHOL PERSPECTIVES    1
                      82 AM PSYCHOL             37   122
  BECKER LJ           78 J APPL PSYCHOL         63   428
  BROWN I             78 J PERS SOC PSYCHOL     36   900
  FEATHER NT          82 EXPECTATIONS ACTIONS
  HECKHAUSEN H        77 MOTIVATION EMOTION      1   283
  KIESLER CA          71 PSYCHOL COMMITMENT E
  LANGER EJ           75 J PERS SOC PSYCHOL     32   311
  LATHAM GP           75 ACADEMY MANAGEMENT J   18   824
  LEWIN K             44 PERSONALITY BEHAVIOR    1
  LOCKE EA            68 ORGANIZATIONAL BEHAV    3   157
                      70 ORG BEHAVIOR HUMAN P    5   135
                      82 EFFECT SELF EFFICACY
  SALOMON G           J EDUC PSYCHOL
  SCHUNK DH           81                        73    93
  STEERS RM           74 PSYCHOL BULL           81   434
  STRANG HR           78 J APPL PSYCHOL         63   446
  WEINBERG RS         79 J SPORT PSYCHOL         1   320
  THE XLVITH ANNUAL CONVENTION OF THE JAPANESE-
  PSYCHOLOGICAL-ASSOCIATION ◊ EDITORIAL
     JPN PSY RES      25(3):170-171              83      NO R
     STANFORD UNIV, STANFORD, CA  94305, USA
  TEMPORAL DYNAMICS AND DECOMPOSITION OF RECIPROCAL
  DETERMINISM - A REPLY ◊ NOTE
     PSYCHOL REV      90(2):166-170              83       7R
     STANFORD UNIV,DEPT PSYCHOL, STANFORD, CA 94305, USA
  BANDURA A           77 SOCIAL LEARNING THEO
                      78 AM PSYCHOL             33   344
                      81 BEHAV THER             12    30
  GUYTON AC           72 ANN REV PHYSL          34
  HALDANE JS         1804 MIND                   9    27
  JAMES W            1804    "                   9   281
  PHILLIPS DC         83 PSYCHOL REV            90   158
BANDURA MM
  see NEWCOMBE N       DEVEL PSYCH             19   215 83
  see      "          SEX ROLES                9   377 83
```

Figure 6: 1983 *SSCI®* Corporate Index, geographic section. The main heading shows the name of the state. All subdivisions are alphabetized. Each city entry includes the name of each institution or departmental subdivision in which authors have published during the indexing period. In this example, "California" is followed by "Stanford," beneath which is found "Stanford Univ," which includes "Dept Psychol." The list of papers published by this department follows. Only the first author of each paper is shown. Bandura's 1983 publications are indicated by the box.

CALIFORNIA
STANFORD
● **STANFORD UNIV**

● *DEPT PSYCHIAT.....................*

GOLDMAN HH	HOSP COMMU		34	129	83
KORAN LM	GEN HOSP PS		5	7	83

● *DEPT PSYCHIAT & BEHAV SCI...*

EMSLIE GJ	AM J PSYCHI		140	708	83
MAGLIOZZ.JR	J NERV MENT	N	171	246	83
REED GL	INT J BEHAV		6	51	83
WARD WH	PSYCHOS MED		45	471	83

● *BEHAV MED PROGRAM*

AGRAS WS	J CONS CLIN	N	51	792	83

● *SOCIAL ECOL LAB*

BILLINGS AG	ADDICT BEHA		8	205	83

● *STUDY BEHAV MED LAB*

GRAHAM LE	J CONS CLIN	N	51	322	83

● *DEPT PSYCHOL.....................*

BANDURA A	J PERS SOC		45	464	83
"			45	1017	83
"	PSYCHOL REV	N	90	166	83

BEAL CR	CHILD DEV		54	148	83
BOWER GH	PHI T ROY B		302	387	83
CARNEY T	PERCEPTION		11	529	82
CLARK HH	J VERB LEAR		22	245	83
"			22	591	83
ELLSWORT.PC	CRIME DELIN		29	116	83
FELDMAN SS	CHILD DEV		54	1628	83
"	DEVEL PSYCH		19	278	83
FLAVELL JH	COG PSYCHOL		15	95	83
"			15	459	83
FRENZEL C	GERONTOL	M	23	110	83
FREYD JJ	BEHAV BRAIN		6	145	83
GERRIG RJ	J EXP PSY L		9	667	83
JACKLIN CN	CONT PSYCHO	B	28	388	83
"	DEVELOP PSY		16	163	83
KAHNEMAN D	BEHAV BRAIN		6	509	83
LAVOND DG	PHARM BIO B	N	19	379	83
MACCOBY EE	AM PSYCHOL		38	80	83
MAUK MD	PHYSL BEHAV	N	30	493	83
MISCHEL HN	CHILD DEV		54	603	83
PODGORNY P	J EXP PSY P		9	380	83
PORRAS JI	J APPL BEH		18	433	82
PRIBRAM K	J SOC BIOL	N	6	147	83
SCHARLAC.AE	GERONTOL	M	6	313	83
SHEPARD RN	SCIENCE		220	632	83
SNOW ME	CHILD DEV		54	227	83
TENENBAU.JM	CONT PSYCHO	B	28	583	83
THOMAS EAC	ORGAN BEH H		32	399	83
THOMPSON RF	ANN R NEUR	R	6	447	83
"	PROG PSYCHB	R	10	167	83
"	TRENDS NEUR	R	6	270	83
TVERSKY A	CC/SOC BEH		1983	22	83
"	J EXP PSY L		9	713	83
"	PSYCHOL REV		90	293	83
WATSON AB	PERC PSYCH		33	113	83
YESAVAGE JA	J GERONTOL		38	197	83

● *DEPT SCI.....................*

CAVALLIS.L	NATURE	E	304	124	83

● *DEPT SOCIOL.....................*

SSCI has indexed about 370,000 book reviews. This is in addition to the 330,000 book reviews indexed in *A&HCI* from 1976 to date. For space and economic reasons, we do not index all book reviews in *SCI*. But we do now include in

SCI all book reviews appearing in *Science* and *Nature*. Unlike the social sciences, there is considerably less interest in book reviews in the sciences.[7]

This primer on how to use *SSCI* does not describe various other strategies for increasing the scope of a literature search, such as *cycling*. These methods are described in detail and fully illustrated in my book on citation indexing.[8] The annual *SSCI Guide* also includes detailed instructions and sample searches, as well as a complete list of journals covered. Our purpose here is limited to helping you use *SSCI* to find a few key current papers.

Any undergraduate can be taught the basic purpose of *SSCI* in minutes. Anyone who can use an alphabetic telephone directory can use either the *Source Index* to determine what an author has published or the *Citation Index* to find out where a particular work has been cited or quoted. If neither of these

Figure 7a: 1983 *SSCI®* Source Index showing a sample entry for a book review. C.N. Jacklin is the reviewer of the book, *Biological Politics—Feminist and Anti-Feminist Perspectives* by J. Sayers. The book review was published in *Contemporary Psychology*, volume 28, issue 5, pages 388 through 389, 1983. The review cited two references, one of which is the book being reviewed (in box). Jacklin's affiliation and address are given beneath the entry.

```
JACKLIN CN
   BIOLOGICAL POLITICS - FEMINIST AND ANTI-FEMINIST
   PERSPECTIVES - SAYERS.J ◆ BOOK REVIEW
   CONT PSYCHO   28(5):388-389              83      2R
   STANFORD UNIV DEPT PSYCHOL STANFORD, CA 94305, USA
   SAYERS J          82 BIOL POLITICS FEMINI
   THOMAS MC         68 ED REV            35   64
```

Figure 7b: 1983 *SSCI®* Citation Index entry for J. Sayer's 1982 book, *Biological Politics—Feminist and Anti-Feminist Perspectives*. The book was cited in four 1983 publications, one editorial and three book reviews. The review by Jacklin, shown in Figure 7a, is indicated by the box.

```
SAYERS G
 71 ENDOCRINOLOGY   88 1063
 SEE SCI FOR 18 ADDITIONAL CITATIONS
 75 KAROLINSKA S RES MET
 77 ANN NY ACAD SCI  297  220
 SEE SCI FOR 4 ADDITIONAL CITATIONS
 MALAMED S       J GERONTOL        38  130 83
 82 BIOL POLITICS FEMINI
 FAUSTOST.A      CONT SOCIOL     B 12  346 83
 "               SIGNS           B  9  307 83
 JACKLIN CN      CONT PSYCHO     B 28  388 83
 ROSE H          SIGNS           E  9   73 83
 82 FEMINIST REV   8   91
 SAYERS J        INT J WOMEN        6   71 83
SAYERS MH
 73 BRIT J HAEMATOL   24 209
 SEE SCI FOR 9 ADDITIONAL CITATIONS
 SZARFARC SC     REV SAUDE P       17  200 83
```

approaches is sufficient, you can do a keyword search in *PSI*.

SSCI is the print version of a computerized data base called *Social SCI-SEARCH®*. The data base can be accessed online through DIALOG, BRS, and DIMDI. You can also access these files by using our *Sci-Mate* ™ software—the *Universal Online Searcher*.[9] Once you've located a relevant record you can "download" it to your personal microcomputer.

Weekly updates of the social sciences literature can be obtained through ISI's *Automatic Subject Citation Alert* (*ASCA®*).[10] This selective dissemination of information service permits you to customize searches to suit your interests. You simply submit a profile of target authors, subjects, journal sets, institutions, etc., and *ASCA* automatically identifies all publications related to it. It is a simple "clipping service" that permits you to identify who is reviewing or citing your work, among other things. *ASCA* covers the totality of journals indexed in *SSCI* and *SCI*.

The one-page summary entitled "How to use the *SSCI*" is provided for those who would like to introduce students to this information retrieval system. Copies of this summary can be made without permission. In addition, you can request a portfolio of sample searches from ISI.

* * * * *

My thanks to Alfred Welljams-Dorof for his help in the preparation of this essay.

REFERENCES

1. **Garfield E.** Journal citation studies. 40. Anthropology journals—what they cite and what cites them. *Current Contents* (37):5-12, 12 September 1983.
2. --------------. The new *Social Sciences Citation Index* (*SSCI*) will add a new dimension to research on man and society. *Essays of an information scientist.* Philadelphia: ISI Press, 1977. Vol. 1. p. 317-9.
3. --------------. Citation indexing: a natural science literature retrieval system for the social sciences. *Amer. Behav. Sci.* 7(10):58-61, 1964.
4. --------------. The 1955-1964 *Science Citation Index* cumulation—a major new bibliographic tool for historians of science and all others who need precise information retrieval for the age of space and molecular biology. *Current Contents* (5):5-8, 31 January 1983.
5. --------------. Citation indexes for science. *Science* 122:108-11, 1955.
6. --------------. How to use *Science Citation Index* (*SCI*). *Current Contents* (9):5-14, 28 February 1983.
7. --------------. A swan song for *IBRS*. *Essays of an information scientist.* Philadelphia: ISI Press, 1983. Vol. 5. p. 327-30.
8. --------------. *Citation indexing—its theory and application in science, technology, and humanities.* Philadelphia: ISI Press, 1983. 274 p.
9. --------------. *Sci-Mate 1.1*: improved customer services and a new version of the software for personal text retrieval and online searching. *Current Contents* (8):3-9, 20 February 1984.
10. --------------. You don't need an online computer to run SDI profiles offline! So why haven't you asked for *ASCA*—the ISI selective citation alert. *Current Contents* (13):5-12, 28 March 1983.

How to Use the
Social Sciences Citation Index
(SSCI)

Social Sciences Citation Index® (*SSCI®*) fully indexes the contents of over 1,400 journals in the social and behavioral sciences, and selectively covers another 3,100 journals in the natural and physical sciences, which publish over 125,000 articles per year. *SSCI* is published in annual and five-year cumulated editions.

Four basic indexes comprise the *SSCI* system.

Source Index. An alphabetical listing of all authors and all papers published during the period covered by the index. Full bibliographic information is provided, including authors, title, journal, volume, issue number, full pagination, year of publication, number of references cited, and address. In addition, condensed citations of all references included in the indexed article are also shown.

Citation Index. An alphabetical listing of first authors of cited papers, books, etc. Listed under each cited item is the condensed citation for each citing paper.

Permuterm® Subject Index (PSI). Uses words appearing in the titles of articles as indexing terms. All significant title words are permuted to create all possible pairs. Each pair then becomes a separate entry in *PSI*.

Corporate Index. Consists of two complementary parts. The geographic section is subdivided by country, city, institution, department, etc. The alphabetic organization section cross-references each institution with its geographic location.

The following examples from the 1983 *SSCI* illustrate how easy it is to use.

To find the most recent information relevant to M.M. Baltes's 1976 paper, "Reestablishing self-feeding in a nursing home resident," *Nursing Research* 25(1):24-26, turn to the *Citation Index*, shown in Figure A. Complete bibliographic information for each citing paper can be obtained from the *Source Index*.

If you know little about research on nursing homes, you can start your search in *PSI*.

As shown in Figure B, a check under the main heading "nursing-home" reveals that the hyphenated term has been used together with many other terms. Among these co-terms are "accidents," "advocacy," "aging," "care," etc., followed in each case by the names of relevant authors. The *Source Index* provides full information on these authors' articles.

You can also check if a particular author has published anything during an indexing period by finding the name in the *Source Index*. For example, Figure C shows that in 1983 Baltes published two articles entitled "On the social ecology of dependence and independence in elderly nursing-home residents—a replication and extension," and "The microecology of residents and staff-behavior mapping in a nursing-home." The former paper is in English, and the latter in German. Baltes also published a comment entitled "Cognitive performance deficits and hospitalization—learned helplessness, instrumental passivity, or what."

The *Corporate Index* identifies all papers published at a given institution. For example, Figure D shows that numerous departments are found following the entry "Free Univ Berlin" under the city heading "Berlin" that follows the main heading "Fed Rep Ger." One of these is the department with which Baltes is affiliated, "Dept Gerontopsychiat."

SSCI's multidisciplinary coverage and cross-referencing are its main advantages for students and scholars. Anatomy, nutrition, dentistry, and instrumentation may all be relevant to anthropology, for example. Conversely, citations in an anthropology article may reveal relationships to other fields.

A detailed schematic explanation of search techniques appears in the front matter of each *SSCI* edition. A complete *Guide and Lists of Source Publications* are also printed separately each year.

©1984 ISI

Sample entries from the 1983 *Social Sciences Citation Index®* (*SSCI®*).

Figure A: Sample entry from *SSCI*'s *Citation Index.*

Figure C: Sample entry from *SSCI*'s *Source Index.*

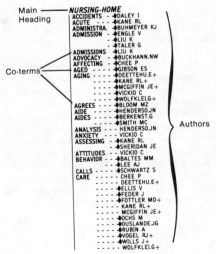

Cited Author — **BALTES MM**
```
            ** J GERONTOL
   BALTES MM        J PERS SOC           45  1013 83
   75 INT J NURS STUD  12    5
     SEE SCI FOR 1 ADDITIONAL CITATION
   HALEY WE       GERONTOL               23    18 83
   WILLIAMS PN    BEHAV MODIF             7   583 83
   76 GERONTOLOGIST  16  428
   HALEY WE       GERONTOL               23    18 83
   76 GERONTOLOGIST  16  429
   WILLIAMS PN    BEHAV MODIF             7   583 83
   76 J APPL PSYCHOL  61  501
   ONEILL GW      HOSP COMMUN R          34   709 83
```
Cited Paper —
```
   76 NURS RES  25  24
   MOSHER PM      EDUC GERON              9    37 83
   SHINNAR SE     J AM DIET A            83   321 83
   77 ED GERONTOLOGY INT Q   2  383
     SEE SCI FOR 1 ADDITIONAL CITATION
   PERONE M       DEVEL PSYCH            19   915 83
   WILLIAMS PN    BEHAV MODIF             7   583 83
   77 OMEGA    3  165
   KUNZ PR        SOCIAL BIOL     N      30   106 83
   77 OMEGA    8  165
   RILEY JW       ANN R SOC               9   191 83
   WELCH CE       OMEGA           N      13   389 83
   80 INT J BEHAV DEV    3  489
   BALTES MM      J GERONTOL             38   556 83
                  J PERS SOC             45  1013 83
                  Z GERONTOL             16    18 83
   82 BASIC PROCESSES HELP
   BALTES MM      J GERONTOL             38   556 83
                  J PERS SOC             45  1013 83
                  Z GERONTOL             16    18 83
   FRIES JF       MILBANK MEM            61   397 83
```
BALTES P
```
   70 LIFE SPAN DEV PSYCHO    3
   FALGER PRJ     Z GERONTOL             16   121 83
   73 LIFE SPAN DEV PSYCHO
   DEMARSH JP     CHILD ST J             13    75 83
   77 LIFE SPAN DEV PSYCHO
   SCHAIE KW      DEVEL PSYCH            19   531 83
   77 LIFE SPAN DEV PSYCHO
   78 MINN S CHILD PSYCHOL  11    1
   79 LIFE SPAN DEV BEHAVI    2  255
   FALGER PRJ     Z GERONTOL             16   121 83
   80 LIFE SPAN DEV BEHAVI    3
   BODEN O        HUMAN DEV              26   308 83
```
BALTES PB
```
   68 HUMAN DEVELOPMENT  11  145
     SEE SCI FOR 1 ADDITIONAL CITATION
   BERZONSK MD    HUMAN DEV              26   213 83
   BIRREN JE      ANN R PSYCH     R      34   543 83
   ELAHI VK       INT J AGING            38   162 83
   ENRIGHT RD     INT J AGING            17   213 83
   KERTZER DI     ANN R SOC       R       9   125 83
```

Citing Papers

Figure B: Sample entry from *SSCI*'s *Permuterm® Subject Index* (*PSI*).

Main Heading — **NURSING-HOME**
```
   ACCIDENTS - ●DALEY I
   ACUTE ----- ●KANE RL
   ADMINISTRA. ●BUHMEYER KJ
   ADMISSION - ●ENGLE V
               ●LIU K
               ●TALER G
   ADMISSIONS ●LIU K
   ADVOCACY - ●BUCKHANN.NW
   AFFECTING - ●CHEE P
   AGED ----- ●GIBSON ES
   AGING ----- ●DEETTEHU.E+
               ●KANE RL+
               ●MCGIFFIN JE+
               ●VICKIO C
               ●WOLFKLEI.G+
   AGREES ---- ●BLOOM MZ
   AIDE ----- ●HENDERSO.JN
   AIDES ----- ●BERKENST.G
               ●SMITH MC
   ANALYSIS -- ●HENDERSO.JN
   ANXIETY --- ●VICKIO C
   ASSESSING - ●KANE RL
               ●SHERIDAN JE
   ATTITUDES - ●VICKIO C
   BEHAVIOR - ●BALTES MM
               ●LEE AJ
   CALLS ---- ●SCHWARTZ S
   CARE ----- ●CHEE P
               ●DEETTEHU.E+
               ●ELLIS V
               ●FEDER J
               ●FOTTLER MD+
               ●KANE RL+
               ●MCGIFFIN JE+
               ●OCHS M
               ●OUSLANDE.JG
               ●RUBIN A
               ●VOGEL RJ+
               ●WILLS J+
               ●WOLFKLEI.G+
```
Co-terms

Authors

BALTER MB
  see MELLINGE.GD PSYCHOL MED 13 607 83
  see UHLENHUT.EH ARCH G PSYC 40 1167 83

BALTES MM
HONN S BARTON EM ORZECH MJ LAGO D—ON THE SOCIAL ECOLOGY OF DEPENDENCE AND INDEPENDENCE IN ELDERLY NURSING-HOME RESIDENTS - A REPLICATION AND EXTENSION
```
J GERONTOL       38(5):556-564              83        18R
  FREE UNIV BERLIN,DEPT GERONTOPSYCHIAT, D-1000 BERLIN 19,
  FED REP GER
ALLISON PD        82 PSYCHOL BULL            91   393
BALTES MM         80 INT J BEHAV DEV          3   489
                  82 BASIC PROCESSES HELP
                  ·83 J PERS SOC PSYCHOL
BARTON EM         80                         38   423
EXTONSMITH AN     77 CARE ELDERLY M CHALL
GOFFMAN E         60 IDENTITY ANXIETY SUR
KALISH RA         60 DEPENDENCIES OLD PEO
LANGER EJ         76 J PERS SOC PSYCHOL     34   191
                  77 CHOICE PERCEIVED CON
LEHR U            77 PSYCHOL ALTERNS
LESTER PB         78 J GERONTOLOGICAL NUR    4    23
MACCOBY EE        70 CARMICHAELS MANUAL C    2
RODIN J           77 J PERS SOC PSYCHOL     35   897
SACKETT GP        79 BEHAVIOR RES METHODS   11   366
SACKETT GT        79 HDB INFANT DEV
SELIGMAN MWP      75 HELPLESSNESS DEPRESS
STEPHENS MAP      79 ENV DESIGN RES THEOR
```
SKINNER EA—COGNITIVE PERFORMANCE DEFICITS AND HOSPITALIZATION - LEARNED HELPLESSNESS, INSTRUMENTAL PASSIVITY, OR WHAT - COMMENT
```
J PERS SOC       45(5):1013-1016            83        12R
  FREE UNIV BERLIN,DEPT GERONTOPSYCHIAT, D-1000 BERLIN 19,
  FED REP GER
ABRAMSON LY       78 J ABNORMAL PSYCHOL     87    49
                  J GERONTOL
BALTES MM         80 INT J BEHAV DEV          3   489
                  82 BASIC PROCESSES HELP
BARTON EM         80 J PERS SOC PSYCHOL     38   423
GOFFMAN E         60 IDENTITY ANXIETY SUR
LANGER EJ         76 J PERS SOC PSYCHOL     36   886
MAIER SF          76 J EXPT PSYCHOL GENER  103     3
MILLER IW         79 PSYCHOL BULL           86    93
RAPS CS           82 J PERS SOC PSYCHOL     42  1036
ROTHBAUM F        82 J PERS SOC PSYCHOL     42     5
ZUROFF DC         80                        79   130
```
BARTON EM ORZECH MJ LAGO D—(GE) THE MICROECOLOGY OF RESIDENTS AND STAFF - BEHAVIOR MAPPING IN A NURSING-HOME
```
Z GERONTOL       16(1):18-26                83        24R
  FREE UNIV BERLIN,KLINIKUM CHARLOTTENBURG,GERONTOPSYCHIAT
  ABT, D-1000 BERLIN 19, FED REP GER
BALTES MM         80 INT J BEHAV DEV          3   489
                  82 BASIC PROCESSES HELP
                  83 J GERONTOL
BALTES PB         81 AGING COGNITIVE PROC
BARKER RG         63 STREAM BEHAVIOR
BARTON EM         80 J PERS SOC PSYCHOL     38   423
BIRREN JE         69 GERONTOLOGIST           9   163
BUTLER RN         71 PSYCHOL TODAY           5    49
ERIKSON EH        74 PSYCHOL ISSUES MONOG    1
FISSENI HJ        76 AKTUELLE GERONTOLOGI    4    29
GOTTESMAN LE      74 GERONTOLOGIST          14   501
ITTELSON WH       76 DESIGNING OPEN NURSI
LARSON JA         79 J GERONTOL            33   109
LARSON R          70 AGING HUMAN DEV         1   330
LAWTON MP         76 GERONTOLOGY M NEW YO
                  78 J AGING HUMAN DE        7    15
                  78 J GERONTOLOGICAL NUR    4    23
LESTER PB         75 J APPL BEHAV ARAL       8   261
MCCLANNAHAN LE    72 THESIS CORNELL U ITH
SNYDER LH         78 GERONTOLOGIST          18   281
SPASOFF RA        76 ENV DESIGN RES THEOR
STEPHENS MAP      77 Z GERONTOL             10   322
TEWS HP
```
BALTES PB
BRANDTSTJ RAUH H SILBEREI.R—(GE) PROMOTION OF POSTGRADUATES IN DEVELOPMENTAL-PSYCHOLOGY - INFORMATION ON A MODEL PLAN EXTENDING BEYOND INSTITUTIONS ● EDITORIAL
```
Z ENTWICK P      15(1):85-87                83        NO R
  see DITTMANN.F    GERONTOL               23   131 83
  see WILLIS SL     J EDUC PSYC            75   257 83
```

Figure D: Sample entry from *SSCI*'s *Corporate Index*, geographic section.

FED REP GER

                       VOL PG YR

City Entry — **BERLIN** ——————— Institutional Subdivision
● **FREE UNIV BERLIN** ——————
```
  ● BOARD FOREIGN STUDENTS....
  AMMON H        INT J POLIT            13    83 83
  ● DEPT ANESTHESIOL & OPERAT INTENS CARE...
  FRUCHT U       INTEN CAR M M          9   227 83
  ● DEPT CHILD & ADOLESCENT PSYCHIAT &
    NEUROL....
  STEINHAU.HC    ACT PSYC SC            68     1 83
                 INT J EAT D             2   221 83
                 J ABN C PSY            10   609 82
                 J AM A CHIL            22   559 83
                 PSYCHOL MED  E         13   239 83
  ● DEPT GERMAN....
  STREECK J      J PRAGMATIC  B          7    93 83
  ● DEPT GERONTOPSYCHIAT....
  BALTES MM      J GERONTOL             38   556 83
                 J PERS SOC             45  1013 83
  ● DEPT INT POLIT....
  ASHKENAS.A     J INT AFF              36   257 83
```
Departmental Subdivisions

212

Current Comments®

A Tribute to Derek John de Solla Price: A Bold, Iconoclastic Historian of Science

Number 28

July 9, 1984

On September 3, 1983, Derek John de Solla Price died suddenly in London. He had been visiting with our mutual friend and colleague, Anthony Michaelis, editor of *Interdisciplinary Science Reviews*. When I heard of Derek's death, I wondered why he had taken the risk of flying to London so soon after recovering from major surgery for an aneurysm. But at a memorial ceremony at Yale University, his son Mark suggested that it could not have been otherwise. It would have been out of character for Derek to refrain from pursuing his work and interests. He is survived by his wife, Ellen; sons, Mark and Jeffrey; daughter, Linda DeMichelle; sister, Joan Cravitz; and three grandchildren.

For me, perhaps one of the most regrettable aspects of Derek's untimely death is the lost opportunity to have co-authored a book or paper with him. But it would do no good to be lugubrious about this matter. Death becomes more prevalent as one grows older and accumulates colleagues the world over. That is a price scholars must pay for the privilege of acceptance into an invisible college. But, somehow, we survive these traumas. However, the loss of a friend such as Derek Price, who was more like a brother to me than a colleague, demands some special attention. Although offering him this posthumous recognition is important to me, it is gratifying to know that Derek was alive to read the special tributes to him which I published

in *Current Contents®* (*CC®*) on at least two occasions.[1,2] I am equally glad that I pressed him to do a commentary[3] on his classic, *Little Science, Big Science*.[4]

Numerous tributes to Derek Price have already been published by colleagues who knew him or his work. Belver Griffith, Drexel University School of Library and Information Science, has praised Derek's contributions to our understanding of the role of science in society.[5] Manfred Kochen, University of Michigan, Ann Arbor, provides a brief review of Derek's career, and credits his influence upon the entire first generation of information scientists.[6] Douglas H. Shaffer, editor, *National Association of Watch and Clock Collectors Bulletin*, praised Price's contributions to the field of horology,[7] the science of measuring time. Susan Crawford, Medical Library Association, wrote of Price's work on the problems of information handling.[8] And in a moving tribute, Alan Mackay, Department of Crystallography, Birkbeck College, University of London, described the multifaceted nature of Price's talent. In an oblique reference to the streak of iconoclasm which Derek possessed, Mackay wrote: "[We] will remember Derek in his accustomed role of expositor of the prospects for the future, the stupidities of the present and of the treasures of the past."[9]

I was asked to write a brief eulogy to Derek for the first issue of *Information Today* in November 1983.[10] Along with many of his friends, I was also asked to contribute an article to a *festschrift* issue of *Scientometrics*, to be published next year. That article discusses the multidisciplinary influence of *Little Science, Big Science*.[11] In these and other publications, I have often spoken of Derek's pioneering role. He uniquely brought together the history of science, scientometrics, and information science, and made an enormous impact on scientific communication. In none of these instances, however, was I able to fully cover the many facets of his creativity. That would take a long-term, collaborative effort by a multidisciplinary research team which would include some of his close colleagues. So what follows will discuss an often-overlooked aspect of Derek's scholarship: his passion for scientific apparatus and his work showing the importance of technology and methodology in the advancement of science.

Derek Price was best known, of course, for his work in scientometrics and the history of science, for which he received a second doctorate in 1954 from the University of Cambridge. But his scientific contributions have not been limited to those fields. His early papers, for instance, were in mathematics and theoretical and experimental physics. Indeed, he had earned his first doctorate in experimental physics in 1947 from the University of London. His lifelong interest, however, was in scientific instruments and hardware.

Born in Leyton, a northeast London suburb, Price was educated in British state schools. His early inclination toward science was derived, at least in part, from a steady diet of science fiction "pulp" magazines. He expanded his scientific horizons during World War II, assisting in military research on optical characteristics of hot and molten metals.[12] He also taught college-level science courses for armed services training programs. In 1947, degree in hand, he accepted a three-year position teaching applied mathematics at Raffles College (now the University of Singapore) in Malaya.

His stay at Raffles was a pivotal point in his career. First, it was during this time that Price made his now-famous discoveries about the exponential growth of science. The college had acquired a complete set of the *Philosophical Transactions of the Royal Society of London*, which had its inception in 1665. Price stored the bound volumes in his home while the college library was under construction. Taking the opportunity to read them cover-to-cover—and thereby gaining his initial education in the history of science—he noticed that the chronologically stacked volumes formed an exponential curve against the wall. Surveying all the other sets of journals he could find, Price found that exponential growth was an apparently universal phenomenon in the scientific literature. He gave a paper presenting his observations to the Sixth International Congress for the History of Science in Amsterdam in 1950.[13] This paper marked his transition from physics and mathematics to the history of science. Although the paper was initially ill-received (in Derek's words, "It went over like a lead balloon"), Price nevertheless entered Cambridge to pursue a doctorate in his newly chosen field.

Price's stay in Singapore also led him to develop an interest in Oriental culture. When he was made honorary curator of Cambridge's Whipple Museum of Antique Scientific Instruments, this interest led him to collaborate with Joseph Needham and Wang Ling on a book and a paper covering the history of medieval Chinese clockwork.[14,15] Published in *Nature* in 1956, the paper stated, "The invention of the mechanical clock was one of the most important points in the history of science and technology," allowing for the first time the accurate measurement of processes over time.[14] The then accepted view was that mechanical timekeepers, powered by a falling weight, were an innovation developed in Europe in the early fourteenth century. However, Price and colleagues, among others, demonstrated that the Chinese tradition of water-powered astronomical clockwork directly contributed to the development of late medieval European mechanical clocks.

Price made an important discovery by accident some years earlier while writing his thesis on the history of scientific instruments. Carefully sifting through medieval literature, he stumbled upon a Middle English manuscript by English poet Geoffrey Chaucer. It described the construction of an instrument for calculating planetary motions. Price identified the beautifully handwritten paper as a companion piece to Chaucer's 1391 *Treatise on the Astrolabe*. He then proved it to be the poet's draft manuscript, the only extensive piece in Chaucer's own hand known to exist.[16,17]

One of Derek's proudest achievements, however, was the solution to the problem of the Greek Antikythera mechanism. An artifact of the first century BC, it was salvaged by the first underwater archaeological expedition in history in 1900. The mechanism featured prominently in all accounts of the history of scientific instruments as the earliest known example of a "technological" tool, but its function was unknown, since it was encrusted within a mass of coral, shells, and other debris. Using the technique of gamma-radiology, however, Price was able to photograph the interior of the corroded mass. A painstaking analysis showed the existence of differential gears. This proved that the Antikythera mechanism was a mechanical calendar exhibiting a level of sophistication and refinement not previously thought possible in such an early culture.[18-20]

Derek's last paper, "Of sealing wax and string,"[21] combined his love of scientific apparatus with his expertise in the history of science. Its posthumous publication in *Natural History* led me to reflect on what may have been one of his most important messages, suggesting that instrumentation has been of far greater importance in the history of scientific achievement than has been suspected. An extensive quote from the article follows:

During the golden age of experimental physics early in this century, all progress seemed to depend on a band of ingenious craftsmen with brains in their fingertips, who exploited a great many little-known properties of materials and other tricks of the trade. These tricks not only made all the difference in what could or could not be done in the laboratory; to a large extent, they determined what was discovered....

The flavor and tradition of this experimentation are markedly different from, and perhaps even in conflict with, the standard view of the role of experiment in science....

The standard view...is that the scientist creates hypotheses and sends them out to be tested by making a trial of the prescribed 'experiment.' Herbert Butterfield and Thomas Kuhn have described the inspired thought that leads to great and revolutionary changes in science as 'shifts in paradigm.' According to this view, the thought is what's important; laboratory instruments...exist only to confirm or invalidate what the thinker has hypothesized.

What actually goes on in laboratories is of a different nature. Since the seventeenth century...experiment has more often meant 'experience' in the use of various techniques. The idea is to find out what will happen when you try certain techniques, and the hope is that in finding out, you will discover facts of nature that fall outside the range of what was known before. The procedure is far from being cut-and-dried, and the theoreticians and experimenters far from being in the master/servant relationship in which they are usually cast.... Skilled experimenters are masters of a...crucially important technology. Their work is at the core of high technology and represents a tradition that is autonomous and did not arise from the cognitive core of science, but from other technologies devised for quite different purposes. Much more often than is commonly believed, the experimenter's craft is the force that moves science forward.

By now, a considerable literature on the importance of methodology and technology in the advancement of the scientific enterprise has accumulated. In our discussions of highly cited papers, we have emphasized that citation analysis highlights the importance of new or improved methods or instruments. Every list of highly cited papers includes a sizable group dealing with new or improved techniques for analysis. Hundreds of the *Citation Classics* ™ we have published illustrate this point. Unfortunately, we do not yet have any systematic data or analyses that would permit one to draw major science policy conclusions. Have we, in fact, given appropriate priority to those seeking support to produce new methods? Or must these techniques be smuggled in under the cloak of basic research?

Without making invidious comparisons between the intellectual value of theoretical or conceptual research and that of instrumentation or methodology, there is a bias in the way the public and the press perceive these two interacting phenomena. And in fact, scientists themselves often use denigrating terminology when speaking of "mere" methodology, or "mere" technique, or "mere" equipment. However, Derek Price produced incontrovertible evidence that technology and methodology open up entirely new areas of science.

The mind and talent of Derek Price were unique. Consider the size of the worldwide scientific enterprise: at least a million scientists are involved in research. Even when we limit discussion to the 100,000 or fewer who contribute the bulk of new knowledge, it is remarkable how unusual each of them is. When the number is reduced by another order of magnitude, and the discussion confined to the 10,000 or so most influential scientists—including some like Derek Price—we realize even more fully how unusual such persons are.

There will never be another Derek Price. It is good to know that others will go on to help illuminate the paradigms he established. But no one is in a position to continue the projects that were uniquely his, to carry on where he left off. Derek himself acknowledged that he, like hundreds of other scholars, had not sufficiently sought or trained candidates for his own replacement. If the National Science Foundation or some other body were to manage science as one tries to manage a large institution or corporation, this important matter of intellectual succession would be given more serious attention.

I have no doubt that the crowning moment of Derek's career was his election, just before his death, to the Royal Swedish Academy of Science. He wrote to me about this with obvious glee and pride. He planned to begin a systematic procedure for nominating candidates for the Nobel prize. His membership entitled him to this privilege. This was not a trivial challenge, but I am sure he would have met it admirably. And we both knew the pitfalls of citation analysis well enough to use the data wisely.

Derek Price was one of the most ardent supporters of the use of unobtrusive methods for identifying significant science. He was often overly zealous in what he had to say on these matters, as any of us who knew him personally had many an occasion to discover. But as with so many of his pronouncements, he always seemed to succeed in drawing attention to ideas and problems that may otherwise have lain fallow. And although his provocative style and bravado caused many a raised eyebrow, whenever he was caught in an outrageous simile or metaphor, he happily corrected himself. When the definitive biography of Derek Price is written, it will surely note his flair for the dramatic.

Derek wrote so much that was original and that truly mattered that it would be a life's work to separate what had ultimately proven right from the rest. The main point is that he got everyone's intellectual juices flowing. And, to say the least, that was always exhilarating. The loss of this exciting and dynamic man, of his ideas and his contributions, is one that will be felt not just by his friends, but by the whole scientific community. Mackay, in particular, stressed Derek's role as a member of the Advisory Board of the *Science Citation Index®*, and his close association with me

and, later, Henry Small and others at ISI®. We both served as founding editors of *Scientometrics*, together with V. V. Nalimov and others. That journal has now established the Derek Price Medal to help perpetuate the memory of this gifted person. While preparing this tribute to Derek, I was informed that I would be the first recipient of the medal bearing his name. This medal will always be symbolic to me of the special relationship Derek and I shared.

* * * * *

My thanks to Stephen A. Bonaduce and Bella Teperov for their help in the preparation of this essay.

©1984 ISI

REFERENCES

1. **Garfield E.** Price's citation cycle. *Essays of an information scientist.* Philadelphia: ISI Press, 1981. Vol. 4. p. 618-33.
2. --------------. J.D. Bernal—the sage of Cambridge. 4S award memorializes his contributions to the social studies of science. *Essays of an information scientist.* Philadelphia: ISI Press, 1983. Vol. 5. p. 511-23.
3. **Price D J D.** Citation Classic. Commentary on *Little science, big science.* New York: Columbia University Press, 1963. 118 p. *Current Contents/Social & Behavioral Sciences* 15(29):18, 18 July 1983.
4. --------------. *Little science, big science.* New York: Columbia University Press, 1963. 118 p.
5. **Griffith B C.** Derek Price (1922-1983) and the social studies of science. *Scientometrics* 6(1):5-7, 1984.
6. **Kochen M.** Toward a paradigm for information science: the influence of Derek de Solla Price. *J. Amer. Soc. Inform. Sci.* 35(3):147-8, 1984.
7. **Shaffer D H.** In recognition of greatness. *Nat. Assn. Watch Clock Collectors Bull.* 25:545, 1983.
8. **Crawford S.** Derek John de Solla Price (1922-1983): the man and the contribution. *Bull. Med. Libr. Assn.* 72(2):238-9, 1984.
9. **Mackay A.** Derek John de Solla Price: an appreciation. *Soc. Stud. Sci.* 14(2):315-20, 1984.
10. **Garfield E.** In memoriam. *Inform. Today* November 1983, p. 31. (Premiere issue.)
11. --------------. A tribute to Derek John de Solla Price: the impact of *Little science, big science.* *Scientometrics* (In press.)
12. **Price D J D & Lowery H.** The emissivity characteristics of hot metals, with special reference to the infrared. *Brit. Iron Steel Res. Assn. Publ.* 7:523-46, 1943.
13. **Price D J D.** Quantitative measures of the development of science. *Arch. Int. Hist. Sci.* (14):85-93, 1951.
14. **Needham J, Ling W & Price D J D.** Chinese astronomical clockwork. *Nature* 177:600-2, 1956.
15. --. *Heavenly clockwork: the great astronomical clocks of medieval China.* Cambridge: Cambridge University Press, 1960. 253 p.
16. **Price D J D.** The equatorie of the planetis. (Abstract.) *Bull. Brit. Soc. Hist. Sci.* 1:223-6, 1953.
17. ----------------. *The equatorie of the planetis.* Cambridge: Cambridge University Press, 1955. 214 p.
18. ----------------. An ancient Greek computer. *Sci. Amer.* 200(6):60-7, 1959.
19. ----------------. The Antikythera mechanism, an ancient Greek computer. *American Philosophical Society Year Book, 1959.* Philadelphia: American Philosophical Society, 1960. p. 618-20.
20. ----------------. *Gears from the Greeks: the Antikythera mechanism, a calendar computer from ca. 80 B.C.* Philadelphia: American Philosophical Society, 1974. 70 p.
21. ----------------. Of sealing wax and string. *Natur. Hist.* 84(1):49-56, 1984.

The Articles Most Cited in 1961-1982. 2.
Another 100 *Citation Classics* Highlight
the Technology of Science

In last week's tribute to Derek Price, the importance of methods and instruments in the advance of science was stressed.[1] Before he died, Derek published several articles and books on this topic.[2] He argued that many conceptual breakthroughs would not have been possible without first developing techniques and instruments to approach basic problems. Indeed, the development of new instruments and methods often leads to unanticipated theoretical innovations.

The importance of technology and methodology in science is further reflected in studies of highly cited articles. We recently published a list of the 100 papers most cited from 1961 to 1982 in *Science Citation Index®* (*SCI®*).[3] We have now extended the list to include 100 additional articles.

Table 1 provides full bibliographic information for these papers. They are arranged in alphabetic order by first author. After the citation count for 1961-1982, we've also included, in parentheses, the number of cites for 1983. A single asterisk indicates that the paper was the subject of a *Citation Classic™* commentary. The issue, year, and edition of *Current Contents®* (*CC®*) in which these commentaries were published follow the reference.

Many of these papers have appeared in earlier studies of most-cited papers. For example, 32 papers were included in a similar study covering 1961-1972.[4]

They are indicated by a number symbol. In comparison, 44 of the 100 papers identified in the first part of this series[3] also appeared in the 1974 study.

These papers were published in 51 journals. Just four journals account for a third of the papers: *Journal of Biological Chemistry* (16 papers), *Biochemistry Journal* (7), *Journal of Chemical Physics* (5), and *Nature* (5). Other high–impact journals that repeatedly turn up in our citation studies include *Science, Lancet, Journal of the American Chemical Society,* etc. But a few "newcomers" are represented, including *Annales de Chimie.* The oldest paper on the list was published in this journal in 1928. P. Job described a method for studying inorganic complexes in solution. That 70 publications cited this paper in 1983 indicates that researchers still have the patience to use Job's method.

Although methods papers dominate these lists of most-cited articles, a large number of high–impact theoretical or conceptual papers are also included. These superstar "idea" papers are widely recognized to be primordial contributions to science. Highly cited methods papers, however, are only grudgingly acknowledged as "useful" even by their authors. Theoretical papers are more highly valued because they usually symbolize major "intellectual" achievements. Methods papers, on the other hand, are "blue collar" efforts, "inevitable" pre-

Table 1. The second 100 most-cited articles, 1961-1982 *SCI®*, arranged in alphabetic order by first author. A=1961-1982 citations. 1983 citations appear in parentheses. B=bibliographic data. An asterisk (*) indicates that the paper was the subject of a *Citation Classic*™ commentary. A number symbol(#) indicates that the paper appeared in the 1974 list of most-cited articles.

A   B

2032 (93)   #*Abell L L, Levy B B, Brodie B B & Kendall F E. A simplified method for the estimation of total cholesterol in serum and demonstration of its specificity. *J. Biol. Chem.* 195:357-66, 1952. (34/79/LS)

1851 (74)   #*Ahlquist R P. A study of the adrenotropic receptors. *Amer. J. Physiol.* 153:586-600, 1948. (45/78)

1916 (102) *Anton A H & Sayre D F. A study of the factors affecting the aluminum oxidetrihydroxyindole procedure for the analysis of catecholamines. *J. Pharmacol. Exp. Ther.* 138:360-75, 1962. (34/77)

1558 (361) Aviv H & Leder P. Purification of biologically active globin messenger RNA by chromatography on oligothymidylic acid-cellulose. *Proc. Nat. Acad. Sci. US* 69:1408-12, 1972.

1554 (90)   Axen R, Porath J & Ernback S. Chemical coupling of peptides and proteins to polysaccharides by means of cyanogen halides. *Nature* 214:1302-4, 1967.

1835 (174) Bauer A W, Kirby W M M, Sherris J C & Turck M. Antibiotic susceptibility testing by a standardized single disk method. *Amer. J. Clin. Pathol.* 45:493-501, 1966.

1589 (79)   Bessey O A, Lowry O H & Brock M J. A method for the rapid determination of alkaline phosphatase with five cubic millimeters of serum. *J. Biol. Chem.* 164:321-9, 1946.

1691 (74)   #*Bloembergen N, Purcell E M & Pound R V. Relaxation effects in nuclear magnetic resonance absorption. *Phys. Rev.* 73:679-712, 1948. (18/77)

1554 (127) *Born G V R. Aggregation of blood platelets by adenosine diphosphate and its reversal. *Nature* 194:927-9, 1962. (37/77)

1558 (36)   #Boyden S V. The adsorption of proteins on erythrocytes treated with tannic acid and subsequent hemagglutination by antiprotein sera. *J. Exp. Med.* 93:107-20, 1951.

1605 (25)   #*Boyer P D. Spectrophotometric study of the reaction of protein sulfhydryl groups with organic mercurials. *J. Amer. Chem. Soc.* 76:4331-7, 1954. (25/79/LS)

1834 (38)   Britten R J & Kohne D E. Repeated sequences in DNA. *Science* 161:529-40, 1968.

1600 (97)   Brunauer S, Emmett P H & Teller E. Adsorption of gases in multimolecular layers. *J. Amer. Chem. Soc.* 60:309-21, 1938.

1823 (54)   Butcher R W & Sutherland E W. Adenosine 3',5'-phosphate in biological materials. I. Purification and properties of cyclic 3',5'-nucleotide phosphodiesterase and use of this enzyme to characterize the adenosine 3',5'-phosphate in human urine. *J. Biol. Chem.* 237:1244-50, 1962.

1675 (65)   *Chance B & Williams G R. The respiratory chain and oxidative phosphorylation. *Advan. Enzymol. Relat. Areas Mol.* 17:65-134, 1956. (49/83/LS)

1738 (144) Chandrasekhar S. Stochastic problems in physics and astronomy. *Rev. Mod. Phys.* 15:1-89, 1943.

1744 (74)   #Clarke D H & Casals J. Techniques for hemagglutination and hemagglutination-inhibition with arthropod-borne viruses. *Amer. J. Trop. Med. Hyg.* 7:561-73, 1958.

1542 (37)   Clementi E. *Ab initio* computations in atoms and molecules. *IBM J. Res. Develop.* 9:2-19, 1965.

1571 (34)   #*Coons A H & Kaplan M H. Localization of antigen in tissue cells. II. Improvements in a method for the detection of antigen by means of fluorescent antibody. *J. Exp. Med.* 91:1-13, 1950. (6/81/LS)

1687 (114) Crestfield A M, Moore S & Stein W H. The preparation and enzymatic hydrolysis of reduced and S-carboxymethylated proteins. *J. Biol. Chem.* 238:622-7, 1963.

1881 (77)   #Davis B D & Mingioli E S. Mutants of *Escherichia coli* requiring methionine or vitamin B_{12}. *J. Bacteriol.* 60:17-28, 1950.

1657 (142) Davis R W, Simon M & Davidson N. Electron microscope heteroduplex methods for mapping regions of base sequence homology in nucleic acids. *Meth. Enzymology* 21:413-28, 1971.

1714 (39)   #Dische Z. A new specific color reaction of hexuronic acids. *J. Biol. Chem.* 167:189-98, 1947.

2024 (119) Dixon M. The determination of enzyme inhibitor constants. *Biochem. J.* 55:170-1, 1953.

1982 (161) Dodge J T, Mitchell C & Hanahan D J. The preparation and chemical characteristics of hemoglobin-free ghosts of human erythrocytes. *Arch. Biochem. Biophys.* 100:119-30, 1963.

1901 (70)   #**Dole V P & Meinertz H.** Microdetermination of long-chain fatty acids in plasma and tissues. *J. Biol. Chem.* 235:2595-9, 1960.

1608 (102) *****Edman P & Begg G.** A protein sequenator. *Eur. J. Biochem.* 1:80-91, 1967. (9/84/LS)

1480 (49)   **Fahey J L & McKelvey E M.** Quantitative determination of serum immunoglobulins in antibody-agar plates. *J. Immunol.* 94:84-90, 1965.

1913 (75)   **Falck B, Hillarp N-A, Thieme G & Torp A.** Fluorescence of catechol amines and related compounds condensed with formaldehyde. *J. Histochem. Cytochem.* 10:348-54, 1962.

1594 (34)   #**Farquhar M G & Palade G E.** Junctional complexes in various epithelia. *J. Cell Biol.* 17:375-412, 1963.

1646 (218) **Feighner J P, Robins E, Guze S B, Woodruff R A, Winokur G & Munoz R.** Diagnostic criteria for use in psychiatric research. *Arch. Gen. Psychiat.* 26:57-63, 1972.

1551 (16)   #**Friedmann T E & Haugen G E.** Pyruvic acid. II. The determination of keto acids in blood and urine. *J. Biol. Chem.* 147:415-42, 1943.

1545 (7)   **Gell-Mann M.** Symmetries of baryons and mesons. *Phys. Rev.* 125:1067-84, 1962.

1750 (48)   *****Gillespie D & Spiegelman S.** A quantitative assay for DNA-RNA hybrids with DNA immobilized on a membrane. *J. Mol. Biol.* 12:829-42, 1965. (11/77)

1528 (189) **Glowinski J & Iversen L L.** Regional studies of catecholamines in the rat brain. I. The disposition of [^{3}H] norepinephrine, of [^{3}H] dopamine, and [^{3}H] dopa in various regions of the brain. *J. Neurochem.* 13:655-69, 1966.

1656 (82)   **Glynn I M & Chappell J B.** A simple method for the preparation of ^{32}P-labelled adenosine triphosphate of high specific activity. *Biochem. J.* 90:147-9, 1964.

1826 (180) *****Haber E, Koerner T, Page L B, Kliman B & Purnode A.** Application of a radioimmunoassay for angiotensin I to the physiologic measurements of plasma renin activity in normal human subjects. *J. Clin. Endocrinol. Metab.* 29:1349-55, 1969. (12/80/CP)

1979 (211) *****Hakomori S.** Letter to editor. (A rapid permethylation of glycolipid and polysaccharide catalyzed by methylsulfinyl carbanion in dimethyl sulfoxide.) *J. Biochem. Tokyo* 55:205-8, 1964. (23/80/LS)

1778 (125) **Hamilton W C.** Significance tests on the crystallographic R factor. *Acta Crystallogr.* 18:502-10, 1965.

1648 (21)   #**Hanes C S & Isherwood F A.** Separation of the phosphoric esters on the filter paper chromatogram. *Nature* 164:1107-12, 1949.

1642 (16)   *****Hanson H P, Herman F, Lea J D & Skillman S.** HFS atomic scattering factors. *Acta Crystallogr.* 17:1040-4, 1964. (30/77)

1531 (80)   **Hatchard C G & Parker C A.** A new sensitive chemical actinometer. II. Potassium ferrioxalate as a standard chemical actinometer. *Proc. Roy. Soc. London Ser. A* 235:518-36, 1956.

2035 (210) *****Havel R J, Eder H A & Bragdon J H.** The distribution and chemical composition of ultracentrifugally separated lipoproteins in human serum. *J. Clin. Invest.* 34:1345-53, 1955. (46/83/LS)

1484 (76)   *****Hayflick L & Moorhead P S.** The serial cultivation of human diploid cell strains. *Exp. Cell Res.* 25:585-621, 1961. (26/78)

1715 (184) **Hehre W J, Stewart R F & Pople J A.** Self-consistent molecular-orbital methods. I. Use of Gaussian expansions of Slater-type atomic orbitals. *J. Chem. Phys.* 51:2657-64, 1969.

1703 (142) **Herbert V, Lau K-S, Gottlieb C W & Bleicher S J.** Coated charcoal immunoassay of insulin. *J. Clin. Endocrinol. Metab.* 25:1375-84, 1965.

1717 (58)   #**Hirs C H W.** The oxidation of ribonuclease with performic acid. *J. Biol. Chem.* 219:611-21, 1956.

1971 (32)   #**Hoffman W S.** A rapid photoelectric process for the determination of glucose in blood and urine. *J. Biol. Chem.* 120:51-5, 1937.

1830 (127) **Hubel D H & Wiesel T N.** Receptive fields, binocular interaction and functional architecture in the cat's visual cortex. *J. Physiol.—London* 160:106-54, 1962.

1605 (160) *****Hughes J, Smith T W, Kosterlitz H W, Fothergill L A, Morgan B A & Morris H R.** Identification of two related pentapeptides from the brain with potent opiate agonist activity. *Nature* 258:577-9, 1975. (38/82/LS)

1549 (156) *****Huzinaga S.** Gaussian-type functions for polyatomic systems. I. *J. Chem. Phys.* 42:1293-302, 1965. (17/80/PC)

2043 (130) *****Jerne N K & Nordin A A.** Plaque formation in agar by single antibody-producing cells. *Science* 140:405, 1963. (35/81/LS)

1546 (67)   **Job P.** Formation and stability of inorganic complexes in solution. *Ann. Chim.—Paris* 9:113-203, 1928.

1502 (6)   **Karnovsky M J.** Simple methods for "staining with lead" at high pH in electron microscopy. *J. Biophys. Biochem. Cytol.* 11:729-32, 1961.

220

1723 (66)   **Kauzmann W.** Some factors in the interpretation of protein denaturation. *Advan. Prot. Chem.* 14:1-63, 1959.

1721 (639)   **Kohler G & Milstein C.** Continuous cultures of fused cells secreting antibody of pre-defined specificity. *Nature* 256:495-7, 1975.

1640 (77)   **Kubo R.** Statistical-mechanical theory of irreversible processes. I. General theory and simple applications to magnetic and conduction problems. *J. Phys. Soc. Jpn.* 12:570-86, 1957.

1999 (59)   **Loening U E.** The fractionation of high-molecular-weight ribonucleic acid by polyacrylamide-gel electrophoresis. *Biochem. J.* 102:251-7, 1967.

1537 (63)   **Lowry O H, Passonneau J V, Hasselberger F X & Schulz D W.** Effect of ischemia on known substrates and cofactors of the glycolytic pathway in brain. *J. Biol. Chem.* 239:18-30, 1964.

1564 (8)   **#Mandell J D & Hershey A D.** A fractioning column for analysis of nucleic acids. *Anal. Biochem.* 1:66-77, 1960.

1654 (84)   **Mans R J & Novelli G D.** Measurement of the incorporation of radioactive amino acids into protein by a filter-paper disk method. *Arch. Biochem. Biophys.* 94:48-53, 1961.

1527 (89)   **Marmur J & Doty P.** Determination of the base composition of deoxyribonucleic acid from its thermal denaturation temperature. *J. Mol. Biol.* 5:109-18, 1962.

1620 (182)   ***Marquardt D W.** An algorithm for least-squares estimation of nonlinear parameters. *J. Soc. Ind. Appl. Math.* 11:431-41, 1963. (27/79/ET)

1740 (144)   **McConahey P J & Dixon F J.** A method of trace iodination of proteins for immunologic studies. *Int. Arch. Allergy Appl. Immunol.* 29:185-9, 1966.

1601 (181)   ***McCord J M & Fridovich I.** Superoxide dismutase. *J. Biol. Chem.* 244:6049-55, 1969. (17/81/LS)

1766 (20)   **Mejbaum W.** Uber die Bestimmung kleiner Pentosemengen insbesondere in Derivaten der Adenylsaure. (Estimation of small amounts of pentose especially in derivatives of adenylic acid.) *Hoppe-Seylers Z. Physiol. Chem.* 258:117-20, 1939.

1942 (38)   **#Millonig G.** Advantages of a phosphate buffer for OsO_4 solutions in fixation. (Abstract.) *J. Appl. Phys.* 32:1637, 1961.

1759 (108)   **Mishell R I & Dutton R W.** Immunization of dissociated spleen cell cultures from normal mice. *J. Exp. Med.* 126:423-42, 1967.

1896 (33)   **#Moore S, Spackman D H & Stein W H.** Chromatography of amino acids on sulfonated polystyrene resins. *Anal. Chem.* 30:1185-90, 1958.

1802 (46)   **#Moore S & Stein W H.** A modified ninhydrin reagent for the photometric determination of amino acids and related compounds. *J. Biol. Chem.* 211:907-13, 1954.

1811 (85)   ***Morgan C R & Lazarow A.** Immunoassay of insulin: two antibody system. *Diabetes* 12:115-26, 1963. (52/77)

1782 (101)   **Mulliken R S.** Electronic population analysis on LCAO-MO molecular wave functions. I. *J. Chem. Phys.* 23:1833-40, 1955.

1464 (44)   ***Nachlas M M, Tsou K-C, De Souza E, Cheng C-S & Seligman A M.** Cytochemical demonstration of succinic dehydrogenase by the use of a new p-nitrophenyl substituted ditetrazole. *J. Histochem. Cytochem.* 5:420-36, 1957. (17/79/LS)

1800 (181)   ***Nash T.** The colorimetric estimation of formaldehyde by means of the Hantzsch reaction. *Biochem. J.* 55:416-21, 1953. (14/81/LS)

1713 (136)   ***Panyim S & Chalkley R.** High resolution acrylamide gel electrophoresis of histones. *Arch. Biochem. Biophys.* 130:337-46, 1969. (33/81/LS)

1526 (31)   **#*Pariser R & Parr R G.** A semi-empirical theory of the electronic spectra and electronic structure of complex unsaturated molecules. II. *J. Chem. Phys.* 21:767-76, 1953. (3/79/PC)

1936 (52)   **Pople J A & Segal G A.** Approximate self-consistent molecular orbital theory. III. CNDO results for AB_2 and AB_3 systems. *J. Chem. Phys.* 44:3289-96, 1966.

1924 (77)   **#Porter R R.** The hydrolysis of rabbit γ-globulin and antibodies with crystalline papain. *Biochem. J.* 73:119-27, 1959.

1694 (75)   **#*Reitman S & Frankel S.** A colorimetric method for the determination of serum glutamic oxalacetic and glutamic pyruvic transaminases. *Amer. J. Clin. Pathol.* 28:56-63, 1957. (10/79/CP)

1623 (84)   **Richardson K C, Jarett L & Finke E H.** Embedding in epoxy resins for ultrathin sectioning in electron microscopy. *Stain Technol.* 35:313-23, 1960.

1587 (894)   **Rigby P W J, Dieckman M, Rhodes C & Berg P.** Labeling deoxyribonucleic acid to high specific activity *in vitro* by nick translation with DNA polymerase I. *J. Mol. Biol.* 113:237-51, 1977.

1885 (156)   *Rodbell M. Metabolism of isolated fat cells. I. Effects of hormones on glucose metabolism and lipolysis. *J. Biol. Chem.* 239:375-80, 1964. (45/80/LS)

1843 (71)   #Roothaan C C J. New developments in molecular orbital theory. *Rev. Mod. Phys.* 23:69-89, 1951.

1890 (46)   Schneider W C. Determination of nucleic acids in tissues by pentose analysis. *Meth. Enzymology* 3:680-4, 1957.

1970 (37)   #*Schneider W C. Phosphorus compounds in animal tissues. I. Extraction and estimation of desoxypentose nucleic acid and of pentose nucleic acid. *J. Biol. Chem.* 161:293-303, 1945. (8/77)

1474 (151)   *Seabright M. Letter to editor. (A rapid banding technique for human chromosomes.) *Lancet* 2:971-2, 1971. (14/81/LS)

1478 (45)   #Seldinger S I. Catheter replacement of the needle in percutaneous arteriography. *Acta Radiol.* 39:368-76, 1953.

1935 (40)   #Sever J L. Application of a microtechnique to viral serological investigations. *J. Immunol.* 88:320-9, 1962.

1650 (131)   *Shannon R D & Prewitt C T. Effective ionic radii in oxides and fluorides. *Acta Crystallogr. B—Struct. Sci.* 25:925-46, 1969. (21/81/PC)

1465 (91)   *Shore P A, Burkhalter A & Cohn V H. A method for the fluorometric assay of histamine in tissues. *J. Pharmacol. Exp. Ther.* 127:182-6, 1959. (40/81/LS)

1720 (50)   *Skou J C. Enzymatic basis for active transport of Na+ and K+ across cell membranes. *Physiol. Rev.* 45:596-617, 1965. (20/81/LS)

1562 (6)   #Smithies O. An improved procedure for starch-gel electrophoresis: further variations in the serum proteins of normal individuals. *Biochem. J.* 71:585-7, 1959.

1646 (33)   #*Sperry W M & Webb M. A revision of the Schoenheimer-Sperry method for cholesterol determination. *J. Biol. Chem.* 187:97-106, 1950. (22/83/LS)

1917 (70)   #*Sweeley C C, Bentley R, Makita M & Wells W W. Gas-liquid chromatography of trimethylsilyl derivatives of sugars and related substances. *J. Amer. Chem. Soc.* 85:2497-507, 1963. (43/77)

2030 (128)   *Till J E & McCulloch E A. A direct measurement of the radiation sensitivity of normal mouse bone marrow cells. *Radiat. Res.* 14:213-22, 1961. (43/79/LS)

1903 (25)   #*Van Handel E & Zilversmit D B. Micromethod for the direct determination of serum triglycerides. *J. Lab. Clin. Med.* 50:152-7, 1957. (16/77)

1662 (148)   Vogel H J & Bonner D M. Acetylornithinase of *Escherichia coli*: partial purification and some properties. *J. Biol. Chem.* 218:97-106, 1956.

1582 (61)   Wachstein M & Meisel E. Histochemistry of hepatic phosphatases at a physiologic pH. *Amer. J. Clin. Pathol.* 27:13-23, 1957.

1880 (148)   Wilkinson G N. Statistical estimations in enzyme kinetics. *Biochem. J.* 80:324-36, 1961.

1694 (60)   #*Yalow R S & Berson S A. Immunoassay of endogenous plasma insulin in man. *J. Clin. Invest.* 39:1157-75, 1960. (14/77)

scriptions or recipes for getting the job done.

Ambiguous feelings about methodological works are often expressed in *Citation Classics* commentaries. Authors of high-impact work usually are pleased to learn that one or more of their papers have become "classics" in their field. But they sometimes are disappointed if their most-cited work is not one of the more theoretical articles they value most.

Although all 100 papers listed in Table 1 are *Citation Classics*, only 37 have been the subject of commentaries published in *CC*. In these commentaries, authors provide interesting background on their work—sources of inspiration, difficulties in obtaining materials or funding, publication delays and rejections, etc. The discussion which follows is based on these commentaries.

As mentioned earlier, many researchers underrate the value of methodological efforts. For example, David Gillespie, National Institutes of Health, Bethesda, Maryland, and the late Sol Spiegelman[5] developed an assay for DNA-RNA hybrids. Gillespie commented on their 1965 paper: "I must admit that...I didn't recognize the potential of what I was doing at the time.... I looked upon the method primarily as a neat trick that would allow me to discover some 'really important' facts of biological interest."[6] The attitude that methods are "neat tricks" while facts and theories are "really important" is echoed in a commentary by S. Hakomori, University of Washington, Seattle: "Life as a scientist is totally unpredictable. Frankly, I have mixed feelings as the paper cited is in my subsidiary interest.... I would be happier if some of my other papers, such as...discovery of cell surface fibronectin, would have been selected...."[7]

Even though researchers tend to trivialize methods papers, they do recognize in hindsight the wide impact these papers have on science. Richard J. Havel, University of California, San Francisco, and colleagues devised a method for isolating lipoproteins from blood serum. Havel commented on this 1955 paper: "None of the authors...felt that it represented a major conceptual advance and we were initially surprised by the wide attention that it received. Evidently, even rather straightforward methodological efforts can sometimes help to open up a fruitful field of research."[8] Havel's method is now routinely used in clinical and epidemiological research.

Devising methods for specific research problems can result in profound advances in basic scientific knowledge. Leonard Hayflick, Children's Hospital Medical Center, Oakland, California, and P.S. Moorhead worked on cultivating human diploid cell strains to study differences between cancerous and normal cells. To their surprise, the normal cell strain died after about 50 population doublings. They suggested that this newly observed phenomenon indicated cellular aging. But their paper was rejected by the *Journal of Experimental Medicine* because the findings conflicted with 50 years of tissue culture research showing that cells multiply *indefinitely*.

Hayflick commented: "Our original suggestion...seems even more tenable today. It has given rise to the new field of 'cytogerontology.' The cells were found to have other properties of immediate practical importance.... [In] 1973, the first poliomyelitis vaccine produced on our normal human cell strain...was distributed...."[9]

A characteristic of classic methods is that they are used by researchers from many different fields. Multidisciplinary methods that can be applied to a variety of research problems will accrue a large number of citations. N. Bloembergen, Harvard University, makes this point in a commentary on a classic 1948 paper he coauthored with E.M. Purcell and R.V. Pound. The paper discussed relaxation effects in nuclear magnetic resonance (NMR) absorption. Commenting on this paper, Bloembergen said: "The exploitation of [NMR spectroscopy] by the chemists and biochemists, who are more numerous...and more prolific in authoring papers than physicists, is...responsible for the higher incidence of citations."[10] D.W. Marquardt, DuPont Company, Wilmington, Delaware, also attributes the large number of citations to his 1963 classic on computing procedures for nonlinear models to its multidisciplinary application: "The growing use of nonlinear models in both the sciences and social sciences...must be a factor in the citation history of this paper."[11]

Another characteristic of classic biomedical methods is that they are applied in clinical practice as well as in basic research laboratories. Albert H. Coons, Harvard Medical School, and Melvin H. Kaplan developed a fluorescent method to localize antigens in tissue cells for basic histological research. In a commentary on this 1950 classic, Coons said: "[The method] also has been applied to the study of autoimmune disease...and in the detection of autoantibodies against tissue components. Immunofluorescence...therefore, became a feature of the diagnostic, as well as the research, laboratory."[12] Many other classic authors attribute the high citation rates of their methods papers to their successful exploitation by clinicians and basic researchers.

These commentators also express surprise that their works are still being cited "after all these years." Indeed, more than half of the classic papers in Table 1 are at least 20 years old. Table 2 shows the age distribution for the 100 most-cited papers in this essay. As you can see, 58 papers were published in the 1960s and 1970s. Exactly the same number of papers in the first part of this series[3] were published in these two decades. It will be interesting to learn whether this pattern holds when we extend these lists in future essays.

Gillespie suggests that classic methods papers continue to be highly cited even after 30 or 40 years because they are "unimprovable."[6] He explained: "[While] attempting to decide why a 'classic' becomes one, especially in...methodology, I keep returning to the notion of developing an unimprovable method.... [The] distinction between a classic and a quickly outmoded method lies in the ability of the investigators to see the uses to which [it] will be put...and, as important, to take heed of the little incongru-

ities that lead to significant improvements."[6]

However, other authors acknowledge that their classic methods have been improved by other researchers, yet the original method is still highly cited for a variety of reasons. Bloembergen commented: "[Many subsequent publications] certainly constitute an improvement on [our] naive experimental and theoretical discussions.... Perhaps new workers, confronted with the complexities of modern NMR and its applications, like the account of our early wrestling with some basic problems...."[10]

In addition, some authors suggest that fewer currently active scientists bother to *explicitly* cite their classic methods because they have become firmly incorporated into the "common knowledge" of their fields. Rosalyn Yalow, Veterans Administration Hospital, Bronx, New York, and the late Solomon Berson developed radioimmunoassay (RIA) in 1960 to measure minute amounts of insulin in plasma and tissue. Yalow commented on this classic: "At present RIA is considered so classic a method that relatively few of the scientific papers based on RIA refer to the original detailed description of the methodology presented in this 1960 paper...."[13] We commented on this "obliteration phenomenon" in 1973 in connection with the work of Albert Wollenberger, German Academy of Sciences, Berlin,[14] and have discussed it in other essays.[15] Nevertheless, the Yalow and Berson paper was explicitly cited in 60 publications in 1983, as can be seen in Table 1, in parentheses. A careful analysis of the number of *implicit*, unreferenced uses of this article is needed before we can determine the degree of its obliteration. Obliteration is probably one of the greatest compliments a researcher can receive.[14]

Table 2: Chronological distribution of publication dates of the second 100 most-cited articles, 1961-1982 *SCI®*. A = publication date. B = number of papers.

A	B
1920s	1
1930s	3
1940s	8
1950s	30
1960s	51
1970s	7
	100

Figure 1: Chronological distribution of citations to two classic papers listed in Table 1. The solid line represents citations to J.T. Dodge's 1963 paper. Dotted line represents citations to M.J. Karnovsky's 1961 paper.

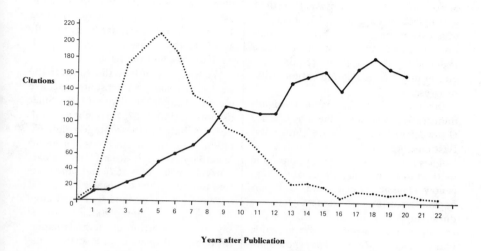

Years after Publication

Of course, citations tend to "decay" over time even for classic papers, whether due to obliteration, obsolescence, or other factors. Many classic papers reach a citation "plateau" and continue to be cited above average for many years. But other high-impact papers enjoy a huge burst of citations soon after publication, followed by a precipitous decline. Figure 1 illustrates the citation patterns for two high-impact papers in this study. The solid line represents 1963-1983 citations to the paper by J.T. Dodge and colleagues describing the preparation and characteristics of hemoglobin-free ghosts of human erythrocytes. The use of this method seems to have peaked in 1981. On the other hand, 1961-1983 citations to M.J. Karnovsky's method for lead staining at high pH in electron microscopy (dotted line) indicate that the method is rarely used anymore.

Before we conclude this study, a few points made by the classic authors on current science policy and funding deserve to be highlighted. Hayflick revealed that his classic method "resulted from the use of resources 'bootlegged' from grants having entirely different purposes. If our work has had any value, it is a tribute to the then prevailing freedom to pursue interesting leads unfettered by preconceived expectations written into grant proposals. Regrettably, in recent years, such opportunities have become increasingly compromised by myopic administrative demands for strict accountability."[9]

Paul D. Boyer, University of California, Los Angeles, also described the restrictions placed on him by narrow-minded administrators. He was to present his now classic method of spectrophotometric analysis of organic mercury compounds at a meeting. Boyer's grant provided for travel to the meeting, but a university administrator forbade him to use the funds because another staff member from a different department had already signed up for the meeting. Boyer commented: "My objections were of no avail, and the paper was presented at my personal expense.... [Such] action was a forerunner of the present condition of science support where the time expended and restrictions required for conformity to regulation often stifle progress."[16]

But the most telling example of administrative neglect is related by Charles C. Sweeley, Michigan State University, East Lansing. In 1963, Sweeley and colleagues innovated a chromatographic method to analyze sugar derivatives that is now a classic. Sweeley said: "It is perhaps noteworthy that we never had any direct support from any source for this research. In retrospect, it is remarkable that such a highly cited paper should not have received direct grant support from any federal agency."[17] Until researchers themselves overcome their bias against methods research, funding will continue to be a low priority for government administrators. I suspect, however, that industrial research directors are quicker to support methods research because innovative processes are often the key to successfully implementing new products.

The fact that 16 Nobel laureates appear in Table 1, many as authors of methods papers, further indicates that the bias against methodological research is misplaced. I am pleased to point out that "Citation Laureate" Oliver Lowry[18] appears twice in Table 1. He is the primary author of an article on the metabolic effects of ischemia, and a coauthor with O.A. Bessey and M.J. Brock of a paper describing a method for the determination of alkaline phosphatases.

As a final note, we would like to invite authors of the papers in Table 1 to contribute *Citation Classics* commentaries, if they have not done so already. We'll follow up this open invitation with letters to the individual authors involved. In the near future, we hope to collect the more than 1,800 commentaries already published in *CC* into a set of bound volumes. Thus, they will be more conveniently available to researchers, students, administrators, and the public.

We plan to continue this series in the weeks to come. At present, we have identified papers cited about 1,500 times or more in 1961-1982. No qualitative value is attributed to these citation data. Citations indicate various types of scientific activity, and they are affected by age, journal coverage in *SCI*, and other factors too numerous to discuss here.

When we extend the list of most-cited articles beyond the top 200 in future essays, the proportion of methods papers probably will decline. Life sciences papers will continue to dominate. This is due to many factors, not the least of which is the amount of publication in the life sciences. This phenomenon is also encountered in our studies of high-impact papers published each year. As pointed out on many occasions, most milestone papers in some fields—biochemistry or molecular biology, for example—are cited very soon after publication. The same is not generally true for papers in other fields, such as mathematics or geosciences. But by basing citation studies on 20 or more years of data, we can overcome the "time lag" that affects such fields.

* * * * *

My thanks to Abigail W. Grissom and Alfred Welljams-Dorof for their help in the preparation of this essay. ©1984 ISI

REFERENCES

1. **Garfield E.** A tribute to Derek John de Solla Price: a bold, iconoclastic historian of science. *Current Contents* (28):3-7, 9 July 1984.
2. **Price D J D.** Of sealing wax and string. *Natur. Hist.* 84(1):49-56, 1984.
3. **Garfield E.** The 100 most-cited papers ever and how we select *Citation Classics.* *Current Contents* (23):3-9, 4 June 1984.
4. --------------. Selecting the all-time citation classics. Here are the fifty most cited papers for 1961-1972; the second fifty papers most cited from 1961-1972. *Essays of an information scientist.* Philadelphia: ISI Press, 1977. Vol. 2. p. 6-9; 21-5.
5. --------------. They stand on the shoulders of giants: Sol Spiegelman, a pioneer in molecular biology. *Current Contents* (21):5-12, 23 May 1983.
6. **Gillespie D.** Citation Classic. Commentary on *J. Mol. Biol.* 12:829-42, 1965. *Current Contents* (11):14, 14 March 1977.
7. **Hakomori S.** Citation Classic. Commentary on *J. Biochem. Tokyo* 55:205-8, 1964. *Current Contents/Life Sciences* 23(23):12, 9 June 1980.
8. **Havel R J.** Citation Classic. Commentary on *J. Clin. Invest.* 34:1345-53, 1955. *Current Contents/Life Sciences* 26(46):23, 14 November 1983.
9. **Hayflick L.** Citation Classic. Commentary on *Exp. Cell Res.* 25:585-621, 1961. *Current Contents* (26):12, 26 June 1978.
10. **Bloembergen N.** Citation Classic. Commentary on *Phys. Rev.* 73:679-712, 1948. *Current Contents* (18):7, 2 May 1977.
11. **Marquardt D W.** Citation Classic. Commentary on *J. Soc. Indust. Appl. Math.* 11:431-41, 1963. *Current Contents/Engineering, Technology & Applied Sciences* 10(27):14, 2 July 1979.
12. **Coons A H.** Citation Classic. Commentary on *J. Exp. Med.* 91:1-13, 1950. *Current Contents/Life Sciences* 24(6):18, 9 February 1981.
13. **Yalow R S.** Citation Classic. Commentary on *J. Clin. Invest.* 39:1157-75, 1960. *Current Contents* (14):9, 4 April 1977.
14. **Garfield E.** Uncitedness III—the importance of *not* being cited. *Essays of an information scientist.* Philadelphia: ISI Press, 1977. Vol. 1. p. 413-4.
15. --------------. The 'obliteration phenomenon' in science—and the advantage of being obliterated! *Essays of an information scientist.* Philadelphia: ISI Press, 1977. Vol. 2. p. 396-8.
16. **Boyer P D.** Citation Classic. Commentary on *J. Amer. Chem. Soc.* 76:4331-7, 1954. *Current Contents/Life Sciences* 22(25):14, 18 June 1979.
17. **Sweeley C C.** Citation Classic. Commentary on *J. Amer. Chem. Soc.* 85:2497-507, 1963. *Current Contents* (43):9, 24 October 1977.
18. **Lowry O H.** Citation Classic. Commentary on *J. Biol. Chem.* 193:265, 1951. *Current Contents* (1):7, 3 January 1977.

Current Comments®

Handfast: The Joys and Frustrations of Parenthood

Number 30   July 23, 1984

Over the years, I've often discussed childhood and children. These discussions have included essays on child care centers,[1] child safety,[2] adolescent depression,[3] and gifted children.[4] All of these subjects are, of course, very important. But equally important, and perhaps more fascinating, is the very special relationship that exists between parents and children. As a parent, I know that this special relationship is not always a smooth one. And it can be difficult to share our parental problems with our friends and relatives. Indeed, I would lament with the British philosopher, Sir Francis Bacon: "The joys of parents are secrets, and so are their griefs and fears."[5] But our children are ours, and even though we may sometimes despair at their behavior, we will always love them. Perhaps the most aggrieved parent is the one whose child's behavior is beyond redemption and forgiveness.

Some parents instinctively feel that their children guarantee immortality. This is a personalized expression of both evolutionary and biblical theories. Other parents need children to attain their own unfulfilled dreams. For others, parenthood is a satisfying way to give and receive unconditional love. After all, as the nineteenth-century essayist, John Ruskin, worded it, "Give a little love to a child and you get a great deal back."[6] Whatever the underlying reasons, the parent-child relationship is fascinating. This is partly because our children are simultaneously extensions of ourselves, yet separate, autonomous human beings.

The following article by Sallie Tisdale, a parent and nurse in Portland, Oregon, describes well the parent-child relationship. It was originally published under the intriguing title "Handfast: the trick of children" in the Winter 1983 issue of *CoEvolution Quarterly*. In the days when arranged marriages were common in the Western world, the archaic word "handfast" described a contract of betrothal.[7] Tisdale describes the parent-child relationship as a "contract [that] cannot be broken." She even intimates that this contract is stronger than that which binds the parents to each other. The child, she writes, is "the flesh of my flesh that lovers promise and can't deliver."

Tisdale's article evoked in me many of the feelings I experienced watching my children grow. Without our usual extensive scientific documentation, it is reprinted here as a poetic expression. Perhaps it will express for *Current Contents®* (*CC®*) readers who are parents their own wonder and trepidation at having brought another human being into the world. Of course, much of the sentiment expressed in Tisdale's article applies more specifically to mothers than to fathers. For that reason, we will reprint in a future issue of *CC* a similar article which presents a "father's view" of parenting.

I cannot fail, however, to point out that Tisdale's feelings are not universal. She, of course, could not imagine unethical parents. By that I mean she assumes that it is universally true that a parent "can't pack a bag, make a break for it, perhaps find a more compatible child." I once told you about my father, Ernest Garofano.[8] He was in fact my stepfather, a word which does such a terrible disservice to all of us who are "stepfathers." Ironically, my biological father did just what Tisdale considers unimaginable. Now that he is dead it does him no harm to mention it. My mother,[9] of course, was the typical parent whom Tisdale imagined as one who could never conceive of calling it quits as a parent. Indeed, as with many parents, she tolerated behavior in her children that went beyond the call of duty.

While I could never understand the rejection of a "natural" father, in my case it made me a better parent. This is not at all universal. For example, the child-abusing parent often proves to have been an abused child too. To para-phrase the Bible,[10] thank goodness the sins of my father were not visited on me.

I need not rhapsodize further on the joys and pains of parenthood. That is why I choose to rely on Tisdale. She stands in a long line of poets and writers who have extolled the special feelings of a mother. But I've also known mothers who had to make terrible choices no less difficult than Sophie's choice when she was forced to select one of her two children for execution.[11]

I have never been overly tolerant of those who insist that there is no parent-child relationship stronger than blood. I have stepchildren who are loved equally with my natural children. Eventually, each child takes on a personality of his or her own and you "like" one a little more than the others or feel more comfortable in his or her presence. But you love them all and nothing you feel for one detracts from the others. Like your good friends, there is no need to grade them. Each one offers a separate and unique relationship.

©1984 ISI

REFERENCES

1. **Garfield E.** Child care: an investment in the future. Part 1. An overview of corporate child care programs and the effects of day care on young children. Part 2. The ISI Caring Center for Children and Parents. *Current Contents* (6):5-11, 7 February 1983 and (7):5-13, 14 February 1983.
2. --------------. Child safety. Part 1. So your children will not be victims. *Current Contents* (48):5-12, 28 November 1983.
3. --------------. What do we know about depression? Part 3. Children and adolescents. *Essays of an information scientist*. Philadelphia: ISI Press, 1983. Vol. 5. p. 157-63.
4. --------------. Will a bright mind make its own way? *Essays of an information scientist*. Philadelphia: ISI Press, 1981. Vol. 4. p. 713-23.
5. **Bacon F.** Of parents and children. *Essays*. London: J.M. Dent, 1972. p. 20.
6. **Ruskin J.** *The crown of wild olive*. New York: Wiley, 1871. p. 40.
7. Handfast. (Woolf H B, ed.) *Webster's new collegiate dictionary*. Springfield, MA: G & C Merriam, 1979. p. 515.
8. **Garfield E.** To remember my father. *Essays of an information scientist*. Philadelphia: ISI Press, 1980. Vol. 3. p. 422-3.
9. --------------. To remember my mother. *Essays of an information scientist*. Philadelphia: ISI Press, 1977. Vol. 2. p. 535-6.
10. Exod. 20:5.
11. **Styron W.** *Sophie's choice*. New York: Random House, 1979. 515 p.

HANDFAST: The Trick of Children

by Sallie Tisdale

Illustrated by B.S. Beaver

One factor determines all else about our relationship with our children: it is irreversible. The contract cannot be broken. Daily we leave jobs, houses, friends, lovers, but the child always comes along.

When the going is rough—when we don't like each other—my son and I can't call it quits and cut our losses. I can't pack a bag, make a break for it, perhaps find a more compatible child. Were it even the remotest of possibilities, everything else would change.

So I take risks with him I would never dare take with anyone else. I treat him badly, with rough impatience, with all the bile I hide from friends and lovers for fear of losing them. I am less tolerant of deviation and idiosyncrasies with him. We fight—bitterly— then, sad and weary of it, make up with a tentative kiss. I demand so much: love, loyalty, obedience, attention, and faith to a degree few adults would allow me to approach. For the most part, in these early years, I get what I demand—deserving or not.

He is tied and bound to me. We are entangled. When I wake from a bad dream without a sound, he wakes in the next room and cries for me. As a baby, his cry could make my breasts run with milk, his weight missing from my arms left

Reprinted with permission of the author from: **Tisdale S.** HANDFAST: the trick of children. *CoEvolution Quarterly* (40):1-2, 1983.

me restless and sore. I watched the baby-fat melt and muscles emerge from the perfect downy skin. I watch the features smooth over, change, gradually hiding the newborn between cheek and chin somewhere. He is the flesh of my flesh that lovers promise and can't deliver.

Yet he is hardly conscious of the intimacy. Later, when he wakes to his own appetites, others' hands—strangers' hands—will stroke where I stroke now. I am jealous of this future secret-sharing apart from me, jealous of the response those hands will provoke.

Between us, yet, is no shame, no inhibition. He thinks me beautiful; he wants to grow to be like me. And I am bound to fail him, and bound to lose him. Daily the gap between us grows. He is not mindful of it—but I am. Oh, I am.

For many years, unremembered years, our children have only the vaguest notion of their separateness from us. We are an immutable and invariable framework in their lives, a perpetual foundation. Therefore they treat us with an abominable negligence and come one day, hat in hand, to claim themselves and leave. They grow into strangers certain to disappoint and perplex us, having long before wakened to disillusionment with us. They seem oblivious to our loss—after all, they've lost nothing. We are only their parents. And haven't we done all this before?

I treat my own mother with an offhand and rather inattentive disregard. She is, after all, my mother. She is always there, and I am always her child, as my son is my child, first, forever and ever.

Could she ever have felt this same fierce protective love for me? It seems she should be grieved, bereft, if that is so. I am far away from her. I cling to my son; this ordinary woman chats of relatives and the weather. What could she be hiding, unarticulate, beneath mundane conversation?

I may never know. Affection embarrasses us. A lump comes to my throat when my mother and I move close to each other; we both feel relief when the contact is averted. Will it be the same for my son and me, who now crawls like a spoiled child-prince across my lap? How could such ease be forgotten, to become the shy silence between my mother and me?—though I know she is like a limb to me, a vital organ.

She shows up, surprising me, in my words to my son. I repeat what she told me, the phrases and platitudes, in the same tone of voice and inflection I heard as a child. We all have vowed to do it differently, to be unlike our parents, and the most we can manage is a variation.

Will my son, then, repeat me, as I my mother and she my grandmother? I become part of his inheritance, and will prevail despite his efforts. Even when he's gone and busy forgetting me I'll show up, surprising him. He'll try to throw me off, the monkey on his back.

I'll grow old on him. The trick of parents through the ages—we turn again into children. "When I grow up," he tells me, "you'll be my baby." Yes, I smile. Yes, if only you knew, my son. I have put my grandmother on the toilet, to bed, consigned to death. Perhaps I'll do the same for my mother in her time. Perhaps one day I'll lie in bed, watching this smooth-faced boy fold my diapers, and see in him a gesture that reminds me of myself once young. But now he remains under my still-strong wing, unconcerned.

This frightful responsibility! I invited it, and I carry it out in a workaday way. But I quail secretly at the number of mistakes I'm bound to make, what I'll saddle him with, what the price for both of us will finally be. I'll give the world a son, heavy with the grief of giving him at all. Then and after, he'll drift in and out of my view, keeping secrets, neglecting me, while I watch from a distance, unrequited.

Current Comments®

The Multidisciplinary Impact of Math and Computer Science Is Reflected in the 100 Most-Cited Articles in CompuMath Citation Index, 1976-1980

Number 31   July 30, 1984

In citation studies of high-impact articles based on data from *Science Citation Index®* (*SCI®*), some fields consistently dominate—biochemistry, immunology, molecular biology, etc. Other fields, such as mathematics or geosciences, usually are underrepresented. One reason is that the average biochemistry paper cites about twice as many references as the average mathematics paper. Thus, the average biochemist will tend to be more highly cited than the average mathematician. Also, biochemists are more prolific than mathematicians in the number of papers they publish. The size of a field's literature will affect the *range* of citation frequencies, but not the *impact* of the average paper. For example, if a body of literature is ten times greater than that of another, it will have a greater chance of producing "superstar" papers.

By focusing on selected portions of ISI®'s data base, we can identify the most-cited publications and authors from the "smaller" sciences that tend to be suppressed in large-scale citation studies. In 1973, we identified 150 books and articles from math journals that were most cited in *SCI* from 1961 to 1972.[1] We also analyzed about 100 pure and applied math journals indexed in the 1980 *SCI* to see what they cited and what cited them.[2] In another study, we identified the 200 mathematicians most cited during 1978-1979 in about 65 *SCI* math journals.[3]

In this essay, we present the 100 articles most cited from 1976 to 1980 in *CompuMath Citation Index®* (*CMCI®*).[4] *CMCI* was launched in 1982 to serve the information needs of pure and applied mathematicians, computer scientists, statisticians, systems analysts, and researchers in related fields. *CMCI* is published every four months and cumulated in annual editions from 1981 onward. The literature from 1976 to 1980 is covered in a five-year cumulation. The *CompuMath* "system" consists of a *Source Index*, *Citation Index*, and *Permuterm® Subject Index*. The organization and uses of these indexes were recently reviewed for *SCI*[5] and *Social Sciences Citation Index®* (*SSCI®*).[6] These essays can serve as "primers" for *CMCI* as well.

Each year, *CMCI* indexes every significant article in about 390 "core" math journals. *CMCI* also selectively covers another 1,800 journals in ISI's data bases. Articles from these journals are *automatically* indexed if they meet the requirements of the selection algorithm. For example, an article is selected for indexing if one or more keywords and phrases in its title matches a dictionary of terms created for *CMCI*. Independent of the title, the algorithm also searches the article's reference list. If it cited two "pure" math journals fully covered in *CMCI*, or one pure *and* two applied math core journals, the article is selected for indexing in *CMCI*. *CompuMath* now provides direct access to 280,000 source articles from 1976 to date and the three million references they cited. This is in addition to coverage of mathematics and computer science in *SCI* from 1955 to 1975.

The present study is based on citation data from the five-year *CMCI* cumulation. The *CMCI* cumulation includes 160,000 articles published from 1976 to 1980 and the two million references they cited. Of these 160,000 articles, about 70 percent were published in 300 "core" math journals fully indexed in *CMCI*. The remaining 50,000 articles were from more than 3,000 journals selectively covered in *CMCI*. Many of these *non-core* articles were from applied physics journals. Thus, we will find that a large number of physics papers are among the most-cited articles in the *CMCI* cumulation. But you should keep in mind that these papers apparently are *of high interest to* math and computer scientists.

Table 1 lists the 100 articles most cited from 1976 to 1980 in *CMCI*. The number of citations each received is shown, followed by full bibliographic information, including the institutional affiliations of the authors. Nineteen of these articles were discussed in *Citation Classics*™ [7] commentaries. They are indicated by asterisks. The issue, year, and edition of *Current Contents*® (*CC*®) in which these commentaries were published follow the reference. A number symbol indicates that the paper was one of the most-cited math articles from 1961 to 1972.[1] The average paper in Table 1 received about 116 citations in the five-year period 1976-1980. Each article was cited at least 77 times. The most-cited paper received 245 citations.

The papers in this study were published in 54 journals. Table 2 lists the journals that published at least two of these papers. The top eight journals account for 38 articles, and they received 4,300 citations. This represents 37 percent of all 12,000 citations to the 100 most-cited *CMCI* articles. Thus, as expected, a small number of journals accounts for the majority of high-impact papers and citations.

It is significant that the *Computer Journal* heads the list in Table 2, accounting for six of the most-cited articles. While *SCI* has always extensively covered the math literature, a systematic effort was made to expand coverage of the computer sciences literature in *CMCI*. About 165 journals and book series never covered in *SCI* are fully indexed in *CMCI*. Most of these newly indexed publications are in the computer sciences. Of the 100 most-cited *CMCI* articles identified here, about 20 are related to various problems in computer science research—algorithms for automatic computation, programming languages, system design, etc.

About 35 physics papers are included in this study. Most of these deal with gauge theories, a mathematical system for describing the four known forces of nature. As explained above, *CMCI* selectively covers many math-dependent journals. The selection algorithm expands *CMCI*'s coverage of the literature *of interest to* math and computer scientists. This includes not only physics but also engineering, psychology, economics, and medical journals.

For example, A.L. Hodgkin and A.F. Huxley, University of Cambridge and University College, London, England, respectively, coauthored a method for measuring current, conduction, and excitation in squid nerves. The paper was published in 1952 in the *Journal of Physiology—London* and was cited 2,400 times in *SCI* from 1961 to 1983. It received about 120 citations between 1976 and 1980 in *CMCI*. Five journals account for half of these *CMCI* citations: *Biological Cybernetics*, *Bulletin of Mathematical Biology*, *Journal of Mathematical Biology*, *Mathematical Biosciences*, and *Biophysical Journal*. Except for the last journal, all of these publica-

Table 1: The 100 articles most cited in 1976-1980 *CMCI*®, in alphabetic order by first author. A number symbol (#) indicates that the article also was one of the most-cited math publications in 1961-1972. An asterisk (*) indicates that the article was the subject of a *Citation Classic*™ commentary.

No. of Cites	Bibliographic Data
128	**Abers E S & Lee B W.** Gauge theories. *Physics Reports C* 9:1-141, 1973. SUNY, Inst. Theor. Phys., Stony Brook, NY.
170	*****Ablowitz M J, Kaup D J, Newell A C & Segur H.** The inverse scattering transform-Fourier analysis for nonlinear problems. *Stud. Appl. Math.* 53:249-315, 1974. Clarkson Coll. Technol., Dept. Math. Comput. Sci., Potsdam, NY. 23/82/ET&AS
134	**#Agmon S, Douglis A & Nirenberg L.** Estimates near the boundary for solutions of elliptic partial differential equations satisfying general boundary conditions. I. *Commun. Pure Appl. Math.* 12:623-727, 1959. Hebrew Univ., Inst. Math., Jerusalem, Israel; Univ. Maryland, College Park, MD; New York Univ., New York, NY.
93	*****Akaike H.** A new look at the statistical model identification. *IEEE Trans. Automat. Contr.* AC-19:716-23, 1974. Inst. Statist. Math., Tokyo, Japan. 51/81/ET&AS
104	*****Astrom K J & Eykhoff P.** System identification—a survey. *Automatica* 7:123-62, 1971. Lund Inst. Technol., Div. Automat. Contr., Lund, Sweden; Eindhoven Univ. Technol., Dept. Elec. Eng., Eindhoven, the Netherlands. 12/80/ET&AS
85	**Atiyah M F & Singer I M.** The index of elliptic operators: III. *Ann. Math.* 87:546-603, 1968. Oxford Univ., Math. Inst., Oxford, UK; Mass. Inst. Technol., Cambridge, MA.
88	**Baskett F, Chandy K M, Muntz R R & Palacios F G.** Open, closed, and mixed networks of queues with different classes of customers. *J. Assn. Comput. Mach.* 22:248-60, 1975. Stanford Univ., Stanford; Univ. California, Los Angeles, CA; Univ. Texas, Austin, TX.
85	**#Bass H.** Finitistic dimension and a homological generalization of semi-primary rings. *Trans. Amer. Math. Soc.* 95:466-88, 1960. Univ. Chicago, Chicago, IL.
216	**Belavin A A, Polyakov A M, Schwartz A S & Tyupkin Yu S.** Pseudoparticle solutions of the Yang-Mills equations. *Phys. Lett. B* 59:85-7, 1975. Acad. Sci., Landau Inst. Theor. Phys., Moscow, USSR.
141	**Box G E P & Cox D R.** An analysis of transformations. *J. Roy. Statist. Soc. Ser. B Metho.* 26:211-43, 1964. Univ. Wisconsin, Madison, WI; Univ. London, Birkbeck Coll., London, UK.
77	**Box G E P & Muller M E.** A note on the generation of random normal deviates. *Ann. Math. Statist.* 29:610-1, 1958. Princeton Univ., Princeton, NJ.
96	**Callan C G, Dashen R F & Gross D J.** The structure of the gauge theory vacuum. *Phys. Lett. B* 63:334-40, 1976. Princeton Univ., Joseph Henry Labs.; Inst. Adv. Study, Princeton, NJ.
93	**Carroll J D & Chang J-J.** Analysis of individual differences in multidimensional scaling via an N-way generalization of "Eckart-Young" decomposition. *Psychometrika* 35:283-319, 1970. Bell Tel. Labs., Murray Hill, NJ.
123	**Chandrasekhar S.** Stochastic problems in physics and astronomy. *Rev. Mod. Phys.* 15:1-89, 1943. Univ. Chicago, Yerkes Observ., Williams Bay, WI.
80	**Ciarlet P G & Raviart P A.** General Lagrange and Hermite interpolation in R^n with applications to finite element methods. *Arch. Ration. Mech. Anal.* 46:177-99, 1972. Road Bridge Central Lab., Serv. Math.; Univ. Paris VI, Dept. Math., Paris, France.
232	**Codd E F.** A relational model of data for large shared data banks. *Commun. ACM* 13:377-87, 1970. IBM Res. Lab., San Jose, CA.
86	**Coleman S.** Quantum sine-Gordon equation as the massive Thirring model. *Phys. Rev. D—Part. Fields* 11:2088-97, 1975. Harvard Univ., Lyman Lab. Phys., Cambridge, MA.
82	**Connes A.** Une classification des facteurs de type III. (A classification of type III factors.) *Ann. Sci. Ecole Norm. Super.* 6:133-252, 1973. CNRS, Ctr. Phys. Theor., Marseille, France.
245	**#Cooley J W & Tukey J W.** An algorithm for the machine calculation of complex Fourier series. *Math. Comput.* 19:297-301, 1965. IBM Watson Res. Ctr., Yorktown Heights, NY; Bell Tel. Labs., Murray Hill; Princeton Univ., Princeton, NJ.
148	**Cox D R.** Regression models and life-tables. *J. Roy. Statist. Soc. Ser. B Metho.* 34:187-202, 1972. Imperial Coll., London, UK.
78	**Dahlquist G G.** A special stability problem for linear multistep methods. *BIT* 3:27-43, 1963. Roy. Inst. Technol., Stockholm, Sweden.
77	**Deser S & Zumino B.** Consistent supergravity. *Phys. Lett. B* 62:335-7, 1976. CERN, Geneva, Switzerland.
88	*****Dijkstra E W.** A note on two problems in connexion with graphs. *Numer. Math.* 1:269-71, 1959. Fdn. Math. Ctr., Amsterdam, the Netherlands. 7/83/ET&AS
83	**Durbin J.** Testing for serial correlation in least-squares regression when some of the regressors are lagged dependent variables. *Econometrica* 38:410-21, 1970. London Sch. Econ. Polit. Sci., London, UK.

81   **Faddeev L D & Popov V N.** Feynman diagrams for the Yang-Mills field. *Phys. Lett. B* 25:29-30, 1967. Inst. Math., Leningrad, USSR.

161   **Fefferman C & Stein E M.** H^p spaces of several variables. *Acta Math.* 129:137-93, 1972. Univ. Chicago, Chicago, IL; Princeton Univ., Princeton, NJ.

86   **Fiedler M & Vlastimil P.** On matrices with non-positive off-diagonal elements and positive principal minors. *Czech. Math. J.* 12:382-400, 1962. Czechoslovak Acad. Sci., Math. Inst., Prague, Czechoslovakia.

102   **Fletcher R.** A new approach to variable metric algorithms. *Comput. J.* 13:317-22, 1970. Atomic Energy Res. Establ. (AERE), Harwell, UK.

234   **#Fletcher R & Powell M J D.** A rapidly convergent descent method for minimization. *Comput. J.* 6:163-8, 1963. Univ. Leeds, Leeds; Atomic Energy Res. Establ. (AERE), Harwell, UK.

96   **#Fletcher R & Reeves C M.** Function minimization by conjugate gradients. *Comput. J.* 7:149-54, 1964. Univ. Leeds, Leeds, Leeds, UK.

78   **#Gabriel P.** Des categories Abeliennes. (Abelian categories.) *Bull. Soc. Math. Fr.* 90:323-448, 1962. Math. Soc. France, Paris, France.

100   **Gardner C S, Greene J M, Kruskal M D & Miura R M.** Korteweg-deVries equation and generalizations. VI. Methods for exact solution. *Commun. Pure Appl. Math.* 27:97-133, 1974. Univ. Texas, Austin, TX; Princeton Univ., Princeton, NJ; Vanderbilt Univ., Nashville, TN.

189   **Gardner C S, Greene J M, Kruskal M D & Miura R M.** Method for solving the Korteweg-deVries equation. *Phys. Rev. Lett.* 19:1095-7, 1967. Princeton Univ., Plasma Phys. Lab., Princeton, NJ.

86   **Glauberman G.** Central elements in core-free groups. *J. Algebra* 4:403-20, 1966. Univ. Chicago, Chicago, IL.

111   **Goldschmidt D M.** 2-fusion in finite groups. *Ann. Math.* 99:70-117, 1974. Univ. California, Berkeley, CA.

78   ***Grizzle J E, Starmer C F & Koch G G.** Analysis of categorical data by linear models. *Biometrics* 25:489-504, 1969. Univ. North Carolina, Depts. Biostat. & Biomath., Chapel Hill, NC. 4/80/PC&ES

113   **Gross D J & Wilczek F.** Asymptotically free gauge theories. I. *Phys. Rev. D—Part. Fields* 8:3633-52, 1973. Natl. Accelerator Lab., Batavia, IL; Princeton Univ., Joseph Henry Labs., Princeton, NJ.

123   **Gross D J & Wilczek F.** Ultraviolet behavior of non-Abelian gauge theories. *Phys. Rev. Lett.* 30:1343-6, 1973. Princeton Univ., Joseph Henry Labs., Princeton, NJ.

122   **Grothendieck A.** Produits tensoriels topologiques et espaces nucleaires. (Topological tensorial products and nuclear spaces.) *Mem. Amer. Math. Soc.* 16:1-140, 1955. Univ. Montpellier II, Dept. Math., Montpellier, France.

89   **Haken H.** Cooperative phenomena in systems far from thermal equilibrium and in nonphysical systems. *Rev. Mod. Phys.* 47:67-121, 1975. Univ. Stuttgart, Inst. Theor. Phys., Stuttgart, FRG.

77   **Harish-Chandra.** Discrete series for semisimple Lie groups. II. *Acta Math.* 116:1-111, 1966. Inst. Adv. Study, Princeton, NJ.

130   **Hoare C A R.** An axiomatic basis for computer programming. *Commun. ACM* 12:576-83, 1969. Queen's Univ. Belfast, Dept. Comput. Sci., Belfast, Northern Ireland.

87   **Hoare C A R.** Monitors: an operating system structuring concept. *Commun. ACM* 17:549-57, 1974. Queen's Univ. Belfast, Dept. Comput. Sci., Belfast, Northern Ireland.

122   ***Hodgkin A L & Huxley A F.** A quantitative description of membrane current and its application to conduction and excitation in nerve. *J. Physiol.—London* 117:500-44, 1952. Univ. Cambridge, Physiol. Lab., Cambridge, UK. 28/81/LS

131   ***Hoerl A E & Kennard R W.** Ridge regression: biased estimation for nonorthogonal problems. *Technometrics* 12:55-67, 1970. Univ. Delaware, Newark; E.I. du Pont de Nemours, Wilmington, DE. 35/82/ET&AS

78   **Hoerl A E & Kennard R W.** Ridge regression: applications to nonorthogonal problems. *Technometrics* 12:69-82, 1970. Univ. Delaware, Newark; E.I. du Pont de Nemours, Wilmington, DE.

157   **Hormander L.** Fourier integral operators. I. *Acta Math.* 127:79-183, 1971. Lund Univ., Lund, Sweden.

78   **Huber P J.** The 1972 Wald lecture. Robust statistics: a review. *Ann. Math. Statist.* 43:1041-67, 1972. Princeton Univ., Dept. Statist., Princeton, NJ.

90   **Huber P J.** Robust estimation of a location parameter. *Ann. Math. Statist.* 35:73-101, 1964. Univ. California, Berkeley, CA.

101   ***Huzinaga S.** Gaussian-type functions for polyatomic systems. I. *J. Chem. Phys.* 42:1293-302, 1965. IBM San Jose Res. Lab., San Jose, CA. 17/80/PC&ES

88   **Jackiw R & Rebbi C.** Vacuum periodicity in a Yang-Mills quantum theory. *Phys. Rev. Lett.* 37:172-5, 1976. Mass. Inst. Technol., Lab. Nucl. Sci. & Phys. Dept., Cambridge, MA.

107   **Johnson S C.** Hierarchical clustering schemes. *Psychometrika* 32:241-54, 1967. Bell Tel. Labs., Murray Hill, NJ.

82   **Kalman R E.** A new approach to linear filtering and prediction problems. *Trans. ASME Ser. D—J. Basic Eng.* 82:35-45, 1960. Res. Inst. Adv. Study, Baltimore, MD.

96   ***Kaplan E L & Meier P.** Nonparametric estimation from incomplete observations. *J. Amer. Statist. Assn.* 53:457-81, 1958. Univ. California, Radiat. Lab., Davis, CA; Univ. Chicago, Chicago, IL. 24/83/LS

86   **Kogut J & Susskind L.** Hamiltonian formulation of Wilson's lattice gauge theories. *Phys. Rev. D—Part. Fields* 11:395-408, 1975. Cornell Univ., Lab. Nucl. Stud., Ithaca; Yeshiva Univ., Belfer Grad. Sch. Sci., New York, NY and Tel Aviv Univ., Ramat Aviv, Israel.

89   **Kohn W & Sham L J.** Self-consistent equations including exchange and correlation effects. *Phys. Rev. A—Gen. Phys.* 140:1133-8, 1965. Univ. California, San Diego, La Jolla, CA.

143   **#*Kruskal J B.** Multidimensional scaling by optimizing goodness of fit to a nonmetric hypothesis. *Psychometrika* 29:1-27, 1964. Bell Tel. Labs., Murray Hill, NJ. 39/79/S&BS

116   **#Kruskal J B.** Nonmetric multidimensional scaling: a numerical method. *Psychometrika* 29:115-29, 1964. Bell Tel. Labs., Murray Hill, NJ.

79   **Kubo R.** Statistical-mechanical theory of irreversible processes. I. *J. Phys. Soc. Jpn.* 12:570-86, 1957. Univ. Tokyo, Dept. Phys., Tokyo, Japan.

108   **Kubo R, Matsuo K & Kitahara K.** Fluctuation and relaxation of macrovariables. *J. Statist. Phys.* 9:51-96, 1973. Univ. Tokyo, Dept. Phys., Tokyo, Japan; Free Univ. Brussels, Sch. Sci., Brussels, Belgium.

170   **Lax P D.** Integrals of nonlinear equations of evolution and solitary waves. *Commun. Pure Appl. Math.* 21:467-90, 1968. New York Univ., Courant Inst., New York, NY.

87   **Li T-Y & Yorke J A.** Period three implies chaos. *Amer. Math. Mon.* 82:985-92, 1975. Univ. Utah, Dept. Math., Salt Lake City, UT; Univ. Maryland, Inst. Fluid Dynam. Appl. Math., College Park, MD.

100   **Lindenstrauss J & Pelczynski A.** Absolutely summing operators in Lp-spaces and their applications. *Stud. Math.* 29:275-326, 1968. Hebrew Univ., Jerusalem, Israel; Poland Acad. Sci., Warsaw, Poland.

132   **Lorenz E N.** Deterministic nonperiodic flow. *J. Atmos. Sci.* 20:130-41, 1963. Mass. Inst. Technol., Cambridge, MA.

80   **Luenberger D G.** Canonical forms for linear multivariable systems. *IEEE Trans. Automat. Contr.* 12:290-3, 1967. Stanford Univ., Stanford, CA.

87   ***Makhoul J.** Linear prediction: a tutorial review. *Proc. IEEE* 63:561-80, 1975. Bolt Beranek and Newman, Inc., Cambridge, MA. 12/82/ET&AS

151   ***Marquardt D W.** An algorithm for least-squares estimation of nonlinear parameters. *J. Soc. Indust. Appl. Math.* 11:431-41, 1963. E.I. du Pont de Nemours, Eng. Dept., Wilmington, DE. 27/79/ET&AS

139   **Metropolis N, Rosenbluth A W, Rosenbluth M N, Teller A H & Teller E.** Equation of state calculations by fast computing machines. *J. Chem. Phys.* 21:1087-92, 1953. Los Alamos Sci. Lab., Los Alamos, NM; Univ. Chicago, Dept. Phys., Chicago, IL.

91   **Milnor J W & Moore J C.** On the structure of Hopf algebras. *Ann. Math.* 81:211-64, 1965. Princeton Univ., Princeton, NJ.

107   **Mori H.** Transport, collective motion, and Brownian motion. *Prog. Theor. Phys. Kyoto* 33:423-55, 1965. Kyoto Univ., Res. Inst. Fundament. Phys., Kyoto, Japan.

81   **Muth J F.** Rational expectations and the theory of price movements. *Econometrica* 29:315-35, 1961. Carnegie Inst. Technol., Pittsburgh, PA.

113   **#*Nelder J A & Mead R.** A simplex method for function minimization. *Comput. J.* 7:308-13, 1965. Natl. Veget. Res. Station, Warwick, UK. 15/79/ET&AS

108   ***Newman E & Penrose R.** An approach to gravitational radiation by a method of spin coefficients. *J. Math. Phys.—NY* 3:566-78, 1962. Univ. Pittsburgh, Pittsburgh, PA; Syracuse Univ., Syracuse, NY. 19/81/PC&ES

113   **Parzen E.** On estimation of a probability density function and mode. *Ann. Math. Statist.* 33:1065-76, 1962. Stanford Univ., Stanford, CA.

135   **Politzer H D.** Reliable perturbative results for strong interactions? *Phys. Rev. Lett.* 30:1346-9, 1973. Harvard Univ., Jefferson Phys. Labs., Cambridge, MA.

77   **Polyakov A M.** Compact gauge fields and the infrared catastrophe. *Phys. Lett. B* 59:82-4, 1975. Landau Inst. Theor. Phys., Moscow, USSR.

96   **Polyakov A M.** Particle spectrum in quantum field theory. *JETP Lett.—Engl. Tr.* 20:194-5, 1974. Landau Inst. Theor. Phys., Moscow, USSR.

117   **#Powell M J D.** An efficient method for finding the minimum of a function of several variables without calculating derivatives. *Comput. J.* 7:155-62, 1964. Atomic Energy Res. Establ. (AERE), Theor. Phys. Div., Harwell, UK.

77   **#*Rosenbrock H H.** An automatic method for finding the greatest or least value of a function. *Comput. J.* 3:175-84, 1960. Constructors John Brown Ltd., Leatherhead, UK. 6/79/ET&AS

131   **Ruelle D & Takens F.** On the nature of turbulence. *Commun. Math. Phys.* 20:167-92, 1971. Inst. Adv. Study, Princeton, NJ; Univ. Amsterdam, Amsterdam, the Netherlands.

232   *****Scott A C, Chu F Y F & McLaughlin D W.** The soliton: a new concept in applied science. *Proc. IEEE* 61:1443-83, 1973. Univ. Wisconsin, Dept. Elec. Comput. Eng., Madison, WI; Iowa State Univ., Dept. Math., Ames, IA. 34/79/ET&AS

138   **#Shannon C E.** A mathematical theory of communication. *Bell Syst. Tech. J.* 27:379-423, 1948. Bell Tel. Labs., Murray Hill, NJ.

102   **#Shannon C E.** A mathematical theory of communication. *Bell Syst. Tech. J.* 27:623-56, 1948. Bell Tel. Labs., Murray Hill, NJ.

187   **Smale S.** Differentiable dynamical systems. *Bull. Amer. Math. Soc.* 73:747-817, 1967. Univ. California, Dept. Math., Berkeley, CA.

105   *****Tarjan R.** Depth-first search and linear graph algorithms. *SIAM J. Comput.* 1:146-60, 1972. Cornell Univ., Dept. Comput. Sci., Ithaca, NY. 30/83/ET&AS

97   **'t Hooft G.** Computation of the quantum effects due to a four-dimensional pseudoparticle. *Phys. Rev. D—Part. Fields* 14:3432-50, 1976. Harvard Univ., Phys. Labs., Cambridge, MA.

79   **'t Hooft G.** Dimensional regularization and the renormalization group. *Nucl. Phys. B* 61:455-68, 1973. CERN, Geneva, Switzerland.

161   **'t Hooft G.** Magnetic monopoles in unified gauge theories. *Nucl. Phys. B* 79:276-84, 1974. CERN, Geneva, Switzerland.

105   **'t Hooft G.** Symmetry breaking through Bell-Jackiw anomalies. *Phys. Rev. Lett.* 37:8-11, 1976. Harvard Univ., Dept. Phys., Cambridge, MA.

118   **'t Hooft G & Veltman M.** Regularization and renormalization of gauge fields. *Nucl. Phys. B* 44:189-213, 1972. Univ. Utrecht, Inst. Theor. Phys., Utrecht, the Netherlands.

80   **Waldhausen F.** On irreducible 3-manifolds which are sufficiently large. *Ann. Math.* 87:56-88, 1968. Univ. Bonn, Bonn, FRG and Inst. Adv. Study, Princeton, NJ.

173   **Weinberg S.** A model of leptons. *Phys. Rev. Lett.* 19:1264-6, 1967. Mass. Inst. Technol., Lab. Nucl. Sci. & Phys. Dept., Cambridge, MA.

89   **Wess J & Zumino B.** Supergauge transformations in four dimensions. *Nucl. Phys. B* 70:39-50, 1974. Karlsruhe Univ., Karlsruhe, FRG; CERN, Geneva, Switzerland.

162   **Wilson K G.** Confinement of quarks. *Phys. Rev. D—Part. Fields* 10:2445-59, 1974. Cornell Univ., Lab. Nucl. Stud., Ithaca, NY.

105   **Wilson K G & Kogut J.** The renormalization group and the ε expansion. *Physics Reports C* 12:75-199, 1974. Inst. Adv. Study, Princeton, NJ; Cornell Univ., Lab. Nucl. Stud., Ithaca, NY.

82   **Wirth N.** The programming language Pascal. *Acta Inform.* 1:35-63, 1971. Swiss Fed. Inst. Technol., Zurich, Switzerland.

145   **Yang C N & Mills R L.** Conservation of isotopic spin and isotopic gauge invariance. *Phys. Rev.* 96:191-5, 1954. Brookhaven Natl. Lab., Upton, NY.

224   *****Zadeh L A.** Fuzzy sets. *Inform. Contr.* 8:338-53, 1965. Univ. California, Dept. Elec. Eng. Comput. Sci., Berkeley, CA. 47/80/ET&AS

151   **Zakharov V E & Shabat A B.** Exact theory of two-dimensional self-focusing and one-dimensional self-modulation of waves in nonlinear media. *Sov. Phys. JETP—Engl. Tr.* 34:62-9, 1972. USSR Acad. Sci., Inst. Hydrodynam., Siberian Div., Novosibirsk, USSR.

112   *****Zellner A.** An efficient method of estimating seemingly unrelated regressions and tests for aggregation bias. *J. Amer. Statist. Assn.* 57:348-68, 1962. Univ. Wisconsin, Madison, WI. 38/82/S&BS

tions are fully indexed in *CMCI*. *Biophysical Journal* is selectively covered in *CMCI*, as is *Journal of Physiology—London*. Clearly, math is a universal language used by researchers in all fields of science and the social sciences—physics, chemistry, biology, psychology, economics, etc. *CMCI*'s multidisciplinary coverage reflects the extensive application of mathematical and computer methods in many fields.

Pure and applied math papers are also well represented in Table 1, accounting for about 45 of the papers listed. Interestingly, the authors of these math papers reiterate the point made here that researchers in other fields find their research very useful. For example, D.W. Marquardt, E.I. du Pont de Nemours & Co., Wilmington, Delaware, described an algorithm for least-squares estimation of nonlinear parameters. In a *Citation Classic* commentary, Marquardt said, "The growing use of nonlinear models in both the sciences and social sciences...must be a factor in the citation history of this paper."[8] E.L. Kaplan, now at Oregon State University, Corvallis, and Paul Meier, University of Chicago, devised a formula for nonpara-

Table 2: Journals that published two or more of the articles most cited from 1976-1980 in *CMCI*®.

Journal	Articles	Journal	Articles
Comput. J.	6	Bell Syst. Tech. J.	2
Phys. Rev. Lett.	6	Econometrica	2
Phys. Lett. B	5	IEEE Trans. Automat. Contr.	2
Phys. Rev. D—Part. Fields	5	J. Amer. Statist. Assn.	2
Ann. Math.	4	J. Chem. Phys.	2
Ann. Math. Statist.	4	J. Roy. Statist. Soc.	2
Nucl. Phys. B	4	Ser. B Metho.	2
Psychometrika	4	Physics Reports C	2
Acta Math.	3	Proc. IEEE	2
Comm. ACM	3	Rev. Mod. Phys.	2
Comm. Pure Appl. Math.	3	Technometrics	2

Table 3: The institutional affiliations of authors in descending order.

Institution	Frequency
Princeton Univ., NJ	10
Univ. California, CA	8
Berkeley (Incl. Los Alamos)	5
Davis	1
Los Angeles	1
San Diego at La Jolla	1
Bell Tel. Labs., Murray Hill, NJ	7
Massachusetts Inst. Technol., Cambridge, MA	6
Univ. Chicago, IL	6
Chicago	5
Yerkes Observ., Williams Bay, WI	1
Inst. Adv. Study, Princeton, NJ	5
Acad. Sci. USSR	4
L.D. Landau Inst. Theor. Phys., Moscow	3
Inst. Hydrodynam., Novosibirsk	1
CERN, Geneva, Switzerland	4
Cornell Univ., Ithaca, NY	4
Harvard Univ., Cambridge, MA	4
E.I. du Pont de Nemours, Wilmington, DE	3
IBM	3
San Jose Res. Lab., CA	2
Watson Res. Ctr., Yorktown Heights, NY	1
Stanford Univ., CA	3
UK Atomic Energy Authority, Atomic Energy Res. Establ. (AERE), Harwell, UK	3
Univ. London, UK	3
Birkbeck Coll.	1
Imperial Coll. Sci. Technol.	1
London Sch. Econ. Polit. Sci.	1
Univ. Wisconsin, Madison, WI	3
Hebrew Univ., Jerusalem, Israel	2
Lund Univ., Sweden	2
New York Univ., NY	2
Queen's Univ. Belfast, Northern Ireland	2
Univ. Delaware, Newark, DE	2
Univ. Leeds, UK	2
Univ. Maryland, College Park, MD	2
Univ. North Carolina, Chapel Hill, NC	2
Univ. Texas, Austin, TX	2
Univ. Tokyo, Japan	2
Bolt Beranek and Newman, Inc., Cambridge, MA	1
Brookhaven Natl. Lab., Upton, NY	1
Carnegie Inst. Technol., Pittsburgh, PA	1
Clarkson Coll. Technol., Potsdam, NY	1
CNRS, Ctr. Phys. Theor., Marseille, France	1
Constructors John Brown Ltd., Leatherhead, UK	1
Czechoslovak Acad. Sci., Prague, Czechoslovakia	1
Eindhoven Univ. Technol., the Netherlands	1
Fdn. Math. Ctr., Amsterdam, the Netherlands	1
Fermi Natl. Accelerator Lab., Batavia, IL	1
Free Univ. Brussels, Belgium	1
Inst. Math., Leningrad, USSR	1
Inst. Statist. Math., Tokyo, Japan	1
Iowa State Univ., Ames, IA	1
Karlsruhe Univ., FRG	1
Kyoto Univ., Japan	1
Math. Soc. France, Paris, France	1
Natl. Veget. Res. Station, Warwick, UK	1
Oxford Univ., UK	1
Poland Acad. Sci., Warsaw, Poland	1

metric estimation from incomplete observations. Kaplan commented that the formula can be applied to problems as diverse as the duration of cancer cells and the lifetimes of vacuum tubes.[9] A.E. Hoerl, University of Delaware, Newark, and R.W. Kennard, formerly of E.I. du Pont de Nemours & Co., explained that their procedure of ridge regression in biased estimation for nonorthogonal problems "pointed out and gave reasons for difficulties in multiple linear regression, a data analysis used in many fields."[10]

Sixty-four institutions were listed in the 100 most-cited *CMCI* articles. They are shown in Table 3. Authors based at US institutions were listed in 62 papers. UK researchers contributed 13 articles. Switzerland and the USSR were listed in five papers each. France, Japan, and the Netherlands follow with four papers each; Federal Republic of Germany, Israel, and Sweden, three each; and Belgium, Czechoslovakia, and Poland, one each.

In a larger population of papers, a number of interesting variables could be analyzed and compared for institutions—impact, or average number of times a given institution's articles were cited; efficiency, or the percentage of its output that was cited and uncited; degree of self-citation, etc. In the future, we'll present a series of institutional citation analyses based on *SCI* data.

Table 4 gives the publication year distribution for the 100 articles in this study. Almost half were published in the

Res. Inst. Adv. Study, Baltimore, MD	1
Road and Bridge Central Lab., Paris, France	1
Roy. Inst. Technol., Stockholm, Sweden	1
SUNY, Stony Brook, NY	1
Swiss Fed. Inst. Technol., Zurich, Switzerland	1
Syracuse Univ., NY	1
Tel Aviv Univ., Ramat Aviv, Israel	1
Univ. Amsterdam, the Netherlands	1
Univ. Bonn, FRG	1
Univ. Cambridge, UK	1
Univ. Montpellier II, France	1
Univ. Paris VI, France	1
Univ. Pittsburgh, PA	1
Univ. Stuttgart, FRG	1
Univ. Utah, Salt Lake City, UT	1
Univ. Utrecht, the Netherlands	1
Vanderbilt Univ., Nashville, TN	1
Yeshiva Univ., New York, NY	1

Table 4: Chronological distribution.

Years	Articles
1940s	3
1950s	9
1960s	40
1970s	48

1970s, all before 1977. Forty papers were published in the 1960s, nine in the 1950s, and three in the 1940s. Before we draw conclusions on the median age of the most-cited publications in *CMCI*, high-impact books also have to be considered. Mathematicians cite books very frequently. For example, the 100 books most cited from 1976 to 1980 in *CMCI* received more than 32,000 citations. In comparison, the 100 journal articles presented here received 12,000 citations. We'll identify and discuss the most-cited *CMCI* books in a separate essay.

Sixteen authors in Table 1 were among the 200 most-cited mathematicians in 1978-1979.[3] Seven of them received the Fields medal, an award comparable in prestige to the Nobel prize.[11] They are: M.F.

Atiyah, A. Connes, C. Fefferman, A. Grothendieck, L. Hormander, J.W. Milnor, and S. Smale. The Fields medal is awarded every four years by the International Mathematical Union. The medal is intended to honor mathematicians under age 40 for their outstanding achievements. Only 27 mathematicians have won the Fields medal since the first two were awarded in 1936.

Six authors in Table 1 were also identified in a study of the 1,000 most-cited authors in the 1965-1978 *SCI*.[12] All six are physicists: D.J. Gross, R. Jackiw, B.W. Lee, S. Weinberg, K.G. Wilson, and B. Zumino. In addition to Weinberg and Wilson, four other authors on the list are Nobel laureates. S. Chandrasekhar and C.N. Yang won the prize for physics in 1983 and 1957, respectively. Hodgkin and Huxley were awarded the prize for physiology or medicine in 1963.

As stated earlier, 19 of the most-cited *CMCI* papers have been commented on by their authors. The majority of these papers qualify as *Citation Classics*. Pending a more comprehensive citation analysis of the math and computer science literature covering the 30-year period from 1955 to date, we will write to the authors and invite them to comment on their classic publications. In making these selections we can, and do, rely on data for individual journals. The most-cited articles for each journal may be chosen regardless of their absolute citation counts.

This concludes our discussion of the most-cited papers in the 1976-1980 *CMCI*. In a continuation of this study, we will analyze the most-cited *books* for the same period. In a few years, we'll follow up these studies by identifying a new crop of most-cited articles and books for 1981-1985.

* * * * *

My thanks to Abigail W. Grissom and Al Welljams-Dorof for their help in the preparation of this essay

©1984 ISI

REFERENCES

1. **Garfield E.** Highly cited works in mathematics. Part 1. "Pure" mathematics. Part 2. "Applied" mathematics. *Essays of an information scientist.* Philadelphia: ISI Press, 1977. Vol. 1. p. 504-13.
2. --------------, Journal citation studies. 36. Pure and applied mathematics journals: what they cite and vice versa. *Essays of an information scientist.* Philadelphia: ISI Press, 1983. Vol. 5. p. 484-92.
3. --------------, The 200 "pure" mathematicians most cited in 1978 and 1979, including a list of most-cited publications for the top 100. *Essays of an information scientist.* Philadelphia: ISI Press, 1983. Vol. 5. p. 666-75.
4. --------------, *ISI/CompuMath,* multidisciplinary coverage of applied and pure mathematics, statistics, and computer science, in print and/or online—take your pick! *Essays of an information scientist.* Philadelphia: ISI Press, 1983. Vol. 5. p. 437-42.
5. --------------, How to use *Science Citation Index (SCI). Current Contents* (9):5-14, 28 February 1983.
6. --------------, How to use *Social Sciences Citation Index (SSCI). Current Contents* (27):3-13, 2 July 1984.
7. --------------, Introducing *Citation Classics:* the human side of scientific reports. *Essays of an information scientist.* Philadelphia: ISI Press, 1980. Vol. 3. p. 1-2.
8. **Marquardt D W.** Citation Classic. Commentary on *J. Soc. Indust. Appl. Math.* 11:431-41, 1963. *Current Contents/Engineering, Technology & Applied Sciences* 10(27):14, 2 July 1979.
9. **Kaplan E L.** Citation Classic. Commentary on *J. Amer. Statist. Assn.* 53:457-81, 1958. *Current Contents/Life Sciences* 26(24):14, 13 June 1983.
10. **Hoerl A E & Kennard R W.** Citation Classic. Commentary on *Technometrics* 12:55-67, 1970. *Current Contents/Engineering, Technology & Applied Sciences* 13(35):18, 30 August 1982.
11. **Mostow G D.** The Fields medals (I): relating the continuous and the discrete. *Science* 202:297-8, 1978.
12. **Garfield E.** The 1,000 contemporary scientists most-cited 1965-1978. Part 1. The basic list and introduction. *Essays of an information scientist.* Philadelphia: ISI Press, 1983. Vol. 5. p. 269-78.

Current Comments®

Anorexia Nervosa: The Enigma of Self-Starvation

Number 32

August 6, 1984

In previous essays, I have discussed fasting.[1] As one who occasionally engages in the practice, I noted that moderate fasting may be a good way for some people to stay trim and keep healthy. But fasting, like anything else, can be taken to extremes. One extreme and dangerous form of fasting, involving virtual self-starvation, is the strange illness known as anorexia nervosa.

Anorexia nervosa is an eating disorder that causes its victims to pursue an obsessive, exaggerated diet—a diet in which food is avoided to the point of emaciation and even death. Since the condition has only recently begun to receive popular attention in magazines and television, it is somewhat surprising to learn that anorexia has been the subject of serious research for more than a century.

One of the first clinical observations of the disorder, in fact, was recorded almost 300 years ago. In 1689, English physician Richard Morton described a woman who inexplicably refused virtually all food, and who resembled "a skeleton only clad with skin."[2] (p. 5) However, the first real recognition of anorexia as a clinical entity occurred in the 1870s. William Gull, an English physician, and Jean Lasegue, a French psychiatrist, made simultaneous observations of the disorder.[3] (p. 1) They observed an affliction of young women which involved refusing to eat, extreme weight loss, amenorrhea (cessation of menstrual periods), constipation, and slow pulse and respira-

tion. Perhaps most significant was an absence of any signs of primary organic disease.

Gull termed the affliction "hysteric apepsia," and later changed the name to "anorexia nervosa," meaning "nervous loss of appetite."[3] (p. 1) Gull's name for the condition has become the accepted term, although it is something of a misnomer. Actually, anorexics retain their appetite but choose to drastically limit their food intake.[4]

At the turn of the century, research on anorexia continued in the wake of Gull and Lasegue's observations. The German pathologist M. Simmonds caused some confusion with his account of the death of an emaciated woman who, on autopsy, was found to have a damaged pituitary gland. From 1914 until the mid-1930s, cases of anorexia were incorrectly identified and treated as a pituitary disorder—as Simmonds's disease.[5] Although Simmonds's theories were discounted, the controversy surrounding anorexia continues, to an extent, up until the present day. There is still some contention as to whether the condition is purely psychological in origin, or whether it is precipitated by a primary disorder of the endocrine system.

In any event, anorexia nervosa, as viewed by Gull, Lasegue, and others, is still very much with us in the modern world. One British study, by A.H. Crisp and colleagues, Department of Psychiatry, St. George's Medical School, London, determined that one out of 200 girls

240

over the age of 12 exhibited the disease in serious form, as did one out of 100 young women between the ages of 16 and 18.[6] A Swedish study reported one serious case per 155 teenage females.[7] Precise statistics on current incidence in the US do not seem to be available, but officials at the National Association of Anorexia Nervosa and Associated Disorders (ANAD) estimate that anorexia strikes one out of every 200 teenagers in this country, nine out of ten of them female.[8] There does seem to be a consensus that the incidence is increasing.[9]

Until recently, the prevailing orthodoxy held that anorexia afflicts white adolescent females, primarily from the middle and upper classes. But anorexia has recently been reported among poor people, and among blacks and other minorities who had not exhibited the condition before. It is possible, however, that these changes merely reflect improved techniques for detecting and diagnosing the disease. There is also evidence that anorexia is increasingly affecting older age groups.[7] (p. 100-19) The incidence of anorexia in males remains rare, generally reported as less than ten percent of total cases.[10]

The American Psychiatric Association's *Diagnostic and Statistical Manual of Mental Disorders (DSM III)* lists specific criteria for the diagnosis of anorexia.[11] The main features, specified as always present, are behavior directed toward losing weight, weight loss, peculiar patterns of handling food, intense fear of gaining weight, disturbance of body image, and, in females, amenorrhea. Secondary features, not always present, include denial of illness and resistance to therapy. The disorder may also delay or stunt psychosexual development in adolescents, and cause adults to lose interest in sexual activity.[11]

There are other, similar sets of diagnostic criteria, such as the one developed by psychiatrist Paul Garfinkel and psychologist David Garner, Toronto General Hospital. They specify a self-inflicted loss of weight, achieved either through avoidance of food, self-induced vomiting, abuse of purgatives, excessive exercise, or some combination of these. Garner and Garfinkel also specify a secondary endocrine disorder which shows up in the female as amenorrhea and in the male as a reduction of sexual interest and activity. Lastly, there is a psychological disturbance that has as its central theme a morbid fear of being unable to control eating and hence becoming too fat.[7] Another set of criteria, developed by John Feighner and colleagues, Department of Psychiatry, Washington University, St. Louis, resembles the above sets, but calls for onset of the illness before age 25 and at least a 25 percent loss of body weight.[12] The Feighner criteria were designed primarily to guarantee compatibility of patients in clinical research studies. Therefore, they are more restrictive than criteria used solely for diagnosis.

Ironically, anorexics may become obsessed with food even as they refuse to eat it. Katherine A. Halmi, Department of Psychiatry, New York Hospital, White Plains, New York, reviewed some psychological aspects of anorexia in a chapter of the *Comprehensive Textbook of Psychiatry/III*. She notes that it is not unusual for anorexics to collect recipes, or even to assume all the family cooking chores.[13] Garfinkel notes that the anorexic also experiences other effects of starvation on thinking, feeling, and behavior. There is poor concentration, indecisiveness, a narrowing of interests, mood fluctuation, and, at times, depression.[14]

Anorexics don't eat normally because they have a morbid fear of gaining weight. This fear can drive an anorexic to ruinous physical consequences. Some patients lose as much as 50 percent of their original body weight. The emaciation can be extreme. Indeed, anorexics experience discomfort caused by their jutting bones even as they insist they need to lose more weight. The skin be-

241

comes dry and cracked. A fine, downy growth of so-called "lanugo" hair will often show on cheeks, neck, forearms, and thighs. The temperature of anorexics is often abnormally low, and they may complain constantly that their hands and feet are cold. Constipation is also common.[15]

The medical effects of anorexia are, of course, serious. Anorexics tend to exhibit bradycardia, an abnormally slow heart rate—60 beats per minute or less. As many as 50 percent of these patients occasionally binge on food and then immediately induce vomiting to protect themselves from any weight gain.[14] This binge-purge syndrome, known as bulimia, affects not only anorexics, but also many persons who otherwise maintain a near-normal body weight. Bulimia, once considered a subcategory of anorexic behavior, has become a separate and serious health hazard in its own right.[16]

In fact, studies comparing bulimic anorexics with nonvomiting anorexics have demonstrated that bulimics exhibit markedly different psychological traits. One study by Garfinkel and colleagues determined that bulimics showed a higher degree of impulsive behavior than fasting anorexics, including kleptomania, drug and alcohol abuse, self-mutilation, and suicide attempts.[16] Another study, by Regina C. Casper, Department of Psychiatry, University of Illinois, and colleagues showed that bulimics manifested greater anxiety, depression, and guilt, and had more somatic complaints than anorexics who did not induce vomiting.[17] Bulimics' overeating episodes appear to have little to do with simple hunger. Gerald Russell, a psychiatrist at Maudsley Hospital, London, has interpreted bulimics' gorging on food as a response to an unfulfilled emotional need.[18] Self-induced vomiting serves to alleviate guilt caused by the binge and neutralize the fattening effects of the food.

The consequences of self-induced vomiting are especially grave. The resulting low serum potassium levels, a condition known as hypokalemia, can lead to cardiac arrhythmia and sudden death. And victims of anorexia and bulimia do die, from heart failure, from the general effects of malnutrition, or from unknown causes.[19] H.-C. Steinhausen, Department of Child and Adolescent Psychiatry and Neurology, Free University of Berlin, Federal Republic of Germany, reviewed mortality statistics from several outcome studies. He found that the figures on mortality in anorexia varied widely, anywhere from one to 25 percent of total cases.[20] Generally, though, the mortality rate is reported at between five and ten percent of cases.[21]

Why do anorexics embark on this destructive course of self-starvation? One early theory, prevalent in the 1940s, held that anorexia involved an unconscious wish to be impregnated through the mouth, which the patient guiltily rejected by avoiding food. According to a Boston group of psychiatrists, the amenorrhea resulted directly from the patient's unconscious desire to be pregnant.[22] This theory has given way to more complex social, psychological, and biochemical hypotheses. Today the precise etiology and ideal course of treatment for anorexia are matters of controversy.

One theory implicates western civilization's version of the "ideal" body shape for women, and the relentless pressure for women to be thin. Garner and Garfinkel undertook a study in which they gauged changes in the measurements of *Playboy* centerfold models and contestants in the Miss America pageant over a 20-year period. They found a trend toward lower weight and a more androgynous, "tubular" figure. The feminine ideal, they conclude, is presented as a slender figure, even though improved nutrition over the years has resulted in higher average weights for women.[23] Garner and Garfinkel also found a high prevalence of anorexia among models and in dance schools, where there is enormous pressure on women to be thin for professional reasons. This finding supports the view that external, societal influences can play a large part in the development of the disease.[14]

But it does not even take a scientific approach to notice the mass media's emphasis on thinness as the ideal feminine shape. Anyone even remotely familiar with magazines and television has noted the prevalence of skinny models in advertising, who no doubt serve as examples for young women.

Some researchers have taken a psychological approach to anorexia. Garfinkel, in reviewing the psychological literature in the field, has assembled a list of possible predisposing factors. Among the factors that may contribute to the development of anorexia in an individual are an impaired sense of personal identity, and subsequent inability to function apart from one's family; a perceptual disturbance which shows up in anorexia as a pronounced inability to perceive one's body size; high birth weight or childhood obesity; perfectionism, or a personality in which self-worth is highly regulated by factors outside the self; and certain family factors including parents who tend to be older when the individual is born and who may have a history of depression.[24]

It is not uncommon for some stressful life situation to precede the onset of anorexia. Halmi and colleagues conducted a study which determined that anorexia commonly occurred in girls at the ages of 14-1/2 and 18. Halmi noted that at these ages a girl may be facing greater independence in the form of a move up to high school or departure from home to college or a job.[25] Other situations which may precipitate anorexia include a death or serious illness in the family, failure at school or work, the necessity to switch jobs, or some kind of sexual conflict. Often the anorexic's obsessive dieting has been initiated by a friend or family member's casual mention that the patient needed to lose a few pounds, or by the teasing of classmates about being overweight.[26] (p. 258)

While a single event may trigger the onset of anorexia in some cases, most researchers believe that complex psychological forces are at work. Crisp views anorexia as a "phobic avoidance" of the demands placed on girls by puberty and maturation.[27] Unable to meet the demands of physical and sexual maturity, girls starve themselves, thereby negating the threatening sexual characteristics (menstruation, which ceases) and regaining an immature, uncurved body.

Hilde Bruch, Department of Psychiatry, Baylor College of Medicine, Houston, has also proposed a psychological theory for the condition. Anorexics and their "relentless pursuit of thinness," says Bruch, are characterized by three main factors: a distortion of body image, misperception of such sensations as hunger and fatigue, and an underlying sense of personal ineffectiveness.[26] (p. 251-4) According to Bruch, anorexia and other eating disorders arise when parents neglect or respond inappropriately to a child's needs. When parental care, such as feeding, is constantly superimposed according to the mother's concept of what the child needs, the child may grow up with a deficient sense of independence and self-awareness, unable to clearly distinguish such basic drives as hunger and satiety. The child's sense of self-value and competence are blunted. Bruch postulates that the child, as a consequence of this constant external control, may come to experience his or her body image in a distorted way.[28]

This matter of anorexia and body image, incidentally, is controversial. Studies in which anorexics were asked to estimate their body sizes have shown that anorexics have a tendency to overestimate their body dimensions. Other studies have found this overestimation to be no more pronounced in anorexics than in control subjects.[29] There have even been suggestions to drop body image misperception from the diagnostic criteria.[30] There is little disagreement that anorexics deny their emaciation, but the exact nature and significance of body image misperception appear to remain unresolved.

In any event, Bruch views anorexia as a misguided compulsion for autonomy and self-control.[28] This compulsion seems to be a central feature of the condition. In one study of female anorexics, 88 percent of the patients said they lost weight because they "liked the feeling of willpower and self-control."[31]

As Bruch indicates, family dynamics plays a major role in the development of anorexia.[28] Others have also examined the role of the family. One of the major proponents of a "family systems" approach to anorexia is Salvador Minuchin, Philadelphia Child Guidance Clinic.

Minuchin has proposed a model for families in which psychosomatic illness, specifically anorexia, seems most likely to occur. These families tend to exhibit "enmeshment," where the family members are overinvolved with one another. "Overprotectiveness" is another feature, where children and parents are highly protective of each other. Minuchin also identified "rigidity," a compulsion to maintain appearances, and "conflict avoidance," a tendency to avoid overt resolution of conflicts. There also may be a high emphasis placed on food and bodily functions.[32] In such a family, the child's autonomy is stifled, and the child fails to develop the skills to deal with others at his or her own age level. Anorexia becomes a means by which to manipulate the parents and perpetuate this overinvolvement with the family.

Such theories of anorexia within a family context are not without their critics, however. Joel Yager, a psychiatrist at School of Medicine, University of California, Los Angeles (UCLA), has pointed out that family models may rely on theories and measurements that are not entirely valid, and may depend on small samples and biased interview techniques.[33]

One intriguing possibility under investigation is that anorexia may be related to affective disorder—that heterogeneous group of illnesses generally lumped under the term "depression."[34] A number of studies have explored the incidence of affective disorder in relatives of anorexia patients. One study, by James I. Hudson and colleagues, Harvard Medical School, investigated the immediate families of patients with anorexia and bulimia. Hudson found that nearly one-quarter of the relatives exhibited signs of major affective disorder, a higher incidence of depression than in families of patients with schizophrenia or borderline personality disorder.[35] Other studies have also found that families of anorexics tend to exhibit a higher incidence of emotional disturbance than control groups.[33] Such results have not only led to the conclusion that there may be a link between affective disorder and anorexia, but have raised the possibility of a genetic predisposition to anorexia.

One study, by Dennis P. Cantwell and colleagues, Neuropsychiatric Institute, UCLA, examined 33 anorexic patients to determine the level of affective disorder among the patients themselves. Cantwell found that one-third of the patients were diagnosed as having affective disorder, and that nearly two-thirds manifested a dysphoric mood, including feelings of worthlessness, death wish, and suicidal ideation. Cantwell concluded that the data suggested "a hypothesis that at least some cases of anorexia nervosa may be a variant of affective disorder."[36] Another study, by Robert L. Hendren, Department of Psychiatry, George Washington University, supported these findings, determining that 56 percent of anorexic patients under study met standard diagnostic criteria for a major depressive disorder.[37]

Still another study, by Elke D. Eckert and colleagues, Department of Psychiatry, University of Minnesota, demonstrated that a higher level of depression in the female anorexic patients under study seemed to be associated with more severe anorexic behavior, such as vomiting, laxative abuse, and resistance to treatment. The study also found that patients who showed the greatest reduction in depression during treatment gained the most weight.[38] In addition to these studies, there is some evidence that antidepressant drugs may be effective in the treatment of anorexics. This link between depression and anorexia is controversial, and clearly requires further exploration.

In addition to exploring the psychological roots of anorexia, researchers have concerned themselves with the physiological causes of the disorder. Here there is some debate. Researchers disagree as to whether anorexia is precipitated by some primary dysfunction of the neuroendocrine system, or whether that dysfunction simply derives from the starvation and weight loss.

A good deal of the debate concerns the amenorrhea in anorexic females, one of the disorder's main features. Menstruation results from a series of hormonal secretions, which originate in the area of the brain known as the hypothalamus. The hypothalamus releases hormones to the pituitary gland, which in turn releases its own hormones to the ovary. Changes in the subsequent levels of ovarian hormones will induce the cyclical changes in the uterus that result in menstruation.

In anorexia, there is a disturbance in this hypothalamic-pituitary-gonadal axis, and menstruation ceases. Some researchers interpret the amenorrhea as evidence of a primary hypothalamic dysfunction in anorexia, while others view the cessation of menses as simply a consequence of the drastic weight loss.

Halmi has written in support of what she calls "indirect evidence" of a primary hypothalamic disturbance in anorexia. She has noted that emaciated anorexic females who've stopped menstruating show decreased levels of hormones called gonadotrophins. These hormones are crucial to the menstrual cycle, and their release from the pituitary is regulated by the hypothalamus. The low gonadotrophin levels in anorexic females do not rise in response to estrogen stimulus or drug treatments as they would in healthy subjects, even after weight gain.[39] In other words, the amenorrhea often continues, for weeks or months, even after normal body weight has been regained.

There are also findings that anorexic patients show an "immature" secretory pattern of a gonadotrophin called luteinizing hormone (LH). One study, by psychiatrist Mark Gold and colleagues, Fair Oaks Hospital, Summit, New Jersey, tested five adult female anorexic patients during their emaciated phase and again at least 60 days after weight gain. After all the patients had regained their ideal body weights, only one patient showed an adult pattern of 24-hour LH secretion, with the others displaying abnormally low LH levels more suggestive of immature, prepubertal subjects.[40]

Halmi also notes that amenorrhea may actually *precede* weight loss in as many as one-third of anorexic patients.[39] All this evidence may point to a defect in the hypothalamus that is not related to the patient's nutritional status. Halmi also claims anorexics may have a "vulnerable" hypothalamus that would predispose them to develop anorexic symptoms.[41]

Russell also believes that a primary hypothalamic disturbance may be behind the amenorrhea. Russell concludes that nonnutritional factors, such as psychological stress and other mechanisms not yet fully understood, contribute to the amenorrhea and the hypothalamic disorder.[42]

One body of opinion, then, holds that a hypothalamic disorder—perhaps an immature pattern of hypothalamic functioning—may be a cause of anorexia.

Other researchers have concluded that the hypothalamic dysfunction and amenorrhea in anorexia are consequences of the malnutrition, and are not necessarily primary features of the disorder. Robert S. Mecklenburg and colleagues, National Institute of Child Health and Human Development, Bethesda, examined hypothalamic dysfunction in anorexia. They noted that other victims of starvation, such as those seen during World War II, also displayed abnormalities in hypothalamic function, including amenorrhea.[43]

Robert A. Vigersky, an endocrinologist at the Walter Reed Army Medical Center, Washington, DC, compared 29 anorexic patients with 19 patients with simple weight loss and 20 normal controls. Vigersky concludes that the hypothalamic changes in anorexia are "secondary to the weight loss, *per se*."[44] In explaining how amenorrhea can precede weight loss, Vigersky points out that such factors as stress and excessive exercise might play a role, particularly since female dancers and athletes have been known to stop menstruating, even though their body weights were not abnormally low. There are also recent findings that normal women placed on markedly restrictive diets exhibit many of the hypothalamic-pituitary-ovarian changes seen in anorexia, including the immature pattern of 24-hour LH secretion.[14]

Two Australian psychiatrists, Peter J.V. Beumont and Janice Russell, University of Sydney, offer a further explanation for amenorrhea occurring before any weight loss. Careful evaluation of the patient's history, they say, will often show that months of erratic eating behavior has preceded—and no doubt helped cause—the amenorrhea. Such erratic eating behavior can continue even after weight has been regained, delaying the return of menses.[45]

The hypothalamus is also of interest to researchers because it controls such functions as appetite and satiety. In a review article on the neurophysiology of feeding, E.T. Rolls, Department of Experimental Psychology, Oxford University, noted that manipulation of the hypothalamus in laboratory animals has been shown to induce irregular feeding behavior.[46] Also, lesions and tumors of the hypothalamus in humans have been associated with behavior that closely resembles anorexia.[43]

Detlev Ploog, Max Planck Institute for Psychiatry, Munich, has postulated that the starvation in anorexia disrupts the neural activity between the brain and the gut. This results, he says, in a constant neural bombardment of the hypothalamus that may cause the anorexic patient to perceive the hunger as pleasant and rewarding.[47] Obviously, this will perpetuate the starvation and lead to a worsening of the illness.

There is, of course, more research being done on the biochemical and psychological aspects of anorexia. One study, for example, by Philip W. Gold and colleagues, Biological Psychiatry Branch, National Institute of Mental Health, Bethesda, studied secretions of a hormone called vasopressin. Vasopressin helps regulate the body's fluid balance, and its level usually rises in response to salt intake. Anorexic patients injected with a saline solution showed erratic, fluctuating vasopressin levels which seemed unresponsive to the saline injections. The defects seemed to be corrected after weight gain. It remains unclear whether the vasopressin defect is peculiar to anorexia or is a nonspecific result of the malnutrition.[48] Other research has dealt with irregularities in pituitary, thyroid, and adrenal functions.[49] But the precise biochemical mechanisms at work in anorexia remain a mystery.

The treatment of anorexia, too, is an area where opinions differ, although many of the methodologies share common features. Practitioners agree that hospitalization is imperative for the most chronic, severely malnourished cases. The immediate goal of treatment is to restore the patient to a normal weight. As the patients are gaining weight, most treatment programs offer therapy to help overcome the morbid fear of obesity that is at the heart of the disorder. Bed rest and a daily caloric intake are usually enforced, with increased freedom and activities serving to reinforce weight gain.

There are differing opinions about the best kind of psychotherapy for anorexic patients. Bruch, for one, has argued against the use of traditional psychotherapy, in which the therapist imposes an interpretation on the private thoughts and emotions of the patient. Such therapy, according to Bruch, will only underscore the patient's sense of ineffectiveness, of being externally controlled.[26] (p. 336) She recommends an altered role for the therapist, in which the patient's thoughts and emotions are accepted supportively and uncritically.

Others share the view that traditional psychotherapy should be avoided. Hans H. Bassøe and Inge Eskeland, endocrinologists at the University of Bergen, Norway, reported a 58 percent success rate in a study of 133 patients. Their program purposely avoided any psychotherapy that would, as the authors state, have "penetrated the sensitive minds of the patients."[50] Instead, the patients received an explanation of the pathophysiology of hunger, and were thereby motivated to use their intelligence and willpower to increase their food intake.

Group therapy, in which anorexic patients can share their fears about weight gain and reinforce one another's progress, has also been used successfully. Often, recovered anorexics will serve as discussion leaders in such groups.[51]

Different treatment paradigms place different emphases on the patient's family. Some researchers agree with Gull's assertion 100 years ago that because the tension and conflict within the family have precipitated and aggravated the disorder, family members are "generally the worst attendants" for an anorexic patient.[3] (p. 47) Ian Story, a psychiatrist at the Austen Riggs Center, Stockbridge, Massachusetts, has stated that the physical separation of the patient from the family should be a vital feature of treatment, in the short and long run.[52]

For others, the family must play a key role in the rehabilitation of an anorexic. Crisp always attempts to engage the parents in the treatment program, and does so in 85 percent of the cases. The presence of the parents, according to Crisp, is essential in unraveling the conflicts which have given rise to anorexia.[53]

Minuchin,[21] Ronald Liebman, and colleagues, Philadelphia Child Guidance Clinic, have developed a treatment program that includes sessions in which the entire family gathers for lunch with a therapist in attendance. These sessions enable the patient to eat in the presence of the parents without the development of a power struggle, and also help to identify structural and dynamic factors within the family that have promoted and prolonged the disease.[54]

Drugs have been used in the treatment of anorexic patients, although there have not been many controlled studies on their effectiveness. Success has been reported with the tranquilizer chlorpromazine, which renders patients less fearful of weight gain.[55] Amitriptyline, a tricyclic antidepressant, has also been used with beneficial effects.[56] Studies with cyproheptadine, an antihistamine, showed that this drug helped anorexics gain weight and also alleviated some of their depressive symptoms.[57] Most of the value of drugs is adjunctive to nutritional rehabilitation and psychological counseling.

Treatment, whatever its form, takes time. Hospitalization or out-patient treatment may take months, with years of follow-up therapy. Unfortunately, not all anorexics fully recover.

One follow-up study, by Crisp, L.K.G. Hsu, and Britta Harding, St. George's Medical School, reports on the outcome of 100 female anorexic patients four to eight years after first presentation. Forty-eight of these patients showed a "good" outcome, with near-normal weight, regular menses, and satisfying social and psychosexual development. Thirty were "intermediate," and 20 were "poor." Two had died. Perhaps more significant was the finding that 49 percent retained the central symptom of a morbid concern about weight gain and becoming fat. Only 28 patients reported being unconcerned about their weight.[58]

Another British follow-up study, by psychiatrist H.G. Morgan, University of Bristol, and Russell, reports on 41 patients four years after discharge. Thirty-nine percent were defined as "good," 27 percent as "intermediate," and 29 percent as "poor." Five percent had died. The authors used the patients' backgrounds to determine factors which might aid in predicting outcome in anorexia. Among the negative predictors of outcome were a later age of initial onset, frequent hospitalization, and a history of disturbed relationships with parents and at school.[59] Another study reviewed data from 12 outcome surveys, and found that over half of the anorexic patients continued to have eating difficulties and almost half showed other signs of psychiatric impairments.[60] Minuchin and colleagues, on the other hand, reported that 86 percent of their patients had been cured of anorexia and related psychological problems.[32]

However, such follow-up studies on anorexics have attracted criticism. Hsu, in particular, has faulted outcome studies, citing a lack of diagnostic and methodological uniformity.[61] Other authors have echoed this charge, claiming that the evaluative criteria in such studies are often inadequately described or incomplete.[20]

But the follow-up studies do demonstrate the enormous difficulty in completely curing anorexic patients in the face of their tendency to maintain their symptoms and suffer relapses.

Scientific interest in anorexia nervosa is demonstrated by the existence of *ISI/BIOMED®* research front #82-1738, "Clinical studies and management of bulimia and anorexia nervosa." There are six core papers in this research front, all of which have been cited in this essay. These include publications by Bruch,[26] Hsu and colleagues,[58] and Morgan and Russell.[59] The other cited core documents, by Garfinkel and colleagues,[16] Casper and colleagues,[17] and Russell,[18] deal with the emergence of bulimia as a separate and distinct syndrome.

A number of journals publish papers on anorexia. *The International Journal of Eating Disorders*, a quarterly, is devoted entirely to the study of anorexia, bulimia, obesity, and related problems. Other journals, among them *Psychological Medicine, Psychosomatic Medicine*, and the *American Journal of Psychiatry*, also publish research on anorexia. All are covered in *Current Contents®/Social & Behavioral Sciences*, *CC®/Life Sciences*, and *CC/Clinical Practice*. As more research is published, and more results from various disciplines synthesized and unified, more will be understood about the psychological and biological causes of anorexia nervosa. Indeed, it is safe to predict that a complete understanding of its causes will have ramifications in many areas of medicine.

* * * * *

My thanks to Christopher King and Amy Stone for their help in the preparation of this essay.   ©1984 ISI

REFERENCES

1. **Garfield E.** To fast or not too much fast. Part 1. The claims for fasting in the popular literature. Part 2. A controversial question gets some scientific answers. *Essays of an information scientist.* Philadelphia: ISI Press, 1983. Vol. 5. p. 313-26.
2. **Thomä H.** *Anorexia nervosa.* New York: International Universities Press, 1967. 342 p.
3. **Dally P.** *Anorexia nervosa.* London: William Heinemann Medical Books, 1969. 137 p.
4. **Halmi K A.** The diagnosis and treatment of anorexia nervosa. (Zales M R, ed.) *Eating, sleeping and sexuality.* New York: Brunner/Mazel, 1982. p. 43-58.
5. **Simmonds M.** Ueber embolische Prozesse in der Hypophysis. (Embolic processes in the pituitary gland.) *Virchows Arch. Pathol. Anat. Physiol.* 217:226-39, 1914.
6. **Crisp A H, Palmer R L & Kalucy R S.** How common is anorexia nervosa? A prevalence study. *Brit. J. Psychiat.* 128:549-54, 1976.
7. **Garfinkel P & Garner D.** *Anorexia nervosa: a multidimensional perspective.* New York: Brunner/Mazel, 1982. 391 p.
8. **Howard H.** Telephone communication. 12 June 1984.
9. **Szmukler G L.** Anorexia nervosa: its entity as an illness and its treatment. *Pharmacol. Ther.* 16:431-46, 1982.
10. **Lucas A R.** Anorexia nervosa. *Contemporary Nutrition* 3(8), 1978. (Newsletter.) Minneapolis, MN: General Mills, 1978.
11. **American Psychiatric Association.** *Diagnostic and statistical manual of mental disorders (DSM-III).* Washington, DC: APA, 1980. p. 67-9.
12. **Feighner J P, Robins E, Guze S B, Woodruff R A, Winokur G & Munoz R.** Diagnostic criteria for use in psychiatric research. *Arch. Gen. Psychiat.* 26:57-63, 1972.
13. **Halmi K A.** Anorexia nervosa. (Kaplan H I, Freedman A M & Sadock B J.) *Comprehensive textbook of psychiatry/III.* Baltimore: Williams & Wilkins, 1980. Vol. 2. p. 1882-91.
14. **Garfinkel P E.** Telephone communication. 3 July 1984.
15. **Boyar R M.** Anorexia nervosa. (Isselbacher K J, Adams R D, Braunwald E, Petersdorf R G & Wilson J D, eds.) *Harrison's principles of internal medicine.* New York: McGraw-Hill, 1980. p. 416-8.
16. **Garfinkel P E, Moldofsky H & Garner D M.** The heterogeneity of anorexia nervosa. *Arch. Gen. Psychiat.* 37:1036-40, 1980.
17. **Casper R C, Eckert E D, Halmi K A, Goldberg S C & Davis J M.** Bulimia. *Arch. Gen. Psychiat.* 37:1030-5, 1980.
18. **Russell G.** Bulimia nervosa: an ominous variant of anorexia nervosa. *Psychol. Med.* 9:429-48, 1979.
19. **Bruch H.** Death in anorexia nervosa. *Psychosom. Med.* 33:135-44, 1971.
20. **Steinhausen H-C.** Follow-up studies of anorexia nervosa: a review of research findings. *Psychol. Med.* 13:239-49, 1983.
21. **Minuchin S.** Telephone communication. 29 June 1984.
22. **Waller J V, Kaufman M R & Deutsch F.** Anorexia nervosa: a psychosomatic entity. *Psychosom. Med.* 2:3-16, 1940.
23. **Garner D M, Garfinkel P E, Schwartz D & Thompson M.** Cultural expectations of thinness in women. *Psychol. Rep.* 47:483-91, 1980.
24. **Garfinkel P E.** Anorexia nervosa: a model for integrating biological and psychodynamic approaches to psychiatry. (Perris C, Struwe G & Jansson B, eds.) *Biological psychiatry 1981. Proceedings of the IIIrd World Congress of Biological Psychiatry,* 28 June-3 July 1981, Stockholm, Sweden. New York: Elsevier/North-Holland Biomedical Press, 1981. p. 550-7.
25. **Halmi K A, Casper R C, Eckert E D, Goldberg S C & Davis J M.** Unique features associated with age onset of anorexia nervosa. *Psychiat. Res.* 1:209-15, 1979.
26. **Bruch H.** *Eating disorders.* New York: Basic, 1973. 396 p.
27. **Crisp A H & Bhat A V.** Personality and anorexia nervosa—the phobic avoidance stance. *Psychother. Psychosom.* 38:178-200, 1982.
28. **Bruch H.** Psychotherapy in anorexia nervosa and developmental obesity. (Goodstein R K, ed.) *Eating and weight disorders.* New York: Springer, 1983. p. 136-46.
29. **Garner D M & Garfinkel P E.** Body image in anorexia nervosa: measurement, theory and clinical implications. *Int. J. Psychiat. Med.* 11:263-84, 1981-82.
30. **Hsu L K G.** Is there a disturbance in body image in anorexia nervosa? *J. Nerv. Ment. Dis.* 170:305-7, 1982.
31. **Leon G R.** Anorexia nervosa: the question of treatment emphasis. (Rosenbaum M, Franks C M & Jaffe Y, eds.) *Perspectives on behavior therapy in the eighties.* New York: Springer, 1983. p. 363-77.
32. **Minuchin S, Rosman B L & Baker L.** *Psychosomatic families.* Cambridge: Harvard University Press, 1978. 351 p.
33. **Yager J.** Family issues in the pathogenesis of anorexia nervosa. *Psychosom. Med.* 44:43-60, 1982.

34. **Garfield E.** What do we know about depression? Part 1: etiology. Part 2: diagnosis and treatment. *Essays of an information scientist.* Philadelphia: ISI Press, 1983. Vol. 5. p. 100-15.
35. **Hudson J I, Pope H G, Jonas J M & Yurgelun-Todd D.** Family history study of anorexia nervosa and bulimia. *Brit. J. Psychiat.* 142:133-8, 1983.
36. **Cantwell D P, Sturzenberger S, Burroughs J, Salkin B & Green J K.** Anorexia nervosa. *Arch. Gen. Psychiat.* 34:1087-93, 1977.
37. **Hendren R L.** Depression in anorexia nervosa. *J. Amer. Acad. Child Psychiat.* 22:59-62, 1983.
38. **Eckert E D, Goldberg S C, Halmi K A, Casper R C & Davis J M.** Depression in anorexia nervosa. *Psychol. Med.* 12:115-22, 1982.
39. **Halmi K A.** Anorexia nervosa. (Hippius H & Winokur G, eds.) *Psychopharmacology 1. Part 2: clinical psychopharmacology.* Princeton: Excerpta Medica, 1983. p. 313-20.
40. **Gold M, Pottash A C, Martin D, Extein I & Howard E.** The 24-hour LH test in the diagnosis and assessment of response to treatment of patients with anorexia nervosa. *Int. J. Psychiat. Med.* 11:245-50, 1981-82.
41. **Halmi K A.** The menstrual cycle in anorexia nervosa. (Friedman R C, ed.) *Behavior and the menstrual cycle.* New York: Dekker, 1982. p. 291-7.
42. **Russell G.** The current status and treatment of anorexia nervosa. (Perris C, Struwe G & Jansson B, eds.) *Biological psychiatry 1981. Proceedings of the IIIrd World Congress of Biological Psychiatry,* 28 June-3 July 1981, Stockholm, Sweden. New York: Elsevier/North-Holland Biomedical Press, 1981. p. 542-9.
43. **Mecklenburg R S, Loriaux D L, Thompson R H, Andersen A E & Lipsett M B.** Hypothalamic dysfunction in patients with anorexia nervosa. *Medicine* 53:147-59, 1974.
44. **Vigersky R A.** Hypothalamic-pituitary function in anorexia nervosa and simple weight loss. (Goodstein R K, ed.) *Eating and weight disorders.* New York: Springer, 1983. p. 105-23.
45. **Beumont P J V & Russell J.** Anorexia nervosa. (Beumont P J V & Burrows G D, eds.) *Handbook of psychiatry and endocrinology.* New York: Elsevier Biomedical Press, 1982. p. 63-96.
46. **Rolls E T.** Neurophysiology of feeding. (Perris C, Struwe G & Jansson B, eds.) *Biological psychiatry 1981. Proceedings of the IIIrd World Congress of Biological Psychiatry,* 28 June-3 July 1981, Stockholm, Sweden. New York: Elsevier/North-Holland Biomedical Press, 1981. p. 1035-8.
47. **Ploog D.** Neuroethological aspects of anorexia nervosa. (Perris C, Struwe G & Jansson B, eds.) *Biological psychiatry 1981. Proceedings of the IIIrd World Congress of Biological Psychiatry,* 28 June-3 July 1981, Stockholm, Sweden. New York: Elsevier/North-Holland Biomedical Press, 1981. p. 1027-34.
48. **Gold P W, Kaye W, Robertson G L & Ebert M.** Abnormalities in plasma and cerebrospinal-fluid arginine vasopressin in patients with anorexia nervosa. *N. Engl. J. Med.* 308:1117-23, 1983.
49. **Weiner H.** Psychobiological and psychosomatic aspects of anorexia nervosa and other eating disorders. (West L J & Stein M, eds.) *Critical issues in behavioral medicine.* Philadelphia: Lippincott, 1982. p. 193-215.
50. **Bassøe H H & Eskeland I.** A prospective study of 133 patients with anorexia nervosa. *Acta Psychiat. Scand.* 65:127-33, 1982.
51. **Piazza E, Carni J D, Kelly J & Plante S K.** Group psychotherapy for anorexia nervosa. *J. Amer. Acad. Child Psychiat.* 22:276-8, 1983.
52. **Story I.** Anorexia nervosa and the psychotherapeutic hospital. *Int. J. Psychoanal. Psychother.* 9:267-302, 1982-83.
53. **Crisp A H.** Treatment and outcome in anorexia nervosa. (Goodstein R K, ed.) *Eating and weight disorders.* New York: Springer, 1983. p. 91-104.
54. **Liebman R, Sargent J & Silver M.** A family systems orientation to the treatment of anorexia nervosa. *J. Amer. Acad. Child Psychiat.* 22:128-33, 1983.
55. **Halmi K A.** Treatment of anorexia nervosa: a discussion. *J. Adolescent Health Care* 4:47-50, 1983.
56. **Needleman H L & Waber D.** The use of amitriptyline in anorexia nervosa. (Vigersky R A, ed.) *Anorexia nervosa.* New York: Raven Press, 1977. p. 357-61.
57. **Halmi K A, Eckert E & Falk J R.** Cyproheptadine, an antidepressant and weight-inducing drug for anorexia nervosa. *Psychopharmacol. Bull.* 11:103-5, 1983.
58. **Hsu L K G, Crisp A H & Harding B.** Outcome of anorexia nervosa. *Lancet* 1:61-5, 1979.
59. **Morgan H G & Russell G F M.** Value of family background and clinical features as predictors of long-term outcome in anorexia nervosa: four-year follow-up study of 41 patients. *Psychol. Med.* 5:355-71, 1975.
60. **Schwartz D M & Thompson M G.** Do anorectics get well? Current research and future needs. *Amer. J. Psychiat.* 138:319-23, 1981.
61. **Hsu L K G.** Outcome of anorexia nervosa. *Arch. Gen. Psychiat.* 37:1041-6, 1980.

Current Comments®

Number 33

August 13, 1984

Over the years, we have published numerous essays examining papers that become highly cited shortly after publication. Presumably, the immediate impact of these papers points to "where the action is." In these studies, however, the life sciences usually dominate, especially such fields as biochemistry, immunology, and molecular biology. In separate studies of the physical sciences, theoretical and experimental particle physics and quantum field theory papers usually predominate. Other fields, such as botany, mathematics, or geosciences, may be underrepresented.

Various factors account for this underrepresentation. In general, the number of citations a paper in a given field is "eligible" to receive depends on the size of that field's literature. Another key factor is the number of references cited in the average paper. For example, the average biochemistry paper cites twice as many references as the average mathematics paper. Thus, a biochemical article has twice the chance of being cited as does a mathematical article. The prolific output of papers by biochemists increases the probability that their papers will dominate a list based on absolute counts. So it would be ludicrous to make direct comparisons between fields without "normalizing" for these variances.

By focusing on selected portions of ISI®'s data base, however, we can identify key articles from fields that would not otherwise turn up. For example, we recently identified the 44 most-cited entomology papers from a list of 36 core journals.[1] Papers from such small fields ordinarily do not achieve the required citation threshold in multidisciplinary studies based on the entire *Science Citation Index®* (*SCI®*). For similar reasons, we used the *CompuMath Citation Index®* to identify 100 highly cited articles in pure and applied mathematics and computer science.[2] By a similar approach, we have now identified geosciences articles published in 1981 which were highly cited from 1981 to 1983.

Data for this essay are from *ISI/ GeoSciTech™*, our online data base for the earth sciences. *ISI/GeoSciTech* includes petroleum science, geochemistry and geophysics, oceanography, metallurgy, mining, meteorology, and many other disciplines related to the Earth's environment.[3]

Each year, *ISI/GeoSciTech* comprehensively indexes more than 400 "core" earth sciences journals. By various selection routines, articles from another 1,500 journals are indexed. Potentially, articles could also be drawn from the over 3,300 publications covered in *SCI*, as well as another 2,700 from the *Social Sciences Citation Index®* (*SSCI®*) and the *Arts & Humanities Citation Index™* (*A&HCI™*) data bases. Items from these journals are automatically indexed if they meet the requirements of the selection algorithm. For example, a current article is selected if it cites two or more articles from core journals. But each automatically selected item is then reviewed by our editors for its relevance to the geosciences.

The present study is based on *ISI/ GeoSciTech* data from 1981 through 1983. This includes 161,000 articles and the 3,000,000 references they cited. About 75 percent, or 120,000, of the articles were published in the fully covered core journals. The remaining 25 percent, or about 41,000 articles, were published in one of the selectively covered journals. Many of these noncore articles were from journals in the astrosciences, crystallography, ecology, and materials science. Consequently, a significant number of the papers identified below come from these journals.

Table 1 includes the 99 papers we identified. They are listed in alphabetic order by first author. Each of the articles in this study received at least 25 citations. Had we lowered the threshold to 24, another 16 papers would have been listed. The number of times each paper was cited is followed by complete bibliographic information, including institutional affiliations. The average paper received 37 citations—4.5 in 1981, 13.9 in 1982, and 18.6 in 1983. The most-cited paper received 136 cites in this three-year period.

Since most of the 4,000,000 papers and books cited each year in *SCI* receive only a few citations, the papers in this study are clearly above average in their impact. We do not claim that these papers represent the "best" or most original geosciences research. Nor is the inclusion of the citation counts meant to suggest that one paper is "better" than another. These papers identify emerging research areas or techniques. Based on experience, there is a strong chance that many will prove to be "important" in the future. But the integration of most new ideas and methods in the earth sciences is relatively slow. It is not unlikely that future analyses will reveal other 1981 papers that subsequently prove to be heavily cited.

Recently, we clustered *SCI* and identified the most active research fronts. Briefly, a research front is established by identifying a group of current papers that collectively cite a cluster of earlier, "core" papers in a specialty. These co-citation clustering procedures have been described previously.[4] Our work with *SCI* research fronts is an extension of those procedures. We expect to report our findings in more detail later. In the meantime, we found that 48 papers in Table 1 are core articles in these 1981, 1982, and 1983 research fronts. The appropriate code numbers follow each reference. Table 2 lists the titles of these research fronts, the number of papers from this study that are core to each one, and the total number of each research front's core papers.

Table 3 shows the number of authors listed on the papers in this study. All but 17 papers were multiauthor works, with nine papers listing ten or more authors.

Forty-six authors appear on more than one paper in Table 1. Thirty-nine authors were listed on two papers each. Seven have three papers each: D.J. DePaolo, R. Hanel, V.G. Kunde, W. Maguire, P.H. Reiff, R.E. Samuelson, and R.W. Spiro.

Table 4 lists the 30 journals in which the geosciences papers were published. The three editions of the *Journal of Geophysical Research* (32 papers) and *Science* (19) account for more than half of the papers. The 51 papers in these two journals received over 2,000 citations, or 55 percent of the 3,662 cites to the 99 articles in this study. Thus, as expected, a

Table 1: The 1981 geosciences articles most cited in 1981-1983, *ISI/GeoSciTech™*, in alphabetic order by first author. Code numbers indicate the ISI® research front specialties for which these are core papers. A=1981 citations. B=1982 citations. C=1983 citations. D=total citations. E=bibliographic data.

A	B	C	D	E
3	13	21	37	**Akasofu S-I.** Energy coupling between the solar wind and the magnetosphere. *Space Sci. Rev.* 28:121-90, 1981. Univ. Alaska, Geophys. Inst., Fairbanks, AK. 83-0390
1	7	20	28	**Angell J K.** Comparison of variations in atmospheric quantities with sea surface temperature variations in the equatorial eastern Pacific. *Mon. Weather Rev.* 109:230-43, 1981. NOAA, Air Resources Labs., Silver Spring, MD; CSIRO, Div. Atmos. Phys., Victoria, Australia. 83-0958
10	7	12	29	**Arnold F, Henschen G & Ferguson E E.** Mass spectrometric measurements of fractional ion abundances in the stratosphere—positive ions. *Planet. Space Sci.* 29:185-93, 1981. Max Planck Inst. Nucl. Phys., Heidelberg, FRG.
2	6	17	25	**Atlas E & Giam C S.** Global transport of organic pollutants: ambient concentrations in the remote marine atmosphere. *Science* 211:163-5, 1981. Texas A & M Univ., Chem. Dept., College Station, TX.
7	20	25	52	**Bagenal F & Sullivan J D.** Direct plasma measurements in the Io torus and inner magnetosphere of Jupiter. *J. Geophys. Res.—Space Phys.* 86:8447-66, 1981. Mass. Inst. Technol., Ctr. Space Res., Cambridge, MA. 83-1538
2	12	12	26	**Baker D N, Hones E W, Payne J B & Feldman W C.** A high time resolution study of interplanetary parameter correlations with AE. *Geophys. Res. Lett.* 8:179-82, 1981. Univ. California, Los Alamos Sci. Lab., Los Alamos, NM.
3	13	14	30	**Balistrieri L, Brewer P G & Murray J W.** Scavenging residence times of trace metals and surface chemistry of sinking particles in the deep ocean. *Deep-Sea Res. Pt. A—Oceanog. Res.* 28:101-21, 1981. Woods Hole Oceanogr. Inst., Woods Hole, MA; Univ. Washington, Dept. Oceanogr., Seattle, WA.
3	11	11	25	**Balluffi R W & Cahn J W.** Mechanism for diffusion induced grain boundary migration. *Acta Met.* 29:493-500, 1981. Mass. Inst. Technol., Dept. Mater. Sci. Eng., Cambridge, MA; Natl. Bur. Stand., Ctr. Mater. Sci., Washington, DC. 83-1708
10	7	11	28	**Barrie L A, Hoff R M & Daggupaty S M.** The influence of mid-latitudinal pollution sources on haze in the Canadian Arctic. *Atmos. Environ.* 15:1407-19, 1981. Atmos. Environ. Serv., Toronto, Canada.
0	11	15	26	**Ben-Avraham Z, Nur A, Jones D & Cox A.** Continental accretion: from oceanic plateaus to allochthonous terranes. *Science* 213:47-54, 1981. Stanford Univ., Dept. Geophys., Stanford; US Geol. Survey, Menlo Park, CA. 83-1145
2	9	18	29	**Benjamin M M & Leckie J O.** Multiple-site adsorption of Cd, Cu, Zn, and Pb on amorphous iron oxyhydroxide. *J. Colloid Interface Sci.* 79:209-21, 1981. Univ. Washington, Seattle, WA; Stanford Univ., Stanford, CA. 83-1353
13	6	8	27	**Boudier F & Coleman R G.** Cross section through the peridotite in the Samail ophiolite, Southeastern Oman Mountains. *J. Geophys. Res.* 86:2573-92, 1981. Univ. Nantes, Tectonophys. Lab., Nantes, France; US Geol. Survey, Menlo Park, CA.
10	17	22	49	**Bridge H S, Belcher J W, Lazarus A J, Olbert S, Sullivan J D, Bagenal F, Gazis P R, Hartle R E, Ogilvie K W, Scudder J D, Sittler E C, Eviatar A, Siscoe G L, Goertz C K & Vasyliunas V M.** Plasma observations near Saturn: initial results from Voyager 1. *Science* 212:217-24, 1981. Mass. Inst. Technol., Ctr. Space Res. & Dept. Phys., Cambridge, MA; NASA/Goddard Space Flight Ctr., Lab. Planet. Atmos. & Lab. Extraterrest. Phys., Greenbelt, MD; Univ. California, Dept. Atmos. Sci., Los Angeles, CA; Max Planck Inst. Aeronom., Katlenburg-Lindau, FRG; Univ. Iowa, Iowa City, IA. 82-1234
16	24	25	65	**Broadfoot A L, Sandel B R, Shemansky D E, Holberg J B, Smith G R, Strobel D F, McConnell J C, Kumar S, Hunten D M, Atreya S K, Donahue T M, Moos H W, Bertaux J L, Blamont J E, Pomphrey R B & Linick S.** Extreme ultraviolet observations from Voyager 1 encounter with Saturn. *Science* 212:206-11, 1981. Univ. S. California, Earth Space Sci. Inst.; Univ. Arizona, Tucson, AZ; Naval Res. Lab., Washington, DC; York Univ., Toronto, Canada; Univ. S. California, Los Angeles; Jet Propulsion Lab., Pasadena, CA; Univ. Michigan, Ann Arbor, MI; Johns Hopkins Univ., Baltimore, MD; CNRS, Serv. Aeronom., Verrieres-le-Buisson, France. 83-3458; 82-1234
7	12	10	29	**Broadfoot A L, Sandel B R, Shemansky D E, McConnell J C, Smith G R, Holberg J B, Atreya S K, Donahue T M, Strobel D F & Bertaux J L.** Overview of the Voyager ultraviolet spectrometry results through Jupiter encounter. *J. Geophys. Res.—Space Phys.* 86:8259-84, 1981. Univ. S. California, Earth Space Sci. Inst., Tucson, AZ; Univ. Michigan, Ann Arbor, MI; Naval Res. Lab., Washington, DC; CNRS, Serv. Aeronom., Verrieres-le-Buisson, France.

A	B	C	D	E

6 14 11 31 **Brown R A.**The Jupiter hot plasma torus: observed electron temperature and energy flows. *Astrophys. J.* 244:1072-80, 1981. Univ. Arizona, Lunar Planet. Lab., Tucson, AZ.

0 3 24 27 **Carlson R W, Lugmair G W & MacDougall J D.** Columbia River volcanism: the question of mantle heterogeneity or crustal contamination. *Geochim. Cosmochim. Acta* 45:2483-99, 1981. Univ. California, San Diego, Scripps Inst. Oceanogr., La Jolla, CA. 83-4040

7 10 9 26 **Cavanaugh C M, Gardiner S L, Jones M L, Jannasch H W & Waterbury J B.** Prokaryotic cells in the hydrothermal vent tube worm *Riftia pachyptila* Jones: possible chemoautotrophic symbionts. *Science* 213:340-2, 1981. Harvard Univ., Museum Compar. Zool., Cambridge; Woods Hole Oceanogr. Inst., Woods Hole, MA; Smithsonian Inst., Natl. Museum Nat. Hist., Washington, DC.

0 16 16 32 **Chase C G.** Oceanic island Pb: two-stage histories and mantle evolution. *Earth Planet. Sci. Lett.* 52:277-84, 1981. Univ. Minnesota, Dept. Geol. Geophys., Minneapolis, MN. 82-0401

3 5 20 28 **Cheney R E & Marsh J G.** Seasat altimeter observations of dynamic topography in the Gulf Stream region. *J. Geophys. Res.—Ocean. Atmos.* 86:473-83, 1981. NASA/Goddard Space Flight Ctr., Geodynam. Branch, Greenbelt, MD.

1 9 16 26 **Coffey M T & Mankin W G.** Simultaneous spectroscopic determination of the latitudinal, seasonal, and diurnal variability of stratospheric N_2O, NO, NO_2, and HNO_3. *J. Geophys. Res.—Ocean. Atmos.* 86:7331-41, 1981. Natl. Ctr. Atmos. Res., Boulder; Univ. Denver, Dept. Phys., Denver, CO. 83-4567

0 10 16 26 **Cook F A, Brown L D, Kaufman S, Oliver J E & Petersen T A.** COCORP seismic profiling of the Appalachian orogen beneath the Coastal Plain of Georgia. *Geol. Soc. Amer. Bull. Pt. 1* 92:738-48, 1981. Cornell Univ., Dept. Geol. Sci., Ithaca, NY.

3 10 13 26 **DePaolo D J.** Nd isotopic studies: some new perspectives on earth structure and evolution. *Eos* 62:137-40, 1981. Univ. California, Dept. Earth Space Sci., Los Angeles, CA.

2 7 17 26 **DePaolo D J.** Neodymium isotopes in the Colorado Front Range and crust-mantle evolution in the Proterozoic. *Nature* 291:193-6, 1981. Univ. California, Dept. Earth Space Sci., Los Angeles, CA.

2 17 28 47 **DePaolo D J.** Trace element and isotopic effects of combined wallrock assimilation and fractional crystallization. *Earth Planet. Sci. Lett.* 53:189-202, 1981. Univ. California, Dept. Earth Space Sci., Los Angeles, CA. 82-1169

5 17 16 38 **Desch M D & Kaiser M L.** Voyager measurement of the rotation period of Saturn's magnetic field. *Geophys. Res. Lett.* 8:253-6, 1981. NASA/Goddard Space Flight Ctr., Lab. Extraterr. Phys., Greenbelt, MD. 83-3458; 82-1234

1 12 24 37 **Dickinson R E, Ridley E C & Roble R G.** A three-dimensional general circulation model of the thermosphere. *J. Geophys. Res.—Space Phys.* 86:1499-512, 1981. Natl. Ctr. Atmos. Res., Boulder, CO. 83-0390

0 19 20 39 **Dresselhaus M S & Dresselhaus G.** Intercalation compounds of graphite. *Advan. Phys.* 30:139-326, 1981. Mass. Inst. Technol., Cambridge, MA. 83-4677

7 14 15 36 **Dunkerton T, Hsu C-P F & McIntyre M E.** Some Eulerian and Lagrangian diagnostics for a model stratospheric warming. *J. Atmos. Sci.* 38:819-43, 1981. Univ. Washington, Dept. Atmos. Sci., Seattle, WA.

0 11 17 28 **Dusenbery P B & Lyons L R.** Generation of ion-conic distribution by upgoing ionospheric electrons. *J. Geophys. Res.—Space Phys.* 86:7627-38, 1981. NOAA/ERL, Space Environ. Lab., Boulder, CO.

2 30 47 79 **Dziewonski A M & Anderson D L.** Preliminary reference Earth model. *Phys. Earth Planet. Interiors* 25:297-356, 1981. Harvard Univ., Dept. Geol. Sci., Cambridge, MA; Calif. Inst. Technol., Seismol. Lab., Pasadena, CA. 83-0408; 83-1921

3 10 14 27 **Dziewonski A M, Chou T-A & Woodhouse J H.** Determination of earthquake source parameters from waveform data for studies of global and regional seismicity. *J. Geophys. Res.* 86:2825-52, 1981. Harvard Univ., Dept. Geol. Sci., Cambridge, MA.

14 18 30 62 **Gorney D J, Clarke A, Croley D, Fennell J, Luhmann J & Mizera P.** The distribution of ion beams and conics below 8000 km. *J. Geophys. Res.—Space Phys.* 86:83-9, 1981. Aerospace Corp., Space Sci. Lab., Los Angeles, CA. 83-0390; 82-1086

8 14 15 37 **Gregory R T & Taylor H P.** An oxygen isotope profile in a section of cretaceous oceanic crust, Samail ophiolite, Oman: evidence for δ^{18}O buffering of the oceans by deep (> 5 km) seawater-hydrothermal circulation at mid-ocean ridges. *J. Geophys. Res.* 86:2737-55, 1981. Calif. Inst. Technol., Div. Geol. Planet. Sci., Pasadena, CA.

11 12 17 40 **Gurnett D A, Kurth W S & Scarf F L.** Plasma waves near Saturn: initial results from Voyager 1. *Science* 212:235-9, 1981. Univ. Iowa, Dept. Phys. Astron., Iowa City, IA; TRW Defense Space Syst. Group, Space Sci. Dept., Redondo Beach, CA.

A	B	C	D	E

13 40 34 87 **Hanel R, Conrath B, Flasar F M, Kunde V, Maguire W, Pearl J, Pirraglia J, Samuelson R, Herath L, Allison M, Cruikshank D, Gautier D, Gierasch P, Horn L, Koppany R & Ponnamperuma C.** Orbits of the small satellites of Saturn. *Science* 212:192-200, 1981. NASA/Goddard Space Flight Ctr., Greenbelt; Univ. Maryland, College Park, MD; Rice Univ., Houston, TX; Univ. Hawaii, Honolulu, HI; Paris Observ., Meudon, France; Cornell Univ., Ithaca, NY; Jet Propulsion Lab., Pasadena, CA. 83-3458; 82-1234

2 25 44 71 **Hansen J, Johnson D, Lacis A, Lebedeff S, Lee P, Rind D & Russell G.** Climate impact of increasing atmospheric carbon dioxide. *Science* 213:957-66, 1981. NASA/Goddard Space Flight Ctr., Greenbelt, MD; Columbia Univ.; Goddard Inst. Space Stud., New York, NY. 83-5753; 82-2384

6 22 19 47 **Harel M, Wolf R A, Reiff P H, Spiro R W, Burke W J, Rich F J & Smiddy M.** Quantitative simulation of a magnetospheric substorm. 1. Model logic and overview. *J. Geophys. Res.—Space Phys.* 86:2217-41, 1981. Rice Univ., Dept. Space Phys. Astron., Houston, TX; Regis Coll. Res. Ctr., Weston; Hanscom Air Force Base, Air Force Geophys. Lab., Bedford, MA. 83-0390; 82-0331

4 15 16 35 **Harel M, Wolf R A, Spiro R W, Reiff P H, Chen C-K, Burke W J, Rich F J & Smiddy M.** Quantitative simulation of a magnetospheric substorm. 2. Comparison with observations. *J. Geophys. Res.—Space Phys.* 86:2242-60, 1981. Rice Univ., Dept. Space Phys. Astron., Houston, TX; Regis Coll. Res. Ctr., Weston; Hanscom Air Force Base, Air Force Geophys. Lab., Bedford, MA.

1 15 22 38 **Haymon R M & Kastner M.** Hot spring deposits on the East Pacific Rise at 21 N: preliminary description of mineralogy and genesis. *Earth Planet. Sci. Lett.* 53:363-81, 1981. Univ. California, San Diego, Scripps Inst. Oceanogr., La Jolla, CA. 83-0867

1 7 34 42 **Hildreth W.** Gradients in silicic magma chambers: implications for lithospheric magmatism. *J. Geophys. Res.* 86:10153-92, 1981. US Geol. Survey, Menlo Park, CA. 83-1213

4 13 18 35 **Hoppe M M, Russell C T, Frank L A, Eastman T E & Greenstadt E W.** Upstream hydromagnetic waves and their association with backstreaming ion populations: ISEE 1 and 2 observations. *J. Geophys. Res.—Space Phys.* 86:4471-92, 1981. Univ. California, Inst. Geophys. Planet. Phys., Los Angeles; TRW Defense Space Syst. Group, Space Sci. Dept., Redondo Beach, CA; Univ. Iowa, Dept. Phys. Astron., Iowa City, IA.

12 8 14 34 **Hopson C A, Coleman R G, Gregory R T, Pallister J S & Bailey E H.** Geologic section through the Samail ophiolite and associated rocks along a Muscat-Ibra transect, Southeastern Oman Mountains. *J. Geophys. Res.* 86:2527-44, 1981. Univ. California, Santa Barbara; US Geol. Survey, Menlo Park; Calif. Inst. Technol., Pasadena, CA.

8 32 46 86 **Horel J D & Wallace J M.** Planetary-scale atmospheric phenomena associated with the Southern Oscillation. *Mon. Weather Rev.* 109:813-29, 1981. Univ. Washington, Dept. Atmos. Sci., Seattle, WA. 83-0958; 82-1054

5 24 30 59 **Hoskins B J & Karoly D J.** The steady linear response of a spherical atmosphere to thermal and orographic forcing. *J. Atmos. Sci.* 38:1179-96, 1981. Univ. Reading, UK Univs. Atmos. Modell. Group & Dept. Meteorol., Reading, UK. 83-0958; 82-1054

3 13 14 30 **Kamide Y, Richmond A D & Matsushita S.** Estimation of ionospheric electric fields, ionospheric currents, and field-aligned currents from ground magnetic records. *J. Geophys. Res.—Space Phys.* 86:801-13, 1981. Kyoto Sangyo (Indust.) Univ., Kyoto, Japan; NOAA Space Environ. Lab.; NCAR High Altitude Observ., Boulder, CO.

1 16 10 27 **Kanamori H & Given J W.** Use of long-period surface waves for rapid determination of earthquake-source parameters. *Phys. Earth Planet. Interiors* 27:8-31, 1981. Calif. Inst. Technol., Seismol. Lab., Pasadena, CA.

8 7 13 28 **Kley D, Drummond J W, McFarland M & Liu S C.** Tropospheric profiles of NO_x. *J. Geophys. Res.—Ocean. Atmos.* 86:3153-61, 1981. Natl. Ocean. Atmos. Admin. (NOAA), Aeronom. Lab., Boulder, CO.

3 12 15 30 **Krimigis S M, Armstrong T P, Axford W I, Bostrom C O, Gloeckler G, Keath E P, Lanzerotti L J, Carbary J F, Hamilton D C & Roelof E C.** Low-energy charged particles in Saturn's magnetosphere: results from Voyager 1. *Science* 212:225-31, 1981. Johns Hopkins Univ., Appl. Phys. Lab., Laurel; Univ. Maryland, Dept. Phys. Astron., College Park, MD; Univ. Kansas, Dept. Phys., Lawrence, KA; Max Planck Inst. Aeronom., Katlenburg-Lindau, FRG; Bell Labs., Murray Hill, NJ.

9 7 15 31 **Krimigis S M, Carbary J F, Keath E P, Bostrom C O, Axford W I, Gloeckler G, Lanzerotti L J & Armstrong T P.** Characteristics of hot plasma in the Jovian magnetosphere: results from the Voyager spacecraft. *J. Geophys. Res.—Space Phys.* 86:8227-57, 1981. Johns Hopkins Univ., Appl. Phys. Lab., Laurel; Univ. Maryland, Dept. Phys. Astron., College Park, MD; Max Planck Inst. Aeronom., Katlenburg-

A	B	C	D		E

Lindau, FRG; Bell Labs., Murray Hill, NJ; Univ. Kansas, Dept. Phys., Lawrence, KS.

0 8 17 25 Kukla G & Gavin J. Summer ice and carbon dioxide. *Science* 214:497-503, 1981. Columbia Univ., Lamont-Doherty Geol. Observ., Palisades, NY.

1 7 19 27 Kunde V G, Aikin A C, Hanel R A, Jennings D E, Maguire W C & Samuelson R E. C_4H_2, HC_3N and C_2N_2 in Titan's atmosphere. *Nature* 292:686-8, 1981. NASA/Goddard Space Flight Ctr., Greenbelt, MD.

1 6 20 27 Lang J K, Baer Y & Cox P A. Study of the 4f and valence band density of states in rare-earth metals: II. Experiment and results. *J. Phys. F—Metal Phys.* 11:121-38, 1981. Swiss Fed. Inst. Technol., Lab. Solid State Phys., Zurich, Switzerland; Oxford Univ., Dept. Inorg. Chem., Oxford, UK. 82-0411

0 7 28 35 Lawrence J M, Riseborough P S & Parks R D. Valence fluctuation phenomena. *Rep. Progr. Phys.* 44:1-84, 1981. Univ. California, Phys. Dept., Irvine, CA; Polytech. Inst. New York, Phys. Dept., New York, NY. 82-0412

5 3 23 31 Lee T N, Atkinson L P & Legeckis R. Observations of a Gulf Stream frontal eddy on the Georgia continental shelf, April 1977. *Deep-Sea Res. Pt. A—Oceanog. Res.* 28:347-78, 1981. Univ. Miami, Rosentiel Sch. Marine Atmos. Sci., Miami, FL; Skidaway Inst. Oceanogr., Savannah, GA; Natl. Ocean. Atmos. Admin. (NOAA), Natl. Environ. Satellite Serv., Washington, DC.

1 17 17 35 Le Pichon X & Sibuet J-C. Passive margins: a model of formation. *J. Geophys. Res.* 86:3708-20, 1981. Univ. Paris VI, Geodynam. Lab., Paris; Ctr. Oceanogr. Bretagne, Brest, France. 83-1537

0 17 21 38 Lindzen R S. Turbulence and stress owing to gravity wave and tidal breakdown. *J. Geophys. Res.—Ocean. Atmos.* 86:9707-14, 1981. Naval Res. Lab., Washington, DC and Harvard Univ., Ctr. Earth Planet. Phys., Cambridge, MA. 83-0924

3 17 37 57 Logan J A, Prather M J, Wofsy S C & McElroy M B. Tropospheric chemistry: a global perspective. *J. Geophys. Res.—Ocean. Atmos.* 86:7210-54, 1981. Harvard Univ., Ctr. Earth Planet. Phys., Cambridge, MA. 83-8298

1 13 24 38 Lowrie W & Alvarez W. One hundred million years of geomagnetic polarity history. *Geology* 9:392-7, 1981. Inst. Geophys., Zurich, Switzerland; Univ. California, Dept. Geol. Geophys., Berkeley, CA. 83-0687

19 21 21 61 Ness N F, Acuna M H, Lepping R P, Connerney J E P, Behannon K W, Burlaga L F & Neubauer F M. Magnetic field studies by Voyager 1: preliminary results at Saturn. *Science* 212:211-7, 1981. NASA/Goddard Space Flight Ctr., Lab. Extraterr. Phys., Greenbelt, MD; Tech. Univ., Braunschweig, FRG. 82-1234

3 11 18 32 North G R, Cahalan R F & Coakley J A. Energy balance climate models. *Rev. Geophys. Space Phys.* 19:91-121, 1981. NASA/Goddard Space Flight Ctr., Lab. Atmos. Sci., Greenbelt, MD; Natl. Ctr. Atmos. Res., Boulder, CO.

0 10 16 26 O'Hara M J & Mathews R E. Geochemical evolution in an advancing, periodically replenished, periodically tapped, continuously fractionated magma chamber. *J. Geol. Soc. London* 138:237-77, 1981. Univ. Wales, Univ. Coll. Wales, Aberystwyth, UK.

1 5 21 27 Okuda H & Ashour-Abdalla M. Formation of a conical distribution and intense ion heating in the presence of hydrogen cyclotron waves. *Geophys. Res. Lett.* 8:811-4, 1981. Univ. California, Dept. Phys. & Inst. Geophys. Planet. Phys., Los Angeles, CA.

12 13 18 43 Pallister J S & Hopson C A. Samail ophiolite plutonic suite: field relations, phase variation, cryptic variation and layering, and a model of a spreading ridge magma chamber. *J. Geophys. Res.* 86:2593-644, 1981. Univ. California, Dept. Geol. Sci., Santa Barbara, CA.

7 9 14 30 Palmer T N. Diagnostic study of a wavenumber-2 stratospheric sudden warming in a transformed Eulerian-mean formalism. *J. Atmos. Sci.* 38:844-55, 1981. Meteorol. Off., Bracknell, UK.

6 12 11 29 Phillips R J, Kaula W M, McGill G E & Malin M C. Tectonics and evolution of Venus. *Science* 212:879-87, 1981. Lunar Planet. Inst., Houston, TX; Univ. California, Dept. Earth Space Sci., Los Angeles, CA; Univ. Massachusetts, Dept. Geol. Geogr., Amherst, MA; Arizona State Univ., Dept. Geol., Tempe, AZ.

0 13 17 30 Ramanathan V. The role of ocean-atmosphere interactions in the CO_2 climate problem. *J. Atmos. Sci.* 38:918-30, 1981. Natl. Ctr. Atmos. Res., Boulder, CO. 83-5753

2 14 10 26 Rasmussen R A & Khalil M A K. Atmospheric methane (CH_4): trends and seasonal cycles. *J. Geophys. Res.—Ocean. Atmos.* 86:9826-32, 1981. Oregon Grad. Ctr., Dept. Environ. Sci., Beaverton, OR. 83-8298

7 6 18 31 Rasmussen R A, Khalil M A K & Dalluge R W. Atmospheric trace gases in Antarctica. *Science* 211:285-7, 1981. Oregon Grad. Ctr., Dept. Environ. Sci., Beaverton, OR.

A B C D
                                                                    E

0 10 26 36 **Reiff P H, Spiro R W & Hill T W.** Dependence of polar cap potential drop on interplanetary parameters. *J. Geophys. Res.—Space Phys.* 86:7639-48, 1981. Rice Univ., Space Phys. Astron. Dept., Houston, TX. 83-0390

2 12 12 26 **Rice A.** Convective fractionation: a mechanism to provide cryptic zoning (macrosegregation), layering, crescumulates, banded tuffs and explosive volcanism in igneous processes. *J. Geophys. Res.* 86:405-17, 1981. Univ. Newcastle upon Tyne, Sch. Phys., Newcastle upon Tyne, UK.

1 12 15 28 **Rice D D & Claypool G E.** Generation, accumulation, and resource potential of biogenic gas. *AAPG Bull.—Amer. Ass. Petrol. G.* 65:5-25, 1981. US Geol. Survey, Denver, CO. 83-1537

0 9 17 26 **Richter F M & McKenzie D P.** On some consequences and possible causes of layered mantle convection. *J. Geophys. Res.* 86:6133-42, 1981. Univ. Chicago, Dept. Geophys. Sci., Chicago, IL; Cambridge Univ., Dept. Earth Sci., Cambridge, UK.

1 11 21 33 **Rothman L S.** AFGL atmospheric absorption line parameters compilation: 1980 version. *Appl. Opt.* 20:791-5, 1981. US Air Force (USAF), Opt. Phys. Div., Hanscom AFB, MA. 83-4567

3 12 13 28 **Ruddiman W F & McIntyre A.** Oceanic mechanisms for amplification of the 23,000-year ice-volume cycle. *Science* 212:617-27, 1981. Columbia Univ., Lamont-Doherty Geol. Observ., Palisades; CUNY, Queens Coll., New York, NY.

3 13 15 31 **Samuelson R E, Hanel R A, Kunde V G & Maguire W C.** Mean molecular weight and hydrogen abundance of Titan's atmosphere. *Nature* 292:688-93, 1981. NASA/Goddard Space Flight Ctr., Greenbelt, MD.

4 12 19 35 **Schuetzle D, Lee F S-C, Prater T J & Tejada S B.** The identification of polynuclear aromatic hydrocarbon (PAH) derivatives in mutagenic fractions of diesel particulate extracts. *Int. J. Environ. Anal. Chem.* 9:93-144, 1981. Ford Motor Co., Anal. Sci. Dept., Dearborn, MI; US Environ. Protect. Agcy., Environ. Sci. Res. Lab., Research Triangle Park, NC. 82-2806

11 10 11 32 **Scudder J D, Sittler E C & Bridge H S.** A survey of the plasma electron environment of Jupiter: a view from Voyager. *J. Geophys. Res.—Space Phys.* 86:8157-79, 1981. NASA/Goddard Space Flight Ctr., Lab. Extraterr. Phys., Greenbelt, MD; Mass. Inst. Technol., Ctr. Space Res., Cambridge, MA.

2 10 13 25 **Sharp R D, Carr D L, Peterson W K & Shelley E G.** Ion streams in the magnetotail. *J. Geophys. Res.—Space Phys.* 86:4639-48, 1981. Lockheed Palo Alto Res. Lab., Palo Alto, CA.

22 62 52 136 **Smith B A, Soderblom L, Beebe R, Boyce J, Briggs G, Bunker A, Collins S A, Hansen C J, Johnson T V, Mitchell J L, Terrile R J, Carr M, Cook A F, Cuzzi J, Pollack J B, Danielson G E, Ingersoll A, Davies M E, Hunt G E, Masursky H, Shoemaker E, Morrison D, Owen T, Sagan C, Veverka J, Strom R & Suomi V E.** Encounter with Saturn: Voyager 1 imaging science results. *Science* 212:163-91, 1981. Univ. Arizona, Dept. Planet. Sci. & Lunar Planet. Lab., Tucson; US Geol. Survey, Flagstaff, AZ; New Mexico State Univ., Dept. Astron., Las Cruces, NM; NASA Headquarters, Washington, DC; Calif. Inst. Technol., Jet Propulsion Lab. & Div. Geol. Planet. Sci., Pasadena; US Geol. Survey, Menlo Park; NASA/Ames Res. Ctr., Moffett Field; Rand Corp., Santa Monica, CA; Ctr. Astrophys., Cambridge, MA; Univ. Coll. London, London, UK; Univ. Hawaii, Inst. Astron., Honolulu, HI; SUNY, Dept. Earth Space Sci., Stony Brook; Cornell Univ., Ithaca, NY; Univ. Wisconsin, Madison, WI. 83-3458; 82-1234

0 15 11 26 **Sorensen J, Christensen D & Jorgensen B B.** Volatile fatty acids and hydrogen as substrates for sulfate-reducing bacteria in anaerobic marine sediment. *Appl. Environ. Microbiol.* 42:5-11, 1981. Univ. Aarhus, Inst. Ecol. Genet., Aarhus, Denmark. 82-0159

1 10 18 29 **Styrt M M, Brackmann A J, Holland H D, Clark B C, Pisutha-Arnond V, Eldridge C S & Ohmoto H.** The mineralogy and the isotopic composition of sulfur in hydrothermal sulfide/sulfate deposits on the East Pacific Rise, 21 N latitude. *Earth Planet. Sci. Lett.* 53:382-90, 1981. Mass. Inst. Technol., Dept. Earth Planet. Sci.; Harvard Univ., Dept. Geol. Sci., Cambridge, MA; Martin Marietta Aerospace, Denver, CO; Penn. State Univ., Dept. Geosci., University Park, PA.

2 12 20 34 **Suresh S, Zamiski G F & Ritchie R O.** Oxide-induced crack closure: an explanation for near-threshold corrosion fatigue crack growth behavior. *Met. Trans. A—Phys. Met. Mater. Sc.* 12:1435-43, 1981. Mass. Inst. Technol., Dept. Mech. Eng., Cambridge, MA; McDonnell-Douglas Corp., Redondo Beach; Univ. California, Dept. Mater. Sci. Mineral Eng. & Lawrence Berkeley Lab., Berkeley, CA. 83-1808

A	B	C	D	E
1	9	19	29	**Taylor S R & McLennan S M.** The composition and evolution of the continental crust: rare earth element evidence from sedimentary rocks. *Phil. Trans. Roy. Soc. London A* 301:381-99, 1981. Australian Natl. Univ., Res. Sch. Earth Sci., Canberra, Australia.
5	14	12	31	**Tipping E.** The adsorption of aquatic humic substances by iron oxides. *Geochim. Cosmochim. Acta* 45:191-9, 1981. Freshwater Biol. Assn., Ambleside, UK.
8	10	9	27	**Tsunoda R T.** Time evolution and dynamics of equatorial backscatter plumes. 1. Growth phase. *J. Geophys. Res.—Space Phys.* 86:139-49, 1981. SRI Intl., Menlo Park, CA.
11	32	36	79	**Tyler G L, Eshleman V R, Anderson J D, Levy G S, Lindal G F, Wood G E & Croft T A.** Radio science investigations of the Saturn system with Voyager 1: preliminary results. *Science* 212:201-6, 1981. Stanford Univ., Ctr. Radar Astron., Stanford; Calif. Inst. Technol., Jet Propulsion Lab., Pasadena; SRI Intl., Radio Phys. Lab., Menlo Park, CA. 83-3458; 82-1234
14	32	1	47	**Vaiana G S, Cassinelli J P, Fabbiano G, Giacconi R, Golub L, Gorenstein P, Haisch B M, Harnden F R, Johnson H M, Linsky J L, Maxson C W, Mewe R, Rosner R, Seward F, Topka K & Zwaan C.** Results from an extensive *Einstein* stellar survey. *Astrophys. J.* 245:163-82, 1981. Harvard-Smithsonian Ctr. Astrophys., Cambridge, MA. 81-1691; 83-0564
3	11	14	28	**van Loon H & Madden R A.** The Southern Oscillation. Part I: global associations with pressure and temperature in northern winter. *Mon. Weather Rev.* 109:1150-62, 1981. Natl. Ctr. Atmos. Res., Boulder, CO.
5	13	13	31	**Vickrey J F, Vondrak R R & Matthews S J.** The diurnal and latitudinal variation of auroral zone ionospheric conductivity. *J. Geophys. Res.—Space Phys.* 86:65-75, 1981. SRI Intl., Radio Phys. Lab., Menlo Park, CA.
5	17	24	46	**Wallace J M & Gutzler D S.** Teleconnections in the geopotential height field during the Northern Hemisphere winter. *Mon. Weather Rev.* 109:784-812, 1981. Univ. Washington, Dept. Atmos. Sci., Seattle, WA. 83-0958
4	18	9	31	**Wallis D D & Budzinski E E.** Empirical models of height integrated conductivities. *J. Geophys. Res.—Space Phys.* 86:125-37, 1981. Natl. Res. Council Canada, Herzberg Inst. Astrophys., Ottawa, Canada. 82-0331
13	16	18	47	**Warwick J W, Pearce J B, Evans D R, Carr T D, Schauble J J, Alexander J K, Kaiser M L, Desch M D, Pedersen M, Lecacheux A, Daigne G, Boischot A & Barrow C H.** Planetary radio astronomy observations from Voyager 1 near Saturn. *Science* 212:239-43, 1981. Radiophys., Inc., Boulder, CO; Univ. Florida, Dept. Astron., Gainesville, FL; NASA/Goddard Space Flight Ctr., Lab. Extraterr. Phys., Greenbelt, MD; Sect. Astrophys. Meudon, Paris Observ., Meudon, France. 83-3458; 82-1234
2	19	20	41	**Webster P J.** Mechanisms determining the atmospheric response to sea surface temperature anomalies. *J. Atmos. Sci.* 38:554-71, 1981. CSIRO, Div. Atmos. Phys., Victoria, Australia. 82-1054
0	10	19	29	**Williamson P G.** Palaeontological documentation of speciation in Cenozoic molluscs from Turkana Basin. *Nature* 293:437-43, 1981. Harvard Univ., Museum Compar. Zool., Cambridge, MA. 83-5706
4	20	15	39	**Willson R C, Gulkis S, Janssen M, Hudson H S & Chapman G A.** Observations of solar irradiance variability. *Science* 211:700-2, 1981. Calif. Inst. Technol., Jet Propulsion Lab., Pasadena; Univ. California, San Diego, Ctr. Astrophys. Space Sci., La Jolla; California State Univ., San Fernando Observ., Northridge, CA.
0	15	13	28	**Woodruff F, Savin S M & Douglas R G.** Miocene stable isotope record: a detailed deep Pacific ocean study and its paleoclimatic implications. *Science* 212:665-8, 1981. Univ. S. California, Dept. Geol. Sci., Los Angeles, CA; Case Western Reserve Univ., Dept. Geol. Sci., Cleveland, OH.
0	10	17	27	**Young D T, Perraut S, Roux A, de Villedary C, Gendrin R, Korth A, Kremser G & Jones D.** Wave-particle interactions near ΩHe^+ observed on GEOS 1 and 2. 1. Propagation of ion cyclotron waves in He$^+$-rich plasma. *J. Geophys. Res.—Space Phys.* 86:6755-72, 1981. Univ. Bern, Phys. Inst., Bern, Switzerland; Ctr. Res. Phys. Environ., Terr. Planet & Ctr. Natl. Stud. Telecommun., Issy-les-Moulineaux, France; Max Planck Inst. Aeronom., Katlenburg-Lindau, FRG; ESTEC, Space Sci. Dept., Noordwijk, Holland.
8	17	1	26	**Zamorani G, Henry J P, Maccacaro T, Tananbaum H, Soltan A, Avni Y, Liebert J, Stocke J, Strittmatter P A, Weymann R J, Smith M G & Condon J J.** X-ray studies of quasars with the *Einstein* observatory. II. *Astrophys. J.* 245:357-74, 1981. Harvard-Smithsonian Ctr. Astrophys., Cambridge, MA; Copernicus Astron. Ctr., Warsaw, Poland; Weizmann Inst. Sci., Rehovot, Israel; Univ. Arizona, Steward Observ., Tucson, AZ; Royal Observ., Edinburgh, UK; Natl. Radio Astron. Observ. & Virginia Polytech. Inst. State Univ., Dept. Phys., Blacksburg, VA. 83-0564; 82-1178

Table 2: 1981, 1982, and 1983 ISI® research fronts for which the papers in this study are core documents. A=research front number. B=research front name. C=number of geosciences papers in the core of each research front. D=total number of core papers in each research front.

A	B	C	D
81-1691	X-ray astrophysics	1	2
82-0159	Kinetics of bacterial methanogenesis and sulfate reduction in estuarine and marine sediments	1	19
82-0331	Relationships between field-aligned currents and auroral phenomena	2	20
82-0401	Isotope geochemistry of oceanic basalts and mantle evolution; isotope geochemistry of oceanic basalts, island arc magmas and continental rocks	1	22
82-0411	Photoemission studies of surface core-level binding energy shifts in rare-earth metal compounds	1	3
82-0412	Photoemission studies of mixed valence and 4F-surface chemical shifts in cerium compounds	1	4
82-1054	Tropical sea-surface temperature-field and surface wind-field variability associated with Southern Oscillation El-Nino	3	7
82-1086	Magnetosphere-ionosphere coupling and auroral plasma	1	15
82-1169	Geochemical studies of volcanic rocks and the mantle	1	3
82-1178	X-ray emission from quasars, Seyfert galaxies and active galactic nuclei	1	12
82-1234	Voyager 1 and Voyager 2 observations of Saturn and Titan and analysis of rings of Saturn, magnetosphere and atmosphere	8	9
82-1921	Seismic wave investigations of mantle and core structure	1	2
82-2384	Effects of increased carbon dioxide in the atmosphere on the climate	1	5
82-2806	Isolation, identification and mutagenic properties of nitrated polycyclic aromatic hydrocarbons	1	4
83-0390	Auroral processes and the magnetosphere and ionosphere	5	33
83-0408	Crustal and mantle velocity structures using earthquake data and inversion techniques	1	14
83-0564	X-ray, radio and optical observations of Seyfert galaxies, stars, quasi-stellar objects and other objects	2	56
83-0687	Cretaceous and early tertiary magnetic stratigraphy and biostratigraphy	1	7
83-0867	Deep-sea drilling project results: hydrothermal mounds of the Galapagos Rift and other spreading centers	1	12
83-0924	Models and observations of baroclinic instability and other middle atmosphere flows	1	34
83-0958	Equatorial Pacific sea-surface temperatures and climate: the El-Nino Southern Oscillation	4	15
83-1145	Paleomagnetic and tectonic studies: determining the structure and evolution of the crust and upper mantle	1	51
83-1213	Origin and geochemistry of granites and other igneous rocks	1	14
83-1353	Adsorption properties and other surface properties of ruthenium dioxide and related oxide catalysts in aqueous solution	1	36
83-1537	Hydrocarbon generation and subsidence, thermal evolution and organic geochemistry of sedimentary basins	2	27
83-1538	Observation and properties of the Io plasma torus and its interaction with the Jovian magnetosphere	1	2
83-1708	Diffusion induced grain-boundary migration and related processes in copper alloys	1	5
83-1808	Fatigue crack growth and fracture toughness in steels and other materials	1	33
83-3458	Voyager observations of Saturn's ring magnetosphere and ice-rich satellites with emphasis on Titan and its atmosphere	6	23
83-4040	Evidence for mantle and crust evolution from mineralogy and trace element chemistry of the Columbia River basalts	1	2
83-4567	Measurements of atmospheric constituents by infrared spectroscopy	2	8
83-4677	Structure and properties of graphite intercalation compounds including those containing potassium and other alkali metals	1	14
83-5706	Systematics, biogeography, cladistic analysis and aspects of phylogenetic relationships in patterns of speciation and evolution	1	20
83-5753	Relationship of atmospheric carbon dioxide and changes in climate and global sea level	2	11
83-8298	Sources and distributions of atmospheric ozone, methane and carbon monoxide	2	3

Table 3: The number of authors on the geosciences papers. A=number of authors. B=number of papers having that number of authors.

A	B
27	1
16	3
15	1
13	1
12	1
10	2
8	3
7	5
6	2
5	5
4	8
3	20
2	30
1	17

Table 4: The 30 journals represented on the list of the 99 geosciences papers most cited 1981-1983. The numbers in parentheses are the impact factors for the journals. (1983 impact factor equals the number of 1983 citations received by 1981-1982 articles, divided by the number of articles published by the journal during the same period.) The figures at the right indicate the number of papers from each journal which appear on the list.

Journal	No. of Papers
*J. Geophys. Res. (3.71)	32
Science (7.41)	19
J. Atmos. Sci. (3.17)	5
Earth Planet. Sci. Lett. (3.34)	4
Mon. Weather Rev. (2.62)	4
Nature (9.26)	4
Astrophys. J. (3.94)	3
Geophys. Res. Lett. (2.93)	3
Deep-Sea Res. Pt. A—Oceanog. Res. (NA)	2
Geochim. Cosmochim. Acta (3.54)	2
Phys. Earth Planet. Interiors (1.75)	2
AAPG Bull.—Amer. Ass. Petrol. G. (1.36)	1
Acta Met. (2.07)	1
Advan. Phys. (12.76)	1
Appl. Environ. Microbiol. (2.08)	1
Appl. Opt. (1.81)	1
Atmos. Environ. (1.97)	1
Eos (NA)	1
Geol. Soc. Amer. Bull. (1.76)	1
Geology (2.37)	1
Int. J. Environ. Anal. Chem. (1.36)	1
J. Colloid Interface Sci. (1.48)	1
J. Geol. Soc. (1.88)	1
J. Phys. F—Metal Phys. (2.24)	1
Met. Trans. A—Phys. Met. Mater. Sc. (1.39)	1
Phil. Trans. Roy. Soc. London A (1.58)	1
Planet. Space Sci. (2.14)	1
Rep. Progr. Phys. (7.18)	1
Rev. Geophys. Space Phys. (4.46)	1
Space Sci. Rev. (1.74)	1

*Includes J. Geophys. Res., J. Geophys. Res—Space Phys., and J. Geophys. Res.—Ocean. Atmos.

small number of journals accounts for the majority of high-impact papers and citations.

Ninety-one institutions were listed on the articles. In Table 5, they are shown in descending order by the number of times they appear in Table 1. Authors based at US institutions appeared on 85 papers. The UK was represented on nine papers, France on seven, and the Federal Republic of Germany (FRG) on six. Australia, Canada, and Switzerland account for three papers each. Denmark, Holland, Israel, Japan, and Poland contributed one paper each.

Of course, many of these papers were multinational collaborations. For example, of the 85 US papers, 15 listed coauthors from Australia, Canada, France, FRG, Israel, Japan, Poland, Switzerland, and the UK. Seventy papers listed *only* US authors. Table 6 shows the total number of papers from each of the 12 nations represented in this study. Also shown are the number that were multinationally coauthored, and the national affiliations of the collaborators. Although these high-impact geosciences papers were from a dozen nations, every one was published in English.

Seven authors in Table 1 were among the 1,000 contemporary scientists most cited from 1965 through 1978.[5] They are: S.-I. Akasofu, E.E. Ferguson, R. Giacconi, X. Le Pichon, M.B. McElroy, N.F. Ness, and R.J. Phillips. Interestingly, Le Pichon was the only geophysicist listed in that study. The specialties of the others include aeronomy, astronomy, inorganic chemistry, and physics.

More than 25 astrosciences papers are in Table 1. Most of these deal with planetary science research, the study of the components of our solar system other than the sun, including the solid, liquid, and gaseous parts of other planets. Indeed, 17 papers report results

Table 5: The institutional affiliations of the authors on the list. Institutions are listed in descending order of the number of times they appear in Table 1.

Institution	Frequency
Univ. California, CA	16
Los Angeles	7
San Diego[1]	3
Berkeley	2
Santa Barbara	2
Irvine	1
Los Alamos, NM	1
NASA	13
Goddard Space Flight Ctr., Greenbelt, MD	11
Ames Res. Ctr., Moffett Field, CA	1
Headquarters, Washington, DC	1
California Inst. Technol., Pasadena, CA	10
Harvard Univ., Cambridge, MA[2]	10
Massachusetts Inst. Technol., Cambridge, MA	7
US Geol. Survey	7
Menlo Park, CA	5
Denver, CO	1
Flagstaff, AZ	1
Natl. Ctr. Atmos. Res. (NCAR), Boulder, CO	6
Max Planck Soc., FRG	5
Inst. Aeronom., Katlenburg-Lindau	4
Inst. Nucl. Phys., Heidelberg	1
Natl. Ocean Atmos. Admin. (NOAA)	5
Boulder, CO	3
Silver Spring, MD	1
Washington, DC	1
Univ. Washington, Seattle, WA	5
Rice Univ., Houston, TX	4
Univ. Arizona, Tucson, AZ	4
Univ. S. California, CA	4
Los Angeles	2
Tucson, AZ	2
Columbia Univ., NY	3
Palisades	2
New York City	1
Cornell Univ., Ithaca, NY	3
Johns Hopkins Univ., MD	3
Laurel	2
Baltimore	1
SRI Intl., Menlo Park, CA	3
Stanford Univ., CA	3
Univ. Iowa, Iowa City, IA	3
Univ. Maryland, College Park, MD	3
USAF, Hanscom AFB, Bedford, MA	3
USN, Naval Res. Lab., Washington, DC	3
Bell Labs., Murray Hill, NJ	2
CNRS, Serv. Aeronom., Verrieres-le-Buisson, France	2
CSIRO, Div. Atmos. Phys., Victoria, Australia	2
Oregon Grad. Ctr., Beaverton, OR	2
Paris Observ., Meudon, France	2
Regis Coll., Weston, MA	2
Swiss Fed. Inst. Technol., Zurich, Switzerland	2
Geophys. Inst. & Swiss Earthquake Serv.	1
Solid State Phys. Lab.	1
TRW Defense Space Syst. Group, Redondo Beach, CA	2
Univ. Hawaii, Honolulu, HI	2
Univ. Kansas, Lawrence, KA	2
Univ. Michigan, Ann Arbor, MI	2
Woods Hole Oceanogr. Inst., MA	2
Aerospace Corp., Los Angeles, CA	1
Arizona State Univ., Tempe, AZ	1
Atmos. Environ. Serv., Toronto, Canada	1
Australian Natl. Univ., Canberra, Australia	1
California State Univ., Northridge, CA	1

Institution	Frequency
Cambridge Univ., UK	1
Case Western Reserve Univ., Cleveland, OH	1
Copernicus Astronom. Ctr., Warsaw, Poland	1
CUNY, New York, NY	1
Earth Planet. Environ. Phys. Res. Ctr., Issy-les-Moulineaux, France	1
ESTEC, Noordwijk, Holland	1
Ford Motor Co., Dearborn, MI	1
Goddard Inst. Space Stud., New York, NY	1
Kyoto Sangyo Univ., Kyoto, Japan	1
Lockheed Palo Alto Res. Lab., CA	1
Lunar Planet. Inst., Houston, TX	1
Martin Marietta Aerospace, Denver, CO	1
McDonnell-Douglas Corp., Redondo Beach, CA	1
Meteorol. Off., Bracknell, UK	1
Natl. Bur. Stand., Washington, DC	1
Natl. Ctr. Telecommun. Stud., Issy-les-Moulineaux, France	1
Natl. Environ. Res. Council (NERC), Freshwater Biol. Assn., Ambleside, UK	1
Natl. Radio Astron. Observ., Green Bank, WV	1
Natl. Res. Council Canada, Ottawa, Canada	1
New Mexico State Univ., Las Cruces, NM	1
ORSTOM, Ctr. Oceanol., Brest, France	1
Oxford Univ., UK	1
Pennsylvania State Univ., University Park, PA	1
Polytech. Inst. New York, NY	1
Radiophys., Inc., Boulder, CO	1
Rand Corp., Santa Monica, CA	1
Royal Observ., Edinburgh, UK	1
Skidaway Inst. Oceanogr., Savannah, GA	1
Smithsonian Inst., Washington, DC	1
SUNY, Stony Brook, NY	1
Tech. Univ., Braunschweig, FRG	1
Texas A&M Univ., College Station, TX	1
Univ. Aarhus, Denmark	1
Univ. Alaska, Fairbanks, AK	1
Univ. Bern, Switzerland	1
Univ. Chicago, IL	1
Univ. Denver, CO	1
Univ. Florida, Gainesville, FL	1
Univ. London, UK	1
Univ. Massachusetts, Amherst, MA	1
Univ. Miami, FL	1
Univ. Minnesota, Minneapolis, MN	1
Univ. Nantes, France	1
Univ. Newcastle upon Tyne, UK	1
Univ. Paris VI, France	1
Univ. Reading, UK	1
Univ. Wales, Aberystwyth, UK	1
Univ. Wisconsin, Madison, WI	1
US Environ. Protection Agcy., Research Triangle Park, NC	1
Virginia Polytech. Inst. State Univ., Blacksburg, VA	1
Weizmann Inst. Sci., Rehovot, Israel	1
York Univ., Toronto, Canada	1

[1]Includes Ctr. Astrophys. Space Sci. & Scripps Inst. Oceanogr., La Jolla, CA
[2]Includes Harvard-Smithsonian Ctr. Astrophys.

based on observations made by the US unmanned spacecraft *Voyager 1*, which flew past Jupiter in March 1979, and past Saturn in November 1980. Nine of these papers were published consecutively in the April 1981 issue of *Science*—includ-

Table 6: National affiliations of the authors of the 1981 geosciences papers most cited in 1981-1983, in order of the total number of papers on which each nation's authors appeared (column A). B=number of papers coauthored with scientists from other countries. C=nationalities of coauthors.

Country	A	B	C
US	85	15	Australia, Canada, France, FRG, Israel, Japan, Poland, Switzerland, UK
UK	9	4	Israel, Poland, Switzerland, US
France	7	6	Canada, FRG, Holland, Switzerland, US
FRG	6	5	France, Holland, Switzerland, US
Australia	3	1	US
Canada	3	1	France, US
Switzerland	3	3	France, FRG, Holland, UK, US
Denmark	1	0	
Holland	1	1	France, FRG, Switzerland
Israel	1	1	Poland, UK, US
Japan	1	1	US
Poland	1	1	Israel, UK, US

ing three of the five most-cited papers in this study. Roughly 25 other papers fall under the category of atmospheric science. Other specialties represented include oceanography, meteorology, geochemistry, and geophysics.

Five papers were cited at least 79 times each. The three papers based on *Voyager 1* data discuss various observations of Saturn and its satellite system. B.A. Smith and a team of 26 other researchers reported on the imaging science results of the *Voyager 1* mission. This paper received 136 citations—22 in 1981, 62 in 1982, and 52 in 1983. R. Hanel and colleagues discussed the orbits of Saturn's small satellites, some of which were first discovered by *Voyager 1*. Cited 87 times, the paper picked up 13 citations in 1981, 40 in 1982, and 34 in 1983. G.L. Tyler and colleagues presented the results of radio science investigations of the Saturn system. The paper received 79 citations—11 in 1981, 32 in 1982, and 36 in 1983.

The other two papers among the top five discuss the atmosphere and internal structure of the Earth itself. J.D. Horel and J.M. Wallace, University of Washington, Seattle, analyzed "Planetary-scale atmospheric phenomena associated with the Southern Oscillation." They discussed some of the effects associated with a global pattern of yearly fluctuations in sea-level air pressure, temperature, and precipitation. The paper was cited 86 times—eight times in 1981, 32 in 1982, and 46 in 1983.

A.M. Dziewonski, Harvard University, Cambridge, Massachusetts, and D.L. Anderson, California Institute of Technology, Pasadena, coauthored the paper entitled "Preliminary reference Earth model." It sets up a computer model of the Earth's internal structure which has numerous applications, including research on tides and the Earth's rotation. The paper was cited 79 times, twice in 1981, 30 times in 1982, and 47 in 1983.

It is interesting to note that at least two of the 99 geosciences papers are in fact directly related to the life sciences. One, by C.M. Cavanaugh, Museum of Comparative Zoology, Harvard University, and colleagues, suggests the existence of, and the symbiotic relationship between, tube worms and a type of sulfur-oxidizing bacteria. Both species thrive at the bottom of the ocean among the lava vents lining tectonic ridges. The other, by J. Sørensen, D. Christensen, and B.B. Jørgensen, all of the Institute of Ecology and Genetics, University of Aarhus, Denmark, describes some of the environmental requirements of coastal marine bacteria that metabolize sulfates. Both papers were cited 26 times each—the former receiving seven citations in 1981, ten in 1982, and nine in 1983, while the latter, published in July 1981, was not cited at all that year, but received 15 cites in 1982 and 11 in 1983. Their relatively quick impact indicates their importance for oceanographers and others who study the ever-changing dynamics of the sea.

This concludes our discussion of the 1981 earth sciences papers. Since a paper's lifetime citation expectancy can be forecasted reasonably well by its citation frequency within the first few years following its publication, it is safe to assume that most of the papers in this study will continue to be well cited in the future. Helmut A. Abt, Kitt Peak National Observatory, Tucson, Arizona, analyzed the citation histories of more than 300 astronomical papers.[6] He found that the highly cited papers did not peak in citations until seven years after publication. In contrast, less fre-quently cited papers reached their peak after four years. In addition, the high-impact papers had a longer citation history, reaching their "half-life" after 27 years. The half-life for the less frequently cited papers was just 16 years.

The composition of this list is, of course, determined by the data base used to identify the most-cited geosciences papers. Even within the relatively "narrow" scope of the earth sciences, there are small fields that produce important work. By examining the individual geoscience research fronts we identify each year, we can pinpoint creative work on specific topics. It will be interesting to see how each of these research fronts develops over the next several years.

* * * * *

My thanks to Stephen A. Bonaduce and Abigail W. Grissom for their help in the preparation of this essay. ©1984 ISI

REFERENCES

1. **Garfield E.** Journal citation studies. 41. Entomology journals—what they cite and what cites them. *Current Contents* (11):3-11, 12 March 1984.
2. --------------. The multidisciplinary impact of math and computer science is reflected in the 100 most-cited articles in *CompuMath Citation Index*, 1976-1980. *Current Contents* (31):3-10, 30 July 1984.
3. -------------. Introducing *ISI/GeoSciTech* and the *GeoSciTech Citation Index*—the 50 most-active research fronts in 1981 in the earth sciences illustrate the unique retrieval capabilities of our new online and print services. *Essays of an information scientist.* Philadelphia: ISI Press, 1983. Vol. 5. p. 607-14.
4. -------------. ABCs of cluster mapping. Parts 1 & 2. Most active fields in the life and physical sciences in 1978. *Essays of an information scientist.* Philadelphia: ISI Press, 1981. Vol. 4. p. 634-49.
5. -------------. The 1,000 contemporary scientists most-cited 1965-1978. Part 1. The basic list and introduction. *Essays of an information scientist.* Philadelphia: ISI Press, 1983. Vol. 5. p. 269-78.
6. **Abt H A.** Long-term citation histories of astronomical papers. *Publ. Astron. Soc. Pac.* 93:207-10, 1981.

Current Comments®

The 100 Most-Cited Books in the *CompuMath Citation Index*, 1976-1980

Number 34   August 20, 1984

We recently identified 100 articles that were most cited in the 1976-1980 *CompuMath Citation Index®* (*CMCI®*) cumulation.[1] We have now identified the 100 *books* most cited during the same five-year period. Although most of these books are on pure and applied mathematics, many come from disciplines such as computer science, mathematical physics, econometrics, and statistics. Available since 1982,[2] *CMCI* covers the literature of these fields as well as systems analysis, biometrics, psychometrics, and numerous medical fields that heavily depend on computers. For example, the index to *Research Fronts in ISI/CompuMath®*[3] includes emerging disciplines such as "Computer-Aided Diagnosis and Clinical Judgement" and "Knowledge Engineering and Computer-Aided Medical Decision Making." In short, *CMCI* accesses the literature *of interest to* researchers who rely heavily on computational theory and methods. More than 280,000 articles and books from 1976 to date, and the 3,000,000 references they cited, are included in the *CompuMath* data base.

Table 1 lists the 100 most-cited *CMCI* books, in alphabetic order by first author. The number of citations each received in *CMCI* is shown, followed by full bibliographic information. Forty-five of these books were previously identified in a study of the most-cited math publications from 1961 to 1972.[4] Six were discussed in *Citation Classic*™[5] commentaries. The issue, year, and edi-

tion of *Current Contents®* (*CC®*) in which these commentaries were published is also provided.

We have unified the varied types of citations to the works in this study. Some authors make only a general reference to a key book, while others clearly cite a particular page or chapter. Also, books may appear in several editions, including translations in different languages. We have combined all citations to these different editions and listed them in Table 1 with the bibliographic information for the earliest edition we could identify. It should be noted that our definition of a book is somewhat restricted. It does not include symposia proceedings or edited monographs in which each chapter is by an author different from the editors. While such publications are indexed in *Current Book Contents®* (*CBC®*)[6] and *Index to Scientific & Technical Proceedings®* (*ISTP®*),[7] citations to them can be found in *Science Citation Index®* (*SCI®*) and *CMCI*. They will be discussed in a separate essay.

The citation frequencies of the books in Table 1 ranged from 1,522 to 181. The average book was cited 382 times. In comparison, the 100 articles we identified[1] averaged 116 cites. Thus, high impact *CompuMath* books were cited three times more often than high impact articles. We found a similar ratio in a study based on *Social Sciences Citation Index®* (*SSCI®*) from 1969 to 1977.[8] However, the opposite situation was reported for the most-cited *SCI* works

Table 1: The 100 books most cited in 1976-1980 *CMCI®*, in alphabetic order by first author. A number symbol (#) indicates that the book also was one of the most-cited math publications in 1961-1972. An asterisk (*) indicates that the book was the subject of a *Citation Classic™* commentary. A=total *CMCI* citations, 1976-1980. B=bibliographic data.

A   B

513   **Aho A V, Hopcroft J E & Ullman J D.** *The design and analysis of computer algorithms.* Reading, MA: Addison-Wesley, 1974. 470 p.

297   **Aho A V & Ullman J D.** *The theory of parsing, translation, and compiling.* Englewood Cliffs, NJ: Prentice-Hall, 1972-73. 2 vols.

391   **#*Anderson T W.** *An introduction to multivariate statistical analysis.* New York: Wiley, 1958. 374 p. 10/79/PC&ES

197   **Barlow R E & Proschan F.** *Mathematical theory of reliability.* New York: Wiley, 1965. 256 p.

244   **Bass H.** *Algebraic K-theory.* New York: W.A. Benjamin, 1968. 762 p.

208   **Bellman R.** *Dynamic programming of continuous processes.* Santa Monica, CA: RAND Corp., 1954. 141 p.

325   **Berge C.** *Graphes et hypergraphes.* (Graphs and hypergraphs.) Paris: Dunod, 1970. 502 p.

519   **#Billingsley P.** *Convergence of probability measures.* New York: Wiley, 1968. 253 p.

319   **Birkhoff G.** *Lattice theory.* New York: American Mathematical Society, 1940. 155 p.

312   **Bourbaki N.** *Groupes et algebres de Lie.* (Lie algebra groups.) Paris: Hermann, 1960. 288 p.

608   **Box G E P & Jenkins G M.** *Time series analysis. Forecasting and control.* San Francisco, CA: Holden-Day, 1970. 553 p.

204   **Breiman L.** *Probability.* Reading, MA: Addison-Wesley, 1968. 421 p.

322   **#Cartan H P & Eilenberg S.** *Homological algebra.* Princeton, NJ: Princeton University Press, 1956. 390 p.

466   **#Clifford A H & Preston G B.** *The algebraic theory of semigroups.* Providence, RI: American Mathematical Society, 1961. 216 p.

408   **#Coddington E A & Levinson N.** *Theory of ordinary differential equations.* New York: McGraw-Hill, 1955. 429 p.

718   **#Courant R & Hilbert D.** *Methoden der mathematischen physik.* (Methods of mathematical physics.) Berlin: J. Springer, 1924. 2 vols.

340   **#*Cramer H.** *Mathematical methods of statistics.* Uppsala, Sweden: Almqvist & Wiksells, 1945. 575 p. 28/83/PC&ES

297   **Curtis C W & Reiner I.** *Representation theory of finite groups and associative algebras.* New York: Interscience, 1962. 685 p.

292   **Dantzig G B.** *Linear programming and extensions.* Princeton, NJ: Princeton University Press, 1963. 627 p.

312   **#Dixmier J.** *Les algebres d'operateurs dans l'espace Hilbertien, algebres de Von Neumann.* (Operator algebras in Hilbert space, Von Neumann algebras.) Paris: Gauthier-Villars, 1957. 368 p.

494   **#Doob J L.** *Stochastic processes.* New York: Wiley, 1953. 654 p.

269   **#*Draper N R & Smith H.** *Applied regression analysis.* New York: Wiley, 1966. 407 p. 1/81/S&BS

258   **Duda R O & Hart P E.** *Pattern classification and scene analysis.* New York: Wiley, 1973. 482 p.

258   **#Dugundji J.** *Topology.* Boston: Allyn and Bacon, 1966. 447 p.

1412   **#Dunford N & Schwartz J T.** *Linear operators.* New York: Interscience, 1958. 3 pts.

206   **Federer H.** *Geometric measure theory.* Berlin: Springer-Verlag, 1969. 679 p.

1522   **#Feller W.** *An introduction to probability theory and its applications.* New York: Wiley, 1950-66. 2 vols.

208   **Fiacco A V & McCormick G P.** *Nonlinear programming: sequential unconstrained minimization techniques.* New York: Wiley, 1968. 210 p.

231   **Ford L R & Fulkerson D R.** *Flows in networks.* Princeton, NJ: Princeton University Press, 1962. 194 p.

395   **#Friedman A.** *Partial differential equations of parabolic type.* Englewood Cliffs, NJ: Prentice-Hall, 1964. 347 p.

333   **Fuchs L.** *Infinite Abelian groups.* New York: Academic Press, 1970. 2 vols.

181   **Gamelin T W.** *Uniform algebras.* Englewood Cliffs, NJ: Prentice-Hall, 1969. 257 p.

607   **Gantmacher F R.** *Teoriya matrits.* (The theory of matrices.) Moscow: Gos. Izd. Tekhniko-Teoreticheskoi Literatury, 1954. 491 p.

206   **Gear C W.** *Numerical initial value problems in ordinary differential equations.* Englewood Cliffs, NJ: Prentice-Hall, 1971. 253 p.

509   **#Gel'fand I M & Shilov G E.** *Obobshchennye funktsii.* (Generalized functions.) Moscow: Fizmatgiz, 1958. 5 vols.

312   **#Gillman L & Jerison M.** *Rings of continuous functions.* Princeton, NJ: D. Van Nostrand, 1960. 300 p.

A

B

406   **#Gorenstein D.** *Finite groups.* New York: Harper & Row, 1967. 527 p.

597   **#Gradshteyn I S & Ryzhik I M.** *Tablitsy integralov, summ, ryadov i proizvedenii.* (Table of integrals, series, and products.) Moscow: Fizmatgiz, 1963. 1100 p.

231   **#Hall M.** *The theory of groups.* New York: Macmillan, 1959. 434 p.

239   **#Halmos P R.** *A Hilbert space problem book.* New York: American Book, 1967. 365 p.

309   **#Halmos P R.** *Measure theory.* New York: Springer-Verlag, 1950. 304 p.

634   **#Harary F.** *Graph theory.* Reading, MA: Addison-Wesley, 1969. 274 p.

395   **#Hardy G H, Littlewood J E & Polya G.** *Inequalities.* Cambridge, UK: Cambridge University Press, 1934. 314 p.

302   **Hardy G H & Wright E M.** *An introduction to the theory of numbers.* Oxford: Clarendon Press, 1938. 403 p.

306   **#Hartman P.** *Ordinary differential equations.* New York: Wiley, 1964. 612 p.

392   **#Helgason S.** *Differential geometry and symmetric spaces.* New York: Academic Press, 1962. 486 p.

426   **#Hewitt E & Ross K A.** *Abstract harmonic analysis.* New York: Springer-Verlag, 1963. 2 vols.

274   **Hille E & Phillips R S.** *Functional analysis and semi-groups.* Providence, RI: American Mathematical Society, 1957. 808 p.

203   **#Hoffman K M.** *Banach spaces of analytic functions.* Englewood Cliffs, NJ: Prentice-Hall, 1962. 217 p.

285   **Hopcroft J E & Ullman J D.** *Formal languages and their relation to automata.* Reading, MA: Addison-Wesley, 1969. 242 p.

228   **Hormander L.** *An introduction to complex analysis in several variables.* Princeton, NJ: D. Van Nostrand, 1966. 208 p.

473   **#Huppert B.** *Endliche Gruppen.* (Finite groups.) Berlin: Springer-Verlag, 1967. 796 p.

294   ***Johnston J.** *Econometric methods.* New York: McGraw-Hill, 1963. 300 p. 16/79/S&BS

227   **Kaplansky I.** *Commutative rings.* London: Dillon's Q.M.C. Bookshop, 1968. 129 p.

885   **#Kato T.** *Perturbation theory for linear operators.* Berlin: Springer-Verlag, 1966. 592 p.

350   **#Kelley J L.** *General topology.* New York: D. Van Nostrand, 1955. 298 p.

678   **#Kendall M G & Stuart A.** *The advanced theory of statistics.* New York: Hafner, 1958-66. 3 vols.

222   **Kleinrock L & Martin D F.** *Queueing systems.* New York: Wiley, 1975-76. 2 vols.

1291   **Knuth D E.** *The art of computer programming.* Reading, MA: Addison-Wesley, 1968. 3 vols.

573   **Kobayashi S & Nomizu K.** *Foundations of differential geometry.* New York: Interscience, 1963. 2 vols.

235   **Krasnosel'skii M A.** *Topologicheskie metody v teorii nelineinykh integral'nykh uravnenii.* (Topological methods in the theory of nonlinear integral equations.) Moscow: Gos. Izd. Tekhniko-Teoreticheskoi Literatury, 1956. 392 p.

538   **Kuratowski C.** *Topologie.* (Topology.) Warszawa-Lwow: Funduszu Kultury Narodowej, 1933. 285 p.

332   **Ladyzhenskaia O A & Ural'tseva N N.** *Lineinye i kvazilineinye uravneniia ellipticheskogo tipa.* (Linear and quasilinear elliptic equations.) Moscow: Nauka, 1964. 538 p.

191   **Lakshmikantham V & Leela S.** *Differential and integral inequalities.* New York: Academic Press, 1969. 2 vols.

279   **#Lehmann E L.** *Testing statistical hypotheses.* New York: Wiley, 1959. 369 p.

331   **Lions J L.** *Quelques methodes de resolution des problemes aux limites non lineaires.* (Some methods for the resolution of problems with nonlinear limits.) Paris: Dunod, 1969. 554 p.

496   **Lions J L & Magenes E.** *Problemes aux limites non homogenes et applications.* (Non-homogeneous boundary value problems and applications.) Paris: Dunod, 1968-70. 3 vols.

433   **#Loeve M.** *Probability theory.* New York: D. Van Nostrand, 1954. 515 p.

239   **Mac Lane S.** *Categories for the working mathematician.* New York: Springer-Verlag, 1971. 262 p.

226   **Mac Lane S.** *Homology.* Berlin: Springer-Verlag, 1963. 422 p.

292   **Meyer P A.** *Probability and potentials.* Waltham, MA: Blaisdell, 1966. 266 p.

384   **Morse P M & Feshbach H.** *Methods of theoretical physics.* Cambridge, MA: Technology Press, MIT, 1946. 497 p.

383   **Ortega J M & Rheinboldt W C.** *Iterative solution of nonlinear equations in several variables.* New York: Academic Press, 1970. 572 p.

225   **#*Papoulis A.** *Probability, random variables, and stochastic processes.* New York: McGraw-Hill, 1965. 583 p. 19/80/ET&AS

238   **Protter M H & Weinberger H F.** *Maximum principles in differential equations.* Englewood Cliffs, NJ: Prentice-Hall, 1967. 261 p.

555   **#*Rao C R.** *Linear statistical inference and its applications.* New York: Wiley, 1965. 625 p. 12/80/S&BS

417   **Reed M & Simon B.** *Methods of modern mathematical physics.* New York: Academic Press, 1972. 4 vols.

A		B

321   #**Richtmyer R D & Morton K W.** *Difference methods for initial-value problems.* New York: Interscience, 1957. 405 p.

302   #**Riesz F & Szokefalvi-Nagy B.** *Lecons d'analyse fonctionnelle.* (Functional analysis.) Budapest: Akademiai Kiado, 1955. 468 p.

474   **Rockafellar R T.** *Convex analysis.* Princeton, NJ: Princeton University Press, 1970. 451 p.

232   **Rogers H.** *Theory of recursive functions and effective computability.* New York: McGraw-Hill, 1967. 482 p.

215   **Rosenbrock H H.** *State-space and multivariable theory.* London: Nelson, 1970. 257 p.

273   **Rudin W.** *Real and complex analysis.* New York: McGraw-Hill, 1966. 412 p.

243   **Ruelle D.** *Statistical mechanics.* New York: W.A. Benjamin, 1969. 219 p.

206   **Salomaa A.** *Formal languages.* New York: Academic Press, 1973. 322 p.

280   #**Schaefer H.** *Topological vector spaces.* New York: Macmillan, 1966. 294 p.

209   #**Scheffe H.** *The analysis of variance.* New York: Wiley, 1959. 477 p.

332   **Schwartz L.** *Theorie des distributions.* (Theory of distributions.) Paris: Hermann, 1950-51. 2 vols.

375   #**Spanier E H.** *Algebraic topology.* New York: McGraw-Hill, 1966. 528 p.

382   **Stein E M.** *Singular integrals and differentiability properties of functions.* Princeton, NJ: Princeton University Press, 1970. 287 p.

326   **Strang W G & Fix G J.** *An analysis of the finite element method.* Englewood Cliffs, NJ: Prentice-Hall, 1973. 306 p.

281   **Theil H.** *Principles of econometrics.* New York: Wiley, 1971. 736 p.

233   **Thom R.** *Stabilite structurelle et morphogenese.* (Structural stability and morphogenesis.) Reading, MA: W.A. Benjamin, 1972. 348 p.

331   #**Varga R S.** *Matrix iterative analysis.* Englewood Cliffs, NJ: Prentice-Hall, 1962. 322 p.

240   **Warner G.** *Harmonic analysis on semi-simple Lie groups I and II.* Berlin: Springer-Verlag, 1972. 2 vols.

411   #**Wilkinson J H.** *The algebraic eigenvalue problem.* Oxford: Clarendon Press, 1965. 662 p.

200   #**Winer B J.** *Statistical principles in experimental design.* New York: McGraw-Hill, 1962. 907 p.

355   #**Zariski O & Samuel P.** *Commutative algebra.* Princeton, NJ: D. Van Nostrand, 1958-60. 2 vols.

557   **Zienkiewicz O C.** *The finite element method in engineering science.* New York: McGraw-Hill, 1971. 521 p.

690   #**Zygmund A.** *Trigonometrical series.* Warszawa-Lwow: Funduszu Kultury Narodowej, 1935. 331 p.

from 1961 to 1972—articles were cited four times as often as books.[9,10]

The 100 books in this study were published by 33 publishing houses. Table 2 lists these publishers and the nations where they are located. Five publishers produced 45 books which received more than 16,000 citations, or 42 percent of the 38,000 total. As expected, the majority of high impact publications are concentrated in a small number of publishing houses.

Nineteen US publishers are listed in Table 2. The UK accounts for four publishers; France and the USSR for three each; and the Federal Republic of Germany, Hungary, Poland, and Sweden have one each.

Eighty-four books were originally published in English, nine in French, five in Russian, and two in German. Many of these books were subsequently translated into other languages not discussed here. Clearly, mathematical computation is a system of universally grasped signs and symbols. As in synthetic chemistry, language may not present as much of a barrier to communication in mathematics as it does in medicine or social science. However, the data indicate that

English is the *lingua franca* of computer science as well as mathematics. The existence of many translations of these works indicates that they are used heavily outside of research.

The 130 authors in Table 1 are from 12 nations. It is significant that Russian authors account for five books in this study. Russian authors also contributed five of the most-cited *CMCI* articles.[1] These data for mathematics from the USSR stand in sharp contrast to the impact of Soviet science in other fields. While Soviet representation among the most-cited life scientists is quite small,[11] there were seven Russians among the 200 most-cited mathematicians in 1978 and 1979.[12]

Although ten French authors are indicated in Table 3, one of them is actually a collective pseudonym for a group of mostly French mathematicians—Nicolas Bourbaki. The Bourbaki "membership" has varied over the years from ten to 20 mathematicians, and they have been affiliated with universities in France and the US.[13] Technically speaking, the Bourbaki book should not have been included in this study, as it can be considered one of a series of multiauthored books. An-

Table 2: Publishers (first edition) of the 100 most-cited books, 1976-1980 *CMCI®*. A=publisher. B=number of books.

A	B
Wiley (US)	14
Springer-Verlag (FRG)	9
McGraw-Hill (US)	8
Prentice-Hall (US)	8
Academic Press (US)	6
Addison-Wesley (US)	5
Princeton University Press (US)	5
D. Van Nostrand (US)	5
Interscience (US)	4
American Mathematical Society (US)	3
W.A. Benjamin (US)	3
Dunod (France)	3
Clarendon Press (UK)	2
Fizmatgiz (State Publishing House for Physical and Mathematical Literature) (USSR)	2
Funduszu Kultury Narodowej (Fund for National Culture) (Poland)	2
Gosudarstvennoe Izdatel'stvo Tekhniko-Teoreticheskoi Literatury (State Publishing House for Technical and Theoretical Literature) (USSR)	2
Hermann (France)	2
Macmillan (US)	2
Akademiai Kiado (Publishing House of the Hungarian Academy of Sciences) (Hungary)	1
Allyn and Bacon (US)	1
Almqvist & Wiksells (Sweden)	1
American Book (US)	1
Blaisdell (US)	1
Cambridge University Press (UK)	1
Dillon's Q.M.C. Bookshop (UK)	1
Gauthier-Villars (France)	1
Hafner (US)	1
Harper & Row (US)	1
Holden-Day (US)	1
Technology Press, MIT	1
Nauka (USSR)	1
Nelson (UK)	1
RAND Corp. (US)	1

Table 3: Current national affiliations of the authors of the 100 books most cited, 1976-1980 *CMCI®*, in order of the total number of authors from each nation. A=country. B=total number of authors from that country.

A	B
US	91
France	10
UK	10
USSR	8
FRG	2
Hungary	2
Sweden	2
Australia	1
Finland	1
India	1
Italy	1
Poland	1
Total	**130**

other work by the Bourbaki group was among the most-cited math publications for 1961-1972.[4]

Including Bourbaki, 55 authors in Table 1 also appeared in a study of the most-cited mathematicians in 1978-1979.[12] In addition, three Fields Medal winners are included in this study—L. Hormander, L. Schwartz, and R. Thom. Thom's book, *Structural Stability and Morphogenesis*, described the principles of his catastrophe theory.[14] It was cited 233 times. The Fields Medal is widely considered to be the equivalent of the Nobel prize in mathematics. It is awarded every four years by the International Mathematical Union to researchers under age 40.[15]

Table 4 shows the publication year distribution for the 100 most-cited *CompuMath* books. Thirty-one of the books were published before 1960, as compared to only 12 for the 100 most-cited *CompuMath* articles.

About 60 of the books are in pure and applied mathematics. Among the many topics they discuss are algebraic functions and equations, graph theory, topology, linear operators, etc. About 15 books are on statistics and probability theory. The most-cited is a two-volume work by W. Feller published in 1950, *An Introduction to Probability Theory and Its Applications*. It was cited in more than 1,500 publications from 1976 to 1980. As an indication of the multidisciplinary impact of statistics and probability theory, five of the most-cited statistics books in this study were also among the 100 books most cited by social scientists from 1969 to 1977.[8]

Several authors have commented on the growth of statistics and its extensive application in the social and natural sciences. Most attribute the increased use of statistical methods to the development of high-speed computers. For example, Theodore W. Anderson, Stanford University, California, made the following observations in a *Citation Classic* commentary on his 1958 book, *An Introduction to Multivariate Statistical Analysis*: "There has been an even greater growth in the use of...statistical methods in the analysis of data in all fields of study due to an increase in mathematical sophistication among social scientists, more comprehensive training of investigators in statistics, and collection of more data. Perhaps the most important factor is the availability of high-speed computers with packages of programs that permit calculation of procedures with hardly more than the effort of entering the data."[16]

Computer science is also well represented in this study, accounting for ten books which

268

Table 4: Publication year distribution (based on the first year of publication) for the 100 most-cited books, 1976-1980 *CMCI®*.

Year	Books
1920s	1
1930s	4
1940s	3
1950s	23
1960s	49
1970s	20
Total	**100**

deal with programming, languages, networks, etc. D.E. Knuth's *The Art of Computer Programming*, published in 1968, was cited about 1,300 times from 1976 to 1980. The book, also available in a 1981 edition, continues to be well cited.

Three books on mathematical physics are listed in Table 1. These include the oldest book in this study, published in German in 1924—R. Courant and D. Hilbert's *Methods of Mathematical Physics*. It is still quoted quite often—more than 150 times in 1983

alone. In addition, two books discuss the principles and methods of econometrics, another field that has grown partly as a result of the increasing availability of powerful computers.

Our analysis of *CompuMath* books and articles has been limited to the period 1976-1980. We'll update these studies upon completion of the five-year cumulation for 1981-1985. In the meantime, we intend to solicit commentaries from authors whose works qualify as *Citation Classics*. For a variety of reasons, math and computer science publications have been underrepresented in our *Citation Classics* series. This is not due to any failing in our journal coverage, but rather to our initial heavy reliance on absolute instead of normalized citation counts.

*   *   *   *   *

My thanks to Abigail W. Grissom and Alfred Welljams-Dorof for their help in the preparation of this essay.

©1984 ISI

REFERENCES

1. **Garfield E.** The multidisciplinary impact of mathematics and computer sciences is reflected in the most-cited articles in the *CompuMath Citation Index*, 1976-1980. *Current Contents* (31):3-10, 30 July 1984.

2. --------------. *ISI/CompuMath*, multidisciplinary coverage of applied and pure mathematics, statistics, and computer science, in print and/or online—take your pick! *Essays of an information scientist*. Philadelphia: ISI Press, 1983. Vol. 5. p. 437-42.

3. **Institute for Scientific Information.** *Research fronts in ISI/CompuMath.* Philadelphia: ISI, 1981. 261 p.

4. **Garfield E.** Highly cited works in mathematics. Part 1. "Pure" mathematics. Part 2. "Applied" mathematics. *Essays of an information scientist*. Philadelphia: ISI Press, 1977. Vol. 1. p. 504-13.

5. --------------. Introducing *Citation Classics*: the human side of scientific reports. *Essays of an information scientist*. Philadelphia: ISI Press, 1980. Vol. 3. p. 1-2.

6. --------------. Five years of *Current Book Contents* and multi-authored book indexing. *Essays of an information scientist*. Philadelphia: ISI Press, 1980. Vol. 3. p. 727-30.

7. --------------. ISI's new *Index to Scientific & Technical Proceedings* lets you know what went on at a conference even if you stayed at home. *Essays of an information scientist*. Philadelphia: ISI Press, 1980. Vol. 3. p. 247-52.

8. --------------. The 100 books most-cited by social scientists, 1969-1977. *Essays of an information scientist*. Philadelphia: ISI Press, 1980. Vol. 3. p. 621-32.

9. --------------. A core research library for developing graduate schools—the 100 books most-cited by researchers. *Essays of an information scientist*. Philadelphia: ISI Press, 1977. Vol. 2. p. 1-5.

10. --------------. Selecting the all-time Citation Classics. Here are the fifty most cited papers for 1961-1972. The second fifty papers most cited from 1961-1972. *Essays of an information scientist*. Philadelphia: ISI Press, 1977. Vol. 2. p. 6-9; 21-5.

11. --------------. The 1,000 contemporary scientists most-cited 1965-1978. Part I. The basic list and introduction. *Essays of an information scientist*. Philadelphia: ISI Press, 1983. Vol. 5. p. 269-78.

12. --------------. The 200 "pure" mathematicians most cited in 1978 and 1979, including a list of most-cited publications for the top 100. *Essays of an information scientist*. Philadelphia: ISI Press, 1983. Vol. 5. p. 666-75.

13. **Halmos P R.** "Nicolas Bourbaki." *Sci. Amer.* 196(5):88-91; 93-4; 96; 99, 1957.

14. Catastrophe theory. *Sci. Amer.* 234(3):60D-1, 1976.

15. **Mostow G D.** The Fields Medals (I): relating the continuous and the discrete. *Science* 202:297-8, 1978.

16. **Anderson T W.** Citation Classic. Commentary on *An introduction to multivariate statistical analysis.* New York: Wiley, 1958. 374 p. *Current Contents/Physical, Chemical & Earth Sciences* 19(10):14, 5 March 1979.

Current Comments®

The Articles Most Cited in 1961-1982. 3.
Another 100 All-Time *Citation Classics*

Number 35   August 27, 1984

In previous essays, we discussed the 200 papers most cited from 1961 through 1982 in *Science Citation Index®* (*SCI®*).[1,2] Another 100 papers in the series for this 22-year period follow. Of the millions of papers cited during this period, less than 500 papers were cited more than 1,000 times. The frequency distribution for articles cited at least 50 times between 1961 and 1982 is given in Table 1. While the average scientific paper is cited less than one time each year over a 20-year period, less than one in 10,000 will be cited over 500 times.

Although each of the papers in this study is by definition a *Citation Classic™*,[3] only 43 have been commented on by their authors in *Current Contents®* (*CC®*). As is explained in each issue of *CC* in the section devoted to their commentaries, we urge authors to provide some hindsight on their work. We invite the authors and/or coauthors of the remaining 59 high-impact papers listed below to submit *Citation Classic* commentaries. For those classic authors who are retired or deceased, we encourage colleagues to submit commentaries, even if they were not a coauthor of the paper identified. Whenever possible, authors are asked to send their essays to coauthors.

The 100 papers in this study are listed in alphabetic order by first author. We use this arrangement to discourage invidious comparisons of individual papers by citation counts alone. Full bibliographic information is given for each paper. We've also included 1983 citation counts, in parentheses, to give you an idea of how frequently these papers are currently cited. An asterisk indicates that the paper was the subject of a *Citation Classic* commentary. The issue, year, and edition of *CC* in which these commentaries appeared follow the reference.

Four of the papers were included in a study published in 1974 covering 1961-1972.[4,5] Of the 200 articles listed in the first two parts of this series, 76 also appeared in the 1974 study.[1,2] Remarkably, 80 out of the 100 identified over ten years ago have continued to rank among the most-cited articles.

The articles were published in 54 journals. *Journal of Biological Chemistry* (*JBC*) published nine. *Physical Review* and *Nature* follow with five papers each. As expected, the majority of classic papers are concentrated in these and other high-impact journals, such as *Lancet* and *Science*.

Eleven Nobel laureates appear in Table 2—P.W. Anderson, C. de Duve, W. Gilbert, A.L. Hodgkin, B. Katz, P. Mitchell, S. Moore, M.F. Perutz, B. Samuelsson, W.H. Stein, and J.H. Van Vleck. Hodgkin received the prize for medicine in 1963 for his work on neuronal physiology. Katz was awarded the prize for medicine in 1970 for work on the chemical transmission of nerve impulses. They coauthored one of the papers in this study, published in the *Journal of Physiology* in 1949. Moore and

Table 1: Citation frequency distribution for papers cited at least 50 times in *SCI*®, 1961-1982. A=number of citations. B=number of items receiving that number of citations. C=approximate percent of items examined (n=226,358).

A	B	C
≥ 5000	20	*
4000-4999	13	*
3000-3999	24	*
2000-2999	48	*
1000-1999	328	.1
900-999	114	.1
800-899	144	.1
700-799	209	.1
600-699	340	.1
500-599	628	.3
400-499	1182	.5
300-399	2767	1.2
200-299	8614	3.8
100-199	47,793	21.1
50-99	164,134	72.5

*equals < .05 percent of items cited at least 50 times in *SCI*, 1961-1982.

Stein, who shared the 1972 Nobel prize for chemistry, also coauthored two papers in this study. In fact, Moore has five papers among the 300 most-cited papers from 1961 to 1982.

Of the 189 authors in this study, 41 were listed among the 1,000 contemporary scientists most cited from 1965 to 1978.[6] In the first two parts of this series, 78 authors were listed. Undoubtedly, a large number of those 1,000 authors will turn up as this series is extended, but not every highly cited author produces a *Citation Classic*. Indeed, we expect to show in the future which scientists *of Nobel class* have not, for whatever reason, been associated with such a classic paper.

The distribution of publication dates for the papers in this study is shown in

Table 2. The third 100 most-cited articles, 1961-1982, arranged in alphabetic order by first author. A=1961-1982 citations. 1983 citations appear in parentheses. B=bibliographic data. An asterisk (*) indicates that the paper was the subject of a *Citation Classic* ™ commentary. A number symbol (#) indicates that the paper appeared in the 1974 list of most-cited articles.

A	B
1244 (40)	**Adelberg E A, Mandel M & Chen G C C.** Optimal conditions for mutagenesis by N-methyl-N¹-nitro-N-nitrosoguanidine in *Escherichia coli* K12. *Biochem. Biophys. Res. Commun.* 18:788-95, 1965.
1438 (39)	#*Allen R J L. The estimation of phosphorus. *Biochem. J.* 34:858-65, 1940. (39/82/LS)
1354 (83)	**Ames B N & Dubin D T.** The role of polyamines in the neutralization of bacteriophage deoxyribonucleic acid. *J. Biol. Chem.* 235:769-75, 1960.
1313 (95)	*Aminoff D. Methods for the quantitative estimation of *N*-acetylneuraminic acid and their application to hydrolysates of sialomucoids. *Biochem. J.* 81:384-92, 1961. (26/80/LS)
1400 (75)	**Anderson P W.** Localized magnetic states in metals. *Phys. Rev.* 124:41-53, 1961.
1295 (75)	**Anson M L.** The estimation of pepsin, trypsin, papain, and cathepsin with hemoglobin. *J. Gen. Physiol.* 22:79-89, 1938.
1361 (63)	**Avrameas S & Ternynck T.** The cross-linking of proteins with glutaraldehyde and its use for the preparation of immunoadsorbents. *Immunochemistry* 6:53-66, 1969.
1232 (32)	*Bachmann B J, Low K B & Taylor A L. Recalibrated linkage map of *Escherichia coli* K-12. *Bacteriol. Rev.* 40:116-67, 1976. (8/82/LS)
1302 (69)	*Barka T & Anderson P J. Histochemical methods for acid phosphatase using hexazonium pararosanilin as coupler. *J. Histochem. Cytochem.* 10:741-53, 1962. (8/78)
1440 (184)	*Berry M N & Friend D S. High-yield preparation of isolated rat liver parenchymal cells. *J. Cell Biol.* 43:506-20, 1969. (3/84/LS)
1305 (50)	*Bianco C, Patrick R & Nussenzweig V. A population of lymphocytes bearing a membrane receptor for antigen-antibody-complement complexes. *J. Exp. Med.* 132:702-20, 1970. (20/81/LS)
1264 (91)	**Black J W, Duncan W A M, Durant C J, Ganellin C R & Parsons E M.** Definition and antagonism of histamine H₂-receptors. *Nature* 236:385-90, 1972.
1419 (34)	#Boas N F. Method for the determination of hexosamines in tissues. *J. Biol. Chem.* 204:553-63, 1953.
1295 (33)	**Brecher G & Cronkite E P.** Morphology and enumeration of human blood platelets. *J. Appl. Physiol.* 3:365-77, 1950.

1263 (14)   #Caulfield J B. Effects of varying the vehicle for OsO_4 in tissue fixation. *J. Biophys. Biochem. Cytol.* 3:827-9, 1957.

1462 (56)   *Cleland W W. The kinetics of enzyme-catalyzed reactions with two or more substrates or products. I. Nomenclature and rate equations. *Biochim. Biophys. Acta* 67:104-37, 1963. (28/77)

1255 (439)   Cleveland D W, Fischer S G, Kirschner M W & Laemmli U K. Peptide mapping by limited proteolysis in sodium dodecyl sulfate and analysis by gel electrophoresis. *J. Biol. Chem.* 252:1102-6, 1977.

1332 (83)   Cooley J W & Tukey J W. An algorithm for the machine calculation of complex Fourier series. *Math. Comput.* 19:297-301, 1965.

1377 (152)   *Cunningham A J & Szenberg A. Further improvements in the plaque technique for detecting single antibody-forming cells. *Immunology* 14:599-600, 1968. (50/81/LS)

1295 (118)   Dahlstrom A & Fuxe K. Evidence for the existence of monoamine-containing neurons in the central nervous system. *Acta Physiol. Scand.* 62(Suppl.232):1-55, 1964.

1459 (43)   de Duve C & Wattiaux R. Functions of lysosomes. *Annu. Rev. Physiol.* 28:435-92, 1966.
1413 (312)   *Denhardt D T. A membrane-filter technique for the detection of complementary DNA. *Biochem. Biophys. Res. Commun.* 23:641-6, 1966. (43/82/LS)

1271 (44)   Dische Z & Shettles L B. A specific color reaction of methylpentoses and a spectrophotometric micromethod for their determination. *J. Biol. Chem.* 175:595-603, 1948.

1291 (63)   Dittmer J C & Lester R L. A simple, specific spray for the detection of phospholipids on thin-layer chromatograms. *J. Lipid Res.* 5:126-7, 1964.

1196 (74)   *Doyle P A & Turner P S. Relativistic Hartree-Fock X-ray and electron scattering factors. *Acta Crystallogr. A* 24:390-7, 1968. (29/80/ET&AS)

1280 (93)   *Druckrey H, Preussmann R, Ivankovic S & Schmahl D. Organotrope carcinogene Wirkungen bei 65 verschiedenen N-Nitroso-Verbindungen an BD-Ratten. (Organotropic carcinogenic effects of 65 different N-nitroso-compounds on BD-rats.) *Z. Krebsforsch.* 69:103-201, 1967. (17/81/LS)

1350 (111)   Edelhoch H. Spectroscopic determination of tryptophan and tyrosine in proteins. *Biochemistry* 6:1948-54, 1967.

1358 (125)   *Fano U. Effects of configuration interaction on intensities and phase shifts. *Phys. Rev.* 124:1866-78, 1961. (27/77)

1212 (56)   Fink R P & Heimer L. Two methods for selective silver impregnation of degenerating axons and their synaptic endings in the central nervous system. *Brain Res.* 4:369-74, 1967.

1252 (100)   Fletcher R & Powell M J D. A rapidly convergent descent method for minimization. *Comput. J.* 6:163-8, 1963.

1188 (51)   *Frank H S & Evans M W. Free volume and entropy in condensed systems. III. Entropy in binary liquid mixtures; partial molal entropy in dilute solutions; structure and thermodynamics in aqueous electrolytes. *J. Chem. Phys.* 13:507-32, 1945. (50/83/PC&ES)

1264 (31)   *Fredrickson D S, Levy R I & Lees R S. Fat transport in lipoproteins—an integrated approach to mechanisms and disorders. Hyperlipoproteinemia. *N. Engl. J. Med.* 276:148-56, 1967. (3/78)

1193 (32)   *Fredrickson D S, Levy R I & Lees R S. Fat transport in lipoproteins—an integrated approach to mechanisms and disorders. Type IV hyperlipoproteinemia. *N. Engl. J. Med.* 276:273-81, 1967. (3/78)

1430 (96)   *Glashow S L, Iliopoulos J & Maiani L. Weak interactions with lepton-hadron symmetry. *Phys. Rev. D—Part. Fields* 2:1285-92, 1970. (20/80/PC&ES)

1283 (47)   *Goodwin T W & Morton R A. The spectrophotometric determination of tyrosine and tryptophan in proteins. *Biochem. J.* 40:628-32, 1946. (28/81/LS)

1383 (39)   Grabar P & Williams C A. Methode permettant l'etude conjuguee des proprietes electrophoretiques et immunochimiques d'un melange de proteines; application au serum sanguin. (Method permitting the combined study of the electrophoretic and the immunochemical properties of protein mixtures; application to blood serum.) *Biochim. Biophys. Acta* 10:193-4, 1953.

1447 (92)   *Gray E G & Whittaker V P. The isolation of nerve endings from brain: an electron-microscopic study of cell fragments derived by homogenization and centrifugation. *J. Anat.* 96:79-87, 1962. (1/81/LS)

1371 (179)   *Hamberg M, Svensson J & Samuelsson B. Thromboxanes: a new group of biologically active compounds derived from prostaglandin endoperoxides. *Proc. Nat. Acad. Sci. US* 72:2994-8, 1975. (2/83/LS)

1333 (208)   Hartree E F. Determination of protein: a modification of the Lowry method that gives a linear photometric response. *Anal. Biochem.* 48:422-7, 1972.

1356 (39)   Hestrin S. The reaction of acetylcholine and other carboxylic acid derivatives with hydroxylamine, and its analytical application. *J. Biol. Chem.* 180:249-61, 1949.

1444 (158) ***Hirt B.** Selective extraction of polyoma DNA from infected mouse cell cultures. *J. Mol. Biol.* 26:365-9, 1967. (33/81/LS)

1319 (77) **Hodgkin A L & Katz B.** The effect of sodium ions on the electrical activity of the giant axon of the squid. *J. Physiol.* 108:37-77, 1949.

1190 (51) ***Huggett A St G & Nixon D A.** Use of glucose oxidase, peroxidase, and O-dianisidine in determination of blood and urinary glucose. *Lancet* 2:368-70, 1957. (21/81/CP)

1292 (372) ***Kaplan E L & Meier P.** Nonparametric estimation from incomplete observations. *J. Amer. Statist. Assn.* 53:457-81. 1958. (24/83/LS)

1280 (23) ***Karle J & Karle I L.** The symbolic addition procedure for phase determination for centrosymmetric and noncentrosymmetric crystals. *Acta Crystallogr.* 21:849-59, 1966. (17/77)

1338 (49) **Karplus M.** Letter to editor. (Vicinal proton coupling in nuclear magnetic resonance.) *J. Amer. Chem. Soc.* 85:2870-1, 1963.

1450 (353) ***Kessler S W.** Rapid isolation of antigens from cells with a staphylococcal protein A-antibody adsorbent: parameters of the interaction of antibody-antigen complexes with protein A. *J. Immunol.* 115:1617-24, 1975. (13/83/LS)

1269 (71) **Koe B K & Weissman A.** *p*-Chlorophenylalanine: a specific depletor of brain serotonin. *J. Pharmacol. Exp. Ther.* 154:499-516, 1966.

1395 (188) **Kohn W & Sham L J.** Self-consistent equations including exchange and correlation effects. *Phys. Rev. A* 40:1133-8, 1965.

1242 (31) **Krishna G, Weiss B & Brodie B B.** A simple, sensitive method for the assay of adenyl cyclase. *J. Pharmacol. Exp. Ther.* 163:379-85, 1968.

1269 (56) **Kunitz M.** Crystalline soybean trypsin inhibitor. II. General properties. *J. Gen. Physiol.* 30:291-310, 1947.

1329 (74) **Lennox E S.** Transduction of linked genetic characters of the host by bacteriophage P1. *Virology* 1:190-206, 1955.

1394 (39) **Martin J B & Doty D M.** Determination of inorganic phosphate. *Anal. Chem.* 21:965-7, 1949.

1390 (29) ***Mattingly D.** A simple fluorimetric method for the estimation of free 11-hydroxycorticoids in human plasma. *J. Clin. Pathol.* 15:374-9, 1962. (8/79/CP)

1209 (1085) **Maxam A M & Gilbert W.** Sequencing end-labelled DNA with base-specific chemical cleavages. *Meth. Enzymology* 65:499-560, 1980.

1457 (219) **McCann J, Choi E, Yamasaki E & Ames B N.** Detection of carcinogens as mutagens in the *Salmonella*/microsome test: assay of 300 chemicals. *Proc. Nat. Acad. Sci. US* 72:5135-9, 1975.

1314 (82) **McFarlane A S.** Efficient trace-labelling of proteins with iodine. *Nature* 182:53, 1958.

1287 (106) **Merrifield R B.** Solid phase peptide synthesis. I. The synthesis of a tetrapeptide. *J. Amer. Chem. Soc.* 85:2149-54, 1963.

1250 (85) ***Miller J A.** Carcinogenesis by chemicals: an overview—G.H.A. Clowes Memorial Lecture. *Cancer Res.* 30:559-76, 1970. (44/81/LS)

1279 (16) **Millonig G.** A modified procedure for lead staining of thin sections. *J. Biophys. Biochem. Cytol.* 11:736-9, 1961.

1310 (63) ***Mitchell P.** Chemiosmotic coupling in oxidative and photosynthetic phosphorylation. *Biol. Rev. Cambridge Phil. Soc.* 41:445-502, 1966. (16/78)

1432 (76) **Mollenhauer H H.** Plastic embedding mixtures for use in electron microscopy. *Stain Technol.* 39:111-4, 1964.

1334 (197) ***Moncada S, Gryglewski R, Bunting S & Vane J R.** An enzyme isolated from arteries transforms prostaglandin endoperoxides to an unstable substance that inhibits platelet aggregation. *Nature* 263:663-5, 1976. (12/84/LS)

1416 (88) **Moore S & Stein W H.** Chromatographic determination of amino acids by the use of automatic recording equipment. *Meth. Enzymology* 6:819-31, 1963.

1242 (48) **Moore S & Stein W H.** Photometric ninhydrin method for use in the chromatography of amino acids. *J. Biol. Chem.* 176:367-88, 1948.

1227 (133) **Morrison W R & Smith L M.** Preparation of fatty acid methyl esters and dimethylacetals from lipids with boron fluoride-methanol. *J. Lipid Res.* 5:600-8, 1964.

1210 (118) ***Nicholson R S & Shain I.** Theory of stationary electrode polarography. *Anal. Chem.* 36:706-23, 1964. (6/81/PC&ES)

1257 (76) ***Niswender G D, Midgley A R, Monroe S E & Reichert L E.** Radioimmunoassay for rat luteinizing hormone with antiovine LH serum and ovine LH-^{131}I. *Proc. Soc. Exp. Biol. Med.* 128:807-11, 1968. (44/80/LS)

1217 (31) ***Nowell P C.** Phytohemagglutinin: an initiator of mitosis in cultures of normal human leukocytes. *Cancer Res.* 20:462-6, 1960. (42/77)

1363 (109) **Ouchterlony O.** Antigen-antibody reactions in gels. *Acta Pathol. Microbiol. Scand.* 26:507-15, 1949.

1241 (55) **Ouchterlony O.** Antigen-antibody reactions in gels. IV. Types of reactions in coordinated systems of diffusion. *Acta Pathol. Microbiol. Scand.* 32:231-40, 1953.

1457 (0)   *Pariser R & Parr R G. A semi-empirical theory of electronic spectra and electronic structure of complex unsaturated molecules. I. *J. Chem. Phys.* 21:466-71, 1953. (3/79/PC&ES)

1360 (34)   Patterson M S & Greene R C. Measurement of low energy beta-emitters in aqueous solution by liquid scintillation counting of emulsions. *Anal. Chem.* 37:854-7, 1965.

1408 (377)   Pelham H R B & Jackson R J. An efficient mRNA-dependent translation system from reticulocyte lysates. *Eur. J. Biochem.* 67:247-56, 1976.

1245 (60)   Perutz M F. Stereochemistry of cooperative effects in haemoglobin. *Nature* 228:726-34, 1970.

1344 (44)   Pople J A. Electron interaction in unsaturated hydrocarbons. *Trans. Faraday Soc.* 49:1375-85, 1953.

1460 (23)   *Poulik M D. Starch gel electrophoresis in a discontinuous system of buffers. *Nature* 180:1477-9, 1957. (15/84/LS)

1211 (50)   Rosen H. A modified ninhydrin colorimetric analysis for amino acids. *Arch. Biochem. Biophys.* 67:10-5, 1957.

1303 (217)   *Salomon Y, Londos C & Rodbell M. A highly sensitive adenylate cyclase assay. *Anal. Biochem.* 58:541-8, 1974. (17/82/LS)

1246 (25)   Schachman H K. Ultracentrifugation, diffusion, and viscometry. *Meth. Enzymology* 4:32-103, 1957.

1351 (44)   Schildkraut C L, Marmur J & Doty P. Determination of the base composition of deoxyribonucleic acid from its buoyant density in CsCl. *J. Mol. Biol.* 4:430-43, 1962.

1222 (33)   Schneider W C & Hogeboom G H. Intracellular distribution of enzymes. V. Further studies on the distribution of cytochrome *c* in rat liver homogenates. *J. Biol. Chem.* 183:123-8, 1950.

1328 (156)   *Seeman P. The membrane actions of anesthetics and tranquilizers. *Pharmacol. Rev.* 24:583-655, 1972. (4/83/LS)

1201 (54)   Smith H W, Finkelstein N, Aliminosa L, Crawford B & Graber M. The renal clearances of substituted hippuric acid derivatives and other aromatic acids in dog and man. *J. Clin. Invest.* 24:388-404, 1945.

1338 (24)   Somogyi M. Determination of blood sugar. *J. Biol. Chem.* 160:69-73, 1945.

1343 (391)   *Sternberger L A, Hardy P H, Cuculis J J & Meyer H G. The unlabeled antibody enzyme method of immunohistochemistry: preparation and properties of soluble antigen-antibody complex (horseradish peroxidase-antihorseradish peroxidase) and its use in identification of spirochetes. *J. Histochem. Cytochem.* 18:315-33, 1970. (4/83/LS)

1405 (132)   Studier F W. Analysis of bacteriophage T7 in early RNAs and proteins on slab gels. *J. Mol. Biol.* 79:237-48, 1973.

1408 (87)   Svennerholm L. Quantitative estimation of sialic acids. II. A colorimetric resorcinol-hydrochloric acid method. *Biochim. Biophys. Acta* 24:604-11, 1957.

1280 (120)   Thiery J-P. Mise en evidence des polysaccharides sur coups fines en microscopie electronique. (Demonstration of polysaccharides on thin sections by electron microscopy.) *J. Microsc.—Paris* 6:987-1018, 1967.

1195 (20)   *Trout D L, Estes E H & Friedberg S J. Titration of free fatty acids of plasma: a study of current methods and a new modification. *J. Lipid Res.* 1:199-202, 1960. (40/77)

1236 (173)   Ungerstedt U. Stereotaxic mapping of the monoamine pathways in the rat brain. *Acta Physiol. Scand.* (Suppl. 367):1-48, 1971.

1368 (44)   *Ussing H H & Zerahn K. Active transport of sodium as the source of electric current in the short-circuited isolated frog skin. *Acta Physiol. Scand.* 23:110-27, 1951. (35/81/LS)

1362 (17)   #Van Slyke D D & Neill J M. The determination of gases in blood and other solutions by vacuum extraction and manometric measurement. I. *J. Biol. Chem.* 61:523-73, 1924.

1361 (43)   *Van Vleck J H. The dipolar broadening of magnetic resonance lines in crystals. *Phys. Rev.* 78:1168-83, 1948. (31/79/PC)

1297 (54)   *Vesterberg O & Svensson H. Isoelectric fractionation, analysis, and characterization of ampholytes in natural pH gradients. IV. Further studies on the resolving power in connection with separation of myoglobins. *Acta Chem. Scand.* 20:820-34, 1966. (40/80/LS)

1304 (34)   Wessells N K, Spooner B S, Ash J F, Bradley M O, Luduena M A, Taylor E L, Wrenn J T & Yamada K M. Microfilaments in cellular and developmental processes. *Science* 171:135-43, 1971.

1193 (29)   *Whitaker J R. Determination of molecular weights of proteins by gel filtration on Sephadex. *Anal. Chem.* 35:1950-3, 1963. (12/81/LS)

1416 (66)   *Woods K R & Wang K-T. Separation of dansyl-amino acids by polyamide layer chromatography. *Biochim. Biophys. Acta* 133:369-70, 1967. (35/84/LS)

1383 (84)   Wroblewski F & LaDue J S. Lactic dehydrogenase activity in blood. *Proc. Soc. Exp. Biol. Med.* 90:210-3, 1955.

1299 (61)   *Zlatkis A, Zak B & Boyle A J. A new method for the direct determination of serum cholesterol. *J. Lab. Clin. Med.* 41:486-92, 1953. (12/81/LS)

Table 3: Chronological distribution of publication dates of the third 100 most-cited articles. A=publication years. B=number of papers.

A	B
1920s	1
1930s	1
1940s	13
1950s	19
1960s	46
1970s	19
1980s	1

Table 3. This is similar to the distribution of publication dates for the 200 most-cited articles. The oldest paper in this segment of the study, published in 1924 in *JBC*, is the classic method by D.D. Van Slyke and J.M. Neill for measuring blood gases. The paper was explicitly cited 17 times in 1983, mainly in clinical journals, indicating that clinical researchers still feel compelled to cite this 60-year-old method.

The most recent paper, by A.M. Maxam and W. Gilbert, was published in *Methods in Enzymology* in 1980. That same year, Gilbert won the Nobel prize for chemistry for his work on the structure of DNA. Their paper on a technique for sequencing DNA received 56 citations in 1980, 387 in 1981, 766 in 1982, and 1,085 in 1983. Clearly, this method attracted immediate attention and has been widely and increasingly used, demonstrating the extensive impact of an important methodology.

We have commented in the first two parts of this series on the dominance of methods papers in citation-based studies. Methods papers describe strategies for studying a particular research problem. Highly cited methods papers represent frequently or widely used strategies, "tried and true" techniques. That is, they can be cited steadily over a long period of time in the literature of such "small" fields as surgery or mathematics. Or they can be cited in the tens of thousands of biochemical articles published each year and achieve high impact in a relatively short time. In any case, while many well-cited methods are regarded as less than ingenious, others like the Maxam and Gilbert paper represent innovations of the highest caliber.

Although many methods papers turn out to be highly cited, they are often undervalued by researchers and journal editors. Yoram Salomon, Weizmann Institute of Science, Rehovot, Israel, discussed the difficulties he and his colleagues had in writing and publishing their classic method for assaying the enzyme adenylate cyclase. In a *Citation Classic* commentary, Salomon said, "We consulted other colleagues who advised us not to waste time on a methods paper. Nevertheless, we could not avoid the feeling that many would welcome an efficient new method.... In its present form, the paper was initially rejected for insufficient advancement. However, our persistence with the editor resulted in its acceptance."[7] The paper has been explicitly cited over 1,500 times since it was published in 1974.

The potential economic value of certain scientific techniques has intensified interest in methods papers. For example, the growth of the genetic engineering industry has had an impact on the citation of pure and applied genetics research. David T. Denhardt, University of Western Ontario, Canada, devised a technique for detecting complementary DNA sequences. In a commentary on this 1966 paper, Denhardt said, "Despite the reprint requests, I saw very few applications of this technique until recombinant DNA technology came into use."[8] The paper was cited 139 times in 1966-1970, 232 in 1971-1975, 546 in 1976-1980, and 808 times in 1981-1983.

Of course, many theoretical works are listed. A characteristic of these high-impact conceptual works is that they raise more questions than they answer. That is, their ideas have consequences for researchers in related fields and initiate further investigations. Mats Hamberg, Karolinska Institutet, Stockholm, Sweden, makes this point in a commentary on the 1975 paper he wrote with Jan

Svensson and recent Nobel laureate Samuelsson. He said, "[It was] the first example of physiological and pathological roles for the prostaglandin-thromboxane system in man.... [This] finding ...has stimulated a large number of biochemical, physiological, and clinical studies."[9]

Relevant reviews of the literature may prove to be highly cited. These papers provide a useful function in defining the consensus of scientific research on a particular topic. By providing such overviews, these papers can provoke fresh insights into the problem. For example, Philip Seeman, University of Toronto, Canada, reviewed the actions of anesthetics and tranquilizers on cell membranes. In a commentary on this 1972 review, Seeman said, "The importance of the review is that it correlates the membrane effects with drug concentrations.... The further reaching importance is that the review prompted the subsequent discovery that alcohol-tolerant tissues have membranes that are more resistant to fluidization by ethanol."[10]

Although the majority of articles in this series come from the life sciences, 19 of the 100 articles listed in Table 2 are from the physical sciences. This is an increase of seven from the first segment of this study, and is equal to the number found in the second segment. As this study is extended, we may see an increase in the number of papers from the physical sciences.

In the weeks to come, we'll continue this series and list additional groups of *Citation Classics*. So far, we've identified 300 papers cited at least 1,188 times from 1961 to 1982. The data in Table 1 show that we can continue this particular series almost indefinitely if we define a *Citation Classic* as any paper cited over 300 times. By the time we would have published 5,000 titles, it would be necessary to resort the file so that we could include the new crop of classics. This would be in addition to those papers we identify by different criteria so that we do not ignore the smaller fields.

* * * * *

My thanks to Thomas Atkins and Linda LaRue for their help in the preparation of this essay. ©1984 ISI

REFERENCES

1. **Garfield E.** The 100 most-cited papers ever and how we select *Citation Classics*. *Current Contents* (23):3-9, 4 June 1984.
2. --------------. The articles most cited in 1961-1982. 2. Another 100 *Citation Classics* highlight the technology of science. *Current Contents* (29):3-12, 16 July 1984.
3. --------------. Introducing *Citation Classics*: the human side of scientific reports. *Essays of an information scientist*. Philadelphia: ISI Press, 1980. Vol. 3. p. 1-2.
4. --------------. Selecting the all-time *Citation Classics*. Here are the fifty most cited papers for 1961-1972. *Essays of an information scientist*. Philadelphia: ISI Press, 1977. Vol. 2. p. 6-9.
5. --------------. The second fifty papers most cited from 1961-1972. *Essays of an information scientist*. Philadelphia: ISI Press, 1977. Vol. 2. p. 21-5.
6. --------------. The 1,000 contemporary scientists most-cited 1965-1978. Part I. The basic list and introduction. *Essays of an information scientist*. Philadelphia: ISI Press, 1983. Vol. 5. p. 269-78.
7. **Salomon Y.** Citation Classic. Commentary on *Anal. Biochem.* 58:541-8, 1974. *Current Contents/Life Sciences* 25(17):20, 26 April 1982.
8. **Denhardt D T.** Citation Classic. Commentary on *Biochem. Biophys. Res. Commun.* 23:641-6, 1966. *Current Contents/Life Sciences* 25(43):22, 25 October 1982.
9. **Hamberg M.** Citation Classic. Commentary on *Proc. Nat. Acad. Sci. US* 72:2994-8, 1975. *Current Contents/Life Sciences* 26(2):19, 10 January 1983.
10. **Seeman P.** Citation Classic. Commentary on *Pharmacol. Rev.* 24:583-655, 1972. *Current Contents/Life Sciences* 26(4):22, 24 January 1983.

Current Comments®

Cystitis and Other Urinary Tract Infections. Part 1. Etiology and Epidemiology

Number 36

September 3, 1984

In the past few years, we have published essays on numerous health problems, including herpes simplex virus infections[1] and trichomoniasis[2]—sexually transmitted diseases that are especially serious for women. This two-part essay reviews a family of closely linked disorders that primarily affect women: urinary tract infections (UTIs). UTIs are among the most common infections encountered by physicians around the world. Although UTIs occur most often in elderly women, they are common in sexually active women as well. Indeed, it is estimated that 10 to 20 percent of all women everywhere will experience at least one episode of UTI.[3]

Most UTIs involve only the lower urinary tract.[4] This consists of the bladder, which stores urine, and the urethra, which carries urine from the body. Lower-tract UTIs are designated by the terms cystitis (inflammation of the bladder) and urethritis (inflammation of the urethra—although some clinicians do not classify urethritis as a UTI). Indications of a lower-tract infection include: a frequent need to urinate, a burning sensation upon urination (dysuria), bacteria in the urine (bacteriuria), and occasional blood and pus in the urine (pyuria).

Occasionally, however, disease-causing bacteria may travel beyond the urethra and bladder to invade the upper urinary tract. The upper tract consists of the kidneys and ureters. The kidneys filter wastes from the blood and concentrate them in the form of urine. The ureters are the fibrous, muscular tubes which carry urine from the kidneys to the bladder. An upper-tract infection, or pyelonephritis, is far more serious than its lower-tract counterpart. It generally combines the symptoms of lower-tract infections with fever, chills, nausea, vomiting, and pain in the lower back. And whereas lower-tract UTIs are virtually never life-threatening, pyelonephritis can cause massive kidney damage in a small percentage of cases. In rare instances, chronic pyelonephritis can lead to a systemic blood infection, which can cause death. One goal of lower-tract treatment is to prevent the spread of the disease to the upper urinary tract—not the mere relief of symptoms.[4,5]

In the past, lower-tract infections were thought to have a single cause, treatable with a few types of therapy.[6] Now, however, many causes have been identified. This has in turn resulted in an increase in the types of therapy available, and in controversies over the best treatment. The causes of lower-tract UTIs are discussed here. Diagnosis and treatment will be covered later.

According to Burke A. Cunha, Department of Medicine, State University of New York School of Medicine, Stony Brook, the most common bacteria responsible for lower-tract UTIs are Enterobacteriaceae, normally found in the intestines.[6] They account for 80 to 95 percent of such infections.[7] Of these, perhaps 80 percent are caused by *Escherichia coli*, which migrate from the bowel to the vagina across the perineum, the fleshy bridge between the anal opening and the vulva. Other bacteria which often cause UTIs include *Proteus mirabilis*, *Klebsiella*, and *Enterobacter*.[6,7]

Marvin Turck, University of Washington, Seattle, and physician-in-chief, Harborview Medical Center, Seattle, suggests that the very structure of the female anatomy may predispose women to lower-tract UTIs.[4] The male urethra is eight to ten inches long—an arduous trip for bacteria trying to reach the bladder. Regular urination will wash them out before they attain their goal. Moreover, since the male urethra opens at the tip of the penis, it is far removed from the main reservoir of the bacteria that cause UTIs—the anus. Turck also speculates that an antimicrobial agent may be present in prostatic fluid, giving men added protection.[4] The female urethra, on the other hand, is a short, straight passage averaging only 1.5 inches. Situated in close proximity to the anus, it provides an easy avenue for bacterial invasion. Once in the urethra, they ascend rapidly into the bladder and begin to multiply.

Physical stress and injury to the urethra can also make it easier for bacteria to invade the urinary tract. Wayne C. Waltzer, Department of Surgery, State University of New York, Stony Brook, notes in a review that changes in the shape of the bladder and urethra during pregnancy and childbirth may prevent invading bacteria from being washed out by the flow of urine.[8] Structural degeneration of the pelvic organs, due to age and changes in hormonal levels, may also make women more susceptible to UTIs, according to urologist Patrick J.B. Smith, United Hospitals, Bath, England.[9,10] Smith found that the linings of both the vagina and the urethra tend to become atrophied, rigid, inelastic, and inflamed as estrogen levels fall in postmenopausal women. This provides bacteria with the opportunity to successfully colonize the tissue.

Little evidence supports the notion that lower-tract infections result primarily from sexual transmission, according to Walter E. Stamm, University of Washington and Harborview Medical Center.[11] Even so, the association between sexual activity and the incidence of lower-tract UTIs is strong enough to have fostered the term, "honeymoon cystitis." A 1968 study by Calvin M. Kunin and Regina C. McCormack, then of the Departments of Preventive Medicine and Internal Medicine, respectively, University of Virginia School of Medicine, Charlottesville, is among the many investigations indirectly linking sexual activity and UTIs. Comparing the incidence of bacteriuria in nuns and married women, they found that in the urine of sexually active women, the bacteria count was almost triple that of nuns.[12] But is intercourse a direct cause of lower-tract infections, or does it merely provoke symptoms? Lindsay E. Nicolle and colleagues, Departments of Medical Microbiology and Medicine, University of Manitoba, Winnipeg, Canada, studied 15 sexually active women who had each experienced at least two lower-tract infections within a six-month interval. They found that most experienced an infection within 24 hours after intercourse. The authors speculate that bacteria from the perineum are massaged into the urethra during foreplay and intercourse.[13]

But to trigger the onset of symptoms and progression to a diseased state, it is not enough for bacteria to merely enter the urinary tract, according to urological surgeon Jack Lapides, University of Michigan Medical Center, Ann Arbor.[14] The urinary tracts of normal, healthy men and women are constantly subjected to bacterial invasions, but the body's defenses and the wash of the urine stream remove the invaders. For infection to occur, Lapides believes that some physical abnormality—whether permanent or transient, systemic or local—must allow the bacteria to remain there.

These abnormalities include outright structural damage, insufficient blood supply to the urinary tract tissues, and the presence of parasites, obstructions, and foreign bodies, including catheters.[14]

According to Lapides, such abnormalities—particularly that of reduced blood supply—are linked to the victim's health and other habits. Lapides theorizes that abnormally infrequent urination results in chronic overdistention of the bladder.[14] This, in turn, constricts the organ's blood vessels, restricting blood supply and increasing the likelihood of infection. To test this theory, Lapides investigated 250 women and 71 girls with histories of recurrent UTIs.[15] Two-thirds were found to void only once in five to ten hours, and most had unusually large bladder capacities. However, Stamm notes that these ideas are not widely accepted and suggests that simply holding the urine for a long period of time—giving bacteria a chance to breed—goes further toward explaining some women's susceptibility to infection than notions about decreased blood supply.[16]

Other factors that may trigger the appearance of symptoms, but do not necessarily lead to UTIs, include the following: allergic reactions to bubble baths, vaginal douches, and aerosol deodorants; tight clothing, especially underwear made of synthetic fibers; lack of personal hygiene as well as excessive washing; the direction in which the perianal region is wiped after defecation; physical injury to the genitalia from frequent or clumsy sexual intercourse without adequate lubrication; and clumsy masturbation with foreign objects.[17]

In 1974, clinicians M. Takahashi, Kaiser-Permanente Contraceptive Drug Study, Walnut Creek, California, and D.B. Loveland, National Institute of Child Health and Human Development, Bethesda, Maryland, investigated the link between UTIs and the use of oral contraceptives. They found that the prevalence of bacteriuria in women using the "pill" was one-and-a-half times the rate among both nonusers and those who had used the pill and stopped.[18] The authors speculate that the estrogen in oral contraceptives contributes to an excess of the hormone in the body, causing physical damage or anatomic changes in the urinary tract which increase susceptibility to infection.

Psychological factors may also contribute to the development of symptoms. Urologist John B. Graham, Northwestern University Medical School, Chicago, and Evanston Hospital, Illinois, speculates that many women may suffer from a "nervous bladder" akin to a host of other, better-known psychosomatic disorders, such as the nervous bowel and the nervous stomach.[19] And in fact, urologists Richard A. Schmidt and Emil A. Tanagho, University of California School of Medicine, San Francisco, found that some women may turn feelings of stress and anxiety inward. This results in muscular spasms of the sphincter controlling the flow of urine, and, thus, more painful and frequent urination.[20]

Although UTIs are primarily a disease of women, men and children can also be victims. The appearance of symptoms and bacteriuria in men, according to Turck, are secondary effects of an obstruction of the urinary tract or of prostatitis (inflammation of the prostate gland).[4] However, clinicians Linda Pead and Rosalind Maskell, Public Health Laboratory, St. Mary's General Hospital, Portsmouth, England, found that UTIs are perhaps not as rare among men as has previously been thought. During a 14-month study of 999 men between the ages of 15 and 50, 223 had bacteriuria and 63 had pyuria—even though most (65 percent) had anatomically normal urinary tracts.[21] They speculate that the site of infection in these men may have been the prostate. Prostate infections seem to be associated with far fewer bacteria in the urine than are infections of the bladder. This may partially account for the lower level of reported incidence of UTIs in men.

In children, the incidence of symptomatic UTIs occurring between the ages of one month and 11 years is approximately 0.7 percent for boys and 2.8 percent for girls.[22] According to Kunin, UTIs in children are commonly associated with vesicoureteral reflux, a condition in which urine backs up from the bladder into the ureters and kidneys.[23] This can cause renal scarring and tissue damage. Obstructions are also commonly found in male children with UTIs. And in a study of 100 infants aged five days to eight months who were hospitalized for acute UTIs, pediatricians Charles M. Ginsburg and George H. McCracken, University of Texas, Southwestern Medical School, Dallas, found that uncircumcised males accounted for 75 percent of those aged three months or less.[24] The immature immune system, the relatively short length of the urethra, and a reservoir of bacteria trapped by the foreskin close to the urethral opening may predispose the male infant to UTIs. Ginsburg and McCracken also found that 45 percent of infant girls with UTIs had unsuspected congenital or other defects of the urinary tract, making them more susceptible to infection.

As mentioned earlier, UTIs are most common among the elderly—especially women. However, the prevalence varies according to whether they live at home, in a nursing care facility, or are under extended care in a hospital. In a review of UTIs in the elderly, Donald Kaye, chairman, Department of Medicine, Medical College of Pennsylvania, Philadelphia, notes that in men aged 65 and older, the incidence of UTIs among those at home was 6 to 13 percent; in nursing homes or extended care facilities, 17 to 26 percent; and among those in the hospital, 30 to 34 percent.[25] For women aged 65 and older, UTIs occurred in 17 to 33 percent of those living at home; 23 to 27 percent of those in extended care facilities; and 32 to 50 percent of those in the hospital.[25] The higher incidence of UTIs among those in hospitals and extended care facilities is due mainly to the bacteria introduced into the urinary tract by catheters.

Other causes of UTIs in the elderly include obstructions, loss of blood flow to the tissues of the urinary tract, and neglected care of invalid patients.[25,26] Prostate disease and the surgery resulting from the disorder, as well as the loss of the bactericidal secretions of the prostate, may predispose elderly men to UTIs.[25] Both elderly men and women have trouble emptying their bladders completely. The residual urine provides a fertile environment for the growth of bacteria. In elderly women, fecal incontinence and the soiling of the perineum may play a role in the development of UTIs. Finally, an increase in UTIs in the elderly is associated with such conditions as cerebrovascular disease, senile brain syndrome, and cardiovascular disease and with those in whom illness or infirmity enforces prolonged bed rest.[25]

The pathogens responsible for UTIs have been identified. But the reason some people seem more susceptible to one or more occurrences of the disease remains elusive. As we have seen, there are a variety of factors and conditions that seem to be associated with either symptoms of UTIs or true bacterial infections. Together with the differences of opinion concerning the etiology and epidemiology of UTIs, this suggests that there is considerably more work to be done in this area. Much the same can be said of the diagnosis and treatment of UTIs. These aspects of cystitis and UTIs will be covered in the second part of this review.

* * * * *

My thanks to Stephen A. Bonaduce and Terri Freedman for their help in the preparation of this essay. ©1984 ISI

REFERENCES

1. **Garfield E.** Herpes simplex virus infections. Part 1. How widespread they are, and who is most threatened. Part 2. Sexually transmitted diseases without a cure. *Essays of an information scientist.* Philadelphia: ISI Press, 1983. Vol. 5. p. 143-56.
2. **------------.** Is research on trichomoniasis commensurate with the prevalence of this STD? *Essays of an information scientist.* Philadelphia: ISI Press, 1983. Vol. 5. p. 524-32.
3. **Kraft J K & Stamey T A.** The natural history of symptomatic recurrent bacteriuria in women. *Medicine* 56:55-60, 1977.
4. **Turck M.** Urinary tract infections. *Hosp. Pract.* 15:49-58, 1980.
5. **Derrick F C.** Urinary tract infection in the adult: a guide to treatment. *Postgrad. Med.* 72:281-8, 1982.
6. **Cunha B A.** Urinary tract infections. 1. Pathophysiology and diagnostic approach. *Postgrad. Med.* 70:141-5, 1981.
7. **Abraham E, Brenner B E & Simon R R.** Cystitis and pyelonephritis. *Ann. Emerg. Med.* 12:228-34, 1983.
8. **Waltzer W C.** The urinary tract in pregnancy. *J. Urol.* 125:271-6, 1981.
9. **Smith P J B.** Age changes in the female urethra. *Brit. J. Urol.* 44:667-76, 1972.
10. **--------------.** The menopause and the lower urinary tract—another case for hormonal replacement therapy? *Practitioner* 218:97-9, 1977.
11. **Stamm W E.** Recent developments in the diagnosis and treatment of urinary tract infections. *West. J. Med.* 137:213-20, 1982.
12. **Kunin C M & McCormack R C.** An epidemiologic study of bacteriuria and blood pressure among nuns and working women. *N. Engl. J. Med.* 278:635-42, 1968.
13. **Nicolle L E, Harding G K M, Preiksaitis J & Ronald A R.** The association of urinary tract infection with sexual intercourse. *J. Infec. Dis.* 146:579-83, 1982.
14. **Lapides J.** Mechanisms of urinary tract infection. *Urology* 14:217-25, 1979.
15. **------------.** Pathophysiology of urinary tract infections. *Univ. Mich. Med. Center J.* 39:103-12, 1973.
16. **Stamm W E.** Telephone communication. 19 July 1984.
17. Acute urethral syndrome in women. *Brit. Med. J.* 282:3-5, 1981.
18. **Takahashi M & Loveland D B.** Bacteriuria and oral contraceptives. *J. Amer. Med. Assn.* 227:762-5, 1974.
19. **Graham J B.** The female urethral syndrome? *Urol. Clin. N. Amer.* 7:59-62, 1980.
20. **Schmidt R A & Tanagho E A.** Urethral syndrome or urinary tract infection? *Urology* 18:424-7, 1981.
21. **Pead L & Maskell R.** Urinary tract infection in adult men. *J. Infection* 3:71-8, 1981.
22. **Winberg J, Andersen H J, Bergstrom T, Jacobsson B, Larson H & Lincoln K.** Epidemiology of symptomatic urinary tract infection in childhood. *Acta Paediat. Scand.* (Suppl.252):1-19, 1974.
23. **Kunin C M.** A ten-year study of bacteriuria in schoolgirls: final report of bacteriologic, urologic, and epidemiologic findings. *J. Infec. Dis.* 122:382-93, 1970.
24. **Ginsburg C M & McCracken G H.** Urinary tract infections in young infants. *Pediatrics* 69:409-12, 1982.
25. **Kaye D.** Urinary tract infections in the elderly. *Bull. NY Acad. Med.* 56:209-20, 1980.
26. **Kurtz S B.** Urinary tract infections in older persons. *Compr. Ther.* 8(2):54-7, 1982.

Current Comments®

Cystitis and Other
Urinary Tract Infections. Part 2.
Diagnosis and Treatment

Number 37   September 10, 1984

Last week, we discussed the etiology and epidemiology of cystitis and other urinary tract infections (UTIs).[1] UTIs are among the most common infections encountered by physicians around the world. They are caused primarily by bacteria from the bowels and most often affect women, especially elderly women. However, men and children are also victims. The onset and progression of UTIs are affected by numerous factors. As will be seen here, the diagnosis and treatment of these infections can also be complex.

Determining the cause of urinary symptoms is a formidable task. Diagnoses of lower- or upper-tract infections based solely on symptoms are frequently inaccurate.[2-4] According to a 1971 study of the sites of UTIs and of the patients' symptoms by K.F. Fairley and colleagues, then at the University Department of Medicine, Royal Melbourne Hospital, Australia, signs of lower-tract disorders were often the only symptoms exhibited by patients with proven renal infections.[2] Moreover, not all symptomatic patients have a UTI. They may be suffering instead from an inflammation of the vagina or vulva (vaginitis and vulvitis, respectively), or even from such sexually transmitted diseases (STDs) as candidiasis, trichomoniasis, gonorrhea, or genital herpes.[5] Indeed, it is estimated that 10 to 20 percent of women suffering from symptoms of UTIs have been infected by the sexually transmitted microorganism *Chlamydia trachomatis*.[6]

Many individuals with a UTI may suffer no symptoms at all.[7] In such cases, the key to an accurate diagnosis, according to Marvin Turck, University of Washington and Harborview Medical Center, Seattle, is detection of bacteriuria.[8] The simplest method is to examine a sample of freshly collected urine under an ordinary light microscope. A more accurate method is the urine culture. But a urine sample can be easily contaminated by bacteria from the vagina, perineum, or pubic hair, according to Walter E. Stamm, University of Washington and Harborview Medical Center.[9] So, in the 1950s, Edward H. Kass, then at the Department of Medicine, Harvard Medical School and Boston City Hospital, Massachusetts, established that a diagnosis of UTI should be made only if two consecutive urine cultures contain more than 100,000 microorganisms per milliliter.[10-12] This ruled out contaminated samples, which rarely contained so many microorganisms.

To reduce the risk of contamination, samples are sometimes collected by inserting a sterile catheter through the patient's urethra into the bladder, or by suprapubic aspiration, in which urine is collected through a large needle plunged through the patient's abdomen. Using the latter method, Stamm and colleagues, Department of Medicine, University of Washington School of Medicine, Seattle Public Health Center, and Harborview Medical Center, found that only 51 percent of the women whose urine samples contained bacteria would have been diagnosed as having UTIs by Kass's criterion.[13] Thus, they recommended that the standard of 100 microorganisms per milliliter be used to diagnose lower-tract UTIs.[13]

But the urine cultures of 30 to 50 percent of all women with symptoms of lower-tract infections contain no evidence of bacteria.[14] Some of these women, when treatment repeatedly fails, may have to undergo a battery of tests, including urinalysis, excretory urography, cystography, urodynamic studies, and cystoscopic examination. Urinalysis consists of a microscopic examination of the urine's physical and chemical makeup.[15] For women whose predominant symptom is urgency or incontinence, urodynamics, the study of the urinary tract in action, may help identify functional irregularities.[15] Using specially designed catheters and recording equipment, the flow rate of the urine, the amount of urine left in the bladder after voiding, the pressure exerted by the urine in the urethra and the bladder, and the tension of the urethral sphincter and pelvic muscles are assessed.[16] In those instances in which abnormalities are found, UTIs are almost always secondary diseases.[15] It should be emphasized, however, that such extensive testing is rarely necessary.

Excretory urography and cystography are used to identify structural abnormalities by outlining the urinary tract with a medium that is opaque to X rays. The routine use of these procedures is not justified, however, since about 90 percent of the patients who undergo these tests have no abnormalities.[15,17] Cystoscopy, the examination of cells scraped from the lining of the urinary tract under a local anesthetic, is also not recommended for routine use. But compared with the other procedures, it is relatively inexpensive, carries little risk for the patient, and occasionally reveals useful information.[15]

Once a UTI has been diagnosed, many practitioners recommend locating the site of the infection, since that, in part, determines how the disease will be treated. One method, the bladder-washout technique, developed by Fairley and colleagues, distinguishes upper- from lower-tract infections.[18] It involves collecting a urine sample through a catheter, emptying the bladder, and pumping back in a solution of sterile saline and antibiotic. After the bladder is again emptied and washed out with sterile water, urine is collected every 10 minutes and bacteria counts are made. If all specimens following the washout contain no microorganisms, then the site of the infection is the bladder itself. Bacteria in specimens immediately following the washout procedure indicate an infection in the ureters or kidneys.

Although highly reliable, the bladder-washout technique is expensive, cumbersome, and invasive. The patient may be catheterized for up to two hours or more.[19] Virginia Thomas, Alexis Shelokov, and Marvin Forland, Departments of Microbiology and Medicine, University of Texas Medical School, San Antonio, have developed a simple, risk-free method, using immunofluorescence, to detect the presence of bacteria coated with antibodies. They found that 34 of 35 patients known to have pyelonephritis had antibody-coated bacteria in their urine, while 19 of 20 patients with cystitis did not.[20] The results of the antibody-coated bacteria test, as it is known, correlate well with those of the bladder-washout technique.[4,21] However, according to Godfrey K.M. Harding and colleagues, University of Manitoba and the Health Sciences Center, Winnipeg, Canada, some women with upper-tract infections have bacteria in their urine that are not coated with antibodies.[4] They advise caution in interpreting negative results from the antibody-coated bacteria test.

In many cases of lower-tract UTIs, symptoms may disappear within 48 hours,[8] and 80 to 90 percent of patients rid their urine of bacteria within 72 hours to one week.[6,8] But symptoms and bacteriuria may not be gone for good, and, in any event, antibiotics will clear them up much more quickly than simply allowing them to run their course.[9] So most clinicians prefer to treat all women with symptoms of UTIs. They also treat asymptomatic infections discovered during evaluations for other complaints, since many subsequently become symptomatic.[4] Since UTIs may be caused by one or more factors, and may be localized in the urethra or bladder or spread throughout the urinary tract, various therapies for UTIs have evolved, with varying degrees of success. The most commonly used treatments include courses of antibiotics. Dilatation of the urethra and surgery have also been common in the past and still have their adherents around the world, but many practitioners doubt their value. More will be said about this later.

Lower-tract UTIs in which the infecting bacteria can be identified usually respond to any broad-spectrum antibiotic, regardless of the patient's age or sex.[7] According to Burke A. Cunha, Department of Medicine, State University of New York School of Medicine, standard therapy consists of suitable dosages of a sulfanomide, ampicillin, trimethoprim, trimethoprim-sulfamethoxazole, or nitrofurantoin for 7 to 14 days.[6] Although symptoms may quickly disappear, Turck recommends a follow-up urine culture one to two weeks after therapy is completed.[8] A patient is said to be "cured" when the urine is sterile.[22] The cure rate immediately following an individual course of antibiotic therapy in uncomplicated UTIs ranges from 95 to nearly 100 percent. When a bacterial infection is secondary to an obstruction or other abnormality, these must be resolved first if the treatment for the UTI is to be successful.[7,8]

In recent years, however, the duration of antimicrobial therapy for uncomplicated, lower-tract UTIs has been reconsidered.[23] To improve patient compliance with therapy, contain costs, and reduce drug-related side effects—which may include rashes, yeast infections of the vagina, nausea, and vomiting—clinicians explored the feasibility of single-dose therapy. In 1978, Leslie S.T. Fang and colleagues, Department of Medicine, Harvard Medical School and the Renal and Infectious Disease Units, Massachusetts General Hospital, Boston, reported the results of the clinical trial of a single, three-gram dose of an antibiotic in each of 22 patients with lower-tract UTIs, as determined by the antibody-coated bacteria test.[24] All were symptom-free within 24 to 48 hours. Although single-dose therapies have proved to be about as effective as conventional therapy under certain circumstances,[25,26] they are by no means a panacea. In conventional therapy, a high concentration of medication builds in the urine, eradicating even antibiotic-resistant bacteria.[23] Preliminary data suggest, according to Stamm, that single-dose therapy is less effective against resistant bacteria than conventional therapy.[23] Stamm notes that using single-dose therapy in place of conventional therapy trades effectiveness for fewer side effects.[9]

As mentioned earlier, no infecting pathogen can be identified in many women with symptoms of lower-tract UTIs, so antibiotics are ineffective.[7] In some of these women, the symptoms may be due to renal tuberculosis,[14] although this is uncommon.[9] In others, highly spiced foods, alcohol, chocolate, and caffeine may irritate the bladder. Analgesics and antispasmodics are effective in such instances.[7] In a few cases, symptoms are due to inflammatory, ulcer-like lesions in the lining of the bladder—a condition called interstitial cystitis. Although its causes are unknown, it is treatable by repeatedly filling the bladder through a catheter with a solution of oxychlorosene sodium.[27] Often, however, the cause of symptoms falls into none of these categories. In such cases, some practitioners resort to surgery to correct a possible structural defect. However, Stamm notes that the overwhelming majority of women with lower-tract UTIs have no demonstrable abnormalities that need to be addressed through surgery.[9]

Almost 90 percent of the women who experience UTIs can expect another infection within 12 months.[28] Eighty percent of these recurrences are due to infections with microorganisms other than the type that caused the original UTI.[22] According to David A. Haase and Allan R. Ronald, Department of Medical Microbiology, University of Manitoba, the other 20 percent are due to numerous factors including: the emergence of an antibiotic-resistant strain of the original infecting organism, poor patient compliance, inadequate levels of medication in the patient's urine due to the kidneys' failure to concentrate the drug in the bladder, and the reemergence of the original infecting organism following successful therapy.[29]

Long-term antibiotic therapy, or prophylaxis, is an attempt to reduce or eliminate altogether the number of recurrences that infection-prone patients develop.[23] The treatment consists of various dosages taken at intervals of twice daily, thrice weekly, or after sexual intercourse for periods ranging from six months to two years.[23,30] Stamm and colleagues reported that 80 percent of infection-prone women given a placebo had another infection within six months of their original course of treatment, whereas women on antibiotics during that time experienced a recurrence rate near zero.[31] Although long-term therapy raises concerns about microbial resistance, its only drawback seems to be that its beneficial effects do not persist once the patient discontinues use of the drug. Still, long-term antibiotic therapy is far more cost-effective than treating each infection as it occurs. Stamm's group reported that the yearly cost of prophylaxis was $85 in 1981, compared with a cost of almost $400 for per-episode treatment.[32]

One of the most common methods of treating recurrent UTIs in the past has been urethral dilatation,[8] the enlarging of the urethral passage. It is still employed by some practitioners. Dilatation is usually performed under some kind of anesthesia. Dilatation is an attempt to reestablish normal urine flow in women whose urethras are thought to be so narrow that turbulence washes bacteria back into the bladder.[33] Its effectiveness, however, is questionable. A study by W.F. Hendry and colleagues, St. Peter's Hospitals and Institute of Urology, London, found that dilatation helps only when combined with antibiotic therapy.[33]

When UTIs are especially unresponsive to treatment, surgery may be an alternative among some practitioners. In a study of 40 women suffering from various combinations of symptoms, ranging from frequency of urination, dysuria, and incontinence to recurrent UTIs, urologist Patrick J.B. Smith, United Hospitals, Bath, England, and colleagues, found that removing one-third of the urethra (urethrectomy) helped 87 percent of those with urgency and dysuria.[34] In women also suffering from incontinence, however, only 14 percent benefited from the procedure. None of the women with recurrent UTIs experienced any improvement. Speculating on these results, Smith suggests that the women experiencing dysuria and urgency had "hypersensitive" urethras. Since the operation results in the partial denervation of the urethra, they felt less pain and experienced the urge to urinate less frequently. However, using a similar procedure, called urethrotomy, Richard D. Hart and Brent J. Murphy, Flint Osteopathic Hospital, Michigan, reported that 70 percent of their patients with recurrent UTIs had complete relief.[35] Twenty-two percent experienced some relief and only eight percent did not experience improvement in symptoms.

Another procedure, called urethroplasty, is sometimes used to treat women whose symptoms are associated with sexual activity. It involves severing the lowest portion of the urethra, including its opening, from its vaginal attachments, and moving it farther away from the vagina. Smith found that of 41 women treated with urethroplasty, 21 had no further symptoms, seven had significant relief, but 13 showed no improvement.[36] And of 40 women between the ages of 40 and 50 who had symptoms of frequency of urination, an interrupted urine stream, and a need to strain when urinating, A.J. Splatt and D. Weedon, Departments of Surgery and Pathology, respectively, Royal Brisbane Hospital, Australia, reported that 38 showed improvement following urethroplasty.[37] The remaining two showed improvement after further surgery.

However, Stamm emphasizes that neither dilatation nor surgery is a common or recommended procedure, and that neither can be justified by any reliable evidence.[9] No substantive evidence supports the idea that a "tight urethra" plays a role in the development of recurrent UTIs.[8] Indeed, according to Ross R. Bailey, Department of Renal Medicine, Christchurch Hospital and Clinical School, New Zealand, "The popular urological practice of dilating the female urethra is unnecessary and unjustified."[38] Joseph N. Corriere, Department of Surgery, University of Texas Medical School, Houston, asserts that most women with UTIs "merely need the cheapest effective antibiotic available."[39] In a comparison of urethrotomy with antibotic therapy in the treatment of recurrent UTIs, N.R. Netto and R. Pimenta da Silva, Department of Urology, Hospital Beneficencia Portuguesa, São Paulo, Brazil, found that two-thirds of the 41 women they treated with antibiotics had relief from their symptoms, whereas only one-third of the other 30 they treated surgically had similar relief.[40] They concluded that antibi-

Table 1: A selected list of organizations that are concerned with urinary tract infections.

American Association of Clinical Urologists (AACU)
21510 South Main Street
Carson, CA 90745

American Association of Genito-Urinary Surgeons (AAGUS)
Mayo Clinic
Rochester, MN 55905

American Urological Association (AUA)
1120 North Charles Street
Baltimore, MD 21201

Association Française d'Urologie
60 Blvd. de Latour-Maubourg
F-75327 Paris, France

Berufsverband der Deutschen Urologen e.V.
c/o Dr. Dieter Heck
Tullastrasse 3
D-6800 Mannheim 1, FRG

British Association of Urological Surgeons (BAUS)
Royal College of Surgeons
35-43 Lincoln's Inn Fields
London WC2A 3PN, UK

Clinical Society of Genito-Urinary Surgeons (CSGUS)
c/o Dr. Jay Gillenwater
Box 422
University of Virginia Hospital
Charlottesville, VA 22908

National Institute of Arthritis, Diabetes, and Digestive and Kidney Diseases (NIADDKD)
c/o Dr. George Brooks
Westwood Bldg., Room 637
Bethesda, MD 20205

National Kidney Foundation (NKF)
Two Park Avenue
New York, NY 10016

Nippon Hinyoki-ka Gakkai
c/o Dr. Tadao Niijima
Taisei Bldg.
3-14-10 Hongo, Bunkyo-ku
Tokyo, Japan

Società Italiana di Urologia (SIU)
c/o Dr. Luciano Giuliani
Viale Cortina d'Ampezzo 49
I-00135 Rome, Italy

Société Française d'Urologie
6 Ave. Constant Coquelin
F-75007 Paris, France

Société Internationale d'Urologie (SIU)
63 Ave. Niel
F-75017 Paris, France

Society for Pediatric Urology (SPU)
c/o Dr. John Woodard
School of Medicine, Division of Urology
Emory University
Atlanta, GA 30322

Society of University Urologists (SUU)
Box 403, Section of Urology
University of Chicago
950 East 59th Street
Chicago, IL 60637

otic treatment was superior to surgery. Moreover, since surgery is always accompanied by antibiotic therapy, any favorable results are actually due to the medication, rather than to the procedure itself.[40]

Although the topic of preventing UTIs is limited, in the scientific literature, to discussions of long-term antibiotic therapy, popular articles in "women's magazines" contain numerous suggestions. Most encourage women to drink at least six glasses of fluid a day and to void regularly and frequently. But there are no systematic studies that demonstrate that anyone is really cured through such measures.[41] A high fluid intake can produce a decreased bacteria count in the urine.[42] Many popular articles go a step further, however, and recommend that drinking large quantities of cranberry or grapefruit juice or taking vitamin C can acidify the urine and thus make it less hospitable to bacteria.[43-46] No evidence exists to support this claim. Yet some of the advice given in these articles is practical: a woman should always wipe from front to back after using the toilet, and both she and her sex partner should be clean before engaging in intercourse.

Table 1 lists the associations in which physicians concerned with the diagnosis and treatment of UTIs may hold membership. These organizations hold annual meetings and continuing education

seminars and some sponsor a journal reflecting the society's interests. For example, the American Urological Association sponsors the *Journal of Urology*.

Journals covered in *Current Contents*® (*CC*®) and *Science Citation Index*® (*SCI*®) that include most of the articles on urinary tract infection are in fact urological journals. These are listed in Table 2 with their associated 1983 impact values. Impact indicates how often, on average, an article published by a certain journal in a given two-year period was cited during a particular year. The impacts given in Table 2 were arrived at by dividing the number of citations received in 1983 by the number of articles published in 1981 and 1982.

Table 2: Some of the main journals publishing research on urinary tract infections. The 1983 impact factor of each is listed.

Journal	Impact Factor
Annales d'Urologie	.17
British Journal of Urology	.66
European Urology	.55
Investigative Urology	1.36
Journal d'Urologie	.13
Journal of Urology	1.32
Kidney International	4.19
Scandinavian Journal of Urology and Nephrology	.71
Urologe-Ausgabe A	.37
Urologic Clinics of North America	1.04
Urologic Radiology	.79
Urological Research	.63
Urology	.72

Table 3: *SCI*® research fronts on urinary tract infections. A=research front number. B=research front name. C=number of core papers in the research front.

A	B	C
83-0493	Use of trimethoprim and other drugs in the treatment of urinary tract infections in women	34
82-0722	Antimicrobial therapy for urinary tract infection	4
82-1305	Clinical and pharmacological comparison of use of trimethoprim alone or in combination as co-trimoxazole in treatment of urinary tract infections and other infections	2
82-2616	Chemical and clinical studies on the role of adherence of *E. coli* to host glycolipid receptors in the pathogenesis of urinary tract infection	2
81-0652	Treatment of urinary tract infection	3
81-1465	Interstitial cystitis and secondary dysfunctions associated with systemic lupus erythematosus	2
81-1953	Diagnosis of urinary tract infections	2
81-2387	Urinary tract infections	2

A number of the papers mentioned in this essay are core documents in several *SCI* research fronts. The titles of these research fronts are listed in Table 3. As I have explained previously, a research front is determined by identifying a group of current papers that collectively cite a cluster of older "core" papers.[47] Papers by Fairley and colleagues,[2,18] Harding and colleagues,[4] Stamm's group,[13] Thomas and colleagues,[20] and Kunin[22] are included in the core literature of the 1983 research front entitled "Use of trimethoprim and other drugs in the treatment of urinary tract infections in women." The papers by Thomas and colleagues,[20] Fang and colleagues,[24] and Bailey and Abbott[25] appear in the core literature of the 1982 front entitled "Antimicrobial therapy for urinary tract infection." Thomas's paper[20] is also among the core articles of the 1981 front on "Diagnosis of urinary tract infections." The papers by Fang,[24] Bailey and Abbott,[25] and A.R. Ronald and colleagues[3] make up the core of the 1981 research front, "Treatment of urinary tract infection."

Although literature on UTIs is abundant, a consensus among clinicians and practitioners on its causes and treatment in women who experience chronic recurrences is elusive. For instance, whereas some physicians believe surgery to be a viable treatment for women suffering from chronic cystitis, others react with horror and disbelief that any competent practitioner would even consider such a course of action. And while comparisons of the efficacy of various treatments are useful, endless debate on such matters may result in the neglect of other promising avenues of research.

Indeed, it is difficult to decide whether cystitis and other UTIs constitute another of the neglected areas of medicine, simply because they are almost never fatal. As such, they will not produce a significant lobby, as do diseases such as lung cancer and heart disease. It is absurd to hope that genetic engineering may provide the desired result.

* * * * *

My thanks to Stephen A. Bonaduce and Terri Freedman for their help in the preparation of this essay.

REFERENCES

1. **Garfield E.** Cystitis and other urinary tract infections. Part 1. Etiology and epidemiology. *Current Contents* (36):3-7, 3 September 1984.
2. **Fairley K F, Carson N E, Gutch R C, Leighton P, Grounds A D, Laird E C, McCallum P H G, Sleeman R L & O'Keefe C M.** Site of infection in acute urinary-tract infection in general practice. *Lancet* 2:615-8, 1971.
3. **Ronald A R, Boutros P & Mourtada H.** Bacteriuria localization and response to single-dose therapy in women. *J. Amer. Med. Assn.* 235:1854-6, 1976.
4. **Harding G K M, Marrie T J, Ronald A R, Hoban S & Muir P.** Urinary tract infection localization in women. *J. Amer. Med. Assn.* 240:1147-50, 1978.
5. **Panja S K.** Urethral syndrome in women attending a clinic for sexually transmitted diseases. *Brit. J. Vener. Dis.* 59:179-81, 1983.
6. **Cunha B A.** Urinary tract infections. 2. Therapeutic approach. *Postgrad. Med.* 70:149-57, 1981.
7. **Derrick F C.** Urinary tract infection in the adult: a guide to treatment. *Postgrad. Med.* 72:281-8, 1982.
8. **Turck M.** Urinary tract infections. *Hosp. Pract.* 15:49-58, 1980.
9. **Stamm W E.** Telephone communication. 19 July 1984.
10. **Kass E H.** Chemotherapeutic and antibiotic drugs in the management of infections of the urinary tract. *Amer. J. Med.* 18:764-81, 1955.
11. ------------. Bacteriuria and the diagnosis of infections of the urinary tract. *Arch. Intern. Med.* 100:709-14, 1957.
12. ------------. The role of asymptomatic bacteriuria in the pathogenesis of pyelonephritis. (Quinn E L & Kass E H, eds.) *Biology of pyelonephritis.* Boston: Little, Brown, 1960. p. 399-412.

13. **Stamm W E, Counts G W, Running K R, Fihn S, Turck M & Holmes K K.** Diagnosis of coliform infection in acutely dysuric women. *N. Engl. J. Med.* 307:463-8, 1982.
14. **Gleckman R A.** Urinary tract infection in women: new perspectives on office management. *Postgrad. Med.* 73:277-82, 1983.
15. **Mabry E W, Carson C C & Older R A.** Evaluation of women with chronic voiding discomfort. *Urology* 18:244-6, 1981.
16. **Schmidt R A & Tanagho E A.** Urethral syndrome or urinary tract infection? *Urology* 18:424-7, 1981.
17. **Fowler J E & Pulaski E T.** Excretory urography, cystography, and cystoscopy in the evaluation of women with urinary-tract infection. *N. Engl. J. Med.* 304:462-5, 1981.
18. **Fairley K F, Bond A G, Brown R B & Habersberger P.** Simple test to determine the site of urinary-tract infection. *Lancet* 2:427-8, 1967.
19. **Sanford J P.** Urinary tract symptoms and infections. *Annu. Rev. Med.* 26:485-98, 1975.
20. **Thomas V, Shelokov A & Forland M.** Antibody-coated bacteria in the urine and the site of urinary-tract infection. *N. Engl. J. Med.* 290:588-90, 1974.
21. **Jones S R, Smith J W & Sanford J P.** Localization of urinary-tract infections by detection of antibody-coated bacteria in urine sediment. *N. Engl. J. Med.* 290:591-3, 1974.
22. **Kunin C M.** Duration of treatment of urinary tract infections. *Amer. J. Med.* 71:849-54, 1981.
23. **Stamm W E.** Recent developments in the diagnosis and treatment of urinary tract infections. *West. J. Med.* 137:213-20, 1982.
24. **Fang L S T, Tolkoff-Rubin N E & Rubin R H.** Efficacy of single-dose and conventional amoxicillin therapy in urinary-tract infection localized by the antibody-coated bacteria technic. *N. Engl. J. Med.* 298:413-6, 1978.
25. **Bailey R R & Abbott G D.** Treatment of urinary tract infection with a single dose of trimethoprim-sulfamethoxazole. *Can. Med. Assn. J.* 118:551-2, 1978.
26. **Buckwold F J, Ludwig P, Harding G K M, Thompson L, Slutchuk M, Shaw J & Ronald A R.** Therapy for acute cystitis in adult women. *J. Amer. Med. Assn.* 247:1839-42, 1982.
27. **Messing E M & Stamey T A.** Interstitial cystitis. *Urology* 12:381-92, 1978.
28. **McGeachie J.** Recurrent infection of the urinary tract: reinfection or recrudescence? *Brit. Med. J.* 1:952-4, 1966.
29. **Haase D A & Ronald A R.** Chronic cystitis: a non-diagnosis. *Can. Fam. Phys.* 28:2193-5, 1982.
30. **Ronald A R & Harding G K M.** Urinary infection prophylaxis in women. *Ann. Intern. Med.* 94:268-70, 1981.
31. **Stamm W E, Counts G W, Wagner K F, Martin D, Gregory D, McKevitt M, Turck M & Holmes K K.** Antimicrobial prophylaxis of recurrent urinary tract infections. *Ann. Intern. Med.* 92:770-5, 1980.
32. **Stamm W E, McKevitt M, Counts G W, Wagner K F, Turck M & Holmes K K.** Is antimicrobial prophylaxis of urinary tract infections cost effective? *Ann. Intern. Med.* 94:251-5, 1981.
33. **Hendry W F, Stanton S L & Williams D I.** Recurrent urinary infections in girls: effects of urethral dilatation. *Brit. J. Urol.* 45:72-83, 1973.
34. **Smith P J B, Powell P H, George N J R & Kirk D.** Urethrolysis in the management of females with recurrent frequency and dysuria. *Brit. J. Urol.* 53:634-6, 1981.
35. **Hart R D & Murphy B J.** Female urethral syndrome: treatment by internal urethrotomy. *J. Amer. Osteopath. Assn.* 82:609-10, 1983.
36. **Smith P J B, Roberts J B M & Ball A J.** "Honeymoon" cystitis: a simple surgical cure. *Brit. J. Urol.* 54:708-10, 1982.
37. **Splatt A J & Weedon D.** The urethral syndrome: experience with the Richardson urethroplasty. *Brit. J. Urol.* 49:173-6, 1977.
38. **Bailey R R.** Management of cystitis in young women. *Drugs* 13:137-41, 1977.
39. **Corriere J N.** Acute cystitis in young women: how much is too much? *Tex. Med.* 77:4, 1981.
40. **Netto N R & da Silva R P.** Treatment of recurrent cystitis in women by internal urethrotomy or antimicrobial agents. *Int. Urol. Nephrol.* 12:211-5, 1980.
41. **Kunin C M.** Cystitis symptoms and fluid intake. *J. Amer. Med. Assn.* 249:1920, 1983.
42. **O'Grady F & Cattell W R.** Kinetics of urinary tract infection. II. The bladder. *Brit. J. Urol.* 38:156-62, 1966.
43. **Brody J E.** What every woman should know about cystitis (including how to prevent it). *Redbook* 157(3):41-4, 1981.
44. **Nolen W A.** Treating a very annoying infection. *McCall's* 109(7):46-8, 1982.
45. **Lake A.** Urinary infections. *Woman's Day* 46(3):47-8; 50; 161-2, 1982.
46. **Gillespie L & Margolis Z.** Cystitis *can* be cured. *Ms.* 11(12):98-101, 1983.
47. **Garfield E.** ABCs of cluster mapping. Parts 1 & 2. Most active fields in the life and physical sciences in 1978. *Essays of an information scientist.* Philadelphia: ISI Press, 1981. Vol. 4. p. 634-49.

Current Comments®

Fine Art Commissioned for ISI's Caring Center for Children and Parents. Part 1. Lilli Ann Killen Rosenberg's "A Celebration of Working Parents and Their Children"

Number 38   September 17, 1984

Since ISI® first commissioned Bill Granizo to do a mural,[1] we have become close friends. Bill has a special place in the hearts of many ISI employees who see his work almost every day. When he heard about our plans for the ISI Caring Center for Children and Parents, he contacted Peter Aborn, then ISI's vice president of administrative services, and the person mainly responsible for the design of our office building as well as the Caring Center. Granizo told us about another muralist whose work he considered very exciting.

Thanks to this introduction by a fellow artist, Peter and I became familiar with the work of Lilli Ann Killen Rosenberg. Calvin Lee of ISI arranged for us to meet, and eventually the work to be described was created.

Like ISI itself, I did not originally "plan" the growth of our art "collection." As explained earlier,[1] we commissioned the first mural because it was part of the deal we made with the City of Philadelphia. But the low budget they required made me realize what a small price any organization needs to pay for permanently valuable and stimulating art. And so we embarked on a program that has now proved to be unusual. But I sincerely hope that the inclusion of art in the design of every building will become commonplace.

A few years ago, I described in some detail the numerous works of art at the ISI headquarters building.[1-4] One of the cumulative effects of the art in our building is to create a cheerful and stimulating work environment for the ISI staff. This alone might justify the program. But it is interesting to note that the art is equally as stimulating to our visitors. Indeed, corporate art plays an important role in community and public relations.

When we planned the Caring Center,[5] we were concerned not only with the quality of the environment for the children, but of equal importance was the impact on the community. So we wanted as much *external*, publicly visible art as possible. Aborn, now senior vice president of the Current Awareness Division, and others at ISI consulted many artists in the early design stages of the new facility. They met with architects, child-care consultants, and building contractors to make certain the building's appearance would contribute to a child's sense of security, comfort, and control.

It was our desire that the experiences of the children there be as rich and multidimensional as possible. Anita Olds, Child Study Department, Tufts University, Medford, Massachusetts, feels children have an innate aesthetic sense that needs nurturing.[6] Art is, therefore, an important aspect of their environment. It can stimulate children to use their imaginations and express their emotions.

The Caring Center now has its own collection of art, perhaps as impressive as that of our main building. Foremost is the spectacular concrete and mosaic bas-relief mural by Lilli Ann which covers the entire exterior west wall of the Caring Center building. Around the perimeter of the playground are four 7′ x 13′ (2.1 m x 3.9 m) ceramic tile murals created independently by husband-and-wife artists Granizo and Lark Lucas. Granizo, by the way, created the tile mural, "Cathedral of Man," for ISI's headquarters.[1] Also within the Caring Center playground stands a life-size cast bronze puma, created by Philadelphia sculptor Eric Berg. Inside the Caring Center building hangs a large Huichol yarn painting by Emeteria Martinez Rios, who also created the yarn painting, "Myths and Rituals of the Huichol Indians," discussed previously.[2]

Since it is impossible for a single essay to do justice to all of these unique works of art, we will discuss them in several essays, so that each may be treated in detail, both in text and in accompanying pictorial inserts. This essay, the first in a series, will describe Lilli Ann's mural, "A Celebration of Working Parents and Their Children," which is by far the largest and most visible work in the entire ISI collection. (See color insert elsewhere in this issue.)

Lilli Ann received her professional training in art and architecture at Cooper Union, New York, and the Cranbrook Academy of Art, Michigan. As a teenager in Southern California, she discovered Simon Rodia's work, "Watts Tower," a mosaic sculpture in Los Angeles. This work, which consists of seven steel and concrete towers,[7] made a lasting impression. The use of variegated pieces of tile, pottery, and glass, which Rodia embedded in his sculpture, appealed to Lilli Ann. Such free use of materials, and the tactile qualities they provide, have since become an enduring feature of her own work.

Working with concrete and mosaic, Lilli Ann's technique is to embed a variety of materials into concrete, sometimes carving into the concrete or casting with it. In this form of sculpture, known as bas-relief, the figures project slightly from the background substance. Her use of rich textures and colors discourages graffiti. Since Lilli Ann creates most of her work for the outdoors, her pieces are extremely durable and presumably resistant to environmental damage. However, under extreme temperature fluctuations, small ceramic pieces may fall off. These can be easily recemented.

Lilli Ann's career began in 1950 as a teacher and director of the art program at the Henry Street Settlement on the Lower East Side of Manhattan. A multiservice social agency serving the residents of the Lower East Side, the Henry Street Settlement also provides cultural and recreational activities for tenants in local housing developments. Lilli Ann felt that art in housing developments would give residents a sense of permanence and belonging, especially if the community participated in the project. Working with children of the LaGuardia Public Housing Development, Lilli Ann placed ceramic murals and sculpture in the community centers. She worked with all age groups in creating concrete play-sculpture gardens adjacent to the housing development. The murals and sculpture, created with Lilli Ann's guidance, helped improve the drab atmosphere and gave each space its own character.

Her work at LaGuardia prompted the Housing Authority to plan similar beautification programs in other housing developments. The Housing Authority established an Art Advisory Council. In 1960, the council received a Rockefeller Foundation grant for improving the appearance of community spaces. Lilli Ann was named art consultant. Her job was to change the institutional atmosphere in the housing developments and to work toward humanizing public spaces with art. She reviewed plans and made suggestions for improving the appearance of all public spaces in New York City housing developments.

Lilli Ann believes that art created *by* children can be beautiful and deserves recognition. When the Henry Street Settlement decided to build a new headquarters, she persuaded the architect to include a mural made by children. The resulting work, entitled "The Friendly Jungle," adorns the front of the Henry Street building on the Lower East Side. In her 1968 book, *Children Make Murals and Sculpture*, Rosenberg described her mural projects involving children. In it she emphasized the need to provide children with avenues of creative expression.[8]

During her years at the Henry Street Settlement, Lilli Ann functioned more as an art teacher than an artist. She had children create a number of murals under her direction. This gave them a sense of accomplishment and self-respect. In time, however, she felt the need to create art of her own. In 1968, she left the Henry Street Settlement, and began creating outdoor murals. She often invited children and other members of the community to contribute small objects for inclusion in these murals, many of which can still be found in New York playgrounds and housing developments.

In 1972, Lilli Ann moved to Boston with her husband and three children, where she continued to produce murals with the participation of the community. For example, in creating a mural for the Judge Baker Clinic, Children's Hospital, Boston, she involved the young patients and hospital staff. The children contributed their own handmade clay pieces. Lilli Ann then embedded them into the mural. This imparted to the children a sense of control in changing their environment.

Concrete mosaic murals created by Lilli Ann with community participation have also been installed at a number of Massachusetts schools. In Boston's predominantly Hispanic Villa Victoria housing development, she produced a mural that honors Ramón Emeterio Betances, a nineteenth-century Puerto Rican patriot.

Five years ago, Lilli Ann completed her largest piece, "Celebration of the Underground," a 110′ x 10′ (33 m x 3 m) mosaic for the Park Street Subway Station in Boston. The 128-section mural tells the story of America's first subway, built in Boston in 1897. The mural consists of concrete embedded with old trolley parts, subway construction tools, seashells, rocks, bones, ceramic pieces,

and colored glass. Part of the mural depicts the origin of the subway as Boston grew from a seaport town into an industrial and commercial center. Another part shows tunnels connecting different neighborhoods of the city.

More recently, Lilli Ann created a mural for blind and handicapped children at the Alfred I. du Pont Institute, an orthopedic pediatric hospital in Wilmington, Delaware. This mural depicts a fantasy garden in which animals and children are interspersed with clouds and plants. Like most of her work, this piece incorporates a "please-touch" quality that children find appealing.

Lilli Ann's work has been exhibited at the Kendall Gallery in Wellfleet, Massachusetts, the Museum of Contemporary Crafts, and the Metropolitan Museum of Art, both in New York City. She has about 40 bas-relief and sculpture creations in Boston and New York City. She even has pieces of sculpture installed in front of the public library in Medellín, Colombia. She created these with her husband, Marvin Rosenberg, who is an artist and social worker. Numerous pieces of her work are in private collections.

It is this experience and dedication to children's art that Lilli Ann brought to the Caring Center mural. The 36′ by 18′ (10.8 m x 5.4 m) mural consists of 72 bas-relief concrete panels that she created in her studio in Newton Centre, Massachusetts. She spent six months creating these panels. Then, with the help of several assistants, she spent four days installing them on the wall of the Caring Center.

The mural can be seen quite clearly from the University City High School located on 36th Street, about 500 yards from the Caring Center. The sun reflects from it and, depending on the angle, it produces a brilliant effect. At night it is clearly visible since it is illuminated by spotlights. My only regret is that this marvelous work is not visible in a more central part of Philadelphia.

"Celebration" depicts four large trees that represent the seasons, their branches filled with an extraordinary variety of exotic birds. At the base of one tree is the prominent figure of a man standing with a child on his shoulders. This symbolizes the often overlooked importance of the father in childraising. On the ground between the trees is a pond, with a panoply of life within and around it. There are fish, turtles, frogs, cats, dogs, dragonflies, butterflies, and other insects. It is this diversity of life that Lilli Ann celebrates in her mural.

On the left side of the mural, in the background behind the trees, Lilli Ann has created a cityscape of Philadelphia, decorated with objects unique to our city: the Liberty Bell, soft pretzels, boat-racing on the Schuylkill River, and of course Benjamin Franklin performing his famous kite-flying experiment. Many of the clay pieces in this collage were created by friends of Lilli Ann who know and love Philadelphia.

Naturally, the mural is adorned everywhere with children. An infant crawls along the banks of the pond, surrounded by alphabet blocks. One child has snared a leaping fish. Other children frolic among the fallen leaves in the foreground or play with adults in the streets of the cityscape.

One theme Lilli Ann sought to incorporate into the mural is that of growth and change. Thus, the left side of the mural depicts the Big Dipper to represent a starry night sky above the leafless trees of winter. The trees in the center are green with spring and summer foliage. On the right of the mural, an autumn sun bursts through trees with leaves of red and gold. Growth and change are also evident in a succession of three handprints impressed into the concrete. These handprints grow successively larger, showing a progression from infancy to childhood to adulthood. Children at the Caring Center like to fill in the hands with their own, and their interaction with the artwork mirrors Lilli Ann's intent that "play leads to discovery."

Lilli Ann has embedded her mural with thousands of brightly colored objects such as coins, seashells, marbles,

and glass. The arrangement of these objects forms the figures in the mural. The one-to-three-inch-thick concrete surface also employs "real life" artifacts to form images. For example, the shells of the turtles consist of round grills from the tops of gas stoves. Scallop shells form the wings of some of the butterflies. Drafting tools, antique keys, and wrought iron fence sections are also part of the mural. And the leaves, more than 1,500 of them, are clay impressions of real leaves, embedded in the concrete. The entire mural is coated with a special weatherproof glaze similar to the anti-graffiti spray used on brick buildings.

One of the most surprising aspects of this work is that there is so much to be seen. For example, you may at first notice the recognizable form of a cat in a tree. As you move closer you can discern the many component objects that make up the cat: mirror fragments, beads, and mosaic tiles. On closer inspection, you see yourself reflected in the mural's fragments. Indeed, you may appreciate the intricately colored beads for their own beauty. Susan Silverstein, Caring Center director, and other members of her staff often observe toddlers trying to articulate the names of the many objects they find in the mural. "I tried to fill it with lots of different objects," says the artist. "Every time people look at it, I hope they'll see things they never saw before. I didn't want people to get tired of it." I suppose this must be the implicit wish of every artist. To further emphasize her theme of growth and change, Lilli Ann designed the work so that it looks different at different times of the day. She suggests that the best time to see it is after noon on bright days. "The colors and the mosaics catch the sun, and everything glitters," she says. Silverstein notes that some parents have made it a daily ritual to visit the mural, where their children search for different objects and designs.

Lilli Ann designed her work so that very small children can find meaningful objects at the bottom of the mural. As they grow taller, they see the mural from different perspectives. Olds believes that Lilli Ann's work is ideally suited for children, attuned as it is to the stages of childhood development. According to Olds, before the age of four, children tend not to perceive the whole, but to focus on subpieces.[6] Lilli Ann's work provides young children with many colorful, small objects to occupy their attention. Moreover, according to Olds, the bas-relief mural allows the child to obtain tactile and kinesthetic information about the structure of its component parts.

Lilli Ann's "Celebration" has been widely praised. Former Philadelphia city planning director, Edmund Bacon, believes that its appeal lies in the familiar objects it contains. "In contrast to more fashionable abstract art," he says, "it gives a much richer evocation to children of the senses and experiences meaningful to them."[9] Robert Campbell, architecture critic for the *Boston Globe*, suggests that children are not the only ones to appreciate the absence of abstraction. Commenting on Lilli Ann's work in general, he noted that her art "can be appreciated by a larger public than the few who attend galleries."[10] This is in sharp contrast to the feelings of Albert C. Barnes, who felt that only those who had studied art could adequately appreciate it.[11]

Through the art at the Caring Center, preschoolers are getting early exposure to a variety of creative folk and fine art. It is important that children identify with the various childhood experiences these artists have portrayed. In future essays, I will discuss the other works at the Caring Center, as well as the new artwork on display in our main offices, which provide parents and toddlers with the kind of daily stimulation that makes life just a little less ordinary.

* * * * *

My thanks to Terri Freedman, Tom Isenberg, and Linda LaRue for their help in the preparation of this essay. ©1984 ISI

REFERENCES

1. **Garfield E.** Fine art enhances ISI's new building: a ceramic mural by Guillermo Wagner Granizo and a sgraffito mural by Joseph Slawinski. *Essays of an information scientist.* Philadelphia: ISI Press, 1983. Vol. 5. p. 15-9.
2. --------------. Huichol mythology and culture. Part 1. World's largest yarn painting is latest in series of ISI-commissioned artworks. *Essays of an information scientist.* Philadelphia: ISI Press, 1983. Vol. 5. p. 164-70.
3. --------------. Works of art at ISI: Jennifer Bartlett's "In the Garden" and "Interpenetrations" by Handel Evans. *Essays of an information scientist.* Philadelphia: ISI Press, 1983. Vol. 5. p. 207-12.
4. --------------. ISI's "World Brain" by Gabriel Liebermann: the world's first holographic engraving. *Essays of an information scientist.* Philadelphia: ISI Press, 1983. Vol. 5. p. 348-54.
5. --------------. Child care: an investment in the future. Part 2. The ISI Caring Center for Children and Parents. *Essays of an information scientist.* Philadelphia: ISI Press, 1984. Vol. 6. p. 38-46.
6. **Olds A.** Telephone communication. 26 June 1984.
7. **Billiter B.** Simon Rodia's incredible towers. *ARTnews* 78(4):92-6, 1979.
8. **Rosenberg L A K.** *Children make murals and sculpture.* New York: Reinhold, 1968. 132 p.
9. **Bacon E.** Telephone communication. 22 June 1984.
10. **Campbell R.** Personal communication. 29 June 1984.
11. **Garfield E.** The legacy of Albert C. Barnes. Part 2. The Barnes Foundation. *Essays of an information scientist.* Philadelphia: ISI Press, 1983. Vol. 5. p. 455-63.

A CELEBRATION
OF Working PARents
And their children

A Mural by Lilli Ann Killen Rosenberg for

THE **iSi**®
CARING CENTER
for CHILDREN & PARENTS

Lilli Ann Killen Rosen berg's mural, "A Celebration of Working Parents and Their Children" is installed on the west wall of the ISI/Caring Center for Children and Parents. The 36′ × 18 (10.8 m × 5.4 m) bas-relief mural consists of 72 concrete panels embedded with thousands of such brightly colored objects as coins, sea shells, marbles, glass, and leaves.

Rosenberg has designed her mural to engage the curiosity of children, and to encourage them to explore objects and themes which they find meaningful. These provide a variety of textures and shapes that appeal to children, who enjoy touching the individual objects. Rosenberg's mural incorporates her feeling that "play leads to discovery". For example, young children can recognize the alphabet blocks in the lower right of the mural, while older children learn from the collage depicting Philadelphia's history and tradition on the left side of the mural.

The theme of the mural is growth and change. The left side depicts the big dipper to represent a starry winter night. Centrally, trees green with spring and summer foliage are filled with a variety of birds. On the right, brightly colored leaves of fall are abundant. Moving from left to right there is also a transition from night into day. The focus of Rosenberg's mural is the figure of a father and child who appear to be moving through the seasons and sharing the process of growth and change.

Handprints of various sizes serve as a template for children at the Caring Center measuring their own growth.

Above, *Artist Lilli Ann Killen Rosenberg adds a layer of sealant to the mural to protect it from the elements.*

"A Celeb
Working
and The

A bas-relief
the ISI Car

Right, *Real leaves are*
leaves are rolled into a cl
clay impression is fired a
concrete mural.

Below, *Full view of "A*
and Their Children" sh
winter to fall.

A view of the Delaware River, separating Philadelphia from Camden, New Jersey, forms a pe
Philadelphia collage.

The figure of Benjamin Franklin is part of a collage within the mural depict-
ing the traditions and vitality of historical Philadelphia.

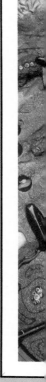

Close inspec
grills from t

The figure of a man with a child on his shoulders is a prominent part of the mural.

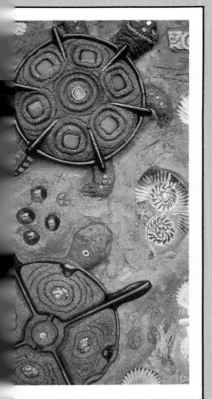

...ion of the mural reveals "found" objects such as the ...e top of a gas stove used in turtle shells.

isi® **Institute for Scientific Information®**

3501 Market St., Philadelphia, PA 19104
Tel: (215) 386-0100, Cable: SCINFO
Telex: 84-5305

©1984 ISI OPC-S/84-143

CC-3501

Current Comments®

100 Classics from *The Lancet*

Number 39   September 24, 1984

We recently initiated a series of essays on the articles most cited in *Science Citation Index®* (*SCI®*) from 1961 to 1982. So far, we've identified 300 of these classic papers,[1-3] and plan to extend the study until at least 1,000 articles are listed. As expected, a significant proportion of the papers discussed to date were published in a small number of multidisciplinary journals—*Proceedings of the National Academy of Sciences of the USA, Science, Nature,* and so on. However, the high-impact articles from clinical and other journals warrant separate discussion. We have already discussed 100 classics from the *New England Journal of Medicine*.[4] This essay covers 100 articles from *The Lancet* that were most cited in *SCI* for the years 1961-1982.

The first issue of *The Lancet* appeared in London on October 5, 1823, making it the oldest weekly medical journal in the UK.[5] Its founder and editor, Thomas Wakley, was a controversial person with a strong desire to reform the British medical establishment. In *The Lancet*, Wakley heaped criticism on the Royal College of Surgeons, inadequate medical education, quackery and malpractice, and the nepotism and patronage governing promotions to hospital surgical teams. At that time, the College determined who could teach in the hospitals and serve as examiners to certify medical students. Teaching positions were highly coveted, because lecturers could earn as much as £20,000 per year in tax-free income from students' fees. These positions were awarded to relatives and close friends of the College's 20-odd ruling administrators, regardless of their qualifications. To make matters worse, no mechanism existed to redress this unfair system. The College's officials were appointed for life, and they named their own successors, also for life.[6,7]

Wakley used *The Lancet* to attack the College's nepotism and patronage. Peter Froggatt, vice chancellor, Queen's University, Belfast, Northern Ireland, noted, "The abscess on the medical body politic required incision: the title *The Lancet* was not idly chosen."[6] In the very first issue, and for many more to come, Wakley published the formal lectures given by the London hospital teachers. By making these lectures public, Wakley threatened the teachers' major source of income and the College's monopolistic authority. Sued 10 times in as many years, Wakley managed to continue publishing the lectures. He carried his fight for reform to Parliament and was elected to the House of Commons in 1835. Wakley's exposure of inadequate education and malpractice within the College led to the enactment of many laws, including the Medical Act of 1858. He also set up a sanitary commission to examine the purity of foods sold in the UK. Wakley's findings of widespread adulteration led to the passage of the Adulteration Act and Sale of Food and Drugs Act.[6-8]

Of course, *The Lancet* was intended to inform as well as reform. *The Lancet* published case reports, updates, medical correspondence, lectures, and society transactions. The consistent high quality of these publications has earned *The*

Lancet its current reputation as one of the most important medical journals in the world. Only nine editors have served *The Lancet* in its 160 years of publication, and they must be credited with building and maintaining *The Lancet*'s enviable position. Keep in mind that, primarily, the editors decide what is published in *The Lancet*. However, according to Ian Munro, *The Lancet*'s current editor, about 20 to 25 percent of the submitted manuscripts are sent to outside referees for advice.[9] Remarkably, accepted manuscripts are usually published within 10 weeks of submission.

Many citation analyses indicate *The Lancet*'s preeminence among medical journals. For example, *The Lancet* ranked among the top 10 journals, *regardless* of discipline, in terms of total citations received and average citations per article (impact) in a study based on the 1974 *SCI*.[10] It also routinely appears in studies of the most-cited articles covering various time periods. By highlighting *The Lancet*'s citation classics in this essay, we pay tribute to its excellent publication record.

Table 1 includes the 100 articles from *The Lancet* that were most cited from 1961 to 1982. They are listed in alphabetic order by first author. Column B gives the number of citations each article received during this 22-year period. For papers published before 1961, we've added citations from the 1955-1964 *SCI* cumulation (column A). The number of 1983 citations are shown in column C to give you an idea of how frequently each article is currently cited. These data are followed by full bibliographic information, including the authors' affiliations. Thirty-five articles have already been featured as *Citation Classics* ™ in *Current Contents*® (*CC*®). They are indicated by asterisks. The issue number, year, and edition of *CC* in which the commentary appeared are shown in parentheses after the reference.

Each paper was cited at least 265 times, and the most cited about 1,600 times. Many hundreds of papers published in *The Lancet* over the past 160

years would qualify as *Citation Classics*. Table 2 shows the frequency distribution for 3,200 papers from *The Lancet* that were cited 50 or more times from 1961 to 1982. About 200 papers have been cited at least 200 times.

Six of *The Lancet* articles in this study were published between 1975 and 1979; 43, 1970-1974; 22, 1965-1969; 21, 1960-1964; 7, 1955-1959; and one paper was published in the 1800s.

The oldest classic from *The Lancet* was published in 1896 by G.T. Beatson, Glasgow Cancer Hospital, Scotland. Beatson found that inoperable breast tumors regressed following surgical removal of the ovaries (oophorectomy) and ingestion of thyroid tablets. Despite its age, the paper was cited between 2 and 40 times per year from 1955 to 1982, for a total of about 350 citations. Remarkably, it was cited in 25 publications in 1983. These current citations acknowledge Beatson as the first researcher to suggest that hormones influence the growth of solid tumors.

The two most recent classics from *The Lancet* were both published in 1977. S. Moncada and colleagues, Wellcome Research Laboratories, Beckenham, England, reported the discovery that prostacyclin is generated in human arterial and venous tissue. Prostacyclin inhibits platelet aggregation on the vessel wall and plays an important role in the genesis and treatment of circulatory diseases, including atherosclerosis. In a 1982 *Citation Classic* commentary, Moncada said, "I think prostacyclin has already established itself as an endogenous substance to be 'reckoned with' if one wants to understand platelet/vessel wall interactions. As very often happens, thinking back to that time, I find myself wondering how it happened that prostacyclin was there for so long and nobody saw it before us."[11] Apparently, many researchers are indeed "reckoning with" prostacyclin—the paper was cited about 600 times from 1977 to 1983.

In the other 1977 classic, N.E. Miller and colleagues, University of Tromsø, Norway, detailed the relationship be-

Table 1: Most-cited articles from *The Lancet*, 1961-1982 *SCI*®, in alphabetic order by first author. A=1955-1960 citations. B=1961-1982 citations. C=1983 citations. D=bibliographic data. An asterisk (*) indicates articles with published *Citation Classic* ™ commentaries. The issue number, year, and edition of *Current Contents*® in which these commentaries appeared are in parentheses.

A	B	C	D
122	299	13	**Ahrens E H, Insull W, Blomstrand R, Hirsch J, Tsaltas T T & Peterson M L.** The influence of dietary fats on serum-lipid levels in man. *Lancet* 1:943-53, 1957. Rockefeller Inst., New York, NY.
	411	31	***Alberti K G M M, Christensen N J, Christensen S E, Prange Hansen Aa, Iversen J, Lundbaek K, Seyer-Hansen K & Orskov H.** Inhibition of insulin secretion by somatostatin. *Lancet* 2:1299-301, 1973. Second Univ. Clin. Intern. Med., Kommunehosp., Aarhus, Denmark. (44/82/LS)
	545	25	***Allison A C, Denman A M & Barnes R D.** Cooperating and controlling functions of thymus-derived lymphocytes in relation to autoimmunity. *Lancet* 2:135-40, 1971. Clin. Res. Ctr., Harrow, England. (24/80/CP)
	344	10	***Almeida J D, Rubenstein D & Stott E J.** New antigen-antibody system in Australia-antigen-positive hepatitis. *Lancet* 2:1225-7, 1971. Roy. Postgrad. Med. Sch., Dept. Virol., London; Northwick Park Hosp., Clin. Res. Ctr., Harrow, England. (9/83/LS)
	373	10	***Almeida J D & Waterson A P.** Immune complexes in hepatitis. *Lancet* 2:983-6, 1969. Roy. Postgrad. Med. Sch., Dept. Virol., London, England. (27/80/CP)
	267	1	**Ardeman S & Chanarin I.** A method for the assay of human gastric intrinsic factor and for the detection and titration of antibodies against intrinsic factor. *Lancet* 2:1350-4, 1963. MRC Exptl. Haematol. Res. Unit; St. Mary's Hosp. Med. Sch., London, England.
	268	18	**Ashbaugh D G, Bigelow D B, Petty T L & Levine B E.** Acute respiratory distress in adults. *Lancet* 2:319-23, 1967. Univ. Colorado Med. Ctr., Denver, CO.
4	571	6	**Astrup P, Jorgensen K, Andersen O S & Engel K.** The acid-base metabolism: a new approach. *Lancet* 1:1035-9, 1960. Rigshosp., Dept. Clin. Chem., Copenhagen, Denmark.
	317	15	**Baum J K, Holtz F, Bookstein J J & Klein E W.** Possible association between benign hepatomas and oral contraceptives. *Lancet* 2:926-9, 1973. Univ. Michigan Hosp.; St. Joseph Mercy Hosp., Dept. Pathol.; Wayne Cty. Gen. Hosp., Ann Arbor, MI.
51	306	25	**Beatson G T.** On the treatment of inoperable cases of carcinoma of the mamma: suggestions for a new method of treatment, with illustrative cases. *Lancet* 2:104-7, 1896. Glasgow Canc. Hosp., Glasgow Western Infirm., Glasgow and Univ. Edinburgh, Edinburgh, Scotland.
	308	8	**Belzer F O, Ashby B S & Dunphy J E.** 24-hour and 72-hour preservation of canine kidneys. *Lancet* 2:536-9, 1967. Univ. California Med. Ctr., San Francisco, CA.
	294	19	**Bishop R F, Davidson G P, Holmes I H & Ruck B J.** Virus particles in epithelial cells of duodenal mucosa from children with acute non-bacterial gastroenteritis. *Lancet* 2:1281-3, 1973. Roy. Child. Hosp., Dept. Gastroenterol.; Univ. Melbourne, Dept. Microbiol., Melbourne, Australia.
	416	7	**Black J W, Crowther A F, Shanks R G, Smith L H & Dornhorst A C.** A new adrenergic beta-receptor antagonist. *Lancet* 1:1080-1, 1964. Imperial Chem. Ind., Ltd., Pharmaceut. Div., Cheshire; St. George's Hosp., Med. Unit, London, England.
	535	10	**Black J W & Stephenson J S.** Pharmacology of a new adrenergic beta-receptor-blocking compound (nethalide). *Lancet* 2:311-4, 1962. Imperial Chem. Ind., Ltd., Pharmaceut. Div., Cheshire, England.
	408	24	**Bloom S R, Mortimer C H, Thorner M O, Besser G M, Hall R, Gomez-Pan A, Roy V M, Russell R C G, Coy D H, Kastin A J & Schally A V.** Inhibition of gastrin and gastric-acid secretion by growth-hormone release-inhibiting hormone. *Lancet* 2:1106-9, 1974. Middlesex Hosp.; St. Bartholomew's Hosp.; St. Mary's Hosp., London; Roy. Victoria Infirm., Newcastle upon Tyne, England; Vet. Admin. Hosp.; Tulane Univ. Sch. Med., New Orleans, LA.
	270	12	**Bloom S R, Polak J M & Pearse A G E.** Vasoactive intestinal peptide and watery-diarrhoea syndrome. *Lancet* 2:14-5, 1973. Middlesex Hosp., Inst. Clin. Res.; Roy. Postgrad. Med. Sch., Dept. Histochem., London, England.
	275	13	**Braithwaite R A, Goulding R, Theano G, Bailey J & Coppen A.** Plasma concentration of amitriptyline and clinical response. *Lancet* 1:1297-300, 1972. Guy's Hosp., Poisons Unit, London; Warlingham Park Hosp., Warlingham; MRC Neuropsychiat. Unit, Carshalton; West Park Hosp., Epsom, England.

A	B	C	D
	494	39	*Brewerton D A, Hart F D, Nicholls A, Caffrey M, James D C O & Sturrock R D. Ankylosing spondylitis and HL-A 27. *Lancet* 1:904-7, 1973. Westminster Hosp., London, England. (29/80/CP)
	380	17	*Brock D J H & Sutcliffe R G. Alpha-fetoprotein in the antenatal diagnosis of anencephaly and spina bifida. *Lancet* 2:197-9, 1972. Univ. Dept. Hum. Gen., Western Gen. Hosp., Edinburgh, Scotland. (16/81/CP)
	357	30	Bryant M G, Polak J M, Modlin I, Bloom S R, Albuquerque R H & Pearse A G E. Possible dual role for vasoactive intestinal peptide as gastrointestinal hormone and neurotransmitter substance. *Lancet* 1:991-3, 1976. Hammersmith Hosp., Roy. Postgrad. Med. Sch., London, England.
	277	2	*Buckton K E, Jacobs P A, Court Brown W M & Doll R. A study of the chromosome damage persisting after X-ray therapy for ankylosing spondylitis. *Lancet* 2:676-82, 1962. MRC Clin. Effects Rad. Res. Unit, Edinburgh, Scotland; Univ. Coll. Hosp. Med. Sch., London, England. (46/82/CP)
	606	36	*Carlson L A & Bottiger L E. Ischaemic heart-disease in relation to fasting values of plasma triglycerides and cholesterol: Stockholm Prospective Study. *Lancet* 1:865-8, 1972. Karolinska Hosp., King Gustaf V Res. Inst., Stockholm; Univ. Uppsala, Dept. Geriat., Uppsala, Sweden. (12/83/LS)
	400	17	*Collins G M, Bravo-Shugarman M & Terasaki P I. Kidney preservation for transportation. *Lancet* 2:1219-22, 1969. Univ. California, Ctr. Hlth. Sci., Los Angeles, CA. (32/80/CP)
	291	15	Combes B, Shorey J, Barrera A, Stastny P, Eigenbrodt E H, Hull A R & Carter N W. Glomerulonephritis with deposition of Australia antigen-antibody complexes in glomerular basement membrane. *Lancet* 2:234-7, 1971. Univ. Texas Southwestern Med. Sch. Dallas; Dallas Vet. Hosp., Dallas, TX.
	330	8	*Connolly J H, Allen I V, Hurwitz L J & Millar J H D. Measles-virus antibody and antigen in subacute sclerosing panencephalitis. *Lancet* 1:542-4, 1967. Queen's Univ. Belfast, Depts. Microbiol. & Pathol.; Roy. Victoria Hosp., Belfast, Northern Ireland. (10/81/CP)
	351	3	*Coulson A S & Chalmers D G. Separation of viable lymphocytes from human blood. *Lancet* 1:468-9, 1964. Univ. Cambridge, Dept. Pathol., Cambridge, England. (35/79/LS)
	543	18	*Dane D S, Cameron C H & Briggs M. Virus-like particles in serum of patients with Australia-antigen-associated hepatitis. *Lancet* 1:695-8, 1970. Middlesex Hosp., Bland-Sutton Inst., London, England. (45/80/CP)
	470	33	*de Groote J, Desmet V J, Gedigk P, Korb G, Popper H, Poulsen H, Scheuer P J, Schmid M, Thaler H, Uehlinger E & Wepler W. A classification of chronic hepatitis. *Lancet* 2:626-8, 1968. Acad. Ziekenhuis St. Rafael, Leuven, Belgium; Univ. Bonn, Bonn; Univ. Marburg, Marburg; City Hosp., Inst. Pathol., Kassel, FRG; Mt. Sinai Sch. Med., New York, NY; Kommunehosp., Inst. Pathol., Copenhagen, Denmark; Roy. Free Hosp. Sch. Med., London, England; Waid City Hosp., Dept. Med.; Univ. Zurich, Zurich, Switzerland; Wilhelminenhosp., Vienna, Austria. (11/80/CP)
	361	26	Dudley F J, Fox R A & Sherlock S. Cellular immunity and hepatitis-associated Australia antigen liver disease. *Lancet* 1:723-6, 1972. Roy. Free Hosp., Dept. Med., London, England.
9	325	2	Edwards J H, Harnden D G, Cameron A H, Crosse V M & Wolff O H. A new trisomic syndrome. *Lancet* 1:787-90, 1960. MRC Pop. Genet. Res. Unit, Oxford & Radiobiol. Res. Unit, Harwell; Child. Hosp.; Birmingham Region. Hosp.; Univ. Birmingham, Birmingham, England.
	655	34	*Epstein M A, Achong B G & Barr Y M. Virus particles in cultured lymphoblasts from Burkitt's lymphoma. *Lancet* 1:702-3, 1964. Middlesex Hosp. Med. Sch., London, England. (14/79/LS)
	268	7	Field E J & Caspary E A. Lymphocyte sensitisation: an in-vitro test for cancer? *Lancet* 2:1337-41, 1970. MRC Demyelinating Dis. Unit, Newcastle upon Tyne, England.
	267	25	Fischer J E & Baldessarini R J. False neurotransmitters and hepatic failure. *Lancet* 2:75-80, 1971. Massachusetts Gen. Hosp., Depts. Gen. Surg. & Psychiat.; Harvard Med. Sch., Boston, MA.
67	334	6	Ford C E, Jones K W, Polani P E, de Almeida J C & Briggs J H. A sex-chromosome anomaly in a case of gonadal dysgenesis (Turner's syndrome). *Lancet* 1:711-3, 1959. MRC Radiobiol. Res. Unit, Harwell; Guy's Hosp., London, England.

A	B	C	D
	426	28	**Franciosa J A, Guiha N H, Limas C J, Rodriguera E & Cohn J N.** Improved left ventricular function during nitroprusside infusion in acute myocardial infarction. *Lancet* 1:650-4, 1972. Vet. Admin. Hosp., Hypertens. Clin. Hemodynam. Sect.; Georgetown Univ. Sch. Med., Washington, DC.
	335	18	**Gardner S D, Field A M, Coleman D V & Hulme B.** New human papovavirus (B.K.) isolated from urine after renal transplantation. *Lancet* 1:1253-7, 1971. Cent. Publ. Hlth. Lab., Virus Ref. Lab.; St. Mary's Hosp., Dept. Histopathol. Cytol. & Med. Unit, London, England.
	629	83	*****Giblett E R, Anderson J E, Cohen F, Pollara B & Meuwissen H J.** Adenosine-deaminase deficiency in two patients with severely impaired cellular immunity. *Lancet* 2:1067-9, 1972. King Cty. Cent. Blood Bank, Inc., Seattle, WA; Child. Hosp. Michigan and Wayne State Univ., Dept. Pediat., Detroit, MI; Albany Med. Coll., Dept. Pediat.; State NY Dept. Hlth., Kidney Dis. & Birth Defects Insts., Albany, NY. (22/82/CP)
	327	44	**Giblett E R, Ammann A J, Sandman R, Wara D W & Diamond L K.** Nucleoside-phosphorylase deficiency in a child with severely defective T-cell immunity and normal B-cell immunity. *Lancet* 1:1010-3, 1975. King Cty. Cent. Blood Bank, Inc., Seattle, WA; Univ. California, San Francisco Med. Ctr., San Francisco, CA.
	380	19	**Gocke D J, Morgan C, Lockshin M, Hsu K, Bombardieri S & Christian C L.** Association between polyarteritis and Australia antigen. *Lancet* 2:1149-53, 1970. Columbia Univ., Coll. Physn. Surg., New York, NY.
32	292	3	*****Gordon R S.** Exudative enteropathy: abnormal permeability of the gastrointestinal tract demonstrable with labelled polyvinylpyrrolidone. *Lancet* 1:325-6, 1959. US Publ. Hlth. Serv., NHI, Bethesda, MD. (13/81/CP)
4	279	5	**Gregory R A, Tracy H J, French J M & Sircus W.** Extraction of a gastrin-like substance from a pancreatic tumor in a case of Zollinger-Ellison syndrome. *Lancet* 1:1045-8, 1960. Univ. Liverpool, Dept. Physiol., Liverpool; Univ. Birmingham, Dept. Med., Birmingham, England; Univ. Edinburgh, Dept. Med. and Western Gen. Hosp., Gastro-Intest. Unit, Edinburgh, Scotland.
	26	6	**Hales C N & Randle P J.** Effects of low-carbohydrate diet and diabetes mellitus on plasma concentrations of glucose, non-esterified fatty acid, and insulin during oral glucose-tolerance tests. *Lancet* 1:790-6, 1963. Univ. Cambridge, Dept. Biochem., Cambridge, England.
	285	14	**Hall R, Schally A V, Evered D, Kastin A J, Mortimer C H, Tunbridge W M G, Besser G M, Coy D H, Goldie D J, McNeilly A S, Phenekos C & Weightman D.** Action of growth-hormone-release inhibitory hormone in healthy men and in acromegaly. *Lancet* 2:581-4, 1973. Roy. Victoria Infirm., Dept. Med., Newcastle upon Tyne; St. Bartholomew's Hosp., Med. Prof. Unit & Dept. Chem. Pathol., London, England; Vet. Admin. Hosp., Dept. Med.; Tulane Univ. Sch. Med., New Orleans, LA.
	394	32	**Hill M J, Drasar B S, Aries V, Crowther J S, Hawksworth G & Williams R E O.** Bacteria and aetiology of cancer of large bowel. *Lancet* 1:95-100, 1971. St. Mary's Hosp. Med. Sch., London, England.
	307	10	**Holmes B, Quie P G, Windhorst D B & Good R A.** Fatal granulomatous disease of childhood. *Lancet* 1:1225-8, 1966. Variety Club Heart Hosp., Pediat. Res. Lab.; Univ. Minnesota, Div. Dermatol., Minneapolis, MN.
	310	11	**Hoofnagle J H, Gerety R J & Barker L F.** Antibody to hepatitis-B-virus core in man. *Lancet* 2:869-73, 1973. Food Drug Admin., Bur. Biologics, Rockville, MD.
	317	27	**Hoover R & Fraumeni J F.** Risk of cancer in renal-transplant recipients. *Lancet* 2:55-7, 1973. NIH, NCI, Bethesda, MD.
60	1190	52	*****Huggett A St G & Nixon D A.** Use of glucose oxidase, peroxidase, and O-dianisidine in determination of blood and urinary glucose. *Lancet* 2:368-70, 1957. St. Mary's Hosp. Med. Sch., London, England. (21/81/CP)
	336	2	**Jacobs P A, Harnden D G, Buckton K E, Brown W M C, King M J, McBride J A, MacGregor T N & Maclean N.** Cytogenetic studies in primary amenorrhoea. *Lancet* 1:1183-9, 1961. MRC Clin. Effects Rad. Res. Unit; Univ. Edinburgh, Dept. Obstet. Gynaecol.; Western Gen. Hosp., Dept. Pathol., Edinburgh, Scotland.
	314	4	**Johansson S G O.** Raised levels of a new immunoglobulin class (IgND) in asthma. *Lancet* 2:951-3, 1967. Univ. Hosp., Blood Ctr., Uppsala, Sweden.
	279	7	*****Johansson S G O, Mellbin T & Vahlquist B.** Immunoglobulin levels in Ethiopian preschool children with special reference to high concentrations of immunoglobulin E (IgND). *Lancet* 1:1118-21, 1968. Univ. Hosp., Dept. Pediat. &

A	B	C	D

Blood Ctr., Uppsala, Sweden.; Child. Nutr. Unit, Addis Ababa, Ethiopia. (50/81/CP)

399 42 **Jones K L, Smith D W, Ulleland C N & Streissguth A P.** Pattern of malformation in offspring of chronic alcoholic mothers. *Lancet* 1:1267-71, 1973. Univ. Washington Sch. Med., Seattle, WA.

293 10 **Kakkar V V, Corrigan T, Spindler J, Fossard D P, Flute P T, Crellin R Q, Wessler S & Yin E T.** Efficacy of low doses of heparin in prevention of deep-vein thrombosis after major surgery. *Lancet* 2:101-6, 1972. King's Coll. Hosp. Med. Sch., London, England; Jewish Hosp. St. Louis, Dept. Med.; Washington Univ. Sch. Med., St. Louis, MO.

0 331 14 ***Kissmeyer-Nielsen F, Olsen S, Posborg Petersen V & Fjeldborg O.** Hyperacute rejection of kidney allografts, associated with pre-existing humoral antibodies against donor cells. *Lancet* 2:662-5, 1960. Aarhus Kommunehosp., Blood Bank Blood Grp. Lab.; Univ. Aarhus, Depts. Pathol. & Intern. Med., Aarhus, Denmark. (23/81/CP)

301 13 **Lapin I P & Oxenkrug G F.** Intensification of the central serotoninergic processes as a possible determinant of the thymoleptic effect. *Lancet* 1:132-6, 1969. Bekhterev Psychoneurol. Res. Inst., Lab. Psychopharmacol., Leningrad, USSR.

341 18 **Lassen N A.** The luxury-perfusion syndrome and its possible relation to acute metabolic acidosis localised within the brain. *Lancet* 2:1113-5, 1966. Bispebjerg Hosp., Dept. Clin. Physiol., Copenhagen, Denmark.

377 25 **Lassen N A, Lindbjerg J & Munck O.** Measurement of blood-flow through skeletal muscle by intramuscular injection of xenon-133. *Lancet* 1:686-9, 1964. Bispebjerg Hosp., Dept. Clin. Physiol.; Glostrup Hosp., Dept. Clin. Physiol. & Med. Dept. C, Copenhagen, Denmark.

297 9 **Lilly F, Boyse E A & Old L J.** Genetic basis of susceptibility to viral leukaemogenesis. *Lancet* 2:1207-9, 1964. Sloan-Kettering Inst. Canc. Res.; Cornell Med. Coll., Sloan-Kettering Div.; NYU Sch. Med., New York, NY.

430 14 ***Marbrook J.** Primary immune response in cultures of spleen cells. *Lancet* 2:1279-81, 1967. Walter and Eliza Hall Inst. Med. Res., Melbourne, Australia. (11/81/LS)

586 21 **Mathe G, Amiel J L, Schwarzenberg L, Schneider M, Cattan A, Schlumberger J R, Hayat M & de Vassal F.** Active immunotherapy for acute lymphoblastic leukaemia. *Lancet* 1:697-9, 1969. Hosp. Paul-Brousse, Inst. Cancerol. Immunogenet.; Inst. Gustave Roussy, Dept. Haematol., Villejuif, France.

455 13 **McDevitt H O & Bodmer W F.** HL-A, immune-response genes, and disease. *Lancet* 1:1269-75, 1974. Stanford Univ. Sch. Med., Stanford, CA; Univ. Oxford, Dept. Biochem., Oxford, England.

298 16 **Miettinen M, Turpeinen O, Karvonen M J, Elosuo R & Paavilainen E.** Effect of cholesterol-lowering diet on mortality from coronary heart-disease and other causes. *Lancet* 2:835-8, 1972. Coll. Vet. Med., Dept. Biochem.; Inst. Occup. Hlth., Helsinki; Kellokoski Hosp., Kellokoski; Nikkila Hosp., Nikkila, Finland.

961 135 ***Miller G J & Miller N E.** Plasma-high-density-lipoprotein concentration and development of ischemic heart-disease. *Lancet* 1:16-9, 1975. MRC Pneumoconiosis Unit, Llandough Hosp., Penarth, Wales; Roy. Infirm., Dept. Cardiol. & Lipid Res. Lab., Edinburgh, Scotland. (15/81/LS)

869 19 ***Miller J F A P.** Immunological function of the thymus. *Lancet* 2:748-9, 1961. Chester Beatty Res. Inst., Inst. Canc. Res., London, England. (24/78)

454 60 **Miller N E, Forde O H, Thelle D S & Mjos O D.** The Tromso heart-study. High-density lipoprotein and coronary heart disease: a prospective case-control study. *Lancet* 1:965-8, 1977. Univ. Tromso, Insts. Clin. Med., Commun. Med. & Med. Biol., Tromso, Norway.

510 83 ***Moncada S, Higgs E A & Vane J R.** Human arterial and venous tissues generate prostacyclin (prostaglandin X), a potent inhibitor of platelet aggregation. *Lancet* 1:18-21, 1977. Wellcome Res. Lab., Beckenham, England. (41/82/LS)

323 11 **Mortimer C H, Carr D, Lind T, Bloom S R, Mallinson C N, Schally A V, Tunbridge W M G, Yeomans L, Coy D H, Kastin A, Besser G M & Hall R.** Effects of growth-hormone release-inhibiting hormone on circulating glucagon, insulin, and growth hormone in normal, diabetic, acromegalic, and hypopituitary patients. *Lancet* 1:697-701, 1974. St. Bartholomew's Hosp., Med. Prof. Unit; Middlesex Hosp., Dept. Med.; Greenwich Dist. Hosp., London; Roy. Victoria Infirm., Dept. Med.; Princess Mary Matern. Hosp., MRC Reprod. Growth Unit, Newcastle upon Tyne, England; Vet. Admin. Hosp.; Tulane Univ. Sch. Med., New Orleans, LA.

A	B	C	D
	267	24	**Moynahan E J.** Letter to editor. (Acrodermatitis enteropathica: a lethal inherited human zinc-deficiency disorder.) *Lancet* 2:399-400, 1974. Hosp. Sick Child., London, England.
	362	15	**Nerup J, Platz P, Ortred Andersen O, Christy M, Lyngsoe J, Poulsen J E, Ryder L P, Thomsen M, Staub Nielsen L & Svejgaard A.** HL-A antigens and diabetes mellitus. *Lancet* 2:864-6, 1974. Gentofte Hosp., Med. Dept. F; State Univ. Hosp., Blood-Grp. Dept.; Frederiksberg Hosp., Med. Dept. E; Steno Mem. Hosp.; Bispebjerg Hosp., Med. Dept. T, Copenhagen, Denmark.
	435	19	***O'Brien J R.** Effects of salicylates on human platelets. *Lancet* 1:779-83, 1968. Portsmouth and Isle of Wight Area Pathol. Serv., Portsmouth, England. (51/80/CP)
	294	19	***Oliver M F, Kurien V A & Greenwood T W.** Relation between serum-free-fatty-acids and arrhythmias and death after acute myocardial infarction. *Lancet* 1:710-5, 1968. Roy. Infirm., Depts. Cardiol., Clin. Chem. & Coron. Care Unit, Edinburgh, Scotland. (45/81/CP)
	274	14	**Ormston B J, Cryer R J, Garry R, Besser G M & Hall R.** Thyrotrophin-releasing hormone as a thyroid-function test. *Lancet* 2:10-4, 1971. Univ. Newcastle upon Tyne, Dept. Med., Newcastle upon Tyne; St. Bartholomew's Hosp., Med. Prof. Unit, London, England.
12	324	10	**Owren P A.** Thrombotest: a new method for controlling anticoagulant therapy. *Lancet* 2:754-8, 1959. Univ. Hosp., Oslo, Norway.
	324	22	**Padgett B L, ZuRhein G M, Walker D L, Eckroade R J & Dessel B H.** Cultivation of papova-like virus from human brain with progressive multifocal leucoencephalopathy. *Lancet* 1:1257-60, 1971. Univ. Wisconsin Med. Sch., Madison; Vet. Admin. Hosp., Wood, WI.
	283	10	***Pantridge J F & Geddes J S.** A mobile intensive-care unit in the management of myocardial infarction. *Lancet* 2:271-3, 1967. Roy. Victoria Hosp., Cardiac Dept., Belfast, North. Ireland. (9/81/CP)
	393	16	**Papamichail M, Brown J C & Holborow E J.** Immunoglobulins on the surface of human lymphocytes. *Lancet* 2:850-2, 1971. MRC Rheumat. Res. Unit, Maidenhead, England.
	532	11	***Park B H, Fikrig S M & Smithwick E M.** Infection and nitroblue-tetrazolium reduction by neutrophils. *Lancet* 2:532-4, 1968. SUNY, Dept. Pediat., Buffalo, NY. (44/81/CP)
10	361	3	***Patau K, Smith D W, Therman E, Inhorn S L & Wagner H P.** Multiple congenital anomaly caused by an extra autosome. *Lancet* 1:790-3, 1960. Univ. Wisconsin Med. Sch., Madison, WI. (48/78)
	437	1	**Pearmain G, Lycette R R & Fitzgerald P H.** Tuberculin-induced mitosis in peripheral blood leucocytes. *Lancet* 1:637-8, 1963. Royston Hosp. Lab., Hastings; Christchurch Hosp., Cytogenet. Unit, Christchurch, New Zealand.
	266	5	**Peterson R D A, Kelly W D & Good R A.** Ataxia-telangiectasia: its association with a defective thymus, immunological-deficiency disease, and malignancy. *Lancet* 1:1189-93, 1964. Variety Club Heart Hosp., Pediat. Res. Lab.; Univ. Minnesota, Dept. Surg., Minneapolis, MN.
	388	22	***Polak J M, Grimelius L, Pearse A G E, Bloom S R & Arimura A.** Growth-hormone release-inhibiting hormone in gastrointestinal and pancreatic D cells. *Lancet* 1:1220-2, 1975. Roy. Postgrad. Med. Sch., London, England; Vet. Admin. Hosp.; Tulane Univ. Sch. Med., New Orleans, LA. (34/82/LS)
	305	18	**Prange A J, Wilson I C, Lara P P, Alltrop L B & Breese G R.** Effects of thyrotropin-releasing hormone in depression. *Lancet* 2:999-1002, 1972. Univ. N. Carolina, Med. Sch.; Biol. Sci. Res. Ctr., Chapel Hill; N. Carolina Mental Hlth. Dept., Div. Res., Raleigh, NC.
	278	20	**Pulvertaft R J V.** Cytology of Burkitt's tumor (African lymphoma). *Lancet* 1:238-40, 1964. Univ. Ibadan, Dept. Pathol., Ibadan, Nigeria.
	801	30	***Randle P J, Hales C N, Garland P B & Newsholme E A.** The glucose fatty-acid cycle: its role in insulin sensitivity and the metabolic disturbances of diabetes mellitus. *Lancet* 1:785-9, 1963. Univ. Cambridge, Dept. Biochem., Cambridge, England. (31/81/LS)
	447	23	**Reye R D K, Morgan G & Baral J.** Encephalopathy and fatty degeneration of the viscera: a disease entity in childhood. *Lancet* 2:749-52, 1963. Roy. Alexandra Hosp. Child., Sydney, Australia.
49	309	5	**Roitt I M & Doniach D.** Human auto-immune thyroiditis: serological studies. *Lancet* 2:1027-33, 1958. Middlesex Hosp., Courtauld Inst. Biochem. & Inst. Clin. Res., London, England.

A	B	C	D
	388	5	**Roitt I M, Torrigiani G, Greaves M F, Brostoff J & Playfair J H L.** The cellular basis of immunological responses. *Lancet* 2:367-71, 1969. Middlesex Hosp. Med. Sch., London, England.
	363	9	**Samols E, Marri G & Marks V.** Promotion of insulin secretion by glucagon. *Lancet* 2:415-6, 1965. Roy. Free Hosp., Med. Unit, London; Area Lab., Epsom, England.
	1474	160	***Seabright M.** Letter to editor. (A rapid banding technique for human chromosomes.) *Lancet* 2:971-2, 1971. Salisbury Gen. Hosp., Dept. Pathol., Wiltshire, England. (14/81/LS)
6	361	8	**Sevitt S & Gallagher N G.** Prevention of venous thrombosis and pulmonary embolism in injured patients. *Lancet* 2:981-9, 1959. Birmingham Accid. Hosp., Birmingham, England.
	329	44	**Smith B R & Hall R.** Thyroid-stimulating immunoglobulins in Graves' disease. *Lancet* 2:427-31, 1974. Univ. Newcastle upon Tyne, Depts. Med. & Clin. Biol., Newcastle upon Tyne, England.
	418	18	***Smythe P M, Schonland M, Brereton-Stiles G G, Coovadia H M, Grace H J, Loening W E K, Mafoyane A, Parent M A & Vos G H.** Thymolympathic deficiency and depression of cell-mediated immunity in protein-calorie malnutrition. *Lancet* 2:939-44, 1971. Univ. Natal, Natal Inst. Immunol.; King Edward VIII Hosp., Durban, S. Africa. (52/80/CP)
	440	6	**Stjernsward J, Vanky F, Jondal M, Wigzell H & Sealy R.** Lymphopenia and change in distribution of human B and T lymphocytes in peripheral blood induced by irradiation for mammary carcinoma. *Lancet* 1:1352-6, 1972. Karolinska Inst., Dept. Tumor Biol., Stockholm, Sweden; Groote Schuur Hosp., Dept. Radiother., Cape Town, S. Africa.
	662	56	***Waldmann T A, Broder S, Blaese R M, Durm M, Blackman M & Strober W.** Role of suppressor T cells in pathogenesis of common variable hypogammaglobulinaemia. *Lancet* 2:609-13, 1974. NIH, NCI, Bethesda, MD. (18/83/LS)
	665	43	**Wide L, Bennich H & Johansson S G O.** Diagnosis of allergy by an in-vitro test for allergen antibodies. *Lancet* 2:1105-7, 1967. Univ. Hosp., Dept. Clin. Chem. & Blood Ctr.; Univ. Uppsala, Inst. Biochem., Uppsala, Sweden.
	301	91	**Wilhelmsson C, Wilhelmsen L, Vedin J A, Tibblin G & Werko L.** Reduction of sudden deaths after myocardial infarction by treatment with alprenolol: preliminary results. *Lancet* 2:1157-60, 1974. Univ. Goteborg, Sahlgren's Hosp., Goteborg, Sweden.
	323	5	***Williams E D, Karim S M M & Sandler M.** Prostaglandin secretion by medullary carcinoma of the thyroid. *Lancet* 1:22-3, 1968. Roy. Postgrad. Med. Sch., Dept. Pathol.; Queen Charlotte's Matern. Hosp., Inst. Obstet. Gynaecol. & Bernhard Baron Mem. Res. Lab., London, England. (36/81/LS)
	416	3	**Wilson J D & Nossal G J V.** Identification of human T & B lymphocytes in normal peripheral blood and in chronic lymphocytic leukaemia. *Lancet* 2:788-91, 1971. Walter and Eliza Hall Inst. Med. Res., Victoria, Australia.
	265	0	**Wright R, McCollum R W & Klatskin G.** Australia antigen in acute and chronic liver disease. *Lancet* 2:117-21, 1969. Yale Univ. Sch. Med., New Haven, CT.
	406	20	***Wybran J, Chantler S & Fudenberg H H.** Isolation of normal T cells in chronic lymphatic leukaemia. *Lancet* 1:126-9, 1973. Univ. California Sch. Med., San Francisco, CA. (21/81/LS)

tween coronary heart disease and plasma levels of high-density lipoprotein (HDL). The paper was cited more than 500 times from 1977 to 1983. While at the Royal Infirmary, Edinburgh, Scotland, Miller also coauthored the third most-cited paper in Table 1 with his brother, G.J. Miller, Llandough Hospital, Penarth, Wales. They discovered an inverse relationship between coronary heart disease and HDL. This finding suggested that HDL is involved in the removal of cholesterol from tissues and the retardation of atherosclerosis. G.J. Miller commented on *The Lancet* editors' reactions to this 1975 work: "I sent my ideas to my brother Norman.... He strengthened the argument considerably and we completed the manuscript over a weekend. Several weeks later I sat at my desk facing the rejected manuscript—returned with apologies. Somewhat bewildered, I was urged by colleagues to seek the editor's advice. To my delight,

Table 2: Frequency distribution of highly cited articles appearing in *The Lancet*, 1961-1982. A= number of citations. B=number of articles receiving that number of citations. C=percent of articles examined (n=3224).

A	B	C
⩾ 500	17	.5
400-499	17	.5
350-399	16	.5
300-349	25	.8
250-299	37	1.1
200-249	81	2.5
150-199	197	6.1
100-149	559	17.3
75-99	755	23.4
50-74	1520	47.1

he recalled the paper, reconsidered his decision, and accepted in little more than 24 hours!"[12] Interestingly, several other authors have noted that their manuscripts were initially rejected and later accepted by the editors. Perhaps because they don't exclusively rely on outside referees as the final authority, *The Lancet*'s editors can exercise the freedom to change their opinions. Of course, an editor of a refereed journal may also choose to do so, but at the risk of losing the services of strong referees.

It is interesting that several of *The Lancet* classics are letters to the editor. These include the most-cited classic, by Marina Seabright, Salisbury General Hospital, Wiltshire, England, which will be discussed in detail later. The important role that letters to the editor play in the progress of science can be seen in an article-by-article citation analysis of journals. For example, Table 3 gives data on the number of *The Lancet* items published in 1977; the number that were cited from 1977 to 1982; the number of 1977-1982 citations they received; cited impact; and total impact. Similar data for the *New England Journal of Medicine* (*NEJM*) are provided for comparison. Total impact is calculated here by simply dividing 1977-1982 citations by the number of 1977 source items. Cited impact is the quotient of 1977-1982 citations divided by *cited* 1977 items.

As you can see, most of the items that *The Lancet* and *NEJM* have published

are letters. About 68 percent of *The Lancet*'s letters were cited, compared with 41 percent for *NEJM* letters. The average letter in *The Lancet* was cited about four times from 1977 to 1982, twice as often as the average *NEJM* letter. About 94 percent of *The Lancet*'s 1977 articles were cited at least once during this six-year period, slightly less than the 97 percent citation rate for *NEJM* articles. The average article from *The Lancet* had a six-year impact of 33, compared with 54 for *NEJM*. Of course, definitions for "articles" are not always consistent between journals, and they may include several different types of publications.

The authors of *The Lancet* classics in this study come from 17 countries. Table 4 lists their national affiliations, in order of the number of papers from each country (column A). Also shown is the number of multinational collaborations each nation's authors were involved in, and the national affiliations of the coauthors. For example, 54 papers listed UK authors. Of these, seven were coauthored with researchers from Austria, Belgium, Denmark, Federal Republic of Germany (FRG), Switzerland, and the US. Forty-seven papers listed *only* UK authors.

The figures in Table 4 and other data confirm that *The Lancet* is an international forum for medical research. For example, we created a country-by-country file that detailed the national affiliations of authors in the 1978 *SCI*. Our analysis of Latin-American research[13] was based on that file. Of the 2,300 source items *The Lancet* published in 1978, 49 percent listed first authors based in the UK. The US accounted for 20 percent; Europe and Scandinavia combined for 19 percent; Third World nations, 3 percent; and Canada, Australia, New Zealand, and Japan accounted for the bulk of the remaining 8 percent. Many journals claim to be international in scope and circulation. It would be interesting to identify the truly international research journals by examining which nations' research they publish. Of course, the nationalities of the *citing* au-

Table 3: Article-by-article analysis of 1977 *The Lancet* and *New England Journal of Medicine* source items and their citations from 1977-1982, *SCI*®. A=number published in 1977. B=number that were cited from 1977 to 1982. C=percent citedness (B/A). D=number of 1977-1982 citations. E=cited impact (D/B). F=total impact (D/A).

The Lancet

	A	B	C	D	E	F
All Items	3149	1937	61.5	26,586	13.7	8.4
Articles	506	473	93.5	16,785	35.5	33.2
Letters	2069	1401	67.7	9043	6.5	4.4
Notes	149	36	24.2	663	18.4	4.4
Rest*	425	27	6.4	95	3.5	0.2

New England Journal of Medicine

	A	B	C	D	E	F
All Items	1772	1054	59.5	26,141	24.8	14.8
Articles	379	369	97.4	20,464	55.5	54.0
Letters	1103	457	41.4	2104	4.6ˈ	1.9
Notes	4	4	100.0	10	2.5	2.5
Rest*	286	224	78.3	3563	15.9	12.5

*Includes corrections, editorials, meeting reports, obituaries, reviews, etc.

thors are another factor to consider in determining whether or not a journal is international in impact. Such a study of international journals might turn up a few surprises.

As noted here, the most-cited classic from *The Lancet* is a 1971 letter from Seabright. She described a method for banding human chromosomes using trypsin. In a *Citation Classic* commentary on this letter, Seabright explained, "The immediate application was to determine the location of break points in naturally occurring chromosome rearrangements...in patients with congenital defects, and to study the lesions and patterns of exchange induced by X-irradiation."[14] The method is now used in routine cytogenetic investigations. It was cited more than 1,600 times from 1971 to 1983.

The second most-cited classic was by A.St.G. Huggett, University of London, and D.A. Nixon, St. Mary's Hospital Medical School, London, England. They described a method for determining glucose levels in blood and urine using a fungal oxidase preparation. Unfortunately, both authors had died before

we were able to contact them about writing a *Citation Classic* commentary. However, their wives were kind enough to comment on the work. Marion Nixon and Helen Huggett wrote, "It is very sad that neither Professor Huggett, FRS, nor Dr. D.A. Nixon is alive to learn of...this *Citation Classic*. By the mid-1960s, both men realised that the paper was often referred to.... The frequent citation of this paper is not difficult to understand for it provided a method [that] has had widespread daily use in clinical medicine."[15] This paper received more than 1,300 citations from 1957 to 1983.

In closing, I'd like to invite the authors listed in Table 1 to submit *Citation Classic* commentaries if they have not done so already. When the original authors are not available, we welcome commentaries by their colleagues, former students, and anyone else who has something relevant to say about their work. These commentaries are valued for the personal and anecdotal background they provide on high-impact research. The humor, frustration, and serendipity of the research process rarely find expression in the dry and impersonal publi-

Table 4: Geographic areas represented by the 100 most-cited papers published in *The Lancet*, listed in descending order of the number of papers produced. A=number of papers. B=number of multinational collaborations. C=nationality of collaborators.

Country	A	B	C
United Kingdom	54	7	Austria,
England	44		Belgium,
Scotland	7		Denmark, FRG,
Northern Ireland	2		Switzerland, US
Wales	1		
United States	32	7	Austria,
			Belgium,
			Denmark, FRG,
			Switzerland, UK
Denmark	7	1	Austria,
			Belgium, FRG,
			Switzerland, UK,
			US
Sweden	6	2	Ethiopia, South
			Africa
Australia	4	0	
Norway	2	0	
South Africa	2	1	Sweden
Austria	1	1	Belgium,
			Denmark, FRG,
			Switzerland, UK,
			US
Belgium	1	1	Austria,
			Denmark, FRG,
			Switzerland, UK,
			US

Country	A	B	C
Ethiopia	1	1	Sweden
Federal Republic of Germany	1	1	Austria, Belgium, Denmark, Switzerland, UK, US
Finland	1	0	
France	1	0	
New Zealand	1	0	
Nigeria	1	0	
Switzerland	1	1	Austria, Belgium, Denmark, FRG, UK, US
USSR	1	0	

cations that usually are the final product. This public call for *Citation Classic* commentaries will be followed up with letters to the individual authors involved. In future essays, we'll identify and discuss the classics published in other leading journals.

* * * * *

My thanks to Thomas Atkins and Alfred Welljams-Dorof for their help in the preparation of this essay.

©1984 ISI

REFERENCES

1. **Garfield E.** The 100 most-cited papers ever and how we select *Citation Classics*. *Current Contents* (23):3-9, 4 June 1984.
2. -------------. The articles most cited in 1961-1982. 2. Another 100 *Citation Classics* highlight the technology of science. *Current Contents* (29):3-12, 16 July 1984.
3. -------------. The articles most cited in 1961-1982. 3. Another 100 all-time *Citation Classics*. *Current Contents* (35):3-9, 27 August 1984.
4. -------------. 100 classics from the *New England Journal of Medicine*. *Current Contents* (25):3-10, 18 June 1984.
5. The Lancet at 150. *NZ Med. J.* 78:308, 1973.
6. **Froggatt P.** Thomas Wakley, The Lancet, and the surgeons. *J. Irish Coll. Physn. Surg.* 7:1-9, 1977.
7. -------------. *The Lancet:* Wakley's instrument for medical education reform. *J. Soc. Occup. Med.* 29:45-53, 1979.
8. **Roland C G.** Doctors afield. Wakley of The Lancet. *N. Engl. J. Med.* 287:231-5, 1972.
9. **Munro I.** Telephone communication. 15 August 1984.
10. **Garfield E.** Significant journals of science. *Nature* 264:609-15, 1976. (Reprinted in: **Garfield E.** *Essays of an information scientist.* Philadelphia: ISI Press, 1984. Vol. 6. p. 573-9.)
11. **Moncada S.** Citation Classic. Commentary on *Lancet* 1:18-21, 1977. *Current Contents/Life Sciences* 25(41):22, 11 October 1982.
12. **Miller G J.** Citation Classic. Commentary on *Lancet* 1:16-9, 1975. *Current Contents/Life Sciences* 24(15):21, 13 April 1981.
13. **Garfield E.** Latin American research. Part 1. Where it is published and how often it is cited. Part 2. Most-cited articles, discipline orientation, and research front concentration. *Current Contents* (19):3-8 and (20):3-10, 7 and 14 May 1984.
14. **Seabright M.** Citation Classic. Commentary on *Lancet* 2:971-2, 1971. *Current Contents/Life Sciences* 24(14):15, 6 April 1981.
15. **Nixon M & Huggett H.** Citation Classic. Commentary on *Lancet* 2:368-70, 1957. *Current Contents/Clinical Practice* 9(21):18, 25 May 1981.

Current Comments®

The Articles Most Cited in 1961-1982. 4. 100 Additional *Citation Classics*

Number 40   October 1, 1984

This essay is a continuation of our multipart series on the papers most cited from 1961 to 1982. Using *Science Citation Index®* (*SCI®*), we've previously identified 300 papers[1-3] cited at least 1,188 times in this 22-year period.

All of the papers we've identified to date can be considered classics in the scientific literature. That they are so frequently referenced indicates their usefulness and relevance to the research of many scientists, for whatever reasons. Certain methodology papers are highly cited because they describe elegant procedures or reliable strategies for attacking research problems. Theoretical works often achieve high impact if they inspire new experiments or when others test the hypotheses they propose. Such papers often symbolize paradigm shifts within a discipline. Timely reviews may also be frequently cited because they provide overviews of various lines of research. Reviews can summarize the consensus of scientific opinion on a given topic and simplify the task of documenting earlier research.

In any event, the papers identified in these studies do not necessarily represent the "best" or most "important" research. That point bears constant repetition to prevent the mistaken impression that these studies encourage overly simplistic criteria for admission to the science "hall of fame." Unlike sports fans, who thrive on statistics about the best athletes, scientists are often reluctant to accept any quantitative indicators. But scientific research is now such a large and widespread enterprise that it

is easy to lose sight of some of the highest-impact achievers.

Table 1 presents full bibliographic information on the 100 classics in this study. They are arranged in alphabetic order by first author. The number of 1961-1982 citations is shown, followed by 1983 citations in parentheses. Each of these papers was cited at least 1,032 times. More than 20 million papers were cited at least once during this 22-year period. Of these, only 433 are "kilo-classics"—i.e., papers that have been cited more than 1,000 times. When books are included in these citation analyses, we'll probably find that no more than 1,000 publications are kilo-classics.

Asterisks indicate the 33 papers that have already been featured as *Citation Classics™* in *Current Contents®* (*CC®*). The issue, year, and edition of *CC* in which the author's commentary appeared are shown after the reference. The authors listed in Table 1 are invited to submit commentaries on their classic papers if they have not done so already.

A number symbol (#) in Table 1 identifies papers that were also included in a 1974 study of the most-cited articles in the 1961-1972 *SCI*.[4] Of the 100 classics identified 10 years ago, 83 are among the 400 most-cited papers presented in this series to date.

Life-sciences papers dominate the list in this and previous studies. We've explained the reason for this before.[2] However, the proportion of life-sciences papers is declining as the series is extended. For example, 85 life-sciences papers were identified in the first group, 77 in the second, and 80 in the third. There are 72 life-sciences papers in this study. The number of physics and chemistry papers is increasing. Physics accounts for 15 papers in Table 1, compared with 6 in the first group of classics we identified, 11 in the second, and 7 in the third. Chemistry accounted for 9 papers in part one, 10 in part two, 10 in part three, and 13 in this study.

I regret that we have never received a commentary from Joel H. Hildebrand, who coauthored with H.A. Benesi the paper on the interaction of iodine with aromatic hydrocarbons. Hildebrand taught chemistry to me and over 100,000 other students.[5] He recently died at the age of 101.[6]

Table 2 shows the publication-year distribution for the 100 classics identified here. It is similar to the distribution reported for the 300 most-cited articles. The oldest paper was published in 1930 in *Physical Review*. J.C. Slater, Harvard University, Cambridge, Massachusetts, described a simple method for approximating wave functions and energy levels of atoms and ions. The paper was cited about 1,200 times from 1961 to 1982. It received 35 citations in 1983, indicating that physicists not only still rely on Slater's atomic shielding constants but also feel compelled to explicitly cite the primordial reference more than 50 years later.

The most recent paper was published in 1977 in *Gene*. F. Bolivar, University of California, San Francisco, and colleagues discussed a method for the construction and characterization of new cloning vehicles. The paper has been referred to in more than 1,500 publications during the past seven years. This unusual rate of citation reflects the rapid growth of genetic engineering and recombinant DNA technology in recent years. It is significant that this paper was cited almost 350 times in 1983, more than any other paper listed.

Perhaps more than in other fields, molecular biology depends on methodological innovations to advance the frontiers of research. P.A. Sharp, Massachusetts Institute of Technology, Cambridge, suggested this point in a commentary on his assay for restriction endonucleases. "Advances in molecular biology are frequently the product of the development of new methodology. Perhaps the most striking recent example of this is the impact that recombinant DNA technology has had. Publications that make novel contributions to the development of new methodology are widely read and frequently referenced. [We] described this type of methodology at a time when the molecular biological community was discovering the multiple uses of restriction endonucleases."[7] Sharp's classic method, coauthored with B. Sugden and J. Sambrook, Cold Spring Harbor Laboratory, New York, was cited more than 1,200 times from 1973 to 1983.

A methodological paper sometimes becomes highly cited after refinements in related technologies make its application more practical. T.F. Anderson, Fox Chase Cancer Center, Philadelphia, noted that his paper on techniques for preserving the three-dimensional structure of specimens prepared for electron microscopes was cited more frequently after these instruments were perfected. "Electron microscopists were very slow to adopt the method, even though everyone knew about it from the beautiful steroscopic pictures...I showed at meetings in both the US and Europe.... It wasn't until late-1960, when scanning electron microscopes became practical and useful, that the method became popular."[8] Anderson's 1951 paper received just 25 citations from 1955 to 1960. It was cited about 1,100 times from 1961 to 1982, and 51 times in 1983.

Although methodology papers commonly appear in citation-based studies, many theoretical works are also included. For example, Leonard Hayflick, then at Wistar Institute of Anatomy and Biology, Philadelphia, expanded on a theory of cellular aging in his 1965 paper published in *Experimental Cell Research* entitled "The limited *in vitro* lifetime of human diploid cell strains." In fact, this

Table 1: The fourth 100 most-cited articles, *SCI®* 1961-1982, arranged in alphabetic order by first author. A = 1961-1982 citations. 1983 citations appear in parentheses. B = bibliographic data. An asterisk (*) indicates that the paper was the subject of a *Citation Classic™* commentary. The issue, year, and edition of *CC®* in which these commentaries appeared are listed in parentheses. A number symbol (#) indicates that the paper appeared in the 1974 list of most-cited articles.

A		B
1112	(92)	**Ames B N, Durston W E, Yamasaki E & Lee F D.** Carcinogens are mutagens: a simple test system combining liver homogenates for activation and bacteria for detection. *Proc. Nat. Acad. Sci. US* 70:2281-5, 1973.
1086	(51)	***Anderson T F.** Techniques for the preservation of three-dimensional structure in preparing specimens for the electron microscope. *Trans. NY Acad. Sci.* 13:130-4, 1951. (49/82/LS)
1060	(146)	**Arunlakshana O & Schild H O.** Some quantitative uses of drug antagonists. *Brit. J. Pharmacol.* 14:48-58, 1959.
1119	(54)	**Benesi H A & Hildebrand J H.** A spectrophotometric investigation of the interaction of iodine with aromatic hydrocarbons. *J. Amer. Chem. Soc.* 71:2703-7, 1949.
1094	(17)	***Bertler A, Carlsson A & Rosengren E.** A method for the fluorimetric determination of adrenaline and noradrenaline in tissues. *Acta Physiol. Scand.* 44:273-92, 1958. (49/79/LS)
1184	(161)	**Blobel G & Dobberstein B.** Transfer of proteins across membranes. I. Presence of proteolytically processed and unprocessed nascent immunoglobulin light chains on membrane-bound ribosomes of murine myeloma. *J. Cell Biol.* 67:835-51, 1975.
1169	(345)	**Bolivar F, Rodriguez R L, Greene P J, Betlach M C, Heyneker H L, Boyer H W, Crosa J H & Fakow S.** Construction and characterization of new cloning vehicles. II. A multipurpose cloning system. *Gene* 2:95-113, 1977.
1048	(123)	**Bondi A.** Van der Waals' volumes and radii. *J. Phys. Chem.* 68:441-51, 1964.
1137	(46)	**Bonsnes R W & Taussky H H.** On the colorimetric determination of creatinine by the Jaffe reaction. *J. Biol. Chem.* 158:581-91, 1945.
1150	(43)	***Bradley T R & Metcalf D.** The growth of mouse bone marrow cells *in vitro. Aust. J. Exp. Biol. Med. Sci.* 44:287-99, 1966. (40/79/LS)
1075	(103)	**Brazeau P, Vale W, Burgus R, Ling N, Butcher M, Rivier J & Guillemin R.** Hypothalamic polypeptide that inhibits the secretion of immunoreactive pituitary growth hormone. *Science* 179:77-9, 1973.
1043	(4)	#***Bush I E.** Methods of paper chromatography of steroids applicable to the study of steroids in mammalian blood tissues. *Biochem. J.* 50:370-8, 1952. (3/84/LS)
1035	(38)	***Carr H Y & Purcell E M.** Effects of diffusion on free precession in nuclear magnetic resonance experiments. *Phys. Rev.* 94:630-8, 1954. (20/83/PC&ES)
1054	(19)	**Ceriotti G.** Determination of nucleic acids in animal tissues. *J. Biol. Chem.* 214:59-70, 1955.
1043	(48)	**Cerottini J-C & Brunner K T.** Cell-mediated cytotoxicity, allograft rejection, and tumor immunity. *Advan. Immunol.* 18:67-132, 1974.
1174	(97)	***Chen R F.** Removal of fatty acids from serum albumin by charcoal treatment. *J. Biol. Chem.* 242:173-81, 1967. (13/82/LS)
1033	(75)	**Cleland W W.** The statistical analysis of enzyme kinetic data. *Advan. Enzymol. Relat. Areas Mol.* 29:1-32, 1967.
1100	(51)	**Clementi E & Raimondi D L.** Atomic screening constants from SCF functions. *J. Chem. Phys.* 38:2686-9, 1963.
1162	(126)	***Cutler S J & Ederer F.** Maximum utilization of the life table method in analyzing survival. *J. Chronic Dis.* 8:699-712, 1958. (16/79/CP)
1070	(127)	**Ditchfield R, Hehre W J & Pople J A.** Self-consistent molecular-orbital methods. IX. An extended Gaussian-type basis for molecular-orbital studies of organic molecules. *J. Chem. Phys.* 54:724-8, 1971.
1032	(152)	**Dunning T H.** Gaussian basis functions for use in molecular calculations. I. Contraction of (9s5p) atomic basis sets for the first-row atoms. *J. Chem. Phys.* 53:2823-33, 1970.
1040	(27)	**Farr R S.** A quantitative immunochemical measure of the primary interaction between I*BSA and antibody. *J. Infec. Dis.* 103:239-62, 1958.
1157	(34)	**Fessenden R W & Schuler R H.** Electron spin resonance studies of transient alkyl radicals. *J. Chem. Phys.* 39:2147-95, 1963.
1144	(26)	***Fredrickson D S, Levy R I & Lees R S.** Fat transport in lipoproteins—an integrated approach to mechanisms and disorders. Glyceride transport. *N. Engl. J. Med.* 276:94-103, 1967. (3/78)
1154	(26)	***Fredrickson D S, Levy R I & Lees R S.** Fat transport in lipoproteins—an integrated approach to mechanisms and disorders. Type II hyperlipoproteinemia. *N. Engl. J. Med.* 276:215-25, 1967. (3/78)

A	B

1182 (96) **Giles K W & Myers A.** An improved diphenylamine method for the estimation of deoxyribonucleic acid. *Nature* 206:93, 1965.

1146 (52) **Glauber R J.** Coherent and incoherent states of the radiation field. *Phys. Rev.* 131:2766-88, 1963.

1068 (54) **Goldman D E.** Potential, impedance, and rectification in membranes. *J. Gen. Physiol.* 27:37-60, 1943.

1167 (47) **Hammond G S.** A correlation of reaction rates. *J. Amer. Chem. Soc.* 77:334-40, 1955.

1069 (76) **Hartley B S.** Strategy and tactics in protein chemistry. *Biochem. J.* 119:805-22, 1970.

1145 (57) **Hayflick L.** The limited *in vitro* lifetime of human diploid cell strains. *Exp. Cell Res.* 37:614-36, 1965.

1114 (69) *****Hedrick J L & Smith A J.** Size and charge isomer separation and estimation of molecular weights of proteins by disc gel electrophoresis. *Arch. Biochem. Biophys.* 126:155-64, 1968. (48/79/LS)

1042 (72) *****Henle G & Henle W.** Immunofluorescence in cells derived from Burkitt's lymphoma. *J. Bacteriol.* 91:1248-56, 1966. (12/84/LS)

1104 (37) *****Huxley H E.** Electron microscope studies on the structure of natural and synthetic protein filaments from striated muscle. *J. Mol. Biol.* 7:281-308, 1963. (29/79/LS)

1051 (20) **Jacob F, Brenner S & Cuzin F.** On the regulation of DNA replication in bacteria. *Cold Spring Harbor Symp.* 28:329-48, 1963.

1046 (10) *****Jacob M & Wick G C.** On the general theory of collisions for particles with spin. *Ann. Phys. NY* 7:404-28, 1959. (21/79/PC&ES)

1095 (40) **Karnovsky M J.** The ultrastructural basis of capillary permeability studied with peroxidase as a tracer. *J. Cell Biol.* 35:213-36, 1967.

1117 (95) **Karnovsky M J & Roots L.** A "direct-coloring" thiocholine method for cholinesterases. *J. Histochem. Cytochem.* 12:219-21, 1964.

1048 (25) *****Kellenberger E, Ryter A & Sechaud J.** Electron microscope study of DNA-containing plasms. II. Vegetative and mature phage DNA as compared with normal bacterial nucleoids in different physiological states. *J. Biophys. Biochem. Cytol.* 4:671-8, 1958. (7/80/LS)

1081 (13) **Kisslinger L S & Sorensen R A.** Spherical nuclei with simple residual forces. *Rev. Mod. Phys.* 35:853-915, 1963.

1050 (65) *****Kramer C Y.** Extension of multiple range tests to group means with unequal numbers of replications. *Biometrics* 12:307-10, 1956. (44/77)

1047 (109) *****Lands A M, Arnold A, McAuliff J P, Luduena F P & Brown T G.** Differentiation of receptor systems activated by sympathomimetic amines. *Nature* 214:597-8, 1967. (47/81/LS)

1141 (81) **Laurell C-B.** Antigen-antibody crossed electrophoresis. *Anal. Biochem.* 10:358-61, 1965.

1041 (51) **Laurent T C & Killander J.** A theory of gel filtration and its experimental verification. *J. Chromatogr.* 14:317-30, 1964.

1160 (164) **Littlefield J W.** Selection of hybrids from matings of fibroblasts *in vitro* and their presumed recombinants. *Science* 145:709-10, 1964.

1068 (16) *****Lowry O H & Lopez J A.** The determination of inorganic phosphate in the presence of labile phosphate esters. *J. Biol. Chem.* 162:421-8, 1946. (31/81/LS)

1119 (98) **Maizel J V.** Polyacrylamide gel electrophoresis of viral proteins. *Meth. Virology* 5:179-246, 1971.

1075 (233) **Maniatis T, Jeffrey A & Kleid D G.** Nucleotide sequence of the rightward operator of phage λ. *Proc. Nat. Acad. Sci. US* 72:1184-8, 1975.

1170 (194) *****Mantel N & Haenszel W.** Statistical aspects of the analysis of data from retrospective studies of disease. *J. Nat. Cancer Inst.* 22:719-48, 1959. (26/81/LS)

1050 (75) **Maroko P R, Kjekshus J K, Sobel B E, Watanabe T, Covell J W, Ross J & Braunwald E.** Factors influencing infarct size following experimental coronary artery occlusions. *Circulation* 43:67-82, 1971.

1124 (70) **McMillan W L.** Transition temperature of strong-coupled superconductors. *Phys. Rev.* 167:331-44, 1968.

1037 (64) *****Miles A A, Misra S S & Irwin J O.** The estimation of the bactericidal power of the blood. *J. Hyg.* 38:732-49, 1938. (37/79/LS)

1149 (85) *****Miller G L.** Protein determination for large numbers of samples. *Anal. Chem.* 31:964, 1959. (9/80/LS)

1107 (53) *****Mittal K K, Mickey M R, Singal D P & Terasaki P I.** Serotyping for homotransplantation. XVIII. Refinement of microdroplet lymphocyte cytotoxicity test. *Transplantation* 6:913-27, 1968. (26/79/LS)

1132 (15) *****Moor H & Muhlethaler K.** Fine structure in frozen-etched yeast cells. *J. Cell Biol.* 17:609-28, 1963. (19/81/LS)

A	B	
1155	(70)	**Mori H.** Transport, collective motion, and Brownian motion. *Prog. Theor. Phys. Kyoto* 33:423-55, 1965.
1065	(36)	**Mulliken R S.** Molecular compounds and their spectra. II. *J. Amer. Chem. Soc.* 74:811-24, 1952.
1085	(121)	**Murphy J & Riley J P.** A modified single solution method for the determination of phosphate in natural waters. *Anal. Chim. Acta* 27:31-6, 1962.
1077	(95)	**Neville D M.** Molecular weight determination of protein-dodecyl sulfate complexes by gel-electrophoresis in a discontinuous buffer system. *J. Biol. Chem.* 246:6328-34, 1971.
1078	(10)	**Nirenberg M W & Leder P.** RNA codewords and protein synthesis. *Science* 145:1399-407, 1964.
1153	(11)	#**Nirenberg M W & Matthaei J H.** The dependence of cell-free protein synthesis in *E. coli* upon naturally occurring or synthetic polyribonucleotides. *Proc. Nat. Acad. Sci. US* 47:1588-602, 1961.
1158	(73)	**Northcliffe L C & Schilling R F.** Range and stopping-power tables for heavy ions. *Nucl. Data Sect. A* 7:233-463, 1970.
1090	(101)	**Omura T & Sato R.** The carbon monoxide-binding pigment of liver microsomes. II. Solubilization, purification, and properties. *J. Biol. Chem.* 239:2379-85, 1964.
1086	(48)	**Onsager L.** Electric moments of molecules in liquids. *J. Amer. Chem. Soc.* 58:1486-93, 1936.
1127	(39)	**Oyama V I & Eagle H.** Measurement of cell growth in tissue culture with a phenol reagent (Folin-Ciocalteau). *Proc. Soc. Exp. Biol. Med.* 91:305-7, 1956.
1048	(35)	**Park J T & Johnson M J.** A submicrodetermination of glucose. *J. Biol. Chem.* 181:149-51, 1949.
1112	(15)	**Partridge S M.** Filter-paper partition chromatography of sugars. 1. General description and application to the qualitative analysis of sugars in apple juice, egg white, and foetal blood of sheep. *Biochem. J.* 42:238-50, 1948.
1178	(10)	****Partridge S M.** Aniline hydrogen phthalate as a spraying reagent for chromatography of sugars. *Nature* 164:443, 1949. (14/79/AB&ES)
1044	(50)	**Peacock A C & Dingman C W.** Molecular weight estimation and separation of ribonucleic acid by electrophoresis in agarose-acrylamide composite gels. *Biochemistry* 7:668-74, 1968.
1083	(44)	****Pearson R G.** Hard and soft acids and bases. *J. Amer. Chem. Soc.* 85:3533-9, 1963. (23/80/PC&ES)
1075	(23)	**Penman S.** RNA metabolism in the HeLa cell nucleus. *J. Mol. Biol.* 17:117-30, 1966.
1039	(21)	****Perey F G.** Optical-model analysis of proton elastic scattering in the range of 9 to 22 MeV. *Phys. Rev.* 131:745-63, 1963. (27/80/PC&ES)
1054	(11)	#**Peterson E A & Sober H A.** Chromatography of proteins. I. Cellulose ion-exchange adsorbents. *J. Amer. Chem. Soc.* 78:751-5, 1956.
1059	(31)	**Pople J A, Beveridge D L & Dobosh P A.** Approximate self-consistent molecular-orbital theory. V. Intermediate neglect of differential overlap. *J. Chem. Phys.* 47:2026-33, 1967.
1054	(7)	****Post R L, Merritt C R, Kinsolving C R & Albright C D.** Membrane adenosine triphosphatase as a participant in the active transport of sodium and potassium in the human erythrocyte. *J. Biol. Chem.* 235:1796-802, 1960. (13/81/LS)
1124	(35)	****Quastler H & Sherman F G.** Cell population kinetics in the intestinal epithelium of the mouse. *Exp. Cell. Res.* 17:420-38, 1959. (48/80/LS)
1035	(69)	****Radloff R, Bauer W & Vinograd J.** A dye-buoyant-density method for the detection and isolation of closed circular duplex DNA: the closed circular DNA in HeLa cells. *Proc. Nat. Acad. Sci. US* 57:1514-21, 1967. (23/81/LS)
1103	(69)	**Reid R V.** Local phenomenological nucleon-nucleon potentials. *Ann. Phys. NY* 50:411-48, 1968.
1101	(42)	****Reissig J L, Strominger J L & Leloir L F.** A modified colorimetric method for the estimation of *N*-acetylamino sugars. *J. Biol. Chem.* 217:959-66, 1955. (28/79/LS)
1065	(18)	****Robison G A, Butcher R W & Sutherland E W.** Cyclic AMP. *Annu. Rev. Biochem.* 37:149-74, 1968. (18/79/LS)
1127	(17)	**Sanger F.** The free amino groups of insulin. *Biochem. J.* 39:507-15, 1945.
1076	(34)	**Sarnoff S J, Braunwald E, Welch G H, Case R B, Stainsby W N & Macruz R.** Hemodynamic determinants of oxygen consumption of the heart with special reference to the tension-time index. *Amer. J. Physiol.* 192:148-56, 1958.
1150	(36)	**Schwert G W & Takenaka Y.** A spectrophotometric determination of trypsin and chymotrypsin. *Biochim. Biophys. Acta* 16:570-5, 1955.
1067	(17)	**Seifter S, Dayton S, Novic B & Muntwyler E.** The estimation of glycogen with the anthrone reagent. *Arch. Biochem.* 25:191-200, 1950.

1151 (68)	*Sharp P A, Sugden B & Sambrook J. Detection of two restriction endonuclease activities in *Haemophilus parainfluenzae* using analytical agarose-ethidium bromide electrophoresis. *Biochemistry* 12:3055-63, 1973. (3/82/LS)
1059 (58)	*Skipski V P, Peterson R F & Barclay M. Quantitative analysis of phospholipids by thin-layer chromatography. *Biochem. J.* 90:374-8, 1964. (1/78)
1147 (23)	Skou J C. The influence of some cations on an adenosine triphosphatase from peripheral nerves. *Biochim. Biophys. Acta* 23:394-401, 1957.
1075 (39)	Slater J C. A simplification of the Hartree-Fock method. *Phys. Rev.* 81:385-90, 1951.
1157 (35)	Slater J C. Atomic shielding constants. *Phys. Rev.* 36:57-64, 1930.
1162 (27)	Somogyi M. A new reagent for the determination of sugars. *J. Biol. Chem.* 160:61-8, 1945.
1056 (10)	Sottocasa G L, Kuylensterna B, Ernster L & Bergstrand A. An electron-transport system associated with the outer membrane of liver mitochondria. *J. Cell Biol.* 32:415-38, 1967.
1047 (163)	Spudich J A & Watt S. The regulation of rabbit skeletal-muscle contraction. I. Biochemical studies of the interaction of the tropomyosin-troponin complex with actin and the proteolytic fragments of myosin. *J. Biol. Chem.* 246:4866-71, 1971.
1044 (8)	Stavitsky A B. Micromethods for the study of proteins and antibodies. I. Procedure and general applications of hemagglutination and hemagglutination-inhibition reactions with tannic acid and protein-treated red blood cells. *J. Immunol.* 72:360-7, 1954.
1085 (107)	Steiner A L, Parker C W & Kipnis D M. Radioimmunoassay for cyclic nucleotides. I. Preparation of antibodies and iodinated cyclic nucleotides. *J. Biol. Chem.* 247:1106-13, 1972.
1077 (63)	Taussky H H & Shorr E. A microcolorimetric method for the determination of inorganic phosphorus. *J. Biol. Chem.* 202:675-85, 1953.
1148 (51)	Taylor R B, Duffus W P H, Raff M C & de Petris S. Redistribution and pinocytosis of lymphocyte surface immunoglobulin molecules induced by anti-immunoglobulin antibody. *Nature New Biol.* 233:225-9, 1971.
1169 (115)	Weber K, Pringle J R & Osborn M. Measurement of molecular weights by electrophoresis on SDS-acrylamide gel. *Meth. Enzymology* 26:3-27, 1972.
1080 (41)	Woodward R B & Hoffmann R. The conservation of orbital symmetry. *Angew. Chem. Int. Ed.* 8:781-853, 1969.
1183 (220)	*Yam L T, Li C Y & Crosby W H. Cytochemical identification of monocytes and granulocytes. *Amer. J. Clin. Pathol.* 55:283-90, 1971. (50/80/CP)
1044 (45)	Yemm E W & Cocking E C. The determination of amino-acids with ninhydrin. *Analyst* 80:209-14, 1955.

Table 2: Chronological distribution of publication dates of the fourth 100 most-cited papers, 1961-1982 *SCI*®. A=publication date. B=number of papers.

A	B
1930s	3
1940s	9
1950s	27
1960s	42
1970s	19
	100

paper updates the research Hayflick and coauthor P.S. Moorhead first reported in 1961 in the same journal.[9] That 1961 paper was listed in the second part of this series.[2] Hayflick, now at the University of Florida, Gainesville, wrote a *Citation Classic* commentary on it,[10] which we quoted extensively earlier.[2]

Another important theoretical work is the 1969 paper by R.B. Woodward, Har-vard University, and R. Hoffmann, Cornell University, New York. The paper described the theory of conservation of orbital symmetry, a basic principle of chemical reactions. It was cited more than 1,100 times from 1969 to 1983.

Both Woodward and Hoffmann received the Nobel prize for chemistry, in 1965 and 1981, respectively. In a previous essay,[11] we reported Hoffmann's assertion that Woodward would have won a second Nobel prize if he were alive today.[12] Eight other Nobel laureates appear in Table 1: R. Guillemin, F. Jacob, R.S. Mulliken, M.W. Nirenberg, L. Onsager, L.F. Leloir, E.W. Sutherland, and F. Sanger. In a forthcoming study, we will discuss in detail how often Nobelists have written classic papers.

Review articles may also become milestone papers in their field. Their impact often equals or exceeds that of classic methodological or theoretical works. For example, G.A. Robison, University of Texas, Houston, coauthored a review on cyclic AMP with R.W. Butcher and Sutherland. For this and other review articles, Robison received the first National Academy of Sciences Award for Excellence in Scientific Reviewing.

When we publish the next essay in this series, we will have identified the 500 most-cited articles in the 1961-1982 *SCI*. In addition to discussing the next group of 100 classics, we'll provide tables summarizing the distribution of all 500 papers by field, journal, year of publication, and so on. Similar summaries will be presented once we've listed the 1,000 most-cited articles.

Even if we continue this series to include the 10,000 most-cited papers, we would not necessarily have identified all of the primordial papers acknowledged to be classic research. A variety of normalizations are necessary to determine the appropriate citation or publication thresholds for each discipline and, indeed, the specific subtopics even within the life sciences. We have selected some small-field papers as *Citation Classics* by relying on analyses of particular journals. Perhaps a better strategy would be to apply our research front clustering techniques. We plan to identify research fronts over a decade or longer so that the core or classic papers for even the smallest specialties will surface.

We invite *CC* readers to recommend to us papers that for one reason or another fall into the category of uncited or rarely cited classics. As in the case of the synthesis of naloxone,[13] some important scientific discoveries are not reported in journals. They may instead be contained in patents, books, or informal communications, for example. If important discoveries are reported in relatively accessible journals, then it is important to understand why, when, and how they remain uncited. With the help of our readers, we can let these "hidden" or delayed-recognition classics stand up and be counted by peer recognition if not by citation analysis.

* * * * *

My thanks to Thomas Atkins and Alfred Welljams-Dorof for their help in the preparation of this essay. ©1984 ISI

REFERENCES

1. **Garfield E.** The 100 most-cited papers ever and how we select *Citation Classics*. *Current Contents* (23):3-9, 4 June 1984.
2. ------------. The articles most cited in 1961-1982. 2. Another 100 *Citation Classics* highlight the technology of science. *Current Contents* (29):3-12, 16 July 1984.
3. ------------. The articles most cited in 1961-1982. 3. Another 100 all-time *Citation Classics*. *Current Contents* (35):3-9, 27 August 1984.
4. ------------. Selecting the all-time Citation Classics. Here are the fifty most cited papers for 1961-1972. The second fifty papers most cited from 1961-1972. *Essays of an information scientist*. Philadelphia: ISI Press, 1977. Vol. 2. p. 6-9; 21-5.
5. **Hildebrand J H.** Pleasures of a nonagenarian. *Chem. Eng. News* 57(11):30-2, 1979.
6. **Turner W.** Joel Hildebrand, 101, chemist; joined U. of California in 1913. (Obituary.) *NY Times* 3 May 1983, p. D27.
7. **Sharp P A.** Citation Classic. Commentary on *Biochemistry* 12:3055-63, 1973. *Current Contents/Life Sciences* 25(3):18, 18 January 1982.
8. **Anderson T F.** Citation Classic. Commentary on *Trans. NY Acad. Sci.* 13:130-4, 1951. *Current Contents/Life Sciences* 25(49):16, 6 December 1982.
9. **Hayflick L & Moorhead P S.** The serial cultivation of human diploid cell strains. *Exp. Cell Res.* 25:585-621, 1961.
10. **Hayflick L.** Citation Classic. Commentary on *Exp. Cell Res.* 25:585-621, 1961. *Current Contents* (26):12, 26 June 1978.
11. **Garfield E.** Were the 1981 Nobel prizewinners in science, economics, and literature anticipated by citation analysis? *Essays of an information scientist*. Philadelphia: ISI Press, 1983. Vol. 5. p. 551-61.
12. **Boffey P M.** 2 share Nobel in chemistry; 3 win in physics. *NY Times* 20 October 1981, p. A1; C2.
13. **Garfield E.** The 1982 John Scott Award goes to Jack Fishman and Harold Blumberg for synthesis and investigation of naloxone. *Essays of an information scientist*. Philadelphia: ISI Press, 1984. Vol. 6. p. 121-30.

Current Comments®

Introducing the *ISI Atlas of Science:*
Biotechnology and Molecular Genetics, 1981/82
and **Bibliographic Update for 1983/84**

Number 41

October 8, 1984

In a poem entitled "A Letter from Caroline Herschel (1750-1848)," the poet and novelist Siv Cedering attributes the following to the sister of astronomer William Herschel:

> I have a way with numbers, so I handle the/necessary reductions and calculations./I also plan every night's observation schedule, for he says my/ intuition helps me turn the telescope to discover/star cluster after star cluster....[1]

And so it is at ISI®. We spend our nights and days trying to discover new and meaningful clusters of scientific events. By clustering the core papers, people, journals, or institutions of science, we attempt to find new relationships not otherwise visible in this very multidimensional world of science. By applying citation and co-citation analyses, among other techniques, we have been able to observe order in the seemingly chaotic universe of scientific literature.

The analogy to astronomy is appropriate. As we gaze out into the night sky, we observe a mass of seemingly disconnected stars. But astronomers tell us that these stars are actually organized into a cluster, our galaxy. Moreover, our galaxy is itself part of a cluster of galaxies, one of many such clusters in our universe. One might say that a goal of astronomers is to perceive order in the superficial chaos of the night sky.

Just as these geographers of the sky map the heavens. we information scientists map the continually changing geography of science, as it is reflected in the scientific literature. With hundreds of thousands of scientists publishing millions of articles and books over several centuries, the universe of science often seems chaotic indeed to the untrained observer. This is compounded because of time warp. More literature is now produced in one or two years than in all previous centuries. As Derek J. de Solla Price would say, 90 percent of the scientists who ever lived are alive today. Articles and books from A to Z appear in great profusion. Yet in a process that can be likened to astronomical events, clusters of literature do appear, drawn together by the gravitational pull of their semantic relationships or connectivities.

This may seem like a romanticized way of introducing you to the *ISI Atlas of Science®*. I must confess that finding order in the scientific literature is as moving to me as finding order in the heavens is to my astroscientific friends. From the earliest times, astronomers have been very successful in maintaining public interest in their craft. We hope to be equally successful in conveying the idea that clusters of literature are not only beautiful and interesting, but also useful in the everyday world.

In 1981, we published the *ISI Atlas of Science: Biochemistry and Molecular Biology, 1978/80* as a prototype of a comprehensive encyclopedic *ISI Atlas of Science*.[2] Each of its 102 chapters covered a distinct subspecialty, or re-

Figure 1: List of research fronts or specialties (classified according to "macrogroup") included in the *ISI Atlas of Science®: Biotechnology and Molecular Genetics, 1981/82.*

Gene Expression, Function, and Controls

1. Ultrastructural-studies of chromatin and nuclear-RNP
2. Transcription initiation and termination in eukaryotes
3. Nucleotide-sequence and transforming agents from murine-sarcoma-virus and other sarcoma-viruses
4. Oncogenic transformation by Harvey and Kirsten strains of murine-sarcoma-virus
5. Structure, function and location of HMG non-histone-proteins
6. Sarcoma-virus transforming-proteins
7. Transcription of adenovirus-genes
8. Proviral-DNA of retrovirus, chromosome, integration and RNA-viral-transformation
9. Polyadenylated and non-polyadenylated m-RNA
10. Genetic characterization of pseudogenes
11. Small molecular-weight nuclear RNA
12. Organization, rearrangement and IG gene-expression
13. Organization of repetitive gene-sequences
14. Studies using polyoma-virus DNA
15. Molecular basis of alpha-thalassemia
16. Avian retrovirus-DNA and retrovirus-RNA
17. Endogenous retrovirus-genes
18. Viral DNA, direct repeated-sequences and terminal redundancy
19. B-cell development
20. Stimulation of protein phosphorylation by epidermal growth-factor
21. Codons for termination of translation in eukaryotes
22. Mouse-mammary-tumor-virus DNA and RNA
23. Nucleosome-organization and chromatin-structure
24. Protein-organization of nucleosomes
25. Ubiquitin-protein and HMG-ubiquitin conjugates
26. Structure of isolated chromatin
27. Histones and chromatin-structure
28. Interaction of histones with DNA
29. Association of replicative DNA with the nuclear matrix
30. Eukaryote gene transcription invitro
31. Chromosome localization of single genes
32. Inhibition of DNA-synthesis by aphidicolin and aphidicolin-resistance

DNA Repair and Recombination

33. Site-specific recombination
34. E-coli recA-protein activities
35. Topoisomerases, gyrases and proteins controlling DNA-structure
36. DNA-repair of interstrand cross-linking and mitotic and meiotic recombination in yeast
37. Protein interaction with single-stranded nucleic-acids

38. Control of transcription in bacteriophage-T-3 and bacteriophage-T-7
39. Yeast mating-type genes

DNA Repair Enzymes

40. Xeroderma-pigmentosum and DNA-repair following UV-light
41. DNA-synthesis and DNA-repair in ataxia-telangiectasia
42. Poly-ADP-ribose-polymerase and DNA-repair
43. DNA-repair and 6-methylguanine
44. DNA-repair in xeroderma-pigmentosum
45. DNA glycosylases and other DNA-repair enzymes
46. Enzymes involved in DNA-repair
47. Excision DNA-repair of UV-light induced pyrimidine-dimers

Transposons

48. Bacteriophage-mu genetics and prokaryotic transposons
49. Mechanism of transposons
50. Transposons and IS-1-elements in bacteria and bacteriophages
51. Studies on gene transposition
52. Transposition of IS-1-elements
53. Mechanism of genetic transpositions

Viral Gene Expression

54. DNase-I-sensitive sites in SV-40 nucleoprotein complexes
55. DNA methylation and cellular differentiation
56. SV-40 and polyoma-virus T-antigens

Mitochondrial Genetics

57. Cytochrome-c-oxidase structure and the mitochondrial genome
58. Primary-structure, secondary-structure and function of r-RNA
59. Electrochemical proton-gradients in mitochondria and liposomes
60. Nucleotide-sequences and secondary-structure of r-DNA and r-RNA from mitochondria, chloroplasts and bacteria
61. Mitochondrial genetics of yeast
62. Mitochondrial DNA of yeasts
63. Thermodynamics and mitochondria

Mitochondrial ATPase

64. Nucleotide-binding-sites of chloroplast-coupling-factor-1
65. Nucleotide-sequence of genes coding for ATPase subunits
66. Affinity-labeling with fluorosulfonylbenzoyl-adenosine and adenine-nucleotide analogs
67. Conformational studies of E-coli and mitochondrial ATPase
68. Studies of mitochondrial ATPase

Immunogenetics

69. Immunological diversity of T-cell-response in radiation-chimeras
70. H-2K mice and IR-gene control of cytotoxic T-cells
71. IR-genes, IA-antigens, and gene complementation

72. T-cell growth-factor
73. T-cell growth-factor and cell-function
74. Alloreactive T-cell clones '
75. T-cell growth-factor interleukin-2
76. Clones of proliferating T-cells
77. Antigen-specific T-cell clones
78. Immunological studies on interleukin-2
79. T-cell-regulation by interleukin-2
80. Production of interleukin-2
81. Invitro growth and maintenance of T-cells

Cytogenetics and Markers of Leukemia and Lymphoma
82. Terminal deoxynucleotidyl-transferase activity
83. Cytogenetics of Burkitts-lymphoma, other lymphomas and other cancers
84. Cytogenetics of preleukemia and acute leukemia
85. Clinical studies of myelogenous and other leukemias
86. Terminal deoxynucleotidyl-transferase during blast crisis in leukemia
87. Cytogenetic markers in acute lymphoblastic leukemia
88. Chromosome-abnormalities in leukemia and lymphoma
89. Cytologic studies on hematopoietic dysplasia

Extrinsic Control of Protein Synthesis
90. Regulation of eukaryote protein-synthesis by heme, RNA and kinases
91. Mechanisms of anti-viral activity of interferon

HSV Gene Expression and Organization
92. Characterization of DNA and HSV and other viruses
93. Mechanism of anti-HSV activity of acyclovir
94. Eukaryote transformation and transfection by DNA and chromosomes

Individual Specialties
95. Structure and function of elongation-factors and studies with the antibiotic kirromycin
96. Regulation of ribosomal-protein-synthesis

97. Genetics of human complement components
98. Structural studies of fibroblast and leukocyte interferon-genes
99. Molecular-genetics of hepatitis-B-virus
100. Folding and binding of lac-repressor
101. DNA exons and functional domains in protein-structure
102. Conformational studies of DNA and synthetic polynucleotides
103. Monoclonal antibodies
104. Defects in the beta-globin-gene in beta-thalassemia
105. Tumor-promotors and transformation
106. Nucleotide-sequences of influenza-virus genes
107. Control of bacterial operon-expression
108. Sister-chromatid-exchange analysis
109. Amplification of dihydrofolate-reductase-genes
110. Studies of plasmids
111. X-linked mental retardation
112. Heat-shock genes and proteins in Drosophila-melanogaster
113. Mitochondrial DNA-sequences and evolution
114. Benzopyrene DNA-adducts
115. HLA-antigens and the genetics of diabetes-mellitus
116. Plasmids of Saccharomyces-cerevisiae
117. Photoreactions between psoralen and DNA
118. HY-antigens and gonadal differentiation
119. T-1-plasmid-DNA of agrobacterium and crown-gall-tumors
120. Modification of coronavirus and mouse hepatitis-virus polypeptides
121. Silver staining of nucleoli and nucleolar-organizer-regions
122. Aflatoxin-B1 DNA-adducts
123. Plasmids and spontaneous mutagenesis
124. Cell-size mutants of yeast
125. Human genetic-factors in ethanol-metabolism
126. Genetics and protein variation of human rotaviruses
127. Regulation of actin gene-expression

---

search front, identified by our clustering procedures. Each chapter consisted of four components: a minireview describing the evolution of the research front, a multidimensionally scaled map showing the "connectedness" among the core papers of the research front, a bibliography of these core papers, and a bibliography of current papers ranked by relevance, that is, the number of core papers they cited.

We have now created a second prototype atlas, the *ISI Atlas of Science: Biotechnology and Molecular Genetics,*

1981/82. Its 127 chapters, whose titles are shown in Figure 1, cover the most active research fronts in these fields, where "most active" is defined in terms of publication productivity. Fifty-two of the chapters consist of the same components found in the earlier *Atlas*: a minireview, a cluster map, a bibliography of core papers, and relevance-ranked lists of key papers published in 1981 and 1982 that cite the core.

The remaining 75 chapters simply provide a bibliography of the core publications and lists of the most relevant current papers for each research front. These chapters generally cover smaller, still-emerging fields. An example of such an emerging field is protein phosphorylation by epidermal growth factor (EGF), which is covered in Chapter 20. Scientists believe that an understanding of EGF will provide insight into the physiology of cell growth. By extension, EGF will also help elucidate disorders of cell growth, such as cancer. Interest in EGF has grown dramatically since 1981. In that year, five core documents were associated with the EGF specialty. By 1982, this had expanded to 34 core papers. By 1983, 51 core documents were identified.

As an example, the figures that follow illustrate the chapter from the new *Atlas* entitled "Structural studies of fibroblast and leukocyte interferon-genes." Keep in mind that the *Atlas* is an 8½" x 11" volume. The figures that follow have been reduced considerably for reasons of space. Figure 2 presents the minireview of this research front. This minireview summarizes work concerning the determination of the amino acid sequences and gene structures of two types of human interferon: alpha-interferon, from leukocytes (a type of white blood cell), and beta-interferon, from fibroblasts (a cell in connective tissue). As before, the minireviews were written by postdoctoral scientists and then refereed by an average of four experts on each subject. Typically, each essay begins with a definition of the specialty and provides an overview of its evolution. The minireview describes the milestone contributions reported in the core documents. The 1981 and 1982 key citing papers are used as the basis for a discussion of recent research and speculations about future trends.

The minireviews contain no jargon, formulas, or undefined abbreviations and acronyms. Thus, they should be comprehensible to research scientists, science administrators, and graduate students alike. We have gone to great lengths to ensure the accuracy of the minireviews.

Until ISI announced its work on our first *Atlas*, the term "minireview" had not, to my knowledge, been widely used in the literature. Of course, numerous publications had published minireviews of one kind or another. All sorts of journals, such as *Science, Nature, Trends in Biochemical Sciences*, and others, provide short reviews in their respective styles. We would contend that when one of our minireviews turns out to look like those that are published by more conventional methods, it will be the ultimate validation of the minireview process itself. Indeed, such review articles will automatically move to the top of the list of current relevant papers we retrieve.

While conventional sources of reviewing may collectively overlap our efforts, the unique role of the *Atlas* is to identify and "review" the worldwide research fronts of science in a comprehensive and systematic manner. That is what makes it encyclopedic. And it is our unique and stated purpose to identify those areas that have not previously been reviewed. Selecting highly active fields may sometimes have thwarted this intent in this particular *Atlas*. But we expect eventually to generate minireviews particularly in those areas not yet covered in the standard review literature. Price once suggested to me that reviews would be necessary after 40 new papers are published on a given topic. But this threshold varies widely across the range of scientific disciplines and depends upon many factors.

Figure 3 includes the multidimensionally scaled map for the chapter on fibroblast- and leukocyte-interferon genes. The numbered boxes identify each paper in the bibliography of core papers. To facilitate scanning, the bibliography is arranged alphabetically by first author. Institutional affiliations appear beneath the name of each first author in

Figure 2: Sample minireview reduced to 50 percent of original size.

Specialty (98)

Structural Studies of Fibroblast and Leukocyte Interferon-Genes

The interferons are a class of small proteins which protect vertebrate cells from viral infections, in addition to having other effects on the cell growth cycle and the immune response. Efforts to purify and characterize the interferons have been spurred on by the possibility that they might prove useful in the treatment of viral disease and cancer. With the advent of recombinant DNA techniques, researchers became very interested in the structure of the interferon genes, with a view to inserting these genes into microorganisms and inducing them to manufacture interferon on a large scale. The core papers of this specialty describe some of the essential work that has led to the attainment of this goal in addition to providing valuable information on the organization and evolution of the interferon gene family.

The structure of a gene can be investigated in several ways. One can isolate and sequence the gene directly, examine the gene at the level of its messenger RNA copy, or determine the amino acid sequence of the protein encoded by the gene.

Early techniques for the purification of interferon only yielded sufficient material for microsequencing techniques. This limited the sequence analysis to the amino-terminal end of the protein ([9], [10], [14], [22]). Allen and Fantes ([1]) subsequently examined the sequence of other regions of interferons by splitting the protein into small peptides whose sequence was then determined. These investigations revealed considerable sequence heterogeneity among the human interferons. The first major differences were noticed between interferon isolated from leukocytes (called alpha-interferon) and that isolated from fibroblasts (beta-interferon). Further sequence variations were then discovered among the alpha-interferons.

The complete amino acid sequence of both alpha- and beta-interferon proteins was first identified by isolating the messenger RNA molecules that direct the manufacture of interferon in the cell. A 'reverse transcriptase' e~zyme was then used to make a DNA copy of the messenger RNA, the nucleotide sequence of this DNA was determined; and, therefore the amino acid sequence of the protein could be deduced ([2], [6], [19]). This approach led to the identification of at least eight distinct chromosomal genes encoding human alpha-interferon ([4], [13], [16]).

These studies identifying the human interferon genes have also yielded interesting information concerning their structure. As would be expected for a secretory protein most of the coding sequences of interferon genes begin with a 'signal peptide' section, marking the protein for transport across the endoplasmic reticulum and out of the cell. Another very interesting finding was that the interferon fibroblast and leukocyte genes do not appear to contain introns, the non-coding sections of DNA found in most eukaryote genes, but not corresponding mRNA, examined to date. Several interferon 'pseudogenes' have also been found. These are interferon genes containing nucleotide alterations in the coding sequence that prevent the genes from producing full-length interferon ([4]).

Comparison of human interferon gene sequences clearly suggests that they have a common ancestry. It has been estimated that the alpha and beta genes probably diverged 500-1000 million years ago, making them as old as the vertebrates([19]). It appears that the alpha gene family probably arose by duplication of the ancestral alpha-interferon gene, beginning 20-80 million years ago (24).

The most studied non-human interferons are those of the mouse. Amino acid sequence analysis has revealed at least two classes of mouse interferon, showing sequence homology with human alpha- and beta-interferon respectively ([17]).

As has already been stated, a major aim of much of the research on interferon genes is to insert these genes into microorganisms and obtain the mass production of interferon for clinical use and further research. Derynck et al.,[1] Goeddel et al. ([3], [5]), Nagata et al. ([12]), Taniguchi et al. ([20]) have inserted interferon genes into Escherichia coli and found that the interferon produced was biologically active.

The interferon system is an area of intensive research and much of the recent work has confirmed the conclusions of the earlier core papers. Thus, several research groups have produced evidence supporting the view that interferon genes do not contain introns (4, 5, 9). Gray and Goeddel (30), however, have determined the structure of human gamma-interferon and shown that it has a sequence unrelated to other interferon species and contains three introns.

Recombinant DNA techniques have allowed hybrid interferon genes to be constructed, in which the beginning of one alpha-interferon gene is attached to the end of another[2] (24). A much more extensive control over the structure of interferon genes has been made possible by Edge (1), with the complete chemical synthesis of the gene for human alpha-interferon. These gene synthesis and hybrid gene construction techniques will provide the ability to modify the structure of interferon genes at will, with the expression of the modified genes being obtained by insertion into a suitable microorganism. This ability will no doubt be used to investigate which regions of the genes are important to particular biological functions, and might eventually lead to the design of a more effective product for clinical use.

1. Derynck R, Remaut E, Saman E, Stanssen P, DeClercq E, Content J & Fiers W. Expression of human fibroblast interferon gene in Escherichia coli. Nature 287 (5779): 193-197, 1980.

2. Weck PK. Antiviral activities of hybrids of two major human leukocyte interferons. Nucl. Acid R. 9: 6153, 1981.

the map. We did not include laboratory names in our first *Atlas*. However, it later became obvious that a map without these names was less useful. Even an ordinary world map needs labels for continents, countries, or cities.

Each map is multidimensionally scaled. That is, it depicts the degree of "connectedness" between pairs of papers. Papers that are frequently co-cited, such as those by Mantei (11) and Taniguchi (18) in Figure 3, appear close together on the map. The problems discussed or elucidated in these papers are co-cited for a variety of reasons. Papers less frequently "connected," such as those by Derynck (2) and Houghton (7), are located farther apart on the map.

Undoubtedly, the "meaning" of these maps is one of the most controversial aspects of the *Atlas*. To give greater meaning to the conceptual associations implied by the clustering procedure, we have added generic captions below the maps. It is significant that even within these already specialized but rapidly changing research fronts, the core papers will form "subclusters" that we can easily identify. These subclusters form the profiles for these topics. In Figure 3, papers numbered 2, 18, and 19 discuss the use of a reverse transcriptase enzyme to aid in identifying the amino acid sequence and, later, eight distinct chromosomal genes encoding human alpha-interferon (papers 4, 13, and 16). The captions provide shorthand descriptions of the subdivisions.

It is important to realize that the map is a snapshot of the status of research in 1981, an arbitrary single frame from what is in reality a continuous reel. For example, in the case of the specialty on fibroblast- and leukocyte-interferon genes, by 1982, only 17 of the 22 original core papers continued to be cited at the minimum threshold of 12. By 1983 only eight remained. More will be said about this expansion and contraction of research fronts later.

To facilitate scanning, the list of core references begins on the same page as the map. Each reference includes the institutional affiliation of the first author. The CF number following the entry for each paper indicates the frequency of its citation by 1981 papers. Since the minimum citation threshold was established at 12 when we identified the 1981 core papers, no core paper listed was cited fewer than 12 times in 1981.

Figure 4 provides part of a list of the most-relevant citing papers from 1981 and 1982. The relevance weight (RW) is shown to the right of each paper. This indicator is the number of core papers cited. For example, Edge *et al.*, ICI Ltd., published a 1981 paper in *Nature* that cited 15 of the core papers. In 1982, Fantes, Wellcome Research Labs, published a review containing 79 references in *Texas Reports in Biology and Medicine*, 19 of which are core papers. There follow more 1982 review papers, by Sehgal, Rockefeller University; Berg, Aarhus University; Dziewanowska, Hoffmann-La Roche, and so on. The system automatically pushes the most-relevant reviews to the top of the list.

Some chapters include a third set of references or footnotes to the minireviews. These are publications that the reviewer or referee believed to merit special mention even though they did not turn up in the core or citing lists. In some cases, they are historically important papers that may no longer be cited explicitly at the minimum threshold required. They might have appeared in clusters for previous years. In the future online version of the *Atlas*, such linkages could be shown.

To test the continuing validity of the core selection, we used the same technique to generate a bibliography of the most up-to-date literature on each topic for 1983 and the first half of 1984. These papers are listed in a supplement to the *Atlas*. In Figure 5, we have listed a few such relevant papers. These 1983-1984

Figure 3: A 50 percent reduced facsimile of a multidimensionally scaled map based on co-citation linkages between core papers. Numbers in boxes identify core papers in the bibliography. Proximity of boxes to one another is a measure of similarity or connectivity between core papers.

Specialty 98 Structural studies of fibroblast and leukocyte interferon-genes

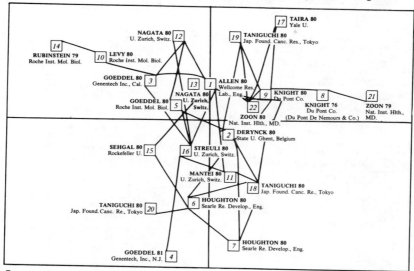

[2], [18], [19] Studies using a reverse transcriptase enzyme to aid in identifying the amino acid
sequence and, later, [4], [13], [16] eight distinct chromosomal genes encoding human alpha-interferon.

Cited Core Documents

CF

[1] ALLEN G, FANTES KH
A FAMILY OF STRUCTURAL GENES FOR HUMAN
LYMPHOBLASTOID (LEUKOCYTE-TYPE) INTERFERON
NATURE 287:408, 1980
WELLCOME RES LABS,DEPT IMMUNOCHEM
BECKENHAM BR3 3BS , KENT , ENGLAND
35

[2] DERYNCK R, CONTENT J, DECLERCQ E,
VOLCKAER. G, TAVERNIE. J, DEVOS R, FIERS W
ISOLATION AND STRUCTURE OF A HUMAN
FIBROBLAST INTERFERON GENE
NATURE 285:542, 1980
STATE UNIV GHENT,MOLEC BIOL LAB
B-9000 GHENT , BELGIUM
34

[3] GOEDDEL DV, YELVERTO. E, ULLRICH A,
HEYNEKER HL, MIOZZARI G, HOLMES W,
SEEBURG PH, DULL T, MAY L, STEBBING N
HUMAN LEUKOCYTE INTERFERON PRODUCED BY E-
COLI IS BIOLOGICALLY ACTIVE
NATURE 287:411, 1980
GENENTECH INC,DEPT MOLEC BIOL
S SAN FRANCISCO , CA 94080
45

[4] GOEDDEL DV, LEUNG DW, DULL TJ, GROSS M,
LAWN RM, MCCANDLI. R, SEEBURG PH,
ULLRICH A, YELVERTO. E, GRAY PW
THE STRUCTURE OF 8 DISTINCT CLONED HUMAN
LEUKOCYTE INTERFERON CDNAS
NATURE 290:20, 1981
GENENTECH INC,DEPT MOLEC BIOL
S SAN FRANCISCO , CA 94080
25

[5] GOEDDEL DV, SHEPARD HM, YELVERTO. E,
LEUNG D, CREA R, SIOMA A, PESTKA S
SYNTHESIS OF HUMAN FIBROBLAST INTERFERON BY
E-COLI
NUCL ACID R 8:2885, 1980
GENENTECH INC,DEPT MOLEC BIOL
S SAN FRANCISCO , CA 94080
29

CF

[6] HOUGHTON M, STEWART AG, DOEL SM,
EMTAGE JS, EATON MAW, SMITH JC, PATEL TP,
LEWIS HM, PORTER AG, BIRCH JR
THE AMINO-TERMINAL SEQUENCE OF HUMAN
FIBROBLAST INTERFERON AS DEDUCED FROM
REVERSE TRANSCRIPTS OBTAINED USING SYNTHETIC
OLIGONUCLEOTIDE PRIMERS
NUCL ACID R 8:1913, 1980
GD SEARLE & CO LTD,SEARLE RES & DEV,DEPT BIOCHEM
HIGH WYCOMBE HP12 4HL , BUCKS , ENGLAND
15

[7] HOUGHTON M, EATON MAW, STEWART AG,
SMITH JC, DOEL SM, CATLIN GH, LEWIS HM,
PATEL TP, EMTAGE JS, CAREY NH
THE COMPLETE AMINO ACID SEQUENCE OF HUMAN
FIBROBLAST INTERFERON AS DEDUCED USING
SYNTHETIC OLIGODEOXYRIBONUCLEOTIDE PRIMERS
OF REVERSE TRANSCRIPTASE
NUCL ACID R 8:2885, 1980
SEARLE RES & DEV
HIGH WYCOMBE , BUCKS , ENGLAND
12

[8] KNIGHT E
INTERFERON - PURIFICATION AND INITIAL
CHARACTERIZATION FROM HUMAN DIPLOID CELLS
P NAS US 73:520, 1976
DUPONT CO,EXPTL STN,DEPT CENT RES & DEV
WILMINGTON , DE 19898
20

[9] KNIGHT E, HUNKAPIL. M, KORANT BD,
HARDY RWF, HOOD LE
HUMAN FIBROBLAST INTERFERON - AMINO ACID
ANALYSIS AND AMINO TERMINAL AMINO ACID
SEQUENCE
SCIENCE 207:525, 1980
DUPONT CO,DEPT CENT RES & DEV
WILMINGTON , DE 19898
40

[10] LEVY WP, SHIVELY J, RUBINSTE. M, DELVALLE U,
PESTKA S
AMINO-TERMINAL AMINO ACID SEQUENCE OF
HUMAN LEUKOCYTE INTERFERON
P NAS BIOL 77:5102, 1980
ROCHE INST MOLEC BIOL
NUTLEY , NJ 07110
14

319

Figure 3 *(cont.)*

Cited Core Documents *(cont.)*

CF

11 MANTEI N, SCHWARZS. M, STREULI M, PANEM S,   32
NAGATA S, WEISSMAN. C
THE NUCLEOTIDE SEQUENCE OF A CLONED HUMAN
LEUKOCYTE INTERFERON CDNA
GENE 10:1, 1980
UNIV ZURICH,INST MOLEK BIOL 1
CH-8093 ZURICH , SWITZERLAND

12 NAGATA S, TAIRA H, HALL A, JOHNSRUD L,   52
STREULI M, ECSODI J, BOLL W, CANTELL K,
WEISSMAN. C
SYNTHESIS IN E-COLI OF A POLYPEPTIDE WITH
HUMAN LEUKOCYTE INTERFERON ACTIVITY
NATURE 284:316, 1980
UNIV ZURICH,INST MOLEK BIOL 1
CH-8093 ZURICH , SWITZERLAND

13 NAGATA S, MANTEI N, WEISSMAN. C   54
THE STRUCTURE OF ONE OF THE 8 OR MORE
DISTINCT CHROMOSOMAL GENES FOR HUMAN
INTERFERON-ALPHA
NATURE 287:401, 1980
UNIV ZURICH,INST MOLEK BIOL 1
CH-8093 ZURICH , SWITZERLAND

14 RUBINSTE.M, RUBINSTE. S, FAMILLET. P,   34
MILLER RS, WALDMAN AA, PESTKA S
HUMAN LEUKOCYTE INTERFERON - PRODUCTION,
PURIFICATION TO HOMOGENEITY, AND INITIAL
CHARACTERIZATION
P NAS US 76:640, 1979
ROCHE INST MOLEC BIOL
NUTLEY , NJ 07110

15 SEHGAL PB, SAGAR AD   16
HETEROGENEITY OF POLY(I).POLY(C)-INDUCED
HUMAN FIBROBLAST INTERFERON MESSENGER RNA
SPECIES
NATURE 288:95, 1980
ROCKEFELLER UNIV
NEW YORK , NY 10021

16 STREULI M, NAGATA S, WEISSMAN. C   33
AT LEAST 3 HUMAN TYPE-ALPHA INTERFERONS -
STRUCTURE OF ALPHA-2
SCIENCE 209:1343, 1980
UNIV ZURICH,INST MOLEK BIOL 1
CH-8093 ZURICH , SWITZERLAND

CF

17 TAIRA H, BROEZE RJ, JAYARAM BM, LENGYEL P,   17
HUNKAPIL. M, HOOD LE
MOUSE INTERFERONS - AMINO TERMINAL AMINO
ACID SEQUENCES OF VARIOUS SPECIES
SCIENCE 207:528, 1980
YALE UNIV,DEPT MOLEC BIOPHYS & BIOCHEM
NEW HAVEN , CT 06520

18 TANIGUCH.T, OHNO S, FUJIIKUR. Y,   31
MURAMATS. M
THE NUCLEOTIDE SEQUENCE OF HUMAN FIBROBLAST
INTERFERON CDNA
GENE 10:11, 1980
JAPANESE FDN CANC RES,INST CANC,DEPT BIOCHEM
TOKYO 170 , JAPAN

19 TANIGUCH.T, MANTEI N, SCHWARZS. M,   35
NAGATA S, MURAMATS. M, WEISSMAN. C
HUMAN LEUKOCYTE AND FIBROBLAST INTERFERONS
ARE STRUCTURALLY RELATED
NATURE 285:547, 1980
JAPANESE FDN CANC RES,INST CANC,DEPT BIOCHEM
TOKYO 170 , JAPAN

20 TANIGUCH.T, GUARENTE L, ROBERTS TM,   12
KIMELMAN D, DOUHAN J, PTASH:NE M
EXPRESSION OF THE HUMAN FIBROBLAST
INTERFERON GENE IN ESCHERICHIA-COLI
P NAS US 77:5230, 1980
JAPANESE FDN CANC RES,INST CANC,TOSHIMA KU
TOKYO 170 , JAPAN

21 ZOON KC, SMITH ME, BRIDGEN PJ, NEDDEN DZ,   12
ANFINSEN CB
PURIFICATION AND PARTIAL CHARACTERIZATION OF
HUMAN LYMPHOBLASTOID INTERFERON
P NAS US 76:5601, 1979
NIAMDD,CHEM BIOL LAB
BETHESDA , MD 20205

22 ZOON KC, SMITH ME, BRIDGEN PJ, ANFINSEN CB,   31
HUNKAPIL. M, HOOD LE
AMINO TERMINAL SEQUENCE OF THE MAJOR
COMPONENT OF HUMAN LYMPHOBLASTOID
INTERFERON
SCIENCE 207:527, 1980
NIAMDD,CHEM BIOL LAB
BETHESDA , MD 20205

Figure 4: 1981 and 1982 key citing papers ranked by relevance. For reasons of space, all 48 key citing papers cannot be shown.

Key Citing Documents

1981

RW

1 EDGE MD, ATKINSON TC, GREENE AR,   15
HEATHCLI.GR, MARKHAM AF, MEACOCK PA,
NEWTON CR, SCANLON DB, SCHUCH W
TOTAL SYNTHESIS OF A HUMAN-LEUKOCYTE
INTERFERON GENE
NATURE 292:756, 1981   55R
ICI LTD,DIV PHARMACEUT
MACCLESFIELD SK10 4TG , CHESHIRE , ENGLAND

2 GOEDDEL DV, DULL TJ, GRAY PW, GROSS M,   15
LAWN RM, LEUNG DW, MCCANDLI.R, SEEBURG PH,
ULLRICH A, YELVERTO.E
THE STRUCTURE OF 8 DISTINCT CLONED HUMAN-
LEUKOCYTE INTERFERON CDNAS
NATURE 290:20, 1981   47R
GENENTECH INC,DEPT MOLEC BIOL
SAN FRANCISCO , CA 94080

3 GORDON J, MINKS MA   15
THE INTERFERON RENAISSANCE - MOLECULAR
ASPECTS OF INDUCTION AND ACTION
MICROBIOL R 45:244, 1981 R   263R
FRIEDRICH MIESCHER INST
CH-4002 BASEL , SWITZERLAND

4 HOUGHTON M, BARBER C, CAREY NH, CATLIN GH,   13
DOEL SM, JACKSON IJ, PORTER AG
THE ABSENCE OF INTRONS WITHIN A HUMAN
FIBROBLAST INTERFERON GENE
NUCL ACID R 9:247, 1981   51R
GD SEARLE & CO LTD,SEARLE RES & DEV,DEPT MOLEC
GENET,POB 53,LANE END RD
HIGH WYCOMBE HP12 4HL , BUCKINGHAMSHIRE , ENGLAND

5 TAVERNIE.J, DERYNCK R, FIERS W   13
EVIDENCE FOR A UNIQUE HUMAN FIBROBLAST
INTERFERON (IFN-BETA-1) CHROMOSOMAL GENE,
DEVOID OF INTERVENING SEQUENCES
NUCL ACID R 9:461, 1981   36R
STATE UNIV GHENT,MOLEC BIOL LAB
B-9000 GHENT , BEL

1982

RW

23 FANTES KH   19
INTERFERONS - CHEMICAL PROPERTIES
TEX REP BIO 41:240, 1982 R   79R
WELLCOME RES LABS,DEPT VIROL RES & DEV
BECKENHAM BR3 3BS, KENT, ENGLAND

24 SEHGAL PB   17
THE INTERFERON GENES
BIOC BIOP A 695:17, 1982 R   108R
ROCKEFELLER UNIV
NEW YORK, NY 10021

25 BERG K   16
PURIFICATION AND CHARACTERIZATION OF MURINE
AND HUMAN INTERFERONS - A REVIEW OF THE LI-
TERATURE OF THE 1970S
ACT PAT M C 1982:1, 1982 R   334R
AARHUS UNIV,INST MED MICROBIOL
DK-8000 AARHUS C. DENMARK

26 DZIEWANO.ZE, PESTKA S   16
THE HUMAN INTERFERONS
MED RES REV 2:325, 1982 R   166R
HOFFMANN LA ROCHE INC,DEPT MED ONCOL & IMMUNOL
NUTLEY, NJ 07110

27 LENGYEL P   16
BIOCHEMISTRY OF INTERFERONS AND THEIR AC-
TIONS
ANN R BIOCH 51:251, 1982 R   257R
YALE UNIV,DEPT MOLEC BIOPHYS & BIOCHEM
NEW HAVEN, CT 06511

28 RUBINSTE.M   16
THE STRUCTURE OF HUMAN INTERFERONS
BIOC BIOP A 695:5, 1982   73R
WEIZMANN INST SCI
IL-76100 REHOVOT, ISRAEL

29 RUBINSTE.M   15
PURIFICATION AND STRUCTURAL-ANALYSIS OF IN-
TERFERON
PHI T ROY B 299:39, 1982   51R
WEIZMANN INST

Figure 5: 1983 and 1984 key citing papers included in the supplemental bibliography, ranked by relevance. For reasons of space, all 23 key citing papers cannot be shown.

Specialty (98)

Structural Studies of Fibroblast and Leukocyte Interferon-Genes

Key Citing Documents

	1983	RW
1	**PESTKA S** THE HUMAN INTERFERONS - FROM PROTEIN- PURIFICATION AND SEQUENCE TO CLONING AND EX- PRESSION IN BACTERIA - BEFORE, BETWEEN, AND BE- YOND *ARCH BIOCH* 221:1, 1983 R 174R ROCHE INST MOLEC BIOL NUTLEY, NJ 07110	18
2	**DWORKINR.E, DWORKIN MB, SWETLY P** MOLECULAR-CLONING OF HUMAN ALPHA- INTERFERON AND BETA-INTERFERON GENES FROM NAMALWA CELLS *J INTERF R* 2:575, 1982 47R ERNST BOEHRINGER INST ARZNEIMITTELFORSCH,BIOCHEM LAB, DR BOEHRINGER GASSE 5-11 A-1121 VIENNA, AUSTRIA	12
3	**MCCULLAG.KG, CATLIN GH, DAVIES JA, DAWSON KM, DOEL SM, HOUGHTON M, ONEILL GJ, SIM IS** BIOLOGICAL PROPERTIES OF HUMAN INTERFERON BETA-1 SYNTHESIZED IN RECOMBINANT BACTERIA *J INTERF R* 3:97, 1983 N 48R SEARLE RES & DEV,DEPT BIOL,POB 53,LANE END RD HIGH WYCOMBE HP12 4HL, BUCKS, ENGLAND	12
4	**ATTALLAH AM, JOHNSON RP, PETRICCI.JC, YEATMAN TJ** BIOLOGICAL RESPONSE MODIFIERS AND THEIR PROM- ISE IN CLINICAL MEDICINE *PHARM THERA* 19:435, 1982 R 148R US BUR BIOL,BLDG 29,ROOM 507,8800 ROCKVILLE PIKE BETHESDA, MD 20205	11
5	**WEISSMAN.C** THE ALPHA-INTERFERONS - SOME ANSWERS AND MANY QUESTIONS *HARVEY LECT* 1983:129, 1983 R 69R UNIV ZURICH,INST MOLEKULARBIOL 1 CH-8006 ZURICH, SWITZERLAND	11
6	**WILSON V, BARRIE PA, BOSELEY PG, BURKE DC, EASTON A, JEFFREYS AJ, SLOCOMBE PM** A COMPARISON OF VERTEBRATE INTERFERON GENE FAMILIES DETECTED BY HYBRIDIZATION WITH HU- MAN INTERFERON DNA *J MOL BIOL* 166:457, 1983 61R UNIV LEICESTER,DEPT GENET LEICESTER LE1 7RH, ENGLAND	10
7	**HAYNES J, WEISSMAN.C** CONSTITUTIVE, LONG-TERM PRODUCTION OF HUMAN INTERFERONS BY HAMSTER-CELLS CONTAINING MUL- TIPLE COPIES OF A CLONED INTERFERON GENE *NUCL ACID R* 11:687, 1983 56R UNIV ZURICH,INST MOLEK BIOL 1 CH-8093 ZURICH, SWITZERLAND	9
8	**KELKER HC, ANDERSON P, VILCEK J, YIP YK** EFFECTS OF GLYCOSIDASE TREATMENT ON THE PHY- SICO-CHEMICAL PROPERTIES AND BIOLOGICAL- ACTIVITY OF HUMAN INTERFERON-GAMMA *J BIOL CHEM* 258:8010, 1983 40R NYU,SCH MED,DEPT MICROBIOL	9

	1984	RW
12	**MENGE U, KULA MR** PURIFICATION TECHNIQUES FOR HUMAN INTERFER- ONS *ENZYME MICR* 6:101, 1984 R 142R GESELL BIOTECHNOL FORSCH MBH,MASCHERODER WEG 1 D-3300 BRUNSWICK, FED REP GER	10
13	**BOWDEN DW, GILL T, HSIAO K, LILLQUIS.JS, MAO JI, TESTA D, VOVIS GF** CLONING OF EUKARYOTIC GENES IN SINGLE-STRAND PHAGE VECTORS - THE HUMAN INTERFERON GENES *GENE* 27:87, 1984 37R COLLABORAT RES INC,128 SPRING ST LEXINGTON, MA 02173	9
14	**YONEHARA S** JA)) RECEPTOR SYSTEM FOR INTERFERON *SEIKAGAKU* 56:184, 1984 R 49R TOKYO METROPOLITAN INST MED SCI,BIOPHYLAXIS SECT, BUNKYO KU TOKYO 113, JAPAN	8
15	**KHESIN YE, AMCHENKO.AM, GULEVICH NE, NAROVLYA.AN, VORONINA FV** RS)) GENETIC MECHANISMS OF THE HUMAN INTER- FERON SYSTEM AS A FACTOR OF THE MAINTENANCE OF CELLULAR HOMEOSTASIS *VA MED NAUK* :80, 1984 R 75R NF GAMALEYA EPIDEMIOL & MICROBIOL INST MOSCOW, USSR	7
16	**DIJKEMA R, DEREUS A, POUWELS P, SCHELLEK.H** STRUCTURE AND EXPRESSION IN ESCHERICHIA-COLI OF A CLONED RAT INTERFERON-ALPHA GENE *NUCL ACID R* 12:1227, 1984 34R TNO,MED BIOL LAB,POB 45 2280 AA RIJSWIJK, NETHERLANDS	6
17	**KELLEY KA, DANDOY F, DEMAEYER E, DEMAEYER.J, KOZAK CA, PITHA PM, SKUP D, SOR F, WINDASS JD** MAPPING OF MURINE INTERFERON-ALPHA GENES TO CHROMOSOME-4 *GENE* 26:181, 1983 36R JOHNS HOPKINS UNIV,SCH MED,CTR ONCOL BALTIMORE, MD 21205	6
18	**OSHEROFF PL, CHIANG TR, TAHARA SM** MONOCLONAL-ANTIBODIES TO A RECOMBINANT HU- MAN-LEUKOCYTE INTERFERON 'RIFN-ALPHA-B *CLIN IMMUN* 30:188, 1984 20R HOFFMANN LA ROCHE INC,ROCHE RES CTR,BIOPOLYMER RES DEPT,340 KINGSLAND ST NUTLEY, NJ 07110	6
19	**BRUNDA MJ, ROSENBAU.D** MODULATION OF MURINE NATURAL-KILLER CELL- ACTIVITY INVITRO AND INVIVO BY RECOMBINANT HUMAN INTERFERONS *CANCER RES* 44:597, 1984 35R HOFFMANN LA ROCHE INC,DEPT EXPTL & APPL BIOL NUTLEY, NJ 07110	5

papers are also ranked by relevance, that is, the number of core papers they cited.

The *Atlas* also includes a foldout "global" map of all 127 specialties, a clustering of clusters. Each research front or specialty is identified in the map by its name and cluster number. We created this map using "residual links." A residual link occurs when two core pa-

pers from different specialties are co-cited, but not frequently enough to place them in the same cluster. In this way we can cluster groups of research fronts.

We have also included a number of indexes to make the information contained in the *Atlas* readily retrievable. The author index includes all authors and coauthors of papers included in the

Atlas. There is also an alphabetic keyword index to the names or titles of the research fronts, and an alphabetic listing of all the significant words from every document title. Finally, we have added an institutional index organized by country and city.

We have also included a 1981 to 1983 chronology for the 52 most-active research fronts to illustrate the dynamic processes of expansion and contraction within the research universe. As was mentioned here earlier, we deliberately chose to minireview the "hottest" fields, and most of these 52 fronts have dramatically changed in terms of core papers, volume of publication, and nomenclature. Thus, having identified a particular 1981 research front in the main *Atlas*, you can observe where that research front had moved in 1982 and 1983.

For example, Figure 6 shows the 1981-1983 chronology for research front #81-0001, which is Specialty 99 in the *Atlas*. The six-digit code number identifies the specialty in the *Index to Research Fronts in ISI/BIOMED®, 1983*. In 1981, this research front, entitled "Non-A-Non-B-Hepatitis-Infections, Hepatitis-A-Infections, and Hepatitis-B-Infections,"

consisted of 39 core papers and 334 citing papers. By 1982, it split into three separate research fronts. Research front #82-0001 deals with the clinical diagnosis and management of hepatitis infections. It included 18 core papers and 116 citing papers. By 1983, this research front contained 43 core papers and 289 citing papers on the immunological aspects of hepatitis as well as rubella viruses.

The other two 1982 research fronts focus on the connection between hepatitis B virus and hepatocellular cancer. Research front #82-0282, which concentrates on the diagnosis, treatment, and immunological features of hepatitis B virus, included 25 core papers and 270 citing papers. Research front #82-1371 contained 10 core papers and 101 citing papers on the sequence, cloning, and expression of hepatitis genes. By 1983, these two research fronts merged and included 41 core papers and 420 citing papers.

In addition to research directors, we anticipate that educators, graduate students, and scientists will be the principal users of the *Atlas*. Historians of science, administrators, and librarians will also find it useful. Teachers can use the lists

Figure 6: Sample 1981-1983 chronology for Specialty 99 in the *Atlas*.

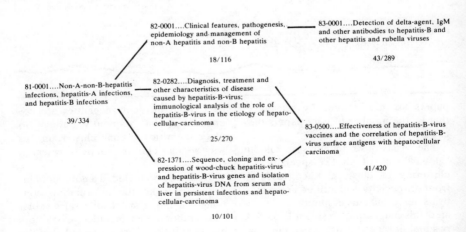

322

of core documents and key citing documents as the basis for preparing reading lists. By using these bibliographies, they can be certain that they've included the papers that have had the greatest impact on the particular topic under discussion. In addition to the bibliographic information, the minireviews could be used when assigning reading for seminars or thesis topics.

In the near future, we will be announcing further developments in the evolution of the *Atlas*. In 1985, we plan to make the same type of encyclopedic information available online. Eventually, we expect to create several thousand minireviews each year. Together with the reference lists for the core and current literature for each research front, the minireviews will become a dynamic, up-to-date account of any topic you choose.

There is a kind of Matthew effect not only with respect to authors[3] but also to subjects. One of the commentators to whom I sent the preliminary *Atlas* material suggested that we were emphasizing those subjects that were already widely discussed in the literature. This is in fact implicit in our definition of "most active" since we chose the first 52 topics to be minireviewed on the basis of the number of articles published. Presumably, there is a large current interest in these topics, because publication productivity is high. However, we realize that less popular topics need reviewing as much as the "hot" ones. We intend to stress such topics in our online *Atlas*.

However, if we restricted our minireviewing to the least "popular" topics, it would diminish the value of our exercise in scientography. In a sense, we would be limiting our discussion to the unexplored parts of the world and omitting world-class science. It would be a strange and perverse type of encyclopedism to begin by reviewing *only* the partially explored areas of science.

The advantage of an online version of the *Atlas* is that lists of references can literally become up-to-the-minute. By combining this information with our *Automatic Subject Citation Alert* (*ASCA®*) service, we can regularly provide weekly bibliographic supplements to the minireviews. In fact, this is how we added the 1983/84 supplement to the *Atlas* just a few weeks ago. We have been able to overcome many of the time limitations involved in printing a volume of more than 700 pages. However, no printed edition can match the ultimate timeliness of an electronic version of the *Atlas*.

Figure 7 shows our so-called "C4 level" map of the 1982 world of biomedicine. The territory covered by the *Atlas* primarily falls into the gray-shaded area. Don't be deceived by the relatively small size of this area. It requires an 11″ x 21″ foldout map, included with the *Atlas*, to detail all the research fronts associated with this rather large and active area of science. The territories we have marked off have no physical significance, that is, they do not measure the size of the field in terms of publications. The research area subtended by each is a measure of distance in a mathematical sense.

We have provided you with examples of both superstar and less brilliant research areas. Among the thousands of areas yet to be minireviewed are stars of varying brilliance. In a reasonable time we hope to have online at least those of maximal brightness. And with the software we are developing, you will eventually be able to zoom in on the faintest of stars in the Universe of Science.

The *ISI Atlas of Science: Biotechnology and Molecular Genetics 1981/82* (ISSN: 0278-2898; ISBN: 0-941708-01-2) including the Bibliographic Update for 1983/84 can now be ordered directly from Jim Shea, ISI, 3501 Market Street, Philadelphia, PA 19104. We expect the first copies of the *Atlas* to be delivered in November. If you are not familiar with

Figure 7: Map of 1982 clusters in the *ISI BIOMED®* database at the C4 level showing the grand divisions of bioscience. The shaded area represents the territory covered in the *ISI Atlas of Science®: Biotechnology and Molecular Genetics, 1981/82.* A=number identifying C3 cluster. B=cluster names.

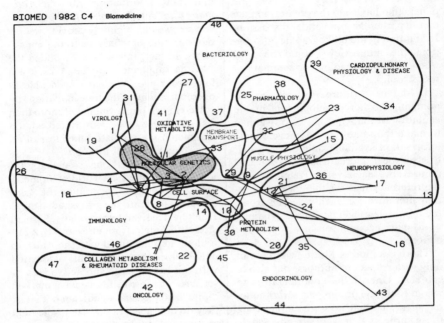

BIOMED 1982 C4   Biomedicine

Each C3 cluster is a cluster of C2 clusters that in turn is a cluster of C1 research fronts. Each forms part of the hierarchy from discipline to subspecialty to core paper.

A   B

1 Immunology and treatment of viral hepatitis
2 DNA structure and factors controlling gene expression
3 Histone and non-histone nuclear proteins
4 Immunoglobulin expression and regulation of the immune response
5 Cellular immunity and diseases of the immune response
6 Chromosome abnormalities and immune response in Hodgkins disease, leukemia and other malignant diseases
7 Collagen genes and collagen synthesis
8 Cell surface composition and effects of various agents on cancer cells
9 Contractile proteins, membrane dynamics, neuronal development and effects of calcium
10 Effects of peptide hormones on cell surface receptors and metabolism
11 Cytotoxicity of oxygen free radicals, macrophages and other substances
12 Peptide hormones and release factors, neurotransmitters and opioid peptides in the CNS
13 Nociception
14 Chemotaxis, histamine release, and purine and pyrimidine metabolism
15 Myosin isoenzymes and innervation patterns in muscle
16 Hypothalamic obesity and the control of food intake
17 Amino acid neurotransmitters
18 Allergies, immunotherapy and cimetidine treatment
19 Regulation of protein synthesis with interferon and other methods in virus infected cells
20 Lipoproteins
21 Receptors for neurotransmitters
22 Collagen metabolism in rheumatoid arthritis and fibroblasts
23 Assessment of ventricular function and management of ventricular disease
24 Hypertension

324

25 Management of ulcers and other gastrointestinal disorders
26 Cyclophosphamide therapy and delayed-type hypersensitivity
27 Lipid peroxidation and oxygen free radical metabolism in liver
28 DNA repair and anti-cancer drugs
29 Treatment of infections, and prostaglandins and related compounds and kidney function
30 Proteases, amino acid metabolism and protein degradation
31 Herpes simplex virus and infections of homosexual men
32 Adult respiratory distress syndrome and pulmonary vascular injuries
33 Protein and proton translocation across membranes
34 Respiration
35 Pituitary hormones
36 Adenosine and GABA receptors and drug analogs
37 Bacterial toxins and diseases of *E-coli* and other enteric bacteria
38 Theophylline and pharmacokinetics of drug therapy in the elderly
39 Sudden infant death syndrome, sleep apnea and esophageal disorders
40 Treatment of infective endocarditis and staphylococcal infections
41 Cytochrome-P-450 and metabolism of cytotoxic aromatic hydrocarbons
42 Treatment of cancer using methotrexate and other drugs
43 Steroid hormones in the pituitary and effects on development and sexual behavior
44 Management of diabetes
45 Hyperparathyroidism and regulation of protein secretion
46 Importance of dietary zinc
47 HLA systems in rheumatic diseases and lupus erythematosus

the earlier *Atlas of Biochemistry*, we can send you a brochure that describes it. The *ISI Atlas of Science: Biochemistry and Molecular Biology, 1978/80* (ISSN: 0278-2898; ISBN: 0-941708-00-4) can still be purchased for $90 while the supply lasts. The new *ISI Atlas of Science: Biotechnology and Molecular Genetics,*

1981/82 is priced at $250. Each includes the maps and indexes described earlier.

* * * * *

My thanks to Brad Schepp for his help in the preparation of this essay.

©1984 ISI

REFERENCES

1. **Cedering S.** A letter from Caroline Herschel (1750-1848). (Poem.) *Science 84* 5(5):65, 1984.
2. **Garfield E.** Introducing the *ISI Atlas of Science: Biochemistry and Molecular Biology, 1978/80. Essays of an information scientist.* Philadelphia: ISI Press, 1983. Vol. 5. p. 279-87.
3. **Merton R K.** The Matthew effect in science. *Science* 159:56-63, 1968.

Current Comments®

The Articles Most Cited in 1961-1982. 5. Another 100 *Citation Classics* and a Summary of the 500 Papers Identified to Date

Number 42   October 15, 1984

Over the past few months, we've published a series of essays on the articles most cited from 1961 to 1982 in *Science Citation Index®* (*SCI®*). So far, we've listed the top 400 papers that were cited at least 1,032 times in this 22-year period.[1-4] In this essay, we'll present another 100 *Citation Classics™*. We'll also discuss the distributions by journal, year of publication, and field for all 500 papers identified to date.

It is interesting to note that these lists of high-impact articles are by no means permanent. Science is a dynamic enterprise with a considerable turnover of highly cited research. For example, 10 years ago, we identified the 100 most-cited articles in the 1961-1972 *SCI*.[5] Of these, 55 were still among the 100 most-cited articles for 1961-1982.[1] Another 28 of these "old" classics reappeared in the second through fourth parts of this series.[2-4] However, none of the papers in that 1974 study appear in this essay. Perhaps the remaining 17 papers identified in the 1974 study will resurface when we extend the list to include the top 1,000 papers for 1961-1982.

Table 1 presents bibliographic information on the 100 classics in this study. The papers are arranged in alphabetic order by first author. The number of 1961-1982 citations is shown for each paper. Citations for 1983 are shown in parentheses to give you an idea of how frequently each paper is currently cited. Each of the papers was cited at least 936 times.

Thirty-nine papers have already been featured in *Current Contents®* (*CC®*) as *Citation Classics*. They are indicated by asterisks. After the reference are shown the issue, year, and edition of *CC* in which the author's commentary appeared. We encourage all of the authors listed in Table 1 to submit commentaries on their papers if they have not done so already.

The 100 classics were published in 53 journals. Just six journals account for one-third of these papers: *Biochemical Journal* and *Science* each published six papers. *Biochimica et Biophysica Acta*, *Journal of Biological Chemistry*, *Journal of Chemical Physics*, and *Proceedings of the National Academy of Sciences of the US* each accounted for five papers.

Table 2 lists 25 journals that published at least 5 of the 500 classics we've identified to date. The 500 papers were published in 130 journals, but the top 25 journals account for 69 percent of them; 50 journals account for 83 percent. Table 2 also shows the 1983 impact factor for each journal. Impact is a measure of how frequently a journal's *current* articles are cited. It is calculated by dividing the number of 1983 citations to a journal's 1981 and 1982 articles by the number of articles it published in those

Table 1: The fifth 100 most-cited articles, 1961-1982 $SCI^®$, arranged in alphabetic order by first author. A=1961-1982 citations. 1983 citations appear in parentheses. B=bibliographic data. An asterisk (*) indicates that the paper was the subject of a *Citation Classic*™ commentary. The issue, year, and edition of $CC^®$ in which these commentaries appeared are listed in parentheses. None of these articles appeared in the 1974 list of most-cited articles.

A   **B**

958 (17)   **Alder K, Bohr A, Huus B, Mottelson B & Winther A.** Study of nuclear structure by electromagnetic excitation with accelerated ions. *Rev. Mod. Phys.* 28:432-542, 1956.

1006 (34)   *****Astrup T & Mullertz S.** The fibrin plate method for estimating fibrinolytic activity. *Arch. Biochem. Biophys.* 40:346-51, 1952. (41/84/LS)

973 (23)   **Baltimore D.** Viral RNA-dependent DNA polymerase. *Nature* 226:1209-11, 1970.

958 (70)   **Becchetti F D & Greenlees G W.** Nucleon-nucleus optical-model parameters, $A > 40$, $E < 50$ MeV. *Phys. Rev.* 182:1190-209, 1969.

994 (35)   **Benacerraf B & McDevitt H O.** Histocompatibility-linked immune response genes. *Science* 175:273-9, 1972.

1000 (7)   **Bogdanski D F, Pletscher A, Brodie B B & Udenfriend S.** Identification and assay of serotonin in brain. *J. Pharmacol. Exp. Ther.* 117:82-8, 1956.

949 (190)   *****Bolton A E & Hunter W M.** The labelling of proteins to high specific radioactivities by conjugation to a ^{125}I-containing acylating agent. *Biochem. J.* 133:529-39, 1973. (29/84/LS)

1024 (12)   **Brenner S & Horne R W.** A negative staining method for high resolution electron microscopy of viruses. *Biochim. Biophys. Acta* 34:103-10, 1959.

984 (60)   **Brown B L, Albano J D M, Ekins R P, Sgherzi A M & Tampion W.** A simple and sensitive saturation assay method for the measurement of adenosine 3':5'-cyclic monophosphate. *Biochem. J.* 121:561-2, 1971.

985 (8)   *****Brown J B.** A chemical method for the determination of oestriol, oestrone and oestradiol in human urine. *Biochem. J.* 60:185-93, 1955. (2/83/LS)

950 (9)   **Burn J H & Rand M J.** The action of sympathomimetic amines in animals treated with reserpine. *J. Physiol.—London* 144:314-36, 1958.

989 (3)   **Chamberlin M & Berg P.** Deoxyribonucleic acid-directed synthesis of ribonucleic acid by an enzyme from *Escherichia coli. Proc. Nat. Acad. Sci. US* 48:81-94, 1962.

989 (25)   **Chauveaʳ J, Moule Y & Rouiller C.** Isolation of pure and unaltered liver nuclei: morphology and biochemical composition. *Exp. Cell Res.* 11:317-21, 1956.

1031 (22)   *****Chrambach A, Reisfeld R A, Wyckoff M & Zaccari J.** A procedure for rapid and sensitive staining of protein fractionated by polyacrylamide gel electrophoresis. *Anal. Biochem.* 20:150-4, 1967. (40/83/LS)

1004 (77)   *****Clegg J B, Naughton M A & Weatherall D J.** Abnormal human haemoglobins. *J. Mol. Biol.* 19:91-108, 1966. (2/82/LS)

980 (4)   *****Clewell D B & Helinski D R.** Supercoiled circular DNA-protein complex in *Escherichia coli*: purification and induced conversion to an open circular DNA form. *Proc. Nat. Acad. Sci. US* 62:1159-66, 1969. (8/83/LS)

1014 (156)   *****Cohen A S, Reynolds W E, Franklin E C, Kulka J P, Ropes M W, Schulman L E & Wallace S L.** Preliminary criteria for the classification of systemic lupus erythematosus. *Bull. Rheumat. Dis.* 21:643-8, 1971. (11/82/CP)

1002 (45)   *****Cole K S & Cole R H.** Dispersion and absorption in dielectrics. I. Alternating current characteristics. *J. Chem. Phys.* 9:341-51, 1941. (3/80/PC&ES)

968 (30)   **Cuatrecasas P, Wilchek M & Anfinsen C B.** Selective enzyme purification by affinity chromatography. *Proc. Nat. Acad. Sci. US* 61:636-43, 1968.

943 (14)   **Dalton A J.** A chrome-osimium fixative for electron microscopy. (Abstract.) *Anat. Rec.* 121:281, 1955.

962 (43)   *****Dexter D L.** A theory of sensitized luminescence in solids. *J. Chem. Phys.* 21:836-50, 1953. (38/77)

936 (107)   **Dunnett C W.** A multiple comparison procedure for comparing several treatments with a control. *J. Amer. Statist. Assn.* 50:1096-121, 1955.

1000 (33)   **Elson L A & Morgan W T J.** A colorimetric method for the determination of glucosamine and chondrosamine. *Biochem. J.* 27:1824-8, 1933.

1005 (74)   *****Erlanger B F, Kokowsky N & Cohen W.** The preparation and properties of two new chromogenic substrates of trypsin. *Arch. Biochem. Biophys.* 95:271-8, 1961. (4/81/LS)

956 (52)   **Feshbach H.** A unified theory of nuclear reactions. II. *Ann. Phys.—NY* 19:287-313, 1962.

946 (30)   **Feynman R P.** Very high-energy collisions of hadrons. *Phys. Rev. Lett.* 23:1415-7, 1969.

973 (8)   **Feynman R P & Gell-Mann M.** Theory of the Fermi interaction. *Phys. Rev.* 109:193-8, 1958.

965 (26)   *****Fisher M E.** The theory of equilibrium critical phenomena. *Rep. Progr. Phys.* 30:615-730, 1967. (46/80/PC&ES)

A | B

948 (40) **Fleck A & Munro H N.** The precision of ultraviolet absorption measurements in the Schmidt-Thannhauser procedure for nucleic acid estimation. *Biochim. Biophys. Acta* 55:571-83, 1962.

1019 (23) **Folin O & Ciocalteu V.** On tyrosine and tryptophane determinations in proteins. *J. Biol. Chem.* 73:627-50, 1927.

964 (21) *****Fredrickson D S, Levy R I & Lees R S.** Fat transport in lipoproteins—an integrated approach to mechanisms and disorders. *N. Engl. J. Med.* 276:34-44, 1967. (3/78)

979 (36) **Garen A & Levinthal C.** A fine-structure genetic and chemical study of the enzyme alkaline phosphatase of *E. coli.* I. Purification and characterization of alkaline phosphatase. *Biochim. Biophys. Acta* 38:470-83, 1960.

983 (41) **Gold P & Freedman S O.** Demonstration of tumor-specific antigens in human colonic carcinomata by immunological tolerance and absorption techniques. *J. Exp. Med.* 121:439-62, 1965.

1005 (42) *****Gold P & Freedman S O.** Specific carcinoembryonic antigens of the human digestive system. *J. Exp. Med.* 122:467-81, 1965. (48/80/CP)

1002 (41) *****Good N E, Winget G D, Winter W, Connolly T N, Izawa S & Singh R M M.** Hydrogen ion buffers for biological research. *Biochemistry—USA* 5:467-77, 1966. (40/83/LS)

943 (60) *****Greenfield N & Fasman G D.** Computed circular dichroism spectra for the evaluation of protein conformation. *Biochemistry—USA* 8:4108-16, 1969. (26/82/LS)

990 (24) **Hager R S & Seltzer E C.** Internal conversion tables. Part I: K-, L-, M-shell conversion coefficients for $Z=30$ to $Z=103$. *Nucl. Data Sect. A* 4:1-235, 1968.

1020 (131) *****Hamilton M.** A rating scale for depression. *J. Neurol. Neurosurg. Psychiat.* 23:56-62, 1960. (33/81/CP)

979 (124) **Helenius A & Simons K.** Solubilization of membranes by detergents. *Biochim. Biophys. Acta* 415:29-79, 1975.

977 (29) **Hinze J & Jaffe H H.** Electronegativity. I. Orbital electronegativity of neutral atoms. *J. Amer. Chem. Soc.* 84:540-6, 1962.

1029 (50) *****Hubbard J.** Electron correlations in narrow energy bands. *Proc. Roy. Soc. London Ser. A* 276:238-57, 1963. (22/80/PC&ES)

962 (67) **Hummel B C W.** A modified spectrophotometric determination of chymotrypsin, trypsin, and thrombin. *Can. J. Biochem. Physiol.* 37:1393-9, 1959.

993 (41) *****Johns E W.** Studies on histones. 7. Preparative methods for histone fractions from calf thymus. *Biochem. J.* 92:55-9, 1964. (11/79/LS)

975 (29) *****Johnson C E & Bovey F A.** Calculation of nuclear magnetic resonance spectra of aromatic hydrocarbons. *J. Chem. Phys.* 29:1012-4, 1958. (23/79/PC&ES)

1007 (78) **Johnson H L.** Astronomical measurements in the infrared. *Annu. Rev. Astron. Astrophys.* 4:193-206, 1966.

961 (28) *****Kalckar H M.** Differential spectrophotometry of purine compounds by means of specific enzymes. III. Studies of the enzymes of purine metabolism. *J. Biol. Chem.* 167:461-75, 1947. (26/84/LS)

1029 (64) **Kane E O.** Band structure of indium antimonide. *J. Phys. Chem. Solids* 1:249-61, 1957.

967 (17) *****Kay E R M, Simmons N S & Dounce A L.** An improved preparation of sodium desoxyribonucleate. *J. Amer. Chem. Soc.* 74:1724-6, 1952. (24/80/LS)

996 (18) **King E J.** The colorimetric determination of phosphorus. *Biochem. J.* 26:292-7, 1932.

949 (44) **Kluver H & Barrera E.** A method for the combined staining of cells and fibers in the nervous system. *J. Neuropathol. Exp. Neurol.* 12:400-10, 1953.

967 (28) **Koshland D E, Nemethy G & Filmer D.** Comparison of experimental binding data and theoretical models in proteins containing subunits. *Biochemistry—USA* 5:365-85, 1966.

972 (31) **Kubo R & Tomita K.** A general theory of magnetic resonance absorption. *J. Phys. Soc. Jpn.* 9:888-919, 1954.

977 (98) *****Lacy P E & Kostianovsky M.** Method for the isolation of intact islets of Langerhans from the rat pancreas. *Diabetes* 16:35-9, 1967. (8/81/LS)

975 (35) **Lamb W E.** Theory of an optical maser. *Phys. Rev. A* 134:1429-50, 1964.

1021 (31) **Lane A M & Thomas R G.** R-matrix theory of nuclear reactions. *Rev. Mod. Phys.* 30:257-353, 1958.

942 (12) *****Lipmann F & Tuttle L C.** A specific micromethod for the determination of acyl phosphates. *J. Biol. Chem.* 159:21-8, 1945. (46/80/LS)

969 (37) **Lyon M F.** Gene action in the X-chromosome of the mouse (*Mus musculus* L.). *Nature* 190:372-3, 1961.

966 (24) **McDaniel D H & Brown H C.** An extended table of Hammett substituent constants based on the ionization of substituted benzoic acids. *J. Org. Chem.* 23:420-7, 1958.

964 (63) *****Melzack R & Wall P D.** Pain mechanisms: a new theory. *Science* 150:971-9, 1965. (23/82/LS)

328

A   B

956 (33)   *Metcalfe L D & Schmitz A A. The rapid preparation of fatty acid esters for gas chromatographic analysis. *Anal. Chem.* 33:363-4, 1961. (2/81/LS)

961 (121) *Miller G J & Miller N E. Plasma-high-density-lipoprotein concentration and development of ischaemic heart-disease. *Lancet* 1:16-9, 1975. (15/81/LS)

1028 (11) Monod J, Changeux J-P & Jacob F. Allosteric proteins and cellular control systems. *J. Mol. Biol.* 6:306-29, 1963.

985 (156) Moretta L, Webb S R, Grossi C E, Lydyard P M & Cooper M D. Functional analysis of two human T-cell subpopulations: help and suppression of B-cell responses by T cells bearing receptors for IgM or IgG. *J. Exp. Med.* 146:184-200, 1977.

1009 (13) Morgan J F, Morton H J & Parker R C. Nutrition of animal cells in tissue culture. I. Initial studies on a synthetic medium. *Proc. Soc. Exp. Biol. Med.* 73:1-8, 1950.

951 (19)   *Moruzzi G & Magoun H W. Brain stem reticular formation and activation of the EEG. *Electroencephalogr. Clin. Neuro.* 1:455-73, 1949. (40/81/LS)

999 (129) Palade G. Intracellular aspects of the process of protein synthesis. *Science* 189:347-58, 1975.

981 (1)   Pedersen C J. Cyclic polyethers and their complexes with metal salts. *J. Amer. Chem. Soc.* 89:7017-36, 1967.

1002 (48) Pople J A & Gordon M. Molecular orbital theory of the electronic structure of organic compounds. I. Substituent effects and dipole moments. *J. Amer. Chem. Soc.* 89:4253-61, 1967.

957 (16)   Pople J A, Santry D P & Segal G A. Approximate self-consistent molecular orbital theory. I. Invariant procedures. *J. Chem. Phys.* 43:S129-35, 1965.

970 (23)   Rasmussen H. Cell communication, calcium ion, and cyclic adenosine monophosphate. *Science* 170:404-12, 1970.

1016 (100) Rittenberg M B & Pratt K L. Antitrinitrophenyl (TNP) plaque assay. *Proc. Soc. Exp. Biol. Med.* 132:575-81, 1969.

944 (95)   Roberts B E & Paterson B M. Efficient translation of tobacco mosaic virus RNA and rabbit globin 9S RNA in a cell-free system from commercial wheat germ. *Proc. Nat. Acad. Sci. US* 70:2330-4, 1973.

940 (42)   Roothaan C C J. Self-consistent field theory for open shells of electronic systems. *Rev. Mod. Phys.* 32:179-85, 1960.

974 (19)   *Sanger F, Brownlee G G & Barrell B G. A two-dimensional fractionation procedure for radioactive nucleotides. *J. Mol. Biol.* 13:373-98, 1965. (3/18/LS)

983 (48)   *Schenkman J B, Remmer H & Estabrook R W. Spectral studies of drug interaction with hepatic microsomal cytochrome. *Mol. Pharmacol.* 3:113-23, 1967. (9/84/LS)

974 (8)   *Scherrer K & Darnell J E. Sedimentation characteristics of rapidly labelled RNA from HeLa cells. *Biochem. Biophys. Res. Commun.* 7:486-90, 1962. (50/80/LS)

985 (19)   Schneider W C. Intracellular distribution of enzymes. III. The oxidation of octanoic acid by rat liver fractions. *J. Biol. Chem.* 176:259-66, 1948.

1018 (38) *Sharon N & Lis H. Lectins: cell-agglutinating and sugar-specific proteins. *Science* 177:949-59, 1972. (21/82/LS)

1013 (83) Siegel L M & Monty K J. Determination of molecular weights and frictional ratios of proteins in impure systems by use of gel filtration and density gradient centrifugation. Application to crude preparations of sulfite and hydroxylamine reductases. *Biochim. Biophys. Acta* 112:346-62, 1966.

941 (36)   Solomon I. Relaxation processes in a system of two spins. *Phys. Rev.* 99:559-65, 1955.

994 (19)   *Spies J R & Chambers D C. Chemical determination of tryptophan in proteins. *Anal. Chem.* 21:1249-66, 1949. (25/77)

937 (50)   *Spizizen J. Transformation of biochemically deficient strains of *Bacillus subtilis* by deoxyribonucleate. *Proc. Nat. Acad. Sci. US* 44:1072-8, 1958. (19/84/LS)

1029 (59) *Stanier R Y, Palleroni N J & Doudoroff M. The aerobic pseudomonads: a taxonomic study. *J. Gen. Microbiol.* 43:159-71, 1966. (31/72)

962 (75)   Steck T L. The organization of proteins in the human red blood cell membrane. *J. Cell Biol.* 62:1-19, 1974.

948 (10)   *Steelman S L & Pohley F M. Assay of the follicle stimulating hormone based on the augmentation with human chorionic gonadotropin. *Endocrinology* 53:604-16, 1953. (21/84/LS)

1003 (10) Sutherland E W & Rall T W. The relation of adenosine-3',5'-phosphate and phosphorylase to the actions of catecholamines and other hormones. *Pharmacol. Rev.* 12:265-99, 1960.

964 (25)   Sutherland E W, Robison G A & Butcher R W. Some aspects of the biological role of adenosine 3',5'-monophosphate (cyclic AMP). *Circulation* 37:279-306, 1968.

988 (97)   Swank R T & Munkres K D. Molecular weight analysis of oligopeptides by electrophoresis in polyacrylamide gel with sodium dodecyl sulfate. *Anal. Biochem.* 39:462-77, 1971.

A		**B**

1019 (24) *Temin H M & Mizutani S. RNA-dependent DNA polymerase in virions of Rous sarcoma virus. *Nature* 226:1211-3, 1970. (47/77)

984 (88) *Tilley J M A & Terry R A. A two-stage technique for the *in vitro* digestion of forage crops. *J. Brit. Grassland Soc.* 18:104-11, 1963. (15/80/AB&ES)

988 (19) Tiselius A, Hjerten S & Levin O. Protein chromatography on calcium phosphate columns. *Arch. Biochem. Biophys.* 65:132-55, 1956.

969 (90) Udenfriend S, Stein S, Bohlen P, Dairman W, Leimgruber W & Weigele M. Fluorescamine: a reagent for assay of amino acids, peptides, proteins, and primary amines in the picomole range. *Science* 178:871-2, 1972.

1019 (57) van de Kamer J H, ten Bokkel Huinink H & Weyers H A. Rapid method for the determination of fat in feces. *J. Biol. Chem.* 177: 347-55, 1949.

1026 (72) van der Pauw L J. A method of measuring specific resistivity and Hall effect of discs of arbitrary shape. *Philips Res. Rep.* 13:1-9, 1958.

993 (79) Weibel E R. Stereological principles for morphometry in electron microscopic cytology. *Int. Rev. Cytol.* 26:235-302, 1969.

955 (63) Westphal O, Luderitz O & Bister F. Uber die Extraktion von Bakterien mit Phenol/Wasser. (Extraction of bacteria with phenol/water.) *Z. Naturforsch. Sect. B* 7:148-55, 1952.

1006 (67) *Winter C A, Risley E A & Nuss G W. Carrageenin-induced edema in hind paw of the rat as an assay for antiinflammatory drugs. *Proc. Soc. Exp. Biol. Med.* 111:544-7, 1962. (6/83/LS)

1028 (31) Wolfsberg M & Helmholz L. The spectra and electronic structure of the tetrahedral ions MnO_4^-, CrO_4^{--}, and ClO_4^-. *J. Chem. Phys.* 20:837-43, 1952.

964 (72) Zacharius R M, Zell T E, Morrison J H & Woodlock J J. Glycoprotein staining following electrophoresis on acrylamide gels. *Anal. Biochem.* 30:148-52, 1969.

1006 (36) *Zubarev D N. Double-time Green functions in statistical physics. *Sov. Phys. Usp.—Engl. Tr.* 3:320-45, 1960. (23/81/PC&ES) (Dvukhvremennue funkstii Greena v statisticheskoi fizike. *Usp. Fiz. Nauk SSSR* 71:71-116, 1960. 918 citations, 1961-1982. 24 citations, 1983.)

Table 2: Journals that published at least 5 of the 500 papers most cited from 1961 to 1982, *SCI*®. A= journal title. B=number of papers. C=1983 impact factor.

A	B	C
J. Biol. Chem.	60	5.8
Biochem. J.	28	3.2
Nature	22	9.3
J. Chem. Phys.	21	3.0
Phys. Rev.	18	2.8
J. Cell Biol.	17	9.2
J. Amer. Chem. Soc.	16	4.5
J. Mol. Biol.	16	6.7
Proc. Nat. Acad. Sci. US	14	8.7
Science	14	7.4
Anal. Biochem.	11	2.9
Anal. Chem.	11	3.4
Biochim. Biophys. Acta	11	2.4
Arch. Biochem. Biophys.	10	2.4
J. Exp. Med.	10	11.1
Acta Crystallogr.	9	1.1
J. Pharmacol. Exp. Ther.	9	3.5
Biochemistry—USA	8	4.1
Meth. Enzymology	7	1.3
Eur. J. Biochem.	6	3.5
J. Histochem. Cytochem.	6	3.9
Proc. Soc. Exp. Biol. Med.	6	1.4
Rev. Mod. Phys.	6	19.9
Exp. Cell Res.	5	2.9
N. Engl. J. Med.	5	16.5

two years. As you can see, the journals that published many classics in the past continue to produce high-impact work.

It is interesting to note that a Russian journal has appeared for the first time in this series. D.N. Zubarev, Steklov Institute of Mathematics, Academy of Sciences of the USSR, Moscow, published his paper, "Double-time Green functions in statistical physics" in 1960. The English translation appeared in *Soviet Physics Uspekhi* that same year. It was cited about 2,000 times in this 23-year period. About half of these citations were to the Russian version published in *Uspekhi Fizicheskikh Nauk*. However, 390 papers cited both versions. Keep in mind that the editors of some journals require authors to cite *all* versions of translated papers, thereby inflating citation counts through "redundancy."

We can use these journal data to get a rough idea of how the 500 classics are

Table 3: Field distributions for the 500 most-cited articles, 1961-1982 *SCI®*

FIELD	TOTAL	Part 1	Part 2	Part 3	Part 4	Part 5
Life Sciences	384	85	77	80	72	70
Biochemistry	147	38	30	26	26	27
Biomedicine	96	17	13	24	21	21
Clinical Medicine	93	16	26	20	14	17
Molecular Biology	43	12	8	9	10	4
Biology	5	2	—	1	1	1
Physics	59	6	11	7	15	20
Chemistry	49	9	10	10	13	7
Mathematics	4	—	1	2	—	1
Engineering/Technology	3	—	1	1	—	1
Earth/Space Sciences	1	—	—	—	—	1
TOTAL	500	100	100	100	100	100

distributed by field. For example, 70 of the papers in this study were published in life-sciences journals, 20 in physics journals, 7 in chemistry journals, and 1 each in mathematics, engineering/technology, and earth/space-sciences journals. Table 3 shows the field distributions for all 500. As we've pointed out before, life-sciences papers dominate this and other citation-based studies, accounting for 384 papers or 77 percent of the 500 classics. Physics follows with 59 papers (12 percent), and chemistry with 49 papers (10 percent). But as the series was extended from 100 to 500 papers, the proportion of life-sciences papers declined from 85 percent to 70 percent. Physics papers increased their share from 6 percent in part one to 20 percent in this study. The proportion of chemistry classics has remained relatively stable, accounting for 7 to 13 percent of the papers in each part of this series. However, biochemistry has been categorized here as a life science. This decision may be considered arbitrary by some chemists, but it is relevant for readers of *CC/Life Sciences*.

It is more difficult to classify papers in this series as being methodological or theoretical. In fact, Leonard Hayflick, University of Florida, Gainesville, recently informed me[6] that his paper on the serial cultivation of human diploid cell strains[7] was mistakenly identified as a methods paper in the second part of this series.[2] Some papers clearly state in their titles that they are discussing a method, technique, or procedure. But other papers refer to measurement, estimation, preparation, isolation, and other terms that may not necessarily be synonymous with "method." Nevertheless, even if we use a broad definition of methods, the proportion of methods papers is declining as this series is extended. About 70 methods papers appeared in part one, 65 in part two, 60 in part three, 55 in part four, and about 50 in this essay.

Table 4 shows the publication-year distributions for both the 100 papers in this study and all 500 classics identified to date. These distributions have been remarkably stable over all five parts of this series. Sixty-one percent of the 500 classics were published in the 1960s and 1970s. Thirty-eight percent were published from 1930 to 1959. It will be interesting to see if this distribution remains stable after we identify the 1,000 most-cited articles. Keep in mind that the citation data reported in this series cover the 22-year period from 1961 to 1982. Additional citations to papers published in 1961 and earlier may be retrieved from the recently published 1955-1964 *SCI* cumulation.

The oldest paper in this study was published in 1927 in the *Journal of Biological Chemistry*. Otto Folin and Vintila Ciocalteu, Harvard Medical School, Boston, Massachusetts, presented a critical analysis of the methods for determining tyrosine and tryptophan that were first described by Folin and J.M. Looney in 1922 in the same journal.[8] In the 1927 paper, the authors noted, "A number of investigators have found the Folin-Looney methods satisfactory, but others have condemned them on general principles, and some have been utterly unable to get any reasonable figures with them.... In these circumstances it seemed well worthwhile to try to clear up any uncertainties or flaws that may legitimately be ascribed to these methods." Folin and Ciocalteu's efforts were indeed worthwhile—their paper became a "kiloclassic" that was cited more than 1,000 times from 1961 to 1982. In 1983, it was still cited explicitly in 23 publications.

The newest paper, by Lorenzo Moretta and colleagues, University of Alabama, Birmingham, was published in 1977 in the *Journal of Experimental Medicine*. The authors examined and discussed the functions of two types of human T cells. T cells are thymus-dependent leukocytes that play an important role in cell-mediated immunity. The paper was cited for having demonstrated

two subpopulations of T cells. Each type of T cell has a specific receptor for either immunoglobulin M (IgM) or IgG, which are distinct antibodies, that is, proteins involved in immune reactions. In addition, the paper was cited for having shown that each type of T cell has a different biological function, to either help or suppress immune reactions. Year-by-year citation data indicate that the explicit citation of this paper has peaked. Though still highly cited, in 1977 it received only 7 citations, 87 in 1978, 186 in 1979, 227 in 1980, 260 in 1981, 218 in 1982, and 156 in 1983.

Throughout this series, we have commented on various aspects of the classic methodology and theory papers—serendipitous events, initial rejections by journal editors, reasons for citations, and so on. One important aspect that we haven't yet discussed is the resistance of the research community to new theories, particularly when these theories are at odds with established dogma. Ronald Melzack, McGill University, Montreal, Canada, and Patrick D. Wall, University College London, England, elaborated on this point in a *Citation Classic* commentary on their 1965 *Science* paper, "Pain mechanisms: a new theory." They said, "A small number of original thinkers had fought hard to replace the old concept of a specific pain pathway by a more dynamic conception in which pain is determined by many factors in addition to injury—by past experiences, culture, attention, and other activities in the nervous system at the time of injury. This small band of courageous people hammered away at the established, traditional theory. But despite occasional lip service to their ingenuity, the field continued unchanged, holding tenaciously on to Descartes' idea, proposed in 1664, that pain is like a bell-ringing alarm system whose sole purpose is to signal injury to the body."[9]

Table 4: Publication-date distributions for the 100 most-cited papers in this study and all 500 classics identified to date. A = publication date. B = number of papers in this study. C = number of papers from all five parts of this series.

A	B	C
1920s	1	4
1930s	2	14
1940s	7	45
1950s	27	131
1960s	47	227
1970s	16	78
1980s	—	1

Figure 1: Year-by-year citations to R. Melzack and P.D. Wall, *Science* 150:971-9, 1965.

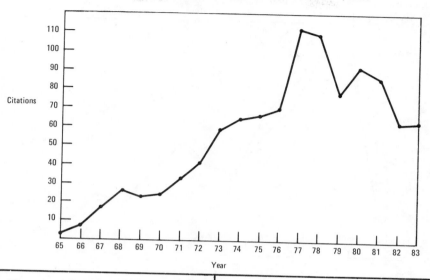

The citation record for Melzack and Wall's paper illustrates the initial resistance to their new theory of pain mechanisms. Figure 1 provides a graph of the citations to this paper from 1965 to 1983. As you can see, the citations gradually increased from 3 in 1965 to peak at 112 in 1977, after which they trail off to 63 in 1983. The paper was cited 1,027 times in this 19-year period. The authors commented, "When we proposed the gate-control theory in 1965, we hardly expected the astonishing increase in research studies and new therapeutic approaches that were stimulated by it.... Naturally, acceptance was not immediate or total, but in spite of continuing controversy about details, the *concept* that injury signals can be radically modified and even blocked at the earliest stages of transmission in the nervous system is now virtually universally accepted. A fortunate aspect of our publication...is the use of the phrase 'gate-control.' It evokes an image that is readily understood even by those who do not grasp the complex physiological mecha-

nisms on which the theory is based. The fact that the theory had relevance to a wide variety of fields in medicine, psychology, and biology also led to its frequent citation."[9]

In a *Citation Classic* commentary on his 1970 *Nature* paper, Howard M. Temin also noted a general resistance to his hypothesis that the replication of RNA tumor viruses involved information transfer from RNA to DNA via an enzyme.[10] In a companion paper published side-by-side with Temin's paper in *Nature*, David Baltimore, Massachusetts Institute of Technology, Boston, reported the simultaneous identification of the enzyme, now called reverse transcriptase. Temin commented, "Since 1963-1964, I had been proposing that the replication of RNA tumor viruses involved a DNA intermediate. This hypothesis, known as the DNA provirus hypothesis, apparently contradicted the so-called 'central dogma' of molecular biology and met with a generally hostile reception. The hypothesis was not generally accepted until the publication of

Figure 2: Year-by-year citations to H.M. Temin and S. Mizutani, *Nature* 226:1211-3, 1970 (broken line) and D. Baltimore, *Nature* 226:1209-11, 1970 (solid line).

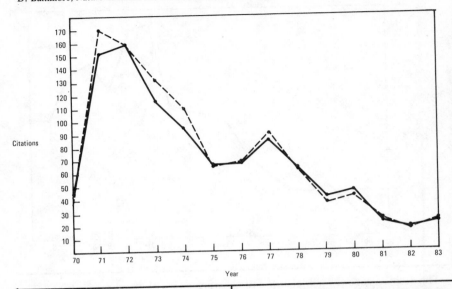

this and the accompanying paper by David Baltimore. These papers demonstrated the existence of an enzyme associated with an RNA template in particles of RNA tumor viruses that could carry out information transfer from RNA to DNA. This result might have been predicted from the previous discovery of polymerases in virus particles and the DNA provirus hypothesis. That the discovery took so many years might indicate the resistance to this hypothesis."[10]

Temin's paper was cited 1,043 times from 1970 to 1983. Baltimore's paper received 996 citations in that 14-year period. Both papers have an almost identical "track record," which can be seen by the graph of their 1970-1983 citations in Figure 2. This should not be surprising, given the nearly identical content of these "companion" papers. In 1970, Temin's paper was cited 40 times and peaked the following year at 170 citations, after which the citations began to decline. Baltimore's paper received 41 citations in 1970, peaked in 1972 with

159 citations, and nearly paralleled the decline in citations observed for Temin's paper. Both papers reached a second peak in citations in 1977. Perhaps this burst of citations is due to Temin and Baltimore having shared the 1975 Nobel prize for physiology or medicine with Renato Dulbecco.

It should come as no surprise that the papers by Temin and Baltimore are highly *co*-cited, when you consider their nearly identical citation records. In fact, these two papers make up the "core" of several current research fronts identified through ISI®'s clustering techniques. For example, they were the core papers in the 1982 research front entitled "Structural Organization and Cellular Origin of Transforming Genes for RNA Tumor Viruses," the 1981 specialty entitled "Alpha-2 Macroglobulin Protease Interactions," and the 1980 research front entitled "DNA and RNA Tumor Viruses."

In addition to Temin and Baltimore, 16 other Nobel laureates are included among the authors listed in Table 1: K.

Alder, C.B. Anfinsen, B. Benacerraf, P. Berg, A. Bohr, H.C. Brown, R.P. Feynman, M. Gell-Mann, F. Jacob, W.E. Lamb, F. Lipmann, J. Monod, B. Mottelson, G. Palade, F. Sanger, and A. Tiselius. In an upcoming essay, we'll report data on the number of classics that the Nobel laureates have authored.

This concludes our essay on the fifth 100 most-cited articles for 1961 to 1982. I'd like again to invite the authors listed in Table 1 who have not yet contributed *Citation Classic* commentaries to do so. These brief comments provide a wealth of insights into high-impact research that students, administrators, and colleagues alike find interesting. In future essays, we'll continue to report on additional groups of 100 most-cited papers until we've covered the top 1,000 at least.

* * * * *

My thanks to Thomas Atkins and Alfred Welljams-Dorof for their help in the preparation of this essay.

©1984 ISI

REFERENCES

1. **Garfield E.** The 100 most-cited papers ever and how we select *Citation Classics.* *Current Contents* (23):3-9, 4 June 1984.
2. -------------. The articles most cited in 1961-1982. 2. Another 100 *Citation Classics* highlight the technology of science. *Current Contents* (29):3-12, 16 July 1984.
3. -------------. The articles most cited in 1961-1982. 3. Another 100 all-time *Citation Classics.* *Current Contents* (35):3-9, 27 August 1984.
4. -------------. The articles most cited in 1961-1982. 4. 100 additional *Citation Classics.* *Current Contents* (40):3-9, 1 October 1984.
5. -------------. Selecting the all-time *Citation Classics.* Here are the fifty most cited papers for 1961-1972. The second fifty papers most cited from 1961-1972. *Essays of an information scientist.* Philadelphia: ISI Press, 1977. Vol. 2. p. 6-9; 21-5.
6. **Hayflick L.** Personal communication. 7 September 1984.
7. **Hayflick L & Moorhead P S.** The serial cultivation of human diploid cell strains. *Exp. Cell Res.* 25:585-621, 1961.
8. **Folin O & Looney J M.** Colorimetric methods for the separate determination of tyrosine, tryptophane, and cystine in proteins. *J. Biol. Chem.* 51:421-34, 1922.
9. **Melzack R & Wall P D.** Citation Classic. Commentary on *Science* 150:971-9, 1965. *Current Contents/Life Sciences* 25(23):22, 7 June 1982.
10. **Temin H M.** Citation Classic. Commentary on *Nature* 226:1211-3, 1970. *Current Contents* (47):14, 21 November 1977.

Current Comments®

Journal Citation Studies. 44.
Citation Patterns in Nursing Journals, and Their Most-Cited Articles

Number 43   October 22, 1984

Current Contents® (*CC®*) readers are by now familiar with ISI®'s series of journal citation studies. In these analyses, groups of journals publishing research in various fields or disciplines are examined to determine what they cite and, in turn, what cites them. Most recently, we've analyzed citation patterns in astrosciences,[1] analytical chemistry,[2] and entomology[3] journals. This essay focuses on the journal literature of nursing, a profession that comprises the largest single group of health-care workers in the world.[4,5]

The origins of nursing are as old as those of medicine and can be traced to ancient civilizations in China, Egypt, Greece, and India. But it wasn't until the late nineteenth century that schools were established to educate nurses as professionals. Florence Nightingale, the renowned British nurse, is credited as the founder of the movement to professionalize nursing. In 1860, she established the Nightingale School for Nursing at St. Thomas' Hospital, London, the first nursing school of its type in the world.[6] Today, there are more than 3,000 programs in the US alone covering a wide spectrum of nursing education, from practical nursing diplomas to advanced doctoral degrees.[7,8] The Rockefeller Archive Center, North Tarrytown, New York, has published two useful sources on the history of nursing and nursing education—*A Survey of Manuscript Sources for the History of Nursing and Nursing Education in the Rockefeller Archive Center, 1984*[9] and the proceedings of the center's conference on *Nursing History: New Perspectives, New Possibilities*.[10]

The great majority of nurses are engaged in providing nursing care to patients in hospitals, extended-care facilities, and home-health and primary-care settings. Only a very small fraction of the nursing population are researchers. In 1979 and 1980, just 0.2 percent of employed nurses had doctoral degrees. Pauline F. Brimmer, American Nurses' Association (ANA), Kansas City, Missouri, and colleagues recently surveyed about 2,000 nurses with doctorates.[11] They found that just 6 to 8 percent were primarily engaged in research. The rest were involved in administration, teaching, clinical practice, and other activities.

We'll now examine a set of nursing journals to determine what the nursing literature cites, and what journals cite it. We'll also identify the most-cited nursing articles. These articles will enable us to determine what current topics are *of interest to* the profession and those who publish in the nursing literature.

Table 1 lists seven nursing journals indexed in *Social Sciences Citation Index®* (*SSCI®*). These journals make up the "core" list included in this study. Also shown is the year each journal began publication. *American Journal of Nursing* is the oldest on the list, having been in publication since 1900. It is the official publication of the ANA, which was founded in 1896. Except for the *International Journal of Nursing Studies* and *Journal of Advanced Nursing*, which are UK publications, all of the core journals are published in the US.

When this study was begun, we did not select *Heart & Lung—the Journal of Critical Care* for the core list. This journal is published by the American Association of Critical-Care Nurses and has been indexed in both *SSCI* and *Science Citation Index®* (*SCI®*) since 1980. Had we included *Heart & Lung* in the core, it would have ranked 12th in terms of the number of core citations it received (Table 2). It ranks eighth in terms of the number of its citations *to* the core nursing journals (Table 3). The 1983 impact factor for *Heart & Lung* is 0.4, equal to the core journals *Nursing Research* and *Research in Nursing & Health* (see column G in Tables 2 and 3). Impact measures how often articles published in the previous two years were cited in the year studied, in this case 1983. The calculation of impact factors will be discussed later in more detail.

However, the papers appearing in *Heart & Lung* undoubtedly concentrate more on cardiovascular research than do the general nursing journals. With hindsight, we would now treat it as a core nursing journal for *CC* selection purposes. What is more important is that the journal citation procedure identifies a relevant journal regardless of its title or language. Just as citation indexing overcomes the terminological barriers to accessing articles, journal citation analyses cluster journals on the basis of their actual subject content and not on what their possibly obsolete titles might imply. For example, you would not know from its title that the *Philosophical Magazine* reports research on the physics of condensed matter. But by determining what journals it cites and, in turn, what journals cite it, the subject content of *Philosophical Magazine* becomes obvious.

Following the convention we use in all our journal citation studies, the core journals analyzed here are treated as if they were a single "Macro Journal of Nursing." We'll provide details on what this macro journal cites, and what cites it. We usually base our analyses on a single publication year for the journals in these citation studies. However, since just seven journals are included in this study, we found that it was necessary to use three years of data because one year of data seemed inconclusive. Data are taken from the 1981-1983 *Journal Citation Reports®* (*JCR™*) for *SSCI*. Keep in mind, however, that the *SSCI JCR* also covers several journals indexed in *SCI*.

The core nursing journals published 1,204 articles from 1981 to 1983. This accounts for just less than 1 percent of the 150,000 articles included in the 1981-1983 *SSCI JCR*. The core journals cited 16,205 references during this three-year period, or 0.5 percent of the three million references processed in the *SSCI JCR*. Thus, the average nursing article cited about 14 references, compared with 20 for the average *SSCI JCR* article.

Articles in the core journals *received* 3,300 citations in 1981-1983. This represents just 0.1 percent of the total references processed in the *SSCI JCR* during this three-year period. *American Jour-*

Table 2: The 51 journals most cited by core nursing journals from 1981 to 1983. An asterisk (*) indicates a core journal. A=citations received from core journals. B=citations received from all journals. C=self-citations. D=percent of citations from all journals that are core journal citations (A/B). E=percent of citations from all journals that are self-citations (self-cited rate, C/B). F=percent of core citations that are self-citations (C/A). G=1983 impact factor (1983 citations to 1981 and 1982 articles of a particular journal divided by the number of articles published in that journal in 1981 and 1982). H=total 1981-1983 source items.

Journal	A	B	C	D	E	F	G	H
*Nurs. Res.	608	1246	292	48.8	23.4	48.0	.40	205
*Amer. J. Nurs.	466	1189	195	39.2	16.4	41.8	.24	476
*J. Nurs. Admin.	240	339	142	70.8	41.9	59.2	—	125
N. Engl. J. Med.	201	157,678	—	.1	—	—	16.47	1149
Nurs. Outlook	194	512	—	37.9	—	—	—	—
Lancet	160	170,462	—	.1	—	—	12.25	1514
Brit. Med. J.	151	90,310	—	.2	—	—	2.77	2796
JAMA—J. Am. Med. Assn.	150	68,986	—	.2	—	—	3.38	1668
Nurs. Times	139	375	—	37.1	—	—	—	—
*J. Adv. Nurs.	127	175	97	72.6	55.4	76.4	.25	176
Amer. J. Obstet. Gynecol.	109	43,603	—	.2	—	—	1.89	1690
Pediatrics	94	34,284	—	.3	—	—	2.56	950
Hospitals—J. Amer. Hosp. Ass.	88	1218	—	7.2	—	—	.23	484
J. Personal. Soc. Psychol.	84	20,236	—	.4	—	—	1.86	680
Psychol. Bull.	82	16,388	—	.5	—	—	3.61	228
J. Health Soc. Behavior	81	3559	—	2.3	—	—	3.39	94
Obstet. Gynecol.	81	19,599	—	.4	—	—	1.66	1016
*J. Nurse-Midwifery	78	113	70	69.0	61.9	89.7	.27	90
Psychosom. Med.	78	7036	—	1.1	—	—	2.24	123
Arch. Gen. Psychiat.	75	29,825	—	.3	—	—	6.11	443
Nurs. Clin. N. Amer.	74	239	—	31.0	—	—	.07	190
Child Develop.	73	13,515	—	.5	—	—	1.58	503
Amer. J. Psychiat.	70	27,523	—	.3	—	—	3.21	980
*Int. J. Nurs. Stud.	70	144	33	48.6	22.9	47.1	.16	69
Amer. J. Public Health	69	7750	—	.9	—	—	1.67	487
J. Pediat.	67	42,934	—	.2	—	—	2.67	1335
*Res. Nurs. Health	63	111	26	56.8	23.4	41.3	.35	63
Amer. J. Orthopsychiat.	60	4201	—	1.4	—	—	.96	193
J. Appl. Psychol.	56	8398	—	.7	—	—	1.55	282
Med. Care	54	3303	—	1.6	—	—	1.15	299
Ann. Intern. Med.	53	58,372	—	.1	—	—	7.00	866
Nurs. Mirror	48	110	—	43.6	—	—	—	—
Science	48	209,576	—	0	—	—	7.41	3032
J. Consult. Clin. Psychol.	47	14,269	—	.3	—	—	2.13	406
J. Nurs. Educ.	47	128	—	36.7	—	—	—	—
Superv. Nurs.	47	72	—	65.3	—	—	—	—
Nurs. Forum	45	119	—	37.8	—	—	—	—
J. Psychosom. Res.	43	4025	—	1.1	—	—	.79	203
Cancer	42	81,994	—	.1	—	—	2.65	2572
Birth Fam. J.	40	178	—	22.5	—	—	.30	23
J. Abnormal Psychol.	40	12,656	—	.3	—	—	2.46	181
J. Marriage Fam.	40	4758	—	.8	—	—	.98	252
Arch. Intern. Med.	39	24,616	—	.2	—	—	1.82	976
Brit. J. Psychiat.	38	15,442	—	.2	—	—	2.39	552
Heart Lung	38	561	—	6.8	—	—	.36	268
J. Chronic Dis.	38	7543	—	.5	—	—	1.37	237
Psychol. Rep.	38	6865	—	.6	—	—	.25	1387
Amer. Sociol. Rev.	37	13,008	—	.3	—	—	2.66	181
Circulation	37	90,721	—	0	—	—	6.90	1359
RN Mag.	36	154	—	23.4	—	—	—	—
Soc. Sci. Med.	36	1985	—	1.8	—	—	.58	440

Table 3: The 48 journals that most frequently cited core nursing journals from 1981 to 1983. An asterisk (*) indicates a core journal. A=citations to core journals. B=citations to all journals. C=self-citations. D=percent of total citations that are core journal citations (A/B). E=percent of total citations that are self-citations (self-*citing* rate, C/B). F=percent of citations to core journals that are self-citations (C/A). G=1983 impact factor. H=total 1981-1983 source items.

Journal	A	B	C	D	E	F	G	H
*Nurs. Res.	445	4258	292	10.5	6.9	65.6	.40	205
*J. Adv. Nurs.	257	3140	97	8.2	3.1	37.7	.25	176
*Amer. J. Nurs.	225	3084	195	7.3	6.3	86.7	.24	476
*J. Nurs. Admin.	221	1122	142	19.7	12.7	64.3	—	125
*Int. J. Nurs. Stud.	177	1494	33	11.8	2.2	18.6	.16	69
*Res. Nurs. Health	139	1647	26	8.4	1.6	18.7	.35	63
*J. Nurse-Midwifery	106	1460	70	7.3	4.8	66.0	.27	90
Heart Lung	84	4993	—	1.7	—	—	.36	268
J. Nurs. Educ.	50	709	—	7.1	—	—	—	—
Soc. Sci. Med.	42	13,582	—	.3	—	—	.58	440
Amer. J. Public Health	41	9271	—	.4	—	—	1.67	487
J. Sch. Health	34	3320	—	1.0	—	—	.18	320
Psychol. Rep.	34	16,290	—	.2	—	—	.25	1387
Med. Care	27	6012	—	.4	—	—	1.15	299
J. Behav. Med.	26	1694	—	1.5	—	—	1.92	90
Soc. Sci. Med.—Med. Soc.	26	2377	—	1.1	—	—	.72	75
Patient Couns. Health Educ.	20	1092	—	1.8	—	—	.20	52
Pain	18	8377	—	.2	—	—	3.32	250
Gerontologist	17	5100	—	.3	—	—	.96	250
J. Amer. Diet. Assn.	17	7554	—	.2	—	—	.77	376
Nurs. Outlook	17	424	—	4.0	—	—	—	—
Int. J. Psychiat. Med.	15	2237	—	.7	—	—	.81	94
J. Health Polit. Policy Law	15	3426	—	.4	—	—	.59	118
Hospitals—J. Amer. Hosp. Ass.	14	1418	—	1.0	—	—	.23	484
N. Engl. J. Med.	14	53,378	—	0	—	—	16.47	1149
Clin. Psychol. Rev.	13	1958	—	.7	—	—	—	—
Gen. Hosp. Psychiat.	12	3188	—	.4	—	—	.70	111
Brit. J. Clin. Psychol.	11	2649	—	.4	—	—	1.20	129
Death Educ.	11	1454	—	.8	—	—	.12	85
J. Amer. Geriat. Soc.	11	8961	—	.1	—	—	.89	384
Soc. Work Health Care	11	847	—	1.3	—	—	.22	89
Acad. Manage. J.	10	4715	—	.2	—	—	1.40	184
Amer. J. Hosp. Pharm.	10	9018	—	.1	—	—	1.04	621
Amer. J. Occup. Ther.	10	3309	—	.3	—	—	.30	179
NY Univ. Law Rev.	10	3918	—	.3	—	—	3.47	70
Arch. Phys. Med. Rehabil.	9	6082	—	.1	—	—	.67	392
Psychiat. Clin. N. Amer.	9	6367	—	.1	—	—	1.45	130
Birth Fam. J.	8	359	—	2.2	—	—	.30	23
Cancer	8	61,812	—	0	—	—	2.65	2572
J. Amer. Dent. Assn.	8	7347	—	.1	—	—	.62	434
J. Clin. Psychol.	8	7713	—	.1	—	—	.43	501
J. Fam. Pract.	8	3429	—	.2	—	—	.65	558
Pediatrics	8	23,574	—	0	—	—	2.56	950
Psychosomatics	8	5452	—	.1	—	—	.89	261
Soc. Sci. Med.—Med. Psychol.	8	1504	—	.5	—	—	.58	33
Annu. Rev. Public Health	7	4239	—	.2	—	—	1.28	58
Fam. Relat.	7	4236	—	.2	—	—	.45	201
Public Health Rep.	7	2905	—	.2	—	—	.49	246

nal of Nursing and *Nursing Research* together account for 73 percent of the citations to the core group, receiving 1,189 and 1,246 citations, respectively. The same two journals also account for 57 percent of all papers published by the core group in 1981-1983. Previous studies of other journal sets show that a small number of publications accounts for the majority of both citations and published articles. This "concentration effect"[12] is also demonstrated for the nursing literature, even though the present study is limited to seven journals.

The 51 journals most cited *by* the core nursing journals from 1981 to 1983 are shown in Table 2. They are listed in descending order of the number of *core* 1981-1983 citations they received (column A). For reasons of space, we try to limit these lists to about 50 journals. However, *RN Magazine* and *Social Science and Medicine* were each cited by the core journals 36 times, the cutoff for inclusion in Table 2. Table 2 also shows the number of citations from *all* journals (column B), each journal's self-citations (column C), 1983 impact factor (column G), and the number of source items published in 1981-1983 (column H).

The 51 journals in Table 2 received 4,800 citations from the core group. This represents about 30 percent of all references cited by the core in 1981-1983. All seven core nursing journals appear in Table 2. They are indicated by asterisks. These core journals received 3,300 citations from all journals, of which 1,650 or about 50 percent were *from* the core group.

Table 2 also includes nine nursing journals that are *not* in the core set because they were not indexed in the 1981-1983 *SSCI* or, in the case of *Heart & Lung*, were purposely excluded from the core. Although *Journal of Nursing Education* was added to the 1983 *SSCI*, we didn't have enough data to include it

in the core group. In addition, several more nursing journals are currently being evaluated for coverage in *SSCI* in the near future—*Nursing Times*, *RN Magazine*, and so on. Incidentally, these journal citation patterns are one of the criteria ISI uses to determine whether or not a journal should be covered in our databases.

A brief scan of the journals in Table 2 indicates that the nursing literature cites research in a variety of medical publications. It will come as no surprise to nurses how many psychology journals are listed—*Journal of Personality and Social Psychology*, *Journal of Applied Psychology*, *Psychological Bulletin*, and so on. The connection between psychology and nursing will be discussed later in this essay when we examine the most-cited nursing articles.

Table 3 lists 48 journals that most frequently cit*ed* the core group from 1981 to 1983. They are shown in order of the number of their citations *to* the core. In Table 3, the inclusion threshold was seven or more citations to the core. Had we lowered the minimum to at least six citations, another 15 journals would have been added to the list. So, for reasons of space, only the top 48 journals are listed.

The top seven journals in Table 3 are all members of the core group. That is, the journals that *most* frequently cited the core in 1981-1983 were the core nursing journals themselves. This is not really remarkable since nursing is a rather small and self-contained research area, as was pointed out earlier. But it is remarkable that only three *other* nursing journals appear in Table 3, including *Heart & Lung*. Remember that nine non-core nursing journals were listed in Table 2. Only *Heart & Lung*, *Journal of Nursing Education*, and *Nursing Outlook* cited any of the core journals at least seven times in 1982. But several psychology journals are among those

Table 4: 1983 *SSCI*® impact factors of selected core nursing journals across various two-year bases. Circles indicate the highest impact factor for each journal. A=1981-1982. B=1980-1981. C=1979-1980. D= 1978-1979. E=1977-1978. F=1976-1977.

Journal	A	B	C	D	E	F
Amer. J. Nurs.	(.24)	.17	.19	.19	.12	.10
Int. J. Nurs. Stud.	.16	.30	.26	.22	.30	(.38)
J. Adv. Nurs.	(.25)	.24	.13	.11	—	—
Nurs. Res.	.40	.36	.34	.40	.39	(.41)
Res. Nurs. Health	.35	.45	.41	(.64)	—	—

that most frequently cited the core. We'll expand on the "overlap" between psychology and nursing later.

Nursing Research and *Research in Nursing & Health* have virtually the same impact—0.4 (see column G in Tables 2 and 3). This is equal to the median impact of all *SSCI* journals in the 1983 *JCR*. *Journal of Advanced Nursing* and *Journal of Nurse-Midwifery* each have an impact of about 0.3, followed by *American Journal of Nursing* and *International Journal of Nursing Studies* at 0.2. Impact data for *Journal of Nursing Administration* are not available because it was added too late to the *SSCI* database for this information to be tabulated.

Impact is determined by dividing the number of 1983 citations to a journal's 1981 and 1982 articles by the combined number of articles it published in those two years. In recent journal studies, we've recalculated impacts using different two-year bases. Papers in "fast moving" fields are cited very soon after publication—in biochemistry or molecular biology, for example. But the same may not be true in other fields, such as geosciences or mathematics. Thus, by using different two-year bases, we can determine what the "peak" citation years may be and derive higher impact factors.

Table 4 shows 1983 impact factors for five of the core nursing journals, using various two-year bases. The highest impact for each journal is circled. As you

can see, two core nursing journals register the highest impact when 1981-1982 publication years are used. Impacts for *Nursing Research* are relatively constant at 0.4 no matter which two-year base is used. But the largest gains in impact are observed for two journals. The *International Journal of Nursing Studies* has an impact of 0.16 when we consider 1983 citations to its 1981-1982 articles. But its impact increases to 0.38 when 1983 citations to its 1976-1977 articles are used instead. And when 1983 citations to 1978-1979 articles from *Research in Nursing & Health* are used, it has an impact of 0.64, the highest of all the core journals. However, its impact is 0.35 when we consider its 1981-1982 articles. For these and other reasons, this journal probably will be added to the *SCI* database in the near future.

In terms of immediacy indexes, that is, how often a journal's articles were cited in the *same* year they were published, the core journals are ranked as follows: *American Journal of Nursing*, 0.23, *Journal of Nursing Administration*, 0.13, *International Journal of Nursing Studies* and *Nursing Research*, 0.08 each, *Journal of Advanced Nursing*, 0.05, and *Research in Nursing & Health*, 0.04. Immediacy for 1983 is calculated by dividing the number of citations a journal's 1983 articles received by the number of articles it published that year. None of the 1983 articles in *Journal of Nurse-Midwifery* were cited that year, so its immediacy index is zero. The median immediacy for all 1983 *SSCI* journals was 0.08.

The *JCR* also gives information on a journal's "half-life"—that is, the median age for a given field's cited and citing literature. Table 5 presents half-lives for the core nursing journals. (Half-life data for *Journal of Nursing Administration* are not available because it was added too late to the *SSCI* for this information to be processed.) Each journal's cit*ed* half-life is given in column A. This indicates the median age of articles from each journal that were cited in 1983. For example, the cited half-life for *Nursing Research* is nine years. Half of the citations this journal *received* in 1983 were to articles it published over the past nine years, from 1975 to 1983. Keep in mind that cited half-life can be affected by the year when a journal began publication. For example, *Research in Nursing & Health* was first published in 1978. Clearly, it cannot have a cited half-life longer than six years. Also, the size of a journal can influence cited half-lives—many journals are now much larger than they were even a decade ago. Thus, one has to be careful in interpreting half-life.

Column B in Table 5 gives each journal's cit*ing* half-life, that is, the median age of the literature cited *by* each journal in 1983. *American Journal of Nursing* and *Journal of Nurse-Midwifery* have the shortest citing half-lives of the core group. Half of their 1983 references were to articles published between 1979 and 1983.

Table 5: 1983 *SSCI*® cit*ed* and cit*ing* half-lives of core nursing journals. A = cit*ed* half-life. B = cit*ing* half-life. C = core nursing journal.

A	B	C
6.4	4.5	Amer. J. Nurs.
6.2	7.0	Int. J. Nurs. Stud.
2.8	6.6	J. Adv. Nurs.
3.5	4.8	J. Nurse-Midwifery
9.0	8.1	Nurs. Res.
4.2	8.2	Res. Nurs. Health

In analyzing journal citation patterns, it is important to examine the "superstar" articles they publish. Table 6 lists the 18 most-cited articles from the core nursing journals, in alphabetic order by first author. Also shown are the number of citations they received from 1966 to 1983 in *SSCI and* from 1963 to 1983 in *SCI*. Only those articles from the core journals that were cited 20 times or more are shown in Table 6. Three core journals met or exceeded this threshold. *Nursing Research* clearly dominates the list, accounting for 14 of the 18 papers shown. *American Journal of Nursing* accounts for three of the most-cited papers, and one was published in *Research in Nursing & Health*.

The most-cited paper, by Mary-'Vesta Marston, Frances Payne Bolton School of Nursing, Case Western Reserve University, Cleveland, Ohio, is a review article published in 1970 in *Nursing Research*. It discussed the literature on compliance, or the extent to which patients follow instructions to take medications. The review has been cited about 180 times. Earlier this year,[13] Marston gave her personal recollections and background information on this paper in a *Citation Classic*™ [14] commentary.

Two papers are tied as the second-most-cited publications. Ben F. Feingold, Kaiser-Permanente Medical Center, San Francisco, California, reported a link between artificial food additives and hyperkinesis and learning disabilities in children. This paper was cited more than 50 times in *SSCI* and *SCI* since its publication in 1975 in *American Journal of Nursing*.

Carol A. Lindeman, director of nursing research, and Betty Van Aernam, Luther Hospital, Eau Claire, Wisconsin, collaborated on the other second-most-cited nursing article. They studied the effectiveness of preoperative deep breathing and coughing exercises on re-

Table 6: Most-cited articles from core nursing journals according to 1966-1983 *SSCI®* and 1963-1983 *SCI®*, in alphabetic order by first author. A=total citations. B=bibliographic data. C=total number of papers from that journal cited 20 or more times.

A	B	C
24	**Campbell M E.** Study of the attitudes of nursing personnel toward the geriatric patient. *Nurs. Res.* 20:147-51, 1971.	14
43	**Dumas R G & Leonard R C.** The effect of nursing on the incidence of postoperative vomiting. *Nurs. Res.* 12:12-5, 1963.	14
54	**Feingold B F.** Hyperkinesis and learning disabilities linked to artificial food flavors and colors. *Amer. J. Nurs.* 75:797-803, 1975.	3
48	**Healy K M.** Does preoperative instruction make a difference? *Amer. J. Nurs.* 68:62-7, 1968.	3
32	**Johnson J E & Dabbs J M.** Enumeration of active sweat glands: a simple physiological indicator of psychological changes. *Nurs. Res.* 16:273-6, 1967.	14
41	**Johnson J E, Dabbs J M & Leventhal H.** Psychosocial factors in the welfare of surgical patients. *Nurs. Res.* 19:18-29, 1970.	14
31	**Johnson J E, Kirchhoff K T & Endress M P.** Altering children's distress behavior during orthopedic cast removal. *Nurs. Res.* 24:404-10, 1975.	14
34	**Johnson J E & Rice V H.** Sensory and distress components of pain. *Nurs. Res.* 23:203-9, 1974.	14
23	**Johnson J E, Rice V H, Fuller S S & Endress M P.** Sensory information, instruction in a coping strategy, and recovery from surgery. *Res. Nurs. Health* 1:4-17, 1978.	1
26	**Katz V.** Auditory stimulation and developmental behavior of the premature infant. *Nurs. Res.* 20:196-201, 1971.	14
35	**Lindeman C A.** Nursing intervention with the presurgical patient. *Nurs. Res.* 21:196-209, 1972.	14
54	**Lindeman C A & Van Aernam B.** Nursing intervention with the presurgical patient—the effects of structured and unstructured preoperative teaching. *Nurs. Res.* 20:319-32, 1971.	14
183	**Marston M-'V.** Compliance with medical regimens: a review of the literature. *Nurs. Res.* 19:312-23, 1970.	14
40	**Neely E & Patrick M L.** Problems of aged persons taking medications at home. *Nurs. Res.* 17:52-5, 1968.	14
27	**Quint J C.** The impact of mastectomy. *Amer. J. Nurs.* 63(11):88-92, 1963.	3
37	**Schmitt F E & Wooldridge P J.** Psychological preparation of surgical patients. *Nurs. Res.* 22:108-16, 1973.	14
40	**Wolfer J A & Davis C E.** Assessment of surgical patients' preoperative emotional condition and postoperative welfare. *Nurs. Res.* 19:402-14, 1970.	14
31	**Wolfer J A & Visintainer M A.** Pediatric surgical patients' and parents' stress responses and adjustment. *Nurs. Res.* 24:244-55, 1975.	14

ducing pulmonary and respiratory complications following surgery. The paper was published in 1971 in *Nursing Research*. In 1972, Lindeman published a follow-up study on this topic in *Nursing Research*, showing that group instruction in these exercises was as effective and more efficient than individual teaching. Both of these papers combined received about 90 citations in 67 articles.

Jean E. Johnson, currently at the School of Nursing, University of Rochester, New York, authored 5 of the 18 most-cited nursing articles with several of her colleagues. All 5 articles deal with various aspects of distress—how it can be measured by sweat glands in the palm, how it can be reduced through cognitive and behavioral training, how it affects the sense of pain, and so on.

In fact, the majority of the most-cited nursing articles deal with the *psychological* preparation of patients facing medical or surgical procedures. By carefully instructing patients about what to expect prior to and following surgery, their stress and pain can be significantly reduced. Many of these studies also show that psychological preparation can reduce postoperative time spent in the hospital. The economic benefits from this type of research are obvious—less time in the hospital means lower health-care costs for the patient, hospital, and insurers. Several other psychological topics are discussed in papers listed in Table 6—nurses' attitudes toward geriatric patients, the social readjustments and self-images of patients with mastectomies, the effect of the maternal voice

Table 7: Sample of highly cited nursing articles published in non-nursing journals, in alphabetic order by first author. A=1966-1983 *SSCI®* and 1964-1983 *SCI®* citations. B=bibliographic data.

A	B
367	**Cobb S.** Social support as a moderator of life stress. *Psychosom. Med.* 38:300-14, 1976.
275	**Egbert L D, Battit G E, Welch C E & Bartlett M K.** Reduction of postoperative pain by encouragement and instruction of patients. *N. Engl. J. Med.* 270:825-7, 1964.
15	**Fuller S S, Endress M P & Johnson J E.** The effects of cognitive and behavioral control on coping with an aversive health examination. *J. Hum. Stress* 4(4):18-25, 1978.
10	**Gatewood T S & Stewart R B.** Obstetricians and nurse-midwives: the team approach in private practice. *Amer. J. Obstet. Gynecol.* 123:35-40, 1975.
76	**Greenberg M & Morris N.** Engrossment: the newborn's impact upon the father. *Amer. J. Orthopsychiat.* 44:520-31, 1974.
1375	**Holmes T H & Rahe R H.** The social readjustment rating scale. *J. Psychosom. Res.* 11:213-8, 1967.
92	**Johnson J E.** Effects of accurate expectations about sensations on the sensory and distress components of pain. *J. Personal. Soc. Psychol.* 27:261-75, 1973.
96	**Johnson J E & Leventhal H.** Effects of accurate expectations and behavioral instructions on reactions during a noxious medical examination. *J. Personal. Soc. Psychol.* 29:710-8, 1974.
112	**Kaplan B H, Cassel J C & Gore S.** Social support and health. *Med. Care* 15(Suppl.):47-58, 1977.
103	**Moos R H.** The development of a menstrual distress questionnaire. *Psychosom. Med.* 30:853-67, 1968.
11	**Peterson G H, Mehl L E & Leiderman P H.** The role of some birth-related variables in father attachment. *Amer. J. Orthopsychiat.* 49:330-8, 1979.
244	**Rizzo J R, House R J & Lirtzman S I.** Role conflict and ambiguity in complex organizations. *Admin. Sci. Quart.* 15:150-63, 1970.
3550	**Rotter J B.** Generalized expectancies for internal versus external control of reinforcement. *Psychol. Monogr.* 80:1-28, 1966.
56	**Wallston K A, Wallston B S & DeVellis R.** Development of the Multidimensional Health Locus of Control (MHLC) scales. *Health Educ. Monogr.* 6:160-70, 1978.

on the developmental behavior of premature infants, and so on.

The link between psychology and nursing is also evident in the sample of articles published in *non*-nursing journals that were highly cited by the core. These articles were selected as follows. We processed all the references cited in the 1982 editions of the core nursing journals. From these data we created a mini citation index. Then we ranked all the cited papers in order of their frequency of citation by the core. Finally, we tabulated the combined number of their citations in the 1966-1983 *SSCI* and 1964-1983 *SCI* and selected those that were cited at least 10 times.

The 14 articles published in non-nursing journals that were identified in this manner are shown in Table 7, in alphabetic order by first author. Almost all of them deal with psychological topics—stress, effects of cognitive and behavioral training on coping with pain, vari-

ous psychological rating scales, role conflicts, father attachment in newborns, and so on. Johnson again appears as the most prolific nurse-researcher on the list, having contributed three papers as a primary or secondary author. It's interesting to note that, following her nursing education, Johnson earned a doctoral degree in social psychology.

Comparing Tables 2 and 3, we see that all seven core nursing journals appear in both tables. Three appear among the top five on both lists. They are *American Journal of Nursing*, *Journal of Nursing Administration*, and *Nursing Research*. These three journals rank highest both in terms of their references *to* the core group and in the number of citations *from* the core. *Nursing Research* was also dominant in terms of impact and the number of "classic" articles published.

Tables 2 and 3 also show that a number of psychology journals were among both those that most frequently cit*ed* and those that were most frequently cited *by* the core nursing journals. The close ties between nursing and psychology are also apparent in a list of the most-cited articles from the core journals. Research topics in psychology also dominated the list of highly cited articles published in *non*-nursing journals. The reduction of stress in medical and surgical patients through cognitive and behavioral training was the most common psychological topic addressed by the authors.

This concludes our study of the nursing literature. In the near future, we will analyze citation patterns in surgery, physical chemistry, and philosophy journals.

* * * * *

My thanks to Abigail W. Grissom for her help in the preparation of this essay.

⁽¹984 ISI

REFERENCES

1. **Garfield E.** Journal citation studies. 43. Astrosciences journals—what they cite and what cites them. *Current Contents* (21):3-14, 21 May 1984.
2. --------------. Journal citation studies. 42. Analytical chemistry journals—what they cite and what cites them. *Current Contents* (13):3-12, 26 March 1984.
3. --------------. Journal citation studies. 41. Entomology journals—what they cite and what cites them. *Current Contents* (11):3-11, 12 March 1984.
4. **Leone L P.** Nursing. *Encyclopaedia Britannica. Macropaedia.* Chicago: H.H. Benton, 1974. Vol. 13. p. 395-401.
5. **US Bureau of the Census.** *Statistical abstract of the United States: 1982-83.* Washington, DC: US Department of Commerce, 1982. p. 388.
6. **Roberts M M.** *American nursing: history and interpretation.* New York: Macmillan, 1954. p. 7.
7. **National League for Nursing.** *Nursing student census with policy implications, 1984.* New York: NLN, 1984. 63 p.
8. -----------------------------------. *State-approved schools of nursing L.P.N./L.V.N., 1984.* New York: NLN, 1984. 120 p.
9. **Rockefeller Archive Center.** *A survey of manuscript sources for the history of nursing and nursing education in the Rockefeller Archive Center, 1984.* North Tarrytown, NY: RAC, 1984. 60 p.
10. **Lagemann E C,** ed. *Nursing history: new perspectives, new possibilities.* New York: Teachers College Press, 1983. 219 p.
11. **Brimmer P F, Skoner M M, Pender N J, Williams C A, Fleming J W & Werley H H.** Nurses with doctoral degrees: education and employment characteristics. *Res. Nurs. Health* 6:157-65, 1983.
12. **Garfield E.** Citation analysis as a tool in journal evaluation. *Science* 178:471-9, 1972.
13. **Marston-Scott M-'V.** Citation Classic. Commentary on *Nurs. Res.* 19:312-23, 1970. *Current Contents/Clinical Practice* 12(4):14, 23 January 1984.
14. **Garfield E.** *Citation Classics*—four years of the human side of science. *Essays of an information scientist.* Philadelphia: ISI Press, 1983. Vol. 5. p. 123-34.

Current Comments®

Scanners of the World Unite:
You Have Nothing to Lose but
Information Overload

Number 44   October 29, 1984

All working scholars live in a world of information overload and its attendant frustration. I am forcefully reminded of this as my file of unread tearsheets and stacks of unread books pile up. Indeed, the pleasure of reading through an entire book has become a rare luxury. So I am constrained to learn about books vicariously or by perusing their contents pages or through surrogates like book reviews. After all, how many books could one read even if there were more time? There would never be enough time. So, to a large extent, in the world of science we must function through surrogates, and we scan a lot.

In a rather poetic description of these problems and other aspects of the information explosion, Kevin Kelly, a science writer and editor for *CoEvolution Quarterly*, reminds us that scientists are inveterate scanners. He describes to the lay reader how scientists use *Current Contents*® (*CC*®) for scanning. And he uses, in a dramatic way, the metaphor of information transfer as an infectious-disease process. "Information as a communicable disease"[1] impressed me so much that I wrote and then called to obtain permission to reprint Kevin's article in *CC*.

Many years ago, I told you about the work of Bill Goffman,[2] a mathematician turned library-school dean, who described the dissemination of scientific ideas as a process similar to the transmission of disease.[3] Using Goffman as his source, Kelly points out, "The behavior of ideas as they jump from person to person has the same pattern as the spread of the Plague." From these remarks he makes an intriguing transition to the computer-assisted programs of ISI®, and in particular, to the *ISI Atlas of Science*®: *Biotechnology and Molecular Genetics, 1981/1982* that I described in *CC* a few weeks ago.[4]

Thanks to *CoEvolution Quarterly* for permission to reprint Kelly's essay. Some of you may not have known this publication of the not-for-profit Point Foundation, Sausalito, California. Its founder, Stewart Brand, conceived and published the *Whole Earth Catalog*, which he says is still available, if somewhat hard to find in bookstores. (He has 50,000 copies on hand and will answer inquiries at the address and phone number given below.) Brand is now the publisher of the bimonthly *Whole Earth Review*, which merges *CoEvolution Quarterly* with the *Whole Earth Software Review*. A subscription to *Whole Earth Review* costs $18 per year; to order, write *Whole Earth Review*, P.O. Box 27956, San Diego, California 92128, or call 1-800-354-8400. I am glad to report that the *New York Times* has also recently discovered Stewart's phenomenal talent, giving an excellent review to the new *Whole Earth Software Catalog* published by Quantum/Doubleday.[5]

©1984 ISI

REFERENCES

1. **Kelly K.** Information as a communicable disease. *CoEvolution Q.* 42:98-103, 1984.
2. **Garfield E.** The epidemiology of knowledge and the spread of scientific information. *Essays of an information scientist.* Philadelphia: ISI Press, 1981. Vol. 4. p. 586-91.
3. **Goffman W & Newill V A.** Generalization of epidemic theory. *Nature* 204:225-8, 1964.
4. **Garfield E.** Introducing the *ISI Atlas of Science: Biotechnology and Molecular Genetics, 1981/82* and Bibliographic Update for 1983/84. *Current Contents* (41):3-15, 8 October 1984.
5. **Lehmann-Haupt C.** Review of "Whole earth software catalog" by S. Brand. *NY Times* 3 October 1984, p. C24.

Information as a Communicable Disease
by Kevin Kelly

The history of science is a house of upsets. Here comes Galileo banging down the doors of astrology, here comes Darwin dragging out the attic furniture, here comes Einstein ripping up curtains to let the light in. To the faraway eye the whole structure is constantly shifting, unfolding, changing its floor plan just when you thought you knew its shape. Even the mathematical basement could overturn. Things don't stay put for more than two minutes in science. There are revolutions brewing in the hallways!

The system makes sense in the end, but who can stand the excitement?

The Truth is not so radical. What actually happens, happens in between the in-betweens. Information growth is so constant and finely textured that it blurs completely when we look back. A hundred years later, only the dramatic gestures are apparent. We can't see the real push and shove of science unless we bend and face it daily from two inches away.

In the research lab where I work, at least, we never see any revolutions, and we've been looking. Things plod along so slowly that, if there's any excitement, it's akin to the beauty of a Japanese play where almost nothing happens. Gloria F. has run the same experiment, with minor variations, nearly a thousand times in the last five months. You can't expect to get your socks blown off with a tame routine like that.

Scientists are driven to do the same old stuff by simple curiosity—the persistent, childlike variety. They are bugged to death when they don't understand something they think they could. The most common refrain I hear in the lab, probably once an hour, is these exact words: "Why does it do this? Why does it go like that? What will happen if we do this?"

The bookkeeping needed to track the answers is regimented and standardized. There is nothing very revolutionary about adding another entry in the ledger. Science is almost uniformly unoriginal because it is incremental by design and derives its value primarily from previous entries. Nothing would be worse than to invent a new number symbol or revise a tallying method in the middle of a book. Things must happen one line at a time.

Life in the lab would flatten out into complete boredom without the little mysteries and hard-to-explain findings which always come up. These give us a chance to ask "Why?" and spend time wondering. Most mysteries are eventually explained, if not by us, then by someone in Massachusetts or Florida. But there are always anomalies that don't go away and that we have to work around. If enough of these pile up in one area so that it becomes awkward to work there, then a curious thing happens: some whipper-snapper butts in with a new way of accounting which everyone reluctantly agrees will take care of the discrepancies. The data is transferred, the whole show is run from a different book, and the new system is the standard until anomalies pile up again.

With keen vision you can see these changes coming like comets. I was inspired to work for a university by a guy I've never met who codiscovered the structure of DNA and won a Nobel prize for it. He was trained as a bird watcher but saw a change coming and shrewdly switched his line of work to biochemistry, perhaps because he lacked preconceived ideas of what the new perspective had to look like. I gathered from this that any normally brilliant fellow who allowed himself to be sensitive to creative ideas could, by being in the right lab at the right time, luck into some awesomely simple insight. It was just a

In addition to traveling all over the globe and founding Nomadics Books in Athens, Georgia, Kevin Kelly has spent a fair amount of his time in college libraries. He wrote this examination of the flow of scientific information following a year working for the University of Georgia, co-producing a medical education and research film about human digestion.
—Jay Kinney

Reprinted from: *CoEvolution Q.* 42:98-103, 1984.

Immunological diversity of T-cell-response in radiation-chimeras

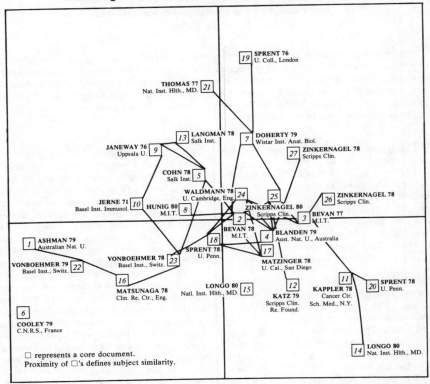

A map showing the principal infectors (cited authors) in the epidemic of current research on the immunological diversity of T-cell response in radiation-chimeras. Through their citations, infectees (citing authors) identify the vectors (cited papers) that communicated the germ of research to them. The most concentrated groups of papers reflect the most similar research subjects. (From *ISI Atlas of Science®: Biotechnology and Molecular Genetics, 1981/82* and Bibliographic Update for 1983/84.)

matter of hanging loose. If you didn't harden your mind and you kept on your toes—ready, like an ace short-stop—you could grab the Big One as it zoomed down from the heavens, and score the gift, just because you were ready! I woke up after six months in the lab and realized that I had as much chance of uncovering some Nobel truth as I did of inadvertently building a finely crafted cabinet or accidentally learning to play the piano. The grain of discovery doesn't run that way.

That there was a texture, a geography, a structure to what we knew, how we knew what to look for and the rules to follow to let us know when we found it was news to me.

Some of the lumpiness in what we know is caused by the special way scientific information is passed along. If every time I passed an idea to you I was required to mention where I first got a hint of it, we'd have a kind of scientific notation. When you passed on the idea I gave you, modified by a few others you picked up from someone else, you would mention that you got some ideas from me. If we did this in writing, and kept all of it, you wouldn't have to mention who gave me my idea, because anyone could find my letter to you and look it up. If we were very orthodox we would do this for every idea, every time. We would soon have whole libraries full of stuff that few people would want to read.

And that's what our libraries have today, whole shelves of books that are never read. Strangely, the better the library, the more complete their records, the more books they have that nobody reads. In a book that hadn't been checked out of the university library in three years I read a study that revealed that only half of the books in a library are checked out in a given year. Another rarely referred-to journal stated that less than half the back journals are referred to each year. And a little-noted paper demonstrated that half of the two million papers published each year are never noted by anyone. The statistics would imply that a few papers might not even be read at all. Yet papers that are never read are kept because their mere existence is valuable. A whole chain of better-read papers is built upon them the way important sums depend on petty figures.

The result is interesting, because papers and books are the presumed currency of information exchange. Most papers are ignored because of the old 20-80 effect, or in this case, more like the 10-90 effect: ten percent of the people do 90 percent of the work. An investigation of documents concerning milkweeds claimed that all the information to be found on the subject was contained in 96 of the four thousand or so papers written on the subject. Until recently the bugaboo was that the researcher wouldn't know which 96 until he finished reading all four thousand.

Scientists won't dump the 39 repetitious papers found in every 40 because redundancy is the sister of accuracy. The price of precision is a cumbersome mess of numbers and papers. So what, the scientist thinks, you just archive it in libraries, which they tend to view as bottomless filing cabinets. Librarians know better. They know they couldn't possibly keep all two million papers published each year.

Books, once ordered, take a long time to arrive, and to be most useful should be in the library shortly after being printed. A couple of librarians will be responsible for securing all the best, newest, most durable information available to science. This means librarians are peeking at the edges, all edges, of science, trying to discern which information is most useful in areas they couldn't possibly be expert in, and to have it ready when we need it.

So many books flow though librarians' hands that they pick up the fabric of what's happening. They know what's hot, what's stagnating ("We're quite rosy in biomass these days"). They learn the rough geography of the expanding terrain from what comes in, and wherever the map is empty they start filling it.

Librarians used to purposely leave blank spots to save money, then borrow information from another library when necessary. These days the real cost of interlibrary loans is so expensive that it is cheaper to buy the book. Our library will automatically purchase any book I request if it costs $100 or less. Science books published last year averaged $51 apiece (some go for $200). That works out to 11 cents per page, which makes the five-cent copy machines in the library an incredible deal.

The two million scientific papers published each year appear in about 80,000 different sources. My friends in the labs each read about 200 of these articles per year. The main method they use to connect with the 200 papers that will do them any good, while weeding out the thousands of redundant ones and the other million or so that have nothing to do with them, and at the same time not missing important ones that slide in at different angles, is to read a tiny, unusual magazine called *Current Contents®*.

This ingenious magazine is compact, about the size of a *TV Guide*. The whole thing is nothing more than the reproduced tables of contents from the several thousand best scientific journals. Table of contents pages in the journals normally list titles and authors of formal, rigorously styled reports. In a single issue of *Current Contents*, about 3,000 papers will be listed. There are seven flavors: life, clinical, social, physical, environmental, engineering, and the arts. The professor I work with eagerly awaits the arrival of *Current Contents* and steals them home to read in bed at night, going through about 1,000 titles each week.

According to a paper recently listed in *Current Contents*, "For every person who reads the whole of a text of a scientific paper, twenty read through the summary, and 500 read the title and stop there. Most papers have their title read and no more." Therefore, a lot must be conveyed by the title. Tremendous energy is spent squeezing the whole message of the study into a brief and appealing headline. In fact, the sensation of reading *Current Contents* (once you have the lingo down) would be similar to reading a weekly Sunday magazine that was composed solely of headlines of the major stories from newspapers around the country. (Not a bad idea for a magazine actually.) Some headlines would be more informative than others, but on the whole you'd get a funky sense of what was going on. You could read the full story by looking up the proper day's paper.

As scientific titles become less of an indication of the paper's content and more of an advertisement, the temptation is toward yellow journalism. In the same vein that supermarket newspapers claim "Study Shows There's Life After Death" or "Lose Weight Eating," so scientists are tempted to work into a title catchy hooks like *cancer* or *cloning* or other best-selling buzz words that are only indirectly connected to the main point of the article. The art of title writing is so important that the title is often the most revised portion of a paper. On occasion, workshops devoted to honing this skill are offered at universities. Some authors completely submit to a pragmatic view and figure that since most folks are going to get no farther than reading the title, the title should give, as much as possible, the results or conclusion of the study. Instead of "A Preliminary Theoretical Model of User Patterns in Scientific Information," just sock it to them: "Texture of Science Is Like Lumpy Gravy."

The author's address is indexed in the back of each *Current Contents*. A researcher baited by the title of a paper mails a post card to the author, requesting a reprint, which the author sends at no charge as long as the supply lasts, which is often not long if the title promises a hot one. The author would like to have an unlimited supply of reprints but he must pay for them himself, as well as often pay to have his article published in the first place. (This is another story.)

Requested reprints trickle back to the research labs, are scanned, and occasionally actually read, and then are filed away in microlibraries according to each scientist's idiosyncratic system. My friend's basic research library is two large filing cabinets that hold all the world knows about pancreatic lipase enzymes. They are within arms' reach sitting down. Half are free reprints, the other half are Xeroxed from back copies of journals in the library.

These latter are acquired by going on a once-a-week or once-a-month library run. Clutching an ongoing grocery list of titles, our hero dashes off to the main library, scurries through the stacks collecting journals, hurries to the copy machines, reproduces them, grabs the copies and runs back to the lab. It is as if scientists didn't like being in libraries. They never read anything there, at least I've never caught one, and it's a rare sight to see one browsing, even for pleasure. Libraries are for students who don't know any better. Yet researchers love to be near libraries. The principal reason why the majority are working at institutions instead of being wired up to an electronic cottage among the cows is because they can run through the big libraries any time they need to.

Some third-world researchers depend on *Current Contents* and the free reprint system for up to 90 percent of their information base. In some disciplines they are the main users of the system. There's a box in the lab overflowing with stamps from around the world. The most exquisite ones were pasted on post cards with polite requests for the latest on "The Hydrolysis of Triacylglycerol Emulsions by Lingual Lipase," a reprint from our lab, to be sent to India or some other distant place.

The future is computers, but they haven't arrived in the science labs, yet.

Certainly the bulk of laboratory apparatus is programmed with computer chips—the scientist couldn't do a thing without them now—but people in the labs are almost unanimously skeptical of the computer's role for their information. They claim that less than 1 percent of their useful stuff is learned by computer networks. The infrequent computer searching they do is chiefly to double-check what they already suspected.

Telephoning is big, however. John P. will be struggling through a poorly written paper, throw up his hands in frustration, and call up the author. How in the world did you come to that conclusion? he demands. Nearly every scientist I've spoken with has praised the casual table-talks following a conference as their most important source of new ideas. That is when the meaty news comes, unburdened by sticky references or cautious statements. Award-winning biology-watcher Lewis Thomas observed, "I have the impression that a great body of information is getting around by a mechanism that can only be termed gossip."

Maybe we're in the middle of a gossip explosion. The facts show that the paper-per-author output has remained steady, implying there is not a literature explosion so much as a population (of scientists) explosion. More scientists, more hubbub. At any rate, there are more papers and more new ideas flying around than before, and it has taken one or two of these new ideas to tame the rest and make them accessible. Let me try to explain one of them.

A scientist studies to prepare his brain for a good idea. He diligently furrows into the field he wishes to have an idea in, getting everything ready for a good idea when it comes. The idea appears all of a sudden, traditionally while he's outside the lab, walking or brushing his teeth, and immediately it grows, feeding on the mental bits and pieces he had been stockpiling for the purpose. As soon as the idea has fruited in his brain it begins to try and replicate itself into other brains.

The behavior of ideas as they jump from person to person has the same pattern as the spread of the Plague. Both are described by the same mathematical model. Under analysis, the booming exponential growth of scientific ideas actually breaks down into a series of recurring epidemics. Information, it seems, is a communicable disease; scientists, mere willing hosts. This is a handy model, because more is currently known about the broadcast of disease than about the workings of information nets.

There's a standard curve for the expansion of an epidemic—slow initial growth, rapid spread, and then tapering off as the population becomes saturated. In the past, scientists relied on intuition for signs of a groundswell in a new field, a hunch of something happening. These days it's important to find the most active areas soon, so the big daddy-os in government and private foundations (who generally aren't scientists) monitor the patterns of scientific papers carefully with computer-assisted programs and graph the resulting curve on the wall. When the curve begins to match the instep slope preceding a full-fledged epidemic, just at the point they figure a little shot of dollars will have maximum effect, they start diverting money in that direction and hope it takes off.

The computer-assisted program they use was developed by Eugene Garfield, who also started *Current Contents* in a converted chicken coop in New Jersey. The tool, called citation indexing, is the first mirror look at the texture of scientific information, a scientific method that examines scientific method.

Among the books in my university's library are several with photographs of Chinese scroll painting. Near the edges of the dark, moody paintings are the "chops" of previous owners of the scroll. These marks have become integral parts of the pictures, and, in fact, bring value to them. In the same way, the marks that an idea carries around, letting you know who else was infected with it, are called citations. They give extra value to the ideas. If a copy of the original was acceptable we could make several, add our own mark, and pass them along. We'd have a branching network of replicating ideas radiating out from the original, each one stamped with citations.

This is where the computer comes in. The computer keeps track of all the pieces being copied and passed around. That's the hard part, especially with several million citations per year. Each time a person mentions he's been infected with an idea, whether it's a recent one or an old one, it goes into the computer with two ends—one under the infectee, one under the infector.

The connections can now be traced both ways, back from an idea, or forward from an idea. Pick a paper at random from the middle of the network. The paper itself is marked with a bibliography that tells where the ideas were one step before this. As mentioned earlier, you can trace it all the way back to the beginning. Going the other way, the citation index traces where each branch of the idea travels afterward.

For instance, it would make a list of any book or paper in the future that acknowledges this text of mine as a source of ideas. A year from now you could follow all the divergent paths these ideas have led to, probably weird offbeat corners you would never have found otherwise. It's like being able to ask someone, "Who's playing with your ideas now?" If you can find the name of any idea, you can find where it came from, using references, and you can find where it's going, using citations.

With all these relationships burned into its brain, the *Science Citation Index®*, as it is properly called, can notice patterns that connect. The index comes either as a large 14-volume series, or in electronic text. Recently it has been taught to paint visual maps of the links within fields of research.

These are the maps of different neighborhoods in science. An experimenter's neighborhood is bounded by the klan of all those who wave to him and everybody he waves to, that is, the set of people who have acknowledged his ideas in their work as well as those he has cited in his work. Usually most of the people down the hall, or sometimes even working in the same lab, belong to a different neighborhood. The group tinkering in the laboratory next to ours is working in another galaxy, while a group in Sweden is our neighbor. The ones living closest together in a neighborhood are the ones bouncing the most ideas off each other. On the map this distance is measured out in units of citations. Nearness means a commonness of ideas.

You enter any neighborhood by dropping names, by citing an author. An individual scientist may be on the fringe of hundreds of communities, and near the heart of a few. In the center of every neighborhood is a nucleus of influential people who set the tone and pace, and occasionally bully the timid. In scientific communities these are the core people others concede as being personal donors of important ideas. A person new to the block doesn't need to unravel the tangled knot of relationships. Just a look at the map hints where the godfathers are. He could begin his research exploring the flock at the center and gather the fattest ideas there. Sweeping outward from the nucleus he would have to cast his net wider and wider, over more and more papers, to haul in the same catch of useful news. The hinterlands of one place, of course, could be the backyard of a different neighborhood.

The maps show only the major landmarks—folks everybody in town knows, and who know everybody else. The "empty" background is, in reality, a solid mass of other, smaller neighborhoods, hangout spots, quiet workers, a few hermits, and people moving around all the time. This is the map of our immediate neighborhood. We're not shown because we're mere peasant laborers in the field, but if we were, you'd see us living somewhere near the edge.

In fact, the map is changing all the time. The ground is not static, but an undulating throb. It's the same growing skin of ideas that foundation directors hold their breaths and run their hands over, searching for a sign of life on the charts. The tissue stirs, the pattern swirls. Maybe when the art is more developed we can make animated movies of ideas as they weave into colonies and every once in a while burst and contaminate everything with their strangeness.

So far we've got a fuzzy snapshot of the rough texture. It took zillions of citations reckoned by a hi-tech computer to verify what my neighbor scientists had been trying to tell me all along. The words they used, when they finally found them, seemed ridiculous, but were as close as any. The texture of scientific information, that is, the terrain of what we know, they kept saying, is a little thick in places, a little thin in others...like lumpy gravy.

BIBLIOGRAPHY

Durack D T. The weight of medical knowledge. *N. Engl. J. Med.* 298:773-75, 1978.

Garfield E. *Essays of an information scientist.* Philadelphia: ISI Press, 1977-1984. 6 vols.

Goffman W & Warren K S. *Scientific information systems and the principle of selectivity.* New York: Praeger, 1980. 189 p.

Kerkut G A. Choosing a title for a paper. *Comp. Biochem. Physiol. Pt. A* 74:1, 1983.

Thomas L. Hubris in science. *Science* 200:1459-62, 1978.

Tullock G. *The organization of inquiry.* Durham, NC: Duke University Press, 1966. 232 p.

Urquart D S. The use of scientific periodicals. *Proceedings of the International Conference on Scientific Information.* Washington, DC: National Academy of Sciences, 1958. p. 277-90.

Ziman J M. Information, communication, and knowledge. *Nature* 224:318-24, 1969.

Current Comments®

The 1982 Articles Most Cited in
1982 and 1983. 1. Life Sciences

Number 45

November 5, 1984

Each year, we list and examine current papers that are highly cited soon after publication. Our last reports covered the 1981 articles in life sciences[1] and physical sciences[2] that were most cited in 1981 and 1982. Papers that attract immediate and widespread attention within the research community often indicate the "hot" areas of science. Indeed, many of these papers form the core literature of new research fronts and specialties that we identify each year for the *Science Citation Index®* (*SCI®*) database. In this essay, we'll identify and discuss the 1982 life-sciences articles that were most cited in 1982 and 1983. The most-cited papers for the physical sciences will be the subject of a separate essay to be published in the near future.

Table 1 lists the 100 articles in this study, in alphabetic order by first author. In a study such as this, citation frequency rankings are relevant only for what they tell us about the emergence of new and active areas of research. However, individual papers should *not* be compared on citations alone. As pointed out many times before, these studies do not necessarily identify the best or most important research. Of course, experts in the life sciences will agree that many papers in Table 1 do represent milestone advances of knowledge. But many papers not included in this study will also eventually achieve high impact. Their recognition is delayed for a variety of reasons. We've discussed such cases of delayed recognition and premature discovery in a separate essay,[3] and will have

much more to report on this topic in the future.

The articles in Table 1 averaged 75 citations in the two-year period: 13 in 1982 and 62 in 1983. In comparison, the most-cited 1981 life-sciences articles[1] averaged 68 citations, and the 1980 life-sciences papers averaged 82.[4] The most-cited paper in Table 1 was cited 158 times, and the least-cited received 52 citations. Keep in mind that most of the four million articles and books cited each year in *SCI* will receive only about one or two citations. Of course, these cited works represent a small fraction of the millions of articles and books published since the invention of printing. Of the 10 million source articles and book chapters that have been indexed in the *SCI* over the past 30 years, probably less than 25 percent are cited each year.

In past studies, we've tried to categorize papers into various research areas—genetics, virology, oncology, and so on. However, these classifications are both subjective and artificial. They also ignore the overlap between fields and specialties that seems to be built into the structure of science. Contrary to the old adage, there is no one place for every paper, and every paper cannot be put in one place.

Nevertheless, it is useful to categorize these papers by broad subject areas. This can be done by considering the journals involved or by other methods. ISI® has developed an algorithm for categorizing papers based on co-citation analysis. This method has been described before,[5] so I won't go into a detailed description. Briefly, when authors cite a paper, they indicate that it is somehow relevant to their research. Furthermore, when several papers are frequently cited together, or co-cited, they presumably share common features—in topics, results, methods, and so on. That is, the citing authors themselves categorize papers into subject-related clusters of research. We use these co-citation groups to identify thousands of research fronts each year. These fronts are named by examining the key words and phrases in the titles of the citing papers. The names we assign are far more detailed and descriptive than are typical broad subject headings. And since the clustering is done systematically, it is more consistent and less ambiguous than traditional indexing methods.

Of the 100 papers in this study, 87 have already been incorporated into the "core" literature of several 1982 and 1983 *SCI* research fronts. The fronts are indicated in Table 1 by the numbers following the references. Numbers with an "82" prefix indicate that the paper was identified as one of several core publications in a 1982 research front. An "83" prefix denotes an article included in the core of a 1983 research front. In 1983, we combined *SCI* data with similar data from *Social Sciences Citation Index®* (*SSCI®*). Of the 13 papers in Table 1 that have not yet been included as core papers in any cluster, many will become part of the core literature of their fields in time, when and if they are co-cited with other high-impact papers. In some cases, however, a key paper may uniquely identify a method or theory for many years, particularly in the social sciences or in smaller pockets of science research.

Table 2 lists the names of the 1982 *SCI* and 1983 *SCI/SSCI* research fronts that include at least two papers from this study as core documents. Forty-four research fronts that included only one paper in Table 1 as a core document are not shown for reasons of space. Readers can obtain the names of these research fronts by contacting ISI. Also shown in Table 2 are the number of papers in this study included in each research front (column C) as well as the total number of core and citing papers (column D).

Scanning the list of research front names gives you a quick impression of the most-active research areas in the life sciences. For example, three papers in this study are core documents in research front #83-0063, "Applications of Nuclear Magnetic Resonance [NMR] Imaging in Medicine." Since their development in the late 1970s, NMR scanners have been increasingly used by radiologists to obtain images of internal organs, much like traditional X-ray machines. However, there are minimal biological risks involved with NMR imaging because the technology relies on magnetic fields rather than on radiation to create images.

Another "hot" topic is research front #83-1973, "Infections of Herpes Simplex and Herpes Zoster Viruses and Their Treatment with Acyclovir and Other Antiviral Drugs." Three papers in this study are included in the core of that research front. They report the results of clinical trials of acyclovir indicating that the new drug is safe and effective in treating herpes infections. As was pointed out in a separate essay on herpes infections,[6] there is no *cure* for this widespread disease. The development of drugs that at least shorten the duration of the painful symptoms of herpes infections is an important advance.

Eighteen papers in this study are core documents in the *SCI/SSCI* research front #83-1740, "Oncogenes and the Genetics of Human Cancer; Viral Transforming Genes and Their DNA Structure." Oncogenes are sequences of DNA that can transform normal cells into malignant cells. Two basic classes of oncogenes have been identified to date. One class is associated with retroviruses and the other is nonviral. Several papers in this study report results indicating that the two classes of oncogenes are homol-, ogous, that is, they share common genetic sequences.

The *SCI/SSCI* research front #83-4277, "Immunoreactivity of the Pituitary and Brain-Related Beta Endorphin, Dynorphin, Enkephalin and Other Opioid Peptides," contains six papers from this study in its core. These include the most-cited paper in this study, published in *Nature*, by Masaharu Noda, Kyoto University, Japan, and colleagues. The paper, entitled "Cloning and sequence analysis of cDNA for bovine adrenal preproenkephalin," reports their success in determining the entire amino acid sequence of bovine preproenkephalin, a protein that is the precursor or "starting point" from which seven smaller opioid peptides are produced by enzymatic cutting of the larger molecules. Opioids are opiate-like substances produced in the body. The paper was cited 46 times in 1982 and 112 times in 1983. In the first nine months of 1984, it was cited 72 times.

The third-most-cited article in this study is a companion paper published side-by-side in *Nature* with Noda's article. Ueli Gubler, Hoffmann-La Roche, Nutley, New Jersey, and colleagues established by DNA sequencing analysis that proenkephalin is indeed the precursor protein for several enkephalins and enkephalin-containing polypeptides (ECPs). The paper received 134 citations—48 in 1982 and 86 in 1983. Interestingly, Noda is one of the coauthors with Hitochi Kakidani, Kyoto University, of a paper in this study that deduced the amino acid sequence of yet another precursor protein for a different set of opioid peptides from porcine hypothalamus, which they called preproenkephalin B. This paper was cited 16 times in 1982 and 91 times in 1983. All three papers are also core documents in the 1982 *SCI* research front #82-1514, "Primary Structure of Human Enkephalins; Location and Regulation of Enkephalin Synthesis in CNS."

The second-most-cited paper was published in *Gene* by Joachim Messing and Jeffrey Vieira, University of Minnesota, St. Paul. The paper describes the construction of two new "bacteriophage vectors," that is, modified bacterial viruses used to produce large quantities of single-stranded bacterial DNA from a particular region of the bacterial chromosome. This "cloned" DNA is used for determinations of the nucleotide sequence of the bacterial DNA. Published in the October issue of *Gene*, the paper was cited just once in 1982 but 145 times in 1983. It has already been cited 150 times in 1984. It is a core paper in the 1983 *SCI/SSCI* research front #83-8552, "Genetic Studies of DNA Nucleotide Sequences, Protein Activation, Messenger RNA Structure, and Related Topics." Messing also coauthored the most-cited 1981 life-sciences paper,[1] which described a "shotgun" method for DNA sequencing.

David D. Sabatini and colleagues, New York University School of Medicine, authored the fourth-most-cited article in this study. This review paper, published in the *Journal of Cell Biology*, considers mechanisms by which newly synthesized proteins are transferred to their functional sites in various membranes and organelles within the eucaryotic cell either during or following synthesis. The authors discuss models that suggest how specific features of proteins can act as signals to direct the proteins to their final destination in the cell. The paper was cited 127 times—33 in 1982 and 94 in 1983. It is a core paper in the 1983 *SCI/SSCI* research front #83-2966, "Membrane Biogenesis and Mechanisms of Protein Insertion and Secretion: Use of cDNA Probes in Protein Processing."

The fifth-most-cited paper is also a review article. Philip Cohen, University of Dundee, Scotland, described how the metabolism of many enzymes and proteins is regulated in the cell by protein phosphorylation, the biochemical process of adding a phosphate group to an organic molecule, and coordinated through this mechanism by neural and hormonal stimuli. Cohen pointed out,

Table 1: The 1982 life-sciences articles most cited in 1982-1983, listed in alphabetic order by first author. The authors' addresses follow each citation. Code numbers indicate the 1982 *SCI®* research front specialties for which these are *core* papers. Code numbers with an asterisk (*) indicate the 1983 *SCI/SSCI®* research front specialties for which these are *core* papers. A=number of citations in 1982. B=number of citations in 1983. C=total number of citations for 1982-1983. D=bibliographic information.

A	B	C	D
4	54	58	**Alfidi R J, Haaga J R, El Yousef S J, Bryan P J, Fletcher B D, LiPuma J P, Morrison S C, Kaufman B, Richey J B, Hinshaw W S, Kramer D M, Yeung H N, Cohen A M, Butler H E, Ament A E & Lieberman J M.** Preliminary experimental results in humans and animals with a superconducting, whole-body, nuclear magnetic resonance scanner. *Radiology* 143:175-81, 1982. Case Western Reserve Univ., Sch. Med.; Univ. Hosps. Cleveland; Technicare Corp., Solon, OH. *83-0063
2	54	56	**Amara S G, Jonas V, Rosenfeld M G, Ong E S & Evans R M.** Alternative RNA processing in calcitonin gene expression generates mRNAs encoding different polypeptide products. *Nature* 298:240-4, 1982. Univ. California, San Diego, Sch. Med., La Jolla; Salk Inst., Tumor Virol. Lab., San Diego, CA.
11	59	70	**Anderson S, de Bruijn M H L, Coulson A R, Eperon I C, Sanger F & Young I G.** Complete sequence of bovine mitochondrial DNA. *J. Mol. Biol.* 156:683-717, 1982. MRC Ctr., Lab. Mol. Biol., Cambridge, UK. *83-0874
10	47	57	**Bittle J L, Houghten R A, Alexander H, Shinnick T M, Sutcliffe J G, Lerner R A, Rowlands D J & Brown F.** Protection against foot-and-mouth disease by immunization with a chemically synthesized peptide predicted from the viral nucleotide sequence. *Nature* 298:30-3, 1982. Scripps Clin., Res. Inst., La Jolla, CA; Anim. Virus Res. Inst., Woking, UK. *83-2152
9	47	56	**Carlson M & Botstein D.** Two differentially regulated mRNAs with different 5' ends encode secreted and intracellular forms of yeast invertase. *Cell* 28:145-54, 1982. MIT, Dept. Biol., Cambridge, MA. *83-4037
9	62	71	**Carroll B J.** The dexamethasone suppression test for melancholia. *Brit. J. Psychiat.* 140:292-304, 1982. Univ. Michigan, Dept. Psychiat., Ann Arbor, MI. *83-0413
2	62	64	**Castagna M, Takai Y, Kaibuchi K, Sano K, Kikkawa U & Nishizuka Y.** Direct activation of calcium-activated, phospholipid-dependent protein kinase by tumor-promoting phorbol esters. *J. Biol. Chem.* 257:7847-51, 1982. Kobe Univ., Sch. Med.; Natl. Inst. Basic Biol., Dept. Cell Biol., Okazaki, Japan.
19	64	83	**Catovsky D, Rose M, Goolden A W G, White J M, Bourikas G, Brownell A I, Blattner W A, Greaves M F, Galton D A G, McCluskey D R, Lampert I, Ireland R, Bridges J M & Galla R C.** Adult T-cell lymphoma-leukaemia in blacks from the West Indies. *Lancet* 1:639-43, 1982. MRC, Leukaemia Unit; Univ. London, Roy. Postgrad. Med. Sch. & King's Coll. Hosp. Med. Sch.; Imperial Cancer Res. Fund, Membrane Immunol. Lab.; Cent. Middlesex Hosp., Dept. Haematol., London; St. James Hosp., Dept. Haematol., Balham; Queen's Univ., Dept. Haematol., Belfast, UK; NIH, NCI, Bethesda, MD. 82-0011; *83-2933
9	57	66	**Chang E H, Furth M E, Scolnick E M & Lowy D R.** Tumorigenic transformation of mammalian cells induced by a normal human gene homologous to the oncogene of Harvey murine sarcoma virus. *Nature* 297:479-83, 1982. NIH, NCI, Bethesda, MD. *83-1740
19	40	59	**Chattopadhyay S K, Cloyd M W, Linemeyer D L, Lander M R, Rands E & Lowy D R.** Cellular origin and role of mink cell focus-forming viruses in murine thymic lymphomas. *Nature* 295:25-31, 1982. NIH, NCI, Bethesda, MD & NIAID, Hamilton, MT. 82-0686; *83-4271
37	75	112	**Chavkin C, James I F & Goldstein A.** Dynorphin is a specific endogenous ligand of the κk opioid receptor. *Science* 215:413-5, 1982. Addiction Res. Fdn.; Stanford Univ., Palo Alto, CA. 82-1512; *83-4277
8	111	119	**Cohen P.** The role of protein phosphorylation in neural and hormonal control of cellular activity. *Nature* 296:613-20, 1982. Univ. Dundee, Dept. Biochem., UK. *83-2196
19	63	82	**Cohen S, Ushiro H, Stoscheck C & Chinkers M.** A native 170,000 epidermal growth factor receptor-kinase complex from shed plasma membrane vesicles. *J. Biol. Chem.* 257:1523-31, 1982. Vanderbilt Univ., Sch. Med., Nashville, TN. 82-0083; *83-0069
2	54	56	**Collins S & Groudine M.** Amplification of endogenous *myc*-related DNA sequences in a human myeloid leukaemia cell line. *Nature* 298:679-81, 1982. Vet. Admin. Hosp.; Fred Hutchinson Cancer Res. Ctr.; Univ. Washington Hosp., Seattle, WA. *83-1740

A	B	C	D

26　84　110　**Comb M, Seeburg P H, Adelman J, Eiden L & Herbert E.** Primary structure of the human Met- and Leu-enkephalin precursor and its mRNA. *Nature* 295:663-6, 1982. Univ. Oregon, Eugene, OR; Genentech, Inc., San Francisco, CA; NIH, NIMH, Bethesda, MD. 82-1514; *83-4277

10　46　56　**Corey L, Nahmias A J, Guinan M E, Benedetti J K, Critchlow C W & Holmes K K.** A trial of topical acyclovir in genital herpes simplex virus infections. *N. Engl. J. Med.* 306:1313-9, 1982. Univ. Washington, Sch. Med.; Child. Orthoped. Hosp. Med. Ctr., Seattle, WA; Emory Univ., Sch. Med.; CDC, Vener. Dis. Control Div., Atlanta, GA. *83-1973

12　42　54　**Craig S W & Pollard T D.** Actin-binding proteins. *Trends Biochem. Sci.* 7:88-92, 1982. Johns Hopkins Univ., Sch. Med., Baltimore, MD. *83-2268

5　55　60　**Crooks L, Arakawa M, Hoenninger J, Watts J, McRee R, Kaufman L, Davis P L, Margulis A R & DeGroot J.** Nuclear magnetic resonance whole-body imager operating at 3.5 KGauss. *Radiology* 143:169-74, 1982. Univ. California, Radiol. Imaging Lab. & Dept. Anat., San Francisco, CA. *83-0063

17　40　57　**Crumpacker C S, Schnipper L E, Marlowe S I, Kowalsky P N, Hershey B J & Levin M J.** Resistance to antiviral drugs of herpes simplex virus isolated from a patient treated with acyclovir. *N. Engl. J. Med.* 306:343-6, 1982. Beth Israel Hosp., Charles A. Dana Res. Inst., Harvard-Thorndike Lab. & Dept. Med.; Sidney Farber Cancer Inst., Lab. Clin. Microbiol.; Harvard Univ., Med. Sch., Boston, MA. 82-1043; *83-1973

0　80　80　**Dalla Favera R, Bregni M, Erikson J, Patterson D, Gallo R C & Croce C M.** Human c-*myc* onc gene is located on the region of chromosome 8 that is translocated in Burkitt lymphoma cells. *Proc. Nat. Acad. Sci. US—Biol. Sci.* 79:7824-7, 1982. NIH, NCI, Bethesda, MD; Wistar Inst. Anat. Biol., Philadelphia, PA; Univ. Colorado, Hlth. Sci. Ctr., Denver, CO. *83-1740

7　62　69　**Darnell J E.** Variety in the level of gene control in eukaryotic cells. *Nature* 297:365-71, 1982. Rockefeller Univ., New York, NY.

14　82　96　**Der C J, Krontiris T G & Cooper G M.** Transforming genes of human bladder and lung carcinoma cell lines are homologous to the *ras* genes of Harvey and Kirsten sarcoma viruses. *Proc. Nat. Acad. Sci. US—Biol. Sci.* 79:3637-40, 1982. Sidney Farber Cancer Inst.; Harvard Univ., Med. Sch., Boston, MA. *83-1740

9　44　53　**Dickerson R E, Drew H R, Conner B N, Wing R M, Fratini A V & Kopka M L.** The anatomy of A-, B-, and Z-DNA. *Science* 216:475-85, 1982. CalTech, Pasadena, CA. *83-1181

11　74　85　**Ek B, Westermark B, Wasteson A & Heldin C-H.** Stimulation of tyrosine-specific phosphorylation by platelet-derived growth factor. *Nature* 295:419-20, 1982. Uppsala Univ., Inst. Med. Physiol. Chem. & Wallenberg Lab., Sweden. *83-0069

20　52　72　**Eva A, Robbins K C, Andersen P R, Srinivasan A, Tronick S R, Reddy E P, Ellmore N W, Galen A T, Lautenberger J A, Papas T S, Westin E H, Wong-Staal F, Gallo R C & Aaronson S A.** Cellular genes analogous to retroviral onc genes are transcribed in human tumour cells. *Nature* 295:116-9, 1982. NIH, NCI, Bethesda, MD. *83-1740

10　53　63　**Evans G A, Margulies D H, Camerini-Otero R D, Ozato K & Seidman J G.** Structure and expression of a mouse major histocompatibility antigen gene, H-2L*ᵈ*. *Proc. Nat. Acad. Sci. US—Biol. Sci.* 79:1994-8, 1982. NIH, NICHHD & NIADDKD, Bethesda, MD. *83-1491

0　60　60　**Farrar J J, Benjamin W R, Hilfiker M L, Howard M, Farrar W L & Fuller-Farrar J.** The biochemistry, biology, and role of interleukin 2 in the induction of cytotoxic T cell and antibody-forming B cell responses. *Immunol. Rev.* 63:129-66, 1982. NIH, NIDR & NIAID, Bethesda; Frederick Cancer Res. Ctr., Biol. Carcinogenesis Program, MD; Cleveland Clin. Fdn., Dept. Mol. Cell Biol., OH.

9　53　62　**Fehr J, Hofmann V & Kappeler U.** Transient reversal of thrombocytopenia in idiopathic thrombocytopenic purpura by high-dose intravenous gamma-globulin. *N. Engl. J. Med.* 306:1254-8, 1982. Univ. Hosp., Dept. Med., Zurich, Switzerland. *83-0336

5　57　62　**Follansbee S E, Busch D F, Wofsy C B, Coleman D L, Gullet J, Aurigemma G P, Ross T, Hadley W K & Drew W L.** An outbreak of *Pneumocystis carinii* pneumonia in homosexual men. *Ann. Intern. Med.* 96:705-13, 1982. Univ. California, Sch. Med., San Francisco, CA. *83-1898

15　44　59　**Friedman-Kien A E, Laubenstein L J, Rubinstein P, Buimovici-Klein E, Marmor M, Stahl R, Spigland I, Kim K S & Zolla-Pazner S.** Disseminated Kaposi's sarcoma in homosexual men. *Ann. Intern. Med.* 96:693-700, 1982. NYU Med. Ctr.; NY Blood

A	B	C	D

Ctr., Lindsley F. Kimball Res. Inst.; St. Luke's-Roosevelt Hosp. Med. Ctr.; NY State Inst. Basic Res. Mental Retardation, Dept. Virol.; Albert Einstein Coll. Med., Montefiore Hosp. Med. Ctr.; NY Vet. Admin. Med. Ctr., New York, NY.

19 39 58 Glenney J R, Glenney P, Osborn M & Weber K. An F-actin- and calmodulin-binding protein from isolated intestinal brush borders has a morphology related to spectrin. *Cell* 28:843-54, 1982. Max Planck Soc. Adv. Sci., Max Planck Inst. Biophys. Chem., Goettingen, FRG. 82-0130

19 44 63 Goedert J J, Neuland C Y, Wallen W C, Greene M H, Mann D L, Murray C, Strong D M, Fraumeni J F & Blattner W A. Amyl nitrite may alter T lymphocytes in homosexual men. *Lancet* 1:412-6, 1982. NIH, NCI & NINCDS; Uniformed Servs. Univ. Hlth. Sci.; Naval Med. Res. Inst., Bethesda; Biomed. Res. Inst., Rockville, MD. 82-1893; *83-1898

20 45 65 Goldfarb M, Shimizu K, Perucho M & Wigler M. Isolation and preliminary characterization of a human transforming gene from T24 bladder carcinoma cells. *Nature* 296:404-9, 1982. Cold Spring Harbor Lab., NY. 82-0131; *83-1740

27 56 83 Gray P W, Leung D W, Pennica D, Yelverton E, Najarian R, Simonsen C C, Derynck R, Sherwood P J, Wallace D M, Berger S L, Levinson A D & Goeddel D V. Expression of human immune interferon cDNA in *E. coli* and monkey cells. *Nature* 295:503-8, 1982. Genentech, Inc., Dept. Mol. Biol., San Francisco, CA; NIH, NCI, Bethesda, MD. *83-0309

22 52 74 Grosveld G C, de Boer E, Shewmaker C K & Flavell R A. DNA sequences necessary for transcription of the rabbit β-globin gene *in vivo. Nature* 295:120-6, 1982. MRC, Natl. Inst. Med. Res., London, UK.

48 86 134 Gubler U, Seeburg P, Hoffman B J, Gage L P & Udenfriend S. Molecular cloning establishes proenkephalin as precursor of enkephalin-containing peptides. *Nature* 295:206-8, 1982. Hoffmann-La Roche, Inc., Dept. Mol. Genet.; Roche Inst. Mol. Biol., Nutley, NJ; Genentech, Inc., Div. Mol. Biol., San Francisco, CA. 82-1514; *83-4277

1 82 83 Guillemin R, Brazeau P, Bohlen P, Esch F, Ling N & Wehrenberg W B. Growth hormone-releasing factor from a human pancreatic tumor that caused acromegaly. *Science* 218:585-7, 1982. Salk Inst. Biol. Stud., Lab. Neuroendocrinol., La Jolla, CA. *83-2888

18 41 59 Hollis G F, Hieter P A, McBride O W, Swan D & Leder P. Processed genes: a dispersed human immunoglobulin gene bearing evidence of RNA-type processing. *Nature* 296:321-5, 1982. NIH, NICHHD & NCI, Bethesda, MD; Harvard Univ., Med. Sch., Boston, MA. 82-0103; *83-7332

16 70 86 Howard M, Farrar J, Hilfiker M, Johnson B, Takatsu K, Hamaoka T & Paul W E. Identification of a T cell-derived B cell growth factor distinct from interleukin 2. *J. Exp. Med.* 155:914-23, 1982. NIH, NIAID & NIDR, Bethesda, MD; Osaka Univ., Med. Sch., Japan. 82-1401; *83-0889

16 91 107 Kakidani H, Furutani Y, Takahashi H, Noda M, Morimoto Y, Hirose T, Asai M, Inayama S, Nakanishi S & Numa S. Cloning and sequence analysis of cDNA for porcine β-neo-endorphin/dynorphin precursor. *Nature* 298:245-9, 1982. Kyoto Univ. Fac. Med.; Keio Univ. Sch. Med., Tokyo, Japan. 82-1514; *83-4277

12 41 53 Kalyanaraman V S, Sarngadharan M G, Nakao Y, Ito Y, Aoki T & Gallo R C. Natural antibodies to the structural core protein (p24) of the human T-cell leukemia (lymphoma) retrovirus found in sera of leukemia patients in Japan. *Proc. Nat. Acad. Sci. US—Biol. Sci.* 79:1653-7, 1982. Litton Bionet., Inc., Dept. Cell Biol., Kensington; NIH, NCI, Bethesda, MD; Kobe Univ., Sch. Med.; Kyoto Univ., Fac. Med.; Shinrakuen Hosp., Res. Div., Niigata, Japan. *83-2933

20 69 89 Kasuga M, Karlsson F A & Kahn C R. Insulin stimulates the phosphorylation of the 95,000-dalton subunit of its own receptor. *Science* 215:185-7, 1982. NIH, NIADDKD, Bethesda, MD. 82-2398; *83-0069

6 57 63 Kasuga M, Zick Y, Blithe D L, Crettaz M & Kahn C R. Insulin stimulates tyrosine phosphorylation of the insulin receptor in a cell-free system. *Nature* 298:667-9, 1982. Harvard Univ., Med. Sch., Boston, MA; NIH, NIADDKD & NICHHD, Bethesda, MD. *83-0069

10 54 64 Kirsch I R, Morton C C, Nakahara K & Leder P. Human immunoglobulin heavy chain genes map to a region of translocations in malignant B lymphocytes. *Science* 216:301-3, 1982. NIH, NICHHD & NCI, Bethesda, MD; Virginia Commonwlth. Univ., Med. Coll. Virginia, Richmond, VA; Harvard Univ., Med. Sch., Boston, MA. *83-1740

3 60 63 Korn E D. Actin polymerization and its regulation by proteins from nonmuscle cells. *Physiol. Rev.* 62:672-737, 1982. NIH, NHLBI, Bethesda, MD. *83-2268

358

A	B	C	D
0	76	76	**Kornfeld H, Vande Stouwe R A, Lange M, Reddy M M & Grieco M H.** T-lymphocyte subpopulations in homosexual men. *N. Engl. J. Med.* 307:729-31, 1982. St. Luke's-Roosevelt Hosp. Med. Ctr., New York, NY. *83-1898
7	45	52	**Kyte J & Doolittle R F.** A simple method for displaying the hydropathic character of a protein. *J. Mol. Biol.* 157:105-32, 1982. Univ. California, San Diego, Dept. Chem., La Jolla, CA.
21	84	105	**Land H, Schutz G, Schmale H & Richter D.** Nucleotide sequence of cloned cDNA encoding bovine arginine vasopressin-neurophysin II precursor. *Nature* 295:299-303, 1982. German Cancer Res. Ctr., Inst. Cell Tumor Biol., Heidelberg; Univ. Hamburg, Inst. Physiol. Chem., FRG. 82-1298; *83-3311
15	52	67	**Lane M-A, Sainten A & Cooper G M.** Stage-specific transforming genes of human and mouse B- and T-lymphocyte neoplasms. *Cell* 28:873-80, 1982. Harvard Univ., Med. Sch.; Sidney Farber Cancer Inst., Boston, MA. *83-1740
3	59	62	**Lazarides E.** Intermediate filaments: a chemically heterogeneous, developmentally regulated class of proteins. *Annu. Rev. Biochem.* 51:219-50, 1982. CalTech, Div. Biol., Pasadena, CA. *83-0671
14	68	82	**Levinson B, Khoury G, Vande Woude G & Gruss P.** Activation of SV40 genome by 72-base pair tandem repeats of Moloney sarcoma virus. *Nature* 295:568-72, 1982. NIH, NCI, Bethesda, MD. *83-1740
4	77	81	**Little J W & Mount D W.** The SOS regulatory system of *Escherichia coli. Cell* 29:11-22, 1982. Univ. Arizona, Arizona Hlth. Sci. Ctr. & Dept. Biochem., Tucson, AZ. *83-0703
13	41	54	**MacGregor G A, Markandu N D, Best F E, Elder D M, Cam J M, Sagnella G A & Squires M.** Double-blind randomised crossover trial of moderate sodium restriction in essential hypertension. *Lancet* 1:351-5, 1982. Univ. London, Charing Cross Hosp. Med. Sch., UK. *83-0703
18	41	59	**Malissen M, Malissen B & Jordon B R.** Exon/intron organization and complete nucleotide sequence of an *HLA* gene. *Proc. Nat. Acad. Sci. US—Biol. Sci.* 79:893-7, 1982. CNRS, INSERM, Marseille, France. *83-1491
10	63	73	**McGrath J C.** Evidence for more than one type of post-junctional α-adrenoceptor. *Biochem. Pharmacol.* 31:467-84, 1982. Univ. Glasgow, Inst. Physiol., UK. *83-0327
6	91	97	**McKnight S L & Kingsbury R.** Transcriptional control signals of a eukaryotic protein-coding gene. *Science* 217:316-24, 1982. Fred Hutchinson Cancer Res. Ctr., Seattle, WA. *83-1740
4	52	56	**Means A R, Tash J S & Chafouleas J G.** Physiological implications of the presence, distribution, and regulation of calmodulin in eukaryotic cells. *Physiol. Rev.* 62:1-39, 1982. Baylor Coll. Med., Dept. Cell Biol., Houston, TX. *83-0824
1	145	146	**Messing J & Vieira J.** A new pair of M13 vectors for selecting either DNA strand of double-digest restriction fragments. *Gene* 19:269-76, 1982. Univ. Minnesota, Dept. Biochem., St. Paul, MN. *83-8552
7	79	86	**Mildvan D, Mathur U, Enlow R W, Romain P L, Winchester R J, Colp C, Singman H, Adelsberg B R & Spigland I.** Opportunistic infections and immune deficiency in homosexual men. *Ann. Intern. Med.* 96:700-4, 1982. Beth Israel Med. Ctr., Dept. Med.; Hosp. Joint Dis. Orthopaed. Inst., Erwin S. and Rose F. Wolfson Lab. Cell. Mechs. Dis.; CUNY, Mount Sinai Sch. Med.; Albert Einstein Coll. Med., Montefiore Hosp. Med. Ctr., New York, NY. *83-1898
22	69	91	**Miller R A, Maloney D G, Warnke R & Levy R.** Treatment of B-cell lymphoma with monoclonal anti-idiotype antibody. *N. Engl. J. Med.* 306:517-22, 1982. Stanford Univ., Depts. Med. & Pathol., CA. *83-3616
13	41	54	**Moore K W, Sher B T, Sun Y H, Eakle K A & Hood L.** DNA sequence of a gene encoding a BALB/c mouse L^d transplantation antigen. *Science* 215:679-82, 1982. DNAX Res. Inst., Palo Alto; CalTech, Div. Biol., Pasadena, CA. *83-1491
19	97	116	**Mount S M.** A catalogue of splice junction sequences. *Nucl. Acid. Res.* 10:459-72, 1982. Yale Univ., Dept. Mol. Biophys. Biochem., New Haven, CT. *83-2424
14	39	53	**Murphy K M M & Snyder S H.** Calcium antagonist receptor binding sites labeled with ^{3}H nitrendipine. *Eur. J. Pharmacol.* 77:201-2, 1982. Johns Hopkins Univ., Sch. Med., Baltimore, MD. *83-1006
46	112	158	**Noda M, Furutani Y, Takahashi H, Toyosato M, Hirose T, Inayama S, Nakanishi S & Numa S.** Cloning and sequence analysis of cDNA for bovine adrenal preproenkephalin. *Nature* 295:202-6, 1982. Kyoto Univ., Fac. Med.; Keio Univ., Sch. Med., Tokyo, Japan. 82-1514; *83-4277
8	46	54	**Okayama H & Berg P.** High-efficiency cloning of full-length cDNA. *Mol. Cell. Biol.* 2:161-70, 1982. Stanford Univ., Sch. Med., CA. *83-7023

A	B	C	D
12	63	75	**Orkin S H, Kazazian H H, Antonarakis S E, Goff S C, Boehm C D, Sexton J P, Waber P G & Giardina P J V.** Linkage of β-thalassaemia mutations and β-globin gene polymorphisms with DNA polymorphisms in human β-globin gene cluster. *Nature* 296:627-31, 1982. Harvard Univ., Med. Sch.; Child. Hosp. Med. Ctr., Div. Hematol. Oncol.; Sidney Farber Cancer Inst., Boston, MA; Johns Hopkins Univ., Sch. Med., & Johns Hopkins Hosp., Baltimore, MD; NY Hosp.-Cornell Med. Ctr., Div. Pediat. Hematol.-Oncol., New York, NY. *83-1010
17	89	106	**Parada L F, Tabin C J, Shih C & Weinberg R A.** Human EJ bladder carcinoma oncogene is homologue of Harvey sarcoma virus *ras* gene. *Nature* 297:474-8, 1982. MIT, Ctr. Cancer Res. & Dept. Biol., Cambridge, MA. 82-0131; *83-1740
30	86	116	**Payne G S, Bishop J M & Varmus H E.** Multiple arrangements of viral DNA and an activated host oncogene in bursal lymphomas. *Nature* 295:209-14, 1982. Univ. California, Depts. Biochem. Biophys. & Microbiol. Immunol., San Francisco, CA. 82-0131; *83-1740
14	46	60	**Pulciani S, Santos E, Lauver A V, Long L K, Robbins K C & Barbacid M.** Oncogenes in human tumor cell lines: molecular cloning of a transforming gene from human bladder carcinoma cells. *Proc. Nat. Acad. Sci. US—Biol. Sci.* 79:2845-9, 1982. NIH, NCI, Bethesda, MD. *83-1740
6	102	108	**Reddy E P, Reynolds R K, Santos E & Barbacid M.** A point mutation is responsible for the acquisition of transforming properties by the T24 human bladder carcinoma oncogene. *Nature* 300:149-52, 1982. NIH, NCI, Bethesda, MD. *83-1740
16	39	55	**Reinherz E L, Morimoto C, Fitzgerald K A, Hussey R E, Daley J F & Schlossman S F.** Heterogeneity of human T⁴⁺ inducer T cells defined by a monoclonal antibody that delineates two functional subpopulations. *J. Immunol.* 128:463-8, 1982. Sidney Farber Cancer Inst., Div. Tumor Immunol.; Harvard Univ., Med. Sch., Boston, MA.
39	78	117	**Rivier C, Brownstein M, Spiess J, Rivier J & Vale W.** *In vivo* corticotropin-releasing factor-induced secretion of adrenocorticotropin, β-endorphin, and corticosterone. *Endocrinology* 110:272-8, 1982. Salk Inst. Biol. Stud., Peptide Biol. Lab., San Diego, CA; NIH, NIMH, Bethesda, MD. 82-2222; *83-2999
0	55	55	**Rivier J, Spiess J, Thorner M & Vale W.** Characterization of a growth hormone-releasing factor from a human pancreatic islet tumour. *Nature* 300:276-8, 1982. Salk Inst. Biol. Stud., Peptide Biol. Lab., San Diego, CA; Univ. Virginia, Sch. Med., Charlottesville, VA. *83-2888
18	55	73	**Robert-Guroff M, Nakao Y, Notake K, Ito Y, Sliski A & Gallo R C.** Natural antibodies to human retrovirus HTLV in a cluster of Japanese patients with adult T cell leukemia. *Science* 215:975-8, 1982. NIH, NCI, Bethesda, MD; Kobe Univ., Sch. Med.; Aichi Med. Univ., Nagoya; Kyoto Univ., Fac. Med., Japan. 82-0011; *83-2933
15	39	54	**Robinson S I, Nelkin B D & Vogelstein B.** The ovalbumin gene is associated with the nuclear matrix of chicken oviduct cells. *Cell* 28:99-106, 1982. Johns Hopkins Univ., Sch. Med., Baltimore, MD.
14	40	54	**Rubin G M, Kidwell M G & Bingham P M.** The molecular basis of P-M hybrid dysgenesis: the nature of induced mutations. *Cell* 29:987-94, 1982. Carnegie Inst. Washington, Dept. Embryol., Baltimore, MD; Brown Univ., Div. Biol. Med., Providence, RI; NIH, NIEHS, Research Triangle Park, NC. *83-2783
33	94	127	**Sabatini D D, Kreibich G, Morimoto T & Adesnik M.** Mechanisms for the incorporation of proteins in membranes and organelles. *J. Cell Biol.* 92:1-22, 1982. NYU, Sch. Med., NY. *83-2966
7	61	68	**Santos E, Tronick S R, Aaronson S A, Pulciani S & Barbacid M.** T24 human bladder carcinoma oncogene is an activated form of the normal human homologue of BALB- and Harvey-MSV transforming genes. *Nature* 298:343-7, 1982. NIH, NCI, Bethesda, MD. *83-1740
9	52	61	**Shih C & Weinberg R A.** Isolation of a transforming sequence from a human bladder carcinoma cell line. *Cell* 29:161-9, 1982. MIT, Ctr. Cancer Res. & Dept. Biol., Cambridge, MA. *83-1740
28	37	65	**Sprinzl M & Gauss D H.** Compilation of tRNA sequences. *Nucl. Acid. Res.* 10(2):r1-55, 1982. Univ. Bayreuth, Dept. Biochem.; Max Planck Soc. Adv. Sci., Max Planck Inst. Exp. Med., Goettingen, FRG.
1	53	54	**Stahl R E, Friedman-Kien A, Dubin R, Marmor M & Zolla-Pazner S.** Immunologic abnormalities in homosexual men. *Amer. J. Med.* 73:171-8, 1982. NY Vet. Admin. Med. Ctr.; NYU, Med. Ctr., NY. *83-1898
2	61	63	**Steinmetz M, Minard K, Horvath S, McNicholas J, Srelinger J, Wake C, Long E, Mach B & Hood L.** A molecular map of the immune response region from the major histocompatibility complex of the mouse. *Nature* 300:35-42, 1982. CalTech, Div.

A	B	C	D
			Biol., Pasadena; Stanford Univ., Dept. Biol. Sci.; USC, Sch. Med., Los Angeles, CA; Univ. Geneva, Med. Sch., Switzerland. *83-1491
20	63	83	**Steinmetz M, Winoto A, Minard K & Hood L.** Clusters of genes encoding mouse transplantation antigens. *Cell* 28:489-98, 1982. CalTech, Div. Biol., Pasadena, CA. 82-1217; *83-1491
8	46	54	**Storb R, Doney K C, Thomas E D, Appelbaum F, Buckner C D, Clift R A, Deeg H J, Goodell B W, Hackman R, Hansen J A, Sanders J, Sullivan K, Weiden P L & Witherspoon R P.** Marrow transplantation with or without donor buffy coat cells for 65 transfused aplastic anemia patients. *Blood* 59:236-46, 1982. Fred Hutchinson Cancer Res. Ctr.; Univ. Washington, Sch. Med., Seattle, WA. *83-1042
3	105	108	**Tabin C J, Bradley S M, Bargmann C I , Weinberg R A, Papageorge A G, Scolnick E M, Dhar R, Lowy D R & Chang E H.** Mechanism of activation of a human oncogene. *Nature* 300:143-9, 1982. Whitehead Inst. Biomed. Res.; MIT, Ctr. Cancer Res. & Dept. Biol., Cambridge, MA; Merck Labs., West Point, PA; NIH, NCI, Bethesda, MD. *83-1740
0	100	100	**Taub R, Kirsch I, Morton C, Lenoir G, Swan D, Tronick S, Aaronson S & Leder P.** Translocation of the c-*myc* gene into the immunoglobulin heavy chain locus in human Burkitt lymphoma and murine plasmacytoma cells. *Proc. Nat. Acad. Sci. US—Biol. Sci.* 79:7837-41, 1982. Harvard Univ., Med. Sch.; Child. Hosp. Med. Ctr., Boston, MA; NIH, NICHHD & NCI, Bethesda, MD; Intl. Agcy. Res. Cancer, Lyon, France. *83-1740
18	48	66	**Tsien R Y, Pozzan T & Rink T J.** T-cell mitogens cause early changes in cytoplasmic free Ca^{2+} and membrane potential in lymphocytes. *Nature* 295:68-71, 1982. Univ. Cambridge, Physiol. Lab., UK; Inst. Gen. Pathol., Padova, Italy. *83-9037
5	53	58	**Tycko B & Maxfield F R.** Rapid acidification of endocytic vesicles containing α_2-macroglobulin. *Cell* 28:643-51, 1982. NYU, Med. Ctr., NY. *83-0860
5	85	90	**Varmus H E.** Form and function of retroviral proviruses. *Science* 216:812-20, 1982. Univ. California, Dept. Microbiol. Immunol., San Francisco, CA.
19	43	62	**Verbi W, Greaves M F, Schneider C, Koubek K, Janossy G, Stein H, Kung P & Goldstein G.** Monoclonal antibodies OKT 11 and OKT 11A have pan-T reactivity and block sheep erythrocyte 'receptors.' *Eur. J. Immunol.* 12:81-6, 1982. Imperial Cancer Res. Fund, Membrane Immunol. Lab.; Univ. London, Roy. Free Hosp., UK; Christian Albrechts Univ., Inst. Pathol., Kiel, FRG; Ortho Pharmaceut. Corp., Raritan, NJ. 82-2290
1	71	72	**Vieira J & Messing J.** The pUC plasmids, an M13mp7-derived system for insertion mutagenesis and sequencing with synthetic universal primers. *Gene* 19:259-68, 1982. Univ. Minnesota, Dept. Biochem., St. Paul, MN.
12	42	54	**Wade J C, Newton B, McLaren C, Flournoy N, Keeney R E & Meyers J D.** Intravenous acyclovir to treat mucocutaneous herpes simplex virus infection after marrow transplantation. *Ann. Intern. Med.* 96:265-9, 1982. Univ. Washington, Sch. Med.; Fred Hutchinson Cancer Res. Ctr., Seattle, WA; Burroughs Wellcome Co., Research Triangle Park, NC. *83-1973
10	47	57	**Wagner G & Wuthrich K.** Sequential resonance assignments in protein ^{1}H nuclear magnetic resonance spectra. *J. Mol. Biol.* 155:347-66, 1982. Swiss Fed. Inst. Technol., Inst. Mol. Biol. Biophys., Zurich, Switzerland. *83-1380
18	47	65	**Watson S J, Akil H, Fischli W, Goldstein A, Zimmerman E, Nilaver G & van Wimersma Greidanus T B.** Dynorphin and vasopressin: common localization in magnocellular neurons. *Science* 216:85-7, 1982. Univ. Michigan, Mental Hlth. Res. Inst., Ann Arbor, MI; Stanford Univ., Dept. Pharmacol., Palo Alto, CA; Columbia Univ., Dept. Neurol., New York, NY; Univ. Utrecht, Rudolf Magnus Inst. Pharmacol., Netherlands. 82-1512; *83-4277
5	56	61	**Weeds A.** Actin-binding proteins—regulators of cell architecture and motility. *Nature* 296:811-6, 1982. MRC, Lab. Mol. Biol., Cambridge, UK. *83-2268
9	66	75	**Weisbrod S.** Active chromatin. *Nature* 297:289-95. Cold Spring Harbor Lab., NY.
14	55	69	**Whitehouse P J, Price D L, Struble R G, Clark A W, Coyle J T & DeLong M R.** Alzheimer's disease and senile dementia: loss of neurons in the basal forebrain. *Science* 215:1237-9, 1982. Johns Hopkins Univ., Sch. Med., Baltimore, MD. *83-1981
12	42	54	**Williams A F & Gagnon J.** Neuronal cell Thy-1 glycoprotein: homology with immunoglobulin. *Science* 216:696-703, 1982. Univ. Oxford, Sir William Dunn Sch. Pathol., Oxford, UK. *83-9006
15	64	79	**Yoshida M, Miyoshi I & Hinuma Y.** Isolation and characterization of retrovirus from cell lines of human adult T-cell leukemia and its implication in the disease. *Proc.*

A B C   D

Nat. Acad. Sci. US—Biol. Sci. 79:2031-5, 1982. Cancer Inst., Dept. Viral Oncol., Tokyo; Kochi Med. Sch., Dept. Intern. Med.; Kyoto Univ., Inst. Virus Res., Japan. *83-2933

11   51   62   **Young I R, Bailes D R, Burl M, Collins A G, Smith D T, McDonnell M J, Orr J S, Banks L M, Bydder G M, Greenspan R H & Steiner R E.** Initial clinical evaluation of a whole body nuclear magnetic resonance (NMR) tomograph. *J. Comput. Assist. Tomogr.* 6:1-18, 1982. Thorn-EMI Ltd., Cent. Res. Lab.; Univ. London, Roy. Postgrad. Med. Sch., UK; Yale Univ., Sch. Med., New Haven, CT. *83-0063

"Almost 35 enzymes and countless other proteins are now known to be regulated in this manner, and protein phosphorylation is clearly the major general mechanism by which intracellular events respond to external physiological stimuli." This paper, published in *Nature*, was cited in 119 publications—8 in 1982 and 111 in 1983. It also is a core document in the 1983 *SCI/SSCI* research front #83-2196, "Studies on Cyclic AMP-Dependent Protein Kinases and Protein Phosphorylation."

The 100 papers in this study were published in 28 journals. These journals are listed in Table 3. Just four journals account for 60 percent of the most-cited 1982 life-sciences papers. They are *Nature* (31 papers), *Science* (12), *Cell* (9), and *Proceedings of the National Academy of Sciences of the USA—Biological Sciences* (8). These journals tend to dominate citation-based studies of the most-cited literature. Also shown in Table 3 are the 1982 impact factors for the listed journals. These impact factors

Table 2: The 1982 *SCI*® and 1983 *SCI/SSCI*® research fronts that contain at least two of the 1982 most-cited life-sciences papers as core documents. A = research front number. B = research front name. C = number of 1982 most-cited life-sciences papers included in the core of each research front. D = number of core/citing documents.

A	B	C	D
82-0011	Pathogenesis, virology and clinical spectrum of T-cell lymphomas and leukemias induced by viruses	2	47/NA
82-0131	Characterization of oncogene activation caused by DNA rearrangement and resulting malignant transformation of cells and role of retroviruses	3	25/NA
82-1512	Immunohistochemical localization and binding of dynorphin to kappa opioid receptors in CNS, ileum and other organs in rodents	2	17/NA
82-1514	Primary structure of human enkephalins; location and regulation of enkephalin synthesis in CNS	4	4/NA
83-0063	Applications of nuclear magnetic resonance imaging in medicine	3	54/551
83-0069	Effects of epidermal growth factor, platelet-derived growth factor and others on tyrosine and protein phosphorylation by protein kinase	4	51/1172
83-1491	Major histocompatibility genes of mouse and man; structure, genetics, polymorphism and their role in T-cell immunocompetency	5	47/931
83-1740	Oncogenes and the genetics of human cancer; viral transforming genes and their DNA structure	18	57/1200
83-1898	Kaposi's sarcoma, cytomegalovirus infection, immunological factors and other aspects of the pathogenesis of acquired immune deficiency syndrome in homosexual men and other populations	5	52/521
83-1973	Infections of herpes simplex and herpes zoster viruses and their treatment with acyclovir and other antiviral drugs	3	47/500
83-2268	Role of actin and actin-binding proteins in polymerization, filament assembly and other aspects of cytoskeletal organization	3	15/361
83-2888	Neurostatin, somatostatin, and growth-hormone releasing peptides; distribution and localization in rat brain	2	23/497
83-2933	Human T-cell lymphoma virus and adult T-cell leukemia; nucleic acid analysis of virus and expression induced by interleukin-2	4	45/843
83-4277	Immunoreactivity of the pituitary and brain-related beta endorphin, dynorphin, enkephalin and other opioid peptides	6	32/672

Table 3: The 28 journals represented on the list of the 100 1982 life-sciences papers most cited in 1982-1983. The numbers in parentheses are the impact factors for the journals. (1982 impact factor equals the number of citations received by 1980-1981 articles in a journal divided by the number of articles published by the journal during the same period.) Data were taken from the 1982 *JCR™*. The figures at the right indicate the number of papers from each journal which appears on the list.

Journal	Number of Papers
Nature (8.75)	31
Science (6.81)	12
Cell (16.44)	9
Proc. Nat. Acad. Sci. US— Biol. Sci. (9.28)	8
N. Engl. J. Med. (15.60)	5
Ann. Intern. Med. (6.44)	4
J. Mol. Biol. (6.32)	3
Lancet (8.76)	3
Gene (4.85)	2
J. Biol. Chem. (5.87)	2
Nucl. Acid. Res. (6.96)	2
Physiol. Rev. (20.65)	2
Radiology (2.79)	2
Amer. J. Med. (4.56)	1
Annu. Rev. Biochem. (29.36)	1
Biochem. Pharmacol. (2.36)	1
Blood (5.20)	1
Brit. J. Psychiat. (2.26)	1
Endocrinology (3.77)	1
Eur. J. Immunol. (5.60)	1
Eur. J. Pharmacol. (3.47)	1
Immunol. Rev. (15.43)	1
J. Cell Biol. (9.42)	1
J. Comput. Assist. Tomogr. (2.61)	1
J. Exp. Med. (11.69)	1
J. Immunol. (6.51)	1
Mol. Cell. Biol. (4.24)	1
Trends Biochem. Sci. (2.74)	1

are calculated by dividing the number of 1982 citations to a journal's 1980 and 1981 articles by the number of articles published in those two years. Clearly, the journals that published the "superstar" life-sciences papers tend to publish articles of higher than average quality in general. The median 1982 impact for all *SCI* journals was 0.6, compared to 8.8 for *Nature*, 6.8 for *Science*, 16.4 for *Cell*, and so on.

The authors of the most-cited life-sciences articles were affiliated with 96 institutions located in nine countries. These institutions are listed in Table 4 in order of the number of times they appeared in Table 1. Sixty-two of these institutions (65 percent) are located in the US. In our study of the 1981 papers, the US accounted for 70 percent of the institutional affiliations.

In Table 1, authors from various divisions of the National Institutes of Health (NIH), Bethesda, Maryland, were listed 35 times on 24 of the 1982 papers. In our study of 1981 papers,[1] the NIH was listed only nine times on eight papers.

Twelve institutions listed in Table 4 are based in the UK, nine in Japan, five in the Federal Republic of Germany (FRG), three in Switzerland, and two in France. Italy, the Netherlands, and Sweden each account for one institution.

Table 4: The institutional affiliations of the authors on the list. Institutions are listed in descending order of the number of times they appear in Table 1.

NIH, Bethesda, MD		35
NCI	17	
NICHHD	5	
NIADDKD	3	
NIAID	3	
Bethesda, MD	2	
Hamilton, MT	1	
NIDR	2	
NIMH	2	
NHLBI	1	
NIEHS, Research Triangle Park, NC	1	
NINCDS	1	
Harvard Univ., Boston, MA		9
Univ. California, CA		6
San Francisco	4	
La Jolla	2	
CalTech, Pasadena, CA		5
Johns Hopkins Univ., Baltimore, MD		5
Sch. Med.	4	
Univ. Hosp.	1	
Kyoto Univ., Japan		5
Sidney Farber Cancer Inst., Boston, MA		5
Stanford Univ., CA		5
Univ. London, UK		5
Roy. Postgrad. Med. Sch.	2	
Charing Cross Hosp.	1	
King's Coll. Hosp.	1	
Roy. Free Hosp.	1	
Fred Hutchinson Cancer Res. Ctr., Seattle, WA		4
MIT, Cambridge, MA		4
MRC, UK		4
Lab. Mol. Biol., Cambridge	2	
Leukaemia Unit, Balham	1	
Natl. Inst. Med. Res., London	1	

NYU, NY	4	Hosp. Joint Dis. Orthopaed. Inst., New York, NY	1
Med. Ctr.	3	Inst. Gen. Pathol., Padova, Italy	1
Sch. Med.	1	Intl. Agcy. Res. Cancer, Lyon, France	1
Salk Inst. Biol. Stud., San Diego, CA	4	Kochi Med. Sch., Japan	1
Univ. Washington, Seattle, WA	4	Litton Bionet., Inc., Kensington, MD	1
Sch. Med.	3	Merck Labs., West Point, PA	1
Univ. Hosp.	1	Natl. Inst. Basic Biol., Okazaki, Japan	1
Beth Israel Hosp., Boston, MA	3	Naval Med. Res. Inst., Bethesda, MD	1
Charles A. Dana Res. Inst.	1	NY Blood Ctr., NY	1
Dept. Med.	1	NY Hosp.– Cornell Med. Ctr., NY	1
Harvard-Thorndike Lab.	1	NY State Inst. Basic Res. Mental Retardation, NY	1
Genentech, Inc., San Francisco, CA	3	Ortho Pharmaceut. Corp., Raritan, NJ	1
Kobe Univ., Japan	3	Osaka Univ., Japan	1
Albert Einstein Coll. Med., New York, NY	2	Queen's Univ., Belfast, UK	1
Children's Hosp. Med. Ctr., Boston, MA	2	Rockefeller Univ., New York, NY	1
Cold Spring Harbor Lab., NY	2	Scripps Clin., Res. Inst., La Jolla, CA	1
Hoffmann-La Roche, Inc., Nutley, NJ	2	Shinrakuen Hosp., Niigata, Japan	1
Dept. Mol. Genet.	1	St. James Hosp., Balham, UK	1
Roche Inst. Mol. Biol.	1	Swiss Fed. Inst. Technol., Zurich, Switzerland	1
Imperial Cancer Res. Fund, UK	2	Technicare Corp., Solon, OH	1
Balham	1	Thorn-EMI, Ltd., London, UK	1
London	1	Uniformed Servs. Univ. Hlth. Sci., Bethesda, MD	1
Keio Univ., Tokyo, Japan	2	Univ. Bayreuth, FRG	1
Max Planck Soc. Adv. Sci., Goettingen, FRG	2	Univ. Cambridge, UK	1
Inst. Biophys. Chem.	1	Univ. Colorado, Denver, CO	1
Inst. Exp. Med.	1	Univ. Dundee, UK	1
NY Vet. Admin. Med. Ctr., NY	2	Univ. Geneva, Switzerland	1
St. Luke's-Roosevelt Hosp. Med. Ctr., New York, NY	2	Univ. Glasgow, UK	1
Univ. Arizona, Tucson, AZ	2	Univ. Hamburg, FRG	1
Arizona Hlth. Sci. Ctr.	1	Univ. Hosps. Cleveland, OH	1
Dept. Biochem.	1	Univ. Oregon, Eugene, OR	1
Univ. Michigan, Ann Arbor, MI	2	Univ. Oxford, UK	1
Univ. Minnesota, St. Paul, MN	2	Univ. Utrecht, the Netherlands	1
Yale Univ., New Haven, CT	2	Univ. Virginia, Charlottesville, VA	1
Addiction Res. Fdn., Palo Alto, CA	1	Univ. Zurich, Switzerland	1
Aichi Med. Univ., Nagoya, Japan	1	USC, Los Angeles, CA	1
Anim. Virus Res. Inst., Woking, UK	1	Uppsala Univ., Sweden	1
Baylor Coll. Med., Houston, TX	1	Vanderbilt Univ., Nashville, TN	1
Beth Israel Med. Ctr., New York, NY	1	Vet. Admin. Hosp., Seattle, WA	1
Biomed. Res. Inst., Rockville, MD	1	Virginia Commonwlth. Univ., Richmond, VA	1
Brown Univ., Providence, RI	1	Whitehead Inst. Biomed. Res., Cambridge, MA	
Burroughs-Wellcome Co., Research Triangle Park, NC	1	Wistar Inst. Anat. Biol., Philadelphia, PA	1
Cancer Inst., Tokyo, Japan	1		
Carnegie Inst. Washington, Baltimore, MD	1		
Case Western Reserve Univ., Cleveland, OH	1		
Cent. Middlesex Hosp., London, UK	1		
Children's Orthoped. Hosp. Med. Ctr., Seattle, WA	1		
Christian Albrechts Univ., Kiel, FRG	1		
Cleveland Clin. Fdn., OH	1		
CNRS, Marseille, France	1		
Columbia Univ., New York, NY	1		
CDC, Atlanta, GA	1		
CUNY, NY	1		
DNAX Res. Inst., Palo Alto, CA	1		
Emory Univ., Atlanta, GA	1		
Frederick Cancer Res. Ctr., MD	1		
German Cancer Res. Ctr., Heidelburg, FRG	1		

Even though authors of nine nationalities appear in this study, all 100 papers were published in English. Table 5 provides information on the number of papers each nation's authors produced. For example, 81 papers listed US authors. Of these, 71 were published by US authors *alone*. Ten were coauthored with researchers from France, the FRG, Japan, the Netherlands, Switzerland, and the UK. It is interesting to note that Japan accounts for seven papers in this study,

Table 5: National affiliations of the authors of the 1982 life-sciences papers most cited in 1982-1983, in order of the total number of papers on which each nation's authors appeared (column A). B= number of papers coauthored with scientists from other countries. C=nationality of coauthors.

Country	A	B	C
US	81	10	France, FRG, Japan, the Netherlands, Switzerland, UK
UK	12	5	FRG, Italy, US
Japan	7	3	US
FRG	4	1	UK, US
Switzerland	3	1	US
France	2	1	US
Italy	1	1	UK
the Netherlands	1	1	US
Sweden	1	0	

three of which were coauthored with US researchers. Japan accounted for only one of the 1981 most-cited papers in the life sciences.[1]

Ten of the papers in Table 1 are single-author works. Fifteen papers list two authors, 12 list three, 15 list four, 11 list five, and 15 list six. Seven authors were listed on three papers, eight on five papers, and nine on seven papers. One paper each listed 10, 11, and 12 authors. Three papers list 14 authors, and one lists 16 authors.

Of the 434 authors in this study, 51 appeared on more than one paper in Table 1. R.C. Gallo, National Cancer Institute, Bethesda, coauthored five papers on retroviruses associated with various human cancers, particularly T cell leukemia. Gallo has received much attention in the media recently for having isolated HTLV-III (human T cell leukemia virus), the virus thought to be responsible for acquired immune deficiency syndrome (AIDS). Eight authors have three papers: S.A. Aaronson, M. Barbacid, L. Hood, P. Leder, D.R. Lowy, E. Santos, S.R. Tronick, and R.A. Weinberg. Forty-two authors each have two papers in this study.

This concludes our report on the 1982 life-sciences papers most cited in 1982 and 1983. In the coming weeks, we'll identify and discuss the most-cited physical-sciences papers for the same time period.

*   *   *   *   *

My thanks to Thomas Atkins and Alfred Welljams-Dorof for their help in the preparation of this essay.

©1984 ISI

REFERENCES

1. **Garfield E.** The 1981 articles most cited in 1981 and 1982. 1. Life sciences. *Essays of an information scientist.* Philadelphia: ISI Press, 1984. Vol. 6. p. 301-11.
2. -------------. The 1981 articles most cited in 1981 and 1982. 2. Physical sciences. *Essays of an information scientist.* Philadelphia: ISI Press, 1984. Vol. 6. p. 373-83.
3. -------------. Premature discovery or delayed recognition—why? *Essays of an information scientist.* Philadelphia: ISI Press, 1981. Vol. 4. p. 488-93.
4. -------------. The 1980 articles most cited in 1980 and 1981. 1. Life sciences. *Essays of an information scientist.* Philadelphia: ISI Press, 1984. Vol. 6. p. 63-73.
5. -------------. ABCs of cluster mapping. Parts 1 & 2. Most active fields in the life and physical sciences in 1978. *Essays of an information scientist.* Philadelphia: ISI Press, 1981. Vol. 4. p. 634-49.
6. -------------. Herpes simplex virus infections. Part 1. How widespread they are, and who is most threatened. Part 2. Sexually transmitted diseases without a cure. *Essays of an information scientist.* Philadelphia: ISI Press, 1983. Vol. 5. p. 143-56.

Current Comments®

Twins. Part 1. The Conception, Development, and Delivery of Twins

Number 46   November 12, 1984

Twins have occupied a prominent place in human imagination and mythology since ancient times. Greek mythology enshrined the twins Castor and Pollux in the heavens as the two stars of the constellation Gemini. Ancient Rome was said to have been founded by twins, Romulus and Remus, raised in the wild by a wolf. The establishment of several North American Indian tribes, such as the Hurons and Iroquois, is also ascribed to twins. Although deified in myths, twins have elicited ambivalent and opposite reactions among human communities. In *Twins and Supertwins*, Amram Scheinfeld, former member of the Genetic and Evolution Seminar of the University Seminars, Columbia University, New York, noted that the birth of twins was sometimes taken to be a bad omen, and one or both twins were killed or allowed to die through neglect.[1] But T.O. Oruene noted that groups such as the Yoruba tribe of Nigeria, who at one time practiced infanticide, today regard twins as special children invested with magical powers.[2]

Twins also occupy a special place in modern science. For example, genetically identical twins provide researchers with a kind of natural laboratory to explore the role that heredity and environment may play in the development of various medical and behavioral problems. In the first part of this essay, we'll discuss the unique biology of conceiving and giving birth to twins. Part two of this essay will focus on the use of twins in medical and behavioral research.

There are two biologically distinct types of twins, monozygotic (MZ) and dizygotic (DZ). MZ twins are genetically identical. They arise from a single fertilized egg (zygote) that splits in two during an early stage of development. These identical twins are always of the same sex. DZ, or fraternal, twins are no more alike genetically than any pair of siblings. They result from a more or less simultaneous double ovulation from the same or opposite ovaries and subsequent fertilization by two different spermatozoa. DZ twins can be of the same or opposite sex.

DZ twin births are more frequent than MZ births. In the US and Europe, for example, Zdenek Hrubec and C. Dennis Robinette, National Academy of Sciences-National Research Council, Washington, DC, noted that 12 of every 1,000 births produce twins.[3] One-third of these are MZ births. Interestingly, the frequency of MZ twinning is constant throughout the world, occurring in about 4 per 1,000 births.[3] But the rate of DZ births is extremely variable. According to P.P.S. Nylander, University College Hospital, Ibadan, Nigeria, the incidence of DZ twinning is highest among the Yoruba, at approximately 50 per 1,000 births.[4] Eiji Inouye, Institute of Brain Research, University of Tokyo, reported that the lowest rate of DZ twinning occurs in Japan at 4 per 1,000 births.[5]

While these figures reflect the incidence of twin *births*, the incidence of twin *conceptions* is thought to be higher. With the recent increased use of ultrasound examination, a technique in which ultrasonic waves are bounced off the fetus and viewed on a television screen, twin pregnancy can be detected as early as the seventh week of gestation. Recent reports of first-trimester ultrasound examinations indicate that far more twins are conceived than are ultimately born. This phenomenon is known as the "vanishing twin." That is, one of the twin embryos is lost during the first trimester of pregnancy. Harris J. Finberg and Jason C. Birnholz, Harvard University Medical School, Peter Bent Brigham Hospital and Boston Hospital for Women, Boston, Massachusetts, examined 19 women with first trimester bleeding. In 14 they found double sacs indicating a twin pregnancy. Ten of these 14 pregnancies resulted in single births.[6] The actual incidence of vanishing twins is difficult to estimate because first-trimester ultrasound examinations are not routine. However, in a review of nine studies on vanishing twins, Helain J. Landy and colleagues, Northwestern University Medical School and Center for Multiple Births, Chicago, Illinois, found "disappearance" rates ranging from 0 to 78 percent.[7]

Maternal inheritance of the tendency to produce DZ twins is generally supported by the research literature. However, there are conflicting reports concerning whether or not women are genetically predisposed to MZ twin births or whether there is a paternal genetic contribution to twinning. The work of P. Parisi and colleagues, School of Medicine, First University of Rome and the Gregor Mendel Institute for Medical Genetics and Twin Studies, Rome, supports both of these possibilities. They found the incidence of twinning to be much higher than average among maternal relatives of both MZ and DZ twins, and also significantly elevated among paternal relatives of DZ twins.[8]

But the stable frequency of MZ twin births around the world suggests that it is a "random" event.[3] Although the precise mechanism for MZ twinning is unknown, M.G. Bulmer, lecturer in biomathematics, University of Oxford, England, notes that one suggestion is that it results from a retardation of the zygote's growth, usually within 10 days of conception.[9]

In MZ twinning, the timing of the single zygote's cleavage into two separate zygotes can be determined by the type of placenta and membrane structure found at birth. The placenta establishes a vascular connection between the mother and fetus through the umbilical cord. Two membranes contiguous with the placenta surround the embryo—the outer chorion and the inner amnion. Each forms at different stages in the developmental process. Doubling of the placenta, chorion, *and* amnion indicates that the zygote split sometime between the first and fifth days after conception. Gerald Corney, Medical Research Council (MRC) Human Biochemical Genetics Unit, Galton Laboratory, University College London, reported that 20 to 30 percent of MZ twins fall into this category.[10] A single placenta and chorion, but double amnion, indicate that the separation took place between the 6th and 9th days. The majority of MZ twins show these features. A single placenta, chorion, *and* amnion indicate that the cleavage occurred between the 9th and 10th days following conception. Ian MacGillivray, University of Aberdeen, Scotland, reported that single-amnion twins occur in only three percent of MZ pregnancies.[11] Further delay in cleavage results in conjoined or Siamese twins, which occur in about 1 of every 400 MZ births.[9]

The case for a hereditary factor is stronger for DZ twinning than for MZ twinning. Several investigators have discovered an association between the conception of DZ twins and maternal height and weight. According to Grace Wyshak, Harvard University Medical School, mothers of DZ twins are relatively taller and heavier than mothers of either singletons or MZ twins.[12] These differences in height and weight, which are strongly influenced by genetics, suggest a genetic influence in DZ twinning.

But Wyshak's finding can also suggest the involvement of a nutritional factor.[12] That is, better fed and, therefore, heavier women may have an increased chance of conceiving DZ twins. D.M. Campbell and colleagues, University of Aberdeen, and Robert Gordon's Institute of Technology, Aberdeen, tested this nutritional hypothesis.[13] They compared mothers of various weights and from different social classes who gave birth to twins. The researchers found no difference in the incidence of twinning between the social classes. Instead, the data support a genetic tendency for taller and heavier women to produce DZ twins.[13]

Hormonal differences between mothers of DZ twins and those who bear singletons also indicate a genetic predisposition for DZ twinning. In a 1964 paper, Samuel Milham, then of New York State Department of Health, Albany, suggested that mothers of DZ twins may have increased levels of pituitary gonadotropic hormones.[14] Pituitary gonadotropins, such as follicle-stimulating hormone (FSH) and luteinizing hormone (LH), are responsible for ovulation, that

is, the maturation and release of the egg from the ovarian follicle. Thus, higher gonadotropin levels may increase the chance of multiple ovulation and result in a higher incidence of DZ twinning. In fact, physicians induce ovulation in some women who have difficulty conceiving by artificially increasing their gonadotropin levels. Most of the recent headline cases of quadruplet and higher-multiple births refer to women under such treatment.

Differences in blood levels of FSH correlate with the variable rates of DZ twinning between the ethnic groups mentioned earlier. For example, Nylander reported that, *on each day* of the menstrual cycle, FSH levels are higher in Yoruba mothers of DZ twins than in Yoruba mothers of singletons.[4] This finding is unusual because FSH levels peak just before ovulation, although they are also high at the early stage of the menstrual cycle when the follicle begins rapid growth. In a multi-institutional study comparing US women who have had two sets of DZ twins with mothers of singletons, Nicholas G. Martin and colleagues, Medical College of Virginia, Richmond, found higher FSH levels in the DZ mothers in this early phase of the menstrual cycle.[15] In Japanese women, who have a very low rate of DZ twinning, Hiroaki Soma and colleagues, Tokyo Medical College, found low FSH levels in *all* stages of the menstrual cycle compared with mothers of singletons in both the US and Nigeria.[16]

Differences in hormone levels may also explain why older women are more likely to bear twins than younger women. The incidence of DZ twinning is highest in women between the ages of 35 and 39.[17] However, if a woman is a twin herself, or the sibling of twins, the tendency to produce twins remains high even until age 44.[17] Pituitary gonadotropins, particularly FSH, are reported by Francisco I. Reyes and coworkers, University of Manitoba, Canada, to be present in greater quantities in older women.[18]

Another factor that predisposes women to produce DZ twins is parity, or the number of live children born. For example, Gordon Allen, Division of Biometry, National Institutes of Mental Health, Rockville, Maryland, analyzed data from 50,000 pregnancies. After correcting for the increase in twinning that is associated with age, he found that the frequency of twinning rises with the number of children born.[19] This finding may be related to an enlargement of the anterior pituitary with successive pregnancies, in addition to this gland's natural enlargement with age.[20] The anterior pituitary produces the gonadotropic hormones responsible for ovulation. Thus, the effect of more frequent twin conceptions with an increasing number of pregnancies might be explained as a fertility phenomenon. But R.G. Record and colleagues, University of Birmingham, England, found results of more direct tests for greater fertility in twin-prone women to be negative.[21]

Compared to a single pregnancy, certain physiological changes associated with multiple pregnancy can confuse an early diagnosis. For example, as early as the first trimester, twin pregnancy is characterized by a weight gain larger than that expected for a single pregnancy.[11] In a single pregnancy, such weight gain could be mistaken for an early sign of pre-eclampsia. Pre-eclampsia is a condition in which the maternal diastolic blood pressure increases to 90 mm Hg or higher after the 26th week of gestation. More will be said about pre-eclampsia later.

Certain maternal blood-composition values are also different between twin and singleton pregnancies. According to Chester Martin, Catholic University, Radboud Hospital, Nijmegen, the Netherlands, twin pregnancy is characterized by a 50 percent greater increase in blood plasma volume compared with a single pregnancy.[22] This is a necessary physiological adaptation to the transport of nutrients to two fetuses, and it may cause anemia, a common problem in multiple pregnancies. An increased alpha-fetoprotein (AFP) value is also not unusual in twin pregnancy.[11] However, in a single pregnancy, elevated AFP may indicate neural-tube defects or malformation of structures related to the central nervous system of the fetus. J.P. Neilson and colleagues, Queen Mother's Hospital, Glasgow, Scotland, recommend ultrasound examinations to investigate the possibility of fetal abnormalities in all cases of elevated AFP.[23]

Ultrasound examination is frequently recommended as a tool for the early diagnosis of multiple pregnancy. By using ultrasound, a multiple pregnancy can be diagnosed as early as the first seven to eight weeks of gestation. By the 7th week, gestational sacs can be seen, and by the end of the 12th week, fetal heads are visible.

According to Joseph G. Schenker and colleagues, Hadassah University Hospital and the Hebrew University, Hadassah Medical School, Jerusalem, a reliable clinical diagnosis of multiple pregnancies can be made only in the latter part of the second trimester.[24] The uterus in a multiple pregnancy, as measured from the top of the uterus to the pubic bone, is larger than expected for gestational age. But a significant size difference is not noticeable before about 12 weeks.[25] Other clinical signs of multiple pregnancy include detection by the mother of increased fetal activity and a larger than normal accumulation of amniotic fluid, a condition, according to Ralph C. Benson, Oregon Health Sciences University, Portland, that is 10 times more common in multiple than single pregnancies.[26] Palpation of the abdomen may also reveal a head that is small in relation to the expected size of a single fetus. Twin pregnancy is also indicated when two separate fetal heartbeats are found, with different rates and at separate points.[25] Fetal heartbeats can be heard as early as the fifth month of gestation by placing a specially adapted stethoscope on the mother's abdomen.

Early diagnosis is essential because complications are more common in twin pregnancies than in those producing single babies. One of the most common problems is pre-eclampsia. Pre-eclampsia is associated with a higher risk of perinatal mortality, that is, death around the time of birth, and of fetal growth retardation. A study by Xavier De Muylder and colleagues, Hôpital Notre-Dame, Montreal, Canada, examined 220 twin deliveries for the years 1969 to 1974. They found a threefold increase in the incidence of pre-eclampsia compared with singleton pregnancies.[27]

In general, twins are more likely than singletons to die around the time of birth. For example, Milada Zahalkova, National Health Institute, Cernopolni, Czechoslovakia, estimates that twins are 11 times more at risk of perinatal death than singletons.[28] Premature birth accounts for much of this increased risk of perinatal mortality for twins. Luigi Gedda and colleagues, Gregor Mendel Institute for Medical Genetics and Twin Studies, reported the time of gestation for twins to be about 20 days shorter than for singletons.[29] In a 1982 study, F. Puissant and F. Leroy, St. Pierre Hospital, Free University, Brussels, Belgium, found that death in twins born between 29 and 38 weeks of gestation was usually due to respiratory distress and cerebral hemorrhage associated with low birth-weight.[30] And 50 percent of stillborn twins delivered after 38 weeks were already decomposed or macerated, indicating that death occurred several days before delivery. Death may have been prevented by artificial termination of the pregnancy at 38 weeks.[30] More will be said about the causes of premature delivery later.

Perinatal mortality in twins is also associated with birth order. In a study of 575 twin deliveries, Puissant and Leroy found the mortality rate for second-born twins to be about 1.4 times that of first-born twins.[31] The second baby is primarily at risk of oxygen deficiency due either to a premature separation of the placenta from the uterus after the birth of the first baby or from reduced placental circulation. The longer the interval between births, therefore, the greater is the threat of oxygen deficiency if a problem exists.

This interval is affected by the position of the second fetus in the womb. Second-born twins are frequently oriented in a breech or transverse position,[31] rather than the normal cephalic presentation in which the head enters the birth canal first. Consequently, the second-born twin faces the possibility of a more traumatic birth.

In addition to their increased risk of perinatal mortality, twins are more likely than singletons to suffer congenital malformation.[31] But this risk is limited *only* to same-sex twins who are most likely MZ. Peter M. Layde and colleagues, Centers for Disease Control and Georgia Mental Health Institute, Atlanta, examined the association between birth defects and same-sex twins.[32] They found that these twins have about a 50 percent greater chance of congenital malformation, including gastrointestinal defects, genital anomalies, and neural-tube defects. Same-sex twins also had an increased incidence of cardiovascular malformation when compared to singletons.[32] A similar study by J. Burn, Institute of Child Health, London, and Corney found the risk of cardiovascular malformation in MZ twins to be approximately twice that of both DZ twins and singletons.[33]

About 90 percent of monochorial twins (twins sharing a single chorion) have some sort of vascular connection between the parts of the placenta supplying each fetus.[9] This can lead to the so-called "transfusion syndrome" in which one twin transfuses blood to the other through the vascular connection. Frank Falkner, University of Michigan, Ann Arbor, and Charles H. Hendricks, University of North Carolina, Chapel Hill, suggest that one-third of all monochorial twins may be affected.[34] As a result of this transfusion, the donor twin is small and anemic while the recipient is large and has an excessive amount of blood. Bulmer, in his frequently cited book *The Biology of Twinning in Man*, suggests that the transfusion syndrome is the main cause of increased mortality in monochorial twins.[9] These twins also run a risk of neonatal death due to cardiovascular complications.

Low birth-weight is another complication of twin pregnancy. Twins are usually born about two pounds lighter than singletons. Premature delivery is the main cause of their low birth-weight. A frequent cause of premature delivery is the early rupture of the fetal membranes. MacGillivray noted that this occurs more frequently in MZ than in DZ twins[35] and is most likely related to the structure of the membranes. Remember that MZ twins usually share a single chorion, sometimes even the same amnion, while each DZ twin is enveloped in its own membranes.

Another factor that contributes to premature delivery is an acute and excessive accumulation of fluid in the amniotic sac. This problem is more common in MZ twins, especially when the twins are males. MacGillivray reported that male twins comprise a greater proportion of preterm MZ deliveries than do females.[35] Warren Newton and colleagues, Northwestern University Medical School, Prentice Women's Hospital, Chicago, confirmed MacGillivray's finding.[36] They suggest that male twins, whether MZ *or* DZ, are unique in this respect. Usually, pairs of male twins have a greater combined weight than female or opposite-sex pairs at any gestational age.

Gedda and colleagues, mentioned earlier, suggest another possible cause of preterm delivery. The early delivery of twins of either sex may be due to an abnormal stimulation of the uterus caused by the increased load of two fetuses.[29] A multiple pregnancy is also characterized

---

Table 1: A selected list of organizations that provide information on twins.

Australian Multiple Birth Association
P.O. Box 105, Coogee
New South Wales 2034
Australia

Center for Study of Multiple Birth
333 E. Superior St.
Suite 463-5
Chicago, IL 60611

International Society for Twin Studies
Gregor Mendel Institute
Piazza Galeno 5
00161 Rome
Italy

International Twins Association
114 N. Lafayette Drive
Muncie, IN 47303

National Organization of Mothers of
Twins Clubs, Inc.
5402 Amberwood Lane
Rockville, MD 20853

Twinline
2131 University Ave.
Suite 204
Berkeley, CA 94704

by increased fetal movement, which might rupture the membranes. In addition, increased concentrations of protein-like substances that mimic the effect of oxytocin may be present in twin pregnancies.[29] Oxytocin is a hormone that stimulates uterine contractions.

Although twins have low birthweights due to premature delivery, they eventually catch up to the normal growth and weight standards for singletons. Ronald S. Wilson, University of Louisville, Kentucky, found that during the first three months, twins make a dramatic jump in weight, gaining as much as five pounds. Only by the time they are eight years old, however, do twins reach the normal weights expected for singletons.[37]

As a consequence of the many potential complications and risks, twin pregnancies are often a financial burden for the family. Prenatally, the mother may be hospitalized for a longer period of time in anticipation of early labor and delivery. Postnatally, the low birthweight infants often require intensive-care nurseries and long-term hospitalization. In a study of the social costs of twins, Emile Papiernik, INSERM, Clamart, France, concluded that a twin pregnancy may be 10 times more costly than a single pregnancy.[38]

Clearly, more research into the special problems associated with twin pregnancies is needed. Early diagnosis is also essential to prevent the complications that delivery poses to both the mother and her twins. Table 1 lists some of the organizations devoted to twins. One is the International Society for Twin Studies, which is supported by the Gregor Mendel Institute for Medical Genetics and Twin Studies. The society promotes twin research and cooperation between scientists and also organizes an international congress every three years.

The society also publishes a journal, *Acta Geneticae Medicae et Gemellologiae—Twin Research*. The term "gemellologiae" is derived from the Latin root "gemel" meaning twin. Data from ISI®'s *Journal Citation Reports®* (*JCR™*), volume 15 of *Science Citation Index®* (*SCI®*), 1983, confirm that this journal is cited by researchers in a variety of fields such as anthropology, biology, genetics, developmental psychology, obstetrics and gynecology, and psychiatry. In short, twin research is not only a multidisciplinary research area, but it also has wide impact. In part two of this essay, we'll review what researchers in the behavioral and medical sciences have learned in their studies of twins.

* * * * *

My thanks to Terri Freedman and Linda LaRue for their help in the preparation of this essay.

©1984 ISI

REFERENCES

1. **Scheinfeld A.** *Twins and supertwins.* Philadelphia: J.B. Lippincott, 1967. 292 p.
2. **Oruene T O.** Cultic powers of Yoruba twins: manifestation of traditional and religious beliefs of the Yoruba. *Acta Genet. Med. Gemellol.* 32:221-8, 1983.
3. **Hrubec Z & Robinette C D.** The study of human twins in medical research. *N. Engl. J. Med.* 310(7):435-41, 1984.
4. **Nylander P P S.** The factors that influence twinning rates. *Acta Genet. Med. Gemellol.* 30:189-202, 1981.
5. **Inouye E.** Frequency of multiple birth in three cities of Japan. *Amer. J. Hum. Genet.* 9:317-20, 1957.
6. **Finberg H J & Birnholz J C.** Ultrasound observations in multiple gestation with first trimester bleeding: the blighted twin. *Radiology* 132:137-42, 1979.
7. **Landy H J, Keith L & Keith D.** The vanishing twin. *Acta Genet. Med. Gemellol.* 31:179-94, 1982.
8. **Parisi P, Gatti M, Prinzi G & Caperna G.** Familial incidence of twinning. *Nature* 304:626-8, 1983.

9. **Bulmer M G.** *The biology of twinning in man.* Oxford: Clarendon Press, 1970. 205 p.
10. **Corney G.** Twin placentation and some effects on twins of known zygosity. *Prog. Clin. Biol. Res.* 24B:9-16, 1978.
11. **MacGillivray I.** Twins and other multiple deliveries. *Clin. Obstet. Gynaecol.* 7:581-600, 1980.
12. **Wyshak G.** Reproductive and menstrual characteristics of mothers of multiple births and mothers of singletons only: a discriminant analysis. *Prog. Clin. Biol. Res.* 69A:95-105, 1981.
13. **Campbell D M, Campbell A J & MacGillivray I.** Maternal characteristics of women having twin pregnancies. *J. Biosoc. Sci.* 6:463-70, 1974.
14. **Milham S.** Pituitary gonadotropin and dizygotic twinning. *Lancet* 2:566, 1964.
15. **Martin N G, Olsen M E, Theile H, El Beaini J L, Handelsman D & Bhatnagar A S.** Pituitary-ovarian function in mothers who have had two sets of dizygotic twins. *Fert. Steril.* 41(6):878-80, 1984.
16. **Soma H, Takayama M, Kiyokawa T, Akaeda T & Tokoro K.** Serum gonadotropin levels in Japanese women. *Obstet. Gynecol.* 46:311-2, 1975.
17. **Wyshak G.** Twinning rates among women at the end of their reproductive span and their relation to age at menopause. *Amer. J. Epidemiol.* 102:170-8, 1975.
18. **Reyes F I, Winter J S D & Faiman C.** Pituitary-ovarian relationships preceding the menopause. I. A cross-sectional study of serum follicle-stimulating hormone, luteinizing hormone, prolactin, estradiol, and progesterone levels. *Amer. J. Obstet. Gynecol.* 129:557-64, 1977.
19. **Allen G.** The parity effect and fertility in mothers of twins. *Prog. Clin. Biol. Res.* 24B:89-97, 1978.
20. **Russell D S.** Pituitary gland (hypophysis). (Anderson W A D, ed.) *Pathology.* St. Louis, MO: Mosby, 1966. Vol 2. p. 1052-73.
21. **Record R G, Armstrong E & Lancashire R J.** A study of the fertility of mothers of twins. *J. Epidemiol. Community Health* 32:183-9, 1978.
22. **Martin C.** Physiologic changes during pregnancy: the mother. (Quilligan E J & Kretchmer N, eds.) *Fetal and maternal medicine.* New York: Wiley, 1980. p. 141-79.
23. **Neilson J P, Hood V D & Cupples W.** Ultrasonic evaluation of twin pregnancies associated with raised serum alpha-fetoprotein levels. *Acta Genet. Med. Gemellol.* 31:229-33, 1982.
24. **Schenker J G, Yarkoni S & Granat M.** Multiple pregnancies following induction of ovulation. *Fert. Steril.* 35:105-23, 1981.
25. **MacGillivray I.** Diagnosis of twin pregnancy. (MacGillivray I, Nylander P P S & Corney G.) *Human multiple reproduction.* Philadelphia: Saunders, 1975. p. 116-23.
26. **Benson R C.** Multiple pregnancy. (Benson R C, ed.) *Current obstetric & gynecologic diagnosis & treatment.* Los Altos, CA: Lange Medical Publications, 1982. p. 755-63.
27. **De Muylder X, Moutquin J-M, Desgranges M F, Leduc B & Lazaro-Lopez F.** Obstetrical profile of twin pregnancies: a retrospective review of 11 years (1969-1979) at Hôpital Notre-Dame, Montreal, Canada. *Acta Genet. Med. Gemellol.* 31:149-55, 1982.
28. **Zahalkova M.** Perinatal and infant mortality in twins. *Prog. Clin. Biol. Res.* 24B:115-20, 1978.
29. **Gedda L, Brenci G & Gatti I.** Low birth weight in twins versus singletons: separate entities and different implications for child growth and survival. *Acta Genet. Med. Gemellol.* 30:1-8, 1981.
30. **Puissant F & Leroy F.** A reappraisal of perinatal mortality factors in twins. *Acta Genet. Med. Gemellol.* 31:213-9, 1982.
31. ------------------------------. The fate of the second twin. *Eur. J. Obstet. Gyn. Reprod. Biol.* 15:275-7, 1983.
32. **Layde P M, Erickson J D, Falek A & McCarthy B J.** Congenital malformation in twins. *Amer. J. Hum. Genet.* 32:69-78, 1980.
33. **Burn J & Corney G.** Congenital heart defects and twinning. *Acta Genet. Med. Gemellol.* 33(1):61-9, 1984.
34. **Falkner F & Hendricks C H.** Clinical aspects of twinning. (Quilligan E J & Kretchmer N, eds.) *Fetal and maternal medicine.* New York: Wiley, 1980. p. 419-41.
35. **MacGillivray I.** Determinants of birthweight of twins. *Acta Genet. Med. Gemellol.* 32:151-7, 1983.
36. **Newton W, Keith L & Keith D.** The Northwestern University multihospital twin study. IV. Duration of gestation according to fetal sex. *Amer. J. Obstet. Gynecol.* 149(6):655-8, 1984.
37. **Wilson R S.** Twin growth: initial deficit, recovery, and trends in concordance from birth to nine years. *Ann. Hum. Biol.* 6:205-20, 1979.
38. **Papiernik E.** Social cost of twin births. *Acta Genet. Med. Gemellol.* 32:105-11, 1983.

Current Comments®

101 Citation Classics from Annals of Internal Medicine

Number 47   November 19, 1984

Recently we identified *Citation Classics*™ from the leading journals of medicine. The first two essays in this series focused on the *New England Journal of Medicine*[1] and *The Lancet*.[2] For this essay, we've identified 101 papers from *Annals of Internal Medicine* using *Science Citation Index*® (*SCI*®) data from 1961 to 1982.

Annals of Internal Medicine is published by the American College of Physicians, which is headquartered in Philadelphia. The College had launched several medical journals that, in effect, were predecessors of *Annals of Internal Medicine*. In 1920, the College published *Annals of Medicine* in association with the American Congress on Internal Medicine. Only four numbers of this journal were issued before it ceased publication due to financial difficulties. *Annals of Clinical Medicine*, the College's second journal, was started in 1922. Publication priority was given to papers presented at the Annual Sessions of the College. As a result, other authors were reluctant to submit manuscripts to the journal, and issues were delayed and published irregularly. The College's Board of Regents also was unhappy with its publisher's contract and decided to publish a journal under the College's direct control. The first issue of this new journal, *Annals of Internal Medicine*, which hereafter I will simply call *Annals*, appeared in July 1927.[3]

In its 57-year history, *Annals* has been served by only five editors, each of whom has made significant contributions to the journal's development and current prestige. Alfred Scott Warthin, the first editor, defined the journal's goals and purposes: "It is not the intention of the editor to make of the *Annals* an ultra-scientific journal directed chiefly to the publication of new experimental investigations, but rather to make of it a practical scientific medium giving to practicing physicians in a concise and usable form the information they should possess as to the new advances and discoveries in the field of internal medicine. It should serve the general practitioners as an index of the progress of the internist's science."[3]

The second editor, Carl V. Weller, helped reduce publication costs by making changes in the style and format of *Annals*. The third editor, Maurice C. Pincoffs, served the journal during the depression of the 1930s and 1940s before retiring in 1960. Pincoffs established the criteria for selecting articles to publish in *Annals*. He also decided to publish transcripts of the National Institutes of Health (NIH) clinical staff conferences as a regular feature. These summaries of research projects were more current and less formal than review articles of the time. J. Russell Elkinton, the fourth editor of *Annals*, developed a peer review system that is still in use today. Elkinton also added the Letters and Comments section to provide readers a forum for communication.[3]

Edward J. Huth, the fifth and present editor, assumed his duties in 1971. In the past 13 years, Huth has also served as a national chairman of the Council of Biology Editors and editor of the Council's style manual. In 1981, the American Medical Writers Association presented Huth with the Harold Swanberg Distinguished Service Award for "unusual and distinguished services to the medical profession." In 1982, ISI Press® published *How to Write and Publish Papers in the Medical Sciences* by Huth, which I described recently.[4]

Under Huth's tenure as editor, *Annals* has almost doubled its circulation, from just over 50,000 in 1970 to more than 90,000 today. Subscribers in the US and Canada account for about 90 percent of the current circulation, but circulation outside North America is close to 10,000. In addition, the number of manuscripts submitted to the journal has also sharply increased. In the early 1930s, an average of 235 manuscripts was submitted each year, compared to more than 2,000 in recent years. *Annals* is able to publish only about 12 percent of these submissions. Each paper is reviewed by Huth and one or more of *Annals'* eight part-time editors. Manuscripts that pass this initial review are sent to several outside referees for final evaluation.[3]

Various indicators show that *Annals* is one of the most important medical journals in the world today. For example, Max D. Miller, Medical College of Georgia, Augusta, recently surveyed several hundred members of the Society of Teachers of Family Medicine. He asked them to identify the top 10 of more than 80 medical journals. The respondents were asked to judge the journals on two points: those in which they would most like to be published and those in which they would expect to find the most important material for educators of family physicians. *Annals* ranked fifth among the top 10 journals. The other nine journals, ranked in descending order, are *Journal of Family Practice, New England Journal of Medicine, American Family Physician, Journal of the American Medical Association, Journal of Medical Education, Postgraduate Medicine, Patient Care, Continuing Education for the Family Physician,* and *The Lancet.*[5]

ISI®'s citation data confirm these subjective ratings of importance and prestige for *Annals*. In the 1982 *Journal Citation Reports®* (*JCR™*), volume 14 of *SCI, Annals* ranked 44th out of more than 4,100 journals in terms of the number of 1982 citations it received, *regardless of discipline*. More significantly, in terms of impact, or the number of times the average article is cited, *Annals* ranked 61st.

Table 1 lists the 101 articles from *Annals* that were most cited from 1961 to 1982 in alphabetic order by first author. The number of citations each article received during this 22-year period is given in column B. Column A shows additional citations from the 1955-1964 *SCI* cumulation for those papers published before 1961. To give you an idea of the current citation frequency for each article, 1983 citations are listed in column C. Full bibliographic information is provided, including the authors' affiliations. The twelve papers with asterisks have already been featured as *Citation Classics*.

Each paper received at least 149 citations—the most cited, 740. The 101 papers in Table 1 represent one-tenth of the 1,100 *Annals* papers cited at least 50 times from 1961 to 1982. (See Table 2.)

Sixteen of the citation classics were published between 1975 and 1979, 32 in 1970-1974, 31 in 1965-1969, 15 in 1960-1964, and 7 in 1959 or earlier. The oldest paper was published in 1948 by William B. Wartman and Herman K. Hellerstein, Case Western Reserve University and University Hospitals of Cleveland, Ohio. The paper provides exhaustive data on the incidence of various types of heart disease—hypertensive, rheumatic, coronary artery, and so on—in 2,000 consecutive autopsies. The paper was cited 185 times from 1955 to 1982—12 times in 1983.

The two most recent papers were published in 1979. Both were identified in our 1982 study of most-cited 1979 papers.[6] Hans R. Brunner, Centre Hospitalier Universitaire, Lausanne, Switzerland, and colleagues assessed the ability of captopril, an inhibitor of the angiotensin-converting enzyme, to lower the blood pressure of patients with hypertension. The authors found "that chronic inhibition of the angiotensin-converting enzyme with [captopril] offers a new, efficient, and well-tolerated approach to the treatment of hypertension." The paper received 213 citations from 1979 to 1982. It was cited in 33 articles in 1983.

The other 1979 *Annals* paper was authored by William B. Kannel, NIH, Bethesda, Maryland, and colleagues. The authors examined the risks of developing atherosclerotic disease that are associated with cholesterol. In particular, they focused on the four different fractions of lipoproteins that are involved in the transport of cholesterol through the blood. These lipoprotein fractions are defined by very-low-density, intermediary-density, low-density, and high-density. Previous research tended to consider only the serum total cholesterol, not the portions of cholesterol in each lipoprotein fraction. Investigators now think that each lipoprotein fraction by itself can contribute to the risk of coronary heart disease. The authors pointed out, "A relatively large amount of cholesterol in the low-density lipoprotein fraction is atherogenic, whereas that in the high-density fraction appears protective.... The previous position that virtually all of the lipid information pertaining to coronary heart disease resided in the serum total cholesterol must be accordingly modified." The paper was cited 171 times from 1979 to 1982, and 58 times in 1983.

Kannel and colleagues authored four additional papers on cholesterol, lipoproteins, and heart disease. Their 1971 *Annals* paper, in fact, is the second-most-cited paper. In a *Citation Classic* commentary on this paper, Kannel observed, "Knowledge of the lipoprotein transport does enhance risk assessment since the serum total cholesterol reflects chiefly the atherogenic LDL-cholesterol component but fails to take into account the protective HDL-cholesterol fraction reflecting removal of cholesterol."[7] This paper was cited 683 times from 1971 to 1983. Taken together, all five papers by Kannel and colleagues were cited in more than 1,800 publications through 1983.

The most-cited *Annals* paper was published in 1970 by Vincent T. DeVita and colleagues, NIH. The authors reported their success in treating patients suffering from advanced Hodgkin's disease with combination chemotherapy. They used four different drugs in full doses, expecting that the drugs would have greater antitumor effects when combined than alone. The combination chemotherapy was administered in 28-day cycles for six months. In a *Citation Classic* commentary, DeVita said, "Although it doesn't seem so now, these were all radical ideas. The intensity and duration of treatment and the use of drugs in combination were not medically sanctioned approaches to the treatment of any disease at the time.... The results...were dramatically different from those previously possible with older approaches.... A 10-year follow-up report has shown that 66 percent of all patients who achieved remission have not developed tumor recurrences. We think these patients are rightfully considered cured of their disease."[8] The combination chemotherapy developed by the authors is now the standard drug regimen used for the treatment of advanced Hodgkin's disease and is used routinely as outpatient therapy. The paper was cited 740 times from 1970 to 1982, and 35 times in 1983.

Two Nobel laureates appear in Table 1—Baruch S. Blumberg and F. Macfarlane Burnet. Blumberg and colleagues, Institute of Cancer Research, Fox Chase Cancer Center, Philadelphia, wrote a 1967 paper in *Annals* that has since become a landmark in its field. In a *Citation Classic* commentary, Blumberg observed, "This is the first paper in which it

Table 1: Most-cited articles from *Annals of Internal Medicine*, 1961-1982 *SCI*®, in alphabetic order by first author. Asterisks (*) indicate articles with *Citation Classics* ™ commentaries. The issue number, year, and edition of *CC*® in which these commentaries appeared are in parentheses. A=1955-1960 citations. B=1961-1982 citations. C=1983 citations. D=bibliographic data.

A	B	C	D
158	5		**Alter H J, Holland P V, Purcell R H, Lander J J, Feinstone S M, Morrow A G & Schmidt P J.** Posttransfusion hepatitis after exclusion of commercial and hepatitis-B antigen-positive donors. *Ann. Intern. Med.* 77:691-9, 1972. NIH, Clin. Ctr., NIAID & NHLI, Bethesda, MD.
202	30		**Austrian R & Gold J.** Pneumococcal bacteremia with especial reference to bacteremic pneumococcal pneumonia. *Ann. Intern. Med.* 60:759-76, 1964. SUNY, Downstate Med. Ctr.; Kings Cty. Hosp., Med. Serv., Brooklyn, NY; Univ. Pennsylvania, Sch. Med., Philadelphia, PA.
236	18		**Bagley C M, DeVita V T, Berard C W & Canellos G P.** Advanced lymphosarcoma: intensive cyclical combination chemotherapy with cyclophosphamide, vincristine, and prednisone. *Ann. Intern. Med.* 76:227-34, 1972. NIH, NCI, Bethesda, MD.
197	14		**Baldwin D S, Lowenstein J, Rothfield N F, Gallo G & McCluskey R T.** The clinical course of the proliferative and membranous forms of lupus nephritis. *Ann. Intern. Med.* 73:929-42, 1970. NYU, Med. Ctr.; Bellevue Hosp., New York, NY.
480	50		**Blum R H & Carter S K.** Adriamycin. *Ann. Intern. Med.* 80:249-59, 1974. NIH, NCI, Bethesda, MD.
479	15		***Blumberg B S, Gerstley B J S, Hungerford D A, London W T & Sutnick A I.** A serum antigen (Australia antigen) in Down's syndrome, leukemia, and hepatitis. *Ann. Intern. Med.* 66:924-31, 1967. Inst. Cancer Res., Fox Chase Cancer Ctr., Philadelphia, PA. (28/83/LS)
181	1		***Bluming A Z, Vogel C L, Ziegler J L, Mody N & Kamya G.** Immunological effects of BCG in malignant melanoma: two modes of administration compared. *Ann. Intern. Med.* 76:405-11, 1972. Uganda Cancer Inst., Solid Tumor Ctr.; Makerere Univ., Med. Sch., Kampala, Uganda. (31/84/CP)
428	28		***Bodey G P, Buckley M, Sathe Y S & Freireich E J.** Quantitative relationships between circulating leukocytes and infection in patients with acute leukemia. *Ann. Intern. Med.* 64:328-40, 1966. NIH, NCI, Bethesda, MD. (36/81/CP)
320	23		***Braunstein G D, Vaitukaitis J L, Carbone P P & Ross G T.** Ectopic production of human chorionic gonadotrophin by neoplasms. *Ann. Intern. Med.* 78:39-45, 1973. NIH, NICHHD & NCI, Bethesda, MD. (43/83/CP)
149	1		**Breen F A & Tullis J L.** Ethanol gelation: a rapid screening test for intravascular coagulation. *Ann. Intern. Med.* 69:1197-206, 1968. N. Engl. Deaconess Hosp., Dept. Med; Blood Res. Inst., Inc., Cytol. Lab., Boston, MA.
266	3		**Brown R S, Haynes H A, Foley H T, Godwin H A, Berard C W & Carbone P P.** Hodgkin's disease. *Ann. Intern. Med.* 67:291-302, 1967. NIH, NCI, Bethesda, MD.
213	33		**Brunner H R, Gavras H, Waeber B, Kershaw G R, Turini G A, Vukovich R A, McKinstry D N & Gavras I.** Oral angiotensin-converting enzyme inhibitor in long-term treatment of hypertensive patients. *Ann. Intern. Med.* 90:19-23, 1979. Ctr. Hosp. Univ., Dept. Med., Lausanne, Switzerland; Boston City Hosp., Thorndike Mem. Labs., MA.
159	7		**Cherubin C E.** The medical sequelae of narcotic addiction. *Ann. Intern. Med.* 67:23-33, 1967. Metropolitan Med. Ctr., NY Med. Coll., NY.
235	10		**Chiang B N, Perlman L V, Ostrander L D & Epstein F H.** Relationship of premature systoles to coronary heart disease and sudden death in the Tecumseh epidemiologic study. *Ann. Intern. Med.* 70:1159-66, 1969. Univ. Michigan, Sch. Publ. Hlth., Ann Arbor, MI.
178	32		**Crystal R G, Fulmer J D, Roberts W C, Moss M L, Line B R & Reynolds H Y.** Idiopathic pulmonary fibrosis. *Ann. Intern. Med.* 85:769-88, 1976. NIH, NHLBI, Bethesda, MD.
740	35		***DeVita V T, Serpick A A & Carbone P P.** Combination chemotherapy in the treatment of advanced Hodgkin's disease. *Ann. Intern. Med.* 73:881-95, 1970. NIH, NCI, Bethesda & NHLBI, Baltimore, MD. (12/79/CP)
189	8		**Doherty J E, Perkins W H & Flanigan W J.** The distribution and concentration of tritiated digoxin in human tissues. *Ann. Intern. Med.* 66:116-24, 1967. Vet. Admin. Hosp.; Univ. Arkansas, Sch. Med., Little Rock, AR.
154	1		**Duncan D A, Drummond K N, Michael A F & Vernier R L.** Pulmonary hemorrhage and glomerulonephritis. *Ann. Intern. Med.* 62:920-38, 1965. Univ. Minnesota Hosps., Minneapolis, MN.

A	B	C	D

201   2   **Kass E H.** Pyelonephritis and bacteriuria. *Ann. Intern. Med.* 56:46-53, 1962. Boston City Hosp., Mallory Inst. Pathol., Thorndike Mem. Lab. & Second and Fourth (Harvard) Med. Servs.; Harvard Univ., Med. Sch., Boston, MA.

260   6   **Kelley W N, Greene M L, Rosenbloom F M, Henderson J F & Seegmiller J E.** Hypoxanthine-guanine phosphoribosyltransferase deficiency in gout. *Ann. Intern. Med.* 70:155-206, 1969. NIH, NIAMD, Bethesda, MD.

34   149   6   **Kemper J W, Baggenstoss A H & Slocumb C H.** The relationship of therapy with cortisone to the incidence of vascular lesions in rheumatoid arthritis. *Ann. Intern. Med.* 46:831-51, 1957. Mayo Clin. and Mayo Fdn., Sects. Med. & Pathol. Anat., Rochester, MN.

161   8   **Keys A, Aravanis C, Blackburn H, Van Buchem F S P, Buzina R, Djordjevic B S, Fidanza F, Karvonen M J, Menotti A, Puddu V & Taylor H L.** Coronary heart disease: overweight and obesity as risk factors. *Ann. Intern. Med.* 77:15-28, 1972. Univ. Minnesota, Lab. Physiol. Hyg., Minneapolis, MN.

26   188   10   **Keys A, Kimura N, Kusukawa A, Bronte-Stewart B, Larsen N & Keys M H.** Lessons from serum cholesterol studies in Japan, Hawaii and Los Angeles. *Ann. Intern. Med.* 48:83-94, 1958. Univ. Minnesota, Lab. Physiol. Hyg., Minneapolis, MN; Univ. Kyushu, Med. Sch., Fukuoka, Japan.

245   16   **Kirkpatrick C H, Rich R R & Bennett J E.** Chronic mucocutaneous candidiasis: model-building in cellular immunity. *Ann. Intern. Med.* 74:955-78, 1971. NIH, NIAID, Bethesda, MD.

186   0   **Kuchel O, Fishman L M, Liddle G W & Michelakis A.** Effect of diazoxide on plasma renin activity in hypertensive patients. *Ann. Intern. Med.* 67:791-9, 1967. Vanderbilt Univ., Sch. Med., Nashville, TN.

188   8   **Kunin C M.** A guide to use of antibiotics in patients with renal disease. *Ann. Intern. Med.* 67:151-8, 1967. Univ. Virginia, Sch. Med., Charlottesville, VA.

153   2   **Kuo P T & Bassett D R.** Dietary sugar in the production of hyperglyceridemia. *Ann. Intern. Med.* 62:1199-212, 1965. Hosp. Univ. Pennsylvania, Philadelphia, PA.

0   160   2   **Lange K, Wasserman E & Slobody L B.** The significance of serum complement levels for the diagnosis and prognosis of acute and subacute glomerulonephritis and lupus erythematosus disseminatus. *Ann. Intern. Med.* 53:636-46, 1960. Metropolitan Med. Ctr., NY Med. Coll., NY.

227   30   **Law D K, Dudrick S J & Abdou N I.** Immunocompetence of patients with protein-calorie malnutrition. *Ann. Intern. Med.* 79:545-50, 1973. Univ. Pennsylvania, Sch. Med.; Vet. Admin. Hosp., Philadelphia, PA.

160   8   **Lee J C, Yamauchi H & Hopper J.** The association of cancer and the nephrotic syndrome. *Ann. Intern. Med.* 64:41-51, 1966. Univ. California, Sch. Med., San Francisco, CA.

49   169   4   **Leinwand I, Duryee A W & Richter M N.** Scleroderma (based on a study of over 150 cases). *Ann. Intern. Med.* 41:1003-41, 1954. NYU, Med. Ctr., NY.

193   7   **Levitt M D, Rapoport M & Cooperband S R.** The renal clearance of amylase in renal insufficiency, acute pancreatitis, and macroamylasemia. *Ann. Intern. Med.* 71:919-25, 1969. Univ. Minnesota, Med. Ctr., Minneapolis, MN; Boston Univ., Sch. Med. & Univ. Hosp., MA.

183   7   **Levy R I, Fredrickson D S, Shulman R, Bilheimer D W, Breslow J L, Stone N J, Lux S E, Sloan H R, Krauss R M & Herbert P N.** Dietary and drug treatment of primary hyperlipoproteinemia. *Ann. Intern. Med.* 77:267-94, 1972. NIH, NHLBI, Bethesda, MD.

149   7   **Lichtman M A, Miller D R, Cohen J & Waterhouse C.** Reduced red cell glycolysis, 2,3-diphosphoglycerate and adenosine triphosphate concentration, and increased hemoglobin-oxygen affinity caused by hypophosphatemia. *Ann. Intern. Med.* 74:562-8, 1971. Univ. Rochester, Sch. Med. Dent., NY.

176   0   **Lipsett M B, Odell W D, Rosenberg L E & Waldmann T A.** Humoral syndromes associated with nonendocrine tumors. *Ann. Intern. Med.* 61:733-56, 1964. NIH, NCI, Bethesda, MD.

194   0   **London W T, Sutnick A I & Blumberg B S.** Australia antigen and acute viral hepatitis. *Ann. Intern. Med.* 70:55-9, 1969. Inst. Cancer Res., Fox Chase Cancer Ctr., Philadelphia, PA.

336   12   **Louria D B, Hensle T & Rose J.** The major medical complications of heroin addiction. *Ann. Intern. Med.* 67:1-22, 1967. Bellevue Hosp., Second (Cornell) Med. Div.; Cornell Univ., Med. Coll., New York, NY.

266   42   **Lutzner M, Edelson R, Schein P, Green I, Kirkpatrick C & Ahmed A.** Cutaneous T-cell lymphomas: the Sezary syndrome, mycosis fungoides, and related disorders. *Ann. Intern. Med.* 83:534-52, 1975. NIH, NCI, Bethesda, MD.

A	B	C	D
	178	20	*Maki D G, Goldmann D A & Rhame F S. Infection control in intravenous therapy. *Ann. Intern. Med.* 79:867-87, 1973. US Dept. HEW, Ctrs. Dis. Control, Atlanta, GA; Boston City Hosp., Harvard Med. Serv., MA. (33/84/CP)
	283	15	Maroko P R & Braunwald E. Modification of myocardial infarction size after coronary occlusion. *Ann. Intern. Med.* 79:720-33, 1973. Peter Bent Brigham Hosp., Dept. Med.; Harvard Univ., Med. Sch., Boston, MA.
	150	8	Massry S G, Coburn J W, Lee D B N, Jowsey J & Kleeman C R. Skeletal resistance to parathyroid hormone in renal failure. *Ann. Intern. Med.* 78:357-64, 1973. Cedars-Sinai Med. Ctr., Renal Hypertens. Serv., Med. Res. Inst. & Dept. Med.; Vet. Admin., Dept. Med.; Wadsworth Hosp. Ctr., Dept. Med.; UCLA, Sch. Med., Los Angeles, CA; Mayo Clin. Mayo Fdn., Sect. Orthoped. Res., Rochester, MN.
	177	6	McCarty D J & Hollander J L. Identification of urate crystals in gouty synovial fluid. *Ann. Intern. Med.* 54:452-60, 1961. Hosp. Univ. Pennsylvania, Philadelphia, PA.
	267	14	McCarty D J, Kohn N N & Faires J S. The significance of calcium phosphate crystals in the synovial fluid of arthritic patients: the "pseudogout syndrome." *Ann. Intern. Med.* 56:711-37, 1962. Hahnemann Univ., Sch. Med. & Hosp., Philadelphia, PA.
	194	2	McDowell F, Lee J E, Swift T, Sweet R D, Ogsbury J S & Kessler J T. Treatment of Parkinson's syndrome with L dihydroxyphenylalanine (levodopa). *Ann. Intern. Med.* 72:29-35, 1970. Cornell Univ., Med. Coll.; NY Hosp., NY.
	227	7	Miller D G. The association of immune disease and malignant lymphoma. *Ann. Intern. Med.* 66:507-21, 1967. Mem. Sloan-Kettering Cancer Ctr., Mem. Hosp. Cancer Allied Dis. & Sloan-Kettering Inst. Cancer Res.; Cornell Univ., Med. Coll., New York, NY.
	191	2	Miller D G. Patterns of immunological deficiency in lymphomas and leukemias. *Ann. Intern. Med.* 57:703-16, 1962. Mem. Sloan-Kettering Cancer Ctr., Sloan-Kettering Inst. Cancer Res. & Mem. Hosp. Cancer Allied Dis.; James Ewing Hosp., Dept. Med.; Cornell Univ., Med. Coll., New York, NY.
	170	2	Morton D L, Holmes E C, Eilber F R & Wood W C. Immunological aspects of neoplasia: a rational basis for immunotherapy. *Ann. Intern. Med.* 74:587-604, 1971. NIH, NCI, Bethesda, MD.
4	211	3	Nelson D H, Meakin J W & Thorn G W. ACTH-producing pituitary tumors following adrenalectomy for Cushing's syndrome. *Ann. Intern. Med.* 52:560-9, 1960. Harvard Univ., Med. Sch.; Peter Bent Brigham Hosp., Boston, MA.
	211	31	Notman D D, Kurata N & Tan E M. Profiles of antinuclear antibodies in systemic rheumatic diseases. *Ann. Intern. Med.* 83:464-9, 1975. Scripps Clin. Res. Fdn., Div. Allergy Immunol., La Jolla, CA.
	149	0	Olson R E. "Excess lactate" and anaerobiosis. *Ann. Intern. Med.* 59:960-2, 1963. Univ. Pittsburgh, Grad. Sch. Publ. Hlth., PA.
	223	6	Ostrander L D, Francis T, Hayner N S, Kjelsberg M O & Epstein F H. The relationship of cardiovascular disease to hyperglycemia. *Ann. Intern. Med.* 62:1188-98, 1965. Univ. Michigan, Sch. Publ. Hlth., Ann Arbor, MI.
	159	3	Pendras J P & Erickson R V. Hemodialysis: a successful therapy for chronic uremia. *Ann. Intern. Med.* 64:293-311, 1966. Swedish Hosp., Seattle Artif. Kidney Ctr., Seattle, WA.
	201	40	Popovich R P, Moncrief J W, Nolph K D, Ghods A J, Twardowski Z J & Pyle W K. Continuous ambulatory peritoneal dialysis. *Ann. Intern. Med.* 88:449-56, 1978. Univ. Texas, Dept. Chem. Eng. & Biomed. Eng. Program; Austin Diagnost. Clin., Dept. Med., TX; Harry S. Truman Vet. Admin. Hosp., Dept Med.; Univ. Missouri, Med. Ctr., Columbia, MO.
6	154	0	Popper H & Schaffner F. Drug-induced hepatic injury. *Ann. Intern. Med.* 51:1230-52, 1959. Mount Sinai Med. Ctr., Mount Sinai Hosp., New York, NY.
	152	3	Posen S. Alkaline phosphatase. *Ann. Intern. Med.* 67:183-203, 1967. Univ. Sydney, Dept. Med., Australia.
	178	3	*Posen S, Neale F C & Clubb J S. Heat inactivation in the study of human alkaline phosphatases. *Ann. Intern. Med.* 62:1234-43, 1965. Univ. Sydney, Dept. Med.; Sydney Hosp., Dept. Biochem., Australia. (17/84/CP)
	247	6	Prockop D J & Kivirikko K I. Relationship of hydroxyproline excretion in urine to collagen metabolism. *Ann. Intern. Med.* 66:1243-66, 1967. Univ. Pennsylvania, Sch. Med.; Philadelphia Gen. Hosp., PA.
	186	3	Rifkind D, Faris T D & Hill R B. *Pneumocystis carinii* pneumonia. *Ann. Intern. Med.* 65:943-56, 1966. Univ. Colorado, Med. Ctr.; Vet. Admin. Hosp., Denver, CO.
	162	4	Rifkind D, Goodman N & Hill R B. The clinical significance of cytomegalovirus infection in renal transplant recipients. *Ann. Intern. Med.* 66:1116-28, 1967. Univ. Colorado, Med. Ctr., Denver, CO.

A	B	C	D
	322	25	**Robbins J H, Kraemer K H, Lutzner M A, Festoff B W & Coon H G.** Xeroderma pigmentosum. *Ann. Intern. Med.* 80:221-48, 1974. NIH, NCI, Bethesda, MD.

| | 165 | 22 | **Rosen S W, Weintraub B D, Vaitukaitis J L, Sussman H H, Hershman J M & Muggia F M.** Placental proteins and their subunits as tumor markers. *Ann. Intern. Med.* 82:71-83, 1975. NIH, NIAMDD, Bethesda, MD. |

| | 179 | 12 | **Rosenow E C.** The spectrum of drug-induced pulmonary disease. *Ann. Intern. Med.* 77:977-91, 1972. Mayo Clin. and Mayo Fdn., Rochester, MN. |

| | 187 | 3 | **Rozencweig M, Von Hoff D D, Slavik M & Muggia F M.** *Cis*-diamminedichloroplatinum (II). *Ann. Intern. Med.* 86:803-12, 1977. NIH, NCI, Bethesda, MD. |

| | 228 | 17 | **Samter M & Beers R F.** Intolerance to aspirin. *Ann. Intern. Med.* 68:975-83, 1968. Univ. Illinois, Coll. Med., Chicago, IL. |

| | 159 | 29 | **Schein P S, DeVita V T, Hubbard S, Chabner B A, Canellos G P, Berard C & Young R C.** Bleomycin, adriamycin, cyclophosphamide, vincristine, and prednisone (BACOP) combination chemotherapy in the treatment of advanced diffuse histiocytic lymphoma. *Ann. Intern. Med.* 85:417-22, 1976. NIH, NCI, Bethesda, MD. |

| | 159 | 16 | **Schimpff S C, Greene W H, Young V M, Fortner C L, Jepsen L, Cusack N, Block J B & Wiernik P H.** Infection prevention in acute nonlymphocytic leukemia. *Ann. Intern. Med.* 82:351-8, 1975. Univ. Maryland Hosp., Baltimore, MD. |

| | 152 | 1 | **Shils M E.** Renal disease and the metabolic effects of tetracycline. *Ann. Intern. Med.* 58:389-408, 1963. Mem. Sloan-Kettering Cancer Ctr., Sloan-Kettering Inst. Cancer Res. & Mem. Hosp. Cancer Allied Dis.; James Ewing Hosp., Dept. Med.; Cornell Univ., Med. Coll., New York, NY. |

| | 171 | 9 | **Smith J W, Seidl L G & Cluff L E.** Studies on the epidemiology of adverse drug reactions. *Ann. Intern. Med.* 65:629-40, 1966. Johns Hopkins Univ., Sch. Med., Baltimore, MD; Univ. Florida, Coll. Med., Gainesville, FL. |

| | 197 | 6 | **Spark R F & Melby J C.** Hypertension and low plasma renin activity: presumptive evidence for mineralocorticoid excess. *Ann. Intern. Med.* 75:831-6, 1971. Harvard Univ., Sch. Med.; Beth Israel Hosp.; Boston Univ., Sch. Med. & Univ. Hosp., MA. |

| | 308 | 17 | *****Tedesco F J, Barton R W & Alpers D H.** Clindamycin-associated colitis. *Ann. Intern. Med.* 81:429-33, 1974. Washington Univ., Sch. Med., St. Louis, MO. (25/84/CP) |

| | 250 | 21 | **Thomson P D, Melmon K L, Richardson J A, Cohn K, Steinbrunn W, Cudihee R & Rowland M.** Lidocaine pharmacokinetics in advanced heart failure, liver disease, and renal failure in humans. *Ann. Intern. Med.* 78:499-508, 1973. Univ. California, Med. Ctr., San Francisco, CA. |

| | 154 | 6 | **Tong M J, Sun S-C, Schaeffer B T, Chang N-K, Lo K-J & Peters R L.** Hepatitis-associated antigen and hepatocellular carcinoma in Taiwan. *Ann. Intern. Med.* 75:687-91, 1971. USN, Naval Med. Res. Unit No. 2, Depts. Clin. Invest. & Pathol.; Chinese Vet. Gen. Hosp., Depts. Gastroenterol. & Med. Res., Taipei, Taiwan; USC, Sch. Med.; John Wesley Hosp., Los Angeles, CA. |

| | 163 | 18 | **Waldmann T A, Blaese R M, Broder S & Krakauer R S.** Disorders of suppressor immunoregulatory cells in the pathogenesis of immunodeficiency and autoimmunity. *Ann. Intern. Med.* 88:226-38, 1978. NIH, NCI, Bethesda, MD. |

| | 182 | 10 | **Waldmann T A, Strober W & Blaese R M.** Immunodeficiency disease and malignancy. *Ann. Intern. Med.* 77:605-28, 1972. NIH, NCI, Bethesda, MD. |

| | 154 | 17 | **Walzer P D, Perl D P, Krogstad D J, Rawson P G & Schultz M G.** *Pneumocystis carinii* pneumonia in the United States. *Ann. Intern. Med.* 80:83-93, 1974. US Dept. HEW, Ctrs. Dis. Control, Atlanta, GA. |

| 28 | 157 | 12 | **Wartman W B & Hellerstein H K.** The incidence of heart disease in 2,000 consecutive autopsies. *Ann. Intern. Med.* 28:41-65, 1948. Case Western Reserve Univ., Inst. Pathol.; Univ. Hosps. Cleveland, OH. |

| | 172 | 3 | **Weil M H, Shubin H & Biddle M.** Shock caused by gram-negative microorganisms. *Ann. Intern. Med.* 60:384-400, 1964. USC, Sch. Med.; Los Angeles Cty. Hosp., CA. |

| 10 | 166 | 0 | **Wiener A S, Unger L J, Cohen L & Feldman J.** Type-specific cold auto-antibodies as a cause of acquired hemolytic anemia and hemolytic transfusion reactions: biologic test with bovine red cells. *Ann. Intern. Med.* 44:221-40, 1956. Jewish Hosp. Brooklyn, Div. Immunohematol.; Off. Chief Med. Examiner NYC, Serolog. Lab.; NYU, Med. Ctr., NY. |

| | 281 | 16 | **Wilson W E C, Kirkpatrick C H & Talmage D W.** Suppression of immunologic responsiveness in uremia. *Ann. Intern. Med.* 62:1-14, 1965. Univ. Colorado, Med. Ctr., Denver, CO. |

| | 152 | 12 | **Yagoda A, Mukherji B, Young C, Etcubanas E, Lamonte C, Smith J R, Tan C T C & Krakoff I H.** Bleomycin, an antitumor antibiotic. *Ann. Intern. Med.* 77:861-70, 1972. Mem. Sloan-Kettering Cancer Ctr., Sloan-Kettering Inst. Cancer Res. & Mem. Hosp. Cancer Allied Dis., New York, NY. |

A	B	C	D

7 256 2 *Zieve L. Jaundice, hyperlipemia and hemolytic anemia: a heretofore unrecognized syndrome associated with alcoholic fatty liver and cirrhosis. *Ann. Intern. Med.* 48:471-96, 1958. Vet. Admin. Hosp., Dept. Med. & Radioisotope Serv.; Univ. Minnesota, Minneapolis, MN. (39/83/CP)

190 35 **Zwillich C W, Sutton F D, Neff T A, Cohn W M, Matthay R A & Weinberger M M.** Theophylline-induced seizures in adults. *Ann. Intern. Med.* 82:784-7, 1975. Univ. Colorado, Med. Ctr. & Univ. Hosps., Denver, CO.

Table 2: Frequency distribution of highly cited articles in *Annals of Internal Medicine*, 1961-1982 *SCI*®. A=number of citations. B=number of articles receiving that number of citations. C=percent of articles examined (n=1098).

A	B	C
≥ 500	2	.2
400-499	4	.4
300-399	4	.4
250-299	11	1.0
200-249	19	1.7
150-199	57	5.2
100-149	181	16.5
75-99	259	23.6
50-74	561	51.1

Table 3: Geographic areas represented by the 101 most-cited articles published in *Annals of Internal Medicine*, listed in descending order of the number of papers produced. A=number of papers. B=number of multinational collaborations. C=nationality of collaborators.

Country	A	B	C
United States	97	3	Japan,
Maryland	31		Switzerland,
Massachusetts	14		Taiwan
New York	14		
Pennsylvania	10		
Minnesota	9		
California	6		
Colorado	4		
Michigan	4		
Georgia	2		
Missouri	2		
Texas	2		
Washington	2		
Alabama	1		
Arkansas	1		
Florida	1		
Illinois	1		
Indiana	1		
Ohio	1		
Tennessee	1		
Virginia	1		
Australia	3	0	
Japan	1	1	US
Switzerland	1	1	US
Taiwan	1	1	US
Uganda	1	0	

was stated that Australia antigen (Au) was the hepatitis virus. This subsequently led to the identification of the hepatitis B virus (HBV), the development of methods for the diagnosis of hepatitis B, the prevention of post-transfusion hepatitis, the control of hepatitis in high-risk environments, a vaccine against hepatitis B, and the recognition of the role of HBV in the causation of primary hepatocellular carcinoma (PHC)."[9] Blumberg also is a coauthor with W.T. London and A.I. Sutnick, Institute of Cancer Research, Fox Chase Cancer Center, of a 1969 *Annals* paper on Australia antigen and acute viral hepatitis. Blumberg and D. Carleton Gajdusek shared the 1976 Nobel prize for their work on the origin and dissemination of infectious disease.

Burnet and Peter Medawar were awarded the 1960 Nobel prize in recognition of their discovery of acquired immunological tolerance. Burnet is the coauthor with M.C. Holmes, Walter and Eliza Hall Institute of Medical Research, Melbourne, Australia, of a 1963 *Annals* paper on autoimmune disease in a particular strain of mice designated as NZB. The authors compared the pattern and manifestation of autoimmune disease in mice with that in humans.

The authors of the *Annals* papers in this study came from six countries, but the overwhelming majority were based in the US. Table 3 lists the authors' national affiliations in order of the number of papers from each country. For the US, we also show the number of papers from individual states. US authors account for 97 of the 101 papers, three of which were coauthored with researchers from Japan, Switzerland, and Taiwan. Of the 97 US papers, 31 were by authors based in Maryland—one each at the

Table 4: Article-by-article analysis of 1977 source items published by *Annals of Internal Medicine*. A=number published in 1977. B=number cited from 1977-1982. C=percent citedness (B/A). D=number of 1977-1982 citations. E=cited impact (D/B). F=total impact (D/A).

	A	B	C	D	E	F
Letters	281	112	39.9	580	5.2	2.1
Articles	135	129	95.6	4992	38.7	37.0
Editorials	35	27	77.1	275	10.2	7.9
Notes	73	66	90.4	1284	19.5	17.6
Reviews	19	19	100.0	1090	57.4	57.4
All Others	15	3	20.0	156	52.0	10.4
TOTAL	558	356	63.8	8377	23.5	15.0

Table 5: Six-year impact factors for 1977 source items published in *Annals of Internal Medicine* and nine other general and internal-medicine journals. Impacts were calculated by dividing 1977-1982 citations to a journal's 1977 source items by the number of 1977 source items it published. The number of 1977 source items follows each journal title in parentheses.

Journal	Six-Year Impact for					
	Articles	Letters	Editorials	Notes	Reviews	All Others
Ann. Intern. Med. (558)	37.0	2.1	7.9	17.6	57.4	10.4
Arch. Intern. Med. (335)	10.7	.8	3.7	2.8	42.3	.5
Brit. Med. J. (3486)	16.6	.9	.3	5.8	11.6	.1
Can. Med. Assn. J. (765)	3.1	.4	.6	2.0	5.0	—
Deut. Med. Wochenschr. (725)	4.3	.5	1.5	.6	3.8	2.0
JAMA—J. Am. Med. Assn. (1605)	14.8	.6	2.1	6.3	23.5	—
Lancet (3149)	33.2	4.4	.2	4.4	—	.2
Med. J. Australia (1228)	3.6	.2	.2	1.1	3.6	.1
N. Engl. J. Med. (1772)	54.0	1.9	8.0	2.5	57.6	9.3
Nouv. Presse Med. (884)	3.7	1.4	1.1	2.7	—	—

University of Maryland and Johns Hopkins University Medical School, Baltimore, and 29 from NIH. Keep in mind that *Annals* regularly publishes transcripts of NIH clinical staff conferences, many of which appear in this study. Although *Annals* is based in Philadelphia, the journal is not obviously biased in favor of papers from Pennsylvania institutions—just 10 papers were by authors from Pennsylvania. However, a more thorough analysis of *all* papers published in *Annals*, not just the most-cited papers, would be required to determine the general validity of this assertion.

Australia accounts for three papers, two from the University of Sydney and one from the Walter and Eliza Hall Institute of Medical Research. One paper was authored by researchers from the Uganda-based Makerere University Medical School and the Uganda Cancer Institute, Kampala.

In these analyses of the most-cited articles from individual journals, it is easy to overlook many other types of communications that are published in them—letters to the editor, notes, corrections, editorials, and so on. For example, Table 4 presents data on the source items published by *Annals* in 1977, the number of items that were cited from 1977 to 1982, the number of 1977-1982 citations, cited impact, and total impact. In this study, total impact is calculated by dividing 1977-1982 citations by the total number of 1977 source items. Cited impact is determined by dividing 1977-1982 citations by the number of *cited* 1977 items.

Clearly, *Annals* has published more letters than any other type of source item. Only 40 percent of the 281 letters it published in 1977 were cited at least once from 1977 to 1982. The average letter in *Annals* had an impact of 2.1. On the other hand, 96 percent of the 1977 research articles in *Annals* were cited, and the average article had a six-year impact of 37.0. All 19 review articles published that year were cited, with an average six-year impact of 57.4.

For purposes of comparison, Table 5 presents six-year impact data for 1977 source items published in several general and internal-medicine journals, including *Annals*. I should caution that these data may not be *directly* comparable. Journals may have different definitions of what they consider to be "articles," "letters," "reviews," and so on. With this caveat in mind, the data confirm that *Annals* is indeed one of the high-impact medical journals. The impact of the average *Annals* letter is second only to that of *The Lancet*. *New England Journal of Medicine* is the only journal with a higher impact than *Annals* for the research articles that they published. When we consider the impact of review articles, *Annals* and *New England Journal of Medicine* share first place among the 10 journals listed.

We will continue to identify citation classics from other significant medical journals in the coming months. This series of essays also will report on journals from other fields, as well as the major multidisciplinary journals of science.

* * * * *

My thanks to Abigail W. Grissom and Alfred Welljams-Dorof for their help in the preparation of this essay. ©1984 ISI

REFERENCES

1. **Garfield E.** 100 classics from the *New England Journal of Medicine. Current Contents* (25):3-10, 18 June 1984.
2. ⸻. 100 classics from *The Lancet. Current Contents* (39):3-13, 24 September 1984.
3. **Huth E J & Van Steenburgh K C.** Annals of Internal Medicine: the first 50 years. *Ann. Intern. Med.* 87:103-10, 1977.
4. **Garfield E.** The history and mission of ISI Press. *Essays of an information scientist.* Philadelphia: ISI Press, 1983. Vol. 5. p. 768-73.
5. **Miller M D.** Ratings of medical journals by family physician educators. *J. Fam. Pract.* 15:517-9, 1982.
6. **Garfield E.** The 1979 articles most cited from 1979 to 1981. 1. Life sciences. *Essays of an information scientist.* Philadelphia: ISI Press, 1983. Vol. 5. p. 575-90.
7. **Kannel W B.** Citation Classic. Commentary on *Ann. Intern. Med.* 74:1-12, 1971. *Current Contents/Life Sciences* (29):18, 18 July 1983.
8. **DeVita V T.** Citation Classic. Commentary on *Ann. Intern. Med.* 73:881-95, 1970. *Current Contents/Clinical Practice* (12):10, 19 March 1979.
9. **Blumberg B S.** Citation Classic. Commentary on *Ann. Intern. Med.* 66:924-31, 1967. *Current Contents/Life Sciences* (28):18, 11 July 1983.

Current Comments®

The 1982 Articles Most Cited in 1982 and 1983. 2. Physical Sciences

Number 48   November 26, 1984

We recently identified and discussed the 1982 life-sciences papers that were most cited in 1982 and 1983.[1] In this essay, we present the most-cited 1982 physical-sciences papers. These studies highlight areas of intense activity in current research, as indicated by rapid citation. That is, by identifying the papers that are highly cited soon after publication, we can get a good idea of the topics that have attracted significant attention within the research community. However, we make no claim that these most-cited papers necessarily represent the "best" or "most important" research. Many papers not included here will achieve high impact over the next few years, and they will be recognized as seminal contributions. Nevertheless, the papers presented in this study will continue to be highly cited for many years. These papers are interesting precisely because their recognition was *immediate*—that is, they are "instant" classics.

Table 1 presents full bibliographic information on the 106 papers in this study. They are arranged in alphabetic order by first author. Column A provides the number of citations each paper received in 1982, and 1983 citations are listed in column B. The total number of citations for this two-year period is given in column C. The average paper received 42 citations: 8 in 1982 and 34 in 1983. The most-cited paper received 105 citations. Ten papers were cited 30 times each, the threshold for inclusion in this study. Keep in mind that the average pa-

per or book chapter cited in *Science Citation Index®* (*SCI®*) each year receives no more than one or two citations.

Clearly, the 106 papers in Table 1 were cited at a rate far above that of the average paper. In fact, many of these have already become part of the "core" literature of research fronts generated from the *SCI* and *Social Sciences Citation Index®* (*SSCI®*) files in 1982 and 1983. Briefly, a research front consists of current papers that cited any of a group of high-impact articles that were frequently cited *together*, or co-cited. ISI®'s co-citation clustering algorithm has been described previously.[2] What you should remember is that research fronts symbolize individual clusters of subject-related research. By examining the titles of the *citing* articles, we get a very clear and concise definition of what the research cluster is about. That is, the citing authors *themselves* categorize the literature into discrete clusters and describe their cognitive content.

Of the 106 papers, 94 are core papers in 53 separate research fronts. These papers are indicated in Table 1 by code-numbers following the reference. Table 2 provides the names of 19 research fronts that include at least two papers from this study in their cores (column C). The total number of core and citing papers for each research front is shown in column D. For reasons of space, we cannot list the 34 research fronts with only one of the most-cited physical-sciences papers in their cores. That infor-

Table 1: The 1982 physical sciences articles most cited in 1982-1983. Articles are listed in alphabetic order by first author. The authors' addresses follow each citation. Code numbers indicate the 1982 *SCI®* research front specialties for which these are core papers. Code numbers with an asterisk (*) indicate the 1983 *SCI/SSCI®* research fronts for which these are core papers. A=citations received, 1982. B=citations received, 1983. C=total citations received, 1982-1983. D=bibliographic data.

A	B	C	D
2	30	32	**Adler S L.** Einstein gravity as a symmetry-breaking effect in quantum field theory. *Rev. Mod. Phys.* 54:729-66, 1982. Inst. Adv. Study, Princeton, NJ.
20	68	88	**Albrecht A & Steinhardt P J.** Cosmology for grand unified theories with radiatively induced symmetry breaking. *Phys. Rev. Lett.* 48:1220-3, 1982. Univ. Pennsylvania, Dept. Phys., Philadelphia, PA. 82-0029; *83-0319
0	36	36	**Alexander S & Orbach R.** Density of states on fractals: 'fractons.' *J. Phys.—Lett.* 43:L625-31, 1982. Hebrew Univ., Racah Inst., Jerusalem, Israel; Inst. Phys. Chem. Ind., Paris, France. *83-0506
11	21	32	**Alvarado S, Campagna M & Hopster H.** Surface magnetism of Ni(100) near the critical region by spin-polarized electron scattering. *Phys. Rev. Lett.* 48:51-4, 1982. Julich Nucl. Res. Ctr., Inst. Solid-State Res., FRG. *83-0683
6	74	80	**Ando T, Fowler A B & Stern F.** Electronic properties of two-dimensional systems. *Rev. Mod. Phys.* 54:437-672, 1982. Univ. Tsukuba, Inst. Appl. Phys., Ibaraki, Japan; IBM, Thomas J. Watson Res. Ctr., Yorktown Heights, NY. *83-0898
2	42	44	**Backer D C, Kulkarni S R, Heiles C, Davis M M & Goss W M.** Letter to editor. (A millisecond pulsar.) *Nature* 300:615-8, 1982. Univ. California, Astron. Dept., Berkeley, CA; Cornell Univ., Natl. Astron. Ionosph. Ctr., Arecibo, PR; Kapteyn Astron. Inst., Groningen, the Netherlands. *83-0638
2	48	50	**Bak P.** Commensurate phases, incommensurate phases and the devil's staircase. *Rep. Progr. Phys.* 45:587-629, 1982. H.C. Oersted Inst., Copenhagen, Denmark. *83-1602
5	55	60	**Barber M, Bordoli R S, Elliot G J, Sedgwick R D & Tyler A N.** Fast atom bombardment mass spectrometry. *Anal. Chem.* 54:645-57A, 1982. Univ. Manchester, Inst. Sci. Technol., UK. *83-0072
7	28	35	**Barbieri R, Ferrara S, Nanopoulos D V & Stelle K S.** Supergravity, R invariance and spontaneous supersymmetry breaking. *Phys. Lett. B* 113:219-22, 1982. Higher Normal Sch.; INFN, Pisa, Italy; CERN, Geneva, Switzerland; Normal Coll., Lab. Theor. Phys., Paris, France.
0	58	58	**Barbieri R, Ferrara S & Savoy C A.** Gauge models with spontaneously broken local supersymmetry. *Phys. Lett. B* 119:343-7, 1982. Higher Normal Sch.; INFN, Pisa, Italy; CERN; Univ. Geneva, Dept. Theor. Phys., Switzerland. *83-1184
6	32	38	**Beall G, Bander M & Soni A.** Constraint on the mass scale of a left-right-symmetric electroweak theory from the K_L-K_S mass difference. *Phys. Rev. Lett.* 48:848-51, 1982. Univ. California, Depts. Phys., Irvine & Los Angeles, CA. *83-2071
7	39	46	**Bhanot G, Heller U M & Neuberger H.** The quenched Eguchi-Kawai model. *Phys. Lett. B* 113:47-50, 1982. Inst. Adv. Study, Princeton, NJ. *83-2705
12	18	30	**Brezin E & Drouffe J M.** Continuum limit of a Z_2 lattice gauge theory. *Nucl. Phys. B* 200:93-106, 1982. CENS, Gif-sur-Yvette, France. *83-0966
8	29	37	**Bridge H S, Bagenal F, Belcher J W, Lazarus A J, McNutt R L, Sullivan J D, Gazis P R, Hartle R E, Ogilvie K W, Scudder J D, Sittler E C, Eviatar A, Siscoe G L, Goertz C K & Vasyliunas V M.** Plasma observations near Saturn: initial results from Voyager 2. *Science* 215:563-70, 1982. MIT, Ctr. Space Res. & Dept. Phys., Cambridge, MA; NASA, Goddard Space Flight Ctr., Greenbelt, MD; Univ. California, Dept. Atmos. Sci., Los Angeles, CA; Univ. Iowa, Dept. Phys. Astron., Iowa City, IA; Max Planck Soc. Adv. Sci., Inst. Aeronom., Katlenburg-Lindau, FRG. *83-3458
12	71	83	**Cabrera B.** First results from a superconductive detector for moving magnetic monopoles. *Phys. Rev. Lett.* 48:1378-81, 1982. Stanford Univ., Phys. Dept., CA. *83-0319
1	44	45	**Callan C G.** Dyon-fermion dynamics. *Phys. Rev. D—Part. Fields* 26:2058-68, 1982. Princeton Univ., Joseph Henry Labs., NJ. *83-0319
2	54	56	**Callan C G.** Disappearing dyons. *Phys. Rev. D—Part. Fields* 25:2141-6, 1982. Princeton Univ., Joseph Henry Labs., NJ. *83-0319
7	25	32	**Cecotti S & Girardello L.** Functional measure, topology and dynamical supersymmetry breaking. *Phys. Lett. B* 110:39-43, 1982. Harvard Univ., Lyman Lab. Phys. & Gordon McKay Lab., Cambridge, MA. *83-1184

A	B	C	D

0 33 33 **Chamseddine A H, Arnowitt R & Nath P.** Locally supersymmetric grand unification. *Phys. Rev. Lett.* 49:970-4, 1982. Northeastern Univ., Dept. Phys., Boston, MA. *83-1184

10 24 34 **Condon J J, Condon M A, Gisler G & Puschell J J.** Strong radio sources in bright spiral galaxies. II. Rapid star formation and galaxy-galaxy interactions. *Astrophys. J.* 252:102-24, 1982. Natl. Radio Astron. Observ., Charlottesville; Virginia Polytech. Inst. State Univ., Blacksburg, VA. *83-4681

12 21 33 **Crabtree R H, Mellea M F, Mihelcic J M & Quirk J M.** Alkane dehydrogenation by iridium complexes. *J. Amer. Chem Soc.* 104:107-13, 1982. Yale Univ., Dept. Chem., New Haven, CT. *83-3652

1 51 52 **Cremmer E, Ferrara S, Girardello L & Van Proeyen A.** Coupling supersymmetric Yang-Mills theories to supergravity. *Phys. Lett. B* 116:231-7, 1982. Normal Coll., Lab. Theor. Phys., Paris, France; CERN, Geneva, Switzerland; Univ. Milan, Inst. Phys.; INFN, Milan, Italy. *83-1184

11 27 38 **Davis M, Huchra J, Latham D W & Tonry J.** A survey of galaxy redshifts. II. The large scale space distribution. *Astrophys. J.* 253:423-45, 1982. Harvard Univ., Harvard-Smithsonian Ctr. Astrophys., Cambridge, MA. *83-1720

5 27 32 **De Marzo C, De Palma M, Distante A, Favuzzi C, Germinario G, Lavopa P, Maggi G, Posa F, Ranieri A, Selvaggi G, Spinelli P, Waldner F, Bialas A, Czyz W, Coghen T, Eskreys A, Eskreys K, Fialkowski K, Kisieliewska D, Madeysky B, Malecki P, Olkiewicz K, Pawlik D, Evans W H, Fry J R, Grant C, Houlden M, Morton A, Muirhead H, Shiers J, Antic M, Baker W, Bechteler H, Derado J, Eckardt V, Fent J, Freund P, Gebauer H J, Kahl T, Kalbach R, Manz A, Meinke R, Polakos P, Pretzl K P, Schmitz N, Seyboth P, Seyerlein J, Stopa C, Vranic D, Wolf G, Crijns F, Metzger W J, Pols C, Spuijbroek T, Schouten T & Sarma N.** A study of deep inelastic hadron-hadron collisions with a large acceptance calorimeter trigger. *Phys. Lett. B* 112:173-7, 1982. Univ. Bari, Inst. Phys.; INFN, Bari, Italy; Stanislaw Staszic Univ. Min. Met., Inst. Nucl. Phys. & Inst. Phys. Nucl. Tech.; Jagiellonian Univ., Kracow, Poland; Univ. Liverpool, UK; Max Planck Soc. Adv. Sci., Inst. Phys. Astrophys., Munich, FRG; Univ. Nijmegen; NIKHEE, the Netherlands; CERN, Geneva, Switzerland. *83-1757

10 28 38 **Dine M & Fischler W.** A phenomenological model of particle physics based on supersymmetry. *Phys. Lett. B* 110:227-31, 1982. Inst. Adv. Stud., Princeton, NJ; Univ. Pennsylvania, Dept. Phys., Philadelphia, PA.

1 34 35 **Dine M & Fischler W.** A supersymmetric GUT. *Nucl. Phys. B* 204:346-64, 1982. Inst. Adv. Stud., Princeton, NJ; Univ. Pennsylvania, Dept. Phys., Philadelphia, PA. *83-1184

1 34 35 **Doddrell D M, Pegg D T & Bendall M R.** Distortionless enhancement of NMR signals by polarization transfer. *J. Magn. Resonance* 48:323-7, 1982. Griffith Univ., Sch. Sci., Nathan, Australia. *83-1189

8 33 41 **Edwards C, Partridge R, Peck C, Porter F C, Antreasyan D, Gu Y E, Kollmann W, Richardson M, Strauch K, Wacker K, Weinstein A, Aschman D, Burnett T, Cavalli-Sforza M, Coyne D, Newman C, Sadrozinski H F W, Gelphman D, Hofstadter R, Horisberger R, Kirkbride I, Kalanoski H, Konigsmann K, Lee R, Liberman A, O'Reilly J, Osterheld A, Pollock B, Tompkins J, Bloom E, Bulos F, Chestnut R, Gaiser J, Godfrey G, Kiesling C, Lockman W, Oreglia M & Scharre D L.** Evidence for 77 resonance in *J/4* radiative decays. *Phys. Rev. Lett.* 48:458-61, 1982. CalTech, Phys. Dept., Pasadena, CA; Harvard Univ., Phys. Dept., Cambridge, MA; Princeton Univ., Phys. Dept., NJ; Stanford Univ., Phys. Dept. & Stanford Linear Accel. Ctr., CA. *83-1583

14 50 64 **Eguchi T & Kawai H.** Reduction of dynamical degrees of freedom in the large-*N* gauge theory. *Phys. Rev. Lett.* 48:1063-6, 1982. Univ. Tokyo, Fac. Sci., Japan. *83-2705

17 24 41 **Einhorn M B & Jones D R T.** The weak mixing angle and unification mass in supersymmetric SU(5). *Nucl. Phys. B* 196:475-88, 1982. Univ. Michigan, Randall Lab. Phys., Ann Arbor, MI. 82-0885

8 54 62 **Ellis J, Ibanez L & Ross G G.** Grand unification with large supersymmetry breaking. *Phys. Lett. B* 113:283-7, 1982. Univ. Oxford, All Souls Coll., Dept. Theor. Phys. & Pembroke Coll.; SERC, Rutherford Appleton Lab., Chilton, UK; Madrid Autonom. Univ., Dept. Theor. Phys., Spain. *83-1184

14 28 42 **Ellis J & Nanopoulos D V.** Flavour-changing neutral interactions in broken supersymmetric theories. *Phys. Lett. B* 110:44-8, 1982. CERN, Geneva, Switzerland. *83-1184

7 26 33 **Emery V J, Bruinsma R & Barisic S.** Electron-electron umklapp scattering in organic superconductors. *Phys. Rev. Lett.* 48:1039-43, 1982. Brookhaven Natl. Lab., Upton, NY; Univ. Paris XI, Lab. Phys. Solid-State, Orsay, France. 82-2192

A	B	C	D

15 32 47 **Fincher C R, Chen C-E, Heeger A J, MacDiarmid A G & Hastings J B.** Structural determination of the symmetry-breaking parameter in $trans$-$(CH)_x$. *Phys. Rev. Lett.* 48:100-4, 1982. Univ. Pennsylvania, Lab. Res. Struct. Mat., Philadelphia, PA; Brookhaven Natl. Lab., Upton, NY. *83-3402

5 25 30 **Fyfe C A, Gobbi G C, Klinowski J, Thomas J M & Ramdas S.** Resolving crystallographically distinct tetrahedral sites in silicalite and ZSM-5 by solid-state NMR. *Nature* 296:530-3, 1982. Univ. Guelph, Dept. Chem., Ontario, Canada; Univ. Cambridge, Dept. Phys. Chem., UK. *83-3408

9 27 36 **Garoche P, Brusetti R, Jerome D & Bechgaard K.** Specific heat measurements of organic superconductivity in $(TMTSF)_2ClO_4$. *J. Phys.—Lett.* 43:L147-52, 1982. Univ. Paris XI, Lab. Phys. Solid-State, Orsay, France; H.C. Oersted Inst., Copenhagen, Denmark. *83-2192

4 30 34 **Giallorenzi T G, Bucaro J A, Dandridge A, Sigel G H, Cole J H, Rashleigh S C & Priest R G.** Optical fiber sensor technology. *IEEE J. Quantum Electron.* 18:626-65, 1982. USN, Naval Res. Lab., Washington, DC. *83-2512

15 41 56 **Girardello L & Grisaru M T.** Soft breaking of supersymmetry. *Nucl. Phys. B* 194:65-76, 1982. Harvard Univ., Gordon McKay Lab., Cambridge, MA; Brandeis Univ., Dept. Phys., Waltham, MA. *83-1184

6 27 33 **Gordon M S, Binkley J S, Pople J A, Pietro W J & Hehre W J.** Self-consistent molecular-orbital methods. 22. Small split-valence basis sets for second-row elements. *J. Amer. Chem. Soc.* 104:2797-803, 1982. N. Dakota State Univ., Dept. Chem., Fargo, ND; Carnegie-Mellon Univ., Dept. Chem., Pittsburgh, PA; Univ. California, Dept. Chem., Irvine, CA. *83-2634

1 29 30 **Grinstein G & Ma S.** Roughening and lower critical dimension in the random-field Ising model. *Phys. Rev. Lett.* 49:685-8, 1982. IBM, Thomas J. Watson Res. Ctr., Yorktown Heights, NY; Univ. California, Dept. Phys. & Inst. Pure Appl. Phys. Sci., San Diego, CA. *83-0316

0 32 32 **Guth A H & Pi S-Y.** Fluctuations in the new inflationary universe. *Phys. Rev. Lett.* 49: 1110-3, 1982. MIT, Dept. Phys.; Harvard Univ., Lyman Lab. Phys., Cambridge, MA; Univ. New Hampshire, Lab. Mech., Durham, NH. *83-0319

4 39 43 **Halperin B I.** Quantized Hall conductance, current-carrying edge states, and the existence of extended states in a two-dimensional disordered potential. *Phys. Rev. B—Condensed Matter* 25:2185-90, 1982. Harvard Univ., Lyman Lab. Phys., Cambridge, MA. *83-0897

11 27 38 **Hamber H, Marinari E, Parisi G & Rebbi C.** Spectroscopy in a lattice gauge theory. *Phys. Lett. B* 108:314-6, 1982. Brookhaven Natl. Lab., Upton, NY; Rome Univ., Inst. Phys.; INFN, Rome & Frascati, Italy. *83-0966

14 31 45 **Hasenfratz A, Kunszt Z, Hasenfratz P & Lang C B.** Hopping parameter expansion for the meson spectrum in SU(3) lattice QCD. *Phys. Lett. B* 110:289-94, 1982. Hungarian Acad. Sci., Cent. Res. Inst. Phys.; Eotvos Lorand Univ., Budapest, Hungary; CERN, Geneva, Switzerland. *83-0966

1 33 34 **Hawking S W.** The development of irregularities in a single bubble inflationary universe. *Phys. Lett. B* 115:295-7, 1982. Univ. Cambridge, Dept. Appl. Math. Theor. Phys., UK. *83-0319

22 39 61 **Hawking S W & Moss I G.** Supercooled phase transitions in the very early universe. *Phys. Lett B* 110:35-8, 1982. Univ. Cambridge, Dept. Appl. Math. Theor. Phys., UK. 82-0029; *83-0319

9 31 40 **Heiney P A, Birgeneau R J, Brown G S, Horn P M, Moncton D E & Stephens P W.** Freezing transition of monolayer xenon on graphite. *Phys. Rev. Lett.* 48:104-8, 1982. MIT, Dept. Phys., Cambridge, MA; Stanford Univ., Synchrotr. Radiat. Lab., CA; IBM, Thomas J. Watson Res. Ctr., Yorktown Heights; SUNY, Dept. Phys., Stony Brook, NY; Bell Labs., Murray Hill, NJ. *83-0707

5 30 35 **Henry C H.** Theory of the linewidth of semiconductor lasers. *IEEE J. Quantum Electron.* 18:259-64, 1982. Bell Labs., Murray Hill, NJ. *83-6088

10 25 35 **Hepburn J W, Northrup F J, Ogram G L, Polanyi J C & Williamson J M.** Rotationally inelastic scattering from surfaces $CO_{(g)} + LiF(001)$. *Chem. Phys. Lett.* 85:127-30, 1982. Univ. Toronto, Dept. Chem., Canada. *83-6088

4 35 39 **Herrmann W A.** The methylene bridge. *Advan. Organometal. Chem.* 20:159-263, 1982. Univ. Regensburg, Inst. Inorg. Chem., FRG. *83-1064

12 38 50 **Herrmann W A.** Organometallic aspects of the Fischer-Tropsch synthesis. *Angew. Chem. Int. Ed.* 21:117-30, 1982. Univ. Regensburg, Inst. Inorg. Chem., FRG. *83-1064

A   B   C   D

11   24   35   **Hirsch J E, Huberman B A & Scalapino D J.** Theory of intermittency. *Phys. Rev. A—Gen. Phys.* 25:519-32, 1982. Univ. California, Inst. Theor. Phys. & Dept. Phys., Santa Barbara; Xerox Palo Alto Res. Ctr., CA. *83-0321

6   24   30   **Hofmann A W & White W M.** Mantle plumes from ancient oceanic crust. *Earth Planet. Sci. Lett.* 57:421-36, 1982. Carnegie Inst. Washington, Dept. Terr. Magnet., Washington, DC.

13   31   44   **Holmes D E, Chen R T, Elliot K R & Kirkpatrick C G.** Stoichiometry-controlled compensation in liquid encapsulated Czochralski GaAs. *Appl. Phys. Lett.* 40:46-8, 1982. Rockwell Intl. Microelectron. Res. Dev. Ctr., Thousand Oaks, CA. *83-0019

0   43   43   **Ibanez L.** Locally supersymmetric SU(5) grand unification. *Phys. Lett. B* 118:73-8, 1982. CERN, Geneva, Switzerland. *83-1184

13   27   40   **Ibanez L & Ross G G.** $SU(2)_L \times U(1)$ symmetry breaking as a radiative effect of supersymmetry breaking in GUTs. *Phys. Lett. B* 110:215-20, 1982. Univ. Oxford, Dept. Theor. Phys., UK.

8   26   34   **Ishikawa K, Teper M & Schierholz G.** The glueball mass spectrum in QCD: first results of a lattice Monte Carlo calculation. *Phys. Lett. B* 110:399-405, 1982. DESY; Hamburg Univ., Inst. Theor. Phys. II, FRG. *83-0966

12   36   48   **Janowicz A H & Bergman R G.** C-H activation in completely saturated hydrocarbons: direct observation of M+R-H→M(R)(H). *J. Amer. Chem. Soc.* 104:352-4, 1982. Univ. California, Dept. Chem. & Lawrence Berkeley Lab., Berkeley, CA. *83-3652

0   44   44   **Jerome D & Schulz H J.** Organic conductors and superconductors. *Advan. Phys.* 31:299-490, 1982. Univ. Paris XI, Lab. Phys. Solid-State, Orsay; Max Von Laue-Paul Langevin Inst., Grenoble, France. *83-2192

7   25   32   **Kobayashi S, Yamamoto Y, Ito M & Kimura T.** Direct frequency modulation in AlGaAs semiconductor lasers. *IEEE J. Quantum Electron.* 18:582-95, 1982. Nippon Telegr. Tel. Publ. Corp., Musashino Elect. Commun. Lab., Tokyo & Ibaraki Elect. Commun. Lab., Japan. *83-0358

8   23   31   **Kroemer H.** Heterostructure bipolar transistors and integrated circuits. *Proc. IEEE* 70:13-25, 1982. Univ. California, Dept. Elect. Comput. Eng., Santa Barbara, CA. *83-0973

9   44   53   **Lagowski J, Gatos H C, Parsey J M, Wada K, Kaminska M & Walukiewicz W.** Origin of the 0.82-eV electron trap in GaAs and its annihilation by shallow donors. *Appl. Phys. Lett.* 40:342-4, 1982. MIT, Dept. Elect. Eng. Comput. Sci., Cambridge, MA. *83-0019

12   28   40   **Lane A L, Hord C W, West R A, Esposito L W, Coffeen D L, Sato M, Simmons K E, Pomphrey R B & Morris R B.** Photopolarimetry from Voyager 2: preliminary results on Saturn, Titan, and the rings. *Science* 215:537-43, 1982. CalTech, Jet Prop. Lab., Pasadena, CA; Univ. Colorado, Lab. Atmos. Space Phys., Boulder, CO; Goddard Inst. Space Stud., New York, NY. *83-3458

10   22   32   **Larson B C, White C W, Noggle T S & Mills D.** Synchrotron X-ray diffraction study of silicon during pulsed-laser annealing. *Phys. Rev. Lett.* 48:337-40, 1982. Oak Ridge Natl. Lab., Solid-State Div., TN; Cornell Univ., High Energy Synchrotr. Source & Sch. Appl. Eng. Phys., Ithaca, NY. *83-1053

33   72   105 **Linde A D.** A new inflationary universe scenario: a possible solution of the horizon, flatness, homogeneity, isotropy and primordial monopole problems. *Phys. Lett. B* 108:389-93, 1982. Acad. Sci. USSR, P.H. Lebedev Phys. Inst., Moscow, USSR. 82-0029; *83-0319

12   20   32   **Masamune S, Hanzawa Y, Murakami S, Bally T & Blount J H.** Cyclotrisilane $(R_2Si)_3$ and disilane ($R_2Si=SiR_2$) systems: synthesis and characterization. *J. Amer. Chem. Soc.* 104:1150-3, 1982. MIT, Dept. Chem., Cambridge, MA; Hoffmann-La Roche, Inc., Nutley, NJ. *83-1039

11   23   34   **Matsuoka T, Nagai H, Itaya Y, Noguchi Y, Suzuki Y & Ikegami T.** CW operation of DFB-BH GaInAsP/InP lasers in 1.5 μm wavelength region. *Electron. Lett.* 18:27-8, 1982. Nippon Telegr. Tel. Publ. Corp., Musashino Elect. Commun. Lab., Tokyo, Japan. *83-0409

7   28   35   **Mayer-Hasselwander H A, Bennett K, Bignami G F, Buccheri R, Caraveo P A, Hermsen W, Kanbach G, Lebrun F, Lichti G G, Masnou J L, Paul J A, Pinkau K, Sacco B, Scarsi L, Swanenburg B N & Wills R D.** Large-scale distribution of galactic gamma radiation observed by COS-B. *Astron. Astrophys.* 105:164-75, 1982. Huygens Lab., Cosm.-Ray Work. Grp., Leiden; Eur. Space Agcy., ESTEC, Noordwijk, the Netherlands; CNR, Cosm. Phys. Inst., Milan & Cosm. Phys. Data Inst., Palermo, Italy; Max Planck Soc. Adv. Sci., Inst. Phys. Astrophys. & Inst. Extraterr. Phys., Munich, FRG; CENS, Serv. Electron. Phys., Gif-sur-Yvette, France. *83-0638

A	B	C	D

10 20 30 **McNeal C J.** Symposium on fast atom and ion induced mass spectrometry of nonvolatile organic solids. *Anal. Chem.* 54:A43-50, 1982. Texas A&M Univ., Dept. Chem., College Station, TX. *83-0072

5 32 37 **Monceau P, Richard J & Renard M.** Charge-density-wave motion in NbSe$_3$. I. Studies of the differential resistance dV/dI. *Phys. Rev. B—Condensed Matter* 25:931-47, 1982. CNRS, Very Low Temp. Res. Ctr., Grenoble, France. *83-1805

11 31 42 **Monod P & Bouchiat H.** Equilibrium magnetization of a spin glass: is mean-field theory valid? *J. Phys.—Lett.* 43:L45-53, 1982. Univ. Paris XI, Lab. Phys. Solid-State, Orsay, France. *83-1782

14 17 31 **Nanopoulos D V & Tamvakis K.** Super cosmology. *Phys. Lett. B* 110:449-55, 1982. CERN, Geneva, Switzerland.

11 21 32 **Ness N F, Acuna M H, Behannon K W, Burlaga L F, Connerney J E P, Lepping R P & Neubauer F M.** Magnetic field studies by Voyager 2: preliminary results at Saturn. *Science* 215:558-63, 1982. NASA, Goddard Space Flight Ctr., Greenbelt, MD; Tech. Univ., Braunschweig, FRG.

5 27 32 **Oset E, Toki H & Weise W.** Pionic modes of excitation in nuclei. *Phys. Rep.* 83:281-380, 1982. Univ. Salamanca, Dept. Atom. Nucl. Phys., Spain; Michigan State Univ., Dept. Phys., East Lansing, MI; Univ. Regensburg, Inst. Theor. Phys., FRG. *83-2664

3 27 30 **Paalanen M A, Tsui D C & Gossard A C.** Quantized Hall effect at low temperatures. *Phys. Rev. B—Condensed Matter* 25:5566-9, 1982. Bell Labs., Murray Hill, NJ. *83-0897

14 17 31 **Pagels H & Primack J R.** Supersymmetry, cosmology, and new physics at teraelectronvolt energies. *Phys. Rev. Lett.* 48:223-6, 1982. Rockefeller Univ., New York, NY; Univ. California, Dept. Phys., Santa Cruz, CA.

1 35 36 **Pandey K C.** Reconstruction of semiconductor surfaces: buckling, ionicity, and π-bonded chains. *Phys. Rev. Lett.* 49:223-6, 1982. IBM, Thomas J. Watson Res. Ctr., Yorktown Heights, NY. *83-2788

1 32 33 **Pandit R, Schick M & Wortis M.** Systematics of multilayer adsorption phenomena on attractive substrates. *Phys. Rev. B—Condensed Matter* 26:5112-40, 1982. Univ. Illinois, Dept. Phys. & Mat. Res. Lab., Urbana, IL; Univ. Washington, Dept. Phys., Seattle, WA. *83-0683

8 35 43 **Parisi G.** A simple expression for planar field theories. *Phys. Lett. B* 112:463-4, 1982. INFN, Natl. Lab., Frascati; Rome Univ., Italy. *83-2705

9 23 32 **Pouget J P, Moret R, Comes R, Bechgaard K, Fabre J M & Giral L.** X-ray diffuse scattering study of some $(TMTSF)_2X$ and $(TMTTF)_2X$ salts. *Mol. Cryst. Liquid Cryst.* 79:129-43, 1982. Univ. Paris XI, Lab. Phys. Solid-State, Orsay; USTL, Lab. Chem. Organ. Struct., Montpellier, France; H.C. Oersted Inst., Copenhagen, Denmark. *83-2192

8 42 50 **Rasmusson E M & Carpenter T H.** Variations in tropical sea surface temperature and surface wind fields associated with the Southern Oscillation/El Nino. *Mon. Weather Rev.* 110:354-84, 1982. NOAA, NMC, Washington, DC. *83-0958

2 28 30 **Reinhardt W P.** Complex coordinates in the theory of atomic and molecular structure and dynamics. *Annu. Rev. Phys. Chem.* 33:223-55, 1982. Univ. Colorado, Dept. Chem. & Joint Inst. Lab. Astrophys. and NBS, Boulder, CO. *83-0311

10 20 30 **Rizzo T G & Senjanovic G.** Grand unification and parity restoration at low energies. II. Unification constraints. *Phys. Rev. D—Part. Fields* 25:235-47, 1982. Brookhaven Natl. Lab., Upton, NY.

0 55 55 **Rubakov V A.** Adler-Bell-Jackiw anomaly and fermion-number breaking in the presence of a magnetic monopole. *Nucl. Phys. B* 203:311-48, 1982. Acad. Sci. USSR, Inst. Nucl. Res., Moscow, USSR. *83-0319

15 31 46 **Sakai N & Yanagida T.** Proton decay in a class of supersymmetric grand unified models. *Nucl. Phys. B* 197:533-42, 1982. Natl. Lab. High Energy Phys., Ibaraki, Japan; Max Planck Soc. Adv. Sci., Inst. Phys. Astrophys., Munich, FRG. *83-1184

1 43 44 **Salam A & Strathdee J.** On Kaluza-Klein theory. *Ann. Phys. NY* 141:316-52, 1982. Intl. Ctr. Theor. Phys., Trieste, Italy; Univ. London, Imperial Coll. Sci. Technol., UK.*83-2796

10 29 39 **Sandage A.** The Oosterhoff period groups and the age of globular clusters. III. The age of the globular cluster system. *Astrophys. J.* 252:553-73, 1982. Carnegie Inst. Washington, Mount Wilson Las Campanas Observs., Pasadena, CA. *83-7090

12 25 37 **Sandel B R, Shemansky D E, Broadfoot A L, Holberg J B, Smith G R, McConnell J C, Strobel D F, Atreya S K, Donahue T M, Moos H W, Hunten D M, Pomphrey R B & Linick S.** Extreme ultraviolet observations from the Voyager 2 encounter with Saturn. *Science* 215:548-53, 1982. USC, Earth Space Sci. Inst.; Univ. Arizona, Lunar Planet.

A	B	C	D

Lab., Tucson, AZ; York Univ., Ontario, Canada; USN, Naval Res. Lab., Washington, DC; Univ. Michigan, Dept. Atmos. Ocean. Sci., Ann Arbor, MI; Johns Hopkins Univ., Baltimore, MD; CalTech, Jet Prop. Lab., Pasadena, CA.

7 23 30 Schuetzle D, Riley T L, Prater T J, Harvey T M & Hunt D F. Analysis of nitrated polycyclic aromatic hydrocarbons in diesel particulates. *Anal. Chem.* 54:265-71, 1982. Ford Motor Co., Analyt. Sci. Dept., Dearborn, MI; Univ. Virginia, Chem. Dept., Charlottesville, VA. *83-4244

9 35 44 Sikivie P. Axions, domain walls, and the early universe. *Phys. Rev. Lett.* 48:1156-9, 1982. Univ. Florida, Dept. Phys., Gainesville, FL. *83-1236

7 28 35 Sinha S K, Crabtree G W, Hinks D G & Mook H. Study of coexistence of ferromagnetism and superconductivity in single-crystal $ErRh_4B_4$. *Phys. Rev. Lett.* 48:950-3, 1982. Argonne Natl. Lab., IL; Oak Ridge Natl. Lab., TN. *83-0140

23 63 86 Smith B A, Soderblom L, Batson R, Bridges P, Inge J, Masursky H, Shoemaker E, Beebe R, Boyce J, Briggs G, Bunker A, Collins S A, Hansen C J, Johnson T V, Mitchell J L, Terrile R J, Cook A F, Cuzzi J, Pollack J B, Danielson G E, Ingersoll A P, Davies M E, Hunt G E, Morrison D, Owen T, Sagan C, Veverka J, Strom R & Suomi V E. A new look at the Saturn system: the Voyager 2 images. *Science* 215:504-37, 1982. Univ. Arizona, Dept. Planet. Sci. & Lunar Planet. Lab., Tucson; US Geol. Survey, Flagstaff, AZ; New Mexico State Univ., Dept. Astron., Las Cruces, NM; NASA Headquarters, Washington, DC & Ames Res. Ctr., Moffett Field; CalTech, Jet Prop. Lab. & Div. Geol. Planet. Sci., Pasadena; Rand Corp., Santa Monica, CA; Univ. London, Univ. Coll., UK; Univ. Hawaii, Inst. Astron., Honolulu, HI; SUNY, Dept. Earth Space Sci., Stony Brook; Cornell Univ., Lab. Planet. Stud., Ithaca, NY; Univ. Wisconsin, Madison, WI. 82-1234; *83-3458

13 23 36 Swiatecki W J. The dynamics of the fusion of two nuclei. *Nucl. Phys. A* 376:275-91, 1982. Univ. California, Lawrence Berkeley Lab., Berkeley, CA. *83-2007

3 33 36 Takahashi T, Jerome D & Bechgaard K. Observation of a magnetic state in the organic superconductor $(TMTSF)_2ClO_4$: influence of the cooling rate. *J. Phys.—Lett.* 43:L565-73, 1982. Univ. Paris XI, Lab. Phys. Solid-State, Orsay, France. *83-2192

12 27 39 Testa J, Perez J & Jeffries C. Evidence for universal chaotic behavior of a driven nonlinear oscillator. *Phys. Rev. Lett.* 48:714-7, 1982. Univ. California, Lawrence Berkeley Lab. & Dept. Phys., Berkeley, CA. *83-0321

6 25 31 Tsui D C, Gossard A C, Field B F, Cage M E & Dziuba R F. Determination of the fine-structure constant using $GaAs-Al_xGa_{1-x}As$ heterostructures. *Phys. Rev. Lett.* 48:3-6, 1982. Bell Labs., Murray Hill, NJ; NBS, Ctr. Absolute Phys. Quants., Washington, DC. *83-0897

1 44 45 Tsui D C, Stormer H L & Gossard A C. Two-dimensional magnetotransport in the extreme quantum limit. *Phys. Rev. Lett.* 48:1559-62, 1982. Bell Labs., Murray Hill, NJ. *83-0897

7 26 33 Uhrberg R I G, Hansson G V, Nicholls J M & Flodstrom S A. Experimental evidence for one highly dispersive dangling-bond band on Si(111) 2×1. *Phys. Rev. Lett.* 48:1032-5, 1982. Linkoping Inst. Technol., Dept. Phys. Measur. Technol., Sweden. *83-2788

12 24 36 Weinberg S. Cosmological constraints on the scale of supersymmetry breaking. *Phys. Rev. Lett.* 48:1303-6, 1982. Univ. Texas, Dept. Phys., Austin, TX.

8 51 59 Weinberg S. Supersymmetry at ordinary energies. Masses and conservation laws. *Phys. Rev. D—Part. Fields* 26:287-302, 1982. Harvard Univ., Lyman Lab. Phys., Cambridge, MA and Univ. Texas, Dept. Phys., Austin, TX. *83-1184

21 51 72 Weingarten D. Monte Carlo evaluation of hadron masses in lattice gauge theories with fermions. *Phys. Lett. B* 109:57-62, 1982. Indiana Univ., Phys. Dept., Bloomington, IN. 82-0032; *83-0966

8 38 46 Wilczek F. Remarks on dyons. *Phys. Rev. Lett.* 48:1146-9, 1982. Univ. California, Inst. Theor. Phys., Santa Barbara, CA. *83-0319

3 41 44 Witten E. Constraints on supersymmetry breaking. *Nucl. Phys B* 202:253-316, 1982. Princeton Univ., Joseph Henry Labs., NJ. *83-1184

22 53 75 Wu F Y. The Potts model. *Rev. Mod. Phys.* 54:235-68, 1982. Julich Nucl. Res. Ctr., Inst. Solid-State Phys., FRG. 82-0376; *83-0506

10 35 45 Yoshizawa H, Cowley R A, Shirane G, Birgeneau R J, Guggenheim H J & Ikeda H. Random-field effects in two- and three-dimensional Ising antiferromagnets. *Phys. Rev. Lett.* 48:438-41, 1982. Brookhaven Natl. Lab., Upton, NY; MIT, Dept. Phys., Cambridge; Bell Labs., Murray Hill, NJ; Ochanomizu Univ., Dept. Phys., Tokyo, Japan. *83-0316

8 22 30 Young A P & Kirkpatrick S. Low-temperature behavior of the infinite-range Ising spin-glass. Exact statistical mechanics for small samples. *Phys. Rev. B—Condensed Matter* 25:440-51, 1982. Univ. London, Imperial Coll. Sci. Technol., UK; IBM, Thomas J. Watson Res. Ctr., Yorktown Heights, NY. *83-1782 mation can be obtained by contacting ISI®. Many of the 12 papers in this study that are *not* in any research front will undoubtedly be incorporated into the core literature of research fronts generated in the next few years.

Research front #83-1184, "Yang-Mills and Other Supersymmetric Grand Unification Theories with Supergravity Effects," includes 12 papers from this study in its core, more than any other research front. The goal of grand unification theories (GUTs) is to devise a single theoretical framework that accounts for the four fundamental forces of nature—weak nuclear, strong nuclear, electromagnetism, and gravity. Scientists have been successful in proposing a "common denominator" for the electromagnetic and weak nuclear forces, the so-called "electroweak" force. Steven Weinberg, Sheldon Glashow, and Abdus Salam shared the 1979 Nobel prize for physics in recognition of their development of the electroweak theory. However, the strong nuclear force and gravity have yet to be described in a comprehensive GUT.

Ten papers in this study are in the core of a closely related research front

Table 2: The 1982 *SCI*® and 1983 *SCI/SSCI*® research fronts that contain at least two of the 1982 most-cited physical sciences papers as core documents. A=research front number. B=research front name. C=number of 1982 most-cited physical sciences papers included in the core of each research front. D=total number of cited/citing documents.

A	B	C	D
82-0029	Phase transitions in the early universe and the inflationary universe scenario	3	39/NA
83-0019	Electronic structure and other properties of EL2 deep level defects in GaAs, metal-doped silicon and other semiconductors	2	37/342
83-0072	Techniques and applications of fast atom bombardment in desorption and secondary ion mass spectrometry	2	38/379
83-0316	Anisotropy, magnetic and random field effects on the critical behavior of Ising systems in amorphous alloys	2	54/383
83-0319	Magnetic monopoles in a supersymmetric inflationary universe; quantum model of grand unification theory and cosmology	10	49/584
83-0321	Transitions to chaos and dynamic models of bifurcations and convection patterns of maps in nonlinear systems	2	54/594
83-0506	Renormalization group approach in Potts models of percolation and critical behavior in fractal lattices	2	19/314
83-0638	High-energy radio emissions and gamma-ray observation from pulsars and supernovas	2	29/321
83-0683	Models of critical wetting transitions at surfaces	2	17/164
83-0897	Theory and analysis of the two-dimensional quantum Hall effect	4	27/297
83-0966	Monte Carlo methods for lattice gauge theory approaches to quantum chromodynamics	5	53/575
83-1064	Fischer-Tropsch syntheses of hydrocarbons and alcohols via the hydrogenation of carbon monoxide on supported iron catalysts	2	35/376
83-1184	Yang-Mills and other supersymmetric grand unification theories with supergravity effects	12	52/516
83-1782	Critical behavior, magnetic order and dynamical properties of Ising spin glasses	2	34/335
83-2192	Organic metals and superconductors based on tetramethyltetraselenafulvalenium salts	4	26/205
83-2705	Twisted Eguchi-Kawai and other reduced models for large-N lattice gauge theory	3	11/108
83-2788	Determination of electronic structure and surface reconstruction of silicon(111) and other semiconductor surfaces	2	14/167
83-3458	Voyager observations of Saturn's ring, magnetosphere and ice rich satellites with emphasis on Titan and its atmosphere	3	23/265
83-3652	Synthesis via the activation of oxygen and carbon-hydrogen bonds using metalloporphyrins and related compounds as catalysts	2	23/223

(#83-0319) entitled "Magnetic Monopoles in a Supersymmetric Inflationary Universe; Quantum Model of Grand Unification Theory and Cosmology." In a recent article in *New Scientist*, John Gribbin noted, "Inflation has become the buzzword of cosmology in the 1980s because it may offer a solution to several serious, related problems physicists face in understanding the Universe. These boil down to the fact that the Universe is incredibly uniform (homogeneous and isotropic). On the scale of clusters of galaxies, the Universe is the same everywhere we look, and it is expanding evenly."[3]

This research front includes the most-cited, second-most-cited, and fourth-most-cited articles in this study as core documents, an indication that inflationary-universe models are indeed hot topics in physics today. The most-cited article was published in *Physics Letters B* by A.D. Linde, P.H. Lebedev Physical Institute, Moscow. The author described a new inflationary universe model that solves the homogeneity and isotropy problems noted by Gribbin as well as related difficulties involving horizon, flatness, and magnetic monopoles. The paper was cited 33 times in 1982 and 72 times in 1983.

The second-most-cited paper suggests another solution to the homogeneity, flatness, and monopole puzzles. Published in *Physical Review Letters* by Andreas Albrecht and Paul J. Steinhardt, University of Pennsylvania, Philadelphia, the paper received 88 citations—20 in 1982 and 68 in 1983. The fourth-most-cited article was also published in *Physical Review Letters*. Blas Cabrera, Stanford University, California, announced the detection for the first time of a moving magnetic monopole and described the instrument used to observe it. This paper was cited 12 times in 1982 and 71 times in 1983. However, Cabrera has since designed a new instrument and hasn't been able to confirm his 1982 finding. According to *New Scientist*, the "event" Cabrera observed was probably a "spurious cause," not a magnetic monopole.[4]

The third-most-cited paper is part of the core of research front #83-3458, "Voyager Observations of Saturn's Ring, Magnetosphere, and Ice-Rich Satellites with Emphasis on Titan and Its Atmosphere." Bradford A. Smith, University of Arizona, Tucson, and 28 colleagues from 14 institutions published their ob-

Table 3: The 31 journals represented on the list of the 106 1982 physical sciences papers most cited in 1982-1983. The numbers in parentheses are the impact factors for the journals. (1982 impact factor equals the number of citations received by 1980-1981 articles in a journal divided by the number of articles published by the journal during the same period.) Data were taken from the 1982 *JCR* ™. The figures at the right indicate the number of papers from each journal that appears on the list.

Journal	Number of Papers
Phys. Rev. Lett. (6.20)	24
Phys. Lett. B (3.66)	20
Nucl. Phys. B (3.82)	7
Phys. Rev. B—Condensed Matter (3.02)	5
Science (6.81)	5
J. Amer. Chem. Soc. (4.72)	4
J. Phys.—Lett. (2.56)	4
Phys. Rev. D—Part. Fields (2.87)	4
Anal. Chem. (3.71)	3
Astrophys. J. (4.07)	3
IEEE J. Quantum Electron. (3.27)	3
Rev. Mod. Phys. (20.71)	3
Appl. Phys. Lett. (3.10)	2
Nature (8.75)	2
Advan. Organometal. Chem. (7.67)	1
Advan. Phys. (10.61)	1
Angew. Chem. Int. Ed. (4.17)	1
Ann. Phys. NY (2.63)	1
Annu. Rev. Phys. Chem. (7.26)	1
Astron. Astrophys. (2.28)	1
Chem. Phys. Lett. (2.19)	1
Earth Planet. Sci. Lett. (2.75)	1
Electron. Lett. (1.51)	1
J. Magn. Resonance (2.22)	1
Mol. Cryst. Liquid Cryst. (1.16)	1
Mon. Weather Rev. (1.61)	1
Nucl. Phys. A (2.43)	1
Phys. Rep. (6.39)	1
Phys. Rev. A—Gen. Phys. (2.58)	1
Proc. IEEE (2.67)	1
Rep. Progr. Phys. (7.08)	1

Table 4: The institutional affiliations of the authors on the list. Institutions are listed in descending order of the number of times they appear in Table 1.

Univ. California, CA	17
Berkeley	6
Santa Barbara	4
Irvine	2
Los Angeles	2
San Diego	2
Santa Cruz	1
CERN, Geneva, Switzerland	8
Harvard Univ., Cambridge, MA[1]	8
INFN, Italy	7
Frascati	2
Pisa	2
Bari	1
Milan	1
Rome	1
MIT, Cambridge, MA	7
Bell Labs, Murray Hill, NJ	6
Univ. Paris XI, Orsay, France	6
Brookhaven Natl. Lab., Upton, NY	5
CalTech, Pasadena, CA	5
IBM, Thomas J. Watson Res. Ctr., Yorktown Heights, NY	5
Max Planck Soc. Adv. Sci., FRG	5
Inst. Phys. Astrophys., Munich	3
Inst. Aeronom., Katlenburg-Lindau	1
Inst. Extraterr. Phys., Munich	1
Cornell Univ., Ithaca, NY[2]	4
Inst. Adv. Stud., Princeton, NJ	4
NASA	4
Goddard Space Flight Ctr., Greenbelt, MD	2
Ames Res. Ctr., Moffett Field, CA	1
Headquarters, Washington, DC	1
Princeton Univ., NJ	4
Stanford Univ., CA	4
Univ. Oxford, UK	4
Univ. Pennsylvania, Philadelphia, PA	4
H.C. Oersted Inst., Copenhagen, Denmark	3
Nippon Telegr. Tel. Publ. Corp., Japan	3
Musashino Elect. Commun. Lab., Tokyo	2
Ibaraki Elect. Commun. Lab.	1
Univ. Arizona, Tucson, AZ	3
Univ. Cambridge, UK	3
Univ. Colorado, CO	3
Boulder	2
Joint Inst. Lab. Astrophys., Boulder[3]	1
Univ. London, UK	3
Imperial Coll. Sci. Technol.	2
Univ. Coll.	1
Univ. Regensburg, FRG	3
Acad. Sci. USSR, Moscow, USSR	2
Inst. Nucl. Res.	1
P.H. Lebedev Phys. Inst.	1
Carnegie Inst. Washington, DC[4]	2
CENS, Gif-sur-Yvette, France	2
CNR, Italy	2
Cosm. Phys. Inst., Milan	1

Cosm. Phys. Data Inst., Palermo	1
Higher Normal Sch., Pisa, Italy	2
Julich Nucl. Res. Ctr., FRG	2
NBS	2
Boulder, CO	1
Washington, DC	1
Normal Coll., Paris, France	2
Oak Ridge Natl. Lab., TN	2
Rome Univ., Italy	2
Stanislaw Staszic Univ. Min. Met., Kracow, Poland	2
SUNY, Stony Brook, NY	2
Univ. Illinois, Urbana, IL	2
Univ. Michigan, Ann Arbor, MI	2
Univ. Texas, Austin, TX	2
USN, Washington, DC	2
Argonne Natl. Lab., IL	1
Brandeis Univ., Waltham, MA	1
Carnegie-Mellon Univ., Pittsburgh, PA	1
CNRS, Grenoble, France	1
DESY, Hamburg, FRG	1
Eotvos Lorand Univ., Budapest, Hungary	1
Eur. Space Agcy., Noordwijk, the Netherlands	1
Ford Motor Co., Dearborn, MI	1
Goddard Inst. Space Stud., New York, NY	1
Griffith Univ., Nathan, Australia	1
Hamburg Univ., FRG	1
Hebrew Univ., Jerusalem, Israel	1
Hoffmann-La Roche, Inc., Nutley, NJ	1
Hungarian Acad. Sci., Budapest, Hungary	1
Huygens Lab., Leiden, the Netherlands	1
Indiana Univ., Bloomington, IN	1
Inst. Phys. Chem. Ind., Paris, France	1
Intl. Ctr. Theor. Phys., Trieste, Italy	1
Jagiellonian Univ., Kracow, Poland	1
Johns Hopkins Univ., Baltimore, MD	1
Kapteyn Astron. Inst., Groningen, the Netherlands	1
Linkoping Inst. Technol., Sweden	1
Madrid Autonom. Univ., Spain	1
Max Von Laue-Paul Langevin Inst., Grenoble, France	1
Michigan State Univ., East Lansing, MI	1
N. Dakota State Univ., Fargo, ND	1
Natl. Lab. High Energy Phys., Ibaraki, Japan	1
Natl. Radio Astron. Observ., Charlottesville, VA	1
New Mexico State Univ., Las Cruces, NM	1
NIKHEE, Nijmegen, the Netherlands	1
NOAA, Washington, DC	1
Northeastern Univ., Boston, MA	1
Ochanomizu Univ., Tokyo, Japan	1
Rand Corp., Santa Monica, CA	1
Rockefeller Univ., New York, NY	1
Rockwell Intl., Thousand Oaks, CA	1
SERC, Chilton, UK	1
Tech. Univ. Braunschweig, FRG	1
Texas A&M Univ., College Station, TX	1
Univ. Bari, Italy	1

Univ. Florida, Gainesville, FL	1
Univ. Geneva, Switzerland	1
Univ. Guelph, Ontario, Canada	1
Univ. Hawaii, Honolulu, HI	1
Univ. Iowa, Iowa City, IA	1
Univ. Liverpool, UK	1
Univ. Manchester, UK	1
Univ. Milan, Italy	1
Univ. New Hampshire, Durham, NH	1
Univ. Nijmegen, the Netherlands	1
Univ. Salamanca, Spain	1
Univ. Tokyo, Japan	1
Univ. Toronto, Canada	1
Univ. Tsukuba, Ibaraki, Japan	1
Univ. Virginia, Charlottesville, VA	1
Univ. Washington, Seattle, WA	1
Univ. Wisconsin, Madison, WI	1
US Geol. Survey, Flagstaff, AZ	1
USC, Tucson, AZ	1
USTL, Montpellier, France	1
Virginia Polytech. Inst. State Univ., Blacksburg, VA	1
Xerox, Palo Alto, CA	1
Yale Univ., New Haven, CT	1
York Univ., Ontario, Canada	1

[1] Includes Harvard-Smithsonian Ctr. Astrophys., Cambridge, MA

[2] Includes Natl. Astron. Ionosph. Ctr., Arecibo, PR

[3] Operated jointly with the Natl. Bureau of Standards, Washington, DC

[4] Includes Mount Wilson Las Campanas Observs., Pasadena, CA

---

servations in *Science* based on the *Voyager 2* space probe. The paper received 86 citations, 23 in 1982 and 63 in 1983. An earlier paper by Smith was the third-most-cited 1981 physical-sciences paper.[5]

Several other papers in this study also deserve mention. Two papers discuss semiconductor lasers. Charles Henry, Bell Laboratories, Murray Hill, New Jersey, describes a theory of the linewidth of semiconductor lasers. Soichi Kobayashi and colleagues, Nippon Telegraph and Telephone Public Corporation, Japan, published their findings on direct frequency modulation characteristics in semiconductor lasers. One of the uses of semiconductor lasers is in optical fiber technology. Thomas G. Giallorenzi and colleagues, USN, Washington, DC, reviewed the current state of the art of optical fiber technology and its future applications, in a paper cited 34 times in 1982 and 1983. All three papers appeared in *IEEE Journal of Quantum Electronics*.

H.T. Fortune, University of Pennsylvania, Philadelphia, points out[6] that the most-cited papers in physical sciences appear to include some of the most-read papers outside their particular specialty. That is, most physicists read papers on cosmology and new elementary particles, even if they are not working in these areas of physical sciences.

The 106 papers in this study were published in the 31 journals listed in Table 3. Just three journals account for 48 percent of the papers: *Physical Review Letters* (24 papers), *Physics Letters B* (20 papers), and *Nuclear Physics B* (7 papers). The same journals dominated our 1981 study.[5]

The authors of the most-cited 1982 physical-sciences papers were affiliated with 105 institutions located in 17 nations (see Table 4). The University of California accounts for 12 papers in the study. CERN, the multinational research organization based in Geneva, was represented in eight papers, an increase over our 1981 study.[5] It is noteworthy that the recent Nobel prize in physics was based on work done at CERN. Carlo Rubbia and Simon van der Meer, CERN, shared the 1984 Nobel prize in physics.

Table 5 lists the national affiliations of the 420 authors in this study, in order of the number of papers on which each nation's authors were listed. For example, 66 papers listed US authors. Of these, 55 were by US authors *only* and 11 were co-authored with researchers based in Canada, France, the Federal Republic of Germany (FRG), Italy, Japan, the Netherlands, Spain, and the UK. Six papers listed authors from Japan. In comparison, Japan accounted for just one of the most-cited 1981 physical-sciences papers.[5] Although authors from 17 nations

Table 5: National affiliations of the authors of the 1982 physical sciences papers most cited in 1982-1983, in order of the total number of papers in which each nation's authors appeared (column A). B=number of papers coauthored with scientists from other countries. C=nationality of coauthors.

Country	A	B	C
US	66	11	Canada, France, FRG, Italy, Japan, the Netherlands, Spain, UK
France	12	7	Denmark, FRG, Israel, Italy, the Netherlands, Switzerland, US
FRG	11	6	France, Italy, Japan, the Netherlands, Poland, Spain, Switzerland, UK, US
UK	10	6	Canada, FRG, Italy, the Netherlands, Poland, Spain, Switzerland, US
Switzerland	8	5	France, FRG, Hungary, Italy, the Netherlands, Poland, UK
Italy	8	7	France, FRG, the Netherlands, Poland, Switzerland, UK, US
Japan	6	3	FRG, US
Canada	3	2	UK, US
Denmark	3	2	France
the Netherlands	3	3	France, FRG, Italy, Poland, Switzerland, UK, US
Spain	2	2	FRG, UK, US
USSR	2	0	
Australia	1	0	
Hungary	1	1	Switzerland
Israel	1	1	France
Poland	1	1	FRG, Italy, the Netherlands, Switzerland, UK
Sweden	1	0	

are represented here, all the articles were in English.

Of the 420 authors in Table 1, 400 contributed one paper and 12 have two papers. Eight authors were listed on three papers each: K. Bechgaard, S. Ferrara, L. Girardello, A.C. Gossard, L. Ibanez, D. Jerome, D.V. Nanopoulos, and D.C. Tsui.

Twenty-seven papers are single-author works. In our study of 1981 papers,[5] just 12 listed one author. Twenty-five papers list two authors, 18 list three, 13 list four, 9 list five, 5 list six, and 2 list seven authors. One paper each lists 9, 13, 15, 16, 29, 38, and 56 authors. It is not unusual for high-energy physics papers to list scores of authors.

This concludes our analysis of the 1982 physical-sciences papers that were most cited in 1982 and 1983. Although several chemistry papers were cited enough to meet the threshold in this study, at least three years of citation data are needed to detect some of the most-significant chemistry papers. Different scientific fields have different "diffusion" rates. That's why we treat each field separately in these studies. More will be said on this point and other forms of delayed recognition in our essay on the 1981 chemistry papers most cited between 1981 and 1983.

* * * * *

My thanks to Thomas Atkins, Alfred Welljams-Dorof, and Abigail Grissom for their help in the preparation of this essay.   ©1984 ISI

REFERENCES

1. **Garfield E.** The 1982 articles most cited in 1982 and 1983. 1. Life sciences. *Current Contents* (45):3-15, 5 November 1984.
2. --------------. ABCs of cluster mapping. Parts 1 & 2. Most active fields in the life and physical sciences in 1978. *Essays of an information scientist.* Philadelphia: ISI Press, 1981. Vol. 4. p. 634-49.
3. **Gribbin J.** One step on from the moment of creation. *New Sci.* 103(1416):30-1, 1984.
4. Now you see me... *New Sci.* 101(1392):19, 1984.
5. **Garfield E.** The 1981 articles most cited in 1981 and 1982. 2. Physical sciences. *Essays of an information scientist.* Philadelphia: ISI Press, 1984. Vol. 6. p. 373-83.
6. **Fortune H T.** Telephone communication. 9 November 1984.

Current Comments®

Twins. Part 2. The Twin Study Method in Behavioral and Clinical Research

There are many anecdotes about identical twins who were separated early in life and later reunited. Although reared in different environments, their remarkable similarities include mannerisms, tastes in food, choices of hobbies, and vocations. Some people even believe that there is an almost extrasensory sympathy between identical twins—shared pain and moods and vague awareness about how the other is doing or what the other is thinking. While these anecdotes receive widespread attention in the media, the truly profound research on twins is not so well known outside the scientific community.

In the first part of this essay,[1] we reviewed the unique biology involved in the conception and birthing of twins. In this part, we'll review what researchers in the behavioral, cognitive, and medical sciences have learned about twins. Much of this research has profound implications for the old philosophical "nature vs. nurture" debate. The extent to which intelligence, personality, and even health and life span are determined by genetics or environmental factors is still very controversial.

As discussed in the first part of this essay, there are two types of twins—monozygotic (MZ) and dizygotic (DZ). DZ twins are like any other siblings—that is, on the average, only *half* of their genes are the same. They can be of the same or opposite sex. MZ twins are genetically *identical*. They have duplicate genes and they are always of the same sex. Thus, by comparing MZ and DZ twins, researchers are able to study the genetic and environmental factors in various human characteristics and diseases. Before we review the results of these twin studies, we'll briefly discuss some of the various ways twins are used in research.

The classic twin study method is a tool for estimating the relative influence of genetic and environmental factors on a specific trait. If one assumes that environmental effects are the same in MZ and DZ twins, then a greater similarity between members of MZ pairs than between members of DZ pairs would indicate that the similarity is a result of their matching genes.

Twins are said to be concordant when both members of the twin pair are alike in a trait or discordant when one twin is different from the other in that trait. The concordance rate, or the percent of MZ and DZ twin pairs sharing similarity for a given trait, is used as a measure of the genetic contribution to that trait. However, if the research is concerned with a continuously variable trait, such as IQ score, a statistical measure known as correlation is used to gauge similarity. The higher the correlation, the more alike are the twins. A correlation of 1.0 indicates complete identity for a given trait.

A major criticism of this classic twin study method is that the childhood environment shared by MZ twins may be more similar than that of DZ twins. For example, parents may treat nonidentical twins differently from the way they treat identical twins. And MZ twins were once thought to spend more time together than DZ twins. However, these speculations are not supported by research. Hugh Lytton, Department of Educational Psychology, University of Calgary, Alberta, Canada, found that parents respond to the differences between DZ pairs, rather than create them by treating the individual twins differently.[2] Nor do parents by their actions introduce greater similarity into the behavior of MZ twins. In fact, when zygosity is unknown to parents, their treatment of the twins is in line with the actual rather than the perceived zygosity of the pair. Steven G. Vandenberg, Institute for Behavioral Genetics, University of Colorado, Boulder, suggested that most twin characteristics, such as having the same friends, do not cause similarity, but result from existing similarity.[3]

Another method, which uses only MZ twins, eliminates this potential environmental bias. By looking at differences between MZ twins separated when they are infants and reared apart, psychologists have been able to examine the extent to which variation in a given trait is environmentally determined. However, use of this method is limited by the small number of MZ twins who are raised apart.

Still another twin study strategy is the co-twin control method. First used in studies of the acquisition of skills, the co-twin control method is more frequently used today in testing various treatments, such as the effectiveness of vitamin C in preventing the common cold. In the co-twin control study, one twin of the MZ pair is treated while the other remains untreated and serves as a control. One variation on this method compares MZ twins discordant for a specific trait. By using MZ twins, genetic

factors are controlled, and the effects of environmental factors can be determined.

Of course, all these methods require accurate knowledge of zygosity; that is, the ability to distinguish MZ from DZ twins. A variety of genetically controlled traits, such as blood type and blood serum antigens, physical appearance, and finger ridge count, can be used to determine zygosity. However, in large twin studies, it may be more feasible to use a questionnaire that assesses early physical resemblance on the basis of selected traits. Discordance for any trait indicates that the pair is dizygotic, but a question arises when concordance occurs. Since they are genetically identical, all MZ pairs will be concordant. However, because approximately half of their genes are the same, concordance may also occur in DZ twins who may be mistaken for MZ.

Although comparison of blood groups and blood-group antigens is often thought to be the most accurate method for determining zygosity, subjective methods are necessary when researchers study large groups of twins. These methods are surprisingly accurate. For example, C. Dennis Robinette, National Academy of Sciences-National Research Council (NAS-NRC), Twin Registry, Washington, DC, noted that he and his colleagues were able to determine zygosity with 96 percent accuracy by asking two questions: (1) "Were you and your twin ever said to be alike as 'two peas in a pod,' or only of ordinary resemblance?" (2) "Did close friends, relatives or school teachers have difficulty telling you and your twin apart?"[4]

Paolo Parisi, University of Rome and Gregor Mendel Institute for Medical Genetics and Twin Studies, Rome, Italy, noted that an experienced observer can classify twins according to zygosity simply by looking at them.[5] This is not surprising, because physical traits such as eye and hair color, ear form and attachment, and the shape of the nose are under strict genetic control. In a 1983 study, Nancy L. Segal, Department of Psychology, University of Minnesota, Minneapolis, compared the accuracy of a skilled observer in determining zygosity with the blood typing procedure. She found the observer's judgments to be the most accurate. Of 53 twin pairs classified by laboratory tests, 5 disagreed with the observer. On retest, researchers found an error in blood typing, and the observer's judgments thus were confirmed in all cases.[6] However, blood typing continues to be the preferred method for an objective diagnosis.

This interesting and important research would be either impossible without twins, or at least difficult and ambiguous. As noted in part one of this essay, twins are a small population, and identical twins occur only in 4 per 1,000 births. Fortunately, twin registries mitigate the relative rarity of twin births. Table 1 presents a selected list of these registries, which maintain extensive databases of demographic and other information about twins. Researchers can use the data in a registry or contact the twins through the registry. One of the largest registries in the US is at the Medical College of Virginia and includes over 29,000 pairs. The NAS-NRC Veterans Twin Registry includes the 16,000 US twins who served in World War II. Registries in the Scandinavian countries are generally based on birth records and include all of the twins who were born in each country. These registries facilitate studies from a wide variety of disciplines.

The first scientific study of twins took place more than 100 years ago when the British anthropologist and eugenicist, Sir Francis Galton, introduced the classic twin study method.[7] Galton's early genetic studies centered on the inheritance of intellectual ability. However, he was unable to distinguish between inherited and environmental factors. Galton realized that twins provided a natural laboratory for studying the nature vs. nurture controversy. Although Galton's studies were based on erroneous ideas about the biology of twinning and zygosity, his general conclusion that there is a genetic component to intelligence was reasonably accurate.

More recent studies of intelligence that used Galton's twin study method found that MZ twins become increasingly similar while DZ twins begin to diverge as they reach school age. Psychologist Ronald S. Wilson, University of Louisville School of Medicine, Kentucky, observed the same children for several years. He reported that prior to the age of 18 months, correlations for intelligence were 0.69 and 0.63 for MZ and DZ pairs, respectively. Between the ages of 18 months and 4 years, these correlations averaged 0.83 and 0.72, respectively. By age 6, correlations stabilized at 0.85 for MZ and 0.63 for DZ twins.[8] Wilson concluded that intelligence is guided by a genetic template that acts throughout childhood and into adolescence.

In a study of intelligence in MZ twins who were reared apart, David T. Lykken, Psychiatry Research Unit, University of Minnesota, Minneapolis, estimated that about 70 percent of intelligence is genetically determined.[9] The largest study of intelligence in MZ twins reared apart was published by the well-known British psychologist Sir Cyril Burt. According to Burt's biographer, L.S. Hearnshaw, University of Liverpool, England, the validity of this work has been questioned, since he chose to create fictitious collaborators with whom he published further confirming studies.[10] To say the least, the question of heritability of intelligence is still hotly debated, there being studies that both support and contradict his studies. However, Burt's work in no way reflects on the more recent studies of MZ twins reared apart.

Table 1: A list of some major twin registries.

Danish Twin Registry
University of Odense
Arvepatologisk Institut
Odense, Denmark

Finnish Twin Registry
Department of Public Health Science
University of Helsinki
Helsinki, Finland

Institute of Medical Genetics
Academy of Medical Sciences of the USSR
Moscow, 115478, USSR

Kaiser-Permanente Twin Registry
Department of Medical Methods Research
Kaiser-Permanente Medical Care Program
Oakland, CA 94611

Medical College of Virginia Twin Registry
Department of Human Genetics
Medical College of Virginia
Richmond, VA 23298

National Academy of Sciences-National
 Research Council Twin Registry
National Research Council
2101 Constitution Avenue, N.W.
Washington, DC 20418

Norwegian Twin Registry
Institute of Medical Genetics
University of Oslo
Blindern, Oslo 3
Norway

Swedish Twin Registry
Department of Environmental Hygiene
Karolinska Institute
Stockholm, Sweden

Language is one means of expressing intelligence. It is a complex function that is influenced both by genetic and environmental factors. Psychologists Patricia L. Mather, Utica College of Syracuse University, New York, and Kathryn N. Black, Purdue University, Lafayette, Indiana, found that in preschool children, vocabulary comprehension is significantly influenced by heredity. Verbal skills are more closely related to the home environment.[11]

Twins are generally slower to speak than singletons. Lytton found that MZ pairs are even slower than DZ pairs to develop speech and vocabulary skills.[12] Verbal interaction with the mother appears to be the most important factor in learning to speak for all children. Dorice Conway and colleagues, Department of Educational Psychology, University of Calgary, Alberta, Canada, found that, because they lack time, mothers speak to twins less frequently and in shorter and less complex utterances than do mothers of singletons.[13] Jennie P. Betton and Lynne S. Koester, Family Research Center, University of North Carolina, Greensboro, observed that twins provide support and encouragement for each other and need their mothers less than singletons do to develop cognitive skills.[14]

Certain speech disorders seem to have a hereditary component. Until recently, few researchers considered stuttering, a disorder in the timing of speech, to be of genetic origin. However, Pauline M. Howie, School of Psychiatry, University of New South Wales, Sydney, Australia, found a concordance of about 63 percent for MZ twins and about 19 percent for DZ twins.[15] To better understand the nature and degree of similarity of symptoms in MZ twins, Howie examined twin pairs with at least one stutterer to determine which characteristics were under genetic control. She found evidence for a genetic contribution to the frequency and type of speech disruption, for example, blocked or prolonged sounds. However, there was little evidence for a genetic influence on the types of speech repetitions and interjections associated with stuttering.[16]

Language skills and intelligence are related to basic brain function. One reflection of basic brain function is the electroencephalogram (EEG). EEG patterns reflect electrical activity within the cerebral cortex, that part of the brain responsible for intelligence. The resulting brain-wave tracings are influenced by factors such as the size and shape of the skull in relation to the underlying cerebral cortex, the anatomy of the cortex, and by the microstructure associated with cognitive and emotional reactions. Generally, each person has a unique brain-wave pattern. However, since MZ twins are genetically identical, it is not surprising that their EEG patterns are very similar, while those of DZ twins are no more alike than those of unrelated individuals. Lykken and colleagues found these patterns to be similar for MZ twins whether they were reared apart or together.[17] This suggests a strong genetic influence on basic neural circuitry.

Certain aspects of personality also seem to be strongly influenced by genetic factors. In a 1980 study of 7- to 10-year-old twin pairs, Adam P. Matheny and Anne B. Dolan, Louisville Twin Study, University of Louisville, Kentucky, found significantly higher MZ correlation than DZ correlation on tests of emotionality, sociability, and activity.[18] Psychologists John C. Loehlin, University of Texas, Austin, and Robert C. Nichols, State University of New York, Buffalo, found a strong genetic contribution to various aspects of personality and measures of general ability in teenagers.[19] Additional evidence comes from studies of MZ twins reared apart. According to psychologist Thomas J. Bouchard, University of Minnesota, Minneapolis, MZ twins who were reared apart are as similar in some personality traits as MZ twins reared together.[20] For example, he reported that aggression, introversion and extroversion, impulse control, and neuroticism are significantly more similar in both types of MZ than in DZ pairs.

Galton also noticed the similar personalities of like-sex twins. He noted that these twins occasionally had similar types of mental disorders.[7] More recent twin studies of mental illness suggest that genetic factors play an important role. One example is schizophrenia. According to Irving I. Gottesman, Department of Psychiatry, Washington University, St. Louis, Missouri, and James Shields, then of the Institute of Psychiatry, London, concordance for schizophrenia in MZ twins is 46 percent while it is only 14 percent for DZ pairs.[21] In her re-analysis of several studies, psychologist Susan L. Farber, then of New York University, New York, reported 67 percent concordance for MZ twins raised apart.[22] Concordant MZ twins also become schizophrenic at similar ages. Although the large difference between MZ and DZ concordance figures provides strong evidence for a genetic contribution, MZ concordance is far less than 100 percent. This indicates that schizophrenia is probably due to a combination of environmental and genetic factors. However, Gottesman and Shields claim that studies of discordant MZ pairs have not provided evidence of a specific environmental factor.[21] Also, David W. Fulker, Institute for Behavioral Genetics, University of Colorado, notes that the provoking environmental circumstances are probably highly specific to the individual.[23]

Some of the most definitive results of twin research have come from the study of diabetes mellitus, a pancreatic disorder that affects carbohydrate metabolism. There are two pathologically distinct types of diabetes: insulin-dependent diabetes (IDD) and noninsulin-dependent diabetes (NIDD). IDD generally develops in childhood while NIDD usually occurs in mid- or late-life. The fact that the occurrence of diabetes is familial has long been known. However, a 1981 study by A.H. Barnett and colleagues, Diabetic Clinic, Kings College Hospital, London, found a little over 50 percent concordance for IDD in MZ twins.[24] This seems to imply that, while there is a genetic tendency to develop the disease, IDD is not entirely of genetic origin. Further support for this is the fact that more discordant than concordant twin pairs between the ages of 20 to 39 years were living apart at the time of diagnosis.

A study of the unaffected members of MZ twin pairs may have provided a marker for early diagnosis of the prediabetic state in IDD. S. Srikanta and colleagues, Department of Medicine, Harvard Medical School, Boston, Massachusetts, periodically examined the unaffected twin in 24 discordant MZ pairs for 21 years. They found that these patients began to produce antibodies to the insulin-producing beta cells of the pancreas several years prior to the onset of IDD.[25] The antibody can be used as a marker for the disease. In the future, susceptible people may be identified early enough to prevent diabetes. Srikanta's findings also suggest that IDD develops slowly, rather than suddenly, as researchers had previously thought.

Apparently there is a stronger genetic component in maturity-onset NIDD than in IDD. Of 53 NIDD twin pairs in Barnett's study, only 5 were discordant for the disease. The interval between the two diagnoses in concordant twins is also short, averaging about five years. These concordant twins had usually been living apart for many years and were often of different weights. This suggests that environmental factors, such as obesity, may be less important in NIDD than previously thought.[24]

Questions about possible environmental factors important to the etiology of neurologic disorders such as multiple sclerosis (MS) may also be answered by long-term follow-up of discordant MZ twins. MS is a degenerative disorder of the central nervous system. Like IDD, concordance rates for MS indicate that factors other than genes contribute to this disease. Neurologist Adrian Williams and colleagues, National Institute of Neurological and Communicative Disorders and Stroke (NINCDS), Bethesda, Maryland, reported concordances of 20 to 40 percent in MZ pairs and 15 percent in DZ twins.[26] Henry F. McFarland and colleagues, also at NINCDS, suggest that discordant twins may also provide an opportunity to evaluate various therapeutic approaches to MS.[27] One approach, based on a hypothesized immunological etiology, was to treat the affected twin with lymphocytes from the unaffected twin. However, this treatment had no long-term effect.[27]

Several recent twin studies examined the genetic contribution to risk factors for heart disease. A 1981 collaborative study between the Institute of Medical Genetics, University of Oslo, Norway, and the Department of Human Genetics, Medical College of Virginia, Richmond, reported by Kare Berg, University of Oslo, found an overall concordance of 66 percent in MZ and 25 percent in DZ twins for coronary heart disease. Studies of several serum lipoproteins associated with coronary artery disease indicate a strong genetic influence.[28]

Longevity and factors that contribute to human life span are of increasing interest to twin researchers. Twins provide a living laboratory for studying the genetics of biological time. In a 1981 study of more than 2,000 twin pairs from the Mormon genealogy born between 1800 and 1899, Dorit Carmelli and Sheree Andersen, Department of Medical Biophysics and Computing, University of Utah, Salt Lake City, reported greater similarity in life span in same-sex twins, who may be MZ, than in opposite-sex pairs, who must be DZ. Females had a higher concordance rate than males.[29] A study of twins who served in World War II, conducted by Zdenek Hrubec, then of NAS-NRC, and geneticist James V. Neel, University of Michigan, Ann Arbor, found greater concordance in MZ than in DZ twins for death due to disease.[30] However, their study group had not reached old age, so much of the full genetic effect could not be measured. Luigi Gedda and Gianni Brenci, Gregor Mendel Institute for Medical Genetics and Twin Studies, concluded from their research on the genetics of the human life span that there is a basic, built-in genetic timetable.[31] They discuss one unusual example: 73-year-old MZ twins who died of the same cause only 10 days apart.[32] Galton described a similar case.[7] Undoubtedly, twin studies will teach us more about the genetic component of the human life span as the populations of the various twin registries reach old age.

A large number of papers on twin research is published each year. For example, we accessed *SCISEARCH®* using the word "twin" as a stem, which retrieves articles containing terms such as "twin," "twins," "twinning," and so on. We found 445 articles published in 1983 that contained such terms.

Some of the journals covered in *Current Contents®* (*CC®*) and *Science Citation Index®* that publish papers on twins are listed in Table 2. We selected for inclusion in the table those journals that most frequently published articles on twin research. The interdisciplinary nature of twin research is indicated by the wide range of disciplines represented in the table. Also included in the table is the 1983 impact factor for each journal. Impact was calculated by dividing the number of citations a journal's 1981 and 1982 articles received in 1983 by the number of articles it published in that two-year period.

Although twin studies do not provide a conclusive or definitive answer to the nature vs. nurture question, they are generally useful in providing a direction for further research. For example, Walter E. Nance and colleagues, Department of Human Genetics, Medical College of Virginia, Richmond, note that by extending twin studies to include families of twins, more detailed information can be obtained on the source of genetic and environmental variation.[33] As we

Table 2: Some of the main journals publishing research on twins. The 1983 impact factor for each has been listed.

Journal	Impact Factor
Acta Geneticae Medicae et Gemellologiae	0.4
Acta Obstetricia et Gynecologica Scandinavica	0.6
American Journal of Human Genetics	4.0
American Journal of Medical Genetics	1.6
American Journal of Obstetrics and Gynecology	1.9
American Journal of Psychiatry	3.2
Annals of Human Biology	0.6
Archives of General Psychiatry	6.1
Behavior Genetics	1.3
British Journal of Obstetrics and Gynaecology	1.5
British Journal of Psychiatry	2.4
Child Development	1.6
Clinical Genetics	1.2
Developmental Psychology	1.7
European Journal of Obstetrics, Gynecology and Reproductive Biology	0.3
Fertility and Sterility	2.4
Human Genetics	2.0
Human Heredity	0.7
Obstetrics and Gynecology	1.7

have seen, most human traits and clinical problems result from a combination of genetic and environmental factors. This brief survey of twin studies is by no means exhaustive. For reasons of space, I cannot review all the areas that use twins in research. However, by highlighting some of the significant twin studies, we realize the impact they have made on our understanding of behavioral genetics and some clinical problems. It would appear some of the folklore about twins is in fact confirmed by science. But clearly there is a great deal more to be learned from this exciting area of research.

* * * * *

My thanks to Terri Freedman and Linda LaRue for their help in the preparation of this essay.

©1984 ISI

REFERENCES

1. **Garfield E.** Twins. Part 1. The conception, development, and delivery of twins. *Current Contents* (46):3-10, 12 November 1984.
2. **Lytton H.** Do parents create, or respond to, differences in twins? *Develop. Psychol.* 13:456-9, 1977.

3. **Vandenberg S G.** Does a special twin situation contribute to similarity for abilities in MZ and DZ twins? *Acta Genet. Med. Gemellol.* 33(2):219-22, 1984.
4. **Robinette C D.** Telephone communication. 29 October 1984.
5. **Parisi P.** Methodology of twin studies: a general introduction. (Johnston F E, Roche A F & Susanne C, eds.) *Human physical growth and maturation.* New York: Plenum Press, 1980. p. 243-63.
6. **Segal N L.** Zygosity diagnosis: the lab is not quicker than the eye. (International Society for Twin Studies.) *Fourth International Congress on Twin Studies: program and abstracts,* 28 June-1 July 1983, London, UK. Rome: ISTS, 1983. p. 91.
7. **Galton F.** The history of twins, as a criterion of the relative powers of nature and nurture. *Fraser's Mag.* 12:566-76, 1875.
8. **Wilson R S.** The Louisville Twin Study: developmental synchronies in behavior. *Child Develop.* 54:298-316, 1983.
9. **Lykken D T.** Research with twins: the concept of emergenesis. *Psychophysiology* 19:361-73, 1982.
10. **Hearnshaw L S.** *Cyril Burt, psychologist.* Ithaca, NY: Cornell University Press, 1979. 370 p.
11. **Mather P L & Black K N.** Hereditary and environmental influences on preschool twins' language skills. *Develop. Psychol.* 20(2):303-8, 1984.
12. **Lytton H.** *Parent-child interaction.* New York: Plenum Press, 1980. 364 p.
13. **Conway D, Lytton H & Pysh F.** Twin-singleton language differences. *Can. J. Behav. Sci.* 12:264-71, 1980.
14. **Betton J P & Koester L S.** The impact of twinship: observed and perceived differences in mothers and twins. *Child Stud. J.* 13:85-93, 1983.
15. **Howie P M.** Concordance for stuttering in monozygotic and dizygotic twin pairs. *J. Speech Hear. Res.* 24:317-21, 1981.
16. --------------. Intrapair similarity in frequency of disfluency in monozygotic and dizygotic twin pairs containing stutterers. *Behav. Genet.* 11:227-38, 1981.
17. **Lykken D T, Tellegen A & Iacono W G.** EEG spectra in twins: evidence for a neglected mechanism of genetic determination. *Physiol. Psychol.* 10:60-5, 1982.
18. **Matheny A P & Dolan A B.** A twin study of personality and temperament during middle childhood. *J. Res. Personal.* 14:224-34, 1980.
19. **Loehlin J C & Nichols R C.** *Heredity, environment, and personality.* Austin, TX: University of Texas Press, 1976. 202 p.
20. **Bouchard T J.** Twins reared together and apart: what they tell us about human diversity. (Fox S W, ed.) *Proceedings of the Liberty Fund Conference on Chemical and Biological Bases for Individuality. Individuality and Determinism,* 1-2 May 1982, Key Biscayne, FL. New York: Plenum Press, 1984. p. 147-84.
21. **Gottesman I I & Shields J.** *Schizophrenia, the epigenetic puzzle.* New York: Cambridge University Press, 1982. 258 p.
22. **Farber S L.** *Identical twins reared apart.* New York: Basic Books, 1981. 383 p.
23. **Fulker D W.** Telephone communication. 29 October 1984.
24. **Barnett A H, Eff C, Leslie R D G & Pyke D A.** Diabetes in identical twins. *Diabetologia* 20:87-93, 1981.
25. **Srikanta S, Ganda O P, Jackson R A, Gleason R E, Kaldany A, Garovoy M R, Milford E L, Carpenter C B, Soeldner J S & Eisenbarth G S.** Type I diabetes mellitus in monozygotic twins: chronic progressive beta cell dysfunction. *Ann. Intern. Med.* 99:320-6, 1983.
26. **Williams A, Eldridge R, McFarland H, Houff S, Krebs H & McFarlin D.** Multiple sclerosis in twins. *Neurology* 30:1139-47, 1980.
27. **McFarland H F, Eldridge R & McFarlin D E.** Studies of multiple sclerosis in twins. *Trends Neurosci.* 6:378-80, 1983.
28. **Berg K.** Twin research in coronary heart disease. *Prog. Clin. Biol. Res.* 69C:117-30, 1981.
29. **Carmelli D & Andersen S.** A longevity study of twins in the Mormon genealogy. *Prog. Clin. Biol. Res.* 69C:187-200, 1981.
30. **Hrubec Z & Neel J V.** Contribution of familial factors to the occurrence of cancer before old age in twin veterans. *Amer. J. Hum. Genet.* 34:658-71, 1982.
31. **Gedda L & Brenci G.** Twin studies and chronogenetics. *Prog. Clin. Biol. Res.* 69C:169-78, 1981.
32. --------------------------. *Chronogenetics.* Springfield, IL: Thomas, 1978. 214 p.
33. **Nance W E, Corey L A & Boughman J A.** Monozygotic twin kinships: a new design for genetic and epidemiologic research. (Morton N E & Chung C S, eds.) *Genetic epidemiology.* New York: Academic Press, 1978. p. 87-131.

Current Comments®

The Awards of Science: Beyond the Nobel Prize. Part 2. The Winners and Their Most-Cited Papers

Number 50

December 10, 1984

In part one of this essay,[1] we provided a list of 52 prizes described as "non-Nobel" awards. The reason for choosing this term was somewhat tongue-in-cheek. The Nobel Prize has attained such a position of prestige with both scientists and the general public that other scientific awards seem to pale in comparison. This generalization is confirmed by the public's attitude toward Nobel Prize winners. Like movie stars, Nobelists are often idolized and consulted by the press on topics for which they have little training. Nobelist Rosalyn Yalow,[2] Veterans Administration Research Center, Bronx, New York, whose name is almost synonymous with radioimmunoassay, notes, "The Nobel Prize gives you the opportunity to make a fool of yourself in public."[3]

Although the Nobel is the most coveted and visible scientific award, hundreds of other prestigious awards recognize excellence in science. Several of these, including the Fields Medal in mathematics and the Holger Crafoord Prizes in mathematics, astronomy, biological science, geological science, and arthritis research, are in a sense "Nobels" for fields the Nobel does not honor. Others are what Harriet Zuckerman, Columbia University, New York, terms "premonitory prizes," which gauge their success by the extent to which they anticipate the Nobel.[4] The Lasker Awards are probably the best-known example. For-

ty Lasker winners have won the Nobel—39 of them before and 1 after winning the Nobel,[5] according to Alice Fordyce, director, Albert Lasker Medical Research Awards.

Another award that has often anticipated the Nobel is the Gairdner Foundation Award. Sally-Anne Hrica, executive director, Gairdner Foundation, notes that 27 Gairdner winners went on to win the Nobel, while 2 received the Gairdner after the Nobel.[6] Recently, the John Scott Award[7] of Philadelphia was given to Georges J.F. Köhler, Basel Institute of Immunology, and Cesar Milstein, Medical Research Council's Laboratory, Cambridge. This selection was made almost a year before the Nobel Prize announcements.

In the first part of this study, we identified the names and sponsors of more than 50 non-Nobel awards. The individuals who received these as well as three other awards are discussed below. One of these additional prizes is the Ernest-Jung-Preis für Medizin, awarded annually since 1976 by Ernest Jung Stiftung in Hamburg, Federal Republic of Germany. This prize carries an honorarium of 100,000 to 300,000 DM ($42,000 to $126,000) for pioneering research that has been translated into clinical practice. The Passano Award for medical research is administered by the Passano Foundation, Baltimore, Maryland. This annual prize has been awarded since

1945 and is accompanied by a cash prize of $15,000. The Badenwerk Foundation and University of Karlsruhe, Federal Republic of Germany, jointly sponsor the triennial Heinrich Hertz Preis. That prize was first awarded in 1975 and includes an honorarium of 50,000 DM ($21,000) for scientific and technical achievements in the generation, distribution, and application of electricity. Two awards listed in part one, the Premio Nacional de Ciencias (Colombia) and the King Faisal International Prize for Science, are not discussed here. We were unable to locate the organization that awards the first of these prizes, and the King Faisal Prize was not awarded in 1983. Also, the two Lasker Awards and the three Gairdner Foundation Awards in Table 2 were each treated as single awards in part one.

The awards discussed in this essay are only a few of the many prizes that recognize scientific excellence. There has been an incredible proliferation of scientific awards. To establish a practical limit for the essay, we set an arbitrary threshold. We have only included those awards that bestow an honorarium of at least $15,000. Although a fairly exhaustive search was conducted, we may have inadvertently omitted some awards. We intend to follow up with additional reports on less remunerative, but perhaps even more prestigious, awards. An alphabetic list of the 1982 award winners appears in Table 1.

When a prize was not awarded in 1982, we included the recipient for the nearest year. Our cutoff point for inclusion in this study was June 1983. We then corresponded with all 94 winners. This proved to be a mammoth task and explains the delay in reporting the results. Following each author's name in Table 1 is a number (or numbers) that identifies the relevant prize (or prizes). Table 2 is

alphabetized by the name of the award. It includes each recipient's most-cited paper during the period from 1961 to 1983 and the number of citations to it. Bibliographic and address information is provided for each paper. The research front for which each paper is a core document is also identified where applicable. A research front is established by identifying a group of current papers that collectively cite a cluster of earlier core papers in a specialty. Fifty-one of the award winners' papers proved to be core papers for 1981, 1982, and 1983 *Science Citation Index®* (*SCI®*) research fronts. Code numbers for seven papers that were identified in 1981 and 1982 *ISI/BIOMED®* research fronts, but not in *SCI* fronts, are also listed.

In assembling the data, we had initially identified papers for which the prize winners were the first authors. However, we asked all 94 winners to verify that the papers we had identified were their most relevant or significant. Of the 76 authors who replied, 58 agreed that the most-cited papers were their most important. Some authors directed us to other papers on which they were not the primary authors. Nineteen of these papers were more highly cited than those we had first identified. So we included them instead of earlier choices. We also added to the list those papers that 39 authors considered to be more important than their most-cited works. These appear after the author's most-cited paper, which is always first in Table 2. Unfortunately, 18 authors did not respond to our letters. They have been denoted by a plus (+) sign in Table 2.

The Humboldt Prize for Senior US Scientists was awarded to 58 individuals in 1982. The award, which was established in 1972 by Willy Brandt, then Chancellor of the Federal Republic of Germany, was created to honor Ameri-

---

Table 1: An alphabetic list of non-Nobel award winners and the award(s) they won. A=winner's name. B=award number (see Table 2).

A	B
Amelinckx, Severin	44
Anderson, Herbert L.	11
Angst, Jules	38
Arnold, Vladimir I.	7
Ashton, Norman	48
Ashwell, Gilbert	13
Atiyah, Michael F.	10
Axel, Richard	53
Becker, Erwin-Willy	20
Berry, R. Stephen	32
Bishop, J. Michael	29,39
Black, James W.	55
Blobel, Gunter	13,31
Brady, Roscoe O.	30
Braun, Armin C.	41
Brown, Michael S.	18
Burkitt, Dennis P.	2,36
Busse, Ewald W.	4
Carlsson, Arvid	13
Castor, Cecil W.	5
Changeux, Jean-Pierre	55
Chantrenne, Hubert	44
Clarke, Arthur C.	35
Cohen, Stanley	49
DeLuca, Hector F.	9
Desty, D.H.	34
Doherty, Peter C.	8
Efron, Bradley	32
El-Shazly, Khalid A.	28
Epstein, Michael A.	2
Erikson, Raymond L.	29
Felten, David L.	32
Gallo, Robert C.	29
Garwin, Richard L.	56
Ghuysen, Jean-Marie	47
Goldstein, Joseph L.	18
Hanafusa, Hidesaburo	29
Hounsfield, Godfrey N.	14
Howell, David S.	5
Hubbert, M. King	52
Hughes, John	43
Janssen, Paul A.J.	13
Johnston, Harold S.	51
Julesz, Bela	32
Kissmeyer-Nielsen, Flemming	24
Kosterlitz, Hans W.	43
Krein, Mark G.	55
Laurens, Paul	42
Lederman, Leon M.	55
Levy, Ronald G.	16
Lower, Richard R.	25
Mayer, Manfred M.	13
McCarty, Daniel J.	5
McClintock, Barbara	21,33,41
Meyer, Paul-Andre	40
Molina, Mario J.	51
Nachbin, Leopoldo	22
Nayfeh, Ali H.	28
Neddermeyer, Seth H.	11
Neufeld, Elizabeth F.	30

A	B
Nirenberg, Louis	7
Okamoto, Shunzo	12
Patz, Arnall	48
Paul, William E.	50
Perl, Martin L.	55
Peskin, Charles S.	32
Peters, Wallace	27
Pimentel, George C.	55
Polanyi, John C.	55
Potter, Michael	8
Puech, Paul	42
Robinson, Julia B.	32
Roelofs, Wendell L.	55
Rowland, F. Sherwood	51
Sandorfy, Camille	46
Sieh, Kerry E.	37
Siminovitch, Louis	15
Skipper, Howard E.	26
Snyder, Solomon H.	55
Spiegelman, Sol	10
Stevenson, George T.	16
Tonegawa, Susuma	21
Trouet, Andre	45
Umezawa, Sumio	12
Varmus, Harold E.	29,39
Verstraete, Marc	47
Weinberg, Alvin M.	17
Weissmann, Charles	19
Westheimer, Frank H.	6,54
Whitney, Hassler	55
Widdowson, Elsie M.	3
Wigler, Michael H.	1
Wrighton, Mark S.	32
Zinkernagel, Rolf M.	8

can scientists with international reputations who have promoted the interchange of ideas between German and American researchers and research institutions. For obvious reasons of space and time, we could not list or contact the 58 recipients, but we feel that this award deserves mention in this essay.

An asterisk in Table 2 indicates the 13 papers that have been discussed in *Citation Classic*™ commentaries. The issue, year, and edition of *Current Contents*® in which each author's commentary appeared follows the reference, after which is given the author's institution. If a paper appeared in ISI®'s study of the 1,000 authors most cited from 1965 to 1978,[8] a dagger (†) follows the author's name.

The list includes 94 authors. Eight of their publications are "kiloclassics"—

Table 2: Awards and recipients. The name of each award and the year it was given are presented as numbered, centered headers. Highly cited publications by the awardees are given after each award. Awardees' names are in bold. Citations to each paper are given in bold in parentheses after the publication information. A plus sign (+) indicates author did not respond. If the recipient was previously identified in ISI®'s study of the 1,000 most-cited scientists, 1965-1978, it is indicated by a dagger (†). A number symbol (#) indicates the article appeared in the study of the articles most cited from 1961 to 1982, Parts 1-5. An asterisk (*) indicates the item was the subject of a *Citation Classic™* commentary. The citation to the *Classic* is given after the item. If the item is a core document in an ISI research front, the number is given. The recipients' current affiliations are listed.

1.   **American Business Cancer Research Foundation Award, 1982**
   +**Wigler M**, Silverstein S, Lee L-S, Pellicer A, Cheng Y & Axel R. Transfer of purified herpes virus thymidine kinase gene to cultured mouse cells. *Cell* 11:223-32, 1977. SCI 83-6764. Cold Spring Harbor Lab., NY **(253)**

2.   **Bristol-Myers Award for Distinguished Achievement in**
                                     Cancer Research, 1982
   *****Burkitt D P.** Epidemiology of cancer of the colon and rectum. *Cancer* 28:3-13, 1971. (12/81/CP) Biomed 81-0273. Univ. London, St. Thomas's Hosp. Med. Sch., UK **(446)**
   *****Epstein M A**, Achong B G & Barr Y M. Virus particles in cultured lymphoblasts from Burkitt's lymphoma. *Lancet* 1:702-3, 1964. (14/79/LS) SCI 83-1209. Univ. Bristol Med. Sch., UK **(625)**

3.   **Bristol-Myers Award for Distinguished Achievement in Nutrition Research, 1982**
   McCance R A, **Widdowson E M**, Paul A A & Southgate D A T. *Composition of foods.* New York: Elsevier/North Holland Biomedical Press, 1978. 417 p. Univ. Cambridge, Addenbrooke's Hosp., UK **(587)**

4.   **Brookdale Awards for Research in Gerontology, 1982**
   Busse E W & Pfeiffer E, eds. *Behavior and adaptation in late life.* Boston, MA: Little, Brown, 1977. 382 p. SCI 83-3874 **(32)**
   Busse E W & Blazer D G, eds. *Handbook of geriatric psychiatry.* New York: Van Nostrand Reinhold, 1980. 542 p. Duke Univ. Med. Ctr., Durham, NC **(10)**

5.   **Ciba-Geigy ILAR Rheumatology Prize, 1982**
   Castor C W & Muirden K D. Collagen formation in monolayer cultures of human fibroblasts. *Lab. Invest.* 13:560-74, 1964. **(73)**
   Castor C W, Miller J W & Walz D A. Structural and biological characteristics of connective tissue activating peptide (CTAP-III), a major human platelet-derived growth factor. *Proc. Nat. Acad. Sci. US—Biol. Sci.* 80:765-9, 1983. Univ. Michigan Med. Sch., Ann Arbor, MI **(2)**
   Howell D S, Pita J C, Marquez J F & Madruga J E. Partition of calcium, phosphate, and protein in the fluid phase aspirated at calcifying sites in epiphyseal cartilage. *J. Clin. Invest.* 47:1121-32, 1968. Vet. Admin. Hosp. Med. Ctr., Miami, FL **(89)**
   McCarty D J, Kohn N N & Faires J S. The significance of calcium phosphate crystals in the synovial fluid of arthritic patients: the "pseudogout syndrome." I. Clinical aspects. *Ann. Intern. Med.* 56:711-37, 1962. SCI 83-0308 **(289)**
   McCarty D J & Hollander J L. Identification of urate crystals in gouty synovial fluid. *Ann. Intern. Med.* 54:452-60, 1961. Med. Coll. Wisconsin, Dept. Med., Milwaukee, WI **(184)**

6.   **Arthur C. Cope Award, 1982**
   Westheimer F H. Pseudo-rotation in the hydrolysis of phosphate esters. *Account. Chem. Res.* 1:70-8, 1968. SCI 83-1156 **(605)**
   Singh A, Thornton E R & **Westheimer F H.** The photolysis of diazo-acetylchymotrypsin. *J. Biol. Chem.* 237:PC3006-8, 1962. Harvard Univ., Dept. Chem., Cambridge, MA **(108)**

7.   **Holger Crafoord Prizes, 1982**
   Arnold V I & Avez A. *Problemes ergodiques de la mecanique classique.* (Ergodic problems of classical mechanics.) Paris: Gauthier-Villars Editeur, 1967. 243 p. SCI 81-0580. Univ. Moscow, Dept. Math., USSR **(265)**
   Nirenberg L. Remarks on strongly elliptic partial differential equations. *Commun. Pure Appl. Math.* 8:649-75, 1955. New York Univ., Courant Inst. Math. Sci., NY **(116)**

8.   **Paul Ehrlich-Ludwig-Darmstaedter Prize, 1983**
   *****Doherty P C**, Blanden R V & **Zinkernagel R M.** Specificity of virus-immune effector T cells for H-2K or H-2D compatible interactions: implications for H-antigen diversity. *Transplant. Rev.* 29:89-124, 1976. (18/83/LS) SCI 81-1438 **(569)**

Zinkernagel R M & Doherty P C. Restriction of *in vitro* T cell-mediated cytotoxicity in lymphocytic choriomeningitis within a syngeneic or semiallogeneic system. *Nature* 248:701-2, 1974. SCI 83-1491. Univ. Zurich, Inst. Pathol., Switzerland; Australian Natl. Univ., John Curtin Sch. Med. Res., Canberra, Australia **(394)**

+**Potter M†.** Immunoglobulin-producing tumors and myeloma proteins of mice. *Physiol. Rev.* 52:631-719, 1972. NIH, NCI, Bethesda, MD **(321)**

9.   **FASEB Award for Research in the Life Sciences, 1982**

Garabedian M, Holick M F, **DeLuca H F†** & Boyle I T. Control of 25-hydroxycholecalciferol metabolism by parathyroid glands. *Proc. Nat. Acad. Sci. US* 69:1673-6, 1972. SCI 83-6203 **(436)**

Holick M F, Schnoes H K, **DeLuca H F†**, Suda T & Cousins R J. Isolation and identification of 1,25-dihydroxycholecalciferol. A metabolite of vitamin D active in intestine. *Biochemistry* 10:2799-804, 1971. Univ. Wisconsin, Dept. Biochem., Madison, WI **(280)**

10.   **Antonio Feltrinelli Prizes, 1982**

Atiyah M F & Singer I M. The index of elliptic operators. *Ann. Math.* 87:484-604, 1968. SCI 83-1324. Univ. Oxford, Math. Inst., UK **(137)**

#*Gillespie D & **Spiegelman S.†** A quantitative assay for DNA-RNA hybrids with DNA immobilized on a membrane. *J. Mol. Biol.* 12:829-42, 1965. (11/77) Columbia Univ., Inst. Cancer Res., New York, NY **(1,755)**

11.   **Enrico Fermi Memorial Award, 1982**

+**Anderson H L,** Bharadwaj V K, Booth N E, Fine R M, Francis W R, Gordon B A, Heisterberg R H, Hicks R G, Kirk T B W, Kirkbride G I, Loomis W A, Matis H S, Mo L W, Myrianthopoulos L C, Pipkin F M, Pordes S H, Quirk T W, Shambroom W D, Skuja A, Verhey L J, Williams W S C, Wilson R & Wright S C. Measurement of nucleon structure function in muon scattering at 147 GeV/*c*. *Phys. Rev. Lett.* 37:4-7, 1976. Univ. Chicago, Dept. Phys., IL **(97)**

Neddermeyer S H & Anderson C D. Note on the nature of cosmic-ray particles. *Phys. Rev.* 51:884-6, 1937. Univ. Washington, Dept. Phys., Seattle, WA **(18)**

12.   **Fujihara Prize, 1982**

Okamoto S. *Introduction to earthquake engineering.* New York: Wiley, 1973. 571 p. Saitama Univ., Urawa City, Japan **(21)**

Umezawa S. Structures and syntheses of aminoglycoside antibiotics. *Advan. Carbohyd. Chem. Biochem.* 30:111-82, 1974. Microbial Chem. Res. Fdn., Inst. Bioorgan. Chem., Kawasaki, Japan **(109)**

13.   **Gairdner Foundation International Awards, 1982**

Ashwell G & Morell A G. The role of surface carbohydrates in the hepatic recognition and transport of circulating glycoproteins. *Advan. Enzymol. Relat. Areas Mol.* 41:99-128, 1974. NIH, NIAMDD, Bethesda, MD **(636)**

#**Blobel G†** & Dobberstein B. Transfer of proteins across membranes. I. Presence of proteolytically processed and unprocessed nascent immunoglobulin light chains on membrane-bound ribosomes of murine myeloma. *J. Cell Biol.* 67:835-51, 1975. SCI 83-2966 **(1,080)**

Blobel G†. Intracellular protein topogenesis. *Proc. Nat. Acad. Sci. US—Biol. Sci.* 77:1496-500, 1980. SCI 83-2966. Rockefeller Univ., New York, NY **(167)**

#*Bertler A, **Carlsson A†** & Rosengren E. A method for the fluorimetric determination of adrenaline and noradrenaline in tissues. *Acta Physiol. Scand.* 44:273-92, 1958. (49/79/LS) SCI 83-2640 **(1,108)**

Carlsson A†, Lindqvist M, Magnusson T & Waldeck B. On the presence of 3-hydroxy-tyramine in brain. *Science* 127:471, 1958. Univ. Gothenburg, Dept. Pharmacol., Sweden **(262)**

Janssen P A J, Niemegeers C J E & Schellekens K H L. Is it possible to predict the clinical effects of neuroleptic drugs (major tranquillizers) from animal data? Part 1. "Neuroleptic activity spectra" for rats. *Arzneim.-Forsch.-Drug Res.* 15:104-17, 1965. **(385)**

Janssen P A J, Niemegeers C J E & Schellekens K H L. Is it possible to predict the clinical effects of neuroleptic drugs (major tranquillizers) from animal data? Part II. "Neuroleptic activity spectra" for dogs. *Arzneim.-Forsch.-Drug Res.* 15:1196-206, 1965. Janssen Pharmaceut., Beerse, Belgium **(103)**

Kabat E A & **Mayer M M.** *Experimental immunochemistry.* Springfield, IL: Thomas, 1961. 905 p. SCI 83-5122 **(6,207)**

Mayer M M. The complement system. *Sci. Amer.* 229(5):54-66, 1973. Johns Hopkins Univ. Sch. Med., Baltimore, MD **(81)**

14.   **Gairdner Foundation International Award of Merit, 1976**
+Hounsfield G N. Computerized transverse axial scanning (tomography). Part I. Description of
system. *Brit. J. Radiol.* 46:1016-22, 1973. SCI 83-0710. EMI Ltd., Middlesex, UK **(748)**

15.   **Gairdner Foundation Wightman Award, 1981**
*Rothfels K H & Siminovitch L†. An air-drying technique for flattening chromosomes in
mammalian cells grown *in vitro. Stain Technol.* 33:73-7, 1958. (43/84/LS) **(510)**
Siminovitch L.† On the nature of hereditable variation in cultured somatic cells. *Cell* 7:1-11, 1976.
SCI 83-9209. Hosp. Sick Child., Toronto, Canada **(281)**

16.   **Armand Hammer Prize in Cancer, 1982**
Levy R & Kaplan H S. Impaired lymphocyte function in untreated Hodgkin's disease. *N. Engl. J.
Med.* 290:181-6, 1974. Biomed 82-1732 **(223)**
Miller R A, Maloney D G, Warnke R & Levy R. Treatment of B-cell lymphoma with monoclonal
anti-idiotype antibody. *N. Engl. J. Med.* 306:517-22, 1982. SCI 83-3616. Stanford Univ. Med.
Ctr., CA **(91)**
Stevenson G T & Dorrington K J. The recombination of dimers of immunoglobulin peptide
chains. *Biochem. J.* 118:703-12, 1970. **(102)**
Stevenson G T & Stevenson F K. Antibody to a molecularly-defined antigen confined to a tumour
cell surface. *Nature* 254:714-6, 1975. Univ. Southampton, Lymphoma Res. Unit, UK **(42)**

17.   **Harvey Prize, 1982**
+Weinberg A M & Wigner E P. *The physical theory of neutron chain reactors.* Chicago: University
of Chicago Press, 1958. 801 p. SCI 83-0471. Inst. Energy Analysis, Oak Ridge, TN **(572)**

18.   **Lita Annenberg Hazen Award for Excellence in Clinical Research, 1982**
Goldstein J L†, Anderson R G W & Brown M S†. Coated pits, coated vesicles, and receptor-
mediated endocytosis. *Nature* 279:679-85, 1979. SCI 83-0860 **(722)**
Goldstein J L† & Brown M S†. The low-density lipoprotein pathway and its relation to
atherosclerosis. *Annu. Rev. Biochem.* 46:897-930, 1977. SCI 83-0776. Univ. Texas Hlth. Sci.
Ctr., Dallas, TX **(619)**

19.   **Dr. H.P. Heineken Prize, 1982**
Schaffner W & Weissmann C. A rapid, sensitive, and specific method for the determination of
protein in dilute solution. *Anal. Biochem.* 56:502-14, 1973. **(601)**
Flavell R A, Sabo D L, Bandle E F & Weissmann C. Site-directed mutagenesis: generation of an
extracistronic mutation in bacteriophage Qβ RNA. *J. Mol. Biol.* 89:255-72, 1974. Univ. Zurich,
Inst. Mol. Biol. I, Switzerland **(78)**

20.   **Heinrich Hertz Preis, 1982**
Becker E W, Bier K & Henkes W. Strahlen aus kondensierten Atomen und Molekeln im
Hochvakuum. (Radiation of condensed atoms and molecules in a high vacuum.) *Z. Phys.*
146:333-8, 1956. **(57)**
Becker E W. Separation nozzle. (Villani S, ed.) *Uranium enrichment.* New York: Springer-Verlag,
1979. p. 245-68. Nucl. Res. Ctr., Karlsruhe Inst. Nucl. Proc. Tech., FRG **(2)**

21.   **Louisa Gross Horwitz Prize, 1982**
+McClintock B. Chromosome organization and genic expression. *Cold Spring Harbor Symp.*
16:13-47, 1951. Cold Spring Harbor Lab., NY **(322)**
+Tonegawa S, Maxam A M, Tizard R, Bernard O & Gilbert W. Sequence of a mouse germ-line
gene for a variable region of an immunoglobulin light chain. *Proc. Nat. Acad. Sci. US*
75:1485-9, 1978. Biomed 82-0015. MIT, Dept. Biol., Cambridge, MA **(238)**

22.   **Bernardo A. Houssay Science Prize, 1982**
Nachbin L. *Topology and order.* Huntington, NY: Krieger, 1976. 122 p. Univ. Rochester,
Dept. Math., NY **(103)**

23.   **Humboldt Prize for Senior US Scientists, 1982**
There were 58 awardees in 1982.

24.   **Anders Jahres Medisinski Priser, 1982**
*Kissmeyer-Nielsen F, Olsen S, Petersen V P & Fjeldborg O. Hyperacute rejection of kidney
allografts, associated with pre-existing humoral antibodies against donor cells. *Lancet* 2:662-5,
1966. (23/81/CP) SCI 83-1704. Univ. Aarhus, Dept. Clin. Immunol., Denmark **(348)**

25. **Ernest-Jung-Preis fur Medizin, 1983**
Lower R R, Stofer R C & Shumway N E. Homovital transplantation of the heart. *J. Thorac. Cardiovasc. Surg.* 41:196-204, 1961. Virginia Commonwealth Univ., Med. Coll. Virginia Hosp., Richmond, VA **(139)**

26. **Charles F. Kettering Prize, 1982**
*Skipper H E, Schabel F M & Wilcox W S. Experimental evaluation of potential anticancer agents. XIII. On the criteria and kinetics associated with "curability" of experimental leukemia. *Cancer Chemother. Rep.* 35:1-111, 1964. (2/81/CP) SCI 83-1333. Southern Res. Inst., Birmingham, AL **(555)**

27. **King Faisal International Prize for Medicine, 1983**
Peters W. *Chemotherapy and drug resistance in malaria.* New York: Academic Press, 1970. 876 p. SCI 83-3315. London Sch. Hyg. Trop. Med., Dept. Med. Protozool., UK **(157)**

28. **Kuwait Foundation for the Advancement of Sciences Prize, 1981**
El-Shazly K. Degradation of protein in the rumen of sheep. 1. Some volatile fatty acids, including branched-chain isomers found *in vivo*. *Biochem. J.* 51:640-7, 1952. Univ. Alexandria, Fac. Agricult., Egypt **(115)**
Nayfeh A H. *Perturbation methods.* New York: Wiley, 1973. 425 p. SCI 83-8712. Yarmouk Univ., Fac. Eng., Irbid, Jordan **(431)**

29. **Albert Lasker Basic Medical Research Award, 1982**
+Collett M S & **Erikson R L.** Protein kinase activity associated with the avian sarcoma virus *src* gene product. *Proc. Nat. Acad. Sci. US* 75:2021-4, 1978. SCI 83-0069. Harvard Univ., Dept. Cell Develop. Biol., Cambridge, MA **(509)**
Morgan D A, Ruscetti F M & **Gallo R C**†. Selective in vitro growth of T lymphocytes from normal human bone marrows. *Science* 193:1007-8, 1976. SCI 83-2933. **(452)**
Poiesz B J, Ruscetti F W, Gazdar A F, Bunn P A, Minna J D & **Gallo R C**†. Detection and isolation of type C retrovirus particles from fresh and cultured lymphocytes of a patient with cutaneous T-cell lymphoma. *Proc. Nat. Acad. Sci. US—Biol. Sci.* 77:7415-9, 1980. SCI 83-2933. NIH, NCI, Bethesda, MD **(210)**
Hanafusa H, Hanafusa T & Rubin H. The defectiveness of Rous sarcoma virus. *Proc. Nat. Acad. Sci. US* 49:572-80, 1963. **(252)**
Hanafusa H, Halpern C C, Buchhagen D L & Kawai S. Recovery of avian sarcoma virus from tumors induced by transformation-defective mutants. *J. Exp. Med.* 146:1735-47, 1977. Biomed 82-0027. Rockefeller Univ., New York, NY **(112)**
Stehelin D, **Varmus H E**, **Bishop J M**† & Vogt P K. DNA related to the transforming gene(s) of avian sarcoma viruses is present in normal avian DNA. *Nature* 260:170-3, 1976. SCI 83-0069. Univ. California Med. Sch., San Francisco, CA **(336)**

30. **Albert Lasker Clinical Medical Research Award, 1982**
Brady R O†, Kanfer J N & Shapiro D. Metabolism of glucocerebrosides. II. Evidence of an enzymatic deficiency in Gaucher's disease. *Biochem. Biophys. Res. Commun.* 18:221-5, 1965. SCI 83-3331 **(231)**
Brady R O†, Kanfer J N, Bradley R M & Shapiro D. Demonstration of a deficiency of glucocerebroside-cleaving enzyme in Gaucher's disease. *J. Clin. Invest.* 45:1112-5, 1966. NIH, NINCDS, Bethesda, MD **(146)**
Hickman S & **Neufeld E F.** A hypothesis for I-cell disease: defective hydrolases that do not enter lysosomes. *Biochem. Biophys. Res. Commun.* 49:992-9, 1972. SCI 83-0860 **(315)**
Fratantoni J C, Hall C W & **Neufeld E F.** The defect in Hurler's and Hunter's syndromes: faulty degradation of mucopolysaccharide. *Proc. Nat. Acad. Sci. US* 60:699-706, 1968. NIH, NIADDK, Bethesda, MD **(276)**

31. **Richard Lounsberry Prize, 1983**
Blobel G. See #13.

32. **MacArthur Prize Fellow Awards, 1982**
+ *Berry R S. Correlation of rates of intramolecular tunneling processes, with application to some group V compounds. *J. Chem. Phys.* 32:933-8, 1960. (8/81/ET&AS,PC&ES) SCI 83-2624. Univ. Chicago, Dept. Chem., IL **(547)**
Efron B & Morris C. Stein's estimation rule and its competitors—an empirical Bayes approach. *J. Amer. Statist. Assn.* 68:117-30, 1973. SCI 83-2497 **(63)**

Efron B. *The jackknife, the bootstrap and other resampling plans.* Philadelphia, PA: SIAM, 1982. 92 p. Stanford Univ., Dept. Stat., Palo Alto, CA **(3)**

Felten D L, Laties A M & Carpenter M B. Monoamine-containing cell bodies in the squirrel monkey brain. *Amer. J. Anat.* 139:153-66, 1974. Biomed 82-1514 **(82)**

Felten D L & Sladek J R. Monoamine distribution in primate brain. V. Monoaminergic nuclei: anatomy, pathways and local organization. *Brain Res. Bull.* 10:171-284, 1983. Univ. Rochester Med. Ctr., NY **(0)**

Julesz B. *Foundations of cyclopean perception.* Chicago: University of Chicago Press, 1971. 406 p. Bell Labs., Sensory Percept. Dept., Murray Hill, NJ **(420)**

+Peskin C S. Flow patterns around heart valves: a numerical method. *J. Comput. Phys.* 10:252-71, 1972. New York Univ., Courant Inst. Math. Sci., NY **(15)**

Davis M, Matijasevic Y & Robinson J. Hilbert's tenth problem. Diophantine equations: positive aspects of a negative solution. *Proc. Symp. Pure Math.* 28:323-78, 1976. Univ. California, Dept. Math., Berkeley, CA **(21)**

Ellis A B, Kaiser S W & **Wrighton M S.** Letter to editor. (Visible light to electrical energy conversion. Stable cadmium sulfide and cadmium selenide photoelectrodes in aqueous electrolytes.) *J. Amer. Chem. Soc.* 98:1635-7, 1976. SCI 83-1775. MIT, Dept. Chem., Cambridge, MA **(131)**

33.   **MacArthur Prize Fellow Laureate Award, 1981**
McClintock B. See #21.

34.   **MacRobert Award, 1982**
Desty D H, Haresnape J N & Whyman B H F. Construction of long lengths of coiled glass capillary. *Anal. Chem.* 2:302-4, 1960. **(119)**
Desty D H. No smoke with fire. *Proc. Inst. Mech. Eng. A—Power* 197:159-70, 1983. British Petroleum Co. Res. Ctr., London, UK **(0)**

35.   **Guglielmo Marconi International Fellowship, 1982**
Clarke A C. Extra-terrestrial relays. *Wireless World* 61:305-8, 1945. Univ. Moratuwa, Sri Lanka **(16)**

36.   **Charles S. Mott Prize, 1982**
Burkitt D P. See #2.

37.   **NAS Award for Initiatives in Research, 1982**
+**Sieh K E.** Prehistoric large earthquakes produced by slip on the San Andreas fault at Pallett Creek, California. *J. Geophys. Res.* 83:3907-39, 1978. CalTech, Div. Geol. Planet. Sci., Pasadena, CA **(31)**

38.   **Otto Naegeli-Preis, 1983**
Angst J. Zur Aetiologie und Nosologie endogener depressiver Psychosen. (On the etiology and nosology of endogenous depressive psychoses.) Berlin: Springer-Verlag, 1966. 118 p. Univ. Zurich, Psychiat. Clin., Switzerland **(256)**

39.   **Passano Award, 1983**
Bishop J M & Varmus H E. See #29.

40.   **Prix Ampere de l'Electricite de France, 1983**
Dellacherie C & **Meyer P-A.** *Probabilities and potential.* New York: North-Holland, 1978. 189 p. SCI 83-0526. Univ. Strasbourg, Dept. Math., France **(576)**

41.   **Prix Charles Leopold-Mayer, 1982**
Braun A C. A demonstration of the recovery of the crown-gall tumor cell with the use of complex tumors of single-cell origin. *Proc. Nat. Acad. Sci.* 45:932-8, 1959. **(119)**
Braun A C. An epigenetic model for the origin of cancer. *Quart. Rev. Biol.* 56:33-60, 1981. Rockefeller Univ., New York, NY **(3)**
McClintock B. See #21.

42.   **Prix Claude-Adolphe Nativelle Pour l'Art et la Medicine, 1977**
+**Laurens P.** Considerations sur l'origine des bruits du coeur. (Considerations of the origin of heart murmurs.) *Acta Cardiol.* 19:327-44, 1964. INSERM, Broussais Hosp., Paris, France **(18)**
+**Puech P** & Grolleau R. *L'activite du faisceau de His normale et pathologique.* (The activity of normal and pathological His bundles.) Paris: Sandoz, 1972. St. Eloi Hosp., Montpellier, France **(69)**

43. Prix de la Fondation Professeur Lucien Dautrebande, 1982

#*Hughes J, Smith T W, Kosterlitz H W, Fothergill L A, Morgan B A & Morris H R. Identification of two related pentapeptides from the brain with potent opiate agonist activity. *Nature* 258:577-9, 1975. (38/82/LS) SCI 83-7424 (1,350)

Lord J A H, Waterfield A A, Hughes J & Kosterlitz H W. Endogenous opioid peptides: multiple agonists and receptors. *Nature* 267:495-9, 1977. SCI 83-3271. Parke-Davis Res. Unit, Cambridge, UK; Univ. Aberdeen, Unit Res. Addictive Drugs, UK (950)

44. Prix Docteur A. de Leeuw-Damry-Bourlart & Prijs Doctor A. de Leeuw-Damry-Bourlart, 1980

+Chantrenne H, Burny A & Marbaix G. The search for the messenger RNA of hemoglobin. *Prog. Nucl. Acid Res. Mol. Biol.* 7:173-94, 1967. Free Univ., Biochem. Lab., Brussels, Belgium (108)

Amelinckx S. *The direct observation of dislocations.* New York: Academic Press, 1964. 487 p. Nucl. Energy Res. Ctr. (SCK/CEN), Brussels, Belgium (294)

45. Prix Franqui, 1981

de Duve C, de Barsy T, Poole B, Trouet A, Tulkens P & Van Hoff F. Lysosomotropic agents. *Biochem. Pharmacol.* 23:2495-531, 1974. SCI 83-0860 (373)

Trouet A, Masquelier M, Baurain R & Deprez-DeCampeneere D. A covalent linkage between daunorubicin and proteins that is stable in serum and reversible by lysosomal hydrolases, as required for a lysosomotropic drug-carrier conjugate: *in vitro* and *in vivo* studies. *Proc. Nat. Acad. Sci. US—Biol. Sci.* 79:626-9, 1982. Intl. Inst. Cell. Mol. Pathol., Brussels, Belgium (13)

46. Prix Marie-Victorin, 1982

Sandorfy C. *Electronic spectra and quantum chemistry.* Englewood Cliffs, NJ: Prentice-Hall, 1964. 385 p. Univ. Montreal, Dept. Chem., Canada (92)

47. Prix Scientifique Joseph Maisin & Wetenschappelijke Prijs Joseph Maisin, 1980

Ghuysen J-M. Use of bacteriolytic enzymes in determination of wall structure and their role in cell metabolism. *Bacteriol. Rev.* 32:425-64, 1968. Univ. Liege, Fac. Med., Belgium (383)

*Verstraete M, Vermylen C, Vermylen J & Vandenbroucke J. Excessive consumption of blood coagulation components as cause of hemorrhagic diathesis. *Amer. J. Med.* 38:899-908, 1965. (46/83/CP) (181)

Verstraete M. Are agents affecting platelet functions clinically useful? *Amer. J. Med.* 61:897-914, 1976. Catholic Univ., Dept. Med. Res., Louvain, Belgium (54)

48. RPB-Jules Stein Award, 1981

Ashton N, Ward B & Serpell G. Effect of oxygen on developing retinal vessels with particular reference to the problem of retrolental fibroplasia. *Brit. J. Ophthalmol.* 38:397-432, 1954. Roy. Coll. Surgs. England, London, UK (126)

Patz A, Eastham A, Higginbotham D H & Kleh T. Oxygen studies in retrolental fibroplasia. II. The production of the microscopic changes of retrolental fibroplasia in experimental animals. *Amer. J. Ophthalmol.* 36:1511-22, 1953. Johns Hopkins Univ., Wilmer Ophthalmol. Inst., Baltimore, MD (94)

49. Alfred P. Sloan Prize, 1982

+Cohen S. Isolation of a mouse submaxillary gland protein accelerating incisor eruption and eyelid opening in the new-born animal. *J. Biol. Chem.* 237:1555-62, 1962. Biomed 82-0310. Vanderbilt Univ. Sch. Med., Nashville, TN (387)

50. Texas Instruments Foundation Founders' Prize, 1979

*Odell W D, Wilber J F & Paul W E†. Radioimmunoassay of thyrotropin in human serum. *J. Clin. Endocrinol.* 25:1179-88, 1965. (43/80/CP) (414)

Paul W E† & Benacerraf B. Functional specificity of thymus-dependent lymphocytes. *Science* 195:1293-300, 1977. Biomed 82-1386. NIH, NIAID, Bethesda, MD (258)

51. John and Alice Tyler Ecology-Energy Prize, 1983

Johnston H S. *Gas phase reaction rate theory.* New York: Ronald Press, 1966. 362 p. SCI 83-6425 (722)

Johnston H S. Reduction of stratospheric ozone by nitrogen oxide catalysts from supersonic transport exhaust. *Science* 173:517-22, 1971. SCI 83-2756. Univ. California, Dept. Chem., Berkeley, CA (301)

Molina M J & Rowland F S. Stratospheric sink for chlorofluoromethanes: chlorine atom-catalysed destruction of ozone. *Nature* 249:810-2, 1974. SCI 83-8321 (373)

Rowland F S & Molina M J. Chlorofluoromethanes in the environment. *Rev. Geophys. Space Phys.* 13:1-35, 1975. Univ. California, Dept. Chem., Irvine, CA; CalTech, Jet Propulsion Lab., Pasadena, CA (237)

52.   **Vetlesen Prize, 1981**
Hubbert M K & Rubey W W. Role of fluid pressure in mechanics of overthrust faulting. I. Mechanics of fluid-filled porous solids and its application to overthrust faulting. *Bull. Geol. Soc. Amer.* 70:115-66, 1959. SCI 83-1145. US Geol. Survey, Reston, VA **(281)**

53.   **Alan T. Waterman Award, 1982**
+**Garel A** & **Axel R**. Selective digestion of transcriptionally active ovalbumin genes from oviduct nuclei. *Proc. Nat. Acad. Sci. US* 73:3966-70, 1976. SCI 83-2808. Columbia Univ., Inst. Cancer Res., New York, NY **(400)**

54.   **Robert A. Welch Award in Chemistry, 1982**
Westheimer F H. See #6.

55.   **Wolf Prizes, 1982**
+#**Black J W**, Duncan W A M, Durant C J, Ganellin C R & Parsons E M. Definition and antagonism of histamine H_2-receptors. *Nature* 236:385-90, 1972. SCI 83-1253. Wellcome Res. Lab., Beckenham, UK **(1,181)**
#**Monod J**, Wyman J & **Changeux J-P**†. On the nature of allosteric transitions: a plausible model. *J. Mol. Biol.* 12:88-118, 1965. SCI 83-1014 **(2,771)**
#**Changeux J-P**†. The acetylcholine receptor: an "allosteric" membrane protein. *Harvey Lectures* 75:85-254, 1981. SCI 83-4227. Inst. Pasteur, Dept. Mol. Neurobiol., Paris, France **(85)**
Krein M G & Rutman M A. Linear operators leaving invariant a cone in a Banach space. *Usp. Mat. Nauk* 3(1):3-95, 1948. SCI 83-0180 **(122)**
Krein M G. *Topics in differential and integral equations and operator theory.* Boston: Birkhauser Verlag, 1983. 302 p. Acad. Sci. UkSSR, Inst. Phys. Chem., Odessa, USSR **(0)**
Herb S W, Hom D C, **Lederman L M**, Sens J C, Snyder H D, Yoh J K, Appel J A, Brown B C, Brown C N, Innes W R, Ueno K, Yamanouchi T, Ito A S, Jostlein H, Kaplan D M & Kephart R D. Observation of a dimuon resonance at 9.5 GeV in 400-GeV proton-nucleus collisions. *Phys. Rev. Lett.* 39:252-5, 1977. SCI 83-0922. Fermi Natl. Accelerat. Lab., Batavia, IL **(413)**
Augustin J-E, Boyarski A M, Breidenbach M, Bulos F, Dakin J T, Feldman G J, Fischer G E, Fryberger D, Hanson G, Jean-Marie B, Larsen R R, Luth V, Lynch H L, Lyon D, Morehouse C C, Paterson J M, **Perl M L**†, Richter B, Rapidis P, Schwitters R F, Tanenbaum W M, Vannucci F, Abrams G S, Briggs D, Chinowsky W, Friedberg C E, Kadyk J A, Lulu B, Pierre F, Trilling G H, Whitaker J S, Wiss J & Zipse J E. Discovery of a narrow resonance in *e+ e−* annihilation. *Phys. Rev. Lett.* 33:1406-8, 1974. SCI 82-0661 **(714)**
Perl M L†, Abrams G S, Boyarski A M, Breidenbach M, Briggs D D, Bulos F, Chinowsky W, Dakin J T, Feldman G J, Friedberg C E, Fryberger D, Goldhaber G, Hanson G, Heile F B, Jean-Marie B, Kadyk J A, Larsen R R, Litke A M, Luke D, Lulu B A, Luth V, Lyon D, Morehouse C C, Paterson J M, Pierre F M, Pun T P, Rapidis P A, Richter B, Sadoulet B, Schwitters R F, Tanenbaum W, Trilling G H, Vannucci F, Whitaker J S, Winkelman F C & Wiss J E. Evidence for anomalous lepton production in *e+ e−* annihilation. *Phys. Rev. Lett.* 35:1489-92, 1975. SCI 81-0183. Stanford Univ., Stanford Linear Accelerat. Ctr., CA **(396)**
*****Pimentel G C** & McClellan A L. *The hydrogen bond.* San Francisco: Freeman, 1960. 475 p. (36/82/PC) **(2,976)**
Kasper J V V & **Pimentel G C**. HCl chemical laser. *Phys. Rev. Lett.* 14:352-4, 1965. Univ. California, Lab. Chem. Biodynam., Berkeley, CA **(183)**
Polanyi J C†. Some concepts in reaction dynamics. *Account. Chem. Res.* 5:161-8, 1972. Univ. Toronto, Dept. Chem., Canada **(235)**
Roelofs W, Comeau A, Hill A & Milicevic G. Sex attractant of the codling moth: characterization with electroantennogram technique. *Science* 174:297-9, 1971. Cornell Univ., New York State Agricult. Exp. Station, Geneva, NY **(116)**
+**Pert C B** & **Snyder S H**†. Opiate receptor: demonstration in nervous tissue. *Science* 179:1011-4, 1973. SCI 83-7424. Johns Hopkins Univ. Sch. Med., Baltimore, MD **(759)**
Whitney H. On the abstract properties of linear dependence. *Amer. J. Math.* 57:509-33, 1935. SCI 83-5525 **(114)**
Whitney H. On the topology of differentiable manifolds. (Wilder R L & Ayres W L, eds.) *Lectures in topology.* Ann Arbor, MI: University of Michigan Press, 1941. p. 101-41. Inst. Advan. Study, Princeton, NJ **(22)**

56.   **Wright Prize, 1983**
Garwin R L, Lederman L M & Weinrich M. Letter to the editor. (Observations of the failure of conservation of parity and charge conjugation in meson decays: the magnetic moment of the free muon.) *Phys. Rev.* 105:1415-7, 1957. IBM, Thomas J. Watson Res. Ctr., Yorktown Heights, NY **(304)**

publications that have received more than 1,000 citations. The most-cited of these is a book entitled *Experimental Immunochemistry*. It was cited over 6,200 times between 1961 and 1983. The late Manfred M. Mayer, Johns Hopkins University School of Medicine, Baltimore, Maryland, honored by a Gairdner Foundation International Award for his work on the complement system, wrote this book with E.A. Kabat, Columbia University. The second edition of this book includes a chapter by Mayer on the complement system, a group of proteins that act in concert with antibodies to protect the body from foreign antigens. Mayer asked that we add his *Scientific American* paper to Table 2 because its reprint distribution exceeds 40,000.

The oldest publication in Table 2 is a 1935 paper by Hassler Whitney, Princeton, New Jersey. Whitney won the Wolf Prize in mathematics for his work in algebraic and differential topology.

In many of the citation studies that ISI publishes, we single out Nobel Prize winners to illustrate that citation frequency often correlates with peer estimates of scientific accomplishment. A paper becomes highly cited because many members of the scientific community have found it valuable. This is not to say that all significant research is highly cited. Some Nobelists do not appear on most-cited lists. And a number of the papers mentioned in this essay received relatively few citations.

In some cases, prize winners' most significant publications may have been so quickly absorbed into the common wisdom of the field that the explicit citation of these works was obliterated. Such cases are rare. Another reason for low citation frequency may be publication in a language not read by most scientists. Shunzo Okamoto, Saitama University, Japan, awarded the 1982 Fujihara Prize, is well-known to earthquake engineers

in both the US and Japan. According to Joseph Penzien, professor of structural engineering, University of California, Berkeley, Okamoto has published primarily in Japanese journals,[9] which may have limited his citation frequency outside his own country.

Papers reporting work in relatively small fields may receive few citations when compared to those in larger fields. In our studies of disciplinary citation rates, we found that geoscientists[10] tend to receive fewer citations than do neuroscientists.[11] Consequently, someone like Kerry E. Sieh, California Institute of Technology, Pasadena, who won the National Academy of Sciences Award for Initiatives in Research for contributions to earthquake engineering, would be expected to receive fewer citations than someone working on opiate receptor research, a field that has attracted many scientists.

Several of the papers in Table 2 received few citations simply because they were published quite recently. These papers were identified when we contacted the prize winners in this study. Some of these authors requested that we include these more recent but less-cited works because they consider them to be more significant.

As mentioned above, prize winning work may not be highly cited because it is "obliterated"—so integrated into a field's common wisdom that scientists neglect to cite it explicitly. For this reason, I was surprised to learn that Arthur C. Clarke's 1945 *Wireless World* article on extraterrestrial relays had been explicitly cited at all. Clarke received the Guglielmo Marconi International Fellowship. He is widely known for his contributions to the invention of the communications satellite, but he is even better known as a master of science fiction.

There isn't always a simple explanation for the paucity of citations to the work of some authors. For a variety of reasons, good research is sometimes unappreciated or ignored by the scientific community. It may achieve delayed recognition.[12] And there may even be cases of systematic citation amnesia,[13] although these are hard to document. However, one must also add the simple explanation that award groups are human and selections may be made for reasons other than purely scientific impact. Many choices, such as earlier Nobel Prizes, are controversial to say the least.

Several awards in Table 2 and their associated core papers have been selected from the same basic research front, for example, oncogenes and the cancervirus connection. Several papers by winners of the 1982 Lasker Basic Medical Research Award helped identify these fronts. Two papers by Robert C. Gallo, National Cancer Institute, Bethesda, Maryland, are core to *SCI* front #83-2933, "Human T-cell lymphoma virus and adult T-cell leukemia: nucleic acid analysis and expression of virus induced by interleukin 2." Gallo won the Lasker for his discovery of the human T-cell leukemia virus, the first retrovirus known to be associated with a human malignancy.

Three of the five Lasker Basic Medical Research Award winners are represented in *SCI* front #83-0069, "Effects of epidermal, platelet-derived, and other growth factors on tyrosine and protein phosphorylation by protein kinase." J. Michael Bishop and Harold E. Varmus, University of California, San Francisco, and Raymond L. Erikson, Harvard University, Cambridge, Massachusetts, shared the Lasker with Gallo for discovering links between viruses and cancer.[14]

Papers by Lasker Clinical Medical Research awardee Elizabeth F. Neufeld, National Institute of Arthritis, Diabetes, Digestive and Kidney Diseases (NIADDKD), Bethesda, and Prix Franqui winner André Trouet, International Institute of Cellular and Molecular Pathology, Brussels, are core in *SCI* front #83-0860, "Receptor-mediated endocytosis and role of coated vesicles in plasma membrane recycling." Prix de la Fondation Professeur Lucien Dautrebande winners John Hughes, ParkeDavis Research Unit, Cambridge, England, and Hans W. Kosterlitz, University of Aberdeen, Scotland, and Solomon H. Snyder, Johns Hopkins University, who won the Wolf Prize in medicine, are classic authors in *SCI* front #83-7424, "Synthesis and properties of beta-endorphins, opioid peptides, enkephalins, and their receptors."

Contributions by Günter Blobel, Rockefeller University, New York, to research on intracellular protein transport are reflected by his two core papers for research front #83-2966, "Membrane biogenesis and mechanism of protein insertion and secretion: use of cDNA probes in protein processing." Blobel received both the Richard Lounsberry Prize and the Gairdner Foundation International Award.

It may not be a surprise that many of the award recipients in Table 2 have won other prestigious awards. For example, Godfrey N. Hounsfield, EMI Ltd., Middlesex, UK, a 1979 Nobelist,[15] had already received the 1976 Gairdner Foundation International Award of Merit for development of the computed axial tomography (CAT) scan. Barbara McClintock, Cold Spring Harbor Laboratory, New York, a 1983 Nobelist, not only received the Louisa Gross Horwitz Prize and the Prix Charles Léopold-Mayer in 1982 but also, in 1981, she won the Lasker Basic Medical Research Award and was named the first MacArthur Prize Fellow Laureate. McClintock is credited with having contributed substantially to our understanding of the "mobility" of genes on chromosomes, so-called "jumping genes." In a subsequent report, I'll have more to say about the mythologies concerning the delayed recognition of her work.

Five of the authors in this list won two awards. As mentioned earlier, Bishop and Varmus won both the Albert Lasker Basic Medical Research Award and the 1983 Passano Award. They were recognized for demonstrating that certain cancer-causing genes from viruses are almost identical to some genes normally found in animals and for thus discovering what are now called oncogenes. Blobel, also mentioned earlier, won both the Gairdner Foundation International Award and the Lounsberry Prize.

Both the Bristol-Myers Award for Distinguished Achievement in Cancer Research and the Charles S. Mott Prize went to Dennis P. Burkitt, St. Thomas's Hospital Medical School, London. Burkitt discovered the role played by a virus in the development of a form of cancer that bears his name, Burkitt's lymphoma. He shared the Bristol-Myers award with Michael A. Epstein, University of Bristol Medical School, who isolated the previously unidentified Epstein-Barr virus from Burkitt's lymphoma. Frank H. Westheimer, Harvard University, received both the Robert A. Welch Award in Chemistry and the Arthur C. Cope Award. Westheimer, a pioneer bio-organic chemist, is probably best known for his contributions to photo-affinity labeling, a method for identifying in membranes those compounds that bind to specific hormones or drugs.

A number of award recipients are past winners of other prizes listed in Table 2. Burkitt won the Gairdner Foundation International Award in 1973 and the Ehrlich Award in 1972. In 1965, Daniel J. McCarty, Medical College of Wisconsin, Milwaukee, also received the Gairdner Foundation International Award. In 1982, he won the Ciba-Geigy ILAR Prize for rheumatology research. Howard E. Skipper, Southern Research Institute, Birmingham, Alabama, who received the 1982 Charles F. Kettering Prize for his research on the treatment of disseminated cancers and Arnall Patz, Johns Hopkins University, who received the 1981 RPB-Jules Stein Award, are previous Lasker awardees. Patz was the first person to discover that oxygen was responsible for retrolental fibroplasia, a disorder that is responsible for blindness in premature infants. Hounsfield won the Lasker Clinical Medical Research Award in 1975.

Hughes and Kosterlitz, won the 1982 Dautrebande Prize for their work on opiate receptors—sites in the brain that bind opiates with a high affinity. Snyder, as I mentioned, was named a Wolf Prize recipient for the development of ways for labeling neurotransmitter receptors. Hughes, Kosterlitz, and Snyder were Lasker Basic Medical Research Award winners in 1978. Kosterlitz and Snyder also received Harvey Prizes in 1981 and 1978, respectively.

Of the 94 scientists identified in this essay, 16 were included in our study of the 1,000 authors most cited from 1965 to 1978.[8] Three of the Gairdner Foundation Award winners are in the 1,000 most-cited author list. Blobel won the award for his work on intracellular protein transport. Arvid Carlsson, University of Gothenburg, Sweden, won it for research on the role of amines, particularly dopamine, as neurotransmitters. Louis Siminovitch, Hospital for Sick Children, Toronto, Canada, received the Gairdner Foundation Wightman Award in 1981 for his many contributions to genetics research. The Wightman Award is given from time to time to a Canadian who has demonstrated leadership in medicine and medical science.

Four of the Wolf Prize winners were on the list of 1,000 most-cited authors: Snyder, mentioned earlier; Martin L. Perl, Stanford Linear Accelerator Center, California, who won the Wolf Prize in physics; John C. Polanyi, University of Toronto, who won the chemistry prize; and Jean-Pierre Changeux, Institut Pasteur, Paris, who won the prize in medicine. Michael S. Brown and Joseph L. Goldstein, University of Texas Health Science Center, Dallas, received the Lita Annenberg Hazen Award for Excellence in Clinical Research for identifying low-density lipoprotein receptor pathways. Three Lasker Award winners were also on the 1,000 most-cited authors list: Gallo, Bishop, and Roscoe O. Brady, National Institute of Neurological and Communicative Disorders and Stroke (NINCDS), Bethesda. Brady shared the Lasker Clinical Medical Research Award with Neufeld for their work on lipid storage diseases and mucopolysaccharide storage diseases, both childhood disorders.

Other scientists who appeared on our list of 1,000 most-cited authors include Hector F. DeLuca, University of Wisconsin, Madison, who won the Federation of American Societies for Experimental Biology (FASEB) Award; William E. Paul, National Institute of Allergy and Infectious Diseases (NIAID), Bethesda, who won the Texas Instruments Foundation Founders' Prize; Michael Potter, National Cancer Institute (NCI), Bethesda, who won the Paul Ehrlich-Ludwig-Darmstaedter Prize; and Sol Spiegelman, Columbia University, who won the Antonio Feltrinelli Prize.

It is significant that six of the award-winning papers were included in our recent study of 500 *Citation Classics*.[16] I would expect that most of these papers would become *Citation Classics*. Blobel and Carlsson, winners of the Gairdner Foundation International Award, are mentioned in that study. So are two Wolf Prize recipients—Changeux and James W. Black. Black, Wellcome Research Laboratory, Beckenham, England, received the prize for developing agents that block beta-adrenergic and histamine receptors. Others identified in that study are Feltrinelli winner Spiegelman and Dautrebande winners Hughes and Kosterlitz.

Although the awards that are discussed in this essay may not receive the same public acclaim as a Nobel Prize, they serve many important and useful functions. The first is to recognize that outstanding work is done by many scientists today. Scientific research can be lonely and frustrating at times, and researchers, no less than Hollywood celebrities, deserve and enjoy recognition from their peers. A second and equally important function concerns interdisciplinary scientific communication. While the papers in Table 2 have generally had widespread impact, as evidenced by the citations they've acquired, most of this influence is or was originally limited to each prize winner's field. By recognizing ideas and discoveries that at first seemed very specialized, awarding committees heighten the visibility and, therefore, the potential applicability of the prize winning work.

Our purpose in this essay has been (a) to identify the many prestigious non-Nobel awards; (b) to name recent recipients of these awards; (c) to identify their most-cited and most-significant papers; and (d) to point out the multiplicity of awards given to the same persons.

Considering that many important scientists never receive any of the prestigious awards we've named, can we dare to suggest that one Nobel Prize ought to be enough for a lifetime? If one assumes that awards are meant to spur the recipients on to even greater heights, then we are caught in a vicious trap. Scientists must either be allowed and encouraged to receive both second Nobels and other prizes or we must create a Super Nobel Prize. I suppose that some of the more recent prizes were created with this need in mind. Science awards benefit both those who receive them and the members of their invisible colleges as well. These prizes provide public recognition of past research frontiers that have become today's accepted wisdom.

Since it is almost two years since we began this study,[1] many readers may not have convenient access to part one. Reprints are available upon request.

* * * * *

My thanks to Joan Lipinsky Cochran, Janet Robertson, and Bella Teperov for their help in the preparation of this essay.

©1984 ISI

REFERENCES

1. **Garfield E.** The awards of science: beyond the Nobel Prize. Part 1. The determinants of prestige. *Essays of an information scientist.* Philadelphia: ISI Press, 1984. Vol. 6. p. 17-26. (Reprinted from: *Current Contents* (4):5-14, 24 January 1983.)
2. --------------. The articles most cited in 1961-1982. 2. Another 100 *Citation Classics* highlight the technology of science. *Current Contents* (29):3-12, 16 July 1984.
3. **Lancaster H & Chase M.** Coveted science prizes bring cash, celebrity but also a few curses. *Wall Street J.* 17 October 1984. p. 1; 27.
4. **Zuckerman H.** *Scientific elite.* New York: Free Press, 1977. 335 p.
5. **Fordyce A.** Telephone communication. 31 October 1984.
6. **Hrica S-A.** Personal communication. 31 October 1984.
7. **Garfield E.** The 1982 John Scott Award goes to Jack Fishman and Harold Blumberg for synthesis and investigation of naloxone. *Essays of an information scientist.* Philadelphia: ISI Press, 1984. Vol. 6. p. 121-30.
8. --------------. The 1,000 contemporary scientists most-cited 1965-1978. Part I. The basic list and introduction. *Essays of an information scientist.* Philadelphia: ISI Press, 1983. Vol. 5. p. 269-78.
9. **Penzien J.** Telephone communication. 5 November 1984.
10. **Garfield E.** The 1981 geosciences articles most cited from 1981 through 1983. *Current Contents* (33):3-15, 13 August 1984.
11. --------------. Journal citation studies. 37. Using citation analysis to study the neuroscience journals. *Essays of an information scientist.* Philadelphia: ISI Press, 1983. Vol. 5. p. 711-20.
12. --------------. Premature discovery or delayed recognition—why? *Essays of an information scientist.* Philadelphia: ISI Press, 1981. Vol. 4. p. 488-93.
13. --------------. More on the ethics of scientific publication: abuses of authorship attribution and citation amnesia undermine the reward system of science. *Essays of an information scientist.* Philadelphia: ISI Press, 1983. Vol. 5. p. 621-6.
14. **Russell C.** Researchers who found virus-cancer link win Lasker Award. *Wash. Post* 18 November 1982. p. A2.
15. **Garfield E.** Are the 1979 prizewinners *of Nobel class? Essays of an information scientist.* Philadelphia: ISI Press, 1981. Vol. 4. p. 609-17.
16. --------------. The articles most cited in 1961-1982. Pts. 1-5. *Current Contents* (23):3-9, 4 June 1984; (29):3-12, 16 July 1984; (35):3-9, 27 August 1984; (40):3-9, 1 October 1984; (42):3-12, 15 October 1984.

Current Comments®

The 1983 Nobel Prizes. Part 1.
Physics and Chemistry Awards
Go to Chandrasekhar, Fowler & Taube

Number 51   December 17, 1984

We have examined each group of annual Nobel Prize winners since 1979. Beginning with the 1982 awards,[1] we included data from the research fronts we identify each year for *Science Citation Index®* (*SCI®*). Briefly, a research front is a group of current papers that cite a cluster of "core" papers identified by co-citation clustering. These procedures have been described previously.[2]

By systematically reviewing our research front data from year to year, one may be able to forecast fields that may eventually be acknowledged with a Nobel Prize. However, it is careless and fallacious to claim that citation analysis or any other method can *predict* the choice of the prize-awarding committees. Citation analysis, however, *will* identify individuals who are *of Nobel class*.[3] From these groups, one might forecast winners for their fields once the prize-awarding committees choose to recognize those areas.

This part of the essay will discuss the 1983 Nobel Prize in physics—awarded to Subrahmanyan Chandrasekhar, University of Chicago, Illinois, and William A. Fowler, California Institute of Technology (CalTech), Pasadena—and the chemistry prize, awarded to Henry Taube, Stanford University, California. Part two will discuss the prizes in physiology or medicine, economics, and literature.

Since we began work on this essay, the 1984 Nobel Prizes have been announced. Carlo Rubbia, Harvard University, Cambridge, Massachusetts, and the Center for European Nuclear Research (CERN), Geneva, and Simon van der Meer, also of CERN, won the physics prize. Their work led to the discovery of the W and Z particles, the communicators of weak nuclear interactions.[4] The 1984 prize in chemistry went to R. Bruce Merrifield, Rockefeller University, New York, for his revolutionary method of protein synthesis. It created completely new possibilities in the fields of peptide and protein chemistry.[5] A future essay will discuss the work of each of these scholars.

Physics

The 1983 Nobel Prize in physics was shared by Subrahmanyan Chandrasekhar and William A. Fowler for their work on the evolution of stars.[6] Fowler's work demonstrated the process by which reactions in the nuclei of stars form sequentially heavier elements. Chandrasekhar's theoretical work deals with a large number of features in stellar evolution relating to equilibrium and stability criteria of stellar configurations. Both astrophysicists are so well known in their field that it comes as no surprise that their works repeatedly appear on our lists of highly cited publications.

Fowler's work on nucleosynthesis—the formation of sequentially heavier elements in the heart of a star—began in 1954 during a Fulbright professorship at Cambridge University, England, where he formed a collaboration with Sir Fred Hoyle. Astrophysicists Geoffrey R. and E. Margaret Burbidge also worked with Fowler and Hoyle at Cambridge, and later at CalTech. Together, the four produced a comprehensive theory of the nucleosynthesis of all the elements and their isotopes. An isotope of an element has the same atomic number and number of protons, as well as similar chemical properties, but a different atomic weight because it contains a larger number of neutrons.

In 1956, the group, then working in Fowler's lab at CalTech, wrote a preliminary paper for *Science* that briefly described the mechanisms of nucleosynthesis in stars.[7] This brief article was published mainly to establish the priority of their work.[8] It was followed in 1957 by a more detailed description in *Reviews of Modern Physics*.[9] This paper is commonly referred to as B²FH—taken from the initials of the four investigators. It describes in detail the stellar synthesis of all naturally occurring chemical elements. These elements are formed by a series of processes that occur in successive generations of stars. Since there is little mixing of material inside most stars, the hot core quickly consumes its hydrogen supply. When this happens, the star becomes a red giant—a bloated, cool star of high luminosity. At the red giant stage, new nuclear reactions occur. As a result, new and heavier elements are made. The most important is the formation of carbon from three helium nuclei. Successive bombardment of carbon nuclei by helium creates other heavier elements, such as iron. The iron group nuclei are then seeds for further synthesis. As stars evolve, some of the matter is returned to interstellar space, either gradually or by supernova. A supernova is a stellar explosion during which a star greatly increases in luminosity while vast quantities of star matter are expelled into space.

According to John Maddox, editor of *Nature*, B²FH is a milestone publication for several reasons.[10] First, it provided a coherent explanation of nucleosynthesis. Second, it settled the dispute about the direction of stellar evolution along the Hertzsprung-Russel diagram, which characterizes stars according to brightness and surface temperature. Finally, B²FH provided the basis for calculating the internal constitutions of stars, as well as for understanding the fate of massive stars in a supernova explosion. In fact, although B²FH was published in 1957, according to the Swedish Academy of Sciences, the work it represents "is still the basis of our knowledge in this field, and the most recent progress in nuclear physics and space research further confirms its correctness."[11]

After publication of B²FH, Fowler continued to work out details of stellar nucleosynthesis. Much of Fowler's theoretical work was done in collaboration with Hoyle. More than 25 of Fowler's 200 papers were coauthored by Hoyle. In 1963, Fowler and Hoyle published a theory suggesting that strong radio waves from certain galaxies resulted from cataclysmic events near the centers of those galaxies.[12] Fowler and Hoyle noted that these radio waves could not be the result of the energy of nuclear fusion. They suggested that they were propagated by the energy released in a supernova, as the gravitational collapse of the star's interior blows off the outer shell of stellar material. This work,[12] published in *Nature*, has been cited in over 100 subsequent publications.

With Hoyle back in Cambridge in 1963-1964, Fowler derived the equations for the binding energy of a super-massive star and published them in 1964 in another article in *Reviews of Modern Physics*. This paper has also been explicitly cited about 100 times.[13]

In 1967, in a letter to the editor of *Nature*, Fowler and Hoyle suggested that the indications that quasars are so distant may be misleading.[14] The objects may in fact be much closer to the Earth than formerly thought. However, this idea is not widely accepted throughout the scientific community.

In another 1967 paper coauthored with R.V. Wagoner, Hoyle and Fowler discuss the synthesis of elements at very high temperatures.[15] This publication, cited more than 300 times, appears in our 1974 study of papers from the *Astrophysical Journal*.[16] Fowler's 1973 paper[17] on light elements appears in the list of papers most cited in that year.[18] That same work, done in collaboration with, among others, French scientist J. Audouze, appeared in our study of French scientists.[19]

From 1955 through 1983, Fowler's collective work has been cited approximately 5,900 times. Not surprisingly, B²FH is the most-cited paper. From its publication in 1957 to date, it has been cited in over 800 publications. In a 1974 interview with Charles Weiner, Center for the History of Physics, New York, directed by Spencer Weart, American Institute of Physics, New York, Fowler commented, "I anticipate that if I am remembered in science it will be as the F in B²FH."[8]

Some of the more recent *SCI* research fronts in which articles by Fowler are core documents appear in Table 1. In the 1981 research front, "Grand unification theories, proton decay, neutrino masses, flavor dynamics, and Higgs boson in the SO(10) model," the 1967 paper by Wagoner, Fowler, and Hoyle[15] discussed above is one of 63 core papers. Of the 682 citing documents in this research front, all were published in 1981. This research front carried through to several

Table 1: *SCI®* research fronts in which articles by William A. Fowler occur as core documents. A=number. B=name. C=number of core papers. D=number of citing papers.

A	B	C	D
81-0312	Grand unification theories, proton decay, neutrino masses, flavor dynamics, and Higgs boson in the SO(10) model	63	682
81-1062	Isotopic anomalies in meteorites in relation to solar system formation	9	140
82-0034	Primordial nucleosynthesis and cosmology	5	68
82-1691	Stellar evolution	2	52
83-0768	Nucleosynthesis and elemental abundances in stellar evolution	10	133

research fronts in 1982. One, "Weak neutral bosons in gauge models and grand unified theories," has 10 core documents. Four of these also are core to the 1981 research front. Another, "Grand unified theories," has six core documents. Five of these also are in the core of the 1981 research front. And "Proton decay" has six core documents, three of which also are core to the 1981 research front. The paper by Wagoner, Fowler, and Hoyle is also among the five that form the core of the 1982 research front, "Primordial nucleosynthesis and cosmology." Figure 1 provides a multidimensional scaling map of these papers. The lengths of the connecting lines are inversely proportional to the co-citation strength.[2]

B[2]FH is one of the core documents in another 1981 research front, "Isotopic anomalies in meteorites in relation to solar system formation." It is interesting to note that this front split into two research fronts in 1982. One was entitled "Noble gases in meteorites," and the other was named "Petrogenesis and other aspects of inclusions in meteorites and chondrites." B[2]FH is also one of 10 core papers in the 1983 front, "Nucleosynthesis and elemental abundances in stellar evolution." So is Fowler's 1975 paper on thermonuclear reaction rates.[20]

While Fowler's work showed how stars during their lifetimes and in their supernova deaths produce all of the chemical elements known today, theoretical physicist Chandrasekhar's work showed that not all stars pass through the white dwarf stage. White dwarfs are very dense stars that have used up their nuclear fuel. They were thought to be the stable end points of stellar evolution for all stars. But Chandrasekhar showed that this was so only if their mass was less than a certain critical value. This maximum, about 1.4 times the mass of the sun, is now called Chandrasekhar's limit. Beyond this limit, stars collapse under their own weight and become black holes.

When Chandrasekhar, at age 24, presented his theory to the Royal Astronomical Society of London in 1935, Sir Arthur Eddington, a preeminent astronomer, denounced the entire theory as absurd.[21] Although some astrophysicists agreed with Chandrasekhar in private, none publicly supported him. Kameshwar C. Wali, Department of Physics, Syracuse University, New York, wrote that Chandrasekhar's work demonstrates the obstacles that affect the acceptance of new scientific theories.[21] Wali noted that contrary to commonly held belief, the human factors such as prestige, personal biases, and authority play as important a role in science as they do in art and literature. It was over 21 years before Chandrasekhar's limit and his theory of stellar evolution were accepted and incorporated into the body of astrophysical knowledge.[21] After publishing his views of stellar evolution in 1939 in *An Introduction to the Study of Stellar Structure*,[22] Chandrasekhar decided that his future in science depended on his going into other areas of research.[23] The book has been cited more than 500 times since 1955, and continues to be cited regularly.

Chandrasekhar's approach to research has followed a distinctive pattern; his field of research changes every 5 to 10 years. In each field, he first publishes a series of papers. When he has accumulated a sufficient body of knowledge, he then publishes it in the form of a book, presenting a coherent self-contained picture of the field. After publishing his theory of stellar evolution, Chandrasekhar began looking at stellar dynamics in terms of the gravitational interactions between stars in a star cluster. The study resulted in another classic publication, *Principles of*

Figure 1: Multidimensional scaling map showing co-citation links between core papers for the 1982 *SCI®* research front, "Primordial nucleosynthesis and cosmology."

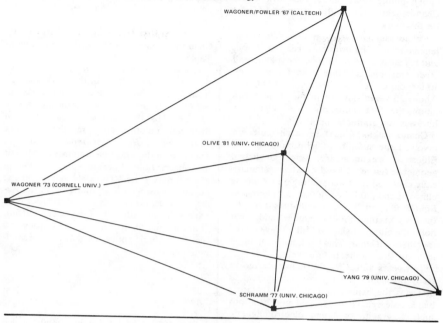

WAGONER/FOWLER '67 (CALTECH)

OLIVE '81 (UNIV. CHICAGO)

WAGONER '73 (CORNELL UNIV.)

YANG '79 (UNIV. CHICAGO)

SCHRAMM '77 (UNIV. CHICAGO)

KEY

Olive K A, Schramm D N, Steigman G, Turner M S & Yang J. Big-bang nucleosynthesis as a probe of cosmology and particle physics. *Astrophys. J.* 246:557-68, 1981.
Schramm D N & Wagoner R V. Element production in the early universe. *Annu. Rev. Nucl. Sci.* 27:37-74, 1977.
Wagoner R V. Big-bang nucleosynthesis revisited. *Astrophys. J.* 179:343-60, 1973.
Wagoner R V, Fowler W A & Hoyle F. On the synthesis of elements at very high temperatures. *Astrophys. J.* 148:3-49, 1967.
Yang J, Schramm D N, Steigman G & Rood R T. Constraints on cosmology and neutrino physics from big-bang nucleosynthesis. *Astrophys. J.* 227:697-704, 1979.

Stellar Dynamics, in 1942.[24] This book has been cited over 400 times since 1955. However, until we have completed *SCI* for the post-war period, we won't know how often the book was cited in the years immediately after publication. Indeed, it is well known that publication and citation counts dip considerably during the post-war period.

During World War II, Chandrasekhar focused on radiation transfer from a star's hot interior to its cooler exterior, and understanding the theory of Brownian movement and its application to stellar encounters. The resulting publication, and Chandrasekhar's second most-cited work, "Stochastic problems in physics and astronomy," was published in 1943 in *Reviews of Modern Phys-*

ics.[25] This work has been cited over 2,100 times since 1955. It appeared in our 1977 study of highly cited articles of the 1940s.[26] Not surprisingly, this paper also turned up in our recent study of superstar *Citation Classics™*.[27] Although published 40 years ago, the article was cited explicitly 158 times in 1983. The paper is also among the 100 articles most cited in the *CompuMath Citation Index®* (*CMCI®*) from 1976 through 1980.[28]

Chandrasekhar's further work in radiation transfer resulted in another book, *Radiative Transfer*, which was published in 1960.[29] During an interview with Weart, Chandrasekhar noted that he chose the field of radiation transfer because it was "fresh ground" and he could do something significant with

423

it.[23] His impact is reflected in over 1,900 citing publications since 1955. In 1957, Chandrasekhar received the Rumford Medal for this work.[30]

Chandrasekhar went on to study turbulence and stability problems. His 1961 book, and his most-cited work, *Hydrodynamic and Hydromagnetic Stability*,[31] sold more than 10,000 copies. It was cited over 2,100 times. About 20 years ago, we included this work among the 100 essential books needed by new libraries and graduate schools.[32]

Chandrasekhar's next research endeavor involved the stability of ellipsoidal figures. Ellipsoids are imaginary, tangerine-shaped geometric figures. Chandrasekhar systematically analyzed the forces acting on a rotating ellipsoid and published *Ellipsoidal Figures of Equilibrium* in 1969.[33] Scientists use the theories in this book to understand what holds the ellipsoid-shaped Milky Way Galaxy together as it spins. This book has been cited in "only" 262 publications as yet.

Ten years ago, Chandrasekhar started to study black holes. Of particular interest to him was the explanation of how a rotating black hole reacts to external perturbations such as gravitational and electromagnetic waves. His most recent book is *The Mathematical Theory of Black Holes*,[34] published in 1983.

In addition to his intensive research efforts, Chandrasekhar also served as the editor of the *Astrophysical Journal* for 19 years—from 1952 to 1971. During that time, he helped put the journal on a sound financial footing. Although Chandrasekhar believes a journal is only as good as the papers it attracts, his influence guided the *Astrophysical Journal* through an exciting period of research.

Chandrasekhar was one of the 50 most-cited authors, 1961-1972.[35] More than one-fourth of those authors were Nobel laureates when the list was compiled in 1973. Since then, two more authors on that list have been awarded the Nobel Prize: Chandrasekhar himself, and H.C. Brown, Purdue University, Lafayette, Indiana, who won the 1979 prize for chemistry. If we could ever claim that citation analysis has forecasting potential, surely that simple experiment gave us good reason to speculate along those lines. Chandrasekhar also appeared in the larger study of the 250 most-cited primary authors from 1961

through 1975.[36] This list included 42 Nobel laureates. Between 1961 and 1975, Chandrasekhar's work received an average of 545 citations annually.

The research fronts in which articles by Chandrasekhar are core documents appear in Table 2.

His book *Radiative Transfer*[29] is one of three core publications in the 1983 research front, "Calculations and applications of radiative transfer in a scattering atmosphere." His 1933 article, "Equilibrium of distorted polytropes,"[37] in the *Monthly Notices of the Royal Astronomical Society*, appeared in the 1983 research front, "Models and observations of periodic perturbations in close binary stars." His 1944 article on the negative hydrogen ion, published in the *Astrophysical Journal*,[38] is one of the four core papers that identified the 1983 research front, "Photoluminescence of bound excitons and biexciton binding energies of direct gap semiconductors."

Chemistry

The 1983 Nobel Prize in chemistry was awarded to Henry Taube for three decades of work "in the mechanism of electron-transfer reactions, especially in metal complexes."[39] Electron transfer is the process by which an atom, during a chemical reaction, gains or loses electrons. The number of electrons transferred determines, to a certain extent, the kind of chemical bond formed. Taube's work was also honored in August 1983 with the Robert A. Welch award, which includes an honorarium of $150,000. The award was founded in 1954 as part of the estate of the Houston, Texas multimillionaire.[30]

Taube's electron-transfer work—including a 1970 monograph[40] cited over 200 times through 1983—provides the basis for understanding the dynamic behavior of inorganic compounds. Indeed, his study of the basic mechanisms of inorganic chemical reactions forms not only the framework upon which much of modern inorganic chemistry is built, but also has led to deeper insights into the chemical processes that maintain life.[41]

The Royal Swedish Academy of Sciences described Taube as "one of the most creative contemporary workers in inorganic chemis-

Table 2: *SCI®* research fronts in which books or articles by Subrahmanyan Chandrasekhar occur as core documents. A=number. B=name. C=number of core papers. D=number of citing papers.

A	B	C	D
83-2063	Models and observations of periodic perturbations in close binary stars	4	37
83-3488	Photoluminescence of bound excitons and biexciton binding energies of direct gap semiconductors	4	26
83-3524	Theory of dynamics, diffusion and rate processes	13	299
83-4213	Calculations and applications of radiative transfer in a scattering atmosphere	3	57

try."[42] He was born in Neudorf, Saskatchewan, Canada, on November 30, 1915. He earned a BS degree in 1935 and an MS degree in 1937 from the University of Saskatchewan, Saskatoon, and then after research with William C. Bray at the University of California, Berkeley, received his PhD there in 1940. Taube's first academic appointment was at Cornell University, Ithaca, New York, but it wasn't until he moved to the University of Chicago in 1946 that he became interested in pursuing a systematic approach to coordination chemistry. This started him down the avenue of research that eventually ended with the Nobel.

Taube's work is broad and basic, yet so diffuse that it may be difficult to grasp. In fact, when Taube was asked to write about his work in layman's terms, he said he found himself writing "the lectures for the first year in general chemistry."[41] Thus, to explain the significance of Taube's work, it is necessary to start with some rather elementary definitions.

Taube's pioneering studies involved the reactions of transition metals, such as iron, copper, cobalt, and molybdenum.[41] Transition metals are well known for their propensity to form coordination complexes. These complexes are compounds that are composed of a metal ion, or electrically charged atom, bonded to a ligand, which is a non-metallic ion or molecule.[41] Ligands—examples of which include water, ammonia, and chloride ions—can donate at least one pair of electrons to a metal ion. The basic theory of coordination compounds was developed at the turn of the century by Alfred Werner, who won the 1913 Nobel Prize.

Taube's great contribution was the careful experimental work that showed how coordination compounds react with one another. In his most-cited paper, published in *Chemical Reviews* in 1952,[43] Taube described a sweep-

ing correlation between ligand substitution rates and electron configuration for coordination compounds of transition metals. This paper was cited at least 300 times from 1955 through 1983. In fact, this paper still dominates research in the reaction chemistry of coordination compounds.

As the Nobel citation indicates, Taube is best known for his pioneering work on oxidation-reduction reactions, known as redox reactions—especially those involving transition metal ions. A 1959 paper in the first issue of *Advances in Inorganic Chemistry and Radiochemistry*[44] describes the mechanisms of these reactions and has been cited about 200 times to date. Figure 2 shows the citation history of this paper from its publication through 1984. The steeply rising curve from 1960 through 1964 illustrates the immediacy of the article's impact, which is atypical of chemistry classics. In another paper,[45] published in 1954 with H. Myers and cited over 175 times, Taube made use of his earlier correlation of ligand exchange rates to demonstrate the principles of "outer sphere," or electron-transfer, and "inner sphere," or atom-transfer, complexes in redox reactions of transition elements.

Taube's study of electron transfer also led him, together with Carol Creutz, Stanford University, to be the first to systematically prepare and characterize a mixed-valence molecule, now commonly known as the Creutz-Taube ion.[46-48] In mixed-valence substances, two similar metals in different oxidation states are linked by a ligand; electron transfer between the two can occur at various rates. Understanding the structural features that control these rates has been an important theme in Taube's work, and has initiated a large, rapidly growing field of chemistry. Their earliest paper in this area,[46] published in 1969, has been cited about 100 times through 1983. And among the papers to

Figure 2: Chronological distribution of articles citing Henry Taube's 1959 *Advances in Inorganic Chemistry and Radiochemistry* paper.

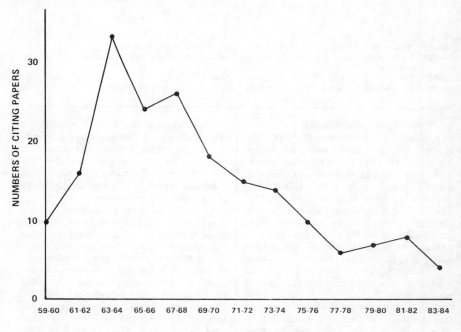

YEARS OF CITING PAPERS

which this research led, the 1973 work on complexes of ruthenium ammines has been cited about 150 times in 10 years.[48]

By measuring reaction rates and charting the paths of electrons as molecules break apart and recombine, Taube has shown how chemical reactions occur. And although most of his research has had little immediate application, it laid the foundation for understanding the chemical reactions that produce the energy required by living organisms. It also led to the development of processes used in the manufacturing of chemicals.[39] Testifying to the extensive usefulness of Taube's research, his work has been cited explicitly over 8,500 times since 1955. Not surprisingly, Taube was among the 1,000 most-cited contemporary authors we identified several years ago.[49]

Table 3 lists the research fronts in which articles by Taube, among others, are core documents. In the 1981 research front, "Electron transfer in chemical and biological systems,"

the Creutz-Taube ion[48] paper is one of three core papers. The other two are papers by M.B. Robin, Bell Telephone Laboratories, Murray Hill, New Jersey, in *Advances in Inorganic Chemistry and Radiochemistry*,[50] and N.S. Hush, University of Bristol, England, in *Progress in Inorganic Chemistry*.[51] The Creutz-Taube ion paper is also among the 10 publications that later formed the core of the 1983 front, "Electron transfer and properties of mixed-valence iron, ruthenium, and related binuclear transition metal complexes studied by Mossbauer and electrochemical methods."

In addition, the paper on "Electron transfer through organic structural units,"[52] coauthored in 1964 with Stanford colleague Edwin S. Gould and cited about 175 times through 1983, is among the three core papers of the 1983 research front, "Kinetics and mechanism of electron transfer in hexaaquochromium (111) and other transition metal complexes with carboxylate ligands." The other

Table 3: $SCI^{®}$ research fronts in which articles by Henry Taube occur as core documents. A=number. B=name. C=number of core papers. D=number of citing papers.

A	B	C	D
81-1323	Electron transfer in chemical and biological systems	3	72
83-0499	Electron transfer and properties of mixed-valence iron, ruthenium, and related binuclear transition metal complexes studied by Mossbauer and electrochemical methods	10	110
83-6736	Kinetics and mechanism of electron transfer in hexaaquochromium (111) and other transition metal complexes with carboxylate ligands	3	20

two papers are by R.E. Hamm,[53] University of Utah, Salt Lake City, and M. Krumpolc,[54] University of Illinois, Chicago, both in the *Journal of the American Chemical Society* (*JACS*). Both papers deal with chromium chemistry.

Quite recently, ISI® has created a *Chemistry Citation Index* (*CCI*) in conjunction with *Index Chemicus Online* ™. We'll have more to report on this file shortly. Not surprisingly, Taube's papers help form the core of several *CCI* research fronts. His 1973 paper[55] is among the six core papers of the 1981 research front, "Synthesis, structure and mechanistic studies of ruthenium, nickel and related transition metal and mixed valence macrocyclic complexes." Taube wrote three of the papers among the 32 core documents for the 1983 research front, "Synthesis, characterization and electron-transfer and other reactions of mixed-valence binuclear complexes containing ruthenium, iron, and other transition metals." Two were coauthored with Creutz.[46,48] The other paper is on experimental approaches to electronic coupling in metal-ion redox systems.[56] The 1964 *JACS* paper coauthored with Gould[52] is also identified as a core paper in the *CCI* front, "Mechanism of inner sphere electron transfer of cobalt (111) complexes," along with Taube's 1969 review paper on the mechanisms of oxidation-reduction reactions.[57]

According to an article in *Science* by Taube's colleagues Harry B. Gray, Division of Chemistry and Chemical Engineering, Cal-Tech, and James P. Collman, Stanford University, Taube is "a rare figure among internationally acclaimed scientists. He does little

or no horn-tooting. Instead, he spends a great deal of time encouraging others, especially young people, to pursue research."[58] Taube's support of students and rising young colleagues is fitting, however, since his groundbreaking work was based on ideas he developed while preparing a series of lectures on coordination chemistry at the University of Chicago: "I knew little about coordination chemistry, and what I knew bored me silly," he said in an interview with C. Norman of *Science*.[59] "I thought I should learn something about it and in preparing my course, I became interested.... My early work in Chicago was really based on what I learned in that course."

In reviewing the 1983 Nobel Prizes in physics and chemistry, we have emphasized not only the pioneering significance of the scientific work involved, but we have demonstrated the three well-established characteristics of most Nobel class work: high productivity, high and long-lasting impact, and work that is not only core to the research fronts that the prize winners helped establish, but work that has led to the proliferation of new and exciting areas of knowledge. I hope readers will understand my delight that all of the winners have been writers of review articles of the highest quality and thus prove once again that the library, personal or otherwise, is the extension of one's laboratory.

* * * * *

My thanks to Stephen A. Bonaduce, Linda LaRue, and Gillian Wilson for their help in the preparation of this essay. ©1984 ISI

REFERENCES

1. **Garfield E.** The 1982 Nobel Prize in physics. *Essays of an information scientist.* Philadelphia: ISI Press, 1984. Vol. 6. p. 413-22.
2. --------------. ABCs of cluster mapping. Parts 1 & 2. Most active fields in the life and physical sciences in 1978. *Essays of an information scientist.* Philadelphia: ISI Press, 1981. Vol. 4. p. 634-49.

3. **Zuckerman H.** *Scientific elite*. New York: Free Press, 1977. 335 p.
4. **Sullivan W.** 2 Europeans win in physics. *NY Times* 18 October 1984. p. A1; B12.
5. **Schmeck H M.** U.S. professor awarded Nobel for chemistry.
   NY Times 18 October 1984. p. A1; B12.
6. **Sullivan W.** 2 Americans share physics Nobel for star theories. *NY Times* 20 October 1983. p. A16.
7. **Hoyle F, Fowler W A, Burbidge G R & Burbidge E M.** Origin of the elements in stars.
   Science 124:611-4, 1956.
8. **American Institute of Physics, Center for History of Physics.** *Oral history interview of William A.
   Fowler by Charles Weiner*. Unpublished, Neils Bohr Library. New York, NY.
9. **Burbidge E M, Burbidge G R, Fowler W A & Hoyle F.** Synthesis of the elements in stars.
   Rev. Mod. Phys. 29:547-650, 1957.
10. **Maddox J.** Final crop of 1983 Nobel awards. *Nature* 305:759, 1983.
11. **Lubkin G B.** Nobel prize to Chandrasekhar and Fowler for astrophysics.
    Phys. Today 37(1):17-20, 1984.
12. **Hoyle F & Fowler W A.** Nature of strong radio sources. *Nature* 197:533-5, 1963.
13. **Fowler W A.** Massive stars, relativistic polytropes and gravitational radiation.
    Rev. Mod. Phys. 36:545-55, 1964.
14. **Hoyle F & Fowler W A.** Letter to editor. (Gravitational red-shifts in quasi-stellar objects.)
    Nature 213:373-4, 1967.
15. **Wagoner R V, Fowler W A & Hoyle F.** On the synthesis of elements at very high
    temperatures. *Astrophys. J.* 148:3-49, 1967.
16. **Garfield E.** Journal citation studies. XII. *Astrophysical Journal* and its *Supplements*. *Essays of an
    information scientist*. Philadelphia: ISI Press, 1977. Vol. 2. p. 120-4.
17. **Reeves H, Audouze J, Fowler W A & Schramm D N.** On the origin of light elements.
    Astrophys. J. 179:909-30, 1973.
18. **Garfield E.** The 1973 papers most cited in 1973. *Essays of an information scientist*.
    Philadelphia: ISI Press, 1977. Vol. 2. p. 422-5.
19. --------------. Do French scientists who publish outside of France and/or in English do better
    research? *Essays of an information scientist*. Philadelphia: ISI Press, 1980. Vol. 3. p. 498-503.
20. **Fowler W A, Caughlan G R & Zimmerman B A.** Thermonuclear reaction rates, II.
    Annu. Rev. Astron. Astrophys. 13:69-112, 1975.
21. **Wali K C.** Chandrasekhar vs. Eddington—an unanticipated confrontation.
    Phys. Today 35(10):33-40, 1982.
22. **Chandrasekhar S.** *An introduction to the study of stellar structure*.
    Chicago: University of Chicago Press, 1939. 509 p.
23. **American Institute of Physics, Center for History of Physics.** *Oral history interview of
    Subrahmanyan Chandrasekhar by Spencer Weart*, Unpublished, Neils Bohr Library.
    New York, NY.
24. **Chandrasekhar S.** *Principles of stellar dynamics*. Chicago: University of Chicago Press, 1942. 251 p.
25. --------------------. Stochastic problems in physics and astronomy. *Rev. Mod. Phys.* 15:1-89, 1943.
26. **Garfield E.** Highly cited articles. 36. Physics, chemistry and mathematics papers published in the
    1940s. *Essays of an information scientist*. Philadelphia: ISI Press, 1980. Vol. 3. p. 54-60.
27. --------------. The articles most cited in 1961-1982. 2. Another 100 *Citation Classics* highlight the
    technology of science. *Current Contents* (29):3-12, 16 July 1984.
28. --------------. The multidisciplinary impact of math and computer science is reflected in the 100 most-
    cited articles in *CompuMath Citation Index*, 1976-1980. *Current Contents* (31):3-10, 30 July 1984.
29. **Chandrasekhar S.** *Radiative transfer*. New York: Dover, 1960. 393 p.
30. **Garfield E.** The awards of science: beyond the Nobel prize. Part 1. The determinants of prestige.
    Essays of an information scientist. Philadelphia: ISI Press, 1984. Vol. 6. p. 17-26.
    (Reprinted from: *Current Contents* (4):5-14, 24 January 1983.)
31. **Chandrasekhar S.** *Hydrodynamic and hydromagnetic stability*.
    Oxford: Clarendon Press, 1961. 652 p.
32. **Garfield E.** A core research library for developing graduate schools—the 100 books
    most-cited by researchers. *Essays of an information scientist*.
    Philadelphia: ISI Press, 1977. Vol. 2. p. 1-5.
33. **Chandrasekhar S.** *Ellipsoidal figures of equilibrium*. New Haven: Yale University Press, 1969. 252 p.
34. ----------------------. *The mathematical theory of black holes*.
    New York: Oxford University Press, 1983. 646 p.
35. **Garfield E.** More on forecasting Nobel prizes and the most cited scientists of 1972!
    Essays of an information scientist. Philadelphia: ISI Press, 1977. Vol. 1. p. 487-8.
36. --------------. The 250 most-cited primary authors, 1961-1975. Parts I-III. *Essays of an
    information scientist*. Philadelphia: ISI Press, 1980. Vol. 3. p. 326-63.
37. **Chandrasekhar S.** Equilibrium of distorted polytropes.
    Mon. Notic. Roy. Astron. Soc. 93:390-405, 1933.
38. ---------------------. Some remarks on the negative hydrogen ion and its absorption coefficient.
    Astrophys. J. 100:176-80, 1944.

39. **Carey J, Mortensen K & Raine G.** The Nobel prizes: an American sweep. *Newsweek* 102(18):90, 1983.
40. **Taube H.** *Electron transfer reactions of complex ions in solution.* New York: Academic Press, 1970. 103 p.
41. **Milgrom L & Anderson I.** Understanding the electron. *New Sci.* 100:253-4, 1983.
42. **Broad W J.** Chemistry Nobel won by coast man. *NY Times* 20 October 1983. p. B13.
43. **Taube H.** Rates and mechanisms of substitution in inorganic complexes in solution. *Chem. Rev.* 50:69-126, 1952.
44. ------------. Mechanism of redox reactions of simple chemistry. *Advan. Inorg. Chem. Radiochem.* 1:1-53, 1959.
45. **Taube H & Myers H.** Evidence for a bridged activated complex for electron transfer reactions. *J. Amer. Chem. Soc.* 76:2103-11, 1954.
46. **Creutz C & Taube H.** Letter to editor. (A direct approach to measuring the Franck-Condon barrier to electron transfer between metal ions.) *J. Amer. Chem. Soc.* 91:3988-9, 1969.
47. ------------------------. Preparation and studies of di-μ- nitrogen-decaaquodiruthenium (II) fluoroborate. *Inorg. Chem.* 10:2664-7, 1971.
48. ------------------------. Binuclear complexes of ruthenium ammines. *J. Amer. Chem. Soc.* 95:1086-94, 1973.
49. **Garfield E.** The 1,000 contemporary scientists most-cited 1965-1978. Part I. The basic list and introduction. *Essays of an information scientist.* Philadelphia: ISI Press, 1983. Vol. 5. p. 269-78.
50. **Robin M B & Day P.** Mixed valence chemistry—a survey and classification. *Advan. Inorg. Chem. Radiochem.* 10:247-422, 1976.
51. **Hush N S.** Intervalence-transfer absorption. Part 2. Theoretical considerations and spectroscopic data. *Prog. Inorg. Chem.* 8:391-443, 1967.
52. **Gould E S & Taube H.** Electron transfer through organic structural units. Aromatic and heterocyclic carboxylates as bridging groups in oxidation-reduction reactions. *J. Amer. Chem. Soc.* 86:1318-28, 1964.
53. **Hamm R E, Johnson R L, Perkins R H & Davis R E.** Complex ions of chromium. VIII. Mechanism of reaction of organic acid anions with chromium (III). *J. Amer. Chem. Soc.* 80:4469-71, 1958.
54. **Krumpolc M & Rocek J.** Synthesis of stable chromium (V) complexes of tertiary hydroxy acids. *J. Amer. Chem. Soc.* 101:3206-9, 1979.
55. **Taube H.** Ruthenium (II) ammines—a study in reactivity. *Surv. Prog. Chem.* 6:1-46, 1973.
56. ------------. Experimental approaches to electronic coupling in metal-ion redox systems. *Ann. NY Acad. Sci.* 313:481-95, 1978.
57. ------------. Mechanisms of oxidation-reduction reactions. *Account. Chem. Res.* 2:321-9, 1969.
58. **Gray H B & Collman J P.** The 1983 Nobel Prize in Chemistry. *Science* 222:986-7, 1983.
59. **Norman C.** The pros and cons of the research-teaching link. (Interview.) *Science* 222:489, 1983.

Current Comments®

Science Books for Children

Number 52   December 24-31, 1984

Many years ago, a delegation of Chinese scientists visited ISI®. During dinner one evening, one of them asked me who was the leading publisher of popular science or children's science books in America. I was stunned when I realized there was no obvious answer to this question. Although I could vaguely recall the Golden Books that I had often read to my children, there was no single publisher that I could identify as the leader for science books for children. Why was there no McGraw-Hill or Academic Press of children's science books? In spite of the passage of many years, there is still no answer to that question. But I thought it would be interesting to communicate these impressions to the readers of *Current Contents®* (*CC®*), some of whom are publishers. In this essay, we'll focus on science books for children and the organizations and magazines that review them and promote their reading in the home and classroom.

Like so many questions to which one assumes at first that there ought to be simple answers, even *defining* a children's science book is not easy. In referring to children, do we simply mean anyone who is not an adult or do we mean those in kindergarten, grade school, or high school? As it turns out, each of these categories warrants a separate investigation. It does not necessarily follow that the existence or lack of science books for children of any age is good or bad, even for the cultivation of future scientists.

As a child, I read very little directly related to science, and yet I eagerly looked forward to attending a science-oriented high school by the time I was 13. Who knows what subtle influences aroused my interest in science? I recall an old theory that suggested a correlation between scientific creativity and the separation of parents.[1] I've often heard the statement that Paul De Kruif's *Microbe Hunters* had caused many a scientific career to be launched. Who knows, maybe Paul Muni playing the movie role of Louis Pasteur or "Dr. Ehrlich's Magic Bullet" did the trick.

On the other hand, through my old friend Watson Davis, who founded the organization that now produces *Science News*, I ordered a subscription to *Things of Science* for my children. Each month, there was some new, fascinating experiment to perform. Who can account for the fact that all but one of my children chose to ignore science? He had an early fascination with dinosaurs, and eventually became a biologist. So without going into a long digression on what motivates young people to pursue scientific careers, let us assume that the writing and publishing of science books for children of all ages is a worthy enterprise. There ought to be more of it. At the least we ought to know, as professional scientists, just exactly what's out there.

I have always felt that science books for children should be created not merely for the benefit of children but also for their parents. Whenever I have had difficulty understanding some scientific phenomenon, I have often sought out the most elementary presentation I could find. This undoubtedly explains why so many scientists hold on to their undergraduate textbooks. And it accounts for the popularity of encyclopedias, dictionaries, and other sources of brief explanations.

Whether or not books motivate youngsters to become scientists, there are many factors that account for their use or disuse. The competition with television is one that cannot be ignored. Anyone who has ever watched "Mr. Wizard" on American TV will appreciate that it is far more appealing to a child or adult to have "difficult" scientific phenomena explained in such an entertaining, graphic manner. But it would take the creativity of a Dr. Seuss to make a child choose a book about science in preference to a televised show. Fortunately, such choices are not required. It has often been demonstrated that books and films have a symbiotic relationship, and even though one may spend several hours watching TV, there is also time to read if one is stimulated to do so.

So it would seem to me that the first task is to create the desire to read and enjoy books before encouraging children to read books about science. Since the young love excitement, books about science, like anything else, should perhaps be written with the sense of adventure. It will not then be a long transition from *The Call of the Wild* or *The Time Machine* to *Microbe Hunters*.

Science-fiction novels are another facet to consider when motivating children to read science "fact" books. There are those, like my friend Maurice Goldsmith, Science Policy Foundation, London, who believe that science fiction is a great spur to science. Clearly the adventures of "Star Trek" and other classics of science fiction have captured the imagination of many of us. While I myself have never been a great consumer of *Analog* magazine or even the work of that superstar Isaac Asimov, I know that many scientists are intrigued—even obsessed—by science fiction. What is today's speculation may be tomorrow's reality. But I would very much like to see the demographic analysis of the readership of *Analog* or other science-fiction magazines. Scientists constitute a small minority of those readers, as is the case for *Omni*, *Discover*, *Science 84*, and other popular science magazines. Some of their most interesting sections are devoted to interviews with scientists.

A child's first exposure to the world of science often comes from popular or "trade" science books, as opposed to textbooks. Science-fiction books, such as those based on the popular "Star Wars" movie series, are entertaining and may stimulate a child's interest in astronomy or space technology. But science-fiction books do not give an accurate picture of what science is really about. Science-*nonfiction* books provide a more realistic introduction to science for young people. Many popular science books are well written, accurate, informative, *and* entertaining to read. There is also evidence that these books are very helpful when used alongside textbooks in the science classroom.

For example, a 1967 study by Louis E. Barrilleaux, Tulane University, New Orleans, Louisiana, compared two groups of eighth-grade students. One group used a standard science textbook. The other group did not have a textbook but was allowed unlimited access to the school library for outside reading in science. At the end of the school year, members of the group that used books in the library scored as high or *higher* than the textbook group on tests measuring science achievement, science attitudes, science writing, and critical thinking.[2] A 1980 study by Becky Fisher, Central Michigan University, Mt. Pleasant, compared seventh-grade students who used either a single science textbook or a variety of outside reading materials. Fisher found that the latter group of students scored higher than the textbook group on science-knowledge tests and also expressed greater interest and enjoyment in what they had learned. She noted that the use of popular science books stimulated talk about science outside the classroom and made the students feel that science was a real part of their lives and not just an academic subject.[3]

Other studies have also concluded that popular science books are effective in stimulating students' interest in science.[4,5] Cathy L. Guerra and DeLores B. Payne, Department of Education, Northwestern State University, Natchitoches, Louisiana, noted that a variety of science books—biographies of scientists, books on science careers, and accounts of discoveries and inventions—enhanced classroom instruction.[5]

It is unclear exactly how many popular science books for children are published in the US each year, but John Donovan, Children's Book Council (CBC), New York, estimates that the number has held steady for the last decade or so, at 300 to 350 books out of the approximately 3,000 children's books published each year.[6] In 1984, says Donovan, the number of juvenile (preschool through eighth grade) science titles was closer to 500. This increase was largely due to a deluge of popular computer books for young readers.

Librarians and educators are faced with the problem of deciding which of these hundreds of titles are "good" science books. Fortunately, there are organizations that aid in the evaluation. The American Association for the Advancement of Science (AAAS), for example, publishes the magazine *Science Books & Films* (*SB&F*) five times a year. Each issue of *SB&F* features hundreds of book reviews, including a section on children's books. The reviews, which also cover science films, videocassettes, and filmstrips, are written by a volunteer corps of scientists, educators, and librarians, most of whom are AAAS members. Reviewers write a brief summary and evaluation, and assign the book or film a rating from "not recommended" to "highly recommended." Subscription inquiries may be sent to *SB&F* Subscriptions, AAAS, 1101 Vermont Ave., NW, 10th Floor, Washington, DC 20005.

Another review publication is *Appraisal: Science Books for Young People*, which is published three times a year in Boston by the New England Roundtable of Children's Librarians. The format of *Appraisal* is similar to *SB&F*, with one important difference—each book is reviewed by a librarian *and* a science specialist. Both reviewers provide a capsule evaluation of the book and assign it a rating from "unsatisfactory" to "excellent." For more information, contact Diane Holzheimer, Editor, *Appraisal*, 605 Commonwealth Ave., Boston, Massachusetts 02215.

Another valuable book list is published each year by a joint committee of the CBC and the National Science Teachers Association (NSTA). The annotated list, "Outstanding Science Trade Books for Children," is published in a spring issue of the NSTA magazine *Science and Children*, which is edited by Phyllis R. Marcuccio. Each issue of *Science and Children*, incidentally, contains a section devoted to the review of children's science books. The NSTA-CBC list may also be obtained by sending a self-addressed, stamped envelope to the Children's Book Council, 67 Irving Place, New York, New York 10003.

All of these organizations have specific criteria for evaluating science books. These criteria provide an insight into what constitutes a good science book for children. Both the AAAS and the NSTA-CBC stress that accuracy is essential.[7,8] Information must be correct, complete, up-to-date, and presented clearly and understandably. Also important, according to AAAS publications manager Kathryn Wolff, are the "quality and relevance of the illustrations, [the book's] appropriateness for particular groups of readers, and the value of the book when compared against similar titles."[7] The NSTA-CBC criteria specify further that "facts and theories must be clearly distinguished, generalizations supported by facts, and significant facts not omitted."[8] Anthropomorphism—talking plants or animals, for example—is inappropriate in the judgment of most *SB&F* and NSTA-CBC reviewers. Books should portray both sexes and a variety of races participating in the activities illustrated. In addition, notes Wolff, authors should convey a sense of excitement about science. But authors, at the same time, should avoid a "gee-whiz" approach that will make science appear magical and fantastic rather than a rational process of inquiry and investigation.[7]

Kathleen Johnston, editor of *SB&F*, claims that a good science book will draw a child into the world of science, and portray the topic as more than a mechanical discipline. Children's books, according to Johnston, should convey the emotive, human aspects of science and scientists.[9]

While not all books manage to meet these standards, many observers agree that there are many excellent books being published for young readers. Glenn Blough, former professor of science education, University of Maryland, College Park, chairs the NSTA-CBC review committee. Each year, his committee of librarians and educators reads hundreds of books and chooses 70 to 80 titles for the outstanding science books list. Blough believes that, generally, the 1984 crop of books is as good as or better than any his committee has ever seen.[10] Zena Sutherland, professor of library science, University of Chicago Graduate Library School, Illinois, shares Blough's belief about the high quality of many children's science books currently published.[11] She points out that publishers, for the most part, are making more of an effort to find qualified authors for their science books. Publishers also now send manuscripts to experts for review.

The 1984 NSTA-CBC list certainly reflects a variety of subject matter, with titles on natural history, astronomy, geology, and biology. A quick scan of the books on the list conveys something of the breadth of topics covered. The recommended grade level is given in parentheses after each title. *First to Fly* (6-up), by Robert R. Moulton, describes the experiences of high-school student Todd Nelson, whose project on zero-gravity insect flight was the first student experiment to fly aboard the space shuttle.[12] *Volcanoes in Our Solar System* (6-up), by G. Jeffrey Taylor, discusses volcanic activity on Earth as well as Mercury, Venus, and Mars.[13] The text is illustrated with drawings and with recent photographs from the US *Mariner* and *Voyager* missions and the Soviet *Venera* spacecraft.

The form and function of animal feet are the subject of *Some Feet Have Noses* (5-up), by Anita Gustafson. Illustrated by April Peters Flory, the book looks at the feet of insects, birds, and mammals, and even at the fin-feet of such land-crawling fish as the mudskipper and the walking catfish.[14] Wyatt Blassingame's *The Strange Armadillo* (4-up) discusses the behavior and habitats of this odd, armored creature.[15] The author includes a chapter on the use of the armadillo as a laboratory animal in the fight against leprosy.[16]

Green Magic: Algae Rediscovered (6-up) by Lucy Kavaler, illustrations by Jean Helmer, talks about the many practical uses of algae as a food source and fertilizer, as well as their possible future uses.[17] Another book, *Viruses* (6-up), by Alan E. Nourse, describes science's battle against viral disease, from the early efforts of Jenner and Pasteur through current research into a viral connection in cancer.[18] In the following excerpt from *Viruses*, it is plain that the author respects the intelligence of his young readers:

Essentially, viruses are nothing more than molecule-size packets of nucleic acid, a complex form of organic compound, surrounded by protective coatings of protein.... It is these nucleic acids that make it possible for cells to reproduce themselves and to pass on their own individual characteristics to new generations of cells. Viruses are really little more than tiny bundles of this hereditary material without the living cell around them. They are sometimes described as "chromosomes on the loose," tiny packets of "infectious heredity," and it is their nucleic acid that is the key to their dangerous power.[18] (p. 10)

Other topics on the NSTA-CBC list include cranberries, hot-air balloons, Ferris wheels, and acid rain.[8]

Perhaps the most effective science books are those that manage to entertain *and* inform the reader. One such book is *Body Magic* by John Fisher. Using simple experiments and tricks that the reader can perform with his or her own body, the book entertainingly illustrates such scientific principles as leverage, vision, perception, and so forth.[19] The reader has fun while learning.

Sutherland has identified several American authors who consistently write excellent, dependable science books for children. For example, Millicent E. Selsam is a trained botanist and former science teacher who has written nearly 100 science books for young readers.[11] Selsam has pointed out that she always attempts, in the course of her books, to acquaint children with basic scientific methodology—observing, gathering facts, and forming and testing theories.[20] She has written on a variety of topics, but has concentrated mostly on biology. One of her recent books, *Catnip*, chosen as a NSTA-CBC outstanding book, tells of the history and various uses of this mint plant.[21]

Sutherland also praises Seymour Simon, another former science teacher who is now a full-time writer. Simon's books, like Selsam's, do not simply list fact after fact to be memorized. His books encourage children to observe, explore, and experiment on their own.[22] Simon has written about animals, the senses, and outer space, among other topics.

Lawrence P. Pringle is another writer recommended by Sutherland. Pringle writes primarily about environmental topics: energy, conservation, and descriptions of various ecosystems. His recent book, *Wolfman: Exploring the World of Wolves*, concerns the exploits of a biologist tracking and researching the often-misunderstood wolf.[23] Another of Pringle's books, *Feral: Tame Animals Gone Wild*, discusses domestic animals, such as pigs, burros, and horses, that have developed significant wild populations.[24]

Sutherland also mentions Franklyn M. Branley, former chairman, American Museum of Natural History-Hayden Planetarium, New York, who writes on astronomy for young readers. One of Branley's recent books, *Saturn*, illustrated by Leonard Kessler, presents the most up-to-date information and images of Saturn from the recent *Voyager* flybys.[25] *Saturn* also appears on the NSTA-CBC outstanding books list.

One notable trend in the improvement of children's science books has been an increased emphasis on graphics and illustration. Blough points out that more publishers are using color photographs and illustrations to complement the text and are paying more attention to format.[10] Margery Cuyler, children's book editor, Holiday House publishers, New York, believes that children have become very conscious of visual presentation as a result of their constant exposure to television and advertising graphics. Therefore, publishers are trying harder to appeal to children visually, with more photographs and more thoughtful graphic design.[26]

One unfortunate consequence of this emphasis on graphics and improved production, as Blough points out, is that science books have become more expensive and thus harder for schools and libraries to obtain.[10] On the other hand, improving the visual aspects of science books allows publishers to reach very young readers. Pamela R. Giller, children's librarian, Cary Public Library,

Lexington, Massachusetts, notes that readers as young as two or three years can be introduced to simple scientific and technical concepts through picture books.[27] Giller points out that publishers have taken into account the work of Jean Piaget, the well-known child psychologist, and other researchers, who have demonstrated that children are capable of learning about virtually any subject if it is presented correctly. Giller mentions such authors as Byron Barton, who has written simple books on housebuilding, animals, and wheels, and Gail Gibbons, whose subjects have included clocks, trucks, and how locks and keys work.[27]

All this is not to say that science book publishing for children is uniformly excellent. Diane Holzheimer, who edits *Appraisal*, notes that quality varies greatly from publisher to publisher and from author to author.[28] A few publishers persist in releasing books that have not been reviewed for accuracy by specialists prior to publication, or books that are hastily assembled, uninspired, and apparently intended more to make a profit than to instruct and amuse the reader.

Even well-intentioned publishers sometimes produce inappropriate science books for children. Blough says he occasionally sees books written by authors who, although they are experts in science, have little or no experience writing for children. These books tend to have complex sentence structures and vocabularies that are above the reading level of the intended audience.[10] This is where *Appraisal* and *SB&F* can be helpful. A judgment of "not recommended" or "unacceptable" in these publications will alert parents or librarians that a particular book is deficient in accuracy, organization, or readability. Generally, though, most observers seem to agree that publishers are producing well-researched, well-written science books for young readers.

One problem that seems to persist, independent of quality, is that science books, and nonfiction books in general, do not get nearly as much attention as fiction does, even though roughly half of the children's books published each year are nonfiction.[29] Librarian and teacher Jo Carr, in the preface to *Beyond Fact: Nonfiction for Children and Young People*, considers the neglect that is suffered by nonfiction. She points out that teachers seldom read nonfiction aloud to their classes. Teachers also fail to encourage students to read nonfiction for enjoyment. Bookstores too, she notes, tend to stock far more children's fiction than nonfiction.[30] (p. IX) Beverly Kobrin, an education specialist who publishes the *Kobrin Newsletter* on juvenile nonfiction, frequently attends conventions of booksellers and educators. She often hears that "nobody wants nonfiction," and finds herself having to convince parents and teachers that nonfiction can be as well-produced, entertaining, and stimulating as fiction.[31]

Science author Vicki Cobb, several of whose books have appeared on NSTA-CBC outstanding books lists, also encounters the bias against nonfiction. In the course of her lectures and science demonstrations at schools and libraries, she is often told that she is the first nonfiction author ever to appear. A common reaction of students and teachers is, "Why didn't we know about these science books?"[32] Holzheimer points out that most children's librarians have humanities backgrounds, and they do not really know how to evaluate science books.[28] That may be one reason why science books do not get the same attention or shelf space as fiction.

The major awards for children's literature also reflect the apparent prejudice against science books and other nonfiction works. Author Milton Meltzer points out that nonfiction books seldom receive the most prestigious prizes. For example, the Newbery Medal is awarded each year by the American Library Association, Chicago, Illinois, for "the most distinguished contribution to American literature for children." But only six nonfiction books have been honored by the Newbery Medal since its inception in 1922. Five of these books were biographies.[33]

Excellence in science writing for children has only recently been recognized by independent awards. Since 1971, the New York Academy of Sciences has sponsored the Annual Children's Science Book Award Program to honor and encourage high-quality science books for young readers. The Academy awards prizes in two age categories of readers—those under 10 years old and those between 10 and 16 years old. The panel of judges includes: William Burrows, Science and Environmental Reporting Program, New York University, New York; Joelle Burrows, picture editor, *The Sciences*, New York; Harry C. Stubbs, Milton Academy, Massachusetts; Philip Morrison, Massachusetts Institute of Technology, Boston; and Phylis Morrison, Workshop for Learning Things, Boston.[34] Incidentally, the Morrisons also present a year-end review of children's science books in each December issue of *Scientific American*.

The 1984 winner of the Academy's award in the Older Category was *Volcano Weather* by Henry and Elizabeth Stommel. The book describes the eruption in 1916 of the volcano Tambora and the subsequent atmospheric effects of volcanic dust and ash on New England weather.[35] The Younger Category winner was *Oak & Company* by Richard Mabey, illustrated by Claire Roberts. This book tells about the life and death of a 283-year-old oak tree and its relation to the surrounding forest and wildlife.[36] Honorable-mention titles included books about dinosaurs, kites, and arithmetic.[34] For more information on the award, write to Ann Collins, New York Academy of Sciences, 2 East 63rd St., New York, New York 10021.

Of course, it would be unfair to limit this discussion of children's science books to the US. In other countries, such as the USSR, these books are also quite popular. Ira Cohen, Imported Publications, Chicago, has made several trips to the USSR. His firm distributes English-language Soviet books in the US, including children's science books. Cohen points out that science books are extremely popular with young readers in the USSR, and that these books cover virtually every imaginable scientific topic.[37] Publishers of children's books, including Malysh and Detskaya Literatura, maintain close ties with the Soviet academic community and compete for the best scientists to participate in the planning and writing of juvenile science books. According to Cohen, most science books in the USSR stress application and emphasize how the science and technology under discussion can be put to use for the improvement of society.

One such book is *From the Bonfire to the Reactor* by Alexei Krylov. As the title implies, the book reviews man's continuous search for the most efficient, economical sources of energy. The author discusses the theory and applications of steam power, the internal combustion engine, and hydroelectricity, as well as solar and nuclear energy. The book's fanciful, almost psychedelic illustrations contrast sharply with its thoughtful, serious text.[38]

Natural history books are also popular. One book, *Builders in the Wild*, by Igor Akimushkin, discusses animals and the often elaborate structures they build for shelter and other purposes. The author describes beaver dams, termite lodges, the tunnel-like nest built by the stickleback fish, and other examples of animal construction.[39] *What the Bat Told Us*, by Boris Zubkov, discusses how the world of nature has influenced man in the concept and design of many inventions. "People learn from the world around them," states the author, and the book attempts to illustrate this point. Zubkov points out that observing a spider's web may have led man to the idea of building bridges, just as the sight of wind-driven leaves may have started man thinking about flight. Scientists, says the author, have learned much from studying animals like the bat, with its sensitive, sonar-like guidance system. The book also discusses animals that can perceive the approach of earthquakes and storms and how man has attempted to emulate this ability.[40]

Imported Publications offers other Soviet science books for children, including titles on transportation, astronomy, and paleontology. In addition, their catalog presents English-language titles from Russian publishers for adult readers, including books on the arts, science, history, and current events. Interested readers should write to Imported Publications, 320 West Ohio Street, Chicago, Illinois 60610.

An excellent source of information about juvenile science books in the UK is *Ways of Knowing: Information Books for 7 to 9 Year Olds*, by Peggy Heeks, assistant county librarian, Royal County of Berkshire, England. The book presents an annotated listing of more than 100 nonfiction titles, including many books on science. The topics that are considered include fossils and prehistory, the human body, natural history, and technology.[41] As in *SB&F* and *Appraisal*, the capsule reviews evaluate the presentation and readability as well as the information content in each book. *Ways of Knowing* is published by the Thimble Press, Lockwood, Station Road, South Woodchester, Stroud, Gloucestershire GL5 5EQ, England. Thimble Press also publishes the *Signal Review*, a yearly guide to children's literature, including science books.

Another good British source is *The Good Book Guide to Children's Books*, published by Penguin Books in association with Braithwaite & Taylor Ltd., London. Like *Ways of Knowing, The Good Book Guide* provides capsule descriptions of a variety of children's titles, including books on the human body, dinosaurs, astronomy, and computers.[42] The book is available from Braithwaite & Taylor Ltd., PO Box 400, Havelock Terrace, London SW8 4AU, England.

As I noted earlier, science nonfiction books can be effective in informing and exciting young people about the world of science. This function is important, especially when one considers the extent to which science and technology increasingly permeate our lives. It seems clear that everyone in the scientific community has an interest in making sure juvenile science books continue to be published, continue to be made available as widely as possible, and continue to reflect the highest standard of accuracy and presentation.

I have always felt that scientific journals tend to dehumanize science. Some of the most interesting books about science are, in fact, biographic. We get glimpses of the personal side of science in almost every issue of *CC* in the section devoted to *Citation Classics*™. What we may need to interest young people in science is more biographic accounts of the early childhood of our most respected scientists.

*   *   *   *   *

My thanks to Terri Freedman and Christopher King for their help in the preparation of this essay.

©1984 ISI

REFERENCES

1. **Schlesinger B.** Children in one-parent families: a review. *Conciliat. Courts Rev.* 19(2):23-31, 1981.
2. **Barrilleaux L E.** An experiment on the effects of multiple library sources as compared to the use of a basic textbook in junior high school science. *J. Exp. Educ.* 35(3):27-35, 1967.
3. **Fisher B.** Using literature to teach science. *J. Res. Sci. Teach.* 17:173-7, 1980.
4. **Janke D & Norton D.** Science trades in the classroom: good tools for teachers. *Sci. Child.* 20(6):46-8, 1983.
5. **Guerra C L & Payne D B.** Using popular books and magazines to interest students in general science. *J. Read.* 24:583-6, 1981.

6. **Donovan J.** Telephone communication. 31 July 1984.
7. **Wolff K.** AAAS science books: a selection tool. *Libr. Trends* 22:453-62, 1974.
8. Outstanding science trade books for children, 1983. *Sci. Child.* 21(6):43-7, 1984.
9. **Johnston K.** Telephone communication. 19 July 1984.
10. **Blough G.** Telephone communication. 18 July 1984.
11. **Sutherland Z.** Science books are better than ever. *Amer. Libr.* 12:535-9, 1981.
12. **Moulton R R.** *First to fly.* Minneapolis, MN: Lerner, 1983. 120 p.
13. **Taylor G J.** *Volcanoes in our solar system.* New York: Dodd, Mead, 1983. 95 p.
14. **Gustafson A.** *Some feet have noses.* New York: Lothrop, Lee & Shepard, 1983. 96 p.
15. **Blassingame W.** *The strange armadillo.* New York: Dodd, Mead, 1983. 64 p.
16. **Garfield E.** Leprosy: down but not out. *Essays of an information scientist.*
    Philadelphia: ISI Press, 1981. Vol. 4. p. 601-8.
17. **Kavaler L.** *Green magic: algae rediscovered.* New York: Thomas Y. Crowell, 1983. 120 p.
18. **Nourse A E.** *Viruses.* New York: Franklin Watts, 1983. 64 p.
19. **Fisher J.** *Body magic.* New York: Stein and Day, 1979. 158 p.
20. **Selsam M E.** Writing about science for children. (Carr J, ed.) *Beyond fact: nonfiction for
    children and young people.* Chicago: American Library Association, 1982. p. 61-5.
21. --------------. *Catnip.* New York: William Morrow, 1983. 48 p.
22. **DeLuca G & Natov R.** Who's afraid of science books? An interview with Seymour Simon.
    Lion Unicorn 6:10-28, 1982.
23. **Pringle L P.** *Wolfman: exploring the world of wolves.* New York: Scribner, 1983. 71 p.
24. --------------. *Feral: tame animals gone wild.* New York: Macmillan, 1983. 110 p.
25. **Branley F M.** *Saturn.* New York: Thomas Y. Crowell, 1983. 57 p.
26. **Cuyler M.** Telephone communication. 26 June 1984.
27. **Giller P R.** Science books for young children. (Carr J, ed.) *Beyond fact: nonfiction for children and
    young people.* Chicago: American Library Association, 1982. p. 65-70.
28. **Holzheimer D.** Telephone communication. 11 July 1984.
29. **Duke J S.** *Children's books and magazines.* White Plains, NY: Knowledge Industry, 1979. p. 77.
30. **Carr J,** ed. *Beyond fact: nonfiction for children and young people.*
    Chicago: American Library Association, 1982. 224 p.
31. **Kobrin B.** Telephone communication. 29 June 1984.
32. **Cobb V.** Telephone communication. 27 June 1984.
33. **Meltzer M.** Where do all the prizes go? *Horn Book Mag.* 52(1):17-23, 1976.
34. **New York Academy of Sciences.** "Oak & Company" and "Volcano Weather" win the New York
    Academy of Sciences Thirteenth Annual Children's Book Awards. (News release.)
    9 March 1984. 2 p.
35. **Stommel H & Stommel E.** *Volcano weather.* Newport, RI: Seven Seas Press, 1983. 177 p.
36. **Mabey R.** *Oak & company.* New York: Greenwillow, 1983. 28 p.
37. **Cohen I.** Telephone communication. 17 October 1984.
38. **Krylov A.** *From the bonfire to the reactor.* Moscow: Raduga, 1983. 80 p.
39. **Akimushkin I.** *Builders in the wild.* Moscow: Malysh, 1978. 24 p.
40. **Zubkov B.** *What the bat told us.* Moscow: Malysh, 1981. 26 p.
41. **Heeks P.** *Ways of knowing: information books for 7 to 9 year olds.*
    Stroud, UK: Thimble Press, 1982. 54 p.
42. **Taylor B & Braithwaite P,** eds. *The good book guide to children's books.*
    London: Penguin, 1984. 79 p.

APPENDIX

APPENDIX

An
Algorithm
for
Translating Chemical Names
to
Molecular Formulas

EUGENE GARFIELD

INSTITUTE FOR SCIENTIFIC INFORMATION
33 SOUTH 17th STREET • PHILADELPHIA 3, PENNSYLVANIA

Originally presented to the Faculty of the Graduate School of Arts and Sciences of the University of Pennsylvania in Partial Fulfillment of the Requirements for the Degree of Doctor of Philosophy, 1961.

Library of Congress Catalog Card Number 61—17455

Institute for Scientific Information
33 South 17th Street • Philadelphia 3, Pennsylvania

PREFACE TO THE FIRST ISI EDITION

This varityped version of my doctoral dissertation has been prepared primarily to satisfy the many requests I received for copies of the original manuscript. With the exception of minor typographical changes and those noted below in the section on Transformations, the only other changes have been in the arrangement of the indexes, bibliography, etc. which had to conform to university conventions. However, in this edition the indexes, etc. have been placed at the end.

The original manuscript was typed primarily by my secretary, Mrs. Sylvia Shapiro. The varityping in this edition was done by Mrs. Joan M. Graham. Proofreading was performed by Mrs. Joan E. Shook and Mr. Walter Fiddler. Mr. Fiddler found errors of omission in the section on Transformations which have been corrected by the addition of footnotes. He also found many errors in the copying of chemical names and formulas in both the original and the final manuscript. This only strengthens my belief that an arduous intellectual task such as naming a chemical or calculating its formula is most consistently performed by a machine.

I also want to thank collectively, the many other persons who helped in the preparation of this work through suggestions and participation. The dissertation, as accepted by the Department of Linguistics of the University of Pennsylvania, went through several revisions before it was accepted. Many of these changes resulted from different interpretations of the *morpheme, allomorph*, etc. Linguistics is not yet so precise that one can prescribe a discovery procedure. Quite simply, this means that linguistic data can be interpreted in many useful ways. For the reader who is interested in pursuing the theoretical background of this statement further, I recommend Noam Chomsky's *Syntactic Structures* (Mouton & Co. 'S-Gravenhage, 1957) especially pages 17 and 56.

Most of the readers of this treatise will not be trained in linguistics. However, I do not feel that anyone interested in learning the procedures described will find the reading too difficult, even though the work was not written as a textbook. It is my intention to supplement this work by a textbook that will enable scientists and librarians to use chemical nomenclature for literature searches and for indexing without getting into the detailed understanding of organic chemical structure and theory. As a follow-up of this dissertation, work is now in progress on the completion of the lexicon of chemical morphemes. In the present work, linguistic analysis was confined primarily to acyclic chemistry while definitely establishing the feasibility of handling cyclics. To complete the linguistic analysis now requires considerable work. For example, the analyses must account for the difference in meaning of *oic acid* when it occurs with *pentanoic acid* and *benzoic acid*. This example also illustrates the futility of any syllabic approach to the study of chemico-linguistics.

I wish to stress that it is not necessary for the reader to wait for the appearance of the above-mentioned lexicon in order to use the algorithm (procedures) described here. This is especially true for those with training in organic chemistry, that is, have already memorized enough chemical nomenclature to carry through the simple calculations.

In closing I should like to encourage my readers to communicate with me concerning any portion of this work.

Eugene Garfield
INSTITUTE FOR SCIENTIFIC INFORMATION
Philadelphia 3, Pa.

July 17, 1961

PREFACE

This dissertation discusses, explains, and demonstrates a new algorithm for translating chemical nomenclature into molecular formulas. In order to place the study in its proper context and perspective, the historical development of nomenclature is first discussed, as well as other related aspects of the chemical information problem. The relationship of nomenclature to modern linguistic studies is then introduced. The relevance of structural linguistic procedures to the study of chemical nomenclature is shown. The methods of the linguist are illustrated by examples from chemical discourse. The algorithm is then explained, first for the human translator and then for use by a computer. Flow diagrams for the computer syntactic analysis, dictionary look-up routine, and formula calculation routine are included. The sampling procedure for testing the algorithm is explained and finally, conclusions are drawn with respect to the general validity of the method and the direction that might be taken for future research. A summary of modern chemical nomenclature practice is appended primarily for use by the reader who is not familiar with chemical nomenclature.

ABSTRACT

An algorithm for translating directly from chemical names to molecular formulas is described. The validity of the algorithm was tested both manually and by computer. Molecular formulas of several hundred randomly selected chemicals were calculated successfully, verifying the linguistic analyses and the logic of the computer program.

The algorithm for manual human translation consists of eight simple operations. The procedure enables non-chemists to compute molecular formulas quickly without drawing structural diagrams. The machine translation routine is rapid and requires a program of less than 1000 instructions. If the experimental dictionary were expanded to include low frequency morphemes, formulas for all chemical names could be handled.

The problem of chemical nomenclature is discussed in terms of the information requirements of chemists. The approach of the linguist to the problem of nomenclature is contrasted with that of the chemist. It is shown that there is only one language of chemical nomenclature though there exist many systems of nomenclature. The difficulties in syntactically analyzing *Chemical Abstracts* *(C. A.)* nomenclature results from C.A.'s ambiguous use of morphemes such as *imino*, not the use of so-called *trivial* nomenclature. The more *systematic I.U.P.A.C.* nomenclature includes idiomatic expressions but eliminates all homonymous expressions.

The structural linguist tries to describe a language compactly. While this study does not not include a complete grammatical description of chemical nomenclature, all of the basic facets of such a grammar have been studied. These linguistic studies include a morphological analysis of the most frequently occurring segments. Approximately forty morphemes such as {o, e, y} and allomorphs such as *thi* and *sulf* were isolated. A list of their 200 actual co-occurrences were compiled. These studies are particularly valuable in identifying idiomatic expressions such as *diaz*, the meaning of which cannot be computed from the referential meanings of *di* and *az*. Morpheme classes are illustrated by the *bonding* morphemes (*an, en, yn, ium*, etc.) and the homologous *alkyl* morphemes *meth, eth, prop, but*, etc.

The syntactic analyses include the demonstration of transformational properties in chemical nomenclature as e.g. in *primary amines* (R–N) where *aminoRane ⇌ Rylamine*. To complete the grammar one would have to expand the inventory of morphemes, morpheme classes, and the list of transformations. Chemical name recognition is not simply a word-for-word translation procedure. Rather the syntactic analysis required is comparable to the procedure employed by Harris, Hiz, et al (Transformations and Discourse Analysis Projects, Univ. of Pennsylvania) for normal English discourse. The structural linguistic data is supported by a summary of *I.U.P.A.C.* rules for generating chemical names.

In order to relate this study to the general problem of chemical information retrieval, the historical development of chemical nomenclature is traced from the 1892 Geneva Conference to the present. The relationship between nomenclature, notation, indexing and searching (retrieval) systems is discussed. In particular, the need for linguistic studies to solve the intellectual facet of the "retrieval" problem is discussed in contrast with the manipulative aspects which are more readily amenable to machine handling. The problem of synonymy in chemical nomenclature must be resolved if computable syntactic analyses of chemical texts are to be used for mechanized indexing. The completion of the detailed grammar of chemical nomenclature would not only permit the calculation of molecular formulas but also the generation of structural diagrams, systematic names, line notations, and other information required in machine searching systems. With suitable modifications the procedures could easily be applied to foreign nomenclature.

The field of chemico-linguistics is of interest to the organic chemist as it can improve methods for teaching nomenclature. Similarly, for the linguist chemical nomenclature is a fertile field of study. One can control the experimental conditions more easily than in normal discourse. However, conclusions can be drawn which may have more general application.

TABLE OF CONTENTS

TABLE OF CONTENTS (continued)

LIST OF TABLES

ORGANIC CHEMICAL NOMENCLATURE --
HISTORICAL AND BACKGROUND INFORMATION

The Contradictory Goals of Chemical Nomenclature

"It is possible in the domain of organic chemistry to give several names to the same compound. This state of affairs has on the one hand the great advantage of permitting clear expression of thought and of rendering it easier to bring out analogies in structure wherever this is useful." [*J Am. Chem. Soc.* 55, 3905(1933)].

These remarks are quite indicative of the general state of affairs of chemical nomenclature. They are the opening sentences of the 1930 "Definitive Report of the Commission on the Reform of the Nomenclature of Organic Chemistry" (opus cited, p. 3905) and like much that is said about nomenclature, the one sentence contradicts the other.

If it is possible to name the same chemical compound in two or more different ways, does this *really* permit clear expression of thought. It depends on one's orientation. For the speaker, synonyms do indeed allow for greater freedom of expression and the ability to bring out subtleties that might otherwise be difficult to make. For the listener, such freedom of expression on the part of the speaker may result in complete loss of comprehension. To complete the round of contradictions we find in the next sentence: "But on the other hand a multiplicity of names for the same substance constitutes a serious obstacle in the preparation of indexes." (opus cited, p. 3905).

Oral Communication Versus Indexing

Thirty years ago it was not yet quite apparent to experts in chemical nomenclature that their attempts to modify prevalent nomenclature for indexing purposes actually might be making oral and written communication even *more* difficult. It is not my purpose or intention to criticize the work of these experts. The purpose of these introductory remarks is to indicate that committees on chemical nomenclature are indeed faced with the baffling dichotomy of trying to serve the purposes of oral *communication* on the one hand and the needs of *indexing* on the other. This is like trying to get people to speak the King's English in order to simplify the task of preparing dictionaries. The inability to make these two functions blend is quite obvious if one examines, briefly, the history of organic nomenclature for the past seventy-five years.

Geneva Nomenclature

Modern chemical nomenclature "officially" began in 1892 [Pictet, *Arch. sci. phy. nat.* 27, 485-520(1892)][Tiemann, *Ber.* 26, 1595-1631(1892)] at the well known Congress of Geneva. All students of elementary organic chemistry are still taught the "Geneva" system though some teachers may now call it the I.U.P.A.C. system. The next major revision of the Geneva system came with the 1930 Report mentioned above. Thirty-eight years later "the intent of the Geneva Congress had not been realized" i.e., Rule I enabled each chemical to be named officially so that it would "be found under only one entry in indexes and dictionaries." (opus cited, p. 3906)

I.U.P.A.C. Nomenclature

The next major report on Organic Chemical Nomenclature came almost thirty years later and is known as the 1957 Report [*J. Am. Chem. Soc.* 82,5545-84(1960)]. It is important to note that the 1957 Report contributed nothing to affect this dissertation. Most of the report is devoted to cyclic compounds. The portion of acyclic chemistry which is discussed, the hydrocarbons, does not in any way affect the linguistic aspects of my research. For that matter, as is noted below, it does not affect the basic description of organic nomenclature.

The nomenclature of so-called simple functions, i.e. substances which contain only one kind of function such as acids, alcohols, etc. are not covered in the 1957 Report. The same is true of the complex functions.

Constant Activity in Nomenclature Field

The failure of the 1957 Report to treat the entire domain of organic nomenclature does not mean that there has not been a great deal of attention devoted to chemical nomenclature during the past thirty years. On the contrary, as Austin M. Patterson noted in 1951 there were so many com-- mittees on nomenclature that it was necessary to compile a directory of them. (*Chem. Eng. News* May 28, page 2181, cited in his "Words about Words" Washington, *Amer. Chem. Soc.*, 1957). This is a collection of nomenclature columns written by Patterson for the weekly organ of the Society, *Chemical and Engineering News.*

No Basic Change

Looking at the development of organic nomenclature from the viewpoint of structural linguist- ics one is forced to conclude that while there are changes in the Geneva System contained in the 1930 Report, the former system is retained basically intact. Only minor details were modified.

The present situation in organic chemistry may be described by posing the following ques- tions. If I had been ignorant of the 1930 and 1957 Reports on organic nomenclature and had compiled the list of morphemes and their corresponding syntactic rules, how accurately would this analysis describe organic nomenclature as it is used today. At least 90% of the new chemicals made each year would be recognized by a grammar based on the Geneva System. It would be an interesting study to make an *exhaustive* analysis of chemical nomenclature prior to 1892. This would determine the basic list of morphemes available to the chemist at the Geneva conference. However, such a comparison was not germane to the particular research involved in this dissertation.

While it is true that "official" nomenclature began at the Geneva conference, examination of the 1892 Report and others (e.g. Armstrong, *Proc. Chem. Soc.* 1892,127-131) and similar examination of earlier nomenclature practice reveals that the morphology of organic chemistry not only remained essentially the same in the 1930 and 1957 Reports, (which were presumably revisions of the 1892 Geneva Report), but even the Geneva conference did not contribute any major morphological changes in organic nomenclature. The Geneva chemists simply accepted the morphological pattern already in use and codified it. In other words, a morphological analysis of organic nomenclature conducted in 1891 would have produced almost exactly the same results as an analysis conducted after the Geneva Conference in 1892.

This is not to underestimate the value of the Geneva Conference. It has served a useful function in teaching nomenclature, as there was not then available any internationally accepted system that teachers could use. However, while the teaching of organic nomenclature was not quite formalized in 1891, the terminology acquired in studying elementary organic chemistry as e.g. by using an 1890 textbook would be not significantly different than that which would be acquired in reading the same textbook in its 1920 edition in which the Geneva system is adopted.

Longest Versus Shortest Chain Structure

The Geneva Conference *did* make some significant contributions to the syntactical description of organic nomenclature, or at least to solidification of syntactical practices used by many but not as universally as was the morphology. Thus, *triethylmethane* became *3-ethylpentane*. The example of *triethylmethane* demonstrates the point well. The morphemes *tri, eth, yl, meth, an, e* were not new. Neither were the morphemes *eth, yl, pent, an, e* in *ethylpentane*. The new rules specified the selection of the latter combination of morphemes for the chemical $CH_3-CH_2-CH(CH_2-CH_3)-CH_2-CH_3$ by establishing the syntactical principle that the "parent" structure shall be the one which contributes the *longest* possible chain of carbon atoms. The older method of naming this chemical had an *implied* syntactic structure where one named chemicals in terms of the *shortest* chain. The same diagram can be written $(CH_3-CH_2)_3-CH$. There are historical r e a s o n s for this change.

Rapid Change in Syntax — Not Morphology

Early organic chemistry naturally was concerned with chemicals of simpler structure such as *methane* gas. As the knowledge of chemical structure increased, chemicals like *pentane* were easier to understand, but still the Geneva chemists could not foresee the rapid development of organic chemistry that would take place, in which it would again become necessary to modify the syntax of nomenclature but not the morphology. This would seem to be the opposite of historical development of languages where it is the morphemes which change more rapidly than syntax.

Reading Organic Chemistry as a Language

Contrary to general belief, organic chemical nomenclature is relatively simple. It is not to the credit of many teachers of organic chemistry that many students are frightened away from organic chemistry because they are confronted too early and quickly with what seem to be very complicated chemical words. Students are not taught the basic elements of organic nomenclature before they begin the formal study of the actual experimental science. This is unfortunate. One can recall that it use to be a requirement for pre-medical students to study Latin. This was really not necessary to the study of medicine. However, having removed Latin from the medical curriculum there remains a vacuum. Special preparation in the language of medicine is needed to fill this vacuum. Similarly, the special language of organic chemistry should be taught first.

Implications for Teaching Organic Chemistry

I believe there *are* implications to be drawn from this dissertation for the teaching of organic chemistry. Teaching chemistry cannot be divorced from the general problem of chemical communication. However, I cannot hope to pursue, in detail, all the derivative problems related to chemical nomenclature.

Increased Volume of Chemical Literature

As was stated in the opening paragraph, the earlier international committees on organic nomenclature tried to resolve *simultaneously* the problem of communicating and indexing chemistry. If the problem of indexing chemicals was already a problem in 1892, it is quite understandable that the emphasis on the indexing implications of nomenclature have increased. Whereas a few thousand new chemicals were prepared each year at the turn of the century, over 75,000 new chemicals were prepared by the world's chemists in 1960 alone (cf. E. Garfield, *Index Chemicus*, 1st Cumulative Index, 1961, 33.)

Notation Systems

This volume has increased the preoccupation of nomenclature experts with indexing requirements. This includes not only conventional indexing systems, but also systems which will employ machines both for listing chemicals in the conventional fashion and also for new types of machine searching. The newer "nomenclature" systems, e.g. G.M. Dyson [(1947) Longmans, N.Y. 1949]and

W.J. Wiswesser (A Line Formula Chemical Notation, Crowell, N.Y., 1954) have completely discarded the semblance of English and employ completely symbolic representations. These so-called cipher or notation systems do undoubtedly simplify the problem of arraying formulas in indexes, just as notation systems simplify the problem of arraying books on a library shelf. However, just as library classification systems cannot place the book on more than one shelf at a time, using a notation system, per se, does not resolve the need to locate chemicals in more than one place in the index.

The various notation systems which have been proposed purport to avoid the pitfalls of nomenclature. None of them have been designed on the basis of a formal linguistic analysis of nomenclature. Rather, their inventors have been preoccupied with such problems as economy of notation and the ability to use the system simultaneously for the unique identification of chemical compounds as well as for generic searching. This now introduces a factor which begins to explain the background purpose of this research program.

Objectives of Linguistic Analysis

One can perform linguistic analysis with many different objectives in mind. Indeed, it is quite possible to visualize a situation in which a language might be analyzed without the linguist acquiring a speaking knowledge of that language. Similarly one can analyze nomenclature either with the idea of mastering the techniques of naming chemicals or one may be more interested in uncovering new methods of classifying chemicals. Since modern formal linguistics certainly helps one to perceive semantic as well as grammatical categories more directly than the older, more intuitive methods, (comparable to *a priori* elucidation of chemical classifications) then it is of interest to explore the possibilities of using formal structural linguistics in studying the problem of chemical information retrieval. I first discussed this possibility with Prof. Z. Harris in 1955 (E. Garfield, private communication "Structural Linguistics and Mechanical Indexing, 1955).

Information Requirements of Chemists

To completely understand the *raison d'etre* of this research, it is necessary to review some of the general information requirements of the chemist and how chemical nomenclature is related to these requirements. The organic chemist may spend years attempting to synthesize a particular chemical. In order to avoid the possibility of repeating experiments which were performed by others, he must have access to comprehensive indexes. Such indexes are typified by the *Chemical Abstracts* (C.A.) Subject and Formula Indexes (Chemical Abstracts, Columbus, Ohio).

In the C.A. indexes one can find a specific chemical by either of two methods. If one understands the C.A. system of chemical nomenclature then one can name a particular chemical in which one is interested and look for it in the alphabetic subject index. On the other hand, if one does not have mastery of the C.A. nomenclature system one still has the option to use the Formula Index. (Incidentally, not more than a few hundred chemists in this country have a complete mastery of the C.A. system. Three years of full-time indexing work are generally required to train a graduate organic chemist to be an indexer for *Chemical Abstracts.*)

Formula Indexes

The Formula Index is a simple device in which each chemical is listed in alpha-numeric order according to the number of carbon and other atoms contained in it. *Ethyl alcohol (ethanol)* is listed under C_2H_6O while *acetic acid (ethanoic acid)* is $C_2H_4O_2$. By simply counting the number of carbon and other atoms in the chemical, the chemist can compute the molecular formula. With no special training he can use the formula index to find the C.A. name of the chemical in which he is interested.

I wish to make clear that these are oversimplified statements for the purpose of explanatory clarity. In actual practice one must be very cautious in calculating a molecular formula as the more complex molecules prepared today can even be difficult to depict in ideographs. This then brings up another vital question, which is, the use of structural diagrams (ideographs).

Structural Diagrams

While a chemist may frequently *not* be able to name a chemical from a structural diagram, according to the I.U.P.A.C. or C.A. systems, he *can* usually draw a diagram from a name. In order to calculate the molecular formula of a complex molecule the chemist will invariably draw its structural diagram and then proceed to add the number of carbon and other atoms. A particularly annoying aspect of working with someone else's diagram is the frequent practice of omitting some of the hydrogen atoms in the diagrams. Hydrogen atoms as such are usually of little interest to the chemist.

All existing methods of naming, indexing, coding and ciphering chemicals are based on the assumption that the chemist will first provide a structural diagram. It is important to keep this in mind when comparing methods of handling chemical information. For example, when a chemical originally reported by name is indexed by *Chemical Abstracts* the indexer will *first* draw a structural diagram. He will then proceed to rename it "systematically". More often than not, the newly assigned name will be completely incomprehensible to the chemist who first prepared the chemical. The indexer will also use the structural diagram to calculate the molecular formula which, as we have seen, is very useful to the chemist in finding a chemical in a formula index.

Molecular Formulas in Analytical Chemistry

The molecular formula also plays another important role in chemical research as it is essential in analyzing chemicals to identify them through molecular or empirical formulas. The empirical formula shows the ratio between carbon, hydrogen and other atoms. For this reason, it is generally required that the chemist report the "calculated" molecular formula of each new compound he prepares when submitting a paper to a scientific journal. It is significant that a large number of the molecular formulas reported by authors contain errors. This statement is based on my personal experience in editing the indexing of more than 100,000 new chemical compounds. Surprisingly few chemists know the "odd-even" rule which requires that the hydrogen count is an odd number if there is an odd number of other atoms present. Most of the errors are in the hydrogen count. "The calculation of correct molecular formulas requires great care and checking is justified." (E. J. Crane: "C A Today — The Production of Chemical Abstracts, Amer. Chem. Soc., Washington, D.C., 1958, p. 86).In this same book Dr. Crane also discusses the frequent errors found in original journal articles (opus cited p. 74).

Generic Searches

While the subject and formula indexes to Chemical Abstracts are designed primarily to help the chemist find a specific chemical in which he is interested, they are not especially useful when he is trying to find a chemical of related structure. Indeed, in this case the chemist may not even know the existence of a particular chemical before he begins his search. Thus he may be interested in learning whether any member of a class of chemicals has been reported in the literature as e. g. hexanols. Generic searching is not always practical with the conventional indexes. For this reason other methods, both manual and machine, are now extensively employed.

Chemical-Biological Coordination Center Code

The most comprehensive classification system designed for searching chemicals generically is the system of the now defunct Chemical-Biological Chemical Coordination Center of the National Research Council. This system is based primarily on the work of Prof. D. Frear of the Pennsylvania State University (CBCC Chemical Code, National Research Council, Washington, 1948.)

Modifications of CBCC Needed

The CBCC chemical code is an elaborate hierarchial system of classification based on a priori assumptions concerning the classes one may wish to search in large files of chemicals. While the CBCC system is quite useful, almost without exception, chemists who employ it must make modifications in particular parts of the classification schedules to differentiate more precisely their particular chemical interests. For example, a steroid chemist would expand certain sections of the code where it is not sufficiently specific to distinguish large numbers of chemicals which might otherwise receive the same code number. This is the same problem that librarians encounter in using systems such as the Dewey Decimal System and the Library of Congress classification system.

Thus the laboratory chemist has two general requirements in searching for chemicals – the search for a *specific* chemical and the *generic* search. Turning from the chemist who is the user of indexes, what is the problem of the chemist who prepares these indexes.

The Indexer's Problem

In attempting to satisfy the information requirements of the lab chemist, the chemical indexer must deal with dozens of foreign languages in which chemical papers are written. He must also deal with the different synonym-producing-systems of naming the same chemical in each foreign language. In other words, French chemists not only have their little devices for naming chemicals, but in France, as in other countries, each chemist has certain preferences for naming chemicals in which he is a specialist.

Nomenclature Requires More Than Cooperation

The last comment may sound strange when one considers the obvious desire and willingness of chemists all over the world to cooperate in using standardized nomenclature. However, nomenclature is a problem that is far beyond the mere question of cooperation. It takes more than good intentions to resolve problems that arise from the vagaries of language. The plethora of chemical synonyms presents a formidable obstacle to the chemical indexer. If some method could be found for indexing chemical names without the many costly and enervating steps now required, a worthwhile step would have been made in documenting the literature of chemistry. This problem has great economic significance to indexer and user alike. The budget of Chemical Abstracts is over five million dollars per year.

Machine Indexing

The use of machines to perform indexing is by now no novel idea. My own investigations on the use of computers to index chemical information began in 1951 as a member of the Johns Hopkins Machine Indexing Project (cf. W.A. Himwich, H. Field, E. Garfield, J. Whittock, S.V. Larkey, Welch Medical Library Indexing Project Reports, Johns Hopkins University: Baltimore, 1951, 1953, 1955.)

Manipulative Versus Analytical Aspects of Indexing

In September of 1952, I presented an oral report on a tentative method for preparing the indexes to *Chemical Abstracts* before the American Chemical Society's Committee on C.A. Mechanization. However, most of the early work in the use of computers for scientific documentation concerned itself with the *manipulative* aspects of the problem rather than the *analytical* aspects. (cf. E. Garfield: Preparation of Printed Indexes by Machines, *Am. Documentation*, 6:68–76, 1955 and Preparation of Subject Heading Lists by Automatic Punched-Card Techniques, *J. Documentation*, 10:1–10, 1954).

In private communication to Prof. Arthur Rose, Pennsylvania State University, then chairman of the American Chemical Society Committee on C.A. Mechanization, the relationship between the problem of mechanical translation of languages and the problem of mechanical analysis of scientific literature was discussed. As the years have passed, the general awareness that the linguistic problems of indexing are far more significant than the manipulative aspects has increased. All workers in the field of information retrieval are now more conscious of the need to concentrate on problems of using computers as a substitute for the costly *intellectual* analysis required to index scientific documents by the conventional criteria as well as new criteria.

Soviet and British Nomenclature

In recent years Soviet scientists have also been devoting more attention to these problems as, for example, in the work of Tsukerman and Vladutz (cf. A.M. Tsukerman & A.P. Terentiev, Chemical Nomenclature Translation, *Proc. Intl. Conf. for Standards on a Common Language for Machine Searching and Translation*; New York, Interscience, 1961). Indeed, what it now a Soviet textbook of organic chemical nomenclature was first published in 1955 (cf. A.P. Terentiev et al, *Nomenklatura Organicheskikh Soedmionii*, Moscow, 1955) (simultaneously published in German translation as *"Vorschlage zur Nomenklature Organischer Verbindungen"*, Moscow, 1955.) It is an excellent treatment of the general subject of nomenclature. There are not too many extant works to which it can be compared. Cahn's recently published work (R.S. Cahn, *An Introduction to Chemical Nomenclature*, London, 1959) is written for the lay chemist. However, as Editor of the *Journal of the Chemical Society of London*, Cahn and Cross also prepared the *"Handbook for Chemical Society Authors"*, (Special Publication No. 14, London, The Chemical Society, 1960) which has many invaluable comments on I.U.P.A.C. as well as British and American nomenclature. It also gives the dates each rule was adopted.

American Nomenclature

The definitive American work on nomenclature is a publication known to most organic chemists — *"The Naming and Indexing of Chemical Compounds by Chemical Abstracts"* (Columbus,

Chemical Abstracts, 1957). The work is simply a reprint with comments of introductory remarks to the 1954 C.A. Subject Index. Neither this work nor that of Cahn can be considered to be a critique of nomenclature. That no really complete critique of chemical nomenclature is available is not surprising. This is a subject which has represented a lifetime of work for several eminent chemists among others A.M. Patterson, E.J. Crane, L.T. Cappell and the staffs of several publications in this country and abroad.

Accelerated Interest in Mechanical Analysis

The increasing availability of high-speed, high-density storage computers has now accelerated interest in the mechanical analysis of texts. It is not surprising that many individuals and teams are working simultaneously on many aspects of this problem. The possible use of computers for mechanical analysis of texts is not just an academic question involving the study of language, information theory, etc., in an academic sense, not that there can be too much research on these subjects. However, as one witnesses the growing volumes of scientific publications and the increasing difficulties of finding qualified personnel with scientific and indexing training one must be tempted to explore the full potential of the computer for every facet of indexing work. As the editor of a chemical index, I am only too well aware of the need for such assistance, even though a complete resolution of all extant problems seems now to be "futuristic". What then are the possibilities of using the computer to perform such intellectual analyses?

INTELLECTUAL INDEXING TASKS REQUIRING STUDY

Mechanical Reading Device

In the first place, one would like to have available a device for mechanically reading the words. This would avoid the costly step of manually creating a computer input in machine language. For example, one would like to index chemical papers merely by underscoring pertinent chemical names in a text. These words then would be analyzed by the computer. This was the basic premise of Frome's experiment (cf. J. Frome, U.S. Patent Office, Report No. 17, 1959).

Selective Word Recognition — Copywriter

In the work of indexing for the *Index Chemicus*, chemists must underscore pertinent chemical names and formulas. At present, there is no device available which would permit one to *selectively* "read" or "sense" printed texts, though the character recognition problem is gradually finding a solution. Large sums are now going into research on character recognition devices. However, the immediate prospect of devices which can simultaneously read the hundreds of different typographical styles now employed is still only on the horizon. Nevertheless, a prototype "reading" unit for selectively copying words for indexing and other purposes has been invented and built by this writer and is called the COPYWRITER (cf. Fourth Annual Report, Council on Library Resources, Washington, 1961, p. 30). This machine might be modified for use in character recognition machines for selected fonts (cf. Z. S. Harris, Intl. Conf. on Scientific Information, p. 949). Since one does know the particular typographical style used by publications regularly indexed, character readers can be built to accommodate these typographical styles (cf. J. Rabinow, *Character Recognition Machines*, 1961).

Chemical Names to Structural Diagrams

Assuming now that we have obtained some form of machine input either by character recognition or by manually creating a record in machine language, what do we wish to have done with this information?

Aside from the use that is made of the structural diagram by the chemist for naming chemicals systematically, and for calculating molecular formulas, one of the primary uses of the structural diagram is for communication. The organic chemist is able to comprehend a chemical most quickly when it is presented to him in the form of a structural diagram. This type of graphic presentation is absolutely necessary because the use of systematic nomenclature is frequently either too difficult or too time consuming. While it is theoretically possible to name any chemical by the Geneva system, it must be understood that this is far from true in practice. What actually happens is that certain complex configurations are assigned either a semi-systematic or trivial name. The chemist therefore overwhelmingly prefers the use of the structural diagram. However, in order to save space journals continue to use nomenclature extensively. One would therefore like to use the computer to convert chemical names back into structural diagrams.

Drawing Diagrams by Machine

At first glance the average chemist considers computer conversion of names to diagrams an impossible task. However, this is by no means the case. It is not true either in the sense of *recognizing* and understanding the chemical name itself nor in the sense that a machine cannot *"draw"*. That structural diagrams can be drawn by machine is an accomplished fact. In two separate reports Opler and Waldo have shown that structural diagrams can be drawn by a computer. (A. Opler and N. Baird, Display of Chemical Structural Formulas as Digital Computer Output, *Am. Documentation* 10: 59 − 63, 1958) (W. H. Waldo and M. de Backer, Printing Chemical Structures Electronically. *Proc. International Conference on Scientific Information*, National Academy of Sciences, Washington, 1959, p. 711−730). In fact, the diagrams drawn by Opler's computer were so realistic, few chemists would believe that it was not a photographic projection technique until they were shown exactly how the illusion was created on the IBM 718 output tube. This particular computer output device has a television type raster. By energizing the appropriate combination of spots, one can obtain drawings of amazing complexity. If the drawings are examined from a distance, one cannot see the spaces between the spots, thereby creating the illusion that they are line drawings. This is basically the technique used in wirephoto facsimile. One can see such patterns of dots on the front page of the daily newspaper, as it is frequently necessary to transmit photos quickly, and the size of the dots consequently must be large and more perceptible to the naked eye. If the transmission rate is slowed down, one can increase the resolution to the point where the human eye cannot easily detect the presence of the dots. There is no question that we can mechanically display and print structural diagrams by computer.

Recognizing Chemical Names by Machine

If we are capable of drawing a structural diagram by machine, then we must determine whether we can indeed find a procedure for "recognizing" a chemical name in such a way that the computer can be properly instructed to draw the correct diagram. I first began to pursue this question years ago. Could a computable procedure be found for *recognizing* chemical names and what type of analysis would be required in order to find this procedure? A further question naturally concerned the design of an experiment which could be completed in a reasonable length of time, with a reasonable chance for success.

Upon examination of the complex computer programming required to reproduce a single *known* and coded chemical on a 718 display tube, it became quite apparent that to recognize a previously unknown, uncoded chemical was not a reasonable task for one person to accomplish. Opler estimated that at least ten man-years would be required *just* to write the necessary computer programs for displaying any type of chemical diagram after suitable linguistic analyses of organic chemistry had been performed (A. Opler, Private Communication 1959). For this reason it was ascertained how much effort would be required to produce conventional line formulas as e.g.

$$C-C-N(CH_3)-C-C:C:O$$

To perform this feat, as in the case of drawing structural diagrams, this requires not only *recognition* routine, but also an extremely sophisticated *generation* routine, i.e. a procedure for generating the correct line-formula. This is further complicated by the fact that most general purpose computers do not have the typographical flexibility required for conventional line-formulas. Other methods of displaying chemicals as e.g. ciphers were also explored. A search of the literature and communication with the proponents of all well known notation systems indicated that such computer routines were not available. (G.M. Dyson and W.J. Wisswisser, Private Communication).

Calculating Molecular Formulas by Machine

Subsequently, I turned to the possibility of calculating the molecular formula. As has been stated above, the molecular formula is not only a widely used method of retrieving chemical information, it is also information that the chemist frequently needs in his laboratory work. In many situations it would not be necessary to draw a diagram if the molecular formula were available. Indeed, this is a very practical problem for every chemical publication or institution which prepares molecular formula indexes. The feasibility of preparing a program for generating molecular formulas seemed reasonable and provided a useful target for research.

While it was desirable to relate the study of finding a recognition routine to some usable output goal, the search for a recognition procedure might still have been undertaken anyhow. However, it is difficult to envision any recognition procedure which would not produce some type of usable output. Even a syntactic analysis of a sentence without regard to ultimate use does produce an output. In the case of chemical nomenclature, any output that results from a recognition routine has some value.

Having limited the scope of the output, it was then necessary to define and limit the recognition capabilities.

The Quagmire of Chemical Nomenclature

Organic chemical nomenclature is at first glance a horrible quagmire that could never be crossed by the most ambitious chemist. Naturally, the average chemist thinks first of the several million chemicals that have already been reported in the literature. There is almost an unlimited number of new chemicals that can be made. New combinations of atoms are uncovered every day. C. A. maintains a cross-reference file consisting of several hundred thousand entries. However, most people are unnecessarily discouraged by this state of affairs. It is necessary to differentiate the various facets of the problem of recognizing chemical names before one comes to the conclusion that it is a problem that is too hopeless to deal with.

There are three basic types of chemical names: (1) Trivial names, (2) Systematic names and (3) Semi-Systematic or Semi-Trivial names.

Trivial Names

The problem of handling trivial names must be dealt with in two parts: (a) names which are known prior to the computer analysis and (b) names which are entirely new. Tsukerman has properly called both types of trivial names "words-provocateurs" (opus cited, p. 4).

From the point of view of machine recognition of known trivial names there exists no problem. The storage of large dictionaries in computers is no longer a serious obstacle. With the improvement of so-called random access memory units we can expect to be able to look up items in large dictionaries quite rapidly at relatively low cost. While I would not underestimate the work involved in analyzing the thousands of trade names and other non-systematic names for chemicals, the problem of trivial names is indeed essentially trivial and of no basic interest to the linguist. This is primarily a problem of locating trade names and other synonyms by reference to standard compendia.

Legislation not a Solution

Similarly new trade names can be dealt with by non-linguistic methods. This may one day require legislative action, though it is extremely doubtful that we will see in our lifetimes the elimination of the practice of naming new chemicals biographically. You don't eliminate the use of terms like *"Richstein's Substance S"* by legislation. Rigid standards might make it very difficult for people to use such names in published journals. However, the use of trivial names or semitrivial names is absolutely essential and *necessary* in chemistry and particularly in biochemistry. Unfortunately, the chemical structure of many chemicals is not completely known for many years. Many chemicals can only be identified by a molecular or empirical formula. The complete chemical *structure* may not be understood for many years as was the case with thousands of chemicals like *insulin*, *penicillin*, etc.

Systematic Names

Systematic names also fall into several categories. The word "systematic" is used very loosely to mean chemical names which are (a) named according to existing nomenclature systems or (b) named on the basis of a very prescribed list of basic terms. As the Geneva system has developed, the various commissions have tried to get chemists to rely on "systematic" nomenclature of the latter type, but this is not always easy. The I.U.P.A.C. rules as they stand today allow for so many exceptions in the selection of lexical items that it is incredible to think that all chemists will ever use it with 100% consistency. Indeed, in using CA or I.U.P.A.C. nomenclature one constantly faces the situation of having to name a chemical in a way which is completely foreign to the chemist. The rules are written primarily for the use of indexers. Consequently, the above distinction which is made by I.U.P.A.C. and by such Soviet authors as Tsukerman (opus cited) between so-called systematic and trivial names almost becomes meaningless. What is a trivial name to one chemist is a systematic name to another. If you are a steroid chemist then *androstane* is not a trivial name. It is amusing to observe that the 1957 Report (opus cited, p. 73) gives up any attempt to get chemists to name *androstane* as a derivative *cyclopentanophenanthrene*, the more systematic description. It is equally ridiculous to call *cyclopentanophenanthrene* a systematic name when one could properly call the phenanthrene portion a derivative of *benzonaphthalene*. Once you are convinced, as I am, that the development of a truly systematic nomenclature for human communication is an impossible absurdity then distinctions between trivial versus systematic names also become absurd. If, on the other hand, one treats nomenclature linguistically chemical names can be classified as idiomatic or non-idiomatic expressions whose meanings can or cannot be computed from the meanings of the participating morphemes.

Treating Nomenclature as a Language

Most difficulties in dealing with nomenclature are due to the failure to recognize, in spite of its being a specialized jargon, that nomenclature is a sub-language of English (or whatever other language is involved). It displays many features of ordinary language. If the study of organic nomenclature is tackled as a linguistic as well as a chemical problem, then you avoid pitfalls such as the trivial-systematic dichotomy. If nomenclature is a linguistic problem then it seems reasonable to analyze the language of chemistry as you might analyze any other language. To completely describe a language is to write the grammar of that language.

Since I assumed chemical nomenclature to be a "language" with complexities or a range of complexities quite different than English or other natural languages, I was prompted to inquire how linguists might deal with such problems. I was further stimulated in this direction by the words of Bloomfield (Language, 1933) and Whorf (Language, Thought and Reality). This type of associative thought and further personal contact with linguists such as Harris inevitably focused my attention on the idea of treating organic chemical nomenclature as the structural linguist would treat a previously undescribed language.

While it was not possible for me to come to the linguistic laboratory with completely clean hands, having as a chemist acquired a general familiarity with chemical nomenclature systems, I was not uncritical of it. I have been reluctant to devote a great deal of time to the complete mastery of nomenclature because I feel that it has certain inherent limitations for communication and retrieval purposes.

In discussing organic chemical nomenclature, I have tried to indicate that as indexing problems have increased, nomenclature systems have tended to become geared more to the requirements of indexers rather than chemists or communicators. Naturally, both of these forces are constantly at work and the example I gave of the change in steroid nomenclature is one which indicates a case where the nomenclature experts had to revise systematic nomenclature to the facts as they already existed. Chemists had not followed the rules and the Commission could not overcome this fact in the in-between meetings. Between the first submission of the 1957 Report and its publication in

1960, there were over twelve thousand new steroid chemicals prepared. This is a fact from personal experience, as I examined that many steroid structures during the three years in question. In the face of such a rapid accumulation of new steroids, it is unreasonable to expect that chemists would do other than follow the principal-of-least-effort in naming chemicals. Even the layman has a good idea of what cholesterol is and it would be folly for scientific commissions to ignore the facts of natural linguistic growth. Creation of names cannot wait for the calling of annual committee meetings.

Designing Nomenclature for Machine Uses

On the other hand, if nomenclature systems can be designed both to help chemists communicate better and to index more consistently, why shouldn't nomenclature be designed so that it can be understood more easily by machines? In fact, it is not at all coincidental that elsewhere in this paper I have raised questions concerning the teaching of organic chemical nomenclature to humans. I suggest that a thorough re-examination of organic chemical nomenclature in terms of simplifying the process of analyzing chemical names by computer also would be most rewarding for teaching humans.

Certain practices are already noticeable in the naming of very complex chemical structures which appear to be accelerating this process anyhow. Chemicals are becoming so complex that chemists are finding it necessary to name them systematically but not in the I.U.P.A.C. or CA sense. This usage of existing terms does make sense to the reader and to the machine. The practice is increasing of adding substituents to the end of parent structures with intervening hyphens, without regard to the established I.U.P.A.C. rules of priority. For example, prefixes and suffixes are being used interchangeably. Most chemists could not care less whether substituents are listed in alphabetical order, by complexity, or by any other criterion. In fact, deviation from these complex ordering rules for multiple prefixes led to the formulation of a new method of filing steroids alphabetically. The system avoids absurdities which result from I.U.P.A.C.'s complex ordering rules [cf. E. Garfield, Steroid Literature Coding Project, *Chem. Literature* 12(3):6(1960)].

For example, it is the general rule in naming a chemical which has a particular function repeated to use the numerical prefix *di*. Thus one encounters *hexanediol* or more specifically *2,4-hexanediol*. If one files another chemical which is also a *hexanediol*, but which also contains an acid function as e.g. *2,4-dihydroxyhexanoic acid*, one obviously must file these two chemicals in entirely different places in an alphabetic scheme. However, the latter chemical could be called *2,4-diol-hexanoic acid* since *hydroxy* equals *ol*. Further simplification of the rules might produce *2-ol,4-ol-hexan-oic acid*. Not only is this easier to learn, it is certainly easier to analyze by machine.

Designing the Experiment

In designing the experiment and limiting its scope, I had to choose some portion of organic chemistry which was sufficiently large as to allow general conclusions to be drawn for chemical nomenclature in general. I chose acyclic chemicals as this class could be easily sub-divided if necessary. The experiment would still be reasonably complete so as to demonstrate the feasibility of tackling, by a team of linguists, chemists, and programmers, the entire domain of chemical nomenclature, especially the cyclics. The present analysis could be expanded to include and deal with more than 90% of the new compounds reported in the literature and a large percentage of the older literature by use of a relatively small number of additional morphemes such as *phen*, *benz*, *cyclo*, and other cyclic co-occurrences such as *aza*, *oxa*, etc. Thus, by a process of elimination the specific objective of my experimental program was established — to find a procedure for the machine translation of chemical names to molecular formulas.

One of the practical by-product results of this research has been to delineate a manual, algorithmic method of calculating the molecular formula of chemical names without resorting to structural diagrams. As I simulated the operations performed by the computer, based on the linguistic analysis, it became readily apparent that the procedure can be used manually. I am confident that most chemists will quickly learn and appreciate the simplicity of the method. One of the greatest values of trying to mechanize is that we are forced to look at a problem in a way that was hitherto difficult. The complete algorithm is summarized in Table V on page 30.

Another practical use of this new algorithm is found in the ability to train a non-chemist clerk to calculate a molecular formula from a chemical name.

Relationship between Nomenclature and Searching

A by-product of this study is the clearer understanding of the relationship between nomenclature and chemical searching requirements. When the computer analysis of the chemical name is completed, the parsed expression that results from the analysis could be used by the computer to perform very adequate *generic* as well as *specific* searches. If the chemists specifies the type of chemical in which he is interested in terms of morphemes instead of conventional chemical class names, generic searches become quite simple. Hence, a search for all *hexenols* becomes a search for all chemicals which contain the morpheme co-occurrence *hexen* and the morpheme *ol*. If he is interested in any six-carbon-chain-alcohol he need only specify the presence of *hex* and *ol*, where *hex* must be the carbon containing morpheme, not the multiplier morpheme as in *hexachlorooctane*.

While the computer program used in this research may be of interest to the reader (and for that reason is included here), it is only incidental to the general program of this research. The general requirements of the program, the basic approach, etc. are the pertinent factors. The specific methodology of particular computers is not of vital concern, though it is certainly an interesting exercise to work with a programmer. All of the actual Univac computer coding work was done in a relatively short time. Any large and several medium sized computers could have been used.

I personally prepared the Unityper tapes both for the input of the chemicals to be tested as well as the program. However, the actual Univac program coding was done by two University programmers, Dr. J. O'Connor and T. Angell. I wish to thank them both for this assistance. The coded Univac I program is omitted for this reason and comprises approximately 1000 code steps. However, the computer operation is described in general terms by flow diagrams in Tables VII to X.

While the study has been limited to acyclic compounds I was interested to explore just how difficult would be the transition to handling cyclic structures. A few cyclic morphemes were added to my testing procedure to simplify the selection of a random sample.

The exciting results of this side excursion over the border between the cyclic and acyclic compounds is that I have found cyclics to present no insurmountable obstacles. Certainly with sufficient, but reasonable manpower, it would be possible to resolve most of the ambiguities in the nomenclature, at least as far as calculation of molecular formulas is concerned. When we enter the realm of mechanically drawing structural diagrams then we are indeed faced with some grave problems in handling cyclics. We cannot ignore positional designations, which we can do in calculating molecular formulas. This is not because the syntactic problems of positional designations is itself difficult, which it is, but because there would appear to be no immediate solutions to the problem of resolving the use, by different chemists, of different systems of numbering well known ring systems. This would be more of a problem for older compounds published before the appearance of CA's Ring Index (Patterson, Cappell, Walker, *Ring Index*, Am. Chem. Soc., Washington, 1960).

Pattern Recognition Devices

This problem leads logically to another facet of the chemical information problem. Is it possible to find a method of "reading" structural diagrams. We have assumed all along that we would usually find our raw information in the form of printed chemical names. However, it is also true one has to deal with the printed structural diagram. Whether for the purpose of calculating a molecular formula or for naming the chemical systematically, a pattern-recognition device would be required in order to completely mechanize recognition. The National Bureau of Standards has been working on this problem using topological techniques. This is an exciting area of research, but we appear to be far from a solution to the problem.

Experiments with Cyclic Compounds

Preliminary experiments involving cyclic chemicals indicate that restricting the experiment to acyclic compounds does not affect the applicability of the procedure to cyclic structures. The greatest additional linguistic work is found, not in expanding from acyclics to cyclics, but from I.U.P.A.C. to less systematized nomenclature such as is used by *Chemical Abstracts*.

STRUCTURAL LINGUISTICS APPROACH TO CHEMICAL NOMENCLATURE

I shall outline below how a structural linguistic analysis of nomenclature differs from a non-linguistic approach. For example, the Soviet chemist Tsukerman (opus cited) uses the "syllabic" approach – a natural course for a chemist with good knowledge of nomenclature to follow. He thinks on terms of prefixes, suffixes, stems or roots, radicals, etc. On the other hand, the linguist studying nomenclature would not begin with the rule book of nomenclature, but rather with the actual discourse, the chemical names created by chemists. From the actual discourse he would discover the existing practices.

In principle, it is possible for a linguist to determine the morphemes of chemistry by interrogating an informant of that language. He can then apply the procedures of structural linguistic analysis to data obtained from the informant. The ultimate objective should be the most compact statement of the morphology. † Table I is a list of morphemes which I compiled for acyclic compounds. The word primary is used to indicate that these are the most frequently occurring – not that it is a preliminary list. In that case it would be a list of morphs.

Linguistic Forms and Their Environments

The basic approach of the structural linguist is to identify forms by examining the environments in which they occur. To obtain a description of a language one must examine a large corpus of that language. Allomorphs, morphemes, etc. are determined by a process of trial and error. Since a morpheme is a linguistic class it is essential that groups of occurrences be examined simultaneously if one is to determine that any particular sequence is or is not an occurrence of a morpheme.

---

†Since the phonemes of English chemical nomenclature were assumed to be the same as those used in normal discourse, it was not considered necessary to study the phonology. (There were very definite problems encountered by chemists in using Geneva nomenclature which could have been avoided if the conference had given some attention to phonetic transcription. Thus, the adoption of *yne* to differentiate acetylenes from *amines* became necessary later on. However, the phonetic identity of *ene* in *alkenes* and *ine* in *amines* is still a problem.) For the problem of translating chemical names to formulas phonology was not investigated. This does not mean that phonological studies are not germane to the problem of analyzing chemical discourse, as indeed they are. Such studies would help uncover ambiguities resulting from suprasegmental morphemes as e.g. in *dimethylphenylamine*.

468

In linguistics you cannot decide that a sequence is a morpheme unless you examine several utterances. Structural linguistics requires that linguistic forms be examined in *various* environments. In applying this technique to chemical nomenclature the procedure is facilitated by the existence of compendia such as Chemical Abstracts [cf. *Chemical Abstracts* 39,5867–5975(1945) for lists of frequently used radicals]. Here one finds occurrences organized by frequently occurring linguistic elements. It therefore becomes relatively simple to locate many occurrences of a particular element.

For example, in scanning a long list of chemical names you find the repetition of the segment *butyl* in names such as *butyl* chloride, *butyl*amine, di*butyl*amine, amino*butyl*decanol, *butyl*-aminohexane, etc. Preliminarily one can classify *butyl* as a morph. A *morph* is defined as a *putative* (tentative)*allomorph*. Further examination of more chemical names reveals the occurrence of *but* in *butane, butene, butynal, butanal, isobutane, aminobutenol*, etc. In addition, one finds the occurrence of *yl* in hex*yl* chloride, hex*yl*amine, dihex*yl*amine, aminohex*yl*dodecanol, hex*yl*aminohexane, etc. On this basis the first trial, testing *butyl* to be a potential allomorph, is found to be in error. We find instead the morphs *but, yl, hex*, etc. If you ask an informant whether there is a difference in the reference meaning of *but* in each of these previous occurrences he will say there is no difference. The same will be true of *yl*. We can now proceed with further tests as to the morphemic character of *but*.

Suppose now the words *nembutal* and *nembutol* are discovered. One may call *nem* a morph. We assume that *but* in *nembutal* is a morph from the previous analyses. Then we check whether we can substitute any other morph for *nem* and we find we cannot. We also try to make a substitution for *but* in *nembutal* and we cannot. This would tend to indicate that the *but* in *nembutal* is not a morph. As additional evidence that *but* in *nembutal* is not a morph we may also ask the informant if there is a difference in the reference meaning of *but* in *nembutal* and *butane*. Should the informant not be able to express strong convictions about *but* in *nembutal* then one would rely on the formal evidence which definitely indicates that it is not the same morph as in *butane*. Thus we have dealt with the fortuitous occurrence of *but* in *nembutal*. We can now proceed with further tests as to the morphemic character of *but*.

To confirm that *but* is a morpheme we find that in most of its occurrences it can be substituted by *hex* as in *hexane, hexene, hexanol*, etc. In addition *but* can replace *pent* in *pentane, pentene, pentanol*, etc. We can now refer to each particular single occurrence of *but* as the morph and to the morpheme {c–c–c–c} when referring to the class of its occurrences. In this fashion we establish a preliminary list of morphemes.

Free Variation and Complementary Distribution

This list may be condensed by looking for allomorphs which occur either in free variation or in complementary distribution. In I. U. P. A. C. nomenclature there is no free variation. While

I.U.P.A.C. has eliminated free variation, it has not eliminated positional variance. We do find that *thi* and *sulf* are allomorphs of the morpheme {S}. *Thi* is in complementary distribution with *sulf*. In addition, the terminal *e* is in complementary distribution with the conjunctives *o* and *y*. These make up the morpheme {e, o, y}. *Ox* and *on* are also *allomorphs*, in complementary distribution, of the morpheme {ox, on}. *Ox* always occurs with the allomorph *o* of the preceding morpheme whereas *on* occurs with the allomorph *e*.

Co-occurrences in Systematic Organic Nomenclature

A list of co-occurrences in organic chemical nomenclature was compiled using the list of morphemes in Table I. The morphemes on this list were permuted with each other. From the total list of 1600 theoretically possible co-occurrences, 199 actual co-occurrences were determined. This was done by finding texts containing the co-occurrence or from personal knowledge of actual occurrences.

Lack of co-occurrence was further tested by using Prof. N. Rubin of the Philadelphia College of Pharmacy as an informant. We systematically went over the preliminary list of theoretical combinations. Many of the eliminations are based, not on their failure to occur in organic chemistry, but their failure to occur in acyclic compounds. Thus, combinations like *aza, oxa, thia, ole, inium, olium*, and *azol*, do in fact occur in chemistry, but only in cyclic structures. The classified list in Table II was compiled first. Then the alphabetic list in Table III was compiled to eliminate repetition.

TABLE I

LIST OF PRIMARY MORPHEMES FOR ACYCLIC ORGANIC CHEMISTRY

1. a	11. di	21. in	31. on**
2. acid	12. e*	22. iod	32. ox**
3. al	13. en	23. it	33. pent
4. am	14. eth	24. ium	34. sulf***
5. an	15. fluor	25. meth	35. tetr
6. at	16. hept	26. nitr	36. thi***
7. az	17. hex	27. o*	37. tri
8. brom	18. hydr	28. oct	38. y*
9. but	19. id	29. oic	39. yl
10. chlor	20. im	30. ol	40. yn

Asterisked items are allomorphs of one of the following morphemes:

* = {o, e, y}   ** = {on, ox}   *** = {sulf, thi}

TABLE II. CLASSIFIED LIST OF CO-OCCURRENCES

a	*at*	*di*	*hept*	*in*	*o*	*ox*	*tri*
hepta	oat	dipent	hepta	azin	oxo	iodox	trien
hexa	sulfat	diprop	heptan	ino	oyl	methox	trieth
octa		disulf	hepten	inyl	sulfo	nitrox	trihept
penta	*az*	dithi	heptyl	sulfin	thio	oxid	trihex
tetra		diyl	heptyn		yno	oxim	trimeth
	azid	diyn	ylhept	*iod*		oxo	trioct
acid	azin				*oct*	oxy	triol
	azo	*e*	*hex*	iodid		pentox	trion
acid amide	azon			iodo	octan	propox	triox
acid halide	azox	ane	hexa	iodox	octen	triox	tripent
oic acid	diaz	ate	hexan		octyl		triprop
	hydraz	ene	hexen	*it*	octyn	*pent*	trithi
al	nitraz	ide	hexyl		yloct		triyn
		ime	hexyn	ite		dipent	
alon	*brom*	ine	ylhex	nitrit	*oic*	pentan	*y*
anal		ite		sulfit		penten	
enal	bromid	one	*hydr*		anoic	pentox	oxy
thial	bromo	yne		*ium*	azoic	pentyl	
ynal			hydrat		dioic	pentyn	yl
	but	*en*	hydraz	idium	enoic	tripent	
am			hydrid	onium	oic acid		butyl
	butan	buten	hydrox		onoic	*sulf*	enyl
amat	buten	enal	sulfhydr	*meth*	thioic		ethyl
amid	butox	enam			ynoic	disulf	methyl
amin	butyl	ene	*id*	dimeth		sulfam	nitryl
amon	butyn	eno		methan	*ol*	sulfhydr	oyl
anam	ylbut	enoic	amid	methox		sulfid	pentyl
diam		enol	azid	methyl	anol	sulfin	propyl
enam	*chlor*	enon	bromid	trimeth	diol	sulfit	ylam
sulfam		enyl	chlorid		enol	sulfo .	ylbut
thiam	chlorid	enyn	fluorid	*nitr*	ol	sulfon	ylen
triam	chloro	ethen	hydrid		olic		yleth
ylam		hepten	ide	dinitr	tetrol	*tetr*	ylhept
	di	hexen	iden	nitrat	thiol		ylhex
an		iden	idin	nitraz	triol	tetra	ylid
	dial	octen	idium	nitrid	ynol	tetrol	ylim
anal	diam	penten	ido	nitrit		tetron	ylmeth
anam	diaz	propen	idox	nitro	*on*	tetrox	yloct
ane	dibrom	thien	idyn	nitroxo			ylpent
ano	dibut	trien	imid	nitryl	amon	*thi*	ylprop
anoic	dichlor	ylen	iodid		anon		ylthi
butan	dien		nitrid	*o*	azon	dithi	ynyl
ethan	dieth	*eth*	oxid		dion	thial	
heptan	difluor		sulfid	ano	enon	thien	*yn*
hexan	dihept	ethan	ylid	ato	onium	thio	
methan	dihex	ethen		azo	onoic	thioic	diyn
octan	diim	ethox	*im*	bromo	onyl	thiol	ethyn
propan	diiod	ethyl		chloro	tetron	thion	idyn
	dimeth	ethyn	ime	eno	thion	trithi	propyn
at	dinitr	yleth	imid	fluoro	trion	ylthi	triyn
	dioat		imin	hydro	ynon		yne
ate	dioct	*fluor*	oxim	ino		*tri*	ynol
nitrat	dioic		ylim	iodo	*ox*		ynon
	diol	fluorid		ito		tribut	ynyl
	dion	fluoro	*in*	nitro	ethox		
	diox			oat	hydrox		
			amin	ono	idox		

471

TABLE III.   ALPHABETICAL LIST OF CO-OCCURRENCES

1. acid amide	51. diox	101. inyl	151. sulfin
2. acid halide	52. dipent	102. ite	152. sulfit
3. amat	53. diprop	103. ito	153. sulfo
4. amid	54. disulf	104. iodid	154. sulfon
5. amin	55. dithi	105. iodo	155. tetra
6. amon	56. diyl	106. iodox	156. tetrol
7. anal	57. diyn	107. methan	157. tetron
8. anam	58. enal	108. methox	158. tetrox
9. ane	59. enam	109. methyl	159. thial
10. ano	60. ene	110. nitrat	160. thiam
11. anoic	61. eno	111. nitraz	161. thien
12. anol	62. enoic	112. nitrid	162. thio
13. anon	63. enol	113. nitrit	163. thioic
14. ate	64. enon	114. nitro	164. thiol
15. ato	65. enyl	115. nitrox	165. thion
16. azid	66. enyn	116. nitryl	166. tribut
17. azin	67. ethan	117. oat	167. trien
18. azo	68. ethen	118. octa	168. trieth
19. azoic	69. ethox	119. octan	169. trihept
20. azon	70. ethyl	120. octen	170. trihex
21. azox	71. ethyn	121. octyl	171. trimeth
22. bromid	72. fluorid	122. octyn	172. trioct
23. bromo	73. fluoro	123. oic acid	173. triol
24. butan	74. hepta	124. ol	174. trion
25. buten	75. heptan	125. olic	175. triox
26. butox	76. hepten	126. one	176. tripent
27. butyl	77. heptyl	127. onium	177. triprop
28. butyn	78. heptyn	128. ono	178. trithi
29. chlorid	79. hexa	129. onoic	179. triyn
30. chloro	80. hexan	130. onyl	180. ylam
31. dial	81. hexen	131. oxid	181. ylbut
32. diam	82. hexyl	132. oxim	182. ylen
33. diaz	83. hexyn	133. oxo	183. yleth
34. dibrom	84. hydrat	134. oxy	184. ylhept
35. dibut	85. hydraz	135. oyl	185. ylhex
36. dichlor	86. hydrid	136. penta	186. ylid
37. dien	87. hydro	137. pentan	187. ylim
38. dieth	88. hydrox	138. penten	188. ylmeth
39. difluor	89. ide	139. pentox	189. yloct
40. dihept	90. iden	140. pentyl	190. ylpent
41. dihex	91. idin	141. pentyn	191. ylprop
42. diim	92. idium	142. propan	192. ylthi
43. diiod	93. ido	143. propen	193. ynal
44. dimeth	94. idox	144. propyl	194. yne
45. dinitr	95. idyn	145. propyn	195. yno
46. dioct	96. ime	146. propox	196. ynoic
47. dioat	97. imid	147. sulfam	197. ynol
48. dioic	98. imin	148. sulfat	198. ynon
49. diol	99. ine	149. sulfhydr	199. ynyl
50. dion	100. ino	150. sulfid	

The Problem of Syntactic Analysis in
Organic Chemical Nomenclature

In analyzing sentences "syntactic analysis" means: a procedure for recognizing the structure of a particular sentence taken as a string of elements. To state the structure of a string is to assign its words to word classes, to divide the word class sequence into substrings and to say what combinations of substrings are admitted. (Z.S. Harris, H. Hiz et al.: Transformations and Discourse Analysis. Univ. of Penna. Computing Center Annual Report. 1960, p. 43)*

By analogy, syntactic analysis of chemical nomenclature is the procedure for recognizing the structure of a particular chemical name taken as a string of elements (morphemes).

Since chemical names are often composed of long continuous strings of morphemes uninterrupted by spaces, hyphens, or brackets, it is necessary to set up a procedure for segmenting chemical words into morphemes. In some instances the chemist does this when he uses hyphens or spaces; however, in a name like *diaminopropylaminobutylhexene* the morphemes *di, amino, prop, yl, amino, but, yl, hex, ene* must be parsed as a continuous string of alphabetic characters. It is further necessary to establish the correct bracketing relationship between adjacent morphemes as e.g. between *di* and *amino* in *diaminopropylbutylhexene* on the one hand and *bis* and *aminopropylbutyl* in *bisaminopropylbutylhexene* on the other hand. In the latter case, the morpheme *bis* has a domain of operations quite distinct from that of its allomorph di. (The reader should remember that chemical morphemes are of two kinds: those which designate calculational values as e.g. *but* = C_4 and those which designate operations performed on them such as *di* = multiply by 2.)

In a comprehensive syntactic procedure for analyzing chemical nomenclature, all bracketing will be determined algorithmically. The computer procedure described in this study does it only in part. This was done to simplify the computer programming. I.U.P.A.C. rules on the use of brackets have been interpreted to mean they are always required when there is a possibility of ambiguity. In the above mentioned case *aminopropylbutyl* would be bracketed during the preparation of the input tape. This is perfectly legitimate use of the rules and I have assumed that all means to be tested are perfectly named. In a more ambitious recognition routine we would have to include additional syntactic procedures that would identify *hexene* as the parent function.

It is significant that neither I.U.P.A.C. nor C.A. accurately prescribe the limits of *bis*. In actual practice *bis* will apply to those morphemes which can be used as substituents and the implied bracketing will end before the "parent" morpheme modified by the substituents. Thus, in the case of *bis-p-methylaminophenylhydrazone* it might refer to $=N-N-(C_6H_4-NHCH_3)_2$ or

---

*For a more detailed treatment see Transformations and Discourse Analysis Project No. 15. Computable Syntactic Analysis. University of Pennsylvania, Dept. of Linguistics, 1959, p. 1.

$(=N-NH-C_6H_4-NHCH_3)_2$ and parentheses become essential. At the present time there appears to be no method for resolving such ambiguity except by pre-editing as was done in this experiment. (A useful function would be served if the computer determined whether *bis* was not followed by a paren. In that event the output would indicate possible ambiguity. In this case the name would not be considered to be well-formed.)

> "The successive words of each sentence are compared with the entries in a dictionary, and each is replaced by its dictionary equivalent, i. e., the class to which it. belongs (e.g. verb.) The sequence of class names which now represent the sentence is scanned for class cleavage, i.e., cases where the word may belong to two or more classes (noun and verb, for example). A program is needed to decide to which class the word belongs in its grammatical context." (Harris, Z.S., Hiz, H. et. al opus cit., p. 44)

In the case of chemical nomenclature, the problem of classification would not appear to be as complex as in normal English discourse. However, in a comprehensive syntactic analysis comparable operations would have to be performed. Otherwise we could not identify *nicotinoyl morpholine* and *pyridyl morpholinyl ketone* as synonyms. In the first case, morpholine is regarded as the parent structure. In the second case, *pyridyl morpholinyl ketone*, the ketonic function is considered the parent structure. This compound could also be regarded as a derivative of pyridine. (see p. 33)

If one seeks to recognize chemical names for the purposes of calculating from them their molecular formulas, then more elaborate forms of syntactic classifications of morphemes would not appear to be necessary. On the other hand, if the routine were designed so that one could both recognize chemical words and produce them according to I.U.P.A.C. rules, it would be very important to assign each morpheme to appropriate "syntactic categories," the sequences of which constitute well-formed chemical names. A cardinal principle of I.U.P.A.C. nomenclature is the selection of the principal functional group. A functional group is "one whose designation can be added at the end of the complete name of a compound without alteration to the name other than, sometimes, elision of terminal *e*." (R.S. Cahn, opus cited, p. 46). In this case, the choice would be quite clear. It must be named as a *ketone*, as this is the only element which is classified as a functional group.

Another important classification will be based on chain length. Hence it will be necessary to identify each member of the homologous series *meth*, *eth*, *prop*, *but*, etc. as such so that it will be possible to decide which of several that may appear in a name will take precedence. The principle of the *longest chain* can only be applied if one can array all members of this class which contribute chain length.

Yet another distinction is made on the basis of selecting chain lengths of greatest unsaturation. Consequently, the classification based on bonding, discussed below under *Bonding Morphemes* takes on even greater significance.

To carry the analogy further, chemical nomenclature also exhibits class cleavage i.e., cases where the morphemes may belong to two or more classes. An algorithm will therefore be required which determines for a particular grammatical context the class assignment of morphemes exhibiting class cleavage. This will be particularly true of expressions which must be classified both as regards chain length and/or functional group. Thus the common element *vinyl* (CH_2=CH–) contributes both to bonding, (unsaturation) as well as to chain length-two conflicting choices according to the circumstances.

Transformations in Organic Chemistry

The analogy between chemical names and normal sentences can be completed by showing that chemical synonyms exhibit transformational relationships similar to those exhibited by sentences. By using an appropriate notation we obtain the following transformations for the class of chemicals known as *diaryl ketones*, Ar_1–(C=O)–Ar_3, where $Ar_2=Ar_1$(C=O) and $Ar_4=Ar_3$(C=O).

$$Ar_1yl\ Ar_3\ yl\ ketone \rightleftarrows Ar_2oylAr_3ene \rightleftarrows Ar_1ylcarbonylAr_3ene \rightleftarrows Ar_3ylcarbonylAr_1ene \rightleftarrows Ar_4Ar_1ene$$

By using these transformations it is possible to generate the following list of perfectly good chemical names. Alongside each group of names is the corresponding structural diagram.

Ar_n	A	B	C	D	E
Ar_1 = phen		pyridin	phen	pyridin	xyl
Ar_2 = benz		nicotin	benz	nicotin	dimethylbenz
Ar_3 = naphthal		morphol	morphol	naphthal	fluoren
Ar_4 = naphthoyl		morpholenecarbonyl		naphthoyl	fluorenecarbonyl

Group A

phenyl naphthyl ketone
benzoylnaphthalene
phenylcarbonylnaphthalene
naphthalylcarbonylphenene*
naphthoylphenene

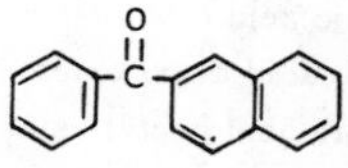

Group B

pyridinyl* morpholyl* ketone
nicotinoylmorpholene*
pyridinylcarbonylmorpholene
morpholylcarbonylpyridinene*
morpholenecarbonylpyridinene

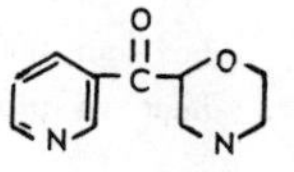

Ar_1, Ar_2, Ar_3, and Ar_4 are class designations. The synonyms for any diaryl ketone can be named by these transformation rules. One can generate well-formed names simply by specifying the values for each Ar group. This means that if one specifies the

Group C

phenyl morpholyl ketone
benzoylmorpholene
phenylcarbonylmorpholene
morpholylcarbonylphenene
morpholenecarbonylphenene

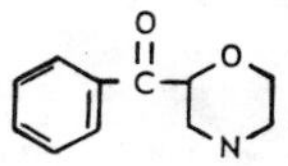

*phenene → benzene (phen → benz)
pyridinyl → pyridyl (inyl → yl)
morpholyl → morpholinyl (yl → inyl)

morpholene → morpholine (ene → ine)
pyridinene → pyridine (inene → ine)

naphthalyl → naphthyl (alyl → yl)
fluorenene → fluorene (enene → ene)

Group D

pyridinyl naphthalyl* ketone
nicotinoylnaphthalene
pyridinylcarbonylnaphthalene
naphthalylcarbonylpyridinene
naphthoylpyridinene

Group E

xylyl fluorenyl ketone
dimethylbenzoylfluorenene*
xylylcarbonylfluorenene
fluorenylcarbonylxylene
fluorenoylxylene

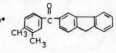

morpheme for Ar_1 and Ar_3 in $Ar_1-(C=O)-Ar_3$ a grammatically correct chemical name will be obtained by replacing Ar_1, Ar_2, etc. in the transformation equations. Prior knowledge of a correct chemical name is not required. In Table IV transformations for other chemical classes are illustrated. A thorough investigation of the transformations of chemical nomenclature would be a *sine qua non* for developing a procedure for the generation of standardized nomenclature. They are mentioned here only to complete the description of the analagous relationship that exists between syntactic analysis of normal English discourse and syntactic analysis of chemical nomenclature.

TABLE IV. TRANSFORMATIONS IN ORGANIC CHEMISTRY

Aldehydes $RCH=O$

R	b_n	R'	Rb_nal	formyl Rb_ne	Rb_ne carboxaldehyde
pent	an		pentanal	formyl pentane	pentane carboxaldehyde
but	en		butenal	formyl butene	butene carboxaldehyde
prop	yn		propynal	formyl propyne	propyne carboxaldehyde

Esters $R\,COOR$

			$Ryl\ R\ b_noate$	$R\ b_noic$ acid Ryl ester	$Ryl\ R\ b_ne$ carboxylate
eth	en	pent	ethyl pentenoate	pentenoic acid ethyl ester	ethyl pentene carboxylate
hex	an	but	hexyl butanoate	butanoic acid hexyl ester	hexyl butane carboxylate
hept	yn	prop	heptyl propynoate	propynoic acid heptyl ester	heptyl propyne carboxylate

Alcohols $R-OH$

		Hydroxy Rb_ne	Rb_nol
pent	en	hydroxypentene	pentenol
but	yn	hydroxybutyne	butynol

Ethers $R-O-R'$

			Roxy $R\ b_ne$	$Ryl\ R\ b_nyl$ ether	
prop	yn	but	propoxy butyne	propyl butynyl ether	(propanyl = propyl)
hex	an	prop	hexoxy propane	hexyl propanyl ether	
eth	en	prop	ethoxy propene	ethyl propenyl ether	

TABLE IV. TRANSFORMATIONS IN ORGANIC CHEMISTRY (continued)

Acids RCOOH

R	b_n	R′	Rb_noic acid	Rb_n carboxylic acid
prop	en		propenoic acid	propene carboxylic acid
but	yn		butynoic acid	butyne carboxylic acid

Amines R–N

			Amino Rane	Rylamine
eth			aminoethane	ethylamine
prop			aminopropane	propylamine

The Value of Structural Linguistics for the
Study of Chemical Nomenclature

The linguistic approach to the study of nomenclature provides an insight to the inconsistencies that have slowly accumulated nomenclature's natural, historical development. Linguistic analysis enables one to uncover, in advance, ambiguities that will result from the imperfect rule book of chemical nomenclature. For example, linguistic analysis indicates the occurrence of the morphemes *di*, *meth*, and *oxy* and their co-occurrence in strings such as *dimeth*, *methoxy*, and *dimethoxy*. This finding uncovers another flaw in the accepted convention of organic nomenclature and renders existing organic nomenclature far from acceptable to the machine and the human. This realization might in turn lead to a readjustment in the rules of organic nomenclature which would stipulate that all numerical prefixes be followed by parentheses. This would make the job of recognition much simpler.

It should be made clear that this study by no means purports to be an exhaustive linguistic analysis of organic nomenclature. My remarks are intended as a summary of the methods that will undoubtedly be required should a completely exhaustive study of chemical nomenclature be undertaken. In that event one would encounter many additional ambiguities in nomenclature and many new interesting morpheme classes. Expanding the scope of the linguistic analysis in this way, e.g. would bring in the cyclic chemicals which account for the majority of new chemicals prepared today. It would also introduce the complexities involved in analyzing chemical names produced not only by the I.U.P.A.C. nomenclature but also by standard British and American nomenclature. This would introduce other complexities such as variations in spelling, use of different "trivial" words, etc. (cf. T. E. R. Singer, U. S. and British Index Entries, *Searching the Chemical Literature Advances in Chemistry No. 4*, Washington: American Chemical Society, 1951.)

The Value of the Study of Chemical
Nomenclature to Linguistics

In a certain sense, the domain of chemistry represents a more strictly controlled experiment for testing linguistic procedures since there are a relatively small number of parameters. It is possible, as was done in this experiment, to vary the number of parameters according to the needs of the experiment. As one gains knowledge of the language, additional morphemes and syntactical relationships can be studied so as to determine their effect on previously established knowledge. Otherwise it becomes necessary to study the language in its entirety and by the time one has even located all occurrences in the language, the natural course of human events has changed some of the relationships. This is particularly true in chemistry, where there is now a very rapid change in terminology as a result of the rapid accumulation of chemical knowledge. Certainly from the point of view of historical linguistics, one can observe changes in chemical nomenclature take place in a period of ten years that might take hundreds in normal discourse.

AN ALGORITHM FOR TRANSLATING CHEMICAL NAMES
INTO MOLECULAR FORMULAS

This dissertation reports the first successful procedure for direct translation of chemical names into molecular formulas.

To test the general validity of this procedure, an experiment was designed in which certain restrictions were placed on the input and output capabilities. These restrictions were made only to facilitate experimentation with an electronic computer. As will be seen, no such restrictions are necessary when the procedure is used by human translators. Indeed, it is one of the more significant aspects of this research that it is now possible, using this procedure, to train a non-chemist to calculate, quickly and accurately, molecular formulas. This could be done by completing, for the entire domain of chemical nomenclature, the dictionary of morphemes, idioms, homonyms, etc. that has been prepared for this experiment.

The dictionary of morphemes contains, for each morpheme, the calculational value and the pertinent operations of addition and/or multiplication for that morpheme or those which precede or follow. While the experimental dictionary of morphemes is small, it is not without interest to note that these morphemes account for a large percentage of all known chemicals. The morphemes that have been eliminated are those which are ordinarily considered to be non-systematic, i.e., trivial.

The procedure was tested on a Univac I computer. However, any medium-sized or large computer could be similarly programmed from the general flow diagram which forms a part of this work.

TABLE V
AN ALGORITHM FOR TRANSLATING CHEMICAL NAMES TO MOLECULAR FORMULAS
SUMMARY OF OPERATIONS FOR HUMAN TRANSLATION

1. Ignore all locants (1, a, N, etc.)
2. Retain all parens.
3. Replace all morphemes by dictionary value.
4. Resolve ambiguity of any penta-octa occurrences.
5. Place + after all morphemes except multipliers.

6. If there is + at far right of parenthesized term, place it outside right paren. If there is + at far right of name, always drop it.
7. Carry out all multiplications.
8. Calculate hydrogen using hydrogen formula: $H = 2 + 2n_C + n_N - n_X - 2n_{DB}$.

Ambiguity Rules

1. You cannot have two multipliers in a row unless separated by paren.
2. If either of the next two morphemes is alkyl ending, it is not multiplier
3. If not, it is multiplier.

TABLE VI
INVENTORY OF MORPHEMES USED IN THE EXPERIMENT

Morpheme	Meaning	Example	Calculation Value						
			p	C	O	N	S	DB	I
al	O=(H)	ethanal	–	–	1	–	–	1	–
amide	ONH$_2$	methanamide	–	–	1	1	–	1	–
amido	C=O(NH$_2$)	methanamidopropane	–	1	1	1	–	1	–
amine	NH$_3$	methylamine	–	–	–	1	–	–	–
amino	NH$_2$	aminobutanol	–	–	–	1	–	–	–
*an	–	propanol	–	–	–	–	–	–	–
*ane	–	propane	–	–	–	–	–	–	–
bis	2X	bis(aminopropyl) amine	2	–	–	–	–	–	–
but	C$_4$	butane	–	4	–	–	–	–	–
di	2X	diaminopropane	2	–	–	–	–	–	–
*en	=	butenol	–	–	–	–	–	1	–
*ene	=	butene	–	–	–	–	–	1	–
eth	C$_2$	ethane	–	2	–	–	–	–	–
hept	C$_7$	heptane	–	7	–	–	–	–	–
hepta	7X	heptaiodohexane	7	–	–	–	–	–	–
hex	C$_6$	hexene	–	6	–	–	–	–	–
hexa	6X	hexaiodoheptane	6	–	–	–	–	–	–
hydroxy	OH	hydroxyethanoic acid	–	–	1	–	–	–	–
*idene	=	butylidenehydroxyamine	–	–	–	–	–	1	–
imino	=NH	iminobutanol	–	–	–	1	–	1	–

*bonding morpheme

TABLE VI (cont.)

Morpheme	Meaning	Example	p	C	O	N	S	DB	I
					Calculation Value				
iodo	I–	iodoethanol	–	–	–	–	–	–	1
iodoso	IO–	iodosoethane	–	–	1	–	–	–	1
iodoxy	IO–O–	iodoxyethane	–	–	2	–	–	–	1
meth	C_1	methane	–	1	–	–	–	–	–
nitrate	$-N=O(O_2)$	methylnitrate	–	–	3	1	–	1	–
nitrile	N≡	methanenitrile	–	–	–	1	–	2	–
nitrilo	N≡	nitriloethanol	–	–	–	1	–	2	–
nitro	N=O(O)	nitrobutane	–	–	2	1	–	1	–
nitroso	N=O	nitrosobutane	–	–	1	1	–	1	–
oate	O=(O)	ethyl pentanoate	–	–	2	–	–	1	–
oct	C_8	octane	–	8	–	–	–	–	–
octa	8X	octaiodooctane	8	–	–	–	–	–	–
oic acid	O=(OH)	pentanoic acid	–	–	2	–	–	1	–
ol	OH	pentanol	–	–	1	–	–	–	–
one	O=	pentanone	–	–	1	–	–	1	–
oxo	O=	oxopentanoic acid	–	–	1	–	–	1	–
oxy	–O–	methoxypropane	–	–	1	–	–	–	–
oyl	O=	pantanoyl iodide	–	–	1	–	–	1	–
pent	5	pentane	–	5	–	–	–	–	–
penta	5X	pentachloropentane	5	–	–	–	–	–	–
peroxide	–O–O	ethylmethyl peroxide	–	–	2	–	–	–	–
prop	C_3	propyne	–	3	–	–	–	–	–
sulfate	$-O-SO_2-O$	methyl sulfate	–	–	4	–	1	–	–
sulfino	HSO_2-	sulfinopropanoic acid	–	–	2	–	1	–	–
sulfinyl	–SO–	ethylsulfinylpropane	–	–	1	–	1	–	–
sulfo	HSO_3	sulfopropanoic acid	–	–	3	–	1	–	–
sulfonyl	$-SO_2-$	methylsulfonylbutane	–	–	2	–	1	–	–
tetra	4X	tetraiodobutane	4	–	–	–	–	–	–
tetrakis	4X	tetrakis(ethylamino)	4	–	–	–	–	–	–
thial	S=(H)	ethanethial	–	–	–	–	1	1	–
thio	–S–	methylthioethane	–	–	–	–	1	–	–
thiol	–SH	ethanethiol	–	–	–	–	1	–	–
thione	S=	propanethione	–	–	–	–	1	1	–
tri	3X	triiodopropane	3	–	–	–	–	–	–
tris	3X	tris(aminopropyl)amine	3	–	–	–	–	–	–
*yl	–	butylamine	–	–	–	–	–	–	–
*ylene	– –	ethylenediamine	–	–	–	–	–	–	–
yn	≡	butynal	–	–	–	–	–	2	–
yne	≡	butyne	–	–	–	–	–	2	–

*bonding morpheme

Generalized Expression for the Molecular Formula

The result of my investigating the requirements for such an algorithm is the following simple generalized expression for a molecular formula in terms of morphemic analysis of its chemical name,

$$(1) \qquad m.f. = \sum_{p=1}^{j} P_j M_{i_n} + H$$

where P_j is the number of occurrences of morpheme M_{i}, i is the element (e.g. carbon, oxygen, nitrogen, etc.) and n is the number of occurrences of i in M. For chemicals which contain only carbon and hydrogen (Hydrocarbons) this expression becomes

$$(2) \qquad \sum_{p=1}^{J} P_j M_{c_n} + H$$

For chemicals containing the elements carbon, oxygen, nitrogen sulfur, and halogen the expression can be expanded as follows:

$$(3) \qquad m.f. = \sum P_j M_{c_n} + \sum P_j M_{O_n} + \sum P_j M_{N_n} + \sum P_j M_{S_n} + \sum P_j M_{X_n} + H$$

This expression covers all chemicals tested in this experiment.

Each of the terms in this latter expression can be expanded, as in the case of morphemes relating to carbon as follows:

$$(4) \qquad \sum P_j M_{C_n} = P_1 M_{C_1} + P_2 M_{C_2} + P_3 M_{C_3} + \ldots P_j M_{C_\infty}$$

where M_{C_1} is the morpheme *meth*, M_{C_2} is the morpheme *eth* and all the other terms are the members of the homologous series $C_1, C_2, C_3, \ldots C_\infty$. Each of the other terms in equation (4) is the summation of all morphemes which contribute to the value of that particular atomic element.

The value for hydrogen is found from the following expression

$$(5) \qquad H = 2 \left[\sum M_C - \sum M_{DB} + 1 \right] + \sum M_N - \sum M_X$$

M_{DB} is the special class of morphemes which contribute double bonds, and cyclics as e.g. *an*, *en*, *yn*, and *cyclo*.

Soffer's Equation for Molecular Formula

This expression is derived in part from Soffer's generalized expression for the molecular formula in terms of cyclic elements of structure. (M.D. Soffer, *Science*, 127:880,1958).

$$(6) \qquad p = 1 + 1/2(2n_C + n_N - n_{H,X})$$

However, Soffer's equation does not take into account such elements as oxygen and sulfur, nor does it provide for chemicals such as quaternary ammonium compounds in a direct fashion. All such compounds are covered by the generalized expression pM_i. The case of quaternary compounds is particularly interesting, as its main morpheme constituent *ium* is classified by its DB value together with *en* and *yn*. *All of these* morphemes are 'bonding' morphemes. This is reasonable as in quaternary ammonium compounds nitrogen is in a pentavalent state and thereby contributes the equivalent of a double bond to trivalent nitrogen. For this reason, its DB value is minus one (−1).

Only One Language of Chemical Nomenclature

Aside from the utility of the algorithm for calculating molecular formulas, it is important to note that there really exists only one language of organic chemistry. It is a sub-language of English, but in spite of all the different "systems" available for naming chemicals, resulting in many synonyms for the same specific chemical, all of these systems draw on the same basic dictionary of morphemes. Two chemists may name the same chemical differently, but they will also be able to reconstruct the structural diagram of the chemical, and from it the molecular formula, with little or no difficulty. Upon cursory examination the chemical *2-(nicotinoyl)morpholine* might not appear to be the same as *3-pyridyl 2-morpholinyl ketone*, but drawing the structure of each, and calculating the formula would snow that they are synonyms. Since there is in fact only one language involved, not several, the algorithm works regardless of the system used. It works equally well for Chemical Abstracts nomenclature as for I.U.P.A.C. nomenclature.

To illustrate the use of the algorithm a series of examples of increasing complexity are discussed. The first will illustrate the dictionary look-up routine, the second and third the use of multipliers and parenthesized expressions, the fourth a chemical requiring the use of an ambiguity-resolving routine. It is particularly interesting to observe that much of the complexity of computer programs for this type of analysis is due to the intricate steps required by the machine to recognize and deal with ambiguity. The human translator combines the ambiguity-resolving routine with the dictionary look-up routine quite easily.

First Example

As a first example consider the simple chemical name *methylaminoethane* in which there are no parenthesized terms, no positional designations (locants) or multiplier morphemes (coefficients).

Methylaminoethane is analyzed morphemically by the human translator as follows –– *meth, yl, amin, o, eth, an, e.* Each morpheme is assigned the following meaning by reference to the dictionary. Since these are the most frequently occurring morphemes in the language they are memorized in the first few minutes.

$$meth = C$$
$$yl = +$$
$$amin = N$$
$$o = +$$
$$eth = 2C$$
$$e = +$$

By the process of simple addition one obtains the partially complete molecular formula as $3C + N$. When written in the conventional chemical subscript notation this becomes C_3N. It now remains to calculate the hydrogen.

$$H = 2 + 2(3) + 1 - 0 - 2(0) = 9$$ The complete formula is C_3H_9N

Second Example

As a second example let us consider the chemical
(3-(diethylamino)propyl)ethyl-3-amino-1,4-butanedioic acid
By a similar morphemic analysis this becomes

$$(O-[2(2C) + N] + 3C) + 2C + O + N + O + 4C + O + 2(2\phi + DB)$$
$$(7C + N) + 6C + N + 4\phi + 2DB = 13C + 2N + 2DB = C_{13}N_2O_2 + 2DB \qquad \phi = \text{oxygen}$$

and where $H = 2 + 2(13) + 2 - 0 - 2(2) = 26$ Final m.f. $= C_{13}H_{26}N_2O_4$

Third Example

As a third example consider *bis(bis[diethylamino]propylamino)butane.*

$$2[2(2[2C] + N) + 3C + N] + 4C + O$$
$$2[2(4C + N) + 3C + N] + 4C$$
$$2(8C + 2N + 3C + N) + 4C$$
$$16C + 4N + 6C + 2N + 4C = 26C + 6N = C_{26}N_6$$
$$H = 2 + 2(26) + 6 - 0 - 0 = 60 \text{ and the m.f.} = C_{26}H_{60}N_6$$

Fourth Example

Finally, consider the example of *hexanitrohexatriene.*

$$6(N + 2\phi + DB) + 6C + 3 DB$$
$$6N + 12\phi + 6DB + 6C + 3DB = 6C + 6N + 12\phi + 9DB = C_6N_6O_{12} + 9DB$$
$$H = 2 + 2(6) + 6 - 0 - 2(9) = 2 \text{ and m.f.} = C_6H_2N_6O_{12}$$

In this particular case the morphemic analysis is not as straightforward since there are several potentially ambiguous morpheme combinations.

Ambiguity and Principal of the Longest Match

The algorithm must account for the fact that the *hexan* in *hexanitro* is not the same as the *hexan* in a compound such as *nitrohexane* or for that matter the *hexane* buried in *hexatriene*. In the latter case the *hexa* in *hexatriene* is not the multiplier found in *hexanitro*. These ambiguities are resolved by a simple ambiguity-resolving sub-routine for the morphemes like *hex* (called *pent-oct* group in experiment). This consists of testing either one and/or two of the morphemes to the right of the ambigous *pent-oct* morpheme as to whether it is an alkyl ending (as e.g. *an, en*), a multiplier-morpheme (as e.g. *tri*) or a morpheme such as *nitro*. In order to understand how the computer procedure differentiates the *hexan* in *hexanitro*, it is necessary to explain the principal of the longest match which is used in the entire recognition procedure for assigning dictionary values to the morphemes. Since the human translator *learns*, he has no difficulty in making the differentiation.

In the experiment, it was found that the longest morpheme in the dictionary was eight letters long. For this reason, matching consists of examining the last eight letters of a chemical name first. In an expanded coverage of chemical nomenclature more letters would be matched as e. g., a morpheme such as *hentriacont*, meaning a thirty-one carbon chain. Consequently, in the example above, *hexanitrohexatriene*, the characters *xatriene* would be examined first. Since no match would be found for this combination of letters, the test would be continued with *atriene*, which again would find no match. There would be no match until *ene* was reached, at which point the last three letters of the name would be stripped and the procedure would continue with *ohexatri*. By a similar procedure, a match would be found for *tri*. Then we would match against *itrohexa* and we would find a match for *hexa*. (To simplify the procedure both *hex* and *hexa* are stored in the dictionary.) Simultaneously the *pent-oct* ambiguity-resolving routine would be called for, as each morpheme is always checked for membership in this list. The correct value of *hexa* in *itrohexa* having been determined, we would then move on to *exantro*, where we would encounter a match for *nitro*, leaving as the final residue, *hexa* which, of course, would go through the same ambiguity-resolving routine as the previous occurrence of this morpheme.

For the human translator, this procedure is by no means as complex, as one can readily perceive that *hexa* is followed by the very common morpheme *nitro* and subsequently by *tri*.

While the reader can apply the algorithm with no difficulty without a computer, the computer program may not be self-evident without reference to a specific example. For this reason, another example has been chosen which will test all of the steps in the program, including the general recognition program, dictionary look-up routine, *pent-oct* ambiguity- resolving routine, and formula calculation routine. In order to test all boxes in the calculation routine it is necessary to select a chemical with several parenthesized expressions, i.e. nested parentheses.

Fifth Example —— Human Procedure

Consider the chemical *2,3,4-tris[3-bis(dibutylamino)propylamino]pentadiene-1,4*
Off computer the algorithm for this compound results simply in $3[2(2 C_4 + N) + C_3 + N] + C_5 + 2$ DB. Carrying out the simple multiplications and additions gives a partial molecular formula of $C_{62}N_9 + DB_2$ and $H = 2 + 2(62) + 9 - 2(2) = 131$. m.f. $= C_{62}H_{131}N_9$. The structural diagram of this chemical is also shown to indicate how time-consuming it can be to go through the procedure of drawing such a diagram in order to calculate the molecular formula.

Fifth Example —— Computer Procedure

The computer procedure for analyzing the same compound is given below. Parenthetical remarks are made to help explain some of the details which would apply to all chemicals. The entire chemical name is punched on an IBM card or typed directly on a Unityper typewriter. The tape or card is then read into the main computer and immediately placed in a working storage unit. Working from right to left each character in the name is brought into the computer register one at a time and processed one at a time. The character in process at any instant is referred to as the *current character.*

Ignorability not Obvious Discovery

The first part of filtering each character consists of the test for 'ignorability', i.e. is it a character which cannot enter any look-up or other operations that will contribute to the molecular formula. It is worth noting that ignorability of positional terms, i.e. locants in chemical names was no obvious discovery and had to be carefully checked for validity.

Current Character Processing

Since the first current character in processing our *pentadiene* example is an *e*, it is not ignorable. It will therefore not be possible to discuss how ignorable characters are handled until later in this example. Since the *e* is not ignorable it is then tested for being a paren and since it is not it is placed in a special storage unit called alpha storage. Immediately we ask whether there are eight characters in the alpha storage; since there aren't, we then test whether we have a sentinel character which signifies the end-of-name. In this experiment, the ampersand symbol was used for this sentinel.

Since we have not reached the end-of-name, the next character is taken out of working storage and processed in exactly the same way. This will continue, in this case, until we do have eight characters in the alpha storage *(ntadiene)*. At this point, we will process the alpha storage, initiating the dictionary match or look-up routine.

Dictionary Match Routine

The dictionary match routine will compare the contents of the alpha storage with the dictionary and will find a match for *ene*. Since this morpheme is not on the pent-oct list the morpheme *ene* will be placed in a special calculation and morpheme storage area along with its appropriate meaning. In this case it will be DB_1. The alpha storage will now be asked whether it is empty. Since it is not, all of the characters in alpha storage that remain will be shifted to the far right leaving *ntadi*. A match will be found for the morpheme *di* and it, too, will then be stored in calculation area. Numerical *multipliers* have a special code digit which is used during the formula calculation routine to differentiate them from *adders*.

Fully Processing Alpha Storage

The alpha storage is now shifted again. This time, when a match is sought for *nta*, there will be no such morpheme. Therefore, current character processing will continue until the first right paren is encountered. This paren will then cause the computer to check if alpha store is empty. Since it is not, the paren will be placed in a paren storage and the contents of the alpha storage will be *fully* processed which means that whatever characters remain in alpha storage must be one or more complete morphemes. In this case *penta* remains in alpha storage and it will go through the dictionary match routine. Since it is on the pent-oct list, it will also go through the pent-oct ambiguity-resolving routine.

Pent-Oct Ambiguity-Resolving Routine

Since the morpheme preceding *penta* is not an alkyl ending, the procedure then determines whether it is a numerical prefix. Since *di* is a numerical prefix, it is determined whether the next morpheme is an alkyl ending. Since *ene* is such an ending, *penta* will be stored in calculation area as would *pentane*, i.e. as a C_5 rather than as a multiplier. The ambiguity has been resolved. Current character processing is now resumed.

The eight characters *pylamino* will go into alpha storage and *amino* will be matched and placed in calculation area. Processing will continue and *yl* will also be matched. Processing will continue until the next right paren is encountered, at which point *prop* will be found in alpha storage, fully processed, and the paren will also be stored in the calculation area as a full word, since the alpha store will have been found to be empty. This was also done with the previous right paren when *penta* was processed. The procedure will continue similarly with *dibutylamino*, until the next paren (a left paren) is encountered. *Bis* will then be processed as a morpheme, the hyphen will be ignorable, as will the 3 and the second left paren will be encountered and placed in the calculation area. *Tris* will then be processed and the remaining characters ignored. When the end-of-name character is encountered, the formula calculation routine will be initiated. Determining whether a character is ignorable is done by a dictionary sub-routine, in which the computer compares each current character with a complete list of ignorable characters consisting of the integers 1 to 8, hyphen, comma, prime, and colon. The presence of an ignorable character will always indicate the beginning or the ending of a portion of the name which can be processed independently of the other portions.

Computer Calculation Routine

The calculation storage area of the computer now contains the following sixteen calculation words. Each morpheme is followed by its appropriate additive or multiplicative value. Note that parens also stored as separate calculation words.

Word	Value	Word	Value	Word	Value	Word	Value
1. tris	3(9)	5. di	2(9)	9.)	---	13.)	---
2. (	---	6. but	C_4	10. prop	C_3	14. penta	C_5
3. bis	2(9)	7. yl	---	11. yl	---	15. di	2(9)
4. (	---	8. amino	N	12. amino	N	16. ene	DB

The first portion of the calculation routine disposes of parentheses and multiplying operations. The first word *tris* is a multiplier, so it is then determined whether the next word is a left paren, which it is. The computer now starts counting left and right parens. We again ask if the next word is a paren. Since it is not, but it is a multiplier, *bis*, multiplication is not yet carried out.

Since the next word is a left paren, the count of left parens will increase to two. However, since the registers for left and right parens are not yet equal, the next word is examined. Since *di* is not a paren, but is a multiplier, it, too, will be ignored. The next word is *but*. Since it is not a numerical prefix, it will be multiplied by the multiplier *tris*. The same will occur for *yl*(7), *amino*(8), *prop*(10), *yl*(11), and *amino*(12) as they are all contained within the parens covered by *tris*(1).

When the right paren following the last *amino*(12) is encountered, the left and right paren registers will be equal. This will signal computer to return to the word immediately following the first left paren — *bis*(3). A similar process will now be followed which will result in multiplying *but*(6), *yl*(7) and *amino*(8) by two. When the paren following the first *amino*(8) is encountered, the computer will be referred back to the first *di*(5). Since it is a multiplier, is not followed by a paren, *but*(6) will be multiplied by two.

Before proceeding, the computer checks whether the last word in calculation area has been reached. Since it has not, *yl*(7) will be processed and ignored as will *amino*(8), right paren(9), *prop*(10), *yl*(11), *amino*(12), right paren (13), and *penta*(14) which had been found, during the ambiguity-resolving routine, to be C_5.

Since *di*(15) is a multiplier the morpheme *ene*(16) is multiplied by two. Since it is the last calculation word, the paren and multiplication operations are completed. All parens and multiplier calculation words are now replaced by zeros. The computer then adds the contents of these registers which now looks as follows:

Word	Value	Word	Value	Word	Value	Word	Value
1. tris	000	5. di	000	9.)	000	13.)	000
2. (	000	6. but	$C_4 \times 3 \times 2 \times 2 = C_{48}$	10. prop	$C_3 \times 3 = C_9$	14. penta	C_5
3. bis	000	7. yl	000	11. yl	000	15. di	000
4. (	000	8. amino	$N \times 3 \times 2 = N_6$	12. amino	$N \times 3 = N_3$	16. ene	$DB \times 2 = DB_2$

The totals are taken and give a partial molecular formula of $C_{62} N_9 DB_2$. The hydrogen calculation is performed using the equation $2 + 2n_C + n_N - n_X - 2n_{DB}$. In this case it is 131 giving a final formula of $C_{62} H_{131} N_9$.

The computer will now test for experimental purposes whether the calculated formula agrees with the formula calculated manually and stored with the original data.

Hydrogen Calculation

The calculation of hydrogen is by no means a simple straightforward or obvious task. There are two ways of solving the problem. There is the method described in this dissertation which derives form Soffer's formula and there is the standard procedure used by chemists. To give the reader an idea of the difficulties of using the conventional method, he is referred to the complex chemical diagram shown on page 36, where the fifth example is discussed. It is obvious that the brute force method of counting 131 hydrogen atoms is likely to generate errors. To duplicate the brute force method of calculating hydrogen by an algorithm is not only difficult but also uneconomic in terms of computer time.

The assignment of computational values (semantic mapping) to a relatively small list of morphemes which also accounts for hydrogen, would at first glance, appear to be a rather trivial task. However, here one must depart from morphology and take into consideration the rules of chemical bond formation. For example, the term *methyl* consists of two morphemes *methyl* and *yl*. This is one of the most commonly occurring terms in organic chemistry and has a calculational value of CH_3. It is invariably CH_3. On the other hand, *propane* is $CH_3CH_2CH_3$. However, *methylpropane* is not merely the summation of the values for methyl and propane. In adding the *methyl* group, one must replace one of the hydrogen atoms on the *propane* nucleus giving a structure $CH_3CH(CH_3)CH_3$ more commonly called isobutane. If in compiling a dictionary of morphemes, we assign the values usually associated with the morpheme, then we must incorporate very sophisticated rules based on a knowledge of chemical formation. The problem increases in complexity when dealing with names containing morphemes such as *oate*, where a chemical reaction is implied as between an acid and an alcohol to form an ester. For example, the simple chemical *ethyl ethanoate (ethyl acetate)* is not the addition of $C_2H_5 + C_2H_6 + O_2$. The formula for this chemical is $C_4H_8O_2$ since an ester is formed from the combination of an alcohol and an acid with the elimination of a molecule of water.

The linguist is prompted to ask whether one has the right to include hydrogen value in the semantic mapping of morphemes such as *meth*. The morpheme *meth* will always contribute one carbon atom to the molecular formula, but it does not always contribute three atoms of hydrogen. It is not at all obvious, even to the chemist, how one resolves the problem of hydrogen calculation. It is well known that the number of hydrogen atoms in a saturated hydrocarbon is derived from the relation $2N_C + 2$ where N_C is the number of carbon atoms. However, the average chemist has no systematic method of quickly solving for hydrogen.

Soffer (opus cited) provides a more sophisticated statement of the relationship between the number of cyclic configurations in a chemical and its molecular formula. I had previously used Soffer's formula in checking the accuracy of several thousand formulas. However, it did not occur to me immediately that it could be modified and used as a means for obtaining the hydrogen value directly. It was observed that each of the terms in Soffer's equation could be replaced by a term representing a morpheme, i.e. a group of allomorphs, particularly the "bonding" morphemes contributing to 'cyclic' configuration. Then it was possible to simplify the syntactic rules for each morpheme.

The value of this approach is more apparent if one considers an example in which hydrogen is determined by the previous method of first identifying the 'parent' structure in a chemical name. The parent morpheme is frequently an alkane ending such as *ane*. The chemical *4-hydroxy-3-heptanone* is derived from *heptane*. You calculate its molecular formula by starting with C_7H_{16}, the molecular formula of heptane. The morpheme *one* adds an oxygen atom and subtracts two hydrogen atoms.

For *hydroxy* you add another atom of oxygen. *Hydroxy* contains one additional hydrogen atom, but this is balanced by the loss of one H atom in adding the *hydroxyl* substituent. This procedure works quite well for chemicals with straightforward substitution of one functional group for hydrogen. However, it breaks down in more complex cases. By confining one's dictionary to morphemes in which hydrogen is excluded and calculated after all other calculations are performed, a more straightforward procedure is possible.

Thus, the assignment of 'meaning' is conditioned by the syntactic methods that are employed for analyzing the chemical name and for generating the correct molecular formula. However, once the new approach is chosen, one must analyze each morpheme a little more closely. It is not sufficient to know that nitro is NO_2. It is necessary to learn that it is one nitrogen atom attached to two oxygen atoms, in which, one of the attachments is by a double bond. The presence of this double bond affects the total hydrogen content of the molecule. It therefore must be recorded in the dictionary along with the remaining semantic information.

Having recorded the semantic value of each morpheme, it is further necessary to provide rules for distinguishing between the homonyms which occur in systematic nomenclature. Thus, there is a class of numerical prefixes which unfortunately are ambiguous with morphemes for alkanes. For example, *pent* may be additive, as in a chain of five carbon atoms, such as pentatriene or it may be a multiplier as in pentachlorohexane. This situation is not unlike the problem of syntactic analysis of English text, in which, one finds two words in a sentence which are part of the same verb, but are separated by an intervening word, e.g. a split infinitive.

TABLE VII. GENERAL PROGRAM FOR CHEMICAL NAME RECOGNITION

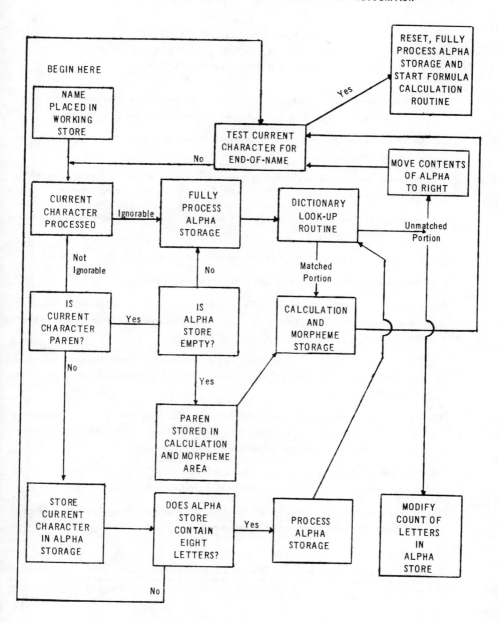

491

TABLE VII
CHEMICAL NOMENCLATURE ANALYSIS
COMPUTER CALCULATION OF MOLECULAR FORMULAS
GENERAL PROGRAM DESCRIPTION

1. Chemical name is typed on Unityper. Only chemical names of sixty characters or less are allowed, to simplify programming. Sixty characters are stored in five Univac words.

2. Chemical name is placed in working storage. (Left-to-right in the name is equivalent to top-to-bottom in storage.)

3. Processing of name starts with bottom character in working storage, i.e. character on the far right of chemical name.

4. Determine whether the current character is ignorable, i.e., a dash (hyphen), number, prime, comma, or delta (space).

5. If it is, then ignore it and fully process* contents of alpha storage.

6. If it is not ignorable character, determine if current character is paren.

7. If current character is a paren, store it in calculation area of storage, unless alpha storage already contains something, in which case, store the paren in paren storage and fully process* alpha storage.

8. If it is not a paren and also not ignorable, then store it in alpha storage. Continue processing until eight characters are stored in alpha storage. This is determined by counting characters as they go into alpha storage.

9. Find a "match" for the contents of the alpha storage, i.e. from the morpheme dictionary, look up value of morpheme in alpha storage. This might be the entire eight letters or just two letters, but no less than two letters, otherwise there is error signal.

10. When the match is found, enter the calculation value of the morpheme in the next available storage location of the calculation storage and the morpheme itself in the morpheme area.

11. Move any remaining unmatched portion to the far right in alpha storage. At the same time this will change the count of the number of letters in alpha storage.

---

*Fully process alpha storage means that whatever alphabetic characters are in alpha storage will be examined so as to identify the morpheme(s) involved. After finding a match for the right end of alpha storage the remainder will be shifted and similarly processed. However, "fully" process cannot be used if alpha storage processing was started as a result of 8 count.

2. Keep on examining more characters in name until there are again eight characters in alpha storage.

3. Continue the process until all characters have been placed in storage. When end-of-name signal (&) is encountered, computer will know that processing of all characters has been completed.

TABLE VIII.   CHEMICAL NOMENCLATURE ANALYSIS

DICTIONARY LOOK-UP ROUTINE

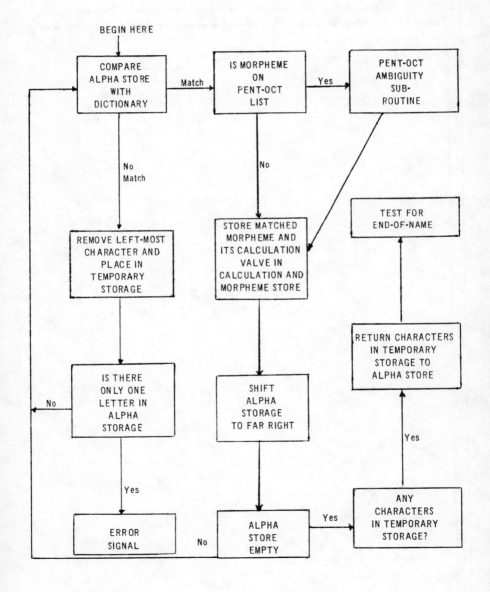

TABLE VIII
CHEMICAL NOMENCLATURE ANALYSIS
DICTIONARY LOOK-UP ROUTINE

1. The longest morpheme match is looked for first. The characters in alpha storage are compared to all morphemes in dictionary.

2. If no match is found, left-most character is dropped and matching process begins again. In this way *thial* is matched before al.

3. Before matched morpheme is stored in calculation area, it is checked for being in pent-oct group of homonyms.

4. If the morpheme is found to be in pent-oct group, then a special ambiguity-resolving routine is initiated.

5. If morpheme is not pent-oct, it is placed in calculation and morpheme storage.

6. If alpha store is not empty, it is shifted to far right and process begins over.

TABLE IX. PENT-OCT AMBIGUITY RESOLVING ROUTINE

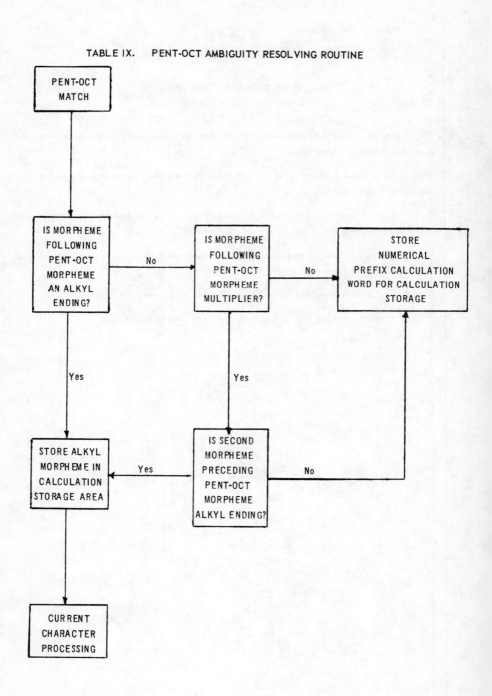

TABLE X. MOLECULAR FORMULA CALCULATION ROUTINE

```
┌─────────────────┐          ┌──────────────────┐         ┌─────────────────┐
│      LAST       │   No     │  REPLACE ALL     │   Yes   │    ADD ALL      │
│  CALCULATION    │◄─────────│  PARENS          │◄────────│   WORDS IN      │
│     WORD?       │          │  & MULTIPLIERS   │         │  CALCULATION    │
└─────────────────┘          │   BY ZERO        │         │     AREA        │
                             └──────────────────┘         └─────────────────┘
```

IS CURRENT CALCULATION WORD A MULTIPLIER?

EXAMINE NEXT CALCULATION WORD

No

Yes

IS NEXT WORD LEFT PAREN?

MULTIPLY NEXT WORD BY MULTIPLIER

No

Yes

PERFORM HYDROGEN CALCULATION

REPLACE DB COUNT BY HYDROGEN

OUTPUT ROUTINE

START COUNTING LEFT AND RIGHT PARENS

DO NOT MULTIPLY

Yes

IS NEXT WORD IN CALCULATION AREA PAREN?

NEXT WORD NUMERICAL PREFIX?

MULTIPLY NEXT WORD BY NUMERICAL PREFIX

No

No

Yes

ADD 1 TO LEFT OR RIGHT PAREN TOTAL

LEFT PARENS EQUAL RIGHT PAREN?

GO TO WORD IMMEDIATELY FOLLOWING FIRST LEFT PAREN

No

Yes

497

TABLE X
MOLECULAR FORMULA CALCULATION ROUTINE

1. Find a word which is a multiplier.

2. If the next word in calculation area is not a left paren, multiply it by the multiplier and continue looking for other multipliers.

3. If the next word is a left paren, starting keeping totals of left and right parens counting this as first left paren.

4. Examine each successive calculation word.

5. If it is not a paren, multiply it by the multiplier, unless it is a numerical prefix.

6. If it is a paren, add one to the left and right paren totals.

7. End process as soon as the left and right paren totals are equal.

8. Now go back to the word immediately following the first left paren and continue looking for multipliers. So process all multipliers in the calculation area.

9. Replace every paren word and every multiplier word in the calculation area by zero. Now add all words in the calculation area.

10. This gives preliminary total formula count. Now calculate II.

11. Replace DB value in preliminary total formula with the calculated II value.

The calculational value of each morpheme is stored as a twelve character number in which each successive pair of numbers represents iodine, double bonds, oxygen, nitrogen, sulfur and carbon. When the final calculation is made, the double bond position is replaced by the hydrogen count. Hence, nitro is stored as +0/01/02/01/00/00, iodo +1/00/00/00/00/00/ and methyl + 0/00/00/00/01. Since the Univac requires one character for sign, no formula containing more than nine iodine atoms can be tested in this equipment.

The manual translation procedure was tested on dozens of chemicals. Some of these were deliberately selected as presenting difficulties. Others were randomly selected. For example, the deliberately chosen names included several that contained pent-oct ambiguous morphemes as e.g. *hexanitrohexadiene*. Others involved complex nesting of parens. The fifth example shown previously is typical of these.

Certain chemicals found in C.A. indexes did not calculate correctly for hydrogen. The morpheme *imino* was found to be used by C.A. quite inconsistently. A basic principle of good nomenclature is that structure and name should correspond. Names should not be based on the origins of compounds. A C.A. example is *1,1'-(ethylenediimino)di-2-propanol* which by I.U.P.A.C. nomenclature is *1,2-bis(2-hydroxy-propylamino)ethane*. C.A. violates the principle that each morpheme should consistently represent the same substituent. This name was omitted from the test as it would give wrong hydrogen count. In any computer program that would attempt to cover all systems, including C.A.'s, *imino* would require a special ambiguity-resolving routine.

When I was satisfied that I had deliberately tested all the morphemes in the dictionary a random sample of chemicals was obtained. This was done by asking a clerk to check the first chemical at the top of each column in the 1958 Subject Index to *Chemical Abstracts*. He was told to keep scanning until a name was located which could be obtained from the morphemes on the test list. This required the elimination of hundreds of chemicals which contain cyclic morphemes rather than acyclic. The following illustrate some of the samples located.

CA Page No.	Molecular Formula	Chemical Name
37	C_5H_9NO	2-hydroxy-2-methyl-butyronitrile
38	$C_5H_{10}N_2S$	2-amino-4-(methyl-thio)butyronitrile
39	$C_5H_{10}O_2$	4-methoxy-2-buten-1-ol
40	$C_5H_{11}NO_3$	methylnitro-2-butanol
52	$C_6H_9N_3$	3,3'-iminodipropionitrile
56	$C_6H_{11}NO_3$	6-amino-4-oxo-hexanoic acid
57	$C_6H_{12}N_2O_4$	2,3-dimethyl-2,3-dinitrobutane
58	$C_6H_{12}O_2S$	3-(propylthio)-propanoic acid
59	$C_6H_{13}NO$	4-dimethylamino-2-butanone
71	C_7H_9NO	3,4-dimethyl-2-oxopentenenitrile
73	$C_7H_{10}O_2$	3-ethylidene-2,4-pentanedione
80	$C_7H_{15}NO$	1-dimethylamino-2-methyl-3-buten-2-ol
80	$C_7H_{15}NO_3$	[bis(2-hydroxyethyl)amino]-2-propanone

I have intentionally listed the compounds for pages 37, 38 and 52 even though they do not come under the purview of this experiment. In spite of my instructions, it was apparently difficult for the person taking the sample to note that the *yro* and *ion* were not on the list of morphemes.

One other interesting example that had to be eliminated from the computer testing, but not the human testing, was the following: *N—[(2-[1,1-dimethyl-2-propynyloxy]ethoxy)methyl]diethylamine*. The use of the *N* as a locant was not anticipated in preparing the computer program. It would have to be added to the list of ignorable characters.

An additional random sample was taken from the *Merck Index*. This was done by taking a continuous series of chemicals in the cross-reference index. This gave quite a scattering of page numbers as is shown below:

Page	M.F.	Chemical Name
178	$C_4H_{11}N$	1-aminobutane
53	$C_4H_9NO_2$	4-aminobutanoic acid
738	$C_9H_{22}N_2$	2-amino-5-diethylaminopentane
1013	$C_2H_7NO_3S$	2-aminoethanesulfonic acid
315	C_2H_7NS	2-aminoethanethiol
4	$C_2H_6N_2$	α-amino-α-iminoethane
666	$C_5H_{11}NO_2S$	2-amino-4-methylthiobutanoic acid

Selections were still made that could not be handled by the experimental dictionary as e.g. sul*fonic* acid. Further, the use of *alpha(α)* as a locant was not anticipated for the computer program, though it could be easily added to the list of ignorable characters.

As a further test of the algorithm several chemists were asked to coin names that might be difficult to handle.

A few of these were 3,7-dimethyl-2,6-octadienal, 3,3´-dithiobis(2-aminopropanoic acid) and 1,4-bis(methanesulfonoxy)butane. The latter is not covered by the experimental dictionary.

Debugging

As a further test of the procedure, fifty of the randomly selected compounds were tested on the Univac I. The so-called debugging procedure uncovered dozens of coding mistakes in the computer program which had to be traced meticulously. Apparently the first twelve deliberately chosen compounds were well selected, as the computer went into loops on each one until the bugs were eliminated.

A More Significant Test

It is obviously important that the absolute validity of the algorithm be proven by more extensive sampling. However, the chemist knows intuitively, once he has used it, that it will work. When it fails, he will find ambiguities in the nomenclature as in the case of *imino*.

Of further importance was an informal test to verify the claim that chemists first draw a diagram in order to calculate molecular formulas. For this reason, I showed about a dozen chemists example *five* and asked each to calculate the formula. Invariably he would draw a diagram. All were surprised that the calculation could be reduced to such a brief algorithm. This confirms my belief that the algorithm can be an extremely useful teaching device. It certainly can be helpful to the indexer. Most graduate organic chemists already have memorized a large enough number of morphemes to calculate quite quickly without learning anything but the DB rules. This includes the more complex cyclic structures. Every steroid chemist knows that the steroid nucleus is C_{17} so it is quite simple for him to calculate steroid formulas no matter how complicated the name may be.
*See page 36.

The Bonding Morphemes

One particularly interesting product of this research has been the more precise definition of a class of so-called *endings* or suffixes.for which, surprisingly enough, the chemist has no generic term. During the entire course of this investigation, difficulties were encountered in keeping programmers aware of the difference between an *alkyl* group and an *alkyl* or *alkane* ending. Neither of the latter two are accurate. Open chain hydrocarbons have the generic name *alkanes*. *Alkyl* is the generic term for hydrocarbon *radicals*. To use these terms to describe *alk-yl* suffixes is quite inaccurate. Furthermore, this does not associate all of the suffixes that can now be properly grouped in what I shall call the *bonding morphemes*. The members of this morpheme class are morphemes such as *ane*, *ene*, *yne*, *idene*, and *ium* since they contribute to the DB value of the chemical. In the pert-oct ambiguity-resolving routine, it would be more accurate to describe the operation in terms of bonding morphemes as the *alkyl* morphemes are really this group of bonding morphemes. It is interesting that to learn the algorithm completely from memory, the chemist need only learn the correct DB values for all morphemes, some of which may not be obvious. The chemist does not usually think of a triple bond as being two double bonds. Thus the DB value for *nitrilo*, *cyano*, *diazo*, and *yne* are the same i.e., DB_2.

Conclusions

I believe there are a number of important conclusions that can be drawn from this work. There can be no doubt that one can calculate molecular formulas from chemical nomenclature. The grammatical work that remains to be completed is still quite large, but it does not appear to be so large that a group of chemists and linguists would have any difficulty completing it within a reasonable length of time. Further, if a computer is at their disposal, there are many shortcuts that could be taken in the analyses. If the grammatical work is expanded to include the type of syntactic analysis in which each morpheme is described as a part-of-speech, i.e. classified according to its membership in various grammatical categories, then it is quite possible to foresee a machine procedure which could generate standardized names. The same would be true of displaying structural diagrams. In fact, the latter problem is less sophisticated, in that there are a relatively small number of topological arrangements required in chemistry. The programming difficulties would arise in making the appropriate additions to the diagrams for substituent atoms. In the case of *nicotinoyl morpholine*, there is only one topological configuration, the hexagon, but the replacement of carbon by nitrogen and/or oxygen in the pyridine and morpholine rings requires considerable programming ingenuity. This work would be aided by the grammatical analyses.

It would also be safe to conclude that by similar procedures, one could analyze the chemical terminology of other languages and by establishing the transformations of that language, arrive at a method for translating chemical terminology quite easily. For certain languages, such as Russian, the work involved should not be very great as one can already, simply by transliteration of Russian nomenclature, understand most of the chemical names.

The linguistic approach to chemistry, i. e. chemico-linguistics holds great promise for chemist and linguist alike. For the chemist, it can mean greater precision in teaching and understanding nomenclature and even chemical classification per se. It is not improbable that a suitably written grammar of organic chemistry could help postulate new and interesting chemical structures. On the other hand, I believe that the field of chemistry offers the linguist a useful model for the study of normal discourse. If the problems of chemical nomenclature cannot be resolved by linguistic analysis, then I suspect that normal discourse will be much too formidable an obstacle. Certainly if we are to find methods of analyzing chemical texts for indexing and other purposes, we cannot expect better than a 50% resolution of the indexing problem in chemistry. More than 50% of the effort that goes into indexing chemistry is in the analysis of chemical names. A large part of the work that is done in reading chemical documents involves the recognition of dozens of chemical names, both new and old. We will have reaped a very poor harvest if we are able to describe the text of a chemical article grammatically without a corresponding ability to deal with the problem of synonymy.

TABLE XI

RANDOM SAMPLE OF CHEMICALS TESTED ON COMPUTER PROGRAM

butane = C_4H_{10}

2-aminoethanol = C_2H_7NO

1,4-bis(ethylamino)butane = $C_8H_{20}N_2$

1,3,5-heptatriene = C_7H_{10}

1,2,3,4,5,6,7-heptaiodooctane = $C_8H_{11}I_7$

2-[(3-aminopropyl)ethylamino]ethanol = $C_7H_{18}N_2O$

1,4-bis[bis(3-diethylaminopropyl)amino]butane = $C_{32}H_{72}N_6$

1-methylsulfonylbutane = $C_5H_{12}O_2S$

2-methylpropanedioic acid = $C_4H_6O_4$

1-propanethiol = C_3H_8S

3-pentanethione = $C_5H_{10}S$

1,6-dinitrohexane = $C_6H_{12}N_2O_4$

2,5-diaminohexanedioic acid = $C_6H_{12}N_2O_4$

4-oxo-heptanedioic acid = $C_7H_{10}O_5$

1-dimethylamino-2-methyl-3-buten-2-ol = $C_7H_{15}NO$

1-ethylamino-2-methyl-3-buten-2-ol = $C_7H_{15}NO$

2-(hydroxymethyl)-2-propyl-1,3-propanediol = $C_7H_{16}O_3$

3-ethyl-2-amino-3-pentanol = $C_7H_{17}NO$

8-hydroxy-6-octene-2,4-diynenitrile = C_8H_5NO

2-propenyl-2-pentenoic acid = $C_8H_{12}O_2$

2-ethylidene-3-methyl-1,5-pentanediol = $C_8H_{16}O_2$

2-nitro-2-pentyl-1,3-propanediol = $C_8H_{17}NO_4$

3-diethylamino-2-methyl-1-propanol = $C_8H_{19}NO$

5,5'-oxybis(2-methyl-2-pentanol) = $C_{12}H_{26}O_3$

1,1-diiodo-2-nitro-1-pentene = $C_5H_7I_2NO_2$

pentyl nitrate = $C_5H_{11}NO_3$

2,5-diiodo-hexanedinitrile = $C_6H_6I_2N_2$

1-aminobutane = $C_4H_{11}N$

4-aminobutanoic acid = $C_4H_9NO_2$

2-amino-1-butanol = $C_4H_{11}NO$

2-amino-5-diethylaminopentane = $C_9H_{22}N_2$

2-aminoethanethiol = C_2H_7NS

2-amino-5-hydroxypentanoic acid = $C_5H_{11}NO_3$

1-amino-1-iminoethane = $C_2H_6N_2$

2-amino-4-methylthiobutanoic acid = $C_5H_{11}NO_2S$

3-methyl-1-pentyn-3-ol = $C_6H_{10}O$

1,3-butadiene = C_4H_6

bis(hydroxyethyl)amine = $C_4H_{11}NO_2$

2,2-bis(hydroxymethyl)-1,3-propanediol = $C_5H_{12}O_4$

TABLE XI (cont.)

2-ethoxyethanol = $C_4H_{10}O_2$
dimethylenimine = C_2H_3N
3,7-dimethyl-2,6-octadienal = $C_{10}H_{16}O$
3,3′-dithiobis-(2-aminopropanoic acid) = $C_6H_{12}N_2O_4S_2$
1-iodo-3-iodomethyl-5-methylheptane = $C_9H_{18}I_2$
1,4-diiodo-2-(methylbutyl)-butane = $C_9H_{18}I_2$
methylsulfonylethane = $C_3H_8O_2S$
(2-hydroxyethyl)-4-hydroxymethyl-3-propyl-1,6-hexanediol = $C_{12}H_{26}O_4$
methylthiopropane = $C_4H_{10}S$
1-(propylsulfinyl)butane = $C_7H_{16}OS$
ethylsulfinylethane = $C_4H_{10}OS$
ethanamide = C_2H_5NO
butanediamide = $C_4H_8N_2O_2$
methylthiopropane = $C_4H_{10}S$
nitrosobutane = C_4H_9NO
ethylmethyl peroxide = $C_3H_8O_2$
iodosoethane = C_2H_5IO
iodoxypropane = $C_3H_7IO_2$
sulfopropanoic acid = $C_3H_6O_5S$
ethanethial = C_2H_4S
trichloromethane = $CHCl_3$
tetranitromethane = CN_4O_8
1-nitro-1,1,2,2,2-pentachloroethane = $C_2Cl_5NO_2$
hexachloroethane = C_2Cl_6
1,1,2-trichloroethane = $C_2H_3Cl_3$
octachloropropane = C_3Cl_8
propylnitrate = $C_3H_7NO_3$
1,1,1,3,3-pentachloro-2,3-dinitro-2-trichloro-methylpropane = $C_4Cl_8N_2O_4$
4-chloro-3-butyn-1-ol = C_4H_5ClO
2-methyl-1,2-dinitropropane = $C_4H_8N_2O_4$
1,4-diamino-2-butanone = $C_4H_{10}N_2O$
1,3,3,4,4-pentachloro-2-methylcyclobutene = $C_5H_3Cl_5$
penten-4-ynol = C_5H_6O
4,5,5-trichloro-4-pentenylamine = $C_5H_8Cl_3N$
dimethylcyclopropane = C_5H_{10}
chloropentanol = $C_5H_{11}ClO$
pentachlorobenzene = C_6HCl_5
2-aminochloronitrophenol = $C_6H_5ClN_2O_3$
benzenediol = $C_6H_6O_2$
2,6-dichlorocyclohexanone = $C_6H_8Cl_2O$
1,1,1-trichloromethyl-3-penten-2-ol = $C_6H_9Cl_3O$
1-cyclopentene-1-methanol = $C_6H_{10}O$
chlorocyclohexane = $C_6H_{11}Cl$
2-amino-4-butyl-6-nitrophenol = $C_{10}H_{14}N_2O_3$
(1-cyclohexen-1-yl) butanone = $C_{10}H_{16}O$
2-phenyl-2,4,6-cycloheptatrien-1-one = $C_{13}H_{10}O$
7-(2,4,5-trichlorophenoxy)heptanoic acid = $C_{13}H_{15}Cl_3O_3$
ethyl 2-cyano-5-phenyl-2,4-pentadienoate = $C_{14}H_{13}NO_2$
7-(4-dimethylaminophenyl)-2,4,6-heptatrienenitrile = $C_{15}H_{16}N_2$
1-3-bis(aminophenoxy)-2-propanol = $C_{15}H_{18}N_2O_3$
4,6-dibutyl-3-methyl-2,4-dinitro-2,5-cyclohexadien-1-one = $C_{15}H_{22}N_2O_5$
2,4-dimethyl-3-octyl-2-cyclopenten-1-one = $C_{15}H_{26}O$
2-nitro-4-phenyl-1-naphthol = $C_{16}H_{11}NO_3$
1-(nitrophenyl)-4-phenyl-2-butene-1,4-dione = $C_{16}H_{11}NO_4$
2-(naphthyl)-2-cyclohexen-1-one = $C_{16}H_{14}O$
diphenyl-3-butynol = $C_{16}H_{14}O$

APPENDIX

I.U.P.A.C. Organic Chemical Nomenclature
A Summary of Principles Including a Detailed Example of its use both in Recognition and Generation of Systematic Names

In summarizing the basic principles of I.U.P.A.C. organic nomenclature for the non-chemist. emphasis has been placed on didactive explanations that will help in the recognition of the meaning of chemical names, rather than complete rules for the generation of names. The latter would require a knowledge of chemistry at least to the extent of understanding structural diagrams. This is not even necessary for the acyclic straight chain hydrocarbons covered in this experiment. Therefore, by following the instructions for naming hydrocarbon derivatives, a non-chemist should have no difficulty creating perfectly reasonable and accurate names for simple chemicals. For the more complex molecules, I suspect he would have no more and possibly less difficulty than the chemist who comes to the subject with certain preferences based on his knowledge of chemistry.

Punctuation

Commas are used between numerals which refer to identical operations as in *1,2,3-tribromo-hexane.*

Colons are used between groups of numerals for similar but distinct operations as in *1,2:5,6-diisopropylidenesorbitol.*

Numerals should be placed immediately in front of the syllables to which they refer as e.g. *2-bromohexane* rather than *bromo-2-hexane; hexan-2-ol* rather than *hexanol-2.* However, in the U.S. 2-hexanol would be rather commonly encountered. The numeral designates the number of the carbon atom in the longest chain of carbon atoms contained in the chemical. The variations in the use of numerals are legion and present a major obstacle to comprehension, especially in French and German literature. In some systems Greek letters are used instead of numerals. Amino acids are popularly numbered this way as in *β-hydroxyalanine,* which is also *2-amino-3-hydroxypropanoic acid* also known as *serine.*

Order of Substituents

Prefixes are arranged in *alphabetical order*. The atoms and groups are alphabetized first and the multiplying prefixes are then inserted as in: *2-bromo-1-chloro-hexane; 4-ethyl-3-methyl-hexane;* and *1,1,1-trifluoro-3,3-dimethylpentane.*

Elision

The terminal *e* is elided before a vowel of an organic suffix, but not in cases where the following letter is a consonant. *Propane* becomes *propanone; hexan-2-one* becomes *hexane-2,3-dione.*

Hyphens

These are used between two identical letters to avoid ambiguity as in tetra-amino. The Chemical Society uses hyphens also when partial names end in a voiced vowel or *y* as e.g. in *amino-*derivative, *thia-*compound, *methoxy-*group, but not after a consonant in such places as methyl derivative, amide group. In English, chemical words do not end in vowels.

Parentheses

Parens are used when necessary to clarify the limits of operations but not unnecessarily. If a string of morphemes is contained in parens which is preceded by a numeral, this means that the entire parenthesized expression is a substituent of a parent structure. For example, *1-(4-amino-2-ethylphenyl)-butanol* means that the entire expression *4-amino-2-ethylphenyl* is attached to the first atom in a four carbon *(but)* chain. The word *mono* is understood but rarely used. However, if the chemical were *1,2 bis-(4-amino-2-ethylphenyl) butanol* the entire parenthesized expression would be multiplied by two, i.e. it occurs at both the first and second carbon atoms in the chain C–C–C–C.

Terminology

Parent is a very ambiguous term in chemical nomenclature, especially when one considers the rules for deciding which morpheme in a name shall be considered the parent morpheme. However, no matter what name is chosen the *parent* morpheme refers to that group of atoms to which all other groups of atoms in the molecule are attached. Thus *benzene* is the parent in *nitrobenzene* and *ethane* is the parent in *ethanol*. This term no longer has any chemical significance which, at one time, was true when chemicals were named on the basis of the shortest chain length.

Group or radical. Any group of atoms commonly occurring together is called a group or radical. Most of these are single morphemes but some are pairs of morphemes. CH_3 is a *methyl* group consisting of the morphemes *meth* and *yl.* However, OH is the hydroxy group.

Function or Functional Group

A *functional group* is a group of atoms which defines the mode of activity of a chemical. The hydroxy group gives alcoholic properties to an alcohol. A ketone owes its properties to the oxygen atom which is doubly bonded to carbon. The distinction between what is functional and what is not is frequently difficult to make, but is an important artefact in naming chemicals regardless of how they act.

Types of Names

There are several types of names encountered in systematic nomenclature aside from the previously discussed *trivial* and semi-systematic names. There are names which involve *substitution,* where one hydrogen atom is replaced by a group or another element, as in *pentanol,* where one hydrogen atom is replaced by the hydroxy radical or group. There are *replacement* names, where one atom such as sulfur replaces another, such as oxygen, as for example *propanol* and *propanethiol,* which are respectively C–C–C–OH and C–C–C–SH.

A *subtractive* name involves the removal of specified atoms as e.g. in aliphatic names ending in *ene* or *yne* exemplified by *hexene* or *hexyne* where hydrogen atoms are removed by the creation of double or triple bonds between carbon atoms –– C–C–C–C–C=C.

There are other types of names such as *radicofunctional,* a name formed from a radical and functional class name such as *ethyl alcohol; additive* names such as *styrene oxide,* conjunctive names such as *naphthaleneacetic acid,* and fusion names such as *benzofuran* and other cyclics. However, in this brief survey, we will be primarily concerned with systematic names, i.e. names "composed wholly of specially coined or selected syllables, with or without numerical prefixes" [cf. I.U.P.A.C.: *Nomenclature of Organic Chemistry.* London: Butterworths, 1958(p. 4)].

What's In a Name?

When the layman sees a chemical name like *7-bis(3-diethylaminopropyl)amino-7´butylamino-4,5,8-trihydroxyoct-3,5-dienoic acid,* he probably wonders how it is possible for chemists to make sense out of it. The structural diagram for this chemical is

507

$$CH_2-CH_2-CH_2-CH_3$$

$$
\begin{array}{c}
\quad\quad OH \quad N-H \quad OH \quad OH \\
\quad\quad | \quad\quad | \quad\quad | \quad\quad | \\
HC-C-C \Rightarrow C - C=C-C-C \overset{\diagup O}{\underset{\diagdown OH}{}} \\
\quad H \quad\quad H \quad\quad\quad H \; H
\end{array}
$$

$$
\begin{array}{c}
\quad\quad H \; H \; H \quad H \; H \; H \\
(CH_3-CH_2)_2N-C-C-C-N-C-C-C-N(CH_2-CH_3)_2 \\
\quad\quad H \; H \; H \quad H \; H \; H
\end{array}
$$

However, chemical names are surprisingly simple to understand and a large number of those made can be derived from a relatively short list of morphemes, such as that which was used in my experiments (see Table VI).

Principal Functional Group

The first thing that must be done in understanding, or for that matter in creating a chemical name is to "*seek out the functional groups.*" (Cahn, opus cited p. 43.) The *senior*, i.e. *principal functional group* sets the whole pattern of nomenclature and numbering. Unfortunately this is not always as simple as it sounds, though in the example above it is quite simple. It is worth noting that among others Degering (cf. *Organic Chemistry — An Outline of the Beginning Course Including Material for Advanced Study*; 6th Ed. New York: Barnes & Noble, 1957) completely avoids a discussion of this problem of naming so-called *complex* functions, that is, chemicals with more than one functional group. He is well advised to do so because there is no rational way of explaining this principle though Chemical Abstracts and others will specify a preferred order of precedence——acid before aldehyde, aldehyde before ketone, ketone before alcohol, etc. Cahn would agree with this order. I.U.P.A.C. does not stipulate a preferred order. Since most chemicals in the U.S. and Great Britain are named by this order one can conclude, in the example shown, that the principal function is the acid function. It is assumed by now that the reader understands that each chemical name can be parsed quite simply into a series of short letter sequences, i.e. morphemes. By reference to Table XII, it will be noted that each of these morphemes has an associated meaning. The *oic acid* at the end of this name is such a morpheme as are *di* and *en* which precede it. *En* is a bonding morpheme, that is, it denotes *unsaturation* in the basic carbon chain of the molecule. Unsaturation refers to the removal of hydrogen atoms attached to carbon atoms to form double bonds. The entire structure of organic nomenclature is based on the theory of covalent bonds.

Most Unsaturated Straight Chain

In naming this chemical no difficulty would arise concerning the next principal group as there is no choice here between two sometimes perplexing alternatives of a shorter chain with greater unsaturation and a longer chain with no or less unsaturation. If there were, then the chain with the most double and triple bonds would be selected. This would be the case, e.g. if there were a side chain containing two additional double bonds. As the second priority item in naming a chemical, the saturation is indicated second from the right. In other words, the so-called principal functions come at the end of the name preceded by bonding morphemes when this is possible.

The Longest Chain

The third criterion for selecting the proper name is the principle of the longest chain. By this is meant not the longest chain of atoms, but the longest chain of consecutive carbon atoms. There is, indeed, a school of thought that prefers the principle whereby the longest chain is used, regardless of the atoms involved. A good case can be made for it in many instances. In this particular chemical, the longest chain of carbon and nitrogen atoms is fourteen. The longest carbon chain is eight atoms long and that is why the next morpheme to the left of *dien* is *octa* signifying an eight carbon chain (C–C–C–C–C–C–C–C).

Numbering

After making the decision as to which sequence of atoms in the molecule will become the *parent*, then one numbers each of the contiguous atoms giving the atom to which the functional group is attached the lowest number. In our example, the *oic acid* function is the principal function, consequently the numbering pattern will be (HO)O=C–C–C=C–C–C=C–C–C. This will explain the numerals preceding diene as the two double bonds are located between carbon atoms 3 and 4 and atoms 5 and 6.

Substituents or Prefixes

Once the selection of the parent chain has been completed, as well as adding as suffixes, the bonding morphemes and the principal functions, it only remains to name the substituents or side chains, all of which may be regarded as radicals, groups, or sub-names depending upon the complexity of the chemical. In this particular case there are three hydroxy groups at the third, fourth, and eighth atoms. They are specified by using the numerals 3,4,8 followed by the numerical prefix *tri* followed in turn by the morpheme *hydroxy*, hence *trihydroxy*. The remaining substituents in this name are themselves substituted as e.g. *butylamino* which means that there is a *nitrogen* atom attached to the seventh atom in the *octane* parent structure. Ordinarily, amino implies the replacement of one hydrogen atom by the amino group (NH_2), but in this case, one of the amino hydrogens is also replaced by a radical, the *butyl* radical, which is composed of a four carbon chain. Hence, *butylamino* is $CH_3CH_2CH_2CH_2NH–$. By a similar building up process, the last portion of this name, *(diethylaminopropyl) amino* is the following: $(C_2H_5)_2-N-CH_2-CH_2-CH_2-N-$. How - ever, since the parenthesized expression is preceded by *bis*, it simply means that the other bond on the right most nitrogen has the same chain repeated, which means we really have, for this side chain $[(C_2H_5)_2-N-CH_2-CH_2-CH_2-]_2N-$, i.e. *bis(diethylaminopropyl) amino*. The 3- preceding diethyl simply specifies that the left most amino group is attached to the third carbon atom in the *propyl* chain.

This sketch of the rules and explanation of this very complex example does not cover all of the problems. Of interest to the linguist is the choice of allomorph to be made e.g. for *OH*, the hydroxy group rather than *ol*. It is only when the principal function is an alcohol that this latter morpheme is used. Were the carboxyl group (oic acid) to be replaced by another hydroxy group, the name of this chemical would change considerably, but primarily by the elimination of the prefix *3,4,8-trihydroxy* and the addition of *tetrol* as a suffix giving us a name ending in *octa-3,5-dien-1, 4,5,8-tetrol*.

Since chemicals can be prepared with a multitude of different permutations and combinations, the reader can well imagine the difficulties one may encounter when having to make a preferred choice. It is no small wonder that chemists arrive at different names. If considerations of cyclic nomenclature are introduced, then the absurdities of nomenclatural logic increase to the point where there is mass confusion. If the principal function is attached to a ring, i.e. cyclic, then it is the cyclic system which is given priority over the acyclic chain, no matter how long, but if the principal functional group is attached to a chain and that in turn to a ring, the British would treat the cyclic radical as a substituent, while the C.A. indexer would take into consideration the complexity of the cyclic substituent and more than likely call it the principal function.

In closing this discussion, it is worth emphasizing that in spite of the variations in naming chemicals, one generally will have no difficulty in figuring out the chemical involved, because it can always be pieced together by reference to the dictionary of morphemes. If that were not the case communication between chemists would have ceased long ago. This is not to underestimate the difficulties of decipherment. In general such difficulties arise from the fact that the distraught chemist trying to use "systematic" nomenclature, invariably forgets one of the rules and in his confused state generates an ambiguous name. He does not always take the trouble to ask another chemist to try deciphering the name he has chosen. Wiser chemists rely strictly on structural diagrams. Perhaps this accounts for the success of the Japanese chemists who are used to working with ideographs. In this connection, a closing quotation from the British Chemical Society's heated disucssion of the Geneva Conference in which it is said "Prof. P.F. Frankland thought names unnecessary, and that it would be better for the purposes of a register to use formulae." (Armstrong, H.E., opus cited p. 130) seems both pertinent and ironically, prophetic.

T a b l e XII can also be used as a condensed review of I.U.P.A.C. nomenclature. It covers twenty-three primary generic groups of chemicals synthesized by the organic chemist. Each type is shown by indicating an *R* group, the conventional symbol for *radical* attached to the appropriate functional group. Following the generic name, the most commonly used morpheme is listed. For any specified value of R and/or R,' one can quickly determine the sort of chemical name to expect. In this experiment, particular attention was given to compounds where the R values would consist of the homologous series *meth, eth, prop, but, pent, hex, hept,* and *oct,* i.e. where R equals one, two, three, etc. carbon atoms.' Finally, the calculational value for each morpheme is shown. This can be used in applying the algorithm for the calculation of molecular formulas. A more complete list of the morphemes used in the experiment is shown in Table VI on pages 30–31.

TABLE XII. SUMMARY OF I.U.P.A.C. NOMENCLATURE

Structure	Generic Name	Morpheme	Value
$R-CH_3$	alkanes	ane	DB_0
$R=CH_2$	alkenes	ene	DB_1
$R\equiv CH$	alkynes	yne	DB_2
$R-OH$	alcohols	ol	O_1
$R-SH$	mercaptans	thiol	S_1
$R-$	radicals	yl	$(+)$
$R-O-R'$	ethers	oxy	O_1
$R-S-R'$	sulfides	thio	S_1
$R-SO-R'$	sulfoxides	sulfinyl	S_1+O_1
$R-SO_2-R'$	sulfones	sulfonyl	S_1+O_2
$R-CH=O$	aldehydes	al	O_1+DB_1
$R-CH=S$	thioaldehydes	thial	S_1+DB_1
$R-C(R')=O$	ketones	one	O_1+DB_1
$R-C(R')=S$	thioketones	thione	S_1+DB_1
$R-COOH$	carboxylic acids	oic acid	O_2+DB_1
RCSOH	thio acids	thioic acid	$S_1+O_1+DB_1$
RCOOR'	salts & esters	oate	O_2+DB_1
$R-COX$	acid halides	oyl halide	$O_1+DB_1+X_1$
$RCONH_2$	amides	amide	$O_1+DB_1+N_1$
$R-CN$	nitriles	nitrile	DB_2+N_1
$R-NO_2$	nitro derivatives	nitro	$O_2+DB_1+N_1$
$R-NO$	nitroso	nitroso	$O_1+DB_1+N_1$
$RONO_2$	nitrates	nitrate	$O_3+DB_1+N_1$

BIBLIOGRAPHY

Armstrong, H. E.: Contributions to an International System of Nomenclature. The Nomenclature of Cycloids. *Proc. Chem. Soc.*, 1892,127.

Bloomfield, L.: *Language.* New York: Holt & Co., 1933.

CA: Naming & Indexing of Chemical Compounds by Chemical Abstracts. Columbus: Chemical Abstracts, 1957.

Cahn, R. S.: *An Introduction to Chemical Nomenclature.* London: Butterworths, 1959.

Cahn, R. S. & Cross, L. C.: *Handbook for Chemical Society Authors.* London: The Chemical Society, 1960.

CLR: *Fourth Annual Report, Council on Library Resources.* Washington: The Council, 1961.

Crane, E.J.: *CA Today — The Production of Chemical Abstracts.* Washington: Amer. Chem. Soc., 1958.

Dyson, G.M.: *A New Notation and Enumeration System for Organic Compounds.* New York: Longmans, 1949.

Frome, J.: *Semi-Automatic Indexing and Encoding. Research and Development Report No. 17.* Washington: U. S. Patent Office, 1959.

Garfield, E.: Communication concerning the use of machines in facilitating documentation. *Chem. Eng. News*, 30:5232,1952.

Garfield, E.: *Preparation of Printed Indexes by Automatic Punched-Card Equipment — A Manual of Procedures.* Baltimore: Johns Hopkins University Medical Indexing Project, 1953.

Garfield, E.: Preliminary Report on the Mechanical Analysis of Information by use of the 101 Statistical Punched-Card Machine. *Am. Documentation*, 5:7, 1954.

Garfield, E.: Preparation of Subject Heading Lists by Automatic Punched-Card Techniques, *J. Documentation*, 10:1, 1954.

Garfield, E.: Forms for Literature Citations, *Science*, 120:1039,1954.

Garfield, E.: Preparation of Printed Indexes by Machines, *Am. Documentation*, 6:68,1955.

Garfield, E.: Citation Indexes for Science, *Science*, 122:108,1955.

Garfield, E.: Breaking the Subject Index Barrier, *J. Pat. Off. Soc.*, 39:583, 1957.

Garfield, E.: A Unified Index to Science, *Proc. Intl. Conf. on Scientific Information, Vol. 1.* Washington: National Academy of Sciences, 1959.

Garfield, E.: The Steroid Literature Coding Project, *Chem. Literature*, 12(3):6,1960.

Garfield, E.: Index Chemicus Molecular Formula Index, *Index Chemicus*, First Cumulative Index Issue:1961,33.

Harris, Z. S.: *Methods in Structural Linguistics.* Chicago: Univ. of Chicago Press, 1951.

Harris, Z.S.: Linguistic Transformations for Information Retrieval, *Proc. Intl. Conf. on Scientific Information, Vol. 2.* Washington: National Academy of Sciences, 1959.

BIBLIOGRAPHY (continued)

Harris, Z.S.: Hiz, H., Joshi, A. K., Kaufman, B., Chomsky, C., and Gleitman, L.: Transformations & Discourse Analysis. *Annual Report of the Computing Center.* Philadelphia: Univ. of Pennsylvania, 1960.

Harris, Z.S.: Hiz, H., et al. *Transformations and Discourse Analysis Projects.* Philadelphia: Univ. of Pennsylvania, Department of Linguistics, 1959–61.

Himwich, W. A., Field, H., Garfield, E., Whittock, J. and Larkey, S. V.: *Welch Medical Library Indexing Project Final Reports.* Baltimore: Johns Hopkins Univ., 1951, 1953, 1955.

I.U.P.A.C.: Definitive Rules for Nomenclature of Organic Chemistry, *J. Am. Chem. Soc.*, 82:5545,1960.

Opler, A., and Baird, N.: Display of Chemical Structural Formulas as Digital Computer Output, *Am. Documentation*, 10:59,1958.

Patterson, A.M.: Definitive Report of the Commission on the Reform of the Nomenclature of Organic Chemistry, *J. Am. Chem. Soc.*, 55:3905,1933.

Patterson, A. M.: *Words about Words.* Washington: American Chemical Society, 1957.

Patterson, A. M., Capell, L. T. and Walker, D. F.: *The Ring Index — A List of Ring Systems used in Organic Chemistry.* 2nd Edition. Washington: American Chemical Society, 1960.

Pictet, A.: Le Congres International de Geneve pour la Reforme de la Nomenclature Chimique, *Arch. Sci. Phys. Nat.*, 27:485,1892.

Rabinow, J.: *Character Recognition Machines.* Washington: Rabinow Engineering Co., 1961.

Soffer, M. D.: The Molecular Formula generalized in terms of cyclic elements of structure. *Science*, 127:880,1958.

Stock, C.C.: *A Method of Coding Chemicals for Correlation and Classification.* Washington: National Academy of Sciences, 1950.

Terentiev, A. P., Kost, A. N., Tsukerman, A. M. and Potapov, V. M.: *Nomenklatura Organicheskikh Soedmionii.* Moscow: Akademiya Nauk SSSR, 1955.

Tiemann, F.: Ueber die Beschlusse des internationalen, in Genf vom 19 bis 22. April 1892 Versammelten Congresses zur Regelung der chemischen nomenclatur, *Ber. d. Deut. Chem. Gesell*, 26:1595,1892.

Tsukerman, A. M. & Terentiev, A. P.: Chemical Nomenclature Translation. *Proc. Intl. Conf. for Standards on a Common Language for Machine Searching & Translation.* Vol. I. New York: Interscience Press, 1961.

Waldo, W.H. and de Backer, M.: Printing Chemical Structures Electronically. *Proc. Intl. Conf. on Scientific Information.* Vol. II. Washington: National Academy of Sciences, 1959.

Wiswesser, W. J.: *A Line Formula Chemical Notation.* New York: Thos. Crowell, 1954.

GENETICS
CITATION
INDEX

Experimental Citation Indexes to Genetics
with Special Emphasis on Human Genetics

Prepared by the

Institute for Scientific Information
Philadelphia 3, Pa.

Eugene Garfield, Ph.D., *Director*
Irving H. Sher, Sc.D., *Project Director*

PREFACE

Dr. Garfield's article on citation indexing which appeared in *Science* in 1955 first brought this technique to my attention and was my first introduction to the organization now known as the Institute for Scientific Information. Citation Indexing seemed a clever idea at the time and I wondered whether it would ever come to fruition.

A few years later the suggestion recurred and I was puzzled how to find out whether there had been any follow-up on Garfield's first suggestion. I had no idea how to look up the literature in the documentation field and from past experience with subject indexing in science had little confidence in the utility of a literature search.

This was the very incident that convinced me of the need for the citation index -- it was parallel to many others in my own research activity. How often I have run across some older reports on methods or on some curiosities of bacterial variations and been frustrated in attempts to find later work on the same subject and, especially, critical enlargement on the earlier work.

For many reasons genetics is an especially apt field for the introduction of citation indexing. It is inherently interdisciplinary, cutting across biochemistry, statistics, agriculture, and medicine so that geneticists need insight into a wide range of scientific literature. While there have been many revolutionary developments, many facets of genetics still rely heavily on older work. The principles of *Drosophila* research of 40 years ago are first finding their application in human cytogenetics today. Geneticists have tended to be perceptive about the historical development of their concept and to fulfill their responsibility in furnishing the appropriate citations in their bibliography. Their concern with parent-offspring relationships perhaps makes geneticists more perceptive to the understanding of the structure of scientific activity that is inherent in citational references. It was, therefore, most gratifying that the review panel of the NIH and NSF concurred in supporting this trial in the field of genetics.

Citation indexing is, of course, only one aspect of literature searching. There will be many disappointments in its use -- but a negative result within the scope of the index is perhaps more meaningful than with any other technique. Other methods generally place great reliance on subjective classification with which the final user can rarely be entirely familiar. Citation indexing can uncover unexpected correlation of scientific work that no other method could hope to find, and a successful match can often be located with great speed and assurance. The chief limitation is perhaps merely the scope of the indexing effort in the sample -- in a given year there may have been no literature on a given reference. A cumulative index to all of science would, of course, be a large undertaking but of course no larger than the problem to which it is addressed. In fact the machine basis of this approach should make it far less costly and more expeditious than any other technique now apparent. Until a complete index is available we may not know the full value of the technique, but the present sample is a noble effort which should give many investigators substantial help in their present retrieval problem and show the way to an ultimate, even more satisfactory, result.

My own contribution to the project has been too limited to inhibit me from commending Dr. Garfield and his associates for organizing and implementing a project which has required an unimaginable attention to detail, technical skill, enthusiasm, and above all, an irrepressible concern for meeting the real need of scientists. To flourish, science has many needs but none are more vital than responsible communication with history, society, and posterity embodied in what we casually call the scientific literature.

Joshua Lederberg
Stanford University

THE GENETICS CITATION INDEX EXPERIMENT

INTRODUCTION

In January 1961, with the partial support of National Institutes of Health grant RG-8050, the Institute for Scientific Information began a research investigation of citation indexing.[1] Since the Genetics Study Section of NIH was particularly interested in new approaches to the documentation of the burgeoning genetics literature, genetics became the focal point of the project. An Advisory Board of geneticists was also selected to guide the project. From the outset it was recognized that a universally acceptable definition of genetics was all but impossible especially since human and biochemical genetics are highly interdisciplinary. Defining the genetics literature was therefore quite difficult. It was decided that a comprehensive and interdisciplinary approach was needed as well as an arbitrary, acceptable definition of the genetics literature to serve as a point of departure for automatic selection.

In May 1961, as a result of contract C-201 with the National Science Foundation, which provided additional partial support, the interdisciplinary and comprehensive approach recommended by our Advisory Board became feasible. A selective approach to the literature, on the other hand, would have required fine judgments as to what is or is not genetics. The comprehensive approach permitted us to begin with an essentially clerical or automatic procedure wherein all references in all articles of each issue of the source journals were processed.

In the comprehensive 1961 Science Citation Index there is, therefore, no question as to what references are or are not covered. However, the reader will always have to distinguish between comprehensiveness of sources and of references. In a citation index, unlike conventional subject or author indexes, one must distinguish source year and reference year. These distinctions are emphasized differently in each of the experimental indexes that follow. The distinction between source and reference diminishes with the passage of time. It becomes apparent that any current source ultimately may become a reference.

The three different sections of this Genetics Citation Index are in fact three different indexes. One reason for including all three is to illustrate the problems in choosing between greater chronological or broader journal coverage in the source material.

The 1961 Genetics Citation Index is based on a single source year and covers 613 source journals. The second index is based on five source years for 38 hard-core genetics journals, while the third index covers more than 14 source years for 3 key genetics journals. The resources of the project did not permit us to control these variables in such a way as to produce three indexes of equal size or information content. Each index stresses certain features. The 14-year citation index presents an historical picture of the field that is not as easily obtained from the other indexes. Nevertheless, an examination of the 1961 Genetics Citation Index reveals that a remarkably comprehensive recapitulation of the genetics literature is provided even by a single year's citation indexing.

In these citation indexes there is no artificial separation of the "old" and "new" literature. Our studies confirm the frequent utilization by scientists of the older literature. Over 50% of the cited references in the 1961 index are more than five years old, in spite of the fact that the literature has grown more voluminous through the years. Certainly the most frequently cited papers are "classical" rather than contemporary.

While the so-called "genetics parcel" is fully explained in the introduction to the 1961 Genetics Citation Index section, let me emphasize in what respects it is selective rather than comprehensive. There is an important distinction between being comprehensively selective (as are the conventional indexes) and being selectively comprehensive. To create the experimental 1961 Science Citation Index we prepared a punched-card for each of 1.4 million cited references appearing in 102,000 source articles. In that respect it is comprehensive. However, our objective here was to produce a genetics citation index in contrast to a general science citation index. Establishment of several basic criteria was necessary. Economic considerations, primarily, determined that up to 20% of the reservoir of literature processed could be included. The genetics citation index parcel (1961 Genetics Citation Index) is therefore derived from a comprehensive, interdisciplinary reservoir of citations. The extraction of 20% *output* from the massive *input* became an exciting and challenging task. The reader will have to judge the validity of the results. To help you in this evaluation, a complete listing of the original 102,000 source articles, arranged alphabetically by first author, immediately follows the 1961 Genetics Citation Index. Though the genetics parcel was derived from the data in these source articles, not all of the sources processed will be found in the extracted parcel of the 1961 Genetics Citation Index.

The genetics parcel contains 19% of the citations in the total 1961 Science Citation Index file, yet these citations refer to only 6.7% of the reference authors in that index. It would appear that the reference authors in the genetics parcel are cited more frequently than those in the total 1961 index. This may, in part, be due to the extensive bio-medical coverage in the index and, in part, to the mechanics of the selection procedures.

The genetics parcel for 1961, therefore, is selective, but if an author is listed then all the citations to those papers in which he was first author are included -- if they were cited in 1961. The limitation to first author holds since, for purely methodological reasons, only the first author in each reference was processed. This in no way affects the value of the citation index for its original purpose -- to locate sources which cite specific reference works. However, any author who is always listed as a second co-author could not be selected in this experiment. Further, those authors who were selected might have co-authored additional papers with first authors who were not selected.

The 5-year and 14-year citation indexes, in contrast to the selective 1961 Genetics Citation Index parcel, are comprehensive. All citations in all papers were not only processed, but also included. However, the same rule concerning first author applies. If this is not kept in mind, one may draw erroneous conclusions concerning the "impact" of an author. Naturally, this attribute would also affect the retrieval value of the index if one expects to find all references to an author's works in one place. This problem could have been overcome by doubling the size of the index through repetition of references under all cited authors -- first, second, etc. For economic and editorial reasons this solution was not practical in these experiments.

Alternatively, a journal citation index arrangement, in contrast to an author citation index, would have placed more emphasis on the individual articles, where it belongs, rather than on the authors. The journal arrangement of the index was seriously considered but would have required excessive editorial effort in standardizing variant journal title abbreviations used in the literature.

However, the lack of standardized reference journal abbreviations in the literature did not essentially affect our accuracy in dealing with multiple sources citing the same reference. Thus, while various abbreviations for a reference journal may appear throughout the index, each easily recognized, the computer program did standardize most variant presentations of the reference journal and/or author for a given reference article. In fact, this so-called "unification" procedure actually corrected many errors in reference journal titles and in reference authors' names and frequently chose the longer and more meaningful variation.

The reader will generally find this experimental Genetics Citation Index quite easy to use and understand. Those of us who helped to prepare it are well aware of features which may prove annoying such as truncated source author names which may be only eight characters in length. Similarly, source journal abbreviations are limited to only eleven characters. We realize that the size of print is much smaller than the average index and that surely it would have been most desirable, though not economically feasible, to include the full titles of citing and cited articles. However, in spite of such short-comings, which can be eliminated in future citation indexes, I am confident that the Genetics Citation Index and the companion 1961 Science Citation Index will justify many times over the cost of preparation--over $400,000.

During the past few years, while these indexes were in preparation, I have had the unique advantage of having at my disposal, not only the files from which this published genetics index is derived, but also earlier experimental files. For example, over 325,000 references from the 1960 literature were processed for various methodological studies.[2] I have rarely been disappointed by a search of these files and on numerous occasions information was uncovered which would otherwise have remained buried. However, the discovery of "buried treasure" in the scientific literature is a function of the user as well as the index. As with a conventional subject index, experience in using a citation index increases one's ability to find information quickly. Unlike the use of a language-oriented index, training in medical, chemical, or other nomenclature is not required to use a citation index effectively. However, it is assumed that the average searcher knows where he wants to begin. At times the user will have to find a "starting point" elsewhere--in a book, encyclopedia, article, or classical index. The citation index can then be used to locate "what has happened since."

Generally one will find a few source papers which cite a particular paper in which one is interested. The citation index is highly specific in that sources retrieved have a direct relationship to the starting point. By various techniques a search may be readily expanded in order to obtain more extensive bibliographies. For instance, one may select relevant articles from the bibliographies of the sources disclosed by the first step of the search and use these erstwhile sources as new entry points into the citation index. This "cycling" procedure may be repeated. You will find that with "cycling" one uncovers relevant material through all the years preceding the citation index. Another technique is to take advantage of the fact that authors will frequently write more than one closely related paper. Therefore, when using the citation index, additional articles by a given author can be checked for relevancy and the sources citing these articles may be picked up. Additional articles by a given author may be found in the list of source articles even if the articles contained no bibliographies.

Starting with a given target reference paper one may find that it is not cited at all. Do not give up! Refer to the target paper and examine the citations contained in it. Locate the most directly related reference citation in the paper. Then, in the citation index, locate new sources which cite this reference. If not, try another relevant reference from the same target paper. Since the average paper has a bibliography of fifteen items it is rare that a pertinent source is not located, provided there has been some work done on the subject.

Naturally a citation index will be most helpful when used in conjunction with a good library. Since the scope of these indexes is quite broad many source articles may be encountered which are not readily available. The Institute for Scientific Information will assist in the procurement of articles in any source publication processed in this experiment.

Since two years have elapsed since the publication of the source articles in the 1961 experiment it should not be surprising if many articles located are known to you. We believe this will confirm the value of the method. Only when citation indexes are issued currently will they compete as a current information sources with *Current Contents*, *Biochemical Titles* or other tools. However, even at this late date, I am confident you will find sources of information that would have been buried or missed in conventional indexes. It is on this basis primarily that citation indexing should be evaluated. Citation indexing is not recommended as a substitute for conventional indexes. Rather, I believe the citation index adds a new dimension to the pursuit of scientific knowledge. The citation index is your road map of the literature. Where it takes you is primarily your decision. What you find depends on you. Only you can measure its relevance. What may be relevant to one man is irrelevant to another. Two otherwise unrelated scientific observations may be correlated in the citation index through a common reference or through a chain of source-reference links. However, you must select the starting point and detect the correlation if it exists.

The detailed history of this project will be covered elsewhere, both in genetics[4] and documentation journals.[5][6] However, the detailed explanatory descriptions of the various experimental indexes contained in this volume will, together with earlier papers,[2,3,7,8,9] provide those interested with a more complete story. In addition, more background information will gladly be provided to anyone who wishes to contact me directly.

Inquiries are cordially invited from journal editors or publishers who would be interested in the use of our files to conduct special studies of citation patterns to and from their journals.

Eugene Garfield, *Director*
Institute for Scientific Information
Philadelphia 3, Pa.

REFERENCES

(1) Garfield, E., "Citation Indexes for Science," *Science* 122, 108-111 (1955).

(2) Garfield, E. and I.H. Sher, "New Factors in the Evaluation of Scientific Literature Through Citation Indexing," *American Documentation* 14, 195-201 (1963).

(3) Garfield, E., "Citation Indexes in Sociological and Historical Research," *American Documentation* (in press), October 1963.

(4) Garfield, E. and I.H. Sher, "Dissemination and Retrieval of Genetics Information Through Interdisciplinary Citation Indexing," *XIth International Congress of Genetics, The Hague,* September 1963.

(5) Garfield, E., I.H. Sher, and C. Voytko, "Citation Index for Genetics: A Programme for Research and Evaluation," in S.R. Ranganathan and A. Neelameghan, *Documentation Periodicals--Coverage, Arrangement, Scatter, Seepage, Compilation,* pp. 181-185, Bangalore, 1963.

(6) Garfield, E., I.H. Sher, and C. Voytko, "Citation Index for Genetics--A Research and Evaluation Program," *Proceedings Second International Congress on Medical Librarianship,* June 1963 (to be published).

(7) Garfield, E., "Citation Indexes--New Paths to Scientific Knowledge," *Chemical Bulletin* 43(4), 11-12, (1956).

(8) Garfield, E., "Breaking the Subject Index Barrier--a Citation Index for Chemical Patents," *Journal of the Patent Office Society* 39, 583-595 (1957).

(9) Garfield, E., "A Unified Index to Science," *Proceedings of the International Conference on Science Information,* November 1958, Vol. 1, pp. 461-474, Washington, 1959.

ADDITIONAL PERTINENT REFERENCES

Adair, W.C., "Citation Indexes for Scientific Literature," *American Documentation* 6, 31-32 (1955).

Seidel, A.H., "Citation System for Patent Office," *Journal of the Patent Office Society* 31, 554 (1949).

Tukey, J.W., "Keeping Research in Contact with Literature: Citation Indices and Beyond," *Journal of Chemical Documentation* 2, 34-37 (1962).

Weinberg, A.M., et al., President's Science Advisory Committee, *Science, Government, and Information (The Responsibilities of the Technical Community and the Government in the Transfer of Information),* Part 3, "Citation Indexing Should be Useful," p. 35, Government Printing Office, 1963.

SYNOPSIS

WHAT IS A CITATION INDEX?

A citation index is a directory of cited references where each reference is accompanied by a list of source documents which cite it. The most characteristic feature of the citation index is that the user begins a search with a specific known paper and from there is brought forward in time to subsequent papers related to the earlier paper.

HOW IS A CITATION INDEX PREPARED?

The 1961 Science Citation Index was prepared by processing 613 journals published in 1961. For *every* reference appearing in *every* article in the 613 source journals a separate IBM punch-card was prepared containing both the reference data and the source data. The 102,000 source articles yielded 1.4 million reference cards. The punched-cards were converted to magnetic tapes. The tapes were sorted and otherwise processed on IBM 1401, 1410, and 7074 computers. While the source data in the 1961 Science Citation Index is limited to the year 1961, references published in any period of recorded history are included. The 1961 Genetics Citation Index was extracted from the total 1961 Science Citation Index by computer selection.

The source coverage of a citation index can be extended by processing sources from additional years. In the 5- and 14-year Citation Indexes produced as part of this experiment, the range of source years is increased but the number of source journals covered is decreased.

HOW IS THE CITATION INDEX USED?

To locate source documents which have cited a particular paper, it will suffice to know the name of the first author, year, and page of the target reference paper. It is generally not necessary to know the title of the publication in which the paper appeared. In the citation index the cited or reference author is easily located on the left. For each paper by that author there is a dashed line which continues to the column reserved for the year of the reference publication. The journal abbreviation (or non-journal acronym), volume and page are found to the right of the reference year. Indented under each dashed line are data identifying source articles which have cited that specific reference. When a given reference has been cited by several sources they are arranged alphabetically by source authors.

The primary use of the citation index is the location of citations to a specific reference work. A secondary application of the index is its use as a conventional author index to help identify an author's publications. Note, however, that only papers in which he appears as first author can be found under a specific author's name in this experimental index, and then only when the work was cited within the source coverage. We therefore caution readers that frequency data for individual scientists can be low since senior investigators may be the last ones named in a paper.

APPLICATIONS OF THE CITATION INDEX

The fundamental question one can answer quickly through the citation index is, "Where and by whom has this paper been cited in the literature?" The significance of the answer lies in the policy of scientific publication that one cites appropriate references--methodological, ideational, historical, or otherwise. We have found this rule is, in general, followed. Naturally there are violations and abuses, but these are the exceptions and not common practice.

The citation index is invaluable in preparing historical introductions to scientific papers and in preparing critical reviews and books. The citation index finds further use in tracing new applications of theories, methods, instruments, chemicals, etc., and in the location of corrections, errata, amendments, refutations, letters, editorials, discussions, translations, reviews, etc.

The sociological applications of citation indexes for personnel evaluation, faculty promotions, awards, etc., are legitimate to the extent that one judiciously uses the citation index, as a retrieval tool, to facilitate the location of criticisms of a man's work. Qualitative judgments must temper quantitative data. The citation index can also be used to quickly identify scientists currently working in special branches of science either for personnel or communication purposes.

A great deal has been said about the use of citation indexes for ego gratification. Though this topic might best be covered in a purely psychological or sociological study of scientists, it is discussed here because well-meaning individuals have "rejected" citation indexing on the grounds that ego gratification is its only value. We do not believe citation indexing will be supported purely for ego gratification of subscribers. Ego gratification is not the only motivation for a scientist who wishes to determine whether his work has been applied or criticized by others. Certainly, each scientist evaluates the citations to his works differently. One man's work stimulates another. The citation index then facilitates feedback in the communication cycle. Any author may choose to ignore citations to his own work. Nevertheless, he may wish to retrieve publications which cite the works of other scientists in whom he is interested.

HOW TO BEGIN A SEARCH

Scientists and librarians are experienced in the use of conventional subject indexes. To find articles on biochemical studies in which a particular dye indicator was used, one would normally expect to look under a subject heading for the dye. In the citation index the "subject" is the information contained in a starting point--the target reference. Using a paper on the synthesis of the dye, or any other known paper involving the use of the dye, one can trace subsequent or previous papers on its use.

Similarly, one can find current modifications of a work, as, for example, the use of Einstein's formulas for measuring molecular dimensions. His 1906 paper was cited in 1959 in the *Journal of Dairy Science* in a study on the molecular properties of milk.

The citation index is a relatively sophisticated searching tool. Some knowledge of a starting point is assumed. A target reference sometimes must be first identified through the use of a conventional encyclopedia, book, or subject index. The citation index is then used to answer the question, "What has happened since?" We believe this question is fundamental to research activity.

Various search strategies are discussed elsewhere but a few actual searches will quickly demonstrate the simplicity of the citation index system. The conventional cross-referencing structure, *see* and *see also* references, is absent because it is not required. Nomenclatural ambiguities and rules are completely eliminated.

The reader who is interested in more detailed information should read the introduction to each of the several sections in this Genetics Citation Index as well as the papers which have been cited in the bibliography.

COMMENTARY: Needed — A Relativistic Theory of Information Science

Eugene Garfield, Chairman

Secondary distribution of information is surely a relative if not an ambiguous term. The variety of topics covered in Theme Session #7 accentuates the recurring difficulty in trying to assign inflexible classifications to any information processing activities. Classically secondary distribution (publication) of information concerns those activities which follow primary publication (distribution) of documents. Thus, the conventional abstracting publications like *Chemical Abstracts* and *Biological Abstracts* are secondary publications. That these are arbitrary descriptions is indicated in relating the role of the newer depository systems to the established systems of distribution. Indeed, the announcement of government research reports, through abstracting publications, reverses the usual publication sequence as far as the consumer is concerned. Primary journals are usually received in libraries many months before abstracting journals appear. Reports, on the other hand, are ordered after their announcement, through abstracts, in various announcement media such as USGRR, STAR, etc. This same reversal of timing occurs in *Current Contents* for a large percentage of foreign journals.

The various systems of so-called Selective Dissemination of Information (SDI) are usually considered a form of secondary distribution. However, this is also arbitrary as the primary-secondary relationship is clearly one of timing. Which comes first—the title, the abstract, or the full report? Like the humans who write them, all possible combinations are possible. Many authors wait until a report is completed before writing an abstract. Others write abstracts of papers that never get presented or written. With the newer automatic methods of dissemination, titles, abstracts, or full papers, or a combination thereof, may be the grist for a selective dissemination or alerting system.

Index Medicus and the *Science Citation Index* illustrate the interesting overlap between a conventional index form, the printed index, and means for automatic alerting an/or current or retrospective searching. The same information (index assignments) is used to produce periodic large published indexes. The index entries are also used for up-to-date matching with customer profiles. In one case, *Index Medicus*, subject headings are the basis of choice. In the other, *Science Citation Index*, the bibliographic citation is the main search or alerting parameter. In both, authors can also be used.

Many of the papers included in this theme session concern the mechanical functions involved in preparing secondary publications. As such, they might easily have been subtended by other sessions. Edmundson's "Com-

Reprinted from AUTOMATION AND SCIENTIFIC COMMUNICATION: Proceedings of the 26th Annual Meeting of the American Documentation Institute, Chicago, October 6-11, 1963. Part 3, pp. 419-420.

puter Abstracting of Russian Text" could obviously fall under translation of scientific information, while Reisner's "Machine Stored Citation Index" paper could come under document storage and display. And surely the same is true of papers in other sessions. Freeman's "Automatic Retrieval from Chemical Titles" could easily have been included in this session.

It is important to note the appearance of citation and KWIC indexes in Part II of the conference proceedings. This is certainly a new and interesting facet of the entire experiment in prompt publication of conference proceedings. Surely Parts I and II, the short papers, represent a limbo between primary and secondary publication in the conventional sense as the material is a necessary combination of rehash of the past, experiments in progress, and future prospects. All of this would seem to indicate that information science needs a relativistic theory to better describe the inseparable dimensions of time and space in information processing. Perhaps the "fifth" dimension for information, in addition to time and space, is the omnipresent human factor which some might call semantic, others sociological, others psychological, others anthropological, and yet others metaphysical. For the time being I propose the following relativitic definition. Any information distribution activity is "secondary" when the activity immediately involved is chronologically later than the predecessor form. By this definition a title, abstract, full paper or even an idea may be considered primary or secondary according to the timing of these respective events. When one considers that all forms can in fact appear simultaneously then the ideal state is truly an equilibrium condition where all forms of information are simultaneously accessible. In another context I called this condition Research Nirvana. (1)

(1) Garfield, E., "Research Nirvana—Total Dissemination and Retrieval of Bio-Medical Information?" Paper presented to the Sixth Annual Session, Medical Writers' Institute, New York City, October 5, 1963.

Reprinted from Science, May 8, 1964, Vol. 144, No. 3619, pages 649-654

"Science Citation Index"— A New Dimension in Indexing

This unique approach underlies versatile bibliographic systems for communicating and evaluating information.

Eugene Garfield

Over a quarter of a century ago H. G. Wells made a magnificent, if premature, plea for the establishment of a world information center, "the World Brain" (1). To Wells, the World Brain became the symbol of international intellectual cooperation in a world at peace. The realization, within our lifetime, of the physical and intellectual achievement envisioned in *World Brain* no longer lies in the realm of science fiction. The ultimate specification for a World Brain must await more fundamental studies and understanding of information science. However, the increasing convergence of such previously unrelated fields as genetics, linguistics, psychology, and chemistry foretells exciting realignments in classical conceptions of the "information" problem. Unquestionably there are many different forms and arrangements which a World Brain could assume. Vannevar Bush's "Memex" was a microfilm version of the universal fingertip library (2); Memex stimulated considerable speculation but also produced some realistic work (3). Tukey's "Information Ledger" is a recent specification of the desiderata for a universal information system (4). More recently, Senders has given an approximate quantitative measure of the information content of the world's libraries (5). Surely the increasing awareness of the science-information problem on the part of both the legis-

lative (6) and executive (7) branches of government will add momentum to the inevitable trend toward establishment of a world information center.

The main purpose of this article is to provide some perspective on the science-information, or science-"indexing," problem; to review briefly the developments in citation indexing that have occurred over the past 10 years; and to indicate why the recently published *Science Citation Index* (8) is a harbinger of things to come—a forerunner of the World Brain.

The average scientist thinks a World Brain would be extremely useful. The possibility of having all recorded knowledge at one's fingertips is fascinating. The librarian, however, eminently more practical on this topic than the scientist, because he has learned to live with bibliographical poverty in the midst of scientific wealth, thinks of the enormously detailed problems of bibliographic control (9). Therefore, the librarian may be the one who best appreciates the implications of the *Science Citation Index* for bibliographic control. It is the first really serious attempt at universal bibliographical control of science literature since the turn of the century (10). On the other hand, the librarian is sometimes too acutely aware of the detailed problems involved in compiling an international inventory of science—precisely what the *Science Citation Index* is. I believe the need for such an inventory, for such bibliographic control, is indisputable (11).

Whether or not citation indexes are useful is a question that has now been

The author is director of the Institute for Scientific Information, Philadelphia, and lecturer in information retrieval at the University of Pennsylvania.

answered. We have enough favorable experience in using them to know they are desirable and useful. However, a citation index must meet the same economic test that all products in our society must meet: Does the cost justify the benefits? To measure its value to the scientific community is not simple. Do the cost and difficulties of retrieving pertinent literature justify bypassing the literature and chancing a replication of research? Or, as Maddox recently phrased the problem: "Is the literature worth keeping?" (12). The Weinberg Committee (7) maintains that the literature is an integral part of the research process. Printed communication still has a long life expectancy as a means of imparting current information and retrieving data; it will be with us at least until we have developed science communication to the point where all indexes, journals, books, and other printed media become obsolete and a World Brain takes over. Meanwhile, the initial bibliographic control necessary for establishing a World Brain is economically justified by the immediate and interim requirements of the expanding complex of science and technology.

If we ever achieve "total communication," a state of research nirvana, then an enormous time-shared, random-access computer memory will augment man's finite memory and replace printed indexes and catalogs. In this condition of nirvana a World Brain will itself have become an auxiliary to man's own brain. Or, as Bernal has stated it (13), "The speculations of the future may then be the speculations, not of one man or of many men, but of all humanity and their machines." But this achievement will require a far greater commitment to the task of accumulating and communicating scientific information than we have ever been willing to make previously. In any event, the direct linking of conceptual information which is made possible for the first time through citation indexing will be a vital part of such total communication.

An Example

In June 1955 a paper appeared in *Science* entitled "Citation indexes for science" (14); it was in part based on suggestions made by Adair (15) and Hart (16). In 1957 there followed a paper on the applicability of the citator system to patents (17), which cited Hart (16) and Seidel (18) in support of arguments for establishing a citation index to patents. In two subsequent papers (19, 20) the a priori nature of conventional indexes was discussed in contrast to the a posteriori character of citation indexing. The relationship of the citation index to the problem of achieving a Unified Science Index was explored at the International Conference on Scientific Information in 1958 (21). Fano (22), Ernst (23), Tukey (24), Savage (25), Lipetz (26), Kessler (27, 28), Atherton (29), and Salton (30) have also pursued various ramifications and possibilities of citation indexing.

The foregoing bibliographic recapitulation is intended to emphasize, to the reader unfamiliar with citation indexes, both the advantages and the simplicity of citation indexing. The 17 papers cited in the preceding paragraph are associated here in this article. A citation index would automatically lead the user to this group of related works, provided he knew of any one of the cited references. With a citation index, this article and the paragraph in question would be retrieved regardless of the date or the journals in which the cited papers originally appeared. The scatter of the 17 references, however, also illustrates some of the complexities of compiling citation indexes. The preceding paragraph is a historical-bibliographic introduction comparable to that provided by many authors in writing scientific papers.

Consider the reader who has never heard the term *citation index* but wants information on this topic. His difficulties in finding the article you are now reading will illustrate the difficulties of finding information by conventional methods. It would be almost impossible for one unfamiliar with the citation-index concept to search for papers under the heading "citation indexing" because the term probably would not occur to him. If the idea of citation indexing did occur to him, the descriptive terminology that he selected in searching for the citation-index "idea" would probably have been different. And yet, previous knowledge of any one of the references cited in this article, or cited in any of the other 17 "citation-index papers," would, through the use of citation indexes, bring to the attention of the requester this "new" concept. Even in this circuitous example there is no paradox involved in calling the results of the search a "new" concept, since the actual search could have been performed by some other person using a citation index, while the requester himself remained unaware of its existence. Thus, interest in Vannevar Bush's paper (2), Avakian's work (3), or any other of the 17 cited references which is relevant to, but does not specifically name, citation indexing would open the door to the idea of citation indexing.

Consider the class of readers who might have thought about the "idea" of a citation index prior to publication of this article. They fall into two subclasses—those who might have called it a citation index or something roughly equivalent, such as a "reference index" or "citator," and those who might not. The latter subclass includes Fano (22) and Ernst (23), whose linguistic conception of the citation-index "idea" was quite different from mine, though the end result was essentially the same. The semantic difference lies in my thinking of a citation index primarily as a printed index, whereas they visualized a "machine" index. This manipu-

lative difference in no way alters the basic commonality of the two systems. The information processed in the two is exactly the same—citations appearing in bibliographies.

To continue our example—the literature searcher interested in finding published articles on "the citation index" by conventional methods faces a basically difficult task. Even though he may have the terminology correct, or nearly correct, he will find that *Science* is one of those journals that is *selectively* indexed by the leading discipline-oriented indexing services. "Chemical" articles are indexed by *Chemical Abstracts*, "physical" articles by *Science Abstracts*, "biological" articles by *Biological Abstracts*, and so on. But even if one assumes that the conventional indexing services do abstract articles such as this, an additional degree of uncertainty is then introduced by the possibility (and too often the probability) that either the indexer or the searcher did not use the "correct" terminology. Concepts or ideas are extremely difficult to handle consistently in classical subject indexes.

For the other papers in the list of 17 citations, effective selection and indexing treatment by the conventional indexing and abstracting services is even more unlikely than it is for the cited article from *Science* (14). The article in the *Journal of the Patent Office Society* (17) illustrates one of the many serious deficiencies of our fragmented, discipline-oriented indexing activities (31). That paper, on indexing chemical patents, was published in a legal journal, and thus the audience of librarians and chemists who might be interested in the paper was sacrificed for an audience of patent attorneys. The situation is even worse with respect to references 20 and 21, both of which are part of the published proceedings of a conference. Hanson and Jones have shown that most papers appearing in the published proceedings of conferences are never indexed (32). Since the number of published conference proceedings is quite large, a considerable amount of important literature would be buried if the participants in these conferences did not cite the same papers in subsequent articles, published in journals which *are* covered by indexing and abstracting services. This is reflected in studies by Touloukian *et al.* (*33*) which show that it is more efficient to use an indexing service to locate a few recent papers and then search bibliographies in these papers than it is to search the indexes exclusively.

The conventional discipline-oriented indexes thus leave much to be desired with respect to breadth of coverage and as means of indexing consistently and by concept. If, instead of searching for papers on the subject of citation indexes, the reader seeks papers on any one of dozens of interdisciplinary subjects investigated today, without knowing the exact headings under which they are indexed, he encounters similar difficulties. This will be apparent if, for example, he tries to compile rapidly a bibliography on one of the following topics: theories on the origin of life; nucleic acid staining techniques; applications of computers to biomedical research.

What Is a Citation Index?

A citation index is an ordered list of cited articles each of which is accompanied by a list of citing articles. The citing article is identified by a source citation, the cited article by a reference citation. The index is arranged by reference citations. Any source citation may subsequently become a reference citation. At the time of indexing, the article you are now reading would be considered a source. In that case it would appear in the citation index under all the reference citations in "References and notes" at the end of the article. It would also appear in the source index which accompanies the citation index proper.

The description of a citation index does not imply a particular order for the list of cited references. We have studied in great detail the many ways one can arrange a citation index. These include arrangement by author, journal, year, document serial number, volume, page, or other parameter. Any fragment of the usual citation might be the basis for organizing a citation index. The decision to arrange the *Science Citation Index* (*8*) by author was based on a total-systems study in which it was determined that the typical user requirement is to find what sources have cited a particular reference, albeit at times the reference citation is incompletely recollected. Our studies have also shown the desirability of providing, with the citation index, a complete source index containing full source-article titles and certain additional data. This source index is similar to an upgraded conventional author index covering all disciplines—the first objective of the Unified Science Index (*21*). Arrangement by author is favored in the citation index and the source index because the research scientist usually approaches the literature first by author.

By using a citation index one determines what *subsequent* papers have cited a particular reference. How would the new citation index help you find articles on the subject "citation index"? I have already shown why it would be difficult to find these with conventional subject indexes. Suppose you have found, by chance, the article by Adair (*15*) by scanning back volumes of *American Documentation*—a not unlikely supposition for someone interested in finding such information. When you have located the Adair article by such browsing you look it up in a cumulated citation index for the source years 1955–64; the index immediately tells you that at least seven papers have appeared on the subject *since* 1955 —*14, 17, 19, 21, 24, 26*, and the article you are now reading—all citing

Adair's paper! However, this is only the beginning. By a technique called "cycling" you can quickly find the other papers on the subject of citation indexes, as well as others related to the use of citations. "Cycling" means examining the bibliographies of the papers you start with, and of the source papers obtained, in order to locate additional relevant works. By looking up the latter in the citation index you find new citing sources.

For example, in my paper in the *Chemical Bulletin* (*19*) the letter by Schoenbach, in which he criticizes citation indexing, is cited (*34*). Schoenbach's paper in turn refers to my original paper (*14*), which, through the citation index, leads to my reply (*35*). Furthermore, by successively checking on whether the "source" articles which cited Adair have themselves appeared later as cited references and following up any secondary sources so located, one quickly generates a complete bibliography.

As the literature of a field increases, the redundancy in bibliographies makes it easier to up-date the search, no matter which of various related articles is located first. This redundancy also reduces loss of information in the citation index through typographical or other errors, including the omission, unwitting or otherwise, of relevant references by authors.

How can we assume that a searcher will find any of the necessary articles to begin his search? The user of the citation index must have a starting point. Here is a major difference between conventional subject indexes and citation indexes.

Proponents of conventional language-oriented subject indexes implicitly assume that the typical reader does not know of any papers on the subject he is investigating. How often is this true of the working scientist? More often, perhaps, it is a librarian or student who seeks information without prior knowledge of the subject. If the user does not know of a previous work on the subject he must find one through a book, an encyclopedia, or a colleague. These can usually supply one or more starting references. If there is little or nothing written on the subject the user will have a difficult time no matter what he does, as no literature search can turn up what doesn't exist!

Too Many Citations or Too Few?

Although the average published paper is cited less than once each year, certain papers are very frequently cited. To take an extreme case, the paper most frequently cited in 1961 was cited over 500 times (*36*). While, by most search standards, this makes a long list of citing papers to scan, even this number is not one bit excessive for the chemist, sociologist, or historian interested in writing a complete review or evaluation of the method cited. Moreover, several of the citing papers introduced procedural modifications.

It is frequently assumed that the usual citation practices lead to an impractical number of sources for a particular reference. In rare instances this may be true, but, as we have seen, for certain purposes the searcher may be only too glad to have a rich and comprehensive bibliography to scan. Experience shows, however, that the number of sources uncovered is in most cases quite manageable. Furthermore, the yield of sources can be reduced by various simple means whenever this is required. One such method involves the use of "bibliographic coupling" (*28*).

In designing the *Science Citation Index* (*8*) it was assumed that the user could specify one or more references as starting points. It may sometimes be necessary or desirable to start with more than one reference. In these cases the searcher can cull the sources by looking up in the index only those sources which cite two or more of the starting references. This is the essence of bibliographic coupling. Or sources may be selected or rejected on the basis of authorship, journal title, article title, number of references, "type" of article, date of publication, and classification numbers.

The refining of a search result by these methods is generally quite unnecessary. In an annual cumulation comprising 1.4 million references (37), the average number of citing sources per reference cited was found to be about 1.5. It is easy to lose sight of the fact that, contrary to the general cliché that there is too much scientific information, there is often little or no information available on a specific point (38). The number of references cited each year is a function of the size of the current and past literature and of the writing habits of the authors. However, it is interesting to note that the average number of citing sources per reference cited did not change appreciably once we exceeded a critical level of several hundred key journals.

In day-to-day research, the citation index will also provide the scientist with useful leads toward an *unspecified* information objective. Frequently the scientist-user of indexes does not have a precise objective in mind. He is simply exploring information pathways that appear to be exciting and interesting. The citation index facilitates this browsing process. On the other hand, the competitive nature of modern research (39) often involves him in negative literature research. Many persons legitimately hope they will *not* find pertinent references—as, for example, in patent searches. In evaluating the citation index and other indexes one must consider the ease with which one can obtain a negative result with a high degree of certainty.

Obviously citation indexes will be effective only to the extent that the bibliographies in published papers are accurate reflections of the earlier literature. In evaluating papers submitted to journals, referees should determine whether all pertinent references have been provided. The citation index will significantly assist the referee in identifying such pertinent references. A paper recently reported as novel a method of analyzing for peptides (40), even though the same work had been reported 4 years earlier (41). There is no question that, had the authors or referees had access to a citation index, the second paper would not have been published, and the subsequent correction (42) would have been unnecessary. The two papers (40, 41) contained four references in common; from any one of these the earlier work could have been pinpointed through the citation index. Our files contain numerous examples of this type.

How serious is the problem of noncitation of pertinent references, for whatever reason, by authors? Most of us have seen examples of what appears to be an obvious omission of a reference to a related piece of work by another author. Such omissions will undoubtedly affect the utility of the citation index for "current awareness" searches. How much cannot yet be determined. The fact that papers which do not cite the earlier literature will not be retrieved directly through citation indexing may exert some influence on authors in the future. However, most papers do contain pertinent bibliographies, and, in time, most papers are cited a few times. It is a rare paper which neither cites nor is cited. However, editors and referees, in accepting or recommending acceptance of a paper, might insist that certain standards of literature search be met by the author, just as similar standards are assumed by anyone applying for a patent. References in patents, however, are supplied by the referee (examiner), not the author (inventor).

Dissemination Problem

I have discussed some of the ways in which the citation index can be used to search literature. If a printed list of sources which cite a particular reference is of use, then a service, through which such citations, or the articles themselves, are automatically and selectively disseminated, will also be useful. It is easier to decide how relevant a citing paper is by quickly scanning the paper itself than by reading a title or an abstract. Through such scanning the starting reference can be considered in context within the source article. This step is aided by the fact that most citations are enumerated and easily traced within the body of the text. A sentence or paragraph thus disclosed may contain vital information which had been completely ignored by an abstractor or subject indexer. The design of just such an automatic weekly alerting service has been completed, and indications are that it will significantly aid the individual in keeping abreast of his specific interests, as defined by his pertinent "question" citations.

Extensions into Subject Indexing

What are the possibilities of using the citation index in conjunction with conventional indexing? In discussions of citation indexes at the Dorking Conference (20) it was correctly concluded that each reference citation is a form of index "heading" or descriptor. A similar conclusion was implied in the statement that each author "indexes" his own papers each time he cites another paper (14). Now, let us assume that the ideas expressed in a particular source article are reflected in the index headings used by some conventional indexing system. In that case, a display of the descriptors or subject headings assigned to that paper by the indexer constitutes a restatement of the subject matter of that paper in the indexer's terminology. When the indexing is automatic and based on article titles, then the key words restate the title and presumably restate the main subjects of the paper. Suppose you now collect and

examine the array of descriptors generated by all the references cited in a particular source paper. How accurately will this list of descriptors describe the contents of the source document? Some preliminary experiments have revealed that the terms selected in indexing a source paper corresponded closely with those used to index the reference citations. The combined array of descriptors for all cited articles characterized the subject matter of the source article in great detail. There are certain exceptions; for example, the nomenclature used to index a previously incompletely described drug is inadequate for the subsequently completely identified chemical structure.

The implications and ramifications of these experiments may prove valuable both in future conventional cerebral indexing and in computer indexing. First, the speed and consistency of conventional indexing would be increased if one could quickly display (by means of computer methods) the earlier indexing terms assigned to the references in a particular source article being indexed. This idea was implicit in the Philco Medlars proposal (43), in which it was suggested that the indexer would be capable of direct communication (online) with the computer. It was also implied in Fano's "matrix," in which the degree of relevance of two documents is determined by comparing the lists of reference citations. In Fano's system, two documents would be considered "identical" if the lists of bibliographical citations were identical. This is a specific case of the more general axiom that two documents are indistinguishable within any retrieval system if all of the assigned descriptors are the same (44). The only way the documents can be differentiated is by the assignment of additional descriptors— that is, by indexing in greater depth.

Machine Citation Index

If the same magnetic-tape files that are used to prepare the nonmanipulative printed citation index were searched by computer, papers could be associated through machine examination of the descriptor patterns of cited papers. In this way one could incorporate and utilize existing indexing of earlier papers in mechanically evaluating the relevance of source papers.

The machine citation index would also facilitate studies on why certain papers are never cited. Kessler reports the existence of a large number of such papers (27). What does this signify? Many factors can contribute to a lack of citations. In addition to the obvious possibility that a paper is relatively worthless, several information concepts come into play. For example, information may remain untransmitted if an article has been published in a relatively obscure journal, in a journal generally devoted to articles in a very different field, or in a language or jargon foreign to potential users. The article may be dry or very long, and thus not widely read. A poorly selected title or bibliography, or both, can also lessen citation of an article. However there is another, and challenging, factor: the timing of a scientific article can be out of step with the general development of science —out of phase with the general communication network. The "time lag" can be positive or negative, depending upon the quality or originality of the message. "Like mutant genes, an idea may be before its time—that is, the social climate may not be right for its acceptance" (45).

A paper may be so far ahead of its time that it is not appreciated or cited for many years. Mendel's experiments with peas in his monastery garden, Fleming's observations of bacterial lysis in mold-contaminated petri dishes, Pressey's reports of "An Apparatus which . . . teaches" all lay buried in dusty tomes for decades before their vast significance for genetics, antimicrobial therapy, and teaching machines became widely recognized. Indeed, the history of science abounds with ex-amples indicating that the scientific community is incapable of quickly absorbing radically new ideas or information. If we assume that the papers which have never been cited include those which were ahead of their time, the citation index may afford a means of ferreting out those papers which might deserve reevaluation, redissemination, or even republication. One experiment contemplated at the Institute for Scientific Information is the identification of genetics papers which were not cited in the *Genetics Citation Index* (46). These would be reappraised by experts with respect to possible "revival" value. It would be gratifying to uncover some hitherto uncited papers buried in the literature which, in the light of more recent scientific discoveries, do deserve republication.

Citation Indexes and Abstracting Services

Recently Bennett (47) has reiterated my earlier recommendation that an index to the abstracts in specialty journals and to abstracts prepared by the smaller abstracting services be compiled (21). Frequently these are abstracts which include criticism. As such, they constitute original publications. Every author should know of such critical abstracts of his papers. In literature searches, abstracts may serve in lieu of the original articles, particularly when the original article is in a foreign language, or when it is not readily available. Citation indexes can be used to locate these abstracts quickly and to identify unabstracted articles (31).

Author Citation Index

A random-access computer memory does not require special ordering for data storage. In such memories the arbitrarily assigned data-addresses need not be known to the user. By contrast, a printed citation index must have a logical order. An alphabetical arrangement of reference citations by cited author has definite advantages and disadvantages. One advantage is that an author arrangement brings into proximity references to different works by the same author. In any other arrangement, citations to the work of a single author would be scattered. A further advantage is that the user who remembers no more than the author's name and the approximate year a paper was published can still usually complete his search. With the author arrangement there is a small but distinct complication: the name of a cited author may appear with different spellings in different journals. This problem is aggravated by the fact that the scientific literature employs many languages, alphabets, and transliterating systems. For instance, when names are transliterated from English into Russian and then back into English, the original spelling may be lost. An American named Wheeler may come through this mill as Viiler. Hilbert comes through as Gilbert. Chinese names present even more bizarre examples. To make things worse, the *Journal of the Chemical Society*, and others, drop authors' initials in citations (48). A Reference to Smith, *Proc. Chem. Soc.* **1953**, 1234, is adequate for most purposes. However, specific identification of the author is made difficult by this practice. Fortunately, only a small percentage of citations present such problems, but these do increase the cost of processing and the difficulties for the user. One solution may ultimately be to prepare brief "contents pages," which contain, for every journal ever published, standardized spelling of the authors' names. The computer can then be used to replace incomplete, incorrect, or variant spellings with this standardized form. The preparation of "contents pages" is also a requisite for the mechanical identification of articles which have never been cited, discussed earlier.

In compiling the *Science Citation Index*, an interim solution to the problem of orthography has been to have the computer use less than the author's full name when first identifying two or more references to the same citation, then to have the computer select one variation of the cited name for use in the index.

Another complication of the author citation index is the problem of multiple authorship. If one expects to find citations to all the work of a given author, then that author must appear as the primary author in the citations, or the index must contain cross references or duplicated entries for all co-authors' names. The average number of authors per paper now exceeds two (49). To list all co-authors in a printed author-citation index would approximately double its size. One partial solution to this cost and space problem has been the compilation of a separate bibliography or index of source articles, with all junior and senior authors listed. Preparation of a cumulated cross-referenced file based on this source index will eventually allow the user to quickly identify all the works to which a given author contributed.

Conclusion

The availability of comprehensive citation indexes now opens new roads to the solution of numerous scientific and documentation problems. Citation indexing bypasses some of the limitations of classical subject indexing, and its techniques can be incorporated in the existing communication system as well as in the World Brain, whatever shape or form that may take. Production of citation indexes has become an eminently practicable procedure, and the results of research on over 2 million citations lead to the conclusion that we cannot afford to neglect this unique and versatile instrument, in view of the accelerating tempo of modern interdisciplinary scientific research. The main objective for the immediate future is to increase the coverage, in terms of chronology and number of source publications, so that we will have a relatively complete inventory of all scientific and related research. To do this will require the support of the entire scientific community.

References and Notes

1. H. G. Wells, *World Brain* (Doubleday, Doran, Garden City, N.Y., 1938).
2. V. Bush, "As we may think," *Atlantic Monthly* **176**, 101 (July, 1945).
3. E. A. Avakian and E. Garfield, "AMFIS—the Automatic Microfilm Information System," *Spec. Libraries* **48**, 145 (1956).
4. J. W. Tukey, "Keeping research in contact with the literature: Citation Indices and beyond," *J. Chem. Doc.* **2**, 34 (1962).
5. J. W. Senders, "Information storage requirements for the contents of the world's libraries," *Science* **141**, 1067 (1963).
6. During the past 7 years numerous Senate hearings on the science-information problem have been conducted by the Committee on Government Operations, Subcommittee on Reorganization and International Organizations (Senator Hubert H. Humphrey, chairman). See, for example, *Interagency Coordination of Information* (published pursuant to Senate Resolution 276, 87th Congress, 21 Sept. 1962) (Government Printing Office, Washington, D.C., 1963). For the House of Representatives, see, among others, *National Information Center* [Hearings on H.R. 1946 before the Committee on Education and Labor, Ad Hoc Subcommittee on Research Data Processing and Information Retrieval (Roman Pucinski, chairman)] (Government Printing Office, Washington, D.C., 1963).
7. A. M. Weinberg *et al.*, "President's Science Advisory Committee," in *Science, Government, and Information* (Responsibilities of the Technical Community in the Transfer of Information) (Government Printing Office, Washington, D.C., 1963).
8. E. Garfield and I. H. Sher, *Science Citation Index* (Institute for Scientific Information, Philadelphia, 1963).
9. J. H. Shera and M. E. Egan, Eds., *Bibliographic Organization* (Univ. of Chicago Press, Chicago, 1951).
10. K. O. Murra, "History of some attempts to organize bibliography internationally," in *Bibliographic Organization*, J. H. Shera and M. E. Egan, Eds. (Univ. of Chicago Press, Chicago, 1951), pp. 24–53.
11. E. Garfield, statement and testimony, Hearings on H.R. 1946 of 19 July 1963 [see *National Information Center* (Government Printing Office, Washington, D.C., 1963), pp. 226–251].
12. J. Maddox, "Is the literature worth keeping?" *Bull. Atomic Scientists* **19**, No. 9, 14 (1963).
13. J. D. Bernal, "The place of speculation in modern technology and science," in *The Scientist Speculates*, I. J. Good, Ed. (Heinemann, London, 1963), pp. 11–28.
14. E. Garfield, "Citation indexes for science," *Science* **122**, 108 (1955).
15. W. C. Adair, "Citation indexes for scientific literature?" *Am. Doc.* **6**, 31 (1955).
16. H. C. Hart, "Re: 'Citation System for Patent Office,'" *J. Patent Office Soc.* **31**, 714 (1949).
17. E. Garfield, "Breaking the subject index barrier—a citation index for chemical patents," *ibid.* **39**, 583 (1957).
18. A. H. Seidel, "Citation system for patent office," *ibid.* **31**, 554 (1949).

19. E. Garfield, "Citation indexes—new paths to scientific knowledge," *Chem. Bull.* **43**, No. 4, 11 (1956).
20. ———, in *Proceedings of the International Study Conference on Classification for Information Retrieval* (Pergamon, New York, 1957), p. 98.
21. ———, "A unified index to science," in *Proceedings of the International Conference on Scientific Information, 1958* (National Academy of Sciences—National Research Council, Washington, D.C., 1959), pp. 461–474.
22. R. M. Fano, private memorandum (1959).
23. H. A. Ernst, "Design and evaluation of a literature retrieval scheme," thesis, Massachusetts Institute of Technology (1959).
24. J. W. Tukey, "The citation index and the information problem," *Princeton Univ. Statistical Techniques Research Group Ann. Rept. for 1962*.
25. I. R. Savage, *Bibliography of Nonparametric Statistics* (Harvard Univ. Press, Cambridge, 1962).
26. B. Lipetz, "Compilation of an experimental citation index from scientific literature," *Am. Doc.* **13**, 251 (1962).
27. M. M. Kessler, "Technical information flow patterns," *Proc. Western Joint Computer Conf.* (1961), pp. 247–257.
28. ———, "Bibliographic coupling between scientific papers," *Am. Doc.* **14**, 10 (1963).
29. P. Atherton and J. C. Yovich, *Three Experiments with Citation Index and Bibliographic Coupling of Physics Literature* (American Institute of Physics, New York, 1962).
30. G. Salton, "Associative document retrieval techniques using bibliographic information," *J. Assoc. Computing Machines* **10**, 440 (1963).
31. E. Garfield, I. H. Sher, P. Sopinsky, "Article-by-article analysis of abstracting services," *Proc. Am. Doc. Inst.* (1963), pt. 1, p. 45.
32. C. W. Hanson, "Lack of indexes in reports of conferences," *J. Doc.* **16**, 65 (1960).
33. P. S. Lykoudis, P. E. Liley, Y. S. Touloukian, "Analytical study of a method for literature search in abstracting journals," in *Proceedings of the International Conference on Scientific Information* (National Academy of Sciences—National Research Council, Washington, D.C., 1959), vol. 1, pp. 351–375; A. O. Cezairliyan, P. S. Lykoudis, Y. S. Touloukian, "Analytical and experimental study of a method for literature search in abstracting journals," *Thermophysical Properties Research Center, Purdue Univ., Rept. No. 11* (1960).
34. U. H. Schoenbach, "Citation indexes for science," *Science* **123**, 61 (1956).
35. E. Garfield, "Citation indexes for science," *ibid.*, p. 62.
36. O. H. Lowry, "Protein measurement with the Folin phenol reagent," *J. Biol. Chem.* **193**, 265 (1951).
37. E. Garfield, "Citation indexes in sociological and historical research," *Am. Doc.* **14**, 289 (1963).
38. S. Herner, "Technical information—too much or too little?" *Sci. Monthly* **83**, 82 (1956).
39. F. Reif, "The competitive world of the pure scientist," *Science* **134**, 1957 (1961).
40. R. H. Mazur, B. W. Ellis, P. S. Cammarata, "A new reagent for detection of peptides,

nucleotides, and other N-H-containing compounds on paper chromatograms," *J. Biol. Chem.* **237**, 1619 (1962).

41. D. P. Schwartz and M. J. Pallansch, "Tert-butyl hypochlorite for detection of nitrogenous compounds on chromatograms," *Anal. Chem.* **30**, 219 (1958).
42. Correction note, *J. Biol. Chem.* **237**, 3315 (1962).
43. *Proposal for MEDLARS* (Philco Corporation Computer Division, Willow Grove, Pa., 1961).
44. E. Garfield, "Information theory and other quantitative factors in code design for document card systems," *J. Chem. Doc.* **1**, 70 (1961).
45. H. Hoagland, "Science and the new humanism," *Science* **143**, 111 (1964); see also E. G. Boring, "Dual role of the Zeitgeist in scientific creativity," *Sci. Monthly* **80**, 101 (1955).
46. E. Garfield and I. H. Sher, *Genetics Citation Index* (Institute for Scientific Information, Philadelphia, 1963).
47. G. Bennett, "Current index to abstracting services," *Sci-Tech News* **15**, 129 (1961).
48. Since preparation of this article I have been advised (personal communication, March 1964) by the editor of the *Journal of the Chemical Society*, L. C. Cross, that by the end of 1964 authors' initials will be included in all reference citations.
49. B. L. Clarke, "Multiple authorship trends in scientific papers," *Science* **143**, 822 (1964).

*Revised version of paper presented under title "What is Relevant in a Patent Search?" at the Joint Meeting of Division of Chemical Literature and Division of Chemical Marketing and Economics, 150th National Meeting of the American Chemical Society, Atlantic City, N. J., September 1965.

Patent Citation Indexing and the Notions of Novelty, Similarity, and Relevance*

EUGENE GARFIELD,
Institute for Scientific Information, 325 Chestnut Street, Philadelphia, Pa.   19106

Received September 15, 1965

The unique features of the "references cited" in U. S. patents are discussed in relation to their use in the patent section of the *Science Citation Index*, which adds a new dimension to patent searching. Citation indexing provides a new basis for clarifying the concepts of similarity, coupling, novelty, and relevance.

The original title of this paper illustrates the inherent ambiguity of natural language. "What is relevant in a patent search?" may refer to the types of documents included in the term "prior art." Many types of published documents are "relevant"—patents, journal articles, books, etc. Whether or not the subject matter of a particular document is relevant, is another question. Furthermore, the specific purpose of a patent search affects relevance. Frequently, only the searcher can determine relevance (*1*). Those who have filed patent applications know too painfully how the inventor and the examiner can disagree on what is relevant. What is relevant to one man may be irrelevant to another. There is no objective measure of relevance.

On the other hand, similarity (*2*) is an objective relationship that exists between two documents. Similarity can be measured in several ways. These are not yet precise measures. They are relative. One measure of similarity is word or descriptor coupling (*3*), another is bibliographic coupling (*4*).

Key words or descriptors are natural language terms used in conventional indexing systems as in the *Uniterm Index to Chemical Patents* or *Chemical Abstracts*. In the Uniterm system, the number of Uniterms shared in common by two patents determines their similarity. If the same set of Uniterms is used to index two different patents, either the patents are essentially the same or the indexing has not been sufficiently deep to reveal their dissimilarity. The same would be true of two patents indexed by *CA*.

Bibliographic coupling is based on citation indexing. In citation indexing, the footnotes or references used by authors in writing technical papers are the indexing terms

(5). The *Science Citation Index*, including its *Patent Citation Index*, is based on citation indexing. In this system, the similarity between two citing documents is a function of the reference citations they share in common. Theoretically, if two different papers contain the same list of "references," then they are essentially the same. If not, as in word indexing, the number of citations is not sufficient to establish their dissimilarity.

Patents, however, are a special case. In patents, there are two kinds of reference citations: those occasionally provided by the inventor, and those provided more frequently by the patent examiner. It is of sociological interest to note that the examiner is comparable to the referee of a technical paper. It is a proper function of the referee (or editor) to determine if an author has cited pertinent prior art. The inventor affirms that to the best of his knowledge his invention is novel. The law does not require that he search the literature or consult his peers to determine the validity of his declaration. This is left to the patent examiner.

The examiner's prior art search frequently turns up a list of pertinent references. These references are usually the basis for disallowing one or more claims. The list of these "references cited," which sometimes includes the inventor's own references, is published at the end of each patent. In the *Science Citation Index*, all of these "references cited" are included as indexing terms. The *Index* does not include all references by the inventor which appear in the body of the specification. To do so would require the expensive task of reading each patent word by word. The inventor's references could be economically included if such references were published in one prescribed location at the beginning or end of the patent. The inventor includes these references to show the state-of-the-art, to identify a priority application, a co-pending application, a continuation, etc.

The majority of references, however, are provided by the examiner and constitute the prior art which the examiner used to disallow one or more claims. Obviously if all claims are disallowed (and about 50% of all patent applications fall in this category), the patent is not issued. The examiner, by definition, cannot cite pertinent anticipatory prior art for the allowed claims, though in fact many cited references are included which did not result in disallowance.

How relevant are these references to the subject matter of any given search? Obviously the examiner considers them relevant "enough" to disallow claims. Anyone interested in learning his reasons can examine the "wrapper" containing the complete file of correspondence. The high frequency of requests for these "references cited" was the reason for listing them from February 4, 1947 to the present. For patents issued before 1947, it is still necessary to consult the wrapper.

In the past few months, the Patent Office has taken another important step in helping the searcher. Next to each cited patent, its classification number is also given.

In using the *Patent Citation Index*, one is not as much concerned with the question, "Is the cited patent relevant to the citing patent?" as the converse and more significant question, "Is the citing or the *retrieved* patent relevant to the cited patent?" The cited patent is the starting point of the citation index search. This is frequently forgotten or misunderstood by those who have not used a citation index. Patent attorneys should not have this difficulty as they are used to the citator systems long established in legal searching—e.g., *Shepard's Citations* (6).

If one has a particular patent in mind, it may be vital to know whether the technology disclosed has been modified, improved, or utilized in any way. This can be done quickly using the *Patent Citation Index*. Arranged in numerical and thereby chronological order, the cited patent is quickly identified. As shown in Figure 1 (sample page of the *PCI*), after each cited patent there is a list of citing patents and/or journal articles. Most of the citing documents will be patents, and all the citing patents are U. S. Patents. However, cited foreign patents are included.

Having found one or more citing patents, the searcher can now turn to the *SCI Source Index* (Figure 2) which provides the full bibliographic description of the citing patent including all inventors, assignees, patent title, classification number, date of issue, and the number of references cited in the patent. He can then decide whether to examine the patent itself or its "abstract," that is, the principal claim in the *Official Gazette*, or its abstract in *Chemical Abstracts*.

Is the retrieved patent or the citing patent relevant? The answer cannot be categorically black or white. It is always some shade of gray which only the searcher can determine. Consider some specific circumstances. A particular 1949 patent describes subject matter which the searcher has determined is relevant. He looks up the patent in the 1964 and 1965 *Patent Citation Indexes* and finds a few 1964 or 1965 patents which have cited it. The examiner cited the 1949 patent because he considered it anticipatory prior art. For this reason, he disallowed one claim which does *not* appear in the list of allowed and published claims. The original claim could be seen in the wrapper. The subject matter of the specification has not been altered one iota. The crux of the question is this: What is the degree of similarity, in any given patent, between the specification and the ungranted claims? It has rarely been my experience to find patents containing completely dissimilar claims. They may be specific embodiments of applications of a general method—

Figure 1. Section of *Patent Citation Index* as
reprinted from 1965 *Science Citation Index.*

German Patent No. 1,163,335, issued to G. Weiss in 1964, has
been cited by R. Paetzold in *Zeit. Anorg. Ang. Chem.* **22,** 338
(1965). The full title of the citing article appears in the *Source
Index.* U. S. Patent No. 1,613,375, issued to Selfridge in 1915,
has been cited by two 1965 patents issued to Grebner and to
Wenthe.

Figure 2. *Source Index* showing full titles, subclasses,
etc. for citing patents or articles.

```
1 163 220----------*15*COREY 112/140------US
1 163 224---------- 319288 5 US           P 65
1 163 PENDLETO.PL  *15*DODGE 34/124----   P 65
1 163 251---------*15*MILJSAUGH 162/217X-US
1 163 296---------*15*WILLIAMS 66/111--US
1 163 335---------*64*WEISS G        65 338 -GER
1 163 PAETZOLD R  Z ANORG A C            P 65
1 163 339---------*15*HAUSS.        65 -US
1 163 SCHNEIDE.KJ 319166 2 US           P 65
1 163 349---------*15*KIMBALL 40/130--- P 65
1 163 350---------*15*LEWIS 24/160----- P 65
1 163 GURIAN SD   321208 0 US           P 65
1 163 PINTAREL.R  320823 9 US           P 65 -FRAN
1 163 358--------*58*                   P 65
      LOWRIE HS   317092 9 US           P 65
      LOWRIE HS   317093 0 US           P 65
1 163 375--------*15*SELFRIDGE          P 65 -US
      GREBNER F   317885 6 US           P 65
      WENTHE RG   321687 5 US           P 65
1 163 401--------*58*                   P 65 -FRAN
      HANEL E     319274 1 US           P 65
1 163 402--------*15*GILLIN             P 65 -US
      SCHLISIN.AE 316760 1 US           P 65
1 163 413--------*58*                   P 65 -FRAN
      PHILLIPS RS 320040 6 US           P 65
1 163 448--------*15*PENKALA 25/17----  P 65 -US
      RAAB HA     321243 2 US           P 65
1 163 465--------*64*                   P 65 -DAS
      ATOMPRAXIS          A 65  11     295
1 163 475--------*58*                   P 65 -FRAN
      SEDDON JW   321620 2 US           P 65
1 163 513--------*58*                   P 65 -FRAN
      KLASS DL    322184 9 US           P 65
1 163 525--------*58*                   P 65 -FRAN
      BROWN EA    319965 0 US           P 65
1 163 539--------         317243 8 US   P 65 -GERM
      GIANELLI L
1 163 MEALS RN    ANN NY ACAD      65 125 137
1 163 541--------*15*HULTIN          65 -US
      WAKEMAN AH  318297 1 US           P 65
```

```
PAETZOLD R   AMDULONG H
Z ANORG A C  337  225  65      24R  N5/6  66190
  UNTERSUCHUNGEN AN SELEN-SAUERSTOFF-
  VERBINDUNGEN .28. DIE SCHWINGUNGSSPEKTREN VON
  KRISTALLISIERTEM FLUSSIGEM UND GASFORMIGEM
  SELENTRIOXID
PAETZOLD R   RONSCH E
Z ANORG A C  338   22  65      14R  N1/2  67121
  DIALKYLAMIDDERIVATE DER SELENIGEN SAURE
PAETZOLD R   RONSCH E
Z ANORG A C  338  195  65      10R  N3/4  67752
  UNTERSUCHUNGEN AN SELEN-SAUERSTOFF-
  VERBINDUNGEN .31. ALKANSELENINSAUREALKYLESTER
PAETZOLD R   AMDULONG H
Z CHEM   5   435  65      M  N11         70270
  KONSTITUTION DER WASSERFREIEN SELENSAURE UND
  VON H2SE04/SE03-LOSUNGEN


GREBNER F   SPINDLER G
317193 US       CL29/155  P   4R   MAR 16
  GIRDER   METHOD OF MANUFACTURING A LATTICE
GREBNER F
317856 US       CL50/293  P  14R   APR 20
  GIRDER CEILING   FORM ARRANGEMENT FOR CASTING
  TRANSVERSE CONNECTING MEMBERS IN A CONCRETE
GREBNER F   KOELSCH W   LAUTERBA.W   RHEINB GMBH
319821 9 US      65   P   7R   AUG    3
  CL140/112  APPARATUS FOR PRODUCING A GIRDER


WENTHE RG   JOHN L SEYM
321687 5 US      65   P  11R   NOV    9
  CL156/154  METHOD OF MAKING STRUCTURAL
  MATERIALS
```

e.g., two different specific chemical compounds or two different generic substituents. But even if we found a patent that had two completely dissimilar subject matters claimed, the information disclosed in the specification is the main question.

In a patent once issued to me on a selective copying device, the examiner cited a seismographic recording device. Would the searcher interested in the seismographic recording device patent consider my patent relevant? The writing unit of a selective copying device is a recording instrument! It is not possible to determine relevance on an *a priori* basis. One can predict a given degree of similarity between the citing and cited patents by examining the primary classifications to which each was assigned. These classifications are included in the *Patent Citation Index* because they are provided, as mentioned earlier, in the published patents.

The provision of the classification numbers in the title of the citing and in the cited patents provides useful information during a *Citation Index* search, but it is perhaps even more helpful in the *ASCA* system. In this current alerting system, the subscriber receives a weekly report informing him where any given patent has been cited in current journal articles or U. S. patents. He can also be notified of all currently issued patents which fall into a particular classification or those assigned to a particular company. He can also use an inventor's name as part of his interest profile or any specific technical paper or book ever published. The scope of this service is quite large, involving at present about 1500 leading journals and all U. S. patents—over 3,000,000 reference citations per year appearing in 235,000 source papers and 60,000 U. S. Patents in 1965. A copy of a typical *ASCA* report is shown in Figure 3.

It has been our experience that users of this system have found a high degree of *pertinence* in the patents and papers disseminated by the *ASCA* service or retrieved by the *Science Citation Index*. Since there is no objective measure of relevance, we would suggest that critics evaluate the system of citation indexing on the basis of *a posteriori* user judgements rather than any *a priori* and ill-conceived notions of relevance.

It has been said that a citator system is necessary and useful for the lawyer because American law is based on the "doctrine of *Stare Decisis* which means that all courts must follow precedents laid down by higher courts and each court generally also follows its own precedents" (6). This has been misconstrued as the raison d'etre for the citator system. On the contrary, it is because the lawyer "must make sure that his authorities are still good law, that is, that the case has not been overruled, reversed, limited or distinguished in some way that makes it no longer useful as a valid authority. Here is where the

```
a s c a

AUTOMATIC  SUBJECT  CITATION  ALERT

DR. ALFRED M. HURST                              M7796 ACCOUNT NUMBER
ELECTROMETRICS, INC.                                43 UNITS USED
RESEARCH DEPT., PHYSICS SECTION                      7 UNITS REMAINING

SAN FRANCISCO, CALIF.   5568

REPORT FOR 25 JUN 65

61,248 citations from current scientific literature and
       current patents were processed for ASCA this week

THE ITEM BY LANGER JS          J PHYS CHEM SOLIDS         12  196 59
REF AUTHOR  OVERHAUSER AW      PHYS REV                  102  676 56
 CITED BY  NAGAI O
         J PHYS JAP    20  509 65      17R   N4      64973
           ELECTRIC FIELD GRADIENT IN CU-AG DILUTE ALLOY

THE BOOK BY BORN M             PRINCIPLES OPTICS                  59
 CITED BY  CHILDER DG
         CAN J PHYS    43 1099 65      31R   N6      65403
           A COVARIANCE (COHERENCY) MATRIX FOR
           BACKSCATTERED AND SPATIAL ELECTROMAGNETIC
           NOISE

THE ITEM BY BRUNNER CA         INDUST ENG CHEM FUND        2  297 63
THE ITEM BY GRIEVES RB         AMER I CHEM ENG J          10  456 64
THE ITEM BY GRIEVES RB         NATURE                    200  332 63
THE ITEM BY HARPER DO          INDUST ENG CHEM FUND        4   13 65
THE ITEM BY LEONARD RA         AMER I CHEM ENG J          11   18 65
THE BOOK BY SCHOEN HM          NEW CHEMICAL ENGINEE               62
 CITED BY  WACE PF      BANFIELD DL
         NATURE       206 1131 65      16R   N4989   65194
           CHEMICAL ENGINEERING OF FOAM SEPARATION

REF AUTHOR  WEIMER             FEB INT SOL STAT CIR            32 62
 CITED BY  WEIMER PK    RAD CORP AM
         3191061 US               65   P   7R   JUN 22
           CL307/88.5 INSULATED GATE FIELD EFFECT DEVICES
           AND ELECTRICAL CIRCUITS EMPLOYING SUCH DEVICES

THE PATENT      1900018        LILLIENFELD 317/258          US    33
 CITED BY  BOYKIN OF    CTS CORP
         3191108 US               65   P  11R   JUN 22
           CL317/258 ELECTRICAL CAPACITOR AND METHOD OF
           MAKING SAME
```

Figure 3. Typical weekly *ASCA* report illustrating citation of a 1933 U. S. Patent by a 1965 Patent. Other profile items include journal articles, books, authors, etc.

use of *Shepard's Citations* comes in.... The amazing efficiency of the citation method is such that once the starting case or statute is found it becomes a key that unlocks the entire store of law on a given point" (*6*).

By analogy, patent searches involve not only what is commonly called "prior at" but also what may be called "subsequent art." Technological innovations are not conceived in a vacuum; nor are they pulled from the air by magic. Every patent involves one or more primordial concepts which the inventor has joined together in a unique way to justify his claim for patent protection. Finding the needles in the haystack—the pertinent patents or publications—rapidly and efficiently, is the function of any index. The *Patent Citation Index*, if properly used in combination with existing tools, can save many valuable hours of search time and also make the time spent in searching productive of information that would otherwise be difficult or impossible to uncover.

ACKNOWLEDGMENT

I should like to acknowledge the help of R. A. Spencer of the U. S. Patent Office (7) in clarifying many points discussed in this paper.

LITERATURE CITED

(1) Taylor, R. S., *Am. Doc.* **13**(4), 31-96 (1962).

(2) Salton, G., *J. Assoc. Computing Machinery* **10**(4), 440-57, (1963).

(3) Garfield, E., "World Brain or Memex?—Mechanical and Intellectual Requirements of Universal Bibliographicl Control." Paper presented at the Symposium on "The Foundations of Access to Knowledge," Syracuse University, Syracuse, N. Y., July 30, 1965, in press.

(4) Kessler, M. M., *Am. Doc.* **14**, 10-25 (1963).

(5) Garfield, E., *Science* **144**(3619), 649-54 (1964).

(6) Adair, W. C., *Am. Doc.* **63**, 31-32 (1955).

(7) Spencer, R. A., private communication to E. Glazer, May 13, 1964.

See also:

(8) Garfield, E., *J. Pat. Off. Soc.* **39**(8), 583-95 (1957).

(9) Seidel, A. H., *ibid.*, **31**, 554 (1949).

(10) Hart, H. C., *ibid.*, **37**, 714 (1949).

(11) Sokal, R. R., and Sneath, P. H. A., "Principles of Numerical Taxonomy," San Francisco, Calif., W. H. Freeman and Co., 1963.

NOTE: Since the presentation of this paper, the *Science Citation Index* service has eliminated the indexing of U. S. Patents as sources. However, the *SCI* continues to index all patents cited in approximately 1500 technical journals as typified by the Paetzold article in Figures 1 and 2.

Reprinted from Science, June 9, 1967, Vol. 156, No. 3780, pages 1398-1401

(Education and Training for) Information Retrieval

The value of educating students in the modern techniques of retrieval and communication of scientific information is no longer disputed. The problem is—how and when. While many educators talk about the need for undergraduate and graduate instruction, very little has been done. This educational need was discussed at a symposium on "The place of information retrieval and scientific communication in the education of the scientist," held at the 133rd AAAS Meeting, Washington, D.C., 27 December 1966. The speakers and panelists at this symposium were selected primarily because none represents the professional information retriever or technical writer. As such, they ought not be accused of grinding an ax with respect to the training of professional information scientists or training scientists to use and prepare information.

Undoubtedly the topic chosen by F. Peter Woodford (Rockefeller University), "Training in scientific thinking through the teaching of scientific writing," attracted the most attention because he dealt with two "truisms." Scientists ought to know how to write. And they ought to know how to think. Woodford convincingly demonstrated that good writing is usually accompanied by clear thinking. Since his report was based on three years of experience teaching a course to students and faculty, it had the ring of authority.

Eugene Garfield (president, Institute for Scientific Information) stated candidly that he had a selfish interest in the symposium topic. His experience in several years of teaching a graduate course in information retrieval at the University of Pennsylvania had clearly demonstrated shocking neglect in the undergraduate education of engineers in the use of libraries. It seemed almost ludicrous for computer scientists and engineers to be discussing automation in libraries when they did not have the slightest acquaintance with the most elementary bibliographic apparatus. Indeed, the lack of training and exposure to such systems may account for the large number of absurd "solutions" offered by hardware-oriented engineers who were not conscious that one might retrieve information in one minute by use of a printed index that would require hours on the most sophisticated computers available.

John Bardeen (University of Illinois) tended to agree with this view, but particularly stressed the absurd waste of valuable technological information available in U.S. patents. His talk, "How can patent literature be made more useful," also provided him an opportunity to report on the recently released report of the President's Commission on the Patent System on which he served. Bardeen implied that academic neglect of the patent literature, in contrast to journals and books, is an unjustifiable form of snobbism. One panelist pointed out that this might also have something to do with an historical aversion in academe towards profit-making, which patents seemed to symbolize. Bardeen agreed that education of scientists should include instruction in information retrieval, though he did not feel too strongly about its potential value for physicists. Physicists tended to ignore the literature much more than their biological confreres who were not only more literature minded, but had a larger literature on which to draw.

If Woodford's theme concerning writing was considered a truism, Bardeen and other panelists pointed out that the value of information retrieval systems is not. There remain many scientists and engineers who would like better and less literature to be published, but they rarely, if ever, make use of systems for information retrieval or selective dissemination. This view was epitomized by a short presentation written by John T. Edsall (editor, *Journal of Biological Chemistry*). He found that he relied less and less on abstracting and indexing services and hardly had enough time to read and digest the hundreds of journal manuscripts that passed before him each year. His paper was read in his absence by Morton V. Malin (Institute for Scientific Information, Bethesda). Malin stated that Edsall surely was atypical. The average graduate student or post-doctoral fellow, even if close to one of the invisible colleges, does not have the opportunity of being on top of the literature as does the editor of a journal like the *Journal of Biological Chemistry*. Furthermore, there was considerable evidence that the multidisciplinary nature of research today makes it all the more imperative that even leaders of invisible colleges or information exchange groups have good knowledge of and access to the literature in ancillary fields or on topics which might seem at first glance to be "peripheral."

Leonard Ornstein (Mt. Sinai Hospital Medical School) not only seconded this view but added comments based on his experience as a referee and member of the Editorial Board of *Journal of Cell Biology*. He felt there was a shocking and disturbing trend to ignore the published literature. Each self-proclaimed expert was "sure" he knew the entire literature of his field without the most routine searches. Ornstein also debated some of the basic issues taken up by Frederick L. Goodman (University of Michigan), the only speaker representing the field of education. Goodman's theme, "The pedagogical politics of educating scientists," contained some sober reflections drawn from his expert knowledge of Dewey's pragmatic philosophy. He was quick to point out that he meant John Dewey and not Melville Dewey of the decimal classification system. Goodman indicated that modern concepts of information retrieval were part of the coming revolution in teaching and the mere introduction of one course in retrieval was barely approaching the solution to the problem. The computer revolution, as is well known, is already having dramatic effects on education. This was quickly confirmed by Dean Sanborn C. Brown (Massachusetts Institute of Technology) who took the position that it was possibly wiser to introduce undergraduate students to time-shared computers to learn information retrieval before they had been exposed to traditional systems. Any bright student would eventually find his way to the university library. Daniel Gore (Asheville-Biltmore College, North Carolina) took issue with this approach to library instruction, stating that it was the primary task of the librarian to instruct students in the use of library materials and retrieval systems. Incidentally, Gore recently created a furor in the library profession by publishing an article in the *Bulletin of the AAUP* which attacked the bureaucrats of the library profession and the proliferation of local cataloging at the eventual sacrifice of book purchases. His paper, "Sweetness and light: A goal for libraries," demonstrated the beauty that can result from the blending of a humanities-trained scholar with a science-oriented theme.

Andrew Lasslo (University of Tennessee) opened the session with "Scientists and literature resources," a presentation of the feelings of a pharmaceutical chemist who had taken the time and energy to do something about training a core of badly needed science librarians.

James D. B. O'Toole (Boston University) provided a fitting parallel in discussing his graduate program for the training of science communicators. His program is designed to increase public understanding of science by equipping science graduates to help unclog the communication channels between science and society.

In opening the session, the chairman read statements by several panelists who could not attend, including Halvor Christensen (University of Michigan),

William Fowler (California Institute of Technology), and Alvin Weinberg (Oak Ridge National Laboratory). Weinberg's remarks would appear to be a fitting conclusion to this report:

"Science's commitment to the handling of scientific information is increasing daily. As science grows, so this commitment must grow.

"What is the nature of this commitment? Obviously, more money will have to be spent for information-handling systems—for computers, new journals, and new retrieval mechanisms. More secondary information handlers will be required: the information center, which was viewed as crucial in the PSAC report 'Science, Government and Information,' is proving to be a dominant element in the new information system. The information center will surely continue to proliferate and develop as science and scientific information increase.

"But the most important commitment of science to information must be the commitment of the individual scientist. Generally, scientists view the handling of scientific information as separate from science itself. They are individually unwilling to devote much of their time to the task of managing the flood of scientific information. This attitude is untenable. Every scientist must accept his share of the responsibility for controlling scientific information. He must realize, as a matter of course, that when he adds to the cascade of scientific information, he assumes a responsibility to participate in the management of the flood.

"I believe the university has a clear duty in this connection. Our coming generations of scientists must be taught to accept their responsibility toward information—not grudgingly and with half heart, but fully and constructively. This attitude represents a change from the prevailing attitude. Scientists generally fail to see why they should be bothered with helping to manage scientific information; this they learn from their professors and colleagues who are similarly disinclined to make the necessary sacrifices.

"But sacrifices will have to be made if science itself is not to collapse. The education of every scientist will have to include instruction in handling the new and ingenious tools of information retrieval. The educational process will even more have to inculcate into all scientists a willingness to contribute time and effort in behalf of the entire scientific communication system."

EUGENE GARFIELD
Institute for Scientific Information, Philadelphia, Pennsylvania 19106

The Permuterm Subject Index: An Autobiographical Review

Eugene Garfield
Institute for Scientific Information
Philadelphia, PA 19106

The *Permuterm Subject Index* (*PSI*) section of the *Science Citation Index* (*SCI*) was designed more than ten years ago and has been published both quarterly and annually since 1966. There is, however, no 'primordial' citable paper about the *PSI*. It has been described and discussed from different standpoints in a number of papers (*1,2*), but none of them provides the formal description usually accorded a new bibliographic tool. This article is intended to provide such a reference point for future workers in information science.

The *PSI* was designed in 1964 at the Institute for Scientific Information (ISI) by myself and Irving Sher, my principal research collaborator at the time. In the subsequent development of the *PSI*, contributions were also made by others, including Arthur W. Elias, who was then in charge of production operations at ISI. In the early sixties we were too preoccupied with the task of convincing the library and information community of the value of citation indexing even to consider the idea of publishing a word index. But it was a logical development once we added the *Source Index* containing full titles.

The value of the *PSI* as a 'natural language' index is now well recognized and exploited by its users, but this was not the original reason for its development. The *PSI* was developed as one solution to a problem commonly faced by uses of the *Citation Index* section of the *Science Citation Index* (*SCI*). While the typical scientist-user could enter the *Citation Index* with a known author or paper, other users with a limited knowledge of the subject often lacked a starting point for their search. Before publication of the *PSI*, we told users whose unfamiliarity with subject matter left them doubtful about a starting point to consult an encyclopedia or the subject index of a book. If these failed, we told them to use another index, such as *Chemical Abstracts*, *Biological Abstracts*, *Physics Abstracts* or *Index Medicus*. Once the user identified a relevant older paper, it could be used to begin a search in the *Citation Index*. Users of the *SCI*—and librarians in particular needed some tool with which a starting point, or what used to be called a target reference, could be quickly and easily identified.

In those days the information community was pre-occupied with Key-Word-in-Context (KWIC) indexes. The development of the KWIC index, which was subsequently vigorously marketed by IBM, undoubtedly had an enormous impact (*3, 4, 5*). But I was never happy with the KWIC system for a number of reasons.

First, Sher and I felt that the KWIC index was highly uneconomical for a printed index. KWIC's use of space is prodigious, and it can be extremely time-consuming to use in searches involving more than one term.

Another aspect of the KWIC system (as used for example by *Chemical Titles*) that disturbed us was its indiscriminate use of stop-lists to eliminate presumably non-significant title words. In our view, it caused considerable loss of information on many subjects of interest to some users, if not to all. Consider the effect of deleting terms like METHOD and BEHAVIOR. In order to retain much of this information, but still prevent the useless entries generated by "terms" like THE and WHICH, we developed the concept of the semi-stop list to be used in addition to a full-stop list.

The full-stop list for the *PSI*, which contains words that are completely suppressed, was and is quite small. The semi-stop words such as METHOD, BEHAVIOR, CAUSE, REPORT and TECHNIQUE are suppressed as primary terms (main entries), but not as secondary or co-terms (subentries). In addition, certain frequently used two-word phrases, which have been identified through statistical analysis of word frequencies, are kept together and treated as a single term rather than being allowed to permute separately. Such phrases as GUINEA-PIG, NEW-YORK, ESCHERICHIA-COLI and BIRTH-CONTROL appear in the *PSI* as hyphenated terms, thus reducing look-up time in many types of searches. This is done by computer in the *PSI*, while in indexes like *Chemical Titles*, it is done by a manual process called "slash and dash."

Finally, the KWIC format was rejected because a number of studies had demonstrated that users of scientific indexes generally specify two or three terms when they use coordinate indexes. We reasoned that the optimum system would precoordinate any two terms, no matter how far apart in the title.

Over ten years of *PSI* experience has confirmed that "specificity" *per se* does not guarantee efficiency of a word as a search term. If used frequently enough, a seemingly highly specific term like DNA becomes as inefficient as more general terms that are used less frequently. The converse also holds; consider the term CREATIVITY. It is general, but because of the comparatively low frequency with which it occurs in the scientific literature, it is an efficient search term. Therefore, pairing—together with precoordination—becomes essential for high-usage terms, and merely convenient for low-usage terms. Triple coordination—and even higher-level coupling—may also be desirable if two terms occur together with a third frequently enough. But the threshold must be correlated with cost of processing and printing, not only with economies in users' time. The ideal system would handle three or more terms, but this proved too costly. We therefore settled on two terms, although recently precoordination of three terms has been built into the five-year cumulative 1965-1969 *PSI*, and an improved three-term precoordination routine will be achieved in the five-year cumulative, *PSI* for 1970-74, to be published by ISI in 1977.

The choice of name for the *Permuterm Subject Index* was quite deliberate. Ohlman suggested the term *permuted* from *cyclic permutation* used in mathematics (*6*). It was in that sense appropriate to KWIC indexes. *Permuterm*, however, is a complete permutation of all title words to produce all possible pairs, including of course, the inversion of every pair. As I and others have noted before, KWIC indexes are more appropriately called *rotated indexes* (*7, 8*). For example, ISI's *Rotaform Index* section of the *Index Chemicus* is a rotated formula index. The *Chemical Substructure Index* (*CSI*) is also a cyclic or rotated index. Using the Wisewesser Line Notation, the *CSI* rotates the line notation to create a main entry for every substantive constituent in each notation.

For each title in the *PSI* with n title words, $n(n-1)$ word-pairs are created by permutation. After applying the full-stop list and semi-stop list, this usually produces about 40 word-pairs for the typical seven-word title. It is by no means unusual for the *PSI* to contain over 100 word-pairs for titles with 11 or more words.

In the *PSI*, every significant word in the title is permuted [not merely rotated, as in a KWIC index (7)] by computer to produce all possible pairs of terms. Every word is potentially both a primary term and a co-term. On the printed page, each permuted word-pair is arranged alphabetically by primary term. All co-terms occurring with a particular primary term are idented as subentries and listed in alphabetical order under the primary term. Dashed lines lead from the co-term to the author, whose name can be used to locate in the *Source Index* section of the *SCI* the complete bibliographic data, including the title for the article.

As part of ISI's quality-control precoordination and spelling-variance unification procedures, every incoming term—that is, every word in every title—is passed against the established *PSI* vocabulary. In this computer comparison, wrong and variant spellings are corrected and coordination tests for accepted word-pairs are applied. Terms which are truly new are selected for human review and added to the vocabulary. Naturally, many author- or ISI-produced errors are identified and corrected in this process.

From the earliest days Sher and I were aware of the enormous potential of the *PSI* vocabulary for scientific lexicography. Besides allowing very specific searches on terms that would never have appeared in thesaurus-controlled indexing systems, the use of actual title-words reflects terminological innovation long before anyone but specialists in the affected field are aware of the changes. Every year nearly two-thirds of the words *added* as primary terms to the *PSI* vocabulary are "new" in the sense that they occurred only once or not at all in titles processed the previous year (*9*). This does not, of course, mean that two-thirds of each year's vocabulary is "new".

The cumulated vocabulary of the *PSI* comprises an author-generated word-index to all the significant articles of science and technology—including letters, technical notes, and proceedings of meetings. It is a pity that the *PSI* vocabulary has not yet been used by lexicographers to identify and define new scientific terms and usages (*10*). A dictionary based on the *PSI*, which could be updated quarterly, would be the first current dictionary of new scientific terms based on primordial sources.

From the outset, we were aware of the shortcomings of title-word indexes: the lack of resolution of obvious (and not-so-obvious) synonyms and the unavoidable fact that morphological variations of the same primary terms, *e.g*, CLASSIFY and CLASSIFICATION, appear separately in the index. Even the plural of a noun may be separated from its singular, *e.g.*, SUGAR and SUGARS. In Ohlman's permutation index to the proceedings of the ICSI 1958 conference, this problem was alleviated somewhat by restricting sorting of the first six characters of each term. However, use of this procedure is impractical for an index as large as the *PSI* (*3*).

Such problems were of minor importance as long as the *PSI* was regarded merely as a supplement to the *Citation Index*. We found that many scientists preferred a title-word index because it enabled them to retrieve a work by a word or phrase remembered from its title, or by subject words they knew to be relevant.

It was inevitable that librarians and others would begin pressuring us to make the *PSI* a search tool in its own right. Our response began with provision of cross-references and eventually led to certain standardizations, especially in the case of spelling variations. Today the so-called source-data edit procedures at ISI are quite systematic and comprehensive (*11*), and the *PSI* does stand on its own as both a current and retrospective subject index.

As early as 1969, I reported at Amsterdam on ISI's efforts to develop automatic procedures for hyphenating word-pairs into phrases, a process we called "precoordination" (*12*) to produce bound terms like BIRTH CONTROL. Such terms would be hyphenated automatically, provided they occurred with sufficient frequency. It was remarkable to discover that punctuation could be ignored if a given word-pair occurred above a certain very low threshold, about two or three times. One would not find too many titles in which the terms BIRTH and CONTROL were separated by a comma, such as "Season of birth, control of disease, and WHO statistics." Linguistic analysts have agonized over the problem of differentiating such items, but it is rarely a real problem.

Besides increasing the specificity and thus the informational value of the *PSI*, the main objective of pre-coordination is to reduce the number of permutations required. This did not prove to be as easy as we had first imagined. We have since found that precoordination is best performed by source-data edits, which requires constant monitoring of term-pair frequencies.

An important objective of permuted index display should be to minimize post-coordination by the user. For example, while BIRTH-CONTROL provides one level of precoordination, the resulting term is of such high frequency that one ought to be able to precoordinate BIRTH-CONTROL at a second level, with terms indicating drugs, devices, methods, etc., so as to narrow the focus of retrieval to less than ten articles for most searches. Obviously, the value of precoordination increases five-fold for a five-year cumulation, in which certain terms might occur dozens or even hundreds of times.

In closing this belated report on *PSI*, we should not overlook the application of the *Permuterm* concept in controlled or manual indexing systems. We first used *Permuterm* in a controlled indexing situation during the production of *Current Contents /Chemical Sciences*. Since then, we have used the method in producing the yearly index of the *Journal of the Electrochemical Society*, and some industrial organizations have used our *Permuterm* programs to generate their own indexes. Further, our on-line searching experience has demonstrated that *PSI* can be (and now *is*) used to facilitate searches of other data bases, such as MEDLINE, precisely because it displays term pairs that one might not think of or cannot find in thesauri such as MeSH. Otherwise, *Permuterm* indexing has had little application outside ISI.

A proper evaluation of *PSI* by the information community has yet to be published. Meanwhile, we can only report that *PSI* has been steadily gaining increasing acceptance among *SCI* subscribers. Most users today know how to optimize their use of the *SCI* with the most appropriate word index available for the time period covered in the search, whether for the period prior to 1965, when *PSI* first became available, or thereafter. Since 80 percent of *SCI* subscribers now also subscribe to *PSI*, it seems reasonable after more than ten year's development, to incorporate *PSI* into the *SCI* system. Thus in the future no user of the *SCI* will lack its complement, the *PSI*.

1. **Weinstock, M.** 1971. "Citation Indexes." *Encyclopedia of Library and Information Science*. 5 Vols. New York: Marcel Dekker, 1971;5:16-40.
2. **Garfield, E.** 1971. "Automation of ISI Services: *Science Citation Index (SCI), Permuterm Subject Index (PSI)*, and *ASCA*." *International Association of Agricultural Librarians and Documentalists, IVth World Congress, Paris, 20-25 April 1970*. Paris: Institut National de la Recherche Agronomique, 1971; p. 107-112.
3. **Citron, J.; Hart, L.; Ohlman, H.** 1959. "A Permutation Index to the Preprints of the International Conference of Scientific Information." Reprint No. SP-44, Revised edition. Santa Monica, CA: System Development Corp. 1959 December 15; 37 pp.
4. "Keyword-in-Context Index for Technical Literature." Report RC 127. New York: IBM Corp., Advanced System Development Division, 1959. Also published in: *American Documentation*. 1959;11:288-295.
5. **Stevens, M.E.** 1965. "Automatic Indexing: a State-of-the-Art Report." National Bureau of Standards Monograph 91. Washington, DC: Government Printing Office. 1965, March 30.
6. **Ohlman, H.** Personal communication, 1975, November.
7. **Garfield, E.** 1972. "Indexing Terminology and Permuted Indexes." *Journal of Documentation*. 1972; 28(4):344-345.
8. **Heumann, K.** et al. 1954. *The Chemical Biological Coordination Center of the National Academy of Sciences*. Washington, DC: National Research Council. 1954: p. 18.
9. **Weinstock, M.; Fenichel, C.; Williams, M.V.V.** 1970. "System Design Implications of the Title Words of Scientific Journal Articles in the *Permuterm Subject Index*." *The Social Impact of Information Retrieval: The Information Bazaar, Seventh Annual National Colloquium on Information Retrieval. May 8-9, 1970*. Philadelphia, PA: The College of Physicians of Philadelphia, 1970;181-200.
10. **Garfield, E.** 1969. "Permuterm Subject Index, the Primordial Dictionary of Science." *Current Contents*. 1969 June 3;22:22.
11. **Fenichel, C.** 1971. "Editing the Permuterm Subject Index." *Proceedings of the American Society for Information Science, 34th Annual Meeting*. Denver, CO. 7-11 November 1971;349-353.
12. **Garfield, E.** 1970. "Citation Indexing, Historio-Bibliography, and the Sociology of Science." *Proceedings of the Third International Congress of Medical Librarianship, Amsterdam, 5-9 May 1969*. Amsterdam, The Netherlands: Excerpta Medica. 1970; p. 187-204.

CITED AUTHOR INDEX

Each author cited in the references of the essays is listed alphabetically with a page and reference number.

Abadzapatero C 20r44

The sample entry indicates that on page 20, reference number 44 is to an item authored by C Abadzapatero.

Cited Author Index

Phila. Inquirer

Mourtada H 288r3
Moutquin J-M 373r27
Muir P 288r4
Mullane K 86r70
Mullaney JA 136r10
Müller H 35r35
Muller U 20r41
Mummery R 127r41,r42
Munoz R 249r12
Munro I 305r9
Murphy BJ 289r35
Murphy RC 85r56
Murra KO 534r10
Myers H 429r45

N

Nance WE 404r33
Narin F 143r11
Nat. Sci. Foundation Bull. 36r47
Nat. Soc. Med. Res. Bull. 35r27
National Academy of Sciences 35r10
National League for Nursing 345r7,r8
National Science Board 143r8
National Society for Medical
        Research 36r52,r53
Natov R 438r22
Nature 36r42
Needham J 217r14,r15
Needleman HL 250r56
Needleman P 86r65,r70
Neel JV 404r30
Neilson JP 373r23
Netto NR 289r40
Neville C 127r23
New Sci. 193r8, 396r4
New York Academy of Sciences 438r34
Newill VA 346r3
Newton W 373r36
Niall HD 20r38
Nichols RC 404r19
Nicholson RS 96r18
Nicolle LE 281r13
Nixon M 305r15
Nolen WA 289r44
Noll M 20r46,r47,r48
Norman C 429r59
Norton D 437r4
Notestein FW 173r14

Nourse AE 438r18
Nowlin J 106r51
Noyes R 136r31
Nugteren DH 86r83
Nuñez A 143r1
NY Times 173r8
Nylander PPS 372r4
NZ Med. J. 305r5

O

Oates JA 84r7
O'Brien GT 137r52
O'Grady F 289r42
Ohlman H 550r3,r6
O'Keefe CM 288r2
Older RA 289r15
Olds A 294r6
Oliveau D 136r14
Olsen ME 373r15
Olson AJ 20r45
Oromaner M 107r55
Oruene TO 372r2
Öst L-G 136r32
Overton WF 107r70,r71

P

Pallansch MJ 535r41
Palmer BI 44r13,r14,r18
Palmer RL 249r6
Panja SK 288r5
Papiernik E 373r38
Parisi P 372r8, 404r5
Parker CA 96r16
Parker K 127r21,r23
Parlett B 174r61
Parsons JA 127r32,r36
Payne DB 437r5
Pead L 281r21
Pender NJ 345r11
Penzias AA 163r14
Penzien J 419r9
Perkins RH 429r53
Perlman RM 106r38
Perlmutter M 106r54
Pernow B 85r48
Perone M 106r48
Phila. Inquirer 19r24

SUBJECT INDEX

A major discussion of a topic in an essay is indicated by a boldface page number. Mention of an individual in an essay often includes reference to one or more of that person's published works. Therefore, readers doing name searches should also consult the Cited Author Index.

Behavior

Gairdner

Michaelis

Subject Index

R

Rabinow, J. 460
Ranganathan, S.R.
    contribution to library science **45**
    life and works **37**
Rapp, Barbara 24
regulation, effects of 108, 110
relativistic theory of information science **523**
Relman, Arnold 186
reprints
    See Garfield E., Kelly, K., and Tisdale, S.
research fronts
    agoraphobia 132
    economics 111
    Latin American research 148
    nucleoproteins 16
    population age 171
    prostaglandins 80
    social gerontology 104
retirement age 168
review articles **182**
reward system 103
Rios, Emeteria Martinez 291
Rodgers, Robert 51
Rogers, Frank Bradway **5**
Roofs or ceilings? (pamphlet) 109
Rose, Arthur 458
Rosenberg, Lilli Ann Killen **290**
Rotaform Index 560
Rothschild, Miriam 68, **120**
Rubin, N. 470

S

saccharin controversy 29
Samuelsson, B.I. **77**, 108
Sayers, W.C. Berwick 38
scanning 346
Sci-Mate 3, **55**
Sci-Mate 1.1 **50**
Science and Children (magazine) 432
Science Books & Films (magazine) 432
science books for children **430**
Science Citation Index
  as new dimension in indexing **525**
  Permuterm Subject Index section of **546**
Science Citation Index, Abridged Edition 57
science in Latin America **138, 144**
Science Indicators 151

scientific reviewing, award for excellence
    in **182**
Scientists' Center for Animal Welfare 34
secondary distribution of information 523
self-covers 1
Sher, Irving 546
Silverstein, Susan 293
Singer, T.E.R. 477
Small, Henry 217
social gerontology **97, 164**
Social Sciences Citation Index **202, 211**
Social SCISEARCH 210
Social Security 169
Soffer, M.D. 482
software
    See computer software
South American research **138, 144**
Stiftung, Ernest Jung 405
Stigler, George J. **108**
Stigler, Stephen M. 108
stop lists 547
Stout, Catherine 51
structural linguistics **468**
students, citation index for 57
subject indexing 524, 531
syntactic analysis of organic chemical
        nomenclature **473**

T

Taine, Seymour I. 7, 8
Taub, Edward 29
Taube, Henry 12, **424**
technology of science **218**
Telesystemes 196
Tenopir, Carol 24
Terentiev, A.P. 458
TERRAP 129, 135
thalidomide 29
Theories of Learning (book) 183
Theory of Price, The (book) 109
Third World research 37
Thomas, Lewis 350
Tisdale, Sallie (reprint) 228
tobacco mosaic virus 13
Tring Museum 120
Tsukerman, A.M. 458
twins
    behavioral and clinical research **397**
    conception, development, and delivery **366**
type size in *Current Contents* 3

United